THE MARX-ENGELS READER

Books by Robert C. Tucker

Philosophy and Myth in Karl Marx
The Soviet Political Mind, *Revised*
The Marxian Revolutionary Idea

THE

MARX-ENGELS

READER

Edited by

ROBERT C. TUCKER

PRINCETON UNIVERSITY

W · W · NORTON & COMPANY · INC ·

NEW YORK

Copyright © 1972 by W. W. Norton & Company, Inc.

FIRST EDITION

SBN 393 05457 8 (Cloth Edition)

SBN 393 09965 2 (Paper Edition)

Library of Congress Catalog Card No. 79-141585

PRINTED IN THE UNITED STATES OF AMERICA

1 2 3 4 5 6 7 8 9 0

Contents

Part IV. Society and Politics in the Nineteenth Century

Part V. The Later Engels: Elaboration and Popularization

Preface

A knowledge of the writings of Marx and Engels is virtually indispensable to an educated person in our time, whatever his political position or social philosophy. For classical Marxism, as the thought of Marx and Engels may be called, has profoundly affected men's views about history, society, economics, ideology, culture, and politics; indeed, about the nature of social inquiry itself. No other intellectual influence has so powerfully shaped the mind of modern left-wing radicalism in most parts of the world. Through classical Marxism, moreover, the left is linked to a greater intellectual tradition extending into the eighteenth-century French Enlightenment, German post-Kantian philosophy, English political economy, and early-nineteenth-century European socialism. Not to be well grounded in the writings of Marx and Engels is to be insufficiently attuned to modern thought, and self-excluded to a degree from the continuing debate by which most contemporary societies live insofar as their members are free and able to discuss the vital issues.

This book offers the original writings needed to acquire a thorough grounding in Marxist thought, together with introductory notes to each selection, a chronology of the careers of the two men, and a concluding bibliographic guide to some of the literature about them and their thought. I have aimed to place between the covers of one volume all or nearly all of what could be considered "the essential Marx and Engels." Since their published writings and correspondence fill more than forty volumes, such an undertaking involves difficult problems of selection. In resolving them I have followed certain established traditions in the anthologizing of Marx and Engels, but also have sought to break fresh ground. The main innovations are the inclusion of the principal early writings of Marx and substantial portions of *Capital*.

The inclusion of the early Marx is a response to the revolution that has taken place in "Marxology" in our time owing to the publication in the 1930s of some previously unknown writings of Marx's formative period. I shall say more about these writings and their significance in the Introduction. The outcome of the new Marx scholarship, as I shall argue, is a deeper and clearer understanding both of Marxism's origins in post-Kantian German philosophy and of its fundamental meaning. The new scholarship has also made plain the basic underlying continuity that exists between the early and later Marx. For these reasons, among others, the most important of the early writings deserve to be represented in any collection of the essential Marx and Engels, and have been included here.

Marx without *Capital* is Kant without *The Critique of Pure Reason* or Darwin without *The Origin of Species*. Even though he completed only the first volume of it, leaving the second and third volumes in unfinished form to be edited and published by Engels after he died, *Capital* was Marx's great work. When he completed and published Volume One in 1867, he described it in a letter to a friend as the book "to which I have sacrificed my health, my happiness and my family." When read closely and in the context of the remainder of his writings, *Capital* turns out to be not simply Marx's major treatise on political economy, but his principal work on man, society, and government—indeed, the fullest expression of his entire world-view. Clearly, there can be no "essential Marx and Engels" with *Capital* missing, yet the book is forbidding on account of its great size—about eight hundred pages—and its complexity. Feeling that token solutions of this problem through the inclusion mainly of Marx's prefaces to *Capital* are unsatisfactory, I have tried to resolve it by putting together sufficiently extensive extracts to convey the book's basic argument, the parts of greatest general interest.

In preparing this anthology, I have tried, wherever possible, to include writings unabridged. In application of this principle, it has seemed better, for example, to include *in toto* two of Marx's major works of political journalism, *The Eighteenth Brumaire of Louis Bonaparte* and *The Civil War in France*, and omit *The Class Struggles in France, 1848–1850*, than to use incomplete versions of all three; in this instance the decision was eased by the circumstance that *The Eighteenth Brumaire* reviews the events of 1848–50 in France. Applying the same principle on a different plane, I have tried to include the most important *sections* of works in their entirety when it was not possible to include the work as a whole. Thus, Part I of *The German Ideology*, containing Marx's only systematic presentation of his theory of history in detail, is given in full. Again, the critically important sections of the *Economic and Philosophic Manuscripts of 1844*—"Estranged Labour," "Private Property and Communism," and others—have been included without abridgement. Such shorter writings as Marx's essays on the Hegelian philosophy of right and the Jewish question, *Wage Labour and Capital*, his first essay on British rule in India, the *Address to the Communist League*, the *Critique of the Gotha Program*, and the *Communist Manifesto*, as well as Engels' booklet

Socialism: Utopian and Scientific, appear here in their entirety. In certain instances, however, particularly some of Engels' later writings, the use of excerpts was unavoidable.

My thanks go first of all to two friends who have been instrumental in making this book a reality. My colleague Professor Stephen Cohen convinced me of the need for the kind of comprehensive anthology of Marx and Engels that the book seeks to provide, and later was generous with his advice on many aspects of the work and gave me the benefit of a searching appraisal of my proposed choice of materials. Mr. James Mairs of W. W. Norton & Company was an unfailing source of encouragement, support, editorial judgment, and practical wisdom on all matters affecting the book.

I am also indebted to Miss Emily Garlin for her editorial assistance; to Professor Ronald Rogowski for translating Marx's letter to Arnold Ruge; to Professor Norman Levine for critical comments and suggestions on the choice of materials; to Professor Steven Marcus for suggesting the inclusion of Engels' description of working-class Manchester; to Mrs. Lorna Giese for her able typing of portions of the manuscript; and to Mr. Jerome Nestor and Mr. Anthony Trenga for assistance in preparing the chronology of the careers of Marx and Engels.

Professor T. B. Bottomore kindly gave permission to reprint his translations of Marx's essays "On the Jewish Question" and "Contribution to the Critique of Hegel's *Philosophy of Right*: Introduction," including the editorial notes, from his book *Karl Marx: Early Writings.* Unless otherwise indicated the remaining texts are translations that have appeared in editions published by the Foreign Languages Publishing House or Progress Publishers in Moscow. Likewise, the editorial notes, save where specifically indicated, are those supplied by the original editor or translator.

R. C. T.

The Careers of Marx and Engels

1818	(May 5) Karl Marx born at Trier, Prussia (now part of West Germany).
1820	(November 28) Friedrich Engels born at Barmen (incorporated into Wuppertal, 1929; now in West Germany).
1830–35	Marx studied in Trier high school.
1834–37	Engels studied in Elberfeld high school.
1835	Marx entered University of Bonn, faculty of law.
1836	Marx transferred to University of Berlin, faculty of law.
1836–38	Marx studied law, philosophy, history, and English and Italian languages at Berlin.
1839–41	Marx studied Greek philosophy and wrote doctoral dissertation, *The Difference Between the Democritean and Epicurean Philosophies of Nature*. Received Ph.D. Departed Berlin for Trier, then moved to Bonn hoping to secure teaching position at University of Bonn.
1838–41	Sent to Bremen for business training, Engels worked as unsalaried clerk in an export business. Continued studies independently and wrote articles for press.
1841–42	Abandoning the idea of university teaching, Marx wrote articles for the Young Hegelian *Deutsche Jahrbücher* and the *Rheinische Zeitung*, an opposition newspaper published in Cologne. Became editor of *Rheinische Zeitung* in October, 1842. Moved to Cologne.
1841–42	Engels served in Household Artillery of Prussian Army, attended lectures at University of Berlin, and joined circle of Young Hegelian radicals, "The Free." Wrote articles for *Rheinische Zeitung*.
1842	(November) First meeting between Marx and Engels, in office of *Rheinische Zeitung* in Cologne. Engels stopped there on way to England.
1842–43	Marx studied French socialist literature.
1842–44	In Manchester to complete his business training in firm of Ermen and Engels, Engels studied English life and literature, read political economists, joined Chartist movement, published in Owenite paper *The New Moral World*, wrote "Outlines of a Critique of Political Economy."

1843   (March 17) Marx resigned as editor of *Rheinische Zeitung* after imposition of strict censorship on paper by Prussian government.

1843   (June 19) Marriage of Marx to Jenny von Westphalen.

1843   Marx undertook with Arnold Ruge to publish *Deutsch-Französische Jahrbücher* and worked on founding of the journal.

1843   (summer) Marx in Kreuznach worked on critique of Hegel's *Philosophy of Right*.

1843   (end of October) Marx moved to Paris.

1843   (fall and winter) Marx wrote "On the Jewish Question" and "Contribution to the Critique of Hegel's *Philosophy of Right*: Introduction" for *Jahrbücher*.

1843   (end of December) Marx became acquainted with Heinrich Heine.

1844   (January-March) Marx studied history of French Revolution and began systematic study of classics of political economy.

1844   (January) Marx received articles from Engels for publication in *Jahrbücher*.

1844   Double issue of *Jahrbücher* published in Paris under editorship of Marx and Ruge. Publication of Engels' "Outlines of a Critique of Political Economy" in it led to correspondence between Marx and Engels.

1844   (April) Marx accused by Prussian government of high treason and *lese majesté* for his articles in *Jahrbücher* and ordered arrested in event of crossing Prussian border.

1844   (July) Marx became acquainted with Proudhon.

1844   (April–August) Marx wrote materials later published as *Economic and Philosophic Manuscripts of 1844.*

1844   (April–August) Engels gathered materials for a social history of England and on condition of English working class.

1844   (around August 28) Returning from Manchester to Germany, Engels visited Paris for second meeting with Marx. Commencement of their collaboration.

1844–45   Engels, in Barmen, wrote *Condition of the Working Class in England* (1845). Marx and Engels collaborated in writing *The Holy Family* (1845).

1845   (January) Banished from Paris by order of French government, acting under Prussian instigation, Marx moved to Brussels.

1845   (spring) Marx wrote "Theses on Feuerbach."

1845   (April) Engels joined Marx in Brussels.

1845   (summer) Marx visited Manchester with Engels, returning to Brussels in late August.

1845–46   Marx and Engels wrote *The German Ideology*.

1845   Marx renounced Prussian citizenship under pressure from Prussian government.

1846–47   Marx wrote *The Poverty of Philosophy* (1847).

1847   Engels took part in First Congress of the Communist League in London. In November both Marx and Engels took part in Second Congress, also in London.

1847   (December) Marx, in Brussels, gave series of lectures later published as *Wage Labour and Capital* (1849).

1848   (February) *Communist Manifesto* published in London.

1848–49   Marx and Engels took active parts in revolution of 1848–49 in Germany, coediting *Neue Rheinische Zeitung* in Cologne.

1849   (June) Engels served as Willich's adjutant in unsuccessful Baden rising.

1849   (fall) Marx and family settled down in London.

1850   Marx resumed his economic studies in British Museum. Engels took up residence in Manchester, where he worked for twenty years in firm of Ermen and Engels, helping to support Marx as well as himself.

1851   Marx began a ten-year period as occasional contributor to *New York Daily Tribune*.

1851–52   Marx wrote *The Eighteenth Brumaire of Louis Bonaparte* (1852). Engels wrote articles on "Revolution and Counter-Revolution in Germany." Latter appeared in *New York Daily Tribune* under Marx's name.

1857   Marx and Engels wrote articles for *New American Encyclopedia*, Engels' on "The History of Artillery."

1857–58   Marx prepared manuscripts on criticism of political economy, the *Grundrisse* (1939–41).

1858–59   Marx wrote *A Contribution to the Critique of Political Economy* (1859).

1862–63   Marx wrote *Theories of Surplus Value*.

1863   Mary Burns, with whom Engels had lived for many years, died.

1864   Founding of International Working Men's Association in London.

1864–71   Marx active in affairs of General Council of International Working Men's Association.

1867   Publication of *Capital*, Volume One.

1867–80   Marx continued work on Volumes Two and Three of *Capital*.

1871   Marx wrote *The Civil War in France* (1871).

1870–95   Engels lived in London.

1872   Appearance of Russian edition of *Capital*.

1874–80   Engels worked intermittently on *Dialectics of Nature*.

1878   Publication of Engels' *Anti-Dühring* in book form.

1881   Death of Jenny Marx.

1883   (March 14) Death of Karl Marx.

1884   Engels wrote *The Origin of the Family, Private Property and the State* (1884).

1885   Publication of Volume Two of *Capital*, edited by Engels.

1886   Engels wrote *Ludwig Feuerbach and the End of Classical German Philosophy* (1886).

1887   Publication of English translation of Volume One of *Capital*, edited by Engels. Publication in New York of first English edition of *The Condition of the Working Class in England in 1844*.

1888   (August–September) Engels traveled in the United States and Canada.

1889   Engels took part in the founding of the Second International.

1893   Engels attended International Socialist Workers' Congress in Zurich. Elected honorary president of Congress.

1894   Publication of Volume Three of *Capital*, edited by Engels.

1895   (August 5) Death of Engels.

Introduction

The Writings of Marx and Engels

ROBERT C. TUCKER

I

Marx, like many writers, published considerably less than he wrote. His early writings, presented in Part I of this book, include some that were published in 1844, soon after he wrote them, and some not destined to appear in print until the 1930s.

The most important of the latter group are the *Economic and Philosophic Manuscripts of 1844* and *The German Ideology* (Part I of which appears to have been one of Marx's contributions to this book written jointly by himself and Engels). He explained the non-publication of *The German Ideology* in the brief history of his opinions that he gave in the Preface to *A Contribution to the Critique of Political Economy*. As for the 1844 manuscripts, which were a very rough first sketch of his theory of history in notes and draft chapters of a projected treatise on the "criticism of political economy," these remained in a raw, unfinished state among his private papers. The papers came into Engels' possession after Marx's death in 1883, and went to the leaders of the German Social Democratic Party after Engels' death in 1895. After the Russian Revolution, the Marx-Engels Institute in Moscow acquired photocopies of the manuscript materials. Its director, the noted Marx scholar David Riazanov, took charge of the editing of the unpublished early writings, and, thanks largely to his labors, these writings finally came out in the 1920s and 1930s.[1] Later, Riazanov, like so many other prominent Russian Marxists, died in Stalin's purges.

Although reactions were somewhat slow in coming, the publication of the previously unknown early writings was a pivotal event in

---

1. The previously unpublished early writings of Marx first appeared in German in Karl Marx and Friedrich Engels, *Historisch-Kritische Gesamtausgabe*, edited by D. Riazanov. Volume I of this work, which is often cited as *MEGA*, came out in 1927 at Frankfurt, Germany. The 1844 manuscripts appeared in *MEGA*, Volume III, published in 1932 under the joint editorship of Riazanov and V. Adoratsky.

the history of Marxism and of scholarship about Marxism. Because they reflected the genesis and growth of the Marxist system of thought in the mind of its principal creator, the 1844 manuscripts and Part I of *The German Ideology* illuminated the origins of the system, its relation to post-Kantian German philosophy, and the meaning of some of Marx's basic concepts. Only then, in fact, did it become possible to trace in depth and detail, stage by stage, the emergence of Marxism.

The manner of Marxism's emergence was a subject that Marx and Engels left in some obscurity although they dealt with it now and then, for example in Engels' *Socialism: Utopian and Scientific*. But what they had to say was enigmatic. In Marxism, which has its foundation in what they variously called the "materialist conception of history" or "historical materialism,"[2] socialist thought had—they said—graduated from its earlier "utopian" stage and become "scientific." Whereas the "utopian" socialists had visualized a socialist reorganization of society as something that *ought* to be realized, the materialist conception of history had conclusively demonstrated that the human historical process was moving toward a worldwide anticapitalist revolution that would usher in socialism or communism (Marx and Engels tended to use these two words interchangeably).

Yet this "scientific socialism" of Marx and Engels was not in a direct line of descent from the teachings of the classical utopian socialists, the early-nineteenth-century fathers of modern socialist thought: Henri de Saint-Simon, Charles Fourier, and Robert Owen. Its immediate intellectual source was, rather, German philosophy, particularly that of Hegel. The materialist conception of history had originated in an inversion of Hegel's idealist conception of history, an intellectual operation whereby the Hegelian dialectic

2. The notion that Marxism has its foundation in "dialectical materialism," a general world-view of which historical materialism is the application to human history, is a later growth particularly associated with Russian and subsequently Communist Marxism, and is not the classical Marxist position. For Marx the prime subject of Marxism was human history, hence historical materialism was the foundation of the teaching. Moreover, historical materialism was itself dialectical in that the human historical process showed a revolutionary pattern of development through opposition and conflict. To this it must be added that Engels, who more than Marx was interested in the progress of natural science in the nineteenth century, did give an initial impetus to the later emergence of a Marxist "dialectical materialism" by his speculations on the presence of dialectical laws in natural processes. He began but never completed a book on this subject, the manuscript of which was first published in the twentieth century under the title *Dialectics of Nature*. The term "dialectical materialism" was put into currency by the Russian Marxist Georgi Plekhanov in one of his writings of the late nineteenth century. For a long while the authoritative version of Communist Marxism on this subject was the essay by Joseph Stalin, "Dialectical and Historical Materialism," published as a part of Chapter Four of the *History of the Communist Party of the Soviet Union (Bolsheviks)*. *Short Course* (Moscow: Foreign Languages Publishing House, many editions).

was, as Engels expressed it in one of his later writings, "placed upon its head; or rather, turned off its head, on which it was standing, and placed upon its feet."[3] This only repeated what Marx himself had written in 1873 in the Afterword to the second German edition of *Capital*, where he observed that thirty years earlier he had criticized the "mystifying side of Hegelian dialectic," and added: "The mystification which dialectic suffers in Hegel's hands, by no means prevents him from being the first to present its general form of working in a comprehensive and conscious manner. With him it is standing on its head. It must be turned right side up again, if you would discover the rational kernel within the mystical shell." So Marx and Engels.

The enigma mentioned above will now be apparent. Social theories normally do not originate through turning metaphysical systems of thought "right side up again." How could Marx's materialist conception of history arise by means of an inversion of Hegel's idealist conception? Hegel represents history as the self-realization of spirit (*Geist*) or God. The fundamental scheme of his theory is as follows. Spirit is self-creative energy imbued with a drive to become fully conscious of itself as spirit. Nature is spirit in its self-objectification in space; history is spirit in its self-objectification as culture—the succession of world-dominant civilizations from the ancient Orient to modern Europe. Spirit actualizes its nature as self-conscious being by the process of knowing. Through the mind of man, philosophical man in particular, the world achieves consciousness of itself as spirit. This process involves the repeated overcoming of spirit's "alienation" (*Entfremdung*) from itself, which takes place when spirit as the knowing mind confronts a world that appears, albeit falsely, as objective, i.e., as *other* than spirit. Knowing is recognition, whereby spirit destroys the illusory otherness of the objective world and recognizes it as actually subjective or *selbstisch*. The process terminates at the stage of "absolute knowledge," when spirit is finally and fully "at home with itself in its otherness," having recognized the whole of creation as spirit—Hegelianism itself being the scientific form of this ultimate self-knowledge on spirit's part. Such is the argument of Hegel's great work *The Phenomenology of Mind* (1807), on which he elaborated further in his later writings.

A philosophical tour de force this, but what does it have to do with Marxism? How could the materialist conception of history and "scientific socialism" be Hegelian in derivation? Marx and Engels asserted such a relationship in terms too clear for misunder-

3. *Ludwig Feuerbach and the End of Classical German Philosophy,* in Karl Marx and Frederick Engels, *Selected Works,* 2 vols. (Moscow: Foreign Languages Publishing House, 1962), vol. II, p. 387.

standing. Engels, to cite a further example, wrote the following about Hegel's system:

> Abstract and idealist though it was in form, yet the development of his thoughts always proceeded parallel with the development of world history and the latter is really meant to be only the test of the former. If, thereby, the real relation was inverted and stood on its head, nevertheless the *real content* entered everywhere into the philosophy; all the more so since Hegel—in contrast to his disciples—did not parade ignorance, but was one of the finest intellects of all time. . . . *This epoch-making conception of history was the direct theoretical premise for the new materialist outlook. . . .*[4]

But nowhere did Marx and Engels adequately explain just *how* Hegel's conception of history had served as the "direct theoretical premise" of Marxism. The materials needed for clarification of the matter did, however, exist—in Marx's desk drawer.

He alluded to this fact when he recalled in the 1873 Afterword to *Capital* that thirty years earlier he had criticized the "mystifying side of Hegelian dialectic." His reference could have been to either or both of two of his still-unpublished early writings: an unfinished commentary of 1843 on Hegel's *Philosophy of Right*, or the section of the 1844 manuscripts entitled "Critique of Hegel's Dialectic and Philosophy in General." Now that these and other early writings of Marx are available, Marxism's Hegelian derivation has ceased to be a mystery. Marx and Engels were correct in saying that Hegelianism had been the "direct theoretical premise" for the materialist conception of history. So great were the philosophical complexities of this transition, however, that the two men understandably refrained in their later years from offering a detailed explanation to their socialist followers, who in their majority were unversed and uninterested in post-Kantian German philosophy.

Briefly, Marx created his theory of history as a conscious act of *translation* of Hegel's theory into what he, Marx, took to be its valid or scientific form. In this he followed the procedure of the German philosopher Ludwig Feuerbach, author of *The Essence of Christianity* (1841), who had argued that Hegel's philosophy could reveal scientific truth if subjected to "transformational criticism." This consisted in the *inverting* of its principal propositions, meaning that one transposed subject and predicate in them. For Hegel man is spirit (or God) in the process of self-alienation and self-realization, i.e., man presents himself in history as self-alienated God. The truth, says Feuerbach, is just the reverse. Instead of seeing man as self-alienated God, we must see God as self-alienated man. That is, when man, the human species, projects an idealized

4. From a review, written in 1859, of *of Political Economy*. Italics added.
Marx's *A Contribution to the Critique*

image of itself into heaven as "God" and worships this imaginary heavenly being, it becomes estranged from itself; its own ungodly earthly reality becomes alien and hateful. To overcome this alienation man must repossess his alienated being, take "God" back into himself, recognize in man—and specifically in other human individuals—the proper object of care, love, and worship. Such is the basic argument of Feuerbach's *Essence of Christianity*. Transformational criticism of Hegel yields the theme that religion is a phenomenon of human self-estrangement. The conception of history as the self-realization of God or spirit through man is transformed into the conception of history as the self-realization of the human species via the detour of alienation in the sphere of religion. Hegelian idealism undergoes a metamorphosis and becomes Feuerbachian "humanism."

For Marx, as for others on the Hegelian left in Germany, Feuerbach's "transformational criticism" of Hegel was an intellectual innovation of epochal importance. The message that Hegelian theory has truth-value if one applies the method of inversion came with a ring of revelation. It meant that one could go on making good use of Hegel while escaping the toils of his colossal and seemingly so otherworldly system. One could discover social reality, the reality of the human predicament in history, by turning Hegel "right side up." Man was not the personification of spirit; rather, spirit was the thought-process taking place in man. But as Feuerbach had shown, this thought-process as depicted by Hegel was a reflection of the actual movement of history. The Hegelian picture of spirit alienated from itself was, on this reading, simply the philosopher's upside-down and hence "mystified" vision of the real social process, namely, *man's* alienation from himself in the material world. Furthermore, man's alienation could be traced out in other spheres than religion. The state, for example, was a sphere of human alienation, and could be exposed as such by applying to Hegel's *political* philosophy the same method of transformational criticism that Feuerbach had applied to his general theory of history. Marx undertook this work in 1843 in a critical commentary on Hegel's *Philosophy of Right*. He did not complete the commentary, but summed up the most important parts of its message in two articles published in 1844. In one of them, the essay "On the Jewish Question," he portrayed the political life of man as analogous to the religious life, as treated in *The Essence of Christianity*. Just as man projects the idealized attributes of the species into his image of a transcendent deity, so he projects social power into a separate sphere—the state—which dominates him. Here, however, the resulting division of man against himself is not a matter of the imagination simply but of institutional reality; and the escape from political alienation, unlike that from religious alienation, requires a real revolution—a collective act whereby the citizens repossess the social power externalized in state institutions.

Applying "transformational criticism" to Hegel's political philosophy, Marx inverted the Hegelian proposition on the relation between the state and "civil society" (*bürgerliche Gesellschaft*, by which Hegel meant the realm of private economic endeavor). Civil society was not an outgrowth of the state, as in Hegel's view; rather, the state was an outgrowth of civil society. The primary sphere of man's being was not his life as a citizen of the state but rather his economic life in civil society; this was the foundation on which all else rested. Having reached this position via the critical commentary on Hegel's *Philosophy of Right*,[5] Marx was approaching the end of the strange road leading him to the formulation of the materialist conception of history. Now he posed for himself the task of investigating the economic life as a sphere of human self-alienation. In pursuit of this aim he undertook an intensive study of Adam Smith and other classical theorists of political economy. In these economic writings, read in conjunction with Hegel, he hoped to find a key to the understanding of man's alienation as a producer of material goods. At some point in the course of these studies he was struck by the thought that was to prove the cornerstone of the Marxian system: the fundamental human reality reflected in a mystified way in Hegel's philosophy of history was the reality of man's alienation in economic life. This was the underlying master theme of the papers that we now know as the *Economic and Philosophic Manuscripts of 1844*.

Deciphering what he conceived to be the hidden meaning-content of Hegel's *Phenomenology of Mind*, Marx here formulated his own conception of history as a process of self-development of the human species culminating in communism. Man, according to this conception, is essentially a producer; and material production is the primary form of his producing activity, industry being the externalized productive powers of the species. In the course of his history, which Marx described as a "history of production," a world of created objects gradually arises around man. Original nature is overlaid with a man-made or "anthropological nature." And Marx believed that this was the true or scientific restatement of the Hegelian conception. For had not Hegel seen the history of the world as a production-history on the part of spirit? His error had been to mystify the process by treating the productive activity as *spirit* activity. To move from mystification to reality, from philosophy to science, one had only to turn Hegel on his head. Then it appeared that the Hegelian image of spirit creating a world was simply a philosopher's distorted picture of the reality of history, namely, that man—working man—creates a world in *material* productive activities over the centuries. Inevitably, therefore, Marx later named his transformed Hegelianism the "materialist conception of history."

Still following Hegel's basic scheme, Marx in the 1844 manuscripts visualized the human history of production as being also a history of estrangement (*Entfremdungsgeschichte*). Man's nature, he postulated, was to be a "free conscious producer," but so far he had not been able to express himself freely in productive activity. He had been driven to produce by need and greed, by a passion for accumulation which in the modern bourgeois age becomes accumulation of capital. His productive activity had always, therefore, been involuntary; it had been "labour." And since man, when he produces involuntarily, is estranged from his human nature, labour is "alienated labour."[6] Escape from alienated labour finally becomes materially possible in the stage of technological development created by modern machine industry. The way of escape lies in the revolutionary seizure and socialization of the productive powers by the proletariat. Repossessed through revolution of his organs of material production externalized in industry, man will at last be able to produce in freedom. Human self-realization will be attained on the scale of all humanity. So Marx defined communism in the 1844 manuscripts as "transcendence of human self-alienation" and "positive humanism." He saw it as the real future situation that Hegel had dimly adumbrated at the close of his *Phenomenology*, where spirit, having attained absolute knowledge, is beyond all alienation and fully "at home with itself in its otherness." Working man would no longer be confronted by an alienated world of objects appropriated as private property. He would dwell in aesthetic communion with an "anthropological nature" transformed into the common possession of all. Man would realize his human nature as a free conscious producer, engaging in a variety of creative activities no longer actuated by the drive to accumulate property.

Such was Marxism in its original formulation in Marx's manuscripts of 1844, for which Hegelianism was indeed the direct theoretical premise. This "original Marxism" was the foundation of the mature Marxist system, the matrix of the materialist conception of history as encountered in the later writings of Marx and Engels. We have evidence of this in the fact that there was no significant hiatus in time between the initial statement of the Marxist position in the manuscripts, which Marx completed in August of 1844, and

6. This is a main theme of the important section of the 1844 manuscripts on *entfremdete Arbeit*. The latter phrase may be translated either "alienated labour" or "estranged labour" (see pp. 56–67, below).

the systematic formulation of the materialist conception of history that he gave in Part One of *The German Ideology*. He laid out some of the underlying main themes of the latter in the spring of 1845 in a set of notes that have come down to us under the title "Theses on Feuerbach." He also expounded the theory to Engels, with whom he met in Brussels at that time. Marx had the theory of history "ready worked out" by then, recalled Engels in a note to the 1890 edition of the *Communist Manifesto*. The theory that Marx was able to set forth orally and in writing by the spring of 1845 must have been the one blocked out in his manuscripts of the previous year.

As the reader will see, there are numerous differences between these two early versions of Marxism. The German philosophical terminology, and therefore also the philosophical foundations, are far more clearly apparent in the manuscripts than in Part One of *The German Ideology*. The concept of man's alienation, which plays so central a part in the first formulation, is no longer an *explicit* centerpiece of the theory as reformulated. Now we are in the more impersonal world of Marxian social theory as made familiar in the later writings, with their characteristic emphasis upon class struggle as the driving force of history. The ethical themes so strikingly present in the manuscripts, such as the notion of "positive humanism" as the goal of human history, are not so salient now. All these changes have presented problems for contemporary scholarship in Marx studies, and should certainly not be dismissed as of small importance. But neither, on the other hand, should they be overemphasized, as though there were some profound rift between original and later Marxism. It appears, for example, that much of the content of the idea of man's alienation lives on in the mature Marx in the meaning that he and Engels assign to the concept "division of labour." The moral theme in Marxism arising out of its view of alienation as an evil, and something destined to be abolished by a final worldwide revolution, remains present in later Marxism's representation of the division of labour as an evil that has plagued man all through his history, in different ways, and will be ended by the proletarian revolution. Scholarly opinion is inclining, and in my opinion will increasingly incline, to the view that there is an underlying basic continuity of thought not only between the 1844 manuscripts and *The German Ideology*, but more broadly between the early Marx and the Marx of the later writings culminating in *Capital*.[7]

But the significance of the now-discovered early Marx goes far

7. The account given here of the origin and development of Marx's thought follows the lines of the interpretation presented in greater length and detail, with supporting evidence, in Robert C. Tucker, *Philosophy and Myth in Karl Marx* (New York: Cambridge University Press, 1961).

beyond these questions of the intellectual development of Marxism and its exegesis. The early writings are of very considerable intrinsic interest. The 1844 manuscripts disclose a strangely modern youthful Marx speaking in accents almost of an existentialist philosopher, a Marx alive to psychological themes of interest to many in the second half of the twentieth century. Some European existentialists have recognized a kindred mind in Marx, and one influential thinker of the psychoanalytic school has made use of some of the ideas of the manuscripts in formulating a neo-Freudian philosophy of man.[8] Many in Russia and Eastern Europe, reacting against Stalinism and the dreary orthodoxy of official Communist Marxism, have found support and inspiration in the early Marx for a new, morally aware, critical Marxism—a Marxism that sees the possibility of alienation not only in bourgeois societies but in those officially called "socialist." For these reasons, among others, the early writings that Marx left unfinished and unpublished are widely read today.

II

The German word *Kritik*, which may be translated as either "criticism" or "critique," is a symbol of great importance for comprehending the mental world of Marx and Engels. It was the watchword of the circle of Young Hegelians with whom they were associated at the end of the 1830s and the beginning of the 1840s. Marx interpreted it in a spirit of radical negation of social reality, as reflected in his letter of 1843 to Arnold Ruge calling for a "ruthless criticism of everything existing." In his essay of 1844, "Contribution to the Critique of Hegel's *Philosophy of Right*," he elaborated his concept and program of criticism and pointed to the proletariat as the real social force destined to carry out criticism's verdict by overthrowing the existing order. In *The Holy Family: A Critique of Critical Criticism* (1845), Marx and Engels proclaimed their break with the Young Hegelian group. But no break with the idea of *Kritik* was intended.

In addition, as we have seen, Marx learned from Feuerbach a specific technique of critical thought involving the use of Hegel. By means of this technique Feuerbach had produced a criticism of religion as a phenomenon of human self-alienation. Taking up the critical enterprise in this sense, Marx produced, first, a criticism of the state as a phenomenon of human self-alienation, and then, in his

8. I am referring to Erich Fromm's *Man for Himself* (New York: Holt, Rinehart & Winston, 1947). See also his autobiographical study, *Beyond the Chains of Illusion: My Encounter with Marx and Freud* (New York: Simon & Schuster, 1962). For a discussion of Marx from an existentialist viewpoint, see F. H. Heinemann, *Existentialism and the Modern Predicament* (New York: Harper & Row, 1958).

manuscripts of 1844, the beginnings of what he called a "criticism of political economy." Engels, who acquired a deep interest in economics still earlier through working in his father's firm and being exposed to economic realities at the site of its English branch in Manchester, preceded Marx in undertaking a criticism of political economy. He produced an essay, "Outlines of a Critique of Political Economy," which appeared, along with Marx's essays on the Jewish question and the Hegelian *Philosophy of Right*, in the *Deutsch-Französische Jahrbücher* of 1844. Marx's references to this essay in the prefaces to his 1844 manuscripts and *A Contribution to the Critique of Political Economy* testify to the influence that it had upon him at the time it appeared.

"This political economy or science of enrichment born of the merchants' mutual envy and greed," wrote Engels at the beginning of his 1844 essay, "bears on its brow the mark of the most loathsome selfishness." The essay addressed itself to this argument through a systematic analysis of the categories of the "science of enrichment." In conclusion Engels referred to the factory system and announced his future intention to "expound in detail the despicable immorality of this system, and to expose mercilessly the economist's hypocrisy which here appears in all its glitter."[9] The projected work did not materialize, but Engels did publish in 1845, based on his English observations, *The Condition of the Working Class in England in 1844*. Strictly descriptive though this work was, it was obviously concerned with exposing the "despicable immorality of this system."[1] It was a work of *Kritik*.

Elsewhere I have suggested that Marx was a writer who spent the greater part of his life writing one important book under a number of different titles. In the 1844 manuscripts he set out to produce a *Kritik* of political economy, seeking to demonstrate, in terms of the categories of political economy, man's alienation as a worker in bourgeois society. Having achieved in these papers a sketch of his entire world-view, he set the manuscripts aside but in a few years time returned to the task he had posed for himself. *Wage Labour and Capital*, written in 1847, was a sort of prospectus for the full-scale *Kritik* of political economy that he was determined to write. In 1859 he published a not very successful beginning of the work under the title *A Contribution to the Critique of Political Economy*. Meanwhile, in 1857–58 he had written a huge new set of manuscripts that would one day be published under the

9. Karl Marx, *The Economic and Philosophic Manuscripts of 1844*, edited by Dirk J. Struik (New York: International Publishers, 1964), pp. 197, 226. Engels' "Outlines of a Critique of Political Economy" appears here as an appendix.

1. See in this connection the selection included here under the title "Working-Class Manchester" (pp. 429–435, below).

title *Fundamentals of the Critique of Political Economy*.[2] When he finally completed the work and published it in 1867 under the title of *Capital*, he subtitled it *Critique of Political Economy*. In short, *Capital* was the form in which Marx finally finished the book on the criticism of political economy that he had originally undertaken in his manuscripts of 1844.

The idea of *Kritik* is, then, a great unifying theme running through the writings of classical Marxism, and a key to the continuity of the thought of Marx and Engels from their youthful philosophical writings to the productions of their mature years. Although they devoted a great deal of energy to economic analysis and contributed writings—especially *Capital*—that constitute a significant and influential chapter in economic thought, they did so not as political economists in the ordinary sense but as *critics* of political economy. As such they wrote from a position that we can variously describe as moral, normative, or philosophical. It would be a great mistake, therefore, to think of the writings gathered in Part II of this volume as belonging to a compartment called "Marxian economics," separate from the remainder of their thought. These writings are in the mainstream of their thought about society and history, their revolutionary outlook, and their socialism. The serious student of Marx must get to know *Capital* as Marx's major book about man. As the attentive reader of these pages will discover, it is the book, too, into which he poured his views on a miscellany of topics of general interest, such as education, the family and its future, the implications of modern technological development, and so on.

For all its tortuous complexity and abstruseness of argument, *Capital* (I refer here to Volume One) is fairly simple in basic theme and design. It could be viewed as an eight-hundred-page elaboration of the passage from *The Holy Family*[3] speaking of private property and the proletariat as opposites forming an antagonistic "whole" that is moving toward its own ultimate dissolution because of private property's inherent tendency to generate more and more proletariat, which in turn is "conscious of itself as a dehumanization and hence abolishes itself." In *Capital* the antagonistic "whole" is presented as wage labour (*Lohnarbeit*) or, alternatively, as the capital-labour relationship—this being the relationship of production constitutive of capitalism itself as a mode of

2. *Grundrisse der Kritik der politischen Ökonomie* (Moscow, 1939–41). A partial English translation of these manuscripts appears in Karl Marx, *The Grundrisse*, edited and translated by David McLellan (New York: Harper & Row, 1971). See also the section contained in Karl Marx, *Pre-Capitalist Economic Formations*, translated by Jack Cohen and edited with an introduction by Eric J. Hobsbawm (New York: International Publishers, 1964). 3. See the selection entitled "Alienation and Social Classes," pp. 104–106, below.

production.[4] For Marx this relationship of production is the "basis" of bourgeois society, over which arises the institutional and ideological "superstructure." The real subject of the book, in his mind, is bourgeois society.

In wage labour, the argument runs, the worker sells to the capitalist employer the only commodity that he possesses, his labour power, and receives in recompense a wage reflecting this commodity's "value." Since, on Marx's assumptions about value, the value of any commodity is equivalent to the amount of average necessary labour time incorporated in it, the value of one day's labour power as a commodity is the monetary equivalent of the amount of resources required to keep the worker alive and at work and able to reproduce his kind, i.e., it is a subsistence wage. But when put to use by the capitalist for a day, this labour power is capable, Marx reasons, of producing a certain amount of value over and above its own value. This Marx calls "surplus value" (*Mehrwert*), and he characterizes capitalism as a system geared to the maximizing of surplus value through intense—and ever-intensifying—exploitation of labour power to the utmost extent sufferable by "that repellent yet elastic natural barrier, man." Further, surplus value has two forms. "Absolute surplus value," meaning the excess of new value created in a day over the value of the labour power bought by the capitalist, can be increased by lengthening the working day itself. "Relative surplus value," arising out of improvements in technology that reduce the necessary labour time invested in labour power, can be obtained by mechanization of production processes and therewith the degree of specialization in the factory, so that the worker becomes a detail labourer performing ever more minute and monotonous operations. The capitalists are driven willy-nilly by the imperatives of their situation to accumulate capital by increasing surplus value along both these lines, so that "in proportion as capital accumulates, the lot of the labourer, be his payment high or low, must grow worse." The "absolute general law of capitalist accumulation," as Marx christens it, "establishes an accumulation of misery, corresponding with accumulation of capital. Accumulation of wealth at one pole is, therefore, at the same time accumulation of misery, agony of toil, slavery, ignorance, brutality, mental degradation, at the opposite pole. . . ." This conclusion of the argument points to the violent breakdown of the "whole" that Marx heralds toward the end of the book, where he speaks of the coming "expropriation of a few usurpers by the mass of the people."

Capital was written by an angry man, and one can hardly read it without sensing the indignation that he felt in the face of the phe-

4. On Marx's use of the terms "mode of production" and "relations of production," see Robert C. Tucker, *The* *Marxian Revolutionary Idea* (New York: W. W. Norton, 1969), chapter 1.

nomena with which he was concerned. The great *Kritik* of political economy is a work of analysis and description, but also of moral condemnation and protest. The word "alienation" may be missing, but the theme is not.[5] *Capital*'s proletarian is still *The Holy Family*'s "dehumanization which is conscious of itself as a dehumanization and hence abolishes itself." What was called "alienated labour" in the manuscripts of 1844 appears here simply as "wage labour." Now the object of study is subjected to endless analysis in terms of the labour theory of value and to lavish documentation out of the annals of British factory inspectors' reports, but it is the same object, and the viewpoint taken toward it is also the same.

The basis of the moral condemnation of wage labour is not that the wages are too low,[6] but that wage labour by its very nature dehumanizes man. This means, for Marx, that it defeats his natural human urge toward spontaneous productive activity, converts his free creativity into forced labour and drudgery, and frustrates his human need for a variety of occupations. The latter theme—the division of labour or occupational specialization as an evil—is a salient one in *Capital*; and the history of the evolution of the modern factory system that Marx gives in Part IV of the book is not presented out of an interest in economic history per se but as a means of describing the horrifying extremes that the division of labour attains under the "machinofacture" developed during the Industrial Revolution. As he expresses his view here, ". . . constant labour of one uniform kind disturbs the intensity and flow of a man's animal spirits, which find recreation and delight in mere change of activity." That this was Engels' view as well, and more generally that the condemnation of division of labour as an evil belongs to the core of classical Marxism, is well illustrated in the section of Engels' *Anti-Dühring* that has been included in the present volume under the heading "On the Division of Labour in Production."

In their later writings, then, Marx and Engels are still writing from the standpoint summed up in Marx's 1844 manuscripts as "positive humanism." They are writing on behalf of a socialism that means to them not a new system of distribution (though that, too, they are sure, will come about) but a new mode of productive activity that is to be achieved through the revolutionary liberation

5. Dirk J. Struik has pointed out that Marx does not completely renounce the term "alienation" in his later economic writings. It makes a reappearance in the *Grundrisse* and in the following passage from *Capital*, Vol. III, Part I, chapter 5, section 1: "The relations of capital conceal indeed the inner connection (of the facts) in the complete indifference, exteriorization and alienation in which it places the worker in relation to the conditions of the reali-

zation of his own labour" (*The Economic and Philosophic Manuscripts of 1844*, p. 235).
6. For Marx's scorn of the distributive orientation in socialist thought, see particularly his comments in *The Critique of the Gotha Program*, pp. 382–398, below. On the problem of distributive justice in Marx, see Tucker, *The Marxian Revolutionary Idea*, chapter 2.

of human productiveness from the bonds of factory toil for the accumulation of "surplus value." They advanced no particular name for this new mode of production, but described it in various places as the free activity of human beings producing in cooperative association. The socialization of the means of production was not, on this view, the essence of socialism or communism, but only its precondition.

III

Although born of German philosophy, Marxism from the beginning eschewed philosophy's contemplative attitude toward the world and adopted as its own the standpoint of the "unity of theory and practice." In the familiar words of Marx's eleventh thesis on Feuerbach, "The philosophers have only *interpreted* the world, in various ways; the point is to *change* it." Apart from being a critical comment on former philosophy, this statement had a biographical meaning. Not content with theorizing about a revolution in the abstract, Marx and Engels concerned themselves deeply with the strategy and tactics of a socialist revolution, the organizing of revolutionary activity, the politics of world-change. In the materials gathered in Part III of this volume, and also in the political journalism represented in Part IV, we see the reflection of this side of their activity.

In Marx's and Engels' own minds, it should be added, there was no clear demarcation line between their theoretical work and their practical and organizing activities. For various reasons they would hardly have agreed with the statement of their future Russian disciple, Lenin, that "without a revolutionary theory there can be no revolutionary movement."[7] They thought of a revolutionary movement as a spontaneous phenomenon of mass rebelliousness generated by conditions of existence that people find intolerable, hence not something dependent on a revolutionary theory for its emergence. Both *The German Ideology* and the *Communist Manifesto* offer unequivocal testimony on this point. But on the other hand, Marx and Engels believed that a correct revolutionary theory could powerfully *assist* a revolutionary movement by providing explanations and orienting its members to the movement's proper ends and means. Their own theorizing appeared to them an historic case in point. The Marxist theory was simply the contemporary proletarian revolutionary movement—an ongoing or incipient phenomenon in every industrial society—come to full programmatic consciousness.

7. *What Is to Be Done*, in V. I. Lenin, *Selected Works* (Moscow: Foreign Languages Publishing House, 1946), p. 165. By "movement" in this context Lenin meant an organized political movement led by a political party.

It was the prospectus of the revolutionary process taking place in bourgeois society, explaining its underlying causes and foretelling its preordained future course and outcome. By their theorizing as such, therefore, they were actively influencing historical events. Such, at any rate, was their view.

An obvious implication of this reasoning was that everything possible should be done to disseminate knowledge of the Marxist revolutionary theory and secure its acceptance by the organized workers' movement. The *Communist Manifesto* is an outstanding example of such effort. Marx's powerful polemical tract on *The Civil War in France*, an account of the Paris Commune and its suppression, may also be seen in this light. To explain the Paris Revolution of September, 1870–May, 1871, according to the canons of Marxist theory and assess its historic meaning in Marxist terms was to show Marxism's cogency as a mode of understanding contemporary historical reality and thereby to enhance its influence on educated minds. So successful was the pamphlet in achieving this purpose that one later historian of the socialist movement dates the widespread impact of Marxism from that time.[8] Much of the political journalism of Marx and Engels appears to have had, at least in part, a similar motivation. They propagated Marxism by seeking to demonstrate its applicability to current events. In *The Eighteenth Brumaire of Louis Bonaparte*, to take a particularly important example, Marx recounted the recent political history of France in a Marxist frame of reference. The result in this instance, as in some others, was a work of journalism that has taken its place also as a classic of Marxist historiography.

The nineteenth century was a birth-time of socialist theories and programs. Since Marxism at mid-century was only one of numerous available versions of socialist thought, its propagation by Marx and Engels was a highly competitive enterprise. In *The German Ideology* they attacked and ridiculed the doctrines of their fellow German "true socialists." A year later, in 1847, Marx published *The Poverty of Philosophy*, a polemic against the theories of the French socialist and anarchist thinker Pierre Joseph Proudhon. In the ensuing decades he and Engels waged a long-drawn-out struggle against Proudhonism and generally against the anarchist persuasion

8. "The work of Marx on the Civil War of 1871 has an extraordinary historical significance: for by this bold step Marx annexed the memory of the Commune. It is only since then that Marxism has possessed a revolutionary tradition in the eyes of mankind. By 1870 Marx had already acquired a reputation as an outstanding theoretician of the labour motivement, but the general public knew nothing of the political and revolutionary activity of the Marxists. . . . It is only since 1871 that Marxism has been clearly associated with the labour revolution. . . . In this manner Marx provided an important tradition for the future movements of the working class, and he placed his own doctrines in the centre of these movements" (Arthur Rosenberg, *Democracy and Socialism* [Boston: Beacon Press, 1965], pp. 204–205).

in socialism, one of whose leading proponents in the later nineteenth century was the Russian revolutionary Mikhail Bakunin. Paradoxically, the Paris Commune of 1871 was, in its decentralizing measures, a victory of the Proudhonian influence, but this in no way inhibited Marx and Engels from hailing the Commune as a harbinger of the realization of the Marxist theory of history and hence claiming it for Marxism.[9] Another arena of their competitive struggle for the dominance of the Marxist theory was German working-class politics, in which a prominent part was played by the gifted political leader Ferdinand Lassalle. Their fight against Lassallean doctrinal influences continued unabated after Lassalle's death in 1864 and finally was immortalized in a set of notes by Marx that was published posthumously under the title *Critique of the Gotha Program* and has since taken its place as one of Marxism's major programmatic statements.

The International Working Men's Association, founded in London in 1864 by representatives of the English, French, German, and Italian workers as an international coordinating body for the working-class movements of these and other countries, offered an important forum for the propagation of Marxism. Although he was present at the founding meeting of the association, now better known as the First International, Marx was not one of its original organizers. Subsequently, however, he played a leading part in its affairs. In drafting the rules of the association, he prefaced them with an "Inaugural Address" written in his characteristically forceful and incisive manner. Although he had to hold the revolutionary rhetoric in check because of constraints arising from the diverse membership of this loose federation of worker groups from different countries, he managed to formulate the Address in the spirit of Marxist doctrine and make of it a kind of successor-document to the *Communist Manifesto*. Later, when the fall of the Paris Commune made European revolutionary prospects and hence those of the International appear dim for the time being, Marx was concerned lest Bakunin and the anarchists acquire a decisive influence in the association. He therefore proposed, at its Hague Congress in 1872, that the headquarters be moved to New York. The ensuing transfer to America signaled the International's demise.

Marxism was not a party doctrine in its inception, nor did Marx and Engels originally envisage it as the formal ideology of a political party. The Communist League, on whose behalf they wrote the *Communist Manifesto*, was not a political party but only a group of a few hundred German journeymen workers living in Paris, Brus-

9. See *ibid.*, pp. 202–205, for further particulars and a discussion of this issue.

sels, and London. In the *Manifesto,* moreover, Marx and Engels explicitly disclaimed the notion that the communists (i.e., the Marxists) should form themselves into a separate party, or that they should "set up any sectarian principles of their own, by which to shape and mould the proletarian movement." The communists, they went on, were simply the most consistently radical representatives of the proletarian movement and those with clear theoretical understanding of its conditions and aims. In later years, however, Marx and Engels shifted their ground in response to the rise of working-class political parties in a number of European countries, Germany in particular. A General German Workers' Society arose in 1863 under Lassalle. Three years later a German Social Democratic Workers' Party was founded under the leadership of Wilhelm Liebknecht, a longtime follower of Marx. The merger of the two groups in 1875 established the German Social Democrats as the leading working-class political party of Western Europe, with Marxist socialism as its ideology; and similar parties emerged in Italy, Austria, France, and elsewhere. Although the name "Social Democrat" did not please them,[1] Marx and Engels welcomed the rise of socialist working-class parties professing Marxism as their platform.

The irony of this development was that Marxism's very success in the struggle for supremacy in working-class politics of the later nineteenth century endangered what Lenin later called its "revolutionary soul." Although officially dedicated to Marxist principles of the revolutionary transformation of society, the Social Democratic parties were not really very radical. In some instances, such as in Germany, they were associated with organized trade union movements whose aims were basically reformist. Finally, increasing electoral success gave them both a place and a stake in the existing order, and encouraged the tendency of the party leaderships to look to the ballot box and the gradual conquest of political power by peaceful parliamentary means as the highroad to a socialist reshaping of society. The concern this aroused in Marx and Engels is clearly shown in their "Circular Letter" of September 17–18, 1879, to Bebel, Liebknecht, and other German Social Democratic leaders.

1. When informed in 1864 that the newspaper of the General German Workers' Society would be called *The Social Democrat,* Engels wrote to Marx: "What a disgusting title—*The Social Democrat!* Why don't those fellows frankly call the thing: *The Proletarian?*" Marx answered: "*Social Democrat* is a bad title. Yet one shouldn't immediately use the best title for something which may turn out to be a failure" (Rosenberg, *Democracy and Socialism,* p. 162). A Russian Social Democratic Workers' Party came into existence in 1898. In 1917, out of disgust with the behavior of the Social Democratic leaders of various countries who had supported their governments in World War I in contravention of Marxist internationalism, Lenin persuaded his Bolshevik branch of the Russian Social Democratic Party to change its name to "Communist Party."

It castigated the spirit of reformism spreading in the German party and insisted upon fidelity to the revolutionary class struggle as the only possible means of freeing the working classes.

Marx died in 1883 and Engels survived him by twelve years during which the German Social Democrats continued their advance at the polls. In an essay published in 1895 that proved to be his own valedictory to the Social Democratic movement,[2] Engels seemed to soften the Circular Letter's insistence on revolutionary class struggle as the only acceptable political strategy for a Marxist party. At any rate, he allowed that classic street-fighting on the barricades had largely been rendered obsolete by technological improvements favoring the military, and hailed the German Social Democrats' two million voters as "the decisive 'shock force' of the international proletarian army." But on close reading, particularly after restoration of those passages excised from the essay by the editors when it was originally published in 1895, Engels' concluding discourse on tactics turns out to be by no means an endorsement of Social Democratic reformism. His commitment to the Marxian revolutionary idea held firm to the end. For the older Engels, no less than for the younger Marx, the point was to change the world radically.

IV

The meetings between Marx and Engels in Paris in August, 1844, and in Brussels in April, 1845, inaugurated a partnership that continued unbroken to Marx's death nearly forty years after. Indeed, it continued beyond that time, for Engels devoted his final years to carrying forward the work on which he and his friend had been engaged together for so long. Intellectual history offers few if any comparable examples of lifelong collaboration between innovative minds. How shall we assess the relative weight of their contributions?

In a footnote to an essay of 1886, Engels answered this question as follows:

> I cannot deny that both before and during my forty years' collaboration with Marx I had a certain independent share in laying the foundations of the theory, and more particularly in its elaboration. But the greater part of its leading basic principles, especially in the realm of economics and history, belong to Marx. What I contributed—at any rate with the exception of my work in a few special fields—Marx could very well have done without me. What Marx accomplished I would not have achieved. Marx stood higher, saw further, and took a wider and quicker view

2. Engels, "The Tactics of Social Democracy," pp. 406–423, below.

than all the rest of us. Marx was a genius; we others were at best talented. Without him the theory would not be by far what it is today. It therefore rightly bears his name.[3]

This generous tribute rightly recognized that Marx's mind was the forge of the system. True, Engels during his first sojourn in Manchester had independently and somewhat earlier than Marx come to the view that economics is the decisively important force in history, and his "Outlines of a Critique of Political Economy" had helped to inspire Marx's first attempt at such a critique. Yet Marxism as a transformed Hegelianism, a theory of history in the grand style, was essentially, as we have seen, Marx's creation. He was the seer and system-builder in relation to whom the merely talented Engels was bound to play a subordinate part.

But after acknowledging this, it must also be said that Engels was misleadingly modest concerning his own contributions. The Marx-Engels correspondence reflects a two-way process of collaboration in which Engels gave theoretical assistance to Marx—for example, on various problems encountered in the writing of *Capital*—as well as vice versa. Engels' independent contributions were substantial too, both in the works that he and Marx wrote jointly and in some that he produced on his own. One of the special fields of his expertise was military affairs and strategy. Another was natural science, and his writings on this subject—including the papers posthumously published under the title *Dialectics of Nature*—gave the impetus to the rise of "dialectical materialism" as a Marxist teaching about nature. Whether one feels that Marxism was enriched or vulgarized by the latter development, its importance is undeniable. Still another area of Engels' work was primitive society. He carried out Marx's unfulfilled plan of writing a treatise based upon the American anthropologist Lewis Henry Morgan's *Ancient Society*. The resulting work on *The Origin of the Family, Private Property and the State*[4] provided Marxism with an anthropology.

As the writings gathered in Part V of this volume show, moreover, one of Engels' greatest services consisted in the systematizing and popularizing of Marxism. Marx was the great system-builder, yet he never managed in the writings published during his lifetime to set forth the fundamentals of the system in easily understandable terms in an essay or short book; *Capital* was not bedtime reading for the masses. Engels made good this deficiency. He lacked the supremely trenchant style of Marx, who wrote as though his pen were dipped in molten anger. But Engels' beautifully clear and free-flowing prose was ideally suited to the popularizing work to

3. Engels, *Ludwig Feuerbach and the End of Classical German Philosophy*, p. 386.

4. A selection from this work appears below, pp. 651–659.

which he applied himself. In a number of letters on historical materialism[5] he attempted to clarify the economic interpretation of history and deal with certain questions that had arisen concerning it. His *Anti-Dühring* gave a running exposition of Marxism in the course of a polemic against one of its critics, and the portion of it published in 1880 under the title *Socialism: Utopian and Scientific* probably did more than any other single book to disseminate knowledge of Marxism. Engels even undertook to bring *Capital* to the wide public by writing nine different reviews of it, seven of which achieved publication at the time.

Paraphrasing Engels, one could say that without him Marxism would not be by far what it became. His gifts and Marx's were in large measure complementary. Classical Marxism is an amalgam in which Engels' work constitutes an essential and inalienable part.

5. See below, pp. 640–650.

PART I

The Early Marx

Marx on the History of His Opinions

This is the preface to Marx's book *A Contribution to the Critique of Political Economy,* first published in 1859. The passage setting forth the materialist conception of history—one of the few general statements of the theory that Marx gave in his middle and later years—is the *locus classicus* of historical materialism. But the preface is also important as an account by Marx himself of the formative period of Marxism. As such it forms an appropriate introduction to the writings of 1843–1846 gathered here in Part I. The "criticism of post-Hegelian philosophy" which he mentions in the third-to-last paragraph is a reference to his work *The German Ideology,* written jointly with Engels.

---

* * * I am omitting a general introduction which I had jotted down because on closer reflection any anticipation of results still to be proved appears to me to be disturbing, and the reader who on the whole desires to follow me must be resolved to ascend from the particular to the general. A few indications concerning the course of my own politico-economic studies may, on the other hand, appear in place here.

I was taking up law, which discipline, however, I only pursued as a subordinate subject along with philosophy and history. In the year 1842–44, as editor of the *Rheinische Zeitung,*[1] I experienced for the first time the embarrassment of having to take part in discussions on so-called material interests. The proceedings of the Rhenish Landtag on thefts of wood and parcelling of landed property, the official polemic which Herr von Schaper, then *Oberpräsident* of the Rhine Province, opened against the *Rheinische Zeitung* on the conditions of the Moselle peasantry, and finally debates on free trade and protective tariffs provided the first occasions for occupying myself with economic questions. On the other hand, at that time when the good will "to go further" greatly outweighed knowledge of the subject, a philosophically weakly tinged echo of French socialism and communism made itself audible in the *Rheinische Zeitung.* I declared myself against this amateurism, but

1. *Rheinische Zeitung* (*Rhenish Gazette*): A daily radical newspaper published in Cologne in 1842–43; from October 15, 1842, to March 18, 1843, its editor was Marx.

3

frankly confessed at the same time in a controversy with the *All-gemeine Augsburger Zeitung*[2] that my previous studies did not permit me even to venture any judgement on the content of the French tendencies. Instead, I eagerly seized on the illusion of the managers of the *Rheinische Zeitung,* who thought that by a weaker attitude on the part of the paper they could secure a remission of the death sentence passed upon it, to withdraw from the public stage into the study.

The first work which I undertook for a solution of the doubts which assailed me was a critical review of the Hegelian philosophy of right, a work the introduction to which appeared in 1844 in the *Deutsch-Französische Jahrbücher,*[3] published in Paris. My investigation led to the result that legal relations as well as forms of state are to be grasped neither from themselves nor from the so-called general development of the human mind, but rather have their roots in the material conditions of life, the sum total of which Hegel, following the example of the Englishmen and Frenchmen of the eighteenth century, combines under the name of "civil society," that, however, the anatomy of civil society is to be sought in political economy. The investigation of the latter, which I began in Paris, I continued in Brussels, whither I had emigrated in consequence of an expulsion order of M. Guizot. The general result at which I arrived and which, once won, served as a guiding thread for my studies, can be briefly formulated as follows: In the social production of their life, men enter into definite relations that are indispensable and independent of their will, relations of production which correspond to a definite stage of development of their material productive forces. The sum total of these relations of production constitutes the economic structure of society, the real foundation, on which rises a legal and political superstructure and to which correspond definite forms of social consciousness. The mode of production of material life conditions the social, political and intellectual life process in general. It is not the consciousness of men that determines their being, but, on the contrary, their social being that determines their consciousness. At a certain stage of their development, the material productive forces of society come in conflict with the existing relations of production, or—what is but a legal expression for the same thing—with the property relations within which they have been at work hitherto. From forms of development of the productive forces these relations turn into their

2. Marx has in mind his article, "Der Kommunismus und die *Augsburger Allgemeine Zeitung*" (Communism and the *Augsburg General Journal*), *Marx-Engels Gesamtausgabe,* Abt. I, B. I, Halbband I, Frankfurt a. M. 1927, S. 260–65.

3. *Deutsch-Französische Jahrbücher* (German-French Annals): Organ of revolutionary and communist propaganda, published by Marx in Paris in 1844.

fetters. Then begins an epoch of social revolution. With the change of the economic foundation the entire immense superstructure is more or less rapidly transformed. In considering such transformations a distinction should always be made between the material transformation of the economic conditions of production, which can be determined with the precision of natural science, and the legal, political, religious, aesthetic or philosophic—in short, ideological forms in which men become conscious of this conflict and fight it out. Just as our opinion of an individual is not based on what he thinks of himself, so can we not judge of such a period of transformation by its own consciousness; on the contrary, this consciousness must be explained rather from the contradictions of material life, from the existing conflict between the social productive forces and the relations of production. No social order ever perishes before all the productive forces for which there is room in it have developed; and new, higher relations of production never appear before the material conditions of their existence have matured in the womb of the old society itself. Therefore mankind always sets itself only such tasks as it can solve; since, looking at the matter more closely, it will always be found that the task itself arises only when the material conditions for its solution already exist or are at least in the process of formation. In broad outlines Asiatic, ancient, feudal, and modern bourgeois modes of production can be designated as progressive epochs in the economic formation of society. The bourgeois relations of production are the last antagonistic form of the social process of production—antagonistic not in the sense of individual antagonism, but of one arising from the social conditions of life of the individuals; at the same time the productive forces developing in the womb of bourgeois society create the material conditions for the solution of that antagonism. This social formation brings, therefore, the prehistory of human society to a close.

Frederick Engels, with whom, since the appearance of his brilliant sketch on the criticism of the economic categories (in the *Deutsch-Französische Jahrbücher*), I maintained a constant exchange of ideas by correspondence, had by another road (compare his *The Condition of the Working Class in England in 1844*) arrived at the same result as I, and when in the spring of 1845 he also settled in Brussels, we resolved to work out in common the opposition of our view to the ideological view of German philosophy, in fact, to settle accounts with our erstwhile philosophical conscience. The resolve was carried out in the form of a criticism of post-Hegelian philosophy. The manuscript, two large octavo volumes, had long reached its place of publication in Westphalia when we received the news that altered circumstances did not allow of its being printed. We abandoned the manuscript to the gnawing criticism of the mice all the more willingly as we had achieved our main purpose—self-clarification. Of the scattered works in which we put our views before the public at that time, now from one aspect, now from another, I will mention only the *Manifesto of the Communist Party*, jointly written by Engels and myself, and *Discours sur le libre échange* published by me. The decisive points of our view were first scientifically, although only polemically, indicated in my work published in 1847 and directed against Proudhon: *Misère de la Philosophie*, etc. A dissertation written in German on *Wage Labour*, in which I put together my lectures on this subject delivered in the Brussels German Workers' Society, was interrupted, while being printed, by the February Revolution and my consequent forcible removal from Belgium.

The editing of the *Neue Rheinische Zeitung* in 1848 and 1849, and the subsequent events, interrupted my economic studies which could only be resumed in the year 1850 in London. The enormous material for the history of political economy which is accumulated in the British Museum, the favourable vantage point afforded by London for the observation of bourgeois society, and finally the new stage of development upon which the latter appeared to have entered with the discovery of gold in California and Australia, determined me to begin afresh from the very beginning and to work through the new material critically. These studies led partly of themselves into apparently quite remote subjects on which I had to dwell for a shorter or longer period. Especially, however, was the time at my disposal curtailed by the imperative necessity of earning my living. My contributions, during eight years now, to the first English-American newspaper, the *New York Tribune*, compelled an extraordinary scattering of my studies, since I occupy myself with newspaper correspondence proper only in exceptional cases. However, articles on striking economic events in England and on the Continent constituted so considerable a part of my contributions that I was compelled to make myself familiar with practical details which lie outside the sphere of the actual science of political economy.

This sketch of the course of my studies in the sphere of political economy is intended only to show that my views, however they may be judged and however little they coincide with the interested prejudices of the ruling classes, are the results of conscientious investigation lasting many years. But at the entrance to science, as at the entrance to hell, the demand must be posted:

> Qui si convien lasciare ogni sospetto;
> Ogni viltà convien che qui sia morta.[4]

4. Here all mistrust must be abandoned
   And here must perish every craven thought.
       (Dante, *The Divine Comedy*)

For a Ruthless Criticism
of Everything Existing

KARL MARX

The watchword of the young Karl Marx, as of his Young Hegelian associates generally, was *Kritik*—criticism. In this early article, printed in the
Deutsch-Französische Jahrbücher in 1844 in the form of a letter to
Arnold Ruge, Marx elaborated the idea of criticism into a program of this
journal, of which he and Ruge were editors. His future strictures on utopian socialist plans, in the *Communist Manifesto* and other later writings,
were prefigured in the dismissal here of the communist utopias of writers
like Étienne Cabet as a "dogmatic abstraction." The *Deutsch-Französische
Jahrbücher* (*German-French Annals*) came out in Paris in February, 1844,
in the German language. Only one double issue of the journal was published.

The translation was made by Dr. Ronald Rogowski for this edition.

M. to R.
Kreuznach
September, 1843

I am delighted that you are resolved and turn your thoughts
from backward glances at the past toward a new undertaking. In
Paris, then, the old university of philosophy (*absit omen!*) and the
new capital of the new world. What is necessary will arrange itself.
I do not doubt, therefore, that all obstacles—whose importance I
do not fail to recognize—will be removed.

The undertaking may succeed, however, or not; in any case I
will be in Paris at the end of this month, since the air here makes
one servile and I see no room at all in Germany for free activity.

In Germany, everything is being forcibly repressed, a true anarchy
of the spirit has burst out, stupidity itself reigns supreme, and
Zürich obeys commands from Berlin; hence it becomes ever clearer
that a new gathering point must be sought for the really thinking
and independent minds. I am convinced that our plan would meet

a real need, and real needs must surely also be able to find real fulfillment. I therefore have no doubts about the enterprise if only we undertake it seriously.

The inner difficulties seem to be almost greater than the external obstacles. For even if there is no doubt about the "whence," all the more confusion reigns about the "whither." Apart from the general anarchy which has erupted among the reformers, each is compelled to confess to himself that he has no clear conception of what the future should be. That, however, is just the advantage of the new trend: that we do not attempt dogmatically to prefigure the future, but want to find the new world only through criticism of the old. Up to now the philosophers had the solution of all riddles lying in their lectern, and the stupid uninitiated world had only to open its jaws to let the roast partridges of absolute science fly into its mouth. Now philosophy has become worldly, and the most incontrovertible evidence of this is that the philosophical consciousness has been drawn, not only externally but also internally, into the stress of battle. But if the designing of the future and the proclamation of ready-made solutions for all time is not our affair, then we realize all the more clearly what we have to accomplish in the present—I am speaking of a *ruthless criticism of everything existing*, ruthless in two senses: The criticism must not be afraid of its own conclusions, nor of conflict with the powers that be.

I am therefore not in favor of setting up any dogmatic flag. On the contrary, we must try to help the *dogmatics* to clarify to themselves the meaning of their own positions. Thus *communism*, to be specific, is a dogmatic abstraction. I do not have in mind here some imaginary, possible communism, but actually existing communism in the form preached by Cabet, Dezamy,[1] Weitling,[2] etc. This communism is only a special manifestation of the humanistic principle which is still infected by its opposite—private being. Elimination of private property is therefore by no means identical with this communism, and it is not accidental but quite inevitable that communism has seen other socialist teachings arise in opposition to it, such as the teachings of Fourier, Proudhon, etc., because it is itself only a special, one-sided realization of the socialist principle.

And the socialist principle itself represents, on the whole, only one side, affecting the *reality* of the true human essence. We have to concern ourselves just as much with the other side, the theoretical existence of man, in other words to make religion, science, etc., the objects of our criticism. Moreover, we want to have an effect on our contemporaries, and specifically on our German contemporaries. The question is, how is this to be approached? Two circum-

1. Theodore Dezamy, author of *Code de la nature* (1842). [*R. T.*]
2. Wilhelm Weitling, a German jour- neyman tailor whose *Guarantees of Harmony and Freedom* (1842) advocated communism. [*R. T.*]

stances cannot be denied. First, religion, and second, politics, arouse predominant interest in contemporary Germany. We must take these two subjects, however they are, for a starting-point, and not set up against them some ready-made system such as the *Voyage en Icarie*.[3]

Reason has always existed, only not always in reasonable form. The critic can therefore start out by taking any form of theoretical and practical consciousness and develop from the *unique* forms of existing reality the true reality as its norm and final goal. Now so far as real life is concerned, precisely the *political state* in all its *modern* forms contains, even where it is not yet consciously imbued with socialist demands, the demands of reason. Nor does the state stop at that. The state everywhere presupposes that reason has been realized. But in just this way it everywhere comes into contradiction between its ideal mission and its real preconditions.

Out of this conflict of the political state with itself, therefore, one can develop social truth. Just as *religion* is the catalogue of the theoretical struggles of mankind, so the *political state* is the catalogue of its practical struggles. The political state thus expresses, within the confines of its form *sub specie rei publicae*,[4] all social struggles, needs, truths. Thus it is not at all beneath the *hauteur des principes* to make the most specific political question—e.g., the difference between the corporative[5] and the representative system—the object of criticism. For this question only expresses in a *political* way the difference between the rule of man and the rule of private property. The critic therefore not only can but must go into these political questions (which the crass kind of socialists consider beneath anyone's dignity). By showing the superiority of the representative system over the corporative system, the critic *affects the practical interests* of a large party. By elevating the representative system from its political form to its general form and by bringing out the true significance underlying this system, the critic at the same time forces this party to go beyond its own confines, since its victory is at the same time its loss.

Nothing prevents us, then, from tying our criticism to the criticism of politics and to a definite party position in politics, and hence from identifying our criticism with real struggles. Then we shall confront the world not as doctrinaires with a new principle: "Here is the truth, bow down before it!" We develop new principles to the world out of its own principles. We do not say to the world: "Stop fighting; your struggle is of no account. We want to

---

3. This is the title of Cabet's utopian novel published in Paris in 1840. At that time Cabet's followers were called "communists." [*R. T.*]
4. From the political point of view. [*R. T.*]

5. The system of representation by estates (classes) as opposed to the system of representation by individuals. [*R. T.*]

shout the true slogan of the struggle at you." We only show the world what it is fighting for, and consciousness is something that the world *must* acquire, like it or not.

The reform of consciousness consists *only* in enabling the world to clarify its consciousness, in waking it from its dream about itself, in *explaining* to it the meaning of its own actions. Our whole task can consist only in putting religious and political questions into self-conscious human form—as is also the case in Feuerbach's criticism of religion.

Our motto must therefore be: Reform of consciousness not through dogmas, but through analyzing the mystical consciousness, the consciousness which is unclear to itself, whether it appears in religious or political form. Then it will transpire that the world has long been dreaming of something that it can acquire if only it becomes conscious of it. It will transpire that it is not a matter of drawing a great dividing line between past and future, but of carrying out the thoughts of the past. And finally, it will transpire that mankind begins no *new* work, but consciously accomplishes its old work.

So, we can express the trend of our journal in one word: the work of our time to clarify to itself (critical philosophy) the meaning of its own struggle and its own desires. This is work for the world and for us. It can only be the work of joint forces. It is a matter of *confession*, no more. To have its sins forgiven mankind has only to declare them to be what they really are.

Contribution to the Critique of Hegel's *Philosophy of Right*: Introduction

KARL MARX

In line with his program of effecting a "ruthless criticism of everything existing," Marx during 1843 took up the criticism of politics. He set about this by working on a critical commentary on Hegel's chief political treatise, *The Philosophy of Right*. Leaving the commentary incomplete and unpublished (it was first published in 1927), he summed up its message in this Introduction, written at the close of 1843 and published in the *Deutsch-Französische Jahrbücher* in the following year. The essay, a consummate expression of the radical mind, proclaims the need for a "radical revolution" as the means of human self-realization. Marx envisages Germany as the focal point of the radical revolution, and the proletariat as its class vehicle. This marks the first appearance of the concept of the proletariat in Marx's writings.

For Germany, the *criticism of religion* has been largely completed; and the criticism of religion is the premise of all criticism.

The *profane* existence of error is compromised once its *celestial oratio pro aris et focis* has been refuted. Man, who has found in the fantastic reality of heaven, where he sought a supernatural being, only his own reflection, will no longer be tempted to find only the *semblance* of himself—a non-human being—where he seeks and must seek his true reality.

The basis of irreligious criticism is this: *man makes religion; religion does not make man.* Religion is indeed man's self-consciousness and self-awareness so long as he has not found himself or has lost himself again. But *man* is not an abstract being, squatting outside the world. Man is *the human world*, the state, society. This state, this society, produce religion which is an *inverted world consciousness*, because they are an *inverted world*. Religion is the general theory of this world, its encyclopedic compendium, its logic in popular form, its spiritual *point d'honneur*, its

11

enthusiasm, its moral sanction, its solemn complement, its general basis of consolation and justification. It is *the fantastic realization* of the human being inasmuch as the *human being* possesses no true reality. The struggle against religion is, therefore, indirectly a struggle against *that world* whose spiritual *aroma* is religion.

Religious suffering is at the same time an *expression* of real suffering and a *protest* against real suffering. Religion is the sigh of the oppressed creature, the sentiment of a heartless world, and the soul of soulless conditions. It is the *opium* of the people.

The abolition of religion as the *illusory* happiness of men, is a demand for their *real* happiness. The call to abandon their illusions about their condition is a *call to abandon a condition which requires illusions*. The criticism of religion is, therefore, *the embryonic criticism of this vale of tears* of which religion is the *halo*.

Criticism has plucked the imaginary flowers from the chain, not in order that man shall bear the chain without caprice or consolation but so that he shall cast off the chain and pluck the living flower. The criticism of religion disillusions man so that he will think, act and fashion his reality as a man who has lost his illusions and regained his reason; so that he will revolve about himself as his own true sun. Religion is only the illusory sun about which man revolves so long as he does not revolve about himself.

It is the *task of history*, therefore, once the *other-world of truth* has vanished, to establish the *truth of this world*. The immediate *task of philosophy*, which is in the service of history, is to unmask human self-alienation in its *secular form* now that it has been unmasked in its *sacred form*. Thus the criticism of heaven is transformed into the criticism of earth, the *criticism of religion* into the *criticism of law*, and the *criticism of theology* into the *criticism of politics*.

The following exposition[1]—which is a contribution to this undertaking—does not deal directly with the original but with a copy, the German *philosophy* of the state and of right, for the simple reason that it deals with Germany.

If one were to begin with the *status quo* itself in Germany, even in the most appropriate way, i.e. negatively, the result would still be an *anachronism*. Even the negation of our political present is already a dusty fact in the historical lumber room of modern nations. I may negate powdered wigs, but I am still left with unpowdered wigs. If I negate the German situation of 1843 I have,

---

1. Marx refers to his intention to publish a critical study of Hegel's *Philosophy of Right*, to which this essay was an introduction. One of Marx's preliminary manuscripts for such a study has been published entitled "Aus der Kritik der Hegelschen Rechtsphilosophie. Kritik des Hegelschen Staatsrechts." (*MEGA* I 11, pp. 403–553).

according to French chronology, hardly reached the year 1789, and still less the vital centre of the present day.

German history, indeed, prides itself upon a development which no other nation had previously accomplished, or will ever imitate in the historical sphere. We have shared in the restorations of modern nations without ever sharing in their revolutions. We have been restored, first because other nations have dared to make revolutions, and secondly because other nations have suffered counter-revolutions; in the first case because our masters were afraid, and in the second case because they were not afraid. Led by our shepherds, we have only once kept company with liberty and that was on the *day of its internment.*

A school of thought, which justifies the infamy of today by that of yesterday, which regards every cry from the serf under the knout as a cry of rebellion once the knout has become time-honoured, ancestral and historical, a school for which history shows only its *a posteriori* as the God of Israel did for his servant Moses—the *Historical school of law*[2]—might be supposed to have invented German history, if it were not in fact itself an invention of German history, A Shylock, but a servile Shylock, it swears upon its bond, its historical, Christian-Germanic bond, for every pound of flesh cut from the heart of the people.

On the other hand, good-natured enthusiasts, German chauvinists by temperament and enlightened liberals by reflection, seek our history of liberty beyond our history, in the primeval Teutonic forests. But how does the history of our liberty differ from the history of the wild boar's liberty, if it is only to be found in the forests? And as the proverb has it: what is shouted into the forest, the forest echoes back. So peace upon the primeval Teutonic forests!

But *war* upon the state of affairs in Germany! By all means! This state of affairs is *beneath the level of history, beneath all criticism;* nevertheless it remains an object of criticism just as the criminal who is beneath humanity remains an object of the *executioner.* In its struggle against this state of affairs criticism is not a passion of the head, but the head of passion. It is not a lancet but a weapon. Its object is an *enemy* which it aims not to refute but to *destroy.* For the spirit of this state of affairs has already been refuted. It is not, in itself, an object worthy of our thought; it is an *existence* as

2. The principal representative of the Historical school was F. K. von Savigny (1779–1861) who outlined its programme in his book *Vom Beruf unserer Zeit für Gesetzgebung und Rechtswissenschaft* (On the Vocation of our Age for Legislation and Jurisprudence), Heidelberg, 1814. Marx attended Savigny's lectures at the University of Berlin in 1836–7; but he was more attracted by the lectures of Eduard Gans (1798–1839), a liberal Hegelian influenced by Saint-Simon, who emphasized in his teaching and writings the part played by reason in the development of law, and who was Savigny's principal opponent in Berlin.

contemptible as it is despised. Criticism itself has no need of any
further elucidation of this object, for it has already understood it.
Criticism is no longer an end in itself, but simply a means; *indignation* is its essential mode of feeling, and *denunciation* its principal
task.

It is a matter of depicting the stifling pressure which the different social spheres exert upon other, the universal but passive
ill-humour, the complacent but self-deluding narrowness of spirit;
all this incorporated in a system of government which lives by con-
serving this paltriness, and is itself *paltriness in government*.

What a spectacle! Society is infinitely divided into the most
diverse races, which confront each other with their petty antipathies, bad conscience and coarse mediocrity; and which, precisely
because of their ambiguous and mistrustful situation, are treated
without exception, though in different ways, as merely tolerated
existences by their masters. And they are forced to recognize and
acknowledge this fact of being *dominated, governed* and *possessed*,
as a *concession from heaven*! On the other side are the rulers themselves, whose greatness is in inverse proportion to their number.

The criticism which deals with this subject-matter is criticism in
a hand-to-hand fight; and in such a fight it is of no interest to know
whether the adversary is of the same rank, is noble or *interesting*—all that matters is to *strike* him. It is a question of denying
the Germans an instant of illusion or resignation. The burden must
be made still more irksome by awakening a consciousness of it, and
shame must be made more shameful still by rendering it public.
Every sphere of German society must be depicted as the *partie
honteuse* of German society; and these petrified social conditions
must be made to dance by singing their own melody to them. The
nation must be taught to be *terrified* of itself, in order to give it
courage. In this way an imperious need of the German nation will
be satisfied, and the needs of nations are themselves the final causes
of their satisfaction.

Even for the modern nations this struggle against the limited
character of the German *status quo* does not lack interest; for the
German *status quo* is the open *consummation of the ancien
régime*, and the *ancien régime* is the *hidden defect of the modern
state*. The struggle against the political present of the Germans is a
struggle against the past of the modern nations, who are still continually importuned by the reminiscences of this past. It is instruc-
tive for the modern nations to see the *ancien régime*, which has
played a *tragic* part in their history, play a *comic* part as a German
ghost. The *ancien régime* had a *tragic* history, so long as it was the
established power in the world while liberty was a personal fancy;
in short, so long as it believed and had to believe in its own valid-

ity. So long as the *ancien régime*, as an existing world order, struggled against a new world which was just coming into existence, there was on its side a historical error but no personal error. Its decline was, therefore, tragic.

The present German régime, on the other hand, which is an anachronism, a flagrant contradiction of universally accepted axioms—the nullity of the *ancien régime* revealed to the whole world—only imagines that it believes in itself and asks the world to share its illusion. If it believed in its own *nature* would it attempt to hide it beneath the *semblance* of an alien nature and look for its salvation in hypocrisy and sophistry? The modern *ancien régime* is the comedian of a world order whose *real heroes* are dead. History is thorough, and it goes through many stages when it conducts an ancient formation to its grave. The last stage of a world-historical formation is comedy. The Greek gods, already once mortally wounded in Aeschylus' tragedy *Prometheus Bound*, had to endure a second death, a comic death, in Lucian's dialogues. Why should history proceed in this way? So that mankind shall separate itself *gladly* from its past. We claim this *joyful* historical destiny for the political powers of Germany.

But as soon as criticism concerns itself with modern social and political reality, and thus arrives at genuine human problems, it must either go outside the German *status quo* or approach its object indirectly. For example, the relation of industry, of the world of wealth in general, to the political world is a major problem of modern times. In what form does this problem begin to preoccupy the Germans? In the form of *protective tariffs*, the *system of prohibition*, the *national economy*. German chauvinism has passed from men to matter, so that one fine day our knights of cotton and heroes of iron found themselves metamorphosed into patriots. The sovereignty of monopoly within the country has begun to be recognized since *sovereignty vis-à-vis foreign countries* was attributed to it. In Germany, therefore, a beginning is made with what came as the conclusion in France and England. The old, rotten order against which these nations revolt in their theories, and which they bear only as chains are borne, is hailed in Germany as the dawn of a glorious future which as yet hardly dares to move from a cunning[3] theory to a ruthless practice. While in France and England the problem is put in the form: *political economy* or the *rule of society over wealth*; in Germany it is put in the form: *national economy* or the *rule of private property over nationality*. Thus, in England and France it is a question of abolishing monop-

---

3. In German, *listigen*; Marx is punning upon the name of Friedrich List (1789–1846), the apostle of industrial capitalism in a nationalist and protec- tionist form, who published in 1840 his influential book, *Das nationale System der politischen Ökonomie*.

oly, which has developed to its final consequences; while in Germany it is a question of proceeding to the final consequences of monopoly. There it is a question of the solution; here, only a question of the collision. We can see very well from this example how modern problems are presented in Germany; the example shows that our history, like a raw recruit, has so far only had to do extra drill on old and hackneyed historical matters.

If the *whole* of German development were at the level of German *political* development, a German could have no greater part in contemporary problems than can a *Russian*. If the individual is not restricted by the limitations of his country, still less is the nation liberated by the liberation of one indivdual. The fact that a Scythian was one of the Greek philosophers[4] did not enable the Scythians to advance a single step towards Greek culture.

Fortunately, we Germans are not Scythians.

Just as the nations of the ancient world lived their pre-history in the imagination, in mythology, so we Germans have lived our post-history in thought, in *philosophy*. We are the *philosophical* contemporaries of the present day without being its *historical* contemporaries. German philosophy is the *ideal prolongation* of German history. When, therefore, we criticize, instead of the *oeuvres incomplètes* of our real history, the *oeuvres posthumes* of our ideal history—*philosophy*, our criticism stands at the centre of the problems of which the present age says: *that is the question.* That which constitutes, for the advanced nations, a *practical* break with modern political conditions, is in Germany where these conditions do not yet exist, virtually a *critical* break with their philosophical reflection.

The German *philosophy of right and of the state* is the only German history which is *al pari* with the *official* modern times. The German nation is obliged, therefore, to connect its dream history with its present conditions, and to subject to criticism not only these existing conditions but also their abstract continuation. Its future cannot be restricted either to the direct negation of its real juridical and political circumstances, or to the direct realization of its ideal juridical and political circumstances. The direct negation of its real circumstances already exists in its ideal circumstances, while it has almost outlived the realization of its ideal circumstances in the contemplation of neighbouring nations. It is with good reason, therefore, that the *practical* political party in Germany demands the *negation of philosophy*. Its error does not consist in formulating this demand, but in limiting itself to a demand which it does not, and cannot, make effective. It supposes that it can achieve this negation by turning its back on philosophy, looking

4. Anacharsis.

elsewhere, and murmuring a few trite and ill-humoured phrases. Because of its narrow outlook it does not take account of philosophy as part of *German* reality, and even regards philosophy as beneath the level of German practical life and its theories. You demand as a point of departure real germs of life, but you forget that the real germ of life of the German nation has so far sprouted only in its *cranium*. In short, *you cannot abolish philosophy without realizing it*.

The same error was committed, but in the opposite direction, by the *theoretical* party which originated in philosophy.

In the present struggle, this party saw *only* the *critical struggle of philosophy against the German world*. It did not consider that *previous philosophy* itself belongs to this world and is its complement, even if only an ideal complement. Critical as regards its counterpart, it was not self-critical. It took as its point of departure the *presuppositions* of philosophy; and either accepted the conclusions which philosophy had reached or else presented as direct philosophical demands and conclusions, demands and conclusions drawn from elsewhere. But these latter—assuming their legitimacy—can only be achieved by the *negation of previous philosophy*, that is, philosophy as philosophy. We shall provide later a more comprehensive account of this party. Its principal defect may be summarized as follows: *it believed that it could realize philosophy without abolishing it*.

The criticism of the *German philosophy of right and of the state* which was given its most logical, profound and complete expression by Hegel, is at once the critical analysis of the modern state and of the reality connected with it, and the definitive negation of all the past *forms of consciousness in German jurisprudence and politics*, whose most distinguished and most general expression, raised to the level of a *science*, is precisely the *speculative philosophy of right*. If it was only Germany which could produce the speculative philosophy of right—this extravagant and abstract thought about the modern state, the reality of which remains in the beyond (even if this beyond is only across the Rhine)—the *German* representative of the modern state, on the contrary, which leaves out of account the *real man* was itself only possible because, and to the extent that, the modern state itself leaves the *real man* out of account or only satisfies the *whole* man in an illusory way. In politics, the Germans have *thought* what other nations have *done*. Germany has been their *theoretical consciousness*. The abstraction and presumption of its philosophy was in step with the partial and stunted character of their reality. If, therefore, the *status quo* of the *German political system* expresses the *consummation of the ancien régime*, the thorn in the flesh of the modern state, the *status quo* of

German political science expresses the *imperfection of the modern state* itself, the degeneracy of its flesh.

As the determined adversary of the previous form of German political consciousness, the criticism of the speculative philosophy of right does not remain within its own sphere, but leads on to *tasks* which can only be solved by *means of practical activity*.

The question then arises: can Germany attain a practical activity *à la hauteur des principes*; that is to say, a revolution which will raise it not only to the *official level* of the modern nations, but to the *human level* which will be the immediate future of those nations.

It is clear that the arm of criticism cannot replace the criticism of arms. Material force can only be overthrown by material force; but theory itself becomes a material force when it has seized the masses. Theory is capable of seizing the masses when it demonstrates *ad hominem*, and it demonstrates *ad hominem* as soon as it becomes radical. To be radical is to grasp things by the root. But for man the root is man himself. What proves beyond doubt the radicalism of German theory, and thus its practical energy, is that it begins from the resolute *positive* abolition of religion. The criticism of religion ends with the doctrine that *man is the supreme being for man*. It ends, therefore, with the *categorical imperative to overthrow all those conditions* in which man is an abased, enslaved, abandoned, contemptible being—conditions which can hardly be better described than in the exclamation of a Frenchman on the occasion of a proposed tax upon dogs: "Wretched dogs! They want to treat you like men!"

Even from the historical standpoint theoretical emancipation has a specific practical importance for Germany. In fact Germany's *revolutionary* past is theoretical—it is the *Reformation*. In that period the revolution originated in the brain of a monk, today in the brain of the philosopher.

Luther, without question, overcame servitude through devotion but only by substituting servitude through *conviction*. He shattered the faith in authority by restoring the authority of faith. He transformed the priests into laymen by turning laymen into priests. He liberated man from external religiosity by making religiosity the innermost essence of man. He liberated the body from its chains because he fettered the heart with chains.

But if Protestantism was not the solution it did at least pose the problem correctly. It was no longer a question, thereafter, of the layman's struggle against the priest outside himself, but of his struggle against his *own internal priest*, against his own *priestly nature*. And if the Protestant metamorphosis of German laymen into priests emancipated the lay popes—the *princes* together with their clergy, the privileged and the philistines—the philosophical metamorphosis of the priestly Germans into men will emancipate the *people*. But just as emancipation will not be confined to princes, so the *secularization* of property will not be limited to the *confiscation of church property*, which was practised especially by hypocritical Prussia. At that time, the Peasant War, the most radical event in German history, came to grief because of theology.

Today, when theology itself has come to grief, the most unfree phenomenon in German history—our *status quo*—will be shattered by philosophy. On the eve of the Reformation official Germany was the most abject servant of Rome. On the eve of its revolution Germany is the abject servant of those who are far inferior to Rome; of Prussia and Austria, of petty squires and philistines.

But a *radical* revolution in Germany seems to encounter a major difficulty.

Revolutions need a *passive* element, a *material* basis. Theory is only realized in a people so far as it fulfils the needs of the people. Will there correspond to the monstrous discrepancy between the demands of German thought and the answers of German reality a similar discrepancy between civil society and the state, and within civil society itself? Will theoretical needs be directly practical needs? It is not enough that thought should seek to realize itself; reality must also strive towards thought.

But Germany has not passed through the intermediate stage of political emancipation at the same time as the modern nations. It has not yet attained in practice those stages which it has transcended in theory. How could Germany, in *salta mortale*, surmount not only its own barriers but also those of the modern nations, that is, those barriers which it must in reality experience and strive for as an emancipation from its own real barriers? A radical revolution can only be a revolution of radical needs, for which the conditions and breeding ground appear to be lacking.

But if Germany accompanied the development of the modern nations only through the abstract activity of thought, without taking an active part in the real struggles of this development, it has also experienced the *pains* of this development without sharing in its pleasures and partial satisfactions. The abstract activity on one side has its counterpart in the abstract suffering on the other. And one fine day Germany will find itself at the level of the European decadence, before ever having attained the level of European emancipation. It will be comparable to a fetishist who is sickening from the diseases of Christianity.

If the *German governments* are examined it will be found that the circumstances of the time, the situation of Germany, the outlook of German culture, and lastly their own fortunate instinct, all drive them to combine the *civilized deficiencies* of the *modern political world* (whose advantages we do not enjoy) with the *barbarous deficiencies* of the *ancien régime* (which we enjoy in full measure); so that Germany must participate more and more, if not in the reason at least in the unreason of those political systems which transcend its *status quo*. Is there, for example, any country in the whole world which shares with such naïveté as so-called constitutional Germany all the illusions of the constitutional régime without sharing its realities? And was it not, of necessity, a German government which had the idea of combining the torments of censorship with the torments of the French September laws[5] which presuppose the liberty of the Press? Just as the gods of all the nations were to be found in the Roman Pantheon, so there will be found in the Holy Roman German Empire all the *sins* of all the forms of State. That this eclecticism will attain an unprecedented degree is assured in particular by the *politico-aesthetic gourmandise* of a German king who proposes to play all the roles of royalty— feudal or bureaucratic, absolute or constitutional, autocratic or democratic—if not in the person of the people at least in his *own* person, and if not for the people, at least for *himself. Germany, as the deficiency of present-day politics constituted into a system,* will not be able to demolish the specific German barriers without demolishing the general barriers of present-day politics.

It is not *radical* revolution, *universal human* emancipation, which is a Utopian dream for Germany, but rather a partial, *merely* political revolution which leaves the pillars of the building standing. What is the basis of a partial, merely political revolution? Simply this: a *section of civil society* emancipates itself and attains universal domination; a determinate class undertakes, from its *particular situation*, a general emancipation of society. This class emancipates society as a whole, but only on condition that the whole of society is in the same situation as this class; for example, that it possesses or can easily acquire money or culture.

No class in civil society can play this part unless it can arouse, in itself and in the masses, a moment of enthusiasm in which it associates and mingles with society at large, identifies itself with it, and is felt and recognized as the *general representative* of this society. Its aims and interests must genuinely be the aims and interests of society itself, of which it becomes in reality the social head and heart. It is only in the name of general interests that a particular class can claim general supremacy. In order to attain this liberating position, and the political direction of all spheres of society, revolutionary energy and consciousness of its own power do

5. The laws of September, 1835, which increased the financial guarantees required from the publishers of news-papers and introduced heavier penalties for "subversive" publications.

not suffice. For a *popular revolution* and the *emancipation of a particular class* of civil society to coincide, for *one* class to represent the whole of society, another class must concentrate in itself all the evils of society, a particular class must embody and represent a general obstacle and limitation. A particular social sphere must be regarded as the *notorious crime* of the whole society, so that emancipation from this sphere appears as a general emancipation. For *one* class to be the liberating class *par excellence*, it is necessary that another class should be openly the oppressing class. The negative significance of the French nobility and clergy produced the positive significance of the bourgeoisie, the class which stood next to them and opposed them.

But in Germany every class lacks the logic, insight, courage and clarity which would make it a negative representative of society. Moreover, there is also lacking in every class the generosity of spirit which identifies itself, if only for a moment, with the popular mind; that genius which pushes material force to political power, that revolutionary daring which throws at its adversary the defiant phrase: *I am nothing and I should be everything*. The essence of German morality and honour, in classes as in individuals, is a *modest egoism* which displays, and allows others to display, its own narrowness. The relation between the different spheres of German society is, therefore, not dramatic, but epic. Each of these spheres begins to be aware of itself and to establish itself beside the others, not from the moment when it is oppressed, but from the moment that circumstances, without any action of its own, have created a new sphere which it can in turn oppress. Even the *moral sentiment of the German middle class* has no other basis than the consciousness of being the representative of the narrow and limited mediocrity of all the other classes. It is not only the German kings, therefore, who ascend their thrones *mal à propos*. Each sphere of civil society suffers a defeat before gaining the victory; it erects its own barrier before having destroyed the barrier which opposes it; it displays the narrowness of its views before having displayed their generosity, and thus every opportunity of playing an important role has passed before it properly existed, and each class, at the very moment when it begins its struggle against the class above it, remains involved in a struggle against the class beneath. For this reason, the princes are in conflict with the monarch, the bureaucracy with the nobility, the bourgeoisie with all of them, while the proletariat is already beginning its struggle with the bourgeoisie. The middle class hardly dares to conceive the idea of emancipation from its own point of view before the development of social conditions, and the progress of political theory, show that this point of view is already antiquated, or at least disputable.

In France it is enough to be something in order to desire to be everything. In Germany no one has the right to be anything without first renouncing everything. In France partial emancipation is a basis for complete emancipation. In Germany complete emancipation is a *conditio sine qua non* for any partial emancipation. In France it is the reality, in Germany the impossibility, of a progressive emancipation which must give birth to complete liberty. In France every class of the population is *politically idealistic* and considers itself first of all, not as a particular class, but as the representative of the general needs of society. The role of liberator can, therefore, pass successively in a dramatic movement to different classes in the population, until it finally reaches the class which achieves social freedom; no longer assuming certain conditions external to man, which are none the less created by human society, but organizing all the conditions of human life on the basis of social freedom. In Germany, on the contrary, where practical life is as little intellectual as intellectual life is practical, no class of civil society feels the need for, or the ability to achieve, a general emancipation, until it is forced to it by its *immediate* situation, by *material* necessity and by its *fetters themselves*.

Where is there, then, a *real* possibility of emancipation in Germany?

This is our reply. A class must be formed which has *radical chains*, a class in civil society which is not a class of civil society, a class which is the dissolution of all classes, a sphere of society which has a universal character because its sufferings are universal, and which does not claim a *particular redress* because the wrong which is done to it is not a *particular wrong* but *wrong in general*. There must be formed a sphere of society which claims no *traditional* status but only a *human* status, a sphere which is not opposed to particular consequences but is totally opposed to the assumptions of the German political system; a sphere, finally, which cannot emancipate itself without emancipating itself from all the other spheres of society, without, therefore, emancipating all these other spheres, which is, in short, a *total loss* of humanity and which can only redeem itself by a *total redemption of humanity*. This dissolution of society, as a particular class, is the *proletariat*.

The proletariat is only beginning to form itself in Germany, as a result of the industrial movement. For what constitutes the proletariat is not *naturally existing* poverty, but poverty *artificially produced*, is not the mass of people mechanically oppressed by the weight of society, but the mass resulting from the *disintegration* of society and above all from the disintegration of the middle class. Needless to say, however, the numbers of the proletariat are also increased by the victims of natural poverty and of Christian-Germanic serfdom.

When the proletariat announces the *dissolution of the existing social order*, it only declares the *secret of its* own existence, for it *is* the *effective* dissolution of this order. When the proletariat demands the *negation of private property* it only lays down as a *principle for society* what society has already made a principle *for the proletariat*, and what the *latter* already involuntarily embodies as the negative result of society. Thus the proletarian has the same right, in relation to the new world which is coming into being, as the *German king* has in relation to the existing world when he calls the people *his* people or a horse *his* horse. In calling the people his private property the king simply declares that the owner of private property is king.

Just as philosophy finds its *material* weapons in the proletariat, so the proletariat finds its *intellectual* weapons in philosophy. And once the lightning of thought has penetrated deeply into this virgin soil of the people, the *Germans* will emancipate themselves and become *men*.

Let us sum up these results. The emancipation of Germany is only possible *in practice* if one adopts the point of view of that theory according to which man is the highest being for man. Germany will not be able to emancipate itself from the *Middle Ages* unless it emancipates itself at the same time from the *partial* victories over the Middle Ages. In Germany *no* type of enslavement can be abolished unless *all* enslavement is destroyed. Germany, which likes to get to the bottom of things, can only make a revolution which upsets *the whole order* of things. The *emancipation of Germany* will be an *emancipation of man. Philosophy* is the *head* of this emancipation and the *proletariat* is its *heart*. Philosophy can only be realized by the abolition of the proletariat, and the proletariat can only be abolished by the realization of philosophy.

On the Jewish Question

KARL MARX

In this essay, written in the autumn of 1843 and published in the *Deutsch-Französische Jahrbücher*, Marx pursued his critical aims through a review of two studies on the Jewish question by another Young Hegelian, Bruno Bauer. The criticism of politics is developed in the first part, leading to the conclusion that human emancipation requires the ending of the division between man as an egoistic being in "civil society" and man as abstract citizen in the state. In the second part, Marx proceeds to the criticism of economics or commerce, which he equates with "Judaism." His concluding call for "the emancipation of society from Judaism" (which has been seen on occasion as a manifesto of anti-Semitism) is in fact a call for the emancipation of society from what he here calls "huckstering," or from what he was subsequently to call "capitalism." This, however, is not to deny that Marx, although he himself was of Jewish origin, harbored anti-Jewish attitudes, nor is it to deny that such attitudes found some expression in this essay.

---

1. Bruno Bauer, *Die Judenfrage*[1]

The German Jews seek emancipation. What kind of emancipation do they want? *Civic, political* emancipation.

Bruno Bauer replies to them: In Germany no one is politically emancipated. We ourselves are not free. How then could we liberate you? You Jews are *egoists* if you demand for yourselves, as Jews, a special emancipation. You should work, as Germans, for the political emancipation of Germany, and as men, for the emancipation of mankind. You should feel the particular kind of oppression and shame which you suffer, not as an exception to the rule but rather as a confirmation of the rule.

Or do the Jews want to be placed on a footing of equality with the *Christian subjects?* If they recognize the *Christian state* as legally established they also recognize the régime of general enslave-

1. The Jewish question. [Braunschweig, 1843.—*Marx*]

ment. Why should their particular yoke be irksome when they accept the general yoke? Why should the German be interested in the liberation of the Jew, if the Jew is not interested in the liberation of the German?

The *Christian* state recognizes nothing but *privileges*. The Jew himself, in this state, has the privilege of being a Jew. As a Jew he possesses rights which the Christians do not have. Why does he want rights which he does not have but which the Christians enjoy?

In demanding his emancipation from the Christian state he asks the Christian state to abandon its *religious* prejudice. But does he, the Jew, give up *his* religious prejudice? Has he then the right to insist that someone else should forswear his religion?

The *Christian* state, *by its very nature*, is incapable of emancipating the Jew. But, adds Bauer, the Jew, by his very nature, cannot be emancipated. As long as the state remains Christian, and as long as the Jew remains a Jew, they are equally incapable, the one of conferring emancipation, the other of receiving it.

With respect to the Jews the Christian state can only adopt the attitude of a Christian state. That is, it can permit the Jew, as a matter of privilege, to isolate himself from its other subjects; but it must then allow the pressures of all the other spheres of society to bear upon the Jew, and all the more heavily since he is in *religious* opposition to the dominant religion. But the Jew likewise can only adopt a Jewish attitude, i.e. that of a foreigner, towards the state, since he opposes his illusory nationality to actual nationality, his illusory law to actual law. He considers it his right to separate himself from the rest of humanity; as a matter of principle he takes no part in the historical movement and looks to a future which has nothing in common with the future of mankind as a whole. He regards himself as a member of the Jewish people, and the Jewish people as the chosen people.

On what grounds, then, do you Jews demand emancipation? On account of your religion? But it is the mortal enemy of the state religion. As citizens? But there are no citizens in Germany. As men? But you are not men any more than are those to whom you appeal.

Bauer, after criticizing earlier approaches and solutions, formulates the question of Jewish emancipation in a new way. What, he asks, is the nature of the Jew who is to be emancipated, and the *nature* of the Christian state which is to emancipate him? He replies by a critique of the Jewish religion, analyses the religious opposition between Judaism and Christianity, explains the essence of the Christian state; and does all this with dash, clarity, wit and profundity, in a style which is as precise as it is pithy and vigorous.

How then does Bauer resolve the Jewish question? What is the result? To formulate a question is to resolve it. The critical study of the Jewish question is the answer to the Jewish question. Here it is in brief: we have to emancipate ourselves before we can emancipate others.

The most stubborn form of the opposition between Jew and Christian is the *religious* opposition. How is an opposition resolved? By making it impossible. And how is *religious* opposition made impossible? By abolishing *religion*. As soon as Jew and Christian come to see in their respective religions nothing more than *stages in the development of the human mind*—snake skins which have been cast off by *history*, and *man* as the snake who clothed himself in them—they will no longer find themselves in religious opposition, but in a purely critical, *scientific* and human relationship. *Science* will then constitute their unity. But scientific oppositions are resolved by science itself.

The *German* Jew, in particular, suffers from the general lack of political freedom and the pronounced Christianity of the state. But in Bauer's sense the Jewish question has a general significance, independent of the specifically German conditions. It is the question of the relations between religion and the state, of the *contradiction between religious prejudice and political emancipation*. Emancipation from religion is posited as a condition, both for the Jew who wants political emancipation, and for the state which should emancipate him and itself be emancipated.

"Very well, it may be said (and the Jew himself says it) but the Jew should not be emancipated because he is a Jew, because he has such an excellent and universal moral creed; the *Jew* should take second place to the citizen, and he will be a *citizen* although he is and desires to remain a Jew. In other words, he is and remains a *Jew*, even though he is a *citizen* and as such lives in a universal human condition; his restricted Jewish nature always finally triumphs over his human and political obligations. The bias persists even though it is overcome by general principles. But if it persists, it would be truer to say that it overcomes all the rest." "It is only in a sophistical and superficial sense that the Jew could remain a Jew in political life. Consequently, if he wanted to remain a Jew, this would mean that the superficial became the essential and thus triumphed. In other words, his life *in the state* would be only a semblance, or a momentary exception to the essential and normal."[2]

Let us see also how Bauer establishes the role of the state.

"France," he says, "has provided us recently,[3] in connexion with

---

2. Bauer, "Die Fähigkeit der heutigen Juden und Christen, frei zu werden," *Einundzwanzig Bogen*, p. 57. [*Marx*]

Emphases added by Marx.
3. Chamber of Deputies. Debate of 26th December, 1840. [*Marx*]

the Jewish question (and for that matter all other *political* questions), with the spectacle of a life which is free but which revokes its freedom by law and so declares it to be merely an appearance; and which, on the other hand, denies its free laws by its acts."[4]

"In France, universal liberty is not yet established by law, nor is the *Jewish question as yet resolved*, because legal liberty, i.e. the equality of all citizens, is restricted in actual life, which is still dominated and fragmented by religious privileges, and because the lack of liberty in actual life influences law in its turn and obliges it to sanction the division of citizens who are by nature free into oppressors and oppressed."[5]

When, therefore, would the Jewish question be resolved in France?

"The Jew would really have ceased to be Jewish, for example, if he did not allow his religious code to prevent his fulfilment of his duties towards the state and his fellow citizens; if he attended and took part in the public business of the Chamber of Deputies on the sabbath. It would be necessary, further, to abolish all *religious privilege,* including the monopoly of a privileged church. If, thereafter, some or many or *even the overwhelming majority felt obliged to fulfil their religious duties,* such practices should be left *to them as an absolutely* private matter."[6] "There is no longer any religion when there is no longer a privileged religion. Take away from religion its power to excommunicate and it will no longer exist."[7] "Mr. Martin du Nord has seen, in the suggestion to omit any mention of Sunday in the law, a proposal to declare that Christianity has ceased to exist. With equal right (and the right is well founded) the declaration that the law of the sabbath is no longer binding upon the Jew would amount to proclaiming the end of Judaism."[8]

Thus Bauer demands, on the one hand, that the Jew should renounce Judaism, and in general that man should renounce religion, in order to be emancipated as a citizen. On the other hand, he considers, and this follows logically, that the political abolition of religion is the abolition of all religion. The state which presupposes religion is not yet a true or actual state. "Clearly, the religious idea gives some assurances to the state. But to what state? *To what kind of state?*"[9]

At this point we see that the Jewish question is considered only from one aspect.

It was by no means sufficient to ask: who should emancipate? who should be emancipated? The critic should ask a third question:

4. Bauer, *Die Judenfrage*, p. 64. [*Marx*]
5. Ibid., p. 65. [*Marx*]
6. Loc. cit. [*Marx*]
7. Ibid., p. 71. [*Marx*]
8. Bauer, *Die Judenfrage*, p. 66. [*Marx*]
9. Ibid., p. 97. [*Marx*]

what kind of emancipation is involved? What are the essential conditions of the emancipation which is demanded? The criticism of *political emancipation* itself was only the final criticism of the Jewish question and its genuine resolution into the *"general question of the age."*

Bauer, since he does not formulate the problem at this level, falls into contradictions. He establishes conditions which are not based upon the nature of *political* emancipation. He raises questions which are irrelevant to his problem, and he resolves problems which leave his question unanswered. When Bauer says of the opponents of Jewish emancipation that "Their error was simply to assume that the Christian state was the only true one, and not to subject it to the same criticism as Judaism,"[1] we see his own error in the fact that he subjects *only* the "Christian state," and not the "state as such" to criticism, that he does not examine *the relation between political emancipation and human emancipation*, and that he, therefore, poses conditions which are only explicable by his lack of critical sense in confusing political emancipation and universal human emancipation. Bauer asks the Jews: Have you, from your standpoint, the right to demand *political emancipation?* We ask the converse question: from the standpoint of *political* emancipation can the Jew be required to abolish Judaism, or man be asked to abolish religion?.

The Jewish question presents itself differently according to the state in which the Jew resides. In Germany, where there is no political state, no state as such, the Jewish question is purely *theological*. The Jew finds himself in *religious* opposition to the state, which proclaims Christianity as its foundation. This state is a theologian *ex professo*. Criticism here is criticism of theology; a double-edged criticism, of Christian and of Jewish theology. And so we move always in the domain of theology, however *critically* we may move therein.

In France, which is a *constitutional* state, the Jewish question is a question of constitutionalism, of the incompleteness *of political emancipation*. Since the *semblance* of a state religion is maintained here, if only in the insignificant and self-contradictory formula of a *religion of the majority*, the relation of the Jews to the state also retains a semblance of religious, theological opposition.

It is only in the free states of North America, or at least in some of them, that the Jewish question loses its *theological* significance and becomes a truly *secular* question. Only where the state exists in its completely developed form can the relation of the Jew, and of the religious man in general, to the political state appear in a pure form, with its own characteristics. The criticism of this relation

1. Bauer, *Die Judenfrage*, p. 3. [*Marx*]

ceases to be theological criticism when the state ceases to maintain a *theological* attitude towards religion, that is, when it adopts the attitude of a state, i.e. a *political* attitude. Criticism then becomes *criticism of the political state*. And at this point, where the question ceases to be *theological*, Bauer's criticism ceases to be critical.

"There is not, in the United States, either a state religion or a religion declared to be that of a majority, or a predominance of one religion over another. The state remains aloof from all religions."[2] There are even some states in North America in which "the constitution does not impose any religious belief or practice as a condition of political rights."[3] And yet, "no one in the United States believes that a man without religion can be an honest man."[4] And North America is pre-eminently the country of religiosity, as Beaumont,[5] Tocqueville[6] and the Englishman, Hamilton,[7] assure us in unison. However, the states of North America only serve as an example. The question is: what is the relation between *complete* political emancipation and religion? If we find in the country which has attained full political emancipation, that religion not only continues to *exist* but is *fresh* and *vigorous*, this is proof that the existence of religion is not at all opposed to the perfection of the state. But since the existence of religion is the existence of a defect, the source of this defect must be sought in the *nature* of the state itself. Religion no longer appears as the basis, but as the *manifestation* of secular narrowness. That is why we explain the religious constraints upon the free citizens by the secular constraints upon them. We do not claim that they must transcend their religious narrowness in order to get rid of their secular limitations. We claim that they will transcend their religious narrowness once they have overcome their secular limitations. We do not turn secular questions into theological questions; we turn theological questions into secular ones. History has for long enough been resolved into superstition; but we now resolve superstition into history. The question of the *relation between political emancipation and religion* becomes for us a question of the *relation between political emancipation and human emancipation*. We criticize the religious failings of the political state by criticizing the political state in its *secular* form, disregarding its religious failings. We express in human terms the contradiction between the state and a *particular religion*, for example *Judaism*, by showing the contradic-

2. Gustave de Beaumont, *Marie ou l'esclavage aux États-Unis*, Bruxelles, 1835, 2 vols., II, p. 207. [*Marx*] Marx refers to another edition, Paris, 1835.
3. Ibid., p. 216. Beaumont actually refers to *all* the States of North America.
4. Ibid., p. 217. [*Marx*]

5. G. de Beaumont, op. cit. [*Marx*]
6. A. de Tocqueville, *De la démocratie en Amérique*. [*Marx*]
7. Thomas Hamilton, *Men and Manners in North America*, Edinburgh, 1833, 2 vols. [*Marx*] Marx quotes from the German translation, Mannheim, 1834.

tion between the state and particular *secular elements,* between the state and *religion in general* and between the state and its general *presuppositions.*

The *political* emancipation of the Jew or the Christian—of the *religious* man in general—is the *emancipation of* the state from Judaism, Christianity, and *religion* in general. The *state* emancipates itself from religion in its own particular way, in the mode which corresponds to its nature, by emancipating itself from the *state religion;* that is to say, by giving recognition to no religion and affirming itself purely and simply as a state. To be *politically* emancipated from religion is not to be finally and completely emancipated from religion, because political emancipation is not the final and absolute form of *human* emancipation.

The limits of political emancipation appear at once in the fact that the *state* can liberate itself from a constraint without man himself being *really* liberated; that a state may be a *free state* without man himself being a *free man.* Bauer himself tacitly admits this when he makes political emancipation depend upon the following condition—

"It would be necessary, moreover, to abolish all religious privileges, including the monopoly of a privileged church. If some people, or even the *immense majority, still felt obliged to fulfil their religious duties,* this practice should be left to them as a *completely private matter.*" Thus the state may have emancipated itself from religion, even though the *immense majority* of people continue to be religious. And the immense majority do not cease to be religious by virtue of being religious *in private.*

The attitude of the state, especially the *free state,* towards religion is only the attitude towards religion of the individuals who compose the state. It follows that man frees himself from a constraint in a *political* way, through the state, when he transcends his limitations, in contradiction with himself, and in an *abstract, narrow* and partial way. Furthermore, by emancipating himself *politically,* man emancipates himself in a *devious way,* through an intermediary, however *necessary* this intermediary may be. Finally, even when he proclaims himself an atheist through the intermediary of the state, that is, when he declares the state to be an atheist, he is still engrossed in religion, because he only recognizes himself as an atheist in a roundabout way, through an intermediary. Religion is simply the recognition of man in a roundabout fashion; that is, through an intermediary. The state is the intermediary between man and human liberty. Just as Christ is the intermediary to whom man attributes all his own divinity and all his religious *bonds,* so the state is the intermediary to which man confides all his non-divinity and all his *human freedom.*

The *political* elevation of man above religion shares the weaknesses and merits of all such political measures. For example, the state as a state abolishes *private property* (i.e. man decrees by *political* means the *abolition* of private property) when it abolishes the *property qualification* for electors and representatives, as has been done in many of the North American States. Hamilton interprets this phenomenon quite correctly from the political standpoint: *The masses have gained a victory over property owners and financial wealth*.[8] Is not private property ideally abolished when the non-owner comes to legislate for the owner of property? The *property qualification* is the last *political* form in which private property is recognized.

But the political suppression of private property not only does not abolish private property; it actually presupposes its existence. The state abolishes, after its fashion, the distinctions established by *birth, social rank, education, occupation*, when it decrees that birth, social rank, education, occupation are *non-political* distinctions; when it proclaims, without regard to these distinctions, that every member of society is an *equal* partner in popular sovereignty, and treats all the elements which compose the real life of the nation from the standpoint of the state. But the state, none the less, allows private property, education, occupation, to *act* after *their* own fashion, namely as private property, education, occupation, and to manifest their *particular* nature. Far from abolishing these *effective* differences, it only exists so far as they are presupposed; it is conscious of being a *political state* and it manifests its *universality* only in opposition to these elements. Hegel, therefore, defines the relation of the political state to religion quite correctly when he says: "In order for the state to come in to existence as the *self-knowing* ethical actuality of spirit, it is essential that it should be distinct from the forms of authority and of faith. But this distinction emerges only in so far as divisions occur within the ecclesiastical sphere itself. It is only in this way that the state, above the *particular* churches, has attained to the universality of thought—its formal principle—and is bringing this universality into existence."[9] To be sure! Only in this manner, *above* the *particular* elements, can the state constitute itself as universality.

The perfected political state is, by its nature, the *species-life*[1] of

8. Hamilton, op. cit., I, pp. 288, 306, 309. [*Marx*]

9. Hegel, *Grundlinien der Philosophie des Rechts*, Ier Aufgabe, 1821, p. 346. [*Marx*] See the English translation by T. M. Knox, *Hegel's Philosophy of Right*, Oxford, 1942, p. 173.

1. The terms "species-life" (*Gattungsleben*) and "species-being" (*Gattungswesen*) are derived from Feuerbach. In

the first chapter of *Das Wesen des Christentums* [*The Essence of Christianity*], Leipzig, 1841, Feuerbach discusses the nature of man, and argues that man is to be distinguished from animals not by "consciousness" as such, but by a particular kind of consciousness. Man is not only conscious of himself as an individual; he is also conscious of himself as a memman as *opposed* to his material life. All the presuppositions of this egoistic life continue to exist in *civil society outside* the political sphere, as qualities of civil society. Where the political state has attained to its full development, man leads, not only in thought, in consciousness, but in *reality*, in *life*, a double existence—celestial and terrestrial. He lives in the *political community*, where he regards himself as a *communal being*, and in *civil society* where he acts simply as a *private individual*, treats other men as means, degrades himself to the role of a mere means, and becomes the plaything of alien powers. The political state, in relation to civil society, is just as spiritual as is heaven in relation to earth. It stands in the same opposition to civil society, and overcomes it in the same manner as religion overcomes the narrowness of the profane world; i.e. it has always to acknowledge it again, re-establish it, and allow itself to be dominated by it. Man, in his *most intimate* reality, in civil society, is a profane being. Here, where he appears both to himself and to others as a real individual he is an *illusory* phenomenon. In the state, on the contrary, where he is regarded as a species-being,[2] man is the imaginary member of an imaginary sovereignty, divested of his real, individual life, and infused with an unreal universality.

The conflict in which the individual, as the professor of a *particular* religion, finds himself involved with his own quality of citizenship and with other men as members of the community, may be resolved into the *secular* schism between the *political* state and *civil society*. For man as a *bourgeois*[3] "life in the state is only an appearance or a fleeting exception to the normal and essential." It is true that the *bourgeois*, like the Jew, participates in political life only in a sophistical way, just as the *citoyen*[4] is a Jew or a *bourgeois* only in a sophistical way. But this sophistry is not personal. It is the *sophistry of the political state* itself. The difference between the religious man and the citizen is the same as that between the shopkeeper and the citizens, between the day-labourer and the citizen, between the landed proprietor and the citizen, between the *living individual* and the *citizen*. The contradiction in which the religious man finds himself with the political man, is the same contradiction in which the *bourgeois* finds himself with the citizen, and the member of civil society with his *political lion's skin*.

---

ber of the human species, and so he apprehends a "human essence" which is the same in himself and in other men. According to Feuerbach this ability to conceive of "species" is the fundamental element in the human power of reasoning: "Science is the consciousness of species." Marx, while not departing from this meaning of the terms, employs them in other contexts; and he insists more strongly than Feuerbach that since this "species-consciousness" defines the nature of man, man is only living and acting authentically (i.e. in accordance with his nature) when he lives and acts deliberately as a "species-being," that is, as a *social* being.
2. See previous note.
3. I.e. as a member of civil society.
4. I.e. the individual with political rights.

This secular opposition, to which the Jewish question reduces itself—the relation between the political state and its presuppositions, whether the latter are material elements such as private property, etc., or spiritual elements such as culture or religion, the conflict between the *general interest* and *private interest*, the schism between the *political* state and *civil society*—these profane contradictions, Bauer leaves intact, while he directs his polemic against their *religious* expression. "It is precisely this basis—that is, the needs which assure the existence of *civil society* and *guarantee its necessity*—which exposes its existence to continual danger, maintains an element of uncertainty in civil society, produces this continually changing compound of wealth and poverty, of prosperity and distress, and above all generates change."[5] Compare the whole section entitled "Civil society,"[6] which follows closely the distinctive features of Hegel's philosophy of right. Civil society, in its opposition to this political state, is recognized as necessary because the political state is recognized as necessary.

Political emancipation certainly represents a great progress. It is not, indeed, the final form of human emancipation, but it is the final form of human emancipation *within* the framework of the prevailing social order. It goes without saying that we are speaking here of real, practical emancipation.

Man emancipates himself *politically* from religion by expelling it from the sphere of public law to that of private law. Religion is no longer the spirit of the *state*, in which man behaves, albeit in a specific and limited way and in a particular sphere, as a species-being, in community with other men. It has become the spirit of *civil society*, of the sphere of egoism and of the *bellum omnium contra omnes*. It is no longer the essence of *community*, but the essence of *differentiation*. It has become what it was at the *beginning*, an expression of the fact that man is *separated* from the *community*, from himself and from other men. It is now only the abstract avowal of an individual folly, a private whim or caprice. The infinite fragmentation of religion in North America, for example, already gives it the *external* form of a strictly private affair. It has been relegated among the numerous private interests and exiled from the life of the community as such. But one should have no illusions about the scope of political emancipation. The division of man into the *public person* and the *private person*, the *displacement* of religion from the state to civil society—all this is not a stage in political emancipation but its consummation. Thus political emancipation does not abolish, and does not even strive to abolish, man's *real* religiosity.

The *decomposition* of man into Jew and citizen, Protestant and citizen, religious man and citizen, is not a deception practised

5. Bauer, *Die Judenfrage*, p. 8. [*Marx*]   6. Ibid., pp. 8–9. [*Marx*]

against the political system nor yet an evasion of political emancipation. It is *political emancipation itself*, the *political* mode of emancipation from religion. Certainly, in periods when the political state as such comes violently to birth in civil society, and when men strive to liberate themselves through political emancipation, the state can, and must, proceed to *abolish and destroy religion*; but only in the same way as it proceeds to abolish private property, by declaring a maximum, by confiscation, or by progressive taxation, or in the same way as it proceeds to abolish life, by the *guillotine*. At those times when the state is most aware of itself, political life seeks to stifle its own prerequisites—civil society and its elements—and to establish itself as the genuine and harmonious species-life of man. But it can only achieve this end by setting itself in *violent* contradiction with its own conditions of existence, by declaring a *permanent* revolution. Thus the political drama ends necessarily with the restoration of religion, of private property, of all the elements of civil society, just as war ends with the conclusion of peace.

In fact, the perfected Christian state is not the so-called *Christian* state which acknowledges Christianity as its basis, as the state religion, and thus adopts an exclusive attitude towards other religions; it is, rather, the *atheistic* state, the democratic state, the state which relegates religion among the other elements of civil society. The state which is still theological, which still professes officially the Christian creed, and which has not yet dared to declare itself a *state*, has not yet succeeded in expressing in a human and *secular* form, in its political *reality*, the human basis of which Christianity is the transcendental expression. The so-called Christian state is simply a *non-state*; since it is not Christianity as a religion, but only the *human core* of the Christian religion which can realize itself in truly human creations.

The so-called Christian state is the Christian negation of the state, but not at all the political realization of Christianity. The state which professes Christianity as a religion does not yet profess it in a political form, because it still has a religious attitude towards religion. In other words, such a state is not the *genuine realization* of the human basis of religion, because it still accepts the *unreal, imaginary* form of this human core. The so-called Christian state is an *imperfect* state, for which the Christian religion serves as the *supplement* and *sanctification* of its imperfection. Thus religion becomes necessarily one of its *means*; and so it is the *hypocritical* state. There is a great difference between saying: (i) that the *perfect* state, owing to a deficiency in the general *nature* of the state, counts religion as one of its *prerequisites*, or (ii) that the *imperfect* state, owing to a deficiency in its *particular existence* as an imperfect state, declares that religion is its *basis*. In the latter, religion becomes *imperfect politics*. In the former, the imperfection even of perfected *politics* is revealed in religion. The so-called Christian state needs the Christian religion in order to complete itself *as a state*. The democratic state, the real state, does not need religion for its political consummation. On the contrary, it can dispense with religion, because in this case the human core of religion is realized in a profane manner. The so-called Christian state, on the other hand, has a political attitude towards religion, and a religious attitude towards politics. It reduces political institutions and religion equally to mere appearances.

In order to make this contradiction clearer we shall examine Bauer's model of the Christian state, a model which is derived from his study of the German-Christian state.

"Quite recently," says Bauer, "in order to demonstrate the *impossibility* or the *non-existence* of a Christian state, those passages in the Bible have been frequently quoted with which the state *does not conform* and *cannot conform unless it wishes to dissolve itself entirely*."

"But the question is not so easily settled. What do these Biblical passages demand? Supernatural renunciation, submission to the authority of revelation, turning away from the state, the abolition of profane conditions. But the Christian state proclaims and accomplishes all these things. It has assimilated the *spirit of the Bible*, and if it does not reproduce it exactly in the terms which the Bible uses, that is simply because it expresses this spirit in political forms, in forms which are borrowed from the political system of this world but which, in the religious rebirth which they are obliged to undergo, are reduced to simple appearances. Man turns away from the state and by this means realizes and completes the political institutions."[7]

Bauer continues by showing that the members of a Christian state no longer constitute a nation with a will of its own. The nation has its true existence in the leader to whom it is subjected, but this leader is, by his origin and nature, alien to it since he has been imposed by God without the people having any part in the matter. The laws of such a nation are not its own work, but are direct revelations. The supreme leader, in his relations with the real nation, the masses, requires privileged intermediaries; and the nation itself disintegrates into a multitude of distinct spheres which are formed and determined by chance, are differentiated from each other by their interests and their specific passions and preju-

7. Bauer, *Die Judenfrage*, p. 55. [*Marx*]

dices, and acquire as a privilege the permission to isolate themselves from each other, etc.[8]

But Bauer himself says: "Politics, if it is to be nothing more than religion, should not be politics; any more than the scouring of pans, if it is treated as a religious matter, should be regarded as ordinary housekeeping."[9] But in the German-Christian state religion is an "economic matter" just as "economic matters" are religion. In the German-Christian state the power of religion is the religion of power.

The separation of the "spirit of the Bible" from the "letter of the Bible" is an *irreligious* act. The state which expresses the Bible in the letter of politics, or in any letter other than that of the Holy Ghost, commits sacrilege, if not in the eyes of men at least in the eyes of its own religion. The state which acknowledges the Bible as its charter and Christianity as its supreme rule must be assessed according to the words of the Bible; for even the language of the Bible is sacred. Such a state, as well as the *human rubbish* upon which it is based, finds itself involved in a painful contradiction, which is insoluble from the standpoint of religious consciousness, when it is referred to those words of the Bible "with which it does not conform and *cannot conform unless it wishes to dissolve itself entirely*." And why does it not wish to dissolve itself entirely? The state itself cannot answer either itself or others. In its own consciousness the official Christian state is an "ought" whose realization is imposible. It cannot affirm the *reality* of its own existence without lying to itself, and so it remains always in its own eyes an object of doubt, an uncertain and problematic object. Criticism is, therefore, entirely within its rights in forcing the state, which supports itself upon the Bible, into a total disorder of thought in which it no longer knows whether it is *illusion* or *reality*; and in which the infamy of its *profane* ends (for which religion serves as a cloak) enter into an insoluble conflict with the probity of its *religious* consciousness (for which religion appears as the goal of the world). Such a state can only escape its inner torment by becoming the *myrmidon* of the Catholic Church. In the face of this Church, which asserts that secular power is entirely subordinate to its commands, the state is powerless; powerless the secular power which claims to be the rule of the religious spirit.

What prevails in the so-called Christian state is not man but alienation. The only man who counts—the *King*—is specifically differentiated from other men and is still a religious being associated directly with heaven and with God. The relations which exist here are relations still based upon *faith*. The religious spirit is still not really secularized.

8. Ibid., p. 56. [*Marx*]   9. Ibid., p. 108. [*Marx*]

But the religious spirit cannot be *really* secularized. For what is it but the *non-secular* form of a stage in the development of the human spirit? The religious spirit can only be realized if the stage of development of the human spirit which it expresses in religious form, manifests and constitutes itself in its *secular* form. This is what happens in the *democratic* state. The basis of this state is not Christianity but the *human basis* of Christianity. Religion remains the ideal, non-secular consciousness of its members, because it is the ideal form of the *stage of human development* which has been attained.

The members of the political state are religious because of the dualism between individual life and species-life, between the life of civil society and political life. They are religious in the sense that man treats political life, which is remote from his own individual existence, as if it were his true life; and in the sense that religion is here the spirit of civil society, and expresses the separation and withdrawal of man from man. Political democracy is Christian in the sense that man, not merely one man but every man, is there considered a sovereign being, a supreme being; but it is uneducated, unsocial man, man just as he is in his fortuitous existence, man as he has been corrupted, lost to himself, alienated, subjected to the rule of inhuman conditions and elements, by the whole organization of our society—in short man who is not yet a *real* species-being. Creations of fantasy, dreams, the postulates of Christianity, the sovereignty of man—but of man as an alien being distinguished from the real man—all these become, in democracy, the tangible and present reality, secular maxims.

In the perfected democracy, the religious and theological consciousness appears to itself all the more religious and theological in that it is apparently without any political significance or terrestrial aims, is an affair of the heart withdrawn from the world, an expression of the limitations of reason, a product of arbitrariness and fantasy, a veritable life in the beyond. Christianity here attains the *practical* expression of its universal religious significance, because the most varied views are brought together in the form of Christianity, and still more because Christianity does not ask that anyone should profess Christianity, but simply that he should have some kind of religion (*see* Beaumont, op. cit.). The religious consciousness runs riot in a wealth of contradictions and diversity.

We have shown, therefore, that political emancipation from religion leaves religion in existence, although this is no longer a privileged religion. The contradiction in which the adherent of a particular religion finds himself in relation to his citizenship is only *one aspect* of the universal *secular contradiction between the political state and* civil society. The consummation of the Christian state is a state which acknowledges itself simply as a state and ignores the religion of its members. The emancipation of the state from religion is not the emancipation of the real man from religion.

We do not say to the Jews, therefore, as does Bauer: you cannot be emancipated politically without emancipating yourselves completely from Judaism. We say rather: it is because you can be emancipated politically, without renouncing Judaism completely and absolutely, that *political emancipation* itself is not *human* emancipation. If you want to be politically emancipated, without emancipating yourselves humanly, the inadequacy and the contradiction is not entirely in yourselves but in the *nature* and the *category* of political emancipation. If you are preoccupied with this category you share the general prejudice. Just as the state *evangelizes* when, although it is a state, it adopts a Christian attitude towards the Jews, the Jew *acts politically* when, though a Jew, he demands civil rights.

But if a man, though a Jew, can be emancipated politically and acquire civil rights, can he claim and acquire what are called the *rights of man?* Bauer *denies* it. "The question is whether the Jew as such, that is, the Jew who himself avows that he is constrained by his true nature to live eternally separate from men, is able to acquire and to concede to others the *universal rights of man.*"

"The idea of the rights of man was only discovered in the Christian world, in the last century. It is not an innate idea; on the contrary, it is acquired in a struggle against the historical traditions in which man has been educated up to the present time. The rights of man are not, therefore, a gift of nature, nor a legacy from past history, but the reward of a struggle against the accident of birth and against the privileges which history has hitherto transmitted from generation to generation. They are the results of culture, and only he can possess them who has merited and earned them."

"But can the Jew really take possession of them? As long as he remains Jewish the limited nature which makes him a Jew must prevail over the human nature which should associate him, as a man, with other men; and it will isolate him from everyone who is not a Jew. He declares, by this separation, that the particular nature which makes him Jewish is his true and supreme nature, before which human nature has to efface itself."

"Similarly, the Christian as such cannot grant the rights of man."[1]

According to Bauer man has to sacrifice the *"privilege of faith"* in order to acquire the general rights of man. Let us consider for a moment the so-called rights of man; let us examine them in their most authentic form, that which they have among those who *dis-*

---

1. Bauer, *Die Judenfrage*, pp. 19–20. [*Marx*]

covered them, the North Americans and the French! These rights of man are, in part, *political rights*, which can only be exercised if one is a member of a community. Their content is *participation* in the *community* life, in the *political* life of the community, the life of the state. They fall in the category of *political liberty*, of *civil rights*, which as we have seen do not at all presuppose the consistent and positive abolition of religion; nor consequently, of Judaism. It remains to consider the other part, namely the *rights of man* as distinct from the *rights of the citizen*.

Among them is to be found the freedom of conscience, the right to practise a chosen religion. The *privilege of faith* is expressly recognized, either as a *right of man* or as a consequence of a right of man, namely liberty. *Declaration of the Rights of Man and of the Citizen*, 1791, Article 10: "No one is to be disturbed on account of his opinions, even religious opinions." There is guaranteed, as one of the rights of man, "the liberty of every man to practise the *religion* to which he adheres."

The *Declaration of the Rights of Man, etc.* 1793, enumerates among the rights of man (Article 7): "The liberty of religious observance." Moreover, it is even stated, with respect to the right to express ideas and opinions, to hold meetings, to practise a religion, that: "The necessity of enunciating these *rights* presupposes either the existence or the recent memory of despotism." Compare the Constitution of 1795, Section XII, Article 354.

Constitution of Pennsylvania, Article 9, § 3: "All men have received from nature the imprescriptible *right* to worship the Almighty according to the dictates of their conscience, and no one can be legally compelled to follow, establish or support against his will any religion or religious ministry. No human authority can, in any circumstances, intervene in a matter of conscience or control the forces of the soul."

Constitution of New Hampshire, Articles 5 and 6: "Among these natural rights some are by nature inalienable since nothing can replace them. The rights of conscience are among them."[2]

The incompatibility between religion and the rights of man is so little manifest in the concept of the rights of man that the *right to be religious*, in one's own fashion, and to practise one's own particular religion, is expressly included among the rights of man. The privilege of faith is a *universal right of man*.

A distinction is made between the rights of man and the rights of the citizen. Who is this *man* distinct from the *citizen*? No one but the *member of civil society*. Why is the member of civil society called "man," simply man, and why are his rights called the "rights of man"? How is this fact to be explained? By the relation between

2. Beaumont, op. cit., II, pp. 206–7. [*Marx*]

the political state and civil society, and by the nature of political emancipation.

Let us notice first of all that the so-called *rights of man*, as distinct from the *rights of the citizen*, are simply the rights of a *member of civil society*, that is, of egoistic man, of man separated from other men and from the community. The most radical constitution, that of 1793, says: *Declaration of the Rights of Man and of the Citizen:* Article 2. "These rights, etc. (the natural and imprescriptible rights) are: *equality, liberty, security, property.*

What constitutes liberty?

Article 6. "Liberty is the power which man has to do everything which does not harm the rights of others."

Liberty is, therefore, the right to do everything which does not harm others. The limits within which each individual can act without harming others are determined by law, just as the boundary between two fields is marked by a stake. It is a question of the liberty of man regarded as an isolated monad, withdrawn into himself. Why, according to Bauer, is the Jew not fitted to acquire the rights of man? "As long as he remains Jewish the limited nature which makes him a Jew must prevail over the human nature which should associate him, as a man, with other men; and it will isolate him from everyone who is not a Jew." But liberty as a right of man is not founded upon the relations between man and man, but rather upon the separation of man from man. It is the right of such separation. The right of the *circumscribed* individual, withdrawn into himself.

The practical application of the right of liberty is the right of private property. What constitutes the right of private property?

Article 16 (Constitution of 1793). "The right of *property* is that which belongs to every citizen of enjoying and disposing *as he will* of his goods and revenues, of the fruits of his work and industry."

The right of property is, therefore, the right to enjoy one's fortune and to dispose of it as one will; without regard for other men and independently of society. It is the right of self-interest. This individual liberty, and its application, form the basis of civil society. It leads every man to see in other men, not the *realization,* but rather the *limitation* of his own liberty. It declares above all the right "to enjoy and to dispose *as one will,* one's goods and revenues, the fruits of one's work and industry."

There remain the other rights of man, equality and security.

The term "equality" has here no political significance. It is only the equal right to liberty as defined above; namely that every man is equally regarded as a self-sufficient monad. The Constitution of 1795 defines the concept of liberty in this sense.

Article 5 (Constitution of 1795). "Equality consists in the fact that the law is the same for all, whether it protects or punishes."

And security?

Article 8 (Constitution of 1793). "Security consists in the protection afforded by society to each of its members for the preservation of his person, his rights, and his property."

Security is the supreme social concept of civil society; the concept of the police. The whole society exists only in order to guarantee for each of its members the preservation of his person, his rights and his property. It is in this sense that Hegel calls civil society "the state of need and of reason."

The concept of security is not enough to raise civil society above its egoism. Security is, rather, the *assurance* of its egoism.

None of the supposed rights of man, therefore, go beyond the egoistic man, man as he is, as a member of civil society; that is, an individual separated from the community, withdrawn into himself, wholly preoccupied with his private interest and acting in accordance with his private caprice. Man is far from being considered, in the rights of man, as a species-being; on the contrary, species-life itself—society—appears as a system which is external to the individual and as a limitation of his original independence. The only bond between men is natural necessity, need and private interest, the preservation of their property and their egoistic persons.

It is difficult enough to understand that a nation which has just begun to liberate itself, to tear down all the barriers between different sections of the people and to establish a political community, should solemnly proclaim (*Declaration* of 1791) the rights of the egoistic man, separated from his fellow men and from the community, and should renew this proclamation at a moment when only the most heroic devotion can save the nation (and is, therefore, urgently called for), and when the sacrifice of all the interests of civil society is in question and egoism should be punished as a crime. (*Declaration of the Rights of Man, etc.* 1793). The matter becomes still more incomprehensible when we observe that the political liberators reduce citizenship, the *political community,* to a mere *means* for preserving these so-called rights of man; and consequently, that the citizen is declared to be the servant of egoistic "man," that the sphere in which man functions as a species-being is degraded to a level below the sphere where he functions as a partial being, and finally that it is man as a bourgeois and not man as a citizen who is considered the *true* and *authentic* man.

"The end of every *political association* is the *preservation* of the natural and imprescriptible rights of man." (*Declaration of the Rights of Man, etc.* 1791, Article 2.) "Government is instituted in

order to guarantee man's enjoyment of his natural and imprescriptible rights." (*Declaration, etc.* 1793, Article 1.) Thus, even in the
period of its youthful enthusiasm, which is raised to fever pitch by
the force of circumstances, political life declares itself to be only a
means, whose end is the life of civil society. It is true that its revolutionary practice is in flagrant contradiction with its theory.
While, for instance, security is declared to be one of the rights of
man, the violation of the privacy of correspondence is openly considered. While the "unlimited freedom of the Press" (*Constitution*
of 1793, Article 122), as a corollary of the right of individual liberty, is guaranteed, the freedom of the Press is completely
destroyed, since "the freedom of the Press should not be permitted
when it endangers public liberty."[3] This amounts to saying: the
right to liberty ceases to be a right as soon as it comes into conflict
with *political* life, whereas in theory political life is no more than
the guarantee of the rights of man—the rights of the individual
man—and should, therefore, be suspended as soon as it comes into
contradiction with its *end*, these rights of man. But practice is only
the exception, while theory is the rule. Even if one decided to
regard revolutionary practice as the correct expression of this relation, the problem would remain as to why it is that in the minds of
political liberators the relation is inverted, so that the end appears
as the means and the means as the end? This optical illusion of
their consciousness would always remain a problem, though a psychological and theoretical one.

But the problem is easily solved.

Political emancipation is at the same time the *dissolution* of the
old society, upon which the sovereign power, the alienated political
life of the people, rests. Political revolution is a revolution of civil
society. What was the nature of the old society? It can be characterized in one word: *feudalism*. The old civil society had a *directly
political* character; that is, the elements of civil life such as property, the family, and types of occupation had been raised, in the
form of lordship, caste and guilds, to elements of political life.
They determined, in this form, the relation of the individual to the
state as a whole; that is, his *political* situation, or in other words, his
separation and exclusion from the other elements of society. For
this organization of national life did not constitute property and
labour as social elements; it rather succeeded in *separating* them
from the body of the state, and made them *distinct* societies within
society. Nevertheless, at least in the feudal sense, the vital functions and conditions of civil society remained political. They
excluded the individual from the body of the state, and transformed the *particular* relation which existed between his corpora-

3. Buchez et Roux, "Robespierre jeune," *Histoire parlementaire de la* *Révolution française*, Tome XXVIII, p. 159. [*Marx*]

tion and the state into a general relation between the individual and social life, just as they transformed his specific civil activity and situation into a general activity and situation. As a result of this organization, the state as a whole and its consciousness, will and activity—the general political power—also necessarily appeared as the *private* affair of a ruler and his servants, separated from the people.

The political revolution which overthrew this power of the ruler, which made state affairs the affairs of the people, and the political state a matter of *general* concern, i.e. a real state, necessarily shattered everything—estates, corporations, guilds, privileges—which expressed the separation of the people from community life. The political revolution therefore *abolished* the *political character of civil society*. It dissolved civil society into its basic elements, on the one hand *individuals*, and on the other hand the *material and cultural elements* which formed the life experience and the civil situation of these individuals. It set free the political spirit which had, so to speak, been dissolved, fragmented and lost in the various culs-de-sac of feudal society; it reassembled these scattered fragments, liberated the political spirit from its connexion with civil life and made of it the community sphere, the *general* concern of the people, in principle independent of these particular elements of civil life. A *specific* activity and situation in life no longer had any but an individual significance. They no longer constituted the general relation between the individual and the state as a whole. Public affairs as such became the general affair of each individual, and political functions became general functions.

But the consummation of the idealism of the state was at the same time the consummation of the materialism of civil society. The bonds which had restrained the egoistic spirit of civil society were removed along with the political yoke. Political emancipation was at the same time an emancipation of civil society from politics and from even the *semblance* of a general content.

Feudal society was dissolved into its basic element, *man*; but into *egoistic* man who was its real foundation.

Man in this aspect, the member of civil society, is now the foundation and presupposition of the *political* state. He is recognized as such in the rights of man.

But the liberty of egoistic man, and the recognition of this liberty, is rather the recognition of the *frenzied* movement of the cultural and material elements which form the content of his life.

Thus man was not liberated from religion; he received religious liberty. He was not liberated from property; he received the liberty to own property. He was not liberated from the egoism of business; he received the liberty to engage in business.

The *formation of the political state*, and the dissolution of civil society into independent *individuals* whose relations are regulated by *law*, as the relations between men in the corporations and guilds were regulated by *privilege*, are accomplished by *one and the same act*. Man as a member of civil society—*non-political* man—necessarily appears as the *natural* man. The rights of man appear as natural rights because *conscious* activity is concentrated upon political *action*. *Egoistic* man is the *passive, given* result of the dissolution of society, an object of *direct apprehension* and consequently a *natural* object. The *political revolution* dissolves civil society into its elements without *revolutionizing* these elements themselves or subjecting them to criticism. This revolution regards civil society, the sphere of human needs, labour, private interests and civil law, as the *basis of its own existence*, as a self-subsistent *precondition*, and thus as its *natural basis*. Finally, man as a member of civil society is identified with *authentic man*, man as distinct from citizen, because he is man in his sensuous, individual and *immediate* existence, whereas *political* man is only abstract, artificial man, man as an *allegorical, moral* person. Thus man as he really is, is seen only in the form of *egoistic* man, and man in his *true* nature only in the form of the *abstract citizen*.

The abstract notion of political man is well formulated by Rousseau: "Whoever dares undertake to establish a people's institutions must feel himself capable of *changing*, as it were, *human nature* itself, of *transforming* each individual who, in isolation, is a complete but solitary whole, into a *part* of something greater than himself, from which in a sense, he derives his life and his being; [of changing man's nature in order to strengthen it;] of substituting a limited and moral existence for the physical and independent life [with which all of us are endowed by nature]. His task, in short, is to take from *a man his own powers*, and to give him in exchange alien powers which he can only employ with the help of other men."[4]

Every emancipation is a *restoration* of the human world and of human relationships to *man himself*.

Political emancipation is a reduction of man, on the one hand to a member of civil society, an *independent* and *egoistic* individual, and on the other hand, to a *citizen*, to a moral person.

Human emancipation will only be complete when the real, individual man has absorbed into himself the abstract citizen; when as an individual man, in his everyday life, in his work, and in his relationships, he has become a *species-being*; and when he has recognized and organized his own powers (*forces propres*) as *social*

4. J. J. Rousseau, *Du contrat social*, Book II. Chapter VII, "The Legislator." Marx quoted this passage in French, and added the emphases; he omitted the portions enclosed in square brackets.

powers so that he no longer separates this social power from himself as *political* power.

2. Bruno Bauer, "Die Fähigkeit der heutigen Juden und Christen frei zu werden"[5]

It is in this form that Bauer studies the relation between the *Jewish and Christian religions*, and also their relation with modern criticism. This latter relation is their relation with "the capacity to become free."

He reaches this conclusion: "The Christian has only to raise himself one degree, to rise above his religion, in order to abolish religion in general," and thus to become free; but "the Jew, on the contrary, has to break not only with his Jewish nature, but also with the process towards the consummation of his religion, a process which has remained alien to him."[6]

Thus Bauer here transforms the question of Jewish emancipation into a purely religious question. The theological doubt about whether the Jew or the Christian has the better chance of attaining salvation is reproduced here in the more enlightened form: which of the two is more *capable of emancipation*? It is indeed no longer asked: which makes free—Judaism or Christianity? On the contrary, it is now asked: which makes free—the negation of Judaism or the negation of Christianity?

"If they wish to become free the Jews should not embrace Christianity as such, but Christianity in dissolution, religion in dissolution; that is to say, the Enlightenment, criticism, and its outcome, a free humanity."[7]

It is still a matter, therefore, of the Jews professing some kind of faith; no longer Christianity as such, but Christianity in dissolution.

Bauer asks the Jews to break with the essence of the Christian religion, but this demand does not follow, as he himself admits, from the development of the Jewish nature.

From the moment when Bauer, at the end of his *Judenfrage*, saw in Judaism only a crude religious criticism of Christianity, and, therefore, attributed to it only a religious significance, it was to be expected that he would transform the emancipation of the Jews into a philosophico-theological act.

Bauer regards the *ideal* and abstract essence of the Jew—his *religion*—as the *whole* of his nature. He, therefore, concludes rightly that "The Jew contributes nothing to mankind when he disregards

5. The capacity of the present-day Jews and Christians to become free. [In *Einundzwanzig Bogen aus der Schweiz* (Ed. G. Herwegh), pp. 56–71.—*Marx*]
6. Loc. cit., p. 71. [*Marx*]
7. Ibid., p. 70. [*Marx*]

his own limited law," when he renounces all his Judaism.[8]

The relation between Jews and Christians thus becomes the following: the only interest which the emancipation of the Jew presents for the Christian is a general human and *theoretical* interest. Judaism is a phenomenon which offends the religious eye of the Christian. As soon as the Christian's eye ceases to be religious the phenomenon ceases to offend it. The emancipation of the Jew is not in itself, therefore, a task which falls to the Christian to perform.

The Jew, on the other hand, if he wants to emancipate himself has to undertake, besides his own work, the work of the Christian—the "criticism of the gospels," of the "life of Jesus," etc.[9]

"It is for them to arrange matters; they will decide their own destiny. But history does not allow itself to be mocked."[1]

We will attempt to escape from the theological formulation of the question. For us, the question concerning the capacity of the Jew for emancipation is transformed into another question: what specific *social* element is it necessary to overcome in order to abolish Judaism? For the capacity of the present-day Jew to emancipate himself expresses the relation of Judaism to the emancipation of the contemporary world. The relation results necessarily from the particular situation of Judaism in the present enslaved world.

Let us consider the real Jew: not the *sabbath Jew*, whom Bauer considers, but the *everyday Jew*.

Let us not seek the secret of the Jew in his religion, but let us seek the secret of the religion in the real Jew.

What is the profane basis of Judaism? *Practical* need, *self-interest*. What is the worldly cult of the Jew? *Huckstering*. What is his worldly god? *Money*.

Very well: then in emancipating itself from *huckstering* and *money*, and thus from real and practical Judaism, our age would emancipate itself.

An organization of society which would abolish the preconditions and thus the very possibility of huckstering, would make the Jew impossible. His religious consciousness would evaporate like some insipid vapour in the real, life-giving air of society. On the other hand, when the Jew recognizes his *practical* nature as invalid and endeavours to abolish it, he begins to deviate from his former path of development, works for general *human emancipation* and

---

8. Loc. cit., p. 65. [*Marx*]
9. Marx alludes here to Bruno Bauer, *Kritik der evangelischen Geschichte der Synoptiker*, Vols. I–II, Leipzig, 1841; Vol. III, Braunschweig, 1842, and David Friedrich Strauss, *Das Leben Jesu*, 2 vols. Tübingen, 1835–6.

An English translation of Strauss' book by Marian Evans (George Eliot) was published in 1846 under the title *Life of Jesus Critically Examined*.
1. Bauer, "Die Fähigkeit . . . etc.," p. 71. [*Marx*]

turns against the *supreme practical* expression of human self-estrangement.

We discern in Judaism, therefore, a universal *antisocial* element of the *present time*, whose historical development, zealously aided in its harmful aspects by the Jews, has now attained its culminating point, a point at which it must necessarily begin to disintegrate.

In the final analysis, the *emancipation of* the Jews is the emancipation of mankind from *Judaism.*

The Jew has already emancipated himself in a Jewish fashion. "The Jew, who is merely tolerated in Vienna for example, determines the fate of the whole Empire by his financial power. The Jew, who may be entirely without rights in the smallest German state, decides the destiny of Europe. While the corporations and guilds exclude the Jew, or at least look on him with disfavour, the audacity of industry mocks the obstinacy of medieval institutions."[2]

This is not an isolated instance. The Jew has emancipated himself in a Jewish manner, not only by acquiring the power of money, but also because *money* has become, through him and also apart from him, a world power, while the practical Jewish spirit has become the practical spirit of the Christian nations. The Jews have emancipated themselves in so far as the Christians have become Jews.

Thus, for example, Captain Hamilton reports that the devout and politically free inhabitant of New England is a kind of Laocoon who makes not the least effort to escape from the serpents which are crushing him. *Mammon* is his idol which he adores not only with his lips but with the whole force of his body and mind. In his view the world is no more than a Stock Exchange, and he is convinced that he has no other destiny here below than to become richer than his neighbour. Trade has seized upon all his thoughts, and he has no other recreation than to exchange objects. When he travels he carries, so to speak, his goods and his counter on his back and talks only of interest and profit. If he loses sight of his own business for an instant it is only in order to pry into the business of his competitors.[3]

In North America, indeed, the effective domination of the Christian world by Judaism has come to be manifested in a common and unambiguous form; the *preaching of the Gospel* itself, Christian preaching, has become an article of commerce, and the bankrupt trader in the church behaves like the prosperous clergyman in business. "This man whom you see at the head of a respectable congregation began as a trader; his business having failed he has become a

2. Bauer, *Die Judenfrage,* p. 14. [*Marx*]   3. Hamilton, op. cit., I, p. 213. [*Marx*] Marx paraphrases this passage.

minister. This other began as a priest, but as soon as he had accumulated some money he abandoned the priesthood for trade. In the eyes of many people the religious ministry is a veritable industrial career."[4]

According to Bauer, it is "a hypocritical situation when, in theory, the Jew is deprived of political rights, while in practice he wields tremendous power and exercises on a wholesale scale the political influence which is denied him in minor matters."[5]

The contradiction which exists between the effective political power of the Jew and his political rights, is the contradiction between politics and the power of money in general. Politics is in principle superior to the power of money, but in practice it has become its bondsman.

Judaism has maintained itself *alongside* Christianity, not only because it constituted the religious criticism of Christianity and embodied the doubt concerning the religious origins of Christianity, but equally because the practical Jewish spirit—Judaism or commerce[6]—has perpetuated itself in Christian society and has even attained its highest development there. The Jew, who occupies a distinctive place in civil society, only manifests in a distinctive way the Judaism of civil society.

Judaism has been preserved, not in spite of history, but by history.

It is from its own entrails that civil society ceaselessly engenders the Jew.

What was, in itself, the basis of the Jewish religion? Practical need, egoism.

The monotheism of the Jews is, therefore, in reality, a polytheism of the numerous needs of man, a polytheism which makes even the lavatory an object of divine regulation. *Practical need, egoism,* is the principle of *civil society,* and is revealed as such in its pure form as soon as civil society has fully engendered the political state. The god of *practical need and self-interest* is *money.*

Money is the jealous god of Israel, beside which no other god may exist. Money abases all the gods of mankind and changes them into commodities. Money is the universal and self-sufficient *value* of all things. It has, therefore, deprived the whole world, both the human world and nature, of their own proper value. Money is the alienated essence of man's work and existence; this essence dominates him and he worships it.

4. Beaumont, op. cit., II, p. 179. [*Marx*]
5. Bauer, *Die Judenfrage*, p. 14. [*Marx*]
6. The German word *Judentum* had, in the language of the time, the secondary meaning of "commerce," and in this and other passages Marx exploits the two senses of the word.

The god of the Jews has been secularized and has become the god of this world. The bill of exchange is the real god of the Jew. His god is only an illusory bill of exchange.

The mode of perceiving nature, under the rule of private property and money, is a real contempt for, and a practical degradation of, nature, which does indeed exist in the Jewish religion but only as a creature of the imagination.

It is in this sense that Thomas Münzer declares it intolerable "that every creature should be transformed into property—the fishes in the water, the birds of the air, the plants of the earth: the creature too should become free."[7]

That which is contained in an abstract form in the Jewish religion—contempt for theory, for art, for history, and for man as an end in himself—is the *real, conscious* standpoint and the virtue of the man of money. Even the species-relation itself, the relation between man and woman, becomes an object of commerce. Woman is bartered away.

The *chimerical* nationality of the Jew is the nationality of the trader, and above all of the financier.

The law, without basis or reason, of the Jew, is only the religious caricature of morality and right in general, without basis or reason; the purely *formal* rites with which the world of self-interest encircles itself.

Here again the supreme condition of man is his *legal* status, his relationship to laws which are valid for him, not because they are the laws of his own will and nature, but because they are dominant and any infraction of them will be *avenged*.

Jewish Jesuitism, the same practical Jesuitism which Bauer discovers in the Talmud, is the relationship of the world of self-interest to the laws which govern this world, laws which the world devotes its principal arts to circumventing.

Indeed, the operation of this world within its framework of laws is impossible without the continual supersession of law.

Judaism could not develop further as a *religion*, in a theoretical form, because the world view of practical need is, by its very nature, circumscribed, and the delineation of its characteristics soon completed.

The religion of practical need could not, by its very nature, find its consummation in theory, but only in *practice*, just because practice is its truth.

Judaism could not create a new world. It could only bring the

---

7. Quoted from Thomas Münzer's pamphlet against Luther, "Hochverrusachte Schutzrede und Antwort wider das geistlose, sanftlebende Fleisch zu Wittenberg, welches mit verkehrter Weise durch den Diebstahl der heiligen Schrift die erbärmliche Christenheit also ganz jammerlich besudelt hat." (p. B. iii. 1524.) [*Marx*]

new creations and conditions of the world within its own sphere of activity, because practical need, the spirit of which is self-interest, is always passive, cannot expand at will, but *finds* itself extended as a result of the continued development of society.

Judaism attains its apogee with the perfection of civil society; but civil society only reaches perfection in the *Christian* world. Only under the sway of Christianity, which *objectifies all* national, natural, moral and theoretical relationships, could civil society separate itself completely from the life of the state, sever all the species-bonds of man, establish egoism and selfish need in their place, and dissolve the human world into a world of atomistic, antagonistic individuals.

Christianity issued from Judaism. It has now been re-absorbed into Judaism.

From the beginning, the Christian was the theorizing Jew; consequently, the Jew is the practical Christian. And the practical Christian has become a Jew again.

It was only in appearance that Christianity overcame real Judaism. It was too *refined*, too spiritual to eliminate the crudeness of practical need except by raising it into the ethereal realm.

Christianity is the sublime thought of Judaism; Judaism is the vulgar practical application of Christianity. But this practical application could only become universal when Christianity as perfected religion had accomplished, in a *theoretical* fashion, the alienation of man from himself and from nature.

It was only then that Judaism could attain universal domination and could turn alienated man and alienated nature into *alienable*, saleable objects, in thrall to egoistic need and huckstering.

Objectification is the practice of alienation. Just as man, so long as he is engrossed in religion, can only objectify his essence by an *alien* and fantastic being; so under the sway of egoistic need, he can only affirm himself and produce objects in practice by subordinating his products and his own activity to the domination of an alien entity, and by attributing to them the significance of an alien entity, namely money.

In its perfected practice the spiritual egoism of Christianity necessarily becomes the material egoism of the Jew, celestial need is transmuted into terrestrial need, subjectivism into self-interest. The tenacity of the Jew is to be explained, not by his religion, but rather by the human basis of his religion—practical need and egoism.

It is because the essence of the Jew was universally realized and secularized in civil society, that civil society could not convince the Jew of the *unreality* of his *religious* essence, which is precisely the ideal representation of practical need. It is not only, therefore, in the Pentateuch and the Talmud, but also in contemporary society, that we find the essence of the present-day Jew; not as an abstract essence, but as one which is supremely empirical, not only as a limitation of the Jew, but as the Jewish narrowness of society.

As soon as society succeeds in abolishing the *empirical* essence of Judaism—huckstering and its conditions—the Jew becomes *impossible*, because his consciousness no longer has an object. The subjective basis of Judaism—practical need—assumes a human form, and the conflict between the individual, sensuous existence of man and his species-existence, is abolished.

The *social* emancipation of the Jew is the *emancipation of society from Judaism.*

Economic and Philosophic
Manuscripts of 1844: Selections

KARL MARX

Soon after moving to Paris in November, 1843, Marx applied himself to the criticism of political economy—the new phase of his critical program foreshadowed in his two essays in the *Deutsch-Französische Jahrbücher*. Between March and August of 1844 he produced the rough draft of what, judging by his preface, was to have been a book. He did not finish it for publication, however, and it lay unpublished for more than eighty years. The surviving parts, comprising four manuscripts, were given the name shown above. An incomplete version in Russian translation was published in Moscow in 1927. The first full edition in German, prepared by D. Riazanov of the Marx-Engels Institute in Moscow, was published in Berlin in 1932, in *Karl Marx, Friedrich Engels, Historisch-kritische Gesamtausgabe*.

The fundamentals of the Marxist interpretation of history are to be found in the 1844 manuscripts, including the notion of the proletarian revolution and future communism as the goal of the historical process. The theory is set forth, however, in terms of philosophical concepts drawn by Marx from Hegel and Feuerbach, most notably the concept of man's "self-alienation" or "self-estrangement." History, particularly under modern capitalism, is seen as a story of man's alienation in his life as producer, and communism is presented as the final transcendence of alienation via a revolution against private property. Because the 1844 manuscripts show us Marxism at the moment of its genesis in Marx's mind and because they help to clarify both the relation of Marxism to earlier German philosophy and its ethical significance, their publication has profoundly affected scholarship on Marx and Marxism in our time.

A portion of the manuscripts consists largely of excerpts from writings of the political economists on such topics as wages of labor, profit of capital, and rent of land. The material reprinted here, comprising in all a little less than half of the manuscripts, consists of the preface and the sections entitled "Estranged Labour," "Private Property and Communism," "The Power of Money in Bourgeois Society," and "Critique of the Hegelian Dialectic and Philosophy as a Whole," all of which are given in full.

The translation and notes are by Martin Milligan.

Preface

I have already given notice in the *Deutsch-Französische Jahrbücher* of the critique of jurisprudence and political science in the form of a critique of the *Hegelian* Philosophy of Right. In the course of elaboration for publication, the intermingling of criticism directed only against speculation with criticism of the various subjects themselves proved utterly unsuitable, hampering the development of the argument and rendering comprehension difficult. Moreover the wealth and diversity of the subjects to be treated, could have been compressed into *one* work only in a purely aphoristic style; whilst an aphoristic presentation of this kind, for its part, would have given the *impression* of arbitrary systematizing. I shall therefore issue the critique of law, ethics, politics, etc., in a series of distinct, independent pamphlets, and at the end try in a special work to present them again as a connected whole showing the interrelationship of the separate parts, and finally, shall make a critique of the speculative elaboration of that material. For this reason it will be found that the interconnection between political economy and the state, law, ethics, civil life, etc., is touched on in the present work only to the extent to which political economy itself *ex professo*[1] touches on these subjects.

It is hardly necessary to assure the reader conversant with political economy that my results have been won by means of a wholly empirical analysis based on a conscientious critical study of political economy.

[Whereas the uninformed reviewer who tries to hide his complete ignorance and intellectual poverty by hurling the *"utopian phrase"* at the positive critic's head, or again such phrases as "pure, resolute, utterly critical criticism," the "not merely legal but social—utterly social—society," the "compact, massy mass," the "oratorical orators of the massy mass,"[2] this reviewer has yet to furnish the first proof that besides his theological family-affairs he has anything to contribute to a discussion of *worldly* matters.][3]

It goes without saying that besides the French and English Social-

---

1. Particularly.
2. Marx refers here to the Young Hegelian Bruno Bauer, who had published in *Allgemeine Literatur-Zeitung* two long reviews dealing with books, articles and pamphlets on the Jewish question. Most of the quoted phrases are taken from these reviews in *Allgemeine Literatur-Zeitung*, vol. 1, December, 1843; vol. 4, March, 1844. The expressions "utopian phrase" and "compact

mass" can be found in Bauer's article "Was ist jetzt der Gegenstand der Kritik?" published in *Allgemeine Literatur-Zeitung*, vol. 8, July, 1844.

Allgemeine Literatur-Zeitung (General Literary Gazette), a German monthly, was published by Bauer in Charlottenburg from December, 1843, to October, 1844.

3. Passages enclosed in brackets were crossed out by Marx in his manuscript.

ists I have made use of German socialist works as well. The only *original* German works of substance in this science, however—other than Weitling's writings—are the essays by Hess published in *Einundzwanzig Bogen*,[4] and Engels' *Umrisse zu einer Kritik der Nationalökonomie*[5] in the *Deutsch-Französische Jahrbücher* where, likewise, I indicated in a very general way the basic elements of this work.

[Besides being indebted to these authors who have given critical attention to political economy, positive criticism as a whole—and therefore also German positive criticism of political economy—owes its true foundation to the discoveries of *Feuerbach*, against whose *Philosophie der Zukunft*[6] and *Thesen zur Reform der Philosophie*[7] in the *Anecdotis*,[8] despite the tacit use that is made of them, the petty envy of some and the veritable wrath of others seem to have instigated a regular conspiracy of *silence*.]

It is only with *Feuerbach* that *positive*, humanistic and naturalistic criticism begins. The less noise they make, the more certain, profound, widespread and enduring is the effect of *Feuerbach*'s writings, the only writings since Hegel's *Phänomenologie* and *Logik* to contain a real theoretical revolution.

In contrast to the *critical theologians*[9] of our day, I have deemed the concluding chapter of the present work—the settling of accounts with *Hegelian dialectic* and Hegelian philosophy as a whole—to be absolutely necessary, a task not yet performed. This *lack of thoroughness* is not accidental, since even the *critical* theologian remains a *theologian*. Hence, either he had to start from certain presuppositions of philosophy accepted as authoritative; or if in the process of criticism and as a result of other people's discoveries doubts about these philosophical presuppositions have arisen in him, he abandons them without vindication and in a cowardly fashion, *abstracts* from them showing his servile dependence on these presuppositions and his resentment at this dependence merely in a negative, unconscious and sophistical manner.

[In this connection the critical theologian is either forever repeat-

4. The full title of this collection of articles is *Einundzwanzig Bogen aus der Schweiz* (*Twenty-One Sheets from Switzerland*), Erster Teil, Zürich and Winterthur, 1843.

5. Engels' "Outlines of a Critique of Political Economy."

6. Ludwig Feuerbach, *Grundsätze der Philosophie der Zukunft* (*Principles of the Philosophy of the Future*), Zürich and Winterthur, 1843.

7. Ludwig Feuerbach, *Vorläufige Thesen zur Reformation der Philosophie* (*Preliminary Theses on the Reformation of Philosophy*) published in *Anekdota*, vol. II.

8. Marx's abbreviation for *Anekdota zur neuesten deutschen Philosophie und Publicistik* (*Unpublished Materials Related to Modern German Philosophy and Writing*), a two-volume collection published by Arnold Ruge in Switzerland. It included Marx's *Notes on the Latest Prussian Instruction to Censors* and *Luther—the Arbiter Between Strauss and Feuerbach*, and articles by Bruno Bauer, Ludwig Feuerbach, Friedrich Köppen, Arnold Ruge, etc.

9. Marx has in mind Bauer and his followers, who were associated with the *Allgemeine Literatur-Zeitung*.

ing assurances about the *purity* of his own criticism, or tries to make it seem as though all that was left for criticism to deal with now was some other immature form of criticism outside itself—say eighteenth-century criticism—and the backwardness of the *masses*, in order to divert the observer's attention as well as his own from the *necessary* task of settling accounts between *criticism* and its point of origin—Hegelian *dialectic* and German philosophy as a whole—from this necessary raising of modern criticism above its own limitation and crudity. Eventually, however, whenever discoveries (such as *Feuerbach's*) are made about the nature of his own philosophic presuppositions, the critical theologian partly makes it appear as if he were the one who had accomplished this, producing that appearance by taking the results of these discoveries and, without being able to develop them, hurling them in the form of *catch-phrases* at writers still caught in the confines of philosophy; partly he even manages to acquire a sense of his own superiority to such discoveries by covertly asserting in a veiled, malicious and sceptical fashion elements of the Hegelian *dialectic* which he still finds lacking in the criticism of that dialectic (which have not yet been critically served up to him for his use) against such criticism—not having tried to bring such elements into their proper relation or having been capable of doing so, asserting, say, the category of mediating proof against the category of positive, self-originating truth, etc., in a way *peculiar* to Hegelian dialectic. For to the theological critic it seems quite natural that everything has to be *done* by philosophy, so that he can *chatter* away about purity, resoluteness, and utterly critical criticism; and he fancies himself the true *conqueror of philosophy* whenever he happens to *feel* some "moment" in Hegel[1] to be lacking in Feuerbach—for however much he practises the spiritual idolatry of *"self-consciousness"* and *"mind"* the theological critic does not get beyond feeling to consciousness.][2]

On close inspection *theological criticism*—genuinely progressive though it was at the inception of the movement—is seen in the final analysis to be nothing but the culmination and consequence of the old *philosophical*, and especially the *Hegelian, transcendentalism*, twisted into a *theological caricature*. This interesting example of the justice in history, which now assigns to theology, ever

1. "Moment" is a technical term in Hegelian philosophy meaning a vital element of thought. The term is used to stress that thought is a process, and thus that elements in a system of thought are also phases in a movement. 2. In Hegel, "feeling" (*Empfindung*) denotes a relatively low form of mental life in which the subjective and the objective are still confused together.

"Consciousness" (*Bewusstein*)—the name given by Hegel to the first major section of his *Phenomenology of Mind*—denotes those forms of mental activity where a subject first seeks to comprehend an object. "Self-consciousness" and "mind" denote subsequent, higher phases in the evolution of "absolute knowledge" or "the absolute".

philosophy's spot of infection, the further role of portraying in itself the negative dissolution of philosophy—i.e., the process of its decay—this historical nemesis I shall demonstrate on another occasion.

How far, on the other hand, *Feuerbach's* discoveries about the nature of philosophy required still, for their *proof* at least, a critical settling of accounts with philosophical dialectic will be seen from my exposition itself.]

Estranged Labour[3]

We have proceeded from the premises of political economy. We have accepted its language and its laws. We presupposed private property, the separation of labour, capital and land, and of wages, profit of capital and rent of land—likewise division of labour, competition, the concept of exchange-value, etc. On the basis of political economy itself, in its own words, we have shown that the worker sinks to the level of a commodity and becomes indeed the most wretched of commodities; that the wretchedness of the worker is in inverse proportion to the power and magnitude of his production; that the necessary result of competition is the accumulation of capital in a few hands, and thus the restoration of monopoly in a more terrible form; that finally the distinction between capitalist and land-rentier, like that between the tiller of the soil and the factory-worker, disappears and that the whole of society must fall apart into the two classes—the property-*owners* and the propertyless *workers*.

Political economy proceeds from the fact of private property, but it does not explain it to us. It expresses in general, abstract formulae the *material* process through which private property actually passes, and these formulae it then takes for *laws*. It does not *comprehend* these laws—i.e., it does not demonstrate how they arise from the very nature of private property. Political economy does not disclose the source of the division between labour and capital, and between capital and land. When, for example, it defines the relationship of wages to profit, it takes the interest of the capitalists to be the ultimate cause; i.e., it takes for granted what it is supposed to evolve. Similarly, competition comes in everywhere. It is explained from external circumstances. As to how far these external and apparently fortuitous circumstances are but the expression of a necessary course of development, political economy teaches us nothing. We have seen how, to it, exchange itself appears to be a

3. *Die Entfremdete Arbeit.* [In some other translations this phrase appears as "alienated labour."—*R. T.*]

fortuitous fact. The only wheels which political economy sets in motion are *avarice* and the *war amongst the avaricious—competition*.

Precisely because political economy does not grasp the connections within the movement, it was possible to counterpose, for instance, the doctrine of competition to the doctrine of monopoly, the doctrine of craft-liberty to the doctrine of the corporation, the doctrine of the division of landed property to the doctrine of the big estate—for competition, craft-liberty and the division of landed property were explained and comprehended only as fortuitous, premeditated and violent consequences of monopoly, the corporation, and feudal property, not as their necessary, inevitable and natural consequences.

Now, therefore, we have to grasp the essential connection between private property, avarice, and the separation of labour, capital and landed property; between exchange and competition, value and the devaluation of men, monopoly and competition, etc.; the connection between this whole estrangement and the *money-system*.

Do not let us go back to a fictitious primordial condition as the political economist does, when he tries to explain. Such a primordial condition explains nothing. He merely pushes the question away into a grey nebulous distance. He assumes in the form of fact, of an event, what he is supposed to deduce—namely, the necessary relationship between two things—between, for example, division of labour and exchange. Theology in the same way explains the origin of evil by the fall of man: that is, it assumes as a fact, in historical form, what has to be explained.

We proceed from an *actual* economic fact.

The worker becomes all the poorer the more wealth he produces, the more his production increases in power and range. The worker becomes an ever cheaper commodity the more commodities he creates. With the *increasing value* of the world of things proceeds in direct proportion the *devaluation* of the world of men. Labour produces not only commodities; it produces itself and the worker as a *commodity*—and does so in the proportion in which it produces commodities generally.

This fact expresses merely that the object which labour produces—labour's product—confronts it as *something alien*, as a *power independent* of the producer. The product of labour is labour which has been congealed in an object, which has become material: it is the *objectification* of labour. Labour's realization is its objectification. In the conditions dealt with by political economy this realization of labour appears as *loss of reality* for the workers; objectification as *loss of the object* and *object-bondage*; appropriation as *estrangement*, as *alienation*.[4]

So much does labour's realization appear as loss of reality that the worker loses reality to the point of starving to death. So much does objectification appear as loss of the object that the worker is robbed of the objects most necessary not only for his life but for his work. Indeed, labour itself becomes an object which he can get hold of only with the greatest effort and with the most irregular interruptions. So much does the appropriation of the object appear as estrangement that the more objects the worker produces the fewer can he possess and the more he falls under the dominion of his product, capital.

All these consequences are contained in the definition that the worker is related to the *product of his labour* as to an *alien* object. For on this premise it is clear that the more the worker spends himself, the more powerful the alien objective world becomes which he creates over-against himself, the poorer he himself—his inner world—becomes, the less belongs to him as his own. It is the same in religion. The more man puts into God, the less he retains in himself. The worker puts his life into the object; but now his life no longer belongs to him but to the object. Hence, the greater this activity, the greater is the worker's lack of objects. Whatever the product of his labour is, he is not. Therefore the greater this product, the less is he himself. The *alienation* of the worker in his product means not only that his labour becomes an object, an *external* existence, but that it exists *outside him*, independently, as something alien to him, and that it becomes a power of its own confronting him; it means that the life which he has conferred on the object confronts him as something hostile and alien.

Let us now look more closely at the *objectification*, at the production of the worker; and therein at the *estrangement*, the *loss* of the object, his product.

The worker can create nothing without *nature*, without the *sensuous external world*. It is the material on which his labor is manifested, in which it is active, from which and by means of which it produces.

But just as nature provides labor with the *means of life* in the sense that labour cannot *live* without objects on which to operate, on the other hand, it also provides the *means of life* in the more restricted sense—i.e., the means for the physical subsistence of the *worker* himself.

Thus the more the worker by his labour *appropriates* the external world, sensuous nature, the more he deprives himself of *means of life* in the double respect: first, that the sensuous external world

---

4. "Alienation"—*Entäusserung*.

more and more ceases to be an object belonging to his labour—to be his labour's *means of life*; and secondly, that it more and more ceases to be *means of life* in the immediate sense, means for the physical subsistence of the worker.

Thus in this double respect the worker becomes a slave of his object, first, in that he receives an *object of labour*, i.e., in that he receives *work*; and secondly, in that he receives *means of subsistence*. Therefore, it enables him to exist, first, as a *worker*; and, second, as a *physical subject*. The extremity of this bondage is that it is only as a *worker* that he continues to maintain himself as a *physical subject*, and that it is only as a *physical subject* that he is a *worker*.

(The laws of political economy express the estrangement of the worker in his object thus: the more the worker produces, the less he has to consume; the more values he creates, the more valueless, the more unworthy he becomes; the better formed his product, the more deformed becomes the worker; the more civilized his object, the more barbarous becomes the worker; the mightier labour becomes, the more powerless becomes the worker; the more ingenious labour becomes, the duller becomes the worker and the more he becomes nature's bondsman.)

Political economy conceals the estrangement inherent in the nature of labour by not considering the direct relationship between the worker (labour) *and production.* It is true that labour produces for the rich wonderful things—but for the worker it produces privation. It produces palaces—but for the worker, hovels. It produces beauty—but for the worker, deformity. It replaces labour by machines—but some of the workers it throws back to a barbarous type of labour, and the other workers it turns into machines. It produces intelligence—but for the worker idiocy, cretinism.

The direct relationship of labour to its produce is the relationship of the worker to the objects of his production. The relationship of the man of means to the objects of production and to production itself is only a *consequence* of this first relationship—and confirms it. We shall consider this other aspect later.

When we ask, then, what is the essential relationship of labour we are asking about the relationship of the *worker* to production.

Till now we have been considering the estrangement, the alienation of the worker only in one of its aspects, i.e., the worker's *relationship to the products of his labour.* But the estrangement is manifested not only in the result but in the *act of production*—within the *producing activity* itself. How would the worker come to face the product of his activity as a stranger, were it not that in the very act of production he was estranging himself from himself? The product is after all but the summary of the activity of production.

If then the product of labour is alienation, production itself must be active alienation, the alienation of activity, the activity of alienation. In the estrangement of the object of labour is merely summarized the estrangement, the alienation, in the activity of labour itself.

What, then, constitutes the alienation of labour?

First, the fact that labour is *external* to the worker, i.e., it does not belong to his essential being; that in his work, therefore, he does not affirm himself but denies himself, does not feel content but unhappy, does not develop freely his physical and mental energy but mortifies his body and ruins his mind. The worker therefore only feels himself outside his work, and in his work feels outside himself. He is at home when he is not working, and when he is working he is not at home. His labour is therefore not voluntary, but coerced; it is *forced labour*. It is therefore not the satisfaction of a need; it is merely a *means* to satisfy needs external to it. Its alien character emerges clearly in the fact that as soon as no physical or other compulsion exists, labour is shunned like the plague. External labour, labour in which man alienates himself, is a labour of self-sacrifice, of mortification. Lastly, the external character of labour for the worker appears in the fact that it is not his own, but someone else's, that it does not belong to him, that in it he belongs, not to himself, but to another. Just as in religion the spontaneous activity of the human imagination, of the human brain and the human heart, operates independently of the individual—that is, operates on him as an alien, divine or diabolical activity—in the same way the worker's activity is not his spontaneous activity. It belongs to another; it is the loss of his self.

As a result, therefore, man (the worker) no longer feels himself to be freely active in any but his animal functions—eating, drinking, procreating, or at most in his dwelling and in dressing-up, etc.; and in his human functions he no longer feels himself to be anything but an animal. What is animal becomes human and what is human becomes animal.

Certainly eating, drinking, procreating, etc., are also genuinely human functions. But in the abstraction which separates them from the sphere of all other human activity and turns them into sole and ultimate ends, they are animal.

We have considered the act of estranging practical human activity, labour, in two of its aspects. (1) The relation of the worker to the *product of labour* as an alien object exercising power over him. This relation is at the same time the relation to the sensuous external world, to the objects of nature as an alien world antagonistically opposed to him. (2) The relation of labour to the *act of production* within the *labour* process. This relation is the relation of the worker to his own activity as an alien activity not belonging to him; it is activity as suffering, strength as weakness, begetting as emasculating, the worker's *own* physical and mental energy, his personal life or what is life other than activity—as an activity which is turned against him, neither depends on nor belongs to him. Here we have *self-estrangement*, as we had previously the estrangement of the *thing*.

We have yet a third aspect of *estranged labour* to deduce from the two already considered.

Man is a species being, not only because in practice and in theory he adopts the species as his object (his own as well as those of other things), but—and this is only another way of expressing it—but also because he treats himself as the actual, living species; because he treats himself as a *universal* and therefore a free being.

The life of the species, both in man and in animals, consists physically in the fact that man (like the animal) lives on inorganic nature; and the more universal man is compared with an animal, the more universal is the sphere of inorganic nature on which he lives. Just as plants, animals, stones, the air, light, etc., constitute a part of human consciousness in the realm of theory, partly as objects of natural science, partly as objects of art—his spiritual inorganic nature, spiritual nourishment which he must first prepare to make it palatable and digestible—so too in the realm of practice they constitute a part of human life and human activity. Physically man lives only on these products of nature, whether they appear in the form of food, heating, clothes, a dwelling, or whatever it may be. The universality of man is in practice manifested precisely in the universality which makes all nature his *inorganic* body—both inasmuch as nature is (1) his direct means of life, and (2) the material, the object, and the instrument of his life-activity. Nature is man's *inorganic body*—nature, that is, in so far as it is not itself the human body. Man *lives* on nature—means that nature is his *body*, with which he must remain in continuous intercourse if he is not to die. That man's physical and spiritual life is linked to nature means simply that nature is linked to itself, for man is a part of nature.

In estranging from man (1) nature, and (2) himself, his own active functions, his life-activity, estranged labour estranges the *species* from man. It turns for him the *life of the species* into a means of individual life. First it estranges the life of the species and individual life, and secondly it makes individual life in its abstract form the purpose of the life of the species, likewise in its abstract and estranged form.

For in the first place labour, *life-activity, productive life* itself, appears to man merely as a *means* of satisfying a need—the need to maintain the physical existence. Yet the productive life is the life of the species. It is life-engendering life. The whole character of a species—its species character—is contained in the character of its life-activity; and free, conscious activity is man's species character. Life itself appears only as *a means to life*.

The animal is immediately identical with its life-activity. It does not distinguish itself from it. It is *its life-activity*. Man makes his life-activity itself the object of his will and of his consciousness. He has conscious life-activity. It is not a determination with which he directly merges. Conscious life-activity directly distinguishes man from animal life-activity. It is just because of this that he is a species being. Or it is only because he is a species being that he is a Conscious Being, i.e., that his own life is an object for him. Only because of that is his activity free activity. Estranged labour reverses this relationship, so that it is just because man is a conscious being that he makes his life-activity, his *essential* being, a mere means to his *existence*.

In creating an *objective world* by his practical activity, in *working-up* inorganic nature, man proves himself a conscious species being, i.e., as a being that treats the species as its own essential being, or that treats itself as a species being. Admittedly animals also produce. They build themselves nests, dwellings, like the bees, beavers, ants, etc. But an animal only produces what it immediately needs for itself or its young. It produces one-sidedly, whilst man produces universally. It produces only under the dominion of immediate physical need, whilst man produces even when he is free from physical need and only truly produces in freedom therefrom. An animal produces only itself, whilst man reproduces the whole of nature. An animal's product belongs immediately to its physical body, whilst man freely confronts his product. An animal forms things in accordance with the standard and the need of the species to which it belongs, whilst man knows how to produce in accordance with the standard of every species, and knows how to apply everywhere the inherent standard to the object. Man therefore also forms things in accordance with the laws of beauty.

It is just in the working-up of the objective world, therefore, that man first really proves himself to be a *species being*. This production is his active species life. Through and because of this production, nature appears as *his* work and his reality. The object of labour is, therefore, the *objectification of man's species life*: for he duplicates himself not only, as in consciousness, intellectually, but also actively, in reality, and therefore he contemplates himself in a world that he has created. In tearing away from man the object of his production, therefore, estranged labour tears from him his *species life*, his real species objectivity, and transforms his advantage over animals into the disadvantage that his inorganic body, nature, is taken from him.

Similarly, in degrading spontaneous activity, free activity, to a means, estranged labour makes man's species life a means to his physical existence.

The consciousness which man has of his species is thus transformed by estrangement in such a way that the species life becomes for him a means.

Estranged labour turns thus:

(3) *Man's species being*, both nature and his spiritual species property, into a being *alien* to him, into a *means* to his *individual existence*. It estranges man's own body from him, as it does external nature and his spiritual essence, his *human* being.

(4) An immediate consequence of the fact that man is estranged from the product of his labour, from his life-activity, from his species being is the *estrangement of man* from *man*. If a man is confronted by himself, he is confronted by the *other* man. What applies to a man's relation to his work, to the product of his labour and to himself, also holds of a man's relation to the other man, and to the other man's labour and object of labour.

In fact, the proposition that man's species nature is estranged from him means that one man is estranged from the other, as each of them is from man's essential nature.[5]

The estrangement of man, and in fact every relationship in which man stands to himself, is first realized and expressed in the relationship in which a man stands to other men.

Hence within the relationship of estranged labour each man views the other in accordance with the standard and the position in which he finds himself as a worker.

We took our departure from a fact of political economy—the estrangement of the worker and his production. We have formulated the concept of this fact—*estranged, alienated* labour. We have analysed this concept—hence analysing merely a fact of political economy.

Let us now see, further, how in real life the concept of estranged, alienated labour must express and present itself.

If the product of labour is alien to me, if it confronts me as an alien power, to whom, then, does it belong?

If my own activity does not belong to me, if it is an alien, a coerced activity, to whom, then, does it belong?

To a being *other* than me.

Who is this being?

The *gods*? To be sure, in the earliest times the principal produc-

5. "Species nature" (and, earlier, "species being")—*Gattungswesen*; "man's essential nature"—*menschlichen Wesen*.

tion (for example, the building of temples, etc., in Egypt, India and Mexico) appears to be in the service of the gods, and the product belongs to the gods. However, the gods on their own were never the lords of labour. No more was *nature*. And what a contradiction it would be if, the more man subjugated nature by his labour and the more the miracles of the gods were rendered superfluous by the miracles of industry, the more man were to renounce the joy of production and the enjoyment of the produce in favour of these powers.

The *alien* being, to whom labour and the produce of labour belongs, in whose service labour is done and for whose benefit the produce of labour is provided, can only be *man* himself.

If the product of labour does not belong to the worker, if it confronts him as an alien power, this can only be because it belongs to some *other man than the worker*. If the worker's activity is a torment to him, to another it must be *delight* and his life's joy. Not the gods, not nature, but only man himself can be this alien power over man.

We must bear in mind the above-stated proposition that man's relation to himself only becomes *objective* and *real* for him through his relation to the other man. Thus, if the product of his labour, his labour *objectified*, is for him an *alien*, hostile, powerful object independent of him, then his position towards it is such that someone else is master of this object, someone who is alien, hostile, powerful, and independent of him. If his own activity is to him an unfree activity, then he is treating it as activity performed in the service, under the dominion, the coercion and the yoke of another man.

Every self-estrangement of man from himself and from nature appears in the relation in which he places himself and nature to men other than and differentiated from himself. For this reason religious self-estrangement necessarily appears in the relationship of the layman to the priest, or again to a mediator, etc., since we are here dealing with the intellectual world. In the real practical world self-estrangement can only become manifest through the real practical relationship to other men. The medium through which estrangement takes place is itself *practical*. Thus through estranged labour man not only engenders his relationship to the object and to the act of production as to powers that are alien and hostile to him; he also engenders the relationship in which other men stand to his production and to his product, and the relationship in which he stands to these other men. Just as he begets his own production as the loss of his reality, as his punishment; just as he begets his own product as a loss, as a product not belonging to him; so he begets the dominion of the one who does not produce over production and over the product. Just as he estranges from himself his own activity, so he confers to the stranger activity which is not his own.

Till now we have only considered this relationship from the standpoint of the worker and later we shall be considering it also from the standpoint of the non-worker.

Through *estranged, alienated labour,* then, the worker produces the relationship to this labour of a man alien to labour and standing outside it. The relationship of the worker to labour engenders the relation to it of the capitalist, or whatever one chooses to call the master of labour. *Private property* is thus the product, the result, the necessary consequence, of *alienated labour,* of the external relation of the worker to nature and to himself.

Private property thus results by analysis from the concept of *alienated labour*—i.e., of *alienated man,* of estranged labour, of estranged life, of *estranged* man.

True, it is as a result of the *movement of private property* that we have obtained the concept of *alienated labour* (*of alienated life*) from political economy. But on analysis of this concept it becomes clear that though private property appears to be the source, the cause of alienated labour, it is really its consequence, just as the gods *in the beginning* are not the cause but the effect of man's intellectual confusion. Later this relationship becomes reciprocal.

Only at the very culmination of the development of private property does this, its secret, re-emerge, namely, that on the one hand it is the *product* of alienated labour, and that secondly it is the *means* by which labour alienates itself, the *realization of this alienation.*

This exposition immediately sheds light on various hitherto unsolved conflicts.

(1) Political economy starts from labour as the real soul of production; yet to labour it gives nothing, and to private property everything. From this contradiction Proudhon has concluded in favour of labour and against private property. We understand, however, that this apparent contradiction is the contradiction of *estranged labour* with itself, and that political economy has merely formulated the laws of estranged labour.

We also understand, therefore, that *wages* and *private property* are identical: where the product, the object of labour pays for labour itself, the wage is but a necessary consequence of labour's estrangement, for after all in the wage of labour, labour does not appear as an end in itself but as the servant of the wage. We shall develop this point later, and meanwhile will only deduce some conclusions.

A *forcing-up of wages* (disregarding all other difficulties, including the fact that it would only be by force, too, that the higher
wages, being an anomaly, could be maintained) would therefore be
nothing but *better payment for the slave*, and would not conquer
either for the worker or for labour their human status and dignity.

Indeed, even the *equality of wages* demanded by Proudhon only
transforms the relationship of the present-day worker to his labour
into the relationship of all men to labour. Society is then conceived
as an abstract capitalist.

Wages are a direct consequence of estranged labour, and
estranged labour is the direct cause of private property. The downfall of the one aspect must therefore mean the downfall of the
other.

(2) From the relationship of estranged labour to private property it further follows that the emancipation of society from private
property, etc., from servitude, is expressed in the *political* form of
the *emancipation of the workers*; not that *their* emancipation alone
was at stake but because the emancipation of the workers contains
universal human emancipation—and it contains this, because the
whole of human servitude is involved in the relation of the worker
to production, and every relation of servitude is but a modification
and consequence of this relation.

Just as we have found the concept of *private property* from the
concept of *estranged, alienated labour* by *analysis*, in the same way
every *category* of political economy can be evolved with the help of
these two factors; and we shall find again in each category, e.g.,
trade, competition, capital, money, only a *definite* and *developed
expression* of the first foundations.

Before considering this configuration, however, let us try to solve
two problems.

(1) To define the general *nature of private property*, as it has
arisen as a result of estranged labour, in its relation to *truly human,
social property*.

(2) We have accepted the *estrangement of labour*, its *alienation*,
as a fact, and we have analysed this fact. How, we now ask, does
man come to *alienate*, to estrange, *his labour*? How is this estrangement rooted in the nature of human development? We have
already gone a long way to the solution of this problem by *transforming* the question as to the *origin of private property* into the
question as to the relation of *alienated labour* to the course of
humanity's development. For when one speaks of *private property*,
one thinks of being concerned with something external to man.
When one speaks of labour, one is directly concerned with man
himself. This new formulation of the question already contains its
solution.

As to (1): The general nature of private property and its relation to truly human property.

Alienated labour has resolved itself for us into two elements which mutually condition one another, or which are but different expressions of one and the same relationship. *Appropriation* appears as *estrangement*, as *alienation;* and *alienation* appears as *appropriation, estrangement* as true *enfranchisement.*

We have considered the one side—*alienated* labour in relation to the *worker* himself, i.e., the *relation of alienated labour to itself.* The *property-relation of the non-worker to the worker and to labour* we have found as the product, the necessary outcome of this relation of alienated labour. *Private property,* as the material, summary expression of alienated labour, embraces both relations—the *relation of the worker to work, to the product of his labour and to the non-worker,* and the relation of the *non-worker to the worker and to the product of his labour.*

Having seen that in relation to the worker who *appropriates* nature by means of his labour, this appropriation *appears* as estrangement, his own spontaneous activity as activity for another and as activity of another, vitality as a sacrifice of life, production of the object as loss of the object to an alien power, to an *alien* person—we shall now consider the relation to the worker, to labour and its object of this person who is *alien* to labour and the worker.

First it has to be noticed, that everything which appears in the worker as an *activity of alienation, of estrangement,* appears in the non-worker as a *state of alienation, of estrangement.*

Secondly, that the worker's *real, practical attitude* in production and to the product (as a state of mind) appears in the non-worker confronting him as a *theoretical* attitude.

Thirdly, the non-worker does everything against the worker which the worker does against himself; but he does not do against himself what he does against the worker.

Let us look more closely at these three relations.[6]

Private Property and Communism

Re. p. XXXIX. The antithesis of *propertylessness* and *property* so long as it is not comprehended as the antithesis of *labour* and *capital,* still remains an antithesis of indifference, not grasped in its *active connection,* its *internal* relation—an antithesis not yet grasped as a *contradiction.* It can find expression in this *first* form even without the advanced development of private property (as in ancient Rome, Turkey, etc.). It does not yet *appear* as having been established by private property itself. But labour, the subjective

6. At this point the first manuscript breaks off unfinished.

essence of private property as exclusion of property, and capital, objective labour as exclusion of labour, constitute *private property* as its developed state of contradiction—hence a dynamic relationship moving inexorably to its resolution.

Re. the same page. The transcendence of self-estrangement follows the same course as self-estrangement. *Private property* is first considered only in its objective aspect—but nevertheless with labour as its essence. Its form of existence is therefore *capital*, which is to be annulled "as such" (Proudhon). Or a *particular form* of labour—labour levelled down, parcelled, and therefore unfree—is conceived as the source of private property's *perniciousness* and of its existence in estrangement from men; for instance, *Fourier*, who, like the physiocrats, also conceived *agricultural labour* to be at least the *exemplary* type, whilst *Saint-Simon* declares in contrast that *industrial labour* as such is the essence, and now also aspires to the *exclusive* rule of the industrialists and the improvement of the workers' condition. Finally, *communism* is the *positive* expression of annulled private property—at first as *universal* private property. By embracing this relation as a *whole*, communism is:

(1) In its first form only a *generalization* and *consummation* of this relationship. It shows itself as such in a twofold form: on the one hand, the dominion of *material* property bulks so large that it wants to destroy *everything* which is not capable of being possessed by all as *private property*. It wants to abstract *by force* from talent, etc. For it the sole purpose of life and existence is direct, physical *possession*. The category of *labourer* is not done away with, but extended to all men. The relationship of private property persists as the relationship of the community to the world of things. Finally, this movement of counterposing universal private property to private property finds expression in the bestial form of counterposing to *marriage* (certainly a *form of exclusive private property*) the *community of women*, in which a woman becomes a piece of *communal* and *common* property. It may be said that this idea of the *community of women* gives away the *secret* of this as yet completely crude and thoughtless communism. Just as the woman passes from marriage to general prostitution,[7] so the entire world of wealth (that is, of man's objective substance) passes from the relationship of exclusive marriage with the owner of private property to a state of universal prostitution with the community. In negating the *personality* of man in every sphere, this type of communism is really nothing but the logical expression of private property, which

7. Prostitution is only a *specific* expression of the *general* prostitution of the *labourer*, and since it is a relationship in which falls not the prostitute alone, but also the one who prostitutes—and the latter's abomination is still greater—the capitalist, etc., also comes under this head. [*Marx*]

is this negation. General *envy* constituting itself as a power is the disguise in which *avarice* re-establishes itself and satisfies itself, only in *another* way. The thoughts of every piece of private property—inherent in each piece as such—are *at least* turnèd against all *wealthier* private property in the form of envy and the urge to reduce to a common level, so that this envy and urge even constitute the essence of competition. The crude communism is only the consummation of this envy and of this levelling-down proceeding from the *preconceived* minimum. It has a *definite, limited* standard. How little this annulment of private property is really an appropriation is in fact proved by the abstract negation of the entire world of culture and civilization, the regression to the *unnatural* simplicity of the *poor and undemanding* man who has not only failed to go beyond private property, but has not yet even attained to it.

The community is only a community of *labour*, and an equality of *wages* paid out by the communal capital—the *community* as the universal capitalist. Both sides of the relationship are raised to an *imagined* universality—*labour* as a state in which every person is put, and *capital* as the acknowledged universality and power of the community.

In the approach to *woman* as the spoil and handmaid of communal lust is expressed the infinite degradation in which man exists for himself, for the secret of this approach has its *unambiguous*, decisive, *plain* and undisguised expression in the relation of *man* to *woman* and in the manner in which the *direct* and *natural* procreative relationship is conceived. The direct, natural, and necessary relation of person to person is the *relation of man to woman*. In this *natural* relationship of the sexes man's relation to nature is immediately his relation to man, just as his relation to man is immediately his relation to nature—his own *natural* function. In this relationship, therefore, is *sensuously manifested*, reduced to an observable *fact*, the extent to which the human essence has become nature to man, or to which nature has to him become the human essence of man. From this relationship one can therefore judge man's whole level of development. It follows from the character of this relationship how much *man* as a *species being*, as *man*, has come to be himself and to comprehend himself; the relation of man to woman is *the most natural* relation of human being to human being. It therefore reveals the extent to which man's *natural* behaviour has become *human*, or the extent to which the *human* essence in him has become a *natural* essence—the extent to which his *human nature* has come to be *nature to him*. In this relationship is revealed, too, the extent to which man's *need* has become a *human* need; the extent to which, therefore, the *other* person as a person has become for him a need—the extent to which he in his individual existence is at the same time a social being. The first positive annulment of private property—*crude* communism—is thus merely one *form* in which the vileness of private property, which wants to set itself up as the *positive community*, *comes to the surface*.

(2) Communism (a) of a political nature still—democratic or despotic; (b) with the annulment of the state, yet still incomplete, and being still affected by private property (i.e., by the estrangement of man). In both forms communism already knows itself to be re-integration or return of man to himself, the transcendence of human self-estrangement; but since it has not yet grasped the positive essence of private property, and just as little the *human* nature of need, it remains captive to it and infected by it. It has, indeed, grasped its concept, but not its essence.

(3) *Communism* as the *positive* transcendence of *private property*, or *human self-estrangement*, and therefore as the real *appropriation of the human* essence by and for man; communism therefore as the complete return of man to himself as a *social* (i.e., human) being—a return become conscious, and accomplished within the entire wealth of previous development. This communism, as fully-developed naturalism, equals humanism, and as fully-developed humanism equals naturalism; it is the *genuine* resolution of the conflict between man and nature and between man and man—the true resolution of the strife between existence and essence, between objectification and self-confirmation, between freedom and necessity, between the individual and the species. Communism is the riddle of history solved, and it knows itself to be this solution.

The entire movement of history is, therefore, both its *actual* act of genesis (the birth act of its empirical existence) and also for its thinking consciousness the *comprehended* and *known* process of its *coming-to-be*. That other, still immature communism, meanwhile, seeks an *historical* proof for itself—a proof in the realm of the existent—amongst disconnected historical phenomena opposed to private property, tearing single phases from the historical process and focussing attention on them as proofs of its historical pedigree (a horse ridden hard especially by Cabet, Villegardelle, etc.). By so doing it simply makes clear that by far the greater part of this process contradicts its claims, and that, if it has once been, precisely its being in the *past* refutes its pretension to being *essential*.

That the entire revolutionary movement necessarily finds both its empirical and its theoretical basis in the movement of *private property*—in that of the economy, to be precise—is easy to see.

This *material*, immediately *sensuous* private property is the material sensuous expression of *estranged human* life. Its movement—production and consumption—is the *sensuous* revelation of the movement of all production hitherto—i.e., the realization or the reality of man. Religion, family, state, law, morality, science, art, etc., are only *particular* modes of production, and fall under its general law. The positive transcendence of *private property* as the appropriation of *human* life is, therefore, the positive transcendence of all estrangement—that is to say, the return of man from religion, family, state, etc., to his *human*, i.e., *social* mode of existence. Religious estrangement as such occurs only in the realm of *consciousness*, of man's inner life, but economic estrangement is that of *real life*; its transcendence therefore embraces both aspects. It is evident that the *initial* stage of the movement amongst the various peoples depends on whether the true and for them *authentic* life of the people manifests itself more in consciousness or in the external world—is more ideal or real. Communism begins from the outset (*Owen*) with atheism; but atheism is at first far from being *communism*; indeed, it is still mostly an abstraction.

The philanthropy of atheism is therefore at first only *philosophical*, abstract, philanthropy, and that of communism is at once *real* and directly bent on *action*.

We have seen how on the premise of positively annulled private property man produces man—himself and the other man; how the object, being the direct embodiment of his individuality, is simultaneously his own existence for the other man, the existence of the other man, and that existence for him. Likewise, however, both the material of labour and man as the subject, are the point of departure as well as the result of the movement (and precisely in this fact, that they must constitute the *point of departure*, lies the historical *necessity* of private property). Thus the *social* character is the general character of the whole movement: *just as* society itself produces *man as man*, so is society *produced* by him. Activity and consumption, both in their content and in their *mode of existence*, are *social*: *social* activity and *social* consumption; the *human* essence of nature first exists only for *social* man; for only here does nature exist for him as a *bond* with *man*—as his existence for the other and the other's existence for him—as the life-element of the human world; only here does nature exist as the *foundation* of his own *human* existence. Only here has what is to him his *natural* existence become his *human* existence, and nature become man for him. Thus *society* is the consummated oneness in substance of man and nature—the true resurrection of nature—the naturalism of man and the humanism of nature both brought to fulfilment.

Social activity and social consumption exist by no means *only* in the form of some *directly* communal activity and directly *commu-*

nal consumption, although *communal* activity and *communal* consumption—i.e., activity and consumption which are manifested and directly confirmed in *real association* with other men—will occur wherever such a *direct* expression of sociality stems from the true character of the activity's content and is adequate to the nature of consumption.

But again when I am active *scientifically,* etc.,—when I am engaged in activity which I can seldom perform in direct community with others—then I am *social,* because I am active as a *man.* Not only is the material of my activity given to me as a social product (as is even the language in which the thinker is active): my *own* existence *is* social activity, and therefore that which I make of myself, I make of myself for society and with the consciousness of myself as a social being.

My *general* consciousness is only the *theoretical* shape of that of which the *living* shape is the *real* community, the social fabric, although at the present day *general* consciousness is an abstraction from real life and as such antagonistically confronts it. Consequently, too, the *activity* of my general consciousness, as an activity, is my *theoretical* existence as a social being.

What is to be avoided above all is the re-establishing of "Society" as an abstraction *vis-à-vis* the individual. The individual *is the social being.* His life, even if it may not appear in the direct form of a *communal* life carried out together with others—is therefore an expression and confirmation of *social life.* Man's individual and species life are not *different,* however much—and this is inevitable—the mode of existence of the individual is a more *particular,* or more *general* mode of the life of the species, or the life of the species is a more *particular* or more *general* individual life.

In his *consciousness of species* man confirms his real *social life* and simply repeats his real existence in thought, just as conversely the being of the species confirms itself in species-consciousness and is for *itself* in its generality as a thinking being.

Man, much as he may therefore be a *particular* individual (and it is precisely his particularity which makes him an individual, and a real *individual* social being), is just as much the *totality*—the ideal totality—the subjective existence of thought and experienced society present for itself; just as he exists also in the real world as the awareness and the real enjoyment of social existence, and as a totality of human life-activity.

Thinking and being are thus no doubt *distinct,* but at the same time they are in *unity* with each other.

Death seems to be a harsh victory of the species over the *definite* individual and to contradict their unity. But the determinate individual is only a *determinate species being,* and as such mortal.

(4) Just as *private property* is only the sensuous expression of the fact that man becomes *objective* for himself and at the same time becomes to himself a strange and inhuman object; just as it expresses the fact that the assertion of his life is the alienation of his life, that his realization is his loss of reality, is an *alien* reality: conversely, the positive transcendence of private property—i.e., the *sensuous* appropriation for and by man of the human essence and of human life, of objective man, of human *achievements*—is not to be conceived merely in the sense of *direct*, one-sided *gratification*—merely in the sense of *possessing*, of *having*. Man appropriates his total essence in a total manner, that is to say, as a whole man. Each of his *human* relations to the world—seeing, hearing, smelling, tasting, feeling, thinking, being aware, sensing, wanting, acting, loving—in short, all the organs of his individual being, like those organs which are directly social in their form, are in their *objective* orientation or in their *orientation to the object*, the appropriation of that object, the appropriation of the *human* world; their orientation to the object is the *manifestation of the human world*;[8] it is human *efficaciousness* and human *suffering*, for suffering, apprehended humanly, is an enjoyment of self in man.

Private property has made us so stupid and one-sided that an object is only *ours* when we have it—when it exists for us as capital, or when it is directly possessed, eaten, drunk, worn, inhabited, etc.,—in short, when it is *used* by us. Although private property itself again conceives all these direct realizations of possession as *means of life*, and the life which they serve as means is the *life of private property*—labour and conversion into capital.

In place of *all* these physical and mental senses there has therefore come the sheer estrangement of *all* these senses—the sense of *having*. The human being had to be reduced to this absolute poverty in order that he might yield his inner wealth to the outer world. (On the category of *"having,"* see Hess in the *Twenty-One Sheets*.)

The transcendence of private property is therefore the complete *emancipation* of all human senses and attributes; but it is this emancipation precisely because these senses and attributes have become, subjectively and objectively, *human*. The eye has become a *human* eye, just as its *object* has become a social, *human* object—an object emanating from man for man. The *senses* have therefore become directly in their practice *theoreticians*. They relate themselves to the *thing* for the sake of the thing, but the thing itself is an *objective human* relation to itself and to man,[9]

8. For this reason it is just as highly priced as the *determinations* of human *essence* and *activities*. [*Marx*]
9. In practice I can relate myself to a thing humanly only if the thing relates itself to the human being humanly. [*Marx*]

and vice versa. Need or enjoyment have consequently lost their *ego-tistical* nature, and nature has lost its mere *utility* by use becoming *human* use.

In the same way, the senses and enjoyments of other men have become my *own* appropriation. Besides these direct organs, there-fore, *social* organs develop in the *form* of society; thus, for instance, activity in direct association with others, etc., has become an organ for *expressing* my own *life*, and a mode of appropriating *human life*.

It is obvious that the *human* eye gratifies itself in a way different from the crude, non-human eye; the human *ear* different from the crude ear, etc.

To recapitulate; man is not lost in his object only when the object becomes for him a *human* object or objective man. This is possible only when the object becomes for him a *social* object, he himself for himself a social being, just as society becomes a being for him in this object.

On the one hand, therefore, it is only when the objective world becomes everywhere for man in society the world of man's essential powers[1]—human reality, and for that reason the reality of his *own* essential powers—that all *objects* become for him the *objectifica-tion of himself*, become objects which confirm and realize his indi-viduality, become *his* objects: that is, *man himself* becomes the object. The manner in which they become *his* depends on the *nature of the objects* and on the nature of the *essential power* cor-responding *to it*; for it is precisely the *determinateness* of this rela-tionship which shapes the particular, *real* mode of affirmation. To the *eye* an object comes to be other than it is to the *ear*, and the object of the eye is another object than the object of the *ear*. The peculiarity of each essential power is precisely its *peculiar essence*, and therefore also the peculiar mode of its objectification, of its *objectively actual* living *being*. Thus man is affirmed in the objec-tive world not only in the act of thinking, but with *all* his senses.

On the other hand, looking at this in its subjective aspect: just as music alone awakens in man the sense of music, and just as the most beautiful music has *no* sense for the unmusical ear—is no object for it, because my object can only be the confirmation of one of my essential powers and can therefore only be so for me as my essential power is present for itself as a subjective capacity, because the sense of an object for me goes only so far as *my* senses go (has only sense for a sense corresponding to that object)—for this reason the *senses* of the social man are *other* senses than those of the non-social man. Only through the objectively unfolded rich-

1. "Essential powers"—*Wesenskräfte:*   my essential nature, my very being.
i.e., powers belonging to me as part of

ness of man's essential being is the richness of subjective *human*
sensibility (a musical ear, an eye for beauty of form—in short,
senses capable of human gratifications, senses confirming themselves as essential powers of *man*) either cultivated or brought into
being. For not only the five senses but also the so-called mental
senses—the practical senses (will, love, etc.)—in a word, *human*
sense—the humanness of the senses—comes to be by virtue of its
object, by virtue of *humanized* nature. The *forming* of the five
senses is a labour of the entire history of the world down to the
present.

The *sense* caught up in crude practical need has only a *restricted*
sense. For the starving man, it is not the human form of food that
exists, but only its abstract being as food; it could just as well be
there in its crudest form, and it would be impossible to say wherein
this feeding-activity differs from that of *animals*. The care-burdened
man in need has no sense for the finest play; the dealer in minerals
sees only the mercantile value but not the beauty and the unique
nature of the mineral: he has no mineralogical sense. Thus, the
objectification of the human essence both in its theoretical and
practical aspects is required to make man's *sense human*, as well as
to create the *human sense* corresponding to the entire wealth of
human and natural substance.

Just as resulting from the movement of *private property*, of its
wealth as well as its poverty—or of its material and spiritual wealth
and poverty—the budding society finds to hand all the material for
this *development*: so *established* society produces man in this
entire richness of his being—produces the *rich* man *profoundly
endowed with all the senses*—as its enduring reality.

It will be seen how subjectivism and objectivism, spiritualism
and materialism, activity and suffering, only lose their antithetical
character, and thus their existence, as such antitheses in the social
condition; it will be seen how the resolution of the *theoretical*
antitheses is *only* possible *in a practical* way, by virtue of the practical energy of men. Their resolution is therefore by no means merely
a problem of knowledge, but a *real* problem of life, which *philosophy* could not solve precisely because it conceived this problem as
merely a theoretical one.

It will be seen how the history of *industry* and the established
objective existence of industry are the *open* book of *man's essential
powers*, the exposure to the senses of human *psychology*. Hitherto
this was not conceived in its inseparable connection with man's
essential being, but only in an external relation of utility, because,
moving in the realm of estrangement, people could only think
man's general mode of being—religion or history in its abstract-
general character as politics, art, literature, etc.,—to be the reality

of man's essential powers and *man's species-activity*. We have before us the *objectified essential powers* of man in the form of *sensuous, alien, useful objects*, in the form of estrangement, displayed in *ordinary material industry* (which can be conceived as a part of that general movement, just as that movement can be conceived as a particular part of industry, since all human activity hitherto has been labour—that is, industry—activity estranged from itself).

A *psychology* for which this, the part of history most contemporary and accessible to sense, remains a closed book, cannot become a genuine, comprehensive and *real* science. What indeed are we to think of a science which *airily* abstracts from this large part of human labour and which fails to feel its own incompleteness, while such a wealth of human endeavour unfolded before it means nothing more to it than, perhaps, what can be expressed in one word—"*need*," "*vulgar need*"?

The *natural sciences* have developed an enormous activity and have accumulated a constantly growing mass of material. Philosophy, however, has remained just as alien to them as they remain to philosophy. Their momentary unity was only a *chimerical illusion*. The will was there, but the means were lacking. Even historiography pays regard to natural science only occasionally, as a factor of enlightenment and utility arising from individual great discoveries. But natural science has invaded and transformed human life all the more *practically* through the medium of industry; and has prepared human emancipation, however directly and much it had to consummate dehumanization. *Industry* is the *actual*, historical relation of nature, and therefore of natural science, to man. If, therefore, industry is conceived as the *exoteric* revelation of man's *essential powers*, we also gain an understanding of the *human* essence of nature or the *natural* essence of man. In consequence, natural science will lose its abstractly material—or rather, its idealistic—tendency, and will become the basis of *human* science, as it has already become the basis of actual human life, albeit in an estranged form. *One* basis for life and another basis for *science* is *a priori* a lie. The nature which comes to be in human history—the genesis of human society—is man's *real* nature; hence nature as it comes to be through industry, even though in an *estranged* form, is true *anthropological* nature.

Sense-perception (see Feuerbach) must be the basis of all science. Only when it proceeds from sense-perception in the twofold form both of *sensuous* consciousness and of *sensuous* need—that is, only when science proceeds from nature—is it *true* science. All history is the preparation for "*man*" to become the object of *sensuous* consciousness, and for the needs of "man as man" to become [natural, sensuous] needs. History itself is a *real* part of *natural his-*

tory—of nature's coming to be man. Natural science will in time subsume under itself the science of man, just as the science of man will subsume under itself natural science: there will be *one* science.

Man is the immediate object of natural science: for immediate, *sensuous nature* for man is, immediately, human sensuousness (the expressions are identical)—presented immediately in the form of the *other* man sensuously present for him. For his own sensuousness first exists as human sensuousness for himself through the *other* man. But *nature* is the immediate object of the *science of man*: the first object of man—man—is nature, sensuousness; and the particular human sensuous essential powers can only find their self-knowledge in the science of the natural world in general, since they can find their objective realization in *natural* objects only. The element of thought itself—the element of thought's living expression—*language*—is of a sensuous nature. The *social* reality of nature, and *human* natural science, or the *natural science about man*, are identical terms.

It will be seen how in place of the *wealth* and *poverty* of political economy come the *rich human being* and rich *human* need. The *rich* human being is simultaneously the human being *in need of* a totality of human life-activities—the man in whom his own realization exists as an inner necessity, as *need*. Not only *wealth*, but likewise the *poverty* of man—given socialism—receives in equal measure a *human* and therefore social significance. Poverty is the passive bond which causes the human being to experience the need of the greatest wealth—the *other* human being. The dominion of the objective being in me, the sensuous outburst of my essential activity, is *emotion*, which thus becomes here the *activity* of my being.

(5) A *being* only considers himself independent when he stands on his own feet; and he only stands on his own feet when he owes his *existence* to himself. A man who lives by the grace of another regards himself as a dependent being. But I live completely by the grace of another if I owe him not only the sustenance of my life, but if he has, moreover, *created* my *life*—if he is the *source* of my life; and if it is not of my own creation, my life has necessarily a source of this kind outside it. The *Creation* is therefore an idea very difficult to dislodge from popular consciousness. The self-mediated being of nature and of man is *incomprehensible* to it, because it contradicts everything *palpable* in practical life.

The creation of the *earth* has received a mighty blow from *geogeny*—i.e., from the science which presents the formation of the earth, the coming-to-be of the earth, as a process, as self-generation. *Generatio aequivoca*[2] is the only practical refutation of the theory of creation.

2. Spontaneous generation.

Now it is certainly easy to say to the single individual what Aristotle has already said. You have been begotten by your father and your mother; therefore in you the mating of two human beings—a species-act of human beings—has produced the human being. You see, therefore, that even physically, man owes his existence to man. Therefore you must not only keep sight of the *one* aspect—the *infinite* progression which leads you further to enquire: "Who begot my father? Who his grandfather?", etc. You must also hold on to the *circular movement* sensuously perceptible in that progression, by which *man* repeats himself in procreation, thus always remaining the subject. You will reply, however: I grant you this circular movement; now grant me the progression which drives me even further until I ask: Who begot the first man, and nature as a whole? I can only answer you: Your question is itself a product of abstraction. Ask yourself how you arrived at that question. Ask yourself whether your question is not posed from a standpoint to which I cannot reply, because it is a perverse one. Ask yourself whether that progression as such exists for a reasonable mind. When you ask about the creation of nature and man, you are abstracting, in so doing, from man and nature. You postulate them as *non-existent*, and yet you want me to prove them to you as *existing*. Now I say to you: Give up your abstraction and you will also give up your question. Or if you want to hold on to your abstraction, then be consistent, and if you think of man and nature as *non-existent*, then think of yourself as non-existent, for you too are surely nature and man. Don't think, don't ask me, for as soon as you think and ask, your *abstraction* from the existence of nature and man has no meaning. Or are you such an egoist that you postulate everything as nothing, and yet want yourself to be?

You can reply: I do not want to postulate the nothingness of nature. I ask you about *its genesis*, just as I ask the anatomist about the formation of bones, etc.

But since for the socialist man the *entire so-called history of the world* is nothing but the begetting of man through human labour, nothing but the coming-to-be of nature for man, he has the visible, irrefutable proof of his *birth* through himself, of his *process* of *coming-to-be*. Since the *real existence* of man and nature has become practical, sensuous and perceptible—since man has become for man as the being of nature, and nature for man as the being of man—the question about an *alien* being, about a being above nature and man—a question which implies the admission of the inessentiality of nature and of man—has become impossible in practice. *Atheism*, as the denial of this inessentiality, has no longer any meaning, for atheism is a *negation of God*, and postulates the *existence of man* through this negation; but socialism as socialism no longer stands in any need of such a mediation. It proceeds from the *practically and theoretically sensuous consciousness* of man and of nature as the *essence*. Socialism is man's *positive self-consciousness* no longer mediated through the annulment of religion, just as *real life* is man's positive reality, no longer mediated through the annulment of private property, through *communism*. Communism is the position as the negation of the negation, and is hence the *actual* phase necessary for the next stage of historical development in the process of human emancipation and recovery. *Communism* is the necessary pattern and the dynamic principle of the immediate future, but communism as such is not the goal of human development—the structure of human society.

The Power of Money in Bourgeois Society

If man's *feelings*, passions, etc., are not merely anthropological phenomena in the [narrower][3] sense, but truly *ontological* affirmations of essential being (of nature), and if they are only really affirmed because their *object* exists for them as an object of *sense*, then it is clear:

(1) That they have by no means merely one mode of affirmation, but rather that the distinctive character of their existence, of their life, is constituted by the distinctive mode of their affirmation. In what manner the object exists for them, is the characteristic mode of their *gratification*.

(2) Whenever the sensuous affirmation is the direct annulment of the object in its independent form (as in eating, drinking, working up of the object, etc.), this is the affirmation of the object.

(3) In so far as man, and hence also his feeling, etc., are *human*, the affirmation of the object by another is likewise his own enjoyment.

(4) Only through developed industry—i.e., through the medium of private property—does the ontological essence of human passion come to be both in its totality and in its humanity; the science of man is therefore itself a product of man's establishment of himself by practical activity.

(5) The meaning of private property—liberated from its estrangement—is the *existence of essential objects* for man, both as objects of enjoyment and as objects of activity.

By possessing the *property* of buying everything, by possessing the property of appropriating all objects, *money* is thus the *object* of eminent possession. The universality of its *property* is the omnipotence of its being. It therefore functions as the almighty being. Money is the *pimp* between man's need and the object,

3. This word is illegible.

between his life and his means of life. But that which mediates *my* life for me, also *mediates* the existence of other people *for me*. For me it is the *other* person.

> "What, man! confound it, hands and feet
> And head and backside, all are yours!
> And what we take while life is sweet,
> Is that to be declared not ours?
> Six stallions, say, I can afford,
> Is not their strength my property?
> I tear along, a sporting lord,
> As if their legs belonged to me."
> (Mephistopheles, in *Faust*)[4]

Shakespeare in *Timon of Athens*:

> "Gold? Yellow, glittering, precious gold? No, Gods,
> I am no idle votarist! . . . Thus much of this will
> make black white, foul fair,
> Wrong right, base noble, old young, coward valiant.
> . . . Why, this
> Will lug your priests and servants from your sides,
> Pluck stout men's pillows from below their heads:
> This yellow *slave*
> Will knit and break religions, bless the accursed;
> Make the hoar leprosy adored, place thieves
> And give them title, knee and approbation
> With senators on the bench: This is it
> That makes the wappen'd widow wed again;
> She, whom the spital-house and ulcerous sores
> Would cast the gorge at, this embalms and spices
> To the April day again. . . . Damned earth,
> Thou common whore of mankind, that putt'st odds
> Among the rout of nations."[5]

And also later:

> "O thou sweet king-killer, and dear divorce
> Twixt natural son and sire! thou bright defiler
> Of Hymen's purest bed! thou valiant Mars!
> Thou ever young, fresh, loved and delicate wooer,
> Whose blush doth thaw the consecrated snow
> That lies on Dian's lap! Thou *visible God*!
> That solder'st *close impossibilities*,
> And mak'st them kiss! That speak'st with every tongue,
> To every purpose! O thou touch of hearts!
> Think thy slave man rebels, and by thy virtue
> Set them into confounding odds, that beasts
> May have the world in empire!"[6]

4. Goethe, *Faust*, (Part I—Faust's Study, III), translated by Philip Wayne (Penguin, 1949), p. 91.
5. Shakespeare, *Timon of Athens*, Act 4, Scene 3. Marx quotes the Schlegel-Tieck German translation. (Marx's emphasis.)
6. Ibid.

Shakespeare excellently depicts the real nature of *money*. To understand him, let us begin, first of all, by expounding the passage from Goethe.

That which is for me through the medium of *money*—that for which I can pay (i.e., which money can buy)—that am *I*, the possessor of the money. The extent of the power of money is the extent of my power. Money's properties are my properties and essential powers—the properties and powers of its possessor. Thus, what I *am* and *am capable* of is by no means determined by my individuality. I am ugly, but I can buy for myself the most *beautiful* of women. Therefore I am not *ugly*, for the effect of *ugliness*—its deterrent power—is nullified by money. I, in my character as an individual, am *lame*, but money furnishes me with twenty-four feet. Therefore I am not lame. I am bad, dishonest, unscrupulous, stupid; but money is honoured, and therefore so is its possessor. Money is the supreme good, therefore its possessor is good. Money, besides, saves me the trouble of being dishonest: I am therefore presumed honest. I am *stupid*, but money is the *real mind* of all things and how then should its possessor be stupid? Besides, he can buy talented people for himself, and is he who has power over the talented not more talented than the talented? Do not I, who thanks to money am capable of *all* that the human heart longs for, possess all human capacities? Does not my money therefore transform all my incapacities into their contrary?

If *money* is the bond binding me to *human* life, binding society to me, binding me and nature and man, is not money the bond of all *bonds*? Can it not dissolve and bind all ties? Is it not, therefore, the universal *agent of divorce*? It is the true *agent of divorce* as well as the true *binding agent*—the [universal][7] *galvano-chemical* power of Society.

Shakespeare stresses especially two properties of money:

(1) It is the visible divinity—the transformation of all human and natural properties into their contraries, the universal confounding and overturning of things: it makes brothers of impossibilities. (2) It is the common whore, the common pimp of people and nations.

The overturning and confounding of all human and natural qualities, the fraternization of impossibilities—the *divine* power of money—lies in its *character* as men's estranged, alienating and self-disposing *species-nature*. Money is the alienated *ability of mankind*.

That which I am unable to do as a *man*, and of which therefore all my individual essential powers are incapable, I am able to do by means of *money*. Money thus turns each of these powers into

7. An end of the page is torn out of the manuscript.

something which in itself it is not—turns it, that is, into its *contrary*.

If I long for a particular dish or want to take the mail-coach because I am not strong enough to go by foot, money fetches me the dish and the mail-coach: that is, it converts my wishes from something in the realm of imagination, translates them from their meditated, imagined or willed existence into their *sensuous, actual* existence—from imagination to life, from imagined being into real being. In effecting this mediation, money is the *truly creative* power.

No doubt *demand* also exists for him who has no money, but his demand is a mere thing of the imagination without effect or existence for me, for a third party, for the others, and which therefore remains for me *unreal* and *objectless*. The difference between effective demand based on money and ineffective demand based on my need, my passion, my wish, etc., is the difference between *being* and *thinking*, between the imagined which *exists* merely within me and the imagined as it is for me outside me as a *real object*.

If I have no money for travel, I have no *need*—that is, no real and self-realizing need—to travel. If I have the *vocation* for study but no money for it, I have *no* vocation for study—that is, no *effective*, no *true* vocation. On the other hand, if I have really *no* vocation for study but have the will *and* the money for it, I have an *effective* vocation for it. Being the external, common *medium* and *faculty* for turning an *image* into *reality* and *reality* into a mere *image* (a faculty not springing from man as man or from human society as society), *money* transforms the *real essential powers of man and nature* into what are merely abstract conceits and therefore *imperfections*—into tormenting chimeras—just as it transforms *real imperfections and chimeras*—essential powers which are really impotent, which exist only in the imagination of the individual—into *real powers* and *faculties*.

In the light of this characteristic alone, money is thus the general overturning of *individualities* which turns them into their contrary and adds contradictory attributes to their attributes.

Money, then, appears as this *overturning* power both against the individual and against the bonds of society, etc., which claim to be *essences* in themselves. It transforms fidelity into infidelity, love into hate, hate into love, virtue into vice, vice into virtue, servant into master, master into servant, idiocy into intelligence and intelligence into idiocy.

Since money, as the existing and active concept of value, confounds and exchanges all things, it is the general *confounding* and *compounding* of all things—the world upside-down—the confounding and compounding of all natural and human qualities.

He who can buy bravery is brave, though a coward. As money is not exchanged for any one specific quality, for any one specific thing, or for any particular human essential power, but for the entire objective world of man and nature, from the standpoint of its possessor it therefore serves to exchange every property for every other, even contradictory, property and object: it is the fraternization of impossibilities. It makes contradictions embrace.

Assume *man* to be *man* and his relationship to the world to be a human one: then you can exchange love only for love, trust for trust, etc. If you want to enjoy art, you must be an artistically-cultivated person; if you want to exercise influence over other people, you must be a person with a stimulating and encouraging effect on other people. Every one of your relations to man and to nature must be a *specific expression*, corresponding to the object of your will, of your *real individual* life. If you love without evoking love in return—that is, if your loving as loving does not produce reciprocal love; if through a *living expression* of yourself as a loving person you do not make yourself a *loved person*, then your love is impotent—a misfortune.

Critique of the Hegelian Dialectic and Philosophy as a Whole

(6) This is perhaps the place at which, by way of explaining and justifying the ideas here presented, we might offer some considerations in regard to the Hegelian dialectic generally and especially its exposition in the *Phenomenology* and *Logic*, and also, lastly, the relation to it of the modern critical movement.

So powerful was modern German criticism's preoccupation with the past—so completely was it possessed in its development by its subject-matter—that there prevailed a completely uncritical attitude to the method of criticizing, together with a complete lack of awareness about the *seemingly formal*, but really *vital* question: how do we now stand as regards the Hegelian *dialectic*? This lack of awareness about the relationship of modern criticism to the Hegelian philosophy as a whole and especially to the Hegelian dialectic has been so great that critics like *Strauss* and *Bruno Bauer* still remain wholly within the confines of the Hegelian *Logic*; the former completely so and the latter at least implicitly so in his *Synoptics*[8] (where, in opposition to Strauss, he replaces the substance of "abstract nature" by the "self-consciousness" of abstract

---

8. Bruno Bauer, *Kritik der evangelischen Geschichte der Synoptiker* (*Critique of the Synoptic Gospels*), vol. 1–2, Leipzig, 1841; vol. 3, Braunschweig, 1842. In religious literature the authors of the first three Gospels are known as the Synoptics.

man) and even in *Christianity Discovered*.[9] Thus in *Christianity Discovered*, for example, you get:

> "As though in positing the world, self-consciousness posits that which is different from itself, and in what it posits it posits itself, because it in turn annuls the difference between what it has posited and itself, inasmuch as it itself has being only in the positing and the movement.—How then can it not have its purpose in this movement?" etc.; or again: "They" (the French materialists) "have not yet been able to see that it is only as the movement of self-consciousness that the movement of the universe has actually come to be for itself, and achieved unity with itself."

Such expressions do not even show any verbal divergence from the Hegelian approach, but on the contrary, repeat it word for word.

How little consciousness there was in relation to the Hegelian dialectic during the act of criticism (Bauer, *The Synoptics*), and how little this consciousness came into being even after the act of material criticism is proved by Bauer when, in his *The Good of Freedom*,[1] he dismisses the brash question put by Herr Gruppe— "What about logic now?"—by referring him to future critics.

But even now—now that *Feuerbach* both in his *Theses* in the *Anecdotis* and, in detail, in *The Philosophy of the Future*, has in principle overthrown the old dialectic and philosophy; now that that school of criticism, on the other hand, which was incapable of accomplishing this has all the same seen it accomplished and has proclaimed itself pure, resolute, absolute criticism—criticism that has come into the clear with itself; now that this criticism, in its spiritual pride, has reduced the whole process of history to the relation between the rest of the world and itself (the rest of the world, in contrast to itself, falling under the category of "the masses") and dissolved all dogmatic antithesis into the *single* dogmatic antithesis of its own cleverness and the stupidity of the world—the antithesis of the critical Christ and Mankind, the *rabble*; now that daily and hourly it has demonstrated its own excellence against the dullness of the masses; now, finally, that it has proclaimed the critical *Last Judgement* in the shape of an announcement that the day is approaching when the whole of expiring humanity will assemble before it and be sorted by it into groups, each particular mob receiving its *testimonium paupertatis*;[2] now that it has made

9. Bruno Bauer, *Das Entdeckte Christentum. Eine Erinnerung des Achtzehnten Jahrhundert und eine Beitrag zur Krisis des Neunzehnten* (*Christianity Discovered: A Memorial of the Eighteenth Century and a Contribution to the Crisis of the Nineteenth*), Zürich and Winterthur, 1843.

1. Bruno Bauer, *Die Gute Sache der Freiheit und meine Eigene Angelegenheit* (*The Good of Freedom and My Own Affair*), Zürich and Winterthur, 1842.

2. Certificate of poverty.

known in print[3] its superiority to human feelings as well as its superiority to the world, over which it sits enthroned in sublime solitude, only letting fall from time to time from its sarcastic lips the ringing laughter of the Olympian Gods—even now, after all these delightful antics of moribund idealism in the guise of criticism (i.e., of Young-Hegelianism)—even now it has not expressed the suspicion that the time was ripe for a critical settling of accounts with the mother of Young-Hegelianism—the Hegelian dialectic—and even had [nothing] to say about its critical attitude towards the Feuerbachian dialectic. Criticism with a completely uncritical attitude to itself!

Feuerbach is the only one who has a *serious, critical* attitude to the Hegelian dialectic and who has made genuine discoveries in this field. He is in fact the true conqueror of the old philosophy. The extent of his achievement, and the unpretentious simplicity with which he, Feuerbach, gives it to the world, stand in striking contrast to the reverse.

Feuerbach's great achievement is:

(1) The proof that philosophy is nothing else but religion rendered into thoughts and thinking expounded, and that it has therefore likewise to be condemned as another form and manner of existence of the estrangement of the essence of man;

(2) The establishment of *true materialism* and of *real science*, since Feuerbach also makes the social relationship "of man to man" the basic principle of the theory;

(3) His opposing to the negation of the negation, which claims to be the absolute positive, the self-supporting positive, positively grounded on itself.

Feuerbach explains the Hegelian dialectic (and thereby justifies starting out from the positive, from sense-certainty) as follows:

Hegel sets out from the estrangement of Substance (in Logic, from the Infinite, the abstractly universal)—from the absolute and fixed abstraction; which means, put popularly, that he sets out from religion and theology.

Secondly, he annuls the infinite, and establishes the actual, sensuous, real, finite, particular (philosophy—annulment of religion and theology).

Thirdly, he again annuls the positive and restores the abstraction, the infinite—restoration of religion and theology.

Feuerbach thus conceives the negation of the negation *only* as a contradiction of philosophy with itself—as the philosophy which affirms theology (the transcendent, etc.) after having denied it, and which it therefore affirms in opposition to itself.

The position or self-affirmation and self-confirmation contained

3. A reference to the *Allgemeine Literatur-Zeitung*.

in the negation of the negation is taken to be a position which is not yet sure of itself, which is therefore burdened with its opposite, which is doubtful of itself and therefore in need of proof, and which, therefore, is not a position establishing itself by its exist-ence—not a position that justifies itself; hence it is directly and immediately confronted by the self-grounded position of sense-certainty.[4]

But because Hegel has conceived the negation of the negation from the point of view of the positive relation inherent in it as the true and only positive, and from the point of view of the negative relation inherent in it as the only true act and self-realizing act of all being, he has only found the *abstract, logical, speculative* expres-sion for the movement of history; and this historical process is not yet the *real* history of man—of man as a given subject, but only man's *act of genesis*—the *story* of man's *origin*. We shall explain both the abstract form of this process and the difference between this process as it is in Hegel in contrast to modern criticism, that is, in contrast to the same process in Feuerbach's *Wesen des Chris-tentums (Essence of Christianity)*, or rather the *critical* form of this in Hegel still uncritical process.

Let us take a look at the Hegelian system. One must begin with Hegel's *Phenomenology*, the true point of origin and the secret of the Hegelian philosophy.

PHENOMENOLOGY[5]

A. *Self-Consciousness*

I. *Consciousness.* (a) Certainty at the level of sense experience; or the "This" and *Meaning.* (b) *Perception*, or the Thing with Its Properties, and *Deception.* (c) Force and Understanding, Appear-ance and the Super-sensible World.

II. *Self-Consciousness.* The Truth of Certainty of Self. (a) Inde-pendence and Dependence of Self-Consciousness; Lordship and Bondage. (b) Freedom of Self-Consciousness: Stoicism, Scepticism, the Unhappy Consciousness.

III. *Reason.* Reason's Certainty and Reason's Truth. (a) Obser-vation as a Process of Reason. Observation of Nature and of Self-Consciousness. (b) Realization of Rational Self-Consciousness

4. Feuerbach views negation of nega-tion, the definite concept as thinking surpassing itself in thinking and as thinking wanting to be directly aware-ness, nature, reality. [*Marx*] Marx is referring to Feuerbach's critical obser-vations about Hegel in § 29–30 of his *Grundsätze der Philosophie zer Zukunft.*
5. What follows here are the main chapter and section-headings of Hegel's *Phenomenology of Mind.* Here and in later quotations from the *Phenomenol-ogy*, the translator has followed Bail-lie's translation very closely, departing from it only on the few occasions where this was necessary to keep the terminology in line with that used throughout the present volume.

through its own Activity. Pleasure and Necessity. The Law of the Heart and the Frenzy of Self-Conceit. Virtue and the Course of the World. (c) The Individuality Which is Real In and For Itself. The Spiritual Animal Kingdom and the Deception, or the Real Fact. Reason as Lawgiver. Reason Which Tests Laws.

B. Mind

I. *True* Mind; the Ethical Order.
II. Mind in Self-Estrangement—Culture.
III. Mind Certain of Itself, Morality.

C. Religion

Natural Religion; *Religion in the Form of Art*; *Revealed* Religion.

D. Absolute Knowledge

Hegel's *Encyclopaedia*,[6] beginning as it does with Logic, with *pure speculative thought*, and ending with *Absolute Knowledge*—with the self-conscious, self-comprehending, philosophic or absolute (i.e., superhuman) abstract mind—is in its entirety nothing but the *display*, the self-objectification, of the *essence* of the philosophic mind, and the philosophic mind is nothing but the estranged mind of the world thinking within its self-estrangement—i.e., comprehending itself abstractly. *Logic* (mind's *coin of the realm*, the speculative or *thought-value* of man and nature—their essence grown totally indifferent to all real determinateness, and hence their unreal essence) is *alienated thinking*, and therefore thinking which abstracts from nature and from real man: *abstract* thinking. Then: *The externality of this abstract thinking . . . nature*, as it is for this abstract thinking. Nature is external to it—its self-loss; and it apprehends nature also in an external fashion, as abstract thinking—but as alienated abstract thinking. Finally, *Mind*, this thinking returning home to its own point of origin—the thinking which, as the anthropological, phenomenological, psychological, ethical, artistic and religious mind, is not valid for itself, until ultimately it finds itself, and relates itself to itself, as

6. G. W. F. Hegel, *Enzyklopädie der Philosophischen Wissenschaften* (Heidelberg, 1st ed., 1817, 3rd ed., 1830). Hegel's *Encyclopaedia of the Philosophical Sciences* is a single volume falling into three main parts: the subject of the first is Logic (cf. *The Logic of Hegel*, trans. William Wallace, 2nd ed., Oxford, 1892); the subject of the second part is the Philosophy of Nature (of which no English translation has been published), and that of the third the Philosophy of Mind. (Cf. Hegel's *Philosophy of Mind*, trans. William Wallace, Oxford, 1894.)

absolute knowledge in the hence absolute, i.e., abstract mind, and so receives its conscious embodiment in a mode of being corresponding to it. For its real mode of being is *abstraction*.

There is a double error in Hegel.

The first emerges most clearly in the *Phenomenology*, the Hegelian philosophy's place of origin. When, for instance, wealth, state-power, etc., are understood by Hegel as entities estranged from the *human* being, this only happens in their form as thoughts. . . . They are thought-entities, and therefore merely an estrangement of *pure*, i.e., abstract, philosophical thinking. The whole process therefore ends with Absolute Knowledge. It is precisely abstract thought from which these objects are estranged and which they confront with their arrogation of reality. The *philosopher* sets up himself (that is, one who is himself an abstract form of estranged man) as the *measuring-rod* of the estranged world. The whole *history of the alienation-process* and the whole *process of the retraction* of the alienation is therefore nothing but the *history of the production* of abstract (i.e., absolute) thought—of logical, speculative thought. The *estrangement*, which therefore forms the real interest of this alienation and of the transcendence of this alienation, is the opposition of *in itself* and *for itself*, of *consciousness* and *self-consciousness*, of *object* and *subject*—that is to say, it is the opposition, within thought itself, between abstract thinking and sensuous reality or real sensuousness. All other oppositions and movements of these oppositions are but the *semblance, the cloak, the exoteric* shape of these oppositions which alone matter, and which constitute the *meaning* of these other, profane oppositions. It is not the fact that the human being *objectifies himself inhumanly*, in opposition to himself, but the fact that he *objectifies himself* in *distinction* from and in *opposition* to abstract thinking, that is the posited essence of the estrangement and the thing to be superseded.

The appropriation of man's essential powers, which have become objects—indeed, alien objects—is thus in the *first place* only an *appropriation* occurring in *consciousness*, in *pure thought*—i.e., in *abstraction*: it is the appropriation of these objects as *thoughts* and as *movements of thought*. Consequently, despite its thoroughly negative and critical appearance and despite the criticism really contained in it, which often anticipates far later development, there is already latent in the *Phenomenology* as a germ, a potentiality, a secret, the uncritical positivism and the equally uncritical idealism of Hegel's later works—that philosophic dissolution and restoration of the existing empirical world. In the *second place*: the vindication of the objective world for man—for example, the realization that *sensuous* consciousness is not an *abstractly* sensuous consciousness but a *humanly* sensuous consciousness—that religion, wealth, etc., are but the estranged world of *human* objectification, of *man's* essential powers given over to work and that they are therefore but the *path* to the true *human* world—this appropriation or the insight into this process consequently appears in Hegel in this form, that *sense, religion,* state-power, etc., are *spiritual* entities; for only *mind* is the *true* essence of man, and the true form of mind is thinking mind, the logical, speculative mind. The *humanness* of nature and of the nature begotten by history—the humanness of man's products—appears in the form that they are *products* of abstract mind and as such, therefore, phases of *mind—thought entities.* The *Phenomenology* is, therefore, an occult critique—still to itself obscure and mystifying criticism; but inasmuch as it keeps steadily in view man's *estrangement,* even though man appears only in the shape of mind, there lie concealed in it *all* the elements of criticism, already *prepared* and *elaborated* in a manner often rising far above the Hegelian standpoint. The "Unhappy Consciousness," the "Honest Consciousness," the struggle of the "Noble and Base Consciousness,"[7] etc., etc.,—these separate sections contain, but still in an estranged form, the *critical* elements of whole spheres such as religion, the state, civil life, etc. Just as *entities, objects,* appear as *thought-entities,* so the *subject* is always *consciousness* or *self-consciousness;* or rather the object appears only as *abstract* consciousness, man only as *self-consciousness*: the distinct forms of estrangement which make their appearance are, therefore, only various forms of consciousness and self-consciousness. Just as *in itself* abstract consciousness (the form in which the object is conceived) is merely a moment of distinction of self-consciousness, what appears as the result of the movement is the identity of self-consciousness with consciousness—absolute knowledge—the movement of abstract thought no longer directed outwards but going on now only within its own self: that is to say, the dialectic of pure thought is the result.

The outstanding thing in Hegel's *Phenomenology* and its final outcome—that is, the dialectic of negativity as the moving and generating principle—is thus first that Hegel conceives the self-genesis of man as a process, conceives objectification as loss of the object, as alienation and as transcendence of this alienation; that he thus grasps the essence of *labour* and comprehends objective man—true, because real man—as the outcome of man's *own labour.* The *real,* active orientation of man to himself as a species being, or his manifestation as a real species being (i.e., as a human being), is only possible by his really bringing out of himself all the *powers* that are his as the *species* man—something which in turn is only possi-

---

7. "The unhappy consciousness," etc.—forms of mind, and phases and factors in human history, distinguished and analysed in particular sections of Hegel's *Phenomenology.*

ble through the totality of man's actions, as the result of history—is only possible by man's treating these generic powers as objects: and this, to begin with, is again only possible in the form of estrangement.

We shall now demonstrate in detail Hegel's one-sidedness and limitations as they are displayed in the final chapter of the *Phenomenology*, "Absolute Knowledge"—a chapter which contains the concentrated spirit of the *Phenomenology*, the relationship of the *Phenomenology* to speculative dialectic, and also Hegel's *consciousness* concerning both and their relationship to one another.

Let us provisionally say just this much in advance: Hegel's standpoint is that of modern political economy. He grasps *labour* as the *essence* of man—as man's essence in the act of proving itself: he sees only the positive, not the negative side of labour. Labour is man's *coming-to-be for himself* within *alienation*, or as *alienated* man. The only labour which Hegel knows and recognizes is *abstractly mental* labour. Therefore, that which constitutes the *essence* of philosophy—the *alienation of man in his knowing of himself*, or *alienated* science *thinking itself*—Hegel grasps as its essence; and he is therefore able *vis-à-vis* preceding philosophy to gather together its separate elements and phases, and to present his philosophy as the philosophy. What the other philosophers did—that they grasped separate phases of nature and of human life as phases of self-consciousness, and indeed of abstract self-consciousness—is *known* to Hegel as the *doings* of philosophy. Hence his science is absolute.

Let us now turn to our subject.

Absolute Knowledge. The last chapter of the "Phenomenology."

The main point is that the *object of consciousness* is nothing else but *self-consciousness*, or that the object is only *objectified self-consciousness*—self-consciousness as object.

(Positing of man=self-consciousness.)

The issue, therefore, is to surmount the *object of consciousness*. Objectivity as such is regarded as an *estranged* human relationship which does not correspond to the *essence of man*, to self-consciousness. The *re-appropriation* of the objective essence of man, begotten in the form of estrangement as something alien, has the meaning therefore not only to annul *estrangement*, but *objectivity* as well. Man, that is to say, is regarded as a *non-objective, spiritual* being.

The movement of *surmounting the object of consciousness* is now described by Hegel in the following way:

The *object* reveals itself not merely as *returning into the self*—for Hegel that is the *one-sided* way of apprehending this movement, the grasping of only one side. Man is posited as equivalent to self. The self, however, is only the *abstractly* conceived man—man begotten by abstraction. Man *is* egotistic. His eye, his ear, etc., are *egotistic*. In him every one of his essential powers has the quality of *selfhood*. But it is quite false to say on that account "*Self-consciousness* has eyes, ears, essential powers." Self-consciousness is rather a quality of human nature, of the human eye, etc.; it is not human nature that is a quality of *self-consciousness*.

The self-abstracted and fixed for itself is man as *abstract egoist*—egoism raised in its pure abstraction to the level of thought. (We shall return to this point later.)

For Hegel the *essence of man—man—*equals *self-consciousness*. All estrangement of the human essence is therefore *nothing but estrangement of self-consciousness*. The estrangement of self-consciousness is not regarded as an *expression* of the *real* estrangement of the human being—its expression reflected in the realm of knowledge and thought. Instead, the *real* estrangement—that which appears real—is from its *innermost*, hidden nature (a nature only brought to light by philosophy) nothing but the *manifestation* of the estrangement of the real essence of man, of *self-consciousness*. The science which comprehends this is therefore called *Phenomenology*. All re-appropriation of the estranged objective essence appears, therefore, as a process of incorporation into self-consciousness: The man who takes hold of his essential being is *merely* the self-consciousness which takes hold of objective essences. Return of the object into the self is therefore the re-appropriation of the object.

The *surmounting of the object of consciousness, comprehensively* expressed, means:[8]

(1) That the object as such presents itself to consciousness as something vanishing. (2) That it is the alienation of self-consciousness which establishes thinghood. (3) That this externalization[9] of self-consciousness has not merely a *negative* but a *positive* significance. (4) That it has this meaning not merely *for us* or *intrinsically*, but *for self-consciousness itself*. (5) For *self-consciousness*, the negative of the object, its annulling of itself, has *positive* significance—self-consciousness *knows* this nullity of the object—because self-consciousness itself alienates itself; for in this alienation it establishes *itself* as object, or, for the sake of the indivisible unity of *being-for-self*, establishes the object as itself. (6) On the other hand, there is also this other moment in the process, that self-consciousness has also just as much annulled and superseded this alienation and objectivity and resumed them into itself, being thus at home with *itself* in *its* other-being *as such*. (7) This is the movement of *consciousness* and in this movement consciousness is the totality of its moments. (8) Consciousness must

8. The paragraph which follows is a transcript of the second and third paragraphs of the last chapter of Hegel's *Phenomenology*, trans. Baillie, 2nd ed., p. 789.
9. "Externalization"—*Entäusserung*.

similarly have taken up a relation to the object in all its aspects and phases, and have comprehended it from the point of view of each of them. This totality of its determinate characteristics makes the object *intrinsically a spiritual being*; and it becomes so in truth for consciousness through the apprehending of each single one of them as *self* or through what was called above the *spiritual* attitude to them.

As to (1): That the object as such presents itself to consciousness as something vanishing—this is the above-mentioned *return of the object into the self.*

As to (2): *The alienation of self-consciousness* establishes *thinghood*. Because man equals self-consciousness, his alienated, objective essence, or *thinghood, equals alienated self-consciousness*, and *thinghood* is thus established through this alienation (thinghood being *that* which is an *object for man* and an object for him is really only that which is to him an essential object, therefore his *objective essence*. And since it is not *real Man*, nor therefore *Nature*—Man being *human Nature*—who as such is made the subject, but only the abstraction of man—self-consciousness—thinghood cannot be anything but alienated self-conciousness). It is only to be expected that a living, natural being equipped and endowed with objective (i.e., material) essential powers should have *real natural objects* of his essence; as is the fact that his self-alienation should lead to the establishing of a *real*, objective world—but a world in the form of *externality*—a world, therefore, not belonging to his own essential being, and an overpowering world. There is nothing incomprehensible or mysterious in this. It would be mysterious, rather, if it were otherwise. But it is equally clear that a *self-consciousness* can only establish *thinghood* through its alienation—i.e., establish something which itself is only an abstract thing, a thing of abstraction and not a *real* thing. It is clear, further, that thinghood is therefore utterly without any *independence*, any *essentiality vis-à-vis* self-consciousness; that on the contrary, it is a mere creature—something *posited* by self-consciousness. And what is posited, instead of confirming itself, is but a confirmation of the act of positing in which is concentrated for a moment the energy of the act as its product, *seeming* to give the de-posit—but only for a moment—the character of an independent, real substance.[1]

Whenever real, corporeal *man*, man with his feet firmly on the solid ground, man exhaling and inhaling all the forces of nature, *establishes* his real, objective *essential powers* as alien objects by his externalization, it is not the *act of positing* which is the subject in this process: it is the subjectivity of *objective* essential powers, whose action, therefore, must also be something *objective*. A being

1. "Substance"—*Wesen*.

who is objective acts objectively, and he would not act objectively if the objective did not reside in the very nature of his being. He creates or establishes only *objects,* *because* he is established by objects—because at bottom he is *nature.* In the act of establishing, therefore, this objective being does not fall from his state of "pure activity" into a *creating of the object*; on the contrary, his *objective* product only confirms his *objective* activity, establishing his activity as the activity of an objective, natural being.

Here we see how consistent naturalism or humanism distinguishes itself both from idealism and materialism, constituting at the same time the unifying truth of both. We see also how only naturalism is capable of comprehending the act of world history.

Man is directly a *natural being.* As a natural being and as a living natural being he is on the one hand furnished with *natural powers of life*—he is an *active* natural being. These forces exist in him as tendencies and abilities—as *impulses.* On the other hand, as a natural, corporeal, sensuous, objective being he is a *suffering,* conditioned and limited creature, like animals and plants. That is to say, the *objects* of his impulses exist outside him, as *objects* independent of him; yet these objects are *objects* of his *need*—essential *objects,* indispensable to the manifestation and confirmation of his essential powers. To say that man is a *corporeal,* living, real, sensuous, objective being full of natural vigour is to say that he has *real, sensuous, objects* as the objects of his being or of his life, or that he can only *express* his life in real, sensuous objects. To be objective, natural and sensuous, and at the same time to have object, nature and sense outside oneself, or oneself to be object, nature and sense for a third party, is one and the same thing. *Hunger* is a natural *need*; it therefore needs a *nature* outside itself, an *object* outside itself, in order to satisfy itself, to be stilled. Hunger is an acknowledged need of my body for an *object* existing outside it, indispensable to its integration and to the expression of its essential being. The sun is the *object* of the plant—an indispensable object to it, confirming its life—just as the plant is an object of the sun, being an *expression* of the life-awakening power of the sun, of the sun's *objective* essential power.

A being which does not have its nature outside itself is not a *natural* being, and plays no part in the system of nature. A being which has no object outside itself is not an objective being. A being which is not itself an object for some third being has no being for its *object*; i.e., it is not objectively related. Its be-ing is not objective.[2]

An unobjective being is a *nullity*—an *un-being.*

Suppose a being which is neither an object itself, nor has an object. Such a being, in the first place, would be the *unique* being:

2. "Being"—*Wesen*; "nature"—*Natur;* "system"—*Wesen*; "be-ing"—*Sein.*

there would exist no being outside it—it would exist solitary and alone. For as soon as there are objects outside me, as soon as I am not *alone*, I am *another—another reality* than the object outside me. For this third object I am thus an *other reality* than it; that is, I am *its* object. Thus, to suppose a being which is not the object of another being is to presuppose that *no* objective being exists. As soon as I have an object, this object has me for an object. But a *non-objective* being is an unreal, nonsensical thing—something merely thought of (merely imagined, that is)—a creature of abstraction. To be *sensuous*, that is, to be an object of sense, to be a *sensuous* object, and thus to have sensuous objects outside oneself—objects of one's sensuousness. To be sensuous is to *suffer*.[3]

Man as an objective, sensuous being is therefore a *suffering* being —and because he feels what he suffers, a *passionate* being. Passion is the essential force of man energetically bent on its object.

But man is not merely a natural being: he is a *human* natural being. That is to say, he is a being for himself. Therefore he is a *species being*, and has to confirm and manifest himself as such both in his being and in his knowing. Therefore, *human* objects are not natural objects as they immediately present themselves, and neither is *human sense* as it immediately *is*—as it is objectively— *human* sensibility, human objectivity. Neither nature objectively nor nature subjectively is directly given in a form adequate to the *human* being. And as everything natural has to have its *beginning*, *man* too has his act of coming-to-be—*history*—which, however, is for him a known history, and hence as an act of coming-to-be it is a conscious self-transcending act of coming-to-be. History is the true natural history of man (on which more later).

Thirdly, because this establishing of thinghood is itself only sham, an act contradicting the nature of pure activity, it has to be cancelled again and thinghood denied.

Re. 3, 4, 5 and 6. (3) This externalization of consciousness has not merely a *negative* but a *positive* significance, and (4) it has this meaning not merely *for us* or intrinsically, but for consciousness itself.[4] (5) *For consciousness* the negative of the object, its annulling of itself, has *positive* significance—consciousness *knows* this nullity of the object because it alienates *itself*; for in this alien-

---

3. "To be sensuous is to suffer" —*Sinnlich sein ist leidend sein.* Here "to suffer" should probably be understood in the sense of "to undergo"—to be the object of another's action. Note the transition in the next sentence from *Leiden* (suffering) to *leidenschaftlich* (passionate).

4. Here Marx has taken the impersonal pronoun *es* (it) to represent *Bewusstsein* (consciousness); but it seems that Baillie is more correct in reading this as standing for *Selbstbewusstsein* (self-consciousness). In the first quotation of this passage (p. 91) Marx simply uses *es* without specifying what it represents, and the translation has followed Baillie in interpreting it as "self-consciousness." In the present repetition of the passage, Marx's specification of the "it" as "consciousness," has been followed in the translation.

ation it *knows* itself as object, or, for the sake of the indivisible unity of *being-for-itself*, the object as itself. (6) On the other hand, there is also this other moment in the process, that consciousness has also just as much annulled and superseded this alienation and objectivity and resumed them into itself, being thus *at home with itself* in its *other-being as such*.

As we have already seen: the appropriation of what is estranged and objective, or the annulling of objectivity in the form of *estrangement* (which has to advance from indifferent foreignness to real, antagonistic estrangement) means equally or even primarily for Hegel that it is *objectivity* which is to be annulled, because it is not the *determinate* character of the object, but rather its *objective* character that is offensive and constitutes estrangement for self-consciousness. The object is therefore something negative, self-annulling—a *nullity*. This nullity of the object has not only a negative but a *positive* meaning for consciousness, for such a *nullity* of the object is precisely the *self-confirmation* of the non-objectivity, of the *abstraction* of itself. For *consciousness itself* this nullity of the object has a positive meaning because it *knows* this nullity, the objective being, as its *self-alienation*; because it knows that it exists only as a result of its own *self-alienation*. ...

The way in which consciousness is, and in which something is for it, is *knowing*. Knowing is its sole act. Something therefore comes to be for consciousness in so far as the latter *knows* this *something*. Knowing is its sole objective relation. Consciousness, then, knows the nullity of the object (i.e., knows the non-existence of the distinction between the object and itself, the non-existence of the object for it) because it knows the object as its *self-alienation*; that is, it knows itself—knows knowing as the object—because the object is only the *semblance* of an object, a piece of mystification, which in its essence, however, is nothng else but knowing itself, which has confronted itself with itself and in so doing has confronted itself with a *nullity*—a something which has *no* objectivity outside the knowing. Or: knowing knows that in relating itself to an object it is only *outside itself*—that it only externalizes itself; that *it itself* appears to itself only *as an object*—or that that which appears to it as an object is only it itself.

On the other hand, says Hegel, there is at the same time this other moment in this process, that consciousness has just as much annulled and superseded this externalization and objectivity and resumed them into itself, being thus *at home* in its *other-being as such*.

In this discussion are brought together all the illusions of speculation.

First of all: consciousness—self-consciousness—is *at home with itself in its other-being as such*. It is therefore—or if we here abstract from the Hegelian abstraction and put the self-consciousness of man instead of Self-consciousness—*it is at home with itself in its other-being, as such*. This implies, for one thing, that consciousness (knowing as knowing, thinking as thinking) pretends to be directly the *other* of itself—to be the world of sense, the real world, life—thought over-reaching itself in thought (Feuerbach).[5] This aspect is contained herein, inasmuch as consciousness as mere consciousness takes offence not at estranged objectivity, but at *objectivity as such*.

Secondly, this implies that self-conscious man, in so far as he has recognized and annulled and superseded the spiritual world (or his world's spiritual, general mode of being) as self-alienation, nevertheless again confirms this in its alienated shape and passes it off as his true mode of being—re-establishes it, and pretends to be *at home in his other-being as such*. Thus, for instance, after annulling and superseding religion, after recognizing religion to be a product of self-alienation, he yet finds confirmation of himself in *religion as religion*. Here *is* the root of Hegel's *false* positivism, or of his merely *apparent* criticism: this is what Feuerbach designated as the positing, negating and re-establishing of religion or theology—but it has to be grasped in more general terms. Thus reason is at home in unreason as unreason. The man who has recognized that he is leading an alienated life in politics, law, etc., is leading his true human life in this alienated life as such. Self-affirmation, *in contradiction* with itself—in contradiction both with the knowledge of and with the essential being of the object—is thus true *knowledge* and *life*.

There can therefore no longer be any question about an act of accommodation on Hegel's part *vis-à-vis* religion, the state, etc., since this lie is *the* lie of his principle.

If I *know* religion as *alienated* human self-consciousness, then what I know in it as religion is not my self-consciousness, but my alienated self-consciousness confirmed in it. I therefore know my own self, the self-consciousness that belongs to its very nature, confirmed not in *religion* but rather in *annihilated* and *superseded* religion.

In Hegel, therefore, the negation of the negation is not the confirmation of the true essence, effected precisely through negation of the pseudo-essence. With him the negation of the negation is the confirmation of the pseudo-essence, or of the self-estranged essence in its denial; or it is the denial of this pseudo-essence as an objec-

5. Marx refers to § 30 of Feuerbach's *Grundsätze der Philosophie der Zukunft*, which says: "Hegel is a thinker who transcends himself in thinking."

tive being dwelling outside man and independent of him, and its transformation into the subject.

A peculiar role, therefore, is played by the act of *superseding* in which denial and preservation—denial and affirmation—are bound together.

Thus, for example, in Hegel's *Philosophy of Right, Private Right* superseded equals *Morality,* Morality superseded equals the *Family,* the Family superseded equals *Civil Society,* Civil Society superseded equals the *State,* the State superseded equals *World History.* In the *actual world* private right, morality, the family, civil society, the state, etc., remain in existence, only they have become *moments* of man—state of his existence and being—which have no validity in isolation, but dissolve and engender one another, etc. They have become *moments of motion.*

In their actual existence this *mobile* nature of theirs is hidden. It first appears and is made manifest in thought, in philosophy. Hence my true religious existence is my existence in the *philosophy of religion;* my true political existence is my existence within the *philosophy of right;* my true natural existence, existence in the *philosophy of nature;* my true artistic existence, existence in the *philosophy of art;* my true *human* existence, my existence in *philosophy.* Likewise the true existence of religion, the state, nature, art is the *philosophy* of religion, of nature, of the state and of art. If, however, the philosophy of religion, etc., is for me the sole true existence of religion, then, too, it is only as a *philosopher of religion* that I am truly religious, and so I deny *real* religious sentiment and the really *religious* man. But at the same time I *assert* them, in part within my own existence or within the alien existence which I oppose to them—for this *is* only their *philosophic* expression—and in part I assert them in their own original shape, for they have validity for me as merely the *apparent* other-being, as allegories, forms of their own true existence (i.e., of my *philosophical* existence) hidden under sensuous disguises.

In just the same way, *Quality* superseded equals *Quantity,* Quantity superseded equals *Measure,* Measure superseded equals *Essence,* Essence superseded equals *Appearance,* Appearance superseded equals *Actuality,* Actuality superseded equals the *Concept,* the Concept superseded equals *Objectivity,* Objectivity superseded equals the *Absolute Idea,* the Absolute Idea superseded equals *Nature,* Nature superseded equals *Ethical* Objective Mind, Ethical Mind superseded equals *Art,* Art superseded equals *Religion,* Religion superseded equals *Absolute Knowledge.*[6]

6. This sequence gives the major "categories" or "thought-forms" of Hegel's *Encyclopaedia* in the order in which they occur and are superseded. Similarly, the sequence above from "private right" to "world history" gives the major categories of Hegel's *Philosophy of Right* in the order in which they appear there.

On the one hand, this act of superseding is a transcending of the thought entity; thus, Private Property *as a thought* is transcended in the *thought* of morality. And because thought imagines itself to be directly the other of itself, to be *sensuous reality*—and therefore takes its own action for *sensuous, real action*—this superseding in thought, which leaves its object standing in the real world, believes that it has really overcome it. On the other hand, because the object has now become for it a moment of thought, thought takes it in its reality too to be self-confirmation of itself—of self-consciousness, of abstraction.

From the one point of view the existent which Hegel *supersedes* in philosophy is therefore not *real* religion, the *real* state, or *real* nature, but religion itself already become an object of knowledge, i.e., *Dogmatics*; the same with *Jurisprudence, Political Science* and *Natural Science*. From the one point of view, therefore, he stands in opposition both to the *real* thing and to immediate, unphilosophic *science* or the unphilosophic *conceptions* of this thing. He therefore contradicts their conventional conceptions.[7]

On the other hand, the religious man, etc., can find in Hegel his final confirmation.

It is now time to lay hold of the *positive* aspects of the Hegelian dialectic within the realm of estrangement.

(a) *Annulling* as an objective movement of *retracting* the alienation *into self*. This is the insight, expressed within the estrangement, concerning the *appropriation* of the objective essence through the annulment of its estrangement; it is the estranged insight into the *real objectification* of man, into the real appropriation of his objective essence through the annihilation of the *estranged* character of the objective world, through the annulment of the objective world in its estranged mode of being—just as atheism, being the annulment of God, is the advent of theoretic humanism, and communism, as the annulment of private property, is the justification of real human life as man's possession and thus the advent of practical humanism (or just as atheism is humanism mediated with itself through the annulment of religion, whilst communism is humanism mediated with itself through the annulment of private property). Only through the annulment of this mediation—which is itself, however, a necessary premise—does positively self-deriving humanism, *positive humanism*, come into being.

But atheism and communism are no flight, no abstraction; they are not a losing of the objective world begotten by man—of man's essential powers given over to the realm of objectivity; they are not a returning in poverty to unnatural, primitive simplicity. On the

7. The conventional conception of the-   natural science, etc.
ology, jurisprudence, political science,

contrary, they are but the first real coming-to-be, the realization become real for man, of man's essence—of the essence of man as something real.

Thus, by grasping the *positive* meaning of self-referred negation (if even again in estranged fashion) Hegel grasps man's self-estrangement, the alienation of man's essence, man's loss of objectivity and his loss of realness as finding of self, change of his nature, his objectification and realization. In short, within the sphere of abstraction, Hegel conceives labour as man's act of *self-genesis*—conceives man's relation to himself as an alien being and the manifesting of himself as an alien being to be the coming-to-be of *species-consciousness* and *species-life*.

(b) However, apart from, or rather in consequence of, the perverseness already described, this act appears in Hegel:

First of all as a *merely formal*, because abstract, act, because the human essence itself is taken to be only an *abstract, thinking essence*, conceived merely as self-consciousness. And,

secondly, because the conception is *formal* and *abstract*, the annulment of the alienation becomes a confirmation of the alienation; or again, for Hegel this movement of *self-genesis* and *self-objectification* in the form of *self-alienation* and *self-estrangement* is the *absolute*, and hence final, *expression of human life*—of life with itself as its aim, of life at rest in itself, of life that has attained oneness with its essence.

This movement, in its abstract form as dialectic, is therefore regarded as *truly human life*, and because it is nevertheless an abstraction—an estrangement of human life—it is regarded as a *divine process*, but as the divine process of man, a process traversed by man's abstract, pure, absolute essence that is distinct from him.

Thirdly, this process must have a bearer, a subject. But the subject first emerges as a result. This result—the subject knowing itself as absolute self-consciousness—is therefore *God—absolute Spirit—the self-knowing and self-manifesting Idea*. Real man and real nature become mere predicates—symbols of this esoteric, unreal man and of this unreal nature. Subject and predicate are therefore related to each other in absolute inversion—a *mystical subject-object* or a *subjectivity reaching beyond* the *object*—the *absolute subject* as a *process*, as *subject alienating* itself and returning from alienation into itself, but at the same time retracting this alienation into itself, and the subject as this process; a pure, *restless* revolving within itself.

First, the *formal and abstract* conception of man's act of self-genesis or self-objectification.

Hegel having posited man as equivalent to self-consciousness, the estranged object—the estranged essential reality of man—is nothing but *consciousness,* the thought of estrangement merely—estrangement's *abstract* and therefore empty and unreal expression, *negation.* The annulment of the alienation is therefore likewise nothing but an abstract, empty annulment of that empty abstraction—the *negation of the negation.* The rich, living, sensuous, concrete activity of self-objectification is therefore reduced to its mere abstraction, *absolute negativity*—an abstraction which is again fixed as such and thought of as an independent activity—as sheer activity. Because this so-called negativity is nothing but the *abstract, empty* form of that real living act, its content can in consequence be merely a *formal* content begotten by abstraction from all content. As a result there are general, abstract *forms of abstraction* pertaining to every content and on that account indifferent to, and, consequently, valid for, all content—the thought-forms or logical categories torn from *real* mind and from *real* nature. (We shall unfold the *logical* content of absolute negativity further on.)

Hegel's positive achievement here, in his speculative logic, is that the *determinate concepts,* the universal *fixed thought-forms* in their independence *vis-à-vis* nature and mind are a necessary result of the general estrangement of the human essence and therefore also of human thought, and that Hegel has therefore brought these together and presented them as moments of the abstraction-process. For example, superseded Being is Essence, superseded Essence is Concept, the Concept superseded is . . . the Absolute Idea. But what, then, is the Absolute Idea? It supersedes its own self again, if it does not want to traverse once more from the beginning the whole act of abstraction, and to acquiesce in being a totality of abstractions or in being the self-comprehending abstraction. But abstraction comprehending itself as abstraction knows itself to be nothing: it must abandon itself—abandon abstraction—and so it arrives at an entity which is its exact contrary —at *nature.* Thus, the entire *Logic* is the demonstration that abstract thought is nothing in itself; that the Absolute Idea is nothing in itself; that only *Nature* is something.

The absolute idea, the *abstract* idea, which "*considered* with regard to its unity with itself is *intuiting,*"[8] (Hegel's *Encyclopaedia,* 3rd edition, p. 222), and which "in its own absolute truth *resolves* to let the moment of its particularity or of initial characterization and other-being—the *immediate idea,* as its reflection, *go forth freely from itself as nature*" (l.c.)—this whole idea

---

8. *The Logic of Hegel,* trans. Wallace, ¶ 244. "Intuiting" is here used to render *Anschauen.* In popular usage *Anschauen* means "to contemplate," but Hegel is here using the word, like Kant, as a technical term in philosophy meaning, roughly, "to be aware through the senses." "Intuiting," likewise, should be understood here not in its popular sense but as the philosophical term which is the recognized English equivalent of *Anschauen.*

which behaves in such a strange and singular way, and which has given the Hegelians such terrible headaches, is from beginning to end nothing else but *abstraction* (i.e., the abstract thinker)—abstraction which, made wise by experience and enlightened concerning its truth, resolves under various (false and themselves still abstract) conditions to *abandon itself* and to replace its self-absorption, nothingness, generality and indeterminateness by its other-being, the particular, and the determinate; resolves to let *nature*, which it held hidden in itself only as an abstraction, as a thought-entity, *go forth freely from itself*: that is to say, abstraction resolves to forsake abstraction and to have a look at nature *free* of abstraction. The abstract idea, which without mediation becomes *intuiting*, is nothing else through-and-through but abstract thinking that gives itself up and resolves on *intuition*. This entire transition from Logic to Natural Philosophy is nothing else but the transition—so difficult to effect for the abstract thinker and therefore so queer in his description of it—from *abstracting* to *intuiting*. The *mystical* feeling which drives the philosopher forward from abstract thinking to intuiting is *boredom*—the longing for a content.

(The man estranged from himself is also the thinker estranged from his *essence*—that is, from the natural and human essence. His thoughts are therefore fixed mental shapes or ghosts dwelling outside nature and man. Hegel has locked up all these fixed mental forms together in his *Logic*, laying hold of each of them first as negation—that is, as an *alienation* of *human* thought—and then as negation of the negation—that is, as a superseding of this alienation, as a *real* expression of human thought. But as even this still takes place within the confines of the estrangement, this negation of the negation is in part the restoring of these fixed forms in their estrangement; in part a stopping-short at the last act—the act of self-reference in alienation—as the true mode of being of these fixed mental forms;[9] and in part, to the extent that this abstraction apprehends itself and experiences an infinite weariness with itself, there makes its appearance in Hegel, in the form of the resolution to recognize *nature* as the essential being and to go over to intuition, the abandonment of abstract thought—the

9. This means that what Hegel does is to put in place of these fixed abstractions the act of abstraction which revolves in its own circle. In so doing, he has the merit, in the first place, of having indicated the source of all these inappropriate concepts which, as originally presented, belonged to disparate philosophies; of having brought them together; and of having created the entire compass of abstraction exhaustively set out as the object of criticism, instead of some specific abstraction. (Why Hegel separates thought from the *subject* we shall see later: at this stage it is already clear, however, that when man is not, his characteristic expression also cannot be human, and so neither could thought be grasped as an expression of man as a human and natural subject endowed with eyes, ears, etc., and living in society, in the world, and in nature.) [*Marx*]

abandonment of thought revolving solely within the orbit of thought, of thought devoid of eyes, of teeth, of ears, of everything.)

But *nature* too, taken abstractly, for itself—nature fixed in isolation from man—is *nothing* for man. It goes without saying that the abstract thinker who has committed himself to intuiting, intuits nature abstractly. Just as nature lay enclosed in the thinker in the form of the absolute idea, in the form of a thought-entity—in a shape which is his and yet is esoteric and mysterious even to him—so what he has let go forth from himself in truth is only this *abstract nature*, only nature as a *thought-entity*—but with the significance now of being the other-being of thought, of being real, intuited nature—of being nature distinguished from abstract thought. Or, to talk a human language, the abstract thinker learns in his intuition of nature that the entities which he thought to create from nothing, from pure abstraction—the entities he believed he was producing in the divine dialectic as pure products of the labour of thought forever weaving in itself and never looking outward—are nothing else but *abstractions* from *characteristics of nature*. To him, therefore, the whole of nature merely repeats the logical abstractions in a sensuous, external form. He *analyses* it and these abstractions over again. Thus, his intuition of nature is only the act of confirming his abstraction from the intuition of nature—is only the conscious repetition by him of the process of begetting his abstraction. Thus, for example, Time equals Negativity referred to itself (l.c., p. 238): to the superseded Becoming as Being there corresponds, in natural form, superseded Movement as Matter. Light is *Reflection-in-Itself*, in *natural* form. Body as *Moon* and *Comet* is the *natural* form of the *antithesis* which according to the *Logic* is on the one side the *Positive resting on itself* and on the other side the *Negative* resting on itself. The Earth is the *natural* form of the logical *Ground*, as the negative unity of the antithesis, etc.[1]

Nature as nature—that is to say, in so far as it is still sensuously distinguished from that secret sense hidden within it—nature isolated, distinguished from these abstractions, is *nothing*—a nothing *proving itself to be nothing*—is *devoid of sense*, or has only the sense of being an externality which has to be annulled.

> "In the finite-*teleological* position is to be found the correct premise that nature does not contain within itself the absolute purpose" (p. 225).

Its purpose is the confirmation of abstraction.

---

1. Time, Motion, Matter, Light, etc., are forms distinguished within Hegel's *Philosophy of Nature*. Becoming, etc., are of course categories of the *Logic*.

"Nature has shown itself to be the Idea in the *form* of *other-being*. Since the *Idea* is in this form the negative of itself or *external to itself*, nature is not just relatively external *vis-à-vis* this idea, but *externality* constitutes the form in which it exists as nature" (p. 227).

Externality here is not to be understood as the *self-externalizing world of sense* open to the light, open to the man endowed with senses. It is to be taken here in the sense of alienation—a mistake, a defect, which ought not to be. For what is true is still the Idea. Nature is only the *form of the Idea's other-being*. And since abstract thought is the *essence*, that which is external to it is by its essence something merely *external*. The abstract thinker recognizes at the same time that *sensuousness—externality* in contrast to thought weaving *within itself*—is the essence of nature. But he expresses his contrast in such a way as to make this *externality of nature*, its *contrast* to thought, its *defect*, so that inasmuch as it is distinguished from abstraction, nature is something defective. Something which is defective not merely for me or in my eyes but in itself—intrinsically—has something outside itself which it lacks. That is, its being is something other than it itself. Nature has therefore to supersede itself for the abstract thinker, for it is already posited by him as a potentially *superseded* being.

"*For us*, Mind has *nature* for its *premise*, being nature's *truth* and for that reason its *absolute prius*. In this truth nature *has vanished*, and mind has resulted as the Idea arrived at being-for-itself, the *object* of which, as well as the *subject*, is the *concept*. This identity is *absolute negativity*, for whereas in nature the concept has its perfect external objectivity, this its alienation has been superseded, and in this alienation the concept has become identical with itself. But it is this identity, therefore, only in being a return out of nature" (p. 392).

"As the *abstract* idea, *revelation* is unmediated transition to, the *coming-to-be* of, nature; as the revelation of the mind, which is free, it is the *establishing* of nature as the *mind's* world—an establishing which at the same time, being reflection, is a *presupposing* of the world as independently-existing nature. Revelation in conception is the creation of nature as the mind's being, in which the mind procures the *affirmation* and the *truth* of its freedom."[2] "*The absolute is mind*. This is the highest definition of the absolute."

2. Cf. Hegel's *Philosophy of Mind*, trans. Wallace, ¶ 381. But in rendering these passages from the *Encyclopaedia*, the present translator has not followed Wallace closely.

Alienation and Social Classes

KARL MARX

A meeting between Marx and Engels in Paris at the end of August, 1844, inaugurated their lifelong collaboration. Their first jointly written work, published in 1845, was *The Holy Family: A Critique of Critical Criticism*, a heavily satirical polemic against Bruno Bauer and the Young Hegelians. The following passage, probably written by Marx, shows the alienation doctrine of the 1844 manuscripts merging into the class struggle doctrine as we encounter it in *The German Ideology* and later Marxist writings. It is also of value as a revelation of Marx's special way of conceiving and explaining historical necessity.

The translation for this edition is by R. C. Tucker.

---

* * * The proletariat and wealth are opposites. As such they form a whole. They are both products of the world of private property. The whole question is what position each of these two elements occupies within the opposition. It does not suffice to proclaim them two sides of one whole.

Private property as private property, as wealth, is compelled to preserve *its own existence* and thereby the existence of its opposite, the proletariat. This is the *positive* side of the antagonism, private property satisfied with itself.

The proletariat, on the other hand, is compelled to abolish itself and thereby its conditioning opposite—private property—which makes it a proletariat. This is the *negative* side of the antagonism, its disturbance within itself, private property abolished and in the process of abolishing itself.

The possessing class and the proletarian class represent one and the same human self-alienation. But the former feels satisfied and affirmed in this self-alienation, experiences the alienation as a sign *of its own power*, and possesses in it the *appearance* of a human existence. The latter, however, feels destroyed in this alienation, seeing in it its own impotence and the reality of an inhuman existence. To use Hegel's expression, this class is, within depravity, an *indignation* against this depravity, an indignation necessarily aroused in this class by the contradiction between its human *nature* and its life-situation, which is a blatant, outright and all-embracing denial of that very nature.

Within the antagonism as a whole, therefore, private property represents the *conservative* side and the proletariat the *destructive* side. From the former comes action aimed at preserving the antagonism; from the latter, action aimed at its destruction.

In its economic movement, it is true, private property presses towards its own dissolution, but it does this only by means of a developmental course that is unconscious and takes place independently of it and against its will, a course determined by the nature of the thing itself. It does this only by giving rise to the proletariat *as* proletariat—this poverty conscious of its own spiritual and physical poverty, this dehumanization which is conscious of itself as a dehumanization and hence abolishes itself. The proletariat executes the sentence that proletariat-producing private property passes upon itself, just as it executes the sentence that wage labour passes upon itself by producing others' wealth and its own poverty. When the proletariat wins victory, it by no means becomes the absolute side of society, for it wins victory only by abolishing itself and its opposite. Both the proletariat itself and its conditioning opposite—private property—disappear with the victory of the proletariat.

If socialist writers attribute this world-historical role to the proletariat, this is by no means, as critical criticism assures us, because they regard the proletarians as *gods*. On the contrary. Since the fully formed proletariat represents, practically speaking, the completed abstraction from everything human, even from the *appearance* of being human; since all the living conditions of contemporary society have reached the acme of inhumanity in the living conditions of the proletariat; since in the proletariat man has lost himself, although at the same time he has both acquired a theoretical consciousness of this loss and has been directly forced into indignation against this inhumanity by virtue of an inexorable, utterly unembellishable, absolutely imperious *need*, that practical expression of *necessity*—because of all this the proletariat itself can and must liberate itself. But it cannot liberate itself without destroying its own living conditions. It cannot do so without destroying *all* the inhuman living conditions of contemporary society which are concentrated in its own situation. Not in vain does it go through the harsh but hardening school of *labour*. It is not a matter of what this or that proletarian or even the proletariat as a whole *pictures* at present as its goal. It is a matter of *what the proletariat is in actuality* and what, in accordance with this *being*, it will historically be compelled to do. Its goal and its historical action are prefigured in the most clear and ineluctable way in its own life-situation as well as in the whole organization of contemporary bourgeois society. There is no need to harp on the fact that a large part of the English and French proletariat is already *conscious* of its historic task and is continually working to bring this consciousness to full clarity.

Theses on Feuerbach

KARL MARX

Marx wrote the "Theses on Feuerbach" in the spring of 1845 as he and Engels were starting their collaborative work *The German Ideology*. More than forty years later, Engels found them in one of the notebooks that had come into his possession after his friend died. He published them as an appendix to his essay of 1888 on *Ludwig Feuerbach and the End of Classical German Philosophy*, and described them in the foreword to this essay as "the brilliant germ of the new world outlook." They have fascinated Marx scholars ever since, and an extensive literature of exegesis of the "Theses" has accumulated. The eleventh thesis, in which Marx proclaims it the task of philosophy not simply to interpret but to change the world, is one of his most frequently quoted statements.

Before resorting to commentaries, however, the reader should apply himself to Marx's own amplification of the "Theses" in Part I of *The German Ideology*—concerning which see below, pp. 111–164.

The "Theses" here appear as edited by Engels and published in the appendix to his *Ludwig Feuerbach* in 1888.

I

The chief defect of all hitherto existing materialism—that of Feuerbach included—is that the thing, reality, sensuousness, is conceived only in the form of the object or of *contemplation*, but not as *human sensuous activity*, *practice*, not subjectively. Hence it happened that the *active* side, in contradistinction to materialism, was developed by idealism—but only abstractly, since, of course, idealism does not know real, sensuous activity as such. Feuerbach wants sensuous objects, really distinct from the thought objects, but he does not conceive human activity itself as *objective* activity. Hence, in *Das Wesen des Christentums*, he regards the theoretical attitude as the only genuinely human attitude, while practice is conceived and fixed only in its dirty-judaical manifestation. Hence he does not grasp the significance of "revolutionary," of practical-critical, activity.

II

The question whether objective truth can be attributed to human thinking is not a question of theory but is a *practical* question. Man must prove the truth, that is, the reality and power, the this-sidedness of his thinking in practice. The dispute over the reality or non-reality of thinking which is isolated from practice is a purely *scholastic* question.

III

The materialist doctrine that men are products of circumstances and upbringing, and that, therefore, changed men are products of other circumstances and changed upbringing, forgets that it is men who change circumstances and that it is essential to educate the educator himself. Hence, this doctrine necessarily arrives at dividing society into two parts, one of which is superior to society (in Robert Owen, for example).

The coincidence of the changing of circumstances and of human activity can be conceived and rationally understood only as revolutionising practice.

IV

Feuerbach starts out from the fact of religious self-alienation, of the duplication of the world into a religious, imaginary world and a real one. His work consists in resolving the religious world into its secular basis. He overlooks the fact that after completing this work, the chief thing still remains to be done. For the fact that the secular basis detaches itself from itself and establishes itself in the clouds as an independent realm can only be explained by the cleavage and self-contradictions within this secular basis. The latter must itself, therefore, first be understood in its contradiction and then, by the removal of the contradiction, revolutionised in practice. Thus, for instance, after the earthly family is discovered to be the secret of the holy family, the former must then itself be criticised in theory and revolutionised in practice.

V

Feuerbach, not satisfied with *abstract thinking*, appeals to *sensuous contemplation*; but he does not conceive sensuousness as practical, human-sensuous activity.

VI

Feuerbach resolves the religious essence into the human essence. But the human essence is no abstraction inherent in each single individual. In its reality it is the ensemble of the social relations.

Feuerbach, who does not enter upon a criticism of this real essence, is consequently compelled:

(1) To abstract from the historical process and to fix the religious sentiment as something by itself and to presuppose an abstract—*isolated*—human individual.

(2) The human essence, therefore, can with him be comprehended only as "genus," as an internal, dumb generality which merely *naturally* unites the many individuals.

VII

Feuerbach, consequently, does not see that the "religious sentiment" is itself a *social product*, and that the abstract individual whom he analyses belongs in reality to a particular form of society.

VIII

Social life is essentially *practical*. All mysteries which mislead theory into mysticism find their rational solution in human practice and in the comprehension of this practice.

IX

The highest point attained by *contemplative* materialism, that is, materialism which does not comprehend sensuousness as practical activity, is the contemplation of single individuals in "civil society."

X

The standpoint of the old materialism is "*civil*" society; the standpoint of the new is *human* society, or socialised humanity.

XI

The philosophers have only *interpreted* the world, in various ways; the point, however, is to *change* it.

The German Ideology: Part I

KARL MARX

Marx and Engels wrote *The German Ideology* in 1845–46 in order (as Marx later recalled) "to settle accounts with our erstwhile philosophical conscience." He further explained: "The manuscript, two large octavo volumes, had long reached its place of publication in Westphalia when we received the news that altered circumstances did not allow of its being printed. We abandoned the manuscript to the gnawing criticism of the mice, all the more willingly as we had achieved our main purpose— self-clarification."* The work was first published in 1932 by the Marx-Engels Institute in Moscow.

The original difficulty of publication was very probably connected with the fact that most of this very bulky work consisted of satirically written, rather arid polemics against Bruno Bauer, Max Stirner, Karl Grün, and others. But Part I (here presented in full) is a different matter. Although polemical at various points, it is basically a work of exposition. It gives every appearance of being the work for which the "Theses on Feuerbach" served as an outline; hence we may infer that it was written by Marx. It is, in essence, a restatement, minus much of the German philosophical terminology, of the theory of history adumbrated in the manuscripts of 1844. Marx now calls it the "materialist conception of history." It is particularly valuable and important to the student of Marxist thought because Marx never again set down a comprehensive statement of his theory of history at such length and in such detail. This point is not contradicted by Engels' remark in the 1888 foreword that the exposition of the materialist conception of history in *The German Ideology* "proves only how incomplete our knowledge of economic history still was at that time."

The German Ideology has recently appeared in a re-edited version containing several previously unknown pages of the manuscript that were discovered in the International Institute of Social History in Amsterdam, where the original manuscript is kept. Part I appears here in this new and fuller version as translated from the German and edited by S. Ryazanskaya, and published in English by the Foreign Languages Publishing House, Moscow, in 1964. In preparing this new translation, the translator made use of an earlier English translation made by W. Lough and edited by R. Pascal.

---

* Preface to *A Contribution to the Critique of Political Economy*. See above, pp. 5–6.

Feuerbach: Opposition of the Materialistic and Idealistic Outlook

As we hear from German ideologists, Germany has in the last few years gone through an unparalleled revolution. The decomposition of the Hegelian philosophy, which began with Strauss, has developed into a universal ferment into which all the "powers of the past" are swept. In the general chaos mighty empires have arisen only to meet with immediate doom, heroes have emerged momentarily only to be hurled back into obscurity by bolder and stronger rivals. It was a revolution beside which the French Revolution was child's play, a world struggle beside which the struggles of the Diadochi appear insignificant. Principles ousted one another, heroes of the mind overthrew each other with unheard-of rapidity, and in the three years 1842–45 more of the past was swept away in Germany than at other times in three centuries.

All this is supposed to have taken place in the realm of pure thought.

Certainly it is an interesting event we are dealing with: the putrescence of the absolute spirit. When the last spark of its life had failed, the various components of this *caput mortuum*[1] began to decompose, entered into new combinations and formed new substances. The industrialists of philosophy, who till then had lived on the exploitation of the absolute spirit, now seized upon the new combinations. Each with all possible zeal set about retailing his apportioned share. This naturally gave rise to competition, which, to start with, was carried on in moderately staid bourgeois fashion. Later when the German market was glutted, and the commodity in spite of all efforts found no response in the world market, the business was spoiled in the usual German manner by fabricated and fictitious production, deterioration in quality, adulteration of the raw materials, falsification of labels, fictitious purchases, bill-jobbing and a credit system devoid of any real basis. The competition turned into a bitter struggle, which is now being extolled and interpreted to us as a revolution of world significance, the begetter of the most prodigious results and achievements.

If we wish to rate at its true value this philosophic charlatanry, which awakens even in the breast of the honest German citizen a glow of national pride, if we wish to bring out clearly the pettiness, the parochial narrowness of this whole Young-Hegelian movement

1. Literally: "dead head"; a term used in chemistry for the residuum left after distillation; here: "remainder," "residue."

and in particular the tragicomic contrast between the illusions of these heroes about their achievements and the actual achievements themselves, we must look at the whole spectacle from a standpoint beyond the frontiers of Germany.

A. IDEOLOGY IN GENERAL, GERMAN IDEOLOGY IN PARTICULAR

German criticism has, right up to its latest efforts, never quitted the realm of philosophy. Far from examining its general philosophic premises, the whole body of its inquiries has actually sprung from the soil of a definite philosophical system, that of Hegel. Not only in their answers but in their very questions there was a mystification. This dependence on Hegel is the reason why not one of these modern critics has even attempted a comprehensive criticism of the Hegelian system, however much each professes to have advanced beyond Hegel. Their polemics against Hegel and against one another are confined to this—each extracts one side of the Hegelian system and turns this against the whole system as well as against the sides extracted by the others. To begin with they extracted pure unfalsified Hegelian categories such as "substance" and "self-consciousness," later they desecrated these categories with more secular names such as "species," "the Unique," "Man," etc.

The entire body of German philosophical criticism from Strauss to Stirner is confined to criticism of *religious* conceptions. The critics started from real religion and actual theology. What religious consciousness and a religious conception really meant was determined variously as they went along. Their advance consisted in subsuming the allegedly dominant metaphysical, political, juridical, moral and other conceptions under the class of religious or theological conceptions; and similarly in pronouncing political, juridical, moral consciousness as religious or theological, and the political, juridical, moral man—"*man*" in the last resort—as religious. The dominance of religion was taken for granted. Gradually every dominant relationship was pronounced a religious relationship and transformed into a cult, a cult of law, a cult of the State, etc. On all sides it was only a question of dogmas and belief in dogmas. The world was sanctified to an ever-increasing extent till at last our venerable Saint Max was able to canonise it *en bloc* and thus dispose of it once for all.

The Old Hegelians had *comprehended* everything as soon as it was reduced to an Hegelian logical category. The Young Hegelians *criticised* everything by attributing to it religious conceptions or by pronouncing it a theological matter. The Young Hegelians are in agreement with the Old Hegelians in their belief in the rule of religion, of concepts, of a universal principle in the existing world. Only, the one party attacks this dominion as usurpation, while the other extols it as legitimate.

Since the Young Hegelians consider conceptions, thoughts, ideas, in fact all the products of consciousness, to which they attribute an independent existence, as the real chains of men (just as the Old Hegelians declared them the true bonds of human society) it is evident that the Young Hegelians have to fight only against these illusions of the consciousness. Since, according to their fantasy, the relationships of men, all their doings, their chains and their limitations are products of their consciousness, the Young Hegelians logically put to men the moral postulate of exchanging their present consciousness for human, critical or egoistic consciousness, and thus of removing their limitations. This demand to change consciousness amounts to a demand to interpret reality in another way, i.e., to recognise it by means of another interpretation. The Young-Hegelian ideologists, in spite of their allegedly "world-shattering" statements, are the staunchest conservatives. The most recent of them have found the correct expression for their activity when they declare they are only fighting against *"phrases."* They forget, however, that to these phrases they themselves are only opposing other phrases, and that they are in no way combating the real existing world when they are merely combating the phrases of this world. The only results which this philosophic criticism could achieve were a few (and at that thoroughly one-sided) elucidations of Christianity from the point of view of religious history; all the rest of their assertions are only further embellishments of their claim to have furnished, in these unimportant elucidations, discoveries of universal importance.

It has not occurred to any one of these philosophers to inquire into the connection of German philosophy with German reality, the relation of their criticism to their own material surroundings.

The premises from which we begin are not arbitrary ones, not dogmas, but real premises from which abstraction can only be made in the imagination. They are the real individuals, their activity and the material conditions under which they live, both those which they find already existing and those produced by their activity. These premises can thus be verified in a purely empirical way.

The first premise of all human history is, of course, the existence of living human individuals. Thus the first fact to be established is the physical organisation of these individuals and their consequent relation to the rest of nature. Of course, we cannot here go either into the actual physical nature of man, or into the natural conditions in which man finds himself—geological, orohydrographical, climatic and so on. The writing of history must always set out from these natural bases and their modification in the course of history through the action of men.

Men can be distinguished from animals by consciousness, by religion or anything else you like. They themselves begin to distinguish themselves from animals as soon as they begin to *produce* their means of subsistence, a step which is conditioned by their physical organisation. By producing their means of subsistence men are indirectly producing their actual material life.

The way in which men produce their means of subsistence depends first of all on the nature of the actual means of subsistence they find in existence and have to reproduce. This mode of production must not be considered simply as being the reproduction of the physical existence of the individuals. Rather it is a definite form of activity of these individuals, a definite form of expressing their life, a definite *mode of life* on their part. As individuals express their life, so they are. What they are, therefore, coincides with their production, both with *what* they produce and with *how* they produce. The nature of individuals thus depends on the material conditions determining their production.

This production only makes its appearance with the *increase of population*. In its turn this presupposes the *intercourse* [*Verkehr*] of individuals with one another. The form of this intercourse is again determined by production.

The relations of different nations among themselves depend upon the extent to which each has developed its productive forces, the division of labour and internal intercourse. This statement is generally recognised. But not only the relation of one nation to others, but also the whole internal structure of the nation itself depends on the stage of development reached by its production and its internal and external intercourse. How far the productive forces of a nation are developed is shown most manifestly by the degree to which the division of labour has been carried. Each new productive force, insofar as it is not merely a quantitative extension of productive forces already known (for instance the bringing into cultivation of fresh land), causes a further development of the division of labour.

The division of labour inside a nation leads at first to the separation of industrial and commercial from agricultural labour, and hence to the separation of *town* and *country* and to the conflict of their interests. Its further development leads to the separation of commercial from industrial labour. At the same time through the division of labour inside these various branches there develop various divisions among the individuals co-operating in definite kinds of labour. The relative position of these individual groups is determined by the methods employed in agriculture, industry and commerce (patriarchalism, slavery, estates, classes). These same conditions are to be seen (given a more developed intercourse) in the relations of different nations to one another.

The various stages of development in the division of labour are just so many different forms of ownership, i.e., the existing stage in the division of labour determines also the relations of individuals to one another with reference to the material, instrument, and product of labour.

The first form of ownership is tribal [*Stammeigentum*] ownership. It corresponds to the undeveloped stage of production, at which a people lives by hunting and fishing, by the rearing of beasts or, in the highest stage, agriculture. In the latter case it presupposes a great mass of uncultivated stretches of land. The division of labour is at this stage still very elementary and is confined to a further extension of the natural division of labour existing in the family. The social structure is, therefore, limited to an extension of the family; patriarchal family chieftains, below them the members of the tribe, finally slaves. The slavery latent in the family only develops gradually with the increase of population, the growth of wants, and with the extension of external relations, both of war and of barter.

The second form is the ancient communal and State ownership which proceeds especially from the union of several tribes into a *city* by agreement or by conquest, and which is still accompanied by slavery. Beside communal ownership we already find movable, and later also immovable, private property developing, but as an abnormal form subordinate to communal ownership. The citizens hold power over their labouring slaves only in their community, and on this account alone, therefore, they are bound to the form of communal ownership. It is the communal private property which compels the active citizens to remain in this spontaneously derived form of association over against their slaves. For this reason the whole structure of society based on this communal ownership, and with it the power of the people, decays in the same measure as, in particular, immovable private property evolves. The division of labour is already more developed. We already find the antagonism of town and country; later the antagonism between those states which represent town interests and those which represent country interests, and inside the towns themselves the antagonism between industry and maritime commerce. The class relation between citizens and slaves is now completely developed.

This whole interpretation of history appears to be contradicted by the fact of conquest. Up till now violence, war, pillage, murder and robbery, etc., have been accepted as the driving force of history. Here we must limit ourselves to the chief points and take, therefore, only the most striking example—the destruction of an old civilisation by a barbarous people and the resulting formation of an entirely new organisation of society. (Rome and the barbarians; feudalism and Gaul; the Byzantine Empire and the Turks.) With the conquering barbarian people war itself is still, as indicated above, a regular form of intercourse, which is the more eagerly exploited as the increase in population together with the traditional and, for it, the only possible, crude mode of production gives rise to the need for new means of production. In Italy, on the other hand, the concentration of landed property (caused not only by buying-up and indebtedness but also by inheritance, since loose living being rife and marriage rare, the old families gradually died out and their possessions fell into the hands of a few)and its conversion into grazing-land (caused not only by the usual economic forces still operative today but by the importation of plundered and tribute corn and the resultant lack of demand for Italian corn) brought about the almost total disappearance of the free population. The very slaves died out again and again, and had constantly to be replaced by new ones. Slavery remained the basis of the whole productive system. The plebeians, midway between freemen and slaves, never succeeded in becoming more than a proletarian rabble. Rome indeed never became more than a city; its connection with the provinces was almost exclusively political and could, therefore, easily be broken again by political events.

With the development of private property, we find here for the first time the same conditions which we shall find again, only on a more extensive scale, with modern private property. On the one hand, the concentration of private property, which began very early in Rome (as the Licinian agrarian law proves) and proceeded very rapidly from the time of the civil wars and especially under the Emperors; on the other hand, coupled with this, the transformation of the plebeian small peasantry into a proletariat, which, however, owing to its intermediate position between propertied citizens and slaves, never achieved an independent development.

The third form of ownership is feudal or estate property. If antiquity started out from the town and its little territory, the Middle Ages started out from the *country*. This different starting-point was determined by the sparseness of the population at that time, which was scattered over a large area and which received no large increase from the conquerors. In contrast to Greece and Rome, feudal development at the outset, therefore, extends over a much wider territory, prepared by the Roman conquests and the spread of agriculture at first associated with them. The last centuries of the declining Roman Empire and its conquest by the barbarians destroyed a number of productive forces; agriculture had declined, industry had decayed for want of a market, trade had died out or been violently suspended, the rural and urban population had decreased. From these conditions and the mode of organisation of the conquest determined by them, feudal property developed under the influence of the Germanic military constitution. Like tribal and communal ownership, it is based again on a community; but the directly producing class standing over against it is not, as in the case of the ancient community, the slaves, but the enserfed small peasantry. As soon as feudalism is fully developed, there also arises antagonism to the towns. The hierarchical structure of landownership, and the armed bodies of retainers associated with it, gave the nobility power over the serfs. This feudal organisation was, just as much as the ancient communal ownership, an association against a subjected producing class; but the form of association and the relation to the direct producers were different because of the different conditions of production.

This feudal system of landownership had its counterpart in the *towns* in the shape of corporative property, the feudal organisation of trades. Here property consisted chiefly in the labour of each individual person. The necessity for association against the organised robber nobility, the need for communal covered markets in an age when the industrialist was at the same time a merchant, the growing competition of the escaped serfs swarming into the rising towns, the feudal structure of the whole country: these combined to bring about the *guilds*. The gradually accumulated small capital of individual craftsmen and their stable numbers, as against the growing population, evolved the relation of journeyman and apprentice, which brought into being in the towns a hierarchy similar to that in the country.

Thus the chief form of property during the feudal epoch consisted on the one hand of landed property with serf labour chained to it, and on the other of the labour of the individual with small capital commanding the labour of journeymen. The organisation of both was determined by the restricted conditions of production—the small-scale and primitive cultivation of the land, and the craft type of industry. There was little division of labour in the heyday of feudalism. Each country bore in itself the antithesis of town and country; the division into estates was certainly strongly marked; but apart from the differentiation of princes, nobility, clergy and peasants in the country, and masters, journeymen, apprentices and soon also the rabble of casual labourers in the towns, no division of importance took place. In agriculture it was rendered difficult by the strip-system, beside which the cottage industry of the peasants themselves emerged. In industry there was no division of labour at all in the individual trades themselves, and very little between them. The separation of industry and commerce was found already in existence in older towns; in the newer it only developed later, when the towns entered into mutual relations.

The grouping of larger territories into feudal kingdoms was a necessity for the landed nobility as for the towns. The organisation of the ruling class, the nobility, had, therefore, everywhere a monarch at its head.

The fact is, therefore, that definite individuals who are productively active in a definite way enter into these definite social and political relations. Empirical observation must in each separate instance bring out empirically, and without any mystification and speculation, the connection of the social and political structure with production. The social structure and the State are continually evolving out of the life process of definite individuals, but of individuals, not as they may appear in their own or other people's imagination, but as they *really* are; i.e., as they operate, produce materially, and hence as they work under definite material limits, presuppositions and conditions independent of their will.

The production of ideas, of conceptions, of consciousness, is at first directly interwoven with the material activity and the material intercourse of men, the language of real life. Conceiving, thinking, the mental intercourse of men, appear at this stage as the direct efflux of their material behaviour. The same applies to mental production as expressed in the language of politics, laws, morality, religion, metaphysics, etc., of a people. Men are the producers of their conceptions, ideas, etc.—real, active men, as they are conditioned by a definite development of their productive forces and of the intercourse corresponding to these, up to its furthest forms. Consciousness can never be anything else than conscious existence, and the existence of men is their actual life-process. If in all ideology men and their circumstances appear upside-down as in a *camera obscura*, this phenomenon arises just as much from their historical life-process as the inversion of objects on the retina does from their physical life-process.

In direct contrast to German philosophy which descends from heaven to earth, here we ascend from earth to heaven. That is to say, we do not set out from what men say, imagine, conceive, nor from men as narrated, thought of, imagined, conceived, in order to arrive at men in the flesh. We set out from real, active men, and on the basis of their real life-process we demonstrate the development of the ideological reflexes and echoes of this life-process. The phantoms formed in the human brain are also, necessarily, sublimates of their material life-process, which is empirically verifiable and bound to material premises. Morality, religion, metaphysics, all the rest of ideology and their corresponding forms of consciousness, thus no longer retain the semblance of independence. They have no history, no development; but men, developing their material production and their material intercourse, alter, along with this their real existence, their thinking and the products of their thinking. Life is not determined by consciousness, but consciousness by life. In the first method of approach the starting-point is consciousness taken as the living individual; in the second method, which conforms to real life, it is the real living individuals themselves, and consciousness is considered solely as *their* consciousness.

This method of approach is not devoid of premises. It starts out from the real premises and does not abandon them for a moment. Its premises are men, not in any fantastic isolation and rigidity, but in their actual, empirically perceptible process of development under definite conditions. As soon as this active life-process is described, history ceases to be a collection of dead facts as it is with the empiricists (themselves still abstract), or an imagined activity of imagined subjects, as with the idealists.

Where speculation ends—in real life—there real, positive science begins: the representation of the practical activity, of the practical process of development of men. Empty talk about consciousness ceases, and real knowledge has to take its place. When reality is depicted, philosophy as an independent branch of knowledge loses its medium of existence. At the best its place can only be taken by a summing-up of the most general results, abstractions which arise from the observation of the historical development of men. Viewed apart from real history, these abstractions have in themselves no value whatsoever. They can only serve to facilitate the arrangement of historical material, to indicate the sequence of its separate strata. But they by no means afford a recipe or schema, as does philosophy, for neatly trimming the epochs of history. On the contrary, our difficulties begin only when we set about the observation and the arrangement—the real depiction—of our historical material, whether of a past epoch or of the present. The removal of these difficulties is governed by premises which it is quite impossible to state here, but which only the study of the actual life-process and the activity of the individuals of each epoch will make evident. We shall select here some of these abstractions, which we use in contradistinction to the ideologists, and shall illustrate them by historical examples.

1. History

Since we are dealing with the Germans, who are devoid of premises, we must begin by stating the first premise of all human existence and, therefore, of all history, the premise, namely, that men must be in a position to live in order to be able to "make history."[2] But life involves before everything else eating and drinking, a habitation, clothing and many other things. The first historical act is thus the production of the means to satisfy these needs, the production of material life itself. And indeed this is an historical act, a fundamental condition of all history, which today, as thousands of years ago, must daily and hourly be fulfilled merely in order to sustain human life. Even when the sensuous world is reduced to a minimum, to a stick as with Saint Bruno, it presupposes the action of producing the stick. Therefore in any interpretation of history one has first of all to observe this fundamental fact in all its significance and all its implications and to accord it its due importance. It is well known that the Germans have never done this, and they have never, therefore, had an *earthly* basis for history and consequently never a historian. The French and the English, even if they have conceived the relation of this fact with so-called history only in an extremely one-sided fashion, particularly as long as they remained in the toils of political ideology, have nevertheless made the first attempts to give the writing of history a materialistic basis by being the first to write histories of civil society, of commerce and industry.

The second point is that the satisfaction of the first need (the action of satisfying, and the instrument of satisfaction which has been acquired) leads to new needs; and this production of new needs is the first historical act. Here we recognise immediately the spiritual ancestry of the great historical wisdom of the Germans who, when they run out of positive material and when they can serve up neither theological nor political nor literary rubbish, assert that this is not history at all, but the "prehistoric era." They do not, however, enlighten us as to how we proceed from this nonsensical "prehistory" to history proper; although, on the other hand, in their historical speculation they seize upon this "prehistory" with especial eagerness because they imagine themselves safe there from interference on the part of "crude facts," and, at the same time, because there they can give full rein to their speculative impulse and set up and knock down hypotheses by the thousand.

The third circumstance which, from the very outset, enters into historical development, is that men, who daily remake their own life, begin to make other men, to propagate their kind: the relation between man and woman, parents and children, the *family*. The family, which to begin with is the only social relationship, becomes later, when increased needs create new social relations and the increased population new needs, a subordinate one (except in Germany), and must then be treated and analysed according to the

2. Marginal note by Marx: "*Hegel.* Geological, hydrographical, etc., conditions. Human bodies. Needs, labour."

existing empirical data, not according to "the concept of the family," as is the custom in Germany.³ These three aspects of social activity are not of course to be taken as three different stages, but just as three aspects or, to make it clear to the Germans, three "moments," which have existed simultaneously since the dawn of history and the first men, and which still assert themselves in history today.

The production of life, both of one's own in labour and of fresh life in procreation, now appears as a double relationship: on the one hand as a natural, on the other as a social relationship. By social we understand the co-operation of several individuals, no matter under what conditions, in what manner and to what end. It follows from this that a certain mode of production, or industrial stage, is always combined with a certain mode of co-operation, or social stage, and this mode of co-operation is itself a "productive force." Further, that the multitude of productive forces accessible to men determines the nature of society, hence, that the "history of humanity" must always be studied and treated in relation to the history of industry and exchange. But it is also clear how in Germany it is impossible to write this sort of history, because the Germans lack not only the necessary power of comprehension and the material but also the "evidence of their senses," for across the Rhine you cannot have any experience of these things since history has stopped happening. Thus it is quite obvious from the start that there exists a materialistic connection of men with one another, which is determined by their needs and their mode of production, and which is as old as men themselves. This connection is ever taking on new forms, and thus presents a "history" independently of the existence of any political or religious nonsense which would especially hold men together.

Only now, after having considered four moments, four aspects of

3. The building of houses. With savages each family has as a matter of course its own cave or hut like the separate family tent of the nomads. This separate domestic economy is made only the more necessary by the further development of private property. With the agricultural peoples a communal domestic economy is just as impossible as a communal cultivation of the soil. A great advance was the building of towns. In all previous periods, however, the abolition of individual economy, which is inseparable from the abolition of private property, was impossible for the simple reason that the material conditions governing it were not present. The setting-up of a communal domestic economy presupposes the development of machinery, of the use of natural forces and of many other productive forces—e.g., of water-supplies, of gas-lighting, steam-heating, etc., the removal [of the antagonism] of town and country. Without these conditions a communal economy would not in itself form a new productive force; lacking any material basis and resting on a purely theoretical foundation, it would be a mere freak and would end in nothing more than a monastic economy.—What was possible can be seen in the towns brought about by condensation and the erection of communal buildings for various definite purposes (prisons, barracks, etc.). That the abolition of individual economy is inseparable from the abolition of the family is self-evident. [*Marx*]

the primary historical relationships, do we find that man also possesses "consciousness";[4] but, even so, not inherent, not "pure" consciousness. From the start the "spirit" is afflicted with the curse of being "burdened" with matter, which here makes its appearance in the form of agitated layers of air, sounds, in short, of language. Language is as old as consciousness, language *is* practical consciousness that exists also for other men, and for that reason alone it really exists for me personally as well; language, like consciousness, only arises from the need, the necessity, of intercourse with other men. Where there exists a relationship, it exists for me: the animal does not enter into *"relations"* with anything, it does not enter into any relation at all. For the animal, its relation to others does not exist as a relation. Consciousness is, therefore, from the very beginning a social product, and remains so as long as men exist at all. Consciousness is at first, of course, merely consciousness concerning the *immediate* sensuous environment and consciousness of the limited connection with other persons and things outside the individual who is growing self-conscious. At the same time it is consciousness of nature, which first appears to men as a completely alien, all-powerful and unassailable force, with which men's relations are purely animal and by which they are overawed like beasts; it is thus a purely animal consciousness of nature (natural religion).

We see here immediately: this natural religion or this particular relation of men to nature is determined by the form of society and vice versa. Here, as everywhere, the identity of nature and man appears in such a way that the restricted relation of men to nature determines their restricted relation to one another, and their restricted relation to one another determines men's restricted relation to nature, just because nature is as yet hardly modified historically; and, on the other hand, man's consciousness of the necessity of associating with the individuals around him is the beginning of the consciousness that he is living in society at all. This beginning is as animal as social life itself at this stage. It is mere herd-consciousness, and at this point man is only distinguished from sheep by the fact that with him consciousness takes the place of instinct or that his instinct is a conscious one. This sheep-like or tribal consciousness receives its further development and extension through increased productivity, the increase of needs, and, what is fundamental to both of these, the increase of population. With these there develops the division of labour, which was originally nothing but the division of labour in the sexual act, then that division of labour which develops spontaneously or "naturally" by

4. Marginal note by Marx: "Men have history because they must *produce* their life, and because they must produce it moreover in a *certain* way: this is determined by their physical organisation; their consciousness is determined in just the same way."

virtue of natural predisposition (e.g., physical strength), needs, accidents, etc., etc. Division of labour only becomes truly such from the moment when a division of material and mental labour appears.[5] From this moment onwards consciousness *can* really flatter itself that it is something other than consciousness of existing practice, that it *really* represents something without representing something real; from now on consciousness is in a position to emancipate itself from the world and to proceed to the formation of "pure" theory, theology, philosophy, ethics, etc. But even if this theory, theology, philosophy, ethics, etc., comes into contradiction with the existing relations, this can only occur because existing social relations have come into contradiction with existing forces of production; this, moreover, can also occur in a particular national sphere of relations through the appearance of the contradiction, not within the national orbit, but between this national consciousness and the practice of other nations,[6] i.e., between the national and the general consciousness of a nation (as we see it now in Germany).

Moreover, it is quite immaterial what consciousness starts to do on its own: out of all such muck we get only the one inference that these three moments, the forces of production, the state of society, and consciousness, can and must come into contradiction with one another, because the *division of labour* implies the possibility, nay the fact that intellectual and material activity—enjoyment and labour, production and consumption—devolve on different individuals, and that the only possibility of their not coming into contradiction lies in the negation in its turn of the division of labour. It is self-evident, moreover, that "spectres," "bonds," "the higher being," "concept," "scruple," are merely the idealistic, spiritual expression, the conception apparently of the isolated individual, the image of very empirical fetters and limitations, within which the mode of production of life and the form of intercourse coupled with it move.

With the division of labour, in which all these contradictions are implicit, and which in its turn is based on the natural division of labour in the family and the separation of society into individual families opposed to one another, is given simultaneously the *distribution*, and indeed the *unequal* distribution, both quantitative and qualitative, of labour and its products, hence property: the nucleus, the first form, of which lies in the family, where wife and children are the slaves of the husband. This latent slavery in the family, though still very crude, is the first property, but even at this early stage it corresponds perfectly to the definition of modern econo-

5. Marginal note by Marx: "The first form of ideologists, *priests*, is concurrent."

6. Marginal note by Marx: "*Religion*. The Germans and *ideology* as such."

mists who call it the power of disposing of the labour-power of others. Division of labour and private property are, moreover, identical expressions: in the one the same thing is affirmed with reference to activity as is affirmed in the other with reference to the product of the activity.

Further, the division of labour implies the contradiction between the interest of the separate individual or the individual family and the communal interest of all individuals who have intercourse with one another. And indeed, this communal interest does not exist merely in the imagination, as the "general interest," but first of all in reality, as the mutual interdependence of the individuals among whom the labour is divided. And finally, the division of labour offers us the first example of how, as long as man remains in natural society, that is, as long as a cleavage exists between the particular and the common interest, as long, therefore, as activity is not voluntarily, but naturally, divided, man's own deed becomes an alien power opposed to him, which enslaves him instead of being controlled by him. For as soon as the distribution of labour comes into being, each man has a particular, exclusive sphere of activity, which is forced upon him and from which he cannot escape. He is a hunter, a fisherman, a shepherd, or a critical critic, and must remain so if he does not want to lose his means of livelihood; while in communist society, where nobody has one exclusive sphere of activity but each can become accomplished in any branch he wishes, society regulates the general production and thus makes it possible for me to do one thing today and another tomorrow, to hunt in the morning, fish in the afternoon, rear cattle in the evening, criticise after dinner, just as I have a mind, without ever becoming hunter, fisherman, shepherd or critic. This fixation of social activity, this consolidation of what we ourselves produce into an objective power above us, growing out of our control, thwarting our expectations, bringing to naught our calculations, is one of the chief factors in historical development up till now.

And out of this very contradiction between the interest of the individual and that of the community the latter takes an independent form as the *State*, divorced from the real interests of individual and community, and at the same time as an illusory communal life, always based, however, on the real ties existing in every family and tribal conglomeration—such as flesh and blood, language, division of labour on a larger scale, and other interests—and especially, as we shall enlarge upon later, on the classes, already determined by the division of labour, which in every such mass of men separate out, and of which one dominates all the others. It follows from this that all struggles within the State, the struggle between democracy, aristocracy, and monarchy, the struggle for the franchise, etc., etc., are merely the illusory forms in which the real struggles of the different classes are fought out among one another (of this the German theoreticians have not the faintest inkling, although they have received a sufficient introduction to the subject in the *Deutsch-Französische Jahrbücher* and *Die heilige Familie*). Further, it follows that every class which is struggling for mastery, even when its domination, as is the case with the proletariat, postulates the abolition of the old form of society in its entirety and of domination itself, must first conquer for itself political power in order to represent its interest in turn as the general interest, which in the first moment it is forced to do. Just because individuals seek *only* their particular interest, which for them does not coincide with their communal interest (in fact the general is the illusory form of communal life), the latter will be imposed on them as an interest "alien" to them, and "independent" of them, as in its turn a particular, peculiar "general" interest; or they themselves must remain within this discord, as in democracy. On the other hand, too, the *practical* struggle of these particular interests, which constantly *really* run counter to the communal and illusory communal interests, makes *practical* intervention and control necessary through the illusory "general" interest in the form of the State. The social power, i.e., the multiplied productive force, which arises through the co-operation of different individuals as it is determined by the division of labour, appears to these individuals, since their co-operation is not voluntary but has come about naturally, not as their own united power, but as an alien force existing outside them, of the origin and goal of which they are ignorant, which they thus cannot control, which on the contrary passes through a peculiar series of phases and stages independent of the will and the action of man, nay even being the prime governor of these.

This *"estrangement"* (to use a term which will be comprehensible to the philosophers) can, of course, only be abolished given two *practical* premises. For it to become an "intolerable" power, i.e., a power against which men make a revolution, it must necessarily have rendered the great mass of humanity "propertyless," and produced, at the same time, the contradiction of an existing world of wealth and culture, both of which conditions presuppose a great increase in productive power, a high degree of its development. And, on the other hand, this development of productive forces (which itself implies the actual empirical existence of men in their *world-historical*, instead of local, being) is an absolutely necessary practical premise because without it *want* is merely made general, and with *destitution* the struggle for necessities and all the old filthy business would necessarily be reproduced; and furthermore, because only with this universal development of productive forces is a *universal* intercourse between men established, which produces in all nations simultaneously the phenomenon of the "propertyless" mass (universal competition), makes each nation dependent on the revolutions of the others, and finally has put *world-historical*, empirically universal individuals in place of local ones. Without this, (1) communism could only exist as a local event; (2) the *forces* of intercourse themselves could not have developed as *universal*, hence intolerable powers: they would have remained home-bred conditions surrounded by superstition; and (3) each extension of intercourse would abolish local communism. Empirically, communism is only possible as the act of the dominant peoples "all at once" and simultaneously, which presupposes the universal development of productive forces and the world intercourse bound up with communism. How otherwise could for instance property have had a history at all, have taken on different forms, and landed property, for example, according to the different premises given, have proceeded in France from parcellation to centralisation in the hands of a few, in England from centralisation in the hands of a few to parcellation, as is actually the case today? Or how does it happen that trade, which after all is nothing more than the exchange of products of various individuals and countries, rules the whole world through the relation of supply and demand—a relation which, as an English economist says, hovers over the earth like the fate of the ancients, and with invisible hand allots fortune and misfortune to men, sets up empires and overthrows empires, causes nations to rise . and to disappear—while with the abolition of the basis of private property, with the communistic regulation of production (and, implicit in this, the destruction of the alien relation between men and what they themselves produce), the power of the relation of supply and demand is dissolved into nothing, and men get exchange, production, the mode of their mutual relation, under their own control again?

Communism is for us not a *state of affairs* which is to be established, an *ideal* to which reality [will] have to adjust itself. We call communism the *real* movement which abolishes the present state of things. The conditions of this movement result from the premises now in existence. Moreover, the mass of *propertyless* workers—the utterly precarious position of labour-power on a mass scale cut off from capital or from even a limited satisfaction and, therefore, no longer merely temporarily deprived of work itself as a secure source of life—presupposes the *world market* through competition. The proletariat can thus only exist *world-historically*, just as communism, its activity, can only have a "world-historical" existence. World-historical existence of individuals, i.e., existence of individuals which is directly linked up with world history.

The form of intercourse determined by the existing productive forces at all previous historical stages, and in its turn determining these, is *civil society*. The latter, as is clear from what we have said above, has as its premises and basis the simple family and the multiple, the so-called tribe, and the more precise determinants of this society are enumerated in our remarks above. Already here we see how this civil society is the true source and theatre of all history, and how absurd is the conception of history held hitherto, which neglects the real relationships and confines itself to high-sounding dramas of princes and states.

Civil society embraces the whole material intercourse of individuals within a definite stage of the development of productive forces. It embraces the whole commercial and industrial life of a given stage and, insofar, transcends the State and the nation, though, on the other hand again, it must assert itself in its foreign relations as nationality, and inwardly must organise itself as State. The term "civil society" [*bürgerliche Gesellschaft*][7] emerged in the eighteenth century, when property relationships had already extricated themselves from the ancient and medieval communal society. Civil society as such only develops with the bourgeoisie; the social organisation evolving directly out of production and commerce, which in all ages forms the basis of the State and of the rest of the idealistic superstructure, has, however, always been designated by the same name.

2. Concerning the Production of Consciousness

In history up to the present it is certainly an empirical fact that separate individuals have, with the broadening of their activity into world-historical activity, become more and more enslaved under a power alien to them (a pressure which they have conceived of as a dirty trick on the part of the so-called universal spirit, etc.), a power which has become more and more enormous and, in the last instance, turns out to be the *world market*. But it is just as empirically established that, by the overthrow of the existing state of society by the communist revolution (of which more below) and the abolition of private property which is identical with it, this power, which so baffles the German theoreticians, will be dissolved; and that then the liberation of each single individual will be accomplished in the measure in which history becomes transformed into world history. From the above it is clear that the real intellectual wealth of the individual depends entirely on the wealth of his real connections. Only then will the separate individuals be liberated from the various national and local barriers, be brought into

7. *Bürgerliche Gesellschaft* can mean either "bourgeois society" or "civil society."

practical connection with the material and intellectual production of the whole world and be put in a position to acquire the capacity to enjoy this all-sided production of the whole earth (the creations of man). *All-round* dependence, this natural form of the *world-historical* co-operation of individuals, will be transformed by this communist revolution into the control and conscious mastery of these powers, which, born of the action of men on one another, have till now overawed and governed men as powers completely alien to them. Now this view can be expressed again in speculative-idealistic, i.e., fantastic, terms as "self-generation of the species" ("society as the subject"), and thereby the consecutive series of interrelated individuals connected with each other can be conceived as a single individual, which accomplishes the mystery of generating itself, It is clear here that individuals certainly make *one another*, physically and mentally, but do not make themselves either in the nonsense of Saint Bruno, or in the sense of the "Unique," of the "made" man.

This conception of history depends on our ability to expound the real process of production, starting out from the material production of life itself, and to comprehend the form of intercourse connected with this and created by this mode of production (i.e., civil society in its various stages), as the basis of all history; and to show it in its action as State, to explain all the different theoretical products and forms of consciousness, religion, philosophy, ethics, etc., etc., and trace their origins and growth from that basis; by which means, of course, the whole thing can be depicted in its totality (and therefore, too, the reciprocal action of these various sides on one another). It has not, like the idealistic view of history, in every period to look for a category, but remains constantly on the real *ground* of history; it does not explain practice from the idea but explains the formation of ideas from material practice; and accordingly it comes to the conclusion that all forms and products of consciousness cannot be dissolved by mental criticism, by resolution into "self-consciousness" or transformation into "apparitions," "spectres," "fancies," etc., but only by the practical overthrow of the actual social relations which gave rise to this idealistic humbug; that not criticism but revolution is the driving force of history, also of religion, of philosophy and all other types of theory. It shows that history does not end by being resolved into "self-consciousness" as "spirit of the spirit," but that in it at each stage there is found a material result: a sum of productive forces, a historically created relation of individuals to nature and to one another, which is handed down to each generation from its predecessor; a mass of productive forces, capital funds and conditions, which, on the one hand, is indeed modified by the new generation, but also on the other prescribes for it its conditions of life and gives it a definite development, a special character. It shows that circumstances make men just as much as men make circumstances. This sum of productive forces, capital funds and social forms of intercourse, which every individual and generation finds in existence as something given, is the real basis of what the philosophers have conceived as "substance" and "essence of man," and what they have deified and attacked: a real basis which is not in the least disturbed, in its effect and influence on the development of men, by the fact that these philosophers revolt against it as "self-consciousness" and the "Unique." These conditions of life, which different generations find in existence, decide also whether or not the periodically recurring revolutionary convulsion will be strong enough to overthrow the basis of the entire existing system. And if these material elements of a complete revolution are not present (namely, on the one hand the existing productive forces, on the other the formation of a revolutionary mass, which revolts not only against separate conditions of society up till then, but against the very "production of life" till then, the "total activity" on which it was based), then, as far as practical development is concerned, it is absolutely immaterial whether the *idea* of this revolution has been expressed a hundred times already, as the history of communism proves.

In the whole conception of history up to the present this real basis of history has either been totally neglected or else considered as a minor matter quite irrelevant to the course of history. History must, therefore, always be written according to an extraneous standard; the real production of life seems to be primeval history, while the truly historical appears to be separated from ordinary life, something extra-superterrestrial. With this the relation of man to nature is excluded from history and hence the antithesis of nature and history is created. The exponents of this conception of history have consequently only been able to see in history the political actions of princes and States, religious and all sorts of theoretical struggles, and in particular in each historical epoch have had to *share the illusion of that epoch.* For instance, if an epoch imagines itself to be actuated by purely "political" or "religious" motives, although "religion" and "politics" are only forms of its true motives, the historian accepts this opinion. The "idea," the "conception" of the people in question about their real practice, is transformed into the sole determining, active force, which controls and determines their practice. When the crude form in which the division of labour appears with the Indians and Egyptians calls forth the caste-system in their State and religion, the historian believes that the caste-system is the power which has produced this crude social form. While the French and the English at least hold by the political illusion, which is moderately close to reality, the Germans move in the realm of the "pure spirit," and make religious illusion the driving force of history. The Hegelian philosophy of history is the last consequence, reduced to its "finest expression," of all this German historiography, for which it is not a question of real, nor even of political, interests, but of pure thoughts, which consequently must appear to Saint Bruno, as a series of "thoughts" that devour one another and are finally swallowed up in "self-consciousness";[8] and even more consistently the course of history appears to the Blessed Max Stirner, who knows not a thing about real history, as a mere tale of "knights," robbers and ghosts, from whose visions he can, of course, only save himself by "unholiness." This conception is truly religious: it postulates religious man as the primitive man, the starting-point of history; and in its imagination puts the religious production of fancies in the place of the real production of the means of subsistence and of life itself. This whole conception of history, together with its dissolution and the scruples and qualms resulting from it, is a purely *national* affair of the Germans and has only *local* interest for the Germans, as for instance the important question treated several times of late: how really we "pass from the realm of God to the realm of Man"—as if this "realm of God" had ever existed anywhere save in the imagination, and the learned gentlemen, without being aware of it, were not constantly living in the "realm of Man" to which they are now seeking the way; and as if the learned pastime (for it is nothing more) of explaining the mystery of this theoretical bubble-blowing did not on the contrary lie in demonstrating its origin in actual earthly conditions. Always, for these Germans, it is simply a matter of resolving the nonsense of earlier writers into some other freak, i.e., of presupposing that all this nonsense has a special *sense* which can be discovered; while really it is only a question of explaining this theoretical talk from the actual existing conditions. The real, practical dissolution of these phrases, the removal of these notions from the consciousness of men, will, as we have already said, be effected by altered circumstances, not by theoretical deductions. For the mass of men, i.e., the proletariat, these theoretical notions do not exist and hence do not require to be dissolved, and if this mass ever had any theoretical notions, e.g., religion, etc., these have now long been dissolved by circumstances.

The purely national character of these questions and solutions is shown again in the way these theorists believe in all seriousness that chimeras like "the God-Man," "Man," etc., have presided over

8. Marginal note by Marx: "So-called *objective* historiography just consists in treating the historical conditions independent of activity. Reactionary character."

individual epochs of history (Saint Bruno even goes so far as to assert that "only criticism and critics have made history") and when they themselves construct historical systems, they skip over all earlier periods in the greatest haste and pass immediately from "Mongolism" to history "with meaningful content," that is to say, to the history of the *Hallische* and *Deutsche Jahrbücher* and the dissolution of the Hegelian school into a general squabble. They forget all other nations, all real events, and the *theatrum mundi* is confined to the Leipzig Book Fair and the mutual quarrels of "Criticism," "Man," and "the Unique." If these theorists treat really historical subjects, as for instance the eighteenth centrry, they merely give a history of the ideas of the times, torn away from the facts and the practical development fundamental to them; and even that merely in order to represent that period as an imperfect preliminary stage, the as yet limited predecessor of the real historical age, i.e., the period of the German philosophic struggle from 1840 to 1844. As might be expected when the history of an earlier period is written with the aim of accentuating the brilliance of an unhistoric person and his fantasies, all the really historic events, even the really historic invasion of politics into history, receive no mention. Instead we get a narrative based not on research but on arbitrary constructions and literary gossip, such as Saint Bruno provided in his now forgotten history of the eighteenth century. These high-falutin and haughty hucksters of ideas, who imagine themselves infinitely exalted above all national prejudices, are thus in practice far more national than the beer-quaffing philistines who dream of a united Germany. They do not recognise the deeds of other nations as historical: they live in Germany, to Germany, and for Germany; they turn the Rhine-song into a religious hymn and conquer Alsace and Lorraine by robbing French philosophy instead of the French State, by Germanising French ideas instead of French provinces. Herr Venedey is a cosmopolitan compared with the Saints Bruno and Max, who, in the universal dominance of theory, proclaim the universal dominance of Germany.

It is also clear from these arguments how grossly Feuerbach is deceiving himself when (*Wigand's Vierteljahrsschrift*, 1845, Volume 2) by virtue of the qualification "common man" he declares himself a communist, transforms the latter into a predicate of "man," and thereby thinks it possible to change the word "communist," which in the real world means the follower of a definite revolutionary party, into a mere category. Feuerbach's whole deduction with regard to the relation of men to one another goes only so far as to prove that men need and *always have needed* each other. He wants to establish consciousness of this fact, that is to say, like the other theorists, merely to produce a correct consciousness about an *existing* fact; whereas for the real communist it is a question of overthrowing the existing state of things. We thoroughly appreciate, moreover, that Feuerbach, in endeavouring to produce consciousness of just *this* fact, is going as far as a theorist possibly can, without ceasing to be a theorist and philosopher. It is characteristic, however, that Saint Bruno and Saint Max seize on Feuerbach's conception of the communist and put it in place of the real communist—which occurs, partly, in order that they can combat communism too as "spirit of the spirit," as a philosophical category, as an equal opponent and, in the case of Saint Bruno, partly also for pragmatic reason. As an example of Feuerbach's acceptance and at the same time misunderstanding of existing reality, which he still shares with our opponents, we recall the passage in the *Philosophie der Zukunft* where he develops the view that the existence of a thing or a man is at the same time its or his essence, that the conditions of existence, the mode of life and activity of an animal or human individual are those in which its "essence" feels itself satisfied. Here every exception is expressly conceived as an unhappy chance, as an abnormality which cannot be altered. Thus if millions of proletarians feel by no means contented with their living conditions, if their "existence" does not in the least correspond to their "essence," then, according to the passage quoted, this is an unavoidable misfortune, which must be borne quietly. The millions of proletarians and communists, however, think differently and will prove this in time, when they bring their "existence" into harmony with their "essence" in a practical way, by means of a revolution. Feuerbach, therefore, never speaks of the world of man in such cases, but always takes refuge in external nature, and moreover in *nature* which has not yet been subdued by men. But every new invention, every advance made by industry, detaches another piece from this domain, so that the ground which produces examples illustrating such Feuerbachian propositions is steadily shrinking. The "essence" of the fish is its "existence," water—to go no further than this one proposition. The "essence" of the freshwater fish is the water of a river. But the latter ceases to be the "essence" of the fish and is no longer a suitable medium of existence as soon as the river is made to serve industry, as soon as it is polluted by dyes and other waste products and navigated by steamboats, or as soon as its water is diverted into canals where simple drainage can deprive the fish of its medium of existence. The explanation that all such contradictions are inevitable abnormalities does not essentially differ from the consolation which the Blessed Max Stirner offers to the discontented, saying that this contradiction is their own contradiction and this predicament their own predicament, whereupon they should either set their minds at ease, keep their disgust to themselves, or revolt against it in some fantastic way. It differs just as little from Saint Bruno's allegation that these unfortunate circumstances are due to the fact that those concerned are stuck in the muck of "substance," have not advanced to "absolute self-consciousness," and do not realise that these adverse conditions are spirit of their spirit.

We shall, of course, not take the trouble[9] to enlighten our wise philosophers by explaining to them that the "liberation" of "man" is not advanced a single step[1] by reducing philosophy, theology, substance and all the trash to "self-consciousness"[2] and by liberating man from the domination of these phrases,[3] which have never held him in thrall.[4] Nor will we explain to them that it is only possible to achieve real liberation in the real world and by employing real means, that slavery cannot be abolished without the steam-engine and the mule and spinning-jenny, serfdom cannot be abolished without improved agriculture, and that, in general, people cannot be liberated as long as they are unable to obtain food and drink, housing and clothing in adequate quality and quantity. "Liberation" is a historical and not a mental act, and it is brought about by historical conditions, the [development] of industry, commerce, [agri]culture, the [conditions of intercourse] * * * [5]

In Germany,[6] a country where only a trivial historical development is taking place, these mental developments, these glorified and ineffective trivialities, naturally serve as a substitute for the lack of historical development, and they take root and have to be combated. But this fight is of local importance.[7]

* * * [8] in reality and for the *practical* materialist, i.e., the *communist*, it is a question of revolutionising the existing world, of practically attacking and changing existing things. When occasionally we find such views with Feuerbach, they are never more than isolated surmises and have much too little influence on his general outlook to be considered here as anything else than embryos capable of development. Feuerbach's "conception" of the sensuous world is confined on the one hand to mere contemplation of it, and on the other to mere feeling; he says "Man" instead of "real historical man." "Man" is really "the German." In the first case, the *contemplation* of the sensuous world, he necessarily lights on things which

9. Marginal note by Marx: *"Feuerbach."*
1. Marginal note by Marx: "Philosophic liberation and real liberation."
2. Marginal note by Marx: *"Man.* The *Unique one.* The *individual."*
3. Marginal note by Marx: "Geological, hydrographical, etc., conditions."
4. Marginal note by Marx: "The human body. Need and labour."
5. The following lines cannot be deciphered, for the sheet of paper is badly damaged.
6. Marginal note by Marx: "The importance of phrases in Germany."
7. Marginal note by Marx: "Language is the language of reality."
8. A gap in the manuscript.

contradict his consciousness and feeling, which disturb the harmony he presupposes, the harmony of all parts of the sensuous world and especially of man and nature.[9] To remove this disturbance, he must take refuge in a double perception, a profane one which only perceives the "flatly obvious" and a higher, philosophical, one which perceives the "true essence" of things. He does not see how the sensuous world around him is, not a thing given direct from all eternity, remaining ever the same, but the product of industry and of the state of society; and, indeed, in the sense that it is an historical product, the result of the activity of a whole succession of generations, each standing on the shoulders of the preceding one, developing its industry and its intercourse, modifying its social system according to the changed needs. Even the objects of the simplest "sensuous certainty" are only given him through social-development, industry and commercial intercourse. The cherry-tree, like almost all fruit-trees, was, as is well known, only a few centuries ago transplanted by *commerce* into our zone, and therefore only *by* this action of a definite society in a definite age it has become "sensuous certainty" for Feuerbach.

Incidentally, when we conceive things thus, as they really are and happened, every profound philosophical problem is resolved, as will be seen even more clearly later, quite simply into an empirical fact. For instance, the important question of the relation of man to nature (Bruno goes so far as to speak of "the antitheses in nature and history" (p. 110), as though these were two separate "things" and man did not always have before him an historical nature and a natural history) out of which all the "unfathomably lofty works" on "substance" and "self-consciousness" were born, crumbles of itself when we understand that the celebrated "unity of man with nature" has always existed in industry and has existed in varying forms in every epoch according to the lesser or greater development of industry, just like the "struggle" of man with nature, right up to the development of his productive powers on a corresponding basis. Industry and commerce, production and the exchange of the necessities of life, themselves determine distribution, the structure of the different social classes and are, in turn, determined by it as to the mode in which they are carried on; and so it happens that in Manchester, for instance, Feuerbach sees only factories and machines, where a hundred years ago only spinning-wheels and weaving-looms were to be seen, or in the Campagna of Rome he finds only pasture lands and swamps, where in the time of Augus-

9. N.B. Feuerbach's failing is not that he subordinates the flatly obvious, the sensuous *appearance*, to the sensuous reality established by more accurate investigation of the sensuous facts, but that he cannot in the last resort cope with the sensuous world except by looking at it with the "eyes," i.e., through the "spectacles" of the philosopher. [*Marx*]

tus he would have found nothing but the vineyards and villas of Roman capitalists. Feuerbach speaks in particular of the perception of natural science; he mentions secrets which are disclosed only to the eye of the physicist and chemist; but where would natural science be without industry and commerce? Even this "pure" natural science is provided with an aim, as with its material, only through trade and industry, through the sensuous activity of men. So much is this activity, this unceasing sensuous labour and creation, this production, the basis of the whole sensuous world as it now exists, that, were it interrupted only for a year, Feuerbach would not only find an enormous change in the natural world, but would very soon find that the whole world of men and his own perceptive faculty, nay his own existence, were missing. Of course, in all this the priority of external nature remains unassailed, and all this has no application to the original men produced by *generatio aequivoca;* [1] but this differentiation has meaning only insofar as man is considered to be distinct from nature. For that matter, nature, the nature that preceded human history, is not by any means the nature in which Feuerbach lives, it is nature which today no longer exists anywhere (except perhaps on a few Australian coral-islands of recent origin) and which, therefore, does not exist for Feuerbach.

Certainly Feuerbach has a great advantage over the "pure" materialists in that he realises how man too is an "object of the senses." But apart from the fact that he only conceives him as an "object of the senses," not as "sensuous activity," because he still remains in the realm of theory and conceives of men not in their given social connection, not under their existing conditions of life, which have made them what they are, he never arrives at the really existing active men, but stops at the abstraction "man," and gets no further than recognising "the true, individual, corporeal man" emotionally, i.e., he knows no other "human relationships" "of man to man" than love and friendship, and even then idealised. He gives no criticism of the present conditions of life. Thus he never manages to conceive the sensuous world as the total living sensuous *activity* of the individuals composing it; and therefore when, for example, he sees instead of healthy men a crowd of scrofulous, overworked and consumptive starvelings, he is compelled to take refuge in the "higher perception" and in the ideal "compensation in the species," and thus to relapse into idealism at the very point where the communist materialist sees the necessity, and at the same time the condition, of a transformation both of industry and of the social structure.

As far as Feuerbach is a materialist he does not deal with history, and as far as he considers history he is not a materialist. With him

1. Spontaneous generation.

materialism and history diverge completely, a fact which incidentally is already obvious from what has been said.

History is nothing but the succession of the separate generations, each of which exploits the materials, the capital funds, the
productive forces handed down to it by all preceding generations,
and thus, on the one hand, continues the traditional activity in
completely changed circumstances and, on the other, modifies the
old circumstances with a completely changed activity. This can be
speculatively distorted so that later history is made the goal of earlier history, e.g., the goal ascribed to the discovery of America is to
further the eruption of the French Revolution. Thereby history
receives its own special aims and becomes "a person ranking with
other persons" (to wit: "Self-Consciousness, Criticism, the
Unique," etc.), while what is designated with the words "destiny,"
"goal," "germ," or "ideal" of earlier history is nothing more than
an abstraction formed from later history, from the active influence
which earlier history exercises on later history.

The further the separate spheres, which act on one another,
extend in the course of this development, the more the original isolation of the separate nationalities is destroyed by the developed
mode of production and intercourse and the division of labour
between various nations naturally brought forth by these, the more
history becomes world history. Thus, for instance, if in England a
machine is invented, which deprives countless workers of bread in
India and China, and overturns the whole form of existence of
these empires, this invention becomes a world-historical fact. Or
again, take the case of sugar and coffee which have proved their
world-historical importance in the nineteenth century by the fact
that the lack of these products, occasioned by the Napoleonic Continental System, caused the Germans to rise against Napoleon, and
thus became the real basis of the glorious Wars of Liberation of
1813. From this it follows that this transformation of history into
world history is not indeed a mere abstract act on the part of the
"self-consciousness," the world spirit, or of any other metaphysical
spectre, but a quite material, empirically verifiable act, an act the
proof of which every individual furnishes as he comes and goes,
eats, drinks and clothes himself.

The ideas of the ruling class are in every epoch the ruling ideas:
i.e., the class which is the ruling *material* force of society, is at the
same time its ruling *intellectual* force. The class which has the
means of material production at its disposal, has control at the
same time over the means of mental production, so that thereby,
generally speaking, the ideas of those who lack the means of mental
production are subject to it. The ruling ideas are nothing more than
the ideal expression of the dominant material relationships, the dom-

inant material relationships grasped as ideas; hence of the relationships which make the one class the ruling one, therefore, the ideas of its dominance. The individuals composing the ruling class possess among other things consciousness, and therefore think. Insofar, therefore, as they rule as a class and determine the extent and compass of an epoch, it is self-evident that they do this in its whole range, hence among other things rule also as thinkers, as producers of ideas, and regulate the production and distribution of the ideas of their age: thus their ideas are the ruling ideas of the epoch. For instance, in an age and in a country where royal power, aristocracy and bourgeoisie are contending for mastery and where, therefore, mastery is shared, the doctrine of the separation of powers proves to be the dominant idea and is expressed as an "eternal law."

The division of labour, which we have already seen above as one of the chief forces of history up till now, manifests itself also in the ruling class as the division of mental and material labour, so that inside this class one part appears as the thinkers of the class (its active, conceptive ideologists, who make the perfecting of the illusion of the class about itself their chief source of livelihood), while the others' attitude to these ideas and illusions is more passive and receptive, because they are in reality the active members of this class and have less time to make up illusions and ideas about themselves. Within this class this cleavage can even develop into a certain opposition and hostility between the two parts, which, however, in the case of a practical collision, in which the class itself is endangered, automatically comes to nothing, in which case there also vanishes the semblance that the ruling ideas were not the ideas of the ruling class and had a power distinct from the power of this class. The existence of revolutionary ideas in a particular period presupposes the existence of a revolutionary class; about the premises for the latter sufficient has already been said above.

If now in considering the course of history we detach the ideas of the ruling class from the ruling class itself and attribute to them an independent existence, if we confine ourselves to saying that these or those ideas were dominant at a given time, without bothering ourselves about the conditions of production and the producers of these ideas, if we thus ignore the individuals and world conditions which are the source of the ideas, we can say, for instance, that during the time that the aristocracy was dominant, the concepts honour, loyalty, etc., were dominant, during the dominance of the bourgeoisie the concepts freedom, equality, etc. The ruling class itself on the whole imagines this to be so. This conception of history, which is common to all historians, particularly since the eighteenth century, will necessarily come up against the phenomenon that increasingly abstract ideas hold sway, i.e., ideas which increasingly take on the form of universality. For each new class which puts itself in the place of one ruling before it, is compelled, merely in order to carry through its aim, to represent its interest as the common interest of all the members of society, that is, expressed in ideal form: it has to give its ideas the form of universality, and represent them as the only rational, universally valid ones. The class making a revolution appears from the very start, if only because it is opposed to a *class*, not as a class but as the representative of the whole of society; it appears as the whole mass of society confronting the one ruling class.[2] It can do this because, to start with, its interest really is more connected with the common interest of all other non-ruling classes, because under the pressure of hitherto existing conditions its interest has not yet been able to develop as the particular interest of a particular class. Its victory, therefore, benefits also many individuals of the other classes which are not winning a dominant position, but only insofar as it now puts these individuals in a position to raise themselves into the ruling class. When the French bourgeoisie overthrew the power of the aristocracy, it thereby made it possible for many proletarians to raise themselves above the proletariat, but only insofar as they became bourgeois. Every new class, therefore, achieves its hegemony only on a broader basis than that of the class ruling previously, whereas the opposition of the non-ruling class against the new ruling class later develops all the more sharply and profoundly. Both these things determine the fact that the struggle to be waged against this new ruling class, in its turn, aims at a more decided and radical negation of the previous conditions of society than could all previous classes which sought to rule.

This whole semblance, that the rule of a certain class is only the rule of certain ideas, comes to a natural end, of course, as soon as class rule in general ceases to be the form in which society is organised, that is to say, as soon as it is no longer necessary to represent a particular interest as general or the "general interest" as ruling.

Once the ruling ideas have been separated from the ruling individuals and, above all, from the relationships which result from a given stage of the mode of production, and in this way the conclusion has been reached that history is always under the sway of ideas, it is very easy to abstract from these various ideas "*the* idea," the notion, etc., as the dominant force in history, and thus to understand all these separate ideas and concepts as "forms of self-determination" on the part of *the* concept developing in history. It

2. Marginal note by Marx: "Universality corresponds to (1) the class versus the estate, (2) the competition, world-wide intercourse, etc., (3) the great numerical strength of the ruling class, (4) the illusion of the *common* interests (in the beginning this illusion is true), (5) the delusion of the ideologists and the division of labour."

follows then naturally, too, that all the relationships of men can be derived from the concept of man, man as conceived, the essence of man, *Man*. This has been done by the speculative philosophers. Hegel himself confesses at the end of the *Geschichtsphilosophie* that he "has considered the progress of the *concept* only" and has represented in history the "true *theodicy*." Now one can go back again to the producers of the "concept," to the theorists, ideologists and philosophers, and one comes then to the conclusion that the philosophers, the thinkers as such, have at all times been dominant in history: a conclusion, as we see, already expressed by Hegel. The whole trick of proving the hegemony of the spirit in history (hierarchy Stirner calls it) is thus confined to the following three efforts.

No. 1. One must separate the ideas of those ruling for empirical reasons, under empirical conditions and as empirical individuals, from these actual rulers, and thus recognise the rule of ideas or illusions in history.

No. 2. One must bring an order into this rule of ideas, prove a mystical connection among the successive ruling ideas, which is managed by understanding them as "acts of self-determination on the part of the concept" (this is possible because by virtue of their empirical basis these ideas are really connected with one another and because, conceived as *mere* ideas, they become self-distinctions, distinctions made by thought).

No. 3. To remove the mystical appearance of this "self-determining concept" it is changed into a person—"Self-Consciousness"—or, to appear thoroughly materialistic, into a series of persons, who represent the "concept" in history, into the "thinkers," the "philosophers," the ideologists, who again are understood as the manufacturers of history, as the "council of guardians," as the rulers.[3] Thus the whole body of materialistic elements has been removed from history and now full rein can be given to the speculative steed.

Whilst in ordinary life every shopkeeper is very well able to distinguish between what somebody professes to be and what he really is, our historians have not yet won even this trivial insight. They take every epoch at its word and believe that everything it says and imagines about itself is true.

This historical method which reigned in Germany and especially the reason why, must be understood from its connection with the illusion of ideologists in general, e.g., the illusions of the jurists, politicians (of the practical statesmen among them, too), from the dogmatic dreamings and distortions of these fellows; this is explained perfectly easily from their practical position in life, their job, and the division of labour.

3. Marginal note by Marx: "Man = the 'rational human spirit.'"

[B. THE REAL BASIS OF IDEOLOGY][4]

1. *Intercourse and Productive Forces*

The greatest division of material and mental labour is the separation of town and country. The antagonism between town and country begins with the transition from barbarism to civilisation, from tribe to State, from locality to nation, and runs through the whole history of civilisation to the present day (the Anti-Corn Law League).

The existence of the town implies, at the same time, the necessity of administration, police, taxes, etc., in short, of the municipality, and thus of politics in general. Here first became manifest the division of the population into two great classes, which is directly based on the division of labour and on the instruments of production. The town already is in actual fact the concentration of the population, of the instruments of production, of capital, of pleasures, of needs, while the country demonstrates just the opposite fact, isolation and separation. The antagonism between town and country can only exist within the framework of private property. It is the most crass expression of the subjection of the individual under the division of labour, under a definite activity forced upon him—a subjection which makes one man into a restricted town-animal, the other into a restricted country-animal, and daily creates anew the conflict between their interests. Labour is here again the chief thing, power *over* individuals, and as long as the latter exists, private property must exist. The abolition of the antagonism between town and country is one of the first conditions of communal life, a condition which again depends on a mass of material premises and which cannot be fulfilled by the mere will, as anyone can see at the first glance. (These conditions have still to be enumerated.) The separation of town and country can also be understood as the separation of capital and landed property, as the beginning of the existence and development of capital independent of landed property—the beginning of property having its basis only in labour and exchange.

In the towns which, in the Middle Ages, did not derive ready-made from an earlier period but were formed anew by the serfs who had become free, each man's own particular labour was his only property apart from the small capital he brought with him, consisting almost solely of the most necessary tools of his craft. The competition of serfs constantly escaping into the town, the con-

4. Brackets indicate a sub-heading added by the editors. [*R. T.*]

stant war of the country against the towns and thus the necessity of an organised municipal military force, the bond of common ownership in a particular kind of labour, the necessity of common buildings for sale of their wares at a time when craftsmen were also traders, and the consequent exclusion of the unauthorised from these buildings, the conflict among the interests of the various crafts, the necessity of protecting their laboriously acquired skill, and the feudal organisation of the whole of the country: these were the causes of the union of the workers of each craft in guilds. We have not at this point to go further into the manifold modifications of the guild-system, which arise through later historical developments. The flight of the serfs into the towns went on without interruption right through the Middle Ages. These serfs, persecuted by their lords in the country, came separately into the towns, where they found an organised community, against which they were powerless and in which they had to subject themselves to the station assigned to them by the demand for their labour and the interest of their organised urban competitors. These workers, entering separately, were never able to attain to any power, since, if their labour was of the guild type which had to be learned, the guild-masters bent them to their will and organised them according to their interest; or if their labour was not such as had to be learned, and therefore not of the guild type, they became day-labourers and never managed to organise, remaining an unorganised rabble. The need for day-labourers in the towns created the rabble.

These towns were true "associations," called forth by the direct need, the care of providing for the protection of property, and of multiplying the means of production and defence of the separate members. The rabble of these towns was devoid of any power, composed as it was of individuals strange to one another who had entered separately, and who stood unorganised over against an organised power, armed for war, and jealously watching over them. The journeymen and apprentices were organised in each craft as it best suited the interest of the masters. The patriarchal relationship existing between them and their masters gave the latter a double power—on the one hand because of their influence on the whole life of the journeymen, and on the other because, for the journeymen who worked with the same master, it was a real bond which held them together against the journeymen of other masters and separated them from these. And finally, the journeymen were bound to the existing order by their simple interest in becoming masters themselves. While, therefore, the rabble at least carried out revolts against the whole municipal order, revolts which remained completely ineffective because of their powerlessness, the journeymen never got further than small acts of insubordination within separate guilds, such as belong to the very nature of the guild system. The great risings of the Middle Ages all radiated from the country, but equally remained totally ineffective because of the isolation and consequent crudity of the peasants.

In the towns, the division of labour between the individual guilds was as yet [quite naturally derived] and, in the guilds themselves, not at all developed between the individual workers. Every workman had to be versed in a whole round of tasks, had to be able to make everything that was to be made with his tools. The limited commerce and the scanty communication between the individual towns, the lack of population and the narrow needs did not allow of a higher division of labour, and therefore every man who wished to become a master had to be proficient in the whole of his craft. Thus there is found with medieval craftsmen an interest in their special work and in proficiency in it, which was capable of rising to a narrow artistic sense. For this very reason, however, every medieval craftsman was completely absorbed in his work, to which he had a contented, slavish relationship, and to which he was subjected to a far greater extent than the modern worker, whose work is a matter of indifference to him.

Capital in these towns was a naturally derived capital, consisting of a house, the tools of the craft, and the natural, hereditary customers; and not being realisable, on account of the backwardness of commerce and the lack of circulation, it descended from father to son. Unlike modern capital, which can be assessed in money and which may be indifferently invested in this thing or that, this capital was directly connected with the particular work of the owner, inseparable from it and to this extent *estate* capital.

The next extension of the division of labour was the separation of production and commerce, the formation of a special class of merchants; a separation which, in the towns bequeathed by a former period, had been handed down (among other things with the Jews) and which very soon appeared in the newly formed ones. With this there was given the possibility of commercial communications transcending the immediate neighbourhood, a possibility, the realisation of which depended on the existing means of communication, the state of public safety in the countryside, which was determined by political conditions (during the whole of the Middle Ages, as is well known, the merchants travelled in armed caravans), and on the cruder or more advanced needs (determined by the stage of culture attained) of the region accessible to intercourse.

With commerce the prerogative of a particular class, with the extension of trade through the merchants beyond the immediate surroundings of the town, there immediately appears a reciprocal action between production and commerce. The towns enter into relations *with one another,* new tools are brought from one town into the other, and the separation between production and commerce soon calls forth a new division of production between the individual towns, each of which is soon exploiting a predominant branch of industry. The local restrictions of earlier times begin gradually to be broken down.

In the Middle Ages the citizens in each town were compelled to unite against the landed nobility to save their skins. The extension of trade, the establishment of communications, led the separate towns to get to know other towns, which had asserted the same interests in the struggle with the same antagonist. Out of the many local corporations of burghers there arose only gradually the burgher *class.* The conditions of life of the individual burghers became, on account of their contradiction to the existing relationships and of the mode of labour determined by these, conditions which were common to them all and independent of each individual. The burghers had created the conditions insofar as they had torn themselves free from feudal ties, and were created by them insofar as they were determined by their antagonism to the feudal system which they found in existence. When the individual towns began to enter into associations, these common conditions developed into class conditions. The same conditions, the same contradiction, the same interests necessarily called forth on the whole similar customs everywhere. The bourgeoisie itself, with its conditions, develops only gradually, splits according to the division of labour into various fractions and finally absorbs all propertied classes it finds in existence[5] (while it develops the majority of the earlier propertyless and a part of the hitherto propertied classes into a new class, the proletariat) in the measure to which all property found in existence is transformed into industrial or commercial capital. The separate individuals form a class only insofar as they have to carry on a common battle against another class; otherwise they are on hostile terms with each other as competitors. On the other hand, the class in its turn achieves an independent existence over against the individuals, so that the latter find their conditions of existence predestined, and hence have their position in life and their personal development assigned to them by their class, become subsumed under it. This is the same phenomenon as the subjection of the separate individuals to the division of labour and can only be removed by the abolition of private property and of labour itself. We have already indicated several times how this subsuming of individuals under the class brings with it their subjection to all kinds of ideas, etc.

5. Marginal note by Marx: "To begin with it absorbs the branches of labour directly belonging to the State and then all ± [more or less] ideological estates."

It depends purely on the extension of commerce whether the productive forces achieved in a locality, especially inventions, are lost for later development or not. As long as there exists no commerce transcending the immediate neighbourhood, every invention must be made separately in each locality, and mere chances such as irruptions of barbaric peoples, even ordinary wars, are sufficient to cause a country with advanced productive forces and needs to have to start right over again from the beginning. In primitive history every invention had to be made daily anew and in each locality independently. How little highly developed productive forces are safe from complete destruction, given even a relatively very extensive commerce, is proved by the Phoenicians,[6] whose inventions were for the most part lost for a long time to come through the ousting of this nation from commerce, its conquest by Alexander and its consequent decline. Likewise, for instance, glass-painting in the Middle Ages. Only when commerce has become world commerce and has as its basis large-scale industry, when all nations are drawn into the competitive struggle, is the permanence of the acquired productive forces assured.

The immediate consequence of the division of labour between the various towns was the rise of manufactures, branches of production which had outgrown the guild-system. Manufactures first flourished, in Italy and later in Flanders, under the historical premise of commerce with foreign nations. In other countries, England and France for example, manufactures were at first confined to the home market. Besides the premises already mentioned manufactures depend on an already advanced concentration of population, particularly in the countryside, and of capital, which began to accumulate in the hands of individuals, partly in the guilds in spite of the guild regulations, partly among the merchants.

That labour which from the first presupposed a machine, even of the crudest sort, soon showed itself the most capable of development. Weaving, earlier carried on in the country by the peasants as a secondary occupation to procure their clothing, was the first labour to receive an impetus and a further development through the extension of commerce. Weaving was the first and remained the principal manufacture. The rising demand for clothing materials, consequent on the growth of population, the growing accumulation and mobilisation of natural capital through accelerated circulation, the demand for luxuries called forth by the latter and favoured generally by the gradual extension of commerce, gave weaving a quantitative and qualitative stimulus, which wrenched it out of the form of production hitherto existing. Alongside the peas-

6. Marginal note by Marx: "and the manufacture of glass in the Middle Ages."

ants weaving for their own use, who continued, and still continue, with this sort of work, there emerged a new class of weavers in the towns, whose fabrics were destined for the whole home market and usually for foreign markets too.

Weaving, an occupation demanding in most cases little skill and soon splitting up into countless branches, by its whole nature resisted the trammels of the guild. Weaving was, therefore, carried on mostly in villages and market centres without guild organisation, which gradually became towns, and indeed the most flourishing towns in each land.

With guild-free manufacture, property relations also quickly changed. The first advance beyond naturally derived estate capital was provided by the rise of merchants whose capital was from the beginning movable, capital in the modern sense as far as one can speak of it, given the circumstances of those times. The second advance came with manufacture, which again made mobile a mass of natural capital, and altogether increased the mass of movable capital as against that of natural capital.

At the same time, manufacture became a refuge of the peasants from the guilds which excluded them or paid them badly, just as earlier the guild-towns had [served] as a refuge for the peasants from [the oppressive landed nobility].

Simultaneously with the beginning of manufactures there was a period of vagabondage caused by the abolition of the feudal bodies of retainers, the disbanding of the swollen armies which had flocked to serve the kings against their vassals, the improvement of agriculture, and the transformation of great strips of tillage into pasture land. From this alone it is clear how this vagabondage is strictly connected with the disintergration of the feudal system. As early as the thirteenth century we find isolated epochs of this kind, but only at the end of the fifteenth and beginning of the sixteenth does this vagabondage make a general and permanent appearance. These vagabonds, who were so numerous that, for instance, Henry VIII of England had 72,000 of them hanged, were only prevailed upon to work with the greatest difficulty and through the most extreme necessity, and then only after long resistance. The rapid rise of manufactures, particularly in England, absorbed them gradually.

With the advent of manufactures, the various nations entered into a competitive relationship, the struggle for trade, which was fought out in wars, protective duties and prohibitions, whereas earlier the nations, insofar as they were connected at all, had carried on an inoffensive exchange with each other. Trade had from now on a political significance.

With the advent of manufacture the relationship between worker and employer changed. In the guilds the patriarchal relationship between journeyman and master continued to exist; in manufacture its place was taken by the monetary relation between worker and capitalist—a relationship which in the countryside and in small towns retained a patriarchal tinge, but in the larger, the real manufacturing towns, quite early lost almost all patriarchal complexion.

Manufacture and the movement of production in general received an enormous impetus through the extension of commerce which came with the discovery of America and the sea-route to the East Indies. The new products imported thence, particularly the masses of gold and silver which came into circulation and totally changed the position of the classes towards one another, dealing a hard blow to feudal landed property and to the workers; the expeditions of adventurers, colonisation; and above all the extension of markets into a world market, which had now become possible and was daily becoming more and more a fact, called forth a new phase of historical development, into which in general we cannot here enter further. Through the colonisation of the newly discovered countries the commercial struggle of the nations amongst one another was given new fuel and accordingly greater extension and animosity.

The expansion of trade and manufacture accelerated the accumulation of movable capital, while in the guilds, which were not stimulated to extend their production, natural capital remained stationary or even declined. Trade and manufacture created the big bourgeoisie; in the guilds was concentrated the petty bourgeoisie, which no longer was dominant in the towns as formerly, but had to bow to the might of the great merchants and manufacturers.[7] Hence the decline of the guilds, as soon as they came into contact with manufacture.

The intercourse of nations took on, in the epoch of which we have been speaking, two different forms. At first the small quantity of gold and silver in circulation involved the ban on the export of these metals; and industry, for the most part imported from abroad and made necessary by the need for employing the growing urban population, could not do without those privileges which could be granted not only, of course, against home competition, but chiefly against foreign. The local guild privilege was in these original prohibitions extended over the whole nation. Customs duties originated from the tributes which the feudal lords exacted as protective levies against robbery from merchants passing through their territories, tributes later imposed likewise by the towns, and which, with the

7. Marginal note by Marx: "Petty bourgeoisie—Middle class—Big bourgeoisie."

rise of the modern states, were the Treasury's most obvious means of raising money.

The appearance of American gold and silver on the European markets, the gradual development of industry, the rapid expansion of trade and the consequent rise of the non-guild bourgeoisie and of money, gave these measures another significance. The State, which was daily less and less able to do without money, now retained the ban on the export of gold and silver out of fiscal considerations; the bourgeois, for whom these masses of money which were hurled on to the market became the chief object of speculative buying, were thoroughly content with this; privileges established earlier became a source of income for the government and were sold for money; in the customs legislation there appeared the export duty, which, since it only [placed] a hindrance in the way of industry, had a purely fiscal aim.

The second period began in the middle of the seventeenth century and lasted almost to the end of the eighteenth. Commerce and navigation had expanded more rapidly than manufacture, which played a secondary role; the colonies were becoming considerable consumers; and after long struggles the separate nations shared out the opening world market among themselves. This period begins with the Navigation Laws and colonial monopolies. The competition of the nations among themselves was excluded as far as possible by tariffs, prohibitions and treaties; and in the last resort the competitive struggle was carried on and decided by wars (especially naval wars). The mightiest maritime nation, the English, retained preponderance in trade and manufacture. Here, already, we find concentration in one country.

Manufacture was all the time sheltered by protective duties in the home market, by monopolies in the colonial market, and abroad as much as possible by differential duties. The working-up of home-produced material was encouraged (wool and linen in England, silk in France), the export of home-produced raw material forbidden (wool in England), and the [working-up] of imported material neglected or suppressed (cotton in England). The nation dominant in sea trade and colonial power naturally secured for itself also the greatest quantitative and qualitative expansion of manufacture. Manufacture could not be carried on without protection, since, if the slightest change takes place in other countries, it can lose its market and be ruined; under reasonably favourable conditions it may easily be introduced into a country, but for this very reason can easily be destroyed. At the same time through the mode in which it is carried on, particularly in the eighteenth century, in the countryside, it is to such an extent interwoven with the vital relationships of a great mass of individuals, that no country dare jeopardise its existence by permitting free competition. Insofar as it manages to export, it therefore depends entirely on the extension or restriction of commerce, and exercises a relatively very small reaction [on the latter]. Hence its secondary [importance] and the influence of [the merchants] in the eighteenth century. It was the merchants and especially the shippers who more than anybody else pressed for State protection and monopolies; the manufacturers also demanded and indeed received protection, but all the time were inferior in political importance to the merchants. The commercial towns, particularly the maritime towns, became to some extent civilised and acquired the outlook of the big bourgeoisie, but in the factory towns an extreme petty-bourgeois outlook persisted. Cf. Aiken, etc. The eighteenth century was the century of trade. Pinto says this expressly: *"Le commerce fait la marotte du siècle"*;[8] and: *"Depuis quelque temps il n'est plus question que de commerce, de navigation et de marine."*[9]

This period is also characterised by the cessation of the bans on the export of gold and silver and the beginning of the trade in money; by banks, national debts, paper money; by speculation in stocks and shares and stockjobbing in all articles; by the development of finance in general. Again capital lost a great part of the natural character which had still clung to it.

The concentration of trade and manufacture in one country, England, developing irresistibly in the seventeenth century, gradually created for this country a relative world market, and thus a demand for the manufactured products of this country, which could no longer be met by the industrial productive forces hitherto existing. This demand, outgrowing the productive forces, was the motive power which, by producing big industry—the application of elemental forces to industrial ends, machinery and the most complex division of labour—called into existence the third period of private ownership since the Middle Ages. There already existed in England the other pre-conditions of this new phase: freedom of competition inside the nation, the development of theoretical mechanics, etc. (Indeed, the science of mechanics perfected by

8. "Commerce is the rage of the century."
9. "For some time now people have been talking only about commerce, navigation and the navy." [The movement of capital, although considerably accelerated, still remained, however, relatively slow. The splitting-up of the world market into separate parts, each of which was exploited by a particular nation, the exclusion of competition among themselves on the part of the nations, the clumsiness of production itself and the fact that finance was only evolving from its early stages, greatly impeded circulation. The consequence of this was a haggling, mean and niggardly spirit which still clung to all merchants and to the whole mode of carrying on trade. Compared with the manufacturers, and above all with the craftsmen, they were certainly big bourgeois; compared with the merchants and industrialists of the next period they remain petty bourgeois. Cf. Adam Smith.—*Marx*]

Newton was altogether the most popular science in France and England in the eighteenth century.) (Free competition inside the nation itself had everywhere to be conquered by a revolution—1640 and 1688 in England, 1789 in France.) Competition soon compelled every country that wished to retain its historical role to protect its manufactures by renewed customs regulations (the old duties were no longer any good against big industry) and soon after to introduce big industry under protective duties. Big industry universalised competition in spite of these protective measures (it is practical free trade; the protective duty is only a palliative, a measure of defence *within* free trade), established means of communication and the modern world market, subordinated trade to itself, transformed all capital into industrial capital, and thus produced the rapid circulation (development of the financial system) and the centralisation of capital. By universal competition it forced all individuals to strain their energy to the utmost. It destroyed as far as possible ideology, religion, morality, etc., and where it could not do this, made them into a palpable lie. It produced world history for the first time, insofar as it made all civilised nations and every individual member of them dependent for the satisfaction of their wants on the whole world, thus destroying the former natural exclusiveness of separate nations. It made natural science subservient to capital and took from the division of labour the last semblance of its natural character. It destroyed natural growth in general, as far as this is possible while labour exists, and resolved all natural relationships into money relationships. In the place of naturally grown towns it created the modern, large industrial cities which have sprung up overnight. Wherever it penetrated, it destroyed the crafts and all earlier stages of industry. It completed the victory of the commercial town over the countryside. [Its first premise] was the automatic system. [Its development] produced a mass of productive forces, for which private [property] became just as much a fetter as the guild had been for manufacture and the small, rural workshop for the developing craft. These productive forces received under the system of private property a one-sided development only, and became for the majority destructive forces; moreover, a great multitude of such forces could find no application at all within this system. Generally speaking, big industry created everywhere the same relations between the classes of society, and thus destroyed the peculiar individuality of the various nationalities. And finally, while the bourgeoisie of each nation still retained separate national interests, big industry created a class, which in all nations has the same interest and with which nationality is already dead; a class which is really rid of all the old world and at the same time stands pitted against it. Big industry makes for the worker not only the relation to the capitalist, but labour itself, unbearable.

It is evident that big industry does not reach the same level of development in all districts of a country. This does not, however, retard the class movement of the proletariat, because the proletarians created by big industry assume leadership of this movement and carry the whole mass along with them, and because the workers excluded from big industry are placed by it in a still worse situation than the workers in big industry itself. The countries in which big industry is developed act in a similar manner upon the more or less non-industrial countries, insofar as the latter are swept by universal commerce into the universal competitive struggle.[1]

These different forms are just so many forms of the organisation of labour, and hence of property. In each period a unification of the existing productive forces takes place, insofar as this has been rendered necessary by needs.

2. *The Relation of State and Law to Property*

The first form of property, in the ancient world as in the Middle Ages, is tribal property, determined with the Romans chiefly by war, with the Germans by the rearing of cattle. In the case of the ancient peoples, since several tribes live together in one town, the tribal property appears as State property, and the right of the individual to it as mere "possession" which, however, like tribal property as a whole, is confined to landed property only. Real private property began with the ancients, as with modern nations, with movable property.—(Slavery and community) (*dominium ex jure Quiritum*[2]). In the case of the nations which grew out of the Middle Ages, tribal property evolved through various stages—feudal landed property, corporative movable property, capital invested in manufacture—to modern capital, determined by big industry and universal competition, i.e., pure private property, which has cast off all semblance of a communal institution and has shut out the State from any influence on the development of property. To this

1. Competition separates individuals from one another, not only the bourgeois but still more the workers, in spite of the fact that it brings them together. Hence it is a long time before these individuals can unite, apart from the fact that for the purposes of this union—if it is not to be merely local—the necessary means, the great industrial cities and cheap and quick communications, have first to be produced by big industry. Hence every organised power standing over against these isolated individuals, who live in relationships daily reproducing this isolation, can only be overcome after long struggles. To demand the opposite would be tantamount to demanding that competition should not exist in this definite epoch of history, or that the individuals should banish from their minds relationships over which in their isolation they have no control. [*Marx*]

2. Ownership in accordance with the law applying to full Roman citizens.

modern private property corresponds the modern State, which, purchased gradually by the owners of property by means of taxation, has fallen entirely into their hands through the national debt, and its existence has become wholly dependent on the commercial credit which the owners of property, the bourgeois, extend to it, as reflected in the rise and fall of State funds on the stock exchange. By the mere fact that it is a *class* and no longer an *estate*, the bourgeoisie is forced to organise itself no longer locally, but nationally, and to give a general form to its mean average interest. Through the emancipation of private property from the community, the State has become a separate entity, beside and outside civil society; but it is nothing more than the form of organisation which the bourgeois necessarily adopt both for internal and external purposes, for the mutual guarantee of their property and interests. The independence of the State is only found nowadays in those countries where the estates have not yet completely developed into classes, where the estates, done away with in more advanced countries, still have a part to play, and where there exists a mixture; countries, that is to say, in which no one section of the population can achieve dominance over the others. This is the case particularly in Germany. The most perfect example of the modern State is North America. The modern French, English and American writers all express the opinion that the State exists only for the sake of private property, so that this fact has penetrated into the consciousness of the normal man.

Since the State is the form in which the individuals of a ruling class assert their common interests, and in which the whole civil society of an epoch is epitomised, it follows that the State mediates in the formation of all common institutions and that the institutions receive a political form. Hence the illusion that law is based on the will, and indeed on the will divorced from its real basis—on *free* will. Similarly, justice is in its turn reduced to the actual laws.

Civil law develops simultaneously with private property out of the disintegration of the natural community. With the Romans the development of private property and civil law had no further industrial and commercial consequences, because their whole mode of production did not alter.[3] With modern peoples, where the feudal community was disintegrated by industry and trade, there began with the rise of private property and civil law a new phase, which was capable of further development. The very first town which carried on an extensive maritime trade in the Middle Ages, Amalfi, also developed maritime law. As soon as industry and trade developed private property further, first in Italy and later in other coun-

3. Marginal note by Engels: "(Usury!)"

tries, the highly developed Roman civil law was immediately adopted again and raised to authority. When later the bourgeoisie had acquired so much power that the princes took up its interests in order to overthrow the feudal nobility by means of the bourgeoisie, there began in all countries—in France in the sixteenth century —the real development of law, which in all countries except England proceeded on the basis of the Roman Codex. In England, too, Roman legal principles had to be introduced to further the development of civil law (especially in the case of movable property). (It must not be forgotten that law has just as little an independent history as religion.)

In civil law the existing property relationships are declared to be the result of the general will. The *jus utendi et abutendi*[4] itself asserts on the one hand the fact that private property has become entirely independent of the community, and on the other the illusion that private property itself is based solely on the private will, the arbitrary disposal of the thing. In practice, the *abuti*[5] has very definite economic limitations for the owner of private property, if he does not wish to see his property and hence his *jus abutendi* pass into other hands, since actually the thing, considered merely with reference to his will, is not a thing at all, but only becomes a thing, true property in intercourse, and independently of the law (a *relationship*, which the philosophers call an idea[6]). This juridical illusion, which reduces law to the mere will, necessarily leads, in the further development of property relationships, to the position that a man may have a legal title to a thing without really having the thing. If, for instance, the income from a piece of land is lost owing to competition, then the proprietor has certainly his legal title to it along with the *jus utendi et abutendi*. But he can do nothing with it: he owns nothing as a landed proprietor if in addition he has not enough capital to cultivate his ground. This illusion of the jurists also explains the fact that for them, as for every code, it is altogether fortuitous that individuals enter into relationships among themselves (e.g., contracts); it explains why they consider that these relationships [can] be entered into or not at will, and that their content rests purely on the individual [free] will of the contracting parties.

Whenever, through the development of industry and commerce, new forms of intercourse have been evolved (e.g., ensurance companies, etc.), the law has always been compelled to admit them among the modes of acquiring property.

4. The right of using and consuming (also: abusing), i.e., of disposing of a thing at will.
5. Consuming or abusing.
6. Marginal note by Marx: *"For the philosophers relationship = idea.* They only know the relation of 'Man' to himself and hence for them all real relations become ideas."

[3. *Natural and Civilised Instruments of Production and Forms of Property*]

* * *[7] From the first, there follows the premise of a highly developed division of labour and an extensive commerce; from the second, the locality. In the first case the individuals must be brought together, in the second they find themselves alongside the given instrument of production as instruments of production themselves. Here, therefore, arises the difference between natural instruments of production and those created by civilisation. The field (water, etc.) can be regarded as a natural instrument of production. In the first case, that of the natural instrument of production, individuals are subservient to nature; in the second, to a product of labour. In the first case, therefore, property (landed property) appears as direct natural domination, in the second, as domination of labour, particularly of accumulated labour, capital. The first case presupposes that the individuals are united by some bond: family, tribe, the land itself, etc.; the second, that they are independent of one another and are only held together by exchange. In the first case, what is involved is chiefly an exchange between men and nature in which the labour of the former is exchanged for the products of the latter; in the second, it is predominantly an exchange of men among themselves. In the first case, average, human common sense is adequate—physical activity is as yet not separated from mental activity; in the second, the division between physical and mental labour must already be practically completed. In the first case, the domination of the proprietor over the propertyless may be based on a personal relationship, on a kind of community; in the second, it must have taken on a material shape in a third party—money. In the first case, small industry exists, but determined by the utilisation of the natural instrument of production and therefore without the distribution of labour among various individuals; in the second, industry exists only in and through the division of labour.

Our investigation hitherto started from the instruments of production, and it has already shown that private property was a necessity for certain industrial stages. In *industrie extractive* private property still coincides with labour; in small industry and all agriculture up till now property is the necessary consequence of the existing instruments of production; in big industry the contradiction between the instrument of production and private property appears for the first time and is the product of big industry; moreover, big industry must be highly developed to produce this contradiction.

7. Four pages of the manuscript are missing here.

And thus only with big industry does the abolition of private property become possible.

In big industry and competition the whole mass of conditions of existence, limitations, biases of individuals, are fused together into the two simplest forms: private property and labour. With money every form of intercourse, and intercourse itself, is considered fortuitous for the individuals. Thus money implies that all previous intercourse was only intercourse of individuals under particular conditions, not of individuals as individuals. These conditions are reduced to two: accumulated labour or private property, and actual labour. If both or one of these ceases, then intercourse comes to a standstill. The modern economists themselves, e.g., Sismondi, Cherbuliez, etc., oppose "association of individuals" to "association of capital." On the other hand, the individuals themselves are entirely subordinated to the division of labour and hence are brought into the most complete dependence on one another. Private property, insofar as within labour itself it is opposed to labour, evolves out of the necessity of accumulation, and has still, to begin with, rather the form of the communality; but in its further development it approaches more and more the modern form of private property. The division of labour implies from the outset the division of the *conditions* of labour, of tools and materials, and thus the splitting-up of accumulated capital among different owners, and thus, also, the division between capital and labour, and the different forms of property itself. The more the division of labour develops and accumulation grows, the sharper are the forms that this process of differentiation assumes. Labour itself can only exist on the premise of this fragmentation.

Thus two facts are here revealed.[8] First the productive forces appear as a world for themselves, quite independent of and divorced from the individuals, alongside the individuals: the reason for this is that the individuals, whose forces they are, exist split up and in opposition to one another, whilst, on the other hand, these forces are only real forces in the intercourse and association of these individuals. Thus, on the one hand, we have a totality of productive forces, which have, as it were, taken on a material form and are for the individuals no longer the forces of the individuals but of private property, and hence of the individuals only insofar as they are owners of private property themselves. Never, in any earlier period, have the productive forces taken on a form so indifferent to the intercourse of individuals *as* individuals, because their intercourse itself was formerly a restricted one. On the other hand, standing over against these productive forces, we have the majority of the individuals from whom these forces have been wrested away,

8. Marginal note by Engels: "Sismondi."

and who, robbed thus of all real life-content, have become abstract individuals, but who are, however, only by this fact put into a position to enter into relation with one another *as individuals.*

The only connection which still links them with the productive forces and with their own existence—labour—has lost all semblance of self-activity and only sustains their life by stunting it. While in the earlier periods self-activity and the production of material life were separated, in that they devolved on different persons, and while, on account of the narrowness of the individuals themselves, the production of material life was considered as a subordinate mode of self-activity, they now diverge to such an extent that altogether material life appears as the end, and what produces this material life, labour (which is now the only possible but, as we see, negative form of self-activity), as the means.

Thus things have now come to such a pass, that the individuals must appropriate the existing totality of productive forces, not only to achieve self-activity, but, also, merely to safeguard their very existence. This appropriation is first determined by the object to be appropriated, the productive forces, which have been developed to a totality and which only exist within a universal intercourse. From this aspect alone, therefore, this appropriation must have a universal character corresponding to the productive forces and the intercourse. The appropriation of these forces is itself nothing more than the development of the individual capacities corresponding to the material instruments of production. The appropriation of a totality of instruments of production is, for this very reason, the development of a totality of capacities in the individuals themselves. This appropriation is further determined by the persons appropriating. Only the proletarians of the present day, who are completely shut off from all self-activity, are in a position to achieve a complete and no longer restricted self-activity, which consists in the appropriation of a totality of productive forces and in the thus postulated development of a totality of capacities. All earlier revolutionary appropriations were restricted; individuals, whose self-activity was restricted by a crude instrument of production and a limited intercourse, appropriated this crude instrument of production, and hence merely achieved a new state of limitation. Their instrument of production became their property, but they themselves remained subordinate to the division of labour and their own instrument of production. In all expropriations up to now, a mass of individuals remained subservient to a single instrument of production; in the appropriation by the proletarians, a mass of instruments of production must be made subject to each individual, and property to all. Modern universal intercourse can be controlled by individuals, therefore, only when controlled by all.

This appropriation is further determined by the manner in which it must be effected. It can only be effected through a union, which by the character of the proletariat itself can again only be a universal one, and through a revolution, in which, on the one hand, the power of the earlier mode of production and intercourse and social organisation is overthrown, and, on the other hand, there develops the universal character and the energy of the proletariat, without which the revolution cannot be accomplished; and in which, further, the proletariat rids itself of everything that still clings to it from its previous position in society.

Only at this stage does self-activity coincide with material life, which corresponds to the development of individuals into complete individuals and the casting-off of all natural limitations. The transformation of labour into self-activity corresponds to the transformation of the earlier limited intercourse into the intercourse of individuals as such. With the appropriation of the total productive forces through united individuals, private property comes to an end. Whilst previously in history a particular condition always appeared as accidental, now the isolation of individuals and the particular private gain of each man have themselves become accidental.

The individuals, who are no longer subject to the division of labour, have been conceived by the philosophers as an ideal, under the name "Man." They have conceived the whole process which we have outlined as the evolutionary process of "Man," so that at every historical stage "Man" was substituted for the individuals and shown as the motive force of history. The whole process was thus conceived as a process of the self-estrangement of "Man," and this was essentially due to the fact that the average individual of the later stage was always foisted on to the earlier stage, and the consciousness of a later age on to the individuals of an earlier. Through this inversion, which from the first is an abstract image of the actual conditions, it was possible to transform the whole of history into an evolutionary process of consciousness.

Finally, from the conception of history we have sketched we obtain these further conclusions: (1) In the development of productive forces there comes a stage when productive forces and means of intercourse are brought into being, which, under the existing relationships, only cause mischief, and are no longer productive but destructive forces (machinery and money); and connected with this a class is called forth, which has to bear all the burdens of society without enjoying its advantages, which, ousted from society, is forced into the most decided antagonism to all other classes; a class which forms the majority of all members of society, and from which emanates the consciousness of the necessity of a fundamental revolution, the communist consciousness, which may, of course, arise among the other classes too through the contemplation of the situation of this class. (2) The conditions under which definite productive forces can be applied, are the conditions of the rule of a definite class of society, whose social power, deriving from its property, has its *practical*-idealistic expression in each case in the form of the State; and, therefore, every revolutionary struggle is directed against a class, which till then has been in power.[9] (3) In all revolutions up till now the mode of activity always remained unscathed and it was only a question of a different distribution of this activity, a new distribution of labour to other persons, whilst the communist revolution is directed against the preceding *mode* of activity, does away with *labour*, and abolishes the rule of all classes with the classes themselves, because it is carried through by the class which no longer counts as a class in society, is not recognised as a class, and is in itself the expression of the dissolution of all classes, nationalities, etc., within present society; and (4) Both for the production on a mass scale of this communist consciousness, and for the success of the cause itself, the alteration of men on a mass scale is necessary, an alteration which can only take place in a practical movement, a *revolution*; this revolution is necessary, therefore, not only because the *ruling* class cannot be overthrown in any other way, but also because the class *overthrowing* it can only in a revolution succeed in ridding itself of all the muck of ages and become fitted to found society anew.

C. COMMUNISM. THE PRODUCTION OF THE FORM OF INTERCOURSE ITSELF

Communism differs from all previous movements in that it overturns the basis of all earlier relations of production and intercourse, and for the first time consciously treats all natural premises as the creatures of hitherto existing men, strips them of their natural character and subjugates them to the power of the united individuals. Its organisation is, therefore, essentially economic, the material production of the conditions of this unity; it turns existing conditions into conditions of unity. The reality, which communism is creating, is precisely the true basis for rendering it impossible that anything should exist independently of individuals, insofar as reality is only a product of the preceding intercourse of individuals themselves. Thus the communists in practice treat the conditions created up to now by production and intercourse as inorganic con-

9. Marginal note by Marx: "The people are interested in maintaining the present state of production."

ditions, without, however, imagining that it was the plan or the destiny of previous generations to give them material, and without believing that these conditions were inorganic for the individuals creating them. The difference between the individual as a person and what is accidental to him is not a conceptual difference but a historical fact. This distinction has a different significance at different times—e.g., the estate as something accidental to the individual in the eighteenth century, the family more or less too. It is not a distinction that we have to make for each age, but one which each age makes itself from among the different elements which it finds in existence, and indeed not according to any theory, but compelled by material collisions in life. What appears accidental to the later age as opposed to the earlier—and this applies also to the elements handed down by an earlier age—is a form of intercourse which corresponded to a definite stage of development of the productive forces. The relation of the productive forces to the form of intercourse is the relation of the form of intercourse to the occupation or activity of the individuals. (The fundamental form of this activity is, of course, material, on which depend all other forms—mental, political, religious, etc. The various shaping of material life is, of course, in every case dependent on the needs which are already developed, and the production, as well as the satisfaction, of these needs is an historical process, which is not found in the case of a sheep or a dog. (Stirner's refractory principal argument *adversus hominem*), although sheep and dogs in their present form certainly, but *malgré eux*, are products of an historical process.) The conditions under which individuals have intercourse with each other, so long as the above-mentioned contradiction is absent, are conditions appertaining to their individuality, in no way external to them; conditions under which these definite individuals, living under definite relations, can alone produce their material life and what is connected with it, are thus the conditions of their self-activity and are produced by this self-activity.[1] The definite condition under which they produce, thus corresponds, as long as the contradiction has not yet appeared, to the reality of their conditioned nature, their one-sided existence, the one-sidedness of which only becomes evident when the contradiction enters on the scene and thus exists for the later individuals. Then this condition appears as an accidental fetter, and the consciousness that it is a fetter is imputed to the earlier age as well.

These various conditions, which appear first as conditions of self-activity, later as fetters upon it, form in the whole evolution of history a coherent series of forms of intercourse, the coherence of which consists in this: in the place of an earlier form of inter-

1. Marginal note by Marx: "Production of the form of intercourse itself."

course, which has become a fetter, a new one is put, corresponding to the more developed productive forces and, hence, to the advanced mode of the self-activity of individuals—a form which in its turn becomes a fetter and is then replaced by another. Since these conditions correspond at every stage to the simultaneous development of the productive forces, their history is at the same time the history of the evolving productive forces taken over by each new generation, and is, therefore, the history of the development of the forces of the individuals themselves.

Since this evolution takes place naturally, i.e., is not subordinated to a general plan of freely combined individuals, it proceeds from various localities, tribes, nations, branches of labour, etc., each of which to start with develops independently of the others and only gradually enters into relation with the others. Furthermore, it takes place only very slowly; the various stages and interests are never completely overcome, but only subordinated to the prevailing interest and trail along beside the latter for centuries afterwards. It follows from this that within a nation itself the individuals, even apart from their pecuniary circumstances, have quite different developments, and that an earlier interest, the peculiar form of intercourse of which has already been ousted by that belonging to a later interest, remains for a long time afterwards in possession of a traditional power in the illusory community (State, law), which has won an existence independent of the individuals; a power which in the last resort can only be broken by a revolution. This explains why, with reference to individual points which allow of a more general summing-up, consciousness can sometimes appear further advanced than the contemporary empirical relationships, so that in the struggles of a latter epoch one can refer to earlier theoreticians as authorities.

On the other hand, in countries which, like North America, begin in an already advanced historical epoch, the development proceeds very rapidly. Such countries have no other natural premises than the individuals, who settled there and were led to do so because the forms of intercourse of the old countries did not correspond to their wants. Thus they begin with the most advanced individuals of the old countries, and, therefore, with the correspondingly most advanced form of intercourse, before this form of intercourse has been able to establish itself in the old countries.[2] This is the case with all colonies, insofar as they are not mere military or trading stations. Carthage, the Greek colonies, and Iceland in the

2. Personal energy of the individuals of various nations—Germans and Americans—energy even through cross-breeding—hence the cretinism of the Germans; in France and England, etc., foreign peoples transplanted to an already developed soil, in America to an entirely new soil; in Germany the natural population quietly stayed where it was. [*Marx*]

eleventh and twelfth centuries, provide examples of this. A similar relationship issues from conquest, when a form of intercourse which has evolved on another soil is brought over complete to the conquered country: whereas in its home it was still encumbered with interests and relationships left over from earlier periods, here it can and must be established completely and without hindrance, if only to assure the conquerors' lasting power. (England and Naples after the Norman conquest, when they received the most perfect form of feudal organisation.)

Nothing is more common than the notion that in history up till now it has only been a question of *taking*. The barbarians *take* the Roman Empire, and this fact of taking is made to explain the transition from the old world to the feudal system. In this taking by barbarians, however, the question is, whether the nation which is conquered has evolved industrial productive forces, as is the case with modern peoples, or whether their productive forces are based for the most part merely on their association and on the community. Taking is further determined by the object taken. A banker's fortune, consisting of paper, cannot be taken at all, without the taker's submitting to the conditions of production and intercourse of the country taken. Similarly the total industrial capital of a modern industrial country. And finally, everywhere there is very soon an end to taking, and when there is nothing more to take, you have to set about producing. From this necessity of producing, which very soon asserts itself, it follows that the form of community adopted by the settling conquerors must correspond to the stage of development of the productive forces they find in existence; or, if this is not the case from the start, it must change according to the productive forces. By this, too, is explained the fact, which people profess to have noticed everywhere in the period following the migration of the peoples, namely, that the servant was master, and that the conquerors very soon took over language, culture and manners from the conquered. The feudal system was by no means brought complete from Germany, but had its origin, as far as the conquerors were concerned, in the martial organisation of the army during the actual conquest, and this only evolved after the conquest into the feudal system proper through the action of the productive forces found in the conquered countries. To what an extent this form was determined by the productive forces is shown by the abortive attempts to realise other forms derived from reminiscences of ancient Rome (Charlemagne, etc.).

Thus all collisions in history have their origin, according to our view, in the contradiction between the productive forces and the form of intercourse. Incidentally, to lead to collisions in a country, this contradiction need not necessarily have reached its extreme limit in this particular country. The competition with industrially more advanced countries, brought about by the expansion of international intercourse, is sufficient to produce a similar contradiction in countries with a backward industry (e.g., the latent proletariat in Germany brought into view by the competition of English industry).

This contradiction between the productive forces and the form of intercourse, which, as we saw, has occurred several times in past history, without, however, endangering the basis, necessarily on each occasion burst out in a revolution, taking on at the same time various subsidiary forms, such as all-embracing collisions, collisions of various classes, contradiction of consciousness, battle of ideas, etc., political conflict, etc. From a narrow point of view one may isolate one of these subsidiary forms and consider it as the basis of these revolutions; and this is all the more easy as the individuals who started the revolutions had illusions about their own activity according to their degree of culture and the stage of historical development.

The transformation, through the division of labour, of personal powers (relationships) into material powers, cannot be dispelled by dismissing the general idea of it from one's mind, but can only be abolished by the individuals again subjecting these material powers to themselves and abolishing the division of labour.[3] This is not possible without the community. Only in community [with others has each] individual the means of cultivating his gifts in all directions; only in the community, therefore, is personal freedom possible. In the previous substitutes for the community, in the State, etc., personal freedom has existed only for the individuals who developed within the relationships of the ruling class, and only insofar as they were individuals of this class. The illusory community, in which individuals have up till now combined, always took on an independent existence in relation to them, and was at the same time, since it was the combination of one class over against another, not only a completely illusory community, but a new fetter as well. In the real community the individuals obtain their freedom in and through their association.

It follows from all we have been saying up till now that the communal relationship into which the individuals of a class entered, and which was determined by their common interests over against a third party, was always a community to which these individuals belonged only as average individuals, only insofar as they lived within the conditions of existence of their class—a relationship in which they participated not as individuals but as members of a class. With the community of revolutionary proletarians, on the

3. Marginal note by Engels: '(Feuerbach: being and essence.)"

other hand, who take their conditions of existence and those of all members of society under their control, it is just the reverse; it is as individuals that the individuals participate in it. It is just this combination of individuals (assuming the advanced stage of modern productive forces, of course) which puts the conditions of the free development and movement of individuals under their control—conditions which were previously abandoned to chance and had won an independent existence over against the separate individuals just because of their separation as individuals, and because of the necessity of their combination which had been determined by the division of labour, and through their separation had become a bond alien to them. Combination up till now (by no means an arbitrary one, such as is expounded for example in the *Contrat social*, but a necessary one) was an agreement upon these conditions, within which the individuals were free to enjoy the freaks of fortune (compare, e.g., the formation of the North American State and the South American republics). This right to the undisturbed enjoyment, within certain conditions, of fortuity and chance has up till now been called personal freedom. These conditions of existence are, of course, only the productive forces and forms of intercourse at any particular time.

If from a *philosophical* point of view one considers this evolution of individuals in the common conditions of existence of estates and classes, which followed on one another, and in the accompanying general conceptions forced upon them, it is certainly very easy to imagine that in these individuals the species, or "Man," has evolved, or that they evolved "Man"—and in this way one can give history some hard clouts on the ear.[4] One can conceive these various estates and classes to be specific terms of the general expression, subordinate varieties of the species, or evolutionary phases of "Man."

This subsuming of individuals under definite classes cannot be abolished until a class has taken shape, which has no longer any particular class interest to assert against the ruling class.

Individuals have always built on themselves, but naturally on themselves within their given historical conditions and relationships, not on the "pure" individual in the sense of the ideologists. But in the course of historical evolution, and precisely through the inevitable fact that within the division of labour social relationships take on an independent existence, there appears a division within the life of each individual, insofar as it is personal and insofar as it

---

4. The statement which frequently occurs with Saint Max that each is all that he is through the State is fundamentally the same as the statement that bourgeois is only a specimen of the bourgeois species; a statement which presupposes that the *class* of bourgeois existed before the individuals constituting it. [*Marx*]

Marginal note by Marx to this sentence: "With the philosophers *pre-existence* of the class."

is determined by some branch of labour and the conditions pertaining to it. (We do not mean it to be understood from this that, for example, the rentier, the capitalist, etc., cease to be persons; but their personality is conditioned and determined by quite definite class relationships, and the division appears only in their opposition to another class and, for themselves, only when they go bankrupt.) In the estate (and even more in the tribe) this is as yet concealed: for instance, a nobleman always remains a nobleman, a commoner always a commoner, apart from his other relationships, a quality inseparable from his individuality. The division between the personal and the class individual, the accidental nature of the conditions of life for the individual, appears only with the emergence of the class, which is itself a product of the bourgeoisie. This accidental character is only engendered and developed by competition and the struggle of individuals among themselves. Thus, in imagination, individuals seem freer under the dominance of the bourgeoisie than before, because their conditions of life seem accidental; in reality, of course, they are less free, because they are more subjected to the violence of things. The difference from the estate comes out particularly in the antagonism between the bourgeoisie and the proletariat. When the estate of the urban burghers, the corporations, etc., emerged in opposition to the landed nobility, their condition of existence—movable property and craft labour, which had already existed latently before their separation from the feudal ties—appeared as something positive, which was asserted against feudal landed property, and, therefore, in its own way at first took on a feudal form. Certainly the refugee serfs treated their previous servitude as something accidental to their personality. But here they only were doing what every class that is freeing itself from a fetter does; and they did not free themselves as a class but separately. Moreover, they did not rise above the system of estates, but only formed a new estate, retaining their previous mode of labour even in their new situation, and developing it further by freeing it from its earlier fetters, which no longer corresponded to the development already attained.[5]

For the proletarians, on the other hand, the condition of their existence, labour, and with it all the conditions of existence governing modern society, have become something accidental, something

5. N.B. It must not be forgotten that the serfs' very need of existing and the impossibility of a large-scale economy, which involved the distribution of the allotments among the serfs, very soon reduced the services of the serfs to their lord to an average of payments in kind and statute-labour. This made it possible for the serf to accumulate movable property and hence facilitated his escape out of possession of his lord and gave him the prospect of making his way as an urban citizen; it also created gradations among the serfs, so that the runaway serfs were already half burghers. It is likewise obvious that the serfs who were masters of a craft had the best chance of acquiring movable property. [*Marx*]

over which they, as separate individuals, have no control, and over which no *social* organisation can give them control. The contradiction between the individuality of each separate proletarian and labour, the condition of life forced upon him, becomes evident to him himself, for he is sacrificed from youth upwards and, within his own class, has no chance of arriving at the conditions which would place him in the other class.

Thus, while the refugee serfs only wished to be free to develop and assert those conditions of existence which were already there, and hence, in the end, only arrived at free labour, the proletarians, if they are to assert themselves as individuals, will have to abolish the very condition of their existence hitherto (which has, moreover, been that of all society up to the present), namely, labour. Thus they find themselves directly opposed to the form in which, hitherto, the individuals, of which society consists, have given themselves collective expression, that is, the State. In order, therefore, to assert themselves as individuals, they must overthrow the State.

PART II

The Critique of Capitalism

Wage Labour and Capital

KARL MARX

Shortly after adumbrating the materialist conception of history in the 1844 manuscripts and formulating it comprehensively in Part I of *The German Ideology*, Marx turned to the economic studies that were going to preoccupy him in the ensuing years. This did not signify any change of interests or outlook but was the logical outgrowth of the position taken in his earlier writings. If the thesis on "alienated labor" was to be made scientifically cogent and if the expectation of coming proletarian revolution was to be based upon it, he needed to show the capital-labor relationship, which he took to be the core of the bourgeois socio-economic system, to be dialectically self-destructive, i.e., transitory by virtue of its inner dynamics of development. The first work in which he attempted this analysis was *Wage Labour and Capital*.

Having first presented it in lectures to a German workers' society in Brussels in December, 1847, Marx printed the work in April, 1849, in the *Neue Rheinische Zeitung*, of which he was editor-in-chief. Several pamphlet editions appeared in later years. In editing it for the German edition of 1891 (the version that appears here), Engels made some changes in the text, mainly centering in the substitution of the phrase "labour power" for the term "labour" in contexts in which Marx had originally spoken of the worker's sale of his labour to the capitalist. This, as Engels explained in his preface to the 1891 edition, brought the reasoning of the pamphlet into line with the analysis of the capital-labor relationship as Marx had refined it by 1859, when he published *A Contribution to the Critique of Political Economy*.

Despite this, it may be said that what Marx produced in the lectures of late 1847 was the future argument of *Capital* in embryo.

I

From various quarters we have been reproached with not having presented the *economic relations* which constitute the material foundation of the present class struggles and national struggles. We have designedly touched upon these relations only where they directly forced themselves to the front in political conflicts.

The point was, above all, to trace the class struggle in current history, and to prove empirically by means of the historical material already at hand and which is being newly created daily, that, with the subjugation of the working class that February and March[1] had wrought, its opponents were simultaneously defeated—the bourgeois republicans in France and the bourgeois and peasant classes which were fighting feudal absolutism throughout the continent of Europe; that the victory of the "honest republic" in France was at the same time the downfall of the nations that had responded to the February Revolution by heroic wars of independence; finally, that Europe, with the defeat of the revolutionary workers, had relapsed into its old double slavery, the *Anglo-Russian* slavery. The June struggle in Paris, the fall of Vienna, the tragicomedy of Berlin's November, 1848, the desperate exertions of Poland, Italy and Hungary, the starving of Ireland into submission—these were the chief factors which characterised the European class struggle between bourgeoisie and working class and by means of which we proved that every revolutionary upheaval, however remote from the class struggle its goal may appear to be, must fail until the revolutionary working class is victorious, that every social reform remains a utopia until the proletarian revolution and the feudalistic counter-revolution measure swords in a *world war*. In our presentation, as in reality, *Belgium* and *Switzerland* were tragicomic genre-pictures akin to caricature in the great historical tableau, the one being the model state of the bourgeois monarchy, the other the model state of the bourgeois republic, both of them states which imagine themselves to be as independent of the class struggle as of the European revolution.

Now, after our readers have seen the class struggle develop in colossal political forms in 1848, the time has come to deal more closely with the economic relations themselves on which the existence of the bourgeoisie and its class rule, as well as the slavery of the workers, are founded.

We shall present in three large sections: (1) the relation of *wage labour to capital*, the slavery of the worker, the domination of the capitalist; (2) *the inevitable destruction of the middle bourgeois classes and of the so-called peasant estate under the present system*; (3) *the commercial subjugation and exploitation of the bourgeois classes of the various European nations* by the despot of the world market—*England*.

We shall try to make our presentation as simple and popular as possible and shall not presuppose even the most elementary notions of political economy. We wish to be understood by the workers.

1. This refers to the Revolutions of February 23–24, 1848, in Paris, March 13 in Vienna, and March 18 in Berlin.

Moreover, the most remarkable ignorance and confusion of ideas prevails in Germany in regard to the simplest economic relations, from the accredited defenders of the existing state of things to the *socialist miracle workers* and the *unrecognised political geniuses* in which fragmented Germany is even richer than in sovereign princes.

Now, therefore, for the first question: *What are wages? How are they determined?*

If workers were asked: "How much are your wages?" one would reply: "I get a mark a day from my employer"; another, "I get two marks," and so on. According to the different trades to which they belong, they would mention different sums of money which they receive from their respective employers for the performance of a particular piece of work, for example, weaving a yard of linen or typesetting a printed sheet. In spite of the variety of their statements, they would all agree on one point: wages are the sum of money paid by the capitalist for a particular labour time or for a particular output of labour.

The capitalist, it seems, therefore, *buys* their labour with money. They *sell* him their labour for money. But this is merely the appearance. In reality what they sell to the capitalist for money is their labour *power*. The capitalist buys this labour power for a day, a week, a month, etc. And after he has bought it, he uses it by having the workers work for the stipulated time. For the same sum with which the capitalist has bought their labour power, for example, two marks, he could have bought two pounds of sugar or a definite amount of any other commodity. The two marks, with which he bought two pounds of sugar, are the *price* of the two pounds of sugar. The two marks, with which he bought twelve hours' use of labour power, are the price of twelve hours' labour. Labour power, therefore, is a commodity, neither more nor less than sugar. The former is measured by the clock, the latter by the scales.

The workers exchange their commodity, labour power, for the commodity of the capitalist, for money, and this exchange takes place in a definite ratio. So much money for so long a use of labour power. For twelve hours' weaving, two marks. And do not the two marks represent all the other commodities which I can buy for two marks? In fact, therefore, the worker has exchanged his commodity, labour power, for other commodities of all kinds and that in a definite ratio. By giving him two marks, the capitalist has given him so much meat, so much clothing, so much fuel, light, etc., in exchange for his day's labour. Accordingly, the two marks express the ratio in which labour power is exchanged for other commodities, the *exchange value* of his labour power. The exchange value of a commodity, reckoned in *money*, is what is called its *price*. *Wages* are only a special name for the price of labour power, commonly called the *price of labour*, for the price of this peculiar commodity which has no other repository than human flesh and blood.

Let us take any worker, say, a weaver. The capitalist supplies him with the loom and yarn. The weaver sets to work and the yarn is converted into linen. The capitalist takes possession of the linen and sells it, say, for twenty marks. Now are the wages of the weaver a *share* in the linen, in the twenty marks, in the product of his labour? By no means. Long before the linen is sold, perhaps long before its weaving is finished, the weaver has received his wages. The capitalist, therefore, does not pay these wages with the money which he will obtain from the linen, but with money already in reserve. Just as the loom and the yarn are not the product of the weaver to whom they are supplied by his employer, so likewise with the commodities which the weaver receives in exchange for his commodity, labour power. It was possible that his employer found no purchaser at all for his linen. It was possible that he did not get even the amount of the wages by its sale. It is possible that he sells it very profitably in comparison with the weaver's wages. All that has nothing to do with the weaver. The capitalist buys the labour power of the weaver with a part of his available wealth, of his capital, just as he has bought the raw material—the yarn—and the instrument of labour—the loom—with another part of his wealth. After he has made these purchases, and these purchases include the labour power necessary for the production of linen, he produces only with the *raw materials and instruments of labour belonging to him.* For the latter include now, true enough, our good weaver as well, who has as little share in the product or the price of the product as the loom has.

Wages are, therefore, not the worker's share in the commodity produced by him. Wages are the part of already existing commodities with which the capitalist buys for himself a definite amount of productive labour power.

Labour power is, therefore, a commodity which its possessor, the wage-worker, sells to capital. Why does he sell it? In order to live.

But the exercise of labour power, labour, is the worker's own life-activity, the manifestation of his own life. And this *life-activity* he sells to another person in order to secure the necessary *means of subsistence.* Thus his life-activity is for him only a means to enable him to exist. He works in order to live. He does not even reckon labour as part of his life, it is rather a sacrifice of his life. It is a commodity which he has made over to another. Hence, also, the product of his activity is not the object of his activity. What he produces for himself is not the silk that he weaves, not the gold that he draws from the mine, not the palace that he builds. What he produces for himself is *wages*, and silk, gold, palace resolve themselves for him into a definite quantity of the means of subsistence, perhaps into a cotton jacket, some copper coins and a lodging in a cellar. And the worker, who for twelve hours weaves, spins, drills, turns, builds, shovels, breaks stones, carries loads, etc.—does he consider this twelve hours' weaving, spinning, drilling, turning, building, shovelling, stone breaking as a manifestation of his life, as life? On the contrary, life begins for him where this activity ceases, at table, in the public house, in bed. The twelve hours' labour, on the other hand, has no meaning for him as weaving, spinning, drilling, etc., but as *earnings*, which bring him to the table, to the public house, into bed. If the silk worm were to spin in order to continue its existence as a caterpillar, it would be a complete wage-worker. Labour power was not always a *commodity*. Labour was not always wage labour, that is, *free labour*. The *slave* did not sell his labour power to the slave owner, any more than the ox sells its services to the peasant. The slave, together with his labour power, is sold once and for all to his owner. He is a commodity which can pass from the hand of one owner to that of another. He is *himself* a commodity, but the labour power is not *his* commodity. The *serf* sells only a part of his labour power. He does not receive a wage from the owner of the land; rather the owner of the land receives a tribute from him.

The serf belongs to the land and turns over to the owner of the land the fruits thereof. The *free labourer*, on the other hand, sells himself and, indeed, sells himself piecemeal. He sells at auction eight, ten, twelve, fifteen hours of his life, day after day, to the highest bidder, to the owner of the raw materials, instruments of labour and means of subsistence, that is, to the capitalist. The worker belongs neither to an owner nor to the land, but eight, ten, twelve, fifteen hours of his daily life belong to him who buys them. The worker leaves the capitalist to whom he hires himself whenever he likes, and the capitalist discharges him whenever he thinks fit, as soon as he no longer gets any profit out of him, or not the anticipated profit. But the worker, whose sole source of livelihood is the sale of his labour power, cannot leave the *whole class of purchasers, that is, the capitalist class*, without renouncing his existence. He belongs not to this or that capitalist but to the *capitalist class*, and, moreover, it is his business to dispose of himself, that is, to find a purchaser within this capitalist class.

Now, before going more closely into the relation between capital and wage labour, we shall present briefly the most general relations which come into consideration in the determination of wages.

Wages, as we have seen, are the *price* of a definite commodity, of labour power. Wages are, therefore, determined by the same laws that determine the price of every other commodity. The question, therefore, is, *how is the price of a commodity determined?*

II

By what is the *price* of a commodity determined?

By competition between buyers and sellers, by the relation of inquiry to delivery, of demand to supply. Competition, by which the price of a commodity is determined, is *three-sided*.

The same commodity is offered by various sellers. With goods of the same quality, the one who sells most cheaply is certain of driving the others out of the field and securing the greatest sale for himself. Thus, the sellers mutually contend among themselves for sales, for the market. Each of them desires to sell, to sell as much as possible and, if possible, to sell alone, to the exclusion of the other sellers. Hence, one sells cheaper than another. Consequently, *competition* takes place *among the sellers*, which *depresses* the price of the *commodities* offered by them.

But *competition* also takes place *among the buyers*, which in its turn *causes* the commodities offered to *rise* in price.

Finally *competition* occurs *between buyers and sellers;* the former desire to buy as cheaply as possible, the latter to sell as dearly as possible. The result of this competition between buyers and sellers will depend upon how the two above-mentioned sides of the competition are related, that is, whether the competition is stronger in the army of buyers or in the army of sellers. Industry leads two armies into the field against each other, each of which again carries on a battle within its own ranks, among its own troops. The army whose troops beat each other up the least gains the victory over the opposing host.

Let us suppose there are 100 bales of cotton on the market and at the same time buyers for 1,000 bales of cotton. In this case, therefore, the demand is ten times as great as the supply. Competition will be very strong among the buyers, each of whom desires to get one, and if possible all, of the hundred bales for himself. This example is no arbitrary assumption. We have experienced periods of cotton crop failure in the history of the trade when a few capitalists in alliance have tried to buy, not one hundred bales, but all the cotton stocks in the world. Hence, in the example mentioned, one buyer will seek to drive the other from the field by offering a relatively higher price per bale of cotton. The cotton sellers, who see that the troops of the enemy army are engaged in the most violent struggle among themselves and that the sale of all their hundred bales is absolutely certain, will take good care not to fall out among themselves and depress the price of cotton at the moment when their adversaries are competing with one another to force it up. Thus, peace suddenly descends on the army of the sellers. They stand facing the buyers as one man, fold their arms philosophically, and there would be no bounds to their demands were it not that the offers of even the most persistent and eager buyers have very definite limits.

If, therefore, the supply of a commodity is lower than the demand for it, then only slight competition, or none at all, takes place among the sellers. In the same proportion as this competition decreases, competition increases among the buyers. The result is a more or less considerable rise in commodity prices.

It is well known that the reverse case with a reverse result occurs more frequently. Considerable surplus of supply over demand; desperate competition among the sellers; lack of buyers; disposal of goods at ridiculously low prices.

But what is the meaning of a rise, a fall in prices; what is the meaning of high price, low price? A grain of sand is high when examined through a microscope, and a tower is low when compared with a mountain. And if price is determined by the relation between supply and demand, what determines the relation between supply and demand?

Let us turn to the first bourgeois we meet. He will not reflect for an instant but, like another Alexander the Great, will cut this metaphysical knot with the multiplication table. If the production of the goods which I sell has cost me 100 marks, he will tell us, and if I get 110 marks from the sale of these goods, within the year of course—then that is sound, honest, legitimate profit. But if I get in exchange 120 or 130 marks, that is a high profit; and if I get as much as 200 marks, that would be an extraordinary, an enormous profit. What, therefore, serves the bourgeois as his *measure* of profit? The *cost of production* of his commodity. If he receives in exchange for this commodity an amount of other commodities which it has cost less to produce, he has lost. If he receives in exchange for his commodity an amount of other commodities the production of which has cost more, he has gained. And he calculates the rise or fall of the profit according to the degree in which the exchange value of his commodity stands above or below zero—the *cost of production*.

We have thus seen how the changing relation of supply and demand causes now a rise and now a fall of prices, now high, now low prices. If the price of a commodity rises considerably because of inadequate supply or disproportionate increase of the demand, the price of some other commodity must necessarily have fallen proportionately, for the price of a commodity only expresses in money the ratio in which other commodities are given in exchange for it. If, for example, the price of a yard of silk material rises from five marks to six marks, the price of silver in relation to silk material has fallen and likewise the prices of all other commodities that have remained at their old prices have fall in relation to the silk. One has to give a larger amount of them in exchange to get the same amount of silks. What will be the consequence of the rising price of a commodity? A mass of capital will be thrown into that flourishing branch of industry and this influx of capital into the domain of the favoured industry will continue until it yields the ordinary profits or, rather, until the price of its products, through overproduction, sinks below the cost of production.

Conversely, if the price of a commodity falls below its cost of production, capital will be withdrawn from the production of this commodity. Except in the case of a branch of industry which has become obsolete and must, therefore, perish, the production of such a commodity, that is, its supply, will go on decreasing owing to this flight of capital until it corresponds to the demand, and consequently its price is again on a level with its cost of production or, rather, until the supply has sunk below the demand, that is, until its price rises again above its cost of production, *for the current price of a commodity is always either above or below its cost of production.*

We see how capital continually migrates in and out, out of the domain of one industry into that of another. High prices bring too great an immigration and low prices too great an emigration.

We could show from another point of view how not only supply but also demand is determined by the cost of production. But this would take us too far away from our subject.

We have just seen how the fluctuations of supply and demand continually bring the price of a commodity back to the cost of production. *The real price of a commodity, it is true, is always above or below its cost of production; but rise and fall reciprocally balance each other*, so that within a certain period of time, taking the ebb and flow of the industry together, commodities are exchanged for one another in accordance with their cost of production, their price, therefore, being determined by their cost of production.

This determination of price by cost of production is not to be understood in the sense of the economists. The economists say that the *average price* of commodities is equal to the cost of production; that this is a *law*. The anarchical movement, in which rise is compensated by fall and fall by rise, is regarded by them as chance. With just as much right one could regard the fluctuations as the law and the determination by the cost of production as chance, as has actually been done by other economists. But it is solely these fluctuations, which, looked at more closely, bring with them the most fearful devastations and, like earthquakes, cause bourgeois society to tremble to its foundations—it is solely in the course of these fluctuations that prices are determined by the cost of production. The total movement of this disorder is its order. In the course of this industrial anarchy, in this movement in a circle, competition compensates, so to speak, for one excess by means of another.

We see, therefore, that the price of a commodity is determined by its cost of production in such manner that the periods in which the price of this commodity rises above its cost of production are compensated by the periods in which it sinks below the cost of production, and vice versa. This does not hold good, of course, for separate, particular industrial products but only for the whole branch of industry. Consequently, it also does not hold good for the individual industrialist but only for the whole class of industrialists.

The determination of price by the cost of production is equivalent to the determination of price by the labour time necessary for the manufacture of a commodity, for the cost of production consists of (1) raw materials and depreciation of instruments, that is, of industrial products the production of which has cost a certain amount of labour days and which, therefore, represent a certain amount of labour time, and (2) of direct labour, the measure of which is, precisely, time.

Now, the same general laws that regulate the price of commodities in general of course also regulate *wages*, the *price of labour*.

Wages will rise and fall according to the relation of supply and demand, according to the turn taken by the competition between the buyers of labour power, the capitalists, and the sellers of labour power, the workers. The fluctuations in wages correspond in general to the fluctuations in prices of commodities. *Within these fluctuations, however, the price of labour will be determined by the cost of production, by the labour time necessary to produce this commodity—labour power.*

What, then, is the cost of production of labour power?

It is the cost required for maintaining the worker as a worker and of developing him into a worker.

The less the period of training, therefore, that any work requires the smaller is the cost of production of the worker and the lower is the price of his labour, his wages. In those branches of industry in which hardly any period of apprenticeship is required and where the mere bodily existence of the worker suffices, the cost necessary for his production is almost confined to the commodities necessary for keeping him alive and capable of working. The *price of his labour* will, therefore, be determined by the *price of the necessary means of subsistence*.

Another consideration, however, also comes in. The manufacturer in calculating his cost of production and, accordingly, the price of the products takes into account the wear and tear of the instruments of labour. If, for example, a machine costs him 1,000 marks and wears out in ten years, he adds 100 marks annually to the price of the commodities so as to be able to replace the worn-out machine by a new one at the end of ten years. In the same way, in calculating the cost of production of simple labour power, there must be included the cost of reproduction, whereby the race of workers is enabled to multiply and to replace worn-out workers by new ones. Thus the depreciation of the worker is taken into account in the same way as the depreciation of the machine.

The cost of production of simple labour power, therefore, amounts to the *cost of existence and reproduction of the worker*. The price of this cost of existence and reproduction constitutes wages. Wages so determined are called the *wage minimum*. This wage minimum, like the determination of the price of commodities by the cost of production in general, does not hold good for the *single individual* but for the *species*. Individual workers, millions of workers, do not get enough to be able to exist and reproduce themselves; *but the wages of the whole working class* level down, within their fluctuations, to this minimum.

Now that we have arrived at an understanding of the most general laws which regulate wages like the price of any other commodity, we can go into our subject more specifically.

III

Capital consists of raw materials, instruments of labour and means of subsistence of all kinds, which are utilised in order to produce new raw materials, new instruments of labour and new means of subsistence. All these component parts of capital are creations of labour, products of labour, *accumulated labour*. Accumulated labour which serves as a means of new production is capital.

So say the economists.

What is a Negro slave? A man of the black race. The one explanation is as good as the other.

A Negro is a Negro. He only becomes a slave in certain relations. A cotton-spinning jenny is a machine for spinning cotton. It becomes *capital* only in certain relations. Torn from these relationships it is no more capital than gold in itself is *money* or sugar the price of sugar.

In production, men not only act on nature but also on one another. They produce only by co-operating in a certain way and mutually exchanging their activities. In order to produce, they enter into definite connections and relations with one another and only within these social connections and relations does their action on nature, does production, take place.

These social relations into which the producers enter with one another, the conditions under which they exchange their activities and participate in the whole act of production, will naturally vary according to the character of the means of production. With the invention of a new instrument of warfare, firearms, the whole internal organisation of the army necessarily changed; the relationships within which individuals can constitute an army and act as an army were transformed and the relations of different armies to one another also changed.

Thus the social relations within which individuals produce, the social relations of production, change, are transformed, with the change and development of the material means of production, the productive forces. The relations of production in their totality constitute what are called the social relations, society, and, specifically, a society at a definite stage of historical development, a society with a peculiar, distinctive character. *Ancient* society, *feudal* society, *bourgeois* society are such totalities of production relations, each of which at the same time denotes a special stage of development in the history of mankind.

Capital, also, is a social relation of production. *It is a bourgeois production relation,* a production relation of bourgeois society. Are not the means of subsistence, the instruments of labour, the raw materials of which capital consists, produced and accumulated under given social conditions, in definite social relations? Are they not utilised for new production under given social conditions, in definite social relations? And is it not just this definite social character which turns the products serving for new production into *capital?*

Capital consists not only of means of subsistence, instruments of labour and raw materials, not only of material products; it consists just as much of *exchange values.* All the products of which it consists are *commodities.* Capital is, therefore, not only a sum of material products; it is a sum of commodities, of exchange values, *of social magnitudes.*

Capital remains the same, whether we put cotton in place of wool, rice in place of wheat or steamships in place of railways, provided only that the cotton, the rice, the steamships—the body of capital—have the same exchange value, the same price as the wool, the wheat, the railways in which it was previously incorporated. The body of capital can change continually without the capital suffering the slightest alteration.

But while all capital is a sum of commodities, that is, of

exchange values, not every sum of commodities, of exchange values, is capital.

Every sum of exchange values is an exchange value. Every separate exchange value is a sum of exchange values. For instance, a house that is worth 1,000 marks is an exchange value of 1,000 marks. A piece of paper worth a pfennig is a sum of exchange values of one-hundred hundredths of a pfennig. Products which are exchangeable for others are commodities. The particular ratio in which they are exchangeable constitutes their *exchange value* or, expressed in money, their *price*. The quantity of these products can change nothing in their quality of being *commodities* or representing an *exchange value* or having a definite price. Whether a tree is large or small it is a tree. Whether we exchange iron for other products in ounces or in hundred-weights, does this make any difference in its character as commodity, as exchange value? It is a commodity of greater or lesser value, of higher or lower price, depending upon the quantity.

How, then, does any amount of commodities, of exchange value, become capital?

By maintaining and multiplying itself as an independent social *power*, that is, as the power *of a portion of society*, by means of its *exchange for direct, living labour power*. The existence of a class which possesses nothing but its capacity to labour is a necessary prerequisite of capital.

It is only the domination of accumulated, past, materialised labour over direct, living labour that turns accumulated labour into capital.

Capital does not consist in accumulated labour serving living labour as a means for new production. It consists in living labour serving accumulated labour as a means of maintaining and multiplying the exchange value of the latter.

What takes place in the exchange between capitalist and wage-worker?

The worker receives means of subsistence in exchange for his labour power, but the capitalist receives in exchange for his means of subsistence labour, the productive activity of the worker, the creative power whereby the worker not only replaces what he consumes but *gives to the accumulated labour a greater value than it previously possessed*. The worker receives a part of the available means of subsistence from the capitalist. For what purpose do these means of subsistence serve him? For immediate consumption. As soon, however, as I consume the means of subsistence, they are irretrievably lost to me unless I use the time during which I am kept alive by them in order to produce new means of subsistence, in order during consumption to create by my labour new values in place of the values which perish in being consumed. But it is just this noble reproductive power that the worker surrenders to the capitalist in exchange for means of subsistence received. He has, therefore, lost it for himself.

Let us take an example: a tenant farmer gives his day labourer five silver groschen a day. For these five silver groschen the labourer works all day on the farmer's field and thus secures him a return of ten silver groschen. The farmer not only gets the value replaced that he has to give the day labourer; he doubles it. He has therefore employed, consumed, the five silver groschen that he gave to the labourer in a fruitful, productive manner. He has bought with the five silver groschen just that labour and power of the labourer which produces agricultural products of double value and makes ten silver groschen out of five. The day labourer, on the other hand, receives in place of his productive power, the effect of which he has bargained away to the farmer, five silver groschen, which he exchanges for means of subsistence, and these he consumes with greater or less rapidity. The five silver groschen have, therefore, been consumed in a double way, *reproductively* for capital, for they have been exchanged for labour power which produced ten silver groschen, *unproductively* for the worker, for they have been exchanged for means of subsistence which have disappeared forever and the value of which he can only recover by repeating the same exchange with the farmer. *Thus capital presupposes wage labour; wage labour presupposes capital. They reciprocally condition the existence of each other; they reciprocally bring forth each other.*

Does a worker in a cotton factory produce merely cotton textiles? No, he produces capital. He produces values which serve afresh to command his labour and by means of it to create new values.

Capital can only increase by exchanging itself for labour power, by calling wage labour to life. The labour power of the wage-worker can only be exchanged for capital by increasing capital, by strengthening the power whose slave it is. *Hence, increase of capital is increase of the proletariat, that is, of the working class.*

The interests of the capitalist and those of the worker are, therefore, *one and the same*, assert the bourgeois and their economists. Indeed! The worker perishes if capital does not employ him. Capital perishes if it does not exploit labour power, and in order to exploit it, it must buy it. The faster capital intended for production, productive capital, increases, the more, therefore, industry prospers, the more the bourgeoisie enriches itself and the better business is, the more workers does the capitalist need, the more dearly does the worker sell himself.

The indispensable condition for a tolerable situation of the worker is, *therefore, the fastest possible growth of productive capital*.

But what is the growth of productive capital? Growth of the power of accumulated labour over living labour. Growth of the domination of the bourgeoisie over the working class. If wage labour produces the wealth of others that rules over it, the power that is hostile to it, capital, then the means of employment, the means of subsistence, flow back to it from this hostile power, on condition that it makes itself afresh into a part of capital, into the lever which hurls capital anew into an accelerated movement of growth.

To say that the interests of capital and those of the workers are one and the same is only to say that capital and wage labour are two sides of one and the same relation. The one conditions the other, just as usurer and squanderer condition each other.

As long as the wage-worker is a wage-worker his lot depends upon capital. That is the much-vaunted community of interests between worker and capitalist.

IV

If capital grows, the mass of wage labour grows, the number of wage-workers grows; in a word, the domination of capital extends over a greater number of individuals. Let us assume the most favourable case: when productive capital grows, the demand for labour grows; consequently, the price of labour, wages, goes up.

A house may be large or small; as long as the surrounding houses are equally small it satisfies all social demands for a dwelling. But let a palace arise beside the little house, and it shrinks from a little house to a hut. The little house shows now that its owner has only very slight or no demands to make; and however high it may shoot up in the course of civilisation, if the neighbouring palace grows to an equal or even greater extent, the occupant of the relatively small house will feel more and more uncomfortable, dissatisfied and cramped within its four walls.

A noticeable increase in wages presupposes a rapid growth of productive capital. The rapid growth of productive capital brings about an equally rapid growth of wealth, luxury, social wants, social enjoyments. Thus, although the enjoyments of the worker have risen, the social satisfaction that they give has fallen in comparison with the increased enjoyments of the capitalist, which are inaccessible to the worker, in comparison with the state of development of society in general. Our desires and pleasures spring from society; we measure them, therefore, by society and not by the objects which serve for their satisfaction. Because they are of a social nature, they are of a relative nature.

In general, wages are determined not only by the amount of

commodities for which I can exchange them. They embody various relations.

What the workers receive for their labour power is, in the first place, a definite sum of money. Are wages determined only by this money price?

In the sixteenth century, the gold and silver circulating in Europe increased as a result of the discovery of richer and more easily worked mines in America. Hence, the value of gold and silver fell in relation to other commodities. The workers received the same amount of coined silver for their labour power as before. The money price of their labour remained the same, and yet their wages had fallen, for in exchange for the same quantity of silver they received a smaller amount of other commodities. This was one of the circumstances which furthered the growth of capital and the rise of the bourgeoisie in the sixteenth century.

Let us take another case. In the winter of 1847, as a result of a crop failure, the most indispensable means of subsistence, cereals, meat, butter, cheese, etc., rose considerably in price. Assume that the workers received the same sum of money for their labour power as before. Had not their wages fallen? Of course. For the same money they received less bread, meat, etc., in exchange. Their wages had fallen, not because the value of silver had diminished, but because the value of the means of subsistence had increased.

Assume, finally, that the money price of labour remains the same while all agricultural and manufactured goods have fallen in price owing to the employment of new machinery, a favourable season, etc. For the same money the workers can now buy more commodities of all kinds. Their wages, therefore, have risen, just because the money value of their wages has not changed.

Thus, the money price of labour, nominal wages, do not coincide with real wages, that is, with the sum of commodities which is actually given in exchange for the wages. If, therefore, we speak of a rise or fall of wages, we must keep in mind not only the money price of labour, the nominal wages.

But neither nominal wages, that is, the sum of money for which the worker sells himself to the capitalist, nor real wages, that is, the sum of commodities which he can buy for this money, exhaust the relations contained in wages.

Wages are, above all, also determined by their relation to the gain, to the profit of the capitalist—comparative, relative wages.

Real wages express the price of labour in relation to the price of other commodities; relative wages, on the other hand, express the share of direct labour in the new value it has created in relation to the share which falls to accumulated labour, to capital.

We said above [page 170]: "Wages are not the worker's share

in the commodity produced by him. Wages are the part of already existing commodities with which the capitalist buys for himself a definite amount of productive labour power." But the capitalist must replace these wages out of the price at which he sells the product produced by the worker; he must replace it in such a way that there remains to him, as a rule, a surplus over the cost of production expended by him, a profit. For the capitalist, the selling price of the commodities produced by the worker is divided into three parts: *first*, the replacement of the price of the raw materials advanced by him together with replacement of the depreciation of the tools, machinery and other means of labour also advanced by him; *secondly*, the replacement of the wages advanced by him, and *thirdly*, the surplus left over, the capitalist's profit. While the first part only replaces *previously existing values*, it is clear that both the replacement of the wages and also the surplus profit of the capitalist are, on the whole, taken from the *new value created by the worker's labour* and added to the raw materials. And *in this sense*, in order to compare them with one another, we can regard both wages and profit as shares in the product of the worker.

Real wages may remain the same, they may even rise, and yet relative wages may fall. Let us suppose, for example, that all means of subsistence have gone down in price by two-thirds while wages per day have only fallen by one-third, that is to say, for example, from three marks to two marks. Although the worker can command a greater amount of commodities with these two marks than he previously could with three marks, yet his wages have gone down in relation to the profit of the capitalist. The profit of the capitalist (for example, the manufacturer) has increased by one mark; that is, for a smaller sum of exchange values which he pays to the worker, the latter must produce a greater amount of exchange values than before. The share of capital relative to the share of labour has risen. The division of social wealth between capital and labour has become still more unequal. With the same capital, the capitalist commands a greater quantity of labour. The power of the capitalist class over the working class has grown, the social position of the worker has deteriorated, has been depressed one step further below that of the capitalist.

What, then, is the general law which determines the rise and fall of wages and profit in their reciprocal relation?

They stand in inverse ratio to each other. Capital's share, profit, rises in the same proportion as labour's share, wages, falls, and vice versa. Profit rises to the extent that wages fall; it falls to the extent that wages rise.

The objection will, perhaps, be made that the capitalist can profit by a favourable exchange of his products with other capitalists, by increase of the demand for his commodities, whether as a result of the opening of new markets, or as a result of a momentarily increased demand in the old markets, etc.; that the capitalist's profit can, therefore, increase by overreaching other capitalists, independently of the rise and fall of wages, of the exchange value of labour power; or that the capitalist's profit may also rise owing to the improvement of the instruments of labour, a new application of natural forces, etc.

First of all, it will have to be admitted that the result remains the same, although it is brought about in reverse fashion. True, the profit has not risen because wages have fallen, but wages have fallen because the profit has risen. With the same amount of other people's labour, the capitalist has acquired a greater amount of exchange values, without having paid more for the labour on that account; that is, therefore, labour is paid less in proportion to the net profit which it yields the capitalist.

In addition, we recall that, in spite of the fluctuations in prices of commodities, the average price of every commodity, the ratio in which it is exchanged for other commodities, is determined by its *cost of production*. Hence the overreachings within the capitalist class necessarily balance one another. The improvement of machinery, new application of natural forces in the service of production, enable a larger amount of products to be created in a given period of time with the same amount of labour and capital, but not by any means a larger amount of exchange values. If, by the use of the spinning jenny, I can turn out twice as much yarn in an hour as before its invention, say, one hundred pounds instead of fifty, then in the long run I will receive for these hundred pounds no more commodities in exchange than formerly for the fifty pounds, because the cost of production has fallen by one-half, or because I can deliver double the product at the same cost.

Finally, in whatever proportion the capitalist class, the bourgeoisie, whether of one country or of the whole world market, shares the net profit of production within itself, the total amount of this net profit always consists only of the amount by which, on the whole, accumulated labour has been increased by direct labour. This total amount grows, therefore, in the proportion in which labour augments capital, that is, in the proportion in which profit rises in comparison with wages.

We see, therefore, that even if we remain *within the relation of capital and wage labour, the interests of capital and the interests of wage labour are diametrically opposed.*

A rapid increase of capital is equivalent to a rapid increase of profit. Profit can only increase rapidly if the price of labour, if relative wages, decrease just as rapidly. Relative wages can fall although real wages rise simultaneously with nominal wages, with the money value of labour, if they do not rise, however, in the same proportion as profit. If, for instance, in times when business is good, wages rise by five per cent, profit on the other hand by thirty per cent, then the comparative, the relative wages, have not *increased* but *decreased*.

Thus if the income of the worker increases with the rapid growth of capital, the social gulf that separates the worker from the capitalist increases at the same time, and the power of capital over labour, the dependence of labour on capital, likewise increases at the same time.

To say that the worker has an interest in the rapid growth of capital is only to say that the more rapidly the worker increases the wealth of others, the richer will be the crumbs that fall to him, the greater is the number of workers that can be employed and called into existence, the more can the mass of slaves dependent on capital be increased.

We have thus seen that:

Even the *most favourable situation* for the working class, the *most rapid possible growth of capital*, however much it may improve the material existence of the worker, does not remove the antagonism between his interests and the interests of the bourgeoisie, the interests of the capitalists. *Profit and wages* remain as before in *inverse porportion*.

If capital is growing rapidly, wages may rise; the profit of capital rises incomparably more rapidly. The material position of the worker has improved, but at the cost of his social position. The social gulf that divides him from the capitalist has widened.

Finally:

To say that the most favourable condition for wage labour is the most rapid possible growth of productive capital is only to say that the more rapidly the working class increases and enlarges the power that is hostile to it, the wealth that does not belong to it and that rules over it, the more favourable will be the conditions under which it is allowed to labour anew at increasing bourgeois wealth, at enlarging the power of capital, content with forging for itself the golden chains by which the bourgeoisie drags it in its train.

V

Are *growth of productive capital and rise of wages* really so inseparably connected as the bourgeois economists maintain? We must not take their word for it. We must not even believe them when they say that the fatter capital is, the better will its slave be fed. The bourgeoisie is too enlightened, it calculates too well, to share the prejudices of the feudal lord who makes a display by the brilliance of his retinue. The conditions of existence of the bourgeoisie compel it to calculate.

We must, therefore, examine more closely:

How does the growth of productive capital affect wages?

If, on the whole, the productive capital of bourgeois society grows, a *more manifold* accumulation of labour takes place. The capitals increase in number and extent. The *numerical increase* of the capitals increases the *competition between the capitalists*. The *increasing extent* of the capitals provides the means for *bringing more powerful labour armies with more gigantic instruments of war into the industrial battlefield.*

One capitalist can drive another from the field and capture his capital only by selling more cheaply. In order to be able to sell more cheaply without ruining himself, he must produce more cheaply, that is, raise the productive power of labour as much as possible. But the productive power of labour is raised, above all, by a *greater division of labour,* by a more universal introduction and continual improvement of *machinery.* The greater the labour army among whom labour is divided, the more gigantic the scale on which machinery is introduced, the more does the cost of production proportionately decrease, the more fruitful is labour. Hence, a general rivalry arises among the capitalists to increase the division of labour and machinery and to exploit them on the greatest possible scale.

If, now, by a greater division of labour, by the utilisation of new machines and their improvement, by more profitable and extensive exploitation of natural forces, one capitalist has found the means of producing with the same amount of labour or of accumulated labour a greater amount of products, of commodities, than his competitors, if he can, for example, produce a whole yard of linen in the same labour time in which his competitors weave half a yard, how will this capitalist operate?

He could continue to sell half a yard of linen at the old market price; this would, however, be no means of driving his opponents from the field and of enlarging his own sales. But in the same measure in which his production has expanded, his need to sell has also increased. The more powerful and costly means of production that he has called into life enable him, indeed, to sell his commodities more cheaply, they *compel* him, however, at the same time *to sell more commodities,* to conquer a much *larger* market for his commodities; consequently, our capitalist will sell his half yard of linen more cheaply than his competitors.

The capitalist will not, however, sell a whole yard as cheaply as his competitors sell half a yard, although the production of the whole yard does not cost him more than the half yard costs the others. Otherwise he would not gain anything extra but only get back the cost of production by the exchange. His possibly greater income would be derived from the fact of having set a larger capital into motion, but not from having made more of his capital than the others. Moreover, he attains the object he wishes to attain, if he puts the price of his goods only a small percentage lower than that of his competitors. He drives them from the field, he wrests from them at least a part of their sales, by *underselling* them. And, finally, it will be remembered that the current price always stands *above or below the cost of production*, according to whether the sale of the commodity occurs in a favourable or unfavourable industrial season. The percentage at which the capitalist who has employed new and more fruitful means of production sells above his real cost of production will vary, depending upon whether the market price of a yard of linen stands below or above its hitherto customary cost of production.

However, the *privileged position* of our capitalist is not of long duration; other competing capitalists introduce the same machines, the same division of labour, introduce them on the same or on a larger scale, and this introduction will become so general that the price of linen *is reduced* not only *below its old*, but *below its new cost of production*.

The capitalists find themselves, therefore, in the same position relative to one another as *before* the introduction of the new means of production, and if they are able to supply by these means double the production at the same price, they are *now* forced to supply the double product *below* the old price. On the basis of this new cost of production, the same game begins again. More division of labour, more machinery, enlarged scale of exploitation of machinery and division of labour. And again competition brings the same counteraction against this result.

We see how in this way the mode of production and the means of production are continually transformed, revolutionised, *how the division of labour is necessarily followed by greater division of labour, the application of machinery by still greater application of machinery, work on a large scale by work on a still larger scale.*

That is the law which again and again throws bourgeois production out of its old course and which compels capital to intensify the productive forces of labour, *because* it has intensified them, it, the law which gives capital no rest and continually whispers in its ear: "Go on! Go on!"

This law is none other than that which, within the fluctuations of trade periods, necessarily *levels out* the price of a commodity to its *cost of production*.

However powerful the means of production which a capitalist brings into the field, competition will make these means of production universal and from the moment when it has made them universal, the only result of the greater fruitfulness of his capital is that he must now supply *for the same price* ten, twenty, a hundred times as much as before. But, as he must sell perhaps a thousand times as much as before in order to outweigh the lower selling price by the greater amount of the product sold, because a more extensive sale is now necessary, not only in order to make more profit but in order to replace the cost of production—the instrument of production itself, as we have seen, becomes more and more expensive—and because this mass sale becomes a question of life and death not only for him but also for his rivals, the old struggle begins again *all the more violently the more fruitful the already discovered means of production are. The division of labour and the application of machinery, therefore, will go on anew on an incomparably greater scale.*

Whatever the power of the means of production employed may be, competition seeks to rob capital of the golden fruits of this power by bringing the price of the commodities back to the cost of production, by thus making cheaper production—the supply of ever greater amounts of products for the same total price—an imperative law to the same extent as production can be cheapened, that is, as more can be produced with the same amount of labour. Thus the capitalist would have won nothing by his own exertions but the obligation to supply more in the same labour time, in a word, *more difficult conditions for the augmentation of the value of his capital.* While, therefore, competition continually pursues him with its law of the cost of production and every weapon that he forges against his rivals recoils against himself, the capitalist continually tries to get the better of competition by incessantly introducing new machines, more expensive, it is true, but producing more cheaply, and new division of labour in place of the old, and by not waiting until competition has rendered the new ones obsolete.

If now we picture to ourselves this feverish simultaneous agitation on the *whole world market*, it will be comprehensible how the growth, accumulation and concentration of capital results in an uninterrupted division of labour, and in the application of new and the perfecting of old machinery precipitately and on an ever more gigantic scale.

But how do these circumstances, which are inseparable from the growth of productive capital, affect the determination of wages?

The greater *division of labour* enables *one* worker to do the work of five, ten or twenty; it therefore multiplies competition among the workers fivefold, tenfold and twentyfold. The workers do not only compete by one selling himself cheaper than another; they compete by *one* doing the work of five, ten, twenty; and the *division of labour*, introduced by capital and continually increased, compels the workers to compete among themselves in this way.

Further, as the *division of labour* increases, labour *is simplified.* The special skill of the worker becomes worthless. He becomes transformed into a simple, monotonous productive force that does not have to use intense bodily or intellectual faculties. His labour becomes a labour that anyone can perform. Hence, competitors crowd upon him on all sides, and besides we remind the reader that the more simple and easily learned the labour is, the lower the cost of production needed to master it, the lower do wages sink, for, like the price of every other commodity, they are determined by the cost of production.

Therefore, as labour becomes more unsatisfying, more repulsive, competition increases and wages decrease. The worker tries to keep up the amount of his wages by working more, whether by working longer hours or by producing more in one hour. Driven by want, therefore, he still further increases the evil effects of the division of labour. The result is that *the more he works the less wages he receives,* and for the simple reason that he competes to that extent with his fellow workers, hence makes them into so many competitors who offer themselves on just the same bad terms as he does himself, and that, therefore, in the last resort he *competes with himself, with himself as a member of the working class.*

Machinery brings about the same results on a much greater scale, by replacing skilled workers by unskilled, men by women, adults by children. It brings about the same results, where it is newly introduced, by throwing the hand workers on to the streets in masses, and, where it is developed, improved and replaced by more productive machinery, by discharging workers in smaller batches. We have portrayed above, in a hasty sketch, the industrial war of the capitalists among themselves; *this war has the peculiarity that its battles are won less by recruiting than by discharging the army of labour. The generals, the capitalists, compete with one another as to who can discharge most soldiers of industry.*

The economists tell us, it is true, that the workers rendered superfluous by machinery find *new* branches of employment.

They dare not assert directly that the same workers who are discharged find places in the new branches of labour. The facts cry out too loudly against this lie. They really only assert that new means of employment will open up for *other component sections of the working class,* for instance, for the portion of the young generation of workers that was ready to enter the branch of industry which has gone under. That is, of course, a great consolation for the disinherited workers. The worshipful capitalists will never want for fresh exploitable flesh and blood, and will let the dead bury their dead. This is a consolation which the bourgeois give themselves rather than one which they give the workers. If the whole class of wage-workers were to be abolished owing to machinery, how dreadful that would be for capital which, without wage labour, ceases to be capital!

Let us suppose, however, that those directly driven out of their jobs by machinery, and the entire section of the new generation that was already on the watch for this employment, *find a new occupation*. Does any one imagine that it will be as highly paid as that which has been lost? *That would contradict all the laws of economics*. We have seen how modern industry always brings with it the substitution of a more simple, subordinate occupation for the more complex and higher one.

How, then, could a mass of workers who have been thrown out of one branch of industry owing to machinery find refuge in another, unless the latter *is lower, worse paid?*

The workers who work in the manufacture of machinery itself have been cited as an exception. As soon as more machinery is demanded and used in industry, it is said, there must necessarily be an increase of machines, consequently of the manufacture of machines, and consequently of the employment of workers in the manufacture of machines; and the workers engaged in this branch of industry are claimed to be skilled, even educated workers.

Since the year 1840 this assertion, which even before was only half true, has lost all semblance of truth because ever more versatile machines have been employed in the manufacture of machinery, no more and no less than in the manufacture of cotton yarn, and the workers employed in the machine factories, confronted by highly elaborate machines, can only play the part of highly unelaborate machines.

But in place of the man who has been discharged owing to the machine, the factory employs maybe *three* children and *one* woman. And did not the man's wages have to suffice for the three children and a woman? Did not the minimum of wages have to suffice to maintain and to propagate the race? What, then, does this favourite bourgeois phrase prove? Nothing more than that now four times as many workers' lives are used up in order to gain a livelihood for *one* worker's family.

Let us sum up: *The more productive capital grows, the more the division of labour and the application of machinery expands. The more the division of labour and the application of machinery expands, the more competition among the workers expands and the more their wages contract.*

In addition, the working class gains recruits from the *higher strata of society* also; a mass of petty industrialists and small rentiers are hurled down into its ranks and have nothing better to do than urgently stretch out their arms alongside those of the workers. Thus the forest of uplifted arms demanding work becomes ever thicker, while the arms themselves become ever thinner.

That the small industrialist cannot survive in a contest one of the first conditions of which is to produce on an ever greater scale, that is, precisely to be a large and not a small industrialist, is self-evident.

That the interest on capital decreases in the same measure as the mass and number of capitals increase, as capital grows; that, therefore, the small rentier can no longer live on his interest but must throw himself into industry, and, consequently, help to swell the ranks of the small industrialists and thereby of candidates for the proletariat—all this surely requires no further explanation.

Finally, as the capitalists are compelled, by the movement described above, to exploit the already existing gigantic means of production on a larger scale and to set in motion all the mainsprings of credit to this end, there is a corresponding increase in industrial earthquakes, in which the trading world can only maintain itself by sacrificing a part of wealth, of products and even of productive forces to the gods of the nether world—in a word, *crises* increase. They become more frequent and more violent, if only because, as the mass of production, and consequently the need for extended markets, grows, the world market becomes more and more contracted, fewer and fewer new markets remain available for exploitation, since every preceding crisis has subjected to world trade a market hitherto unconquered or only superficially exploited. But capital does not *live* only on labour. A lord, at once aristocratic and barbarous, it drags with it into the grave the corpses of its slaves, whole hecatombs of workers who perish in the crises. Thus we see: *if capital grows rapidly, competition among the workers grows incomparably more rapidly, that is, the means of employment, the means of subsistence, of the working class decrease proportionately so much the more, and, nevertheless, the rapid growth of capital is the most favourable condition for wage labour.*

Capital: Selections

KARL MARX

Capital (*Das Kapital*) was Marx's life work, a project begun in 1848, when he turned thirty, and continued for thirty years. Volume One, published in 1867, is the book generally referred to simply as *Capital* and is relatively complete in itself. The projected Volumes Two and Three, left in raw and incomplete manuscript form on his death in 1883, were subsequently edited and brought out by Engels.

The following selections from Volume One, together with Marx's Preface to the first German edition and Afterword to the second, are taken from the text of the English edition of 1887, as translated from the third German edition by Samuel Moore and Edward Aveling and edited by Engels. An attempt has been made here to provide those sections of the book that collectively convey the basic argument and the most characteristic themes. Breaks in the text have been indicated by means of three asterisks. In some instances Marx's footnotes have been deleted in the interest of saving space.

Preface to the First German Edition

The work, the first volume of which I now submit to the public, forms the continuation of my "Zur Kritik der Politischen Oekonomie" (A Contribution to the Criticism of Political Economy) published in 1859. The long pause between the first part and the continuation is due to an illness of many years' duration that again and again interrupted my work.

The substance of that earlier work is summarised in the first three chapters of this volume. This is done not merely for the sake of connexion and completeness. The presentation of the subject-matter is improved. As far as circumstances in any way permit, many points only hinted at in the earlier book are here worked out more fully, whilst, conversely, points worked out fully there are only touched upon in this volume. The sections on the history of the theories of value and of money are now, of course, left out altogether. The reader of the earlier work will find, however, in the notes to the first chapter additional sources of reference relative to the history of those theories.

That every beginning is difficult holds in all sciences. To understand the first chapter, especially the section that contains the analysis of commodities, will, therefore, present the greatest difficulty. That which concerns more especially the analysis of the substance of value and the magnitude of value, I have, as much as it was possible, popularised.[1] The value-form, whose fully developed shape is the money-form, is very elementary and simple. Nevertheless, the human mind has for more than 2,000 years sought in vain to get to the bottom of it, whilst on the other hand, to the successful analysis of much more composite and complex forms, there has been at least an approximation. Why? Because the body, as an organic whole, is more easy of study than are the cells of that body. In the analysis of economic forms, moreover, neither microscopes nor chemical reagents are of use. The force of abstraction must replace both. But in bourgeois society the commodity-form of the product of labour—or the value-form of the commodity—is the economic cell-form. To the superficial observer, the analysis of these forms seems to turn upon minutiæ. It does in fact deal with minutiæ, but they are of the same order as those dealt with in microscopic anatomy.

With the exception of the section on value-form, therefore, this volume cannot stand accused on the score of difficulty. I presuppose, of course, a reader who is willing to learn something new and therefore to think for himself.

The physicist either observes physical phenomena where they occur in their most typical form and most free from disturbing influence, or, wherever possible, he makes experiments under conditions that assure the occurrence of the phenomenon in its normality. In this work I have to examine the capitalist mode of production, and the conditions of production and exchange corresponding to that mode. Up to the present time, their classic ground is England. That is the reason why England is used as the chief illustration in the development of my theoretical ideas. If, however, the German reader shrugs his shoulders at the condition of the English

1. This is the more necessary, as even the section of Ferdinand Lassalle's work against Schulze-Delitzsch, in which he professes to give "the intellectual quintessence" of my explanations on these subjects, contains important mistakes. If Ferdinand Lassalle has borrowed almost literally from my writings, and without any acknowledgement, all the general theoretical propositions in his economic works, e.g., those on the historical character of capital, on the connexion between the conditions of production and the mode of production, &c., &c., even to the terminology created by me, this may perhaps be due to purposes of propaganda. I am here, of course, not speaking of his detailed working out and application of these propositions, with which I have nothing to do. [*Marx*]

industrial and agricultural labourers, or in optimist fashion comforts himself with the thought that in Germany things are not nearly so bad; I must plainly tell him, *"De te fabula narratur!"*[2]

Intrinsically, it is not a question of the higher or lower degree of development of the social antagonisms that result from the natural laws of capitalist production. It is a question of these laws themselves, of these tendencies working with iron necessity towards inevitable results. The country that is more developed industrially only shows, to the less developed, the image of its own future.

But apart from this. Where capitalist production is fully naturalised among the Germans (for instance, in the factories proper) the condition of things is much worse than in England, because the counterpoise of the Factory Acts is wanting. In all other spheres, we, like all the rest of Continental Western Europe, suffer not only from the development of capitalist production, but also from the incompleteness of that development. Alongside of modern evils, a whole series of inherited evils oppress us, arising from the passive survival of antiquated modes of production, with their inevitable train of social and political anachronisms. We suffer not only from the living, but from the dead. *Le mort saisit le vif!*[3]

The social statistics of Germany and the rest of Continental Western Europe are, in comparison with those of England, wretchedly compiled. But they raise the veil just enough to let us catch a glimpse of the Medusa head behind it. We should be appalled at the state of things at *home*, if, as in England, our governments and parliaments appointed periodically commissions of inquiry into economic conditions; if these commissions were armed with the same plenary powers to get at the truth; if it was possible to find for this purpose men as competent, as free from partisanship and respect of persons as are the English factory-inspectors, her medical reporters on public health, her commissioners of inquiry into the exploitation of women and children, into housing and food. Perseus wore a magic cap that the monsters he hunted down might not see him. We draw the magic cap down over eyes and ears as a make-believe that there are no monsters.

Let us not deceive ourselves on this. As in the 18th century, the American war of independence sounded the tocsin for the European middle-class, so in the 19th century, the American Civil War sounded it for the European working-class. In England the progress of social disintegration is palpable. When it has reached a certain point, it must re-act on the Continent. There it will take a form more brutal or more humane, according to the degree of development of the working-class itself. Apart from higher motives, therefore, their own most important interests dictate to the classes that

2. This story is about you.　　　　3. The dead man seizes the living one.

are for the nonce the ruling ones, the removal of all legally remov-able hindrances to the free development of the working-class. For this reason, as well as others, I have given so large a space in this volume to the history, the details, and the results of English factory legislation. One nation can and should learn from others. And even when a society has got upon the right track for the discovery of the natural laws of its movement—and it is the ultimate aim of this work, to lay bare the economic law of motion of modern socie-ty—it can neither clear by bold leaps, nor remove by legal enact-ments, the obstacles offered by the successive phases of its normal development. But it can shorten and lessen the birth-pangs.

To prevent possible misunderstanding, a word. I paint the capi-talist and the landlord in no sense *couleur de rose*.[4] But here indi-viduals are dealt with only in so far as they are the personifications of economic categories, embodiments of particular class-relations and class-interests. My standpoint, from which the evolution of the economic formation of society is viewed as a process of natural his-tory, can less than any other make the individual responsible for relations whose creature he socially remains, however much he may subjectively raise himself above them.

In the domain of Political Economy, free scientific inquiry meets not merely the same enemies as in all other domains. The peculiar nature of the material it deals with, summons as foes into the field of battle the most violent, mean and malignant passions of the human breast, the Furies of private interest. The English Established Church, *e.g.*, will more readily pardon an attack on 38 of its 39 articles than on 1/39 of its income. Now-a-days atheism itself is *culpa levis*, as compared with criticism of existing property relations. Nevertheless, there is an unmistakable advance. I refer, *e.g.*, to the Blue book published within the last few weeks: "Corre-spondence with Her Majesty's Missions Abroad, regarding Industrial Questions and Trades' Unions." The representatives of the English Crown in foreign countries there declare in so many words that in Germany, in France, to be brief, in all the civilised states of the European Continent, a radical change in the existing relations between capital and labour is as evident and inevitable as in Eng-land. At the same time, on the other side of the Atlantic Ocean, Mr. Wade, vice-president of the United States, declared in public meetings that, after the abolition of slavery, a radical change of the relations of capital and of property in land is next upon the order of the day. These are signs of the times, not to be hidden by purple mantles or black cassocks. They do not signify that tomorrow a miracle will happen. They show that, within the ruling-classes themselves, a foreboding is dawning, that the present society is no

4. Rose-coloured.

solid crystal, but an organism capable of change, and is constantly changing.

The second volume of this work will treat of the process of the circulation of capital (Book II.), and of the varied forms assumed by capital in the course of its development (Book III.), the third and last volume (Book IV.), the history of the theory.

Every opinion based on scientific criticism I welcome. As to the prejudices of so-called public opinion, to which I have never made concessions, now as aforetime the maxim of the great Florentine is mine:

"*Segui il tuo corso, e lascia dir le genti.*"[5]

London, July 25, 1867   *Karl Marx*

From the Afterword to the Second German Edition

That the method employed in "Das Kapital" has been little understood, is shown by the various conceptions, contradictory one to another, that have been formed of it.

Thus the Paris *Revue Positiviste* reproaches me in that, on the one hand, I treat economics metaphysically, and on the other hand—imagine!—confine myself to the mere critical analysis of actual facts, instead of writing receipts (Comtist ones?) for the cook-shops of the future. In answer to the reproach *in re* metaphysics, Professor Sieber has it: "In so far as it deals with actual theory, the method of Marx is the deductive method of the whole English school, a school whose failings and virtues are common to the best theoretic economists." M. Block—"Les Théoriciens du Socialisme en Allemagne. Extrait du Journal des Economistes, Juillet et Août 1872"—makes the discovery that my method is analytic and says: "Par cet ouvrage M. Marx se classe parmi les esprits analytiques les plus éminents."[6] German reviews, of course, shriek out at "Hegelian sophistics." The *European Messenger* of St. Petersburg in an article dealing exclusively with the method of "Das Kapital" (May number, 1872, pp. 427–436), finds my method of inquiry severely realistic, but my method of presentation, unfortunately, German-dialectical. It says: "At first sight, if the judgment is based on the external form of the presentation of the subject, Marx is the most ideal of ideal philosophers, always in the German, *i.e.*, the bad sense of the word. But in point of fact he is infinitely more realistic than all his fore-runners in the work of economic criticism. He can in no sense be called an idealist." I cannot answer the writer better than by aid of a few extracts from his own criticism, which may

5. Follow your own course, no matter what people say.

6. With this work Marx takes his place among the most eminent analytic minds.

interest some of my readers to whom the Russian original is inaccessible.

After a quotation from the preface to my "Criticism of Political Economy," Berlin, 1859, pp. IV–VII, where I discuss the materialistic basis of my method, the writer goes on: "The one thing which is of moment to Marx, is to find the law of the phenomena with whose investigation he is concerned; and not only is that law of moment to him, which governs these phenomena, in so far as they have a definite form and mutual connexion within a given historical period. Of still greater moment to him is the law of their variation, of their development, *i.e.*, of their transition from one form into another, from one series of connexions into a different one. This law once discovered, he investigates in detail the effects in which it manifests itself in social life. Consequently, Marx only troubles himself about one thing: to show, by rigid scientific investigation, the necessity of successive determinate orders of social conditions, and to establish, as impartially as possible, the facts that serve him for fundamental starting-points. For this it is quite enough, if he proves, at the same time, both the necessity of the present order of things, and the necessity of another order into which the first must inevitably pass over, and this all the same, whether men believe or do not believe it, whether they are conscious or unconscious of it. Marx treats the social movement as a process of natural history, governed by laws not only independent of human will, consciousness and intelligence, but rather, on the contrary, determining that will, consciousness and intelligence. . . . If in the history of civilisation the conscious element plays a part so subordinate, then it is self-evident that a critical inquiry whose subject-matter is civilisation, can, less than anything else, have for its basis any form of, or any result of, consciousness. That is to say, that not the idea, but the material phenomenon alone can serve as its starting-point. Such an inquiry will confine itself to the confrontation and the comparison of a fact, not with ideas, but with another fact. For this inquiry, the one thing of moment is, that both facts be investigated as accurately as possible, and that they actually form, each with respect to the other, different momenta of an evolution; but most important of all is the rigid analysis of the series of successions, of the sequences and concatenations in which the different stages of such an evolution present themselves. But it will be said, the general laws of economic life are one and the same, no matter whether they are applied to the present or the past. This Marx directly denies. According to him, such abstract laws do not exist. On the contrary, in his opinion every historical period has laws of its own. . . . As soon as society has outlived a given period of development, and is passing over from one given stage to another, it begins to be subject also to other laws. In a word, economic life offers us a phenomenon analogous to the history of evolution in other branches of biology. The old economists misunderstood the nature of economic laws when they likened them to the laws of physics and chemistry. A more thorough analysis of phenomena shows that social organisms differ among themselves as fundamentally as plants or animals. Nay, one and the same phenomenon falls under quite different laws in consequence of the different structure of those organisms as a whole, of the variations of their individual organs, of the different conditions in which those organs function, &c. Marx, *e.g.*, denies that the law of population is the same at all times and in all places. He asserts, on the contrary, that every stage of development has its own law of population.... With the varying degree of development of productive power, social conditions and the laws governing them vary too. Whilst Marx sets himself the task of following and explaining from this point of view the economic system established by the sway of capital, he is only formulating, in a strictly scientific manner, the aim that every accurate investigation into economic life must have. The scientific value of such an inquiry lies in the disclosing of the special laws that regulate the origin, existence, development, death of a given social organism and its replacement by another and higher one. And it is this value that, in point of fact, Marx's book has."

Whilst the writer pictures what he takes to be actually my method, in this striking and [as far as concerns my own application of it] generous way, what else is he picturing but the dialectic method?

Of course the method of presentation must differ in form from that of inquiry. The latter has to appropriate the material in detail, to analyse its different forms of development, to trace out their inner connexion. Only after this work is done, can the actual movement be adequately described. If this is done successfully, if the life of the subject-matter is ideally reflected as in a mirror, then it may appear as if we had before us a mere a priori construction.

My dialectic method is not only different from the Hegelian, but is its direct opposite. To Hegel, the life-process of the human brain, *i.e.*, the process of thinking, which, under the name of "the Idea," he even transforms into an independent subject, is the demiurgos of the real world, and the real world is only the external, phenomenal form of "the Idea." With me, on the contrary, the ideal is nothing else than the material world reflected by the human mind, and translated into forms of thought.

The mystifying side of Hegelian dialectic I criticised nearly thirty years ago, at a time when it was still the fashion. But just as I was working at the first volume of "Das Kapital," it was the good pleasure of the peevish, arrogant, mediocre epigones who now talk large in cultured Germany, to treat Hegel in the same way as the brave Moses Mendelssohn in Lessing's time treated Spinoza, *i.e.*, as a "dead dog." I therefore openly avowed myself the pupil of that mighty thinker, and even here and there, in the chapter on the theory of value, coquetted with the modes of expression peculiar to him. The mystification which dialectic suffers in Hegel's hands, by no means prevents him from being the first to present its general form of working in a comprehensive and conscious manner. With him it is standing on its head. It must be turned right side up again, if you would discover the rational kernel within the mystical shell.

In its mystified form, dialectic became the fashion in Germany, because it seemed to transfigure and to glorify the existing state of things. In its rational form it is a scandal and abomination to bourgeoisdom and its doctrinaire professors, because it includes in its comprehension an affirmative recognition of the existing state of things, at the same time also, the recognition of the negation of that state, of its inevitable breaking up; because it regards every historically developed social form as in fluid movement, and therefore takes into account its transient nature not less than its momentary existence; because it lets nothing impose upon it, and is in its essence critical and revolutionary.

The contradictions inherent in the movement of capitalist society impress themselves upon the practical bourgeois most strikingly in the changes of the periodic cycle, through which modern industry runs, and whose crowning point is the universal crisis. That crisis is once again approaching, although as yet but in its preliminary stage; and by the universality of its theatre and the intensity of its action it will drum dialectics even into the heads of the mushroom-upstarts of the new, holy Prusso-German empire.

London, January 24, 1873   *Karl Marx*

Part I. Commodities and Money

CHAPTER I. COMMODITIES

Section 1. The Two Factors of a Commodity: Use-Value and Value (The Substance of Value and the Magnitude of Value)

The wealth of those societies in which the capitalist mode of production prevails, presents itself as "an immense accumulation of commodities,"[1] its unit being a single commodity. Our investigation must therefore begin with the analysis of a commodity.

A commodity is, in the first place, an object outside us, a thing that by its properties satisfies human wants of some sort or another. The nature of such wants, whether, for instance, they spring from the stomach or from fancy, makes no difference.[2] Neither are we here concerned to know how the object satisfies these wants, whether directly as means of subsistence, or indirectly as means of production.

Every useful thing, as iron, paper, &c., may be looked at from the two points of view of quality and quantity. It is an assemblage of many properties, and may therefore be of use in various ways. To discover the various uses of things is the work of history.[3] So also is the establishment of socially-recognised standards of measure for the quantities of these useful objects. The diversity of these measures has its origin partly in the diverse nature of the objects to be measured, partly in convention.

The utility of a thing makes it a use-value.[4] But this utility is not a thing of air. Being limited by the physical properties of the commodity, it has no existence apart from that commodity. A commodity, such as iron, corn, or a diamond, is therefore, so far as it is a material thing, a use-value, something useful. This property of a commodity is independent of the amount of labour required to appropriate its useful qualities. When treating of use-value, we always assume to be dealing with definite quantities, such as dozens of watches, yards of linen, or tons of iron. The use-values of commodities furnish the material for a special study, that of the commercial knowledge of commodities.[5] Use-values become a reality only by use or consumption: they also constitute the substance of all wealth, whatever may be the social form of that wealth. In the

1. Karl Marx, "Zur Kritik der Politischen Oekonomie." Berlin, 1859, p. 3. [*Marx*]

2. "Desire implies want; it is the appetite of the mind, and as natural as hunger to the body. . . . The greatest number (of things) have their value from supplying the wants of the mind." Nicholas Barbon: "A Discourse Concerning Coining the New Money Lighter. In Answer to Mr. Locke's Considerations," &c., London, 1696, pp. 2, 3. [*Marx*]

3. "Things have an intrinsick vertue" (this is Barbon's special term for value in use) "which in all places have the same vertue; as the loadstone to attract iron" (l. c., p. 6). The property which the magnet possesses of attracting iron, became of use only after by means of that property the polarity of the magnet had been discovered. [*Marx*]

4. "The natural worth of anything consists in its fitness to supply the necessities, or serve the conveniences of human life." (John Locke, "Some Considerations on the Consequences of the Lowering of Interest, 1691," in Works Edit. Lond., 1777, Vol. II., p. 28.) In English writers of the 17th century we frequently find "worth" in the sense of value in use, and "value" in the sense of exchange-value. This is quite in accordance with the spirit of a language that likes to use a Teutonic word for the actual thing, and a Romance word for its reflexion. [*Marx*]

5. In bourgeois societies the economic fictio juris prevails, that every one, as a buyer, possesses an encyclopaedic knowledge of commodities. [*Marx*]

form of society we are about to consider, they are, in addition, the material depositories of exchange-value.

Exchange-value, at first sight, presents itself as a quantitative relation, as the proportion in which values in use of one sort are exchanged for those of another sort,[6] a relation constantly changing with time and place. Hence exchange-value appears to be something accidental and purely relative, and consequently an intrinsic value, *i.e.*, an exchange-value that is inseparably connected with, inherent in commodities, seems a contradiction in terms.[7] Let us consider the matter a little more closely.

A given commodity, *e.g.*, a quarter of wheat is exchanged for x blacking, y silk, or z gold, &c.—in short, for other commodities in the most different proportions. Instead of one exchange-value, the wheat has, therefore, a great many. But since x blacking, y silk, or z gold, &c., each represent the exchange-value of one quarter of wheat, x blacking, y silk, z gold, &c., must, as exchange-values, be replaceable by each other, or equal to each other. Therefore, first: the valid exchange-values of a given commodity express something equal; secondly, exchange-value, generally, is only the mode of expression, the phenomenal form, of something contained in it, yet distinguishable from it.

Let us take two commodities, *e.g.*, corn and iron. The proportions in which they are exchangeable, whatever those proportions may be, can always be represented by an equation in which a given quantity of corn is equated to some quantity of iron: *e.g.*, 1 quarter corn $=$ x cwt. iron. What does this equation tell us? It tells us that in two different things—in 1 quarter of corn and x cwt. of iron, there exists in equal quantities something common to both. The two things must therefore be equal to a third, which in itself is neither the one nor the other. Each of them, so far as it is exchange-value, must therefore be reducible to this third.

A simple geometrical illustration will make this clear. In order to calculate and compare the areas of rectilinear figures, we decompose them into triangles. But the area of the triangle itself is expressed by something totally different from its visible figure, namely, by half the product of the base into the altitude. In the same way the exchange-values of commodities must be capable of being expressed in terms of something common to them all, of which thing they represent a greater or less quantity.

This common "something" cannot be either a geometrical, a chemical, or any other natural property of commodities. Such prop-

6. "La valeur consiste dans le rapport d'échange qui se trouve entre telle chose et telle autre, entre telle mesure d'une production, et telle mesure d'une autre." (Le Trosne: "De l'Intérêt Social." Physiocrates, Ed. Daire. Paris, 1846. P. 889.) [*Marx*]

7. "Nothing can have an intrinsick value." (N. Barbon, l. c., p. 6); or as Butler says—
   "The value of a thing
   is just as much as it will bring."
   [*Marx*]

erties claim our attention only in so far as they affect the utility of those commodities, make them use-values. But the exchange of commodities is evidently an act characterised by a total abstraction from use-value. Then one use-value is just as good as another, provided only it be present in sufficient quantity. Or, as old Barbon says, "one sort of wares are as good as another, if the values be equal. There is no difference or distinction in things of equal value. ... An hundred pounds' worth of lead or iron, is of as great value as one hundred pounds' worth of silver or gold." As use-values, commodities are, above all, of different qualities, but as exchange-values they are merely different quantities, and consequently do not contain an atom of use-value.

If then we leave out of consideration the use-value of commodities, they have only one common property left, that of being products of labour. But even the product of labour itself has undergone a change in our hands. If we make abstraction from its use-value, we make abstraction at the same time from the material elements and shapes that make the product a use-value; we see in it no longer a table, a house, yarn, or any other useful thing. Its existence as a material thing is put out of sight. Neither can it any longer be regarded as the product of the labour of the joiner, the mason, the spinner, or of any other definite kind of productive labour. Along with the useful qualities of the products themselves, we put out of sight both the useful character of the various kinds of labour embodied in them, and the concrete forms of that labour; there is nothing left but what is common to them all; all are reduced to one and the same sort of labour, human labour in the abstract.

Let us now consider the residue of each of these products; it consists of the same unsubstantial reality in each, a mere congelation of homogeneous human labour, of labour-power expended without regard to the mode of its expenditure. All that these things now tell us is, that human labour-power has been expended in their production, that human labour is embodied in them. When looked at as crystals of this social substance, common to them all, they are —Values.

We have seen that when commodities are exchanged, their exchange-value manifests itself as something totally independent of their use-value. But if we abstract from their use-value, there remains their Value as defined above. Therefore, the common substance that manifests itself in the exchange-value of commodities, whenever they are exchanged, is their value. The progress of our investigation will show that exchange-value is the only form in which the value of commodities can manifest itself or be expressed. For the present, however, we have to consider the nature of value independently of this, its form.

A use-value, or useful article, therefore, has value only because human labour in the abstract has been embodied or materialised in it. How, then, is the magnitude of this value to be measured? Plainly, by the quantity of the value-creating substance, the labour, contained in the article. The quantity of labour, however, is measured by its duration, and labour-time in its turn finds its standard in weeks, days, and hours.

Some people might think that if the value of a commodity is determined by the quantity of labour spent on it, the more idle and unskillful the labourer, the more valuable would his commodity be, because more time would be required in its production. The labour, however, that forms the substance of value, is homogeneous human labour, expenditure of one uniform labour-power. The total labour-power of society, which is embodied in the sum total of the values of all commodities produced by that society, counts here as one homogeneous mass of human labour-power, composed though it be of innumerable individual units. Each of these units is the same as any other, so far as it has the character of the average labour-power of society, and takes effect as such; that is, so far as it requires for producing a commodity, no more time than is needed on an average, no more than is socially necessary. The labour-time socially necessary is that required to produce an article under the normal conditions of production, and with the average degree of skill and intensity prevalent at the time. The introduction of power-looms into England probably reduced by one-half the labour required to weave a given quantity of yarn into cloth. The hand-loom weavers, as a matter of fact, continued to require the same time as before; but for all that, the product of one hour of their labour represented after the change only half an hour's social labour, and consequently fell to one-half its former value.

We see then that that which determines the magnitude of the value of any article is the amount of labour socially necessary, or the labour-time socially necessary for its production.[8] Each individual commodity, in this connexion, is to be considered as an average sample of its class.[9] Commodities, therefore, in which equal quantities of labour are embodied, or which can be produced in the same time, have the same value. The value of one commodity is to the value of any other, as the labour-time necessary for the production of the one is to that necessary for the production of the other.

8. "The value of them (the necessaries of life), when they are exchanged the one for another, is regulated by the quantity of labour necessarily required and commonly taken in producing them." ("Some Thoughts on the Interest of Money in General, and Particularly in the Publick Funds, &c." Lond., p. 36.) This remarkable anonymous work, written in the last century, bears no date. It is clear, however, from internal evidence, that it appeared in the reign of George II. about 1739 or 1740. [*Marx*]

9. "Toutes les productions d'un même genre ne forment proprement qu'une masse, dont le prix se détermine en général et sans égard aux circonstances particulières." (Le Trosen, l. c., p. 893.) [*Marx*]

"As values, all commodities are only definite masses of congealed labour-time."

The value of a commodity would therefore remain constant, if the labour-time required for its production also remained constant. But the latter changes with every variation in the productiveness of labour. This productiveness is determined by various cicumstances, amongst others, by the average amount of skill of the workmen, the state of science, and the degree of its practical application, the social organisation of production, the extent and capabilities of the means of production, and by physical conditions. For example, the same amount of labour in favourable seasons is embodied in 8 bushels of corn, and in unfavourable, only in four. The same labour extracts from rich mines more metal than from poor mines. Diamonds are of very rare occurrence on the earth's surface, and hence their discovery costs, on an average, a great deal of labour-time. Consequently much labour is represented in a small compass. Jacob doubts whether gold has ever been paid for at its full value. This applies still more to diamonds. According to Eschwege, the total produce of the Brazilian diamond mines for the eighty years, ending in 1823, had not realised the price of one-and-a-half years' average produce of the sugar and coffee plantations of the same country, although the diamonds cost much more labour, and therefore represented more value. With richer mines, the same quantity of labour would embody itself in more diamonds, and their value would fall. If we could succeed at a small expenditure of labour, in converting carbon into diamonds, their value might fall below that of bricks. In general, the greater the productiveness of labour, the less is the labour-time required for the production of an article, the less is the amount of labour crystallised in that article, and the less is its value; and *vice versa*, the less the productiveness of labour, the greater is the labour-time required for the production of an article, and the greater is its value. The value of a commodity, therefore, varies directly as the quantity, and inversely as the productiveness, of the labour incorporated in it.

A thing can be a use-value, without having value. This is the case whenever its utility to man is not due to labour. Such are air, virgin soil, natural meadows, &c. A thing can be useful, and the product of human labour, without being a commodity. Whoever directly satisfies his wants with the produce of his own labour, creates, indeed, use-values, but no commodities. In order to produce the latter, he must not only produce use-values, but use-values for others, social use-values. (And not only for others, without more. The mediæval peasant produced quit-rent-corn for his feudal lord and tithe-corn for his parson. But neither the quit-rent-corn nor the tithe-corn became commodities by reason of the fact that they had been produced for others. To become a commodity a product must be transferred to another, whom it will serve as a use-value, by means of an exchange.)[1] Lastly nothing can have value, without being an object of utility. If the thing is useless, so is the labour contained in it; the labour does not count as labour, and therefore creates no value.

Section 2. The Two-fold Character of the Labour Embodied in Commodities

At first sight a commodity presented itself to us as a complex of two things—use-value and exchange-value. Later on, we saw also that labour, too, possesses the same two-fold nature; for, so far as it finds expression in value, it does not possess the same characteristics that belong to it as a creator of use-values. I was the first to point out and to examine critically this two-fold nature of the labour contained in commodities. As this point is the pivot on which a clear comprehension of Political Economy turns, we must go more into detail.

Let us take two commodities such as a coat and 10 yards of linen, and let the former be double the value of the latter, so that, if 10 yards of linen $= W$, the coat $= 2W$.

The coat is a use-value that satisfies a particular want. Its existence is the result of a special sort of productive activity, the nature of which is determined by its aim, mode of operation, subject, means, and result. The labour, whose utility is thus represented by the value in use of its product, or which manifests itself by making its product a use-value, we call useful labour. In this connexion we consider only its useful effect.

As the coat and the linen are two qualitatively different use-values, so also are the two forms of labour that produce them, tailoring and weaving. Were these two objects not qualitatively different, not produced respectively by labour of different quality, they could not stand to each other in the relation of commodities. Coats are not exchanged for coats, one use-value is not exchanged for another of the same kind.

To all the different varieties of values in use there correspond as many different kinds of useful labour, classified according to the order, genus, species, and variety to which they belong in the social division of labour. This division of labour is a necessary condition for the production of commodities, but it does not follow, conversely, that the production of commodities is a necessary condition for the division of labour. In the primitive Indian community there

1. I am inserting the parenthesis because its omission has often given rise to the misunderstanding that every product that is consumed by some one other than its producer is considered in Marx a commodity. [*Engels, 4th German edition*]

is social division of labour, without production of commodities. Or, to take an example nearer home, in every factory the labour is divided according to a system, but this division is not brought about by the operatives mutually exchanging their individual products. Only such products can become commodities with regard to each other, as result from different kinds of labour, each kind being carried on independently and for the account of private individuals.

To resume, then: In the use-value of each commodity there is contained useful labour, *i.e.*, productive activity of a definite kind and exercised with a definite aim. Use-values cannot confront each other as commodities, unless the useful labour embodied in them is qualitatively different in each of them. In a community, the produce of which in general takes the form of commodities, *i.e.*, in a community of commodity producers, this qualitative difference between the useful forms of labour that are carried on independently by individual producers, each on their own account, develops into a complex system, a social division of labour.

Anyhow, whether the coat be worn by the tailor or by his customer, in either case it operates as a use-value. Nor is the relation between the coat and the labour that produced it altered by the circumstance that tailoring may have become a special trade, an independent branch of the social division of labour. Wherever the want of clothing forced them to it, the human race made clothes for thousands of years, without a single man becoming a tailor. But coats and linen, like every other element of material wealth that is not the spontaneous produce of Nature, must invariably owe their existence to a special productive activity, exercised with a definite aim, an activity that appropriates particular nature-given materials to particular human wants. So far therefore as labour is a creator of use-value, is useful labour, it is a necessary condition, independent of all forms of society, for the existence of the human race; it is an eternal nature-imposed necessity, without which there can be no material exchanges between man and Nature, and therefore no life.

The use-values, coat, linen, &c., *i.e.*, the bodies of commodities, are combinations of two elements—matter and labour. If we take away the useful labour expended upon them, a material substratum is always left, which is furnished by Nature without the help of man. The latter can work only as Nature does, that is by changing the form of matter. Nay more, in this work of changing the form he is constantly helped by natural forces. We see, then, that labour is not the only source of material wealth, of use-values produced by labour. As William Petty puts it, labour is its father and the earth its mother.

Let us now pass from the commodity considered as a use-value to the value of commodities.

By our assumption, the coat is worth twice as much as the linen.

But this is a mere quantitative difference, which for the present does not concern us. We bear in mind, however, that if the value of the coat is double that of 10 yds. of linen, 20 yds. of linen must have the same value as one coat. So far as they are values, the coat and the linen are things of a like substance, objective expressions of essentially identical labour. But tailoring and weaving are, qualitatively, different kinds of labour. There are, however, states of society in which one and the same man does tailoring and weaving alternately, in which case these two forms of labour are mere modifications of the labour of the same individual, and no special and fixed functions of different persons; just as the coat which our tailor makes one day, and the trousers which he makes another day, imply only a variation in the labour of one and the same individual. Moreover, we see at a glance that, in our capitalist society, a given portion of human labour is, in accordance with the varying demand, at one time supplied in the form of tailoring, at another in the form of weaving. This change may possibly not take place without friction, but take place it must.

Productive activity, if we leave out of sight its special form, viz., the useful character of the labour, is nothing but the expenditure of human labour-power. Tailoring and weaving, though qualitatively different productive activities, are each a productive expenditure of human brains, nerves, and muscles, and in this sense are human labour. They are but two different modes of expending human labour-power. Of course, this labour-power, which remains the same under all its modifications, must have attained a certain pitch of development before it can be expended in a multiplicity of modes. But the value of a commodity represents human labour in the abstract, the expenditure of human labour in general. And just as in society, a general or a banker plays a great part, but mere man, on the other hand, a very shabby part,[2] so here with human labour. It is the expenditure of simple labour-power, *i.e.*, of the labour-power which, on an average, apart from any special development, exists in the organism of every ordinary individual. Simple average labour, it is true, varies in character in different countries and at different times, but in a particular society it is given. Skilled labour counts only as simple labour intensified, or rather, as multiplied simple labour, a given quantity of skilled being considered equal to a greater quantity of simple labour. Experience shows that this reduction is constantly being made. A commodity may be the product of the most skilled labour, but its value, by equating it to the product of simple unskilled labour, represents a definite quantity of the latter labour alone.[3] The different proportions in which

2. Comp. Hegel, "Philosophie des Rechts." Berlin, 1840. P. 250, § 190. [*Marx*]

different sorts of labour are reduced to unskilled labour as their standard, are established by a social process that goes on behind the backs of the producers, and, consequently, appear to be fixed by custom. For simplicity's sake we shall henceforth account every kind of labour to be unskilled, simple labour; by this we do no more than save ourselves the trouble of making the reduction.

Just as, therefore, in viewing the coat and linen as values, we abstract from their different use-values, so it is with the labour represented by those values: we disregard the difference between its useful forms, weaving and tailoring. As the use-values, coat and linen, are combinations of special productive activities with cloth and yarn, while the values, coat and linen, are, on the other hand, mere homogeneous congelations of undifferentiated labour, so the labour embodied in these latter values does not count by virtue of its productive relation to cloth and yarn, but only as being expenditure of human labour-power. Tailoring and weaving are necessary factors in the creation of the use-values, coat and linen, precisely because these two kinds of labour are of different qualities; but only in so far as abstraction is made from their special qualities, only in so far as both possess the same quality of being human labour, do tailoring and weaving form the substance of the values of the same article.

Coats and linen, however, are not merely values, but values of definite magnitude, and according to our assumption, the coat is worth twice as much as the ten yards of linen. Whence this difference in their values? It is owing to the fact that the linen contains only half as much labour as the coat, and consequently, that in the production of the latter, labour-power must have been expended during twice the time necessary for the production of the former.

While, therefore, with reference to use-value, the labour contained in a commodity counts only qualitatively, with reference to value it counts only quantitatively, and must first be reduced to human labour pure and simple. In the former case, it is a question of How and What, in the latter of How much? How long a time? Since the magnitude of the value of a commodity represents only the quantity of labour embodied in it, it follows that all commodities, when taken in certain proportions, must be equal in value.

If the productive power of all the different sorts of useful labour required for the production of a coat remains unchanged, the sum of the values of the coats produced increases with their number. If one coat represents x days' labour, two coats represent 2x days'

3. The reader must note that we are not speaking here of the wages or value that the labourer gets for a given labour-time, but of the value of the commodity in which that labour-time is materialised. Wages is a category that, as yet, has no existence at the present stage of our investigation. [*Marx*]

labour, and so on. But assume that the duration of the labour necessary for the production of a coat becomes doubled or halved. In the first case, one coat is worth as much as two coats were before; in the second case, two coats are only worth as much as one was before, although in both cases one coat renders the same service as before, and the useful labour embodied in it remains of the same quality. But the quantity of labour spent on its production has altered.

An increase in the quantity of use-values is an increase of material wealth. With two coats two men can be clothed, with one coat only one man. Nevertheless, an increased quantity of material wealth may correspond to a simultaneous fall in the magnitude of its value. This antagonistic movement has its origin in the two-fold character of labour. Productive power has reference, of course, only to labour of some useful concrete form, the efficacy of any special productive activity during a given time being dependent on its productiveness. Useful labour becomes, therefore, a more or less abundant source of products, in proportion to the rise or fall of its productiveness. On the other hand, no change in this productiveness affects the labour represented by value. Since productive power is an attribute of the concrete useful forms of labour, of course it can no longer have any bearing on that labour, so soon as we make abstraction from those concrete useful forms. However then productive power may vary, the same labour, exercised during equal periods of time, always yields equal amounts of value. But it will yield, during equal periods of time, different quantities of values in use; more, if the productive power rise, fewer, if it fall. The same change in productive power, which increases the fruitfulness of labour, and, in consequence, the quantity of use-values produced by that labour, will diminish the total value of this increased quality of use-values, provided such change shorten the total labour-time necessary for their production; and *vice versa*.

On the one hand all labour is, speaking physiologically, an expenditure of human labour-power, and in its character of identical abstract human labour, it creates and forms the value of commodities. On the other hand, all labour is the expenditure of human labour-power in a special form and with a definite aim, and in this, its character of concrete useful labour, it produces use-values.

Section 3. *The Form of Value or Exchange-Value*

Commodities come into the world in the shape of use-values, articles, or goods, such as iron, linen, corn, &c. This is their plain, homely, bodily form. They are, however, commodities, only because they are something two-fold, both objects of utility, and, at the same time, depositories of value. They manifest themselves therefore as commodities, or have the form of commodities, only in so far as they have two forms, a physical or natural form and a value-form.

The reality of the value of commodities differs in this respect from Dame Quickly, that we don't know "where to have it." The value of commodities is the very opposite of the coarse materiality of their substance, not an atom of matter enters into its composition. Turn and examine a single commodity, by itself, as we will, yet in so far as it remains an object of value, it seems impossible to grasp it. If, however, we bear in mind that the value of commodities has a purely social reality, and that they acquire this reality only in so far as they are expressions or embodiments of one identical social substance, viz., human labour, it follows as a matter of course, that value can only manifest itself in the social relation of commodity to commodity. In fact we started from exchange-value, or the exchange relation of commodities, in order to get at the value that lies hidden behind it. We must now return to this form under which value first appeared to us.

Every one knows, if he knows nothing else, that commodities have a value-form common to them all, and presenting a marked contrast with the varied bodily forms of their use-values. I mean their money-form. Here, however, a task is set us, the performance of which has never yet even been attempted by *bourgeois* economy, the task of tracing the genesis of this money-form, of developing the expression of value implied in the value-relation of commodities, from its simplest, almost imperceptible outline, to the dazzling money-form. By doing this we shall, at the same time, solve the riddle presented by money.

The simplest value-relation is evidently that of one commodity to some one other commodity of a different kind. Hence the relation between the values of two commodities supplies us with the simplest expression of the value of a single commodity.

A. ELEMENTARY OR ACCIDENTAL FORM OF VALUE

x commodity A = y commodity B, or
x commodity A is worth y commodity B.
20 yards of linen = 1 coat, or
20 yards of linen are worth 1 coat.

1. *The Two Poles of the Expression of Value: Relative Form and Equivalent Form*

The whole mystery of the form of value lies hidden in this elementary form. Its analysis, therefore, is our real difficulty.

Here two different kinds of commodities (in our example the linen and the coat), evidently play two different parts. The linen expresses its value in the coat; the coat serves as the material in which that value is expressed. The former plays an active, the latter a passive, part. The value of the linen is represented as relative value, or appears in relative form. The coat officiates as equivalent, or appears in equivalent form.

The relative form and the equivalent form are two intimately connected, mutually dependent and inseparable elements of the expression of value; but, at the same time, are mutually exclusive, antagonistic extremes—*i.e.*, poles of the same expression. They are allotted respectively to the two different commodities brought into relation by that expression. It is not possible to express the value of linen in linen. 20 yards of linen = 20 yards of linen is no expression of value. On the contrary, such an equation merely says that 20 yards of linen are nothing else than 20 yards of linen, a definite quantity of the use-value linen. The value of the linen can therefore be expressed only relatively—*i.e.*, in some other commodity. The relative form of the value of the linen pre-supposes, therefore, the presence of some other commodity—here the coat—under the form of an equivalent. On the other hand, the commodity that figures as the equivalent cannot at the same time assume the relative form. That second commodity is not the one whose value is expressed. Its function is merely to serve as the material in which the value of the first commodity is expressed.

No doubt, the expression 20 yards of linen = 1 coat, or 20 yards of linen are worth 1 coat, implies the opposite relation: 1 coat = 20 yards of linen, or 1 coat is worth 20 yards of linen. But, in that case, I must reverse the equation, in order to express the value of the coat relatively; and, so soon as I do that, the linen becomes the equivalent instead of the coat. A single commodity cannot, therefore, simultaneously assume, in the same expression of value, both forms. The very polarity of these forms makes them mutually exclusive.

Whether, then, a commodity assumes the relative form, or the opposite equivalent form, depends entirely upon its accidental position in the expression of value—that is, upon whether it is the commodity whose value is being expressed or the commodity in which value is being expressed.

2. The Relative Form of Value

a. The Nature and Import of This Form

In order to discover how the elementary expression of the value of a commodity lies hidden in the value-relation of two commodities, we must, in the first place, consider the latter entirely apart from its quantitative aspect. The usual mode of procedure is generally the reverse, and in the value-relation nothing is seen but the proportion between definite quantities of two different sorts of commodities that are considered equal to each other. It is apt to be forgotten that the magnitudes of different things can be compared quantitatively, only when those magnitudes are expressed in terms of the same unit. It is only as expressions of such a unit that they are of the same denomination, and therefore commensurable.

Whether 20 yards of linen = 1 coat or = 20 coats or = x coats—that is, whether a given quantity of linen is worth few or many coats, every such statement implies that the linen and coats, as magnitudes of value, are expressions of the same unit, things of the same kind. Linen = coat is the basis of the equation.

But the two commodities whose identity of quality is thus assumed, do not play the same part. It is only the value of the linen that is expressed. And how? By its reference to the coat as its equivalent, as something that can be exchanged for it. In this relation the coat is the mode of existence of value, is value embodied, for only as such is it the same as the linen. On the other hand, the linen's own value comes to the front, receives independent expression, for it is only as being value that it is comparable with the coat as a thing of equal value, or exchangeable with the coat. To borrow an illustration from chemistry, butyric acid is a different substance from propyl formate. Yet both are made up of the same chemical substances, carbon (C), hydrogen (H), and oxygen (O), and that, too, in like proportions—namely $C_4H_8O_2$. If now we equate butyric acid to propyl formate, then, in the first place, propyl formate would be, in this relation, merely a form of existence of $C_4H_8O_2$; and in the second place, we should be stating that butyric acid also consists of $C_4H_8O_2$. Therefore, by thus equating the two substances, expression would be given to their chemical composition., while their different physical forms would be neglected.

If we say that, as values, commodities are mere congelations of human labour, we reduce them by our analysis, it is true, to the abstraction, value; but we ascribe to this value no form apart from their bodily form. It is otherwise in the value-relation of one commodity to another. Here, the one stands forth in its character of value by reason of its relation to the other.

By making the coat the equivalent of the linen, we equate the labour embodied in the former to that in the latter. Now, it is true that the tailoring, which makes the coat, is concrete labour of a different sort from the weaving which makes the linen. But the act of equating it to the weaving, reduces the tailoring to that which is really equal in the two kinds of labour, to their common character of human labour. In this roundabout way, then, the fact is expressed, that weaving also, in so far as it weaves value, has nothing to distinguish it from tailoring, and, consequently, is abstract human labour. It is the expression of equivalence between different sorts of commodities that alone brings into relief the specific character of value-creating labour, and this it does by actually reducing the different varieties of labour embodied in the different kinds of commodities to their common quality of human labour in the abstract.[4]

There is, however, something else required beyond the expression of the specific character of the labour of which the value of the linen consists. Human labour-power in motion, or human labour, creates value, but is not itself value. It becomes value only in its congealed state, when embodied in the form of some object. In order to express the value of the linen as a congelation of human labour, that value must be expressed as having objective existence, as being a something materially different from the linen itself, and yet a something common to the linen and all other commodities. The problem is already solved.

When occupying the position of equivalent in the equation of value, the coat ranks qualitatively as the equal of the linen, as something of the same kind, because it is value. In this position it is a thing in which we see nothing but value, or whose palpable bodily form represents value. Yet the coat itself, the body of the commodity, coat, is a mere use-value. A coat as such no more tells us it is value, than does the first piece of linen we take hold of. This shows that when placed in value-relation to the linen, the coat signifies more than when out of that relation, just as many a man strutting about in a gorgeous uniform counts for more than when in mufti.

In the production of the coat, human labour-power, in the shape of tailoring, must have been actually expended. Human labour is therefore accumulated in it. In this aspect the coat is a depository of value, but though worn to a thread, it does not let this fact show through. And as equivalent of the linen in the value equation, it exists under this aspect alone, counts therefore as embodied value, as a body that is value. A, for instance, cannot be "your majesty" to B, unless at the same time majesty in B's eyes assumes the

4. The celebrated Franklin, one of the first economists, after Wm. Petty, who saw through the nature of value, says: "Trade in general being nothing else but the exchange of labour for labour, the value of all things is . . . most justly measured by labour." ("The works of B. Franklin, &c.," edited by Sparks. Boston, 1836, Vol. II., p. 267.) Franklin is unconscious that by estimating the value of everything in labour, he makes abstraction from any difference in the sorts of labour exchanged, and thus reduces them all to equal human labour. But although ignorant of this, yet he says it. He speaks first of "the one labour," then of "the other labour," and finally of "labour," without further qualification, as the substance of the value of everything. [*Marx*]

bodily form of A, and, what is more, with every new father of the people, changes its features, hair, and many other things besides.

Hence, in the value equation, in which the coat is the equivalent of the linen, the coat officiates as the form of value. The value of the commodity linen is expressed by the bodily form of the commodity coat, the value of one by the use-value of the other. As a use-value, the linen is something palpably different from the coat; as value, it is the same as the coat, and now has the appearance of a coat. Thus the linen acquires a value-form different from its physical form. The fact that it is value, is made manifest by its equality with the coat, just as the sheep's nature of a Christian is shown in his resemblance to the Lamb of God.

We see, then, all that our analysis of the value of commodities has already told us, is told us by the linen itself, so soon as it comes into communication with another commodity, the coat. Only it betrays its thoughts in that language with which alone it is familiar, the language of commodities. In order to tell us that its own value is created by labour in its abstract character of human labour, it says that the coat, in so far as it is worth as much as the linen, and therefore is value, consists of the same labour as the linen. In order to inform us that its sublime reality as value is not the same as its buckram body, it says that value has the appearance of a coat, and consequently that so far as the linen is value, it and the coat are as like as two peas. We may here remark, that the language of commodities has, besides Hebrew, many other more or less correct dialects. The German "Wertsein," to be worth, for instance, expresses in a less striking manner than the Romance verbs "valere," "valer," "valoir," that the equating of commodity B to commodity A, is commodity A's own mode of expressing its value. Paris vaut bien une messe.

By means, therefore, of the value-relation expressed in our equation, the bodily form of commodity B becomes the value-form of commodity A, or the body of commodity B acts as a mirror to the value of commodity A.[5] By putting itself in relation with commodity B, as value *in propria persona*, as the matter of which human labour is made up, the commodity A converts the value in use, B, into the substance in which to express its, A's, own value. The value of A, thus expressed in the use-value of B, has taken the form of relative value.

5. In a sort of way, it is with man as with commodities. Since he comes into the world neither with a looking glass in his hand, nor as a Fichtian philosopher, to whom "I am I" is sufficient, man first sees and recognises himself in other men. Peter only establishes his own identity as a man by first comparing himself with Paul as being of like kind. And thereby Paul, just as he stands in his Pauline personality, becomes to Peter the type of the genus homo. [*Marx*]

b. Quantitative Determination of Relative Value

Every commodity, whose value it is intended to express, is a useful object of given quantity, as 15 bushels of corn, or 100 lbs. of coffee. And a given quantity of any commodity contains a definite quantity of human labour. The value-form must therefore not only express value generally, but also value in definite quantity. Therefore, in the value-relation of commodity A to commodity B, of the linen to the coat, not only is the latter, as value in general, made the equal in quality of the linen, but a definite quantity of coat (1 coat) is made the equivalent of a definite quantity (20 yards) of linen.

The equation, 20 yards of linen=1 coat, or 20 yards of linen are worth one coat, implies that the same quantity of value-substance (congealed labour) is embodied in both; that the two commodities have each cost the same amount of labour of the same quantity of labour-time. But the labour-time necessary for the production of 20 yards of linen or 1 coat varies with every change in the productiveness of weaving or tailoring. We have now to consider the influence of such changes on the quantitative aspect of the relative expression of value.

I. Let the value of the linen vary,[6] that of the coat remaining constant. If, say in consequence of the exhaustion of flax-growing soil, the labour-time necessary for the production of the linen be doubled, the value of the linen will also be doubled. Instead of the equation, 20 yards of linen=1 coat, we should have 20 yards of linen=2 coats, since 1 coat would now contain only half the labour-time embodied in 20 yards of linen. If, on the other hand, in consequence, say, of improved looms, this labour-time be reduced by one-half, the value of the linen would fall by one-half. Consequently, we should have 20 yards of linen=½ coat. The relative value of commodity A, *i.e.*, its value expressed in commodity B, rises and falls directly as the value of A, the value of B being supposed constant.

II. Let the value of the linen remain constant, while the value of the coat varies. If, under these circumstances, in consequence, for instance, of a poor crop of wool, the labour-time necessary for the production of a coat becomes doubled, we have instead of 20 yards of linen=1 coat, 20 yards of linen=½ coat. If, on the other hand, the value of the coat sinks by one-half, then 20 yards of linen=2 coats. Hence, if the value of commodity A remain constant, its relative value expressed in commodity B rises and falls inversely as the value of B.

6. Value is here, as occasionally in the preceding pages, used in sense of value determined as to quantity, or of magnitude of value. [*Marx*]

If we compare the different cases in I. and II., we see that the same change of magnitude in relative value may arise from totally opposite causes. Thus, the equation, 20 yards of linen=1 coat, becomes 20 yards of linen=2 coats, either, because the value of the linen has doubled, or because the value of the coat has fallen by one-half; and it becomes 20 yards of linen=½ coat, either, because the value of the linen has fallen by one-half, or because the value of the coat has doubled.

III. Let the quantities of labour-time respectively necessary for the production of the linen and the coat vary simultaneously in the same direction and in the same proportion. In this case 20 yards of linen continue equal to 1 coat, however much their values may have altered. Their change of value is seen as soon as they are compared with a third commodity, whose value has remained constant. If the values of all commodities rose or fell simultaneously, and in the same proportion, their relative values would remain unaltered. Their real change of value would appear from the diminished or increased quantity of commodities produced in a given time.

IV. The labour-time respectively necessary for the production of the linen and the coat, and therefore the value of these commodities may simultaneously vary in the same direction, but at unequal rates, or in opposite directions, or in other ways. The effect of all these possible different variations, on the relative value of a commodity, may be deduced from the results of I., II., and III.

Thus real changes in the magnitude of value are neither unequivocally nor exhaustively reflected in their relative expression, that is, in the equation expressing the magnitude of relative value. The relative value of a commodity may vary, although its value remains constant. Its relative value may remain constant, although its value varies; and finally, simultaneous variations in the magnitude of value and in that of its relative expression by no means necessarily correspond in amount. * * *

Section 4. The Fetishism of Commodities and the Secret Thereof

A commodity appears, at first sight, a very trivial thing, and easily understood. Its analysis shows that it is, in reality, a very queer thing, abounding in metaphysical subtleties and theological niceties. So far as it is a value in use, there is nothing mysterious about it, whether we consider it from the point of view that by its properties it is capable of satisfying human wants, or from the point that those properties are the product of human labour. It is as clear as noon-day, that man, by his industry, changes the forms of the materials furnished by Nature, in such a way as to make them useful to him. The form of wood, for instance, is altered, by making a table out of it. Yet, for all that, the table continues to be that common, every-day thing, wood. But, so soon as it steps forth as a commodity, it is changed into something transcendent. It not only stands with its feet on the ground, but, in relation to all other commodities, it stands on its head, and evolves out of its wooden brain grotesque ideas, far more wonderful than "table-turning" ever was.

The mystical character of commodities does not originate, there-fore, in their use-value. Just as little does it proceed from the nature of the determining factors of value. For, in the first place, however varied the useful kinds of labour, or productive activities, may be, it is a physiological fact, that they are functions of the human organism, and that each such function, whatever may be its nature or form, is essentially the expenditure of human brain, nerves, muscles, &c. Secondly, with regard to that which forms the ground-work for the quantitative determination of value, namely, the duration of that expenditure, or the quantity of labour, it is quite clear that there is a palpable difference between its quantity and quality. In all states of society, the labour-time that it costs to produce the means of subsistence, must necessarily be an object of interest to mankind, though not of equal interest in different stages of development.[7] And lastly, from the moment that men in any way work for one another, their labour assumes a social form.

Whence, then, arises the enigmatical character of the product of labour, so soon as it assumes the form of commodities? Clearly from this form itself. The equality of all sorts of human labour is expressed objectively by their products all being equally values; the measure of the expenditure of labour-power by the duration of that expenditure, takes the form of the quantity of value of the products of labour; and finally, the mutual relations of the producers, within which the social character of their labour affirms itself, take the form of a social relation between the products.

A commodity is therefore a mysterious thing, simply because in it the social character of men's labour appears to them as an objective character stamped upon the product of that labour; because the relation of the producers to the sum total of their own labour is presented to them as a social relation, existing not between themselves, but between the products of their labour. This is the reason why the products of labour become commodities, social things whose qualities are at the same time perceptible and imperceptible

---

7. Among the ancient Germans the unit for measuring land was what could be harvested in a day, and was called Tagwerk, Tagwanne (jurnale, or terra jurnalis, or diornalis), Mannsmaad, &c. (See G. L. von Maurer. "Einleitung zur Geschichte der Mark—, &c. Verfassung," München, 1854, p. 129 sq.) [*Marx*]

by the senses. In the same way the light from an object is perceived by us not as the subjective excitation of our optic nerve, but as the objective form of something outside the eye itself. But, in the act of seeing, there is at all events, an actual passage of light from one thing to another, from the external object to the eye. There is a physical relation between physical things. But it is different with commodities. There, the existence of the things *quâ* commodities, and the value-relation between the products of labour which stamps them as commodities, have absolutely no connexion with their physical properties and with the material relations arising therefrom. There it is a definite social relation between men, that assumes, in their eyes, the fantastic form of a relation between things. In order, therefore, to find an analogy, we must have recourse to the mist-enveloped regions of the religious world. In that world the productions of the human brain appear as independent beings endowed with life, and entering into relation both with one another and the human race. So it is in the world of commodities with the products of men's hands. This I call the Fetishism which attaches itself to the products of labour, so soon as they are produced as commodities, and which is therefore inseparable from the production of commodities.

This Fetishism of commodities has its origin, as the foregoing analysis has already shown, in the peculiar social character of the labour that produces them.

As a general rule, articles of utility become commodities, only because they are products of the labour of private individuals or groups of individuals who carry on their work independently of each other. The sum total of the labour of all these private individuals forms the aggregate labour of society. Since the producers do not come into social contact with each other until they exchange their products, the specific social character of each producer's labour does not show itself except in the act of exchange. In other words, the labour of the individual asserts itself as a part of the labour of society, only by means of the relations which the act of exchange establishes directly between the products, and indirectly, through them, between the producers. To the latter, therefore, the relations connecting the labour of one individual with that of the rest appear, not as direct social relations between individuals at work, but as what they really are, material relations between persons and social relations between things. It is only by being exchanged that the products of labour acquire, as values, one uniform social status, distinct from their varied forms of existence as objects of utility. This division of a product into a useful thing and a value becomes practically important, only when exchange has acquired such an extension that useful articles are produced for the

purpose of being exchanged, and their character as values has therefore to be taken into account, beforehand, during production.
From this moment the labour of the individual producer acquires
socially a two-fold character. On the one hand, it must, as a
definite useful kind of labour, satisfy a definite social want, and
thus hold its place as part and parcel of the collective labour of all,
as a branch of a social division of labour that has sprung up spontaneously. On the other hand, it can satisfy the manifold wants of
the individual producer himself, only in so far as the mutual
exchangeability of all kinds of useful private labour is an
established social fact, and therefore the private useful labour of
each producer ranks on an equality with that of all others. The
equalisation of the most different kinds of labour can be the result
only of an abstraction from their inequalities, or of reducing them
to their common denominator, viz., expenditure of human
labour-power or human labour in the abstract. The two-fold social
character of the labour of the individual appears to him, when
reflected in his brain, only under those forms which are impressed
upon that labour in every-day practice by the exchange of products.
In this way, the character that his own labour possesses of being
socially useful takes the form of the condition, that the product
must be not only useful, but useful for others, and the social character that his particular labour has of being the equal of all other
particular kinds of labour, takes the form that all the physically different articles that are the products of labour, have one common
quality, viz., that of having value.

Hence, when we bring the products of our labour into relation
with each other as values, it is not because we see in these articles
the material receptacles of homogeneous human labour. Quite the
contrary: whenever, by an exchange, we equate as values our different products, by that very act, we also equate, as human labour,
the different kinds of labour expended upon them. We are not
aware of this, nevertheless we do it. Value, therefore, does not stalk
about with a label describing what it is. It is value, rather, that converts every product into a social hieroglyphic. Later on, we try to
decipher the hieroglyphic, to get behind the secret of our own
social products; for to stamp an object of utility as a value, is just as
much a social product as language. The recent scientific discovery,
that the products of labour, so far as they are values, are but material expressions of the human labour spent in their production,
marks, indeed, an epoch in the history of the development of the
human race, but, by no means, dissipates the mist through which
the social character of labour appears to us to be an objective character of the products themselves. The fact, that in the particular
form of production with which we are dealing, viz., the production

of commodities, the specific social character of private labour carried on independently, consists in the equality of every kind of that labour, by virtue of its being human labour, which character, therefore, assumes in the product the form of value—this fact appears to the producers, notwithstanding the discovery above referred to, to be just as real and final, as the fact, that, after the discovery by science of the component gases of air, the atmosphere itself remained unaltered.

What, first of all, practically concerns producers when they make an exchange, is the question, how much of some other product they get for their own? in what proportions the products are exchangeable? When these proportions have, by custom, attained a certain stability, they appear to result from the nature of the products, so that, for instance, one ton of iron and two ounces of gold appear as naturally to be of equal value as a pound of gold and a pound of iron in spite of their different physical and chemical qualities appear to be of equal weight. The character of having value, when once impressed upon products, obtains fixity only by reason of their acting and re-acting upon each other as quantities of value. These quantities vary continually, independently of the will, foresight and action of the producers. To them, their own social action takes the form of the action of objects, which rule the producers instead of being ruled by them. It requires a fully developed production of commodities before, from accumulated experience alone, the scientific conviction springs up, that all the different kinds of private labour, which are carried on independently of each other, and yet as spontaneously developed branches of the social division of labour, are continually being reduced to the quantitative proportions in which society requires them. And why? Because, in the midst of all the accidental and ever fluctuating exchange-relations between the products, the labour-time socially necessary for their production forcibly asserts itself like an over-riding law of Nature. The law of gravity thus asserts itself when a house falls about our ears.[8] The determination of the magnitude of value by labour-time is therefore a secret, hidden under the apparent fluctuations in the relative values of commodities. Its discovery, while removing all appearance of mere accidentality from the determination of the magnitude of the values of products, yet in no way alters the mode in which that determination takes place.

Man's reflections on the forms of social life, and consequently, also, his scientific analysis of those forms, take a course directly

8. "What are we to think of a law that asserts itself only by periodical revolutions? It is just nothing but a law of Nature, founded on the want of knowledge of those whose action is the subject of it." (Friedrich Engels: "Umrisse zu einer Kritik de Nationalökonomie," in the "Deutsch-Französische Jahrbücher," edited by Arnold Ruge and Karl Marx. Paris, 1844.) [*Marx*]

opposite to that of their actual historical development. He begins, post festum, with the results of the process of development ready to hand before him. The characters that stamp products as commodities, and whose establishment is a necessary preliminary to the circulation of commodities, have already acquired the stability of natural, self-understood forms of social life, before man seeks to decipher, not their historical character, for in his eyes they are immutable, but their meaning. Consequently it was the analysis of the prices of commodities that alone led to the determination of the magnitude of value, and it was the common expression of all commodities in money that alone led to the establishment of their characters as values. It is, however, just this ultimate money-form of the world of commodities that actually conceals, instead of disclosing, the social character of private labour, and the social relations between the individual producers. When I state that coats or boots stand in a relation to linen, because it is the universal incarnation of abstract human labour, the absurdity of the statement is self-evident. Nevertheless, when the producers of coats and boots compare those articles with linen, or, what is the same thing, with gold or silver, as the universal equivalent, they express the relation between their own private labour and the collective labour of society in the same absurd form.

The categories of bourgeois economy consist of such like forms. They are forms of thought expressing with social validity the conditions and relations of a definite, historically determined mode of production, viz., the production of commodities. The whole mystery of commodities, all the magic and necromancy that surrounds the products of labour as long as they take the form of commodities, vanishes therefore, so soon as we come to other forms of production.

Since Robinson Crusoe's experiences are a favourite theme with political economists, let us take a look at him on his island. Moderate though he be, yet some few wants he has to satisfy, and must therefore do a little useful work of various sorts, such as making tools and furniture, taming goats, fishing and hunting. Of his prayers and the like we take no account, since they are a source of pleasure to him, and he looks upon them as so much recreation. In spite of the variety of his work, he knows that his labour, whatever its form, is but the activity of one and the same Robinson, and consequently, that it consists of nothing but different modes of human labour. Necessity itself compels him to apportion his time accurately between his different kinds of work. Whether one kind occupies a greater space in his general activity than another, depends on the difficulties, greater or less as the case may be, to be overcome in attaining the useful effect aimed at. This our friend

Robinson soon learns by experience, and having rescued a watch, ledger, and pen and ink from the wreck, commences, like a true-born Briton, to keep a set of books. His stock-book contains a list of the objects of utility that belong to him, of the operations necessary for their production; and lastly, of the labour-time that definite quantities of those objects have, on an average, cost him. All the relations between Robinson and the objects that form this wealth of his own creation, are here so simple and clear as to be intelligible without exertion, even to Mr. Sedley Taylor. And yet those relations contain all that is essential to the determination of value.

Let us now transport ourselves from Robinson's island bathed in light to the European middle ages shrouded in darkness. Here, instead of the independent man, we find everyone dependent, serfs and lords, vassals and suzerains, laymen and clergy. Personal dependence here characterises the social relations of production just as much as it does the other spheres of life organised on the basis of that production. But for the very reason that personal dependence forms the ground-work of society, there is no necessity for labour and its products to assume a fantastic form different from their reality. They take the shape, in the transactions of society, of services in kind and payments in kind. Here the particular and natural form of labour, and not, as in a society based on production of commodities, its general abstract form is the immediate social form of labour. Compulsory labour is just as properly measured by time, as commodity-producing labour, but every serf knows that what he expends in the service of his lord, is a definite quantity of his own personal labour-power. The tithe to be rendered to the priest is more matter of fact than his blessing. No matter, then, what we may think of the parts played by the different classes of people themselves in this society, the social relations between individuals in the performance of their labour, appear at all events as their own mutual personal relations, and are not disguised under the shape of social relations between the products of labour.

For an example of labour in common or directly associated labour, we have no occasion to go back to that spontaneously developed form which we find on the threshold of the history of all civilised races. We have one close at hand in the patriarchal industries of a peasant family, that produces corn, cattle, yarn, linen, and clothing for home use. These different articles are, as regards the family, so many products of its labour, but as between themselves, they are not commodities. The different kinds of labour, such as tillage, cattle tending, spinning, weaving and making clothes, which result in the various products, are in themselves, and such as they are, direct social functions, because functions of the family, which, just as much as a society based on the production of commodities, possesses a spontaneously developed system of division of labour. The distribution of the work within the family, and the regulation of the labour-time of the several members, depend as well upon differences of age and sex as upon natural conditions varying with the seasons. The labour-power of each individual, by its very nature, operates in this case merely as a definite portion of the whole labour-power of the family, and therefore, the measure of the expenditure of individual labour-power by its duration, appears here by its very nature as a social character of their labour.

Let us now picture to ourselves, by way of change, a community of free individuals, carrying on their work with the means of production in common, in which the labour-power of all the different individuals is consciously applied as the combined labour-power of the community. All the characteristics of Robinson's labour are here repeated, but with this difference, that they are social, instead of individual. Everything produced by him was exclusively the result of his own personal labour, and therefore simply an object of use for himself. The total product of our community is a social product. One portion serves as fresh means of production and remains social. But another portion is consumed by the members as means of subsistence. A distribution of this portion amongst them is consequently necessary. The mode of this distribution will vary with the productive organisation of the community, and the degree of historical development attained by the producers. We will assume, but merely for the sake of a parallel with the production of commodities, that the share of each individual producer in the means of subsistence is determined by his labour-time. Labour-time would, in that case, play a double part. Its apportionment in accordance with a definite social plan maintains the proper proportion between the different kinds of work to be done and the various wants of the community. On the other hand, it also serves as a measure of the portion of the common labour borne by each individual, and of his share in the part of the total product destined for individual consumption. The social relations of the individual producers, with regard both to their labour and to its products, are in this case perfectly simple and intelligible, and that with regard not only to production but also to distribution.

The religious world is but the reflex of the real world. And for a society based upon the production of commodities, in which the producers in general enter into social relations with one another by treating their products as commodities and values, whereby they reduce their individual private labour to the standard of homogeneous human labour—for such a society, Christianity with its *cultus* of abstract man, more especially in its bourgeois developments, Protestantism, Deism, &c., is the most fitting form of religion. In the ancient Asiatic and other ancient modes of production, we find that the conversion of products into commodities, and therefore the conversion of men into producers of commodities, holds a subordinate place, which, however, increases in importance as the primitive communities approach nearer and nearer to their dissolution. Trading nations, properly so called, exist in the ancient world only in its interstices, like the gods of Epicurus in the Intermundia, or like Jews in the pores of Polish society. Those ancient social organisms of production are, as compared with bourgeois society, extremely simple and transparent. But they are founded either on the immature development of man individually, who has not yet severed the umbilical cord that unites him with his fellowmen in a primitive tribal community, or upon direct relations of subjection. They can arise and exist only when the development of the productive power of labour has not risen beyond a low stage, and when, therefore, the social relations within the sphere of material life, between man and man, and between man and Nature, are correspondingly narrow. This narrowness is reflected in the ancient worship of Nature, and in the other elements of the popular religions. The religious reflex of the real world can, in any case, only then finally vanish, when the practical relations of every-day life offer to man none but perfectly intelligible and reasonable relations with regard to his fellowmen and to Nature.

The life-process of society, which is based on the process of material production, does not strip off its mystical veil until it is treated as production by freely associated men, and is consciously regulated by them in accordance with a settled plan. This, however, demands for society a certain material ground-work or set of conditions of existence which in their turn are the spontaneous product of a long and painful process of development.

Political Economy has indeed analysed, however incompletely, value and its magnitude, and has discovered what lies beneath these forms. But it has never once asked the question why labour is represented by the value of its product and labour-time by the magnitude of that value. These formulæ, which bear it stamped upon them in unmistakeable letters that they belong to a state of society, in which the process of production has the mastery over man, instead of being controlled by him, such formulæ appear to the bourgeois intellect to be as much a self-evident necessity imposed by Nature as productive labour itself. Hence forms of social production that preceded the bourgeois form, are treated by the bourgeoisie in much the same way as the Fathers of the Church treated pre-Christian religions.

To what extent some economists are misled by the Fetishism inherent in commodities, or by the objective appearance of the social characteristics of labour, is shown, amongst other ways, by the dull and tedious quarrel over the part played by Nature in the formation of exchange-value. Since exchange-value is a definite social manner of expressing the amount of labour bestowed upon object, Nature has no more to do with it, than it has in fixing the course of exchange.

The mode of production in which the product takes the form of a commodity, or is produced directly for exchange, is the most general and most embryonic form of bourgeois production. It therefore makes its appearance at an early date in history, though not in the same predominating and characteristic manner as now-a-days. Hence its Fetish character is comparatively easy to be seen through. But when we come to more concrete forms, even this appearance of simplicity vanishes. Whence arose the illusions of the monetary system? To it gold and silver, when serving as money, did not represent a social relation between producers but were natural objects with strange social properties. And modern economy, which looks down with such disdain on the monetary system, does not its superstition come out as clear as noon-day, whenever it treats of capital? How long is it since economy discarded the physiocratic illusion, that rents grow out of the soil and not out of society?

But not to anticipate, we will content ourselves with yet another example relating to the commodity-form. Could commodities themselves speak, they would say: Our use-value may be a thing that interests men. It is no part of us as objects. What, however, does belong to us as objects, is our value. Our natural intercourse as commodities proves it. In the eyes of each other we are nothing but exchange-values. Now listen how those commodities speak through the mouth of the economist. "Value"—(*i.e.*, exchange-value) "is a property of things, riches"—(*i.e.*, use-value) "of man. Value, in this sense, necessarily implies exchanges, riches do not." "Riches" (use-value) "are the attribute of men, value is the attribute of commodities. A man or a community is rich, a pearl or a diamond is valuable. . . . A pearl or a diamond is valuable" as a pearl or diamond. So far no chemist has ever discovered exchange-value either in a pearl or a diamond. The economic discoverers of this chemical element, who by-the-by lay special claim to critical acumen, find however that the use-value of objects belongs to them independently of their material properties, while their value, on the other hand, forms a part of them as objects. What confirms them in this view, is the peculiar circumstance that the use-value of objects is realised without exchange, by means of a direct relation between the objects and man, while, on the other hand, their value is realised only by exchange, that is, by means of a social process. Who fails here to call to mind our good friend, Dogberry, who informs neighbour Seacoal, that, "To be a well-favoured man is the gift of fortune; but reading and writing comes by Nature."

Part II. The Transformation of Money into Capital

CHAPTER IV. THE GENERAL FORMULA FOR CAPITAL

The circulation of commodities is the starting-point of capital. The production of commodities, their circulation, and that more developed form of their circulation called commerce, these form the historical ground-work from which it rises. The modern history of capital dates from the creation in the 16th century of a world-embracing commerce and a world-embracing market.

If we abstract from the material substance of the circulation of commodities, that is, from the exchange of the various use-values, and consider only the economic forms produced by this process of circulation, we find its final result to be money: this final product of the circulation of commodities is the first form in which capital appears.

As a matter of history, capital, as opposed to landed property, invariably takes the form at first of money; it appears as moneyed wealth, as the capital of the merchant and of the usurer. But we have no need to refer to the origin of capital in order to discover that the first form of appearance of capital is money. We can see it daily under our very eyes. All new capital, to commence with, comes on the stage, that is, on the market, whether of commodities, labour, or money, even in our days, in the shape of money that by a definite process has to be transformed into capital.

The first distinction we notice between money that is money only, and money that is capital, is nothing more than a difference in their form of circulation.

The simplest form of the circulation of commodities is C—M—C, the transformation of commodities into money, and the change of the money back again into commodities; or selling in order to buy. But alongside of this form we find another specifically different form: M—C—M, the transformation of money into commodities, and the change of commodities back again into money; or buying in order to sell. Money that circulates in the latter manner is thereby transformed into, becomes capital, and is already potentially capital.

Now let us examine the circuit M—C—M a little closer. It consists, like the other, of two antithetical phases. In the first phase, M—C, or the purchase, the money is changed into a commodity.

In the second phase, C—M, or the sale, the commodity is changed back again into money. The combination of these two phases constitutes the single movement whereby money is exchanged for a commodity, and the same commodity is again exchanged for money; whereby a commodity is bought in order to be sold, or, neglecting the distinction in form between buying and selling, whereby a commodity is bought with a commodity. The result, in which the phases of the process vanish, is the exchange of money for money, M—M. If I purchase 2,000 lbs. of cotton for £100, and resell the 2,000 lbs. of cotton for £110, I have, in fact, exchanged £100 for £110, money for money.

Now it is evident that the circuit M—C—M would be absurd and without meaning if the intention were to exchange by this means two equal sums of money, £100 for £100. The miser's plan would be far simpler and surer; he sticks to his £100 instead of exposing it to the dangers of circulation. And yet, whether the merchant who has paid £100 for his cotton sells it for £110, or lets it go for £100, or even £50, his money has, at all events, gone through a characteristic and original movement, quite different in kind from that which it goes through in the hands of the peasant who sells corn, and with the money thus set free buys clothes. We have therefore to examine first the distinguishing characteristics of the forms of the circuits M—C—M and C—M—C, and in doing this the real difference that underlies the mere difference of form will reveal itself.

Let us see, in the first place, what the two forms have in common.

Both circuits are resolvable into the same two antithetical phases, C—M, a sale, and M—C, a purchase. In each of these phases the same material elements—a commodity, and money, and the same economic dramatis personæ, a buyer and a seller—confront one another. Each circuit is the unity of the same two antithetical phases, and in each case this unity is brought about by the intervention of three contracting parties, of whom one only sells, another only buys, while the third both buys and sells.

What, however, first and foremost distinguishes the circuit C—M—C from the circuit M—C—M, is the inverted order of succession of the two phases. The simple circulation of commodities begins with a sale and ends with a purchase, while the circulation of money as capital begins with a purchase and ends with a sale. In the one case both the starting-point and the goal are commodities, in the other they are money. In the first form the movement is brought about by the intervention of money, in the second by that of a commodity.

In the circulation C—M—C, the money is in the end converted into a commodity, that serves as a use-value; it is spent once for all.

In the inverted form, M—C—M, on the contrary, the buyer lays out money in order that, as a seller, he may recover money. By the purchase of his commodity he throws money into circulation, in order to withdraw it again by the sale of the same commodity. He lets the money go, but only with the sly intention of getting it back again. The money, therefore, is not spent, it is merely advance.

In the circuit C—M—C, the same piece of money changes its place twice. The seller gets it from the buyer and pays it away to another seller. The complete circulation, which begins with the receipt, concludes with the payment, of money for commodities. It is the very contrary in the circuit M—C—M. Here it is not the piece of money that changes its place twice, but the commodity. The buyer takes it from the hands of the seller and passes it into the hands of another buyer. Just as in the simple circulation of commodities the double change of place of the same piece of money effects its passage from one hand into another, so here the double change of place of the same commodity brings about the reflux of the money to its point of departure.

Such reflux is not dependent on the commodity being sold for more than was paid for it. This circumstance influences only the amount of the money that comes back. The reflux itself takes place, so soon as the purchased commodity is resold, in other words, so soon as the circuit M—C—M is completed. We have here, therefore, a palpable difference between the circulation of money as capital, and its circulation as mere money.

The circuit C—M—C comes completely to an end, so soon as the money brought in by the sale of one commodity is abstracted again by the purchase of another.

If, nevertheless, there follows a reflux of money to its starting-point, this can only happen through a renewal or repetition of the operation. If I sell a quarter of corn of £3, and with this £3 buy clothes, the money, so far as I am concerned, is spent and done with. It belongs to the clothes merchant. If I now sell a second quarter of corn, money indeed flows back to me, not however as a sequel to the first transaction, but in consequence of its repetition. The money again leaves me, so soon as I complete this second transaction by a fresh purchase. Therefore, in the circuit C—M—C, the expenditure of money has nothing to do with its reflux. On the other hand, in M—C—M, the reflux of the money is conditioned by the very mode of its expenditure. Without this reflux, the operation fails, or the process is interrupted and incomplete, owing to the absence of its complementary and final phase, the sale.

The circuit C—M—C starts with one commodity, and finishes with another, which falls out of circulation and into consumption. Consumption, the satisfaction of wants, in one word, use-value, is its end and aim. The circuit M—C—M, on the contrary, com-

mences with money and ends with money. Its leading motive, and
the goal that attracts it, is therefore mere exchange-value.

In the simple circulation of commodities, the two extremes of
the circuit have the same economic form. They are both commodities, and commodities of equal value. But they are also use-values
differing in their qualities, as, for example, corn and clothes. The
exchange of products, of the different materials in which the labour
of society is embodied, forms here the basis of the movement. It is
otherwise in the circulation M—C—M, which at first sight appears
purposeless, because tautological. Both extremes have the same
economic form. They are both money, and therefore are not qualitatively different use-values; for money is but the converted form of
commodities, in which their particular use-values vanish. To
exchange £100 for cotton, and then this same cotton again for
£110, is merely a roundabout way of exchanging money for money,
the same for the same, and appears to be an operation just as purposeless as it is absurd. One sum of money is distinguishable from
another only by its amount. The character and tendency of the
process M—C—M, is therefore not due to any qualitative difference between its extremes, both being money, but solely to their
quantitative difference. More money is withdrawn from circulation
at the finish than was thrown into it at the start. The cotton that
was bought for £100 is perhaps resold for £100+£10 or £110. The
exact form of this process is therefore M—C—M', where M'
$= M+\triangle M =$ the original sum advanced, plus an increment. This
increment or excess over the original value I call "surplus-value." The
value originally advanced, therefore, not only remains intact while
in circulation, but adds to itself a surplus-value or expands itself.
It is this movement that converts it into capital.

Of course, it is also possible, that in C—M—C, the two extremes C—C, say corn and clothes, may represent different quantities of value. The farmer may sell his corn above its value, or may
buy the clothes at less than their value. He may, on the other
hand, "be done" by the clothes merchant. Yet, in the form of circulation now under consideration, such differences in value are
purely accidental. The fact that the corn and the clothes are equivalents, does not deprive the process of all meaning, as it does in
M—C—M. The equivalence of their values is rather a necessary
condition to its normal course.

The repetition or renewal of the act of selling in order to buy, is
kept within bounds by the very object it aims at, namely, consumption or the satisfaction of definite wants, an aim that lies altogether outside the sphere of circulation. But when we buy in order
to sell, we, on the contrary, begin and end with the same thing,
money, exchange-value; and thereby the movement becomes interminable. No doubt, M becomes $M+\triangle M$, £100 become £110. But

when viewed in their qualitative aspect alone, £110 are the same as £100, namely money; and considered quantitatively, £110 is, like £100, a sum of definite and limited value. If now, the £110 be spent as money, they cease to play their part. They are no longer capital. Withdrawn from circulation, they become petrified into a hoard, and though they remained in that state till doomsday, not a single farthing would accrue to them. If, then, the expansion of value is once aimed at, there is just the same inducement to augment the value of the £110 as that of the £100; for both are but limited expressions for exchange-value, and therefore both have the same vocation to approach, by quantitative increase, as near as possible to absolute wealth. Momentarily, indeed, the value originally advanced, the £100, is distinguishable from the surplus-value of £10 that is annexed to it during circulation; but the distinction vanishes immediately. At the end of the process, we do not receive with one hand the original £100, and with the other, the surplus-value of £10. We simply get a value of £110, which is in exactly the same condition and fitness for commencing the expanding process, as the original £100 was. Money ends the movement only to begin it again.[9] Therefore, the final result of every separate circuit, in which a purchase and consequent sale are completed, forms of itself the starting-point of a new circuit. The simple circulation of commodities—selling in order to buy—is a means of carrying out a purpose unconnected with circulation, namely, the appropriation of use-values, the satisfaction of wants. The circulation of money as capital is, on the contrary, an end in itself, for the expansion of value takes place only within this constantly renewed movement. The circulation of capital has therefore no limits.[1]

9. "Capital is divisible ... into the original capital and the profit, the increment to the capital ... although in practice this profit is immediately turned into capital, and set in motion with the original." (F. Engels, "Umrisse zu einer Kritik der Nationalökonomie, in the "Deutsch-Französische Jahrbücher," edited by Arnold Ruge and Karl Marx." Paris, 1844, p. 99.) [*Marx*]
1. Aristotle opposes Oeconomic to Chrematistic. He starts from the former. So far as it is the art of gaining a livelihood, it is limited to procuring those articles that are necessary to existence, and useful either to a household or the state. "True wealth consists of such values in use; for the quantity of possessions of this kind, capable of making life pleasant, is not unlimited. There is, however, a second mode of acquiring things, to which we may by preference and with correctness give the name of Chrematistic, and in this case there appear to be no limits to riches and possessions. Trade (literally re-

tail trade, and Aristotle takes this kind because in it values in use predominate) does not in its nature belong to Chrematistic, for here the exchange has reference only to what is necessary to themselves (the buyer or seller)." Therefore, as he goes on to show, the original form of trade was barter, but with the extension of the latter, there arose the necessity for money. On the discovery of money, barter of necessity developed into trading in commodities, and this again, in opposition to its original tendency, grew into Chrematistic, into the art of making money. Now Chrematistic is distinguishable from Oeconomic in this way, that "in the case of Chrematistic circulation is the source of riches. And it appears to revolve about money, for money is the beginning and end of this kind of exchange. Therefore also riches, such as Chrematistic strives for, are unlimited. Just as every art that is not a means to an end, but an end in itself, has no limit to its aims, because it seeks constantly to approach nearer and nearer to that end, while those arts that

As the conscious representative of this movement, the possessor of money becomes a capitalist. His person, or rather his pocket, is the point from which the money starts and to which it returns. The expansion of value, which is the objective basis or main-spring of the circulation M—C—M, becomes his subjective aim, and it is only in so far as the appropriation of ever more and more wealth in the abstract becomes the sole motive of his operations, that he functions as a capitalist, that is, as capital personified and endowed with consciousness and a will. Use-values must therefore never be looked upon as the real aim of the capitalist; neither must the profit on any single transaction. The restless never-ending process of profit-making alone is what he aims at. This boundless greed after riches, this passionate chase after exchange-value, is common to the capitalist and the miser; but while the miser is merely a capitalist gone mad, the capitalist is a rational miser. The never-ending augmentation of exchange-value, which the miser strives after, by seeking to save his money from circulation, is attained by the more acute capitalist, by constantly throwing it afresh into circulation.

The independent form, *i.e.*, the money-form, which the value of commodities assumes in the case of simple circulation, serves only one purpose, namely, their exchange, and vanishes in the final result of the movement. On the other hand, in the circulation M—C—M, both the money and the commodity represent only different modes of existence of value itself, the money its general mode, and the commodity its particular, or, so to say, disguised mode. It is constantly changing from one form to the other without thereby becoming lost, and thus assumes an automatically active character. If now we take in turn each of the two different forms which self-expanding value successively assumes in the course of its life, we then arrive at these two propositions: Capital is money: Capital is commodities. In truth, however, value is here the active factor in a process, in which, while constantly assuming the form in turn of money and commodities, it at the same time changes in magnitude, differentiates itself by throwing off surplus-value from itself; the original value, in other words, expands spontaneously. For the movement, in the course of which it adds surplus-value, is its own movement, its expansion, therefore, is automatic expansion. Because it is value, it has acquired the occult quality of being able

---

pursue means to an end, are not boundless, since the goal itself imposes a limit upon them, so with Chrematistic, there are no bounds to its aims, these aims being absolute wealth. Oeconomic not Chrematistic has a limit . . . the object of the former is something different from money, of the latter the augmenta-tion of money. . . . By confounding these two forms, which overlap each other, some people have been led to look upon the preservation and increase of money ad infinitum as the end and aim of Oeconomic." (Aristoteles, "De-Rep." edit. Bekker. lib. I. c. 8, 9. passim.) [*Marx*] to add value to itself. It brings forth living offspring, or, at the least, lays golden eggs.

Value, therefore, being the active factor in such a process, and assuming at one time the form of money, at another that of commodities, but through all these changes preserving itself and expanding, it requires some independent form, by means of which its identity may at any time be established. And this form it possesses only in the shape of money. It is under the form of money that value begins and ends, and begins again, every act of its own spontaneous generation. It began by being £100, it is now £110, and so on. But the money itself is only one of the two forms of value. Unless it takes the form of some commodity, it does not become capital. There is here no antagonism, as in the case of hoarding, between the money and commodities. The capitalist knows that all commodities, however scurvy they may look, or however badly they may smell, are in faith and in truth money, inwardly circumcised Jews, and what is more, a wonderful means whereby out of money to make more money.

In simple circulation, C—M—C, the value of commodities attained at the most a form independent of their use-values, *i.e.*, the form of money; but that same value now in the circulation M—C—M, or the circulation of capital, suddenly presents itself as an independent substance, endowed with a motion of its own, passing through a life-process of its own, in which money and commodities are mere forms which it assumes and casts off in turn. Nay, more: instead of simply representing the relations of commodities, it enters now, so to say, into private relations with itself. It differentiates itself as original value from itself as surplus-value; as the father differentiates himself from himself quâ the son, yet both are one and of one age: for only by the surplus-value of £10 does the £100 originally advanced become capital, and so soon as this takes place, so soon as the son, and by the son, the father, is begotten, so soon does their difference vanish, and they again become one, £110.

Value therefore now becomes value in process, money in process, and, as such, capital. It comes out of circulation, enters into it again, preserves and multiplies itself within its circuit, comes back out of it with expanded bulk, and begins the same round ever afresh. M—M', money which begets money, such is the description of Capital from the mouths of its first interpreters, the Mercantilists.

Buying in order to sell, or, more accurately, buying in order to sell dearer, M—C—M', appears certainly to be a form peculiar to one kind of capital alone, namely merchants' capital. But industrial capital too is money, that is changed into commodities, and by the sale of these commodities, is re-converted into more money.

The events that take place outside the sphere of circulation, in the interval between the buying and selling, do not affect the form of this movement. Lastly, in the case of interest-bearing capital, the circulation M—C—M' appears abridged. We have its result without the intermediate stage, in the form M—M', "en style lapidaire" so to say, money that is worth more money, value that is greater than itself.

M—C—M' is therefore in reality the general formula of capital as it appears prima facie within the sphere of circulation. * * *

Part III. The Production of Absolute Surplus-Value

CHAPTER VII. THE LABOUR-PROCESS AND THE PROCESS OF PRODUCING SURPLUS-VALUE

Section 1. *The Labour-Process or the Production of Use-Values*

The capitalist buys labour-power in order to use it; and labour-power in use is labour itself. The purchaser of labour-power consumes it by setting the seller of it to work. By working, the latter becomes actually, what before he only was potentially, labour-power in action, a labourer. In order that his labour may re-appear in a commodity, he must, before all things, expend it on something useful, on something capable of satisfying a want of some sort. Hence, what the capitalist sets the labourer to produce, is a particular use-value, a specified article. The fact that the production of use-values or goods, is carried on under the control of a capitalist and on his behalf, does not alter the general character of that production. We shall, therefore, in the first place, have to consider the labour-process independently of the particular form it assumes under given social conditions.

Labour is, in the first place, a process in which both man and Nature participate, and in which man of his own accord starts, regulates, and controls the material re-actions between himself and Nature. He opposes himself to Nature as one of her own forces, setting in motion arms and legs, head and hands, the natural forces of his body, in order to appropriate Nature's productions in a form adapted to his own wants. By thus acting on the external world and changing it, he at the same time changes his own nature. He develops his slumbering powers and compels them to act in obedience to his sway. We are not now dealing with those primitive instinctive forms of labour that remind us of the mere animal. An immeasurable interval of time separates the state of things in which a man brings his labour-power to market for sale as a commodity, from that state in which human labour was still in its first instinctive stage. We pre-suppose labour in a form that stamps it as exclusively human. A spider conducts operations that resemble those of a weaver, and a bee puts to shame many an architect in the construction of her cells. But what distinguishes the worst architect from the best of bees is this, that the architect raises his structure in imagination before he erects it in reality. At the end of every labour-process, we get a result that already existed in the imagination of the labourer at its commencement. He not only effects a change of form in the material on which he works, but he also realises a purpose of his own that gives the law to his modus operandi, and to which he must subordinate his will. And this subordination is no mere momentary act. Besides the exertion of the bodily organs, the process demands that, during the whole operation, the workman's will be steadily in consonance with his purpose. This means close attention. The less he is attracted by the nature of the work, and the mode in which it is carried on, and the less, therefore, he enjoys it as something which gives play to his bodily and mental powers, the more close his attention is forced to be.

The elementary factors of the labour-process are (1), the personal activity of man, *i.e.*, work itself, (2), the subject of that work, and (3), its instruments.

The soil (and this, economically speaking, includes water) in the virgin state in which it supplies man with necessaries or the means of subsistence ready to hand, exists independently of him, and is the universal subject of human labour. All those things which labour merely separates from immediate connexion with their environment, are subjects of labour spontaneously provided by Nature. Such are fish which we catch and take from their element, water, timber which we fell in the virgin forest, and ores which we extract from their veins. If, on the other hand, the subject of labour has, so to say, been filtered through previous labour, we call it raw material; such is ore already extracted and ready for washing. All raw material is the subject of labour, but not every subject of labour is raw material: it can only become so, after it has undergone some alteration by means of labour.

An instrument of labour is a thing, or a complex of things, which the labourer interposes between himself and the subject of his labour, and which serves as the conductor of his activity. He makes use of the mechanical, physical, and chemical properties of some substances in order to make other substances subservient to his aims.[1] Leaving out of consideration such ready-made means of

1. "Reason is just as cunning as she is powerful. Her cunning consists principally in her mediating activity, which, by causing objects to act and re-act on each other in accordance with their own nature, in this way, without any direct interference in the process, carries out reason's intentions." (Hegel: "Enzyklopädie, Erster Theil, Die Logik," Berlin, 1840, p. 382.) [*Marx*]

subsistence as fruits, in gathering which a man's own limbs serve as the instruments of his labour, the first thing of which the labourer possesses himself is not the subject of labour but its instrument. Thus Nature becomes one of the organs of his activity, one that he annexes to his own bodily organs, adding stature to himself in spite of the Bible. As the earth is his original larder, so too it is his original tool house. It supplies him, for instance, with stones for throwing, grinding, pressing, cutting, &c. The earth itself is an instrument of labour, but when used as such in agriculture implies a whole series of other instruments and a comparatively high development of labour. No sooner does labour undergo the least development, than it requires specially prepared instruments. Thus in the oldest caves we find stone implements and weapons. In the earliest period of human history domesticated animmals, *i.e.*, animals which have been bred for the purpose, and have undergone modifications by means of labour, play the chief part as instruments of labour along with specially prepared stones, wood, bones, and shells. The use and fabrication of instruments of labour, although existing in the germ among certain species of animals, is specifically characteristic of the human labour-process, and Franklin therefore defines man as a tool-making animal. Relics of bygone instruments of labour possess the same importance for the investigation of extinct economic forms of society, as do fossil bones for the determination of extinct species of animals. It is not the articles made, but how they are made, and by what instruments, that enables us to distinguish different economic epochs. Instruments of labour not only supply a standard of the degree of development to which human labour has attained, but they are also indicators of the social conditions under which that labour is carried on. Among the instruments of labour, those of a mechanical nature, which, taken as a whole, we may call the bone and muscles of production, offer much more decided characteristics of a given epoch of production, than those which, like pipes, tubs, baskets, jars, &c., serve only to hold the materials for labour, which latter class, we may in a general way, call the vascular system of production. The latter first begins to play an important part in the chemical industries.

In a wider sense we may include among the instruments of labour, in addition to those things that are used for directly transferring labour to its subject, and which therefore, in one way or another, serve as conductors of activity, all such objects as are necessary for carrying on the labour-process. These do not enter directly into the process, but without them it is either impossible for it to take place at all, or possible only to a partial extent. Once more we find the earth to be a universal instrument of this sort, for it furnishes a locus standi to the labourer and a field of employment for his activity. Among instruments that are the result of previous labour and also belong to this class, we find workshops, canals, roads, and so forth.

In the labour-process, therefore, man's activity, with the help of the instruments of labour, effects an alteration, designed from the commencement, in the material worked upon. The process disappears in the product; the latter is a use-value, Nature's material adapted by a change of form to the wants of man. Labour has incorporated itself with its subject: the former is materialised, the latter transformed. That which in the labourer appeared as movement, now appears in the product as a fixed quality without motion. The blacksmith forges and the product is a forging.

If we examine the whole process from the point of view of its result, the product, it is plain that both the instruments and the subject of labour, are means of production, and that the labour itself is productive labour.

Though a use-value, in the form of a product, issues from the labour-process, yet other use-values, products of previous labour, enter into it as means of production. The same use-value is both the product of a previous process, and a means of production in a later process. Products are therefore not only results, but also essential conditions of labour.

With the exception of the extractive industries, in which the material for labour is provided immediately by Nature, such as mining, hunting, fishing, and agriculture (so far as the latter is confined to breaking up virgin soil), all branches of industry manipulate raw material, objects already filtered through labour, already products of labour. Such is seed in agriculture. Animals and plants, which we are accustomed to consider as products of Nature, are in their present form, not only products of, say last year's labour, but the result of a gradual transformation, continued through many generations, under man's superintendence, and by means of his labour. But in the great majority of cases, instruments of labour show even to the most superficial observer, traces of the labour of past ages.

Raw material may either form the principal substance of a product, or it may enter into its formation only as an accessory. An accessory may be consumed by the instruments of labour, as coal under a boiler, oil by a wheel, hay by draft-horses, or it may be mixed with the raw material in order to produce some modification thereof, as chlorine into unbleached linen, coal with iron, dye-stuff with wool, or again, it may help to carry on the work itself, as in the case of the materials used for heating and lighting workshops. The distinction between principal substance and accessory vanishes in the true chemical industries, because there none of the raw material re-appears, in its original composition, in the substance of the product.

Every object possesses various properties, and is thus capable of being applied to different uses. One and the same product may therefore serve as raw material in very different processes. Corn, for example, is a raw material for millers, starch-manufacturers, distillers, and cattle-breeders. It also enters as raw material into its own production in the shape of seed; coal, too, is at the same time the product of, and a means of production in, coal-mining.

Again, a particular product may be used in one and the same process, both as an instrument of labour and as raw material. Take, for instance, the fattening of cattle, where the animal is the raw material, and at the same time an instrument for the production of manure.

A product, though ready for immediate consumption, may yet serve as raw material for a further product, as grapes when they become the raw material for wine. On the other hand, labour may give us its product in such a form, that we can use it only as raw material, as is the case with cotton, thread, and yarn. Such a raw material, though itself a product, may have to go through a whole series of different processes: in each of these in turn, it serves, with constantly varying form, as raw material, until the last process of the series leaves it a perfect product, ready for individual consumption, or for use as an instrument of labour.

Hence we see, that whether a use-value is to be regarded as raw material, as instrument of labour, or as product, this is determined entirely by its function in the labour-process, by the position it there occupies: as this varies, so does its character.

Whenever therefore a product enters as a means of production into a new labour-process, it thereby loses its character of product, and becomes a mere factor in the process. A spinner treats spindles only as implements for spinning, and flax only as the material that he spins. Of course it is impossible to spin without material and spindles; and therefore the existence of these things as products, at the commencement of the spinning operation, must be presumed: but in the process itself, the fact that they are products of previous labour, is a matter of utter indifference; just as in the digestive process, it is of no importance whatever, that bread is the produce of the previous labour of the farmer, the miller, and the baker. On the contrary, it is generally by their imperfections as products, that the means of production in any process assert themselves in their character of products. A blunt knife or weak thread forcibly remind us of Mr. A., the cutler, or Mr. B., the spinner. In the finished product the labour by means of which it has acquired its useful qualities is not palpable, has apparently vanished.

A machine which does not serve the purposes of labour, is useless. In addition, it falls a prey to the destructive influence of natural forces. Iron rusts and wood rots. Yarn with which we neither weave nor knit, is cotton wasted. Living labour must seize upon these things and rouse them from their death-sleep, change them from mere possible use-values into real and effective ones. Bathed in the fire of labour, appropriated as part and parcel of labour's organism, and, as it were, made alive for the performance of their functions in the process, they are in truth consumed, but consumed with a purpose, as elementary constituents of new use-values, of new products, ever ready as means of subsistence for individual consumption, or as means of production for some new labour-process.

If then, on the one hand, finished products are not only results, but also necessary conditions, of the labour-process, on the other hand, their assumption into that process, their contact with living labour, is the sole means by which they can be made to retain their character of use-values, and be utilised.

Labour uses up its material factors, its subject and its instruments, consumes them, and is therefore a process of consumption. Such productive consumption is distinguished from individual consumption by this, that the latter uses up products, as means of subsistence for the living individual; the former, as means whereby alone, labour, the labour-power of the living individual, is enabled to act. The product, therefore, of individual consumption, is the consumer himself; the result of productive consumption, is a product distinct from the consumer.

In so far then, as its instruments and subjects are themselves products, labour consumes products in order to create products, or in other words, consumes one set of products by turning them into means of production for another set. But, just as in the beginning, the only participators in the labour-process were man and the earth, which latter exists independently of man, so even now we still employ in the process many means of production, provided directly by Nature, that do not represent any combination of natural substances with human labour.

The labour-process, resolved as above into its simple elementary factors, is human action with a view to the production of use-values, appropriation of natural substances to human requirements; it is the necessary condition for effecting exchange of matter between man and Nature; it is the everlasting Nature-imposed condition of human existence, and therefore is independent of every social phase of that existence, or rather, is common to every such phase. It was, therefore, not necessary to represent our labourer in connexion with other labourers; man and his labour on one side,

Nature and its materials on the other, sufficed. As the taste of the porridge does not tell you who grew the oats, no more does this simple process tell you of itself what are the social conditions under which it is taking place, whether under the slave-owner's brutal lash, or the anxious eye of the capitalist, whether Cincinnatus carries it on in tilling his modest farm or a savage in killing wild animals with stones.

Let us now return to our would-be capitalist. We left him just after he had purchased, in the open market, all the necessary factors of the labour-process; its objective factors, the means of production, as well as its subjective factor, labour-power. With the keen eye of an expert, he has selected the means of production and the kind of labour-power best adapted to his particular trade, be it spinning, bootmaking, or any other kind. He then proceeds to consume the commodity, the labour-power that he has just bought, by causing the labourer, the impersonation of that labour-power, to consume the means of production by his labour. The general character of the labour-process is evidently not changed by the fact, that the labourer works for the capitalist instead of for himself; moreover, the particular methods and operations employed in bootmaking or spinning are not immediately changed by the intervention of the capitalist. He must begin by taking the labour-power as he finds it in the market, and consequently be satisfied with labour of such a kind as would be found in the period immediately preceding the rise of capitalists. Changes in the methods of production by the subordination of labour to capital, can take place only at a later period, and therefore will have to be treated of in a later chapter.

The labour-process, turned into the process by which the capitalist consumes labour-power, exhibits two characteristic phenomena. First, the labourer works under the control of the capitalist to whom his labour belongs; the capitalist taking good care that the work is done in a proper manner, and that the means of production are used with intelligence, so that there is no unnecessary waste of raw material, and no wear and tear of the implements beyond what is necessarily caused by the work.

Secondly, the product is the property of the capitalist and not that of the labourer, its immediate producer. Suppose that a capitalist pays for a day's labour-power at its value; then the right to use that power for a day belongs to him, just as much as the right to use any other commodity, such as a horse that he has hired for the day. To the purchaser of a commodity belongs its use, and the seller of labour-power, by giving his labour, does no more, in reality, than part with the use-value that he has sold. From the instant he steps into the workshop, the use-value of his labour-power, and therefore also its use, which is labour, belongs to the capitalist. By the purchase of labour-power, the capitalist incorporates labour, as a living ferment, with the lifeless constituents of the product. From his point of view, the labour-process is nothing more than the consumption of the commodity purchased, *i.e.*, of labour-power; but this consumption cannot be effected except by supplying the labour-power with the means of production. The labour-process is a process between things that the capitalist has purchased, things that have become his property. The product of this process belongs, therefore, to him, just as much as does the wine which is the product of a process of fermentation completed in his cellar.

Section 2. *The Production of Surplus-Value*

The product appropriated by the capitalist is a use-value, as yarn, for example, or boots. But, although boots are, in one sense, the basis of all social progress, and our capitalist is a decided "progressist," yet he does not manufacture boots for their own sake. Use-value is, by no means, the thing "qu'on aime pour lui-même" in the production of commodities. Use-values are only produced by capitalists, because, and in so far as, they are the material substratum, the depositories of exchange-value. Our capitalist has two objects in view: in the first place, he wants to produce a use-value that has a value in exchange, that is to say, an article destined to be sold, a commodity; and secondly, he desires to produce a commodity whose value shall be greater than the sum of the values of the commodities used in its production, that is, of the means of production and the labour-power, that he purchased with his good money in the open market. His aim is to produce not only a use-value, but a commodity also; not only use-value, but value; not only value, but at the same time surplus-value.

It must be borne in mind, that we are now dealing with the production of commodities, and that, up to this point, we have only considered one aspect of the process. Just as commodities are, at the same time, use-values and values, so the process of producing them must be a labour-process, and at the same time, a process of creating value.

Let us now examine production as a creation of value.

We know that the value of each commodity is determined by the quantity of labour expended on and materialised in it, by the working-time necessary, under given social conditions, for its production. This rule also holds good in the case of the product that accrued to our capitalist, as the result of the labour-process carried on for him. Assuming this product to be 10 lbs. of yarn, our first step is to calculate the quantity of labour realised in it.

For spinning the yarn, raw material is required; suppose in this case 10 lbs. of cotton. We have no need at present to investigate the value of this cotton, for our capitalist has, we will assume, bought it at its full value, say of ten shillings. In this price the labour required for the production of the cotton is already expressed in terms of the average labour of society. We will further assume that the wear and tear of the spindle, which, for our present purpose, may represent all other instruments of labour employed, amounts to the value of 2s. If, then, twenty-four hours' labour, or two working-days are required to produce the quantity of gold represented by twelve shillings, we have here, to begin with, two days' labour already incorporated in the yarn.

We must not let ourselves be misled by the circumstance that the cotton has taken a new shape while the substance of the spindle has to a certain extent been used up. By the general law of value, if the value of 40 lbs. of yarn = the value of 40 lbs. of cotton + the value of a whole spindle, *i.e.*, if the same working-time is required to produce the commodities on either side of this equation, then 10 lbs. of yarn are an equivalent for 10 lbs. of cotton, together with one-fourth of a spindle. In the case we are considering the same working-time is materialised in the 10 lbs. of yarn on the one hand, and in the 10 lbs. of cotton and the fraction of a spindle on the other. Therefore, whether value appears in cotton, in a spindle, or in yarn, makes no difference in the amount of that value. The spindle and cotton, instead of resting quietly side by side, join together in the process, their forms are altered, and they are turned into yarn; but their value is no more affected by this fact than it would be if they had been simply exchanged for their equivalent in yarn.

The labour required for the production of the cotton, the raw material of the yarn, is part of the labour necessary to produce the yarn, and is therefore contained in the yarn. The same applies to the labour embodied in the spindle, without whose wear and tear the cotton could not be spun.

Hence, in determining the value of the yarn, or the labour-time required for its production, all the special processes carried on at various times and in different places, which were necessary, first to produce the cotton and the wasted portion of the spindle, and then with the cotton and spindle to spin the yarn, may together be looked on as different and successive phases of one and the same process. The whole of the labour in the yarn is past labour; and it is a matter of no importance that the operations necessary for the production of its constituent elements were carried on at times which, referred to the present, are more remote than the final operation of spinning. If a definite quantity of labour, say thirty days, is requisite to build a house, the total amount of labour incorporated in it is not altered by the fact that the work of the last day is done twenty-nine days later than that of the first. Therefore the labour contained in the raw material and the instruments of labour can be treated just as if it were labour expended in an earlier stage of the spinning process, before the labour of actual spinning commenced.

The values of the means of production, *i.e.*, the cotton and the spindle, which values are expressed in the price of twelve shillings, are therefore constituent parts of the value of the yarn, or, in other words, of the value of the product.

Two conditions must nevertheless be fulfilled. First, the cotton and spindle must concur in the production of a use-value; they must in the present case become yarn. Value is independent of the particular use-value by which it is borne, but it must be embodied in a use-value of some kind. Secondly, the time occupied in the labour of production must not exceed the time really necessary under the given social conditions of the case. Therefore, if no more than 1 lb. of cotton be requisite to spin 1 lb. of yarn, care must be taken that no more than this weight of cotton is consumed in the production of 1 lb. of yarn; and similarly with regard to the spindle. Though the capitalist have a hobby, and use a gold instead of a steel spindle, yet the only labour that counts for anything in the value of the yarn is that which would be required to produce a steel spindle, because no more is necessary under the given social conditions.

We now know what portion of the value of the yarn is owing to the cotton and the spindle. It amounts to twelve shillings or the value of two days' work. The next point for our consideration is, what portion of the value of the yarn is added to the cotton by the labour of the spinner.

We have now to consider this labour under a very different aspect from that which it had during the labour-process; there, we viewed it solely as that particular kind of human activity which changes cotton into yarn; there, the more the labour was suited to the work, the better the yarn, other circumstances remaining the same. The labour of the spinner was then viewed as specifically different from other kinds of productive labour, different on the one hand in its special aim, viz., spinning, different, on the other hand, in the special character of its operations, in the special nature of its means of production and in the special use-value of its product. For the operation of spinning, cotton and spindles are a necessity, but for making rifled cannon they would be of no use whatever. Here, on the contrary, where we consider the labour of the spinner only so far as it is value-creating, *i.e.*, a source of value, his labour differs in no respect from the labour of the man who bores cannon, or (what here more nearly concerns us), from the labour of the cotton-planter and spindle-maker incorporated in the means of production. It is solely by reason of this identity, that cotton planting, spindle making and spinning, are capable of forming the component parts, differing only quantitatively from each other, of one whole, namely, the value of the yarn. Here, we have nothing more to do with the quality, the nature and the specific character of the labour, but merely with its quantity. And this simply requires to be calculated. We proceed upon the assumption that spinning is simple, unskilled labour, the average labour of a given state of society. Hereafter we shall see that the contrary assumption would make no difference.

While the labourer is at work, his labour constantly undergoes a transformation: from being motion, it becomes an object without motion; from being the labourer working, it becomes the thing produced. At the end of one hour's spinning, that act is represented by a definite quantity of yarn; in other words, a definite quantity of labour, namely that of one hour, has become embodied in the cotton. We say labour, *i.e.*, the expenditure of his vital force by the spinner, and not spinning labour, because the special work of spinning counts here, only so far as it is the expenditure of labour-power in general, and not in so far as it is the specific work of the spinner.

In the process we are now considering it is of extreme importance, that no more time be consumed in the work of transforming the cotton into yarn than is necessary under the given social conditions. If under normal, *i.e.*, average social conditions of production, *a* pounds of cotton ought to be made into *b* pounds of yarn by one hour's labour, then a day's labour does not count as 12 hours' labour unless 12 *a* pounds of cotton have been made into 12 *b* pounds of yarn; for in the creation of value, the time that is socially necessary alone counts.

Not only the labour, but also the raw material and the product now appear in quite a new light, very different from that in which we viewed them in the labour-process pure and simple. The raw material serves now merely as an absorbent of a definite quantity of labour. By this absorption it is in fact changed into yarn, because it is spun, because labour-power in the form of spinning is added to it; but the product, the yarn, is now nothing more than a measure of the labour absorbed by the cotton. If in one hour $1\frac{2}{3}$ lbs. of cotton can be spun into $1\frac{2}{3}$ lbs. of yarn, then 10 lbs. of yarn indicate the absorption of 6 hours' labour. Definite quantities of product, these quantities being determined by experience, now represent nothing but definite quantities of labour, definite masses of crystallised labour-time. They are nothing more than the materialisation of so many hours or so many days of social labour.

We are here no more concerned about the facts, that the labour is the specific work of spinning, that its subject is cotton and its product yarn, than we are about the fact that the subject itself is already a product and therefore raw material. If the spinner, instead of spinning, were working in a coal mine, the subject of his labour, the coal, would be supplied by Nature; nevertheless, a definite quantity of extracted coal, a hundredweight for example, would represent a definite quantity of absorbed labour.

We assumed, on the occasion of its sale, that the value of a day's labour-power is three shillings, and that six hours' labour is incorporated in that sum; and consequently that this amount of labour is requisite to produce the necessaries of life daily required on an average by the labourer. If now our spinner by working for one hour, can convert 1⅔ lbs. of cotton into 1⅔ lbs. of yarn,[2] it follows that in six hours he will convert 10 lbs. of cotton into 10 lbs. of yarn. Hence, during the spinning process, the cotton absorbs six hours' labour. The same quantity of labour is also embodied in a piece of gold of the value of three shillings. Consequently by the mere labour of spinning, a value of three shillings is added to the cotton.

Let us now consider the total value of the product, the 10 lbs. of yarn. Two and a half days' labour has been embodied in it, of which two days were contained in the cotton and in the substance of the spindle worn away, and half a day was absorbed during the process of spinning. This two and a half days' labour is also represented by a piece of gold of the value of fifteen shillings. Hence, fifteen shillings is an adequate price for the 10 lbs. of yarn, or the price of one pound is eighteenpence.

Our capitalist stares in astonishment. The value of the product is exactly equal to the value of the capital advanced. The value so advanced has not expanded, no surplus-value has been created, and consequently money has not been converted into capital. The price of the yarn is fifteen shillings, and fifteen shillings were spent in the open market upon the constituent elements of the product, or, what amounts to the same thing, upon the factors of the labour-process; ten shillings were paid for the cotton, two shillings for the substance of the spindle worn away, and three shillings for the labour-power. The swollen value of the yarn is of no avail, for it is merely the sum of the values formerly existing in the cotton, the spindle, and the labour-power: out of such a simple addition of existing values, no surplus-value can possibly arise. These separate values are now all concentrated in one thing; but so they were also in the sum of fifteen shillings, before it was split up into three parts, by the purchase of the commodities.

There is in reality nothing very strange in this result. The value

2. These figures are quite arbitrary. [*Marx*]

of one pound of yarn being eighteenpence, if our capitalist buys 10 lbs. of yarn in the market, he must pay fifteen shillings for them. It is clear that, whether a man buys his house ready built, or gets it built for him, in neither case will the mode of acquisition increase the amount of money laid out on the house.

Our capitalist, who is at home in his vulgar economy, exclaims: "Oh! but I advanced my money for the express purpose of making more money." The way to Hell is paved with good intentions, and he might just as easily have intended to make money, without producing at all. He threatens all sorts of things. He won't be caught napping again. In future he will buy the commodities in the market, instead of manufacturing them himself. But if all his brother capitalists were to do the same, where would he find his commodities in the market? And his money he cannot eat. He tries persuasion. "Consider my abstinence; I might have played ducks and drakes with the 15 shillings; but instead of that I consumed it productively, and made yarn with it." Very well, and by way of reward he is now in possession of good yarn instead of a bad conscience; and as for playing the part of the miser; it would never do for him to relapse into such bad ways as that; we have seen before to what results such asceticism leads. Besides, where nothing is, the king has lost his rights; whatever may be the merit of his abstinence, there is nothing wherewith specially to remunerate it, because the value of the product is merely the sum of the values of the commodities that were thrown into the process of production. Let him therefore console himself with the reflection that virtue is its own reward. But no, he becomes importunate. He says: "The yarn is of no use to me: I produced it for sale." In that case let him sell it, or, still better, let him for the future produce only things for satisfying his personal wants, a remedy that his physician MacCulloch has already prescribed as infallible against an epidemic of over-production. He now gets obstinate. "Can the labourer," he asks, "merely with his arms and legs, produce commodities out of nothing? Did I not supply him with the materials, by means of which, and in which alone, his labour could be embodied? And as the greater part of society consists of such ne'er-do-wells, have I not rendered society incalculable service by my instruments of production, my cotton and my spindle, and not only society, but the labourer also, whom in addition I have provided with the necessaries of life? And am I to be allowed nothing in return for all this service?" Well, but has not the labourer rendered him the equivalent service of changing his cotton and spindle into yarn? Moreover, there is here no question of service. A service is nothing more than the useful effect of a use-value, be it of a commodity, or be it of labour. But here we are dealing with exchange-value. The capitalist paid to the labourer a value of 3 shillings, and the labourer gave him back an exact equivalent in the value of 3 shillings, added by him to the cotton: he gave him value for value. Our friend, up to this time so purse-proud, suddenly assumes the modest demeanour of his own workman, and exclaims: "Have I myself not worked? Have I not performed the labour of superintendence and of overlooking the spinner? And does not this labour, too, create value?" His overlooker and his manager try to hide their smiles. Meanwhile, after a hearty laugh, he re-assumes his usual mien. Though he chanted to us the whole creed of the economists, in reality, he says, he would not give a brass farthing for it. He leaves this and all such like subterfuges and juggling tricks to the professors of Political Economy, who are paid for it. He himself is a practical man; and though he does not always consider what he says outside his business, yet in his business he knows what he is about.

Let us examine the matter more closely. The value of a day's labour-power amounts to 3 shillings, because on our assumption half a day's labour is embodied in that quantity of labour-power, *i.e.*, because the means of subsistence that are daily required for the production of labour-power, cost half a day's labour. But the past labour that is embodied in the labour-power, and the living labour that it can call into action; the daily cost of maintaining it, and its daily expenditure in work, are two totally different things. The former determines the exchange-value of the labour-power, the latter is its use-value. The fact that half a day's labour is necessary to keep the labourer alive during 24 hours, does not in any way prevent him from working a whole day. Therefore, the value of labour-power, and the value which that labour-power creates in the labour-process, are two entirely different magnitudes; and this difference of the two values was what the capitalist had in view, when he was purchasing the labour-power. The useful qualities that labour-power possesses, and by virtue of which it makes yarn or boots, were to him nothing more than a *conditio sine qua non*; for in order to create value, labour must be expended in a useful manner. What really influenced him was the specific use-value which this commodity possesses of being *a source not only of value, but of more value than it has itself*. This is the special service that the capitalist expects from labour-power, and in this transaction he acts in accordance with the "eternal laws" of the exchange of commodities. The seller of labour-power, like the seller of any other commodity, realises its exchange-value, and parts with its use-value. He cannot take the one without giving the other. The use-value of labour-power, or in other words, labour, belongs just as little to its seller, as the use-value of oil after it has been sold belongs to the dealer who has sold it. The owner of the money has paid the value of a day's labour-power; his, therefore, is the use of it for a day; a day's labour belongs to him. The circumstance, that on the one hand the daily sustenance of labour-power costs only half a day's labour, while on the other hand the very same labour-power can work during a whole day, that consequently the value which its use during one day creates, is double what he pays for that use, this circumstance is, without doubt, a piece of good luck for the buyer, but by no means an injury to the seller.

Our capitalist foresaw this state of things, and that was the cause of his laughter. The labourer therefore finds, in the workshop, the means of production necessary for working, not only during six, but during twelve hours. Just as during the six hours' process our 10 lbs. of cotton absorbed six hours' labour, and became 10 lbs. of yarn, so now, 20 lbs. of cotton will absorb 12 hours' labour and be changed into 20 lbs. of yarn. Let us now examine the product of this prolonged process. There is now materialised in this 20 lbs. of yarn the labour of five days, of which four days are due to the cotton and the lost steel of the spindle, the remaining day having been absorbed by the cotton during the spinning process. Expressed in gold, the labour of five days is thirty shillings. This is therefore the price of the 20 lbs. of yarn, giving, as before, eighteenpence as the price of a pound. But the sum of the values of the commodities that entered into the process amounts to 27 shillings. The value of the yarn is 30 shillings. Therefore the value of the product is 1/9 greater than the value advanced for its production; 27 shillings have been transformed into 30 shillings; a surplus-value of 3 shillings has been created. The trick has at last succeeded; money has been converted into capital.

Every condition of the problem is satisfied, while the laws that regulate the exchange of commodities, have been in no way violated. Equivalent has been exchanged for equivalent. For the capitalist as buyer paid for each commodity, for the cotton, the spindle and the labour-power, its full value. He then did what is done by every purchaser of commodities; he consumed their use-value. The consumption of the labour-power, which was also the process of producing commodities, resulted in 20 lbs. of yarn, having a value of 30 shillings. The capitalist, formerly a buyer, now returns to market as a seller, of commodities. He sells his yarn at eighteenpence a pound, which is its exact value. Yet for all that he withdraws 3 shillings more from circulation than he originally threw into it. This metamorphosis, this conversion of money into capital, takes place both within the sphere of circulation and also outside it; within the circulation, because conditioned by the purchase of the labour-power in the market; outside the circulation, because what is done within it is only a stepping-stone to the production of surplus-value, a process which is entirely confined to the sphere of production. Thus "tout est pour le mieux dans le meilleur des mondes possibles."

By turning his money into commodities that serve as the material elements of a new product, and as factors in the labour-process, by incorporating living labour with their dead substance, the capitalist at the same time converts value, *i.e.*, past, materialised, and dead labour into capital, into value big with value, a live monster that is fruitful and multiplies.

If we now compare the two processes of producing value and of creating surplus-value, we see that the latter is nothing but the continuation of the former beyond a definite point. If on the one hand the process be not carried beyond the point, where the value paid by the capitalist for the labour-power is replaced by an exact equivalent, it is simply a process of producing value; if, on the other hand, it be continued beyond that point, it becomes a process of creating surplus-value.

If we proceed further, and compare the process of producing value with the labour-process, pure and simple, we find that the latter consists of the useful labour, the work, that produces use-values. Here we contemplate the labour as producing a particular article; we view it under its qualitative aspect alone, with regard to its end and aim. But viewed as a value-creating process, the same labour-process presents itself under its quantitative aspect alone. Here it is a question merely of the time occupied by the labourer in doing the work; of the period during which the labour-power is usefully expended. Here, the commodities that take part in the process, do not count any longer as necessary adjuncts of labour-power in the production of a definite, useful object. They count merely as depositories of so much absorbed or materialised labour; that labour, whether previously embodied in the means of production, or incorporated in them for the first time during the process of the action of labour-power, counts in either case only according to its duration; it amounts to so many hours or days as the case may be.

Moreover, only so much of the time spent in the production of any article is counted, as, under the given social conditions, is necessary. The consequences of this are various. In the first place, it becomes necessary that the labour should be carried on under normal conditions. If a self-acting mule is the implement in general use for spinning, it would be absurd to supply the spinner with a distaff and spinning wheel. The cotton too must not be such rubbish as to cause extra waste in being worked, but must be of suitable quality. Otherwise the spinner would be found to spend more time in producing a pound of yarn than is socially necessary, in which case the excess of time would create neither value nor money. But whether the material factors of the process are of normal quality or not, depends not upon the labourer, but entirely upon the capitalist. Then again, the labour-power itself must be of average efficacy. In the trade in which it is being employed, it must possess the average skill, handiness and quickness prevalent in that trade, and our capitalist took good care to buy labour-power of such normal goodness. This power must be applied with the average amount of exertion and with the usual degree of intensity; and the capitalist is as careful to see that this is done, as that his workmen are not idle for a single moment. He has bought the use of the labour-power for a definite period, and he insists upon his rights. He has no intention of being robbed. Lastly, and for this purpose our friend has a penal code of his own, all wasteful consumption of raw material or instruments of labour is strictly forbidden, because what is so wasted, represents labour superfluously expended, labour that does not count in the product or enter into its value.

We now see, that the difference between labour, considered on the one hand as producing utilities, and on the other hand, as creating value, a difference which we discovered by our analysis of a commodity, resolves itself into a distinction between two aspects of the process of production.

The process of production, considered on the one hand as the unity of the labour-process and the process of creating value, is production of commodities; considered on the other hand as the unity of the labour-process and the process of producing surplus-value, it is the capitalist process of production, or capitalist production of commodities.

We stated, on a previous page, that in the creation of surplus-value it does not in the least matter, whether the labour appropriated by the capitalist be simple unskilled labour of average quality or more complicated unskilled labour. All labour of a higher or more complicated character than average labour is expenditure of labour-power of a more costly kind, labour-power whose production has cost more time and labour, and which therefore has a higher value, than unskilled or simple labour-power. This power being of higher value, its consumption is labour of a higher class, labour that creates in equal times proportionally higher values than unskilled labour does. Whatever difference in skill there may be between the labour of a spinner and that of a jeweller, the portion of his labour by which the jeweller merely replaces the value of his own labour-power, does not in any way differ in quality from the additional portion by which he creates surplus-value. In the making of jewellery, just as in spinning, the surplus-value results only from a quantitative excess of labour, from a lengthening-out of one and the same labour-process, in the one case, of the process of making jewels, in the other of the process of making yarn.

But on the other hand, in every process of creating value, the reduction of skilled labour to average social labour, *e.g.*, one day of skilled to six days of unskilled labour, is unavoidable. We therefore save ourselves a superfluous operation, and simplify our analysis, by the assumption, that the labour of the workman employed by the capitalist is unskilled average labour.

CHAPTER X. THE WORKING-DAY

Section 1. *The Limits of the Working-Day*

We started with the supposition that labour-power is bought and sold at its value. Its value, like that of all other commodities, is determined by the working-time necessary to its production. If the production of the average daily means of subsistence of the labourer takes up 6 hours, he must work, on the average, 6 hours every day, to produce his daily labour-power, or to reproduce the value received as the result of its sale. The necessary part of his working-day amounts to 6 hours, and is, therefore, *caeteris paribus*, a given quantity. But with this, the extent of the working-day itself is not yet given.

Let us assume that the line A B represents the length of the necessary working-time, say 6 hours. If the labour be prolonged 1, 3, or 6 hours beyond A B, we have 3 other lines:

Working-day I.   Working-day II.   Working-day III.
A ——— B — C.   A ——— B —— C.   A——— B ———C.

representing 3 different working-days of 7, 9, and 12 hours. The extension B C of the line A B represents the length of the surplus-labour. As the working-day is A B+B or A C, it varies with the variable quantity B C. Since A B is constant, the ratio of B C to A B can always be calculated. In working-day I, it is 1/6, in working-day II, 3/6, in working-day III, 6/6 of A B. Since, further, the ratio $\frac{\text{surplus working-time,}}{\text{necessary working-time,}}$ determines the rate of the surplus-value, the latter is given by the ratio of B C to A B. It amounts in the 3 different working-days respectively to 16 2/3, 50 and 100 per cent. On the other hand, the rate of surplus-value alone would not give us the extent of the working-day. If this rate, *e.g.*, were 100 per cent, the working-day might be of 8, 10, 12, or more hours. It would indicate that the 2 constituent parts of the working-day, necessary-labour and surplus-labour time, were equal in extent, but not how long each of these two constituent parts was.

The working-day is thus not a constant, but a variable quantity. One of its parts, certainly, is determined by the working-time required for the reproduction of the labour-power of the labourer himself. But its total amount varies with the duration of the surplus-labour. The working-day is, therefore, determinable, but is, *per se*, indeterminate.

Although the working-day is not a fixed, but a fluent quantity, it can, on the other hand, only vary within certain limits. The minimum limit is, however, not determinable; of course, if we make the extension line B C or the surplus-labour = o, we have a minimum limit, *i.e.*, the part of the day which the labourer must necessarily work for his own maintenance. On the basis of capitalist production, however, this necessary labour can form a part only of the working-day; the working-day itself can never be reduced to this minimum. On the other hand, the working-day has a maximum limit. It cannot be prolonged beyond a certain point. This maximum limit is conditioned by two things. First, by the physical bounds of labour-power. Within the 24 hours of the natural day a man can expend only a definite quantity of his vital force. A horse, in like manner, can only work from day to day, 8 hours. During part of the day this force must rest, sleep; during another part the man has to satisfy other physical needs, to feed, wash, and clothe himself. Besides these purely physical limitations, the extension of the working-day encounters moral ones. The labourer needs time for satisfying his intellectual and social wants, the extent and number of which are conditioned by the general state of social advancement. The variation of the working-day fluctuates, therefore, within physical and social bounds. But both these limiting conditions are of a very elastic nature, and allow the greatest latitude. So we find working-days of 8, 10, 12, 14, 16, 18 hours, *i.e.*, of the most different lengths.

The capitalist has bought the labour-power at its day-rate. To him its use-value belongs during one working-day. He has thus acquired the right to make the labourer work for him during one day. But, what is a working-day?

At all events, less than a natural day. By how much? The capitalist has his own views of this *ultima Thule*, the necessary limit of the working-day. As capitalist, he is only capital personified. His soul is the soul of capital. But capital has one single life impulse, the tendency to create value and surplus-value, to make its constant factor, the means of production, absorb the greatest possible amount of surplus-labour.

Capital is dead labour, that, vampire-like, only lives by sucking living labour, and lives the more, the more labour it sucks. The time during which the labourer works, is the time during which the capitalist consumes the labour-power he has purchased of him.

If the labourer consumes his disposable time for himself, he robs the capitalist.

The capitalist then takes his stand on the law of the exchange of commodities. He, like all other buyers, seeks to get the greatest possible benefit out of the use-value of his commodity. Suddenly the voice of the labourer, which had been stifled in the storm and stress of the process of production, rises:

The commodity that I have sold to you differs from the crowd of other commodities, in that its use creates value, and a value greater than its own. That is why you bought it. That which on your side appears a spontaneous expansion of capital, is on mine extra expenditure of labour-power. You and I know on the market only one law, that of the exchange of commodities. And the consumption of the commodity belongs not to the seller who parts with it, but to the buyer, who acquires it. To you, therefore, belongs the use of my daily labour-power. But by means of the price that you pay for it each day, I must be able to reproduce it daily, and to sell it again. Apart from natural exhaustion through age, &c., I must be able on the morrow to work with the same normal amount of force, health and freshness as to-day. You preach to me constantly the gospel of "saving" and "abstinence." Good! I will, like a sensible saving owner, husband my sole wealth, labour-power, and abstain from all foolish waste of it. I will each day spend, set in motion, put into action only as much of it as is compatible with its normal duration, and healthy development. By an unlimited extension of the working-day, you may in one day use up a quantity of labour-power greater than I can restore in three. What you gain in labour I lose in substance. The use of my labour-power and the spoliation of it are quite different things. If the average time that (doing a reasonable amount of work) an average labourer can live, is 30 years, the value of my labour-power, which you pay me from day to day is $\frac{1}{365 \times 30}$ or $\frac{1}{10950}$ of its total value. But if you consume it in 10 years, you pay me daily $\frac{1}{10950}$ instead of $\frac{1}{3650}$ of its total value, *i.e.*, only 1/3 of its daily value, and you rob me, therefore, every day of 2/3 of the value of my commodity. You pay me for one day's labour-power, whilst you use that of 3 days. That is against our contract and the law of exchanges. I demand, therefore, a working-day of normal length, and I demand it without any appeal to your heart, for in money matters sentiment is out of place. You may be a model citizen, perhaps a member of the Society for the

Prevention of Cruelty to Animals, and in the odour of sanctity to boot; but the thing that you represent face to face with me has no heart in its breast. That which seems to throb there is my own heart-beating. I demand the normal working-day because I, like every other seller, demand the value of my commodity.

We see then, that, apart from extremely elastic bounds, the nature of the exchange of commodities itself imposes no limit to the working-day, no limit to surplus-labour. The capitalist maintains his rights as a purchaser when he tries to make the working-day as long as possible, and to make, whenever possible, two working-days out of one. On the other hand, the peculiar nature of the commodity sold implies a limit to its consumption by the purchaser, and the labourer maintains his right as seller when he wishes to reduce the working-day to one of definite normal duration. There is here, therefore, an antinomy, right against right, both equally bearing the seal of the law of exchanges. Between equal rights force decides. Hence is it that in the history of capitalist production, the determination of what is a working-day, presents itself as the result of a struggle, a struggle between collective capital, *i.e.*, the class of capitalists, and collective labour, *i.e.*, the working-class.

Section 2. The Greed for Surplus-Labour. Manufacturer and Boyard

Capital has not invented surplus-labour. Wherever a part of society possesses the monopoly of the means of production, the labourer, free or not free, must add to the working-time necessary for his own maintenance an extra working-time in order to produce the means of subsistence for the owners of the means of production, whether this proprietor be the Athenian nobleman, Etruscan theocrat, civis Romanus, Norman baron, American slave-owner, Wallachian Boyard, modern landlord or capitalist. It is, however, clear that in any given economic formation of society, where not the exchange-value but the use-value of the product predominates, surplus-labour will be limited by a given set of wants which may be greater or less, and that here no boundless thirst for surplus-labour arises from the nature of the production itself. Hence in antiquity over-work becomes horrible only when the object is to obtain exchange-value in its specific independent money-form; in the production of gold and silver. Compulsory working to death is here the recognised form of over-work. Only read Diodorus Siculus. Still these are exceptions in antiquity. But as soon as people, whose production still moves within the lower forms of slave-labour, corvée-labour, &c., are drawn into the whirlpool of an international market dominated by the capitalistic mode of production, the sale of their products for export becoming their principal interest, the civilised horrors of over-work are grafted on the barbaric horrors of slavery, serfdom, &c. Hence the negro labour in the Southern States of the American Union preserved something of a patriarchal charactor, so long as production was chiefly directed to immediate local consumption. But in proportion, as the export of cotton became of vital interest to these states, the over-working of the negro and sometimes the using up of his life in 7 years of labour became a factor in a calculated and calculating system. It was no longer a question of obtaining from him a certain quantity of useful products. It was now a question of production of surplus-labour itself. So was it also with the corvée, *e.g.*, in the Danubian Principalities (now Roumania).

The comparison of the greed for surplus-labour in the Danubian Principalities with the same greed in English factories has a special interest, because surplus-labour in the corvée has an independent and palpable form.

Suppose the working-day consists of 6 hours of necessary labour, and 6 hours of surplus-labour. Then the free labourer gives the capitalist every week 6×6 or 36 hours of surplus-labour. It is the same as if he worked 3 days in the week for himself, and 3 days in the week gratis for the capitalist. But this is not evident on the surface. Surplus-labour and necessary labour glide one into the other. I can, therefore, express the same relationship by saying, *e.g.*, that the labourer in every minute works 30 seconds for himself, and 30 for the capitalist, etc. It is otherwise with the corvée. The necessary labour which the Wallachian peasant does for his own maintenance is distinctly marked off from his surplus-labour on behalf of the Boyard. The one he does on his own field, the other on the seignorial estate. Both parts of the labour-time exist, therefore, independently, side by side one with the other. In the corvée the surplus-labour is accurately marked off from the necessary labour. This, however, can make no difference with regard to the quantitative relation of surplus-labour to necessary labour. Three days' surplus-labour in the week remain three days that yield no equivalent to the labourer himself, whether it be called corvée or wage-labour. But in the capitalist the greed for surplus-labour appears in the straining after an unlimited extension of the working-day, in the Boyard more simply in a direct hunting after days of corvée. * * *

The Factory Act of 1850 now in force (1867) allows for the average working-day 10 hours, *i.e.*, for the first 5 days 12 hours from 6 a.m. to 6 p.m., including ½ an hour for breakfast, and an hour for dinner, and thus leaving 10½ working-hours, and 8 hours for Saturday, from 6 a.m. to 2 p.m., of which ½ an hour is subtracted for breakfast. 60 working-hours are left, 10½ for each of the first 5 days, 7½ for the last. Certain guardians of these laws are appointed, Factory Inspectors, directly under the Home Secretary, whose reports are published half-yearly, by order of Parliament. They give regular and official statistics of the capitalistic greed for surplus-labour.

Let us listen, for a moment, to the Factory Inspectors. "The fraudulent mill-owner begins work a quarter of an hour (sometimes more, sometimes less) before 6 a.m., and leaves off a quarter of an hour (sometimes more, sometimes less) after 6 p.m. He takes 5 minutes from the beginning and from the end of the half hour nominally allowed for breakfast, and 10 minutes at the beginning and end of the hour nominally allowed for dinner. He works for a quarter of an hour (sometimes more, sometimes less) after 2 p.m. on Saturday. Thus his gain is—

Before 6 a.m., ...	15 minutes.
After 6 p.m., ...	15 minutes.
At breakfast time, ...	10 minutes.
At dinner time, ...	20 minutes.
Five days—300 minutes,	60 minutes.
On Saturday before 6 a.m., ...	15 minutes.
At breakfast time, ...	10 minutes.
After 2 p.m., ...	15 minutes.
	40 minutes.
Total weekly, ...	340 minutes.

Or 5 hours and 40 minutes weekly, which multiplied by 50 working weeks in the year (allowing two for holidays and occasional stoppages) is equal to 27 working-days."

"Five minutes a day's increased work, multiplied by weeks, are equal to two and a half days of produce in the year."

"An additional hour a day gained by small instalments before 6 a.m., after 6 p.m., and at the beginning and end of the times nominally fixed for meals, is nearly equivalent to working 13 months in the year." * * *

These "small thefts" of capital from the labourer's meal and recreation time, the factory inspectors also designate as "petty pilferings of minutes," "snatching a few minutes," or, as the labourers technically called them, "nibbling and cribbling at meal-times."

It is evident that in this atmosphere the formation of surplus-value by surplus-labour, is no secret. "If you allow me," said a highly respectable master to me, "to work only ten minutes in the day over-time, you put one thousand a year in my *pocket*." "Moments are the elements of profit."

Nothing is from this point of view more characteristic than the designation of the workers who work full time as "full-timers," and the children under 13 who are only allowed to work 6 hours as "half-timers." The worker is here nothing more than personified labour-time. All individual distinctions are merged in those of "full-timers" and "half-timers."

Section 3. Branches of English Industry Without Legal Limits to Exploitation

We have hitherto considered the tendency to the extension of the working-day, the were-wolf's hunger for surplus-labour in a department where the monstrous exactions, not surpassed, says an English bourgeois economist, by the cruelties of the Spaniards to the American red-skins, caused capital at last to be bound by the chains of legal regulations. Now, let us cast a glance at certain branches of production in which the exploitation of labour is either free from fetters to this day, or was so yesterday.

Mr. Broughton Charlton, county magistrate, declared, as chairman of a meeting held at the Assembly Rooms, Nottingham, on the 14th of January, 1860, "that there was an amount of privation and suffering among that portion of the population connected with the lace trade, unknown in other parts of the kingdom, indeed, in the civilised world. . . . Children of nine or ten years are dragged from their squalid beds at two, three, or four o'clock in the morning and compelled to work for a bare subsistence until ten, eleven, or twelve at night, their limbs wearing away, their frames dwindling, their faces whitening, and their humanity absolutely sinking into a stone-like torpor, utterly horrible to contemplate. . . . We are not surprised that Mr. Mallett, or any other manufacturer, should stand forward and protest against discussion. . . . The system, as the Rev. Montagu Valpy describes it, is one of unmitigated slavery, socially, physically, morally, and spiritually. . . . What can be thought of a town which holds a public meeting to petition that the period of labour for men shall be diminished to eighteen hours a day? . . . We declaim against the Virginian and Carolinian cotton-planters. Is their black-market, their lash, and their barter of human flesh more detestable than this slow sacrifice of humanity which takes place in order that veils and collars may be fabricated for the benefit of capitalists?" * * *

The manufacture of lucifer matches dates from 1833, from the discovery of the method of applying phosphorus to the match itself. Since 1845 this manufacture has rapidly developed in England, and has extended especially amongst the thickly populated parts of London as well as in Manchester, Birmingham, Liverpool, Bristol, Norwich, Newcastle and Glasgow. With it has spread the form of lockjaw, which a Vienna physician in 1845 discovered to be a disease peculiar to lucifer-matchmakers. Half the workers are children under thirteen, and young persons under eighteen. The manufacture is on account of its unhealthiness and unpleasantness in such bad odour that only the most miserable part of the labouring class, half-starved widows and so forth, deliver up their children to it, "the ragged, half-starved, untaught children."

Of the witnesses that Commissioner White examined (1863), 270 were under 18, 50 under 10, 10 only 8, and 5 only 6 years old. A range of the working-day from 12 to 14 or 15 hours, night-labour, irregular meal-times, meals for the most part taken in the very workrooms that are pestilent with phosphorus. Dante would have found the worst horrors of his Inferno surpassed in this manufacture. * * *

No branch of industry in England (we do not take into account the making of bread by machinery recently introduced) has preserved up to the present day a method of production so archaic, so—as we see from the poets of the Roman Empire—pre-christian, as baking. But capital, as was said earlier, is at first indifferent as to the technical character of the labour-process; it begins by taking it just as it finds it.

The incredible adulteration of bread, especially in London, was first revealed by the House of Commons Committee "on the adulteration of articles of food" (1855–56), and Dr. Hassall's work, "Adulterations detected." The consequence of these revelations was the Act of August 6th, 1860, "for preventing the adulteration of articles of food and drink," an inoperative law, as it naturally shows the tenderest consideration for every Free-trader who determines by the buying or selling of adulterated commodities "to turn an honest penny." The Committee itself formulated more or less naïvely its conviction that Free-trade meant essentially trade with adulterated, or as the English ingeniously put it, "sophisticated" goods. In fact this kind of sophistry knows better than Protagoras how to make white black, and black white, and better than the Eleatics how to demonstrate *ad oculos* that everything is only appearance.

At all events the Committee had directed the attention of the public to its "daily bread," and therefore to the baking trade. At the same time in public meetings and in petitions to Parliament rose the cry of the London journeymen bakers against their overwork, &c. The cry was so urgent that Mr. H. S. Tremenheere, also a member of the Commission of 1863 several times mentioned, was appointed Royal Commissioner of Inquiry. His report, together with the evidence given, roused not the heart of the public but its stomach. Englishmen, always well up in the Bible, knew well enough that man, unless by elective grace a capitalist, or landlord, or sinecurist, is commanded to eat his bread in the sweat of his brow, but they did not know that he had to eat daily in his bread a certain quantity of human perspiration mixed with the discharge of abscesses, cobwebs, dead black-beetles, and putrid German yeast, without counting alum, sand, and other agreeable mineral ingredients. Without any regard to his holiness, Free-trade, the free baking-trade was therefore placed under the supervision of the State inspectors (Close of the Parliamentary session of 1863), and by the same Act of Parliament, work from 9 in the evening to 5 in the morning was forbidden for journeymen bakers under 18. The last clause speaks volumes as to the over-work in this old-fashioned, homely line of business.

"The work of a London journeyman baker begins, as a rule, at about eleven at night. At that hour he 'makes the dough,'—a laborious process, which lasts from half an hour to three quarters of an hour, according to the size of the batch or the labour bestowed upon it. He then lies down upon the kneading-board, which is also the covering of the trough in which the dough is 'made'; and with a sack under him, and another rolled up as a pillow, he sleeps for about a couple of hours. He is then engaged in a rapid and continuous labour for about five hours—throwing out the dough, 'scaling if off,' moulding it, putting it into the oven, preparing and baking rolls and fancy bread, taking the batch bread out of the oven, and up into the shop, &c., &c. The temperature of a bakehouse ranges from about 75 to upwards of 90 degrees, and in the smaller bakehouses approximates usually to the higher rather than to the lower degree of heat. When the business of making the bread, rolls, &c., is over, that of its distribution begins, and a considerable proportion of the journeymen in the trade, after working hard in the manner described during the night, are upon their legs for many hours during the day, carrying baskets, or wheeling hand-carts, and sometimes again in the bakehouse, leaving off work at various hours between 1 and 6 p.m. according to the season of the year, or the amount and nature of their master's business; while others are again engaged in the bakehouse in 'bringing out' more batches until late in the afternoon. . . . During what is called 'the London season,' the operatives belonging to the 'full-priced' bakers at the West End of the town, generally begin work at 11 p.m., and are engaged in making the bread, with one or two short (sometimes very short) intervals of rest, up to 8 o'clock the next morning. They are then engaged all day long, up to 4, 5, 6, and as late as 7 o'clock in the evening carrying out bread, or sometimes in the afternoon in the bakehouse again, assisting in the biscuit-baking. They may have, after they have done their work, sometimes five or six, sometimes only four or five hours' sleep before they begin again. On Fridays they always begin sooner, some about ten o'clock, and continue in some cases, at work, either in making or delivering the bread up to 8 p.m. on Saturday night, but more generally up to 4 or 5 o'clock, Sunday morning. On Sundays the men must attend twice or three times during the day for an hour or two to make preparations for the next day's bread. . . . The men employed by the underselling masters (who sell their bread under the 'full price,' and who, as already pointed out, comprise three-fourths of the London bakers) have not only to work on the average longer hours, but their work is almost entirely confined to the bakehouse. The underselling masters generally sell their bread. . . . in the shop. If they send it out, which is not common, except as supplying chandler's shops, they usually employ other hands for that purpose. It is not their practice to deliver bread from house to house. Towards the end of the week . . . the men begin on Thursday night at 10 o'clock, and continue on with only slight intermission until late on Saturday evening."

Even the bourgeois intellect understands the position of the "underselling" masters. "The unpaid labour of the men was made the source whereby the competition was carried on." And the "full-priced" baker denounces his underselling competitors to the Commission of Inquiry as thieves of foreign labour and adulterators. "They only exist now by first defrauding the public, and next getting 18 hours' work out of their men for 12 hours' wages."

The adulteration of bread and the formation of a class of bakers that sells the bread below the full price, date from the beginning of the 18th century, from the time when the corporate character of the trade was lost, and the capitalist in the form of the miller or flour-factor, rises behind the nominal master baker. Thus was laid the foundation of capitalistic production in this trade, of the unlimited extension of the working-day and of night-labour, although the latter only since 1824 gained a serious footing, even in London.

After what has just been said, it will be understood that the Report of the Commission classes journeymen bakers among the short-lived labourers, who, having by good luck escaped the normal decimation of the children of the working-class, rarely reach the age of 42. Nevertheless, the baking trade is always overwhelmed with applicants. The sources of the supply of these labour-powers to London are Scotland, the western agricultural districts of England, and Germany. * * *

From the motley crowd of labourers of all callings, ages, sexes, that press on us more busily than the souls of the slain on Ulysses, on whom—without referring to the Blue books under their arms—we see at a glance the mark of over-work, let us take two more figures whose striking contrast proves that before capital all men are alike—a milliner and a blacksmith.

In the last week of June, 1863, all the London daily papers published a paragraph with the "sensational" heading, "Death from simple over-work." It dealt with the death of the milliner, Mary Anne Walkley, 20 years of age, employed in a highly-respectable dressmaking establishment, exploited by a lady with the pleasant name of Elise. The old, often-told story, was once more recounted. This girl worked, on an average, 16½ hours, during the season often 30 hours, without a break, whilst her failing labour-power was revived by occasional supplies of sherry, port, or coffee. It was just now the height of the season. It was necessary to con-jure up in the twinkling of an eye the gorgeous dresses for the noble ladies bidden to the ball in honour of the newly-imported Princess of Wales. Mary Anne Walkley had worked without inter-mission for 26½ hours, with 60 other girls, 30 in one room, that only afforded ⅓ of the cubic feet of air required for them. At night, they slept in pairs in one of the stifling holes into which the bedroom was divided by partitions of board. And this was one of the best millinery establishments in London. Mary Anne Walkley fell ill on the Friday, died on Sunday, without, to the astonishment of Madame Elise, having previously completed the work in hand. The doctor, Mr. Keys, called too late to the death-bed, duly bore witness before the coroner's jury that "Mary Anne Walkley had died from long hours of work in an over-crowded workroom, and a too small and badly-ventilated bedroom." In order to give the doctor a lesson in good manners, the coroner's jury thereupon brought in a verdict that "the deceased had died of apoplexy, but there was reason to fear that her death had been accelerated by over-work in an over-crowded workroom, &c." "Our white slaves," cried the *Morning Star*, the organ of the Free-traders, Cobden and Bright, "our white slaves, who are toiled into the grave, for the most part silently pine and die."

"It is not in dressmakers' rooms that working to death is the order of the day, but in a thousand other places; in every place I had almost said, where 'a thriving business' has to be done. . . . We will take the blacksmith as a type. If the poets were true, there is no man so hearty, so merry, as the blacksmith; he rises early and strikes his sparks before the sun; he eats and drinks and sleeps as no other man. Working in moderation, he is, in fact, in one of the best of human positions, physically speaking. But we follow him into the city or town, and we see the stress of work on that strong man, and what then is his position in the death-rate of his country. In Marylebone, blacksmiths die at the rate of 31 per thousand per annum, or 11 above the mean of the male adults of the country in its entirety. The occupation, instinctive almost as a portion of human art, unobjectionable as a branch of human industry, is made by mere excess of work, the destroyer of the man. He can strike so many blows per day, walk so many steps, breathe so many breaths, produce so much work, and live an average, say of fifty years; he is made to strike so many more blows, to walk so many more steps, to breathe so many more breaths per day, and to increase altogether a fourth of his life. He meets the effort; the result is, that producing for a limited time a fourth more work, he dies at 37 for 50."

Section 4. Day and Night Work. The Relay System

Constant capital, the means of production, considered from the standpoint of the creation of surplus-value, only exist to absorb labour, and with every drop of labour a proportional quantity of surplus-labour. While they fail to do this, their mere existence causes a relative loss to the capitalist, for they represent during the time they lie fallow, a useless advance of capital. And this loss becomes positive and absolute as soon as the intermission of their employment necessitates additional outlay at the recommencement of work. The prolongation of the working-day beyond the limits of the natural day, into the night, only acts as a palliative. It quenches only in a slight degree the vampire thirst for the living blood of labour. To appropriate labour during all the 24 hours of the day is, therefore, the inherent tendency of capitalist production. But as it is physically impossible to exploit the same individual labour-power constantly during the night as well as the day, to overcome this physical hindrance, an alternation becomes necessary between the workpeople whose powers are exhausted by day, and those who are used up by night. This alternation may be effected in various ways; *e.g.*, it may be so arranged that part of the workers are one week employed on day-work, the next week on night-work. It is well known that this relay system, this alternation of two sets of workers, held full sway in the full-blooded youth-time of the English cotton manufacture, and that at the present time it still flourishes, among others, in the cotton spinning of the Moscow district. This 24 hours' process of production exists to-day as a system in many of the branches of industry of Great Britain that are still "free," in the blast-furnaces, forges, plate-rolling mills, and other metallurgical establishments in England, Wales, and Scotland. The working-time here includes, besides the 24 hours of the 6 working-days, a great part also of the 24 hours of Sunday. The workers consist of men and women, adults and children of both sexes. The ages of the children and young persons run through all intermediate grades, from 8 (in some cases from 6) to 18.

In some branches of industry, the girls and women work through the night together with the males. * * *

Section 5. The Struggle for a Normal Working-Day. Compulsory Laws for the Extension of the Working-Day from the Middle of the 14th to the End of the 17th Century

"What is a working-day? What is the length of time during which capital may consume the labour-power whose daily value it buys? How far may the working-day be extended beyond the working-time necessary for the reproduction of labour-power itself?" It has been seen that to these questions capital replies: the working-day contains the full 24 hours, with the deduction of the few hours of repose without which labour-power absolutely refuses its services again. Hence it is self-evident that the labourer is nothing else, his whole life through, than labour-power, that therefore all his disposable time is by nature and law labour-time, to be devoted to the self-expansion of capital. Time for education, for intellectual development, for the fulfilling of social functions and for social intercourse, for the free-play of his bodily and mental activity, even the rest time of Sunday (and that in a country of Sabbatarians!)—moonshine! But in its blind unrestrainable passion, its were-wolf hunger for surplus-labour, capital oversteps not only the moral, but even the merely physical maximum bounds of the working-day. It usurps the time for growth, development, and healthy maintenance of the body. It steals the time required for the consumption of fresh air and sunlight. It higgles over a meal-time, incorporating it where possible with the process of production itself, so that food is given to the labourer as to a mere means of production, as coal is supplied to the boiler, grease and oil to the machinery. It reduces the sound sleep needed for the restoration, reparation, refreshment of the bodily powers to just so many hours of torpor as the revival of an organism, absolutely exhausted, renders essential. It is not the normal maintenance of the labour-power which is to determine the limits of the working-day; it is the greatest possible daily expenditure of labour-power, no matter how diseased, compulsory, and painful it may be, which is to determine the limits of the labourers' period of repose. Capital cares nothing for the length of life of labour-power. All that concerns it is simply and solely the maximum of labour-power, that can be rendered fluent in a working-day. It attains this end by shortening the extent of the labourer's life, as a greedy farmer snatches increased produce from the soil by robbing it of its fertility.

The capitalistic mode of production (essentially the production of surplus-value, the absorption of surplus-labour), produces thus, with the extension of the working-day, not only the deterioration of human labour-power by robbing it of its normal, moral and physical, conditions of development and function. It produces also the premature exhaustion and death of this labour-power itself. It extends the labourer's time of production during a given period by shortening his actual life-time.

But the value of the labour-power includes the value of the commodities necessary for the reproduction of the worker, or for the keeping up of the working-class. If then the unnatural extension of the working-day, that capital necessarily strives after in its unmeasured passion for self-expansion, shortens the length of life of the individual labourer, and therefore the duration of his labour-power, the forces used up have to be replaced at a more rapid rate and the sum of the expenses for the reproduction of labour-power will be greater; just as in a machine the part of its value to be reproduced every day is greater the more rapidly the machine is worn out. It would seem therefore that the interest of capital itself points in the direction of a normal working-day.

The slave-owner buys his labourer as he buys his horse. If he loses his slave, he loses capital that can only be restored by new outlay in the slave-mart. But "the rice-grounds of Georgia, or the swamps of the Mississippi may be fatally injurious to the human constitution; but the waste of human life which the cultivation of these districts necessitates, is not so great that it cannot be repaired from the teeming preserves of Virginia and Kentucky. Considerations of economy, moreover, which, under a natural system, afford some security for human treatment by identifying the master's interest with the slave's preservation, when once trading in slaves is practised, become reasons for racking to the uttermost the toil of the slave; for, when his place can at once be supplied from foreign preserves, the duration of his life becomes a matter of less moment than its productiveness while it lasts. It is accordingly a maxim of slave management, in slave-importing countries, that the most effective economy is that which takes out of the human chattel in the shortest space of time the utmost amount of exertion it is capable of putting forth. It is in tropical culture, where annual profits often equal the whole capital of plantations, that negro life is most recklessly sacrificed. It is the agriculture of the West Indies, which has been for centuries prolific of fabulous wealth, that has engulfed millions of the African race. It is in Cuba, at this day, whose revenues are reckoned by millions, and whose planters are princes, that we see in the servile class, the coarsest fare, the most exhausting and unremitting toil, and even the absolute destruction of a portion of its numbers every year."

Mutato nomine de te fabula narratur. For slave-trade read labour-market, for Kentucky and Virginia, Ireland and the agricultural districts of England, Scotland, and Wales, for Africa, Germany. We heard how over-work thinned the ranks of the bakers in London. Nevertheless, the London labour-market is always overstocked with German and other candidates for death in the bakeries. Pottery, as we saw, is one of the shortest-lived industries. Is there any want therefore of potters? Josiah Wedgwood, the inventor of modern pottery, himself originally a common workman, said in 1785 before the House of Commons that the whole trade employed from 15,000 to 20,000 people. In the year 1861 the population alone of the town centres of this industry in Great Britain numbered 101,302. "The cotton trade has existed for ninety years. . . . It has existed for three generations of the English race, and I believe I may safely say that during that period it has destroyed nine generations of factory operatives." * * *

What experience shows to the capitalist generally is a constant excess of population, *i.e.*, an excess in relation to the momentary requirements of surplus-labour-absorbing capital, although this excess is made up of generations of human beings stunted, short-lived, swiftly replacing each other, plucked, so to say, before maturity. And, indeed, experience shows to the intelligent observer with what swiftness and grip the capitalist mode of production, dating, historically speaking, only from yesterday, has seized the vital power of the people by the very root—shows how the degeneration of the industrial population is only retarded by the constant absorption of primitive and physically uncorrupted elements from the country—shows how even the country labourers, in spite of fresh air and the principle of natural selection, that works so powerfully amongst them, and only permits the survival of the strongest, are already beginning to die off. Capital that has such good reasons for denying the sufferings of the legions of workers that surround it, is in practice moved as much and as little by the sight of the coming degradation and final depopulation of the human race, as by the probable fall of the earth into the sun. In every stock-jobbing swindle every one knows that some time or other the crash must come, but every one hopes that it may fall on the head of his neighbour, after he himself has caught the shower of gold and placed it in safety. *Après moi le déluge!* is the watchword of every capitalist and of every capitalist nation. Hence Capital is reckless of the health or length of life of the labourer, unless under compulsion from society. To the out-cry as to the physical and mental degradation, the premature death, the torture of over-work, it answers: Ought these to trouble us since they increase our profits? But looking at things as a whole, all this does not, indeed, depend on the good or ill will of the individual capitalist. Free competition brings out the inherent laws of capitalist production, in the shape of external coercive laws having power over every individual capitalist.

The establishment of a normal working-day is the result of centuries of struggle between capitalist and labourer. The history of this struggle shows two opposed tendencies. Compare, *e.g.*, the English factory legislation of our time with the English Labour Statutes from the 14th century to well into the middle of the 18th. Whilst the modern Factory Acts compulsorily shortened the working-day, the earlier statutes tried to lengthen it by compulsion. Of course the pretensions of capital in embryo—when, beginning to grow, it secures the right of absorbing a *quantum sufficit* of surplus-labour, not merely by the force of economic relations, but by the help of the State—appear very modest when put face to face with the concessions that, growling and struggling, it has to make in its adult condition. It takes centuries ere the "free" labourer, thanks to the development of capitalistic production, agrees, *i.e.*, is compelled by social conditions, to sell the whole of his active life, his very capacity for work, for the price of the necessaries of life, his birthright for a mess of pottage. Hence it is natural that the lengthening of the work-day, which capital, from the middle of the 14th to the end of the 17th century, tries to impose by State-measures on adult labourers, approximately coincides with the shortening of the working-day which, in the second half of the 19th century, has here and there been effected by the State to prevent the coining of children's blood into capital. That which to-day, *e.g.*, in the State of Massachusetts, until recently the freest State of the North-American Republic, has been proclaimed as the statutory limit of the labour of children under 12, was in England, even in the middle of the 17th century, the normal working-day of able-bodied artisans, robust labourers, athletic blacksmiths. * * *

Part IV. Production of Relative Surplus-Value

CHAPTER XII. THE CONCEPT OF RELATIVE SURPLUS-VALUE

That portion of the working-day which merely produces an equivalent for the value paid by the capitalist for his labour-power, has, up to this point, been treated by us as a constant magnitude, and such in fact it is, under given conditions of production and at a given stage in the economic development of society. Beyond this, his necessary labour-time, the labourer, we saw, could continue to work for 2, 3, 4, 6, &c., hours. The rate of surplus-value and the length of the working-day depended on the magnitude of this prolongation. Though the necessary labour-time was constant, we saw, on the other hand, that the total working-day was variable. Now suppose we have a working-day whose length, and whose apportionment between necessary labour and surplus-labour, are given. Let the whole line a c, a————b—c represent, for example, a working-day of 12 hours; the portion of a b 10 hours of necessary labour, and the portion b c 2 hours of surplus-labour. How now can the production of surplus-value be increased, *i.e.*, how can the surplus-labour be prolonged, without, or independently of, any prolongation of a c?

Although the length of a c is given, b c appears to be capable of prolongation, if not by extension beyond its end c, which is also the end of the working-day a c, yet, at all events, by pushing back its starting-point b in the direction of a. Assume that b'—b in the line a b' b c is equal to half of b c

a————————————b'—b——c

or to one hour's labour-time. If now, in a c, the working-day of 12 hours, we move the point b to b', b c becomes b' c; the surplus-labour increases by one half, from 2 hours to 3 hours, although the working-day remains as before at 12 hours. This extension of the surplus labour-time from b c to b' c, from 2 hours to 3 hours, is, however, evidently impossible, without a simultaneous contraction of the necessary labour-time from a b into a b', from 10 hours to 9 hours. The prolongation of the surplus-labour would correspond to a shortening of the necessary labour; or a portion of the labour-time previously consumed, in reality, for the labourer's own benefit, would be converted into labour-time for the benefit of the capitalist. There would be an alteration, not in the length of the working-day, but in its division into necessary labour-time and surplus labour-time.

On the other hand, it is evident that the duration of the surplus-labour is given, when the length of the working-day, and the value of labour-power, are given. The value of labour-power, *i.e.*, the labour-time requisite to produce labour-power, determines the labour-time necessary for the reproduction of that value. If one working-hour be embodied in sixpence, and the value of a day's labour-power be five shillings, the labourer must work 10 hours a day, in order to replace the value paid by capital for his labour-power, or to produce an equivalent for the value of his daily necessary means of subsistence. Given the value of these means of subsistence, the value of his labour-power is given; and given the value of his labour-power, the duration of his necessary labour-time is given. The duration of the surplus-labour, however, is arrived at, by subtracting the necessary labour-time from the total working-day. Ten hours subtracted from twelve, leave two, and it is not easy to see, how, under the given conditions, the surplus-labour can possibly be prolonged beyond two hours. No doubt, the capitalist can, instead of five shillings, pay the labourer four shillings and sixpence or even less. For the reproduction of this value of four shillings and sixpence, nine hours' labour-time would suffice; and consequently three hours of surplus-labour, instead of two, would accrue to the capitalist, and the surplus-value would rise from one shilling to eighteenpence. This result, however, would be obtained only by lowering the wages of the labourer below the value of his labour-power. With the four shillings and sixpence which he produces in nine hours, he commands one-tenth less of the necessaries of life than before, and consequently the proper reproduction of his labour-power is crippled. The surplus-labour would in this case be prolonged only by an overstepping of its normal limits; its domain would be extended only by a usurpation of part of the domain of necessary labour-time. Despite the important part which this method plays in actual practice, we are excluded from considering it in this place, by our assumption, that all commodities, including labour-power, are bought and sold at their full value. Granted this, it follows that the labour-time necessary for the production of labour-power, or for the reproduction of its value, cannot be lessened by a fall in the labourer's wages below the value of his labour-power, but only by a fall in this value itself. Given the length of the working-day, the prolongation of the surplus-labour must of necessity originate in the curtailment of the necessary labour-time; the latter cannot arise from the former. In the example we have taken, it is necessary that the value of labour-power should actually fall by one-tenth, in order that the necessary labour-time may be diminished by one-tenth, *i.e.*, from ten hours to nine, and in order that the surplus-labour may consequently be prolonged from two hours to three.

Such a fall in the value of labour-power implies, however, that the same necessaries of life which were formerly produced in ten hours, can now be produced in nine hours. But this is impossible without an increase in the productiveness of labour. For example, suppose a shoemaker, with given tools, makes in one working-day of twelve hours, one pair of boots. If he must make two pairs in the same time, the productiveness of his labour must be doubled; and this cannot be done, except by an alteration in his tools or in his mode of working, or in both. Hence, the conditions of production, *i.e.*, his mode of production, and the labour-process itself, must be revolutionised. By increase in the productiveness of labour, we mean, generally, an alteration in the labour-process, of such a kind as to shorten the labour-time socially necessary for the production of a commodity, and to endow a given quantity of labour with the power of producing a greater quantity of use-value. Hitherto in treating of surplus-value, arising from a simple prolongation of the working-day, we have assumed the mode of production to be given and invariable. But when surplus-value has to be produced by the conversion of necessary labour into surplus-labour, it by no means suffices for capital to take over the labour-process in the form under which it has been historically handed down, and then simply to prolong the duration of that process. The technical and social conditions of the process, and consequently the very mode of production must be revolutionised, before the productiveness of labour can be increased. By that means alone can the value of labour-power be made to sink, and the portion of the working-day necessary for the reproduction of that value, be shortened.

The surplus-value produced by prolongation of the working-day, I call *absolute surplus-value*. On the other hand, the surplus-value arising from the curtailment of the necessary labour-time, and from the corresponding alteration in the respective lengths of the two components of the working-day, I call *relative surplus-value*.

In order to effect a fall in the value of labour-power, the increase in the productiveness of labour must seize upon those branches of industry, whose products determine the value of labour-power, and consequently either belong to the class of customary means of subsistence, or are capable of supplying the place of those means. But the value of a commodity is determined, not only by the quantity of labour which the labourer directly bestows upon that commodity, but also by the labour contained in the means of production. For instance, the value of a pair of boots depends, not only on the cobbler's labour, but also on the value of the leather, wax, thread, &c. Hence, a fall in the value of labour-power is also brought about by an increase in the productiveness of labour, and by a corresponding cheapening of commodities in those industries which supply the instruments of labour and the raw material, that form the material elements of the constant capital required for producing the necessaries of life. But an increase in the productiveness of labour in those branches of industry which supply neither the necessaries of life, nor the means of production for such necessaries, leaves the value of labour-power undisturbed.

The cheapened commodity, of course, causes only a pro tanto fall in the value of labour-power, a fall proportional to the extent of that commodity's employment in the reproduction of labour-power. Shirts, for instance, are a necessary means of subsistence, but are only one out of many. The totality of the necessaries of life consists, however, of various commodities, each the product of a distinct industry; and the value of each of those commodities enters as a component part into the value of labour-power. This latter value decreases with the decrease of the labour-time necessary for its reproduction; the total decrease being the sum of all the different curtailments of labour-time effected in those various and distinct industries. This general result is treated, here, as if it were the immediate result directly aimed at in each individual case. Whenever an individual capitalist cheapens shirts, for instance, by increasing the productiveness of labour, he by no means necessarily aims at reducing the value of labour-power and shortening, pro tanto, the necessary labour-time. But it is only in so far as he ultimately contributes to this result, that he assists in raising the general rate of surplus-value. The general and necessary tendencies of capital must be distinguished from their forms of manifestation.

It is not our intention to consider, here, the way in which the laws, immanent in capitalist production, manifest themselves in the movements of individual masses of capital, where they assert themselves as coercive laws of competition, and are brought home to the mind and consciousness of the individual capitalist as the directing motives of his operations. But this much is clear; a scientific analysis of competition is not possible, before we have a conception of the inner nature of capital, just as the apparent motions of the heavenly bodies are not intelligible to any but him, who is acquainted with their real motions, motions which are not directly perceptible by the senses. Nevertheless, for the better comprehension of the production of relative surplus-value, we may add the following remarks, in which we assume nothing more than the results we have already obtained.

If one hour's labour is embodied in sixpence, a value of six shillings will be produced in a working-day of 12 hours. Suppose, that with the prevailing productiveness of labour, 12 articles are produced in these 12 hours. Let the value of the means of production used up in each article be sixpence. Under these circumstances, each article costs one shilling: sixpence for the value of the means of production, and sixpence for the value newly added in working with those means. Now let some one capitalist contrive to double the productiveness of labour, and to produce in the working-day of 12 hours, 24 instead of 12 such articles. The value of the means of production remaining the same, the value of each article will fall to ninepence, made up of sixpence for the value of the means of production and threepence for the value newly added by the labour. Despite the doubled productiveness of labour, the day's labour creates, as before, a new value of six shillings and no more, which, however, is now spread over twice as many articles. Of this value each article now has embodied in it 1/24th, instead of 1/12th, three-pence instead of sixpence; or, what amounts to the same thing, only half an hour's instead of a whole hour's labour-time, is now added to the means of production while they are being transformed into each article. The individual value of these articles is now below their social value; in other words, they have cost less labour-time than the great bulk of the same article produced under the average social conditions. Each article costs, on an average, one shilling, and represents 2 hours of social labour; but under the altered mode of production it costs only ninepence, or contains only 1½ hours' labour. The real value of a commodity is, however, not its individual value, but its social value; that is to say, the real value is not measured by the labour-time that the article in each individual case costs the producer, but by the labour-time socially required for its production. If therefore, the capitalist who applies the new method, sells his commodity at its social value of one shilling, he sells it for threepence above its individual value, and thus realises an extra surplus-value of threepence. On the other hand, the working-day of 12 hours is, as regards him, now represented by 24 articles instead of 12. Hence, in order to get rid of the product of one working-day, the demand must be double what it was, *i.e.*, the market must become twice as extensive. Other things being equal, his commodities can command a more extended market only by a diminution of their prices. He will therefore sell them above their individual but under their social value, say at tenpence each. By this means he still squeezes an extra surplus-value of one penny out of each. This augmentation of surplus-value is pocketed by him, whether his commodities belong or not to the class of necessary means of subsistence that participate in determining the general value of labour-power. Hence, independently of this latter circumstance, there is a motive for each individual capitalist to cheapen his commodities, by increasing the productiveness of labour.

Nevertheless, even in this case, the increased production of surplus-value arises from the curtailment of the necessary labour-time, and from the corresponding prolongation of the surplus-labour. Let the necessary labour-time amount to 10 hours, the value of a day's labour-power to five shillings, the surplus labour-time to 2 hours, and the daily surplus-value to one shilling. But the capitalist now produces 24 articles, which he sells at tenpence a-piece, making twenty shillings in all. Since the value of the means of production is twelve shillings, 14 2/5 of these articles merely replace the constant capital advanced. The labour of the 12 hours' working-day is represented by the remaining 9 3/5 articles. Since the price of the labour-power is five shillings, 6 articles represent the necessary labour-time, and 3 3/5 articles the surplus-labour. The ratio of the necessary labour to the surplus-labour, which under average social conditions was 5:1, is now only 5:3. The same result may be arrived at in the following way. The value of the product of the working-day of 12 hours is twenty shillings. Of this sum, twelve shillings belong to the value of the means of production, a value that merely re-appears. There remain eight shillings, which are the expression in money, of the value newly created during the working-day. This sum is greater than the sum in which average social labour of the same kind is expressed: twelve hours of the latter labour are expressed by six shillings only. The exceptionally productive labour operates as intensified labour; it creates in equal periods of time greater values than average social labour of the same kind. But our capitalist still continues to pay as before only five shillings as the value of a day's labour-power. Hence, instead of 10 hours, the labourer need now work only 7 4/5 hours, in order to reproduce this value. His surplus-labour is, therefore, increased by 2 4/5 hours, and the surplus-value he produces grows from one, into three shillings. Hence, the capitalist who applies the improved method of production, appropriates to surplus-labour a greater portion of the working-day, than the other capitalists in the same trade. He does individually, what the whole body of capitalists engaged in producing relative surplus-value, do collectively. On the other hand, however, this extra surplus-value vanishes, so soon as the new method of production has become general, and has consequently caused the difference between the individual value of the cheapened commodity and its social value to vanish. The law of the determination of value by labour-time, a law which brings under its sway the individual capitalist who applies the new method of production, by compelling him to sell his goods under their social value, this same law, acting as a coercive law of competition, forces his competitors to adopt the new method. The general rate of surplus-value is, therefore, ultimately affected by the whole process, only when the increase in the productiveness of labour, has seized upon those branches of production that are connected with, and has cheapened those commodities that form part of, the necessary means of subsistence, and are therefore elements of the value of labour-power.

The value of commodities is in inverse ratio to the productiveness of labour. And so, too, is the value of labour-power, because it depends on the values of commodities. Relative surplus-value is, on the contrary, directly proportional to that productiveness. It rises with rising and falls with falling productiveness. The value of money being assumed to be constant, an average social working-day of 12 hours always produces the same new value, six shillings, no matter how this sum may be apportioned between surplus-value and wages. But if, in consequence of increased productiveness, the value of the necessaries of life fall, and the value of a day's labour-power be thereby reduced from five shillings to three, the surplus-value increases from one shilling to three. Ten hours were necessary for the reproduction of the value of the labour-power; now only six are required. Four hours have been set free, and can be annexed to the domain of surplus-labour. Hence there is immanent in capital an inclination and constant tendency, to heighten the productiveness of labour, in order to cheapen commodities, and by such cheapening to cheapen the labourer himself.

The value of a commodity is, in itself, of no interest to the capitalist. What alone interests him, is the surplus-value that dwells in it, and is realisable by sale. Realisation of the surplus-value necessarily carries with it the refunding of the value that was advanced. Now, since relative surplus-value increases in direct proportion to the development of the productiveness of labour, while, on the other hand, the value of commodities diminishes in the same proportion; since one and the same process cheapens commodities, and augments the surplus-value contained in them; we have here the solution of the riddle: why does the capitalist, whose sole concern is the production of exchange-value, continually strive to depress the exchange-value of commodities? A riddle with which Quesnay, one of the founders of Political Economy, tormented his opponents, and to which they could give him no answer. "You acknowledge," he says, "that the more expenses and the cost of labour can, in the manufacture of industrial products, be reduced without injury to production, the more advantageous is such reduction, because it diminishes the price of the finished article. And yet, you believe that the production of wealth, which arises from the labour of the workpeople, consists in the augmentation of the exchange-value of their products."

The shortening of the working-day is, therefore, by no means what is aimed at, in capitalist production, when labour is economised by increasing its productiveness. It is only the shortening of the labour-time, necessary for the production of a definite quantity of commodities, that is aimed at. The fact that the workman, when the productiveness of his labour has been increased, produces, say 10 times as many commodities as before, and thus spends one-tenth as much labour-time on each, by no means prevents him from continuing to work 12 hours as before, nor from producing in those 12 hours 1,200 articles instead of 120. Nay, more, his working-day may be prolonged at the same time, so as to make him produce, say, 1,400 articles in 14 hours. In the treatises, therefore, of economists of the stamp of MacCulloch, Ure, Senior, and tutti quanti, we may read upon one page, that the labourer owes a debt of gratitude to capital for developing his productiveness, because the necessary labour-time is thereby shortened, and on the next page, that he must prove his gratitude by working in future for 15 hours instead of 10. The object of all development of the productiveness of labour, within the limits of capitalist production, is to shorten that part of the working-day, during which the workman must labour for his own benefit, and by that very shortening, to lengthen the other part of the day, during which he is at liberty to work gratis for the capitalist. How far this result is also attainable, without cheapening commodities, will appear from an examination of the particular modes of producing relative surplus-value, to which examination we now proceed.

CHAPTER XIII. CO-OPERATION

Capitalist production only then really begins, as we have already seen, when each individual capital employs simultaneously a comparatively large number of labourers; when consequently the labour-process is carried on on an extensive scale and yields, relatively, large quantities of products. A greater number of labourers working together, at the same time, in one place (or, if you will, in the same field of labour), in order to produce the same sort of commodity under the mastership of one capitalist, constitutes, both historically and logically, the starting-point of capitalist production. With regard to the mode of production itself, manufacture, in its strict meaning, is hardly to be distinguished, in its earliest stages, from the handicraft trades of the guilds, otherwise than by the greater number of workmen simultaneously employed by one and the same individual capital. The workshop of the mediæval master handicraftsman is simply enlarged. * * *

We saw in a former chapter, that a certain minimum amount of capital was necessary, in order that the number of labourers simultaneously employed, and consequently, the amount of surplus-value produced, might suffice to liberate the employer himself from manual labour, to convert him from a small master into a capitalist, and thus formally to establish capitalist production. We now see that a certain minimum amount is a necessary condition for the conversion of numerous isolated and independent processes into one combined social process.

We also saw that at first, the subjection of labour to capital was only a formal result of the fact, that the labourer, instead of working for himself, works for and consequently under the capitalist. By the co-operation of numerous wage-labourers, the sway of capital develops into a requisite for carrying on the labour-process itself, into a real requisite of production. That a capitalist should command on the field of production, is now as indispensable as that a general should command on the field of battle.

All combined labour on a large scale requires, more or less, a directing authority, in order to secure the harmonious working of the individual activities, and to perform the general functions that have their origin in the action of the combined organism, as distinguished from the action of its separate organs. A single violin player is his own conductor; an orchestra requires a separate one. The work of directing, superintending, and adjusting, becomes one of the functions of capital, from the moment that the labour under the control of capital, becomes co-operative. Once a function of capital, it acquires special characteristics.

The directing motive, the end and aim of capitalist production, is to extract the greatest possible amount of surplus-value, and consequently to exploit labour-power to the greatest possible extent. As the number of the co-operating labourers increases, so too does their resistance to the domination of capital, and with it, the necessity for capital to overcome this resistance by counter-pressure. The control exercised by the capitalist is not only a special function, due to the nature of the social labour-process, and peculiar to that process, but it is, at the same time, a function of the exploitation of a social labour-process, and is consequently rooted in the unavoidable antagonism between the exploiter and the living and labouring raw material he exploits.

Again, in proportion to the increasing mass of the means of production, now no longer the property of the labourer, but of the capitalist, the necessity increases for some effective control over the proper application of those means. Moreover, the co-operation of wage-labourers is entirely brought about by the capital that employs them. Their union into one single productive body and the establishment of a connexion between their individual functions, are matters foreign and external to them, are not their own act, but the act of the capital that brings and keeps them together. Hence the connexion existing between their various labours appears to them, ideally, in the shape of a preconceived plan of the capitalist, and practically in the shape of the authority of the same capitalist, in the shape of the powerful will of another, who subjects their activity to his aims. If, then, the control of the capitalist is in substance two-fold by reason of the two-fold nature of the process of production itself,—which, on the one hand, is a social process for producing use-values, on the other, a process for creating surplus-value—in form that control is despotic. As co-operation extends its scale, this despotism takes forms peculiar to itself. Just as at first the capitalist is relieved from actual labour so soon as his capital has reached that minimum amount with which capitalist production, as such, begins, so now, he hands over the work of direct and constant supervision of the individual workmen, and groups of workmen, to a special kind of wage-labourer. An industrial army of workmen, under the command of a capitalist, requires, like a real army, officers (managers), and sergeants (foremen, overlookers), who, while the work is being done, command in the name of the capitalist. The work of supervision becomes their established and exclusive function. When comparing the mode of production of isolated peasants and artisans with production by slave-labour, the political economist counts this labour of superintendence among the *faux frais* of production. But, when considering the capitalist mode of production, he, on the contrary, treats the work of control made necessary by the co-operative character of the labour-process as identical with the different work of control, necessitated by the capitalist character of that process and the antagonism of interests between capitalist and labourer. It is not because he is a leader of industry that a man is a capitalist; on the contrary, he is a leader of industry because he is a capitalist. The leadership of industry is an attribute of capital, just as in feudal times the functions of general and judge, were attributes of landed property.

The labourer is the owner of his labour-power until he has done bargaining for its sale with the capitalist; and he can sell no more than what he has—*i.e.*, his individual, isolated labour-power. This state of things is in no way altered by the fact that the capitalist, instead of buying the labour-power of one man, buys that of 100, and enters into separate contracts with 100 unconnected men instead of with one. He is at liberty to set the 100 men to work, without letting them co-operate. He pays them the value of 100 independent labour-powers, but he does not pay for the combined labour-power of the hundred. Being independent of each other, the labourers are isolated persons, who enter into relations with the capitalist, but not with one another. This co-operation begins only with the labour-process, but they have then ceased to belong to themselves. On entering that process, they become incorporated with capital. As co-operators, as members of a working organism they are but special modes of existence of capital. Hence, the productive power developed by the labourer when working in co-operation, is the productive power of capital. This power is developed gratuitously, whenever the workmen are placed under given conditions, and it is capital that places them under such conditions. Because this power costs capital nothing, and because, on the other hand, the labourer himself does not develop it before his labour belongs to capital, it appears as a power with which capital is endowed by Nature—a productive power that is immanent in capital.

The colossal effects of simple co-operation are to be seen in the gigantic structures of the ancient Asiatics, Egyptians, Etruscans, &c.

"It has happened in times past that these Oriental States, after supplying the expenses of their civil and military establishments, have found themselves in possession of a surplus which they could apply to works of magnificence or utility and in the construction of these their command over the hands and arms of almost the entire non-agricultural population has produced stupendous monuments which still indicate their power. The teeming valley of the Nile . . . produced food for a swarming non-agricultural population, and this food, belonging to the monarch and the priesthood, afforded the means of erecting the mighty monuments which filled the land. . . . In moving the colossal statues and vast masses of which the transport creates wonder, human labour almost alone, was prodigally used. . . . The number of the labourers and the concentration of their efforts sufficed. We see mighty coral reefs rising from the depths of the ocean into islands and firm land, yet each individual depositor is puny, weak, and contemptible. The non-agricultural labourers of an Asiatic monarchy have little but their individual bodily exertions to bring to the task, but their number is their strength, and the power of directing these masses gave rise to the palaces and temples, the pyramids, and the armies of gigantic statues of which the remains astonish and perplex us. It is that confinement of the revenues which feed them, to one or a few hands, which makes such undertakings possible." This power of Asiatic and Egyptian kings, Etruscan theocrats, &c., has in modern society been transferred to the capitalist, whether he be an isolated, or as in joint-stock companies, a collective capitalist.

Co-operation, such as we find it at the dawn of human development, among races who live by the chase, or, say, in the agriculture of Indian communities, is based, on the one hand, on ownership in common of the means of production, and on the other hand, on the fact, that in those cases, each individual has no more torn himself off from the navel-string of his tribe or community, than each bee has freed itself from connexion with the hive. Such co-operation is distinguished from capitalistic co-operation by both of the above characteristics. The sporadic application of co-operation on a large scale in ancient times, in the middle ages, and in modern colonies, reposes on relations of dominion and servitude, principally on slavery. The capitalistic form, on the contrary, pre-supposes from first to last, the free wage-labourer, who sells his labour power to capital. Historically, however, this form is developed in opposition to peasant agriculture and to the carrying on of independent handicrafts whether in guilds or not. From the standpoint of these, capitalistic co-operation does not manifest itself as a particular historical form of co-operation, but co-operation itself appears to be a historical form peculiar to, and specifically distinguishing, the capitalist process of production.

Just as the social productive power of labour that is developed by co-operation, appears to be the productive power of capital, so co-operation itself, contrasted with the process of production carried on by isolated independent labourers, or even by small employers, appears to be a specific form of the capitalist process of production. It is the first change experienced by the actual labour-process, when subjected to capital. This change takes place spontaneously. The simultaneous employment of a large number of wage-labourers, in one and the same process, which is a necessary condition of this change, also forms the starting-point of capitalist production. This point coincides with the birth of capital itself. If then, on the one hand, the capitalist mode of production presents itself to us historically, as a necessary condition to the transformation of the labour-process into a social process, so, on the other hand, this social form of the labour-process presents itself, as a method employed by capital for the more profitable exploitation of labour, by increasing that labour's productiveness.

In the elementary form, under which we have hitherto viewed it, co-operation is a necessary concomitant of all production on a large scale, but it does not, in itself, represent a fixed form characteristic of a particular epoch in the development of the capitalist mode of production. At the most it appears to do so, and that only approximately, in the handicraft-like beginnings of manufacture, and in that kind of agriculture on a large scale, which corresponds to the epoch of manufacture, and is distinguished from peasant agriculture, mainly by the number of the labourers simultaneously employed, and by the mass of the means of production concentrated for their use. Simple co-operation is always the prevailing form, in those branches of production in which capital operates on a large scale, and division of labour and machinery play but a subordinate part.

Co-operation ever constitutes the fundamental form of the capitalist mode of production; nevertheless the elementary form of co-operation continues to subsist as a particular form of capitalist production side by side with the more developed forms of that mode of production.

CHAPTER XIV. DIVISION OF LABOUR AND MANUFACTURE

Section 1. Two-fold Origin of Manufacture

That co-operation which is based on division of labour, assumes its typical form in manufacture, and is the prevalent characteristic form of the capitalist process of production throughout the manufacturing period properly so called. That period, roughly speaking, extends from the middle of the 16th to the last third of the 18th century.

Manufacture takes its rise in two ways:—

(1) By the assemblage, in one workshop under the control of a single capitalist, of labourers belonging to various independent handicrafts, but through whose hands a given article must pass on its way to completion. A carriage, for example, was formerly the product of the labour of a great number of independent artificers, such as wheelwrights, harness-makers, tailors, locksmiths, upholsterers, turners, fringe-makers, glaziers, painters, polishers, gilders, &c. In the manufacture of carriages, however, all these different artificers are assembled in one building where they work into one another's hands. * * *

(2) Manufacture also arises in a way exactly the reverse of this—namely, by one capitalist employing simultaneously in one workshop a number of artificers, who all do the same, or the same kind of work, such as making paper, type, or needles. This is co-operation in its most elementary form. Each of these artificers (with the help, perhaps, of one or two apprentices), makes the entire commodity, and he consequently performs in succession all the operations necessary for its production. He still works in his old handicraft-like way. But very soon external circumstances cause a different use to be made of the concentration of the workmen on one spot, and of the simultaneousness of their work. An increased quantity of the article has perhaps to be delivered within a given time. The work is therefore re-distributed. Instead of each man being allowed to perform all the various operations in succession, these operations are changed into disconnected, isolated ones, carried on side by side; each is assigned to a different artificer, and the whole of them together are performed simultaneously by the co-operating workmen. * * *

The mode in which manufacture arises, its growth out of handicrafts, is therefore two-fold. On the one hand, it arises from the union of various independent handicrafts, which become stripped of their independence and specialised to such an extent as to be reduced to mere supplementary partial processes in the production of one particular commodity. On the other hand, it arises from the co-operation of artificers of one handicraft; it splits up that particular handicraft into its various detail operations, isolating, and making these operations independent of one another up to the point where each becomes the exclusive function of a particular labourer. On the one hand, therefore, manufacture either introduces division of labour into a process of production, or further develops that division; on the other hand, it unites together handicrafts that were formerly separate. But whatever may have been its particular starting-point, its final form is invariably the same—a productive mechanism whose parts are human beings. * * *

Section 2. The Detail Labourer and His Implements

If we now go more into detail, it is, in the first place, clear that a labourer who all his life performs one and the same simple operation, converts his whole body into the automatic, specialised implement of that operation. Consequently, he takes less time in doing it, than the artificer who performs a whole series of operations in succession. But the collective labourer, who constitutes the living mechanism of manufacture, is made up solely of such specialised detail labourers. Hence, in comparison with the independent handicraft, more is produced in a given time, or the productive power of labour is increased. Moreover, when once this fractional work is established as the exclusive function of one person, the methods it employs become perfected. The workman's continued repetition of the same simple act, and the concentration of his attention on it, teach him by experience how to attain the desired effects with the minimum of exertion. But since there are always several generations of labourers living at one time, and working together at the manufacture of a given article, the technical skill, the tricks of the trade thus acquired, become established, and are accumulated and handed down. Manufacture, in fact, produces the skill of the detail labourer, by reproducing, and systematically driving to an extreme within the workshop, the naturally developed differentiation of trades, which it found ready to hand in society at large. On the other hand, the conversion of fractional work into the life-calling of one man, corresponds to the tendency shown by earlier societies, to make trades hereditary; either to petrify them into castes, or whenever definite historical conditions beget in the individual a tendency to vary in a manner incompatible with the nature of castes, to ossify them into guilds. * * *

An artificer, who performs one after another the various fractional operations in the production of a finished article, must at one time change his place, at another his tools. The transition from one operation to another interrupts the flow of his labour, and creates, so to say, gaps in his working-day. These gaps close up so soon as he is tied to one and the same operation all day long; they vanish in proportion as the changes in his work diminish. The resulting increased productive power is owing either to an increased expenditure of labour-power in a given time—i.e., to increased intensity of labour—or to a decrease in the amount of labour-power unproductively consumed. The extra expenditure of power, demanded by every transition from rest to motion, is made up for by prolonging the duration of the normal velocity when once acquired. On the other hand, constant labour of one uniform kind disturbs the intensity and flow of a man's animal spirits, which find recreation and delight in mere change of activity. * * *

Early in the manufacturing period, the principle of lessening the necessary labour-time in the production of commodities, was accepted and formulated: and the use of machines, especially for certain simple first processes that have to be conducted on a very large scale, and with the application of great force, sprang up here and there. Thus, at an early period in paper manufacture, the tearing up of the rags was done by paper-mills; and in metal works, the pounding of the ores was effected by stamping mills. The Roman Empire had handed down the elementary form of all machinery in the water-wheel.

The handicraft period bequeathed to us the great inventions of the compass, of gunpowder, of type-printing, and of the automatic clock. But, on the whole, machinery played that subordinate part which Adam Smith assigns to it in comparison with division of labour. The sporadic use of machinery in the 17th century was of the greatest importance, because it supplied the great mathematicians of that time with a practical basis and stimulant to the creation of the science of mechanics.

The collective labourer, formed by the combination of a number of detail labourers, is the machinery specially characteristic of the manufacturing period. The various operations that are performed in turns by the producer of a commodity, and coalesce one with another during the progress of production, lay claim to him in various ways. In one operation he must exert more strength, in another more skill, in another more attention; and the same individual does not possess all these qualities in an equal degree. After Manufacture has once separated, made independent, and isolated the various operations, the labourers are divided, classified, and grouped according to their predominating qualities. If their natural endowments are, on the one hand, the foundation on which the division of labour is built up, on the other hand, Manufacture, once introduced, develops in them new powers that are by nature fitted only for limited and special functions. The collective labourer now possesses, in an equal degree of excellence, all the qualities requisite for production, and expends them in the most economical manner, by exclusively employing all his organs, consisting of particular labourers, or groups of labourers, in performing their special functions. The one-sidedness and the deficiencies of the detail labourer become perfections when he is a part of the collective labourer. The habit of doing only one thing converts him into a never failing instrument, while his connexion with the whole mechanism compels him to work with the regularity of the parts of a machine.

Since the collective labourer has functions, both simple and complex, both high and low, his members, the individual labour-powers, require different degrees of training, and must therefore have different values. Manufacture, therefore, develops a hierarchy of labour-powers, to which there corresponds a scale of wages. If, on the one hand, the individual labourers are appropriated and annexed for life by a limited function; on the other hand, the various operations of the hierarchy are parcelled out among the labourers according to both their natural and their acquired capabilities. Every process of production, however, requires certain simple manipulations, which every man is capable of doing. They too are now severed from their connexion with the more pregnant moments of activity, and ossified into exclusive functions of specially appointed labourers. Hence, Manufacture begets, in every handicraft that it seizes upon, a class of so-called unskilled labourers, a class which handicraft industry strictly excluded. * * *

Section 4. Division of Labour in Manufacture, and Division of Labour in Society

We first considered the origin of Manufacture, then its simple elements, then the detail labourer and his implements, and finally, the totality of the mechanism. We shall now lightly touch upon the relation between the division of labour in manufacture, and the social division of labour, which forms the foundation of all production of commodities.

If we keep labour alone in view, we may designate the separation of social production into its main divisions or *genera*—viz., agriculture, industries, &c., as division of labour in general, and the splitting up of these families into species and sub-species, as division of labour in particular, and the division of labour within the workshop as division of labour in singular or in detail.

Division of labour in a society, and the corresponding tying down of individuals to a particular calling, develops itself, just as does the division of labour in manufacture, from opposite starting-points. Within a family, and after further development with a tribe, there springs up naturally a division of labour, caused by differences of sex and age, a division that is consequently based on a purely physiological foundation, which division enlarges its materials by the expansion of the community, by the increase of population, and more especially, by the conflicts between different tribes, and the subjugation of one tribe by another. On the other hand, as I have before remarked, the exchange of products springs up at the points where different families, tribes, communities, come in contact; for, in the beginning of civilisation, it is not private individuals but families, tribes, &c., that meet on an independent footing. Different communities find different means of production, and different means of subsistence in their natural environment. Hence, their modes of production, and of living, and their products are different. It is this spontaneously developed difference which, when different communities come in contact, calls forth the mutual exchange of products, and the consequent gradual conversion of those products into commodities. * * *

The foundation of every division of labour that is well developed, and brought about by the exchange of commodities, is the separation between town and country. It may be said, that the whole economic history of society is summed up in the movement of this antithesis. We pass it over, however, for the present.

Just as a certain number of simultaneously employed labourers are the material pre-requisites for division of labour in manufacture, so are the number and density of the populations, which here correspond to the agglomeration in one workshop, a necessary condition for the division of labour in society. Nevertheless, this density is more or less relative. A relatively thinly populated country, with well-developed means of communication, has a denser population than a more numerously populated country, with badly-developed means of communication; and in this sense the Northern States of the American Union, for instance, are more thickly populated than India.

Since the production and the circulation of commodities are the general pre-requisites of the capitalist mode of production, division of labour in manufacture demands, that · division of labour in society at large should previously have attained a certain degree of development. Inversely, the former division reacts upon and develops and multiplies the latter. Simultaneously, with the differentiation of the instruments of labour, the industries that produce these instruments, become more and more differentiated. If the manufacturing system seize upon an industry, which, previously, was carried on in connexion with others, either as a chief or as a subordinate industry, and by one producer, these industries immediately separate their connexion, and become independent. If it seize upon a particular stage in the production of a commodity, the other stages of its production become converted into so many independent industries. It has already been stated, that where the finished article consists merely of a number of parts fitted together, the detail operations may re-establish themselves as genuine and separate handicrafts. In order to carry out more perfectly the division of labour in manufacture, a single branch of production is, according to the varieties of its raw material, or the various forms that one and the same raw material may assume, split up into numerous, and to some extent, entirely new manufactures. Accordingly, in France alone, in the first half of the 18th century, over 100 different kinds of silk stuffs were woven, and, in Avignon, it was law, that "every apprentice should devote himself to only one sort of fabrication, and should not learn the preparation of several kinds of stuff at once." The territorial division of labour, which confines special branches of production to special districts of a country, acquires fresh stimulus from the manufacturing system, which exploits every special advantage. The Colonial system and the opening out of the markets of the world, both of which are included in the general conditions of existence of the manufacturing period, furnish rich material for developing the division of labour in society. It is not the place, here, to go on to show how division of labour seizes upon, not only the economic, but every other sphere of society, and everywhere lays the foundation of that all engrossing system of specialising and sorting men, that development in a man of one single faculty at the expense of all other faculties, which caused A. Ferguson, the master of Adam Smith, to exclaim: "We make a nation of Helots, and have no free citizens."

But, in spite of the numerous analogies and links connecting them, division of labour in the interior of a society, and that in the interior of a workshop, differ not only in degree, but also in kind. The analogy appears most indisputable where there is an invisible bond uniting the various branches of trade. For instance the cattle-breeder produces hides, the tanner makes the hides into leather, and the shoemaker, the leather into boots. Here the thing produced by each of them is but a step towards the final form, which is the product of all their labours combined. There are, besides, all the various industries that supply the cattle-breeder, the tanner, and the shoemaker with the means of production. Now it is quite possible to imagine, with Adam Smith, that the difference between the above social division of labour, and the division in manufacture, is merely subjective, exists merely for the observer, who, in a manufacture, can see with one glance, all the numerous operations being performed on one spot, while in the instance given above, the spreading out of the work over great areas, and the great number of people employed in each branch of labour, obscure the connexion. But what is it that forms the bond between the independent labours of the cattle-breeder, the tanner, and the shoemaker? It is the fact that their respective products are commodities. What, on the other hand, characterises division of labour in manufactures? The fact that the detail labourer produces no commodities. It is only the common product of all the detail labourers that becomes a commodity. Division of labour in society is brought about by the purchase and sale of the products of different branches of industry, while the connexion between the detail operations in a workshop, is due to the sale of the labour-power of several workmen to one capitalist, who applies it as combined labour-power. The division of labour in the workshop implies concentration of the means of production in the hands of one capitalist; the division of labour in society implies their dispersion among many independent producers of commodities. While within the workshop, the iron law of proportionality subjects definite numbers of workmen to definite functions, in the society outside the workshop, chance and caprice have full play in distributing the producers and their means of production among the various branches of industry. The different spheres of production, it is true, constantly tend to an equilibrium: for, on the one hand, while each producer of a commodity is bound to produce a use-value, to satisfy a particular social want, and while the extent of these wants differs quantitatively, still there exists an inner relation which settles their proportions into a regular system, and that system one of spontaneous growth; and, on the other hand, the law of the value of commodities ultimately determines how much of its disposable working-time society can expend on each particular class of commodities. But this constant tendency to equilibrium, of the various spheres of production, is exercised, only in the shape of a reaction against the constant upsetting of this equilibrium. The *a priori* system on which the division of labour, within the workshop, is regularly carried out, becomes in the division of labour within the society, an *a posteriori*, nature-imposed necessity, controlling the lawless caprice of the producers, and perceptible in the barometrical fluctuations of the market-prices. Division of labour within the workshop implies the undisputed authority of the capitalist over men, that are but parts of a mechanism that belongs to him. The division of labour within the society brings into contact independent commodity-producers, who acknowledge no other authority but that of competition, of the coercion exerted by the pressure of their mutual interests; just as in the animal kingdom, the *bellum omnium contra omnes* more or less preserves the conditions of existence of every species. The same bourgeois mind which praises division of labour in the workshop, life-long annexation of the labourer to a partial operation, and his complete subjection to capital, as being an organisation of labour that increases its productiveness—that same bourgeois mind denounces with equal vigour every conscious attempt to socially control and regulate the process of production, as an inroad upon such sacred things as the rights of property, freedom and unrestricted play for the bent of the individual capitalist.

It is very characteristic that the enthusiastic apologists of the factory system have nothing more damning to urge against a general organisation of the labour of society, than that it would turn all society into one immense factory.

If, in a society with capitalist production, anarchy in the social division of labour and despotism in that of the workshop are mutual conditions the one of the other, we find, on the contrary, in those earlier forms of society in which the separation of trades has been spontaneously developed, then crystallised, and finally made permanent by law, on the one hand, a specimen of the organisation of the labour of society, in accordance with an approved and authoritative plan, and on the other, the entire exclusion of division of labour in the workshop, or at all events a mere dwarf-like or sporadic and accidental development of the same.

Those small and extremely ancient Indian communities, some of which have continued down to this day, are based on possession in common of the land, on the blending of agriculture and handicrafts, and on an unalterable division of labour, which serves, whenever a new community is started, as a plan and scheme ready cut and dried. * * * The law that regulates the division of labour in the community acts with the irresistible authority of a law of Nature, at the same time that each individual artificer, the smith, the carpenter, and so on, conducts in his workshop all the operations of his handicraft in the traditional way, but independently, and without recognising any authority over him. The simplicity of the organisation for production in these self-sufficing communities that constantly reproduce themselves in the same form, and when accidentally destroyed, spring up again on the spot and with the same name—this simplicity supplies the key to the secret of the unchangeableness of Asiatic societies, an unchangeableness in such striking contrast with the constant dissolution and refounding of Asiatic States, and the never-ceasing changes of dynasty. The structure of the economic elements of society remains untouched by the storm-clouds of the political sky.

The rules of the guilds, as I have said before, by limiting most strictly the number of apprentices and journeymen that a single master could employ, prevented him from becoming a capitalist. Moreover, he could not employ his journeymen in many other handicrafts than the one in which he was a master. The guilds zealously repelled every encroachment by the capital of merchants, the only form of free capital with which they came in contact. A merchant could buy every kind of commodity, but labour as a commodity he could not buy. He existed only on sufferance, as a dealer in the products of the handicrafts. If circumstances called for a further division of labour, the existing guilds split themselves up into varieties, or founded new guilds by the side of the old ones; all this, however, without concentrating various handicrafts in a single workshop. Hence, the guild organisation, however much it may have contributed by separating, isolating, and perfecting the handicrafts, to create the material conditions for the existence of manufacture, excluded division of labour in the workshop. On the whole, the labourer and his means of production remained closely united, like the snail with its shell, and thus there was wanting the principal basis of manufacture, the separation of the labourer from his means of production, and the conversion of these means into capital.

While division of labour in society at large, whether such division be brought about or not by exchange of commodities, is common to economic formations of society the most diverse, division of labour in the workshop, as practised by manufacture, is a special creation of the capitalist mode of production alone.

Section 5. The Capitalistic Character of Manufacture

An increased number of labourers under the control of one capitalist is the natural starting-point, as well of co-operation generally, as of manufacture in particular. But the division of labour in manufacture makes this increase in the number of workmen a technical necessity. The minimum number that any given capitalist is bound to employ is here prescribed by the previously established division of labour. On the other hand, the advantages of further division are obtainable only by adding to the number of workmen, and this can be done only by adding multiples of the various detail groups. But an increase in the variable component of the capital employed necessitates an increase in its constant component, too, in the workshops, implements, &c., and, in particular, in the raw material, the call for which grows quicker than the number of workmen. The quantity of it consumed in a given time, by a given amount of labour, increases in the same ratio as does the productive power of that labour in consequence of its division. Hence, it is a law, based on the very nature of manufacture, that the minimum amount of capital, which is bound to be in the hands of each capitalist, must keep increasing; in other words, that the transformation into capital of the social means of production and subsistence must keep extending.

In manufacture, as well as in simple co-operation, the collective working organism is a form of existence of capital. The mechanism that is made up of numerous individual detail labourers belongs to the capitalist. Hence, the productive power resulting from a combination of labours appears to be the productive power of capital. Manufacture proper not only subjects the previously independent workman to the discipline and command of capital, but, in addition, creates a hierarchic gradation of the workmen themselves.

While simple co-operation leaves the mode of working by the individual for the most part unchanged, manufacture thoroughly revolutionises it, and seizes labour-power by its very roots. It converts the labourer into a crippled monstrosity, by forcing his detail dexterity at the expense of a world of productive capabilities and instincts; just as in the States of La Plata they butcher a whole beast for the sake of his hide or his tallow. Not only is the detail work distributed to the different individuals, but the individual himself is made the automatic motor of a fractional operation, and the absurd fable of Menenius Agrippa, which makes man a mere fragment of his own body, becomes realised. If, at first, the workman sells his labour-power to capital, because the material means of producing a commodity fail him, now his very labour-power refuses its services unless it has been sold to capital. Its functions can be exercised only in an environment that exists in the workshop of the capitalist after the sale. By nature unfitted to make anything independently, the manufacturing labourer develops productive activity as a mere appendage of the capitalist's workshop. As the chosen people bore in their features the sign manual of Jehovah, so division of labour brands the manufacturing workman as the property of capital.

The knowledge, the judgment, and the will, which, though in ever so small a degree, are practised by the independent peasant or handicraftsman, in the same way as the savage makes the whole art of war consist in the exercise of his personal cunning—these faculties are now required only for the workshop as a whole. Intelligence in production expands in one direction, because it vanishes in many others. What is lost by the detail labourers, is concentrated in the capital that employs them. It is a result of the division of labour in manufactures, that the labourer is brought face to face with the intellectual potencies of the material process of production, as the property of another, and as a ruling power. This separation begins in simple co-operation, where the capitalist represents to the single workman, the oneness and the will of the associated labour. It is developed in manufacture which cuts down the labourer into a detail labourer. It is completed in modern industry, which makes science a productive force distinct from labour and presses it into the service of capital.

In manufacture, in order to make the collective labourer, and through him capital, rich in social productive power, each labourer must be made poor in individual productive powers. "Ignorance is the mother of industry as well as of superstition. Reflection and fancy are subject to err; but a habit of moving the hand or the foot is independent of either. Manufactures, accordingly, prosper most where the mind is least consulted, and where the workshop may . . . be considered as an engine, the parts of which are men." As a matter of fact, some few manufacturers in the middle of the 18th century preferred for certain operations that were trade secrets, to employ half-idiotic persons.

"The understandings of the greater part of men," says Adam Smith, "are necessarily formed by their ordinary employments. The man whose whole life is spent in performing a few simple operations . . . has no occasion to exert his understanding. . . . He generally becomes as stupid and ignorant as it is possible for a human creature to become." After describing the stupidity of the detail labourer he goes on: "The uniformity of his stationary life naturally corrupts the courage of his mind. . . . It corrupts even the activity of his body and renders him incapable of exerting his strength with vigour and perseverance in any other employments than that to which he has been bred. His dexterity at his own particular trade seems in this manner to be acquired at the expense of his intellectual, social, and martial virtues. But in every improved and civilised society, this is the state into which the labouring poor, that is, the great body of the people, must necessarily fall." For preventing the complete deterioration of the great mass of the people by division of labour, A. Smith recommends education of the people by the State, but prudently, and in homœopathic doses. G. Garnier, his French translator and commentator, who, under the first French Empire, quite naturally developed into a senator, quite as naturally opposes him on this point. Education of the masses, he urges, violates the first law of the division of labour, and with it "our whole social system would be proscribed." "Like all other divisions of labour," he says, "that between hand labour and head labour is more pronounced and decided in proportion as society (he rightly uses this word, for capital, landed property and their State) becomes richer. This division of labour, like every other, is an effect of past, and a cause of future progress . . . ought the government then to work in opposition to this division of labour, and to hinder its natural course? Ought it to expend a part of the public money in the attempt to confound and blend together two classes of labour, which are striving after division and separation?"[3]

Some crippling of body and mind is inseparable even from division of labour in society as a whole. Since, however, manufacture carries this social separation of branches of labour much further, and also, by its peculiar division, attacks the individual at the very roots of his life, it is the first to afford the materials for, and to give a start to, industrial pathology.

"To subdivide a man is to execute him, if he deserves the sentence, to assassinate him if he does not. . . . The subdivision of labour is the assassination of a people."

3. G. Garnier, Vol. V of his translation of A. Smith, pp. 4–5. [*Marx*]

Co-operation based on division of labour, in other words, manufacture, commences as a spontaneous formation. So soon as it attains some consistence and extension, it becomes the recognised methodical and systematic form of capitalist production. History shows how the division of labour peculiar to manufacture, strictly so called, acquires the best adapted form at first by experience, as it were behind the backs of the actors, and then, like the guild handicrafts, strives to hold fast that form when once found, and here and there succeeds in keeping it for centuries. Any alteration in this form, except in trivial matters, is solely owing to a revolution in the instruments of labour. Modern manufacture wherever it arises—I do not here allude to modern industry based on machinery—either finds the disjecta membra poetæ ready to hand, and only waiting to be collected together, as is the case in the manufacture of clothes in large towns, or it can easily apply the principle of division, simply by exclusively assigning the various operations of a handicraft (such as book-binding) to particular men. In such cases, a week's experience is enough to determine the proportion between the numbers of the hands necessary for the various functions.[4]

By decomposition of handicrafts, by specialisation of the instruments of labour, by the formation of detail labourers, and by grouping and combining the latter into a single mechanism, division of labour in manufacture creates a qualitative gradation, and a quantitative proportion in the social process of production; it consequently creates a definite organisation of the labour of society, and thereby develops at the same time new productive forces in the society. In its specific capitalist form—and under the given conditions, it could take no other form than a capitalistic one—manufacture is but a particular method of begetting relative surplus-value, or of augmenting at the expense of the labourer the self-expansion of capital—usually called social wealth, "Wealth of Nations," &c. It increases the social productive power of labour, not only for the benefit of the capitalist instead of for that of the labourer, but it does this by crippling the individual labourers. It creates new conditions for the lordship of capital over labour. If, therefore, on the one hand, it presents itself historically as a progress and as a necessary phase in the economic development of society, on the other hand, it is a refined and civilised method of exploitation.

4. The simple belief in the inventive genius exercised a priori by the individual capitalist in division of labour, exists now-a-days only among German professors, of the stamp of Herr Roscher, who, to recompense the capitalist from whose Jovian head division of labour sprang ready formed, dedicates to him "various wages" (diverse Arbeitslöhne). The more or less extensive application of division of labour depends on length of purse, not on greatness of genius. [*Marx*]

Political Economy, which as an independent science, first sprang into being during the period of manufacture, views the social division of labour only from the standpoint of manufacture, and sees in it only the means of producing more commodities with a given quantity of labour, and, consequently, of cheapening commodities and hurrying on the accumulation of capital. In most striking contrast with this accentuation of quantity and exchange-value, is the attitude of the writers of classical antiquity, who hold exclusively by quality and use-value. In consequence of the separation of the social branches of production, commodities are better made, the various bents and talents of men select a suitable field, and without some restraint no important results can be obtained anywhere. Hence both product and producer are improved by division of labour. If the growth of the quantity produced is occasionally mentioned, this is only done with reference to the greater abundance of use-values. There is not a word alluding to exchange-value or to the cheapening of commodities. This aspect, from the standpoint of use-value alone, is taken as well by Plato,[5] who treats division of labour as the foundation on which the division of society into classes is based, as by Xenophon, who with characteristic bourgeois instinct, approaches more nearly to division of labour within the workshop. Plato's Republic, in so far as division of labour is treated in it, as the formative principle of the State, is merely the Athenian idealisation of the Egyptian system of castes, Egypt having served as the model of an industrial country to many of his contemporaries also, amongst others to Isocrates, and it continued to have this importance to the Greeks of the Roman Empire.

During the manufacturing period proper, *i.e.*, the period during which manufacture is the predominant form taken by capitalist production, many obstacles are opposed to the full development of the peculiar tendencies of manufacture. Although manufacture creates, as we have already seen, a simple separation of the labourers

5. With Plato, division of labour within the community is a development from the multifarious requirements, and the limited capacities of individuals. The main point with him is, that the labourer must adapt himself to the work, not the work to the labourer; which latter is unavoidable, if he carries on several trades at once, thus making one or the other of them subordinate. So in Thucydides: "Seafaring is an art like any other, and cannot, as circumstances require, be carried on as a subsidiary occupation; nay, other subsidiary occupations cannot be carried on alongside of this one." If the work, says Plato, has to wait for the labourer, the critical point in the process is missed and the article spoiled. The same Platonic idea is found recurring in the protest of the English bleachers against the clause in the Factory Act that provides fixed meal-times for all operatives. Their business cannot wait the convenience of the workmen, for "in the various operations of singeing, washing, bleaching, mangling, calendering, and dyeing, none of them can be stopped at a given moment without risk of damage . . . to enforce the same dinner hour for all the workpeople might occasionally subject valuable goods to the risk of danger by incomplete operations." Le platonisme où va-t-il se nicher! [*Marx*]

into skilled and unskilled, simultaneously with their hierarchic arrangement in classes, yet the number of the unskilled labourers, owing to the preponderating influence of the skilled, remains very limited. Although it adapts the detail operations to the various degrees of maturity, strength, and development of the living instruments of labour, thus conducing to exploitation of women and children, yet this tendency as a whole is wrecked on the habits and the resistance of the male labourers. Although the splitting up of handicrafts lowers the cost of forming the workman, and thereby lowers his value, yet for the more difficult detail work, a longer apprenticeship is necessary, and, even where it would be superfluous, is jealously insisted upon by the workmen. In England, for instance, we find the laws of apprenticeship, with their seven years' probation, in full force down to the end of the manufacturing period; and they are not thrown on one side till the advent of Modern Industry. Since handicraft skill is the foundation of manufacture, and since the mechanism of manufacture as a whole possesses no framework, apart from the labourers themselves, capital is constantly compelled to wrestle with the insubordination of the workmen. "By the infirmity of human nature," says friend Ure, "it happens that the more skilful the workman, the more self-willed and intractable he is apt to become, and of course the less fit a component of a mechanical system in which . . . he may do great damage to the whole." Hence throughout the whole manufacturing period there runs the complaint of want of discipline among the workmen. And had we not the testimony of contemporary writers, the simple facts, that during the period between the 16th century and the epoch of Modern Industry, capital failed to become the master of the whole disposable working-time of the manufacturing labourers, that manufacturers are short-lived, and change their locality from one country to another with the emigrating or immigrating workmen, these facts would speak volumes. "Order must in one way or another be established," exclaims in 1770 the oft-cited author of the "Essay on Trade and Commerce." "Order," re-echoes Dr. Andrew Ure 66 years later, "Order" was wanting in manufacture based on "the scholastic dogma of division of labour," and "Arkwright created order."

At the same time manufacture was unable, either to seize upon the production of society to its full extent, or to revolutionise that production to its very core. It towered up as an economic work of art, on the broad foundation of the town handicrafts, and of the rural domestic industries. At a given stage in its development, the narrow technical basis on which manufacture rested, came into conflict with requirements of production that were created by manufacture itself.

One of its most finished creations was the workshop for the

production of the instruments of labour themselves, including especially the complicated mechanical apparatus then already employed. A machine-factory, says Ure, "displayed the division of labour in manifold gradations—the file, the drill, the lathe, having each its different workman in the order of skill." (P. 21.) This workshop, the product of the division of labour in manufacture, produced in its turn—machines. It is they that swept away the handicraftsman's work as the regulating principle of social production. Thus, on the one hand, the technical reason for the life-long annexation of the workman to a detail function is removed. On the other hand, the fetters that this same principle laid on the dominion of capital, fall away.

Part IV. (Continued). Production of Relative Surplus-Value

CHAPTER XV. MACHINERY AND MODERN INDUSTRY

Section 1. The Development of Machinery

John Stuart Mill says in his "Principles of Political Economy": "It is questionable if all the mechanical inventions yet made have lightened the day's toil of any human being."[6] That is, however, by no means the aim of the capitalistic application of machinery. Like every other increase in the productiveness of labour, machinery is intended to cheapen commodities, and, by shortening that portion of the working-day, in which the labourer works for himself, to lengthen the other portion that he gives, without an equivalent, to the capitalist. In short, it is a means for producing surplus-value.

In manufacture, the revolution in the mode of production begins with the labour-power, in modern industry it begins with the instruments of labour. Our first inquiry then is, how the instruments of labour are converted from tools into machines, or what is the difference between a machine and the implements of handicraft? We are only concerned here with striking and general characteristics; for epochs in the history of society are no more separated from each other by hard and fast lines of demarcation, than are geological epochs. * * *

Section 3. The Proximate Effects of Machinery on the Workman

The starting-point of Modern Industry is, as we have shown, the revolution in the instruments of labour, and this revolution attains its most highly developed form in the organised system of machin-

6. Mill should have said, "of any human being not fed by other people's labour," for, without doubt, machinery has greatly increased the number of well-to-do idlers. [*Marx*]

ery in a factory. Before we inquire how human material is incorporated with this objective organism, let us consider some general effects of this revolution on the labourer himself.

A. APPROPRIATION OF SUPPLEMENTARY LABOUR-POWER BY CAPITAL. THE EMPLOYMENT OF WOMEN AND CHILDREN

In so far as machinery dispenses with muscular power, it becomes a means of employing labourers of slight muscular strength, and those whose bodily development is incomplete, but whose limbs are all the more supple. The labour of women and children was, therefore, the first thing sought for by capitalists who used machinery. That mighty substitute for labour and labourers was forthwith changed into a means for increasing the number of wage-labourers by enrolling, under the direct sway of capital, every member of the workman's family, without distinction of age or sex. Compulsory work for the capitalist usurped the place, not only of the children's play, but also of free labour at home within moderate limits for the support of the family.

The value of labour-power was determined, not only by the labour-time necessary to maintain the individual adult labourer, but also by that necessary to maintain his family. Machinery, by throwing every member of that family on to the labour-market, spreads the value of the man's labour-power over his whole family. It thus depreciates his labour-power. To purchase the labour-power of a family of four workers may, perhaps, cost more than it formerly did to purchase the labour-power of the head of the family, but, in return, four days' labour takes the place of one, and their price falls in proportion to the excess of the surplus-labour of four over the surplus-labour of one. In order that the family may live, four people must now, not only labour, but expend surplus-labour for the capitalist. Thus we see, that machinery, while augmenting the human material that forms the principal object of capital's exploiting power, at the same time raises the degree of exploitation. * * *

B. PROLONGATION OF THE WORKING-DAY

If machinery be the most powerful means for increasing the productiveness of labour—*i.e.*, for shortening the working-time required in the production of a commodity, it becomes in the hands of capital the most powerful means, in those industries first invaded by it, for lengthening the working-day beyond all bounds set by human nature. It creates, on the one hand, new conditions by which capital is enabled to give free scope to this its constant tendency, and on the other hand, new motives with which to whet capital's appetite for the labour of others.

In the first place, in the form of machinery, the implements of labour become automatic, things moving and working independent of the workman. They are thenceforth an industrial *perpetuum mobile*, that would go on producing forever, did it not meet with certain natural obstructions in the weak bodies and the strong wills of its human attendants. The automaton, as capital, and because it is capital, is endowed, in the person of the capitalist, with intelligence and will; it is therefore animated by the longing to reduce to a minimum the resistance offered by that repellent yet elastic natural barrier, man. This resistance is moreover lessened by the apparent lightness of machine work, and by the more pliant and docile character of the women and children employed on it. * * *

Machinery produces relative surplus-value; not only by directly depreciating the value of labour-power, and by indirectly cheapening the same through cheapening the commodities that enter into its reproduction, but also, when it is first introduced sporadically into an industry, by converting the labour employed by the owner of that machinery, into labour of a higher degree and greater efficacy, by raising the social value of the article produced above its individual value, and thus enabling the capitalist to replace the value of a day's labour-power by a smaller portion of the value of a day's product. During this transition period, when the use of machinery is a sort of monopoly, the profits are therefore exceptional, and the capitalist endeavours to exploit thoroughly "the sunny time of this his first love," by prolonging the working-day as much as possible. The magnitude of the profit whets his appetite for more profit.

As the use of machinery becomes more general in a particular industry, the social value of the product sinks down to its individual value, and the law that surplus-value does not arise from the labour-power that has been replaced by the machinery, but from the labour-power actually employed in working with the machinery, asserts itself. Surplus-value arises from variable capital alone, and we saw that the amount of surplus-value depends on two factors, viz., the rate of surplus-value and the number of the workmen simultaneously employed. Given the length of the working-day, the rate of surplus-value is determined by the relative duration of the necessary labour and of the surplus-labour in a day. The number of the labourers simultaneously employed depends, on its side, on the ratio of the variable to the constant capital. Now, however much the use of machinery may increase the surplus-labour at the expense of the necessary labour by heightening the productiveness of labour, it is clear that it attains this result, only by diminishing the number of workmen employed by a given amount of capital. It converts what was formerly variable capital, invested in labour-power, into machinery which, being constant capital, does not produce surplus-value. It is impossible, for instance, to squeeze as much surplus-value out of 2 as out of 24 labourers. If each of these 24 men gives only one hour of surplus-labour in 12, the 24 men give together 24 hours of surplus-labour, while 24 hours is the total labour of the two men. Hence, the application of machinery to the production of surplus-value implies a contradiction which is imma-nent in it, since of the two factors of the surplus-value created by a given amount of capital, one, the rate of surplus-value, cannot be increased, except by diminishing the other, the number of work-men. This contradiction comes to light, as soon as by the general employment of machinery in a given industry, the value of the machine-produced commodity regulates the value of all commodi-ties of the same sort; and it is this contradiction, that in its turn, drives the capitalist, without his being conscious of the fact, to excessive lengthening of the working-day, in order that he may compensate the decrease in the relative number of labourers exploited, by an increase not only of the relative, but of the abso-lute surplus-labour.

If, then, the capitalistic employment of machinery, on the one hand, supplies new and powerful motives to an excessive lengthen-ing of the working-day, and radically changes, as well the methods of labour, as also the character of the social working organism, in such a manner as to break down all opposition to this tendency, on the other hand it produces, partly by opening out to the capitalist new strata of the working-class, previously inaccessible to him, partly by setting free the labourers it supplants, a surplus working population, which is compelled to submit to the dictation of capi-tal. Hence that remarkable phenomenon in the history of Modern Industry, that machinery sweeps away every moral and natural re-striction on the length of the working-day. Hence, too, the eco-nomic paradox, that the most powerful instrument for shortening labour-time, becomes the most unfailing means for placing every moment of the labourer's time and that of his family, at the dis-posal of the capitalist for the purpose of expanding the value of his capital. "If," dreamed Aristotle, the greatest thinker of antiquity, "if every tool, when summoned, or even of its own accord, could do the work that befits it, just as the creations of Dædalus moved of themselves, or the tripods of Hephæstos went of their own accord to their sacred work, if the weavers' shuttles were to weave of them-selves, then there would be no need either of apprentices for the master workers, or of slaves for the lords." And Antipatros, a Greek poet of the time of Cicero, hailed the invention of the water-wheel for grinding corn, an invention that is the elementary form of all machinery, as the giver of freedom to female slaves, and the bringer back of the golden age. Oh! those heathens! They understood, as the learned Bastiat, and before him the still wiser MacCulloch have discovered, nothing of Political Economy and Christianity. They did not, for example, comprehend that machinery is the surest means of lengthening the working-day. They perhaps excused the slavery of one on the ground that it was a means to the full development of another. But to preach slavery of the masses, in order that a few crude and half-educated parvenus, might become "eminent spinners," "extensive sausage-makers," and "influential shoe-black dealers," to do this, they lacked the bump of Christianity.

C. INTENSIFICATION OF LABOUR

The immoderate lengthening of the working-day, produced by machinery in the hands of capital, leads to a reaction on the part of society, the very sources of whose life are menaced; and, thence, to a normal working-day whose length is fixed by law. Thenceforth a phenomenon that we have already met with, namely, the intensification of labour, develops into great importance. Our analysis of absolute surplus-value had reference primarily to the extension or duration of the labour, its intensity being assumed as given. We now proceed to consider the substitution of a more intensified labour for labour of more extensive duration, and the degree of the former. * * *

Section IV. The Factory

At the commencement of this chapter we considered that which we may call the body of the factory, *i.e.*, machinery organised into a system. We there saw how machinery, by annexing the labour of women and children, augments the number of human beings who form the material for capitalistic exploitation, how it confiscates the whole of the workman's disposable time, by immoderate extension of the hours of labour, and how finally its progress, which allows of enormous increase of production in shorter and shorter periods, serves as a means of systematically getting more work done in a shorter time, or of exploiting labour-power more intensely. We now turn to the factory as a whole, and that in its most perfect form. * * *

So far as division of labour re-appears in the factory, it is primarily a distribution of the workmen among the specialised machines; and of masses of workmen, not however organised into groups, among the various departments of the factory, in each of which they work at a number of similar machines placed together; their co-operation, therefore, is only simple. The organised group, peculiar to manufacture, is replaced by the connexion between the head workman and his few assistants. The essential division is, into workmen who are actually employed on the machines (among whom are included a few who look after the engine), and into mere attendants (almost exclusively children) of these workmen. Among the attendants are reckoned more or less all "Feeders" who supply the machines with the material to be worked. In addition to these two principal classes, there is a numerically unimportant class of persons, whose occupation it is to look after the whole of the machinery and repair it from time to time; such as engineers, mechanics, joiners, &c. This is a superior class of workmen, some of them scientifically educated, others brought up to a trade; it is distinct from the factory operative class, and merely aggregated to it. This division of labour is purely technical.

To work at a machine, the workman should be taught from childhood, in order that he may learn to adapt his own movements to the uniform and unceasing motion of an automaton. When the machinery, as a whole, forms a system of manifold machines, working simultaneously and in concert, the co-operation based upon it, requires the distribution of various groups of workmen among the different kinds of machines. But the employment of machinery does away with the necessity of crystallising this distribution after the manner of Manufacture, by the constant annexation of a particular man to a particular function. Since the motion of the whole system does not proceed from the workman, but from the machinery, a change of persons can take place at any time without an interruption of the work. The most striking proof of this is afforded by the *relays system*, put into operation by the manufacturers during their revolt from 1848 to 1850. Lastly, the quickness with which machine work is learnt by young people, does away with the necessity of bringing up for exclusive employment by machinery, a special class of operatives. With regard to the work of the mere attendants, it can, to some extent, be replaced in the mill by machines, and owing to its extreme simplicity, it allows of a rapid and constant change of the individuals burdened with this drudgery.

Although then, technically speaking, the old system of division of labour is thrown overboard by machinery, it hangs on in the factory, as a traditional habit handed down from Manufacture, and is afterwards systematically re-moulded and established in a more hideous form by capital, as a means of exploiting labour-power. The life-long speciality of handling one and the same tool, now becomes the life-long speciality of serving one and the same machine. Machinery is put to a wrong use, with the object of transforming the workman, from his very childhood, into a part of a detail-machine. In this way, not only are the expenses of his reproduction considerably lessened, but at the same time his helpless dependence upon the factory as a whole, and therefore upon the capitalist, is rendered complete. Here as everywhere else, we must distinguish between the increased productiveness due to the development of the social process of production, and that due to the capitalist exploitation of that process. In handicrafts and manufacture, the workman makes use of a tool, in the factory, the machine makes use of him. There the movements of the instrument of labour proceed from him, here it is the movements of the machine that he must follow. In manufacture the workmen are parts of a living mechanism. In the factory we have a lifeless mechanism independent of the workman, who becomes its mere living appendage. "The miserable routine of endless drudgery and toil in which the same mechanical process is gone through over and over again, is like the labour of Sisyphus. The burden of labour, like the rock, keeps ever falling back on the worn-out labourer."[7] At the same time that factory work exhausts the nervous system to the uttermost, it does away with the many-sided play of the muscles, and confiscates every atom of freedom, both in bodily and intellectual activity. The lightening of the labour, even, becomes a sort of torture, since the machine does not free the labourer from work, but deprives the work of all interest. Every kind of capitalist production, in so far as it is not only a labour-process, but also a process of creating surplus-value, has this in common, that it is not the workman that employs the instruments of labour, but the instruments of labour that employ the workman. But it is only in the factory system that this inversion for the first time acquires technical and palpable reality. By means of its conversion into an automaton, the instrument of labour confronts the labourer, during the labour-process, in the shape of capital, of dead labour, that dominates, and pumps dry, living labour-power. The separation of the intellectual powers of production from the manual labour, and the conversion of those powers into the might of capital over labour, is, as we have already shown, finally completed by modern industry erected on the foundation of machinery. The special skill of each individual insignificant factory operative vanishes as an infinitesimal quantity before the science, the gigantic physical forces, and the mass of labour that are embodied in the factory mechanism and, together with that mechanism, constitute the power of the "master." This "master," therefore, in whose brain the machinery and his monopoly of it are inseparably united, whenever he falls out with his

7. F. Engels, *The Condition of the Working Class in England in 1844*, p. 217.—Even an ordinary optimistic freetrader like Mr. Molinari goes so far as to say: "A man will become exhausted sooner if he watches over the uniform motion of a mechanism fifteen hours day than if he exercises his physical force over the same interval of time. This work of watching over something, which could be useful perhaps as mental gynmastics provided it were not too prolonged, will, in the long run, destroy both body and mind through excess."—G. de Molinari, *Études économiques*, Paris, 1846.

"hands," contemptuously tells them: "The factory operatives should keep in wholesome remembrance the fact that theirs is really a low species of skilled labour; and that there is none which is more easily acquired, or of its quality more amply remunerated, or which by a short training of the least expert can be more quickly, as well as abundantly, acquired. ... The master's machinery really plays a far more important part in the business of production than the labour and the skill of the operative, which six months' education can teach, and a common labourer can learn." The technical subordination of the workman to the uniform motion of the instruments of labour, and the peculiar composition of the body of workpeople, consisting as it does of individuals of both sexes and of all ages, give rise to a barrack discipline, which is elaborated into a complete system in the factory, and which fully develops the before mentioned labour of overlooking, thereby dividing the workpeople into operatives and overlookers, into private soldiers and sergeants of an industrial army. "The main difficulty [in the automatic factory] ... lay ... above all in training human beings to renounce their desultory habits of work, and to identify themselves with the unvarying regularity of the complex automaton. To devise and administer a successful code of factory discipline, suited to the necessities of factory diligence, was the Herculean enterprise, the noble achievement of Arkwright! Even at the present day, when the system is perfectly organised and its labour lightened to the utmost, it is found nearly impossible to convert persons past the age of puberty, into useful factory hands." The factory code in which capital formulates, like a private legislator, and at his own good will, his autocracy over his workpeople, unaccompanied by that division of responsibility, in other matters so much approved of by the bourgeoisie, and unaccompanied by the still more approved representative system, this code is but the capitalistic caricature of that social regulation of the labour-process which becomes requisite in co-operation on a great scale, and in the employment in common, of instruments of labour and especially of machinery. The place of the slave-driver's lash is taken by the overlooker's book of penalties. All punishments naturally resolve themselves into fines and deductions from wages, and the law-giving talent of the factory Lycurgus so arranges matters, that a violation of his laws is, if possible, more profitable to him than the keeping of them.

We shall here merely allude to the material conditions under which factory labour is carried on. Every organ of sense is injured in an equal degree by artificial elevation of the temperature, by the dust-laden atmosphere, by the deafening noise, not to mention danger to life and limb among the thickly crowded machinery, which, with the regularity of the seasons, issues its list of the killed and wounded in the industrial battle. Economy of the social means of production, matured and forced as in a hothouse by the factory system, is turned, in the hands of capital, into systematic robbery of what is necessary for the life of the workman while he is at work, robbery of space, light, air, and of protection to his person against the dangerous and unwholesome accompaniments of the productive process, not to mention the robbery of appliances for the comfort of the workman. Is Fourier wrong when he calls factories "tempered bagnos"?

Section 5. The Strife Between Workman and Machine

The contest between the capitalist and the wage-labourer dates back to the very origin of capital. It raged on throughout the whole manufacturing period. But only since the introduction of machinery has the workman fought against the instrument of labour itself, the material embodiment of capital. He revolts against this particular form of the means of production, as being the material basis of the capitalist mode of production. * * *

Section 9. The Factory Acts. Sanitary and Educational Clauses of the Same. Their General Extension in England

Factory legislation, that first conscious and methodical reaction of society against the spontaneously developed form of the process of production, is, as we have seen, just as much the necessary product of modern industry as cotton yarn, self-actors, and the electric telegraph. Before passing to the consideration of the extension of that legislation in England, we shall shortly notice certain clauses contained in the Factory Acts, and not relating to the hours of work.

Apart from their wording, which makes it easy for the capitalist to evade them, the sanitary clauses are extremely meagre, and, in fact, limited to provisions for whitewashing the walls, for insuring cleanliness in some other matters, for ventilation, and for protection against dangerous machinery. In the third book we shall return again to the fanatical opposition of the masters to those clauses which imposed upon them a slight expenditure on appliances for protecting the limbs of their workpeople, an opposition that throws a fresh and glaring light on the Free-trade dogma, according to which, in a society with conflicting interests, each individual necessarily furthers the common weal by seeking nothing but his own personal advantage! * * *

Paltry as the education clauses of the Act appear on the whole, yet they proclaim elementary education to be an indispensable condition to the employment of children. The success of those clauses proved for the first time the possibility of combining education and gymnastics with manual labour, and, consequently, of combining manual labour with education and gymnastics. The factory inspectors soon found out by questioning the schoolmasters, that the factory children, although receiving only one half the education of the regular day scholars, yet learnt quite as much and often more. "This can be accounted for by the simple fact that, with only being at school for one half of the day, they are always fresh, and nearly always ready and willing to receive instruction. The system on which they work, half manual labour, and half school, renders each employment a rest and a relief to the other; consequently, both are far more congenial to the child, than would be the case were he kept constantly at one. It is quite clear that a boy who has been at school all the morning, cannot (in hot weather particularly) cope with one who comes fresh and bright from his work." Further information on this point will be found in Senior's speech at the Social Science Congress at Edinburgh in 1863. He there shows, amongst other things, how the monotonous and uselessly long school hours of the children of the upper and middle classes, uselessly add to the labour of the teacher, "while he not only fruitlessly but absolutely injuriously, wastes the time, health, and energy of the children." From the Factory system budded, as Robert Owen has shown us in detail, the germ of the education of the future, an education that will, in the case of every child over a given age, combine productive labour with instruction and gymnastics, not only as one of the methods of adding to the efficiency of production, but as the only method of producing fully developed human beings.

Modern Industry, as we have seen, sweeps away by technical means the manufacturing division of labour, under which each man is bound hand and foot for life to a single detail-operation. At the same time, the capitalistic form of that industry reproduces this same division of labour in a still more monstrous shape; in the factory proper, by converting the workman into a living appendage of the machine; and everywhere outside the Factory, partly by the sporadic use of machinery and machine workers, partly by re-establishing the division of labour on a fresh basis by the general introduction of the labour of women and children, and of cheap unskilled labour.

The antagonism between the manufacturing division of labour and the methods of Modern Industry makes itself forcibly felt. It manifests itself, amongst other ways, in the frightful fact that a great part of the children employed in modern factories and manufactures, are from their earliest years riveted to the most simple manipulations, and exploited for years, without being taught a single sort of work that would afterwards make them of use, even in the same manufactory or factory.

Modern Industry never looks upon and treats the existing form of a process as final. The technical basis of that industry is therefore revolutionary, while all earlier modes of production were essentially conservative. By means of machinery, chemical processes and other methods, it is continually causing changes not only in the technical basis of production, but also in the functions of the labourer, and in the social combinations of the labour-process. At the same time, it thereby also revolutionises the division of labour within the society, and incessantly launches masses of capital and of workpeople from one branch of production to another. But if Modern Industry, by its very nature, therefore necessitates variation of labour, fluency of function, universal mobility of the labourer, on the other hand, in its capitalistic form, it reproduces the old division of labour with its ossified particularisations. We have seen how this absolute contradiction between the technical necessities of Modern Industry, and the social character inherent in its capitalistic form, dispels all fixity and security in the situation of the labourer; how it constantly threatens, by taking away the instruments of labour, to snatch from his hands his means of subsistence, and, by suppressing his detail-function, to make him superfluous. We have seen, too, how this antagonism vents its rage in the creation of that monstrosity, an industrial reserve army, kept in misery in order to be always at the disposal of capital; in the incessant human sacrifices from among the working-class, in the most reckless squandering of labour-power, and in the devastation caused by a social anarchy which turns every economic progress into a social calamity. This is the negative side. But if, on the one hand, variation of work at present imposes itself after the manner of an overpowering natural law, and with the blindly destructive action of a natural law that meets with resistance at all points, Modern Industry, on the other hand, through its catastrophes imposes the necessity of recognising, as a fundamental law of production, variation of work, consequently fitness of the labourer for varied work, consequently the greatest possible development of his varied aptitudes. It becomes a question of life and death for society to adapt the mode of production to the normal functioning of this law. Modern Industry, indeed, compels society, under penalty of death, to replace the detail-worker of to-day, crippled by life-long repetition of one and the same trivial operation, and thus reduced to the mere fragment of a man, by the fully developed individual, fit for a variety of labours, ready to face any change of production, and to whom the different social functions he performs, are but so many modes of giving free scope to his own natural and acquired powers.

One step already spontaneously taken towards effecting this revolution is the establishment of technical and agricultural schools, and of "écoles d'enseignement professionnel," in which the children of the working-men receive some little instruction in technology and in the practical handling of the various implements of labour. Though the Factory Act, that first and meagre concession wrung from capital, is limited to combining elementary education with work in the factory, there can be no doubt that when the working-class comes into power, as inevitably it must, technical instruction, both theoretical and practical, will take its proper place in the working-class schools. There is also no doubt that such revolutionary ferments, the final result of which is the abolition of the old division of labour, are diametrically opposed to the capitalistic form of production, and to the economic status of the labourer corresponding to that form. But the historical development of the antagonisms, immanent in a given form of production, is the only way in which that form of production can be dissolved and a new form established. "Ne sutor ultra crepidam"—this ne plus ultra of handicraft wisdom became sheer nonsense, from the moment the watchmaker Watt invented the steam-engine, the barber Arkwright, the throstle, and the working-jeweller, Fulton, the steamship.

So long as Factory legislation is confined to regulating the labour in factories, manufactories, &c., it is regarded as a mere interference with the exploiting rights of capital. But when it comes to regulating the so-called "home-labour," it is immediately viewed as a direct attack on the patria potestas, on parental authority. The tender-hearted English Parliament long affected to shrink from taking this step. The force of facts, however, compelled it at last to acknowledge that modern industry, in overturning the economic foundation on which was based the traditional family, and the family labour corresponding to it, had also unloosened all traditional family ties. The rights of the children had to be proclaimed. The final report of the Ch. Empl. Comm. of 1866, states: "It is unhappily, to a painful degree, apparent throughout the whole of the evidence, that against no persons do the children of both sexes so much require protection as against their parents." The system of unlimited exploitation of children's labour in general and the so-called home-labour in particular is "maintained only because the parents are able, without check or control, to exercise this arbitrary and mischievous power over their young and tender offspring. . . . Parents must not possess the absolute power of making their children mere 'machines to earn so much weekly wage.' . . . The children and young persons, therefore, in all such cases may justifiably claim from the legislature, as a natural right, that an exemption should be secured to them, from what destroys prematurely their physical strength, and lowers them in the scale of intellectual and moral beings." It was not, however, the misuse of parental authority that created the capitalistic exploitation, whether direct or indirect, of children's labour; but, on the contrary, it was the capitalistic mode of exploitation which, by sweeping away the economic basis of parental authority, made its exercise degenerate into a mischievous misuse of power. However terrible and disgusting the dissolution, under the capitalist system, of the old family ties may appear, nevertheless, modern industry, by assigning as it does an important part in the process of production, outside the domestic sphere, to women, to young persons, and to children of both sexes, creates a new economic foundation for a higher form of the family and of the relations between the sexes. It is, of course, just as absurd to hold the Teutonic-Christian form of the family to be absolute and final as it would be to apply that character to the ancient Roman, the ancient Greek, or the Eastern forms which, moreover, taken together form a series in historical development. Moreover, it is obvious that the fact of the collective working group being composed of individuals of both sexes and all ages, must necessarily, under suitable conditions, become a source of humane development; although in its spontaneously developed, brutal, capitalistic form, where the labourer exists for the process of production, and not the process of production for the labourer, that fact is a pestiferous source of corruption and slavery. * * *

Part V. The Production of Absolute and of Relative Surplus-Value

CHAPTER XVI. ABSOLUTE AND RELATIVE SURPLUS-VALUE

In considering the labour-process, we began by treating it in the abstract, apart from its historical forms, as a process between man and Nature. We stated: "If we examine the whole labour-process, from the point of view of its result, it is plain that both the instruments and the subjects of labour are means of production, and that the labour itself is productive labour." And we further added: "This method of determining, from the standpoint of the labour-process alone, what is productive labour, is by no means directly applicable to the case of the capitalist process of production." We now proceed to the further development of this subject.

So far as the labour-process is purely individual, one and the same labourer unites in himself all the functions, that later on become separated. When an individual appropriates natural objects for his livelihood, no one controls him but himself. Afterwards he is controlled by others. A single man cannot operate upon Nature without calling his own muscles into play under the control of his own brain. As in the natural body head and hand wait upon each other, so the labour-process unites the labour of the hand with that of the head. Later on they part company and even become deadly foes. The product ceases to be the direct product of the individual, and becomes a social product, produced in common by a collective labourer, *i.e.*, by a combination of workmen, each of whom takes only a part, greater or less, in the manipulation of the subject of their labour. As the co-operative character of the labour-process becomes more and more marked, so, as a necessary consequence, does our notion of productive labour, and of its agent the productive labourer, become extended. In order to labour productively, it is no longer necessary for you to do manual work yourself; enough, if you are an organ of the collective labourer, and perform one of its subordinate functions. The first definition given above of productive labour, a definition deduced from the very nature of the production of material objects, still remains correct for the collective labourer, considered as a whole. But it no longer holds good for each member taken individually.

On the other hand, however, our notion of productive labour becomes narrowed. Capitalist production is not merely the production of commodities, it is essentially the production of surplus-value. The labourer produces, not for himself, but for capital. It no longer suffices, therefore, that he should simply produce. He must produce surplus-value. That labourer alone is productive, who produces surplus-value for the capitalist, and thus works for the self-expansion of capital. If we may take an example from outside the sphere of production of material objects, a schoolmaster is a productive labourer, when, in addition to belabouring the heads of his scholars, he works like a horse to enrich the school proprietor. That the latter has laid out his capital in a teaching factory, instead of in a sausage factory, does not alter the relation. Hence the notion of a productive labourer implies not merely a relation between work and useful effect, between labourer and product of labour, but also a specific, social relation of production, a relation that has sprung up historically and stamps the labourer as the direct means of creating surplus-value. To be a productive labourer is, therefore, not a piece of luck, but a misfortune. * * *

The prolongation of the working-day beyond the point at which the labourer would have produced just an equivalent for the value of his labour-power, and the appropriation of that surplus-labour by capital, this is production of absolute surplus-value. It forms the general groundwork of the capitalist system, and the starting-point for the production of relative surplus-value. The latter pre-supposes that the working-day is already divided into two parts, necessary labour, and surplus-labour. In order to prolong the surplus-labour, the necessary labour is shortened by methods whereby the equivalent for the wages is produced in less time. The production of absolute surplus-value turns exclusively upon the length of the working-day; the production of relative surplus-value, revolutionises out and out the technical processes of labour, and the composition of society. It therefore pre-supposes a specific mode, the capitalist mode of production, a mode which, along with its methods, means, and conditions, arises and develops itself spontaneously on the foundation afforded by the formal subjection of labour to capital. In the course of this development, the formal subjection is replaced by the real subjection of labour to capital. * * *

From one standpoint, any distinction between absolute and relative surplus-value appears illusory. Relative surplus-value is absolute, since it compels the absolute prolongation of the working-day beyond the labour-time necessary to the existence of the labourer himself. Absolute surplus-value is relative, since it makes necessary such a development of the productiveness of labour, as will allow of the necessary labour-time being confined to a portion of the working-day. But if we keep in mind the behaviour of surplus-value, this appearance of identity vanishes. Once the capitalist mode of production established and become general, the difference between absolute and relative surplus-value makes itself felt, whenever there is a question of raising the rate of surplus-value. Assuming that labour-power is paid for at its value, we are confronted by this alternative: given the productiveness of labour and its normal intensity, the rate of surplus-value can be raised only by the actual prolongation of the working-day; on the other hand, given the length of the working-day, that rise can be effected only by a change in the relative magnitudes of the components of the working-day, viz., necessary labour and surplus-labour; a change which, if the wages are not to fall below the value of labour-power, pre-supposes a change either in the productiveness or in the intensity of the labour.

If the labourer wants all his time to produce the necessary means of subsistence for himself and his race, he has no time left in which

to work gratis for others. Without a certain degree of productiveness in his labour, he has no such superfluous time at his disposal;
without such superfluous time, no surplus-labour, and therefore no
capitalists, no slave-powers, no feudal lords, in one word, no class of
large proprietors. * * *

CHAPTER XXV. THE GENERAL LAW OF CAPITALIST ACCUMULATION

*Section 1. The Increased Demand for Labour-Power That Accom-
panies Accumulation, the Composition of Capital Remaining the
Same*

In this chapter we consider the influence of the growth of capital
on the lot of the labouring class. The most important factor in this
inquiry, is the composition of capital and the changes it undergoes
in the course of the process of accumulation.

The composition of capital is to be understood in a two-fold
sense. On the side of value, it is determined by the proportion in
which it is divided into constant capital or value of the means of
production, and variable capital or value of labour-power, the sum
total of wages. On the side of material, as it functions in the process of production, all capital is divided into means of production
and living labour-power. This latter composition is determined by
the relation between the mass of the means of production
employed, on the one hand, and the mass of labour necessary for
their employment on the other. I call the former the *value-
composition*, the latter the *technical composition* of capital.
Between the two there is a strict correlation. To express this, I call
the value-composition of capital, in so far as it is determined by its
technical composition and mirrors the changes of the latter, the
organic composition of capital. Wherever I refer to the composition of capital, without further qualification, its organic composition is always understood.

The many individual capitals invested in a particular branch of
production have, one with another, more or less different compositions. The average of the individual compositions gives us the composition of the total capital in this branch of production. Lastly,
the average of these averages, in all branches of production, gives
us the composition of the total social capital of a country, and with
this alone are we, in the last resort, concerned in the following investigation.

Growth of capital involves growth of its variable constituent or
of the part invested in labour-power. A part of the surplus-value
turned into additional capital must always be re-transformed into
variable capital, or additional labour-fund. If we suppose that, all

other circumstances remaining the same, the composition of capital also remains constant (*i.e.*, that a definite mass of means of production constantly needs the same mass of labour-power to set it in motion), then the demands for labour and the subsistence-fund of the labourers clearly increase in the same proportion as the capital, and the more rapidly, the more rapidly the capital increases. Since the capital produces yearly a surplus-value, of which one part is yearly added to the original capital; since this increment itself grows yearly along with the augmentation of the capital already functioning; since lastly, under special stimulus to enrichment, such as the opening of new markets, or of new spheres for the outlay of capital in consequence of newly developed social wants, &c., the scale of accumulation may be suddenly extended, merely by a change in the division of the surplus-value or surplus-product into capital and revenue, the requirements of accumulating capital may exceed the increase of labour-power or of the number of labourers; the demand for labourers may exceed the supply, and, therefore, wages may rise. This must, indeed, ultimately be the case if the conditions supposed above continue. For since in each year more labourers are employed than in its predecessor, sooner or later a point must be reached, at which the requirements of accumulation begin to surpass the customary supply of labour, and, therefore, a rise of wages takes place. A lamentation on this score was heard in England during the whole of the fifteenth, and the first half of the eighteenth centuries. The more or less favourable circumstances in which the wage-working class supports and multiplies itself, in no way alter the fundamental character of capitalist production. As simple reproduction constantly reproduces the capital-relation itself, *i.e.*, the relation of capitalists on the one hand, and wage-workers on the other, so reproduction on a progressive scale, *i.e.*, accumulation, reproduces the capital-relation on a progressive scale, more capitalists or larger capitalists at this pole, more wage-workers at that. The reproduction of a mass of labour-power, which must incessantly re-incorporate itself with capital for that capital's self-expansion; which cannot get free from capital, and whose enslavement to capital is only concealed by the variety of individual capitalists to whom it sells itself, this reproduction of labour-power forms, in fact, an essential of the reproduction of capital itself. Accumulation of capital is, therefore, increase of the proletariat. * * *

The law of capitalist production, that is at the bottom of the pretended "natural law of population," reduces itself simply to this: The correlation between accumulation of capital and rate of wages is nothing else than the correlation between the unpaid labour transformed into capital, and the additional paid labour necessary for the setting in motion of this additional capital. It is therefore in no way a relation between two magnitudes, independent one of the other: on the one hand, the magnitude of the capital; on the other, the number of the labouring population; it is rather, at bottom, only the relation between the unpaid and the paid labour of the same labouring population. If the quantity of unpaid labour supplied by the working-class, and accumulated by the capitalist class, increases so rapidly that its conversion into capital requires an extraordinary addition of paid labour, then wages rise, and, all other circumstances remaining equal, the unpaid labour diminishes in proportion. But as soon as this diminution touches the point at which the surplus-labour that nourishes capital is no longer supplied in normal quantity, a reaction sets in: a smaller part of revenue is capitalised, accumulation lags, and the movement of rise in wages receives a check. The rise of wages therefore is confined within limits that not only leave intact the foundations of the capitalistic system, but also secure its reproduction on a progressive scale. The law of capitalistic accumulation, metamorphosed by economists into a pretended law of Nature, in reality merely states that the very nature of accumulation excludes every diminution in the degree of exploitation of labour, and every rise in the price of labour, which could seriously imperil the continual reproduction, on an ever-enlarging scale, of the capitalistic relation. It cannot be otherwise in a mode of production in which the labourer exists to satisfy the needs of self-expansion of existing values, instead of, on the contrary, material wealth existing to satisfy the needs of development on the part of the labourer. As, in religion, man is governed by the products of his own brain, so in capitalistic production, he is governed by the products of his own hand. * * *

The industrial reserve army, during the periods of stagnation and average prosperity, weighs down the active labour-army; during the periods of over-production and paroxysm, it holds its pretensions in check. Relative surplus-population is therefore the pivot upon which the law of demand and supply of labour works. It confines the field of action of this law within the limits absolutely convenient to the activity of exploitation and to the domination of capital. * * *

Section 4. Different Forms of the Relative Surplus-Population. The General Law of Capitalistic Accumulation

The relative surplus-population exists in every possible form. Every labourer belongs to it during the time when he is only partially employed or wholly unemployed. Not taking into account the great periodically recurring forms that the changing phases of the industrial cycle impress on it, now an acute form during the crisis, then again a chronic form during dull times—it has always three forms, the floating, the latent, the stagnant. * * *

The lowest sediment of the relative surplus-population finally dwells in the sphere of pauperism. Exclusive of vagabonds, criminals, prostitutes, in a word, the "dangerous" classes, this layer of society consists of three categories. First, those able to work. One need only glance superficially at the statistics of English pauperism to find that the quantity of paupers increases with every crisis, and diminishes with every revival of trade. Second, orphans and pauper children. These are candidates for the industrial reserve army, and are, in times of great prosperity, as 1860, *e.g.*, speedily and in large numbers enrolled in the active army of labourers. Third, the demoralised and ragged, and those unable to work, chiefly people who succumb to their incapacity for adaptation, due to the division of labour; people who have passed the normal age of the labourer; the victims of industry, whose number increases with the increase of dangerous machinery, of mines, chemical works, &c., the mutilated, the sickly, the widows, &c. Pauperism is the hospital of the active labour-army and the dead weight of the industrial reserve army. Its production is included in that of the relative surplus-population, its necessity in theirs; along with the surplus-population, pauperism forms a condition of capitalist production, and of the capitalist development of wealth. It enters into the *faux frais* of capitalist production; but capital knows how to throw these, for the most part, from its own shoulders on to those of the working-class and the lower middle class.

The greater the social wealth, the functioning capital, the extent and energy of its growth, and, therefore, also the absolute mass of the proletariat and the productiveness of its labour, the greater is the industrial reserve army. The same causes which develop the expansive power of capital, develop also the labour-power at its disposal. The relative mass of the industrial reserve army increases therefore with the potential energy of wealth. But the greater this reserve army in proportion to the active labour-army, the greater is the mass of a consolidated surplus-population, whose misery is in inverse ratio to its torment of labour. The more extensive, finally, the lazarus-layers of the working-class, and the industrial reserve army, the greater is official pauperism. *This is the absolute general law of capitalist accumulation.* Like all other laws it is modified in its working by many circumstances, the analysis of which does not concern us here.

The folly is now patent of the economic wisdom that preaches to the labourers the accommodation of their number to the requirements of capital. The mechanism of capitalist production and accumulation constantly effects this adjustment. The first word of this adaptation is the creation of a relative surplus-population, or industrial reserve army. Its last word is the misery of constantly extending strata of the active army of labour, and the dead weight of pauperism.

The law by which a constantly increasing quantity of means of production, thanks to the advance in the productiveness of social labour, may be set in movement by a progressively diminishing expenditure of human power, this law, in a capitalist society—where the labourer does not employ the means of production, but the means of production employ the labourer—undergoes a complete inversion and is expressed thus: the higher the productiveness of labour, the greater is the pressure of the labourers on the means of employment, the more precarious, therefore, becomes their condition of existence, viz., the sale of their own labour-power for the increasing of another's wealth, or for the self-expansion of capital. The fact that the means of production, and the productiveness of labour, increase more rapidly than the productive population, expresses itself, therefore, capitalistically in the inverse form that the labouring population always increases more rapidly than the conditions under which capital can employ this increase for its own self-expansion.

We saw in Part IV., when analysing the production of relative surplus-value: within the capitalist system all methods for raising the social productiveness of labour are brought about at the cost of the individual labourer; all means for the development of production transform themselves into means of domination over, and exploitation of, the producers; they mutilate the labourer into a fragment of a man, degrade him to the level of an appendage of a machine, destroy every remnant of charm in his work and turn it into a hated toil; they estrange from him the intellectual potentialities of the labour-process in the same proportion as science is incorporated in it as an independent power; they distort the conditions under which he works, subject him during the labour-process to a despotism the more hateful for its meanness; they transform his life-time into working-time, and drag his wife and child beneath the wheels of the Juggernaut of capital. But all methods for the production of surplus-value are at the same time methods of accumulation; and every extension of accumulation becomes again a means for the development of those methods. It follows therefore that in proportion as capital accumulates, the lot of the labourer, be his payment high or low, must grow worse. The law, finally, that always equilibrates the relative surplus-population, or industrial reserve army, to the extent and energy of accumulation, this law rivets the labourer to capital more firmly than the wedges of Vulcan did Prometheus to the rock. It establishes an accumulation of misery, corresponding with accumulation of capital. Accumulation of wealth at one pole is, therefore, at the same time accumulation of misery, agony of toil, slavery, ignorance, brutality, mental degradation, at the opposite pole, *i.e.*, on the side of the class that produces its own product in the form of capital. * * *

Part VIII. The So-Called Primitive Accumulation

CHAPTER XXVI. THE SECRET OF PRIMITIVE ACCUMULATION

We have seen how money is changed into capital; how through capital surplus-value is made, and from surplus-value more capital. But the accumulation of capital pre-supposes surplus-value; surplus-value pre-supposes capitalistic production; capitalistic production pre-supposes the pre-existence of considerable masses of capital and of labour-power in the hands of producers of commodities. The whole movement, therefore, seems to turn in a vicious circle, out of which we can only get by supposing a primitive accumulation (previous accumulation of Adam Smith) preceding capitalistic accumulation; an accumulation not the result of the capitalist mode of production but its starting point.

This primitive accumulation plays in Political Economy about the same part as original sin in theology. Adam bit the apple, and thereupon sin fell on the human race. Its origin is supposed to be explained when it is told as an anecdote of the past. In times long gone by there were two sorts of people; one, the diligent, intelligent, and above all, frugal élite; the other, lazy rascals, spending their substance, and more, in riotous living. The legend of theological original sin tells us certainly how man came to be condemned to eat his bread in the sweat of his brow; but the history of economic original sin reveals to us that there are people to whom this is by no means essential. Never mind! Thus it came to pass that the former sort accumulated wealth, and the latter sort had at last nothing to sell except their own skins. And from this original sin dates the poverty of the great majority that, despite all its labour, has up to now nothing to sell but itself, and the wealth of the few that increases constantly although they have long ceased to work. Such insipid childishness is every day preached to us in the defence of property. M. Thiers, *e.g.*, had the assurance to repeat it with all the solemnity of a statesman, to the French people, once so *spiri-*

tuel. But as soon as the question of property crops up, it becomes a sacred duty to proclaim the intellectual food of the infant as the one thing fit for all ages and for all stages of development. In actual history it is notorious that conquest, enslavement, robbery, murder, briefly force, play the great part. In the tender annals of Political Economy, the idyllic reigns from time immemorial. Right and "labour" were from all time the sole means of enrichment, the present year of course always excepted. As a matter of fact, the methods of primitive accumulation are anything but idyllic.

In themselves money and commodities are no more capital than are the means of production and of subsistence. They want transforming into capital. But this transformation itself can only take place under certain circumstances that centre in this, viz., that two very different kinds of commodity-possessors must come face to face and into contact; on the one hand, the owners of money, means of production, means of subsistence, who are eager to increase the sum of values they possess, by buying other people's labour-power; on the other hand, free labourers, the sellers of their own labour-power, and therefore the sellers of labour. Free labourers, in the double sense that neither they themselves form part and parcel of the means of production, as in the case of slaves, bondsmen, &c., nor do the means of production belong to them, as in the case of peasant-proprietors; they are, therefore, free from, unencumbered by, any means of production of their own. With this polarisation of the market for commodities, the fundamental conditions of capitalist production are given. The capitalist system presupposes the complete separation of the labourers from all property in the means by which they can realise their labour. As soon as capitalist production is once on its own legs, it not only maintains this separation, but reproduces it on a continually extending scale. The process, therefore, that clears the way for the capitalist system, can be none other than the process which takes away from the labourer the possession of his means of production; a process that transforms, on the one hand, the social means of subsistence and of production into capital, on the other, the immediate producers into wage-labourers. The so-called primitive accumulation, therefore, is nothing else than the historical process of divorcing the producer from the means of production. It appears as primitive, because it forms the pre-historic stage of capital and of the mode of production corresponding with it.

The economic structure of capitalistic society has grown out of the economic structure of feudal society. The dissolution of the latter set free the elements of the former.

The immediate producer, the labourer, could only dispose of his own person after he had ceased to be attached to the soil and ceased to be the slave, serf, or bondman of another. To become a free seller of labour-power, who carries his commodity wherever he finds a market, he must further have escaped from the regime of the guilds, their rules for apprentices and journeymen, and the impediments of their labour regulations. Hence, the historical movement which changes the producers into wage-workers, appears, on the one hand, as their emancipation from serfdom and from the fetters of the guilds, and this side alone exists for our bourgeois historians. But, on the other hand, these new freedmen became sellers of themselves only after they had been robbed of all their own means of production, and of all the guarantees of existence afforded by the old feudal arrangements. And the history of this, their expropriation, is written in the annals of mankind in letters of blood and fire.

The industrial capitalists, these new potentates, had on their part not only to displace the guild masters of handicrafts, but also the feudal lords, the possessors of the sources of wealth. In this respect their conquest of social power appears as the fruit of a victorious struggle both against feudal lordship and its revolting prerogatives, and against the guilds and the fetters they laid on the free development of production and the free exploitation of man by man. The chevaliers d'industrie, however, only succeeded in supplanting the chevaliers of the sword by making use of events of which they themselves were wholly innocent. They have risen by means as vile as those by which the Roman freedman once on a time made himself the master of his *patronus*.

The starting-point of the development that gave rise to the wage-labourer as well as to the capitalist, was the servitude of the labourer. The advance consisted in a change of form of this servitude, in the transformation of feudal exploitation into capitalist exploitation. To understand its march, we need not go back very far. Although we come across the first beginnings of capitalist production as early as the 14th or 15th century, sporadically, in certain towns of the Mediterranean, the capitalistic era dates from the 16th century. Wherever it appears, the abolition of serfdom has been long effected, and the highest development of the middle ages, the existence of sovereign towns, has been long on the wane.

In the history of primitive accumulation, all revolutions are epoch-making that act as levers for the capitalist class in course of formation; but, above all, those moments when great masses of men are suddenly and forcibly torn from their means of subsistence, and hurled as free and "unattached" proletarians on the labour-market. The expropriation of the agricultural producer, of the peasant, from the soil, is the basis of the whole process. The history of this expropriation, in different countries, assumes different aspects, and runs through its various phases in different orders of succession, and at different periods. In England alone, which we take as our example, has it the classic form.

CHAPTER XXVII. EXPROPRIATION OF THE AGRICULTURAL POPULATION FROM THE LAND

In England, serfdom had practically disappeared in the last part of the 14th century. The immense majority of the population consisted then, and to a still larger extent, in the 15th century, of free peasant proprietors, whatever was the feudal title under which their right of property was hidden. * * *

The prelude of the revolution that laid the foundation of the capitalist mode of production, was played in the last third of the 15th, and the first decade of the 16th century. A mass of free proletarians was hurled on the labour-market by the breaking-up of the bands of feudal retainers, who, as Sir James Steuart well says, "everywhere uselessly filled house and castle." Although the royal power, itself a product of bourgeois development, in its strife after absolute sovereignty forcibly hastened on the dissolution of these bands of retainers, it was by no means the sole cause of it. In insolent conflict with king and parliament, the great feudal lords created an incomparably larger proletariat by the forcible driving of the peasantry from the land, to which the latter had the same feudal right as the lord himself, and by the usurpation of the common lands. The rapid rise of the Flemish wool manufactures, and the corresponding rise in the price of wool in England, gave the direct impulse to these evictions. The old nobility had been devoured by the great feudal wars. The new nobility was the child of its time, for which money was the power of all powers. Transformation of arable land into sheep-walks was, therefore, its cry. * * *

With the development of capitalist production during the manufacturing period, the public opinion of Europe had lost the last remnant of shame and conscience. The nations bragged cynically of every infamy that served them as a means to capitalistic accumulation. Read, *e.g.*, the naïve Annals of Commerce of the worthy A. Anderson. Here it is trumpeted forth as a triumph of English statecraft that at the Peace of Utrecht, England extorted from the Spaniards by the Asiento Treaty the privilege of being allowed to ply the negro-trade, until then only carried on between Africa and the English West Indies, between Africa and Spanish America as well. England thereby acquired the right of supplying Spanish America until 1743 with 4,800 negroes yearly. This threw, at the same time, an official cloak over British smuggling. Liverpool waxed fat on the slave-trade. This was its method of primitive accumulation. And, even to the present day, Liverpool "respectability" is the Pindar of the slave-trade which—compare the work of Aikin [1795] already quoted—"has coincided with that spirit of bold adventure which has characterised the trade of Liverpool and rapidly carried it to its present state of prosperity; has occasioned vast employment for shipping and sailors, and greatly augmented the demand for the manufactures of the country" (p. 339). Liverpool employed in the slave-trade, in 1730, 15 ships; in 1751, 53; in 1760, 74; in 1770, 96; and in 1792, 132.

Whilst the cotton industry introduced child-slavery in England, it gave in the United States a stimulus to the transformation of the earlier, more or less patriarchal slavery, into a system of commercial exploitation. In fact, the veiled slavery of the wage-workers in Europe needed, for its pedestal, slavery pure and simple in the new world.

Tantæ molis erat, to establish the "eternal laws of Nature" of the capitalist mode of production, to complete the process of separation between labourers and conditions of labour, to transform, at one pole, the social means of production and subsistence into capital, at the opposite pole, the mass of the population into wage-labourers, into "free labouring poor," that artificial product of modern society. If money, according to Augier, "comes into the world with a congenital blood-stain on one cheek," capital comes dripping from head to foot, from every pore, with blood and dirt.

CHAPTER XXXII. HISTORICAL TENDENCY OF CAPITALIST ACCUMULATION

What does the primitive accumulation of capital, *i.e.*, its historical genesis, resolve itself into? In so far as it is not immediate transformation of slaves and serfs into wage-labourers, and therefore a mere change of form, it only means the expropriation of the immediate producers, *i.e.*, the dissolution of private property based on the labour of its owner. Private property, as the antithesis to social, collective property, exists only where the means of labour and the external conditions of labour belong to private individuals. But according as these private individuals are labourers or not labourers, private property has a different character. The numberless shades, that it at first sight presents, correspond to the intermediate stages lying between these two extremes. The private property of the labourer in his means of production is the foundation of petty industry, whether agricultural, manufacturing, or both; petty industry, again, is an essential condition for the development of social production and of the free individuality of the labourer himself. Of course, this petty mode of production exists also under slavery, serfdom, and other states of dependence. But it flourishes, it lets loose its whole energy, it attains its adequate classical form, only where the labourer is the private owner of his own means of labour set in action by himself: the peasant of the land which he cultivates, the artisan of the tool which he handles as a virtuoso. This mode of production pre-supposes parcelling of the soil, and scattering of the other means of production. As it excludes the concentration of these means of production, so also it excludes co-operation, division of labour within each separate process of production, the control over, and the productive application of the forces of Nature by society, and the free development of the social productive powers. It is compatible only with a system of production, and a society, moving within narrow and more or less primitive bounds. To perpetuate it would be, as Pecqueur rightly says, "to decree universal mediocrity." At a certain stage of development it brings forth the material agencies for its own dissolution. From that moment new forces and new passions spring up in the bosom of society; but the old social organisation fetters them and keeps them down. It must be annihilated; it is annihilated. Its annihilation, the transformation of the individualised and scattered means of production into socially concentrated ones, of the pigmy property of the many into the huge property of the few, the expropriation of the great mass of the people from the soil, from the means of subsistence, and from the means of labour, this fearful and painful expropriation of the mass of the people forms the prelude to the history of capital. It comprises a series of forcible methods, of which we have passed in review only those that have been epoch-making as methods of the primitive accumulation of capital. The expropriation of the immediate producers was accomplished with merciless Vandalism, and under the stimulus of passions the most infamous, the most sordid, the pettiest, the most meanly odious. Self-earned private property, that is based, so to say, on the fusing together of the isolated, independent labouring-individual with the conditions of his labour, is supplanted by capitalistic private property, which rests on exploitation of the nominally free labour of others, *i.e.*, on wage-labour.

As soon as this process of transformation has sufficiently decomposed the old society from top to bottom, as soon as the labourers are turned into proletarians, their means of labour into capital, as soon as the capitalist mode of production stands on its own feet, then the further socialisation of labour and further transformation of the land and other means of production into socially exploited and, therefore, common means of production, as well as the further expropriation of private proprietors, takes a new form. That which is now to be expropriated is no longer the labourer working for himself, but the capitalist exploiting many labourers. This expropriation is accomplished by the action of the immanent laws of capitalistic production itself, by the centralisation of capital. One capitalist always kills many. Hand in hand with this centralisation, or this expropriation of many capitalists by a few, develop, on an ever-extending scale, the co-operative form of the labour-process, the conscious technical application of science, the methodical cultivation of the soil, the transformation of the instruments of labour into instruments of labour only usable in common, the economising of all means of production by their use as the means of production of combined, socialised labour, the entanglement of all peoples in the net of the world-market, and with this, the international character of the capitalistic régime. Along with the constantly diminishing number of the magnates of capital, who usurp and monopolise all advantages of this process of transformation, grows the mass of misery, oppression, slavery, degradation, exploitation; but with this too grows the revolt of the working-class, a class always increasing in numbers, and disciplined, united, organised by the very mechanism of the process of capitalist production itself. The monopoly of capital becomes a fetter upon the mode of production, which has sprung up and flourished along with, and under it. Centralisation of the means of production and socialisation of labour at last reach a point where they become incompatible with their capitalist integument. This integument is burst asunder. The knell of capitalist private property sounds. The expropriators are expropriated.

The capitalist mode of appropriation, the result of the capitalist mode of production, produces capitalist private property. This is the first negation of individual private property, as founded on the labour of the proprietor. But capitalist production begets, with the inexorability of a law of Nature, its own negation. It is the negation of negation. This does not re-establish private property for the producer, but gives him individual property based on the acquisitions of the capitalist era: *i.e.*, on co-operation and the possession in common of the land and of the means of production.

The transformation of scattered private property, arising from individual labour, into capitalist private property is, naturally, a process, incomparably more protracted, violent, and difficult, than the transformation of capitalistic private property, already practically resting on socialised production, into socialised property. In the former case, we had the expropriation of the mass of the people by a few usurpers; in the latter, we have the expropriation of a few usurpers by the mass of the people.

On the Realm of Necessity
and the Realm of Freedom

KARL MARX

This short excerpt from Volume Three of *Capital* is an important formulation of Marx's futurology, his vision of man in a future condition of creative leisure made possible, first, by the enormous productive powers inherent in modern machine industry, and, second, by the worldwide proletarian
revolution that, in Marx's view, was destined to liberate humanity's productive activity from the bonds of capitalist acquisitiveness. There would still
remain, as he saw it, a residual realm of necessity—the labor time required
to produce needed goods under the most advanced system of technology.

We have seen that the capitalist process of production is a historically determined form of the social process of production in
general. The latter is as much a production process of material conditions of human life as a process taking place under specific historical and economic production relations, producing and reproducing
these production relations themselves, and thereby also the bearers
of this process, their material conditions of existence and their
mutual relations, i.e., their particular socio-economic form. For the
aggregate of these relations, in which the agents of this production
stand with respect to Nature and to one another, and in which
they produce, is precisely society, considered from the standpoint of
its economic structure. Like all its predecessors, the capitalist process of production proceeds under definite material conditions,
which are, however, simultaneously the bearers of definite social
relations entered into by individuals in the process of reproducing
their life. Those conditions, like these relations, are on the one
hand prerequisites, on the other hand results and creations of the
capitalist process of production; they are produced and reproduced
by it. We saw also that capital—and the capitalist is merely capital
personified and functions in the process of production solely as the
agent of capital—in its corresponding social process of production,

pumps a definite quantity of surplus labour out of the direct producers, or labourers; capital obtains this surplus labour without an equivalent, and in essence it always remains forced labour—no matter how much it may seem to result from free contractual agreement. This surplus labour appears as surplus value, and this surplus value exists as a surplus product. Surplus labour in general, as labour performed over and above the given requirements, must always remain. In the capitalist as well as in the slave system, etc., it merely assumes an antagonistic form and is supplemented by complete idleness of a stratum of society. A definite quantity of surplus labour is required as insurance against accidents, and by the necessary and progressive expansion of the process of reproduction in keeping with the development of the needs and the growth of population, which is called accumulation from the viewpoint of the capitalist. It is one of the civilizing aspects of capital that it enforces this surplus labour in a manner and under conditions which are more advantageous to the development of the productive forces, social relations, and the creation of the elements for a new and higher form than under the preceding forms of slavery, serfdom, etc. Thus it gives rise to a stage, on the one hand, in which coercion and monopolization of social development (including its material and intellectual advantages) by one portion of society at the expense of the other are eliminated; on the other hand, it creates the material means and embryonic conditions, making it possible in a higher form of society to combine this surplus labour with a greater reduction of time devoted to material labour in general. For, depending on the development of labour productivity, surplus labour may be large in a small total working day, and relatively small in a large total working day. If the necessary labour time $= 3$ and the surplus labour $= 3$, then the total working day $= 6$ and the rate of surplus labour $= 100\%$. If the necessary labour $= 9$ and the surplus labour $= 3$, then the total working day $= 12$ and the rate of surplus labour only $33\frac{1}{3}\%$. In that case, it depends upon the labour productivity how much use value shall be produced in a definite time, hence also in a definite surplus labour time. The actual wealth of society, and the possibility of constantly expanding its reproduction process, therefore, do not depend upon the duration of surplus labour, but upon its productivity and the more or less copious conditions of production under which it is performed. In fact, the realm of freedom actually begins only where labour which is determined by necessity and mundane considerations ceases; thus in the very nature of things it lies beyond the sphere of actual material production. Just as the savage must wrestle with Nature to satisfy his wants, to maintain and reproduce life, so must civilized man, and he must do so in all social formations and under all possible modes of production. With his development this realm of physical necessity expands as a result of his wants; but, at the same time, the forces of production which satisfy these wants also increase. Freedom in this field can only consist in socialized man, the associated producers, rationally regulating their interchange with Nature, bringing it under their common control, instead of being ruled by it as by the blind forces of Nature; and achieving this with the least expenditure of energy and under conditions most favourable to, and worthy of, their human nature. But it nonetheless still remains a realm of necessity. Beyond it begins that development of human energy which is an end in itself, the true realm of freedom, which, however, can blossom forth only with the realm of necessity as its basis. The shortening of the working day is its basic prerequisite.

On the Division of Labour in Production

FRIEDRICH ENGELS

This discussion of production is taken from Engels' work of 1878, *Herr Eugen Dühring's Revolution in Science*, better known as *Anti-Dühring* (English translation issued by the Foreign Languages Publishing House, Moscow, 1947). It clearly shows that the dehumanizing nature of the division of labour was a central theme in the thought of Marx and Engels, linking their early philosophical communism with *Capital* and other later writings in an unbroken line of continuity. The socialism of Marx and Engels, unlike that of some other socialist theorists of their time and after, placed principal emphasis upon production rather than distribution. Its central concern, that is, was with man as a producer and the conditions of his productive activity. It saw the division of labour in production as an enslaving situation that had been characteristic of all hitherto existing modes of production—capitalism particularly—and it looked to future socialism as a mode of production in which the division of labour in production would be transcended.

---

* * * In every society in which production has developed spontaneously—and our present society is of this type—the situation is not that the producers control the means of production, but that the means of production control the producers. In such a society each new lever of production is necessarily transformed into a new means for the subjection of the producers to the means of production. This is most of all true of that lever of production which, prior to the introduction of modern industry, was by far the most powerful—the division of labour. The first great division of labour, the separation of town and country, condemned the rural population to thousands of years of mental torpidity, and the people of the towns each to subjection to his own individual trade. It destroyed the basis of the intellectual development of the former and the physical development of the latter. When the peasant appropriates his land, and the townsman his trade, his land appropriates the peasant and his trade the townsman to the very same extent. In the division of labour, man is also divided. All other physical and mental faculties are sacrificed to the development of one single activity. This stunting of man grows in the same measure as the division of labour, which attains its highest development in manufacture. Manufacture splits up each trade into its separate partial operations, allots each of these to an individual labourer as his life calling, and thus chains him for life to a particular detail function and a particular tool. "It converts the labourer into a crippled monstrosity, by forcing his detail dexterity at the expense of a world of productive capabilities and instincts. . . . The individual himself is made the automatic motor of a fractional operation" (Marx)[1]—a motor which in many cases is perfected only by literally crippling the labourer physically and mentally. The machinery of modern industry degrades the labourer from a machine to the mere appendage of a machine. "The life-long speciality of handling one and the same tool, now becomes the lifelong speciality of serving one and the same machine. Machinery is put to a wrong use, with the object of transforming the workman, from his very childhood, into a part of a detail-machine" (Marx).[2] And not only the labourers, but also the classes directly or indirectly exploiting the labourers are made subject, through the divison of labour, to the tool of their function: the empty-minded bourgeois to his own capital and his own insane craving for profits; the lawyer to his fossilized legal conceptions, which dominate him as an independent power; the "educated classes" in general to their manifold species of local narrow-mindedness and one-sidedness, to their own physical and mental short-sightedness, to their stunted growth due to their narrow specialized education and their being chained for life to this specialized activity—even when this specialized activity is merely to do nothing.

The utopians were already perfectly clear in their minds as to the effects of the division of labour, the stunting on the one hand of the labourer, and on the other of the labour function, which is restricted to the lifelong, uniform, mechanical repetition of one and the same operation. The abolition of the antithesis between town and country was demanded by Fourier, as by Owen, as the first prerequisite for the abolition of the old division of labour altogether. Both of them thought that the population should be scattered through the country in groups of sixteen hundred to three thousand persons; each group was to occupy a gigantic palace, with a household run on communal lines, in the centre of their area of land. It is true that Fourier occasionally refers to towns, but these were to consist in turn of only four or five such palaces situated near each other. Both writers would have each member of society

1. See *Capital*, p. 286, above. [R. T.]   2. See *Capital*, p. 296, above. [R. T.]

occupied in agriculture as well as in industry; with Fourier, industry covers chiefly handicrafts and manufacture, while Owen assigns the main role to modern industry and already demands the introduction of steam-power and machinery in domestic work. But within agriculture as well as industry both of them also demand the greatest possible variety of occupation for each individual, and in accordance with this, the training of the youth for the utmost possible all-round technical functions. They both consider that man should gain universal development through universal practical activity and that labour should recover the attractiveness of which the division of labour has despoiled it, in the first place through this variation of occupation, and through the correspondingly short duration of the "sitting"—to use Fourier's expression—devoted to each particular kind of work. Both Fourier and Owen are far in advance of the mode of thought of the exploiting classes inherited by Herr Dühring, according to which the antithesis between town and country is inevitable in the nature of things; the narrow view that a number of "entities" must in any event be condemned to the production of *one single* article, the view that desires to perpetuate the "economic species" of men distinguished by their way of life—people who take pleasure in the performance of precisely this and no other thing, who have therefore sunk so low that they *rejoice* in their own subjection and one-sidedness. In comparison with the basic conceptions even of the "idiot" Fourier's most recklessly bold fantasies; in comparison even with the paltriest ideas of the "crude, feeble, and paltry" Owen—Herr Dühring, himself still completely dominated by the division of labour, is no more than an impertinent dwarf.

In making itself the master of all the means of production to use them in accordance with a social plan, society puts an end to the former subjection of men to their own means of production. It goes without saying that society cannot free itself unless every individual is freed. The old mode of production must therefore be revolutionized from top to bottom, and in particular the former division of labour must disappear. Its place must be taken by an organization of production in which, on the one hand, no individual can throw on the shoulders of others his share in productive labour, this natural condition of human existence; and in which, on the other hand, productive labour, instead of being a means of subjugating men, will become a means of their emancipation, by offering each individual the opportunity to develop all his faculties, physical and mental, in all directions and exercise them to the full—in which, therefore, productive labour will become a pleasure instead of being a burden.

Today this is no longer a fantasy, no longer a pious wish. With the present development of the productive forces, the increase in production that will follow from the very fact of the socialization of the productive forces, coupled with the abolition of the barriers and disturbances, and of the waste of products and means of production, resulting from the capitalist mode of production, will suffice, with everybody doing his share of work, to reduce the time required for labour to a point which, measured by our present conceptions, will be small indeed.

Nor is the abolition of the old division of labour a demand which could only be carried through to the detriment of the productivity of labour. On the contrary. Thanks to modern industry it has become a condition of production itself. "The employment of machinery does away with the necessity of crystallizing this distribution after the manner of Manufacture, by the constant annexation of a particular man to a particular function. Since the motion of the whole system does not proceed from the workman, but from the machinery, a change of persons can take place at any time without an interruption of the work. . . . Lastly, the quickness with which machine work is learnt by young people does away with the necessity of bringing up for exclusive employment by machinery, a special class of operatives."[3] But while the capitalist mode of employment of machinery necessarily perpetuates the old division of labour with its fossilized specialization, although it has become superfluous from a technical standpoint, the machinery itself rebels against this anachronism. The technical basis of modern industry is revolutionary. "By means of machinery, chemical processes and other methods, it is continually causing changes not only in the technical basis of production, but also in the functions of the labourer, and in the social combinations of the labour process. At the same time, it thereby also revolutionizes the division of labour within the society, and incessantly launches masses of capital and of workpeople from one branch of production to another. Modern industry, by its very nature, therefore necessitates variation of labour, fluency of function, universal mobility of the labourer. . . . We have seen how this absolute contradiction . . . vents its rage . . . in the incessant human sacrifices from among the working class, in the most reckless squandering of labour-power, and in the devastation caused by social anarchy. This is the negative side. But, if, on the one hand, variation of work at present imposes itself after the manner of an overpowering natural law, and with the blindly destructive action of a natural law that meets with resistance at all points, modern industry, on the other hand, through its catastrophes imposes the necessity of recognizing, as a fundamental law of production, variation of work, consequently fitness of the

3. See *Capital*, p. 296, above. [*R. T.*]

labourer for varied work, consequently the greatest possible development of his varied aptitudes. It becomes a question of life and death for society to adapt the mode of production to the normal functioning of this law. Modern industry, indeed, compels society, under penalty of death, to replace the detail-worker of today, crippled by lifelong repetition of one and the same trivial operation, and thus reduced to the mere fragment of a man, by the fully developed individual, fit for a variety of labours, ready to face any change of production, and to whom the different social functions he performs, are but so many modes of giving free scope to his own natural and acquired powers" (Marx, *Capital*).[4]

Modern industry, which has taught us to convert the movement of molecules, something more or less universally feasible, into the movement of masses for technical purposes, has thereby to a considerable extent freed production from restrictions of locality. Water-power was local; steam-power is free. While water-power is necessarily rural, steam-power is by no means necessarily urban. It is capitalist utilization which concentrates it mainly in the towns and changes factory villages into factory towns. But in so doing it at the same time undermines the conditions under which it operates. The first requirement of the steam-engine, and a main requirement of almost all branches of production in modern industry, is relatively pure water. But the factory town transforms all water into stinking manure. However much therefore urban concentration is a basic condition of capitalist production, each individual industrial capitalist is constantly striving to get away from the large towns necessarily created by this concentration, and to transfer his plant to the countryside. This process can be studied in detail in the textile industry districts of Lancashire and Yorkshire; modern capitalist industry is constantly bringing new large towns into being there by constant flight from the towns into the country. The situation is similar in the metal-working districts where, in part, other causes produce the same effects.

Once more, only the abolition of the capitalist character of modern industry can bring us out of this new vicious circle, can resolve this contradiction in modern industry, which is constantly reproducing itself. Only a society which makes it possible for its productive forces to dovetail harmoniously into each other on the basis of one single vast plan can allow industry to be distributed over the whole country in the way best adapted to its own development, and to the maintenance and development of the other elements of production.

Accordingly, abolition of the antithesis between town and country is not merely possible. It has become a direct necessity of indus-

4. See pp. 301–302, above. [*R. T.*]

trial production itself, just as it has become a necessity of agricultural production and, besides, of public health. The present poisoning of the air, water and land can be put an end to only by the fusion of town and country; and only such fusion will change the situation of the masses now languishing in the towns, and enable their excrement to be used for the production of plants instead of for the production of disease.

Capitalist industry has already made itself relatively independent of the local limitations arising from the location of sources of the raw materials it needs. The textile industry works up, in the main, imported raw materials. Spanish iron ore is worked up in England and Germany and Spanish and South-American copper ores, in England. Every coal-field now supplies fuel to an industrial area beyond its own borders, an area which is widening every year. Along the whole of the European coast steam-engines are driven by English and to some extent also by German and Belgian coal. Society liberated from the barriers of capitalist production can go much further still. By generating a race of producers with an all-round training who understand the scientific basis of industrial production as a whole, and each of whom has had practical experience in a whole series of branches of production from start to finish, this society will bring into being a new productive force which will abundantly compensate for the labour required to transport raw materials and fuel from great distances.

The abolition of the separation of town and country is therefore not utopian, also, in so far as it is conditioned on the most equal distribution possible of modern industry over the whole country. It is true that in the huge towns civilization has bequeathed us a heritage which it will take much time and trouble to get rid of. But it must and will be got rid of, however protracted a process it may be. Whatever destiny may be in store for the German Empire of the Prussian nation, Bismarck can go to his grave proudly aware that the desire of his heart is sure to be fulfilled: the great towns will perish.

And now see how puerile Herr Dühring's notions are—that society can take possession of all means of production in the aggregate without revolutionizing from top to bottom the old method of production and first of all putting an end to the old division of labour; that everything will be in order once "natural aptitudes and personal capabilities are taken into account"—that therefore whole masses of entities will remain, as in the past, subjected to the production of *one single* article; whole "populations" will be engaged in a single branch of production, and humanity continue divided, as in the past, into a number of different crippled "economic species," for there still are "porters" and "architects." Society is to become master of the means of production as a whole, in order that each individual may remain the slave of his means of production, and have only a choice as to *which* means of production are to enslave him. And see also how Herr Dühring considers the separation of town and country as "inevitable in the nature of things," and can find only a tiny palliative in schnaps-distilling and beet-sugar manufacturing—two, in their connection specifically Prussian, branches of industry; how he makes the distribution of industry over the country dependent on certain future inventions and on the *necessity* of associating industry directly with the procurement of raw materials—raw materials which are already used at an ever increasing distance from their place of origin! And Herr Dühring finally tries to cover his retreat by assuring us that in the long run social wants will carry through the union between agriculture and industry even *against* economic considerations, as if this would be some economic sacrifice!

Certainly, to be able to see that the revolutionary elements, which will do away with the old division of labour, along with the separation of town and country, and will revolutionize the whole of production; see that these elements are already contained in embryo in the productive conditions of modern large-scale industry and that their development is hindered by the existing capitalist mode of production—to be able to see these things, it is necessary to have a somewhat wider horizon than the sphere of jurisdiction of the Prussian *Landrecht,* than the country where production of schnaps and beet-sugar are the key industries, and where commercial crises can be studied on the book market. To be able to see these things it is necessary to have some knowledge of real large-scale industry in its historical growth and in its present actual form, especially in the one country where it has its home and where alone it has attained its classical development. Then no one will think of attempting to vulgarize modern scientific socialism and to degrade it into Herr Dühring's *specifically Prussian socialism.*

PART III

Revolutionary Program and Strategy

Manifesto of the Communist Party

MARX AND ENGELS

In 1836 German radical workers living in Paris formed a secret association called "League of the Just." At congresses in London in 1847 it changed its name to "Communist League" and commissioned Marx and Engels, who had recently become members, to draw up a manifesto on its behalf. Both men prepared first drafts. Engels' draft, preserved under the title "The Principles of Communism," was in the form of a catechism with twenty-five questions and answers. Marx is believed to have had the greater hand in giving the *Communist Manifesto* its final form as both a programmatic statement and a compressed summary of the Marxian theory of history. It was originally published in London in February, 1848, and brought out in a French translation in Paris shortly before the insurrection of June, 1848, there. It has become the most widely read and influential single document of modern socialism. The text given here is that of the English edition of 1888, edited by Engels.

Preface to the German Edition of 1872

The Communist League, an international association of workers, which could of course be only a secret one under the conditions obtaining at the time, commissioned the undersigned, at the Congress held in London in November 1847, to draw up for publication a detailed theoretical and practical programme of the Party. Such was the origin of the following Manifesto, the manuscript of which travelled to London, to be printed, a few weeks before the February Revolution.[1] First published in German, it has been republished in that language in at least twelve different editions in Germany, England and America. It was published in English for the first time in 1850 in the *Red Republican*, London, translated by Miss Helen Macfarlane, and in 1871 in at least three different translations in America. A French version first appeared in Paris shortly before the June insurrection of 1848 and recently in *Le Soci-*

1. The February Revolution in France, 1848.

aliste of New York. A new translation is in the course of preparation. A Polish version appeared in London shortly after it was first published in German. A Russian translation was published in Geneva in the sixties. Into Danish, too, it was translated shortly after its first appearance.

However much the state of things may have altered during the last twenty-five years, the general principles laid down in this Manifesto are, on the whole, as correct today as ever. Here and there some detail might be improved. The practical application of the principles will depend, as the Manifesto itself states, everywhere and at all times, on the historical conditions for the time being existing, and, for that reason, no special stress is laid on the revolutionary measures proposed at the end of Section II. That passage would, in many respects, be very differently worded today. In view of the gigantic strides of Modern Industry in the last twenty-five years, and of the accompanying improved and extended party organisation of the working class, in view of the practical experience gained, first in the February Revolution, and then, still more, in the Paris Commune, where the proletariat for the first time held political power for two whole months, this programme has in some details become antiquated. One thing especially was proved by the Commune, *viz.*, that "the working class cannot simply lay hold of the ready-made State machinery, and wield it for its own purposes." (See *The Civil War in France; Address of the General Council of the International Working Men's Association*, London, Trulove, 1871, p. 15, where this point is further developed.)[2] Further, it is self-evident that the criticism of socialist literature is deficient in relation to the present time, because it comes down only to 1847; also, that the remarks on the relation of the Communists to the various opposition parties (Section IV), although in principle still correct, yet in practice are antiquated, because the political situation has been entirely changed, and the progress of history has swept from off the earth the greater portion of the political parties there enumerated.

But, then, the Manifesto has become a historical document which we have no longer any right to alter. A subsequent edition may perhaps appear with an introduction bridging the gap from 1847 to the present day; this reprint was too unexpected to leave us time for that.

Karl Marx   Friedrich Engels

London, June 24, 1872

2. See Engels' comment, p. 535, below. [*R. T.*]

Preface to the Russian Edition of 1882

The first Russian edition of the *Manifesto of the Communist Party*, translated by Bakunin, was published early in the sixties[3] by the printing office of the *Kolokol*. Then the West could see in it (the *Russian* edition of the Manifesto) only a literary curiosity. Such a view would be impossible today.

What a limited field the proletarian movement still occupied at that time (December 1847) is most clearly shown by the last section of the Manifesto: the position of the Communists in relation to the various opposition parties in the various countries. Precisely Russia and the United States are missing here. It was the time when Russia constituted the last great reserve of all European reaction, when the United States absorbed the surplus proletarian forces of Europe through immigration. Both countries provided Europe with raw materials and were at the same time markets for the sale of its industrial products. At that time both were, therefore, in one way or another, pillars of the existing European order.

How very different today! Precisely European immigration fitted North America for a gigantic agricultural production, whose competition is shaking the very foundations of European landed property—large and small. In addition it enabled the United States to exploit its tremendous industrial resources with an energy and on a scale that must shortly break the industrial monopoly of Western Europe, and especially of England, existing up to now. Both circumstances react in revolutionary manner upon America itself. Step by step the small and middle landownership of the farmers, the basis of the whole political constitution, is succumbing to the competition of giant farms; simultaneously, a mass proletariat and a fabulous concentration of capitals are developing for the first time in the industrial regions.

And now Russia! During the Revolution of 1848-49 not only the European princes, but the European bourgeois as well, found their only salvation from the proletariat, just beginning to awaken, in Russian intervention. The tsar was proclaimed the chief of European reaction. Today he is a prisoner of war of the revolution, in Gatchina, and Russia forms the vanguard of revolutionary action in Europe.

The Communist Manifesto had as its object the proclamation of the inevitably impending dissolution of modern bourgeois property. But in Russia we find, face to face with the rapidly developing capitalist swindle and bourgeois landed property, just beginning to

3. The date is not correct; the edition referred to appeared in 1869.

develop, more than half the land owned in common by the peasants. Now the question is: Can the Russian *obshchina*,[4] though greatly undermined, yet a form of the primeval common ownership of land, pass directly to the higher form of communist common ownership? Or, on the contrary, must it first pass through the same process of dissolution as constitutes the historical evolution of the West?

The only answer to that possible today is this: If the Russian Revolution becomes the signal for a proletarian revolution in the West, so that both complement each other, the present Russian common ownership of land may serve as the starting-point for a communist development.

Karl Marx   Friedrich Engels

London, January 21, 1882

Preface to the German Edition of 1883

The preface to the present edition I must, alas, sign alone. Marx, the man to whom the whole working class of Europe and America owes more than to anyone else, rests at Highgate Cemetery and over his grave the first grass is already growing. Since his death, there can be even less thought of revising or supplementing the Manifesto. All the more do I consider it necessary again to state here the following expressly:

The basic thought running through the Manifesto—that economic production and the structure of society of every historical epoch necessarily arising therefrom constitute the foundation for the political and intellectual history of that epoch; that consequently (ever since the dissolution of the primeval communal ownership of land) all history has been a history of class struggles, of struggles between exploited and exploiting, between dominated and dominating classes at various stages of social development; that this struggle, however, has now reached a stage where the exploited and oppressed class (the proletariat) can no longer emancipate itself from the class which exploits and oppresses it (the bourgeoisie), without at the same time forever freeing the whole of society from exploitation, oppression and class struggles—this basic thought belongs solely and exclusively to Marx.

I have already stated this many times; but precisely now it is necessary that it also stand in front of the Manifesto itself.

Friedrich Engels

London, June 28, 1883

4. *Obshchina:* Village community.

MANIFESTO
OF THE COMMUNIST PARTY

A spectre is haunting Europe—the spectre of Communism. All the Powers of old Europe have entered into a holy alliance to exorcise this spectre: Pope and Czar, Metternich and Guizot, French Radicals and German police-spies.

Where is the party in opposition that has not been decried as Communistic by its opponents in power? Where the Opposition that has not hurled back the branding reproach of Communism, against the more advanced opposition parties, as well as against its reactionary adversaries?

Two things result from this fact.

I. Communism is already acknowledged by all European Powers to be itself a Power.

II. It is high time that Communists should openly, in the face of the whole world, publish their views, their aims, their tendencies, and meet this nursery tale of the Spectre of Communism with a Manifesto of the party itself.

To this end, Communists of various nationalities have assembled in London, and sketched the following Manifesto, to be published in the English, French, German, Italian, Flemish and Danish languages.

I. Bourgeois and Proletarians[5]

The history of all hitherto existing society[6] is the history of class struggles.

Freeman and slave, patrician and plebeian, lord and serf,

5. By bourgeoisie is meant the class of modern Capitalists, owners of the means of social production and employers of wage-labour. By proletariat, the class of modern wage-labourers who, having no means of production of their own, are reduced to selling their labour-power in order to live. [*Engels, English edition of 1888*]

6. That is, all *written* history. In 1847, the pre-history of society, the social organisation existing previous to recorded history, was all but unknown. Since then, Haxthausen discovered common ownership of land in Russia, Maurer proved it to be the social foundation from which all Teutonic races started in history, and by and by village communities were found to be, or to have

been the primitive form of society everywhere from India to Ireland. The inner organisation of this primitive Communistic society was laid bare, in its typical form, by Morgan's crowning discovery of the true nature of the *gens* and its relation to the *tribe*. With the dissolution of these primaeval communities society begins to be differentiated into separate and finally antagonistic classes. I have attempted to retrace this process of dissolution in: "Der Ursprung der Familie, des Privateigenthums und des Staats" [*The Origin of the Family, Private Property and the State*], 2nd edition, Stuttgart 1886. [*Engels, English edition of 1888*] guild-master[7] and journeyman, in a word, oppressor and oppressed, stood in constant opposition to one another, carried on an uninterrupted, now hidden, now open fight, a fight that each time ended, either in a revolutionary re-constitution of society at large, or in the common ruin of the contending classes.

In the earlier epochs of history, we find almost everywhere a complicated arrangement of society into various orders, a manifold gradation of social rank. In ancient Rome we have patricians, knights, plebeians, slaves; in the Middle Ages, feudal lords, vassals, guild-masters, journeymen, apprentices, serfs; in almost all of these classes, again, subordinate gradations.

The modern bourgeois society that has sprouted from the ruins of feudal society has not done away with clash antagonisms. It has but established new classes, new conditions of oppression, new forms of struggle in place of the old ones.

Our epoch, the epoch of the bourgeoisie, possesses, however, this distinctive feature: it has simplified the class antagonisms: Society as a whole is more and more splitting up into two great hostile camps, into two great classes directly facing each other: Bourgeoisie and Proletariat.

From the serfs of the Middle Ages sprang the chartered burghers of the earliest towns. From these burgesses the first elements of the bourgeoisie were developed.

The discovery of America, the rounding of the Cape, opened up fresh ground for the rising bourgeoisie. The East-Indian and Chinese markets, the colonisation of America, trade with the colonies, the increase in the means of exchange and in commodities generally, gave to commerce, to navigation, to industry, an impulse never before known, and thereby, to the revolutionary element in the tottering feudal society, a rapid development.

The feudal system of industry, under which industrial production was monopolised by closed guilds, now no longer sufficed for the growing wants of the new markets. The manufacturing system took its place. The guild-masters were pushed on one side by the manufacturing middle class; division of labour between the different corporate guilds vanished in the face of division of labour in each single workshop.

Meantime the markets kept ever growing, the demand ever rising. Even manufacture no longer sufficed. Thereupon, steam and machinery revolutionised industrial production. The place of manufacture was taken by the giant, Modern Industry, the place of the industrial middle class, by industrial millionaires, the leaders of whole industrial armies, the modern bourgeois.

---

7. Guild-master, that is, a full member of a guild, a master within, not a head of a guild. [*Engels, English edition of 1888*]

Modern industry has established the world-market, for which the discovery of America paved the way. This market has given an immense development to commerce, to navigation, to communication by land. This development has, in its turn, reacted on the extension of industry; and in proportion as industry, commerce, navigation, railways extended, in the same proportion the bourgeoisie developed, increased its capital, and pushed into the background every class handed down from the Middle Ages.

We see, therefore, how the modern bourgeoisie is itself the product of a long course of development, of a series of revolutions in the modes of production and of exchange.

Each step in the development of the bourgeoisie was accompanied by a corresponding political advance of that class. An oppressed class under the sway of the feudal nobility, an armed and self-governing association in the mediaeval commune;[8] here independent urban republic (as in Italy and Germany), there taxable "third estate" of the monarchy (as in France), afterwards, in the period of manufacture proper, serving either the semi-feudal or the absolute monarchy as a counterpoise against the nobility, and, in fact, corner-stone of the great monarchies in general, the bourgeoisie has at last, since the establishment of Modern Industry and of the world-market, conquered for itself, in the modern representative State, exclusive political sway. The executive of the modern State is but a committee for managing the common affairs of the whole bourgeoisie.

The bourgeoisie, historically, has played a most revolutionary part.

The bourgeoisie, wherever it has got the upper hand, has put an end to all feudal, patriarchal, idyllic relations. It has pitilessly torn asunder the motley feudal ties that bound man to his "natural superiors," and has left remaining no other nexus between man and man than naked self-interest, than callous "cash payment." It has drowned the most heavenly ecstasies of religious fervour, of chivalrous enthusiasm, of philistine sentimentalism, in the icy water of egotistical calculation. It has resolved personal worth into exchange value, and in place of the numberless indefeasible chartered freedoms, has set up that single, unconscionable freedom—Free Trade. In one word, for exploitation, veiled by religious and political illusions, it has substituted naked, shameless, direct, brutal exploitation.

8. "Commune" was the name taken, in France, by the nascent towns even before they had conquered from their feudal lords and masters local self-government and political rights as the "Third Estate." Generally speaking, for the economical development of the bourgeoisie, England is here taken as the typical country; for its political development, France. [*Engels, English edition of 1888*]

This was the name given their urban communities by the townsmen of Italy and France, after they had purchased or wrested their initial rights of self-government from their feudal lords. [*Engels, German edition of 1890*]

The bourgeoisie has stripped of its halo every occupation hitherto honoured and looked up to with reverent awe. It has converted the physician, the lawyer, the priest, the poet, the man of science, into its paid wage-labourers.

The bourgeoisie has torn away from the family its sentimental veil, and has reduced the family relation to a mere money relation.

The bourgeoisie has disclosed how it came to pass that the brutal display of vigour in the Middle Ages, which Reactionists so much admire, found its fitting complement in the most slothful indolence. It has been the first to show what man's activity can bring about. It has accomplished wonders far surpassing Egyptian pyramids, Roman aqueducts, and Gothic cathedrals; it has conducted expeditions that put in the shade all former Exoduses of nations and crusades.

The bourgeoisie cannot exist without constantly revolutionising the instruments of production, and thereby the relations of production, and with them the whole relations of society. Conservation of the old modes of production in unaltered form, was, on the contrary, the first condition of existence for all earlier industrial classes. Constant revolutionising of production, uninterrupted disturbance of all social conditions, everlasting uncertainty and agitation distinguish the bourgeois epoch from all earlier ones. All fixed, fast-frozen relations, with their train of ancient and venerable prejudices and opinions, are swept away, all new-formed ones become antiquated before they can ossify. All that is solid melts into air, all that is holy is profaned, and man is at last compelled to face with sober senses, his real conditions of life, and his relations with his kind.

The need of a constantly expanding market for its products chases the bourgeoisie over the whole surface of the globe. It must nestle everywhere, settle everywhere, establish connexions everywhere.

The bourgeoisie has through its exploitation of the world-market given a cosmopolitan character to production and consumption in every country. To the great chagrin of Reactionists, it has drawn from under the feet of industry the national ground on which it stood. All old-established national industries have been destroyed or are daily being destroyed. They are dislodged by new industries, whose introduction becomes a life and death question for all civilised nations, by industries that no longer work up indigenous raw material, but raw material drawn from the remotest zones; industries whose products are consumed, not only at home, but in every quarter of the globe. In place of the old wants, satisfied by the productions of the country, we find new wants, requiring for their satisfaction the products of distant lands and climes. In place of the old local and national seclusion and self-sufficiency, we have intercourse in every direction, universal inter-dependence of nations. And as in material, so also in intellectual production. The intellectual creations

of individual nations become common property. National one-sidedness and narrow-mindedness become more and more impossible,
and from the numerous national and local literatures, there arises a
world literature.

The bourgeoisie, by the rapid improvement of all instruments of
production, by the immensely facilitated means of communication,
draws all, even the most barbarian, nations into civilisation. The
cheap prices of its commodities are the heavy artillery with which it
batters down all Chinese walls, with which it forces the barbarians'
intensely obstinate hatred of foreigners to capitulate. It compels all
nations, on pain of extinction, to adopt the bourgeois mode of production; it compels them to introduce what it calls civilisation into
their midst, *i.e.*, to become bourgeois themselves. In one word, it
creates a world after its own image.

The bourgeoisie has subjected the country to the rule of the
towns. It has created enormous cities, has greatly increased the
urban population as compared with the rural, and has thus rescued
a considerable part of the population from the idiocy of rural life.
Just as it has made the country dependent on the towns, so it has
made barbarian and semi-barbarian countries dependent on the civilised ones, nations and peasants on nations of bourgeois, the East
on the West.

The bourgeoisie keeps more and more doing away with the scattered state of the population, of the means of production, and of
property. It has agglomerated population, centralised means of production, and has concentrated property in a few hands. The necessary consequence of this was political centralisation. Independent,
or but loosely connected provinces, with separate interests, laws,
governments and systems of taxation, became lumped together into
one nation, with one government, one code of laws, one national
class-interest, one frontier and one customs-tariff.

The bourgeoisie, during its rule of scarce one hundred years, has
created more massive and more colossal productive forces than have
all preceding generations together. Subjection of Nature's forces to
man, machinery, application of chemistry to industry and agriculture, steam-navigation, railways, electric telegraphs, clearing of
whole continents for cultivation, canalisation of rivers, whole populations conjured out of the ground—what earlier century had even a
presentiment that such productive forces slumbered in the lap of
social labour?

We see then: the means of production and of exchange, on
whose foundation the bourgeoisie built itself up, were generated in
feudal society. At a certain stage in the development of these means
of production and of exchange, the conditions under which feudal
society produced and exchanged, the feudal organisation of agriculture and manufacturing industry, in one word, the feudal relations

of property became no longer compatible with the already developed productive forces; they became so many fetters. They had to be burst asunder; they were burst asunder.

Into their place stepped free competition, accompanied by a social and political constitution adapted to it, and by the economical and political sway of the bourgeois class.

A similar movement is going on before our own eyes. Modern bourgeois society with its relations of production, of exchange and of property, a society that has conjured up such gigantic means of production and of exchange, is like the sorcerer, who is no longer able to control the powers of the nether world whom he has called up by his spells. For many a decade past the history of industry and commerce is but the history of the revolt of modern productive forces against modern conditions of production, against the property relations that are the conditions for the existence of the bourgeoisie and of its rule. It is enough to mention the commercial crises that by their periodical return put on its trial, each time more threateningly, the existence of the entire bourgeois society. In these crises a great part not only of the existing products, but also of the previously created productive forces, are periodically destroyed. In these crises there breaks out an epidemic that, in all earlier epochs, would have seemed an absurdity—the epidemic of over-production. Society suddenly finds itself put back into a state of momentary barbarism; it appears as if a famine, a universal war of devastation had cut off the supply of every means of subsistence; industry and commerce seem to be destroyed; and why? Because there is too much civilisation, too much means of subsistence, too much industry, too much commerce. The productive forces at the disposal of society no longer tend to further the development of the conditions of bourgeois property; on the contrary, they have become too powerful for these conditions, by which they are fettered, and so soon as they overcome these fetters, they bring disorder into the whole of bourgeois society, endanger the existence of bourgeois property. The conditions of bourgeois society are too narrow to comprise the wealth created by them. And how does the bourgeoisie get over these crises? On the one hand by enforced destruction of a mass of productive forces; on the other, by the conquest of new markets, and by the more thorough exploitation of the old ones. That is to say, by paving the way for more extensive and more destructive crises, and by diminishing the means whereby crises are prevented.

The weapons with which the bourgeoisie felled feudalism to the ground are now turned against the bourgeoisie itself.

But not only has the bourgeoisie forged the weapons that bring death to itself; it has also called into existence the men who are to wield those weapons—the modern working class—the proletarians.

In proportion as the bourgeoisie, *i.e.*, capital, is developed, in the same proportion is the proletariat, the modern working class, developed—a class of labourers, who live only so long as they find work, and who find work only so long as their labour increases capital. These labourers, who must sell themselves piece-meal, are a commodity, like every other article of commerce, and are consequently exposed to all the vicissitudes of competition, to all the fluctuations of the market.

Owing to the extensive use of machinery and to division of labour, the work of the proletarians has lost all individual character, and consequently, all charm for the workman. He becomes an appendage of the machine, and it is only the most simple, most monotonous, and most easily acquired knack, that is required of him. Hence, the cost of production of a workman is restricted, almost entirely, to the means of subsistence that he requires for his maintenance, and for the propagation of his race. But the price of a commodity, and therefore also of labour,[9] is equal to its cost of production. In proportion, therefore, as the repulsiveness of the work increases, the wage decreases. Nay more, in proportion as the use of machinery and division of labour increases, in the same proportion the burden of toil also increases, whether by prolongation of the working hours, by increase of the work exacted in a given time or by increased speed of the machinery, etc.

Modern industry has converted the little workshop of the patriarchal master into the great factory of the industrial capitalist. Masses of labourers, crowded into the factory, are organised like soldiers. As privates of the industrial army they are placed under the command of a perfect hierarchy of officers and sergeants. Not only are they slaves of the bourgeois class, and of the bourgeois State; they are daily and hourly enslaved by the machine, by the over-looker, and, above all, by the individual bourgeois manufacturer himself. The more openly this despotism proclaims gain to be its end and aim, the more petty, the more hateful and the more embittering it is.

The less the skill and exertion of strength implied in manual labour, in other words, the more modern industry becomes developed, the more is the labour of men superseded by that of women. Differences of age and sex have no longer any distinctive social validity for the working class. All are instruments of labour, more or less expensive to use, according to their age and sex.

No sooner is the exploitation of the labourer by the manufacturer, so far, at an end, that he receives his wages in cash, than he is set upon by the other portions of the bourgeoisie, the landlord, the shopkeeper, the pawnbroker, etc.

The lower strata of the middle class—the small tradespeople, shopkeepers, and retired tradesmen generally, the handicraftsmen

9. Subsequently Marx pointed out that the worker sells not his labour but his labour power.

and peasants—all these sink gradually into the proletariat, partly because their diminutive capital does not suffice for the scale on which Modern Industry is carried on, and is swamped in the competition with the large capitalists, partly because their specialised skill is rendered worthless by new methods of production. Thus the proletariat is recruited from all classes of the population.

The proletariat goes through various stages of development. With its birth begins its struggle with the bourgeoisie. At first the contest is carried on by individual labourers, then by the workpeople of a factory, then by the operatives of one trade, in one locality, against the individual bourgeois who directly exploits them. They direct their attacks not against the bourgeois conditions of production, but against the instruments of production themselves; they destroy imported wares that compete with their labour, they smash to pieces machinery, they set factories ablaze, they seek to restore by force the vanished status of the workman of the Middle Ages.

At this stage the labourers still form an incoherent mass scattered over the whole country, and broken up by their mutual competition. If anywhere they unite to form more compact bodies, this is not yet the consequence of their own active union, but of the union of the bourgeoisie, which class, in order to attain its own political ends, is compelled to set the whole proletariat in motion, and is moreover yet, for a time, able to do so. At this stage, therefore, the proletarians do not fight their enemies, but the enemies of their enemies, the remnants of absolute monarchy, the landowners, the non-industrial bourgeois, the petty bourgeoisie. Thus the whole historical movement is concentrated in the hands of the bourgeoisie; every victory so obtained is a victory for the bourgeoisie.

But with the development of industry the proletariat not only increases in number; it becomes concentrated in greater masses, its strength grows, and it feels that strength more. The various interests and conditions of life within the ranks of the proletariat are more and more equalised, in proportion as machinery obliterates all distinctions of labour, and nearly everywhere reduces wages to the same low level. The growing competition among the bourgeois, and the resulting commercial crises, make the wages of the workers ever more fluctuating. The unceasing improvement of machinery, ever more rapidly developing, makes their livelihood more and more precarious; the collisions between individual workmen and individual bourgeois take more and more the character of collisions between two classes. Thereupon the workers begin to form combinations (Trades Unions) against the bourgeois; they club together in order to keep up the rate of wages; they found permanent associations in order to make provision beforehand for these occasional revolts. Here and there the contest breaks out into riots.

Now and then the workers are victorious, but only for a time. The real fruit of their battles lies, not in the immediate result, but in the ever-expanding union of the workers. This union is helped on by the improved means of communication that are created by modern industry and that place the workers of different localities in contact with one another. It was just this contact that was needed to centralise the numerous local struggles, all of the same character, into one national struggle between classes. But every class struggle is a political struggle. And that union, to attain which the burghers of the Middle Ages, with their miserable highways, required centuries, the modern proletarians, thanks to railways, achieve in a few years.

This organisation of the proletarians into a class, and consequently into a political party, is continually being upset again by the competition between the workers themselves. But it ever rises up again, stronger, firmer, mightier. It compels legislative recognition of particular interests of the workers, by taking advantage of the divisions among the bourgeoisie itself. Thus the ten-hours' bill in England was carried.

Altogether collisions between the classes of the old society further, in many ways, the course of development of the proletariat. The bourgeoisie finds itself involved in a constant battle. At first with the aristocracy; later on, with those portions of the bourgeoisie itself, whose interests have become antagonistic to the progress of industry; at all times, with the bourgeoisie of foreign countries. In all these battles it sees itself compelled to appeal to the proletariat, to ask for its help, and thus, to drag it into the political arena. The bourgeoisie itself, therefore, supplies the proletariat with its own elements of political and general education, in other words, it furnishes the proletariat with weapons for fighting the bourgeoisie.

Further, as we have already seen, entire sections of the ruling classes are, by the advance of industry, precipitated into the proletariat, or are at least threatened in their conditions of existence. These also supply the proletariat with fresh elements of enlightenment and progress.

Finally, in times when the class struggle nears the decisive hour, the process of dissolution going on within the ruling class, in fact within the whole range of society, assumes such a violent, glaring character, that a small section of the ruling class cuts itself adrift, and joins the revolutionary class, the class that holds the future in its hands. Just as, therefore, at an earlier period, a section of the nobility went over to the bourgeoisie, so now a portion of the bourgeoisie goes over to the proletariat, and in particular, a portion of the bourgeois ideologists, who have raised themselves to the level of comprehending theoretically the historical movement as a whole.

Of all the classes that stand face to face with the bourgeoisie today, the proletariat alone is a really revolutionary class. The other classes decay and finally disappear in the face of Modern Industry; the proletariat is its special and essential product.

The lower middle class, the small manufacturer, the shopkeeper, the artisan, the peasant, all these fight against the bourgeoisie, to save from extinction their existence as fractions of the middle class. They are therefore not revolutionary, but conservative. Nay more, they are reactionary, for they try to roll back the wheel of history. If by chance they are revolutionary, they are so only in view of their impending transfer into the proletariat, they thus defend not their present, but their future interests, they desert their own standpoint to place themselves at that of the proletariat.

The "dangerous class," the social scum, that passively rotting mass thrown off by the lowest layers of old society, may, here and there, be swept into the movement by a proletarian revolution; its conditions of life, however, prepare it far more for the part of a bribed tool of reactionary intrigue.

In the conditions of the proletariat, those of old society at large are already virtually swamped. The proletarian is without property; his relation to his wife and children has no longer anything in common with the bourgeois family-relations; modern industrial labour, modern subjection to capital, the same in England as in France, in America as in Germany, has stripped him of every trace of national character. Law, morality, religion, are to him so many bourgeois prejudices, behind which lurk in ambush just as many bourgeois interests.

All the preceding classes that got the upper hand, sought to fortify their already acquired status by subjecting society at large to their conditions of appropriation. The proletarians cannot become masters of the productive forces of society, except by abolishing their own previous mode of appropriation, and thereby also every other previous mode of appropriation. They have nothing of their own to secure and to fortify; their mission is to destroy all previous securities for, and insurances of, individual property.

All previous historical movements were movements of minorities, or in the interests of minorities. The proletarian movement is the self-conscious, independent movement of the immense majority, in the interests of the immense majority. The proletariat, the lowest stratum of our present society, cannot stir, cannot raise itself up, without the whole superincumbent strata of official society being sprung into the air.

Though not in substance, yet in form, the struggle of the proletariat with the bourgeoisie is at first a national struggle. The proletariat of each country must, of course, first of all settle matters with its own bourgeoisie.

In depicting the most general phases of the development of the proletariat, we traced the more or less veiled civil war, raging within existing society, up to the point where that war breaks out into open revolution, and where the violent overthrow of the bourgeoisie lays the foundation for the sway of the proletariat.

Hitherto, every form of society has been based, as we have already seen, on the antagonism of oppressing and oppressed classes. But in order to oppress a class, certain conditions must be assured to it under which it can, at least, continue its slavish existence. The serf, in the period of serfdom, raised himself to membership in the commune, just as the petty bourgeois, under the yoke of feudal absolutism, managed to develop into a bourgeois. The modern labourer, on the contrary, instead of rising with the progress of industry, sinks deeper and deeper below the conditions of existence of his own class. He becomes a pauper, and pauperism develops more rapidly than population and wealth. And here it becomes evident, that the bourgeoisie is unfit any longer to be the ruling class in society, and to impose its conditions of existence upon society as an over-riding law. It is unfit to rule because it is incompetent to assure an existence to its slave within his slavery, because it cannot help letting him sink into such a state, that it has to feed him, instead of being fed by him. Society can no longer live under this bourgeoisie, in other words, its existence is no longer compatible with society.

The essential condition for the existence, and for the sway of the bourgeois class, is the formation and augmentation of capital; the condition for capital is wage-labour. Wage-labour rests exclusively on competition between the labourers. The advance of industry, whose involuntary promoter is the bourgeoisie, replaces the isolation of the labourers, due to competition, by their revolutionary combination, due to association. The development of Modern Industry, therefore, cuts from under its feet the very foundation on which the bourgeoisie produces and appropriates products. What the bourgeoisie, therefore, produces, above all, is its own grave-diggers. Its fall and the victory of the proletariat are equally inevitable.

II. Proletarians and Communists

In what relation do the Communists stand to the proletarians as a whole?

The Communists do not form a separate party opposed to other working-class parties.

They have no interests separate and apart from those of the proletariat as a whole.

They do not set up any sectarian principles of their own, by which to shape and mould the proletarian movement.

The Communists are distinguished from the other working-class parties by this only: (1) In the national struggles of the proletarians of the different countries, they point out and bring to the front the common interests of the entire proletariat, independently of all nationality. (2) In the various stages of development which the struggle of the working class against the bourgoisie has to pass through, they always and everywhere represent the interests of the movement as a whole.

The Communists, therefore, are on the one hand, practically, the most advanced and resolute section of the working-class parties of every country, that section which pushes forward all others; on the other hand, theoretically, they have over the great mass of the proletariat the advantage of clearly understanding the line of march, the conditions, and the ultimate general results of the proletarian movement.

The immediate aim of the Communists is the same as that of all the other proletarian parties: formation of the proletariat into a class, overthrow of the bourgeois supremacy, conquest of political power by the proletariat.

The theoretical conclusions of the Communists are in no way based on ideas or principles that have been invented, or discovered, by this or that would-be universal reformer.

They merely express, in general terms, actual relations springing from an existing class struggle, from a historical movement going on under our very eyes. The abolition of existing property relations is not at all a distinctive feature of Communism.

All property relations in the past have continually been subject to historical change consequent upon the change in historical conditions.

The French Revolution, for example, abolished feudal property in favour of bourgeois property.

The distinguishing feature of Communism is not the abolition of property generally, but the abolition of bourgeois property. But modern bourgeois private property is the final and most complete expression of the system of producing and appropriating products, that is based on class antagonisms, on the exploitation of the many by the few.

In this sense, the theory of the Communists may be summed up in the single sentence: Abolition of private property.

We Communists have been reproached with the desire of abolishing the right of personally acquiring property as the fruit of a man's own labour, which property is alleged to be the groundwork of all personal freedom, activity and independence.

Hard-won, self-acquired, self-earned property! Do you mean the property of the petty artisan and of the small peasant, a form of property that preceded the bourgeois form? There is no need to abolish that; the development of industry has to a great extent already destroyed it, and is still destroying it daily.

Or do you mean modern bourgeois private property?

But does wage-labour create any property for the labourer? Not a bit. It creates capital, *i.e.*, that kind of property which exploits wage-labour, and which cannot increase except upon condition of begetting a new supply of wage-labour for fresh exploitation. Property, in its present form, is based on the antagonism of capital and wage-labour. Let us examine both sides of this antagonism.

To be a capitalist, is to have not only a purely personal, but a social *status* in production. Capital is a collective product, and only by the united action of many members, nay, in the last resort, only by the united action of all members of society, can it be set in motion.

Capital is, therefore, not a personal, it is a social power.

When, therefore, capital is converted into common property, into the property of all members of society, personal property is not thereby transformed into social property. It is only the social character of the property that is changed. It loses its class-character.

Let us now take wage-labour.

The average price of wage-labour is the minimum wage, *i.e.*, that quantum of the means of subsistence, which is absolutely requisite to keep the labourer in bare existence as a labourer. What, therefore, the wage-labourer appropriates by means of his labour, merely suffices to prolong and reproduce a bare existence. We by no means intend to abolish this personal appropriation of the products of labour, an appropriation that is made for the maintenance and reproduction of human life, and that leaves no surplus wherewith to command the labour of others. All that we want to do away with, is the miserable character of this appropriation, under which the labourer lives merely to increase capital, and is allowed to live only in so far as the interest of the ruling class requires it.

In bourgeois society, living labour is but a means to increase accumulated labour. In Communist society, accumulated labour is but a means to widen, to enrich, to promote the existence of the labourer.

In bourgeois society, therefore, the past dominates the present; in Communist society, the present dominates the past. In bourgeois society capital is independent and has individuality, while the living person is dependent and has no individuality.

And the abolition of this state of things is called by the bourgeois, abolition of individuality and freedom! And rightly so. The abolition of bourgeois individuality, bourgeois independence, and bourgeois freedom is undoubtedly aimed at.

By freedom is meant, under the present bourgeois conditions of production, free trade, free selling and buying.

But if selling and buying disappears, free selling and buying disappears also. This talk about free selling and buying, and all the other "brave words" of our bourgeoisie about freedom in general, have a meaning, if any, only in contrast with restricted selling and buying, with the fettered traders of the Middle Ages, but have no meaning when opposed to the Communistic abolition of buying and selling, of the bourgeois conditions of production, and of the bourgeoisie itself.

You are horrified at our intending to do away with private property. But in your existing society, private property is already done away with for nine-tenths of the population; its existence for the few is solely due to its non-existence in the hands of those nine-tenths. You reproach us, therefore, with intending to do away with a form of property, the necessary condition for whose existence is the non-existence of any property for the immense majority of society.

In one word, you reproach us with intending to do away with your property. Precisely so; that is just what we intend.

From the moment when labour can no longer be converted into capital, money, or rent, into a social power capable of being monopolised, *i.e.*, from the moment when individual property can no longer be transformed into bourgeois property, into capital, from that moment, you say, individuality vanishes.

You must, therefore, confess that by "individual" you mean no other person than the bourgeois, than the middle-class owner of property. This person must, indeed, be swept out of the way, and made impossible.

Communism deprives no man of the power to appropriate the products of society; all that it does is to deprive him of the power to subjugate the labour of others by means of such appropriation.

It has been objected that upon the abolition of private property all work will cease, and universal laziness will overtake us.

According to this, bourgeois society ought long ago to have gone to the dogs through sheer idleness; for those of its members who work, acquire nothing, and those who acquire anything, do not work. The whole of this objection is but another expression of the tautology: that there can no longer be any wage-labour when there is no longer any capital.

All objections urged against the Communistic mode of producing and appropriating material products, have, in the same way, been urged against the Communistic modes of producing and appropriating intellectual products. Just as, to the bourgeois, the disappearance of class property is the disappearance of production itself, so the disappearance of class culture is to him identical with the disappearance of all culture.

That culture, the loss of which he laments, is, for the enormous majority, a mere training to act as a machine.

But don't wrangle with us so long as you apply, to our intended abolition of bourgeois property, the standard of your bourgeois notions of freedom, culture, law, &c. Your very ideas are but the outgrowth of the conditions of your bourgeois production and bourgeois property, just as your jurisprudence is but the will of your class made into a law for all, a will, whose essential character and direction are determined by the economical conditions of existence of your class.

The selfish misconception that induces you to transform into eternal laws of nature and of reason, the social forms springing from your present mode of production and form of property—historical relations that rise and disappear in the progress of production—this misconception you share with every ruling class that has preceded you. What you see clearly in the case of ancient property, what you admit in the case of feudal property, you are of course forbidden to admit in the case of your own bourgeois form of property.

Abolition of the family! Even the most radical flare up at this infamous proposal of the Communists.

On what foundation is the present family, the bourgeois family, based? On capital, on private gain. In its completely developed form this family exists only among the bourgeoisie. But this state of things finds its complement in the practical absence of the family among the proletarians, and in public prostitution.

The bourgeois family will vanish as a matter of course when its complement vanishes, and both will vanish with the vanishing of capital.

Do you charge us with wanting to stop the exploitation of children by their parents? To this crime we plead guilty.

But, you will say, we destroy the most hallowed of relations, when we replace home education by social.

And your education! Is not that also social, and determined by the social conditions under which you educate, by the intervention, direct or indirect, of society, by means of schools, &c.? The Communists have not invented the intervention of society in education; they do but seek to alter the character of that intervention, and to rescue education from the influence of the ruling class.

The bourgeois clap-trap about the family and education, about the hallowed co-relation of parent and child, becomes all the more disgusting, the more, by the action of Modern Industry, all family ties among the proletarians are torn asunder, and their children transformed into simple articles of commerce and instruments of labour.

But you Communists would introduce community of women, screams the whole bourgeoisie in chorus.

The bourgeois sees in his wife a mere instrument of production. He hears that the instruments of production are to be exploited in common, and, naturally, can come to no other conclusion than that the lot of being common to all will likewise fall to the women.

He has not even a suspicion that the real point aimed at is to do away with the status of women as mere instruments of production.

For the rest, nothing is more ridiculous than the virtuous indignation of our bourgeois at the community of women which, they pretend, is to be openly and officially established by the Communists. The Communists have no need to introduce community of women; it has existed almost from time immemorial.

Our bourgeois, not content with having the wives and daughters of their proletarians at their disposal, not to speak of common prostitutes, take the greatest pleasure in seducing each other's wives.

Bourgeois marriage is in reality a system of wives in common and thus, at the most, what the Communists might possibly be reproached with, is that they desire to introduce, in substitution for a hypocritically concealed, an openly legalised community of women. For the rest, it is self-evident that the abolition of the present system of production must bring with it the abolition of the community of women springing from that system, *i.e.*, of prostitution both public and private.

The Communists are further reproached with desiring to abolish countries and nationality.

The working men have no country. We cannot take from them what they have not got. Since the proletariat must first of all acquire political supremacy, must rise to be the leading class of the nation, must constitute itself *the* nation, it is, so far, itself national, though not in the bourgeois sense of the word.

National differences and antagonisms between peoples are daily more and more vanishing, owing to the development of the bourgeoisie, to freedom of commerce, to the world-market, to uniformity in the mode of production and in the conditions of life corresponding thereto.

The supremacy of the proletariat will cause them to vanish still faster. United action, of the leading civilised countries at least, is one of the first conditions for the emancipation of the proletariat.

In proportion as the exploitation of one individual by another is put an end to, the exploitation of one nation by another will also be put an end to. In proportion as the antagonism between classes within the nation vanishes, the hostility of one nation to another will come to an end.

The charges against Communism made from a religious, a philosophical, and, generally, from an ideological standpoint, are not deserving of serious examination.

Does it require deep intuition to comprehend that man's ideas, views and conceptions, in one word, man's consciousness, changes with every change in the conditions of his material existence, in his social relations and in his social life?

What else does the history of ideas prove, than that intellectual production changes its character in proportion as material production is changed? The ruling ideas of each age have ever been the ideas of its ruling class.

When people speak of ideas that revolutionise society, they do but express the fact, that within the old society, the elements of a new one have been created, and that the dissolution of the old ideas keeps even pace with the dissolution of the old conditions of existence.

When the ancient world was in its last throes, the ancient religions were overcome by Christianity. When Christian ideas succumbed in the 18th century to rationalist ideas, feudal society fought its death battle with the then revolutionary bourgeoisie. The ideas of religious liberty and freedom of conscience merely gave expression to the sway of free competition within the domain of knowledge.

"Undoubtedly," it will be said, "religious, moral, philosophical and juridical ideas have been modified in the course of historical development. But religion, morality, philosophy, political science, and law, constantly survived this change."

"There are, besides, eternal truths, such as Freedom, Justice, etc., that are common to all states of society. But Communism abolishes eternal truths, it abolishes all religion, and all morality, instead of constituting them on a new basis; it therefore acts in contradiction to all past historical experience."

What does this accusation reduce itself to? The history of all past society has consisted in the development of class antagonisms, antagonisms that assumed different forms at different epochs.

But whatever form they may have taken, one fact is common to all past ages, *viz.*, the exploitation of one part of society by the other. No wonder, then, that the social consciousness of past ages, despite all the multiplicity and variety it displays, moves within certain common forms, or general ideas, which cannot completely vanish except with the total disappearance of class antagonisms.

The Communist revolution is the most radical rupture with traditional property relations; no wonder that its development involves the most radical rupture with traditional ideas.

But let us have done with the bourgeois objections to Communism.

We have seen above, that the first step in the revolution by the working class, is to raise the proletariat to the position of ruling class, to win the battle of democracy.

The proletariat will use its political supremacy to wrest, by degrees, all capital from the bourgeoisie, to centralise all instruments of production in the hands of the State, *i.e.*, of the proletariat organised as the ruling class; and to increase the total of productive forces as rapidly as possible.

Of course, in the beginning, this cannot be effected except by means of despotic inroads on the rights of property, and on the conditions of bourgeois production; by means of measures, therefore, which appear economically insufficient and untenable, but which, in the course of the movement, outstrip themselves, necessitate further inroads upon the old social order, and are unavoidable as a means of entirely revolutionising the mode of production.

These measures will of course be different in different countries.

Nevertheless in the most advanced countries, the following will be pretty generally applicable.

1. Abolition of property in land and application of all rents of land to public purposes.

2. A heavy progressive or graduated income tax.

3. Abolition of all right of inheritance.

4. Confiscation of the property of all emigrants and rebels.

5. Centralisation of credit in the hands of the State, by means of a national bank with State capital and an exclusive monopoly.

6. Centralisation of the means of communication and transport in the hands of the State.

7. Extension of factories and instruments of production owned by the State; the bringing into cultivation of waste-lands, and the improvement of the soil generally in accordance with a common plan.

8. Equal liability of all to labour. Establishment of industrial armies, especially for agriculture.

9. Combination of agriculture with manufacturing industries; gradual abolition of the distinction between town and country, by a more equable distribution of the population over the country.

10. Free education for all children in public schools. Abolition of children's factory labour in its present form. Combination of education with industrial production, &c., &c.

When, in the course of development, class distinctions have disappeared, and all production has been concentrated in the hands of a vast association of the whole nation, the public power will lose its political character. Political power, properly so called, is merely the organised power of one class for oppressing another. If the proletariat during its contest with the bourgeoisie is compelled, by the force of circumstances, to organise itself as a class, if, by means of a revolution, it makes itself the ruling class, and, as such, sweeps away by force the old conditions of production, then it will, along with these conditions, have swept away the conditions for the existence of class antagonisms and of classes generally, and will thereby have abolished its own supremacy as a class.

In place of the old bourgeois society, with its classes and class antagonisms, we shall have an association, in which the free development of each is the condition for the free development of all.

III. Socialist and Communist Literature

1. REACTIONARY SOCIALISM

A. *Feudal Socialism*

Owing to their historical position, it became the vocation of the aristocracies of France and England to write pamphlets against modern bourgeois society. In the French revolution of July 1830, and in the English reform agitation, these aristocracies again succumbed to the hateful upstart. Thenceforth, a serious political contest was altogether out of the question. A literary battle alone remained possible. But even in the domain of literature the old cries of the restoration period[1] had become impossible.

In order to arouse sympathy, the aristocracy were obliged to lose sight, apparently, of their own interests, and to formulate their indictment against the bourgeoisie in the interest of the exploited working class alone. Thus the aristocracy took their revenge by singing lampoons on their new master, and whispering in his ears sinister prophecies of coming catastrophe.

In this way arose Feudal Socialism: half lamentation, half lampoon; half echo of the past, half menace of the future; at times, by its bitter, witty and incisive criticism, striking the bourgeoisie to the very heart's core; but always ludicrous in its effect, through total incapacity to comprehend the march of modern history.

The aristocracy, in order to rally the people to them, waved the proletarian alms-bag in front for a banner. But the people, so often as it joined them, saw on their hindquarters the old feudal coats of arms, and deserted with loud and irreverent laughter.

One section of the French Legitimists[2] and "Young England"[3] exhibited this spectacle.

1. Not the English Restoration 1660 to 1689, but the French Restoration 1814 to 1830. [*Engels, English edition of 1888*]
2. *The Legitimists*: The party of the noble landowners, who advocated the restoration of the Bourbon dynasty.
3. *"Young England"*: A group of British Conservatives—aristocrats and men of politics and literature—formed about 1842. Prominent among them were Disraeli, Thomas Carlyle and others.

In pointing out that their mode of exploitation was different to that of the bourgeoisie, the feudalists forget that they exploited under circumstances and conditions that were quite different, and that are now antiquated. In showing that, under their rule, the modern proletariat never existed, they forget that the modern bourgeoisie is the necessary offspring of their own form of society.

For the rest, so little do they conceal the reactionary character of their criticism that their chief accusation against the bourgeoisie amounts to this, that under the bourgeois *régime* a class is being developed, which is destined to cut up root and branch the old order of society.

What they upbraid the bourgeoisie with is not so much that it creates a proletariat, as that it creates a *revolutionary* proletariat.

In political practice, therefore, they join in all coercive measures against the working class; and in ordinary life, despite their high falutin phrases, they stoop to pick up the golden apples dropped from the tree of industry, and to barter truth, love, and honour for traffic in wool, beetroot-sugar, and potato spirits.[4]

As the parson has ever gone hand in hand with the landlord, so has Clerical Socialism with Feudal Socialism.

Nothing is easier than to give Christian asceticism a Socialist tinge. Has not Christianity declaimed against private property, against marriage, against the State? Has it not preached in the place of these, charity and poverty, celibacy and mortification of the flesh, monastic life and Mother Church? Christian Socialism is but the holy water with which the priest consecrates the heart-burnings of the aristocrat.

B. Petty-Bourgeois Socialism

The feudal aristocracy was not the only class that was ruined by the bourgeoisie, not the only class whose conditions of existence pined and perished in the atmosphere of modern bourgeois society. The mediaeval burgesses and the small peasant proprietors were the precursors of the modern bourgeoisie. In those countries which are but little developed, industrially and commercially, these two classes still vegetate side by side with the rising bourgeoisie.

In countries where modern civilisation has become fully developed, a new class of petty bourgeois has been formed, fluctuating between proletariat and bourgeoisie and ever renewing itself as a

4. This applies chiefly to Germany where the landed aristocracy and squirearchy have large portions of their estates cultivated for their own account by stewards, and are, moreover, extensive beetroot-sugar manufacturers and distillers of potato spirits. The wealthier British aristocracy are, as yet, rather above that; but they, too, know how to make up for declining rents by lending their names to floaters of more or less shady joint-stock companies. [*Engels, English edition of 1888*]

supplementary part of bourgeois society. The individual members of this class, however, are being constantly hurled down into the proletariat by the action of competition, and, as modern industry develops, they even see the moment approaching when they will completely disappear as an independent section of modern society, to be replaced, in manufactures, agriculture and commerce, by overlookers, bailiffs and shopmen.

In countries like France, where the peasants constitute far more than half of the population, it was natural that writers who sided with the proletariat against the bourgeoisie, should use, in their criticism of the bourgeois *régime*, the standard of the peasant and petty bourgeois, and from the standpoint of these intermediate classes should take up the cudgels for the working class. Thus arose petty-bourgeois Socialism. Sismondi was the head of this school, not only in France but also in England.

This school of Socialism dissected with great acuteness the contradictions in the conditions of modern production. It laid bare the hypocritical apologies of economists. It proved, incontrovertibly, the disastrous effects of machinery and division of labour; the concentration of capital and land in a few hands; overproduction and crises; it pointed out the inevitable ruin of the petty bourgeois and peasant, the misery of the proletariat, the anarchy in production, the crying inequalities in the distribution of wealth, the industrial war of extermination between nations, the dissolution of old moral bonds, of the old family relations, of the old nationalities.

In its positive aims, however, this form of Socialism aspires either to restoring the old means of production and of exchange, and with them the old property relations, and the old society, or to cramping the modern means of production and of exchange, within the framework of the old property relations that have been, and were bound to be, exploded by those means. In either case, it is both reactionary and Utopian.

Its last words are: corporate guilds for manufacture, patriarchal relations in agriculture.

Ultimately, when stubborn historical facts had dispersed all intoxicating effects of self-deception, this form of Socialism ended in a miserable fit of the blues.

C. German, or "True," Socialism

The Socialist and Communist literature of France, a literature that originated under the pressure of a bourgeoisie in power, and that was the expression of the struggle against this power, was introduced into Germany at a time when the bourgeoisie, in that country, had just begun its contest with feudal absolutism.

German philosophers, would-be philosophers, and *beaux esprits*, eagerly seized on this literature, only forgetting, that when these writings immigrated from France into Germany, French social conditions had not immigrated along with them. In contact with German social conditions, this French literature lost all its immediate practical significance, and assumed a purely literary aspect. Thus, to the German philosophers of the eighteenth century, the demands of the first French Revolution were nothing more than the demands of "Practical Reason" in general, and the utterance of the will of the revolutionary French bourgeoisie signified in their eyes the law of pure Will, of Will as it was bound to be, of true human Will generally.

The work of the German *literati* consisted solely in bringing the new French ideas into harmony with their ancient philosophical conscience, or rather, in annexing the French ideas without deserting their own philosophic point of view.

This annexation took place in the same way in which a foreign language is appropriated, namely, by translation.

It is well known how the monks wrote silly lives of Catholic Saints *over* the manuscripts on which the classical works of ancient heathendom had been written. The German *literati* reversed this process with the profane French literature. They wrote their philosophical nonsense beneath the French original. For instance, beneath the French criticism of the economic functions of money, they wrote "Alienation of Humanity," and beneath the French criticism of the bourgeois State they wrote "dethronement of the Category of the General," and so forth.

The introduction of these philosophical phrases at the back of the French historical criticisms they dubbed "Philosophy of Action," "True Socialism," "German Science of Socialism," "Philosophical Foundation of Socialism," and so on.

The French Socialist and Communist literature was thus completely emasculated. And, since it ceased in the hands of the German to express the struggle of one class with the other, he felt conscious of having overcome "French one-sidedness" and of representing, not true requirements, but the requirements of truth; not the interests of the proletariat, but the interests of Human Nature, of Man in general, who belongs to no class, has no reality, who exists only in the misty realm of philosophical fantasy.

This German Socialism, which took its schoolboy task so seriously and solemnly, and extolled its poor stock-in-trade in such mountebank fashion, meanwhile gradually lost its pedantic innocence.

The fight of the German, and especially, of the Prussian bourgeoisie, against feudal aristocracy and absolute monarchy, in other words, the liberal movement, became more earnest.

By this, the long wished-for opportunity was offered to "True" Socialism of confronting the political movement with the Socialist demands, of hurling the traditional anathemas against liberalism, against representative government, against bourgeois competition, bourgeois freedom of the press, bourgeois legislation, bourgeois liberty and equality, and of preaching to the masses that they had nothing to gain, and everything to lose, by this bourgeois movement. German Socialism forgot, in the nick of time, that the French criticism, whose silly echo it was, presupposed the existence of modern bourgeois society, with its corresponding economic conditions of existence, and the political constitution adapted thereto, the very things whose attainment was the object of the pending struggle in Germany.

To the absolute governments, with their following of parsons, professors, country squires and officials, it served as a welcome scarecrow against the threatening bourgeoisie.

It was a sweet finish after the bitter pills of floggings and bullets with which these same governments, just at that time, dosed the German working-class risings.

While this "True" Socialism thus served the governments as a weapon for fighting the German bourgeoisie, it, at the same time, directly represented a reactionary interest, the interest of the German Philistines. In Germany the *petty-bourgeois* class, a relic of the sixteenth century, and since then constantly cropping up again under various forms, is the real social basis of the existing state of things.

To preserve this class is to preserve the existing state of things in Germany. The industrial and political supremacy of the bourgeoisie threatens it with certain destruction; on the one hand, from the concentration of capital; on the other, from the rise of a revolutionary proletariat. "True" Socialism appeared to kill these two birds with one stone. It spread like an epidemic.

The robe of speculative cobwebs, embroidered with flowers of rhetoric, steeped in the dew of sickly sentiment, this transcendental robe in which the German Socialists wrapped their sorry "eternal truths," all skin and bone, served to wonderfully increase the sale of their goods amongst such a public.

And on its part, German Socialism recognised, more and more, its own calling as the bombastic representative of the petty-bourgeois Philistine.

It proclaimed the German nation to be the model nation, and the German petty Philistine to be the typical man. To every villainous meanness of this model man it gave a hidden, higher, Socialistic interpretation, the exact contrary of its real character. It went to the extreme length of directly opposing the "brutally destructive" tendency of Communism, and of proclaiming its supreme and impartial contempt of all class struggles. With very few exceptions, all the so-called Socialist and Communist publications that now (1847) circulate in Germany belong to the domain of this foul and enervating literature.[5]

2. CONSERVATIVE, OR BOURGEOIS, SOCIALISM

A part of the bourgeoisie is desirous of redressing social grievances, in order to secure the continued existence of bourgeois society.

To this section belong economists, philanthropists, humanitarians, improvers of the condition of the working class, organisers of charity, members of societies for the prevention of cruelty to animals, temperance fanatics, hole-and-corner reformers of every imaginable kind. This form of Socialism has, moreover, been worked out into complete systems.

We may site Proudhon's *Philosophie de la Misère* as an example of this form.

The Socialistic bourgeois want all the advantages of modern social conditions without the struggles and dangers necessarily resulting therefrom. They desire the existing state of society minus its revolutionary and disintegrating elements. They wish for a bourgeoisie without a proletariat. The bourgeoisie naturally conceives the world in which it is supreme to be the best; and bourgeois Socialism develops this comfortable conception into various more or less complete systems. In requiring the proletariat to carry out such a system, and thereby to march straightway into the social New Jerusalem, it but requires in reality, that the proletariat should remain within the bounds of existing society, but should cast away all its hateful ideas concerning the bourgeoisie.

A second and more practical, but less systematic, form of this Socialism sought to depreciate every revolutionary movement in the eyes of the working class, by showing that no mere political reform, but only a change in the material conditions of existence, in economical relations, could be of any advantage to them. By changes in the material conditions of existence, this form of Socialism, however, by no means understands abolition of the bourgeois relations of production, an abolition that can be effected only by a revolution, but administrative reforms, based on the continued existence of these relations; reforms, therefore, that in no respect affect the

5. The revolutionary storm of 1848 swept away this whole shabby tendency and cured its protagonists of the desire to dabble further in Socialism. The chief representative and classical type of this tendency is Herr Karl Grün. [*Engels, German edition of 1890*]

relations between capital and labour, but, at the best, lessen the cost, and simplify the administrative work, of bourgeois government.

Bourgeois Socialism attains adequate expression, when, and only when, it becomes a mere figure of speech.

Free trade: for the benefit of the working class. Protective duties: for the benefit of the working class. Prison Reform: for the benefit of the working class. This is the last word and the only seriously meant word of bourgeois Socialism.

It is summed up in the phrase: the bourgeois is a bourgeois—for the benefit of the working class.

3. CRITICAL-UTOPIAN SOCIALISM AND COMMUNISM

We do not here refer to that literature which, in every great modern revolution, has always given voice to the demands of the proletariat, such as the writings of Babeuf and others.

The first direct attempts of the proletariat to attain its own ends, made in times of universal excitement, when feudal society was being overthrown, these attempts necessarily failed, owing to the then undeveloped state of the proletariat, as well as to the absence of the economic conditions for its emancipation, conditions that had yet to be produced, and could be produced by the impending bourgeois epoch alone. The revolutionary literature that accompanied these first movements of the proletariat had necessarily a reactionary character. It inculcated universal asceticism and social levelling in its crudest form.

The Socialist and Communist systems properly so called, those of Saint-Simon, Fourier, Owen and others, spring into existence in the early undeveloped period, described above, of the struggle between proletariat and bourgeoisie (see Section I. Bourgeois and Proletarians).

The founders of these systems see, indeed, the class antagonisms, as well as the action of the decomposing elements, in the prevailing form of society. But the proletariat, as yet in its infancy, offers to them the spectacle of a class without any historical initiative or any independent political movement.

Since the development of class antagonism keeps even pace with the development of industry, the economic situation, as they find it, does not as yet offer to them the material conditions for the emancipation of the proletariat. They therefore search after a new social science, after new social laws, that are to create these conditions.

Historical action is to yield to their personal inventive action, historically created conditions of emancipation to fantastic ones, and the gradual, spontaneous class-organisation of the proletariat to the organisation of society specially contrived by these inventors. Future history resolves itself, in their eyes, into the propaganda and the practical carrying out of their social plans.

In the formation of their plans they are conscious of caring chiefly for the interests of the working class, as being the most suffering class. Only from the point of view of being the most suffering class does the proletariat exist for them.

The undeveloped state of the class struggle, as well as their own surroundings, causes Socialists of this kind to consider themselves far superior to all class antagonisms. They want to improve the condition of every member of society, even that of the most favoured. Hence, they habitually appeal to society at large, without distinction of class; nay, by preference, to the ruling class. For how can people, when once they understand their system, fail to see in it the best possible plan of the best possible state of society?

Hence, they reject all political, and especially all revolutionary, action; they wish to attain their ends by peaceful means, and endeavour, by small experiments, necessarily doomed to failure, and by the force of example, to pave the way for the new social Gospel.

Such fantastic pictures of future society, painted at a time when the proletariat is still in a very undeveloped state and has but a fantastic conception of its own position correspond with the first instinctive yearnings of that class for a general reconstruction of society.

But these Socialist and Communist publications contain also a critical element. They attack every principle of existing society. Hence they are full of the most valuable materials for the enlightenment of the working class. The practical measures proposed in them —such as the abolition of the distinction between town and country, of the family, of the carrying on of industries for the account of private individuals, and of the wage system, the proclamation of social harmony, the conversion of the functions of the State into a mere superintendence of production, all these proposals, point solely to the disappearance of class antagonisms which were, at that time, only just cropping up, and which, in these publications, are recognised in their earliest, indistinct and undefined forms only. These proposals, therefore, are of a purely Utopian character.

The significance of Critical-Utopian Socialism and Communism bears an inverse relation to historical development. In proportion as the modern class struggle develops and takes definite shape, this fantastic standing apart from the contest, these fantastic attacks on it, lose all practical value and all theoretical justification. Therefore, although the originators of these systems were, in many respects, revolutionary, their disciples have, in every case, formed mere reactionary sects. They hold fast by the original views of their masters, in opposition to the progressive historical development of the proletariat. They, therefore, endeavour, and that consistently, to deaden the class struggle and to reconcile the class antagonisms. They still dream of experimental realisation of their social Utopias, of founding isolated *"phalanstères,"* of establishing "Home Colonies," of setting up a "Little Icaria"[6]—duodecimo editions of the New Jerusalem—and to realise all these castles in the air, they are compelled to appeal to the feelings and purses of the bourgeois. By degrees they sink into the category of the reactionary conservative Socialists depicted above, differing from these only by more systematic pedantry, and by their fanatical and superstitious belief in the miraculous effects of their social science.

They, therefore, violently oppose all political action on the part of the working class; such action, according to them, can only result from blind unbelief in the new Gospel.

The Owenites in England, and the Fourierists in France, respectively, oppose the Chartists and the *Réformistes*.[7]

IV. Position of the Communists in Relation to the Various Existing Opposition Parties

Section II has made clear the relations of the Communists to the existing working-class parties, such as the Chartists in England and the Agrarian Reformers in America.

The Communists fight for the attainment of the immediate aims, for the enforcement of the momentary interests of the working class; but in the movement of the present, they also represent and take care of the future of that movement. In France the Communists ally themselves with the Social-Democrats,[8] against the conservative and radical bourgeoisie, reserving, however, the right to

6. *Phalanstères* were Socialist colonies on the plan of Charles Fourier; *Icaria* was the name given by Cabet to his Utopia and, later on, to his American Communist colony. [*Engels, English edition of 1888*]

"Home colonies" were what Owen called his Communist model societies. *Phalanstères* was the name of the public palaces planned by Fourier. *Icaria* was the name given to the Utopian land of fancy, whose Communist institutions Cabet portrayed. [*Engels, German edition of 1890*]

7. This refers to the adherents of the newspaper *La Réforme*, which was published in Paris from 1843 to 1850.

8. The party then represented in Parliament by Ledru-Rollin, in literature by Louis Blanc, in the daily press by the *Réforme*. The name of Social-Democracy signified, with these its inventors, a section of the Democratic or Republican party more or less tinged with Socialism. [*Engels, English edition of 1888*]

The party in France which at that time called itself Socialist-Democratic was represented in political life by Ledru-Rollin and in literature by Louis Blanc; thus it differed immeasurably from present-day German Social-Democracy. [*Engels, German edition of 1890*] take up a critical position in regard to phrases and illusions traditionally handed down from the great Revolution.

In Switzerland they support the Radicals, without losing sight of the fact that this party consists of antagonistic elements, partly of Democratic Socialists, in the French sense, partly of radical bourgeois.

In Poland they support the party that insists on an agrarian revolution as the prime condition for national emancipation, that party which fomented the insurrection of Cracow in 1846.

In Germany they fight with the bourgeoisie whenever it acts in a revolutionary way, against the absolute monarchy, the feudal squirearchy, and the petty bourgeoisie.[9]

But they never cease, for a single instant, to instil into the working class the clearest possible recognition of the hostile antagonism between bourgeoisie and proletariat, in order that the German workers may straightway use, as so many weapons against the bourgeoisie, the social and political conditions that the bourgeoisie must necessarily introduce along with its supremacy, and in order that, after the fall of the reactionary classes in Germany, the fight against the bourgeoisie itself may immediately begin.

The Communists turn their attention chiefly to Germany, because that country is on the eve of a bourgeois revolution that is bound to be carried out under more advanced conditions of European civilisation, and with a much more developed proletariat, than that of England was in the seventeenth, and of France in the eighteenth century, and because the bourgeois revolution in Germany will be but the prelude to an immediately following proletarian revolution.

In short, the Communists everywhere support every revolutionary movement against the existing social and political order of things.

In all these movements they bring to the front, as the leading question in each, the property question, no matter what its degree of development at the time.

Finally, they labour everywhere for the union and agreement of the democratic parties of all countries.

The Communists disdain to conceal their views and aims. They openly declare that their ends can be attained only by the forcible overthrow of all existing social conditions. Let the ruling classes tremble at a Communistic revolution. The proletarians have nothing to lose but their chains. They have a world to win.

WORKING MEN OF ALL COUNTRIES, UNITE!

9. *Kleinbürgerei* in the German original. Marx and Engels used this term to describe the reactionary elements of the urban petty bourgeoisie.

Address of the Central Committee
to the Communist League

MARX AND ENGELS

In 1848 most of the German workers in the Communist League returned to their homeland, and some played prominent parts in the revolutionary events there. In early 1850, when the wave of revolution had subsided but hope still existed for a new wave, Marx and Engels wrote this Address and dispatched it with an emissary to Germany for circulation among League members. In it they presented a radical political strategy for use in event of a resurgence of revolution in Germany, a strategy aimed at "making the revolution permanent." This meant preventing the "petty bourgeois democracy," which would inevitably lead the initial phase of a new revolutionary wave, from consolidating its ascendancy and keeping the movement in purely reformist channels. Looking back in 1885, in his essay "On the History of the Communist League," Engels wrote that the Address "is still of interest today, because petty-bourgeois democracy is even now the party which must certainly be the first to come to power in Germany as the savropean upheaval now soon due (the European revolutions, 1815, 1830, ior of society from the communist workers on the occasion of the next Eu-1848–52, 1870, have occurred at intervals of fifteen to eighteen years in our century)."

Brothers! In the two revolutionary years 1848–49 the League proved itself in double fashion: first, in that its members energetically took part in the movement in all places, that in the press, on the barricades and on the battlefields, they stood in the front ranks of the only decidedly revolutionary class, the proletariat. The League further proved itself in that its conception of the movement as laid down in the circulars of the congresses and of the Central Committee of 1847 as well as in the *Communist Manifesto* turned out to be the only correct one, that the expectations expressed in those documents were completely fulfilled and the conception of present-day social conditions, previously propagated only in secret by the League, is now on everyone's lips and is openly preached in the market places. At the same time the former firm organisation of the League was considerably slackened. A large part of the members who directly participated in the revolutionary movement believed the time for secret societies to have gone by and public activities alone sufficient. The individual circles and communities allowed their connections with the Central Committee to become loose and gradually dormant. Consequently, while the democratic party, the party of the petty bourgeoisie, organised itself more and more in Germany, the workers' party lost its only firm foothold, remained organised at the most in separate localities for local purposes and in the general movement thus came completely under the domination and leadership of the petty-bourgeois democrats. An end must be put to this state of affairs, the independence of the workers must be restored. The Central Committee realised this necessity and therefore already in the winter of 1848–49 it sent an emissary, Josef Moll, to Germany for the reorganisation of the League. Moll's mission, however, was without lasting effect, partly because the German workers at that time had not acquired sufficient experience and partly because it was interrupted by the insurrection of the previous May. Moll himself took up the musket, entered the Baden-Palatinate army and fell on July 19 in the encounter at the Murg. The League lost in him one of its oldest, most active and most trustworthy members, one who had been active in all the congresses and Central Committees and even prior to this had carried out a series of missions with great success. After the defeat of the revolutionary parties of Germany and France in July 1849, almost all the members of the Central Committee came together again in London, replenished their numbers with new revolutionary forces and set about the reorganisation of the League with renewed zeal.

Reorganisation can only be carried out by an emissary, and the Central Committee considers it extremely important that the emissary should leave precisely at this moment when a new revolution is impending, when the workers' party, therefore, must act in the most organised, most unanimous and most independent fashion possible if it is not to be exploited and taken in tow again by the bourgeoisie as in 1848.

Brothers! We told you as early as 1848 that the German liberal bourgeois would soon come to power and would immediately turn their newly acquired power against the workers. You have seen how this has been fulfilled. In fact it was the bourgeois who, immediately after the March movement of 1848, took possession of the state power and used this power to force back at once the workers, their allies in the struggle, into their former oppressed position.

Though the bourgeoisie was not able to accomplish this without uniting with the feudal party, which had been disposed of in March, without finally even surrendering power once again to this feudal absolutist party, still it has secured conditions for itself which, in the long run, owing to the financial embarrassment of the government, would place power in its hands and would safeguard all its interests, if it were possible for the revolutionary movement to assume already now a so-called peaceful development. The bourgeoisie, in order to safeguard its rule, would not even need to make itself obnoxious by violent measures against the people, since all such violent steps have already been taken by the feudal counter-revolution. Developments, however, will not take this peaceful course. On the contrary, the revolution, which will accelerate this development, is near at hand, whether it will be called forth by an independent uprising of the French proletariat or by an invasion of the Holy Alliance against the revolutionary Babylon.[1]

And the role, this so treacherous role which the German liberal bourgeois played in 1848 against the people, will in the impending revolution be taken over by the democratic petty bourgeois, who at present occupy the same position in the opposition as the liberal bourgeois before 1848. This party, the democratic party, which is far more dangerous to the workers than the previous liberal one, consists of three elements:

I. Of the most advanced sections of the big bourgeoisie, which pursue the aim of the immediate complete overthrow of feudalism and absolutism. This faction is represented by the one-time Berlin compromisers, by the tax resisters.

II. Of the democratic-constitutional petty bourgeois, whose main aim during the previous movement was the establishment of a more or less democratic federal state as striven for by their representatives, the Lefts in the Frankfort Assembly, and later by the Stuttgart parliament, and by themselves in the campaign for the Reich Constitution.

III. Of the republican petty bourgeois, whose ideal is a German federative republic after the manner of Switzerland, and who now call themselves Red and social-democratic because they cherish the pious wish of abolishing the pressure of big capital on small capital, of the big bourgeois on the small bourgeois. The representatives of this faction were the members of the democratic congresses and committees, the leaders of the democratic associations, the editors of the democratic newspapers.

Now, after their defeat, all these factions call themselves Republicans or Reds, just as the republican petty bourgeois in France now

1. *Revolutionary Babylon*: The reference is to Paris, which ever since the French bourgeois revolution of the end of the eighteenth century was considered the hotbed of the revolution.

call themselves Socialists. Where, as in Württemberg, Bavaria, etc., they still find opportunity to pursue their aims constitutionally, they seize the occasion to retain their old phrases and to prove by deeds that they have not changed in the least. It is evident, moreover, that the altered name of this party does not make the slightest difference in its attitude to the workers, but merely proves that they are now obliged to turn against the bourgeoisie, which is united with absolutism, and to seek support in the proletariat.

The petty-bourgeois democratic party in Germany is very powerful; it comprises not only the great majority of the bourgeois inhabitants of the towns, the small people in industry and trade and the guild masters; it numbers among its followers also the peasants and the rural proletariat, in so far as the latter has not yet found a support in the independent urban proletariat.

The relation of the revolutionary workers' party to the petty-bourgeois democrats is this: it marches together with them against the faction which it aims at overthrowing, it opposes them in everything whereby they seek to consolidate their position in their own interests.

Far from desiring to revolutionise all society for the revolutionary proletarians, the democratic petty bourgeois strive for a change in social conditions by means of which existing society will be made as tolerable and comfortable as possible for them. Hence they demand above all diminution of state expenditure by a curtailment of the bureaucracy and shifting the chief taxes on to the big landowners and bourgeois. Further, they demand the abolition of the pressure of big capital on small, through public credit institutions and laws against usury, by which means it will be possible for them and the peasants to obtain advances, on favourable conditions, from the state instead of from the capitalists; they also demand the establishment of bourgeois property relations in the countryside by the complete abolition of feudalism. To accomplish all this they need a democratic state structure, either constitutional or republican, that will give them and their allies, the peasants, a majority; also a democratic communal structure that will give them direct control over communal property and over a series of functions now performed by the bureaucrats.

The domination and speedy increase of capital is further to be counteracted partly by restricting the right of inheritance and partly by transferring as many jobs of work as possible to the state. As far as the workers are concerned, it remains certain above all that they are to remain wage-workers as before; the democratic petty bourgeois only desire better wages and a more secure existence for the workers and hope to achieve this through partial employment by the state and through charity measures; in short, they hope to bribe the workers by more or less concealed alms and to break their revolutionary potency by making their position tolerable for the moment. The demands of the petty-bourgeois democracy here summarised are not put forward by all of its factions at the same time and only a very few members of them consider that these demands constitute definite aims in their entirety. The further separate individuals or factions among them go, the more of these demands will they make their own, and those few who see their own programme in what has been outlined above might believe that thereby they have put forward the utmost that can be demanded from the revolution. But these demands can in nowise suffice for the party of the proletariat. While the democratic petty bourgeois wish to bring the revolution to a conclusion as quickly as possible, and with the achievement, at most, of the above demands, it is our interest and our task to make the revolution permanent, until all more or less possessing classes have been forced out of their position of dominance, until the proletariat has conquered state power, and the association of proletarians, not only in one country but in all the dominant countries of the world, has advanced so far that competition among the proletarians of these countries has ceased and that at least the decisive productive forces are concentrated in the hands of the proletarians. For us the issue cannot be the alteration of private property but only its annihilation, not the smoothing over of class antagonisms but the abolition of classes, not the improvement of existing society but the foundation of a new one. That during the further development of the revolution, the petty-bourgeois democracy will for a moment obtain predominating influence in Germany is not open to doubt. The question, therefore, arises as to what the attitude of the proletariat and in particular of the League will be in relation to it:

1. During the continuance of the present conditions where the petty-bourgeois democrats are likewise oppressed;

2. In the next revolutionary struggle, which will give them the upper hand;

3. After this struggle, during the period of preponderance over the overthrown classes and the proletariat.

1. At the present moment, when the democratic petty bourgeois are everywhere oppressed, they preach in general unity and reconciliation to the proletariat, they offer it their hand and strive for the establishment of a large opposition party which will embrace all shades of opinion in the democratic party, that is, they strive to entangle the workers in a party organisation in which general social-democratic phrases predominate, behind which their special inter-

ests are concealed and in which the particular demands of the proletariat may not be brought forward for the sake of beloved peace.
Such a union would turn out solely to their advantage and altogether to the disadvantage of the proletariat. The proletariat would
lose its whole independent, laboriously achieved position and once
more sink down to being an appendage of official bourgeois democracy. This union must, therefore, be most decisively rejected.
Instead of once again stooping to serve as the applauding chorus of
the bourgeois democrats, the workers, and above all the League,
must exert themselves to establish an independent, secret and
public organisation of the workers' party alongside of the official
democrats and make each section the central point and nucleus of
workers' societies in which the attitude and interests of the proletariat will be discussed independently of bourgeois influences. How far
the bourgeois democrats are from seriously considering an alliance in
which the proletarians would stand side by side with them with
equal power and equal rights is shown, for example, by the Breslau
democrats who, in their organ, the *Neue Oder-Zeitung*,[2] most
furiously attack the independently organised workers, whom they
style Socialists. In the case of a struggle against a common adversary
no special union is required. As soon as such an adversary has to be
fought directly, the interests of both parties, for the moment, coincide, and, as previously, so also in the future, this connection, calculated to last only for the moment, will arise of itself. It is self-evident that in the impending bloody conflicts, as in all earlier ones, it
is the workers who, in the main, will have to win the victory by
their courage, determination and self-sacrifice. As previously, so also
in this struggle, the mass of the petty bourgeois will as long as possible remain hesitant, undecided and inactive, and then, as soon as
the issue has been decided, will seize the victory for themselves, will
call upon the workers to maintain tranquillity and return to their
work, will guard against so-called excesses and bar the proletariat
from the fruits of victory. It is not in the power of the workers to
prevent the petty-bourgeois democrats from doing this, but it is in
their power to make it difficult for them to gain the upper hand as
against the armed proletariat, and to dictate such conditions to
them that the rule of the bourgeois democrats will from the outset
bear within it the seeds of their downfall, and that their subsequent extrusion by the rule of the proletariat will be considerably
facilitated. Above all things, the workers must counteract, as much
as is at all possible, during the conflict and immediately after the
struggle, the bourgeois endeavours to allay the storm, and must

2. *Neue Oder-Zeitung* (*New Oder Gazette*): Appeared daily in Breslau in 1849–55.

compel the democrats to carry out their present terrorist phrases. Their actions must be so aimed as to prevent the direct revolutionary excitement from being suppressed again immediately after the victory. On the contrary, they must keep it alive as long as possible. Far from opposing so-called excesses, instances of popular revenge against hated individuals or public buildings that are associated only with hateful recollections, such instances must not only be tolerated but the leadership of them taken in hand. During the struggle and after the struggle, the workers must, at every opportunity, put forward their own demands alongside of the demands of the bourgeois democrats. They must demand guarantees for the workers as soon as the democratic bourgeois set about taking over the government. If necessary they must obtain these guarantees by force and in general they must see to it that the new rulers pledge themselves to all possible concessions and promises—the surest way to compromise them. In general, they must in every way restrain as far as possible the intoxication of victory and the enthusiasm for the new state of things, which make their appearance after every victorious street battle, by a calm and dispassionate estimate of the situation and by unconcealed mistrust in the new government. Alongside of the new official governments they must establish simultaneously their own revolutionary workers' governments, whether in the form of municipal committees and municipal councils or in the form of workers' clubs or workers' committees, so that the bourgeois-democratic governments not only immediately lose the support of the workers but from the outset see themselves supervised and threatened by authorities which are backed by the whole mass of the workers. In a word, from the first moment of victory, mistrust must be directed no longer against the conquered reactionary party, but against the workers' previous allies, against the party that wishes to exploit the common victory for itself alone.

2. But in order to be able energetically and threateningly to oppose this party, whose treachery to the workers will begin from the first hour of victory, the workers must be armed and organised. The arming of the whole proletariat with rifles, muskets, cannon and munitions must be put through at once, the revival of the old Citizens' Guard directed against the workers must be resisted. However, where the latter is not feasible the workers must attempt to organise themselves independently as a proletarian guard with commanders elected by themselves and with a general staff of their own choosing, and to put themselves at the command not of the state authority but of the revolutionary community councils which the workers will have managed to get adopted. Where workers are employed at the expense of the state they must see that they are

armed and organised in a separate corps with commanders of their own choosing or as part of the proletarian guard. Arms and ammunition must not be surrendered on any pretext; any attempt at disarming must be frustrated, if necessary by force. Destruction of the influence of the bourgeois democrats upon the workers, immediate independent and armed organisation of the workers and the enforcement of conditions as difficult and compromising as possible upon the inevitable momentary rule of the bourgeois democracy—these are the main points which the proletariat and hence the League must keep in view during and after the impending insurrection.

3. As soon as the new governments have consolidated their positions to some extent, their struggle against the workers will begin. Here, in order to be able to offer energetic opposition to the democratic petty bourgeois, it is above all necessary that the workers shall be independently organised and centralised in clubs. After the overthrow of the existing governments, the Central Committee will, as soon as it is at all possible, betake itself to Germany, immediately convene a congress and put before the latter the necessary proposals for the centralisation of the workers' clubs under a leadership established in the chief seat of the movement. The speedy organisation of at least a provincial interlinking of the workers' clubs is one of the most important points for the strengthening and development of the workers' party; the immediate consequence of the overthrow of the existing governments will be the election of a national representative assembly. Here the proletariat must see to it:

I. That no groups of workers are barred on any pretext or by any kind of trickery on the part of local authorities or government commissioners.

II. That everywhere workers' candidates are put up alongside of the bourgeois-democratic candidates, that they should consist as far as possible of members of the League, and that their election is promoted by all possible means. Even where there is no prospect whatsoever of their being elected, the workers must put up their own candidates in order to preserve their independence, to count their forces and to bring before the public their revolutionary attitude and party standpoint. In this connection they must not allow themselves to be seduced by such arguments of the democrats as, for example, that by so doing they are splitting the democratic party and making it possible for the reactionaries to win. The ultimate intention of all such phrases is to dupe the proletariat. The advance which the proletarian party is bound to make by such independent action is infinitely more important than the disadvantage that might be incurred by the presence of a few reactionaries in the representative body. If the democracy from the outset comes out resolutely and terroristically against the reaction, the influence of the latter in the elections will be destroyed in advance.

The first point on which the bourgeois democrats will come into conflict with the workers will be the abolition of feudalism. As in the first French Revolution, the petty bourgeois will give the feudal lands to the peasants as free property, that is to say, try to leave the rural proletariat in existence and form a petty-bourgeois peasant class which will go through the same cycle of impoverishment and indebtedness which the French peasant is now still going through.

The workers must oppose this plan in the interest of the rural proletariat and in their own interest. They must demand that the confiscated feudal property remain state property and be converted into workers' colonies cultivated by the associated rural proletariat with all the advantages of large-scale agriculture, through which the principle of common property immediately obtains a firm basis in the midst of the tottering bourgeois property relations. Just as the democrats combine with the peasants so must the workers combine with the rural proletariat. Further, the democrats will work either directly for a federative republic, or, if they cannot avoid a single and indivisible republic, they will at least attempt to cripple the central government by the utmost possible autonomy and independence for the communities[3] and provinces. The workers, in opposition to this plan, must not only strive for a single and indivisible German republic, but also within this republic for the most determined centralisation of power in the hands of the state authority. They must not allow themselves to be misguided by the democratic talk of freedom for the communities, of self-government, etc. In a country like Germany where there are still so many relics of the Middle Ages to be abolished, where there is so much local and provincial obstinacy to be broken, it must under no circumstances be permitted that every village, every town and every province should put a new obstacle in the path of revolutionary activity, which can proceed with full force only from the centre. It is not to be tolerated that the present state of affairs should be renewed, that Germans must fight separately in every town and in every province for one and the same advance. Least of all is it to be tolerated that a form of property, namely, communal property, which still lags behind modern private property and which everywhere is necessarily passing into the latter, together with the quarrels resulting from it between poor and rich communities, as well as communal civil law, with its trickery against the workers, that exists alongside of state civil law, should be perpetuated by a so-called free communal constitution. As in France in 1793 so today in Germany it is the task of

3. *Community* (*Gemeinde*): This term is employed here in a wide sense to embrace both urban municipalities and rural communities.

the really revolutionary party to carry through the strictest central-isation.[4]

We have seen how the democrats will come to power with the next movement, how they will be compelled to propose more or less socialistic measures. It will be asked what measures the workers ought to propose in reply. At the beginning of the movement, of course, the workers cannot yet propose any directly communistic measures. But they can:

1. Compel the democrats to interfere in as many spheres as possible of the hitherto existing social order, to disturb its regular course and to compromise themselves as well as to concentrate the utmost possible productive forces, means of transport, factories, railways, etc., in the hands of the state;

2. They must drive the proposals of the democrats, who in any case will not act in a revolutionary but in a merely reformist manner, to the extreme and transform them into direct attacks upon private property; thus, for example, if the petty bourgeois propose purchase of the railways and factories, the workers must demand that these railways and factories shall be simply confiscated by the state without compensation as being the property of reactionaries. If the democrats propose proportional taxes, the workers must demand progressive taxes; if the democrats themselves put forward a moderately progressive tax, the workers must insist on a tax with rates that rise so steeply that big capital will be ruined by it; if the democrats demand the regulation of state debts, the workers must demand state bankruptcy. Thus, the demands of the workers must everywhere be governed by the concessions and measures of the democrats.

If the German workers are not able to attain power and achieve their own class interests without completely going through a

4. It must be recalled today that this passage is based on a misunderstanding. At that time—thanks to the Bonapartist and liberal falsifiers of history —it was considered as established that the French centralised machine of administration had been introduced by the Great Revolution and in particular that it had been operated by the Convention as an indispensable and decisive weapon for defeating the royalist and federalist reaction and the external enemy. It is now, however, a well-known fact that throughout the whole revolution up to the eighteenth Brumaire the whole administration of the departments, arrondissements and communes consisted of authorities elected by the respective constituents themselves, and that these authorities acted with complete freedom within the general state laws; that precisely this provincial and local self-government, similar to the American, became the most powerful lever of the revolution and indeed to such an extent that Napoleon, immediately after his *coup d'état* of the eighteenth Brumaire, hastened to replace it by an administration by prefects, which still exists and which, therefore, was a pure instrument of reaction from the beginning. But just as little as local and provincial self-government is in contradiction to political, national centralisation, so is it to an equally small extent necessarily bound up with that narrow-minded, cantonal or communal self-seeking which strikes us as so repulsive in Switzerland, and which all the South German federal republicans wanted to make the rule in Germany in 1849. [*Engels, 1885 edition*]

lengthy revolutionary development, they at least know for a certainty this time that the first act of this approaching revolutionary drama will coincide with the direct victory of their own class in France and will be very much accelerated by it.

But they themselves must do the utmost for their final victory by clarifying their minds as to what their class interests are, by taking up their position as an independent party as soon as possible and by not allowing themselves to be seduced for a single moment by the hypocritical phrases of the democratic petty bourgeois into refraining from the independent organisation of the party of the proletariat. Their battle cry must be: The Revolution in Permanence.

Inaugural Address of the
Working Men's International Association

KARL MARX

Marx wrote the Inaugural Address in October, 1864, as a charter document
for the Working Men's International Association (otherwise known as the
First International), which was established on September 28, 1864, at a
meeting in St. Martin's Hall in London. It was both a review of the work-
ing-class movement since 1848 and a program. Despite the echo of the
Communist Manifesto in the closing words ("Proletarians of all countries,
Unite!"), some have seen the Inaugural Address, with its salute to the
English Ten Hours' Bill, as a herald of the decreasingly revolutionary
Marxist Social Democratic movement of the late nineteenth century.
Against this interpretation must be set Marx's shorthand recapitulation of
his theory of history and proletarian revolution in the statement here that
"hired labor is but a transitory and inferior form, destined to disappear before associated labour plying its toil with a willing hand, a ready mind, and
a joyous heart." Given the disparate character of the various national con-
tingents of the new association, some less radical than others, there was
also a tactical reason for restraint on revolutionary rhetoric. As Marx wrote
to Engels, "Time is necessary before the revived movement can permit itself the old audacious language. The need of the moment is: bold in matter, but mild in manner."

Working Men,

It is a great fact that the misery of the working masses has not
diminished from 1848 to 1864, and yet this period is unrivalled for
the development of its industry and the growth of its commerce. In
1850, a moderate organ of the British middle class, of more than
average information, predicted that if the exports and imports of
England were to rise 50 per cent, English pauperism would sink to
zero. Alas! on April 7, 1864, the Chancellor of the Exchequer
delighted his parliamentary audience by the statement that the total

import and export trade of England had grown in 1863 "to £443,955,000! that astonishing sum about three times the trade of the comparatively recent epoch of 1843!" With all that, he was eloquent upon "poverty." "Think," he exclaimed, "of those who are on the border of that region," upon "wages . . . not increased"; upon "human life . . . in nine cases out of ten but a struggle of existence!" He did not speak of the people of Ireland, gradually replaced by machinery in the north, and by sheep-walks in the south, though even the sheep in that unhappy country are decreasing, it is true, not at so rapid a rate as the men. He did not repeat what then had been just betrayed by the highest representatives of the upper ten thousand in a sudden fit of terror. When the garotte[1] panic had reached a certain height, the House of Lords caused an inquiry to be made into, and a report to be published upon, transportation and penal servitude. Out came the murder in the bulky Blue Book of 1863, and proved it was, by official facts and figures, that the worst of the convicted criminals, the penal serfs of England and Scotland, toiled much less and fared far better than the agricultural labourers of England and Scotland. But this was not all. When, consequent upon the Civil War in America, the operatives of Lancashire and Cheshire were thrown upon the streets, the same House of Lords sent to the manufacturing districts a physician commissioned to investigate into the smallest possible amount of carbon and nitrogen, to be administered in the cheapest and plainest from, which on an average might just suffice to "avert starvation diseases." Dr. Smith, the medical deputy, ascertained that 28,000 grains of carbon, and 1,330 grains of nitrogen were the weekly allowance that would keep an average adult . . . just over the level of starvation diseases, and he found furthermore that quantity pretty nearly to agree with the scanty nourishment to which the pressure of extreme distress had actually reduced the cotton operatives.[2] But now mark! The same learned Doctor was later on again deputed by the medical officer of the Privy Council to inquire into the nourishment of the poorer labouring classes. The results of his researches are embodied in the "Sixth Report on Public Health," published by order of Parliament in the course of the present year. What did the Doctor discover? That the silk weavers, the needle women, the kid glovers, the stocking weavers, and so forth, received, on an average, not even the distress pittance of the cotton

1. *Garotters*: Street robbers whose attacks increased in London in the beginning of the sixties to such an extent that Parliament was compelled to take up the matter.
2. We need hardly remind the reader that, apart from the elements of water and certain inorganic substances, carbon and nitrogen form the raw materials of human food. However, to nourish the human system, those simple chemical constituents must be supplied in the form of vegetable or animal substances. Potatoes, for instance, contain mainly carbon, while wheaten bread contains carbonaceous and nitrogenous substances in a due proportion. [*Marx*]

operatives, not even the amount of carbon and nitrogen "just sufficient to avert starvation diseases."

"Moreover," we quote from the report, "as regards the examined families of the agricultural population, it appeared that more than a fifth were with less than the estimated sufficiency of carbonaceous food, that more than one-third were with less than the estimated sufficiency of nitrogenous food, and that in three counties (Berkshire, Oxfordshire and Somersetshire) insufficiency of nitrogenous food was the average local diet." "It must be remembered," adds the official report, "that privation of food is very reluctantly borne, and that, as a rule, great poorness of diet will only come when other privations have preceded it. . . . Even cleanliness will have been found costly or difficult, and if there still be self-respectful endeavours to maintain it, every such endeavour will represent additional pangs of hunger." "These are painful reflections, especially when it is remembered that the poverty to which they advert is not the deserved poverty of idleness; in all cases it is the poverty of working populations. Indeed, the work which obtains the scanty pittance of food is for the most part excessively prolonged." The report brings out the strange, and rather unexpected fact: "That of the divisions of the United Kingdom," England, Wales, Scotland, and Ireland, "the agricultural population of England," the richest division, "is considerably the worst fed"; but that even the agricultural labourers of Berkshire, Oxfordshire, and Somersetshire, fare better than great numbers of skilled indoor operatives of the East of London.

Such are the official statements published by order of Parliament in 1864, during the millennium of free trade, at a time when the Chancellor of the Exchequer told the House of Commons that "the average condition of the British labourer has improved in a degree we know to be extraordinary and unexampled in the history of any country or any age." Upon these official congratulations jars the dry remark of the official Public Health Report: "The public health of a country means the health of its masses, and the masses will scarcely be healthy unless, to their very base, they be at least moderately prosperous."

Dazzled by the "Progress of the Nation" statistics dancing before his eyes, the Chancellor of the Exchequer exclaims in wild ecstasy: "From 1842 to 1852 the taxable income of the country increased by 6 per cent; in the eight years from 1853 to 1861, it has increased from the basis taken in 1853 20 per cent! the fact is so astonishing as to be almost incredible! . . . This intoxicating augmentation of wealth and power," adds Mr. Gladstone, "is entirely confined to classes of property!"

If you want to know under what conditions of broken health, tainted morals and mental ruin, that "intoxicating augmentation of wealth and power entirely confined to classes of property" was, and is being produced by the classes of labour, look to the picture hung up in the last "Public Health Report" of the workshops of tailors, printers and dressmakers! Compare the "Report of the Children's Employment Commission" of 1863, where it is stated, for instance, that: "The potters as a class, both men and women, represent a much degenerated population, both physically and mentally," that "the unhealthy child is an unhealthy parent in his turn," that "a progressive deterioration of the race must go on," and that "the degenerescence of the population of Staffordshire would be even greater were it not for the constant recruiting from the adjacent country, and the intermarriages with more healthy races." Glance at Mr. Tremenheere's Blue Book on the "Grievances complained of by the Journeymen Bakers"! And who has not shuddered at the paradoxical statement made by the inspectors of factories, all illustrated by the Registrar General, that the Lancashire operatives, while put upon the distress pittance of food, were actually improving in health, because of their temporary exclusion by the cotton famine from the cotton factory, and that the mortality of the children was decreasing, because their mothers were now at last allowed to give them, instead of Godfrey's cordial, their own breasts.

Again reverse the medal! The Income and Property Tax Returns laid before the House of Commons on July 20, 1864, teach us that the persons with yearly incomes, valued by the tax-gatherer at £50,000 and upwards, had, from April 5, 1862, to April 5, 1863, been joined by a dozen and one, their number having increased in that single year from 67 to 80. The same returns disclose the fact that about 3,000 persons divide amongst themselves a yearly income of about £25,000,000 sterling, rather more than the total revenue doled out annually to the whole mass of the agricultural labourers of England and Wales. Open the census of 1861, and you will find that the number of the male landed proprietors of England and Wales had decreased from 16,934 in 1851, to 15,066 in 1861, so that the concentration of land had grown in 10 years 11 per cent. If the concentration of the soil of the country in a few hands proceeds at the same rate, the land question will become singularly simplified, as it had become in the Roman empire, when Nero grinned at the discovery that half the Province of Africa was owned by six gentlemen.

We have dwelt so long upon these "facts so astonishing to be almost incredible," because England heads the Europe of commerce and industry. It will be remembered that some months ago one of the refugee sons of Louis Philippe publicly congratulated the English agricultural labourer on the superiority of his lot over that of his less florid comrade on the other side of the Channel. Indeed, with local colours changed, and on a scale somewhat contracted, the English acts reproduce themselves in all the industrious and progressive countries of the Continent. In all of them there has taken place, since 1848, an unheard-of development of industry, and an undreamed-of expansion of imports and exports. In all of them "the augmentation of wealth and power entirely confined to classes of property" was truly "intoxicating." In all of them, as in England, a minority of the working classes got their real wages somewhat advanced; while in most cases the monetary rise of wages denoted no more a real access of comforts than the inmate of the metropolitan poor-house or orphan asylum, for instance, was in the least benefited by his first necessaries costing £9 15s. 8d. in 1861 against £7 7s. 4d. in 1852. Everywhere the great mass of the working classes were sinking down to a lower depth, at the same rate at least, that those above them were rising in the social scale. In all countries of Europe it has now become a truth demonstrable to every unprejudiced mind, and only denied by those, whose interest it is to hedge other people in a fool's paradise, that no improvement of machinery, no appliance of science to production, no contrivances of communication, no new colonies, no emigration, no opening of markets, no free trade, nor all these things put together, will do away with the miseries of the industrious masses; but that, on the present false base, every fresh development of the productive powers of labour must tend to deepen social contrasts and point social antagonisms. Death of starvation rose almost to the rank of an institution, during this intoxicating epoch of economical progress, in the metropolis of the British Empire. That epoch is marked in the annals of the world by the quickened return, the widening compass, and the deadlier effects of the social pest called a commercial and industrial crisis.

After the failure of the Revolutions of 1848, all party organisations and party journals of the working classes were, on the Continent, crushed by the iron hand of force, the most advanced sons of labour fled in despair to the Transatlantic Republic, and the short-lived dreams of emancipation vanished before an epoch of industrial fever, moral marasme, and political reaction. The defeat of the Continental working classes, partly owed to the diplomacy of the English Government, acting then as now in fraternal solidarity with the Cabinet of St. Petersburg, soon spread its contagious effects to this side of the Channel. While the rout of their Continental brethren unmanned the English working classes, and broke their faith in their own cause, it restored to the landlord and the money-lord their somewhat shaken confidence. They insolently withdrew concessions already advertised. The discoveries of new goldlands led to an immense exodus, leaving an irreparable void in the ranks of the

British proletariat. Others of its formerly active members were caught by the temporary bribe of greater work and wages, and turned into "political blacks." All the efforts made at keeping up, or remodeling, the Chartist Movement, failed signally; the press organs of the working class died one by one of the apathy of the masses, and, in point of fact, never before seemed the English working class so thoroughly reconciled to a state of political nullity. If, then, there had been no solidarity of action between the British and the Continental working classes, there was, at all events, a solidarity of defeat.

And yet the period passed since the Revolutions of 1848 has not been without its compensating features. We shall here only point to two great facts.

After a thirty years' struggle, fought with most admirable perseverance, the English working classes, improving a momentaneous split between the landlords and money-lords, succeeded in carrying the Ten Hours' Bill. The immense physical, moral and intellectual benefits hence accruing to the factory operatives, half-yearly chronicled in the reports of the inspectors of factories, are now acknowledged on all sides. Most of the Continental governments had to accept the English Factory Act in more or less modified forms, and the English Parliament itself is every year compelled to enlarge its sphere of action. But besides its practical import, there was something else to exalt the marvellous success of this working men's measure. Through their most notorious organs of science, such as Dr. Ure, Professor Senior, and other sages of that stamp, the middle class had predicted, and to their heart's content proved, that any legal restriction of the hours of labour must sound the death knell of British industry, which, vampyre like, could but live by sucking blood, and children's blood, too. In olden times, child murder was a mysterious rite of the religion of Moloch, but it was practised on some very solemn occasions only, once a year perhaps, and then Moloch had no exclusive bias for the children of the poor. This struggle about the legal restriction of the hours of labour raged the more fiercely since, apart from frightened avarice, it told indeed upon the great contest between the blind rule of the supply and demand laws which form the political economy of the middle class, and social production controlled by social foresight, which forms the political economy of the working class. Hence the Ten Hours' Bill was not only a great practical success; it was the victory of a principle; it was the first time that in broad daylight the political economy of the middle class succumbed to the political economy of the working class.

But there was in store a still greater victory of the political economy of labour over the political economy of property. We speak of the co-operative movement, especially the co-operative factories raised by the unassisted efforts of a few bold "hands." The value of these great social experiments cannot be over-rated. By deed, instead of by argument, they have shown that production on a large scale, and in accord with the behests of modern science, may be carried on without the existence of a class of masters employing a class of hands; that to bear fruit, the means of labour need not be monopolised as a means of dominion over, and of extortion against, the labouring man himself; and that, like slave labour, like serf labour, hired labour is but a transitory and inferior form, destined to disappear before associated labour plying its toil with a willing hand, a ready mind, and a joyous heart. In England, the seeds of the co-operative system were sown by Robert Owen; the working men's experiments, tried on the Continent, were, in fact, the practical upshot of the theories, not invented, but loudly proclaimed, in 1848.

At the same time, the experience of the period from 1848 to 1864 has proved beyond doubt that, however excellent in principle, and however useful in practice, co-operative labour, if kept within the narrow circle of the casual efforts of private workmen, will never be able to arrest the growth in geometrical progression of monopoly, to free the masses, nor even to perceptibly lighten the burden of their miseries. It is perhaps for this very reason that plausible noblemen, philanthropic middle-class spouters, and even keen political economists, have all at once turned nauseously complimentary to the very co-operative labour system they had vainly tried to nip in the bud by deriding it as the Utopia of the dreamer, or stigmatising it as the sacrilege of the Socialist. To save the industrious masses, co-operative labour ought to be developed to national dimensions, and consequently, to be fostered by national means. Yet, the lords of land and the lords of capital will always use their political privileges for the defence and perpetuation of their economical monopolies. So far from promoting, they will continue to lay every possible impediment in the way of the emancipation of labour. Remember the sneer with which, last session, Lord Palmerston put down the advocates of the Irish Tenants' Right Bill. The House of Commons, cried he, is a house of landed proprietors. To conquer political power has therefore become the great duty of the working classes. They seem to have comprehended this, for in England, Germany, Italy, and France there have taken place simultaneous revivals, and simultaneous efforts are being made at the political reorganisation of the working men's party.

One element of success they possess—numbers; but numbers weigh only in the balance, if united by combination and led by knowledge. Past experience has shown how disregard of that bond of brotherhood which ought to exist between the workmen of different countries, and incite them to stand firmly by each other in all their struggles for emancipation, will be chastised by the common discomfiture of their incoherent efforts. This thought prompted the working men of different countries assembled on September 28, 1864, in public meeting at St. Martin's Hall, to found the International Association.

Another conviction swayed that meeting.

If the emancipation of the working classes requires their fraternal concurrence, how are they to fulfil that great mission with a foreign policy in pursuit of criminal designs, playing upon national prejudices, and squandering in piratical wars the people's blood and treasure? It was not the wisdom of the ruling classes, but the heroic resistance to their criminal folly by the working classes of England that saved the West of Europe from plunging headlong into an infamous crusade for the perpetuation and propagation of slavery on the other side of the Atlantic. The shameless approval, mock sympathy, or idiotic indifference, with which the upper classes of Europe have witnessed the mountain fortress of the Caucasus falling a prey to, and heroic Poland being assassinated by, Russia; the immense and unresisted encroachments of that barbarous power, whose head is at St. Petersburg, and whose hands are in every cabinet of Europe, have taught the working classes the duty to master themselves the mysteries of international politics; to watch the diplomatic acts of their respective Governments; to counteract them, if necessary, by all means in their power; when unable to prevent, to combine in simultaneous denunciations, and to vindicate the simple laws of morals and justice, which ought to govern the relations of private individuals, as the rules paramount of the intercourse of nations.

The fight for such a foreign policy forms part of the general struggle for the emancipation of the working classes.

Proletarians of all countries, Unite!

Critique of the Gotha Program

KARL MARX

Marx's most detailed pronouncement on programmatic matters was made in this letter of early May, 1875, to the leaders of the so-called Eisenach faction of the German Social Democratic movement, with whom he and Engels were in close association. At the forthcoming party congress in the town of Gotha, the Eisenachers planned to unite with the Lassallean faction to form a unified German Social Democratic Party, and they sent the draft program for a united party to Marx and Engels for their comments. They found it fundamentally flawed by the influence of ideas of Ferdinand Lassalle, and Marx's lengthy reply to the Eisenachers, a letter in the form of marginal notes on the draft program, was vitriolic in this regard. Practical political interests were involved in the unification movement, however, and the Gotha Congress, held in late May, 1875, adopted the draft program with only minor alterations. Much later, in 1891, when the party had declared its intention of adopting a new program, Engels caused Marx's programmatic letter to be published in the party organ *Neue Zeit*, and gave it the title "Critique of the Gotha Program."

I

1. "Labour is the source of all wealth and all culture, *and since* useful labour is possible only in society and through society, the proceeds of labour belong undiminished with equal right to all members of society."

First Part of the Paragraph: "Labour is the source of all wealth and all culture."

Labour is *not the source* of all wealth. *Nature* is just as much the source of use values (and it is surely of such that material wealth consists!) as labour, which itself is only the manifestation of a force of nature, human labour power. The above phrase is to be found in all children's primers and is correct in so far as it is *implied* that labour is performed with the appurtenant subjects and instruments.

But a socialist programme cannot allow such bourgeois phrases to pass over in silence the *conditions* that alone give them meaning. And in so far as man from the beginning behaves towards nature, the primary source of all instruments and subjects of labour, as an owner, treats her as belonging to him, his labour becomes the source of use values, therefore also of wealth. The bourgeois have very good grounds for falsely ascribing *supernatural creative power* to labour; since precisely from the fact that labour depends on nature it follows that the man who posseses no other property than his labour power must, in all conditions of society and culture, be the slave of other men who have made themselves the owners of the material conditions of labour. He can work only with their permission, hence live only with their permission.

Let us now leave the sentence as it stands, or rather limps. What would one have expected in conclusion? Obviously this:

"Since labour is the source of all wealth, no one in society can appropriate wealth except as the product of labour. Therefore, if he himself does not work, he lives by the labour of others and also acquires his culture at the expense of the labour of others."

Instead of this, by means of the verbal rivet *"and since"* a second proposition is added in order to draw a conclusion from this and not from the first one.

Second Part of the Paragraph: "Useful labour is possible only in society and through society."

According to the first proposition, labour was the source of all wealth and all culture; therefore no society is possible without labour. Now we learn, conversely, that no "useful" labour is possible without society.

One could just as well have said that only in society can useless and even socially harmful labour become a branch of gainful occupation, that only in society can one live by being idle, etc., etc.—in short, one could just as well have copied the whole of Rousseau.

And what is "useful" labour? Surely only labour which produces the intended useful result. A savage—and man was a savage after he had ceased to be an ape—who kills an animal with a stone, who collects fruits, etc., performs "useful" labour.

Thirdly. The Conclusion: "And since useful labour is possible only in society and through society, the proceeds of labour belong undiminished with equal right to all members of society."

A fine conclusion! If useful labour is possible only in society and through society, the proceeds of labour belong to society—and only so much therefrom accrues to the individual worker as is not required to maintain the "condition" of labour, society.

In fact, this proposition has at all times been made use of by the champions of the *state of society prevailing at any given time*. First come the claims of the government and everything that sticks to it, since it is the social organ for the maintenance of the social order; then come the claims of the various kinds of private property, for the various kinds of private property are the foundations of society, etc. One sees that such hollow phrases can be twisted and turned as desired.

The first and second parts of the paragraph have some intelligible connection only in the following wording:

"Labour becomes the source of wealth and culture only as social labour," or, what is the same thing, "in and through society."

This proposition is incontestably correct, for although isolated labour (its material conditions presupposed) can create use values, it can create neither wealth nor culture.

But equally incontestable is this other proposition:

"In proportion as labour develops socially, and becomes thereby a source of wealth and culture, poverty and destitution develop among the workers, and wealth and culture among the non-workers."

This is the law of all history hitherto. What, therefore, had to be done here, instead of setting down general phrases about "labour" and "society," was to prove concretely how in present capitalist society the material, etc., conditions have at last been created which enable and compel the workers to lift this social curse.

In fact, however, the whole paragraph, bungled in style and content, is only there in order to inscribe the Lassallean catchword of the "undiminished proceeds of labour" as a slogan at the top of the party banner. I shall return later to the "proceeds of labour," "equal right," etc., since the same thing recurs in a somewhat different form further on.

2. "In present-day society, the instruments of labour are the monopoly of the capitalist class; the resulting dependence of the working class is the cause of misery and servitude in all its forms."

This sentence, borrowed from the Rules of the International, is incorrect in this "improved" edition.

In present-day society the instruments of labour are the monopoly of the landowners (the monopoly of property in land is even the basis of the monopoly of capital) *and* the capitalists. In the passage in question, the Rules of the International do not mention either the one or the other class of monopolists. They speak of the *"monopoliser of the means of labour, that is, the sources of life."* The addition, *"sources of life,"* makes it sufficiently clear that land is included in the instruments of labour.

The correction was introduced because Lassalle, for reasons now generally known, attacked *only* the capitalist class and not the landowners. In England, the capitalist is usually not even the owner of the land on which his factory stands.

3. "The emancipation of labour demands the promotion of the instruments of labour to the common property of society and the co-operative regulation of the total labour with a fair distribution of the proceeds of labour."

"Promotion of the instruments of labour to the common property" ought obviously to read their "conversion into the common property"; but this only in passing.

What are "proceeds of labour"? The product of labour or its value? And in the latter case, is it the total value of the product or only that part of the value which labour has newly added to the value of the means of production consumed?

"Proceeds of labour" is a loose notion which Lassalle has put in the place of definite economic conceptions.

What is "a fair distribution"?

Do not the bourgeois assert that the present-day distribution is "fair"? And is it not, in fact, the only "fair" distribution on the basis of the present-day mode of production? Are economic relations regulated by legal conceptions or do not, on the contrary, legal relations arise from economic ones? Have not also the socialist sectarians the most varied notions about "fair" distribution?

To understand what is implied in this connection by the phrase "fair distribution," we must take the first paragraph and this one together. The latter presupposes a society wherein "the instruments of labour are common property and the total labour is cooperatively regulated," and from the first paragraph we learn that "the proceeds of labour belong undiminished with equal right to all members of society."

"To all members of society"? To those who do not work as well? What remains then of the "undiminished proceeds of labour"? Only to those members of society who work? What remains then of the "equal right" of all members of society?

But "all members of society" and "equal right" are obviously mere phrases. The kernel consists in this, that in this communist society every worker must receive the "undiminished" Lassallean "proceeds of labour."

Let us take first of all the words "proceeds of labour" in the sense of the product of labour; then the co-operative proceeds of labour are the *total social product*.

From this must now be deducted:

First, cover for replacement of the means of production used up.

Secondly, additional portion for expansion of production.

Thirdly, reserve or insurance funds to provide against accidents, dislocations caused by natural calamities, etc.

These deductions from the "undiminished proceeds of labour" are an economic necessity and their magnitude is to be determined according to available means and forces, and partly by computation of probabilities, but they are in no way calculable by equity.

There remains the other part of the total product, intended to serve as means of consumption.

Before this is divided among the individuals, there has to be deducted again, from it:

First, the general costs of administration not belonging to production.

This part will, from the outset, be very considerably restricted in comparison with present-day society and it diminishes in proportion as the new society develops.

Secondly, that which is intended for the common satisfaction of needs, such as schools, health services, etc.

From the outset this part grows considerably in comparison with present-day society and it grows in proportion as the new society develops.

Thirdly, funds for those unable to work, etc., in short, for what is included under so-called official poor relief today.

Only now do we come to the "distribution" which the programme, under Lassallean influence, alone has in view in its narrow fashion, namely, to that part of the means of consumption which is divided among the individual producers of the co-operative society.

The "undiminished proceeds of labour" have already unnoticeably become converted into the "diminished" proceeds, although what the producer is deprived of in his capacity as a private individual benefits him directly or indirectly in his capacity as a member of society.

Just as the phrase of the "undiminished proceeds of labour" has disappeared, so now does the phrase of the "proceeds of labour" disappear altogether.

Within the co-operative society based on common ownership of the means of production, the producers do not exchange their products; just as little does the labour employed on the products appear here *as the value* of these products, as a material quality possessed by them, since now, in contrast to capitalist society, individual labour no longer exists in an indirect fashion but directly as a component part of the total labour. The phrase "proceeds of labour," objectionable also today on account of its ambiguity, thus loses all meaning.

What we have to deal with here is a communist society, not as it has *developed* on its own foundations, but, on the contrary, just as it *emerges* from capitalist society; which is thus in every respect, economically, morally and intellectually, still stamped with the birth marks of the old society from whose womb it emerges. Accordingly, the individual producer receives back from society—after the deductions have been made—exactly what he gives to it. What he has given to it is his individual quantum of labour. For example, the social working day consists of the sum of the individual hours of work; the individual labour time of the individual producer is the part of the social working day contributed by him, his share in it. He receives a certificate from society that he has furnished such and such an amount of labour (after deducting his labour for the common funds), and with this certificate he draws from the social stock of means of consumption as much as costs the same amount of labour. The same amount of labour which he has given to society in one form he receives back in another.

Here obviously the same principle prevails as that which regulates the exchange of commodities, as far as this is exchange of equal values. Content and form are changed, because under the altered circumstances no one can give anything except his labour, and because, on the other hand, nothing can pass to the ownership of individuals except individual means of consumption. But, as far as the distribution of the latter among the individual producers is concerned, the same principle prevails as in the exchange of commodity equivalents: a given amount of labour in one form is exchanged for an equal amount of labour in another form.

Hence, *equal right* here is still in principle—*bourgeois right*, although principle and practice are no longer at loggerheads, while the exchange of equivalents in commodity exchange only exists *on the average* and not in the individual case.

In spite of this advance, this *equal right* is still constantly stigmatised by a bourgeois limitation. The right of the producers is *proportional* to the labour they supply; the equality consists in the fact that measurement is made with an *equal standard*, labour.

But one man is superior to another physically or mentally and so supplies more labour in the same time, or can labour for a longer time; and labour, to serve as a measure, must be defined by its duration or intensity, otherwise it ceases to be a standard of measurement. This *equal* right is an unequal right for unequal labour. It recognises no class differences, because everyone is only a worker like everyone else; but it tacitly recognises unequal individual endowment and thus productive capacity as natural privileges. *It is, therefore, a right of inequality, in its content, like every right.* Right by its very nature can consist only in the application of an equal standard; but unequal individuals (and they would not be different individuals if they were not unequal) are measurable only by an equal standard in so far as they are brought under an equal point of view, are taken from one *definite* side only, for instance, in the present case, are regarded *only as workers* and nothing more is seen in them, everything else being ignored. Further, one worker is married, another not; one has more children than another, and so on and so forth. Thus, with an equal performance of labour, and hence an equal share in the social consumption fund, one will in fact receive more than another, one will be richer than another, and so on. To avoid all these defects, right instead of being equal would have to be unequal.

But these defects are inevitable in the first phase of communist society as it is when it has just emerged after prolonged birth pangs from capitalist society. Right can never be higher than the economic structure of society and its cultural development conditioned thereby.

In a higher phase of communist society, after the enslaving subordination of the individual to the division of labour, and therewith also the antithesis between mental and physical labour, has vanished; after labour has become not only a means of life but life's prime want; after the productive forces have also increased with the all-round development of the individual, and all the springs of co-operative wealth flow more abundantly—only then can the narrow horizon of bourgeois right be crossed in its entirety and society inscribe on its banner: From each according to his ability, to each according to his needs!

I have dealt more at length with the "undiminished proceeds of labour," on the one hand, and with "equal right" and "fair distribution," on the other, in order to show what a crime it is to attempt, on the one hand, to force on our Party again, as dogmas, ideas which in a certain period had some meaning but have now become obsolete verbal rubbish, while again perverting, on the other, the realistic outlook, which it cost so much effort to instil into the Party but which has now taken root in it, by means of ideological nonsense about right and other trash so common among the democrats and French Socialists.

Quite apart from the analysis so far given, it was in general a mistake to make a fuss about so-called *distribution* and put the principal stress on it.

Any distribution whatever of the means of consumption is only a consequence of the distribution of the conditions of production themselves. The latter distribution, however, is a feature of the mode of production itself. The capitalist mode of production, for example, rests on the fact that the material conditions of production are in the hands of non-workers in the form of property in capital and land, while the masses are only owners of the personal condition of production, of labour power. If the elements of production are so distributed, then the present-day distribution of the means of consumption results automatically. If the material conditions of production are the co-operative property of the workers themselves, then there likewise results a distribution of the means of consumption different from the present one. Vulgar socialism (and from it in turn a section of the democracy) has taken over from the bourgeois economists the consideration and treatment of distribution as independent of the mode of production and hence the presentation of socialism as turning principally on distribution. After the real relation has long been made clear, why retrogress again?

4. "The emancipation of labour must be the work of the working class, relatively to which all other classes are *only one reactionary mass*."

The first strophe is taken from the introductory words of the Rules of the International, but "improved." There it is said: "The emancipation of the working class must be the act of the workers themselves"; here, on the contrary, the "working class" has to emancipate—what? "Labour." Let him understand who can.

In compensation, the antistrophe, on the other hand, is a Lassallean quotation of the first water: "relatively to which (the working class) all other classes are *only one reactionary mass*."

In the *Communist Manifesto* it is said: "Of all the classes that stand face to face with the bourgeoisie today, the proletariat alone is a *really revolutionary class*. The other classes decay and finally disappear in the face of modern industry; the proletariat is its special and essential product."

The bourgeoisie is here conceived as a revolutionary class—as the bearer of large-scale industry—relatively to the feudal lords and the lower middle class, who desire to maintain all social positions that are the creation of obsolete modes of production. Thus they do not form *together* with the *bourgeoisie* only one reactionary mass.

On the other hand, the proletariat is revolutionary relatively to the bourgeoisie because, having itself grown up on the basis of large-scale industry, it strives to strip off from production the capitalist character that the bourgeoisie seeks to perpetuate. But the *Manifesto* adds that the "lower middle class" is becoming revolutionary "in view of [its] impending transfer into the proletariat."

From this point of view, therefore, it is again nonsense to say that it, together with the bourgeoisie, and with the feudal lords into the bargain, "form only one reactionary mass" relatively to the working class.

Has one proclaimed to the artisans, small manufacturers, etc., and *peasants* during the last elections: Relatively to us you, together with the bourgeoisie and feudal lords, form only one reactionary mass?

Lassalle knew the *Communist Manifesto* by heart, as his faithful followers know the gospels written by him. If, therefore, he has falsified it so grossly, this has occurred only to put a good colour on his alliance with absolutist and feudal opponents against the bourgeoisie.

In the above paragraph, moreover, his oracular saying is dragged in by main force without any connection with the botched quotation from the Rules of the International. Thus is it here simply an impertinence, and indeed not at all displeasing to Herr Bismarck, one of those cheap pieces of insolence in which the Marat of Berlin[1] deals.

5. "The working class strives for its emancipation first of all *within the framework of the present-day national state*, conscious that the necessary result of its efforts, which are common to the workers of all civilised countries, will be the international brotherhood of peoples."

Lassalle, in opposition to the *Communist Manifesto* and to all earlier socialism, conceived the workers' movement from the narrowest national standpoint. He is being followed in this—and that after the work of the International!

It is altogether self-evident that, to be able to fight at all, the working class must organise itself at home *as a class* and that its own country is the immediate arena of its struggle. In so far its class struggle is national, not in substance, but, as the *Communist Manifesto* says, "in form." But the "framework of the present-day national state," for instance, the German Empire, is itself in its turn economically "within the framework" of the world market, politically "within the framework" of the system of states. Every businessman knows that German trade is at the same time foreign trade, and the greatness of Herr Bismarck consists, to be sure, precisely in his pursuing a kind of *international* policy.

And to what does the German workers' party reduce its internationalism? To the consciousness that the result of its efforts will be *"the international brotherhood of peoples"*—a phrase borrowed from the bourgeois League of Peace and Freedom[2] which is intended to pass as equivalent to the international brotherhood of the working classes in the joint struggle against the ruling classes and their governments. Not a word, therefore, *about the international functions* of the German working class! And it is thus that it is to challenge its own bourgeoisie—which is already linked up in brotherhood against it with the bourgeois of all other countries—and Herr Bismarck's international policy of conspiracy!

In fact, the internationalism of the programme stands *even*

1. The "Marat of Berlin" is obviously an ironical reference to Hasselmann, the chief editor of the *Neuer Social-Demokrat,* the central organ of the Lassalleans.

2. The *International League of Peace and Freedom* was organised in Geneva in 1867 by bourgeois democrats and pacifists.

infinitely below that of the Free Trade Party. The latter also asserts that the result of its efforts will be "the international brotherhood of peoples." But it also *does* something to make trade international and by no means contents itself with the consciousness—that all peoples are carrying on trade at home.

The international activity of the working classes does not in any way depend on the existence of the *International Working Men's Association*. This was only the first attempt to create a central organ for that activity; an attempt which was a lasting success on account of the impulse which it gave but which was no longer realisable in its *first historical form* after the fall of the Paris Commune.

Bismarck's *Norddeutsche* was absolutely right when it announced, to the satisfaction of its master, that the German workers' party had sworn off internationalism in the new programme.[3]

II

"Starting from these basic principles, the German workers' party strives by all legal means for the *free state—and—*socialist society: the abolition of the wage system *together with* the *iron law of wages*—and—exploitation in every form; the elimination of all social and political inequality."

I shall return to the "free" state later.

So, in future, the German workers' party has got to believe in Lassalle's "iron law of wages"! That this may not be lost, the nonsense is perpetrated of speaking of the "abolition of the wage system" (it should read: system of wage labour) "*together with* the iron law of wages." If I abolish wage labour, then naturally I abolish its laws also, whether they are of "iron" or sponge. But Lassalle's attack on wage labour turns almost solely on this so-called law. In order, therefore, to prove that Lassalle's sect has conquered, the "wage system" must be abolished "*together with* the iron law of wages" and not without it.

It is well known that nothing of the "iron law of wages" is Lassalle's except the word "iron" borrowed from Goethe's "great eternal iron laws." The word *iron* is a label by which the true believers recognise one another. But if I take the law with Lassalle's stamp on it and, consequently, in his sense, then I must also take it with his substantiation for it. And what is that? As Lange already showed, shortly after Lassalle's death, it is the Malthusian theory of population (preached by Lange himself). But if this theory is

3. Marx refers to the editorial which appeared in No. 67 of the *Norddeutsche Allgemeine Zeitung* (*North German General Newspaper*) of March 20, 1875. It stated with regard to Article 5 of the Social-Democratic Programme that "Social-Democratic agitation had in many respects become more prudent" and that it was "repudiating the International."

correct, then again I *cannot* abolish the law even if I abolish wage labour a hundred times over, because the law then governs not only the system of wage labour but *every* social system. Basing themselves directly on this, the economists have been proving for fifty years and more that socialism cannot abolish poverty, *which has its basis in nature*, but can only make it *general*, distribute it simultaneously over the whole surface of society!

But all this is not the main thing. *Quite apart* from the *false* Lassallean formulation of the law, the truly outrageous retrogression consists in the following.

Since Lassalle's death there has asserted itself in *our* Party the scientific understanding that wages are not what they *appear* to be, namely, the *value*, or *price, of labour*, but only a masked form for the *value*, or *price, of labour power*. Thereby the whole bourgeois conception of wages hitherto, as well as all the criticism hitherto directed against this conception, was thrown overboard once for all and it was made clear that the wage-worker has permission to work for his own subsistence, that is, *to live*, only in so far as he works for a certain time gratis for the capitalist (and hence also for the latter's co-consumers of surplus value); that the whole capitalist system of production turns on the increase of this gratis labour by extending the working day or by developing the productivity, that is, increasing the intensity of labour power, etc; that, consequently, the system of wage labour is a system of slavery, and indeed of a slavery which becomes more severe in proportion as the social productive forces of labour develop, whether the worker receives better or worse payment. And after this understanding has gained more and more ground in our Party, one returns to Lassalle's dogmas, although one must have known that Lassalle *did not know* what wages were, but following in the wake of the bourgeois economists took the appearance for the essence of the matter.

It is as if, among slaves who have at last got behind the secret of slavery and broken out in rebellion, a slave still in thrall to obsolete notions were to inscribe on the programme of the rebellion: Slavery must be abolished because the feeding of slaves in the system of slavery cannot exceed a certain low maximum!

Does not the mere fact that the representatives of our Party were capable of perpetrating such a monstrous attack on the understanding that has spread among the mass of our Party prove by itself with what criminal levity and with what lack of conscience they set to work in drawing up this compromise programme!

Instead of the indefinite concluding phrase of the paragraph, "the elimination of all social and political inequality," it ought to have been said that with the abolition of class distinctions all social and political inequality arising from them would disappear of itself.

III

"The German workers' party, in order *to pave the way to the solution of the social question*, demands the establishment of producers' co-operative societies *with state aid under the democratic control of the toiling people*. The producers' co-operative societies *are to be called into being* for industry and agriculture on such a scale *that the socialist organisation of the total labour will arise from them*."

After the Lassallean "iron law of wages," the physic of the prophet. The way to it is "paved" in worthy fashion. In place of the existing class struggle appears a newspaper scribbler's phrase: "the social *question*," to the "*solution*" of which one "paves the way." Instead of arising from the revolutionary process of transformation of society, the "socialist organisation of the total labour" "arises" from the "state aid" that the state gives to the producers' co-operative societies and which the *state*, not the worker, "*calls into being*." It is worthy of Lassalle's imagination that with state loans one can build a new society just as well as a new railway!

From the remnants of a sense of shame, "state aid" has been put —under the democratic control of the "toiling people."

In the first place, the majority of the "toiling people" in Germany consists of peasants, and not of proletarians.

Secondly, "democratic" means in German "*volksherrschaftlich*" ["by the rule of the people"]. But what does "control by the rule of the people of the toiling people" mean? And particularly in the case of a toiling people which, through these demands that it puts to the state, expresses its full consciousness that it neither rules nor is ripe for ruling!

It would be superfluous to deal here with the criticism of the recipe prescribed by Buchez in the reign of Louis Philippe in *opposition* to the French Socialists and accepted by the reactionary workers of the *Atelier*.[4] The chief offence does not lie in having inscribed this specific nostrum in the programme, but in taking, in general, a retrograde step from the standpoint of a class movement to that of a sectarian movement.

That the workers desire to establish the conditions for co-operative production on a social scale, and first of all on a national scale in their own country, only means that they are working to revolutionise the present conditions of production, and it has nothing in common with the foundation of co-operative societies with state aid. But as far as the present co-operative societies are concerned, they are of value *only* in so far as they are the independent crea-

4. *Atelier* (Workshop). A workers' monthly which appeared in Paris in 1840–50. It was under the influence of the Catholic socialism of Buchez.

tions of the workers and not protégés either of the government or of the bourgeois.

IV

I come now to the democratic section.

A. *"The free basis of the state."*

First of all, according to II, the German workers' party strives for "the free state."

Free state—what is this?

It is by no means the aim of the workers, who have got rid of the narrow mentality of humble subjects, to set the state free. In the German Empire the "state" is almost as "free" as in Russia. Freedom consists in converting the state from an organ superimposed upon society into one completely subordinate to it, and today, too, the forms of state are more free or less free to the extent that they restrict the "freedom of the state."

The German workers' party—at least if it adopts the programme —shows that its socialist ideas are not even skin-deep; in that, instead of treating existing society (and this holds good for any future one) as the *basis* of the existing state (or of the future state in the case of future society), it treats the state rather as independent entity that possesses its own *intellectual, ethical and libertarian bases.*

And what of the riotous misuse which the programme makes of the words *"present-day state," "present-day society,"* and of the still more riotous misconception it creates in regard to the state to which it addresses its demands?

"Present-day society" is capitalist society, which exists in all civilised countries, more or less free from medieval admixture, more or less modified by the special historical development of each country, more or less developed. On the other hand, the "present-day state" changes with a country's frontier. It is different in the Prusso-German Empire from what it is in Switzerland, it is different in England from what it is in the United States. The "present-day state" is, therefore, a fiction.

Nevertheless, the different states of the different civilised countries, in spite of their manifold diversity of form, all have this in common, that they are based on modern bourgeois society, only one more or less capitalistically developed. They have, therefore, also certain essential features in common. In this sense it is possible to speak of the "present-day state," in contrast with the future, in which its present root, bourgeois society, will have died off.

The question then arises: what transformation will the state undergo in communist society? In other words, what social functions will remain in existence there that are analogous to present functions of the state? This question can only be answered scientifically, and one does not get a flea-hop nearer to the problem by a thousandfold combination of the word people with the word state.

Between capitalist and communist society lies the period of the revolutionary transformation of the one into the other. There corresponds to this also a political transition period in which the state can be nothing but *the revolutionary dictatorship of the proletariat*.

Now the programme does not deal with this nor with the future state of communist society.

Its political demands contain nothing beyond the old democratic litany familiar to all: universal suffrage, direct legislation, popular rights, a people's militia, etc. They are a mere echo of the bourgeois People's Party, of the League of Peace and Freedom. They are all demands which, in so far as they are not exaggerated in fantastic presentation, have already been *realised*. Only the state to which they belong does not lie within the borders of the German Empire, but in Switzerland, the United States, etc. This sort of "state of the future" is a present-day state, although existing outside the "framework" of the German Empire.

But one thing has been forgotten. Since the German workers' party expressly declares that it acts within "the present-day national state," hence within *its own* state, the Prusso-German Empire—its demands would indeed otherwise be largely meaningless, since one only demands what one has not got—it should not have forgotten the chief thing, namely, that all those pretty little gewgaws rest on the recognition of the so-called sovereignty of the people and hence are appropriate only in a *democratic republic*.

Since one has not the courage—and wisely so, for the circumstances demand caution—to demand the democratic republic, as the French workers' programmes under Louis Philippe and under Louis Napoleon did, one should not have resorted, either, to the subterfuge, neither "honest"[5] nor decent, of demanding things which have meaning only in a democratic republic from a state which is nothing but a police-guarded military despotism, embellished with parliamentary forms, alloyed with a feudal admixture, already influenced by the bourgeoisie and bureaucratically carpentered, and then to assure this state into the bargain that one imagines one will be able to force such things upon it "by legal means."

Even vulgar democracy, which sees the millennium in the democratic republic and has no suspicion that it is precisely in this last form of state of bourgeois society that the class struggle has to be

5. *"Honest"* was the epithet applied to the Eisenachers. Here a play upon words.

fought out to a conclusion—even it towers mountains above this kind of democratism which keeps within the limits of what is permitted by the police and not permitted by logic.

That, in fact, by the word "state" is meant the government machine, or the state in so far as it forms a special organism separated from society through division of labour, is shown by the words "the German worker's party demands *as the economic basis of the state*: a single progressive income tax," etc. Taxes are the economic basis of the government machinery and of nothing else. In the state of the future, existing in Switzerland, this demand has been pretty well fulfilled. Income tax presupposes various sources of income of the various social classes, and hence capitalist society. It is, therefore, nothing remarkable that the Liverpool financial reformers, bourgeois headed by Gladstone's brother, are putting forward the same demand as the programme.

B. "The German workers' party demands as the intellectual and ethical basis of the state:

"1. Universal and *equal elementary education* by the state. Universal compulsory school attendance. Free instruction."

Equal elementary education? What idea lies behind these words? Is it believed that in present-day society (and it is only with this one has to deal) education can be *equal* for all classes? Or is it demanded that the upper classes also shall be compulsorily reduced to the modicum of education—the elementary school—that alone is compatible with the economic conditions not only of the wage-workers but of the peasants as well?

"Universal compulsory school attendance. Free instruction." The former exists even in Germany, the second in Switzerland and in the United States in the case of elementary schools. If in some states of the latter country higher educational institutions are also "free" that only means in fact defraying the cost of the education of the upper classes from the general tax receipts. Incidentally, the same holds good for "free administration of justice" demanded under A, 5. The administration of criminal justice is to be had free everywhere; that of civil justice is concerned almost exclusively with conflicts over property and hence affects almost exclusively the possessing classes. Are they to carry on their litigation at the expense of the national coffers?

The paragraph on the schools should at least have demanded technical schools (theoretical and practical) in combination with the elementary school.

"*Elementary education by the state*" is altogether objectionable. Defining by a general law the expenditures on the elementary schools, the qualifications of the teaching staff, the branches of instruction, etc., and, as is done in the United States, supervising the fulfilment of these legal specifications by state inspectors, is a very different thing from appointing the state as the educator of the people! Government and Church should rather be equally excluded from any influence on the school. Particularly, indeed, in the Prusso-German Empire (and one should not take refuge in the rotten subterfuge that one is speaking of a "state of the future"; we have seen how matters stand in this respect) the state has need, on the contrary, of a very stern education by the people.

But the whole programme, for all its democratic clang, is tainted through and through by the Lassallean sect's servile belief in the state, or, what is no better, by a democratic belief in miracles, or rather it is a compromise between these two kinds of belief in miracles, both equally remote from socialism.

"Freedom of science" says a paragraph of the Prussian Constitution. Why, then, here?

"Freedom of conscience"! If one desired at this time of the *Kulturkampf*[6] to remind liberalism of its old catchwords, it surely could have been done only in the following form: Everyone should be able to attend to his religious as well as his bodily needs without the police sticking their noses in. But the workers' party ought at any rate in this connection to have expressed its awareness of the fact that bourgeois "freedom of conscience" is nothing but the toleration of all possible kinds of *religious freedom of conscience,* and that for its part it endeavours rather to liberate the conscience from the witchery of religion. But one chooses not to transgress the "bourgeois" level.

I have now come to the end, for the appendix that now follows in the programme does not constitute a characteristic component part of it. Hence I can be very brief here.

2. *"Normal working day."*

In no other country has the workers' party limited itself to such an indefinite demand, but has always fixed the length of the working day that it considers normal under the given circumstances.

3. "Restriction of female labour and prohibition of child labour."

The standardisation of the working day must include the restriction of female labour, in so far as it relates to the duration, intermissions, etc., of the working day; otherwise it could only mean the

6. *Kulturkampf* (Struggle for culture): Bismarck's struggle in the seventies against the German Catholic Party, the Party of the "Centre," by means of police persecution of Catholicism.

exclusion of female labour from branches of industry that are especially unhealthy for the female body or are objectionable morally for the female sex. If that is what was meant, it should have been said so.

"*Prohibition of child labour.*" Here it was absolutely essential to state the age limit.

A *general prohibition* of child labour is incompatible with the existence of large-scale industry and hence an empty, pious wish. Its realisation—if it were possible—would be reactionary, since, with a strict regulation of the working time according to the different age groups and other safety measures for the protection of children, an early combination of productive labour with education is one of the most potent means for the transformation of present-day society.

4. "State supervision of factory, workshop and domestic industry."

In consideration of the Prusso-German state it should definitely have been demanded that the inspectors are to be removable only by a court of law; that any worker can have them prosecuted for neglect of duty; that they must belong to the medical profession.

5. "Regulation of prison labour."

A petty demand in a general workers' programme. In any case, it should have been clearly stated that there is no intention from fear of competition to allow ordinary criminals to be treated like beasts, and especially that there is no desire to deprive them of their sole means of betterment, productive labour. This was surely the least one might have expected from Socialists.

6. "An effective liability law."

It should have been stated what is meant by an "effective" liability law.

Be it noted, incidentally, that in speaking of the normal working day the part of factory legislation that deals with health regulations and safety measures, etc., has been overlooked. The liability law only comes into operation when these regulations are infringed.

In short, this appendix also is distinguished by slovenly editing.

Dixi et salvavi animam meam.[7]

7. I have spoken and saved my soul.

Circular Letter to Bebel, Liebknecht, Bracke, and Others

KARL MARX

Movements in radical opposition to an existing order must often contend with voices within their midst that urge a toning down of the radical program in the interests of piecemeal reform and collaboration with liberal elements who desire only gradual and partial change of the society. The German socialist movement of the 1870's was a case in point. In this circular letter to the Social Democratic Party leaders, Marx and Engels registered their strong protest against reformist voices within the movement. They still stood firm in their radical opposition to the existing order and their commitment to class struggle as the means of overthrowing it, and they wished the party to do likewise. The "three Zurichers" referred to in the letter were Höchberg, Bernstein, and Schramm; the article attacked by Marx and Engels in the letter was published in the *Jahrbuch für Sozialwissenschaft und Sozialpolitik*.[1]

London, September 17–18, 1879

The Manifesto of the Three Zurichers

In the meantime Höchberg's *Jahrbuch* has reached us, containing an article, "The Socialist Movement in Germany in Retrospect," which, as Höchberg himself tells me, has been written by precisely the three members of the Zurich Commission. Here we have their authentic criticism of the movement up till now and with it their authentic programme for the line of the new organ in so far as this depends on them.

Right at the beginning we read:

"The movement, which Lassalle regarded as an eminently political one, to which he summoned not only the workers but all honest

1. *Annual for Social Sciences and Social Policy.* [*R. T.*]

399

democrats, *at the head of which* were to march the independent representatives of science and *all men imbued with true love of humanity*, was diminished under the presidency of Johann Baptist Schweitzer to a *one-sided struggle of the industrial workers in their own interests.*"

I shall not examine whether or how far this is historically accurate. The special reproach here levelled against Schweitzer is that he *diminished* Lassalleanism, which is here taken as a bourgeois-democratic-philanthropic movement, to a one-sided struggle in the interest of the industrial workers, by *deepening* its character as a class struggle of the industrial workers against the bourgeois. He is further reproached with having "rejected bourgeois democracy." What business has bourgeois democracy within the Social-Democratic Party anyway? If it consists of "honest men" it cannot wish for admission, and if it does nevertheless wish to be admitted this can only be in order to start a row.

The Lassallean party "chose to conduct itself *in the most one-sided* way as a *workers' party.*" The gentlemen who write that are themselves members of the party which conducts itself in the most one-sided way as a workers' party, they are at present invested with offices and dignities in this party. Here there is an absolute incompatibility. If they mean what they write they must leave the party, or at least resign their offices and dignities. If they do not do so, they admit that they are proposing to utilise their official position in order to combat the proletarian character of the Party. Thus, if the Party leaves them their offices and dignities it will be betraying itself.

In the opinion of these gentlemen, then, the Social-Democratic Party should *not* be a one-sided workers' party but an all-sided party of "all men imbued with true love of humanity." It must prove this above all by laying aside coarse proletarian passions and placing itself under the guidance of educated, philanthropic bourgeois "in order to cultivate good taste" and "learn good form" (p. 85). Then the "disreputable behaviour" of some of the leaders will give way to a thoroughly respectable "bourgeois behaviour." (As if the externally disreputable appearance of those here referred to were not the least they can be reproached with!) Then, too, "*numerous adherents* from the circles of the *educated* and *propertied* classes will make their appearance. But *these* must first be won if the . . . agitation conducted is to attain *tangible successes.*" German socialism has "attached too much importance to the winning of the *masses* and in so doing has neglected energetic [!] propaganda among the so-called upper strata of society." For "the Party still lacks men fit to represent it in the Reichstag." It is, however, "desirable and necessary to entrust the mandates to men who have the time and opportunity to make themselves thoroughly acquainted with the relevant material. The simple worker and small master craftsman . . . have necessary leisure for this only in rare and exceptional cases." So elect bourgeois!

In short: the working class of itself is incapable of its own emancipation. For this purpose it must place itself under the leadership of "educated and propertied" bourgeois who alone possess the "time and opportunity" to acquaint themselves with what is good for the workers. And secondly, the bourgeoisie is on no account to be fought against but—to be *won over* by energetic propaganda.

But if one wants to win over the upper strata of society or only its well-disposed elements one must not frighten them on any account. And here the three Zurichers think they have made a reassuring discovery:

"Precisely at the present time, under the pressure of the Anti-Socialist Law, the Party is showing that it *is not inclined* to pursue the path of violent bloody revolution but is determined . . . to follow the path of legality, that is, of *reform*." So if the 500,000 to 600,000 Social-Democratic voters—between a tenth and an eighth of the whole electorate and, besides, dispersed over the length and breadth of the land—have the sense not to run their heads against a wall and to attempt a "bloody revolution" of one against ten, this proves that they for ever *renounce* taking advantage of some tremendous external event, a sudden revolutionary upsurge arising from it or even a *victory* of the people gained in a conflict resulting from it. If Berlin should ever again be so uneducated as to have another March 18[2] the Social-Democrats, instead of taking part in the fight as "riff-raff with a mania for barricades" (p. 88), must rather "follow the path of legality," put on the brakes, clear away the barricades and if necessary march with the glorious army against the one-sided, coarse, uneducated masses. Or if the gentlemen assert that this is not what they meant, what then did they mean?

But still better follows.

"Hence, the more quiet, objective and deliberate it [the Party] is in its criticism of existing conditions and in its proposals to change them, the less possible will it be to repeat the present successful move [when the Anti-Socialist Law was introduced] by which the conscious reactionaries intimidated the bourgeoisie by conjuring up the Red bogey" (p. 88).

In order to relieve the bourgeoisie of the last trace of anxiety it must be clearly and convincingly proved to it that the Red bogey is really only a bogey, and does not exist. But what is the secret of the Red bogey if not the bourgeoisie's dread of the inevitable life-and-

2. This refers to the revolutionary barricade fighting in Berlin on March 18–19, 1848.

death struggle between it and the proletariat? Dread of the inevitable outcome of the modern class struggle? Do away with the class struggle and the bourgeoisie and "all independent people" will "not be afraid to go hand in hand with the proletarians"! And the ones to be cheated would be precisely the proletarians.

Let the Party, therefore, prove by its humble and lowly manner that it has once and for all laid aside the "improprieties and excesses" which occasioned the Anti-Socialist Law. If it voluntarily promises that it only intends to act within the limits of this law, Bismarck and the bourgeoisie will surely have the kindness to repeal it, as it will then be superfluous!

"Let no one misunderstand us"; we do not want "to give up our Party and our programme, but think that for years hence we shall have enough to do if we concentrate our whole strength and energy upon the attainment of certain immediate aims which must in any case be achieved before the realisation of the more far-reaching aspirations can be thought of." Then those bourgeois, petty bourgeois and workers who are "at present frightened away . . . by our far-reaching demands" will join us in masses.

The programme is not to be *given up* but only *postponed*—for an indefinite period. One accepts it, though not really for oneself and one's own lifetime but posthumously, as an heirloom to be handed down to one's children and grandchildren. In the meantime one devotes one's "whole strength and energy" to all sorts of petty rubbish and the patching up of the capitalist order of society in order at least to produce the appearance of something happening without at the same time scaring the bourgeoisie. There I must really praise the "Communist" Miquel, who proves his unshakable belief in the inevitable overthrow of capitalist society in the course of the next few hundred years by swindling for all he's worth, contributing his honest best to the crash of 1873[3] and so *really* doing something to help along the collapse of the existing order.

Another offence against good form was the "exaggerated attacks on the company promoters," who were after all "only children of their time"; it would therefore "have been better to abstain . . . from abusing Strousberg and similar people." Unfortunately everyone is only a "child of his time" and if this is a sufficient excuse nobody ought ever to be attacked any more, all controversy, all struggle on our part ceases; we quietly accept all the kicks our adversaries give us because we, who are so wise, know that these adversaries are "only children of their time" and cannot act otherwise. Instead of repaying their kicks with interest we ought rather to pity these unfortunates.

3. The crash of 1873 ended the so-called *"Grunder taumel"* (the promoting frenzy), a period of furious speculation and stock-exchange gambling which followed on the termination of the Franco-Prussian War of 1870–71.

Then again the support of the Commune had the disadvantage, nevertheless, that "people who were otherwise well disposed to us were alienated and in general the *hatred of the bourgeoisie* against us was increased." Furthermore, the Party "is not wholly without blame for the passage of the October Law,[4] for it had increased the *hatred of the bourgeoisie* unnecessarily."

There you have the programme of the three censors of Zurich. In clarity it leaves nothing to be desired. Least of all to us, who are very familiar with the whole of this phraseology from the 1848 days. It is the representatives of the petty bourgeoisie who are here presenting themselves, full of anxiety that the proletariat, under the pressure of its revolutionary position, may "go too far." Instead of determined political opposition, general mediation; instead of struggle against the government and the bourgeoisie, an attempt to win over and persuade them; instead of defiant resistance to ill treatment from above, humble submission and confession that the punishment was deserved. Historically necessary conflicts are all interpreted as misunderstandings, and all discussion ends with the assurance that after all we are all agreed on the main point. The people who came out as bourgeois democrats in 1848 could just as well call themselves Social-Democrats now. To the former the democratic republic was as unattainably remote as the overthrow of the capitalist system is to the latter, and therefore is of absolutely no importance in present-day politics; one can mediate, compromise and philanthropise to one's heart's content. It is just the same with the class struggle because its existence can no longer be denied, but in practice it is hushed up, diluted, attenuated, The Social-Democratic Party *is not* to be a workers' party, is not to incur the odium of the bourgeoisie or of anyone else; it should above all conduct energetic propaganda among the bourgeoisie; instead of laying stress on far-reaching aims which frighten away the bourgeoisie and after all are not attainable in our generation, it should rather devote its whole strength and energy to those petty-bourgeois patchwork reforms which, by providing the old order of society with new props, may perhaps transform the ultimate catastrophe into a gradual, piecemeal and as far as possible peaceful process of dissolution. These are the same people who, ostensibly engaged in indefatigable activity, not only do nothing themselves but try to prevent anything happening at all except—chatter; the same people whose fear of every form of action in 1848 and 1849 obstructed the movement at every step and finally brought about its downfall, the same people who never see reaction and are then quite astonished to find themselves in the end in a blind alley where neither resistance nor flight is possible,

4. The reference is to the Exceptional Law against the Socialists, introduced by Bismarck in October 1878.

the same people who want to confine history within their narrow
Philistine horizon and over whose heads history invariably proceeds
to the order of the day.

As to their socialist convictions, this has been adequately criticised already in the *Manifesto*, the chapter on "German, or 'True,'
Socialism." Where the class struggle is pushed aside as a disagreeable "coarse" phenomenon, nothing remains as a basis for socialism
but "true love of humanity" and empty phraseology about "justice."

It is an inevitable phenomenon, rooted in the course of development, that people from what have hitherto been the ruling classes
should also join the militant proletariat and supply it with educative
elements. We clearly stated this in the *Manifesto*. But here two
points are to be noted:

First, in order to be of use to the proletarian movement these
people must bring real educative elements into it. But with the
great majority of the German bourgeois converts that is not the
case. Neither the *Zukunft* nor the *Neue Gesellschaft*[5] have contributed anything which could advance the movement one step further. Here there is an absolute lack of real education material,
whether factual or theoretical. In its place there are attempts to
bring superficially mastered socialist ideas into harmony with the
exceedingly varied theoretical standpoints which these gentlemen
have brought with them from the university or elsewhere and of
which, owing to the process of decomposition which the remnants
of German philosophy are at present undergoing, one is more confused than the other. Instead of thoroughly studying the new science themselves to begin with, each of them preferred to trim
it to fit the point of view he already had brought along, made himself forthwith a private science of his own and at once came forward
with the pretension of wanting to teach it. Hence, there are about
as many points of view among these gentry as there are heads; instead of producing clarity in a single case they have only produced
desperate confusion—fortunately almost exclusively among themselves. Educative elements whose first principle is to teach what they
have not learnt can very well be dispensed with by the Party.

Secondly. If people of this kind from other classes join the proletarian movement, the first condition must be that they should not
bring any remnants of bourgeois, petty-bourgeois, etc., prejudices
with them but should whole-heartedly adopt the proletarian outlook. But these gentlemen, as has been proved, are chock-full of
bourgeois and petty-bourgeois ideas. In such a petty-bourgeois coun-

5. *Zukunft* [*Future*] and *Neue Gesellschaft* [*New Society*]: Social-reformist
journals. The former appeared in Zurich in 1877–80; the latter in Berlin
in 1877–78.

try as Germany these ideas certainly have their justification. But only *outside* the Social-Democratic Workers' Party. If these gentlemen constitute themselves into a Social-Democratic petty-bourgeois party they have a perfect right to do so; one could then negotiate with them, form a *bloc* according to circumstances, etc. But in a workers' party they are an adulterating element. If reasons exist for tolerating them there for the moment it is also duty *only* to tolerate them, to allow them no influence in the Party leadership and to remain aware that a break with them is only a matter of time. That time, moreover, seems to have come. How the Party can tolerate the authors of this article in its midst any longer is incomprehensible to us. But if even the leadership of the Party should fall more or less into the hands of such people, the Party would simply be castrated and there would be an end of proletarian snap.

As for ourselves, in view of our whole past there is only one path open to us. For almost forty years we have stressed the class struggle as the immediate driving power of history and in particular the class struggle between bourgeoisie and proletariat as the great lever of the modern social revolution; it is, therefore, impossible for us to co-operate with people who wish to expunge this class struggle from the movement. When the International was formed we expressly formulated the battle cry: The emancipation of the working class must be the work of the working class itself. We cannot, therefore, co-operate with people who openly state that the workers are too uneducated to emancipate themselves and must first be freed from above by philanthropic big bourgeois and petty bourgeois. If the new Party organ adopts a line corresponding to the views of these gentlemen, a line that is bourgeois and not proletarian, then nothing remains for us, much though we should regret it, but publicly to declare our opposition to it, and to dissolve the solidarity with which we have hitherto represented the German Party abroad. But it is to be hoped that things will not come to *that* pass.

The Tactics of Social Democracy

FRIEDRICH ENGELS

In 1850 Marx published in his journal *Neue Rheinische Zeitung* a series of articles entitled "The Class Struggles in France 1848–1850," in which he gave a narrative account of the revolution of 1848 and after in France. Here he proclaimed the point of view of "revolutionary socialism" or "communism" as follows: "This socialism is the *declaration of the permanence of the revolution,* the *class dictatorship* of the proletariat as the necessary transit point to the *abolition of class distinctions generally,* to the abolition of all the relations of production on which they rest, to the abolition of all the social relations that correspond to these relations of production, to the revolutionizing of all the ideas that result from these social relations." In 1895 Engels put out the articles as a separate pamphlet with a long Introduction, which proved to be his valedictory to the Social Democratic movement, as he died later that year. Surveying changes in the European scene over the more than forty years since Marx's pamphlet was written, Engels hailed the steady progress made by Social Democracy, particularly in Germany, through the electoral process. His endorsement of peaceful political tactics was further accentuated when, in March, 1895, *Vorwärts,* the central organ of the German Social Democratic Party, printed an abbreviated version of the Introduction featuring those portions of it which, as Engels complained in a private letter, could serve to "defend the tactics of peace at all costs and of the abhorrence of force. . . ." On April 1, 1895, Engels wrote further to Karl Kautsky: ". . . I see today in the *Vorwärts* an extract from my Introduction, printed without my prior knowledge and trimmed in such a fashion that I appear as a peaceful worshipper of legality *quand même.* So much the more would I like the Introduction to appear unabridged in the *Neue Zeit,* so that this disgraceful impression will be wiped out." Even in its unabridged form, however, as printed here, the Introduction is notable for its hearty approval of the tactics that had evolved in Social Democratic practice in the late nineteenth century.

The work here republished was Marx's first attempt to explain a section of contemporary history by means of his materialist conception, on the basis of the given economic situation. In the *Commu-*

nist Manifesto, the theory was applied in broad outline to the whole of modern history; in the articles by Marx and myself in the *Neue Rheinische Zeitung*, it was constantly used to interpret political events of the day. Here, on the other hand, the question was to demonstrate the inner causal connection in the course of a development which extended over some years, a development as critical, for the whole of Europe, as it was typical; hence, in accordance with the conception of the author, to trace political events back to effects of what were, in the final analysis, economic causes.

If events and series of events are judged by current history, it will never be possible to go back to the *ultimate* economic causes. Even today, when the specialised press concerned provides such rich material, it still remains impossible even in England to follow day by day the movement of industry and trade in the world market and the changes which take place in the methods of production in such a way as to be able to draw a general conclusion, for any point of time, from these manifold, complicated and ever-changing factors, the most important of which, into the bargain, generally operate a long time in secret before they suddenly make themselves violently felt on the surface. A clear survey of the economic history of a given period can never be obtained contemporaneously, but only subsequently, after a collecting and sifting of the material has taken place. Statistics are a necessary auxiliary means here, and they always lag behind. For this reason, it is only too often necessary, in current history, to treat this, the most decisive, factor as constant, and the economic situation existing at the beginning of the period concerned as given and unalterable for the whole period, or else to take notice of only such changes in this situation as arise out of the patently manifest events themselves, and are, therefore, likewise patently manifest. Hence, the materialist method has here quite often to limit itself to tracing political conflicts back to the struggles between the interests of the existing social classes and fractions of classes created by the economic development, and to prove the particular political parties to be the more or less adequate political expression of these same classes and fractions of classes.

It is self-evident that this unavoidable neglect of contemporaneous changes in the economic situation, the very basis of all the processes to be examined, must be a source of error. But all the conditions of a comprehensive presentation of current history unavoidably include sources of error—which, however, keeps nobody from writing current history.

When Marx undertook this work, the source of error mentioned was even more unavoidable. It was simply impossible during the period of the Revolution of 1848–49 to follow up the economic transformations taking place at the same time or even to keep them it view. It was the same during the first months of exile in London, in the autumn and winter of 1849–50. But that was just the time when Marx began this work. And in spite of these unfavourable circumstances, his exact knowledge both of the economic situation in France before, and of the political history of that country after the February Revolution made it possible for him to give a picture of events which laid bare their inner connections in a way never attained ever since, and which later brilliantly stood the double test applied by Marx himself.

The first test resulted from the fact that after the spring of 1850 Marx once again found leisure for economic studies, and first of all took up the economic history of the last ten years. Thereby what he had hitherto deduced, half *a priori*, from sketchy material, became absolutely clear to him from the facts themselves, namely, that the world trade crisis of 1847 had been the true mother of the February and March Revolutions, and that the industrial prosperity, which had been returning gradually since the middle of 1848 and attained full bloom in 1849 and 1850, was the revitalising force of the newly strengthened European reaction. That was decisive. Whereas in the first three articles (which appeared in the January, February and March issues of the *Neue Rheinische Zeitung, Politisch-ökonomische Revue*,[1] Hamburg, 1850) there was still the expectation of a early new upsurge of revolutionary energy, the historical review written by Marx and myself for the last issue, a double issue (May to October), which was published in the autumn of 1850, breaks once and for all with these illusions: "A new revolution is possible only in the wake of a new crisis. It is, however, just as certain as this crisis." But that was the only essential change which had to be made. There was absolutely nothing to alter in the interpretation of events given in the earlier chapters, or in the causal connections established therein, as the continuation of the narrative from March 10 up to the autumn of 1850 in the review in question proves. I have, therefore, included this continuation as the fourth article in the present new edition.

The second test was even more severe. Immediately after Louis Bonaparte's *coup d'état* of December 2, 1851, Marx worked out anew the history of France from February 1848 up to this event, which concluded the revolutionary period for the time being. (*The Eighteenth Brumaire of Louis Bonaparte*. Third edition, Hamburg, Meissner, 1885). In this pamphlet the period depicted in our present publication is again dealt with, although more briefly. Compare this second presentation, written in the light of the decisive event which happened over a year later, with ours and it will be found that the author had very little to change.

1. *New Rhenish Gazette, Politico-Economic Review*, a journal published by   Marx and Engels in January–October 1850.

What, besides, gives our work quite special significance is the circumstance that it was the first to express the formula which, by common agreement, the workers' parties of all countries in the world briefly summarise their demand for economic transformation: the appropriation of the means of production by society. In the second chapter, in connection with the "right to work," which is characterised as "the first clumsy formula wherein the revolutionary demands of the proletariat are summarised," it is said: "But behind the right to work stands the power over capital; behind the power over capital, the *appropriation of the means of production*, their subjection to the associated working class and, therefore, the abolition of wage labour as well as of capital and of their mutual relations." Thus, here, for the first time, the proposition is formulated by which modern workers' socialism is equally sharply differentiated both from all the different shades of feudal, bourgeois, petty-bourgeois, etc., socialism and also from the confused community of goods of utopian and of spontaneous workers' communism. If, later, Marx extended the formula to include appropriation of the means of exchange, this extension, which in any case was self-evident after the *Communist Manifesto*, only expressed a corollary to the main proposition. A few wiseacres in England have of late added that the "means of distribution" should also be handed over to society. It would be difficult for these gentlemen to say what these economic means of distribution are, as distinct from the means of production and exchange; unless *political* means of distribution are meant, taxes, poor relief, including the *Sachsenwald*[2] and other endowments. But, first, these are already now means of distribution in possession of society in the aggregate, either of the state or of the community, and secondly, it is precisely the abolition of these that we desire.

When the February Revolution broke out, all of us, as far as our conceptions of the conditions and the course of revolutionary movements were concerned, were under the spell of previous historical experience, particularly that of France. It was, indeed, the latter which had dominated the whole of European history since 1789, and from which now once again the signal had gone forth for general revolutionary change. It was, therefore, natural and unavoidable that our conceptions of the nature and the course of the "social" revolution proclaimed in Paris in February 1848, of the revolution of the proletariat, should be strongly coloured by memories of the prototypes of 1789 and 1830. Moreover, when the Paris uprising found its echo in the victorious insurrections in Vienna, Milan and Berlin; when the whole of Europe right up to the Russian frontier was swept into the movement; when thereupon in Paris, in June,

2. *Sachsenwald:* A vast estate granted to Bismarck by William I in 1871.

the first great battle for power between the proletariat and the bourgeoisie was fought; when the very victory of its class so shook the bourgeoisie of all countries that it fled back into the arms of the monarchist-feudal reaction which had just been overthrown—there could be no doubt for us, under the circumstances then obtaining, that the great decisive combat had commenced, that it would have to be fought out in a single, long and vicissitudinous period of revolution, but that it could only end in the final victory of the proletariat.

After the defeats of 1849 we in no way shared the illusions of the vulgar democracy grouped around the future provisional governments *in partibus*.[3] This vulgar democracy reckoned on a speedy and finally decisive victory of the "people" over the "tyrants"; we looked to a long struggle, after the removal of the "tyrants," among the antagonistic elements concealed within this "people" itself. Vulgar democracy expected a renewed outbreak any day; we declared as early as autumn 1850 that at least the *first* chapter of the revolutionary period was closed and that nothing was to be expected until the outbreak of a new world economic crisis. For which reason we were excommunicated, as traitors to the revolution, by the very people who later, almost without exception, made their peace with Bismarck—so far as Bismarck found them worth the trouble.

But history has shown us too to have been wrong, has revealed our point of view of that time to have been an illusion. It has done even more: it has not merely dispelled the erroneous notions we then held; it has also completely transformed the conditions under which the proletariat has to fight. The mode of struggle of 1848 is today obsolete in every respect, and this is a point which deserves closer examination on the present occasion.

All revolutions up to the present day have resulted in the displacement of one definite class rule by another; but all ruling classes up to now have been only small minorities in relation to the ruled mass of the people. One ruling minority was thus overthrown; another minority seized the helm of state in its stead and refashioned the state institutions to suit its own interests. This was on every occasion the minority group qualified and called to rule by the given degree of economic development; and just for that reason, and only for that reason, it happened that the ruled majority either participated in the revolution for the benefit of the former or else calmly acquiesced in it. But if we disregard the concrete content in each case, the common form of all these revolutions was that they were minority revolutions. Even when the majority took part, it did

---

3. *In partibus infidelium:* literally, in the lands of the infidels, that is, beyond the frontiers of one's own country, in emigration.

so—whether wittingly or not—only in the service of a minority; but because of this, or even simply because of the passive, unresisting attitude of the majority, this minority acquired the appearance of being the representative of the whole people.

As a rule, after the first great success, the victorious minority divided; one half was satisfied with what had been gained, the other wanted to go still further, and put forward new demands, which, partly at least, were also in the real or apparent interest of the great mass of the people. In individual cases these more radical demands were actually forced through, but often only for the moment; the more moderate party would regain the upper hand, and what had last been won would wholly or partly be lost again; the vanquished would then shriek of treachery or ascribe their defeat to accident. In reality, however, the truth of the matter was largely this: the achievements of the first victory were only safeguarded by the second victory of the more radical party; this having been attained, and, with it, what was necessary for the moment, the radicals and their achievements vanished once more from the stage.

All revolutions of modern times, beginning with the great English Revolution of the seventeenth century, showed these features, which appeared inseparable from every revolutionary struggle. They appeared applicable, also, to the struggle of the proletariat for its emancipation; all the more applicable, since precisely in 1848 there were but a very few people who had any idea at all of the direction in which this emancipation was to be sought. The proletarian masses themselves, even in Paris, after the victory, were still absolutely in the dark as to the path to be taken. And yet the movement was there, instinctive, spontaneous, irrepressible. Was not this just the situation in which a revolution had to succeed, led, true, by a minority, but this time not in the interest of the minority, but in the veriest interest of the majority? If, in all the longer revolutionary periods, it was so easy to win the great masses of the people by the merely plausible false representations of the forward-thrusting minorities, why should they be less susceptible to ideas which were the truest reflection of their economic condition, which were nothing but the clear, rational expression of their needs, of needs not yet understood but merely vaguely felt by them? To be sure, this revolutionary mood of the masses had almost always, and usually very speedily, given way to lassitude or even to a revulsion of feeling as soon as illusion evaporated and disappointment set in. But here it was not a question of false representations, but of giving effect to the highest special interests of the great majority itself, interests which, true, were at that time by no means clear to this great majority, but which soon enough had to become clear to it, in the course of giving practical effect to them, by their convincing obviousness. And when, as Marx showed in this third article, in the spring of 1850, the development of the bourgeois republic that arose out of the "social" Revolution of 1848 had even concentrated real power in the hands of the big bourgeoisie—monarchistically inclined as it was into the bargain—and, on the other hand, had grouped all the other social classes, peasantry as well as petty bourgeoisie, round the proletariat, so that, during and after the common victory, not they but the proletariat grown wise by experience had to become the decisive factor—was there not every prospect then of turning the revolution of the minority into a revolution of the majority?

History has proved us, and all who thought like us, wrong. It has made it clear that the state of economic development on the Continent at that time was not, by a long way, ripe for the elimination of capitalist production; it has proved this by the economic revolution which, since 1848, has seized the whole of the Continent, and has caused big industry to take real root in France, Austria, Hungary, Poland and, recently, in Russia, while it has made Germany positively an industrial country of the first rank—all on a capitalist basis, which in the year 1848, therefore, still had great capacity for expansion. But it is just this industrial revolution which has everywhere produced clarity in class relations, has removed a number of intermediate forms handed down from the period of manufacture and in Eastern Europe even from guild handicraft, has created a genuine bourgeoisie and a genuine large-scale industrial proletariat and has pushed them into the foreground of social development. However, owing to this, the struggle between these two great classes, a struggle which, apart from England, existed in 1848 only in Paris and, at the most, in a few big industrial centres, has spread over the whole of Europe and reached an intensity still inconceivable in 1848. At that time the many obscure evangels of the sects, with their panaceas; today the *one* generally recognised, crystal-clear theory of Marx, sharply formulating the ultimate aims of the struggle. At that time the masses, sundered and differing according to locality and nationality, linked only by the feeling of common suffering, undeveloped, helplessly tossed to and fro from enthusiasm to despair; today the *one* great international army of Socialists, marching irresistibly on and growing daily in number, organisation, discipline, insight and certainty of victory. If even this mighty army of the proletariat has still not reached its goal, if, far from winning victory by one mighty stroke, it has slowly to press forward from position to position in a hard, tenacious struggle, this only proves, once and for all, how impossible it was in 1848 to win social transformation by a simple surprise attack.

A bourgeoisie split into two dynastic-monarchist sections,[4] a bourgeoisie, however, which demanded, above all, peace and security for its financial operations, faced by a proletariat vanquished, indeed, but still always a menace, a proletariat round which petty bourgeois and peasants grouped themselves more and more—the continual threat of a violent outbreak, which, nevertheless, offered absolutely no prospect of a final solution—such was the situation, as if specially created for the *coup d'état* of the third, the pseudo-democratic pretender, Louis Bonaparte. On December 2, 1851, by means of the army, he put an end to the tense situation and secured Europe domestic tranquillity in order to confer upon it the blessing of a new era of wars.[5] The period of revolutions from below was concluded for the time being; there followed a period of revolutions from above.

The reversion to the empire in 1851 gave new proof of the unripeness of the proletarian aspirations of that time. But it was itself to create the conditions under which they were bound to ripen. Internal tranquillity ensured the full development of the new industrial boom; the necessity of keeping the army occupied and of diverting the revolutionary currents outwards produced the wars in which Bonaparte, under the pretext of asserting "the principle of nationality," sought to hook annexations for France. His imitator, Bismarck, adopted the same policy for Prussia; he made his *coup d'état*, his revolution from above, in 1866, against the German Confederation and Austria, and no less against the Prussian *Konfliktskammer*.[6] But Europe was too small for two Bonapartes and the irony of history so willed it that Bismarck overthrew Bonaparte, and King William of Prussia not only established the little German empire,[7] but also the French republic. The general result, however, was that in Europe the independence and internal unity of the great nations, with the exception of Poland, had become a fact. Within relatively modest limits, it is true, but, for all that, on a scale large enough to allow the development of the working class to proceed without finding national complications any longer a serious

4. The parties referred to are the *Legitimists*, the supporters of the "legitimate," Bourbon, dynasty, who were in power in France up to 1792 and also during the epoch of the Restoration (1814–30), and the *Orleanists*, the supporters of the Orléans dynasty, who came to power during the July Revolution of 1830 and were overthrown by the Revolution of 1848.
5. During the reign of Napoleon III, France took part in the Crimean Campaign (1854–55), carried on war with Austria on account of Italy (1859),

participated together with England in the wars against China (1856–58 and 1860), began the conquest of Indo-China, organised an expedition into Syria (1860–61) and Mexico (1862–67), and finally, in 1870–71, waged war against Prussia.
6. *Konfliktskammer*, that is, the Prussian Chamber then in conflict with the government.
7. This term is applied to the German Empire (without Austria) that arose in 1871 under Prussia's hegemony.

obstacle. The grave-diggers of the Revolution of 1848 had become the executors of its will. And alongside of them already rose threateningly the heir of 1848, the proletariat, in the shape of the *International*.

After the war of 1870–71, Bonaparte vanishes from the stage and Bismarck's mission is fulfilled, so that he can now sink back again into the ordinary *Junker*. The period, however, is brought to a close by the Paris Commune. An underhand attempt by Thiers to steal the cannon of the Paris National Guard called forth a victorious rising. It was shown once more that in Paris none but a proletarian revolution is any longer possible. After the victory power fell, quite of itself and quite undisputed, into the hands of the working class. And once again it was proved how impossible even then, twenty years after the time described in our work, this rule of the working class still was. On the one hand, France left Paris in the lurch, looked on while it bled profusely from the bullets of MacMahon; on the other hand, the Commune was consumed in unfruitful strife between the two parties which split it, the Blanquists (the majority) and the Proudhonists (the minority), neither of which knew what was to be done. The victory which came as a gift in 1871 remained just as unfruitful as the surprise attack of 1848.

It was believed that the militant proletariat had been finally buried with the Paris Commune. But, completely to the contrary, it dates its most powerful resurgence from the Commune and the Franco-Prussian War. The recruitment of the whole of the population able to bear arms into armies that henceforth could be counted only in millions, and the introduction of fire-arms, projectiles and explosives of hitherto undreamt-of efficacy, created a complete revolution in all warfare. This revolution, on the one hand, put a sudden end to the Bonapartist war period and ensured peaceful industrial development by making any war other than a world war of unheard-of cruelty and absolutely incalculable outcome an impossibility. On the other hand, it caused military expenditure to rise in geometrical progression and thereby forced up taxes to exorbitant levels and so drove the poorer classes of people into the arms of socialism. The annexation of Alsace-Lorraine, the immediate cause of the mad competition in armaments, was able to set the French and German bourgeoisie chauvinistically at each other's throats; for the workers of the two countries it became a new bond of unity. And the anniversary of the Paris Commune became the first universal day of celebration of the whole proletariat.

The war of 1870–71 and the defeat of the Commune transferred the centre of gravity of the European workers' movement for the time being from France to Germany, as Marx had foretold. In France it naturally took years to recover from the blood-letting of

May 1871. In Germany, on the other hand, where industry—fostered, in addition, in positively hothouse fashion by the blessing of the French milliards[8]—developed more and more rapidly, Social-Democracy experienced a still more rapid and enduring growth. Thanks to the intelligent use which the German workers made of the universal suffrage introduced in 1866, the astonishing growth of the party is made plain to all the world by incontestable figures: 1871, 102,000; 1874, 352,000; 1877, 493,000 Social-Democratic votes. Then came recognition of this advance by high authority in the shape of the Anti-Socialist Law; the party was temporarily broken up, the number of votes dropped to 312,000 in 1881. But that was quickly overcome, and then, under the pressure of the Exceptional Law, without a press, without a legal organisation and without the right of combination and assembly, rapid expansion really began: 1884, 550,000; 1887, 763,000; 1890, 1,427,000 votes. Thereupon the hand of the state was paralysed. The Anti-Socialist Law disappeared; socialist votes rose to 1,787,000, over a quarter of all the votes cast. The government and the ruling classes had exhausted all their expedients—uselessly, purposelessly, unsuccessfully. The tangible proofs of their impotence, which the authorities, from night watchman to the imperial chancellor, had had to accept—and that from the despised workers!—these proofs were counted in millions. The state was at the end of its tether, the workers only at the beginning of theirs.

But, besides, the German workers rendered a second great service to their cause in addition to the first, a service performed by their mere existence as the strongest, best disciplined and most rapidly growing Socialist Party. They supplied their comrades in all countries with a new weapon, and one of the sharpest, when they showed them how to make use of universal suffrage.

There had long been universal suffrage in France, but it had fallen into disrepute through the misuse to which the Bonapartist government had put it. After the Commune there was no workers' party to make use of it. It also existed in Spain since the republic, but in Spain boycott of elections was ever the rule of all serious opposition parties. The experience of the Swiss with universal suffrage was also anything but encouraging for a workers' party. The revolutionary workers of the Latin countries had been wont to regard the suffrage as a snare, as an instrument of government trickery. It was otherwise in Germany. The *Communist Manifesto* had already proclaimed the winning of universal suffrage, of democracy, as one of the first and most important tasks of the militant proletariat, and Lassalle had again taken up this point. Now, when Bis-

8. The reference is to the payment of the five-billion-franc indemnity by France to Germany under the terms of the Frankfurt Peace Treaty of May 10, 1871.

marck found himself compelled to introduce this franchise as the only means of interesting the mass of the people in his plans, our workers immediately took it in earnest and sent August Bebel to the first, constituent Reichstag. And from that day on, they have used the franchise in a way which has paid them a thousandfold and has served as a model to the workers of all countries. The franchise has been, in the words of the French Marxist programme, *transformé, de moyen de duperie qu'il a été jusqu'ici, en instrument d'émancipation*—transformed by them from a means of deception, which it was before, into an instrument of emancipation.[9] And if universal suffrage had offered no other advantage than that it allowed us to count our numbers every three years; that by the regularly established, unexpectedly rapid rise in the number of our votes it increased in equal measure the workers' certainty of victory and the dismay of their opponents, and so became our best means of propaganda; that it accurately informed us concerning our own strength and that of all hostile parties, and thereby provided us with a measure of proportion for our actions second to none, safeguarding us from untimely timidity as much as from untimely foolhardiness—if this had been the only advantage we gained from the suffrage, it would still have been much more than enough. But it did more than this by far. In election agitation it provided us with a means, second to none, of getting in touch with the mass of the people where they still stand aloof from us; of forcing all parties to defend their views and actions against our attacks before all the people; and, further, it provided our representatives in the Reichstag with a platform from which they could speak to their opponents in parliament, and to the masses without, with quite other authority and freedom than in the press or at meetings. Of what avail was their Anti-Socialist Law to the government and the bourgeoisie when election campaigning and socialist speeches in the Reichstag continually broke through it?

With this successful utilisation of universal suffrage, however, an entirely new method of proletarian struggle came into operation, and this method quickly developed further. It was found that the state institutions, in which the rule of the bourgeoisie is organised, offer the working class still further opportunities to fight these very state institutions. The workers took part in elections to particular Diets, to municipal councils and to trades courts; they contested with the bourgeoisie every post in the occupation of which a sufficient part of the proletariat had a say. And so it happened that the bourgeoisie and the government came to be much more afraid

9. This phrase was taken from the preamble, written by Marx, of the programme of the French Workers' Party. The programme was adopted in 1880, at the Havre Congress of the Party.

of the legal than of the illegal action of the workers' party, of the results of elections than of those of rebellion.

For here, too, the conditions of the struggle had essentially changed. Rebellion in the old style, street fighting with barricades, which decided the issue everywhere up to 1848, was to a considera-

Let us have no illusions about it: a real victory of an insurrection ble extent obsolete.

over the military in street fighting, a victory as between two armies, is one of the rarest exceptions. And the insurgents counted on it just as rarely. For them it was solely a question of making the troops yield to moral influences which, in a fight between the armies of two warring countries, do not come into play at all or do so to a much smaller extent. If they succeed in this, the troops fail to respond, or the commanding officers lose their heads, and the insurrection wins. If they do not succeed in this, then, even where the military are in the minority, the superiority of better equipment and training, of single leadership, of the planned employment of the military forces and of discipline makes itself felt. The most that an insurrection can achieve in the way of actual tactical operations is the proper construction and defence of a single barricade. Mutual support, the disposition and employment of reserves—in short, concerted and co-ordinated action of the individual detachments, indispensable even for the defence of one section of a town, not to speak of the whole of a large town, will be attainable only to a very limited extent, and most of the time not at all. Concentration of the military forces at a decisive point is, of course, out of the question here. Hence passive defence is the prevailing form of fighting; the attack will rise here and there, but only by way of exception, to occasional thrusts and flank assaults; as a rule, however, it will be limited to occupation of positions abandoned by retreating troops. In addition, the military have at their disposal artillery and fully equipped corps of trained engineers, resources of war which, in nearly every case, the insurgents entirely lack. No wonder, then, that even the barricade fighting conducted with the greatest heroism—Paris, June 1848; Vienna, October 1848; Dresden, May 1849—ended in the defeat of the insurrection as soon as the leaders of the attack, unhampered by political considerations, acted from the purely military standpoint, and their soldiers remained reliable.

The numerous successes of the insurgents up to 1848 were due to a great variety of causes. In Paris, in July 1830 and February 1848, as in most of the Spanish street fighting, a citizens' guard stood between the insurgents and the military. This guard either sided directly with the insurrection, or else by its lukewarm, indecisive attitude caused the troops likewise to vacillate, and supplied the insurrection with arms into the bargain. Where this citizens' guard opposed the insurrection from the outset, as in June 1848 in Paris, the insurrection was vanquished. In Berlin in 1848, the people were victorious partly through a considerable accession of new fighting forces during the night and the morning of [March] the 19th, partly as a result of the exhaustion and bad victualling of the troops, and, finally, partly as a result of the paralysis that was seizing the command. But in all cases the fight was won because the troops failed to respond, because the commanding officers lost the faculty to decide or because their hands were tied.

Even in the classic time of street fighting, therefore, the barricade produced more of a moral than a material effect. It was a means of shaking the steadfastness of the military. If it held out until this was attained, victory was won; if not, there was defeat. This is the main point, which must be kept in view, likewise, when the chances of possible future street fighting are examined.

Already in 1849, these chances were pretty poor. Everywhere the bourgeoisie had thrown in its lot with the governments, "culture and property" had hailed and feasted the military moving against insurrection. The spell of the barricade was broken; the soldier no longer saw behind it "the people," but rebels, agitators, plunderers, levellers, the scum of society; the officer had in the course of time become versed in the tactical forms of street fighting, he no longer marched straight ahead and without cover against the improvised breastwork, but went round it through gardens, yards and houses. And this was now successful, with a little skill, in nine cases out of ten.

But since then there have been very many more changes, and all in favour of the military. If the big towns have become considerably bigger, the armies have become bigger still. Paris and Berlin have, since 1848, grown less than fourfold, but their garrisons have grown more than that. By means of the railways, these garrisons can, in twenty-four hours, be more than doubled, and in forty-eight hours they can be increased to huge armies. The arming of this enormously increased number of troops has become incomparably more effective. In 1848 the smooth-bore, muzzle-loading percussion gun, today the small-calibre, breech-loading magazine rifle, which shoots four times as far, ten times as accurately and ten times as fast as the former. At that time the relatively ineffective round shot and grape-shot of the artillery; today the percussion shells, of which one is sufficient to demolish the best barricade. At that time the pick-axe of the sapper for breaking through fire-walls; today the dynamite cartridge.

On the other hand, all the conditions of the insurgents' side have grown worse. An insurrection with which all sections of the people sympathise will hardly recur; in the class struggle all the middle strata will probably never group themselves round the proletariat so exclusively that in comparison the party of reaction gathered round the bourgeoisie will well-nigh disappear. The "people," therefore, will always appear divided, and thus a most powerful lever, so extraordinarily effective in 1848, is gone. If more soldiers who have seen service came over to the insurrectionists, the arming of them would become so much the more difficult. The hunting and fancy guns of the munitions shops—even if not previously made unusable by removal of part of the lock by order of the police—are far from being a match for the magazine rifle of the soldier, even in close fighting. Up to 1848 it was possible to make the necessary ammunition oneself out of powder and lead; today the cartridges differ for each gun, and are everywhere alike only in one point, namely, that they are a complicated product of big industry, and therefore not to be manufactured *ex tempore*, with the result that most guns are useless as long as one does not possess the ammunition specially suited to them. And, finally, since 1848 the newly built quarters of the big cities have been laid out in long, straight, broad streets, as though made to give full effect to the new cannon and rifles. The revolutionist would have to be mad who himself chose the new working-class districts in the North or East of Berlin for a barricade fight.

Does that mean that in the future street fighting will not longer play any role? Certainly not. It only means that the conditions since 1848 have become far more unfavourable for civilian fighters and far more favourable for the military. In future, street fighting can, therefore, be victorious only if this disadvantageous situation is compensated by other factors. Accordingly, it will occur more seldom in the beginning of a great revolution than in its further progress, and will have to be undertaken with greater forces. These, however, may then well prefer, as in the whole great French Revolution or on September 4 and October 31, 1870,[1] in Paris, the open attack to the passive barricade tactics.

Does the reader now understand why the powers that be positively want to get us to go where the guns shoot and the sabres slash? Why they accuse us today of cowardice, because we do not betake ourselves without more ado into the street, where we are certain of defeat in advance? Why they so earnestly implore us to play for once the part of cannon fodder?

The gentlemen pour out their prayers and their challenges for nothing, for absolutely nothing. We are not so stupid. They might just as well demand from their enemy in the next war that he

1. On September 4, 1870, the government of Louis Bonaparte was overthrown and the republic proclaimed, and on October 31 of the same year there took place the unsuccessful attempt of the Blanquists to make an insurrection against the Government of "National Defence."

should accept battle in the line formation of old Fritz,[2] or in the columns of whole divisions *à la* Wagram and Waterloo, and with the flint-lock in his hands at that. If conditions have changed in the case of war between nations, this is no less true in the case of the class struggle. The time of surprise attacks, of revolutions carried through by small conscious minorities at the head of unconscious masses, is past. Where it is a question of a complete transformation of the social organisation, the masses themselves must also be in it, must themselves already have grasped what is at stake, what they are going in for, body and soul. The history of the last fifty years has taught us that. But in order that the masses may understand what is to be done, long, persistent work is required, and it is just this work that we are now pursuing, and with a success which drives the enemy to despair.

In the Latin countries, also, it is being realised more and more that the old tactics must be revised. Everywhere the German example of utilising the suffrage, of winning all posts accessible to us, has been imitated; everywhere the unprepared launching of an attack has been relegated to the background. In France, where for more than a hundred years the ground has been undermined by revolution after revolution, where there is not a single party which has not done its share in conspiracies, insurrections and all other revolutionary actions; in France, where, as a result, the government is by no means sure of the army and where, in general, the conditions for an insurrectionary *coup de main* are far more favourable than in Germany—even in France the Socialists are realising more and more that no lasting victory is possible for them, unless they first win the great mass of the people, that is, in this case, the peasants. Slow propaganda work and parliamentary activity are recognised here, too, as the immediate tasks of the party. Successes were not lacking. Not only have a whole series of municipal councils been won; fifty Socialists have seats in the Chambers, and they have already overthrown three ministries and a president of the republic. In Belgium last year the workers forced the adoption of the franchise, and have been victorious in a quarter of the constituencies. In Switzerland, in Italy, in Denmark, yes, even in Bulgaria and Rumania the Socialists are represented in the parliaments. In Austria all parties agree that our admission to the *Reichsrat* can no longer be withheld. We will get in, that is certain; the only question still in dispute is: by which door? And even in Russia, when the famous *Zemsky Sobor* meets —that National Assembly to which young Nicholas offers such vain resistance—even there we can reckon with certainty on being represented in it.

Of course, our foreign comrades do not thereby in the least re-

2. Frederick II, King of Prussia (1740–86).

nounce their right to revolution. The right to revolution is, after all, the only *really* "historical right," the only right on which all modern states without exception rest, Mecklenburg included, whose aristocratic revolution was ended in 1755 by the "hereditary settlement" ["Erbvergleich"], the glorious charter of feudalism still valid today. The right to revolution is so incontestably recognised in the general consciousness that even General von Boguslawski derives the right to a *coup d'état*, which he vindicates for his Kaiser, solely from this popular right.

But whatever may happen in other countries, the German Social-Democracy occupies a special position and therewith, at least in the immediate future, has a special task. The two million voters whom it sends to the ballot box, together with the young men and women who stand behind them as non-voters, form the most numerous, most compact mass, the decisive "shock force" of the international proletarian army. This mass already supplies over a fourth of the votes cast; and as the by-elections to the *Reichstag*, the Diet elections in individual states, the municipal council and trades court elections demonstrate, it increases incessantly. Its growth proceeds as spontaneously, as steadily, as irresistibly, and at the same time as tranquilly as a natural process. All government intervention has proved powerless against it. We can count even today on two and a quarter million voters. If it continues in this fashion, by the end of the century we shall conquer the greater part of the middle strata of society, petty bourgeois and small peasants, and grow into the decisive power in the land, before which all other powers will have to bow, whether they like it or not. To keep this growth going without interruption until it of itself gets beyond the control of the prevailing governmental system, not to fritter away this daily increasing shock force in vanguard skirmishes, but to keep it intact until the decisive day, that is our main task. And there is only one means by which the steady rise of the socialist fighting forces in Germany could be temporarily halted, and even thrown back for some time: a clash on a big scale with the military, a blood-letting like that of 1871 in Paris. In the long run that would also be overcome. To shoot a party which numbers millions out of existence is too much even for all the magazine rifles of Europe and America. But the normal development would be impeded, the shock force would, perhaps, not be available at the critical moment, the decisive combat would be delayed, protracted and attended by heavier sacrifices.

The irony of world history turns everything upside down. We, the "revolutionists," the "overthrowers"—we are thriving far better on legal methods than on illegal methods and overthrow. The parties of Order, as they call themselves, are perishing under the legal conditions created by themselves. They cry despairingly with

Odilon Barrot: *la légalité nous tue*, legality is the death of us; whereas we, under this legality, get firm muscles and rosy cheeks and look like life eternal. And if *we* are not so crazy as to let ourselves be driven to street fighting in order to please them, then in the end there is nothing left for them to do but themselves break through this fatal legality.

Meanwhile they make new laws against overthrows. Again everything is turned upside down. These anti-overthrow fanatics of today, are they not themselves the overthrowers of yesterday? Have *we* perchance evoked the civil war of 1866? Have *we* driven the King of Hanover, the Elector of Hesse, and the Duke of Nassau from their hereditary lawful domains and annexed these hereditary domains? And these overthrowers of the German Confederation and three crowns by the grace of God complain of overthrow! *Quis tulerit Gracchos de seditione queretes?*[3] Who could allow the Bismarck worshippers to rail at overthrow?

Let them, nevertheless, put through their anti-overthrow bills, make them still worse, transform the whole penal law into indiarubber, they will gain nothing but new proof of their impotence. If they want to deal Social-Democracy a serious blow they will have to resort to quite other measures in addition. They can cope with the Social-Democratic overthrow, which just now is doing so well by keeping the law, only by an overthrow on the part of the parties of Order, an overthrow which cannot live without breaking the law. Herr Rössler, the Prussian bureaucrat, and Herr von Boguslawski, the Prussian general, have shown them the only way perhaps still possible of getting at the workers, who simply refuse to let themselves be lured into street fighting. Breach of the constitution, dictatorship, return to absolutism, *regis voluntas suprema lex!*[4] Therefore, take courage, gentlemen; here half measures will not do; here you must go the whole hog!

But do not forget that the German empire, like all small states and generally all modern states, is a *product of contract*; of the contract, first, of the princes with one another and, second, of the princes with the people. If one side breaks the contract, the whole contract falls to the ground; the other side is then also no longer bound, as Bismarck demonstrated to us so beautifully in 1866. If, therefore, you break the constitution of the Reich, the Social-Democracy is free, and can do as it pleases with regard to you. But it will hardly blurt out to you today what it is going to do then.

It is now, almost to the year, sixteen centuries since a dangerous party of overthrow was likewise active in the Roman empire. It undermined religion and all the foundations of the state; it flatly

3. Who would suffer the Gracchi to complain of sedition?   4. The King's will is the supreme law!

denied that Caesar's will was the supreme law; it was without a fatherland, was international; it spread over all countries of the empire, from Gaul to Asia, and beyond the frontiers of the empire. It had long carried on seditious activities in secret, underground; for a considerable time, however, it had felt itself strong enough to come out into the open. This party of overthrow, which was known by the name of Christians, was also strongly represented in the army; whole legions were Christian. When they were ordered to attend the sacrificial ceremonies of the pagan established church, in order to do the honours there, the subversive soldiers had the audacity to stick peculiar emblems—crosses—on their helmets in protest. Even the wonted barrack bullying of their superior officers was fruitless. The Emperor Diocletian could no longer quietly look on while order, obedience and discipline in his army were being undermined. He interfered energetically, while there was still time. He promulgated an anti-Socialist—beg pardon, I meant to say anti-Christian —law. The meetings of the overthrowers were forbidden, their meeting halls were closed or even pulled down, the Christian emblems, crosses, etc., were, like the red handkerchiefs in Saxony, prohibited. Christians were declared incapable of holding public office; they were not to be allowed to become even corporals. Since there were not available at that time judges so well trained in "respect of persons" as Herr von Köller's anti-overthrow bill[5] assumes, Christians were forbidden out of hand to seek justice before a court. This exceptional law was also without effect. The Christians tore it down from the walls with scorn; they are even supposed to have burnt the Emperor's palace in Nicomedia over his head. Then the latter revenged himself by the great persecution of Christians in the year 303 of our era. It was the last of its kind. And it was so effective that seventeen years later the army consisted overwhelmingly of Christians, and the succeeding autocrat of the whole Roman empire, Constantine, called the Great by the priests, proclaimed Christianity the state religion.

5. A new bill against the Socialists, introduced in the Reichstag on December 5, 1894, and rejected on May 11, 1895.

PART IV

Society and Politics in the Nineteenth Century

Speech at the Anniversary
of the *People's Paper*

KARL MARX

This speech is a vivid expression of Marx's sense of proletarian revolution
as a volcanic presence in European society of the mid-nineteenth century,
and also of his intensely moralistic vision of the coming revolution as capital punishment of a society that deserved to die. He gave the speech in
English on April 14, 1856, and it was published a few days later in the
People's Paper. This was a Chartist paper, published in London from 1852
to 1858, for which Marx occasionally wrote articles.

The so-called Revolutions of 1848 were but poor incidents—
small fractures and fissures in the dry crust of European society.
However, they denounced the abyss. Beneath the apparently solid
surface, they betrayed oceans of liquid matter, only needing expansion to rend into fragments continents of hard rock. Noisily and
confusedly they proclaimed the emancipation of the Proletarian,
i.e., the secret of the nineteenth century, and of the revolution of
that century. That social revolution, it is true, was no novelty
invented in 1848. Steam, electricity, and the self-acting mule were
revolutionists of a rather more dangerous character than even citizens Barbès, Raspail and Blanqui. But, although the atmosphere in
which we live, weighs upon every one with a 20,000 lb. force, do
you feel it? No more than European society before 1848 felt the
revolutionary atmosphere enveloping and pressing it from all sides.
There is one great fact, characteristic of this our nineteenth century, a fact which no party dares deny. On the one hand, there have
started into life industrial and scientific forces, which no epoch of
the former human history had ever suspected. On the other hand,
there exist symptoms of decay, far surpassing the horrors recorded
of the latter times of the Roman empire. In our days everything
seems pregnant with its contrary. Machinery, gifted with the won-

derful power of shortening and fructifying human labour, we behold starving and overworking it. The new-fangled sources of wealth, by some strange weird spell, are turned into sources of want. The victories of art seem bought by the loss of character. At the same pace that mankind masters nature, man seems to become enslaved to other men or to his own infamy. Even the pure light of science seems unable to shine but on the dark background of ignorance. All our invention and progress seem to result in endowing material forces with intellectual life, and in stultifying human life into a material force. This antagonism between modern industry and science on the one hand, modern misery and dissolution on the other hand; this antagonism between the productive powers, and the social relations of our epoch is a fact, palpable, overwhelming, and not to be controverted. Some parties may wail over it; others may wish to get rid of modern arts, in order to get rid of modern conflicts. Or they may imagine that so signal a progress in industry wants to be completed by as signal a regress in politics. On our part, we do not mistake the shape of the shrewd spirit that continues to mark all these contradictions. We know that to work well the new-fangled forces of society, they only want to be mastered by new-fangled men—and such are the working men. They are as much the invention of modern time as machinery itself. In the signs that bewilder the middle class, the aristocracy and the poor prophets of regression, we do recognise our brave friend, Robin Goodfellow,[1] the old mole that can work in the earth so fast, that worthy pioneer —the Revolution. The English working men are the first born sons of modern industry. They will then, certainly, not be the last in aiding the social revolution produced by that industry, a revolution, which means the emancipation of their own class all over the world, which is as universal as capital-rule and wages-slavery. I know the heroic struggles the English working class have gone through since the middle of the last century—struggles no less glorious, because they are shrouded in obscurity, and buried by the middle class historian. To revenge the misdeeds of the ruling class, there existed in the middle ages, in Germany, a secret tribunal, called the *"Vehmgericht."* If a red cross was seen marked on a house, people knew that its owner was doomed by the *"Vehm."* All the houses of Europe are now marked with the mysterious red cross. History is the judge —its executioner, the proletarian.

1. *Robin Goodfellow*: A sprite, who was popularly believed in England during the sixteenth and seventeenth centuries to lend people a helping hand. He is one of the chief characters in Shakespeare's comedy *A Midsummer Night's Dream.*

Working-Class Manchester

FRIEDRICH ENGELS

Engels, the son of a well-to-do German manufacturer, was sent to England in 1842, at the age of twenty-two, to learn business in the office of the Ermen and Engels paper mill in the industrial city of Manchester. He remained in England for nearly two years and while there gathered material for his first book, *The Condition of the Working Class in England in 1844*, which was published in German in 1845. The extract below, from the chapter on "The Great Towns," is taken from the English translation published by the Foreign Languages Publishing House, Moscow, in 1962.

---

* * * I now proceed to describe Manchester's worker districts. First of all, there is the Old Town, which lies between the northern boundary of the commercial district and the Irk. Here the streets, even the better ones, are narrow and winding, as Todd Street, Long Millgate, Withy Grove, and Shude Hill, the houses dirty, old, and tumble-down, and the construction of the side streets utterly horrible. Going from the Old Church to Long Millgate, the stroller has at once a row of old-fashioned houses at the right, of which not one has kept its original level; these are remnants of the old pre-manufacturing Manchester, whose former inhabitants have removed with their descendants into better-built districts, and have left the houses, which were not good enough for them, to a working-class population strongly mixed with Irish blood. Here one is in an almost undisguised working-men's quarter, for even the shops and beerhouses hardly take the trouble to exhibit a trifling degree of cleanliness. But all this is nothing in comparison with the courts and lanes which lie behind, to which access can be gained only through covered passages, in which no two human beings can pass at the same time. Of the irregular cramming together of dwellings in ways which defy all rational plan, of the tangle in which they are crowded literally one upon the other, it is impossible to convey an idea. And it is not the buildings surviving from the old times of Manchester which are to blame for this; the confusion has only recently reached its height when every scrap of space left by the old way of building has been filled up and patched over until not a foot of land is left to be further occupied.

To confirm my statement I have drawn here a small section of the plan of Manchester—not the worst spot and not one-tenth of the whole Old Town.

This drawing will suffice to characterise the irrational manner in which the entire district was built, particularly the part near the Irk.

The south bank of the Irk is here very steep and between fifteen and thirty feet high. On this declivitous hillside there are planted three rows of houses, of which the lowest rise directly out of the river, while the front walls of the highest stand on the crest of the hill in Long Millgate. Among them are mills on the river, in short, the method of construction is as crowded and disorderly here as in the lower part of Long Millgate. Right and left a multitude of covered passages lead from the main street into numerous courts, and he who turns in thither gets into a filth and disgusting grime, the equal of which is not be found—especially in the courts which lead down to the Irk, and which contain unqualifiedly the most horrible

dwellings which I have yet beheld. In one of these courts there stands directly at the entrance, at the end of the covered passage, a privy without a door, so dirty that the inhabitants can pass into and out of the court only by passing through foul pools of stagnant urine and excrement. This is the first court on the Irk above Ducie Bridge—in case any one should care to look into it. Below it on the river there are several tanneries which fill the whole neighborhood with the stench of animal putrefaction. Below Ducie Bridge the only entrance to most of the houses is by means of narrow, dirty stairs and over heaps of refuse and filth. The first court below Ducie Bridge, known as Allen's Court, was in such a state at the time of the cholera that the sanitary police ordered it evacuated, swept and disinfected with chloride of lime. Dr. Kay gives a terrible description of the state of this court at that time.[1] Since then, it seems to have been partially torn away and rebuilt; at least looking down from Ducie Bridge, the passer-by sees several ruined walls and heaps of *débris* with some newer houses. The view from this bridge, mercifully concealed from mortals of small stature by a parapet as high as a man, is characteristic for the whole district. At the bottom flows, or rather stagnates, the Irk, a narrow, coal-black, foul-smelling stream, full of *débris* and refuse, which it deposits on the shallower right bank. In dry weather, a long string of the most disgusting blackish-green slime pools are left standing on this bank, from the depths of which bubbles of miasmatic gas constantly arise and give forth a stench unendurable even on the bridge forty or fifty feet above the surface of the stream. But besides this, the stream itself is checked every few paces by high weirs, behind which slime and refuse accumulate and rot in thick masses. Above the bridge are tanneries, bonemills, and gasworks, from which all drains and refuse find their way into the Irk, which receives further the contents of all the neighbouring sewers and privies. It may be easily imagined, therefore, what sort of residue the stream deposits. Below the bridge you look upon the piles of *débris*, the refuse, filth, and offal from the courts on the steep left bank; here each house is packed close behind its neighbour and a piece of each is visible, all black, smoky, crumbling, ancient, with broken panes and window-frames. The background is furnished by old barrack-like factory buildings. On the lower right bank stands a long row of houses and mills; the second house being a ruin without a roof, piled with *débris*; the third stands so low that the lowest floor is uninhabitable, and therefore without windows or doors. Here the background embraces the pauper burial-ground, the station of the Liverpool and Leeds railway, and, in the rear of this, the Workhouse, the "Poor-Law Bastille" of Manchester, which, like a citadel, looks threateningly down from behind its high walls and parapets on the hilltop, upon the working-people's quarter below.

Above Ducie Bridge, the left bank grows more flat and the right bank steeper, but the condition of the dwellings on both banks grows worse rather than better. He who turns to the left here from the main street, Long Millgate, is lost; he wanders from one court

---

1. "The Moral and Physical Condition of the Working-Class employed in the Cotton Manufacture in Manchester." By James Ph. Kay, M.D. 2nd Ed. 1832. Dr. Kay confuses the working-class in general with the factory workers; otherwise, an excellent pamphlet.

to another, turns countless corners, passes nothing but narrow, filthy nooks and alleys, until after a few minutes he has lost all clue, and knows not whither to turn. Everywhere half or wholly ruined buildings, some of them actually uninhabited, which means a great deal here; rarely a wooden or stone floor to be seen in the houses, almost uniformly broken, ill-fitting windows and doors, and a state of filth! Everywhere heaps of *débris*, refuse, and offal; standing pools for gutters, and a stench which alone would make it impossible for a human being in any degree civilised to live in such a district. The newly-built extension of the Leeds railway, which crosses the Irk here, has swept away some of these courts and lanes, laying others completely open to view. Immediately under the railway bridge there stands a court, the filth and horrors of which surpass all the others by far, just because it was hitherto so shut off, so secluded that the way to it could not be found without a good deal of trouble. I should never have discovered it myself, without the breaks made by the railway, though I thought I knew this whole region thoroughly. Passing along a rough bank, among stakes and washing-lines, one penetrates into this chaos of small one-storied, one-roomed huts, in most of which there is no artificial floor; kitchen, living and sleeping-room all in one. In such a hole, scarcely five feet long by six broad, I found two beds—and such bedsteads and beds! —which, with a staircase and chimney-place, exactly filled the room. In several others I found absolutely nothing, while the door stood open, and the inhabitants leaned against it. Everywhere before the doors refuse and offal; that any sort of pavement lay underneath could not be seen but only felt, here and there, with the feet. This whole collection of cattle-sheds for human beings was surrounded on two sides by houses and a factory, and on the third by the river, and besides the narrow stair up the bank, a narrow doorway alone led out into another almost equally ill-built, ill-kept labyrinth of dwellings.

Enough! The whole side of the Irk is built in this way, a planless, knotted chaos of houses, more or less on the verge of uninhabitableness, whose unclean interiors fully correspond with their filthy external surroundings. And how could the people be clean with no proper opportunity for satisfying the most natural and ordinary wants? Privies are so rare here that they are either filled up every day, or are too remote for most of the inhabitants to use. How can people wash when they have only the dirty Irk water at hand, while pumps and water pipes can be found in decent parts of the city alone? In truth, it cannot be charged to the account of these helots of modern society if their dwellings are not more clean than the pig sties which are here and there to be seen among them. The landlords are not ashamed to let dwellings like the six or seven cellars on the quay directly below Scotland Bridge, the floors of which stand at least two feet below the low-water level of the Irk that flows not six feet away from them; or like the upper floor of the corner-house on the opposite shore directly above the bridge, where the ground-floor, utterly uninhabitable, stands deprived of all fittings for doors and windows, a case by no means rare in this region, when this open ground-floor is used as a privy by the whole neighbourhood for want of other facilities!

If we leave the Irk and penetrate once more on the opposite side from Long Millgate into the midst of the working-men's dwellings, we shall come into a somewhat newer quarter, which stretches from St. Michael's Church to Withy Grove and Shude Hill. Here there is somewhat better order. In place of the chaos of buildings, we find at least long straight lanes and alleys or courts, built according to a plan and usually square. But if, in the former case, every house was built according to caprice, here each lane and court is so built, without reference to the situation of the adjoining ones. The lanes run now in this direction, now in that, while every two minutes the wanderer gets into a blind alley, or on turning a corner, finds himself back where he started from; certainly no one who has not lived a considerable time in this labyrinth can find his way through it.

If I may use the word at all in speaking of this district, the ventilation of these streets and courts is, in consequence of this confusion, quite as imperfect as in the Irk region; and if this quarter may, nevertheless, be said to have some advantage over that of the Irk, the houses being newer and the streets occasionally having gutters, nearly every house has, on the other hand, a cellar dwelling, which is rarely found in the Irk district, by reason of the greater age and more careless construction of the houses. As for the rest, the filth, *débris*, and offal heaps, and the pools in the streets are common to both quarters, and in the district now under discussion, another feature most injurious to the cleanliness of the inhabitants, is the multitude of pigs walking about in all the alleys, rooting into the offal heaps, or kept imprisoned in small pens. Here, as in most of the working-men's quarters of Manchester, the pork-raisers rent the courts and build pig-pens in them. In almost every court one or even several such pens may be found, into which the inhabitants of the court throw all refuse and offal, whence the swine grow fat; and the atmosphere, confined on all four sides, is utterly corrupted by putrefying animal and vegetable substances. Through this quarter, a broad and measurably decent street has been cut, Millers Street, and the background has been pretty successfully concealed. But if any one should be led by curiosity to pass through one of the numerous passages which lead into the courts, he will find this piggery repeated at every twenty paces.

Such is the Old Town of Manchester, and on re-reading my description, I am forced to admit that instead of being exaggerated, it is far from black enough to convey a true impression of the filth, ruin, and uninhabitableness, the defiance of all considerations of cleanliness, ventilation, and health which characterise the construction of this single district, containing at least twenty to thirty thousand inhabitants. And such a district exists in the heart of the second city of England, the first manufacturing city of the world. If any one wishes to see in how little space a human being can move, how little air—and *such* air!—he can breathe, how little of civilisation he may share and yet live, it is only necessary to travel hither. True, this is the *Old* Town, and the people of Manchester emphasise the fact whenever any one mentions to them the frightful condition of this Hell upon Earth; but what does that prove? Everything which here arouses horror and indignation is of recent origin, belongs to the *industrial epoch*. The couple of hundred houses, which belong to old Manchester, have been long since abandoned by their original inhabitants; the industrial epoch alone has crammed into them the swarms of workers whom they now shelter; the industrial epoch alone has built up every spot between these old houses to win a covering for the masses whom it has conjured hither from the agricultural districts and from Ireland; the industrial epoch alone enables the owners of these cattlesheds to rent them for high prices to human beings, to plunder the poverty of the workers, to undermine the health of thousands, in order that they *alone*, the owners, may grow rich. In the industrial epoch alone has it become possible that the worker scarcely freed from feudal servitude could be used as mere material, a mere chattel; that he must let himself be crowded into a dwelling too bad for every other, which he for his hard-earned wages buys the right to let go utterly to ruin. This manufacture has achieved, which, without these workers, this poverty, this slavery could not have lived. True, the original construction of this quarter was bad, little good could have been made out of it; but, have the landowners, has the municipality done anything to improve it when rebuilding? On the contrary, wherever a nook or corner was free, a house has been run up; where a superfluous passage remained, it has been built up; the value of land rose with the blossoming out of manufacture, and the more it rose, the more madly was the work of building up carried on, without reference to the health or comfort of the inhabitants, with sole reference to the highest possible profit on the principle that *no hole is so bad but that some poor creature must take it who can pay for nothing better*. However, it is the Old Town, and with this reflection the bourgeoisie is comforted. Let us see, therefore, how much better it is in the New Town.

The New Town, known also as Irish Town, stretches up a hill of clay, beyond the Old Town, between the Irk and St. George's Road. Here all the features of a city are lost. Single rows of houses or groups of streets stand, here and there, like little villages on the naked, not even grassgrown clay soil; the houses, or rather cottages, are in bad order, never repaired, filthy, with damp, unclean, cellar dwellings; the lanes are neither paved nor supplied with sewers, but harbour numerous colonies of swine penned in small sties or yards, or wandering unrestrained through the neighbourhood. The mud in the streets is so deep that there is never a chance, except in the dryest weather, of walking without sinking into it ankle deep at every step. In the vicinity of St. George's Road, the separate groups of buildings approach each other more closely, ending in a continuation of lines, blind alleys, back lanes and courts, which grow more and more crowded and irregular the nearer they approach the heart of the town. True, they are here oftener paved or supplied with paved sidewalks and gutters; but the filth, the bad odor of the houses, and especially of the cellars, remain the same. *   *   *

The Eighteenth Brumaire
of Louis Bonaparte

KARL MARX

This pamphlet, a stylistic masterpiece, shows Marx in his most brilliant form as a social and political historian, treating actual historical events—those leading up to Louis Bonaparte's *coup d'état* of December 2, 1851—from the viewpoint of the materialist conception of history. In a preface to the second edition, he himself said it was the intention of the work to "demonstrate how the *class struggle* in France created circumstances and relationships that made it possible for a grotesque mediocrity to play a hero's part." Since Louis Bonaparte's rise and rule have been seen as a forerunner of the phenomenon that was to become known in the twentieth century as fascism, Marx's interpretation of it is of interest, among other ways, as a sort of prologue to later Marxist thought on the nature and meaning of fascism.

The Eighteenth Brumaire was written by Marx in late 1851 and early 1852, and originally appeared in 1852 in a magazine entitled *Die Revolution*, published in New York.

I

Hegel remarks somewhere that all great, world-historical facts and personages occur, as it were, twice. He has forgotten to add: the first time as tragedy, the second as farce. Caussidière for Danton, Louis Blanc for Robespierre, the Mountain of 1848 to 1851 for the Mountain of 1793 to 1795, the Nephew for the Uncle. And the same caricature occurs in the circumstances in which the second edition of the Eighteenth Brumaire is taking place.[1]

1. On the Eighteenth Brumaire (according to the calendar introduced in the period of the first French burgeois revolution), or November 9, 1799, Napoleon I carried out the *coup d'état* whereby as First Consul he concentrated supreme power in his hands; in 1804 he declared himself emperor. By "the second edition of the Eighteenth Brumaire," Marx means the *coup d'état* accomplished by Louis Bonaparte, the nephew of Napoleon I, on December 2, 1851. For an explanation of "the Mountain," see p. 458.

Men make their own history, but they do not make it just as they please; they do not make it under circumstances chosen by themselves, but under circumstances directly found, given and transmitted from the past. The tradition of all the dead generations weighs like a nightmare on the brain of the living. And just when they seem engaged in revolutionising themselves and things, in creating something entirely new, precisely in such epochs of revolutionary crisis they anxiously conjure up the spirits of the past to their service and borrow from them names, battle slogans and costumes in order to present the new scene of world history in this time-honoured disguise and this borrowed language. Thus Luther donned the mask of the Apostle Paul, the Revolution of 1789 to 1814 draped itself alternately as the Roman Republic and the Roman Empire, and the Revolution of 1848 knew nothing better to do than to parody, in turn, 1789 and the revolutionary tradition of 1793 to 1795. In like manner the beginner who has learnt a new language always translates it back into his mother tongue, but he has assimilated the spirit of the new language and can produce freely in it only when he moves in it without remembering the old and forgets in it his ancestral tongue.

Consideration of this world-historical conjuring up of the dead reveals at once a salient difference. Camille Desmoulins, Danton, Robespierre, Saint-Just, Napoleon, the heroes, as well as the parties and the masses of the old French Revolution, performed the task of their time in Roman costume and with Roman phrases, the task of releasing and setting up modern *bourgeois* society. The first ones knocked the feudal basis to pieces and mowed off the feudal heads which had grown from it. The other created inside France the conditions under which free competition could first be developed, the parcelled landed property exploited, the unfettered productive power of the nation employed, and outside the French borders he everywhere swept the feudal formations away, so far as was necessary to furnish bourgeois society in France with a suitable up-to-date environment on the European Continent. The new social formation once established, the antediluvian Colossi disappeared and with them the resurrected Romans—the Brutuses, Gracchi, Publicolas, the tribunes, the senators and Caesar himself. Bourgeois society in its sober reality had begotten its true interpreters and mouthpieces in the Says, Cousins, Royer-Collards, Benjamin Constants and Guizots; its real military leaders sat behind the office desks, and the hogheaded Louis XVIII was its political chief. Wholly absorbed in the production of wealth and in the peaceful struggle of competition, it no longer comprehended that ghosts from the days of Rome had watched over its cradle. But unheroic as bourgeois society is, yet it had need of heroism, of sacrifice, of terror, of civil war and of national battles to bring it into being. And in the classically austere traditions of the Roman Republic its gladiators found the ideals and the art forms, the self-deceptions that they needed in order to conceal from themselves the bourgeois limitations of the content of their struggles and to keep their passion at the height of the great historical tragedy. Similarly, at another stage of development, a century earlier, Cromwell and the English people had borrowed speech, passions and illusions from the Old Testament for their bourgeois revolution.[2] When the real aim had been achieved, when the bourgeois transformation of English society had been accomplished, Locke supplanted Habakkuk.

The awakening of the dead in those revolutions therefore served the purpose of glorifying the new struggles, not of parodying the old; of magnifying the given tasks in imagination, not of taking flight from their solution in reality; of finding once more the spirit of revolution, not of making its ghost walk again.

From 1848 to 1851 only the ghost of the old revolution walked, from Marrast, the *republicain en gants jaunes*,[3] who disguised himself as the old Bailly, to the adventurer who hides his trivially repulsive features under the iron death mask of Napoleon. An entire people, which had imagined that by a revolution it had increased its power of action, suddenly finds itself set back into a dead epoch and, in order that no doubt as to the relapse may be possible, the old data again arise, the old chronology, the old names, the old edicts, which have long become a subject of antiquarian erudition, and the old henchmen, who had long seemed dead and decayed. The nation appears to itself like that mad Englishman in Bedlam, who fancies that he lives in the times of the ancient Pharaohs and daily bemoans the hard labour that he must perform in the Ethiopian mines as a gold digger, immured in this subterranean prison, a dimly burning lamp fastened to his head, the overseer of the slaves behind him with a long whip, and at the exits a confused mass of barbarian mercenaries, who understand neither the forced labourers in the mines nor one another, since they have no common speech. "And all this is expected of me," groans the mad Englishman, "of me, a free-born Briton, in order to make gold for the old Pharaohs." "In order to pay the debts of the Bonaparte family," sighs the French nation. The Englishman, so long as he was in his right mind, could not get rid of the fixed idea of making gold. The French, so long as they were engaged in revolution, could not get rid of the memory of Napoleon, as the election of December 10, 1848,[4] proved. From the perils of revolution their longings went back to the flesh-pots of Egypt, and December 2, 1851, was the

---

2. The bourgeoisie was allied with the new nobility against the monarchy, the feudal nobility, and the ruling church. [*Marx*]

3. Republican in yellow gloves.
4. The day Louis Bonaparte was elected president of the republic.

answer. They have not only a caricature of the old Napoleon, they have the old Napoleon himself, caricatured as he would inevitably appear in the middle of the nineteenth century.

The social revolution of the nineteenth century cannot draw its poetry from the past, but only from the future. It cannot begin with itself, before it has stripped off all superstition in regard to the past. Earlier revolutions required world-historical recollections in order to drug themselves concerning their own content. In order to arrive at its content, the revolution of the nineteenth century must let the dead bury their dead. There the phrase went beyond the content; here the content goes beyond the phrase.

The February Revolution was a sudden attack, a taking of the old society by *surprise*, and the people proclaimed this unhoped for *stroke* as a world-historic deed, opening the new epoch. On December 2 the February Revolution is conjured away by a card-sharper's trick, and what seems overthrown is no longer the monarchy; it is the liberal concessions that were wrung from it by century-long struggles. Instead of *society* having conquered a new content for itself, the *state* only appears to have returned to its oldest form, to the shamelessly simple domination of the sabre and the cowl. This is the answer to the *coup de main* of February 1848, given by the *coup de tête* of December 1851. Easy come, easy go. Meanwhile the interval has not passed by unused. During the years 1848 to 1851 French society has made up, and that by an abbreviated, because revolutionary, method, for the studies and experiences which, in a regular, so to speak, text-book development would have had to precede the February Revolution, if the latter was to be more than a disturbance of the surface. Society now seems to have fallen back behind its point of departure; it has in truth first to create for itself the revolutionary point of departure, the situation, the relationships, the conditions, under which modern revolution alone becomes serious.

Bourgeois revolutions, like those of the eighteenth century, storm more swiftly from success to success; their dramatic effects outdo each other; men and things seem set in sparkling brilliants; ecstasy is the everyday spirit: but they are short lived; soon they have attained their zenith, and a long depression lays hold of society before it learns soberly to assimilate the results of its storm and stress period. Proletarian revolutions, on the other hand, like those of the nineteenth century, criticise themselves constantly, interrupt themselves continually in their own course, come back to the apparently accomplished in order to begin it afresh, deride with unmerciful thoroughness the inadequacies, weaknesses and paltrinesses of their first attempts, seem to throw down their adversary only in order that he may draw new strength from the earth and rise again more gigantic before them, recoil ever and anon from the indefinite prodigiousness of their own aims, until the situation has been created which makes all turning back impossible, and the conditions themselves cry out:

Hic Rhodus, hic salta!
Hier ist die Rose, hier tanze![5]

For the rest, every fairly competent observer, even if he had not followed the course of French development step by step, must have had a presentiment that a terrible fiasco was in store for the revolution. It was enough to hear the self-complacent howl of victory with which Messieurs the Democrats congratulated each other on the gracious consequences of May 2, 1852.[6] In their minds May 2, 1852, had become a fixed idea, a dogma, like the day on which Christ should reappear and the millennium begin, in the minds of the Chiliasts.[7] As ever, weakness had taken refuge in a belief in miracles, had fancied the enemy overcome when he was only conjured away in imagination, and lost all understanding of the present in a passive glorification of the future that was in store for it and of the deeds it had *in petto*,[8] but merely did not want to carry out as yet. Those heroes, who seek to disprove their demonstrated incapacity by mutually offering each other their sympathy and getting together in a crowd, had tied up their bundles, collected their laurel wreaths in advance and were just then engaged in discounting on the exchange market the republics *in partibus*,[9] for which they had already thoughtfully organised the government personnel with all the calm of their unassuming disposition. December 2 struck them like a thunderbolt from a clear sky, and the peoples that in epochs of pusillanimous depression gladly let their inward apprehension be drowned by the loudest bawlers will perchance have convinced themselves that the times are past when the cackle of geese could save the Capitol.[1]

The Constitution, the National Assembly, the dynastic parties,[2] the blue and the red republicans,[3] the heroes of Africa,[4] the thun-

5. Here is Rhodes, leap here! Here is the rose, dance here! The words are from a fable by Aesop about a braggart who claimed he could produce witnesses to prove he had once made a remarkable leap in Rhodes, to which claim he received the reply: "Why cite witnesses if it is true? Here is Rhodes, leap here!" That is, "Show us right here what you can do." The German paraphrase of the Greek quotation (*Rhodus* means *rose*) was used by Hegel in the preface to his *Philosophy of Right*.
6. The day on which new presidential elections were to be held. Louis Bonaparte would have had to retire on this day, as the constitution did not permit anyone to be elected to the presidency for a second time, except after an interval of four years.
7. The adherents of an ancient Christian sect, who believed in the second coming of Christ and in the establishment of the millennium, a thousand years of paradise on earth.
8. In reserve.
9. *In partibus infidelium*: literally, "in the country of the infidels." An expression often used by Marx and Engels to describe émigré governments formed abroad without regard to the real situation in a country.

der from the platform, the sheet lightning of the daily press, the entire literature, the political names and the intellectual reputations, the civil law and penal code, the *liberté, egalité, fraternité* and the second of May 1852—all have vanished like a phantasmagoria before the spell of a man whom even his enemies do not make out to be a magician. Universal suffrage seems to have survived only for a moment, in order that with its own hand it may make its last will and testament before the eyes of all the world and declare in the name of the people itself: Everything that exists has this much worth, that it will perish.

It is not enough to say, as the French do, that their nation has been taken by surprise. A nation and a woman are not forgiven the unguarded hour in which the first adventurer that came along could violate them. The riddle is not solved by such terms of speech, but merely formulated in another way. It remains to be explained how a nation of thirty-six millions can be surprised and delivered unresisting into captivity by three high class swindlers.

Let us recapitulate in their general outlines the phases that the French Revolution has gone through from February 24, 1848, to December 1851.

Three main periods are unmistakable: the *February period*; the *period of the constituting of the republic or of the Constituent National Assembly,* May 4, 1848, to May 29, 1849; the *period of the constitutional republic or of the Legislative National Assembly,* May 29, 1849, to December 2, 1851.

The first period, from February 24, or the overthrow of Louis Philippe, to May 4, 1848, the meeting of the Constituent Assembly, the *February period proper,* may be described as the *prologue* of the Revolution. Its character was officially expressed in the fact that the government improvised by it declared itself to be *provisional* and, like the government, everything that was instigated, attempted or enunciated during this period, proclaimed itself to be *provisional.* Nothing and nobody ventured to lay claim to the right of existence and of real action. All the elements that had prepared or determined the Revolution, the dynastic opposition, the republican bourgeoisie, the democratic-republican petty bourgeoisie and the social-democratic workers, provisionally found their place in the February *government.*

It could not be otherwise. The February days originally intended

---

1. An old Roman story tells that once, when Rome was besieged, the sacred geese in the Roman fortress, the Capitol, wakened the garrison with their cackling; thanks to this, the garrison was able to beat off the attack of the enemies who had stolen up in the night.

2. For these parties see pp. 452 ff.
3. The blue (bourgeois) and the red (socialist) republican parties.
4. This refers to the generals distinguished for their savage deeds in Africa during the conquest of Algeria (Cavaignac, Changarnier and others).

an electoral reform, by which the circle of the politically privileged among the possessing class itself was to be widened and the exclusive domination of the aristocracy of finance overthrown. When it came to the actual conflict, however, when the people mounted the barricades, the National Guard maintained a passive attitude, the army offered no serious resistance and the monarchy ran away, the republic appeared to be a matter of course. Every party construed it in its own sense. Having been won by the proletariat by force of arms, the proletariat impressed its stamp on it and proclaimed it to be a *social republic.* There was thus indicated the general content of the modern revolution, which stood in most singular contradiction to everything that, with the material at hand, with the degree of education attained by the masses, under the given circumstances and relationships, could be immediately realised in practice. On the other hand, the claims of all the remaining elements that had participated in the February Revolution were recognised by the lion's share that they obtained in the government. In no period do we therefore find a more confused mixture of high-flown phrases and actual uncertainty and clumsiness, of more enthusiastic striving for innovation and more deeply rooted domination of the old routine, of more apparent harmony of the whole society and more profound estrangement of its elements. While the Paris proletariat still revelled in the vision of the wide prospects that had opened before it and indulged in seriously-meant discussions on social problems, the old powers of society had grouped themselves, assembled, reflected and found an unexpected support in the mass of the nation, the peasants and petty bourgeois, who all at once stormed on to the political stage, after the barriers of the July monarchy had fallen.

The *second period,* from May 4, 1848, to the end of May 1849, is the period of the *constitution,* of the *foundation of the bourgeois republic.* Directly after the February days the dynastic opposition had not only been surprised by the republicans, the republicans by the socialists, but all France had been surprised by Paris. The National Assembly, which had met on May 4, 1848, having emerged from the national elections, represented the nation. It was a living protest against the presumptuous aspirations of the February days and was to reduce the results of the Revolution to the bourgeois scale. In vain the Paris proletariat, which immediately grasped the character of this National Assembly, attempted on May 15, a few days after it met, forcibly to deny its existence, to dissolve it, to disintegrate once more into its constituent parts the organic form in which the proletariat was threatened by the reactionary spirit of the nation. As is known, May 15 had no other result save that of removing Blanqui and his comrades, that is, the real leaders of the proletarian party [the revolutionary communists],[5] from the public stage for the entire duration of the cycle we are considering.

The *bourgeois monarchy* of Louis Philippe can only be followed by the *bourgeois republic*, that is, if a limited section of the bourgeoisie formerly ruled in the name of the king, the whole of the bourgeoisie will now rule in the name of the people. The demands of the Paris proletariat are utopian nonsense to which an end must be put. To this declaration of the Constituent National Assembly the Paris proletariat replied with the *June Insurrection*, the most colossal event in the history of European civil wars. The bourgeois republic triumphed. On its side stood the aristocracy of finance, the industrial bourgeoisie, the middle class, the petty bourgeois, the army, the *lumpenproletariat* organised as the Mobile Guard, the intellectual lights, the clergy, and the rural population. On the side of the Paris proletariat stood none but itself. More than three thousand insurgents were butchered after the victory, and fifteen thousand were transported without trial. With this defeat the proletariat passes into the background of the revolutionary stage. It attempts to press forward again on every occasion, as soon as the movement appears to make a fresh start, but with ever decreased expenditure of strength and always more insignificant results. As soon as one of the social strata situated above it gets into revolutionary ferment, it enters into an alliance with it and so shares all the defeats that the different parties suffer one after another. But these subsequent blows become steadily weaker, the more they are distributed over the entire surface of society. Its more important leaders in the Assembly and the press successively fall victims to the courts, and ever more equivocal figures come to the fore. In part it throws itself into *doctrinaire experiments, exchange banks and workers' associations, hence into a movement in which it renounces the revolutionising of the old world by means of its own great, combined resources, and seeks, rather, to achieve its salvation behind society's back, in private fashion, within its limited conditions of existence, and hence inevitably suffers shipwreck.* It seems to be unable either to rediscover revolutionary greatness in itself or to win new energy from the alliances newly entered into, until *all classes* with which it contended in June themselves lie prostrate beside it. But at least it succumbs with the honours of the great, world-historic struggle; not only France, but all Europe trembles at the June earthquake, while the ensuing defeats of the upper classes

5. Here and elsewhere the square brackets in the text denote passages of the first edition omitted in subsequent editions.

are so cheaply bought that they require bare-faced exaggeration by the victorious party to be able to pass for events at all and become the more ignominious the further the defeated party is removed from the proletariat.

The defeat of the June insurgents, to be sure, had now prepared and levelled the ground on which the bourgeois republic could be founded and built up, but it had shown at the same time that in Europe there are other questions involved than that of "republic or monarchy." It had revealed that here *bourgeois republic* signifies the unlimited despotism of one class over other classes. It had proved that in lands with an old civilisation, with a developed formation of classes, with modern conditions of production and with an intellectual consciousness into which all traditional ideas have been absorbed by the work of centuries, *the republic* signifies *in general only the political form of the revolution of bourgeois society* and not its *conservative form of life*, as, for example, in the United States of North America, where, though classes, indeed, already exist, they have not yet become fixed, but continually change and interchange their elements in a constant state of flux, where the modern means of production, instead of coinciding with a stagnant surplus population, rather supply the relative deficiency of heads and hands and where, finally, the feverishly youthful movement of material production, that has a new world to make its own, has left neither time nor opportunity for abolishing the old spirit world.

During the June days all classes and parties had united in the *Party of Order* against the proletarian class as the *party of anarchy*, of socialism, of communism. They had "saved" society from "*the enemies of society*." They had given out the watchwords of the old society, "*property, family, religion, order*," to their army as passwords and had proclaimed to the counter-revolutionary crusaders: "In this sign you will conquer!" From that moment, as soon as one of the numerous parties which had gathered under this sign against the June insurgents seeks to hold the revolutionary battlefield in its own class interests it goes down before the cry: "Property, family, religion, order." Society is saved just as often as the circle of its rulers contracts, as a more exclusive interest is maintained against a wider one. Every demand of the simplest bourgeois financial reform, of the most ordinary liberalism, of the most formal republicanism, of the most insipid democracy, is simultaneously castigated as an "attempt on society" and stigmatised as "socialism." And, finally, the high priests of "religion and order" themselves are driven wtih kicks from their Pythian tripods, hauled out of their beds in the darkness of night, put in prison-vans, thrown into dungeons or sent into exile; their temple is razed to the ground, their mouths are sealed, their pens broken, their law torn to pieces in the name of religion, of property, of family, of order. Bourgeois fanatics for order are shot down on their balconies by mobs of drunken soldiers, their domestic sanctuaries profaned, their houses bombarded for amusement—in the name of property, of family, of religion and of order. Finally the scum of bourgeois society forms *the holy phalanx of order* and the hero Crapulinsky[6] installs himself in the Tuileries[7] as the "*saviour of society.*"

II

Let us pick up the threads of the development once more.

The history of the *Constituent National Assembly* since the June days is the *history of the domination and the liquidation of the republican section of the bourgeoisie*, of that section which is known by the names of tricolour republicans, pure republicans, political republicans, formalist republicans, etc.

Under the bourgeois monarchy of Louis Philippe it had formed the *official* republican *opposition* and consequently a recognised, component part of the political world of the day. It had its representatives in the Chambers and a considerable sphere of influence in the press. Its Paris organ, the *National*, was considered just as respectable in its way as the *Journal des Débats*. Its character corresponded to this position under the constitutional monarchy. It was not a section of the bourgeoisie held together by great, common interests and marked off by specific conditions of production. It was a coterie of republican-minded bourgeois—writers, lawyers, officers and officials—that owed its influence to the personal antipathies of the country to Louis Philippe, to memories of the old republic, to the republican faith of a number of enthusiasts, above all, however, to *French nationalism*, whose hatred of the Vienna treaties and of the alliance with England it stirred up perpetually. A large part of the following that the *National* had under Louis Philippe was due to this concealed imperialism, which could consequently confront it later, under the republic, as a deadly rival in the person of Louis Bonaparte. It fought the aristocracy of finance, as did all the rest of the bourgeois opposition. Polemics against the budget, which were closely connected in France with fighting the aristocracy of finance, procured popularity too cheaply, and material for puritanical leading articles too plentifully, not to be exploited. The industrial bourgeoisie was grateful to it for its slavish defence of the French protec-

6. The hero of Heine's poem, *Two Knights*. In this character, Heine ridicules the spendthrift Polish nobleman ("Crapulinsky" comes from the French word *crapule*—gluttony, greediness). Here Marx means Louis Bonaparte.
7. The residence of the head of the government in France.

tionist system, which it accepted, however, more on national grounds than on grounds of political economy; the bourgeoisie as a whole was grateful to it for its vicious denunciation of communism and socialism. For the rest, the party of the *National* was purely republican, that is, it demanded a republican instead of a monarchist form of bourgeois rule and, above all, the lion's share of this rule. Concerning the conditions of this transformation it was by no means clear. On the other hand, what was clear as daylight to it and was publicly acknowledged at the reform banquets in the last days of Louis Philippe, was its unpopularity with the democratic petty bourgeois and, in particular, with the revolutionary proletariat. These pure republicans, as is, indeed, the way with pure republicans, were already on the point of contenting themselves in the first instance with a regency of the Duchess of Orléans,[8] when the February Revolution broke out and assigned their best known representatives a place in the Provisional Government. From the start, they naturally had the confidence of the bourgeoisie and a majority in the Constituent National Assembly. The *Socialist* elements of the Provisional Government were excluded forthwith from the Executive Commission which the National Assembly formed when it met, and the party of the *National* took advantage of the outbreak of the June Insurrection to discharge the *Executive Commission* also, and therewith to get rid of its immediate rivals, the *petty-bourgeois* or *democratic republicans* (Ledru-Rollin, etc.). Cavaignac, the general of the bourgeois republican party, who commanded the June battle, took the place of the Executive Commission with a sort of dictatorial power. Marrast, former editor-in-chief of the *National*, became the perpetual president of the Constituent Assembly, and the ministries, as well as all other important posts, fell to the portion of the pure republicans.

The republican bourgeois section, which had long regarded itself as the legitimate heir of the July monarchy, thus found itself successful beyond its hopes; it attained power, however, not as it had dreamed under Louis Philippe, through a liberal revolt of the bourgeoisie against the throne, but through a rising of the proletariat against capital, a rising laid low with grape-shot. What it had pictured to itself as the *most revolutionary* happening, turned out in reality to be the *most counter-revolutionary*. The fruit fell into its lap, but it fell from the tree of knowledge, not from the tree of life.

The exclusive *rule of the bourgeois republicans* lasted only from June 24 to December 10, 1848. It is summed up in the *drafting of a republican constitution* and in the *state of siege of Paris*.

8. On February 24, 1848, Louis Philippe, frightened at the revolutionary uprising, signed his abdication from the throne in favour of his grandson, the Count of Paris. Since the latter was a minor, it was proposed that his mother, the Duchess of Orléans, act as regent.

The new *Constitution* was at bottom only the republicanised edition of the constitutional Charter of 1830. The narrow electoral qualification of the July monarchy,[9] which even excluded a large part of the bourgeoisie from political rule, was incompatible with the existence of the bourgeois republic. In lieu of this qualification, the February Revolution had at once proclaimed direct universal suffrage. The bourgeois republicans could not revoke this event. They had to content themselves with adding the limiting proviso of a six months' domicile in the constituency. The old organisation of government, of the municipal system, of the administration of law, of the army, etc., continued to exist inviolate, or, where the Constitution changed them, the change concerned the table of contents, not the contents; the name, not the thing.

The inevitable general staff of the liberties of 1848, personal liberty, liberty of the press, of speech, of association, of assembly, of education and of religion, etc., received a constitutional uniform, which made them invulnerable. Each of these liberties, namely, is proclaimed as the *absolute* right of the French *citoyen*, but always with the marginal note that it is unlimited so far as it is not restricted by the *"equal rights of others* and the *public safety"* or by "laws" which are intended to secure just this harmony of the individual liberties with one another and with the public safety. For example: "The citizens have the right of association, of peaceful and unarmed assembly, of petition and of the free expression of opinions, whether in the press or otherwise. *The enjoyment of these rights has no limit save the equal rights of others and the public safety.*" (Chapter II of the French Constitution, § 8.)—"Education is free. Freedom of education shall be *enjoyed* under the conditions fixed by law and under the general supervision of the state." (*Ibidem*, § 9.)—"The domicile of every citizen is inviolable *except* in the forms prescribed by law." (Chapter II, § 3.) Etc., etc.—The Constitution, therefore, constantly refers to future *organic* laws, which are to put into effect those marginal notes and regulate the enjoyment of these unrestricted liberties so that they collide neither with one another nor with the public safety. And later, the organic laws were brought into being by the friends of order and all those liberties regulated in such a way that the bourgeoisie in its enjoyment of them does not come into collision with the equal rights of the other classes. Where it forbids these liberties entirely to "the others" or permits enjoyment of them under conditions that are just so many police traps, this always happens solely

9. After the July Revolution in 1830, the revision of the constitution made almost no changes in the formerly existing suffrage. The electoral qualification was lowered only to 200 francs; and the age qualification was lowered from 40 to 30. Only 250,000 of the 34,000,000 persons in France had the right to vote.

in the interest of the "public safety," that is, the safety of the bourgeoisie, as the Constitution prescribes. In the sequel, both sides accordingly appeal with complete justice to the Constitution, the friends of order, who suspended all these liberties, as well as the democrats, who demanded them back. Each paragraph of the Constitution, namely, contains in itself its own antithesis, its own Upper and Lower House, namely liberty in the general phrase, suspension of liberty in the marginal note. So long, therefore, as the *name* of freedom was respected and only its actual realisation prevented, of course in a legal way, the constitutional existence of liberty remained intact and inviolate, however mortal the blows dealt to its *everyday* existence.

This Constitution, made inviolable in so ingenious a manner, was nevertheless, like Achilles, vulnerable in one point, not in the heel, but in the head, or rather in the two heads in which it issued—the *Legislative Assembly*, on the one hand, the *President*, on the other. Glance through the Constitution and you will find that only the paragraphs in which the relationship of the President to the Legislative Assembly is determined are absolute, positive, non-contradictory, incapable of distortion. Here, that is to say, the issue for the bourgeois republicans was to safeguard themselves. Sections 45–70 of the Constitution are so worded that the National Assembly can remove the President constitutionally, whereas the President can only remove the National Assembly unconstitutionally, only by setting aside the constitution itself. Here, therefore, it challenges its overthrow by force. It not only sanctifies the division of powers, like the Charter of 1830, it widens it into an intolerable contradiction. *The play of the constitutional powers*, as Guizot termed the parliamentary squabble between the legislative and executive authorities, is in the Constitution of 1848 continually played *va-banque*.[1] On one side are seven hundred and fifty representatives of the people, elected by universal suffrage and eligible for re-election; they form an uncontrollable, indissoluble, indivisible National Assembly, a National Assembly that enjoys legislative omnipotence, decides in the last instance on war, peace and commercial treaties, alone possesses the right of amnesty and, by its permanence, perpetually holds the front of the stage. On the other side is the President, with all the attributes of royal power, with authority to appoint and dismiss his ministers independently of the National Assembly, with all the resources of the executive power in his hands, bestowing all posts and disposing thereby in France over at least a million and a half existences, for so many depend on the five hundred thousand officials and officers of every rank. He has the whole of the armed forces behind him. He enjoys the privilege of pardoning individual

1. Staking all on one chance.

criminals, of suspending National Guards, of discharging, in agreement with the Council of State, the general cantonal and municipal councils elected by the citizens themselves. Initiative and direction are reserved to him in all treaties with foreign countries. While the Assembly constantly performs on the boards and is exposed to the searching light of day, he leads a hidden life in the Elysian fields, and that with Article 45 of the Constitution before his eyes and in his heart, crying to him daily: *"Frère, il faut mourir!"*[2] Your power ceases on the second Sunday of the lovely month of May in the fourth year after your election! Then the glory is at an end, the piece is not played twice and if you have debts, look to it betimes that you pay them off with the six hundred thousand francs granted you by the Constitution, unless, perchance, you should prefer to go to Clichy,[3] on the second Monday of the lovely month of May!— Thus, if the Constitution assigns actual power to the President, it seeks to secure moral power for the National Assembly. Apart from the fact that it is impossible to create a moral power by paragraphs of law, the Constitution here suspends itself once more, by having the President elected by all Frenchmen through direct suffrage. While the votes of France are split up among the seven hundred and fifty members of the National Assembly, they are, on the contrary, here concentrated on a single individual. While each separate representative of the people represents only this or that party, this or that town, this or that bridge-head, or even the mere necessity of electing one of the seven hundred and fifty, in which neither the cause nor the man is closely examined, the President is the elect of the nation and the act of his election is the trump that the sovereign people plays once every four years. The elected National Assembly stands in a metaphysical relation, but the elected President in a personal relation to the nation. The National Assembly indeed, exhibits in its individual representatives the manifold aspects of the national spirit, but in the President this national spirit finds its incarnation. As against the Assembly, he possesses a sort of divine right, he is President, by grace of the people.

Thetis, the sea goddess, had prophesied to Achilles that he would die in the bloom of youth. The Constitution, which, like Achilles, had its weak spot, had also, like Achilles, its presentiment that it must go to an early death. It was sufficient for the constitution-making, pure republicans to cast a glance from the cloud-kingdom of their ideal republic at the profane world, in order to perceive how the arrogance of the royalists, the Bonapartists, the democrats, the communists as well as their own discredit grew daily in the same measure as they approached the completion of their great legislative work of art, without Thetis on this account having to leave the sea

2. Brother you must die!   3. The debtors' prison in Paris.

and communicate the secret to them. They sought to cheat destiny by constitutional cunning, through § 111 of the Constitution, according to which every motion for the *revision of the Constitution* must have at least three-quarters of the votes cast for it in three successive debates between which an entire month must always lie, with the added proviso that not less than five hundred members of the National Assembly must vote. Thereby they merely made the impotent attempt to exercise as a parliamentary minority, as which they already saw themselves prophetically in their mind's eye, a power which at the moment when they commanded a parliamentary majority and all the resources of governmental authority was slipping daily more and more from their feeble hands.

Finally the Constitution, in a melodramatic paragraph, entrusts itself "to the vigilance and the patriotism of the whole French people and every single Frenchman," after it had previously entrusted the "vigilant" and "patriotic" in another paragraph to the tender, painstaking care of the High Court of Justice, of the *"haute cour,"* established by it for the purpose.

Such was the Constitution of 1848, which on December 2, 1851, was overthrown not by a head, but fell at the touch of a mere hat; this hat, to be sure, was a three-cornered, Napoleonic hat.

While the bourgeois republicans in the Assembly were busy elaborating, discussing and voting this Constitution, outside the Assembly Cavaignac maintained the *state of seige of Paris.* The state of siege of Paris was the *accoucheur*[4] of the Constituent Assembly in its travail of republican creation. If the Constitution is subsequently put out of existence by bayonets, it must not be forgotten that it was likewise by bayonets, and these turned against the people, that it had to be protected in its mother's womb and by bayonets that it had to be brought into existence. The forefathers of the "honest republicans" had sent their symbol, the tricolour, on a tour round Europe. They now, in turn, also produced an invention that made its way by itself over the whole continent, but returned to France with ever renewed love until it has now acquired citizen rights in half her departments—*the state of siege.* It was a splendid invention, periodically employed in every ensuing crisis in the course of the French Revolution. But barrack and bivouac, which were periodically laid on French society's head to compress its brain and make a quiet man of it; sabre and musket, which were periodically allowed to direct and administer, hold in tutelage and act as censor, play policeman and do night-watchman's duties; moustache and uniform, which were periodically trumpeted as the highest wisdom and master of society—were not barrack and bivouac, sabre and musket, moustache and uniform, finally bound to hit upon the idea

4. Midwife.

of saving society, rather, once and for all, by proclaiming their own regime as the highest and freeing bourgeois society from all the trouble of governing itself? Barrack and bivouac, sabre and musket, moustache and uniform, were bound to hit upon the idea all the more as they might then also expect better cash payment for their higher services, whereas from the merely periodical state of siege and the transient rescues of society at the bidding of this or that bourgeois faction they gained little of substance beyond some killed and wounded and some friendly bourgeois grimaces. Should not the military, at length, likewise one day play the state of siege in their own interest and for their own interest and at the same time besiege the bourgeois *bourses?* Moreover, be it remarked in passing, one must not forget that *Colonel Bernard,* the same president of the military commission who under Cavaignac had 15,000 insurgents deported without trial, is at this moment again at the head of the military commissions active in Paris.

If, with the state of siege in Paris, the honest, the pure republicans founded the nursery in which the praetorians[5] of December 2, 1851, were to grow up, on the other hand they deserve praise for the reason that, instead of exaggerating the national sentiment as under Louis Philippe, they now, when they have command of the national power, crawl before foreign countries, and, instead of setting Italy free, let her be reconquered by Austrians and Neapolitans. Louis Bonaparte's election as president on December 10, 1848, put an end to the dictatorship of Cavaignac and the Constituent Assembly.

In § 44 of the Constitution it is stated: "The President of the French Republic must never have lost his status as a French citizen." The first President of the French Republic, L. N. Bonaparte, had not merely lost his status as a French citizen, had not only been an English special constable, he was even a naturalised Swiss.

I have worked out elsewhere the significance of the election of December 10. I will not revert to it here. It is sufficient to remark here that it was a *reaction of the peasants,* who had had to pay the costs of the February Revolution, against the remaining classes of the nation, a *reaction of the countryside against the town.* It met with great approval in the army, for which the republicans of the *National* had provided neither glory nor additional pay, among the big bourgeoisie, which hailed Bonaparte as a bridge to monarchy, among the proletarians and petty bourgeois, who hailed him as a scourge for Cavaignac. I shall have an opportunity later of going

5. Praetorians was the name given in ancient Rome to the personal bodyguard of any general or emperor; this guard was in his pay, and was given various privileges. Mercenary, corrupt praetorians usually played a large part in the various palace revolutions. Here Marx is referring to the "Society of December 10," the bodyguard of Louis Bonaparte.

more closely into the relationship of the peasants to the French Revolution.

The period from December 20, 1848,[6] until the dissolution of the Constituent Assembly in May 1849, comprises the history of the downfall of the bourgeois republicans. After having founded a republic for the bourgeoisie, driven the revolutionary proletariat out of the field and reduced the democratic petty bourgeoisie to silence for the time being, they are themselves thrust aside by the mass of the bourgeoisie, which justly impounds this republic as *its property*. This bourgeois mass was, however, *royalist*. One section of it, the large landowners, had ruled during the *Restoration* and was accordingly *Legitimist*.[7] The other, the aristocrats of finance and big industrialists, had ruled during the July Monarchy and was consequently *Orleanist*. The high dignitaries of the army, the university, the church, the bar, the academy and the press were to be found on either side, though in different proportions. Here in the bourgeois republic, which bore neither the name *Bourbon* nor the name *Orleans*, but the name *capital*, they had found the form of state in which they could rule *conjointly*. The June Insurrection had already united them in the "Party of Order." Now it was necessary, in the first place, to remove the coterie of bourgeois republicans, who still occupied seats in the National Assembly. Just as these pure republicans were brutal in their misuse of physical force against the people, to the same degree were they now cowardly, downcast, broken-spirited and incapable of fighting in their retreat, when it was a question of maintaining their republicanism and their legislative rights against the executive power and the royalists. I do not have to relate here the ignominious story of their dissolution. They were not destroyed; they passed away. Their history has come to an end forever, and, both inside and outside the Assembly, they figure in the following period only as memories, memories that again seem to become living whenever the mere name, republic, is once more the issue and as often as the revolutionary conflict threatens to sink down to the lowest level. I may remark in passing that the journal which gave its name to this party, the *National*, went over to socialism in the following period.

Before we finish with this period we must still cast a retrospective glance at the two powers, one of which annihilates the other on

6. On December 20, 1848, Louis Bonaparte appointed his first ministry, headed by Odilon Barrot.
7. The Restoration—the period from the downfall of Napoleon I (1814) to the July Revolution of 1830, when the dynasty of the Bourbons, which had been overthrown by the French Revolution, was again in power. The supporters of this dynasty, which represented the interests of the big landowners, called themselves Legitimists (they considered the Bourbon monarchy the only legitimate government). The Orleanists were the supporters of the Orleans dynasty, which represented the interests of the bankers, the financial aristocracy, and which came into power after the July Revolution of 1830.

December 2, 1851, whereas from December 10, 1848, until the exit of the Constituent Assembly they lived in conjugal relations. We mean Louis Bonaparte, on the one hand, and the party of the royalist coalition, the Party of Order, of the big bourgeoisie, on the other. On his entry into the presidency, Bonaparte at once formed a ministry of the Party of Order, at the head of which he placed Odilon Barrot, the old leader, *nota bene*, of the most liberal section of the parliamentary bourgeoisie. M. Barrot had at last secured the portfolio, the spectre of which had haunted him since 1830, and what is more, the premiership in the ministry; but not, as he had imagined under Louis Philippe, as the most advanced leader of the parliamentary opposition, but with the task of killing a parliament, and as the confederate of all his arch-enemies, Jesuits and Legitimists. He brought the bride home at last, but only after she had become a prostitute. Bonaparte appeared to efface himself completely. This party acted for him.

The first council of ministers at once resolved on the expedition to Rome, which they agreed to undertake behind the back of the National Assembly and the means for which they agreed to obtain from it by false pretences. Thus they began by swindling the National Assembly and secretly conspiring with the absolutist powers abroad against the revolutionary Roman republic. In the same manner and with the same manœuvres Bonaparte prepared his coup of December 2 against the royalist Legislative Assembly and its constitutional republic. Let us not forget that the same party which formed Bonaparte's ministry on December 20, 1848, formed the majority of t he Legislative National Assembly on December 2, 1851.

In August the Constituent Assembly had decided to dissolve only after it had worked out and promulgated a whole series of organic laws that were to supplement the Constitution. On January 6, 1849, the Party of Order had a deputy named Rateau move that it should let the organic laws go and, rather, decide on its *own dissolution*. Not merely the ministry, with Odilon Barrot at its head, but all the royalist members of the National Assembly bullyingly told it at this moment that its dissolution was necessary for the restoration of credit, for the consolidation of order, for putting an end to the indefinite provisional arrangements and for establishing a definite state of affairs; that it hampered the productivity of the new government and sought to prolong its existence merely out of malice; that the country was tired of it. Bonaparte took note of all this invective against the legislative power, learnt it by heart and proved to the parliamentary royalists on December 2, 1851, that he had learnt from them. He reiterated their own catchwords against them.

The Barrot ministry and the Party of Order went further. They caused *petitions to the National Assembly* to be made throughout France, in which this body was most politely requested to disappear. Against the National Assembly, the constitutionally organised expression of the people, they thus led its unorganised masses into the fire. They taught Bonaparte to appeal from the parliamentary assemblies to the people. At length, on January 29, the day had come on which the Constituent Assembly was to decide concerning its own dissolution. The National Assembly found the building where its sessions were held occupied by the military; Changarnier, the general of the Party of Order, in whose hands the supreme command of the National Guard and troops of the line had been united, held a great review in Paris, as if a battle were impending, and the royalists in coalition threateningly declared to the Constituent Assembly that force would be employed if it were not docile. It was docile and only bargained for a short extra term of life. What was January 29 but the *coup d'état* on December 2, 1851, only carried out by the royalists with Bonaparte against the republican National Assembly? The gentlemen did not observe or did not wish to observe that Bonaparte availed himself of January 29, 1848, to have a portion of the troops march past him in front of the Tuileries and seized with avidity on just this first public calling out of the military power against the parliamentary power to foreshadow Caligula.[8] They, to be sure, saw only their Changarnier.

One motive, in particular, that actuated the Party of Order in forcibly cutting short the duration of the Constituent Assembly's life consisted in the *organic* laws supplementing the Constitution, such as the education law, the law on religious worship, etc. To the royalists in coalition it was most important that they should make these laws themselves and not let them be made by the republicans, who had grown mistrustful. Among these organic laws, however, was also a law on the responsibility of the President of the republic. In 1851 the Legislative Assembly was occupied with the drafting of just such a law, when Bonaparte anticipated this coup with the coup of December 2. In their parliamentary winter compaign of 1851 what would the royalists in coalition not have given to have found the Responsibility Law ready to hand, and drawn up, at that, by a mistrustful malicious republican Assembly!

After the Constituent Assembly had itself shattered its last weapon on January 29, 1849, the Barrot ministry and the friends of order hounded it to death, left nothing undone that could humiliate it and wrested from its self-despairing weakness laws that cost it the last remnant of respect in the eyes of the public. Bonaparte, occupied with his fixed Napoleonic idea, was bold enough to exploit

8. Gaius Caligula—the third Roman emperor (37–41). A crazy despot, put on the throne by the army. To humili-ate the Senate—the shadowy remnant of the institutions of Republican Rome—he made his horse a senator.

publicly this degradation of the parliamentary power. That is to say, when on May 8, 1849, the National Assembly passed a vote of censure on the ministry because of the occupation of Civita Vecchia by Oudinot, and ordered it to bring back the Roman expedition to its ostensible purpose, Bonaparte published the same evening in the *Moniteur* a letter to Oudinot, in which he congratulated him on his heroic exploits and, in contrast to the ink-slinging parliamentarians, already posed as the generous protector of the army. The royalists smiled at this. They regarded him simply as their dupe. Finally, when Marrast, the President of the Constituent Assembly, believed for a moment that the safety of the National Assembly was endangered and, relying on the Constitution, requisitioned a colonel and his regiment, the colonel declined, took refuge in discipline and referred Marrast to Changarnier, who scornfully refused him with the remark that he did not like *baionettes intelligentes*. In November 1851, when the royalists in coalition wished to begin the decisive struggle with Bonaparte, they sought to push through in their notorious *Quæstors' Bill*[9] the principle of the direct requisition of troops by the President of the National Assembly. One of their generals, Leflô, had signed the bill. In vain did Changarnier vote for it and Thiers pay homage to the far-sighted wisdom of the former Constituent Assembly. The *War Minister, Saint-Arnaud,* answered him as Changarnier had answered Marrast—and to the acclamation of the Mountain!

Thus the *Party of Order,* when it was not yet the National Assembly, when it was still only the ministry, had itself stigmatised the *parliamentary regime.* And it makes an outcry when December 2, 1851, banished this regime from France!

We wish it a happy journey.

III

On May 29, 1849, the Legislative National Assembly met. On December 2, 1851, it was forcibly dissolved. This period covers the life of the *constitutional or parliamentary republic.*

[It is subdivided into three main periods: *May 29, 1849, to June 13, 1849,* struggle of the democracy and the bourgeoisie, *defeat of the petty-bourgeois or democratic party; June 13, 1849, to May 31, 1850,* parliamentary dictatorship of the bourgeoisie, that is, of the Orleanists and Legitimists in coalition or the Party of

---

9. The quæstors (deputies of the National Assembly entrusted with the finance and safeguarding of the National Assembly), generals Leflô and Baze, brought in a bill by which the President of the National Assembly was to be entrusted with the preservation of the safety of the National Assembly, for which purpose he was to receive the right to call out military forces. This *Quæstors' Bill* was rejected on October 17, 1851, by a majority of 408 votes to 300.

Order, dictatorship that is completed by the *abolition of universal suffrage; May 31, 1850, up to December 2, 1851,* struggle of the bourgeoisie and Bonaparte, *overthrow of bourgeois rule, downfall of the constitutional or parliamentary republic.*][1]

In the first French Revolution the rule of the *Constitutionalists* is followed by the rule of the *Girondins* and the rule of the *Girondins* by the rule of the *Jacobins*. Each of these parties supported itself on the more progressive party. As soon as it has brought the revolution far enough to be unable to follow it further, still less to go ahead of it, it is thrust aside by the bolder ally that stands behind it and sent to the guillotine. The revolution thus moves along an ascending line.

It is the reverse with the Revolution of 1848. The proletarian party appears as an appendage of the petty-bourgeois democratic party. It is betrayed and dropped by the latter on April 16, May 15, and in the June days. The democratic party, in its turn, leans on the shoulders of the bourgeois-republican party. The bourgeois-republicans no sooner believe themselves well established than they shake off the troublesome comrade and support themselves on the shoulders of the Party of Order. The Party of Order hunches its shoulders, lets the bourgeois-republicans tumble and throws itself on the shoulders of armed force. It fancies it is still sitting on its shoulders when, one fine morning, it perceives that the shoulders have transformed themselves into bayonets. Each party strikes from behind at that pressing further and leans from in front on that pressing back. No wonder that in this ridiculous posture it loses its balance and, having made the inevitable grimaces, collapses with curious capers. The revolution thus moves in a descending line. It finds itself in this state of retrogressive motion before the last February barricade has been cleared away and the first revolutionary authority constituted.

The period that we have before us comprises the most motley mixture of crying contradictions: constitutionalists who conspire openly against the Constitution; revolutionaries who are confessedly constitutional; a National Assembly that wants to be omnipotent and always remains parliamentary; a Mountain that finds its vocation in patience and counters its present defeats by prophesying future victories; royalists who form the *patres conscripti*[2] of the republic and are forced by the situation to keep the hostile royal houses, to which they adhere, abroad, and the republic, which they hate, in France; an executive power that finds its strength in its very weakness and its respectability in the contempt that it calls forth; a republic that is nothing but the combined infamy of two monar-

1. This paragraph was omitted in the third German edition (1883).
2. Conscript fathers. In ancient Rome

Senate with this appellation.
every Senator began his speech to the

chies, the Restoration and the July Monarchy, with an imperial label—combinations, whose first proviso is separation; struggles, whose first law is indecision; wild, empty agitation in the name of revolution; passions without truth, truth without passion; heroes without heroic deeds, history without events; development, whose sole driving force seems to be the calendar, wearying with constant repetition of the same tensions and relaxations; antagonisms that periodically seem to reach a high pitch only in order to lose their acuteness and fall away without being able to find a solution; pretentiously paraded exertions and bourgeois terror at the danger of the downfall of the world and at the same time the pettiest intrigues and court comedies played by the world redeemers, who in their *laisser aller*[3] remind us less of the Day of Judgment than of the times of the Fronde[4]—the official collective genius of France brought to naught by the artful stupidity of a single individual; the collective will of the nation, as often as it speaks through universal suffrage, seeking its appropriate expression through the ancient enemies of the mass interests, until at length it finds it in the self-will of a filibuster. If any section of history has been painted grey on grey, it is this. Men and events appear inverted Schlemihls,[5] as shadows that have lost their substance. The revolution itself paralyses its own bearers and endows only its adversaries with passionate forcefulness. When the "red spectre," continually conjured up and exorcised by the counter-revolutionaries, finally appears, it appears not with the Phrygian cap of anarchy on its head, but in the uniform of order, in *red breeches*.

We have seen that the ministry which Bonaparte installed on December 20, 1848, on his Ascension Day, was a ministry of the Party of Order, of the Legitimist and Orleanist coalition. This Barrot-Falloux ministry had outlived the republican Constituent Assembly, whose term of life it had more or less violently cut short, and found itself still at the helm. Changarnier, the general of the allied royalists, continued to unite in his person the general command of the first division of the army and the National Guard of Paris. The general elections had finally secured the Party of Order a large majority in the National Assembly. Here the deputies and peers of Louis Philippe encountered a hallowed host of Legitimists, for whom numerous ballot papers of the nation had become transformed into admission cards to the political stage. The Bonapartist

3. Letting things take their course.
4. The Fronde period in France (1648–53). The period of the regency of Anne of Austria before Louis XIV came of age—a period characterised by the opposition movement of the so-called parliamentary Fronde and the Fronde princes. This movement, which was directed against the absolute power of the king, was extremely weak, petty and irresolute.
5. Schlemihl—the hero of "Peter Schlemihl," by Chamisso (1781–1838). He sold his shadow for wealth, and went seeking it all over the world.

representatives of the people were too few to be able to form an independent parliamentary party. They appear merely as the *mauvaise queue*[6] of the Party of Order. Thus the Party of Order was in possession of the governmental power, the army and the legislative body, in short, of the whole power of the state, while it had been morally strengthened by the general elections which made its rule appear as the will of the people and by the simultaneous triumph of counter-revolution over the whole continent of Europe.

Never did a party open its campaign with greater resources or under more favourable auspices.

The shipwrecked *pure republicans* found themselves reduced to a clique of some fifty men in the National Assembly, the African generals—Cavaignac, Lamoricière and Bedau—at their head. The great opposition party, however was formed by the *Mountain*. The *Social-Democratic* Party had given itself this parliamentary name. It commanded more than two hundred of the seven hundred and fifty votes of the National Assembly and was consequently at least as powerful as any one of the three factions of the Party of Order taken by itself. Its relative minority compared with the entire royalist coalition seemed compensated by special circumstances. Not only did the elections in the Departments show that it had gained a considerable following among the rural population. It counted in its ranks almost all the deputies from Paris; the army had made a confession of democratic faith by the election of three non-commissioned officers, and the leader of the Mountain, Ledru-Rollin, in contradistinction to all the representatives of the Party of Order, had been raised to the parliamentary peerage by five Departments, which had pooled their votes for him. In view of the inevitable clashes of the royalists among themselves and of the whole Party of Order with Bonaparte, the Mountain seemed to have all the elements of success before it on May 29, 1849. A fortnight later it had lost everything, honour included.

Before we pursue parliamentary history further, some remarks are necessary to avoid common misunderstandings regarding the whole character of the period that lies before us. Looked at in the democratic way, the period of the Legislative National Assembly is concerned with what the period of the Constituent Assembly was concerned, *viz.*, the simple struggle between republicans and royalists. The movement itself, however, they sum up in the stock word "reaction"—a night in which all cats are grey and which permits them to reel off their night-watchman's commonplaces. And, to be sure, at first sight the Party of Order reveals a maze of different royalist factions, which not only intrigue against each other so that each may elevate its own pretender to the throne and

6. Evil appendage.

exclude the pretender of the opposing party, but also all unite in common hatred of and common onslaughts on the "republic." In opposition to this royalist conspiracy the Mountain, for its part, appears as the representative of the "republic." The Party of Order appears to be perpetually engaged in a "reaction," which directs itself against press, association and the like, neither more nor less than in Prussia, and which, as in Prussia, is carried out in the form of brutal police intervention by the bureaucracy, the *gendarmerie* and the law courts. The "Mountain," for its part, is again just as continually occupied in warding off these attacks and thus defending the "eternal rights of man," as every so-called people's party has done, more or less, for a century and a half. Looking at the situation and the parties more closely, however, this superficial appearance which veils the *class struggle* and the peculiar physiognomy of this period disappears.

Legitimists and Orleanists, as we have said, formed the two great sections of the Party of Order. Was that which held these sections fast to their pretenders and kept them apart from one another nothing but lily and tricolour, house of Bourbon and house of Orléans, different shades of royalty, was it the confession of faith in royalty at all? Under the Bourbons, *large landed property* had governed with its priests and lackeys; under the Orléans, high finance, large-scale industry, wholesale trade, that is, *capital* governed with its retinue of lawyers, professors and orators. The Legitimate Monarchy was merely the political expression of the hereditary rule of the lords of the soil, as the July Monarchy was only the political expression of the usurping rule of the bourgeois *parvenus*. What kept the two sections apart, therefore, was not any so-called principles, it was their material conditions of existence, two different kinds of property, it was the old contrast of town and country, the rivalry between capital and landed property. That at the same time old memories, personal enmities, fears and hopes, prejudices and illusions, sympathies and antipathies, convictions, articles of faith and principles bound them to one or the other royal house, who is there that denies this? Upon the different forms of property, upon the social conditions of existence rises an entire superstructure of distinct and characteristically formed sentiments, illusions, modes of thought and views of life. The entire class creates and forms them out of its material foundations and out of the corresponding social relations. The single individual who derives them through tradition and education may imagine that they form the real motives and the starting point of his activity. If Orleanists and Legitimists, if each section sought to make itself and the other believe that loyalty to their two royal houses separated them, it later proved to be the case that it was rather their divided interests which forbade the uniting of the two royal houses. And as in private life one distinguishes between what a man thinks and says of himself and what he really is and does, still more in historical struggles must one distinguish the phrases and fancies of the parties from their real organism and their real interests, their conception of themselves with their reality. Orleanists and Legitimists found themselves side by side in the republic with equal claims. If each side wished to effect the *restoraion* of its *own* royal house against the other, that merely signifies that the *two great interests* into which the *bourgeoisie* is split—landed property and capital—sought each to restore its own supremacy and the subordination of the other. We speak of two interests of the bourgeoisie, for large landed property, despite its feudal coquetry and pride of race, has been rendered thoroughly bourgeois by the development of modern society. Thus the Tories in England long imagined that they were enthusiastic about the monarchy, the church and the beauties of the old English Constitution, until the day of danger wrung from them the confession that they are only enthusiastic about *ground rent*.

The royalists in coalition carried on their intrigues against one another in the press, in Ems, in Claremont, outside parliament. Behind the scenes they donned their old Orleanist and Legitimist liveries again and engaged in their old tourneys once more. But on the public stage, in their principal and state actions, as a great parliamentary party, they put off their respective royal houses with formal obeisances and adjourn the restoration of the monarchy *in infinitum*. They do their real business as the *Party of Order*, that is, under a *social*, not under a *political* title; as representatives of the bourgeois world-order, not as knights of errant princesses; as the bourgeois class against other classes, not as royalists against the republicans. And as the Party of Order they exercised more absolute and sterner domination over the other classes of society than ever previously during the Restoration or during the July Monarchy, a domination which, in general, was only possible under the form of the parliamentary republic, for only under this form could the two great divisions of the French bourgeoisie unite, and therefore put the rule of their class instead of the regime of a privileged section of it on the order of the day. If, nevertheless, they, as the Party of Order, also insult the republic and express their repugnance to it, this happens not merely from royalist memories. Instinct taught them that the republic, indeed, perfects their political rule, but at the same time undermines its social foundation, since they must now confront the subjugated classes and contend against them without intermediation, without the concealment afforded by the crown, without being able to divert the national interest through their subordinate struggles with one another and with the monarchy. It was a feeling of weakness that caused them to recoil from the pure conditions of their own class rule and to sigh for the more incomplete, more undeveloped and consequently less dangerous forms of this rule. On the other hand, as often as the royalists in coalition come in conflict with the pretender that confronts them, with Bonaparte, as often as they believe their parliamentary omnipotence endangered by the executive power, as often therefore, as they must put forward the political title to their rule, they come forward as *republicans* and not as *royalists*, from the Orleanist Thiers, who warns the National Assembly that the republic divides them least, to the Legitimist Berryer, who, as a tribune swathed in a tricoloured sash, harangues the people assembled before the town hall of the tenth *arrondissement*[7] on December 2, 1851, in the name of the republic. To be sure, a mocking echo calls back to him: Henry V! Henry V!

As against the coalition of the bourgeoisie, a coalition between petty bourgeois and workers had been formed, the so-called *Social-Democratic* Party. The petty bourgeoisie saw that they were badly rewarded after the June days of 1848, their material interests imperilled and the democratic guarantees which were to ensure the enforcement of these interests endangered by the counter-revolution. Accordingly, they came closer to the workers. On the other hand, their parliamentary representation, the Mountain, thrust aside during the dictatorship of the bourgeois republicans, had in the last half of the life of the Constituent Assembly reconquered its lost popularity through the struggle with Bonaparte and the royalist ministers. It had concluded an alliance with the socialist leaders. In February 1849, banquets celebrated the reconciliation. A joint programme was drafted, joint election committees were set up and joint candidates put forward. From the social demands of the proletariat the revolutionary point was broken off and a democratic turn given to them; from the democratic claims of the petty bourgeoisie the purely political form was stripped off and their socialist point thrust forward. Thus arose *Social-Democracy*. The new *Mountain*, the result of this combination, apart from some supernumeraries from the working class and some socialist sectarians, contained the same elements as the old Mountain, only numerically stronger. But in the course of development it had changed with the class that it represented. The peculiar character of Social-Democracy is epitomised in the fact that democratic-republican institutions are demanded not as a means of doing away with both the extremes, capital and wage labour, but of weakening their antagonism and transforming it into harmony. However different the means proposed for the attainment of this end may be, however much it

7. District of a French Department; in Paris, a city ward.

may be trimmed with more or less revolutionary notions, the content remains the same. This content is the transformation of society in a democratic way, but a transformation within the bounds of the petty bourgeoisie. Only one must not form the narrow-minded notion that the petty bourgeoisie, on principle, wishes to enforce an egoistic class interest. Rather, it believes that the *special* conditions of its emancipation are the *general* conditions under which modern society can alone be saved and the class struggle avoided. Just as little must one imagine that the democratic representatives are all shopkeepers or enthusiastic champions of shopkeepers. According to their education and their individual position they may be separated from them as widely as heaven from earth. What makes them representatives of the petty bourgeoisie is the fact that in their minds they do not go beyond the limits which the latter do not go beyond in life, that they are consequently driven theoretically to the same tasks and solutions to which material interest and social position practically drive the latter. This is in general the relationship of the *political and literary representatives* of a class to the class that they represent.

After the analysis given, it is obvious that if the Mountain continually contends with the Party of Order for the republic and the so-called rights of man, neither the republic nor the rights of man are its final end, any more than an army which it is desired to deprive of its weapons and which sets about defending itself has taken the field in order to remain in possession of its own weapons.

Immediately, as soon as the National Assembly met, the Party of Order provoked the Mountain. The bourgeoisie now felt the necessity of making an end of the democratic petty bourgeois, as a year before it had realised the necessity of settling with the revolutionary proletariat. Only the situation of the adversary was a different one. The strength of the proletarian party lay in the streets, that of the petty bourgeois in the National Assembly itself. It was therefore a question of decoying them out of the National Assembly into the streets and causing them to smash their parliamentary power themselves, before time and circumstances could consolidate it. The Mountain rushed headlong into the trap.

The bombardment of Rome by the French troops was the bait that was thrown to it. It violated Article 54 of the Constitution, which forbids the French republic to employ its military forces against the freedom of another people. In addition to this, Article IV also prohibited any declaration of war on the part of the executive power without the assent of the National Assembly, and by its resolution of May 8, the Constituent Assembly had disapproved of the Roman expedition. On these grounds Ledru-Rollin brought in a bill of impeachment against Bonaparte and his ministers on June

11, 1849. Provoked by the wasp stings of Thiers, he actually let himself be carried away to the point of threatening that he would defend the Constitution by every means, even by force of arms. The Mountain arose as *one* man and repeated this call to arms. On June 12, the National Assembly rejected the bill of impeachment, and the Mountain left the parliament. The events of June 13 are known: the proclamation issued by a section of the Mountain, declaring Bonaparte and his ministers "outside the Constitution"; the street processions of the democratic National Guards, who, unarmed as they were, were dispersed in the encounter with the troops of Changarnier, etc., etc. A part of the Mountain fled abroad; another part was arraigned before the High Court at Bourges, and a parliamentary regulation subjected the remainder to the schoolmasterly surveillance of the President of the National Assembly. Paris was again declared in a state of siege and the democratic section of its National Guard dissolved. Thus the influence of the Mountain in parliament and the power of the petty bourgeois in Paris were broken.

Lyons, where June 13 had given the signal for a bloody insurrection of the workers, was, along with the five surrounding Departments, likewise declared in a state of siege, a condition that has continued up to the present moment.

The bulk of the Mountain had left its advance guard in the lurch, having refused to subscribe to its proclamation. The press had deserted, only two journals having dared to publish the *pronunciamento*. The petty bourgeois betrayed their representatives, in that the National Guards either stayed away or, where they appeared, hindered the erection of barricades. The representatives had duped the petty bourgeois, in that the alleged allies from the army were nowhere to be seen. Finally, instead of gaining an accession of strength from it, the democratic party had infected the proletariat with its own weakness and, as is usual with the great deeds of democrats, the leaders had the satisfaction of being able to charge their "people" with desertion, and the people the satisfaction of being able to charge its leaders with selling it.

Seldom had an action been announced with more noise than the impending campaign of the Mountain, seldom had an event been trumpeted with greater certainty or longer in advance than the inevitable victory of democracy. Most assuredly, the democrats believe in the trumpets before whose blasts the walls of Jericho fell down. And as often as they stand before the ramparts of despotism, they seek to imitate the miracle. If the Mountain wished to triumph in parliament, it should not have called to arms. If it called to arms in parliament, it should not have acted in parliamentary fashion on the streets. If the peaceful demonstration was seriously intended, then it was folly not to foresee that it would be given a warlike reception. If a real struggle was intended, then it was a queer idea to lay down the weapons with which it must be waged. But the revolutionary threats of the petty bourgeois and their democratic representatives are mere attempts to intimidate the antagonist. And when they have run into a blind alley, when they have sufficiently compromised themselves to make it necessary to give effect to their threats, then this happens in an ambiguous fashion that avails nothing so much as the means to the end and tries to find an excuse for defeat. The blaring overture that announced the struggle dies away in a dejected snarl as soon as the struggle has to begin, the actors cease to take themselves *au sérieux*, and the action collapses completely, like a pricked balloon.

No party exaggerates its powers more than the democrats, none deludes itself more irresponsibly over the situation. When a section of the army had voted for it, the Mountain was now convinced that the army would revolt for it. And on what grounds? On grounds which, from the standpoint of the troops, had no other meaning than that the revolutionaries took the side of the Roman soldiers against the French soldiers. On the other hand, the recollections of June 1848 were still too fresh to allow of anything but a profound aversion on the part of the proletariat towards the National Guard and a thorough-going mistrust of the democratic chiefs on the part of the leaders of the secret societies. To make up for these differences, it was necessary for great, common interests to be at stake. The violation of an abstract paragraph of the Constitution could not provide these interests. Had not the Constitution been repeatedly violated, according to the assurance of the democrats themselves? Had not the most popular journals branded it as counter-revolutionary botch-work? But the democrat, because he represents the petty bourgeoisie, therefore a *transition class*, in which the interests of two classes are simultaneously deadened, imagines himself elevated above class antagonism generally. The democrats concede that a privileged class confronts them, but they, along with all the rest of the surrounding nation, form the *people*. What they represent are the *people's rights*; what interests them are the *people's interests*. Accordingly, when a struggle is impending, they do not need to examine the interests and positions of the different classes. They do not need to consider their own resources too critically. They have merely to give the signal and the people, with all its inexhaustible resources, will fall upon the *oppressors*. If in the performance their interests now prove to be uninteresting and their power to be impotence, then either the fault lies with pernicious sophists, who split the *indivisible people* into different hostile camps, or the army was too brutalised and blinded to apprehend the pure aims of democracy as best for itself, or the whole thing has been wrecked by a detail in its execution, or else an unforeseen accident has for this time spoilt the game. In any case, the democrat comes out of the most disgraceful defeat just as immaculate as he went into it innocent, with the newly-won conviction that he is bound to conquer, not that he himself and his party have to give up the old standpoint, but, on the contrary, that conditions have to ripen in his direction.

Accordingly, one must not imagine the Mountain, decimated and broken though it was, and humiliated by the new parliamentary regulation, as being particularly miserable. If June 13 had removed its chiefs, on the other hand it made room for men of lesser calibre, whom this new position flattered. If their powerlessness in parliament could no longer be doubted, they were also entitled now to confine their actions to outbursts of moral indignation and blustering declamation. If the Party of Order affected to see embodied in them, as the last official representatives of the revolution, all the terrors of anarchy, they could in reality be all the more insipid and moderate. They consoled themselves, however, for June 13 with the profound utterance: But if they dare to attack universal suffrage, ah then—then we'll show them what we are made of! *Nous verrons!*[8]

So far as the *Montagnards* who fled abroad are concerned, it is sufficient to remark here that Ledru-Rollin, because in barely a fortnight he had succeeded in ruining irretrievably the powerful party at whose head he stood, now found himself called upon to form a French government *in partibus*; that to the extent that the level of the revolution sank and the official stalwarts of official France became more dwarflike, his figure in the distance, removed from the scene of action, seemed to grow in stature; that he could figure as the republican pretender for 1852, and that he issued periodical circulars to the Wallachians and other peoples, in which the despots of the Continent are threatened with the deeds of himself and his confederates. Was Proudhon altogether wrong when he cried to these gentlemen: *"Vous n'êtes que des blagueurs"*?[9]

On June 13, the Party of Order had not only broken the Mountain, it had effected the *subordination of the Constitution to the majority decisions of the National Assembly*. And so it understood the republic: that the bourgeoisie rules here in parliamentary forms, without, as in the monarchy, any limitations such as the veto of the executive power or the fact that parliament could be dissolved. This was the *parliamentary republic*, as Thiers termed it. But if on June 13 the bourgeoisie secured its omnipotence within the house of par-

8. We shall see.   9. You are nothing but windbags.

liament, did it not afflict parliament itself with incurable weakness as compared with the executive power and the people by excluding its most popular part?[1] By surrendering numerous deputies without further ado on the demand of the public prosecutor, it abolished its own parliamentary inviolability. The humiliating regulations[2] to which it subjected the Mountain exalted the President of the republic in the same measure as it degraded the individual representative of the people. By branding the insurrection for the protection of the constitutional charter as an anarchic act aiming at the overthrow of society, it prohibited an appeal to insurrection in its own case as soon as, in relation to it, the executive power should violate the Constitution. And by the irony of history, the general who on Bonaparte's instructions bombarded Rome and thus provided the immediate occasion for the constitutional revolt of June 13, that very *Oudinot* was the man offered by the Party of Order imploringly and unavailingly to the people as general on behalf of the Constitution against Bonaparte on December 2, 1851. Another hero of June 13, *Vieyra*, who was lauded from the tribune of the National Assembly for the brutalities that he had committed in the democratic newspaper offices at the head of a troop of National Guards in the pay of the high financiers, this same Vieyra had been initiated into Bonaparte's conspiracy and he essentially contributed to depriving the National Assembly in the hour of its death of any protection by the National Guard.

June 13 had still another meaning. The Mountain had wanted to force the impeachment of Bonaparte. Its defeat was therefore a direct victory for Bonaparte, his personal triumph over his democratic enemies. The Party of Order gained the victory; Bonaparte had only to profit by it. He did so. On June 14 a proclamation could be read on the walls of Paris in which the President, reluctantly and against his will, as it were, compelled by the mere force of events, comes forth from his cloistered seclusion and, posing as misunderstood virtue, complains of the calumnies of his opponents and, while he seems to identify his person with the cause of order, rather identifies the cause of order with his person. Moreover, the National Assembly had, it is true, subsequently approved the expedition against Rome, but Bonaparte had taken the initiative in the matter. After having installed the High Priest Samuel in the Vatican once more, he could hope to enter the Tuileries as King David. He had won over the priests.

1. After the events of June 13, forty deputies were brought to trial, one after the other. Some of the leaders of the Mountain fled (Ledru-Rollin, Felix Pyat and others); others were put into prison.
2. In order to silence the republican opposition, a new ruling was adopted by the majority of the Assembly, limiting freedom of speech and subjecting the deputies to the direction of the President. Deputies could now be excluded from the Assembly and deprived of their salaries.

The revolt of June 13, as we have seen, was confined to a peaceful street procession. No war laurels were therefore to be won against it. Nevertheless, at a time as poor as this in heroes and events the Party of Order transformed this bloodless battle into a second Austerlitz.[3] Platform and press praised the army as the power of order, in contrast to the popular masses representing the impotence of anarchy, and extolled Changarnier as the "bulwark of society," a deception in which he himself finally came to believe. Surreptitiously, however, the troops that seemed doubtful were transferred from Paris, the regiments whose elections had turned out most democratically were banished from France to Algiers, the turbulent spirits among the troops were relegated to penal detachments and finally the isolation of the press from the barracks and of the barracks from bourgeois society was systematically carried out.

Here we have reached the decisive turning point in the history of the French National Guard. In 1830 it was decisive in the overthrow of the Restoration. Under Louis Philippe every rising miscarried in which the National Guard stood on the side of the troops. When in the February days of 1848 it evinced a passive attitude towards the insurrection and an equivocal one towards Louis Philippe, he gave himself up for lost and actually was lost. Thus the conviction took root that the revolution could not conquer *without* the National Guard, nor the army *against it*. This was the superstition of the army in regard to bourgeois omnipotence. The June days of 1848, when the entire National Guard, with the troops of the line, put down the insurrection, had strengthened the superstition. After Bonaparte's assumption of office, the position of the National Guard was to some extent weakened by the unconstitutional uniting in the person of Changarnier of the command of its forces with the command of the first military division.

Just as here the command of the National Guard appeared as a subsidiary function of the military commander-in-chief, so the National Guard itself appeared as only an appendage of the troops of the line. Finally, on June 13 its power was broken, and not only by its partial dissolution, which from this time on was periodically repeated all over France, until mere fragments of it were left behind. The demonstration of June 13 was, above all, a demonstration of the democratic National Guards. They had not indeed borne their arms, but had worn their uniforms against the army; precisely in this uniform, however, lay the talisman. The army convinced itself that this uniform was a piece of woollen cloth like any other. The spell was broken. In the June days of 1848, bourgeoisie and petty bourgeoisie as the National Guard had been united with the

3. Near Austerlitz, Napoleon I won a great victory over the combined Russian and Austrian armies in 1805.

army against the proletariat; on June 13, 1849, the bourgeoisie let the petty-bourgeois National Guard be scattered by the army; on December 2, 1851, the National Guard of the bourgeoisie itself had vanished, and Bonaparte merely registered this fact when he subsequently signed the decree for its dissolution. Thus the bourgeoisie had itself smashed its last weapon against the army, but it had to smash it the moment the petty bourgeoisie no longer stood behind it as a vassal, but before it as a rebel, as in general it was bound to destroy all its means of defence against absolutism with its own hand, as soon as it had itself become absolute.

Meanwhile, the Party of Order celebrated the reconquest of a power that seemed lost in 1848 only to be found again, freed from its restraints, in 1849, with invective against the republic and the Constitution, with curses on all future, present and past revolutions, including those which its own leaders had made, and with laws by which the press was muzzled, association abolished and the state of siege regulated as an organic institution.[4] The National Assembly then adjourned from the middle of August to the middle of October, after having appointed a permanent commission for the period of its absence. During this recess the Legitimists intrigued with Ems, the Orleanists with Claremont, Bonaparte by princely tours, and the Departmental Councils in deliberations on the revision of the Constitution—incidents which regularly recur in the periodical recesses of the National Assembly and which I only propose to discuss when they become events. Here it may merely be remarked that it was impolitic for the National Assembly to disappear for considerable intervals from the stage and leave only a single, albeit a sorry, figure to be seen at the head of the republic, that of Louis Bonaparte, while to the scandal of the public the Party of Order fell asunder into its royalist component parts and followed its conflicting desires for Restoration. As often as the confused noise of parliament grew silent during these recesses and its body dissolved in the nation, it became unmistakably clear that only one thing was still wanting to complete the true form of this republic, to make the parliamentary recess permanent and replace the republic's *Liberté, Egalité, Fraternité* by the unambiguous words, Infantry, Cavalry, Artillery!

4. The temporary law against the press was issued on July 27. This law forbade the retail sale of newspapers without the permission of the administration; the latter could refuse this permission without giving any reasons. Any insult to the President of the republic was officially prosecuted. Any criticism of the laws was punished by fines, imprisonment, etc. The right of association—one of the most essential of the political victories of the February days—was abolished. By the new law on clubs, the government had the right to "close down clubs and existing unions which might be dangerous to public order." The state of siege was declared not only in Paris and its environs, but also in Lyons with five Departments and in Strasbourg, Rheims, and other cities with sixteen Departments. Military courts functioned everywhere in place of the usual courts during the state of siege.

IV

In the middle of October 1849, the National Assembly met once more. On November 1, Bonaparte surprised it with a message in which he announced the dismissal of the Barrot-Falloux ministry and the formation of a new ministry. No one has ever sacked lackeys with less ceremony than Bonaparte his ministers. The kicks that were intended for the National Assembly were given in the meantime to Barrot and Co.

The Barrot ministry, as we have seen, had been composed of Legitimists and Orleanists, a ministry of the Party of Order. Bonaparte had needed it to dissolve the republican Constituent Assembly, to bring about the expedition against Rome and to break the democratic party. Behind this ministry he had seemingly eclipsed himself, surrendered governmental power into the hands of the Party of Order and donned the modest character-mask that the legally responsible editor of a newspaper wore under Louis Philippe, the mask of the *homme de paille*.[5] He now threw off his mask, which was no longer a light veil behind which he could hide his face, but an iron mask which prevented him from displaying his own features. He had appointed the Barrot ministry so as to force the dissolution of the republican National Assembly in the name of the Party of Order; he dismissed it in order to declare his own name independent of the National Assembly of the Party of Order.

Plausible pretexts for this dismissal were not lacking. The Barrot ministry neglected even the forms of politeness that would have let the President of the republic appear as a power side by side with the National Assembly. During the recess of the National Assembly Bonaparte published a letter to Edgar Ney in which he seemed to disapprove of the illiberal attitude of the Pope, just as in opposition to the Constituent Assembly he had published a letter in which he commended Oudinot for the attack on the Roman republic. When the national Assembly now voted the budget for the Roman expedition, Victor Hugo, ostensibly out of liberalism, brought up this letter for discussion. The Party of Order with scornfully incredulous outcries stifled the idea that Bonaparte's ideas could have any political importance. Not one of the ministers took up the gauntlet for him. On another occasion Barrot, with his well-known hollow rhetoric, let fall from the platform words of indignation concerning the "abominable machinations" that, according to his assertion, went on in the immediate entourage of the President. Finally, while the ministry obtained from the National Assembly a widow's pension for the Duchess of Orléans it refused to submit any motion to

5. Man of straw.

increase the Civil List of the President. And in Bonaparte the imperial pretender was so intimately bound up with the adventurer down on his luck, that the *one* great idea, that he was called on to restore the Empire, was always supplemented by the other, that it was the mission of the French people to pay his debts.

The Barrot-Falloux ministry was the first and last *parliamentary ministry* that Bonaparte brought into being. Its dismissal forms, accordingly, a decisive turning point. With it the Party of Order lost, never to reconquer it, an indispensable post for the maintenance of the parliamentary regime, the lever of executive power. It is immediately obvious that in a country like France, where the executive power commands an army of officials numbering more than half a million individuals and therefore constantly maintains an immense mass of interests and existences in the most absolute dependence; where the state enmeshes, controls, punishes, superintends and tutors bourgeois society from its most comprehensive manifestations of life down to its most insignificant stirrings, from its most general modes of being to the private existence of individuals; where through the most extraordinary centralisation this parasitic body acquires an ubiquity, an omniscience, a capacity for swifter motion and an elasticity which has an analogy only in the helpless dependence, in the utter shapelessness of the actual body of society —it is obvious that in such a country the National Assembly forfeited all real influence when it lost command of the ministerial posts, if it did not at the same time simplify the administration of the state, reduce the army of officials as far as possible and, finally, let bourgeois society and public opinion create organs of their own, independent of the governmental power. But it is with the maintenance of that extensive state machine in its numerous ramifications that the *material interests* of the French bourgeoisie are interwoven in precisely the closest fashion. Here it finds posts for its surplus population and makes up in the form of state salaries for what it cannot pocket in the form of profits, interest, rents and honorariums. On the other hand, its *political interests* compelled it to increase daily the repressive measures and therefore the means and the personnel of the state power, while at the same time it had to wage an uninterrupted war against public opinion and mistrustfully mutilate and cripple society's organs of independent movement, where it did not succeed in amputating them wholly. Thus the French bourgeoisie was compelled by its class position to annihilate, on the one hand, the vital conditions of all parliamentary-power, and therefore of its own, likewise, and to render irresistible, on the other hand, the executive power hostile to it.

The new ministry was called the d'Hautpoul ministry. Not in the sense that General d'Hautpoul had received the rank of Prime Minister. Rather, simultaneously with Barrot's dismissal, Bonaparte abolished this dignity, which certainly condemned the President of the republic to the status of a legal nonentity, of a constitutional monarch, but of a constitutional monarch without a throne or a crown, without a sceptre or a sword, without irresponsibility, without imprescriptible possession of the highest state dignity, and worst of all, without a Civil List. The d'Hautpoul ministry contained only one man of parliamentary standing, the Jew *Fould*, one of the most notorious of the high financiers. To his lot fell the ministry of finance. Look up the quotations of the Paris *bourse* and you will find that from November 1849 onwards the French *Fonds*[6] rise and fall with the rise and fall of Bonapartist stocks. While Bonaparte had thus found his ally in the *bourse*, at the same time he took possession of the police by appointing Carlier Chief of Police in Paris.

Only in the course of development, however, could the consequences of the change of ministers come to light. To begin with, Bonaparte had only taken a step forward in order to be driven backward all the more obviously. His brusque message was followed by the most servile declaration of submissiveness to the National Assembly. As often as the ministers dared to make a diffident attempt to introduce his personal fads as legislative proposals, they themselves seemed only to carry out, against their will and compelled by their position, comic instructions of whose fruitlessness they were persuaded in advance. As often as Bonaparte blurted out his intentions behind the ministers' backs and played with his "*idées napoléoniennes*,"[7] his own ministers disavowed him from the tribune of the National Assembly. His usurpatory longings seemed to make themselves heard only in order that the malicious laughter of his opponents might not be muted. He behaved like a misunderstood genius, whom all the world takes for a simpleton. Never did he enjoy the contempt of all classes in fuller measure than during this period. Never did the bourgeoisie rule more absolutely, never did it display more ostentatiously the insignia of domination.

I have not here to write the history of its legislative activity, which is summarised during this period in two laws: in the law re-establishing the *wine tax*[8] and the *education law* abolishing unbe-

6. Consolidated government stocks.
7. Napoleonic ideas.
8. The *wine tax*, a burden falling on the poorest sections of the population, was repealed by the National Assembly with the intention of replacing it by an income tax. The first measure of the Fould ministry, appointed on November 1, 1849, was the re-establishment of the wine tax, in its former scandalous form, which made the tax fall mainly on the small consumers.

lief. If wine drinking was made harder for the French, they were presented all the more plentifully with the water of truer life. If in the law on the wine tax the bourgeoisie declared the old, hateful French tax system to be inviolable, through the education law it sought to ensure among the masses the old state of mind that put up with the tax system. One is astonished to see the Orleanists, the liberal bourgeois, these old apostles of Voltairianism and eclectic philosophy, entrust to their hereditary enemies, the Jesuits, the superintendence of the French mind. But if, in regard to the pretenders to the throne, Orleanists and Legitimists could part company, they understood that to secure their united rule necessitated the uniting of the means of repression of two epochs, that the means of subjugation of the July Monarchy had to be supplemented and strengthened by the means of subjugation of the Restoration.

The peasants, disappointed in all their hopes, crushed more than ever by the low level of corn prices on the one hand, and by the growing burden of taxes and mortgage debts on the other, began to bestir themselves in the Departments. They were answered by attacks on the schoolmasters, who were subjected to the clergy, by attacks on the mayors, who were subjected to the prefects, and by a system of espionage, to which all were subjected. In Paris and the large towns reaction has the very physiognomy of its epoch and challenges more than it strikes down. In the countryside it is dull, coarse, petty, tiresome and vexatious, in a word, the *gendarme*. One comprehends how three years of the regime of the *gendarme*, consecrated by the regime of the priest, were bound to demoralise immature masses.

Whatever amount of passion and declamation might be employed by the Party of Order against the minority from the tribune of the National Assembly, its speech remained as monosyllabic as that of the Christians, whose words were to be: Yea, yea; nay, nay! As monosyllabic on the platform as in the press. Flat as a riddle whose answer is known in advance. Whether it was a question of the right of petition or the tax on wine, freedom of the press or free trade, the clubs or the municipal constitution, protection of personal liberty or regulation of the state budget, the watchword constantly recurs, the theme remains always the same, the verdict is ever ready and invariably runs: "*Socialism!*" Even bourgeois liberalism is declared *socialistic*, bourgeois enlightenment socialistic, bourgeois financial reform socialistic. It was socialistic to build a railway, where a canal already existed, and it was socialistic to defend oneself with a stick, when one was attacked with a dagger.

This was not merely a figure of speech, fashion or party tactics. The bourgeoisie had true insight into the fact that all the weapons which it had forged against feudalism turned their points against itself, that all the means of education which it had produced rebelled against its own civilisation, that all the gods which it had created had fallen away from it. It understood that all the so-called bourgeois liberties and organs of progress attacked and menaced its *class rule* at its social foundation and its political summit simultaneously, and had therefore become *"socialistic."* In this menace and this attack it rightly discerned the secret of socialism, whose import and tendency it judges more correctly than so-called socialism knows how to judge itself; the latter can, accordingly, not comprehend why the bourgeoisie callously hardens its heart against it, whether it sentimentally bewails the sufferings of mankind, or in Christian spirit prophesies the millennium and universal brotherly love, or in humanistic style twaddles about mind, education and freedom, or in doctrinaire fashion devises a system for the conciliation and welfare of all classes. What the bourgeoisie did not grasp, however, was the logical conclusion that its *own parliamentary regime*, that its *political rule* in general was now bound to meet with the general verdict of condemnation as being likewise *socialistic*. As long as the rule of the bourgeois class had not been organised completely, as long as it had not acquired its pure political expression, the antagonism of the other classes, likewise, could not appear in its pure form, and where it did appear, could not take the dangerous turn that transforms every struggle against the power of the state into a struggle against capital. If in every stirring of life in society it saw "tranquillity" imperilled, how could it want to maintain at the head of society the *regime of unrest*, its own regime, the *parliamentary regime*, this regime that, according to the expression of one of its orators, lives in struggle and by struggle? The parliamentary regime lives by discussion; how shall it forbid discussion? Every interest, every social institution is here transformed into general ideas debated as ideas; how shall any interest, any institution sustain itself as above thought and impose itself as an article of faith? The struggle of the orators on the platform evokes the struggle of the scribblers of the press; the debating club in parliament is inevitably supplemented by debating clubs in the salons and the pot-houses; the representatives who constantly appeal to public opinion give public opinion the right to speak its real mind in petitions. The parliamentary regime leaves everything to the decision of majorities; how shall the great majorities outside parliament not want to decide? When you play the fiddle at the top of the state, what else is to be expected but that those down below dance?

By now stigmatising as *"socialistic"* what it had previously extolled as *"liberal,"* the bourgeoisie therefore confesses that its own interest dictates that it should be delivered from the danger of *governing in its own name*; that, in order to restore tranquillity in the land, its bourgeois parliament must, first of all, be given its quietus; that in order to preserve its social power inviolate, its political power must be broken; that the private bourgeois can only continue to exploit the other classes and to enjoy undisturbed property, family, religion and order on condition that their class be condemned along with the other classes to a like political nullity; that in order to save its purse, it must abandon the crown, and the sword that is to safeguard it must at the same time be hung over its own head like the sword of Damocles.

In the domain of general bourgeois interests the National Assembly showed itself so unproductive that, for example, the discussions on the Paris-Avignon railway, which began in the winter of 1850, were still not ripe for conclusion on December 2, 1851. Where it did not repress or react it was stricken with incurable barrenness.

While Bonaparte's ministry partly took the initiative in framing laws in the spirit of the Party of Order, and partly outdid its harshness in their execution and administration, he, on the other hand, by childishly silly proposals sought to win popularity to bring out the contrast between himself and the National Assembly, and to hint at a secret reserve that was only temporarily prevented by conditions from making its hidden treasures available to the French people. Of this character was the proposal to decree a bonus of four *sous* a day to the non-commissioned officers. Of this character was the proposal of an honour loan bank for the workers. Money as a gift and money on loan, it was with prospects such as these that he hoped to allure the masses. Donations and loans—the financial science of the *lumpenproletariat*, whether high or low, is restricted to this. Such were the only springs which Bonaparte knew how to set in action. Never has a Pretender speculated more stupidly on the stupidity of the masses.

The National Assembly flared up repeatedly over these unmistakable attempts to gain popularity at its expense, over the growing danger that this adventurer, whom his debts spurred on and no established reputation held back, would venture a desperate coup. The discord between the Party of Order and the President had taken on a threatening character when an unexpected event threw him back repentant into its arms. We mean the *by-elections of March 10, 1850*. These elections were held with the object of filling once more the representatives' seats that after June 13 had been rendered vacant by imprisonment or exile. Paris elected only Social-Democratic candidates. It even concentrated most of the votes on an insurgent of June 1848, on Deflotte. Thus did the Parisian petty bourgeoisie, in alliance with the proletariat, revenge itself for its defeat on June 13, 1849. It seemed to have disappeared from the battlefield at the moment of danger only to reappear there on a more propitious occasion with more numerous fighting forces and with a bolder battle-cry. One circumstance seemed to heighten the peril of this election victory. The army voted in Paris for the June insurgent against Lahitte, a minister of Bonaparte's, and in the Departments largely for the *Montagnards*, who here, too, though not indeed so decisively as in Paris, maintained the ascendancy over their adversaries.

Bonaparte saw himself suddenly confronted with revolution once more. As on January 29, 1849, as on June 13, 1849, on March 10, 1850, he disappeared behind the Party of Order. He made obeisance, he pusillanimously begged pardon, he offered to appoint any ministry it pleased at the behest of the parliamentary majority, he even implored the Orleanist and Legitimist party leaders, the Thiers, the Berryers, the Broglies, the Molés, in brief, the so-called burgraves[9] themselves to take the helm of state. The Party of Order did not know how to take advantage of this moment that would never return. Instead of boldly possessing itself of the power offered, it did not even compel Bonaparte to reinstate the ministry dismissed on November 1; it contented itself with humiliating him by its forgiveness and adding M. *Baroche* to the d'Hautpoul ministry. As public prosecutor this Baroche had stormed and raged before the High Court at Bourges, the first time against the revolutionaries of May 15, the second time against the democrats of June 13, both times because of an *attentat*[1] on the National Assembly. None of Bonaparte's ministers subsequently contributed more to the degradation of the National Assembly, and after December 2, 1851, we meet him once more as the comfortably installed and highly paid vice-president of the Senate. He had spat in the revolutionaries' soup in order that Bonaparte might eat it up.

The Social-Democratic Party, for its part, seemed only to try to find pretexts for putting its victory once again in doubt and blunting the point of its victory. Vidal, one of the newly elected representatives of Paris, had been elected simultaneously in Strasbourg. He was induced to decline election for Paris and accept it for Strasbourg. Instead, therefore, of giving its victory at the polls a definite character and thereby compelling the Party of Order at once to contest it in parliament, instead of thus forcing the adversary to fight at the moment of popular enthusiasm and favourable state of feeling in the army, the democratic party wearied Paris during the months of March and April with a new election agitation, let the popular

9. A sarcastic nickname, which referred to the impotent love of power and feudal ambitions of the royalists; bor- rowed from a play by Victor Hugo.
1. Attempt, attack.

passions aroused wear themselves out in this provisional election interlude, let the revolutionary energy satiate itself with constitutional successes, dissipate itself in petty intrigues, hollow declamations and sham movements, let the bourgeoisie rally and make their preparations, and, lastly, allowed the meaning of the March elections to find a sentimentally softening commentary in the subsequent April election by the return of Eugène Sue. In a word, it made an April Fool of March 10.

The parliamentary majority understood the weakness of its antagonist. Its seventeen burgraves—for Bonaparte had left to it the direction of and responsibility for the attack—worked out a new electoral law, the introduction of which was entrusted to M Faucher, who solicited this honour for himself. On May 8 he introduced the law by which universal suffrage was abolished, a residence of three years in the locality of the election imposed as a condition on the electors and, finally, the proof of this residence made dependent in the case of the workers on a certificate from their employers.

In the same measure as the democrats had agitated and raged in revolutionary fashion during the constitutional election contest, equally constitutionally did they now, when it was requisite to prove the serious nature of that victory arms in hand, preach order, majestic calm (*calme majestueux*), a legal attitude, that is to say, blind subjection to the will of the counter-revolution, which imposed itself as the law. During the debate the Mountain put the Party of Order to shame by asserting against its revolutionary passionateness the dispassionate standpoint of the philistine who keeps within the law, and by felling it to earth with the fearful reproach that it proceeded in a revolutionary manner. Even the newly elected deputies were at pains to prove by their decorous and discreet action what a misconception it was to decry them as anarchists and construe their election as a victory for revolution. On May 31, the new electoral law went through. The Mountain contented itself with smuggling a protest into the pocket of the President. The electoral law was followed by a new press law, by which the revolutionary newspaper press was entirely suppressed. It had deserved its fate. The *National* and *La Presse*, two bourgeois organs, were left behind after this deluge as the most advanced outposts of the revolution.

We have seen how during March and April the democratic leaders had done everything to embroil the people of Paris in a sham fight, and how after May 8 they did everything to restrain them from a real fight. In addition to this, we must not forget that the year 1850 was one of the most splendid years of industrial and commercial prosperity, and the Paris proletariat was therefore fully employed. But the election law of May 31, 1850, excluded it from any participation in political power. It cut away from it the very ground of the struggle. It threw the workers back into the position of pariahs, just as they had been before the February Revolution. Since in face of such an event they could let themselves be led by the democrats and could forget the revolutionary interests of their class for a momentary ease and comfort, they renounced the honour of being a conquering power, surrendered themselves to their fate, proved that the defeat of June 1848 had made them incapable of fighting for years and that the historical process would first of all have to go forward again *over* their heads. So far as the petty-bourgeois democracy is concerned, which on June 13 had cried: "But if once universal suffrage is attacked, then we'll show them," it now consoled itself with the contention that the counter-revolutionary blow which had struck it was no blow and the law of May 31 no law. On May 2, 1852, every Frenchman would appear at the polling-place with ballot-paper in one hand and sword in the other. With this prophecy it rested content. Finally, just as for the elections of May 29, 1849, so for those of March and April 1850, the army was punished by its chiefs. This time, however, it said decidedly: "The revolution shall not dupe us a third time."

The law of May 31, 1850, was the *coup d'état* of the bourgeoisie. All its conquests over the revolution hitherto had only a provisional character. They were endangered as soon as the existing National Assembly retired from the stage. They depended on the hazards of a new general election, and the history of elections since 1848 irrefutably proved that in the same measure as the actual domination of the bourgeoisie developed in fact, its moral domination over the mass of the people was lost. On March 10, universal suffrage declared itself directly against the domination of the bourgeoisie; the bourgeoisie answered by outlawing universal suffrage. The law of May 31 was therefore one of the necessities of the class struggle. On the other hand, the Constitution required a minimum of two million votes in order that the election of the President of the republic might be valid. If none of the candidates for the presidency received this minimum, the National Assembly was then to choose the President from among the three candidates to whom the largest number of votes would fall. At the time when the Constituent Assembly made this law, ten million electors were registered on the rolls of voters. In its view therefore, a fifth of the people entitled to vote was sufficient to make the presidential election valid. The law of May 31 struck at least three million votes off the electoral rolls, reduced the number of people entitled to vote to seven millions and, nevertheless, retained the legal minimum of two millions for the presidential election. It therefore raised the legal minimum from a fifth to nearly a third of the effective votes, that is, it did everything to smuggle the election of the President out of the hands of the people and into the hands of the National Assembly. Through the electoral law of May 31 the Party of Order thus seemed to have made its rule doubly secure, since it left the election of the National Assembly and that of the President of the republic to the stationary section of society.

V

As soon as the revolutionary crisis had been weathered and universal suffrage abolished, the struggle between the National Assembly and Bonaparte immediately broke out again.

The Constitution had fixed Bonaparte's salary at 600,000 francs. Barely six months after his installation he succeeded in increasing this sum to twice as much, for Odilon Barrot wrung from the Constituent National Assembly an extra allowance of 600,000 francs a year for so-called representation monies. After June 13, Bonaparte had caused similar requests to be voiced, this time without getting a response from Barrot. Now, after May 31, he at once availed himself of the favourable moment and caused his ministers to propose a Civil List of three millions in the National Assembly. A long life of adventurous vagabondage had endowed him with the most developed antennae for feeling out the weak moments when he might squeeze money from his bourgeois. He practised regular *chantage*.[2] The National Assembly had violated the sovereignty of the people with his assistance and his cognisance. He threatened to denounce its crime to the tribunal of the people unless it loosened its pursestrings and purchased his silence with three million a year. It had robbed three million Frenchmen of their franchise. He demanded, for every Frenchman put out of currency, a franc having currency, precisely three million francs. He, the elect of six millions, claims damages for the votes out of which he has subsequently been cheated. The Commission of the National Assembly refused the importunate one. The Bonapartist press threatened. Could the National Assembly break with the President of the republic at a moment when in principle it had definitely broken with the mass of the nation? It rejected the annual Civil List, it is true, but it granted, for this once, an extra allowance of two million one hundred and sixty thousand francs. It thus rendered itself guilty of the double weakness of granting the money and of showing at the same time by its vexation that it only granted it unwillingly. We shall see later for what purpose Bonaparte needed the money. After this vexatious aftermath, which followed on the heels of the abolition of universal suffrage and in which Bonaparte exchanged his

2. Blackmail.

humble attitude during the crisis of March and April for challenging impudence to the usurpatory parliament, the National Assembly adjourned for three months, from August 11 to November 11. In its place it left behind a Permanent Commission of eighteen members, which contained no Bonapartists, but did contain some moderate republicans. The Permanent Commission of 1849 had included only men of the Party of Order and Bonapartists. But at that time the Party of Order declared itself in permanence against the revolution. This time the parliamentary republic declared itself in permanence against the President. After the law of May 31, this was the only rival that still confronted the Party of Order.

When the National Assembly met once more in November 1850, it seemed that, instead of the petty skirmishes it had hitherto had with the President, a great and ruthless struggle, a life-and-death struggle between the two powers, had become inevitable.

As in 1849, so during this year's parliamentary recess the Party of Order had broken up into its separate sections, each occupied with its own Restoration intrigues, which obtained fresh nutriment through the death of Louis Philippe. The Legitimist king, Henry V, had even nominated a formal ministry which resided in Paris and in which members of the Permanent Commission held seats. Bonaparte, in his turn, was therefore entitled to make tours of the French Departments, and according to the disposition of the town that he favoured with his presence, now covertly, now more openly, divulge his own restoration plans and canvass votes for himself. On these processions, which the great official *Moniteur* and the little private *Moniteurs* of Bonaparte were naturally bound to celebrate as triumphal processions, he was constantly accompanied by associates of the *Society of December 10*. This society dates from the year 1849. On the pretext of founding a benevolent society, the *lumpenproletariat* of Paris had been organised into secret sections, each section being led by Bonapartist agents, with a Bonapartist general at the head of the whole. Alongside decayed *roués* with doubtful means of subsistence and of doubtful origin, alongside ruined and adventurous offshoots of the bourgeoisie, were vagabonds, discharged soldiers, discharged jail-birds, escaped galley-slaves, swindlers, mountebanks, *lazzaroni*,[3] pickpockets, tricksters, gamblers, *maquereaux*,[4] brothel-keepers, porters, *literati*, organ-grinders, ragpickers, knife-grinders, tinkers, beggars, in short the whole indefinite, disintegrated mass thrown hither and thither, which the French term *la Bohème*; from this kindred element Bonaparte formed the basis of the Society of December 10. A "benevolent society"—in so far as, like Bonaparte, all its members felt the need

3. The name given to the idlers and beggars of Naples.   4. Procurers.

of benefiting themselves at the expense of the working nation. This Bonaparte, who constitutes himself chief of the *lumpenproletariat*, who here alone rediscovers in mass form the interests which he personally pursues, who recognises in this scum, offal, refuse of all classes, the only class weapon upon which he can base himself unconditionally, he is the real Bonaparte, the Bonaparte *sans phrase*. An old crafty *roué*, he conceives the historical life of the nations and their principal and state actions as comedy in the most vulgar sense, as a masquerade where the grand costumes, words and postures merely serve to mask the pettiest knavishness. Thus on his expedition to Strasbourg,[5] when a trained Swiss vulture had played the art of the Napoleonic eagle. For his irruption into Boulogne he puts some London lackeys into French uniforms. They represent the army. In his Society of December 10, he assembles ten thousand rascally fellows, who must play the part of the people, as Klaus Zettel[6] that of the lion. At a moment when the French bourgeoisie itself played the most complete comedy, but in the most serious manner in the world, without infringing any of the pedantic conditions of French dramatic etiquette, and was itself half deceived, half convinced by the solemnity of its own principal and state actions, the adventurer who took the comedy as plain comedy was bound to conquer. Only when he has eliminated his solemn opponent, when he himself now takes his imperial role seriously and with the Napoleonic mask thinks to play the part of the real Napoleon, does he become the victim of his own conception of the world, the serious buffoon, who no longer takes world history for a comedy, but his comedy for world history. What the *National Ateliers*[7] were for the socialist workers, what the *Gardes Mobiles*[8] were for the bourgeois republicans, the Society of December 10 was for Bonaparte, the party fighting force peculiar to him. On his journeys the detachments of this society packing the railways had to improvise a public for him, display the public enthusiasm, howl *vive l'Empereur*,[9] insult and thrash the republicans, of course under the protection of the police. On his return journeys to Paris they had to form the advance guard, forestall counter-demonstrations or disperse them. The Society of December 10 belonged to him, it was *his* work, his very own idea. Whatever else he appropriates is put into his hands by the forces of circumstance; whatever else he does, the circumstances do for him or he is content to copy from the deeds of others. But Bonaparte in public before the citizens, with the official phrases of order, religion, family, property, and with the secret society of

5. Louis Bonaparte's first unsuccessful attempt at a *coup d'état* took place in 1836, in Strasbourg. The invasion of Boulogne—his second unsuccessful attempt to proclaim himself emperor—was in 1840.

6. The reference is to Nick Bottom, the weaver (Klaus Zettel) in Shakespeare's comedy *A Midsummer Night's Dream*.
7. Workshops.
8. Mobile Guards.
9. Long live the Emperor.

the Schufterles and Spiegelbergs,[1] the society of disorder, prostitution and theft, behind him—that is Bonaparte himself as original author, and the history of the Society of December 10 is his own history. Now it had happened by way of exception that popular representatives belonging to the Party of Order came under the cudgels of the Decembrists. Still more. Yon, the police-inspector assigned to the National Assembly and charged with watching over its safety, acting on the information given by a certain Alais, advised the Permanent Commission that a section of the Decembrists had determined to assassinate General Changarnier and Dupin, the President of the National Assembly, and had already fixed the individuals who were to do it. One comprehends the terror of M. Dupin. A parliamentary enquiry into the Society of December 10, that is, the profanation of the Bonapartist secret world, seemed inevitable. Just before the meeting of the National Assembly Bonaparte providently disbanded his society, naturally only on paper, for in a detailed memoir at the end of 1851 Police-Prefect Carlier still sought in vain to move him to a real dispersal of the Decembrists.

The Society of December 10 was thus to remain the private army of Bonaparte until he succeeded in transforming the public army into a Society of December 10. Bonaparte made the first attempt at this shortly after the adjournment of the National Assembly, and indeed with the money just wrested from it. As a fatalist, he lives in the conviction that there are certain higher powers which man, and the soldier in particular, cannot withstand. Among these powers he counts, first and foremost, cigars and champagne, cold poultry and garlic sausage. To begin with, in the apartments of the Elysée he accordingly treats officers and non-commissioned officers to cigars and champagne, to cold poultry and garlic sausage. On October 3 he repeats this manœuvre with the mass of the troops at the review at St. Maur and on October 10 the same manœuvre on a still larger scale at the army parade at Satori. The Uncle remembered the campaigns of Alexander[2] in Asia, the Nephew the triumphal marches of Bacchus[3] in the same land. Alexander was a demi-god, to be sure, but Bacchus was a god and moreover the tutelary deity of the Society of December 10.

After the review of October 3, the Permanent Commission summoned the War Minister d'Hautpoul before it. He promised that these breaches of discipline should not recur. We know how on October 10 Bonaparte kept d'Hautpoul's word. As Commander-in-Chief of the Paris army, Changarnier had commanded at both reviews. He, at once a member of the Permanent Commission,

---

1. Rascally characters in Schiller's drama *Die Räuber* (The Robbers).
2. Alexander of Macedon made a number of conquering expeditions into Asia.

3. According to the Greek myth *Bacchus* (or Dionysus), the ancient Greek god of the vine, went all over Asia with a drunken retinue.

chief of the National Guard, the "saviour" of January 29 and June 13, the "bulwark of society," the candidate of the Party of Order for presidential honours, the suspected Monk[4] of two monarchies, had hitherto never acknowledged himself as the subordinate of the War Minister, had always openly derided the republican Constitution and had pursued Bonaparte with an ambiguous, lordly protection. Now he was consumed with zeal for discipline against the War Minister and for the Constitution against Bonaparte. While on October 10 a section of the cavalry raised the shout: "*Vive Napoleon! Vivent les saucissons!*"[5] Changarnier arranged that at least the infantry marching past under the command of his friend Neumayer should preserve an icy silence. As a punishment, the War Minister relieved General Neumayer of his post in Paris at Bonaparte's instigation, on the pretext of appointing him commanding general of the fourteenth and fifteenth military divisions. Neumayer refused this exchange of posts and so had to resign. Changarnier, for his part, published an order of the day on November 2, in which he forbade the troops to indulge in political outcries or demonstrations of any kind while under arms. The Elysée papers[6] attacked Changarnier; the papers of the Party of Order attacked Bonaparte; the Permanent Commission held repeated secret sessions in which it was repeatedly proposed to declare the country in danger; the army seemed divided into two hostile camps, with two hostile general staffs, one in the Elysée, where Bonaparte resided, the other in the Tuileries, the quarters of Changarnier. It seemed that only the meeting of the National Assembly was needed to give the signal for battle. The French public judged this friction between Bonaparte and Changarnier like that English journalist who has characterised it in the following words: "The political housemaids of France are sweeping away the glowing lava of the revolution with old brooms and wrangle with one another while they do their work."

Meanwhile, Bonaparte hastened to remove the War Minister, d'Hautpoul, to pack him off in a hurry to Algiers and to appoint General Schramm War Minister in his place. On November 12, he sent to the National Assembly a message of American prolixity, overloaded with detail, redolent of order, desirous of reconciliation, constitutionally acquiescent, treating of all and sundry, but not of the *questions brûlantes*[7] of the moment. As if in passing, he made the remark that according to the express provisions of the Constitution the President alone disposed over the army. The message closed with the following lofty words:

4. General Monk who served under Charles I, then under Cromwell and later under Charles II.
5. Hurrah for Napoleon! Hurrah for the sausages!
6. Bonapartist newspapers.
7. Burning questions.

"Above all things, France demands tranquillity. . . . But bound by an oath, I shall keep within the narrow limits that it has set for me. . . . As far as I am concerned, elected by the people and owing my power to it alone, I shall always bow to its lawfully expressed will. Should you resolve in this session on the revision of the Constitution, a Constituent Assembly will then regulate the position of the executive power. If not, then the people will solemnly pronounce its decision in 1852. But whatever the solutions of the future may be, let us come to an understanding, so that passion, surprise or violence may never decide the destiny of a great nation. . . . What occupies my attention, above all, is not who will rule France in 1852, but how to employ the time which remains at my disposal so that the intervening period may pass by without agitation or disturbance. I have opened my heart to you with sincerity; you will answer my frankness with your trust, my good endeavours with your co-operation, and God will do the rest."*

The respectable, hypocritically moderate, virtuously common-place language of the bourgeoisie reveals its deepest meaning in the mouth of the autocrat of the Society of December 10 and the picnic hero of Saint-Maur and Satori.

The burgraves of the Party of Order did not delude themselves for a moment concerning the trust that this opening of the heart deserved. About oaths they had long been blasé; they numbered in their midst veterans and virtuosos of political perjury; they had not failed to hear the passage about the army. They observed with annoyance that in its discursive enumeration of lately enacted laws the message passed over the most important law, the electoral law, in studied silence, and moreover, in the event of there being no revision of the Constitution, left the election of the President in 1852 in the hands of the people. The electoral law was the leaden ball chained to the feet of the Party of Order, which hindered it in walking and now even prevented it from storming forward! Moreover, by the official disbanding of the Society of December 10 and the dismissal of the War Minister d'Hautpoul, Bonaparte had with his own hand sacrificed the scapegoats on the altar of the country. He had deprived the expected collision of its sharpness. Finally, the Party of Order itself anxiously sought to avoid, to mitigate, to palliate any decisive conflict with the executive power. From fear of losing their conquests over the revolution, they allowed their rivals to carry off the fruits of these. "Above all things, France demands tranquillity." This was what the Party of Order had cried to the revolution since February, this was what Bonaparte cried to the Party of Order in his message. "Above all things, France demands tranquillity." Bonaparte perpetrated acts that aimed at usurpation, but the Party of Order was guilty of "unrest" if it raised the alarm about these acts and construed them hypochondriacally. The sausages of Satori were quiet as mice when no one spoke of them. "Above all things, France demands tranquillity." Bonaparte demanded, therefore, that he be left in peace to do as he liked and the parliamentary party was paralysed by a double fear, by the fear of again evoking revolutionary unrest and by the fear of itself appearing as the instigator of unrest in the eyes of its own class, in the eyes of the bourgeoisie. Consequently, since France demanded tranquillity above all things, the Party of Order dared not answer "war" after Bonaparte had talked "peace" in his message. The public, which had flattered itself that there would be scenes of great scandal on the opening of the National Assembly, was cheated of its expectations. The opposition deputies, who demanded the submission of the Permanent Commission's minutes on the October events, were outvoted by the majority. On principle, all debates that might cause excitement were avoided. The activities of the National Assembly during November and December 1850 were without interest.

At last, towards the end of December, guerilla warfare began over individual prerogatives of parliament. The movement got bogged in petty chicaneries regarding the prerogatives of the two powers, since the bourgeoisie had done away with the class struggle for the moment by abolishing universal suffrage.

A judgment for debt had been obtained from the court against Manguin, one of the representatives of the people. In answer to the inquiry of the chief magistrate, the Minister for Justice, Rouher, declared that an order of arrest was to be executed against the debtor without further ado. Manguin, therefore, was thrown into the debtors' gaol. The National Assembly flared up when it learned of the assault. Not only did it order his immediate release, but it even had him fetched forcibly from Clichy the same evening, by its clerk. In order, however, to confirm its faith in the sanctity of private property and with the idea at the back of its mind of opening, in case of need, an asylum for *Montagnards* who had become troublesome, it declared imprisonment of the people's representatives for debt permissible after previously obtaining its consent. It forgot to decree that the President of the republic might also be locked up for debt. It destroyed the last semblance of immunity that surrounded the members of its own body.

It will be remembered that, acting on the information given by a certain Alais, Police-Inspector Yon had denounced a section of the Decembrists for planning the murder of Dupin and Changarnier. In reference to this, at the very first sitting the *quæstors* made the proposal that parliament should form a police force of its own, paid out of the private budget of the National Assembly and absolutely independent of the police-prefect. The Minister for Home Affairs, Baroche, had protested against this invasion of his domain. A miserable compromise on this matter was concluded, according to which the police-inspector of the Assembly was indeed to be paid out of its private budget and to be appointed and dismissed by its *quæstors*, but after previous agreement with the Minister for Home Affairs. Meanwhile criminal proceedings had been taken by the government against Alais, and here it was easy to represent his information as a hoax and through the mouth of the public prosecutor to cast ridicule upon Dupin, Changarnier, Yon and the whole National Assembly. On December 29 the Minister Baroche now writes a letter to Dupin, in which he demands Yon's dismissal. The Bureau of the National Assembly decides to retain Yon in his position, but the National Assembly, alarmed by its violence in the Manguin affair and accustomed when it has ventured a blow at the executive power, to receive two blows from it in return, does not sanction this decision. It dismisses Yon as a reward for his zeal in service and robs itself of a parliamentary prerogative indispensable against a man who does not decide something in the night in order to carry it out by day, but who decides by day and carries it out in the night.

We have seen how on great and striking occasions during November and December the National Assembly avoided or quashed the struggle with the executive power. Now we see it compelled to take it up on the pettiest occasions. In the Manguin affair it confirms the principle of imprisoning the representatives of the people for debt, but reserves the right to have it applied only to representatives obnoxious to itself and wrangles over this infamous privilege with the Minister for Justice. Instead of availing itself of the alleged murder plot to decree an inquiry into the Society of December 10 and irredeemably unmasking Bonaparte before France and Europe in his true character of chief of the Paris *lumpenproletariat*, it lets the collision be degraded to a point where the only issue between it and the Minister for Home Affairs is one as to which of them has the authority to appoint and dismiss a police-inspector. Thus, during the whole of this period, we see the Party of Order compelled by its equivocal position to dissipate and disintegrate its struggle with the executive power in petty squabbles concerning competency, in chicaneries, legal squabbles, and border-line disputes, and to make the most ridiculous matters of form the substance of its activity. It does not dare to take up the conflict at the moment when this has significance from the standpoint of principle, when the executive power has really exposed itself and the cause of the National Assembly would be the cause of the nation.

By so doing it would give the nation its marching orders, and it fears nothing more than that the nation should be set in motion. On such occasions it accordingly rejects the motions of the Mountain and proceeds to the order of the day. The question at issue in its larger aspects having thus been dropped, the executive power calmly awaits the time when it can again take up the same question on petty and insignificant occasions, when this has, so to speak, only a parliamentary local interest. Then the repressed rage of the Party of Order breaks out, then it tears away the curtain from the *coulisses,* then it denounces the President, then it declares the republic in danger, but then, also, its fervour appears absurd and the occasion for the struggle seems a hypocritical pretext or not at all worth fighting about. The parliamentary storm becomes a storm in a teacup; the fight becomes an intrigue; the collision becomes a scandal. While the revolutionary classes gloat with malicious joy over the humiliation of the National Assembly, for they are just as enthusiastic about the parliamentary prerogatives of this Assembly as the latter is about the public liberties, the bourgeoisie outside parliament does not understand how the bourgeoisie inside parliament can fritter away time over such petty squabbles and imperil tranquillity by such pitiful rivalries with the President. It becomes confused by a strategy that makes peace at the moment when all the world is expecting battles, and attacks at the moment when all the world believes peace has been made.

On December 20, Pascal Duprat put a question to the Minister for Home Affairs concerning the Gold Bar Lottery. This lottery was a "daughter of Elysium." Bonaparte with his faithful followers had brought her into the world and Police-Prefect Carlier had placed her under his official protection, although French law forbids all lotteries with the exception of raffles for charitable purposes. Seven million lottery tickets at a franc apiece, the profits ostensibly to be devoted to shipping Parisian vagabonds to California. On the one hand, dreams of gold were to supplant the socialist dreams of the Paris proletariat, the seductive prospect of the first lottery prize, the doctrinaire right to work. Naturally, the Paris workers did not recognise in the glitter of the California gold bars the inconspicuous francs that were enticed out of their pockets. In the main, however, the matter involved a direct swindle. The vagabonds who wanted to open the California gold mines without troubling to leave Paris were Bonaparte himself and his debt-ridden Round Table. The three millions voted by the National Assembly had been squandered; in one way or another the treasury had to be replenished. In vain had Bonaparte opened a national subscription for the foundation of so-called *cités ouvrières*[8] and figured at the head of the

8. Workers' cities.

list himself with a considerable sum. The hardhearted bourgeois waited mistrustfully for him to pay up his share and since this, naturally, did not ensue, the speculation in socialist castles in the air fell straightaway to the ground. The gold bars proved a better draw. Bonaparte and company were not content to pocket part of the excess of the seven millions over the gold bars to be allotted in prizes, they manufactured false lottery-tickets, they issued ten, fifteen and even twenty tickets with the same number, financial operations quite in the spirit of the Society of December 10! Here the National Assembly was confronted not with the fictitious President of the republic, but with Bonaparte in flesh and blood. Here it could catch him in the act, in conflict not with the Constitution but with the *Code Pénal*. If on Duprat's interpellation it proceeded to the order of the day, this did not happen merely because Girardin's motion that it should declare itself *satisfait* reminded the Party of Order of its own systematic corruption. The bourgeois and, above all, the bourgeois inflated to become a statesman, supplements his practical meanness by theoretical extravagance. As a statesman he becomes, like the state power that confronts him, a higher being, that can only be fought in a higher, consecrated fashion.

The Assembly itself having guided him with its own hand across the slippery ground of the military banquets, the reviews, the Society of December 10, and finally, the *Code Pénal*, Bonaparte, who precisely because he was a Bohemian, a princely *lumpenproletarian*, had the advantage over a rascally bourgeois in that he could conduct the struggle meanly, now saw that the moment had come when he could pass from an apparent defensive to the offensive. The minor defeats meanwhile sustained by the Minister for Justice, the Minister for War, the Minister for the Navy and the Minister for Finance, through which the National Assembly signified its snarling displeasure, troubled him little. He not only prevented the ministers from resigning and thus recognising the sovereignty of parliament over the executive power, he could now consummate what he had begun during the recess of the National Assembly, the separation of the military power from parliament, the *removal of Changarnier*.

An Elysée paper published an order of the day alleged to have been addressed during the month of May to the first military division, and therefore proceeding from Changarnier, in which the officers were recommended, in the event of an insurrection, to give no quarter to the traitors in their own ranks, but to shoot them immediately and refuse the National Assembly the troops, should it requisition them. On January 3, 1851, the Cabinet was interpellated concerning this order of the day. For the investigation of this matter it requests a breathing-space first of three months, then of a week, finally of only twenty-four hours. The Assembly insists on an immediate explanation. Changarnier rises and declares that this order of the day never existed. He adds that he will always hasten to comply with the demands of the National Assembly and that in case of a collision it can count on him. It receives his declaration with indescribable applause and passes a vote of confidence in him. It abdicates, it decrees its own impotence and the omnipotence of the army by placing itself under the private protection of a general; but the general deceives himself when he puts at its command against Bonaparte a power that he only holds in fee from the same Bonaparte and when, in his turn, he expects to be protected by this parliament, by his own protégé in need of protection. But Changarnier believes in the mysterious power with which the bourgeoisie has endowed him since January 29, 1849. He considers himself the third power, existing side by side with both the other state powers. He shares the fate of the rest of this epoch's heroes or rather saints whose greatness consists precisely in the great opinion of them that their party exhibits in its own interests and who shrink into everyday figures as soon as circumstances call on them to perform miracles. Unbelief is, in general, the mortal enemy of these reputed heroes and real saints. Hence their majestically moral indignation at unenthusiastic wits and scoffers.

The same evening, the ministers were summoned to the Elysée; Bonaparte insists on the dismissal of Changarnier; five ministers refuse to sign it; the *Moniteur* announces a ministerial crisis, and the Party of Order threatens to form a parliamentary army under Changarnier's command. The Party of Order had constitutional authority to take this step. It merely had to appoint Changarnier President of the National Assembly and requisition any number of troops it pleased for its protection. It could do so all the more safely as Changarnier still really stood at the head of the army and the Paris National Guard and was only waiting to be requisitioned together with the army. The Bonapartist press did not as yet even dare to question the right of the National Assembly directly to requisition troops, a legal scruple that in the given circumstances did not promise any success. That the army would have obeyed the orders of the National Assembly seems probable when one reflects that Bonaparte had to search all Paris for eight days in order, finally, to find two generals—Baraguey d'Hilliers and Saint-Jean d'Angely—who declared themselves ready to countersign Changarnier's dismissal. That the Party of Order, however, would have found in its own ranks and in parliament the necessary number of votes for such a resolution seems more than doubtful, when one considers that eight days later two hundred and eighty-six votes detached themselves from the party and that in December 1851, at the last hour for decision, the Mountain still rejected a similar proposal. Nevertheless, the burgraves might, perhaps, still have succeeded in spurring the mass of their party to a heroism that consisted in feeling themselves secure behind a forest of bayonets and accepting the services of an army that had deserted to their camp. Instead of this, on the evening of January 6 the Messrs. Burgraves betook themslves to the Elysée in order to make Bonaparte desist from Changarnier's dismissal by means of statesmanlike phrases and considerations of statecraft. Whomever one seeks to persuade, one acknowledges as master of the situation. On January 12, Bonaparte, made secure by this step, appoints a new ministry in which the leaders of the old ministry, Fould and Baroche, remain members. Saint-Jean d'Angely becomes War Minister, the *Moniteur* publishes the decree dismissing Changarnier and his command is divided between Baraguey d'Hilliers, who receives the first military division, and Perrot, who receives the National Guard. The bulwark of society has been discharged, and if it does not cause any tiles to fall from the roof, on the other hand the quotations on the *Bourse* rise.

By repulsing the army, which places itself in the person of Changarnier at the disposal of the Party of Order, and so surrendering it irrevocably to the President, the Party of Order declares that the bourgeoisie has lost its vocation to rule. Already a parliamentary ministry no longer existed. Having now lost, in addition, the lever of the army and National Guard, what forcible means remained to it with which simultaneously to maintain the usurped authority of parliament over the people and its constitutional authority against the President? None. Only the appeal to impotent principles remained to it now, to principles that it had itself always interpreted merely as general rules, which one prescribes for others in order to be able to move all the more freely oneself. The dismissal of Changarnier and the falling of the military power into Bonaparte's hands closes the first part of the period we are considering, the period of struggle between the Party of Order and the executive power. War between the two powers has now been openly declared, is openly waged, but only after the Party of Order has lost arms and soldiers. Without the ministry, without the people, without public opinion, no longer after its Electoral Law of May 31 the representative of the sovereign nation, *sans* eyes, *sans* ears, *sans* teeth, *sans* everything, the National Assembly had undergone a gradual transformation into an *old French Parliament*,[9] that has to leave action

9. Marx is referring to the parliaments of pre-revolutionary France, which were supreme courts. They had the right to register new royal decrees; in case of disagreement, they could only present a remonstrance to the king, requesting that the decree be revoked. In reality the old French parliament had no power.

to the government and content itself with growling remonstrances *post festum.*[1]

The Party of Order receives the new ministry with a storm of indignation. General Bedeau recalls to mind the mildness of the Permanent Commission during the recess and the excess of consideration owing to which it has refrained from the publication of its minutes. The Minister for Home Affairs now himself insists on publication of these minutes which by this time have naturally become as dull as ditch-water, disclose no fresh facts and have not the slightest effect on the blasé public. Upon Rémusat's proposal the National Assembly retires into its committees and appoints a "Committee for Extraordinary Measures." Paris departs the less from the rut of its everyday routine, since at this moment trade is prosperous, manufactures are busy, corn prices are low, foodstuffs are overflowing and the savings banks receive fresh deposits daily. The "extraordinary measures" that parliament has announced with so much noise fizzle out on January 18 in a no-confidence vote against the ministry without General Changarnier even being mentioned. The Party of Order had been forced to frame its motion in this way, in order to secure the votes of the republicans, as of all the measures of the ministry Changarnier's dismissal is precisely the only one which the republicans approve of, while the Party of Order is in fact not in a position to censure the other ministerial acts which it had itself dictated.

The no-confidence vote of January 18 was passed by four hundred and fifteen votes to two hundred and eighty-six. Thus, it was only carried by a *coalition* of the extreme Legitimists and Orleanists with the pure republicans and the Mountain. It proved, therefore, that the Party of Order had lost in conflicts with Bonaparte not only the ministry, not only the army, but also its independent parliamentary majority, that a body of representatives had deserted from its camp, out of fanaticism for conciliation, out of fear of the struggle, out of lassitude, out of family regard for the state salaries of relatives, out of speculation on ministerial posts becoming vacant (Odilon Barrot), out of the shallow egoism which makes the ordinary bourgeois always inclined to sacrifice the general interest of his class for this or that private motive. From the first, the Bonapartist representatives adhered to the Party of Order only in the struggle against revolution. The leader of the Catholic party, Montalembert, had already at that time thrown his influence into the Bonapartist scale, since he despaired of the parliamentary party's prospects of life. Lastly, the leaders of this party, Thiers and Berryer, the Orleanist and the Legitimist, were compelled openly to proclaim themselves republicans, to confess that their hearts were

1. After the event.

royalist, but their heads republican, that their parliamentary republic was the sole possible form for the rule of the whole bourgeoisie. Thus, they were compelled, before the eyes of the bourgeois class itself, to stigmatise the Restoration plans, which they continued indefatigably to pursue behind parliament's back, as an intrigue as dangerous as it was brainless.

The no-confidence vote of January 18 hit the ministers and not the President. But it was not the ministry, it was the President who had dismissed Changarnier. Should the Party of Order impeach Bonaparte himself? On account of his restoration desires? The latter merely supplemented their own. On account of his conspiracy in connection with the military reviews and the Society of December 10? They had buried these themes long since under simple orders of the day. On account of the dismissal of the hero of January 29 and June 13, the man who in May 1850 threatened to set fire to all four corners of Paris in the event of a rising? Their allies of the Mountain and Cavaignac did not even allow them to raise the fallen bulwark of society by means of an official attestation of sympathy. They themselves could not deny the President the constitutional authority to dismiss a general. They only raged because he made an unparliamentary use of his constitutional right. Had they not continually made an unconstitutional use of their parliamentary prerogative, and particularly in regard to the abolition of universal suffrage? They were therefore reduced to moving within strictly parliamentary limits. And this involved that peculiar malady which since 1848 has spread all over the Continent, *parliamentary cretinism*, which holds those infected by it fast in an imaginary world and robs them of all sense, all memory, all understanding of the rude external world—it involved this parliamentary cretinism when those who had destroyed all the conditions of parliamentary power with their own hands, and were bound to destroy them in their struggle with the other classes, still took their parliamentary triumphs for victories and believed they hit the President by striking at his ministers. They merely gave him the opportunity to humiliate the National Assembly afresh in the eyes of the nation. On January 20 the *Moniteur* announced that the resignation of the entire ministry had been accepted. On the pretext that no parliamentary party any longer had a majority, as the vote of January 18, this fruit of the coalition between Mountain and royalists, proved, and pending the formation of a new majority, Bonaparte appointed a so-called transition ministry, not one member of which was a member of parliament, all being absolutely unknown and insignificant individuals, a ministry of mere clerks and copyists. The Party of Order could now work to exhaustion playing with these marionettes; the executive power no longer thought it worth while to be seriously represented in the

National Assembly. The more his ministers were pure dummies, the more manifestly Bonaparte concentrated the whole executive power in his own person and the more scope he had for exploiting it for his own ends.

In coalition with the Mountain, the Party of Order revenged itself by rejecting the presidential grant of one million eight hundred thousand francs, which the chief of the Society of December 10 had compelled his ministerial clerks to propose. This time a majority of only a hundred and two votes decided the matter; twenty-seven fresh votes had therefore fallen away since January 18; the dissolution of the Party of Order was going forward. At the same time, in order that there might not for a moment be any mistake about the meaning of its coalition with the Mountain, it scorned even to consider a proposal signed by a hundred and eighty-nine members of the Mountain for a general amnesty for political offenders. It sufficed for the Minister for Home Affairs, a certain Vaïsse, to declare that the tranquillity was only apparent, in secret great agitation prevailed, in secret ubiquitous societies were being organised, the democratic papers were preparing to come out again, the reports from the Departments were unfavourable, the Geneva refugees were directing a conspiracy spreading by way of Lyons over all the south of France. France was on the verge of an industrial and commercial crisis, the manufacturers of Roubaix had reduced working hours, the prisoners of Belle Isle were in revolt—it sufficed for even a mere Vaïsse to conjure up the red spectre and the Party of Order rejected without discussion a motion that would certainly have won the National Assembly immense popularity and thrown Bonaparte back into its arms. Instead of letting itself be intimidated by the executive power with the prospect of fresh disturbances, it ought rather to have allowed the class struggle a little elbowroom, so as to keep the executive power dependent on it. But it did not feel equal to the task of playing with fire.

Meanwhile, the so-called transition ministry continued to vegetate until the middle of April. Bonaparte wearied and befooled the National Assembly with continual new ministerial combinations. Now he seemed to want to form a republican ministry with Lamartine and Billault, now a parliamentary one with the inevitable Odilon Barrot, whose name may never be missing when a dupe is necessary, then a Legitimist ministry with Vatimesnil and Benoît d'Azy, and again an Orleanist one with Maleville. While he thus keeps the different sections of the Party of Order in tension against one another and alarms them as a whole with the prospect of a republican ministry and the consequent inevitable restoration of universal suffrage, at the same time he engenders in the bourgeoisie the conviction that his honest efforts to form a parliamentary ministry are frustrated by the irreconcilability of the royalist factions.

The bourgeoisie, however, cried out all the louder for a "strong government." It found it all the more unpardonable to leave France "without administration," the more a general commercial crisis seemed now to be approaching and won recruits for socialism in the towns, just as the ruinously low price of corn did the countryside. Trade became daily slacker, the unemployed hands considerably increased, ten thousand workers, at least, were without bread in Paris, innumerable factories stood idle in Rouen, Mühlhausen, Lyons, Roubaix, Tourcoing, St. Etienne, Elbeuf, etc. Under these circumstances, on April 11 Bonaparte could venture to restore the ministry of January 18, Messrs. Rouher, Fould, Baroche, etc., reinforced by M. Léon Faucher, whom the Constituent Assembly during its last days had, with the exception of five votes cast by ministers, unanimously stigmatised with a vote of no-confidence for sending out false telegrams. The National Assembly had therefore gained a victory over the ministry on January 18, it had struggled with Bonaparte for three months, in order that on April 11 Fould and Baroche might admit the puritan Faucher as a third party in their ministerial alliance.

In November 1849, Bonaparte had contented himself with an *unparliamentary* ministry, in January 1851 with an *extra-parliamentary* one, and on April 11 he felt strong enough to form an *anti-parliamentary* ministry, which harmoniously combined in itself the no-confidence votes of both Assemblies, the Constituent and the Legislative, the republican and the royalist. This gradation of ministries was the thermometer with which parliament could measure the decrease of its own vital heat. By the end of April the latter had fallen so low that Persigny, in a personal interview, could urge Changarnier to go over to the camp of the President. Bonaparte, he assures him, regards the influence of the National Assembly as completely destroyed, and the proclamation is already prepared that is to be published after the *coup d'état*, which was kept steadily in view but was by chance again postponed. Changarnier informed the leaders of the Party of Order of the death warrant, but who believes that bug-bites are fatal? And the parliament, stricken, disintegrated and death-tainted as it was, could not prevail on itself to see in its duel with the grotesque chief of the Society of December 10 anything other than a duel with a bug. But Bonaparte answered the Party of Order as Agesilaus did King Agis: "*I seem to you an ant, but I shall one day be a lion.*"

VI

The coalition with the Mountain and the pure republicans, to which the Party of Order saw itself condemned in its unavailing efforts to maintain possession of the military power and to reconquer supreme control of the executive power, proved incontrovertibly that it had lost its independent *parliamentary majority*. On May 29, the mere power of the calendar, of the hour-hand of the clock gave the sign for its complete disintegration. With May 29, the last year of the life of the National Assembly began. It had now to decide for continuing the Constitution unaltered or for revising it. But revision of the Constitution, that implied not only rule of the bourgeoisie or of petty-bourgeois democracy, democracy or proletarian anarchy, parliamentary republic or Bonaparte, it implied at the same time Orleans or Bourbon! Thus the apple of discord fell in the midst of parliament, whereupon the conflict of interests, which split the Party of Order into hostile sections, was bound to blaze up in the open. The Party of Order was a combination of heterogeneous social substances. The question of revision generated a political temperature at which the product again decomposed into its original constituents.

The interest of the Bonapartists in a revision was simple. For them it was above all a question of abolishing Article 45, which forbade Bonaparte's re-election, and the prolongation of his authority. No less simple appeared the position of the republicans. They unconditionally rejected any revision, they saw in it a universal conspiracy against the republic. Since they commanded *more than a quarter of the votes* in the National Assembly and, according to the Constitution, three-quarters of the votes were required for a resolution for revision to be legally valid and for convocation of a revising Assembly, they only needed to count their votes to be sure of victory. And they were sure of victory.

As against these clear positions, the Party of Order found itself caught in inextricable contradictions. If it rejected revision, then it imperilled the *status quo*, since it left Bonaparte only one way out, that of force, and since on May 2, 1852, at the decisive moment, it surrendered France to revolutionary anarchy, with a President who lost his authority, with a parliament which had for a long time not possessed it and with a people that thought to reconquer it. If it voted for constitutional revision, then it knew that it voted in vain and would be bound to fail because of the veto of the republicans. If it unconstitutionally declared a simple majority vote to be binding, then it could only hope to dominate the revolution if it subjected itself unconditionally to the sovereignty of the executive power, then it made Bonaparte master of the Constitution, of the revision and of itself. An only partial revision, which prolonged the authority of the President, paved the way for imperial usurpation. A general revision which shortened the existence of the republic, brought the dynastic claims into unavoidable conflict, for the conditions of a Bourbon and the conditions of an Orleanist Restoration were not only different, they were mutually exclusive.

The *parliamentary republic* was more than the neutral territory on which the two factions of the French bourgeoisie, Legitimists and Orleanists, large landed property and industry, could dwell side by side with equality of rights. It was the unavoidable condition of their *common* rule, the sole form of state in which their general class interest subjected to itself at the same time both the claims of their particular sections and all the remaining classes of society. As royalists they fell back into their antagonism, into the struggle for the supremacy of landed property or of money, and the highest expression of this antagonism, its personification, was their kings themselves, their dynasties. Hence the resistance of the Party of Order to the *recall of the Bourbons*.

The Orleanist and representative of the people, Creton, had in 1849, 1850 and 1851 periodically introduced a motion for the revocation of the decree exiling the royal families. Just as regularly parliament presented the spectacle of an Assembly of royalists that obdurately barred the gates through which their exiled kings might return home. Richard III had murdered Henry VI with the remark that he was too good for this world and belonged in heaven. They declared France too bad to possess her kings again. Constrained by force of circumstances, they had become republicans and repeatedly sanctioned the plebiscite that banished their kings from France.

The revision of the Constitution—and circumstances compelled taking it into consideration—called in question the common rule of the two bourgeois sections along with the republic, and revived, with the possibility of a monarchy, the rivalry of the interests which had alternately predominated in representing it, the struggle for the supremacy of one section over the other. The diplomats of the Party of Order believed they could settle the struggle by a unification of two dynasties, by a so-called *fusion* of the royalist parties and their royal houses. The real fusion of the Restoration and the July Monarchy was the parliamentary republic, in which Orleanist and Legitimist colours were obliterated and the various species of bourgeois disappeared in the bourgeois as such, in the bourgeois genus. Now, however, Orleanist was to become Legitimist and Legitimist Orleanist. Monarchy, in which their antagonism was personified, was to embody their unity, the expression of their exclusive factional interests to become the expression of their common class interest, the monarchy to do that which only the abolition of two monarchies, the republic, could do and had done. This was the philosopher's stone, to produce which the doctors of the Party of Order racked their brains. As if the Legitimist monarchy could ever become the monarchy of the industrial bourgeois or the bourgeois monarchy ever become the monarchy of the hereditary landed aristocracy. As if landed property and industry could fraternise under one crown, when the crown could only descend to one head, the head of the elder brother or of the younger. As if industry could come to terms with landed property at all, so long as landed property does not decide itself to become industrial. If Henry V should die tomorrow, the Count of Paris would not on that account become the king of the Legitimists unless he ceased to be the king of the Orleanists. The philosophers of fusion, however, who became more vociferous in proportion as the revision question came to the fore, who had provided themselves with an official daily organ in the *Assemblée Nationale* and who are again at work even at this very moment (February 1852), explained the whole difficulty to themselves by the opposition and rivalry of the two dynasties. The attempts to reconcile the Orléans family with Henry V, begun since the death of Louis Philippe,[2] but, like the dynastic intrigues generally, only played at while the National Assembly was in recess, during the *entr'actes* behind the scenes and having rather the character of sentimental coquetry with the old superstition than of seriously-meant business—these attempts now became principal and state actions and were enacted by the Party of Order on the public stage, instead of amateur theatricals as hitherto. The couriers sped from Paris to Venice, from Venice to Claremont, from Claremont to Paris. The Count of Chambord issues a manifesto in which "with the help of all the members of his family" he announces not his, but the "national" Restoration. The Orleanist, Salvandy, throws himself at the feet of Henry V. The Legitimist chiefs, Berryer, Benoît d'Azy and Saint-Priest, travel to Claremont in order to persuade the Orléans, but in vain. The fusionists perceive too late that the interests of the two bourgeois sections neither lose in exclusiveness nor gain in pliancy when they become accentuated in the form of family interests, interests of two royal houses. If Henry V recognised the Count of Paris as his successor—the sole success that the fusion could achieve at best—the House of Orléans did not in this way win any claim that the childlessness of Henry V had not already secured to it, but it lost all claim that it had conquered through the July Revolution. It waived its original claims, all the titles that it had wrested from the Bourbons in almost a hundred years of struggle with the older branch; it bartered away its historical prerogative, the prerogative of the modern kingdom, for the prerogative of its genealogical tree. The fusion was therefore nothing but a voluntary abdication of the House of Orléans, its resignation

2. Louis Philippe died on August 26, 1850, in Claremont (England).

to Legitimacy, repentant withdrawal from the Protestant state church into the Catholic. A withdrawal, moreover, that did not even bring it to the throne which it had lost, but to the throne's steps, on which it had been born. The old Orleanist ministers, Guizot, Duchâtel, etc., who likewise hastened to Claremont to advocate the fusion, in fact represented merely the *Katzenjammer*[3] over the July Revolution, the despair felt in regard to the bourgeois monarchy and the monarchical rule of the bourgeois, the superstitious belief in Legitimacy as the last amulet against anarchy. Imagining themselves mediators between Orléans and Bourbon, in reality they were merely Orleanist deserters, and the Prince of Joinville received them as such. On the other hand, the vital, bellicose section of Orleanists, Thiers, Baze, etc., persuaded Louis Philippe's family all the more easily that if any immediate monarchist restoration presupposed the fusion of the two dynasties, any such fusion, however, presupposed abdication of the House of Orléans; it was on the contrary, wholly in accord with the tradition of their forefathers to recognise the republic for the moment and wait until events permitted the conversion of the presidential chair into a throne. Rumours of Joinville's candidature were circulated, public curiosity was kept in suspense and, a few months later, in September after the rejection of revision, his candidature was publicly proclaimed.

The attempt at a royalist fusion of Orleanists with Legitimists had thus not only failed, it had destroyed their *parliamentary fusion*, their common republican form, and had split the Party of Order into its original component parts; but the more the estrangement between Claremont and Venice grew, the more their agreement broke down and the more the Joinville agitation gained ground, so much the more eager and earnest became the negotiations between Bonaparte's minister, Faucher, and the Legitimists.

The disintegration of the Party of Order did not stop at its original elements. Each of the two great sections, in its turn, underwent decomposition anew. It was as if all the old nuances that had formerly fought and jostled one another within each of the two circles, whether Orleanist or Legitimist, had thawed again like dry infusoria on contact with water, as if they had acquired a new sufficient vital energy to form groups of their own and independent antagonisms. The Legitimists dreamed that they were back among the controversies between the Tuileries and the Pavillon Marsan,[4] between Villèle and Polignac. The Orleanists relived the golden days of the

3. The "morning-after" feeling.
4. This refers to the conflict during the restoration period between Louis XVIII, who resided in the Palace of the Tuileries, and the representative of even more reactionary policy, Comte d'Artois (afterwards King Charles X), who lived in the Pavillon Marsan, in the Tuileries.

tourneys between Guizot, Molé, Broglie, Thiers and Odilon Barrot.

That part of the Party of Order which was eager for revision, but was divided again on the limits to revision, a section composed of the Legitimists led by Berryer and Falloux, on the one hand, and by Larochejaquelein, on the other, and of the conflict-weary Orleanists led by Molé, Broglie, Montalembert and Odilon Barrot, agreed with the Bonapartist representatives on the following indefinite and broadly framed motion: "With the object of restoring to the nation the full exercise of its sovereignty, the undersigned representatives move that the Constitution be revised." At the same time, however, they unanimously declared through their reporter Tocqueville that the National Assembly had not the right to move the *abolition of the republic*, that this right belonged solely to the Revising Chamber. For the rest, the Constitution might only be revised *in a "legal" manner*, hence only if the constitutionally prescribed three-quarters of the number of votes were cast in favour of revision. On June 19, after six days of stormy debate, revision was rejected, as was to be anticipated. Four hundred and forty-six votes were cast for it, but two hundred and seventy-eight against. The extreme Orleanists, Thiers, Changarnier, etc., voted with the republicans and the Mountain.

Thus, the majority of parliament declared against the Constitution, but this Constitution itself declared for the minority and that its vote was binding. But had not the Party of Order subordinated the Constitution to the parliamentary majority on May 31, 1850,[5] and on June 13, 1849? Up to now, was not its whole policy based on the subordination of the paragraphs of the Constitution to the votes of the parliamentary majority? Had it not left to the democrats the Old Testament superstition in the letter of the law, and scolded the democrats for it? At the present moment, however, revision of the Constitution meant nothing but continuation of the presidential authority, just as continuation of the Constitution meant nothing but Bonaparte's deposition. Parliament had declared for him, but the Constitution declared against parliament. He therefore acted in the sense of parliament when he tore up the Constitution, and he acted in the sense of the Constitution when he dispersed parliament.

Parliament had declared the Constitution and, with the latter, its own rule to be "beyond the majority"; by its vote it had suspended the Constitution and prolonged the presidential power, while declaring at the same time that neither the one can die nor the other live so long as it itself continues to exist. Those who were to bury it were standing at the door. While it debated on revision,

5. May 31, 1850—the day the Legislative Assembly revoked universal suffrage.

Bonaparte removed General Baraguey d'Hilliers, who had proved irresolute, from the command of the first military division and appointed in his place General Magnan, the victor of Lyons, the hero of the December days, one of his creatures, who under Louis Philippe had already compromised himself more or less in Bonaparte's favour on the occasion of the Boulogne expedition.

The Party of Order proved by its vote on revision that it knew neither how to rule nor how to serve; neither how to live nor how to die; neither how to suffer the republic nor how to overthrow it; neither how to uphold the Constitution nor how to throw it overboard; neither how to co-operate with the President, nor how to break with him. To what, then, did it look for the solution of all the contradictions? To the calendar, to the course of events. It ceased to presume to sway the events. It therefore challenged the events to assume sway over it, and thereby the power to which in the struggle against the people it had surrendered one attribute after another until before this power it itself stood impotent. In order that the head of the executive power might be able the more undisturbed to draw up his plan of campaign against it, strengthen his means of attack, select his tools and fortify his positions, it resolved precisely at this critical moment to retire from the stage and adjourn for three months, from August 10 to November 4.

The parliamentary party was not only dissolved into its two great sections, each of these sections was not only split up within itself, but the Party of Order in parliament had fallen out with the Party of Order *outside* parliament. The spokesmen and scribes of the bourgeoisie, its platform and its press, in short, the ideologists of the bourgeoisie and the bourgeoisie itself, the representatives and the represented, faced one another in estrangement and no longer understood one another.

The Legitimists in the provinces, with their limited horizon and their unlimited enthusiasm, accused their parliamentary leaders, Berryer and Falloux, of deserting Henry V and going over to the Bonapartist camp. Their lily minds[6] believed in the fall of man, but not in diplomacy.

Far more fateful and decisive was the breach of the commercial bourgeoisie with its politicians. It reproached them, not as the Legitimists reproached theirs, with having abandoned their principles, but, on the contrary, with clinging to principles that had become unprofitable.

I have already indicated that since the entry of Fould into the ministry the section of the commercial bourgeoisie which had held the lion's share of power during Louis Philippe's reign, that of the *aristocracy of finance*, had become Bonapartist. Fould represented not only Bonaparte's interests in the *Bourse*, he represented at the

6. The lily was the emblem of the Bourbons.

same time the interests of the *Bourse* in Bonaparte. The position of the aristocracy of finance is most strikingly depicted by the passage from its European organ, the London *Economist*. In its number of February 1, 1851, its Paris correspondent writes:

> "Now we have it stated from numerous quarters that France wishes above all things for repose. The President declares it in his message to the Legislative Assembly; it is echoed from the tribune; it is asserted in the journals; it is announced from the pulpit; *it is demonstrated by the sensitiveness of the public funds at the least prospect of disturbance, and their firmness the instant it is made manifest that the executive is far superior in wisdom and power to the factious ex-officials of all former governments.*"

In its issue of November 29, 1851, *The Economist* declares in its own name: *"the president . . . is the guardian of order, and . . . is now recognised as such on every Stock Exchange of Europe."*

The aristocracy of finance therefore condemned the parliamentary struggle of the Party of Order with the executive power as a disturbance of order, and celebrated every victory of the President over its ostensible representatives as a *victory of order*. By the aristocracy of finance must here be understood not merely the great loan promoters and speculators in government securities, in regard to whom it is immediately obvious that their interests coincide with the interests of the state power. All modern finance, the whole of banking business, is interwoven in the closest fashion with public credit. A part of their business capital is necessarily invested and put out at interest in quickly convertible government securities. Their deposits, the capital placed at their disposal and distributed by them among merchants and industrialists, is partly derived from the dividends of holders of government securities. If for the entire money market and the priests of this money market, the stability of the state power has in every epoch signified Moses and the prophets, why not all the more so today, when every deluge threatens to sweep away the old states, and the old state debts with them.

The *industrial bourgeoisie*, too, in its fanaticism for order, was angered by the squabbles of the parliamentary Party of Order with the executive power. After their vote of January 18 on the occasion of Changarnier's dismissal, Thiers, Anglas, St. Beuve, etc., received from their voters in precisely the industrial districts public reproofs in which particularly their coalition with the Mountain was scourged as high treason to order. If we have seen that the boastful taunts, the petty intrigues, which marked the struggle of the Party of Order with the President, merited no better reception, then, on the other hand, this bourgeois party, which required its representatives to allow the military power to go out of the hands of its own parliament into those of an adventurous pretender without offering resistance, was not even worth the intrigues that were squandered on its interests. It proved that the struggle to maintain its *public* interests, its own *class interests*, its *political power*, only troubled and upset it as a disturbance of private business.

With barely an exception, the bourgeois dignitaries of the towns in the Departments, the municipal authorities, the judges of the Commercial Court, etc., everywhere received Bonaparte on his tours in the most servile manner, even when, as in Dijon, he made an unrestrained attack on the National Assembly and especially on the Party of Order.

When trade was good, as it still was at the beginning of 1851, the commercial bourgeoisie raged against any parliamentary struggle, lest indeed trade be put out of humour. When trade was bad, as it continually was from the end of February 1851, the commercial bourgeoisie accused the parliamentary struggles of being the cause of stagnation and cried out for them to be ended, that trade might become lively again. The revision debates came on just in this bad period. Since the question here was whether the existing form of state was to be or not to be, the bourgeoisie felt itself all the more justified in demanding from its representatives the ending of this torturing provisional arrangement and at the same time the maintainance of the *status quo*. There was no contradiction in this. By the end of the provisional arrangement it understood precisely its continuation, the postponement to a distant future of the moment when it had to reach a decision. The *status quo* could be maintained in only two ways: prolongation of Bonaparte's authority or his constitutional retirement and the election of Cavaignac. A section of the bourgeoisie desired the latter solution and knew no better advice to give its representatives than to keep silent and leave the burning question untouched. They were of the opinion that if their representatives did not speak, Bonaparte would not act. They wanted an ostrich parliament that hid its head in order to remain unseen. Another section of the bourgeoisie, because Bonaparte was already in the presidential chair, desired to leave him sitting in it, so that everything might remain on the old lines. They were indignant because their parliament did not openly infringe the Constitution and abdicate without ceremony.

The General Councils of the Departments, those provincial representative bodies of the big bourgeoisie, which met from August 25 onwards during the recess of the National Assembly, declared almost unanimously for revision, therefore against parliament and in favour of Bonaparte.

Still more unequivocally than over the falling out with its *parliamentary representatives* the bourgeoisie displayed its wrath in regard to its literary representatives, its own press. The verdicts of the bourgeois juries, sentencing to ruinous fines and shameless imprisonments for every attack of the bourgeois journalists on Bonaparte's usurpationist desires, for every attempt of the press to defend the political rights of the bourgeoisie against the executive power, astonished not merely France, but all Europe.

If by its clamour for tranquillity the *parliamentary Party of Order*, as I have shown, committed itself to quiescence, if it declared the political rule of the bourgeoisie to be incompatible with the safety and stability of the bourgeoisie, by destroying with its own hands in the struggle against the other classes of society all the conditions for its own regime, the parliamentary regime, then the *extra-parliamentary* mass of the bourgeoisie, on the other hand, by its servility towards the President, by its vilification of parliament, by the brutal maltreatment of its own press, invited Bonaparte to suppress and annihilate its speaking and writing section, its politicians and its *literati*, its platform and its press, in order that it might then be able to pursue its private affairs with full confidence in the protection of a strong and unrestricted government. It declared unequivocally that it longed to get rid of its own political rule in order to get rid of the troubles and dangers of ruling.

And this mass, that had already rebelled against the purely parliamentary and literary struggle for the rule of its own class and betrayed the leaders of this struggle, now dares after the event to indict the proletariat for not having risen in a bloody struggle, a life-and-death struggle on its behalf! This mass, that every moment sacrificed its general class interests, that is, its political interests, to the narrowest and dirtiest private interests, and demanded a similar sacrifice from its representatives, now moans that the proletariat has sacrificed its ideal political interests to its material interests. It poses as a lovely soul that has been misunderstood and deserted in the decisive hour by the proletariat misled by socialists. And it finds a general echo in the bourgeois world. Naturally, I do not speak here of obscure German politicians and riff-raff of this persuasion. I refer, for example, to the same *Economist* that as late as November 29, 1851, consequently four days prior to the *coup d'état*, had declared Bonaparte to be the "guardian of order," but Thiers and Berryer to be "anarchists," and already on December 27, 1851, after Bonaparte had quieted these anarchists, is already vociferous concerning the treason to "the skill, knowledge, discipline, mental influence, intellectual resources and moral weight of the middle and upper ranks" of society committed by "ignorant, untrained, and stupid, *prolétaires*." The stupid, ignorant and vulgar mass was none other than the bourgeois mass itself.

In the year 1851, France, to be sure, had passed through a kind of minor trade crisis. The end of February showed a decline in exports compared with 1850; in March trade suffered and factories closed down; in April the position of the industrial Departments appeared as desperate as after the February days; in May business had still not revived; as late as June 28, the holdings of the Bank of France showed, by the enormous growth of deposits and the equally great decrease in advances on bills of exchange, that production was at a standstill, and it was not until the middle of October that a progressive improvement of business again set in. The French bourgeoisie explained this trade stagnation by purely political causes, by the struggle between parliament and the executive power, by the precariousness of a merely provisional form of state, by the terrifying prospect of May 2, 1852. I will not deny that all these circumstances had a depressing effect on some branches of industry in Paris and the Departments. But in any case this influence of the political conditions was only local and inconsiderable. Does this .require further proof than the fact that the improvement of trade set in towards the middle of October, at the very moment when the political situation grew worse, the political horizon darkened and a thunderbolt from Elysium was expected at any moment? For the rest, a French bourgeois, whose skill, knowledge, spiritual insight and intellectual resources, reach no further than his nose, could throughout the period of the Industrial Exhibition in London have found under his nose the cause of his commercial miseries. While in France factories were closed down, in England commercial bankruptcies broke out. While in April and May the industrial panic reached a climax in France, in April and May the commercial panic reached a climax in England. Like the French woollen industry, the English woollen industry suffered, and as French silk manufacture, so did English silk manufacture. If the English cotton factories continued working, this no longer resulted in the same profits as in 1849 and 1850. The only difference was that the crisis in France was industrial, in England commercial; that while in France the factories stood idle, in England they extended operations, but under less favourable conditions than in preceding years; that in France it was exports, in England imports which were hardest hit. The common cause, which is naturally not to be sought within the bounds of the French political horizon, was obvious. The years 1849 and 1850 were years of the greatest material prosperity and of an overproduction that appeared as such only in 1851. At the beginning of this year it was given a further special impetus by the prospect of the Industrial Exhibition. In addition there came as special circumstances: first the partial failure of the cotton crop in 1850 and 1851, then the certainty of a bigger cotton crop than had been expected; first the rise, then the sudden fall, in short, the fluctuations in the price of cotton. The supply of raw silk, in France at least, had turned out to be below the average yield. Woollen manufacture, finally, had expanded so much since 1848 that the production of wool could not keep pace with it and the price of raw wool rose out of all proportion to the price of woollen manufactures. Here, then, in the raw material of three industries for the world market, we have already threefold material for a stagnation in trade. Apart from these special circumstances, the apparent crisis of 1851 was nothing more than the halt which overproduction and overspeculation invariably make in describing the industrial cycle, before they gather all their forces in order to rush feverishly through the final phase of this cycle and arrive once more at their starting point, the *general trade crisis.* During such intervals in trade history commercial bankruptcies break out in England, while in France industry itself is reduced to idleness, being partly forced into retreat by the competition of the English in all markets, just then becoming intolerable, and being partly singled out for attack as a luxury indus-, try by every business depression. Thus, besides the general crisis, France goes through national trade crises of her own, which are nevertheless determined and conditioned far more by the general state of the world market than by French local influences. It will not be without interest to contrast the judgment of the English bourgeois with the prejudice of the French bourgeois. In its annual trade report for 1851, one of the largest Liverpool houses writes:

"Few years have more thoroughly belied the anticipations formed at their commencement than the one just closed, or shown the fallacy of human calculations more completely, and instead of the great prosperity which was almost unanimously looked for at its opening, it has proved, with the single exception of '47, one of the most discouraging that has been seen for the last quarter of a century—this, of course, refers to the *mercantile,* not to the *manufacturing* classes. And yet there certainly were grounds for anticipating the reverse at the beginning of the year—stocks of produce were moderate, money was abundant, and has continued so throughout; food was cheap, and no apprehension has ever arisen to the contrary; a plentiful harvest well secured, unbroken peace on the Continent, and no political or fiscal disturbances at home; indeed the wings of commerce were never more unfettered. . . . To what source then, is this disastrous result to be attributed? We believe to overtrading both in imports and exports. . . . Unless they [our merchants] will put more stringent limits to their freedom of action, nothing but a *triennial* panic can keep us in check."[7]

Now picture to yourself the French bourgeois, think how in the throes of this business panic his trade-sick brain is tortured, set in a whirl and stunned by rumours concerning *coups d'état* and the restoration of universal suffrage, by the struggle between parliament and the executive power, by the Fronde war between Orleanists and Legitimists, by the communist conspiracies in the south of France, by alleged *Jacqueries*[8] in the Departments of Nièvre and Cher, by the advertising of the different candidates for the presidency, by the cheapjack slogans of the journals, by the threats of the republicans to uphold the Constitution and universal suffrage by force of arms, by the gospel preaching of the *émigré* heroes *in partibus*, who announced that the world would end on May 2, 1852—think of all this and you will comprehend why in this unspeakable, uproarious confusion of fusion, revision, prorogation, Constitution, conspiracy, coalition, emigration, usurpation and revolution the bourgeoisie madly snorts to this parliamentary republic: *"Rather an end with terror than a terror without end!"*

Bonaparte understood this cry. His powers of comprehension were sharpened by the growing turbulence of creditors who, in each sunset which brought settling day, May 2, 1852, nearer, saw a movement of the stars protesting against their earthly bills of exchange. They become veritable astrologers. The National Assembly had blighted Bonaparte's hopes of a constitutional prorogation of his authority; the candidature of the Prince of Joinville for further vacillation.

If ever an event has, well in advance of its coming, cast its shadow before, it was Bonaparte's *coup d'état*. As early as January 29, 1849, barely a month after his election, he had made a proposal about it to Changarnier. In the summer of 1849 his own Prime Minister, Odilon Barrot, had covertly denounced the policy of *coups d'état*; in the winter of 1850 Thiers had openly done so. In May 1851, Persigny had sought once more to win Changarnier for the coup; the *Messager de l'Assemblée* had published an account of their conversation. During every parliamentary storm, the Bonapartist journals threatened a *coup d'état*, and the nearer the crisis drew, the louder grew their tones. In the orgies that Bonaparte kept up every night with men and women of the "swell mob," as soon as the hour of midnight approached and copious potations had loosened tongues and fired imaginations, the *coup d'état* was fixed for the following morning. Swords were drawn, glasses clinked, the representatives were thrown out of the window, the imperial mantle fell upon Bonaparte's shoulders, until the following morning banished the spook once more and astonished Paris learned from vestals of little reticence and from indiscreet paladins[9] of the danger it

---

7. Quoted from *The Economist*, January 10, 1852, pp. 29–30.
8. Peasant risings. "Jacques Bonhomme" (John Goodfellow) was the nickname given to the French peasant.

had once again escaped. During the months of September and October rumours of a *coup d'état* followed fast one after the other. The shadow took on colour, like a variegated daguerreotype. Look up the events of the month for September and October in the organs of the European daily press and you will find, work for word, intimations like the following: "Paris is full of rumours of a *coup d'état*. The capital is to be filled with troops during the night and the next morning is to bring decress which dissolve the National Assembly, declare the Department of the Seine in a state of siege, restore universal suffrage and appeal to the people. Bonaparte is said to be seeking ministers for the execution of these illegal decrees." The letters that bring these tidings always end with the fateful word *"postponed."* The *coup d'état* was ever the fixed idea of Bonaparte. With this idea he had again set foot on French soil. He was so obsessed by it that he continually betrayed it and blurted it out. He was so weak that, just as continally, he gave it up again. The shadow of the *coup d'état* had become so familiar to the Parisians as a spectre, that they were not willing to believe in it when it finally appeared in flesh and blood. It was therefore neither the reticent reserve of the chief of the Society of December 10 nor an unanticipated surprise attack by the National Assembly which allowed the *coup d'état* to succeed. If it succeeded, it succeeded despite his indiscretion and with its foreknowledge, a necessary, inevitable result of the preceding development.

On October 10 Bonaparte announced to his ministers his decision to restore universal suffrage; on the sixteenth they handed in their resignations; on the twenty-sixth Paris learned of the formation of the Thorigny ministry. The Police-Prefect, Carlier, was simultaneously replaced by Maupas; the head of the first military division, Magnan, concentrated the most reliable regiments in the capital. On November 4, the National Assembly resumed its sittings. It had nothing better to do than to recapitulate in a short, succinct form the course it had gone through and to prove that it was buried only after it had died.

The first post that it had forfeited in the struggle with the executive power was the ministry. It had solemnly to admit this loss by accepting the Thorigny ministry, a mere shadow cabinet, as genuine. The permanent Commission had received M. Giraud with laughter when he presented himself in the name of the new ministers. Such a weak ministry for such strong measures as the restoration of universal suffrage! But the precise object was to accomplish nothing *in* parliament, everything *against* parliament.

9. Marx's ironic term for the corrupt court ladies and gentlemen. Vestals was the name given in the ancient world to the priestesses of the goddess Vesta, who took the vow of chastity. The Paladins were knights of the Middle Ages who were shining examples of knightly valour.

On the very first day of its re-opening, the National Assembly received the message from Bonaparte in which he demanded the restoration of universal suffrage and the abolition of the law of May 31, 1850. The same day his ministers introduced a decree to this effect. The National Assembly at once rejected the ministry's motion of urgency and rejected the law itself on November 13 by three hundred and fifty-five votes to three hundred and forty-eight. Thus, it tore up its mandate once more; it once more confirmed the fact that it had transformed itself from the freely elected representatives of the people into the usurpatory parliament of a class; it acknowledged once more that it had itself cut in two the muscles which connected the parliamentary head with the body of the nation.

If by its motion to restore universal suffrage the executive power appealed from the National Assembly to the people, by its Quæstors' Bill the legislative power appealed from the people to the army. The Quæstors' Bill was to establish its right of immediate requisition of troops, of forming a parliamentary army. If it thus designated the army as the arbitrator between itself and the people, between itself and Bonaparte, if it recognised the army as the decisive state power, on the other hand it had to admit the fact that it had long given up its claim to command this power. By debating its right to requisition troops, instead of requisitioning them at once, it betrayed the doubt about its own powers. By rejecting the Quæstors' Bill, it made public confession of its impotence. This bill was defeated by a hundred and eight votes, the Mountain had thus determined the issue. It found itself in the position of Buridan's ass, not, indeed, between two bundles of hay with the problem of deciding which was the more attractive, but between two showers of blows with the problem of deciding which was the harder. On the one hand, there was the fear of Changarnier; on the other, the fear of Bonaparte. It must be confessed that the position was no heroic one.

On November 18, an amendment was moved to the law introduced by the Party of Order on the municipal elections, to the effect that, instead of three years', one year's domicile should suffice for the municipal electors. The amendment was lost by a single vote, but this one vote immediately proved to be a mistake. Through splitting up into its hostile sections, the Party of Order had long ago lost its independent parliamentary majority. It showed now that there was no majority in parliament at all. The National Assembly had become *incapable of decision.* Its atomic constituents were no longer held together by any force of cohesion; it had drawn its last breath; it was dead.

Finally, a few days before the catastrophe, the extra-parliamentary mass of the bourgeoisie was solemnly to confirm once more its breach with the bourgeoisie in parliament. Thiers, as a parliamentary hero infected more than the rest with the incurable disease of parliamentary cretinism, had, after the death of parliament, hatched out a new parliamentary intrigue with the Council of State, a responsibility law by which the President was to be firmly held within the limits of the Constitution. Just as, in laying the foundation stone of the new market halls in Paris on September 15, Bonaparte, like a second Masaniello,[1] had enchanted the *dames des halles*,[2] the fishwives—to be sure, one fishwife outweighed seventeen burgraves in real power—just as after the introduction of the Quæstors' Bill he enraptured the lieutenants whom he entertained in the Elysée, so now, on November 25, he swept off their feet the industrial bourgeoisie, who had gathered at the circus to receive at his hands prize medals for the London Industrial Exhibition.[3] I give the significant portion of his speech as reported in the *Journal des Débats*:

"With such unhoped for successes, I am justified in reiterating how great the French republic would be if it were permitted to pursue its real interests and reform its institutions, instead of being constantly disturbed by demagogues, on the one hand, and by monarchist hallucinations, on the other. [Loud, stormy and repeated applause from every part of the amphitheatre.] The monarchist hallucinations hinder all progress and all important branches of industry. In place of progress, nothing but struggle. One sees men who were formerly the most zealous supporters of the royal authority and prerogative become partisans of a Convention, merely in order to weaken the authority that has sprung from universal suffrage. [Loud and repeated applause.] We see men who have suffered most from the Revolution and have deplored it most, provoke a new one, and merely in order to fetter the nation's will. . . . I promise you tranquility for the future, etc. [Bravo, bravo, stormy bravos.]"

Thus did the industrial bourgeoisie applaud with servile bravos the *coup d'état* of December 2, the annihilation of parliament, the downfall of its own rule, the dictatorship of Bonaparte. The thunder of applause on November 25 had its answer in the thunder of cannon on December 4, and the house of M. Sallandrouze, who had been most lavish with bravos, was the most battered by bombs.

Cromwell, when he dissolved the Long Parliament, went alone into its midst, drew out his watch in order that it should not continue to exist a minute after the period fixed by him, and drove out

1. Masaniello (1623–47). A fisherman, the leader of an uprising against the Spanish dominion in Naples, in 1647.
2. Market women.

3. The first world-wide Industrial Exhibition took place in London May 1 to October 11, 1851.

each one of the members of parliament with hilariously humorous taunts. Napoleon, smaller than his prototype, at least betook himself on the eighteenth Brumaire to the legislative body and read out to it, though in an anxious voice, its sentence of death. The second Bonaparte, who, moreover, found himself in possession of an executive power very different from that of Cromwell or Napoleon, sought his model, not in the annals of world history, but in the annals of the Society of December 10, in the annals of criminal jurisdiction. He robs the Bank of France of twenty-five million francs, buys General Magnan with a million, the soldiers with fifteen francs apiece and liquor, comes together with his accomplices secretly like a thief in the night, has the houses of the most dangerous parliamentary leaders broken into and Cavaignac, Lamoricière, Leflô, Changarnier, Charras, Thiers, Baze, etc., dragged from their beds, the chief squares of Paris and the parliamentary buildings occupied by troops, and cheapjack placards posted early in the morning on all the walls, proclaiming the dissolution of the National Assembly and the Council of State, the restoration of universal suffrage and the placing of the Seine Department in a state of siege. In like manner, he inserted a little later in the *Moniteur* a false document, according to which influential parliamentarians had grouped themselves round him as state advisers.

The rump parliament, assembled in the mayoral building of the tenth *arrondissement* and consisting mainly of Legitimists and Orleanists, votes the deposition of Bonaparte amid repeated cries of "Long live the republic," unavailingly harangues the gaping crowds before the building and is finally led off in the custody of African sharpshooters, first of all to the d'Orsay barracks, and later packed into prison vans and transported to the prisons of Mazas, Ham and Vincennes. Thus ended the Party of Order, the Legislative Assembly and the February Revolution. Before hastening to a close, let us briefly summarise its history:

I. *First Period.* From February 24 to May 4, 1848. February period. Prologue. Universal brotherhood swindle.

II. *Second Period.* Period of constituting the republic and of the Constituent National Assembly.

    1. May 4 to June 25, 1848. Struggle of all classes against the proletariat. Defeat of the proletariat in the June days.

    2. June 25 to December 10, 1848. Dictatorship of the pure bourgeois-republicans. Drafting of the Constitution. Proclamation of the state of seige in Paris. The bourgeois dictatorship set aside on December 10 by the election of Bonaparte as President.

3. December 20, 1848, to May 29, 1849. Struggle of the Constituent Assembly with Bonaparte and with the Party of Order in alliance with him. Passing of the Constituent Assembly. Downfall of the republican bourgeoisie.

III. *Third Period.* Period of the *constitutional republic* and of the *Legislative National Assembly.*

1. May 29, 1849, to June 13, 1849. Struggle of the petty bourgeoisie with the bourgeoisie and with Bonaparte. Defeat of the petty-bourgeois democracy.

2. June 13, 1849, to May 31, 1850. Parliamentary dictatorship of the Party of Order. It completes its rule by abolishing universal suffrage, but loses the parliamentary ministry.

3. May 31, 1850, to December 2, 1851. Struggle between the parliamentary bourgeoisie and Bonaparte.

(a) May 31, 1850, to January 12, 1851. Parliament loses the supreme command of the army.

(b) January 12 to April 11, 1851. It is worsted in the attempts to regain the administrative power. The Party of Order loses its independent parliamentary majority. Its coalition with the republicans and the Mountain.

(c) April 11, 1851, to October 9, 1851. Attempts at revision, fusion, prorogation. The Party of Order decomposes into its separate constituents. The breach widens between the bourgeois mass and the bourgeois parliament and press.

(d) October 9 to December 2, 1851. Open breach between parliament and the executive power. Parliament performs its dying act and succumbs, left in the lurch by its own class, by the army and by all the remaining classes. Passing of the parliamentary regime and of bourgeois rule. Victory of Bonaparte. Parody of imperial restoration.

VII

On the threshold of the February Revolution, the *social republic* appeared as a phrase, as a prophecy. In the June days of 1848, it was drowned in the blood of the *Paris proletariat*, but it haunts the subsequent acts of the drama like a ghost. The *democratic republic* makes its appearance. On June 13, 1849, it is dissipated together with its *petty bourgeois*, who take to their heels, but in its flight it blows its own trumpet with redoubled boastfulness. The *parliamentary republic*, together with the bourgeoisie, takes possession of the entire stage; it lives out its existence to the full, but December 2, 1851, buries it to the accompaniment of the cry of terror of the royalists in coalition: "Long live the republic!"

The French bourgeoisie offered resistance to the domination of the working proletariat; it has brought the *lumpenproletariat* to domination, with the chief of the Society of December 10 at the head. The bourgeoisie kept France in breathless fear of the future terrors of red anarchy; Bonaparte discounted this future for it when, on December 4, he had the eminent bourgeois of the Boulevard Montmartre and the Boulevard des Italiens shot down at their windows by the army of order, whose enthusiasm was inspired by liquor. It apotheosised the sword; the sword rules it. It destroyed the revolutionary press; its own press has been destroyed. It placed public meetings under police supervision; its salons are under the supervision of the police. It disbanded the democratic National Guard; its own National Guard has been disbanded. It imposed the state of siege; the state of siege has been imposed on it. It supplanted the juries by military commissions; its juries are supplanted by military commissions; it subjected public education to the priests; the priests subject it to their own education. It transported people without trial; it is transported without trial. It suppressed every stirring in society by means of the state power; every stirring in its society is repressed by means of the state power. Out of enthusiasm for its purse, it rebelled against its own politicians and men of letters; its politicians and men of letters are swept aside, but its purse is plundered now that its mouth has been gagged and its pen broken. The bourgeoisie never wearied of crying out to the revolution what Saint Arsenius cried out to the Christians: *"Fuge, tace, quiesce!"* Flee, be silent, keep quiet! Bonaparte cries to the bourgeoisie: *"Fuge, tace, quiesce!"* Flee, be silent, keep quiet!

The French bourgeoisie had long since found the solution to Napoleon's dilemma: *"Dans cinquante ans l'Europe sera républicaine ou cosaque."*[4] It had found the solution to it in the *"république cosaque."* No Circe, by means of black magic, has distorted that work of art, the bourgeois republic, into a monstrous shape. That republic has nothing but the semblance of respectability. The present-day France was contained in a finished state within the parliamentary republic. It only required a bayonet thrust for the bubble to burst and the monster to spring forth before our eyes.

[The immediate aim of the February Revolution was to overthrow the Orleans dynasty and the section of the bourgoisie that ruled during its reign. This aim was only attained on December 2, 1851. The immense possessions of the house of Orleans, the real basis of its influence, were now confiscated and what had been expected after the February Revolution came to pass after the December coup—prison, fight, dismissal, banishment, disarming, derision for the men who since 1830 had wearied France with their renown. But under Louis Philippe only a part of the commercial bourgeoisie

4. Within fifty years Europe will be republican or Cossack.

ruled. Its other sections formed a dynastic and a republican opposition or were altogether disfranchised. Only the parliamentary republic accepted all sections of the commercial bourgeoisie into its sphere of state. Under Louis Philippe, moreover, the commercial bourgeoisie excluded the landowning bourgeoisie. Only the parliamentary republic set them side by side, with equal rights, married the July monarchy to the Legitimist monarchy and fused two epochs of property rule into one. Under Louis Philippe, the favoured section of the bourgeoisie concealed its rule under cover of the crown; in the parliamentary republic the rule of the bourgeoisie, after it had united all its elements and extended its realm to be the realm of its class, revealed its uncovered head. Thus the revolution itself had first to create the form in which the rule of the bourgeoisie could obtain its broadest, most general and final expression, and therefore could also be overthrown without being able to arise again.

Only now was the judgment, passed in February, executed on the Orleanist bourgeoisie, that is, on the most vital section of the French bourgeoisie. Now it was defeated in its parliament, its bar, its commercial courts, its provincial representative bodies, its notaries, its university, its tribune and its tribunals, its press and its literature, its administrative revenues and its court fees, its army pay and its state incomes, in its mind and in its body. *Blanqui* had made the disbandment of the bourgeois guards the first demand on the revolution, and the bourgeois guards, who in February offered the revolution their hand in order to hinder its progress, vanished from the scene in December. The Pantheon itself becomes transformed into an ordinary church. With the final form of the bourgeois regime the spell is likewise broken which transfigured its initiators of the eighteenth century into saints.][5]

Why did not the Paris proletariat rise in revolt after December?

The overthrow of the bourgeoisie had as yet only been decreed; the decree had not been carried out. Any serious insurrection of the proletariat would at once have put fresh life into the bourgeoisie, would have reconciled it with the army and would have ensured a second June defeat for the workers.

On December 4 the proletariat was incited to fight by the bourgeois and the small shopkeepers. On the evening of that day several legions of the National Guard promised to appear, armed and uniformed, on the scene of action. For the bourgeois and the small shopkeepers had found out that in one of his decrees of December 2 Bonaparte abolished the secret ballot and enjoined them to record

---

5. The sentences in square brackets were omitted by Engels from the third   German edition because of censorship restrictions.

their "yes" or "no" in the official registers after their names. The resistance of December 4 intimidated Bonaparte. During the night he caused placards to be posted on all the street corners of Paris, announcing the restoration of the secret ballot. The bourgeois and the small shopkeepers believed that they had gained their end. Those who failed to appear next morning were the bourgeois and the small shopkeepers.

By a *coup de main* during the night of December 1 to 2, Bonaparte had robbed the Paris proletariat of its leaders, the barricade commanders. An army without officers, made disinclined to fight under the banner of the *Montagnards* by the memories of June 1848 and 1849 and May 1850, it left to its vanguard, the secret societies, the task of saving the insurrectionary honour of Paris, which the bourgeoisie had so spinelessly surrendered to the soldiers that, later on, Bonaparte could sneeringly give as his motive for disarming the National Guard—his fear that its arms would be turned against itself by anarchists!

"C'est le triomphe complet et définitif du socialisme!"[6]

Thus Guizot characterised December 2. But if the overthrow of the parliamentary republic contains within itself the germ of the triumph of the proletarian revolution, its immediate and obvious result was *the victory of Bonaparte over parliament, of the executive power over the legislative power, of force without phrases over the force of phrases*. In parliament the nation made its general will the law, that is, it made the law of the ruling class its general will. Before the executive power it renounces all will of its own and surrenders itself to the superior orders of something alien, of authority. The executive power, in contrast to the legislative power, expresses the heteronomy[7] of the nation, in contrast to its autonomy. France, therefore, seems to have escaped the despotism of a class only to fall back beneath the despotism of an individual and, what is more, beneath the authority of an individual without authority. The struggle seems to be settled in such a way that all classes, equally impotent and equally mute, fall on their knees before the club.

But the revolution is thorough-going. It is still in process of passing through purgatory. It does its work methodically. By December 2, 1851, it had completed one half of its preparatory work; it is now completing the other half. First it perfected the parliamentary power, in order to be able to overthrow it. Now that it has attained this, it perfects the *executive power*, reduces it to its purest expression, isolates it, sets it up against itself as the sole target, in order to

6. "This is the complete and final triumph of socialism."

7. *I.e.*, dependence on foreign authority.

concentrate all its forces of destruction against it. And when it has done this second half of its preliminary work, Europe will leap from her seat and exultantly exclaim: Well grubbed, old mole![8]

This executive power with its enormous bureaucratic and military organisation, with its artificial state machinery embracing wide strata, with a host of officials numbering half a million, besides an army of another half million, this appalling parasitic growth, which enmeshes the body of French society like a net and chokes all its pores, sprang up in the days of the absolute monarchy, with the decay of the feudal system, which it helped to hasten. The seigniorial privileges of the landowners and towns became transformed into so many attributes of the state power, the feudal dignitaries into paid officials and the motley pattern of conflicting mediæval plenary powers into the regulated plan of a state authority, whose work is divided and centralised as in a factory. The first French Revolution, with its task of breaking all local, territorial, urban and provincial independent powers in order to create the bourgeois unity of the nation, was bound to develop what the absolute monarchy had begun—centralisation, but at the same time the extent, the attributes and the agents of governmental authority. Napoleon perfected this state machinery. The Legitimist monarchy and the July monarchy added nothing but a greater division of labour, growing in the same measure that the division of labour within bourgeois society created new groups of interests, and, therefore, new material for state administration. Every *common* interest was straightaway severed from society, counter-posed to it as a higher, *general* interest, snatched from the self-activity of society's members and made an object of governmental activity from the bridge, the school-house and the communal property of a village community to the railways, the national wealth and the national university of France. The parliamentary republic, finally, in its struggle against the revolution, found itself compelled to strengthen, along with the repressive measures, the resources and centralisation of governmental power. All the revolutions perfected this machine instead of smashing it. The parties that contended in turn for domination regarded the possession of this huge state edifice as the principal spoils of the victor.

But under the absolute monarchy, during the first revolution, and under Napoleon, bureaucracy was only the means of preparing the class rule of the bourgeoisie. Under the Restoration, under Louis Philippe and under the parliamentary republic, it was the instrument of the ruling class, however much it strove for power of its own.

8. A reference to Shakespeare's *Hamlet*. The actual words are: "Old mole! Canst work i' the earth so fast? A worthy pioneer!"

Only under the second Bonaparte does the state seem to have made itself completely independent. As against bourgeois society, the state machine has consolidated its position so thoroughly that the chief of the Society of December 10 suffices for its head, an adventurer blown in from abroad, elevated on the shield by a drunken soldiery, which he has bought with liquor and sausages, and which he must continually ply with sausage anew. Hence the downcast despair, the feeling of most dreadful humiliation and degradation that oppresses the breast of France and makes her catch her breath. She feels herself dishonoured.

And yet the state power is not suspended in mid-air. Bonaparte represents a class, and the most numerous class of French society at that, the *small peasants*.

Just as the Bourbons were the dynasty of large landed property and just as the Orleans were the dynasty of money, so the Bonapartes are the dynasty of the peasants, that is, the mass of the French people. Not the Bonaparte who submitted to the bourgeois parliament, but the Bonaparte who dispersed it is the chosen of the peasantry. For three years the towns had succeeded in falsifying the meaning of the election of December 10 and in cheating the peasants out of the restoration of the Empire. The election of December 10, 1848, was consummated only by the *coup d'état* of December 2, 1851.

The small peasants form a vast mass, the members of which live in similar conditions, but without entering into manifold relations with one another. Their mode of production isolates them from one another, instead of bringing them into mutual intercourse. The isolation is increased by France's bad means of communication and by the poverty of the peasants. Their field of production, the small holding, admits of no division of labour in its cultivation, no application of science and, therefore, no multiplicity of development, no diversity of talents, no wealth of social relationships. Each individual peasant family is almost self-sufficient; it itself directly produces the major part of its consumption and thus acquires its means of life more through exchange with nature than in intercourse with society. The small holding, the peasant and his family; alongside them another small holding, another peasant and another family. A few score of these make up a village, and a few score of villages make up a Department. In this way, the great mass of the French nation is formed by simple addition of homologous magnitudes, much as potatoes in a sack form a sackful of potatoes. In so far as millions of families live under economic conditions of existence that divide their mode of life, their interests and their culture from those of the other classes, and put them in hostile contrast to the latter, they form a class. In so far as there is merely a local interconnection

among these small peasants, and the identity of their interests begets no unity, no national union and no political organisation, they
do not form a class. They are consequently incapable of enforcing
their class interest in their own name, whether through a parliament or through a convention. They cannot represent themselves,
they must be represented. Their representative must at the same
time appear as their master, as an authority over them, as an unlimited governmental power that protects them against the other
classes and sends them the rain and the sunshine from above. The
political influence of the small pesasants, therefore, finds its final expression in the executive power subordinating society to itself.

Historical tradition gave rise to the faith of the French peasants
in the miracle that a man named Napoleon would bring all the
glory back to them. And an individual was found who gives himself
out as the man because he bears the name of Napoleon, in consequence of the *Code Napoléon*,[9] which lays down that *la recherche
de la paternité est interdite*.[1] After being a vagabond for twenty
years and after a series of grotesque adventures, the legend finds fulfilment and the man becomes Emperor of the French. The fixed
idea of the nephew was realised, because it coincided with the fixed
idea of the most numerous class of the French people.

But, it may be objected, what about the peasant risings in half of
France, the hounding of masses of peasants by the army, the mass
incarceration and transportation of the peasants?

Since Louis XIV, France has experienced no similar persecution
of the peasants "on account of demagogic intrigues."

But let there be no misunderstanding. The Bonaparte dynasty
represents not the revolutionary, but the conservative peasant; not
the peasant that strikes out beyond the condition of his social existence, the small holding, but rather the peasant who wants to consolidate it; not the country folk who want to overthrow the old
order through their own energies linked up with the towns, but on
the contrary those who, in stupefied bondage to this old order, want
to see themselves with their small holding saved and favoured by
the ghost of the empire. It represents not the enlightenment, but
the superstition of the peasant; not his judgment, but his prejudice;
not his future, but his past; not his modern Cevennes,[2] but his
modern Vendée.[3]

The three years' rigorous rule of the parliamentary republic had
freed a part of the French peasants from the Napoleonic illusion

9. The French code of civil law, promulgated on March 31, 1804.
1. Inquiry into fatherhood is forbidden.
2. In Cevennes (Southern France, Lan-
guedoc), at the beginning of the eighteenth century, there was an uprising
of peasants under the slogans, "Down

with taxes! Freedom of faith!"
3. The Vendée peasantry was the most
politically backward at the time of the
first French bourgeois revolution; it
supported the royalist counter-
revolution.

and had revolutionised them, even if only superficially, but the bourgoisie violently repressed them, as often as they set themselves in motion. Under the parliamentary republic the modern and the traditional consciousness of the French peasant contended for mastery. The contest proceeded in the form of an incessant struggle between the schoolmasters and the priests. The bourgeoisie struck down the schoolmasters. For the first time, the peasants made efforts to behave independently in the face of governmental activity. This was shown in the continual conflict between the mayors and the prefects. The bourgeoisie deposed the mayors. Finally, during the period of the parliamentary republic, the peasants of different localities rose against their own offspring, the army. The bourgeoisie punished them with states of siege and distraints on their goods. And this same bourgeoisie now cries out about the stupidity of the masses, the vile multitude, that has betrayed it to Bonaparte. It has itself forcibly strengthened the imperialism[4] of the peasant class, it held fast to the conditions that form the birthplace of this peasant religion. The bourgeoisie, to be sure, is bound to fear the stupidity of the masses, as long as they remain conservative, and the insight of the masses, as soon as they become revolutionary.

In the risings after the *coup d'état*, a part of the French peasants protested, arms in hand, against their own vote of December 10, 1848. The school they had gone through since 1848 had sharpened their wits. But they had made themselves over to the underworld of history; history held them to their word, and the majority was still so bound that in precisely the reddest Departments the peasant population voted openly for Bonaparte.[5] In its view, the National Assembly had hindered his progress. He had now merely broken the fetters that the town had imposed on the will of the countryside. In some parts the peasants even entertained the grotesque notion of a Convention[6] side by side with a Napoleon.

After the first revolution had transformed the peasants from semi-villeins into freeholders, Napoleon confirmed and regulated the conditions on which they could exploit undisturbed the soil of France which had only just come into their possession and slake their youthful passion for property. But what is now causing the ruin of the French peasant is his dwarf holding itself, the division of the land, the form of property which Napoleon consolidated in

---

4. In the sense of imperial sentiments.
5. In the plebiscite that ratified the *coup d'état*, by voting Bonaparte back as President with a huge majority.
6. The Convention. The revolutionary representative assembly of the first French bourgeois revolution. It was convened in September 1792, after the overthrow of the monarchy and the establishment of the republic. After the expulsion of the Girondins (May 31–June 2, 1893), the majority of its members were Jacobins—the representatives of the revolutionary petty bourgeoisie.

France. It is precisely the material conditions which made the feudal peasant into a small peasant and Napoleon into an emperor. Two generations have sufficed to produce the inevitable result: progressive deterioration of agriculture, progressive indebtedness of the agriculturist. The "Napoleonic" form of property, which at the beginning of the nineteenth century was the condition for the liberation and enrichment of the French country folk, has developed in the course of this century as the law of their enslavement and pauperisation. And it is just this law which is the first of the *"idées napoléoniennes"* which the second Bonaparte has to uphold. If he still shares with the peasants the illusion that the cause of their ruin is to be sought not in this small holding property itself but outside it in the influence of secondary causes, then his experiments will burst like soap bubbles when they come into contact with the relations of production.

The economic development of this small holding property has turned the relation of the peasants to the remaining classes of society completely upside down. Under Napoleon, the fragmentation of the land in the countryside supplemented free competition and the beginning of big industry in the towns. [Even the favouring of the peasant class was in the interest of the new bourgeois order. This newly-created class was the many-sided extension of the bourgeois regime beyond the gates of the towns, its realisation on a national scale.][7] This class was the ubiquitous protest against the landed aristocracy which had just been overthrown.

[If it was favoured above all, it, above all, offered the point of attack for the restoration of the feudal lands.]

The roots that this small holding property struck in French soil deprived feudalism of all nutriment. Its landmarks formed the natural fortifications of the bourgeoisie against any *coup de main* on the part of its old overlords. But in the course of the nineteenth century the feudal lords were replaced by urban usurers; the feudal obligation that went with the land was replaced by the mortgage; aristocratic landed property was replaced by bourgeois capital. The small holding of the peasant is now only the pretext that allows the capitalist to draw profits, interest and rent from the soil, while leaving it to the tiller of the soil himself to see how he can extract his wages. The mortgage debt burdening the soil of France imposes on the French peasantry payment of an amount of interest equal to the annual interest on the entire British national debt. Small-holding property, in this enslavement by capital to which its development inevitably pushes forward, has transformed the mass of the French

7. The sentences in square brackets on this and the following pages were omitted by Engels from the third German edition because of censorship restrictions.

nation into troglodytes. Sixteen million peasants (including women and children) dwell in hovels, a large number of which have but one opening, others only two and the most favoured only three. And windows are to a house what the five senses are to the head. The bourgeois order, which at the beginning of the century set the state to stand guard over the newly arisen small holding and manured it with laurels, has become a vampire that sucks out its blood and marrow and throws them into the alchemistic cauldron of capital. The *Code Napoléon* is now nothing but a *codex* of distraints, forced sales and compulsory auctions. To the four million (including children, etc.) officially recognised paupers, vagabonds, criminals and prostitutes in France must be added five millions who hover on the margin of existence and either have their haunts in the countryside itself or, with their rags and their children, continually desert the countryside for the towns and the towns for the countryside. The interests of the peasants, therefore, are no longer, as under Napoleon, in accord with, but in opposition to the interests of the bourgeoisie, to capital. Hence the peasants find their natural ally and leader in the *urban proletariat*, whose task is the overthrow of the bourgeois order. But *strong and unlimited government* —and this is the second *"idée napoléonienne,"* which the second Napoleon has to carry out—is called upon to defend by force this "material" order. This "material order" also serves as the catchword in all Bonaparte's proclamations against the rebellious peasants.

Besides the mortgage which capital imposes on it, the small holding is burdened by *taxes*. Taxes are the source of life for the bureaucracy, the army, the priests and the court, in short, for the whole apparatus of the executive power. Strong government and heavy taxes are identical. By its very nature, small holding property forms a suitable basis for an all-powerful and innumerable bureaucracy. It creates a uniform level of relationships and persons over the whole surface of the land. Hence it also permits of uniform action from a supreme centre on all points of this uniform mass. It annihilates the aristocratic intermediate grades between the mass of the people and the state power. On all sides, therefore, it calls forth the direct interference of this state power and the intervention of its immediate organs. Finally, it produces an unemployed surplus population for which there is no place either on the land or in the towns, and which accordingly reaches out for state offices as a sort of respectable alms, and provokes the creation of state posts.

[Under Napoleon this numerous governmental personnel was not merely immediately productive, inasmuch as, through the means of compulsion of the state, it executed on behalf of the newly arisen peasantry, in the form of public works, etc., what the bourgeoisie could not yet accomplish by way of private industry.

State taxes were a necessary means of compulsion to maintain exchange between town and country. Otherwise, the owner of a dwarf holding would in his rustic self-sufficiency have severed his connection with the townsman, as in Norway and a part of Switzerland.]

By the new markets which he opened at the point of the bayonet, and by the plundering of the Continent, Napoleon repaid the compulsory taxes with interest. These taxes were a spur to the industry of the peasant, whereas now they rob his industry of its last sources of aid and complete his powerlessness to resist pauperism. And an enormous bureaucracy, well-dressed and well-fed, is the *"idée napoléonienne"* which is most congenial of all to the second Bonaparte. How could it be otherwise, seeing that alongside the actual classes of society, he is forced to create an artificial caste, for which the maintenance of his regime becomes a bread-and-butter question? Accordingly, one of his first financial operations was the raising of officials' salaries to their old level again and the creation of new sinecures.

Another *"idée napoléonienne"* is the domination of the *priests* as a means of government. But if in its accord with society, in its dependence on natural forces and its subjection to the authority which protected it from above, the small holding that had newly come into being was naturally religious, the small holding that is ruined by debts, at odds with society and authority, and driven beyond its own limitations, naturally becomes irreligious. Heaven was quite a pleasing accessory to the narrow strip of land just won, more particularly as it makes the weather; it becomes an insult as soon as it is thrust forward as substitute for the small holding. The priest then appears as only the anointed bloodhound of the earthly police —another *"idée napoléonienne*[—whose mission under the second Bonaparte is to keep watch over, not the enemies of the peasant regime in the towns, as under Napoleon, but the enemies of Bonaparte in the country]. On the next occasion, the expedition against Rome will take place in France itself, but in a sense opposite to that of M. de Montalembert.[8]

Finally, the culminating point of the *"idées napoléoniennes"* is the preponderance of the *army*. The army was the *point d'honneur* of the peasants, it was they themselves transformed into heroes, defending their new possessions against the outer world, glorifying their recently won nationality, plundering and revolutionising the world. The uniform was their own state dress; war was their poetry; the small holding, extended and rounded off in imagination, was

8. Montalembert, the head of the militant Catholic Party, spoke, during the discussions on the repeal of universal suffrage, on the necessity of undertaking a Roman expedition "within" France—meaning support of the Roman Pope and the Catholic clergy. Marx, on the other hand, is speaking of an expedition against Rome in the sense of a struggle *against* the clergy.

their fatherland, and patriotism the ideal form of the property sense. But the enemies against whom the French peasant has now to defend his property are not the Cossacks; they are the *hussiers*[9] and the tax collectors. The small holding lies no longer in the so-called fatherland, but in the register of mortgages. The army itself is no longer the flower of the peasant youth; it is the swamp-flower of the peasant *lumpenproletariat*. It consists in large measure of *remplaçants*, of substitutes, just as the second Bonaparte is himself only a *remplaçant*, the substitute for Napoleon. It now performs its deeds of valour by hounding the peasants in masses like chamois, by discharging *gendarme* duties, and when the internal contradictions of his system chase the chief of the Society of December 10 over the French border, his army, after some acts of brigandage, will reap, not laurels, but thrashings.

One sees: *all* idées napoléoniennes *are the ideas of the undeveloped small holding in the freshness of its youth*: for the small holding that has outlived its day they are an absurdity. They are only the hallucinations of its death struggle, words that are reduced to phrases, spirits reduced to ghosts. But the parody of imperialism was necessary to free the mass of the French nation from the weight of tradition and to work out in pure form the opposition between the state power and society. With the progressive undermining of this small holding property, the state structure erected upon it collapses. The state centralisation that modern society requires arises only on the ruins of the military-bureaucratic governmental machinery which was forged in opposition to feudalism.

[The demolition of the state machine will not endanger centralisation. Bureaucracy is only the low and brutal form of a centralisation that is still afflicted with its opposite, with feudalism. On coming to despair of the Napoleonic Restoration, the French peasant parts with his belief in his small holding, the entire state edifice erected on this small holding falls to the ground and the *proletarian revolution* obtains *that chorus without which its solo song in all peasant nations becomes a swan song*.]

French peasant relationships provide us with the answer to the riddle of the general elections of December 20 and 21, which bore the second Napoleon up Mount Sinai, not to receive laws, but to give them.

[To be sure, on those fateful days the French nation committed a deadly sin against democracy, which is on its knees and prays daily: Holy universal suffrage, intercede for us! Naturally, the believers in universal suffrage do not want to renounce a miraculous power that has accomplished such great things in regard to them-

9. Bailiffs.

selves, which has transformed Bonaparte II into a Napoleon, a Saul into a Paul and a Simon into a Peter. The spirit of the people speaks to them through the ballot-box as the god of the prophet Ezekiel spoke to the marrowless bones: *"Haec dicit dominus deus ossibus suis: Ecce, ego intromittam in vos spiritum et vivetis."* "Thus saith the Lord God unto these bones: Behold, I will cause breath to enter into you, and ye shall live."]

Manifestly, the bourgeoisie had now no choice but to elect Bonaparte. [Despotism or anarchy. Naturally, it voted for despotism.] When the puritans at the Council of Constance complained of the dissolute lives of the popes and wailed about the necessity of moral reform, Cardinal Pierre d'Ailly thundered to them: "Only the devil in person can now save the Catholic Church, and you ask for angels." In like manner, after the *coup d'état*, the French bourgeoisie cried: Only the chief of the Society of December 10 can now save bourgeois society! Only theft can now save property; only perjury, religion; only bastardy, the family; only disorder, order!,

As the executive authority which has made itself an independent power, Bonaparte feels it to be his mission to safeguard "civil order." But the strength of this civil order lies in the middle class. He looks on himself, therefore, as the representative of the middle class and issues decrees in this sense. Nevertheless, he is somebody solely due to the fact that he has broken the political power of this middle class and daily breaks it anew. Consequently, he looks on himself as the adversary of the political and literary power of the middle class. But by protecting its material power, he generates its political power anew. The cause must accordingly be kept alive; but the effect, where it manifests itself, must be done away with. But this cannot pass off without slight confusions of cause and effect, since in their interaction both lose their distinguishing features. New decrees, that obliterate the border-line. At the same time, Bonaparte looks on himself as the representative of the peasants, and of the people in general, against the bourgeoisie, who wants to make the lower classes of the people happy within the frame of bourgeois society. New decrees, that cheat the "true socialists" of their statecraft in advance. But, above all, Bonaparte looks on himself as the chief of the Society of December 10, as the representative of the *lumpenproletariat* to which he himself, his *entourage*, his government and his army belong, and for which the prime consideration is to benefit itself and draw California lottery prizes from the state treasury. And he makes good his position as chief of the Society of December 10 with decrees, without decrees and despite decrees.

This contradictory task of the man explains the contradictions of his government, the confused groping hither and thither which seeks now to win, now to humiliate first one class and then another and arrays all of them uniformly against him, whose practical uncertainty forms a highly comical contrast to the imperious categorical style of the government decrees, a style which is copied obsequiously from the Uncle.

Industry and trade, hence the business affairs of the middle class, are to prosper in hot-house fashion under the strong government. Granting of innumerable railway concessions. But the Bonapartist *lumpenproletariat* is to enrich itself. Trickery with the railway concessions on the *Bourse* by those previously initiated. But no capital is forthcoming for the railways. Obligation of the Bank to make advances on railway shares. But, at the same time, the Bank is to be exploited for personal ends and therefore must be cajoled. Release of the Bank from the obligation to publish its report weekly. Leonine agreement[1] of the Bank with the government. The people are to be given employment. Inauguration of public works. But the public works increase the obligations of the people in respect of taxes. Therefore, reduction of the taxes by an onslaught on the *rentiers*,[2] by conversion of the five per cent bonds to four-and-a-half per cent. But, once more, the middle class must receive a sop. Therefore doubling of the wine tax for the people, who buy it *en détail*,[3] and halving of the wine tax for the middle class, who drink it *en gros*.[4] Dissolution of the actual workers' associations, but promises of miracles of association in the future. The peasants are to be helped. Mortgage banks, that expedite their getting into debt and accelerate the concentration of property. But these banks are to be used to make money out of the confiscated estates of the house of Orleans. No capitalist wants to agree to this condition, which is not in the decrees, and the mortgage bank remains a mere decree, etc., etc.

Bonaparte would like to appear as the patriarchal benefactor of all classes. But he cannot give to one class without taking from another. Just as at the time of the Fronde it was said of the Duke of Guise that he was the most *obligeant* man in France because he had turned all his possessions into his partisans' obligations to him, so Bonaparte would fain be the most *obligeant* man in France and turn all the property, all the labour of France into a personal obligation to himself. He would like to steal the whole of France in order to be able to make a present of her to France or, rather, in order to be able to buy France anew with French money, for as the chief of the Society of December 10 he must needs buy what ought to belong to him. And all the state institutions, the Senate, the Council

1. Meaning an agreement by which one gets the lion's share.
2. Persons drawing income from bonds and investments.
3. Retail.
4. Wholesale.

of State, the legislative body, the Legion of Honour, the soldiers'
medals, the wash-houses, the public works, the railways, the *état
major*[5] of the National Guard to the exclusion of privates, and the
confiscated estates of the house of Orleans—all become parts of the
institution of purchase. Every place in the army and in the government machine becomes a means for purchase. But the most important feature of this process, whereby France is taken in order to give
to her, is the percentages that find their way to the head and the
members of the Society of December 10 during the turnover. The
witticism with which Countess L., the mistress of M. de Morny,
characterised the confiscation of the Orleans estates: "*C'est le pre-
mier vol de l'aigle,*"[6] is applicable to every flight of the *eagle*,
which is more like a *raven*. He himself and his adherents call out to
one another daily like that Italian Carthusian admonishing the
miser who, with boastful display, counted up the goods on which
he could yet live for years to come: "*Tu fai conto sopra i beni,
bisogna prima far il conto sopra gli anni.*"[7] Lest they make a mistake in the years, they count the minutes. At the court, in the ministries, at the head of the administration and the army, a crowd of
fellows pushes forward, of the best of whom it can be said that no
one knows whence he comes, a noisy, disreputable, rapacious
Bohéme that dresses itself in gallooned coats with the same caricature of dignity as the high dignitaries of Soulouque. One can
visualise clearly this upper stratum of the Society of December 10,
if one reflects that *Veron-Crevel*[8] is its preacher of morals and
Granier de Cassagnac its thinker. When Guizot, at the time of his
ministry, utilised this Granier on a hole-and-corner newspaper
against the dynastic opposition, he used to boast of him with the
quip: "*C'est le roi des drôles,*" "he is the king of buffoons." One
would do wrong to recall the Regency of Louis XV in connection
with Louis Bonaparte's court and clique. For "often already, France
has experienced a government of mistresses; but never before, a
government of *hommes entretenus.*"[9]

Driven by the contradictory demands of his situation, and, at the
same time, like a conjurer under the necessity of keeping the public
gaze fixed on himself, as Napoleon's subsitute, by constant surprises,
hence of executing a *coup d'état en miniature* every day, Bonaparte throws the entire bourgeois economy into confusion, lays
hands on everything that seemed inviolable to the revolution of

5. General Staff.
6. "It is the first flight (theft) of the
eagle." *Vol* means flight and theft.
7. Thou countest thy goods, thou
shouldst first count thy years.
8. In his work, *La Cousine Bette,* Bal-
zac delineates the thoroughly dissolute
Parisian philistine in the character of
Crevel, which he draws after the model
of Dr. Veron, the proprietor of the
Constitutionnel. [*Marx*]
9. Kept men. The words quoted are the
words of Madame Girardin. [*Marx*]

1848, makes some tolerant of revolution, others desirous of revolution, and produces actual anarchy in the name of order, while at the same time he divests the whole state machine of its halo, profanes it and makes it at once loathsome and ridiculous. The cult of the Holy Coat of Treves[1] he duplicates at Paris in the cult of the Napoleonic imperial mantle. But if the imperial mantle finally falls on the shoulders of Louis Bonaparte, the iron statue of Napoleon will crash from the top of the Vendôme column.

1. One of the "sacred" relics ("the vestment of the Lord"), exhibited in the Treves cathedral in 1844 for public worship.

The Civil War in France

KARL MARX

This, the last of Marx's great political pamphlets, was composed during the Paris Revolution of September, 1870–May, 1871, and read by Marx to the General Council of the International Working Men's Association on May 30, 1871, only two days after the last resistance of the Paris Commune's fighters was overcome. In addition to providing an immensely vivid and trenchant account of the Commune and its fate, the Address was a major contribution to Marxist theory of the state and of the revolutionary process itself from the political point of view. It treated the Paris Commune as the short-lived but momentous first example in history of a "dictatorship of the proletariat." In preparing the document for publication as a separate pamphlet on the twentieth anniversary of the Paris Commune in 1891, Engels included in the publication two shorter addresses by Marx on the Franco-Prussian War, in which the Paris Revolution had its origin.

Introduction

I did not anticipate that I would be asked to prepare a new edition of the Address of the General Council of the International on *The Civil War in France,* and to write an introduction to it. Therefore I can only touch briefly here on the most important points.

I am prefacing the longer work mentioned above by the two shorter Addresses of the General Council on the Franco-Prussian War. In the first place, because the second of these, which itself cannot be fully understood in full without the first, is referred to in *The Civil War.* But also because these two Addresses, likewise drafted by Marx, are, no less than *The Civil War,* outstanding examples of the author's remarkable gift, first proved in *The Eighteenth Brumaire of Louis Bonaparte,* for grasping clearly the character, the import and the necessary consequences of great historical events, at a time when these events are still in progress before our eyes or have only just taken place. And, finally, because today we in Germany are still having to endure the consequences which Marx predicted would follow from these events.

Has that which was declared in the first Address not come to pass: that if Germany's defensive war against Louis Bonaparte degenerated into a war of conquest against the French people, all the misfortunes which befell Germany after the so-called wars of liberation[1] would revive again with renewed intensity? Have we not had a further twenty years of Bismarck's rule, the Exceptional Law and Socialist-baiting taking the place of the prosecutions of demagogues, with the same arbitrary action of the police and with literally the same staggering interpretations of the law?

And has not the prediction been proved to the letter, that the annexation of Alsace-Lorraine would "force France into the arms of Russia," and that after this annexation Germany must either become the avowed servant of Russia, or must, after some short respite, arm for a new war, and, moreover, "a race war against the combined Slavonic and Roman races"? Has not the annexation of the French provinces driven France into the arms of Russia? Has not Bismarck for fully twenty years vainly wooed the favour of the tsar, wooed it with services even more lowly than those which little Prussia, before it became the "first Power in Europe," was wont to lay at Holy Russia's feet? And is there not every day still hanging over our heads the Damocles' sword of war, on the first day of which all the chartered covenants of princes will be scattered like chaff; a war of which nothing is certain but the absolute uncertainty of its outcome; a race war which will subject the whole of Europe to devastation by fifteen or twenty million armed men, and which is not raging already only because even the strongest of the great military states shrinks before the absolute incalculability of its final result?

All the more is it our duty to make again accessible to the German workers these brilliant proofs, now half-forgotten, of the far-sightedness of international working-class policy in 1870.

What is true of these two Addresses is also true of *The Civil War in France*. On May 28, the last fighters of the Commune succumbed to superior forces on the slopes of Belleville; and only two days later, on May 30, Marx read to the General Council the work in which the historical significance of the Paris Commune is delineated in short, powerful strokes, but with such trenchancy, and above all such truth as has never again been attained in all the mass of literature on this subject.

Thanks to the economic and political development of France since 1789, Paris has been placed for the last fifty years in such a position that no revolution could break out there without assuming a proletarian character, that is to say, without the proletariat, which had bought victory with its blood, advancing its own

1. The wars against Napoleon I in 1813–15.

demands after victory. These demands were more or less unclear and even confused, corresponding to the state of development reached by the workers of Paris at the particular period, but in the last resort they all amounted to the abolition of the class antagonism between capitalists and workers. It is true that no one knew how this was to be brought about. But the demand itself, however indefinitely it still was couched, contained a threat to the existing order of society; the workers who put it forward were still armed; therefore, the disarming of the workers was the first commandment for the bourgeois, who were at the helm of the state. Hence, after every revolution won by the workers, a new struggle, ending with the defeat of the workers.

This happened for the first time in 1848. The liberal bourgeois of the parliamentary opposition held banquets for securing a reform of the franchise, which was to ensure supremacy for their party. Forced more and more, in their struggle with the government, to appeal to the people, they had gradually to yield precedence to the radical and republican strata of the bourgeoisie and petty bourgeoisie. But behind these stood the revolutionary workers, and since 1830 these had acquired far more political independence than the bourgeois, and even the republicans, suspected. At the moment of the crisis between the government and the opposition, the workers began street-fighting; Louis Philippe vanished, and with him the franchise reform; and in its place arose the republic, and indeed one which the victorious workers themselves designated as a "social" republic. No one, however, was clear as to what this social republic was to imply; not even the workers themselves. But they now had arms and were a power in the state. Therefore, as soon as the bourgeois republicans in control felt something like firm ground under their feet, their first aim was to disarm the workers. This took place by driving them into the insurrection of June 1848 by direct breach of faith, by open defiance and the attempt to banish the unemployed to a distant province. The government had taken care to have an overwhelming superiority of force. After five days' heroic struggle, the workers were defeated. And then followed a blood-bath among the defenceless prisoners, the like of which has not been seen since the days of the civil wars which ushered in the downfall of the Roman republic. It was the first time that the bourgeoisie showed to what insane cruelties of revenge it will be goaded the moment the proletariat dares to take its stand against the bourgeoisie as a separate class, with its own interests and demands. And yet 1848 was only child's play compared with the frenzy of the bourgeoisie in 1871.

Punishment followed hard at heel. If the proletariat was not yet able to rule France, the bourgeoisie could no longer do so. At least

not at that period, when the greater part of it was still monarchi-
cally inclined, and it was divided into three dynastic parties and a
fourth, republican party. It internal dissensions allowed the adventurer Louis Bonaparte to take possession of all the commanding
points—army, police, administrative machinery—and, on December
2, 1851, to explode the last stronghold of the bourgeoisie, the
National Assembly. The Second Empire began—the exploitation of
France by a gang of political and financial adventurers, but at the
same time also an industrial development such as had never been
possible under the narrow-minded and timorous system of Louis
Philippe, with the exclusive domination of only a small section of
the big bourgeoisie. Louis Bonaparte took the political power from
the capitalists under the pretext of protecting them, the bourgeois,
from the workers, and on the other hand the workers from them;
but in return his rule encouraged speculation and industrial activity
—in a word, the upsurgence and enrichment of the whole bourgeoisie to an extent hitherto unknown. To an even greater extent, it is
true, corruption and mass thievery developed, clustering around the
imperial court, and drawing their heavy percentages from this
enrichment.

But the Second Empire was the appeal to French chauvinism,
was the demand for the restoration of the frontiers of the First
Empire, which had been lost in 1814, or at least those of the First
Republic. A French empire within the frontiers of the old monarchy and, in fact, within the even more amputated frontiers of
1815—such a thing was impossible for any length of time. Hence
the necessity for occasional wars and extensions of frontiers. But no
extension of frontiers was so dazzling to the imagination of the
French chauvinists as the extension to the German left bank of the
Rhine. One square mile on the Rhine was more to them than ten
in the Alps or anywhere else. Given the Second Empire, the
demand for the restoration of the left bank of the Rhine, either all
at once or piecemeal, was merely a question of time. The time came
with the Austro-Prussian War of 1866; cheated of the anticipated
"territorial compensation" by Bismarck and by his own over-cun-
ning, hesitant policy, there was now nothing left for Napoleon but
war, which broke out in 1870 and drove him first to Sedan, and
thence to Wilhelmshöhe.[2]

The necessary consequence was the Paris Revolution of September 4, 1870. The empire collapsed like a house of cards, and the
republic was again proclaimed. But the enemy was standing at the
gates; the armies of the empire were either hopelessly encircled at

2. At Sedan, on September 2, 1870, the
French army was defeated and captured together with the emperor. He was
detained at Wilhelmshöhe, a Prussian
castle near Kassel.

Metz or held captive in Germany. In this emergency the people allowed the Paris deputies to the former legislative body to constitute themselves into a "Government of National Defence." This was the more readily conceded, since, for the purposes of defence, all Parisians capable of bearing arms had enrolled in the National Guard and were armed, so that now the workers constituted a great majority. But very soon the antagonism between the almost completely bourgeois government and the armed proletariat broke into open conflict. On October 31, workers' battalions stormed the town hall and captured part of the membership of the government. Treachery, the government's direct breach of its undertakings, and the intervention of some petty-bourgeois battalions set them free again, and in order not to occasion the outbreak of civil war inside a city besieged by a foreign military power, the former government was left in office.

At last, on January 28, 1871, starved Paris capitulated. But with honours unprecedented in the history of war. The forts were surrendered, the city wall stripped of guns, the weapons of the regiments of the line and of the Mobile Guard were handed over, and they themselves considered prisoners of war. But the National Guard kept its weapons and guns, and only entered into an armistice with the victors. And these did not dare enter Paris in triumph. They only dared to occupy a tiny corner of Paris, which, into the bargain, consisted partly of public parks, and even this they only occupied for a few days! And during this time they, who had maintained their encirclement of Paris for 131 days, were themselves encircled by the armed workers of Paris, who kept a sharp watch that no "Prussian" should overstep the narrow bounds of the corner ceded to the foreign conqueror. Such was the respect which the Paris workers inspired in the army before which all the armies of the empire had laid down their arms; and the Prussian *Junkers*, who had come to take revenge at the home of the revolution, were compelled to stand by respectfully, and salute precisely this armed revolution!

During the war the Paris workers had confined themselves to demanding the vigorous prosecution of the fight. But now, when peace had come after the capitulation of Paris, now Thiers, the new supreme head of the government, was compelled to realise that the rule of the propertied classes—big landowners and capitalists—was in constant danger so long as the workers of Paris had arms in their hands. His first action was an attempt to disarm them. On March 18, he sent troops of the line with orders to rob the National Guard of the artillery belonging to it, which had been constructed during the siege of Paris and had been paid for by public subscription. The attempt failed; Paris mobilised as one man for resistance, and war between Paris and the French Government sitting at Versailles was declared. On March 26 the Paris Commune was elected and on March 28 it was proclaimed. The Central Committee of the National Guard, which up to then had carried on the government, handed in its resignation to the Commune after it had first decreed the abolition of the scandalous Paris "Morality Police." On March 30 the Commune abolished conscription and the standing army, and declared the sole armed force to be the National Guard, in which all citizens capable of bearing arms were to be enrolled. It remitted all payments of rent for dwelling houses from October 1870 until April, the amounts already paid to be booked as future rent payments, and stopped all sales of articles pledged in the municipal loan office. On the same day the foreigners elected to the Commune were confirmed in office, because "the flag of the Commune is the flag of the World Republic." On April 1 it was decided that the highest salary to be received by any employee of the Commune, and therefore also by its members themselves, was not to exceed 6,000 francs (4,800 marks). On the following day the Commune decreed the separation of the church from the state, and the abolition of all state payments for religious purposes as well as the transformation of all church property into national property; as a result of which, on April 8, the exclusion from the schools of all religious symbols, pictures, dogmas, prayers—in a word, "of all that belongs to the sphere of the individual's conscience"—was ordered and gradually put into effect. On the 5th, in reply to the shooting, day after day, of captured Commune fighters by the Versailles troops, a decree was issued for the imprisonment of hostages, but it was never carried into execution. On the 6th, the guillotine was brought out by the 137th battalion of the National Guard, and publicly burnt, amid great popular rejoicing. On the 12th, the Commune decided that the Victory Column on the *Place Vendôme*, which had been cast from captured guns by Napoleon after the war of 1809, should be demolished as a symbol of chauvinism and incitement to national hatred. This was carried out on May 16. On April 16 it ordered a statistical tabulation of factories which had been closed down by the manufacturers, and the working out of plans for the operation of these factories by the workers formerly employed in them, who were to be organised in co-operative societies, and also plans for the organisation of these co-operatives in one great union. On the 20th it abolished night work for bakers, and also the employment offices, which since the Second Empire had been run as a monopoly by creatures appointed by the police—labour exploiters of the first rank; these offices were transferred to the mayoralties of the twenty *arrondissements* of Paris. On April 30 it ordered the closing of the pawnshops, on the ground that they were a private exploitation of the workers, and were in contradiction with the right of the workers to their instruments of labour and to credit. On May 5 it ordered the razing of the Chapel of Atonement, which had been built in expiation of the execution of Louis XVI.

Thus from March 18 onwards the class character of the Paris movement, which had previously been pushed into the background by the fight against the foreign invaders, emerged sharply and clearly. As almost only workers, or recognised representatives of the workers, sat in the Commune, its decisions bore a decidedly proletarian character. Either these decisions decreed reforms which the republican bourgeoisie had failed to pass solely out of cowardice, but which proveded a necessary basis for the free activity of the working class—such as the realisation of the principle that *in relation to the state,* religion is a purely private matter—or the Commune promulgated decrees which were in the direct interest of the working class and in part cut deeply into the old order of society. In a beleaguered city, however, it was possible to make at most a start in the realisation of all this. And from the beginning of May onwards all their energies were taken up by the fight against the armies assembled by the Versailles government in ever-growing numbers.

On April 7 the Versailles troops had captured the Seine crossing at Neuilly, on the western front of Paris; on the other hand, in an attack on the southern front on the 11th they were repulsed with heavy losses by General Eudes. Paris was continually bombarded and, moreover, by the very people who had stigmatised as a sacrilege the bombardment of the same city by the Prussians. These same people now begged the Prussian government for the hasty return of the French soldiers taken prisoner at Sedan and Metz, in order that they might recapture Paris for them. From the beginning of May the gradual arrival of these troops gave the Versailles forces a decided superiority. This already became evident when, on April 23, Thiers broke off the negotiations for the exchange, proposed by the Commune, of the Archbishop of Paris and a whole number of other priests held as hostages in Paris, for only one man, Blanqui, who had twice been elected to the Commune but was a prisoner in Clairvaux. And even more from the changed language of Thiers; previously procrastinating and equivocal, he now suddenly became insolent, threatening, brutal. The Versailles forces took the redoubt of Moulin Saquet on the southern front, on May 3; on the 9th, Fort Issy, which had been completely reduced to ruins by gunfire; on the 14th, Fort Vanves. On the western front they advanced gradually, capturing the numerous villages and buildings which extended up to the city wall, until they reached the main defences; on the 21st, thanks to treachery and the carelessness of the National Guards stationed there, they succeeded in forcing their way into the city. The Prussians, who held the northern and eastern forts, allowed the Versailles troops to advance across the land north of the city, which was forbidden ground to them under the armistice, and thus to march forward, attacking on a wide front, which the Parisians naturally thought covered by the armistice, and therefore held only weakly. As a result of this, only a weak resistance was put up in the western half of Paris, in the luxury city proper; it grew stronger and more tenacious the nearer the incoming troops approached the eastern half, the working-class city proper. It was only after eight days' fighting that the last defenders of the Commune succumbed on the heights of Belleville and Menilmontant; and then the massacre of defenceless men, women and children, which had been raging all through the week on an increasing scale, reached its zenith. The breechloaders could no longer kill fast enough; the vanquished were shot down in hundreds by *mitrailleuse*[3] fire. The "Wall of the Federals" at the Père Lachaise cemetery, where the final mass murder was consummated, is still standing today, a mute but eloquent testimony to the frenzy of which the ruling class is capable as soon as the working class dares to stand up for its rights. Then, when the slaughter of them all proved to be impossible, came the mass arrests, the shooting of victims arbitrarily selected from the prisoners' ranks, and the removal of the rest to great camps where they awaited trial by courts-martial. The Prussian troops surrounding the northeastern half of Paris had orders not to allow any fugitives to pass; but the officers often shut their eyes when the soldiers paid more obedience to the dictates of humanity than to those of the Supreme Command; particular honour is due to the Saxon army corps, which behaved very humanely and let through many who were obviously fighters for the Commune.

If today, after twenty years, we look back at the activity and historical significance of the Paris Commune of 1871, we shall find it necessary to make a few additions to the account given in *The Civil War in France*.

The members of the Commune were divided into a majority, the Blanquists, who had also been predominant in the Central Committee of the National Guard; and a minority, members of the International Working Men's Association, chiefly consisting of adherents of the Proudhon school of socialism. The great majority of the Blanquists were at that time Socialists only by revolutionary, proletarian instinct; only a few had attained greater clarity on principles, through Vaillant, who was familiar with German scientific social-

3. *Mitrailleuse*: Machine-gun. *Wall of*   Wall of the Communards.
the Federals: Now usually called the

ism. It is therefore comprehensible that in the economic sphere much was left undone which, according to our view today, the Commune ought to have done. The hardest thing to understand is certainly the holy awe with which they remained standing respectfully outside the gates of the Bank of France. This was also a serious political mistake. The bank in the hands of the Commune—this would have been worth more than ten thousand hostages. It would have meant the pressure of the whole of the French bourgeoisie on the Versailles government in favour of peace with the Commune. But what is still more wonderful is the correctness of much that nevertheless was done by the Commune, composed as it was of Blanquists and Proudhonists. Naturally, the Proudhonists were chiefly responsible for the economic decrees of the Commune, both for their praiseworthy and their unpraiseworthy aspects; as the Blanquists were for its political commissions and omissions. And in both cases the irony of history willed—as is usual when doctrinaires come to the helm—that both did the opposite of what the doctrines of their school prescribed.

Proudhon, the Socialist of the small peasant and mastercraftsman, regarded association with positive hatred. He said of it that there was more bad than good in it; that it was by nature sterile, even harmful, because it was a fetter on the freedom of the worker; that it was a pure dogma, unproductive and burdensome, in conflict as much with the freedom of the worker as with economy of labour; that its disadvantages multiplied more swiftly than its advantages; that, as compared with it, competition, division of labour and private property were economic forces. Only in the exceptional cases —as Proudhon called them—of large-scale industry and large establishments, such as railways, was the association of workers in place. (See *General Idea of the Revolution, 3rd sketch.*)

By 1871, large-scale industry had already so much ceased to be an exceptional case even in Paris, the centre of artistic handicrafts, that by far the most important decree of the Commune instituted an organisation of large-scale industry and even of manufacture which was not only to be based on the association of the workers in each factory, but also to combine all these associations in one great union; in short, an organisation which, as Marx quite rightly says in *The Civil War*, must necessarily have led in the end to communism, that is to say, the direct opposite of the Proudhon doctrine. And, therefore, the Commune was the grave of the Proudhon school of socialism. Today this school has vanished from French working-class circles; here, among the Possibilists[4] no less than among the "Marxists," Marx's theory now rules unchallenged. Only among the "radical" bourgeoisie are there still Proudhonists.

4. *Possibilism*: The opportunist trend in the French labour movement at the end of the nineteenth century.

The Blanquists fared no better. Brought up in the school of conspiracy, and held together by the strict discipline which went with it, they started out from the viewpoint that a relatively small number of resolute, well-organised men would be able, at a given favourable moment, not only to seize the helm of state, but also by a display of great, ruthless energy, to maintain power until they succeeded in sweeping the mass of the people into the revolution and ranging them round the small band of leaders. This involved, above all, the strictest, dictatorial centralisation of all power in the hands of the new revolutionary government. And what did the Commune, with its majority of these same Blanquists, actually do? In all its proclamations to the French in the provinces, it appealed to them to form a free federation of all French Communes with Paris, a national organisation which for the first time was really to be created by the nation itself. It was precisely the oppressing power of the former centralised government, army, political police, bureaucracy, which Napoleon had created in 1798 and which since then had been taken over by every new government as a welcome instrument and used against its opponents—it was precisely this power which was to fall everywhere, just as it had already fallen in Paris.

From the very outset the Commune was compelled to recognise that the working class, once come to power, could not go on managing with the old state machine; that in order not to lose again its only just conquered supremacy, this working class must, on the one hand, do away with all the old repressive machinery previously used against it itself, and, on the other, safeguard itself against its own deputies and officials, by declaring them all, without exception, subject to recall at any moment. What had been the characteristic attribute of the former state? Society had created its own organs to look after its common interests, originally through simple division of labour. But these organs, at whose head was the state power, had in the course of time, in pursuance of their own special interests, transformed themselves from the servants of society into the masters of society. This can be seen, for example, not only in the hereditary monarchy, but equally so in the democratic republic. Nowhere do "politicians" form a more separate and powerful section of the nation than precisely in North America. "There, each of the two major parties which alternately succeed each other in power is itself in turn controlled by people who make a business of politics, who speculate on seats in the legislative assemblies of the Union as well as of the separate states, or who make a living by carrying on agitation for their party and on its victory are rewarded with positions. It is well known how the Americans have been trying for thirty years to shake off this yoke, which has become intolerable, and how in spite of it all they continue to sink ever deeper in this swamp of corruption. It is precisely in America that we see best how there takes place this process of the state power making itself independent in relation to society, whose mere instrument it was originally intended to be. Here there exists no dynasty, no nobility, no standing army, beyond the few men keeping watch on the Indians, no bureaucracy with permanent posts or the right to pensions. And nevertheless we find here two great gangs of political speculators, who alternately take possession of the state power and exploit it by the most corrupt means and for the most corrupt ends—and the nation is powerless against these two great cartels of politicians, who are ostensibly its servants, but in reality dominate and plunder it.

Against this transformation of the state and the organs of the state from servants of society into masters of society—an inevitable transformation in all previous states—the Commune made use of two infallible means. In the first place, it filled all posts—administrative, judicial and educational—by election on the basis of universal suffrage of all concerned, subject to the right of recall at any time by the same electors. And, in the second place, all officials, high or low, were paid only the wages received by other workers. The highest salary paid by the Commune to anyone was 6,000 francs. In this way an effective barrier to place-hunting and careerism was set up, even apart from the binding mandates to delegates to representative bodies which were added besides.

This shattering [Sprengung] of the former state power and its replacement by a new and truly democratic one is described in detail in the third section of The Civil War. But it was necessary to dwell briefly here once more on some of its features, because in Germany particularly the superstitious belief in the state has been carried over from philosophy into the general consciousness of the bourgeoisie and even of many workers. According to the philosophical conception, the state is the "realisation of the idea," or the Kingdom of God on earth, translated into philosophical terms, the sphere in which eternal truth and justice is or should be realised. And from this follows a superstitious reverence for the state and everything connected with it, which takes root the more readily since people are accustomed from childhood to imagine that the affairs and interests common to the whole of society could not be looked after otherwise than as they have been looked after in the past, that is, through the state and its lucratively positioned officials. And people think they have taken quite an extraordinarily bold step forward when they have rid themselves of belief in hereditary monarchy and swear by the democratic republic. In reality, however, the state is nothing but a machine for the oppression of one class by another, and indeed in the democratic republic no less than in the monarchy; and at best an evil inherited by the proletariat after its victorious struggle for class supremacy, whose worst sides the victorious proletariat, just like the Commune, cannot avoid having to lop off at once as much as possible until such time as a generation reared in new, free social conditions is able to throw the entire lumber of the state on the scrap heap.

Of late, the Social-Democratic philistine has once more been filled with wholesome terror at the words: Dictatorship of the Proletariat. Well and good, gentlemen, do you want to know what this dictatorship looks like? Look at the Paris Commune. That was the Dictatorship of the Proletariat.

Friedrich Engels
London, on the twentieth anniversary of the Paris Commune, March 18, 1891

I

On the 4th of September, 1870, when the working men of Paris proclaimed the Republic, which was almost instantaneously acclaimed throughout France, without a single voice of dissent, a cabal of place-hunting barristers, with Thiers for their statesman and Trochu for their general, took hold of the Hôtel de Ville.[5] At that time they were imbued with so fanatical a faith in the mission of Paris to represent France in all epochs of historical crisis, that, to legitimate their usurped titles as governors of France, they thought it quite sufficient to produce their lapsed mandates as representatives of Paris. In our second address on the late war, five days after the rise of these men, we told you who they were. Yet, in the turmoil of surprise, with the real leaders of the working class still shut up in Bonapartist prisons and the Prussians already marching upon Paris, Paris bore with their assumption of power, on the express condition that it was to be wielded for the single purpose of national defence. Paris, however, was not to be defended without arming its working class, organising them into an effective force, and training their ranks by the war itself. But Paris armed was the Revolution armed. A victory of Paris over the Prussian aggressor would have been a victory of the French workman over the French capitalist and his State parasites. In this conflict between national duty and class interest, the Government of National Defence did not hesitate one moment to turn into a Government of National Defection.

The first step they took was to send Thiers on a roving tour to all the courts of Europe, there to beg mediation by offering the barter of the Republic for a king. Four months after the commencement of the siege, when they thought the opportune moment come for

5. The seat of city government.

breaking the first word of capitulation, Trochu, in the presence of Jules Favre and others of his colleagues, addressed the assembled mayors of Paris in these terms:

"The first question put to me by my colleagues on the very evening of the 4th of September was this: Paris, can it with any chance of success stand a siege by the Prussian army? I did not hesitate to answer in the negative. Some of my colleagues here present will warrant the truth of my words and the persistence of my opinion. I told them, in these very terms, that, under the existing state of things, the attempt of Paris to hold out a siege by the Prussian army would be a folly. Without doubt, I added, it would be an heroic folly; but that would be all. . . . The events (managed by himself) have not given the lie to my prevision."

This nice little speech of Trochu was afterwards published by M. Corbon, one of the mayors present.

Thus, on the very evening of the proclamation of the republic, Trochu's "plan" was known to his colleagues to be the capitulation of Paris. If national defence had been more than a pretext for the personal government of Thiers, Favre, and Co., the upstarts of the 4th of September would have abdicated on the 5th—would have initiated the Paris people into Trochu's "plan," and called upon them to surrender at once, or to take their own fate into their own hands. Instead of this, the infamous impostors resolved upon curing the heroic folly of Paris by a regimen of famine and broken heads, and to dupe her in the meanwhile by ranting manifestoes, holding forth that Trochu, "the governor of Paris, will never capitulate," and Jules Favre, the foreign minister, will "not cede an inch of our territory, nor a stone of our fortresses." In a letter to Gambetta, that very same Jules Favre avows that what they were "defending" against were not the Prussian soldiers, but the working men of Paris. During the whole continuance of the siege the Bonapartist cut-throats, whom Trochu had wisely intrusted with the command of the Paris army, exchanged, in their intimate correspondence, ribald jokes at the well-understood mockery of defence. (See, for instance, the correspondence of Alphonse Simon Guiod, supreme commander of the artillery of the Army of Defence of Paris and Grand Cross of the Legion of Honour, to Susane, general of division of artillery, a correspondence published by the *Journal Officiel* of the Commune.) The mask of imposture was at last dropped on the 28th of January, 1871. With the true heroism of utter self-debasement, the Government of National Defence, in their capitulation, came out as the government of France by Bismarck's prisoners —a part so base that Louis Bonaparte himself had, at Sedan, shrunk from accepting it. After the events of the 18th of March, on their wild flight to Versailles, the *capitulards* left in the hands of

Paris the documentary evidence of their treason, to destroy which, as the Commune says in its manifesto to the provinces, "those men would not recoil from battering Paris into a heap of ruins washed by a sea of blood."

To be eagerly bent upon such a consummation, some of the leading members of the Government of Defence had, besides, most peculiar reasons of their own.

Shortly after the conclusion of the armistice, M. Millière, one of the representatives of Paris to the National Assembly, now shot by express order of Jules Favre, published a series of authentic legal documents in proof that Jules Favre, living in concubinage with the wife of a drunkard resident at Algiers, had, by a most daring concoction of forgeries, spread over many years, contrived to grasp, in the name of the children of his adultery, a large succession, which made him a rich man, and that, in a lawsuit undertaken by the legitimate heirs, he only escaped exposure by the connivance of the Bonapartist tribunals. As these dry legal documents were not to be got rid of by any amount of rhetorical horse-power, Jules Favre, for the first time in his life, held his tongue, quietly awaiting the outbreak of the civil war, in order, then, frantically to denounce the people of Paris as a band of escaped convicts in utter revolt against family, religion, order and property. This same forger had hardly got into power, after the 4th of September, when he sympathetically let loose upon society Pic and Taillefer, convicted, even under the empire, of forgery, in the scandalous affair of the "Étendard." One of these men, Taillefer, having dared to return to Paris under the Commune, was at once reinstated in prison; and then Jules Favre exclaimed, from the tribune of the National Assembly, that Paris was setting free all her jailbirds!

Ernest Picard, the Joe Miller[6] of the government of National Defence, who appointed himself Finance Minister of the Republic after having in vain striven to become the Home Minister of the Empire, is the brother of one Arthur Picard, an individual expelled from the Paris *Bourse* as a blackleg (see report of the Prefecture of Police, dated the 13th of July, 1867), and convicted, on his own confession, of a theft of 300,000 francs, while manager of one of the branches of the *Société Générale*, rue Palestro, No. 5 (see report of the Prefecture of Police, 11th December, 1868). This Arthur Picard was made by Ernest Picard the editor of his paper, *l'Electeur Libre*. While the common run of stockjobbers were led astray by the official lies of this Finance office paper, Arthur was running backwards and forwards between the Finance office and the

6. The German edition has Karl Vogt; the French, Falstaff.
Joe Miller: Celebrated English actor of the eighteenth century. *Karl Vogt*: German bourgeois democrat who became an agent of Napoleon III.

Bourse, there to discount the disaster of the French Army. The whole financial correspondence of that worthy pair of brothers fell into the hands of the Commune.

Jules Ferry, a penniless barrister before the 4th of September, contrived, as Mayor of Paris during the siege, to job a fortune out of famine. The day on which he would have to give an account of his maladministration would be the day of his conviction.

These men, then, could find, in the ruins of Paris only, their tickets-of-leave: they were the very men Bismarck wanted. With the help of some shuffling of cards, Thiers, hitherto the secret prompter of the Government, now appeared at its head, with ticket-of-leave-men[7] for his Ministers.

Thiers, that monstrous gnome, has charmed the French bourgeoisie for almost half a century, because he is the most consummate intellectual expression of their own class-corruption. Before he became a statesman he had already proved his lying powers as an historian. The chronicle of his public life is the record of the misfortunes of France. Banded, before 1830, with the republicans, he slipped into office under Louis Philippe by betraying his protector Laffitte, ingratiating himself with the king by exciting mob-riots against the clergy, during which the church of Saint Germain l'Auxerrois and the Archbishop's palace were plundered, and by acting the minister-spy upon, and the jail-*accoucheur* of, the Duchess de Berry. The massacre of the republicans in the rue Transnonain, and the subsquent infamous laws of September against the press and the right of association, were his work. Reappearing as the chief of the Cabinet in March, 1840, he astonished France with his plan of fortifying Paris. To the Republicans, who denounced this plan as a sinister plot against the liberty of Paris, he replied from the tribune of the Chamber of Deputies:

"What! to fancy that any works of fortification could ever endanger liberty! And first of all you calumniate any possible Government in supposing that it could some day attempt to maintain itself by bombarding the capital; ... but that government would be a hundred times more impossible after its victory than before." Indeed, no Government would ever have dared to bombard Paris from the forts, but that Government which had previously surrendered these forts to the Prussians.

When King Bomba[8] tried his hand at Palermo, in January, 1848, Thiers, then long since out of office, again rose in the Chamber of Deputies: "You know, gentlemen, what is happening at Palermo.

---

7. In England common criminals are often discharged on parole after serving the greater part of their term, and are placed under police surveillance. On such discharge they receive a certificate called ticket-of-leave, their possessors being referred to as ticket-of-leave-men. [*Engels, German edition of 1871*]

8. *King Bomba*: Sobriquet of King Ferdinand II of the Two Sicilies.

You, all of you, shake with horror (in the parliamentary sense) on hearing that during forty-eight hours a large town has been bombarded—by whom? Was it by a foreign enemy exercising the rights of war? No, gentlemen, it was by its own Government. And why? Because that unfortunate town demanded its rights. Well, then, for the demand of its rights it has got forty-eight hours of bombardment. . . . Allow me to appeal to the opinion of Europe. It is doing a service to mankind to arise, and to make reverberate, from what is perhaps the greatest tribune in Europe, some words (indeed words) of indignation against such acts. . . . When the Regent Espartero, who had rendered services to his country (which M. Thiers never did), intended bombarding Barcelona, in order to suppress its insurrection, there arose from all parts of the world a general outcry of indignation."

Eighteen months afterwards, M. Thiers was amongst the fiercest defenders of the bombardment of Rome by a French army.[9] In fact, the fault of King Bomba seems to have consisted in this only, that he limited his bombardment to forty-eight hours.

A few days before the Revolution of February, fretting at the long exile from place and pelf to which Guizot had condemned him, and sniffing in the air the scent of an approaching popular commotion, Thiers, in that pseudo-heroic style which won him the nickname of *Mirabeau-mouche*,[1] declared to the Chamber of Deputies: "I am of the party of Revolution, not only in France, but in Europe. I wish the Government of the Revolution to remain in the hands of moderate men . . . but if that Government should fall into the hands of ardent minds, even into those of Radicals, I shall, for all that, not desert my cause. I shall always be of the party of the Revolution." The Revolution of February came. Instead of displacing the Guizot Cabinet by the Thiers Cabinet, as the little man had dreamt, it superseded Louis Philippe by the Republic. On the first day of the popular victory he carefully hid himself, forgetting that the contempt of the working men screened him from their hatred. Still, with his legendary courage, he continued to shy the public stage, until the June massacres[2] had cleared it for his sort of action. Then he became the leading mind of the "Party of Order" and its Parliamentary Republic, that anonymous interregnum, in which all the rival factions of the ruling class conspired together to crush the people, and conspired against each other to restore each of them its own monarchy. Then, as now,

9. In April, 1849, French troops were sent to Italy to suppress the Italian Revolution. They bombarded revolutionary Rome, in glaring violation of the French constitution, which provided that the republic would never employ its forces to suppress the liberty of any people.
1. Mirabeau the fly.
2. This refers to the suppression of the June insurrection of the Paris proletariat in 1848.

Thiers denounced the Republicans as the only obstacle to the consolidation of the Republic; then, as now, he spoke to the Republic
as the hangman spoke to Don Carlos:—"I shall assassinate thee,
but for thy own good." Now, as then, he will have to exclaim on
the day after his victory: *"L'Empire est fait"*—the Empire is consummated. Despite his hypocritical homilies about necessary liberties and his personal grudge against Louis Bonaparte, who had
made a dupe of him, and kicked out parliamentarism—and outside
of its factitious atmosphere the little man is conscious of withering
into nothingness—he had a hand in all the infamies of the Second
Empire, from the occupation of Rome by French troops to the war
with Prussia, which he incited by his fierce invective against
German unity—not as a cloak of Prussian despotism, but as an
encroachment upon the vested right of France in German disunion.
Fond of brandishing, with his dwarfish arms, in the face of Europe
the sword of the first Napoleon, whose historical shoe-black he had
become, his foreign policy always culminated in the utter humiliation of France, from the London convention of 1841 to the Paris
capitulation of 1871, and the present civil war, where he hounds on
the prisoners of Sedan and Metz against Paris by special permission
of Bismarck. Despite his versatility of talent and shiftiness of purpose, this man has his whole lifetime been wedded to the most
fossil routine. It is self-evident that to him the deeper under-cur-
rents of modern society remained forever hidden; but even the most
palpable changes on its surface were abhorrent to a brain all the
vitality of which had fled to the tongue. Thus he never tired of
denouncing as a sacrilege any deviation from the old French protective system. When a minister of Louis Philippe, he railed at railways as a wild chimera; and when in opposition under Louis Bonaparte, he branded as a profanation every attempt to reform the
rotten French army system. Never in his long political career has he
been guilty of a single—even the smallest—measure of any practical
use. Thiers was consistent only in his greed for wealth and his
hatred of the men that produce it. Having entered his first ministry
under Louis Philippe poor as Job, he left it a millionaire. His last
ministry under the same king (of the 1st of March, 1840) exposed
him to public taunts of peculation in the Chamber of Deputies, to
which he was content to reply by tears—a commodity he deals in as
freely as Jules Favre, or any other crocodile. At Bordeaux his first
measure for saving France from impending financial ruin was to
endow himself with three millions a year, the first and the last word
of the "Economical Republic," the vista of which he had opened to
his Paris electors in 1869. One of his former colleagues of the
Chamber of Deputies of 1830, himself a capitalist and, nevertheless, a devoted member of the Paris Commune, M. Beslay, lately

addressed Thiers thus in a public placard: "The enslavement of labour by capital has always been the corner-stone of your policy, and from the very day you saw the Republic of Labour installed at the Hôtel de Ville, you have never ceased to cry out to France: 'These are criminals!' " A master in small state roguery, a virtuoso in perjury and treason, a craftsman in all the petty stratagems, cunning devices, and base perfidies of parliamentary party-warfare; never scrupling, when out of office, to fan a revolution, and to stifle it in blood when at the helm of the state; with class prejudices standing him in the place of ideas, and vanity in the place of a heart; his private life as infamous as his public life is odious—even now, when playing the part of a French Sulla, he cannot help setting off the abomination of his deeds by the ridicule of his ostentation.

The capitulation of Paris, by surrendering to Prussia not only Paris, but all France, closed the long-continued intrigues of treason with the enemy, which the usurpers of the 4th of September had begun, as Trochu himself said, on that very same day. On the other hand, it initiated the civil war they were now to wage, with the assistance of Prussia, against the Republic and Paris. The trap was laid in the very terms of the capitulation. At that time above one-third of the territory was in the hands of the enemy, the capital was cut off from the provinces, all communications were disorganised. To elect under such circumstances a real representation of France was impossible unless ample time were given for preparation. In view of this, the capitulation stipulated that a National Assembly must be elected within eight days; so that in many parts of France the news of the impending election arrived on its eve only. This assembly, moreover, was, by an express clause of the capitulation, to be elected for the sole purpose of deciding on peace or war, and, eventually, to conclude a treaty of peace. The population could not but feel that the terms of the armistice rendered the continuation of the war imposible, and that for sanctioning the peace imposed by Bismarck, the worst men in France were the best. But not content with these precautions, Thiers, even before the secret of the armistice had been broached to Paris, set out for an electioneering tour through the provinces, there to galvanise back into life the Legitimist party, which now, along with the Orleanists, had to take the place of the then impossible Bonapartists. He was not afraid of them. Impossible as a government of modern France, and, therefore, contemptible as rivals, what party were more eligible as tools of counter-revolution than the party whose action, in the words of Thiers himself (Chamber of Deputies, 5th January, 1833), "had always been confined to the three resources of foreign invasion, civil war, and anarchy"? They verily believed in the advent of their long-expected retrospective millennium. There were the heels of foreign invasion trampling upon France; there was the downfall of an empire, and the captivity of a Bonaparte; and there they were themselves. The wheel of history had evidently rolled back to stop at the *Chambre introuvable* of 1816. In the assemblies of the republic, 1848 to 51, they had been represented by their educated and trained parliamentary champions; it was the rank-and-file of the party which now rushed in—all the Pourceaugnacs[3] of France.

As soon as this Assembly of "Rurals" had met at Bordeaux, Thiers made it clear to them that the peace preliminaries must be assented to at once, without even the honours of a Parliamentary debate, as the only condition on which Prussia would permit them to open the war against the Republic and Paris, its stronghold. The counter-revolution had, in fact, no time to lose. The Second Empire had more than doubled the national debt, and plunged all the large towns into heavy municipal debts. The war had fearfully swelled the liabilities, and mercilessly ravaged the resources of the nation. To complete the ruin, the Prussian Shylock was there with his bond for the keep of half a million of his soldiers on French soil, his indemnity of five milliards, and interest at 5 per cent on the unpaid instalments thereof. Who was to pay the bill? It was only by the violent overthrow of the Republic that the appropriators of wealth could hope to shift on the shoulders of its producers the cost of a war which they, the appropriators, had themselves originated. Thus, the immense ruin of France spurred on these patriotic representatives of land and capital, under the very eyes and patronage of the invader, to graft upon the foreign war a civil war—a slave-holders' rebellion.

There stood in the way of this conspiracy one great obstacle— Paris. To disarm Paris was the first condition of success. Paris was therefore summoned by Thiers to surrender its arms. Then Paris was exasperated by the frantic anti-republican demonstrations of the "Rural" Assembly and by Thiers' own equivocations about the legal status of the Republic; by the threat to decapitate and decapitalise Paris; the appointment of Orleanist ambassadors; Dufaure's laws on overdue commercial bills and house-rent, inflicting ruin on the commerce and industry of Paris; Pouyer-Quertier's tax of two centimes upon every copy of every imaginable publication; the sentences of death against Blanqui and Flourens; the suppression of the Republican journals; the transfer of the National Assembly to Versailles; the renewal of the state of siege declared by Palikao, and expired on the 4th of September; the appointment of Vinoy, the

---

3. *Pourceaugnac*: A character in one of Molière's comedies, typifying the dull-witted, narrow-minded landed gentry. *Assembly of Rurals*: The National Assembly, which opened in Bordeaux on February 12, 1871, had a vast majority of royalists (450 out of 750 deputies)—representatives of the landlords and reactionary elements of town and country. Hence its name of "Assembly of Rurals" or Landlord Chamber.

Décembriseur,[4] as governor of Paris—of Valentin, the imperialist *gendarme*, as its prefect of police—and of D'Aurelle de Paladines, the Jesuit general, as the commander-in-chief of its National Guard.

And now we have to address a question to M. Thiers and the men of national defence, his under-strappers. It is known that, through the agency of M. Pouyer-Quertier, his finance minister, Thiers had contracted a loan of two milliards. Now, is it true, or not,—

1. That the business was so managed that a consideration of several hundred millions was secured for the private benefit of Thiers, Jules Favre, Ernest Picard, Pouyer-Quertier, and Jules Simon? and—

2. That no money was to be paid down until after "pacification" of Paris?

At all events, there must have been something very pressing in the matter, for Thiers and Jules Favre, in the name of the majority of the Bordeaux Assembly, unblushingly solicited the immediate occupation of Paris by Prussian troops. Such, however, was not the game of Bismarck, as he sneeringly, and in public, told the admiring Frankfort philistines on his return to Germany.

II

Armed Paris was the only serious obstacle in the way of the counter-revolutionary conspiracy. Paris was, therefore, to be disarmed. On this point the Bordeaux Assembly was sincerity itself. If the roaring rant of its Rurals had not been audible enough, the surrender of Paris by Thiers to the tender mercies of the triumvirate of Vinoy the *Décembriseur*, Valentin the Bonapartist *gendarme*, and Aurelle de Paladines the Jesuit general, would have cut off even the last subterfuge of doubt. But while insultingly exhibiting the true purpose of the disarmament of Paris, the conspirators asked her to lay down her arms on a pretext which was the most glaring, the most barefaced of lies. The artillery of the Paris National Guard, said Thiers, belonged to the State, and to the State it must be returned. The fact was this: From the very day of the capitulation, by which Bismarck's prisoners had signed the surrender of France, but reserved to themselves a numerous body-guard for the express purpose of cowing Paris, Paris stood on the watch. The National Guard reorganised themselves and intrusted their supreme control to a Central Committee elected by their whole body, save some fragments of the old Bonapartist formations. On the eve of the entrance of the Prussians into Paris, the Central Committee took measures for the removal to Montmartre, Belleville, and La Villette

4. Participant in the December 2, 1851, *coup d'état* of Louis Bonaparte (see p. 436, above). [*R. T.*]

of the cannon and *mitrailleuses* treacherously abandoned by the *capitulards* in and about the very quarters the Prussians were to occupy. That artillery had been furnished by the subscriptions of the National Guard. As their private property, it was officially recognised in the capitulation of the 28th of January, and on that very title exempted from the general surrender, into the hands of the conqueror, of arms belonging to the government. And Thiers was so utterly destitute of even the flimsiest pretext for initiating the war against Paris, that he had to resort to the flagrant lie of the artillery of the National Guard being State property!

The seizure of her artillery was evidently but to serve as the preliminary to the general disarmament of Paris, and, therefore, of the Revolution of the 4th of September. But that Revolution had become the legal status of France. The republic, its work, was recognised by the conqueror in the terms of the capitulation. After the capitulation, it was acknowledged by all the foreign Powers, and in its name the National Assembly had been summoned. The Paris working men's revolution of the 4th of September was the only legal title of the National Assembly seated at Bordeaux, and of its executive. Without it, the National Assembly would at once have to give way to the *Corps Législatif*, elected in 1869 by universal suffrage under French, not under Prussian, rule, and forcibly dispersed by the arm of the Revolution. Thiers and his ticket-of-leave-men would have had to capitulate for safe conducts signed by Louis Bonaparte, to save them from a voyage to Cayenne.[5] The National Assembly, with its power of attorney to settle the terms of peace with Prussia, was but an incident of that Revolution, the true embodiment of which was still armed Paris, which had initiated it, undergone for it a five months' siege, with its horrors of famine, and made her prolonged resistance, despite Trochu's plan, the basis of an obstinate war of defence in the provinces. And Paris was now either to lay down her arms at the insulting behest of the rebellious slaveholders of Bordeaux, and acknowledge that her Revolution of the 4th of September meant nothing but a simple transfer of power from Louis Bonaparte to his Royal rivals; or she had to stand forward as the self-sacrificing champion of France, whose salvation from ruin, and whose regeneration were impossible, without the revolutionary overthrow of the political and social conditions that had engendered the Second Empire, and, under its fostering care, matured into utter rottenness. Paris, emaciated by a five months' famine, did not hesitate one moment. She heroically resolved to run all the hazards of a resistance against the French conspirators, even with Prussian cannon frowning upon her from her own forts. Still,

5. *Cayenne*: Capital of French Guiana in South America; penal settlement and place of exile.

in its abhorrence of the civil war into which Paris was to be goaded, the Central Committee continued to persist in a merely defensive attitude, despite the provocations of the Assembly, the usurpations of the Executive, and the menacing concentration of troops in and around Paris.

Thiers opened the civil war by sending Vinoy, at the head of a multitude of *sergents-de-ville* and some regiments of the line, upon a nocturnal expedition against Montmartre, there to seize, by surprise, the artillery of the National Guard. It is well known how this attempt broke down before the resistance of the National Guard and the fraternisation of the line with the people. Aurelle de Paladines had printed beforehand his bulletin of victory, and Thiers held ready the placards announcing his measures of *coup d'état*. Now these had to be replaced by Thiers' appeals, imparting his magnanimous resolve to leave the National Guard in the possession of their arms, with which, he said, he felt sure they would rally round the Government against the rebels. Out of 300,000 National Guards only 300 responded to this summons to rally round little Thiers against themselves. The glorious working men's Revolution of the 18th March took undisputed sway of Paris. The Central Committee was its provisional government. Europe seemed, for a moment, to doubt whether its recent sensational performances of state and war had any reality in them, or whether they were the dreams of a long bygone past.

From the 18th of March to the entrance of the Versailles troops into Paris, the proletarian revolution remained so free from the acts of violence in which the revolutions, and still more the counter-revolutions, of the "better classes" abound, that no facts were left to its opponents to cry out about but the execution of Generals Lecomte and Clément Thomas, and the affair of the Place Vendôme.

One of the Bonapartist officers engaged in the nocturnal attempt against Montmartre, General Lecomte, had four times ordered the 81st line regiment to fire at an unarmed gathering in the Place Pigalle, and on their refusal fiercely insulted them. Instead of shooting women and children, his own men shot him. The inveterate habits acquired by the soldiery under the training of the enemies of the working class are, of course, not likely to change the very moment these soldiers changed sides. The same men executed Clément Thomas.

"General" Clément Thomas, a malcontent ex-quartermaster-sergeant, had in the latter times of Louis Philippe's reign, enlisted at the office of the Republican newspaper *Le National*, there to serve in the double capacity of responsible man-of-straw (*gérant résponsable*) and of duelling bully to that very combative journal.

After the revolution of February, the men of the *National* having got into power, they metamorphosed this old quartermaster-sergeant into a general on the eve of the butchery of June, of which he, like Jules Favre, was one of the sinister plotters, and became one of the most dastardly executioners. Then he and his generalship disappeared for a long time, to again rise to the surface on the 1st November, 1870. The day before the Government of Defence, caught at the Hôtel de Ville, had solemnly pledged their parole to Blanqui, Flourens, and other representatives of the working class, to abdicate their usurped power into the hands of a commune to be freely elected by Paris. Instead of keeping their word, they let loose on Paris the Bretons of Trochu, who now replaced the Corsicans of Bonaparte. General Tamisier alone, refusing to sully his name by such a breach of faith, resigned the commandership-in-chief of the National Guard, and in his place Clément Thomas for once became again a general. During the whole of his tenure of command, he made war, not upon the Prussians, but upon the Paris National Guard. He prevented their general armament, pitted the bourgeois battalions against the working men's battalions, weeded out the officers hostile to Trochu's "plan," and disbanded, under the stigma of cowardice, the very same proletarian battalions whose heroism has now astonished their most inveterate enemies. Clément Thomas felt quite proud of having reconquered his June pre-eminence as the personal enemy of the working class of Paris. Only a few days before the 18th of March, he laid before the War Minister, Le Flô, a plan of his own for "finishing off *la fine fleur* [the cream] of the Paris *canaille*." After Vinoy's rout, he must needs appear upon the scene of action in the quality of an amateur spy. The Central Committee and the Paris working men were as much responsible for the killing of Clément Thomas and Lecomte as the Princess of Wales was for the fate of the people crushed to death on the day of her entrance into London.

The massacre of unarmed citizens in the Place Vendôme is a myth which M. Thiers and the Rurals persistently ignored in the Assembly, intrusting its propagation exclusively to the servants' hall of European journalism. "The men of order," the reactionists of Paris, trembled at the victory of the 18th of March. To them it was the signal of popular retribution at last arriving. The ghosts of the victims assassinated at their hands from the days of June, 1848, down to the 22nd of January, 1871, arose before their faces. Their panic was their only punishment. Even the *sergents-de-ville*, instead of being disarmed and locked up, as ought to have been done, had the gates of Paris flung wide open for their safe retreat to Versailles. The men of order were left not only unharmed, but allowed to rally and quietly to seize more than one stronghold in the very centre of Paris. This indulgence of the Central Committee—this magnanimity of the armed working men—so strangely at variance with the habits of the "Party of Order," the latter misinterpreted as mere symptoms of conscious weakness. Hence their silly plan to try, under the cloak of an unarmed demonstration, what Vinoy had failed to perform with his cannon and *mitrailleuses*. On the 22nd of March a riotous mob of swells started from the quarters of luxury, all the *petits crevés*[6] in their ranks, and at their head the notorious familiars of the Empire—the Heckeren, Coëtlogon, Henri de Pène, etc. Under the cowardly pretence of a pacific demonstration, this rabble, secretly armed with the weapons of the bravo, fell into marching order, ill-treated and disarmed the detached patrols and sentries of the National Guards they met with on their progress, and, on debouching from the Rue de la Paix, with the cry of "Down with the Central Committee! Down with the assassins! The National Assembly for ever!" attempted to break through the line drawn up there, and thus to carry by a surprise the headquarters of the National Guard in the Place Vendôme. In reply to their pistol-shots, the regular *sommations* (the French equivalent of the English Riot Act) were made, and, proving ineffective, fire was commanded by the general of the National Guard. One volley dispersed into wild flight the silly coxcombs, who expected that the mere exhibition of their "respectability" would have the same effect upon the Revolution of Paris as Joshua's trumpets upon the wall of Jericho. The runaways left behind them two National Guards, nine severely wounded (among them a member of the Central Committee), and the whole scene of their exploit strewn with revolvers, daggers, and sword-canes, in evidence of the "unarmed" character of their "pacific" demonstration. When, on the 13th of June, 1849, the National Guard made a really pacific demonstration in protest against the felonious assault of French troops upon Rome, Changarnier, then general of the Party of Order, was acclaimed by the National Assembly, and especially by M. Thiers, as the saviour of society, for having launched his troops from all sides upon these unarmed men, to shoot and sabre them down, and to trample them under their horses' feet. Paris, then, was placed under a state of siege. Dufaure hurried through the Assembly new laws of repression. New arrests, new proscriptions—a new reign of terror set in. But the lower orders manage these things otherwise. The Central Committee of 1871 simply ignored the heroes of the "pacific demonstration"; so much so that only two days later they were enabled to muster under Admiral Saisset for that *armed* demonstration, crowned by the famous stampede to Versailles. In their reluctance to continue the civil war opened by Thiers' burglarious attempt on

6. Fops.

Montmartre, the Central Committee made itself, this time, guilty of a decisive mistake in not at once marching upon Versailles, then completely helpless, and thus putting an end to the conspiracies of Thiers and his Rurals. Instead of this, the Party of Order was again allowed to try its strength at the ballot box, on the 26th of March, the day of the election of the Commune. Then, in the *mairies*[7] of Paris, they exchanged bland words of conciliation with their too generous conquerors, muttering in their hearts solemn vows to exterminate them in due time.

Now look at the reverse of the medal. Thiers opened his second campaign against Paris in the beginning of April. The first batch of Parisian prisoners brough into Versailles was subjected to revolting atrocities, while Ernest Picard, with his hands in his trousers' pockets, strolled about jeering them, and while Mesdames Thiers and Favre, in the midst of their ladies of honour (?) applauded, from the balcony, the outrages of the Versailles mob. The captured soldiers of the line were massacred in cold blood; our brave friend, General Duval, the iron-founder, was shot without any form of trial. Galliffet, the kept man of his wife, so notorious for her shameless exhibitions at the orgies of the Second Empire, boasted in a proclamation of having commanded the murder of a small troop of National Guards, with their captain and lieutenant, surprised and disarmed by his Chasseurs. Vinoy, the runaway, was appointed by Thiers Grand Cross of the Legion of Honour, for his general order to shoot down every soldier of the line taken in the ranks of the Federals. Desmarêt, the gendarme, was decorated for the treacherous butcher-like chopping in pieces of the high-souled and chivalrous Flourens, who had saved the heads of the Government of Defence on the 31st of October, 1870. "The encouraging particulars" of his assassination were triumphantly expatiated upon by Thiers in the National Assembly. With the elated vanity of a parliamentary Tom Thumb, permitted to play the part of a Tamerlane, he denied the rebels against his littleness every right of civilised warfare, up to the right of neutrality for ambulances. Nothing more horrid than that monkey, allowed for a time to give full fling to his tigerish instincts, as foreseen by Voltaire.[8]

After the decree of the Commune of the 7th April, ordering reprisals and declaring it to be its duty "to protect Paris against the cannibal exploits of the Versailles banditti, and to demand an eye for an eye, a tooth for a tooth," Thiers did not stop the barbarous treatment of prisoners, moreover insulting them in his bulletins as follows:—"Never have more degraded countenances of a degraded democracy met the afflicted gazes of honest men,"—honest like Thiers himself and his ministerial ticket-of-leave-men. Still the

7. Local administrative offices.   8. See below, pp. 574–575. [*R. T.*]

shooting of prisoners was suspended for a time. Hardly, however, had Thiers and his Decembrist generals become aware that the Communal decree of reprisals was but an empty threat, that even their gendarme spies caught in Paris under the disguise of National Guards, that even *sergents-de-ville*, taken with incendiary shells upon them, were spared,—when the wholesale shooting of prisoners was resumed and carried on uninterruptedly to the end. Houses to which National Guards had fled were surrounded by gendarmes, inundated with petroleum (which here occurs for the first time in this war), and then set fire to, the charred corpses being afterwards brought out by the ambulance of the Press at the Ternes. Four National Guards having surrendered to a troop of mounted Chasseurs at Belle Epine, on the 25th of April, were afterwards shot down, one after another, by the captain, a worthy man of Galliffet's. One of his four victims, left for dead, Scheffer, crawled back to the Parisian outposts, and deposed to this fact before a commission of the Commune. When Tolain interpellated the War Minister upon the report of this commission, the Rurals drowned his voice and forbade Le Flô to answer. It would be an insult to their "glorious" army to speak of its deeds. The flippant tone in which Thiers' bulletins announced the bayoneting of the Federals surprised asleep at Moulin Saquet, and the wholesale fusillades at Clamart shocked the nerves even of the not over-sensitive London *Times*. But it would be ludicrous today to attempt recounting the merely preliminary atrocities committed by the bombarders of Paris and the fomenters of a slaveholders' rebellion protected by foreign invasion. Amidst all these horrors, Thiers, forgetful of his parliamentary laments on the terrible responsibility weighing down his dwarfish shoulders, boasts in his bulletin that *l'Assemblée siège paisiblement* (the Assembly continues meeting in peace), and proves by his constant carousals, now with Decembrist generals, now with German princes, that his digestion is not troubled in the least, not even by the ghosts of Lecomte and Clément Thomas.

III

On the dawn of the 18th of March, Paris arose to the thunderburst of "Vive la Commune!" What is the Commune, that sphinx so tantalising to the bourgeois mind?

"The proletarians of Paris," said the Central Committee in its manifesto of the 18th March, "amidst the failures and treasons of the ruling classes, have understood that the hour has struck for them to save the situation by taking into their own hands the direction of public affairs. . . . They have understood that it is their imperious duty and their absolute right to render themselves masters of their own destinies, by seizing upon the governmental power." But the working class cannot simply lay hold of the ready-made state machinery, and wield it for its own purposes.

The centralised State power, with its ubiquitous organs of standing army, police, bureaucracy, clergy, and judicature—organs wrought after the plan of a systematic and hierarchic division of labour,—originates from the days of absolute monarchy, serving nascent middle-class society as a mighty weapon in its struggles against feudalism. Still, its development remained clogged by all manner of mediaeval rubbish, seignorial rights, local privileges, municipal and guild monopolies and provincial constitutions. The gigantic broom of the French Revolution of the eighteenth century swept away all these relics of bygone times, thus clearing simultaneously the social soil of its last hindrances to the superstructure of the modern State edifice raised under the First Empire, itself the offspring of the coalition wars of old semi-feudal Europe against modern France. During the subsequent *régimes* the Government, placed under parliamentary control—that is, under the direct control of the propertied classes—became not only a hotbed of huge national debts and crushing taxes; with its irresistible allurements of place, pelf, and patronage, it became not only the bone of contention between the rival factions and adventurers of the ruling classes; but its political character changed simultaneously with the economic changes of society. At the same pace at which the progress of modern industry developed, widened, intensified the class antagonism between capital and labour, the State power assumed more and more the character of the national power of capital over labour, of a public force organised for social enslavement, of an engine of class despotism. After every revolution marking a progressive phase in the class struggle, the purely repressive character of the State power stands out in bolder and bolder relief. The Revolution of 1830, resulting in the transfer of Government from the landlords to the capitalists, transferred it from the more remote to the more direct antagonists of the working men. The bourgeois Republicans, who, in the name of the Revolution of February, took the State power, used it for the June massacres, in order to convince the working class that "social" republic meant the Republic ensuring their social subjection, and in order to convince the royalist bulk of the bourgeois and landlord class that they might safely leave the cares and emoluments of Government to the bourgeois "Republicans." However, after their one heroic exploit of June, the bourgeois Republicans had, from the front, to fall back to the rear of the "Party of Order"—a combination formed by all the rival fractions and factions of the appropriating class in their now openly declared antagonism to the producing classes. The proper form of their joint-stock

Government was the *Parliamentary Republic*, with Louis Bonaparte for its President. Theirs was a *régime* of avowed class terrorism and deliberate insult toward the "vile multitude." If the Parliamentary Republic, as M. Thiers said, "divided them (the different fractions of the ruling class) least," it opened an abyss between that class and the whole body of society outside their spare ranks. The restraints by which their own divisions had under former *régimes* still checked the State power, were removed by their union; and in view of the threatening upheaval of the proletariat, they now used that State power mercilessly and ostentatiously as the national war-engine of capital against labour. In their uninterrupted crusade against the producing masses they were, however, bound not only to invest the executive with continually increased powers of repression, but at the same time to divest their own parliamentary stronghold —the National Assembly—one by one, of all its own means of defence against the Executive. The Executive, in the person of Louis Bonaparte, turned them out. The natural offspring of the "Party-of-Order" Republic was the Second Empire.

The empire, with the *coup d'état* for its certificate of birth, universal suffrage for its sanction, and the sword for its sceptre, professed to rest upon the peasantry, the large mass of producers not directly involved in the struggle of capital and labour. It professed to save the working class by breaking down Parliamentarism, and, with it, the undisguised subserviency of Government to the propertied classes. It professed to save the propertied classes by upholding their economic supremacy over the working class; and, finally, it professed to unite all classes by reviving for all the chimera of national glory. In reality, it was the only form of government possible at a time when the bourgeoisie had already lost, and the working class had not yet acquired, the faculty of ruling the nation. It was acclaimed throughout the world as the saviour of society. Under its sway, bourgeois society, freed from political cares, attained a development unexpected even by itself. Its industry and commerce expanded to colossal dimensions; financial swindling celebrated cosmopolitan orgies; the misery of the masses was set off by a shameless display of gorgeous, meretricious and debased luxury. The State power, apparently soaring high above society, was at the same time itself the greatest scandal of that society and the very hotbed of all its corruptions. Its own rottenness, and the rottenness of the society it had saved, were laid bare by the bayonet of Prussia, herself eagerly bent upon transferring the supreme seat of that *régime* from Paris to Berlin. Imperialism is, at the same time, the most prostitute and the ultimate form of the State power which nascent middle-class society had commenced to elaborate as a means of its own emancipation from feudalism, and which full-grown bourgeois society had finally transformed into a means for the enslavement of labour by capital.

The direct antithesis to the empire was the Commune. The cry of "social republic," with which the revolution of February was ushered in by the Paris proletariat, did but express a vague aspiration after a Republic that was not only to supersede the monarchical form of class-rule, but class-rule itself. The Commune was the positive form of that Republic.

Paris, the central seat of the old governmental power, and, at the same time, the social stronghold of the French working class, had risen in arms against the attempt of Thiers, and the Rurals to restore and perpetuate that old governmental power bequeathed to them by the empire. Paris could resist only because, in consequence of the siege, it had got rid of the army, and replaced it by a National Guard, the bulk of which consisted of working men. This fact was now to be transformed into an institution. The first decree of the Commune, therefore, was the suppression of the standing army, and the substitution for it of the armed people.

The Commune was formed of the municipal councillors, chosen by universal suffrage in the various wards of the town, responsible and revocable at short terms. The majority of its members were naturally working men, or acknowledged representatives of the working class. The Commune was to be a working, not a parliamentary, body, executive and legislative at the same time. Instead of continuing to be the agent of the Central Government, the police was at once stripped of its political attributes, and turned into the responsible and at all times revocable agent of the Commune. So were the officials of all other branches of the Administration. From the members of the Commune downwards, the public service had to be done at *workmen's wages*. The vested interests and the representation allowances of the high dignitaries of State disappeared along with the high dignitaries themselves. Public functions ceased to be the private property of the tools of the Central Government. Not only municipal administration, but the whole initiative hitherto exercised by the State was laid into the hands of the Commune.

Having once got rid of the standing army and the police, the physical force elements of the old Government, the Commune was anxious to break the spiritual force of repression, the "parson-power," by the disestablishment and disendowment of all churches as proprietary bodies. The priests were sent back to the recesses of private life, there to feed upon the alms of the faithful in imitation of their predecessors, the Apostles. The whole of the educational institutions were opened to the people gratuitously, and at the same time cleared of all interference of Church and State. Thus, not only was education made accessible to all, but science itself freed from the fetters which class prejudice and governmental force had imposed upon it.

The judicial functionaries were to be divested of that sham independence which had but served to mask their abject subserviency to all succeeding governments to which, in turn, they had taken, and broken, the oaths of allegiance. Like the rest of public servants, magistrates and judges were to be elective, responsible, and revocable.

The Paris Commune was, of course, to serve as a model to all the great industrial centres of France. The communal *régime* once established in Paris and the secondary centres, the old centralised Government would in the provinces, too, have to give way to the self-government of the producers. In a rough sketch of national organisation which the Commune had no time to develop, it states clearly that the Commune was to be the political form of even the smallest country hamlet, and that in the rural districts the standing army was to be replaced by a national militia, with an extremely short term of service. The rural communes of every district were to administer their common affairs by an assembly of delegates in the central town, and these district assemblies were again to send deputies to the National Delegation in Paris, each delegate to be at any time revocable and bound by the *mandat impératif* (formal instructions) of his constituents. The few but important functions which still would remain for a central government were not to be suppressed, as has been intentionally mis-stated, but were to be discharged by Communal, and therefore strictly responsible agents. The unity of the nation was not to be broken, but, on the contrary, to be organised by the Communal Constitution and to become a reality by the destruction of the State power which claimed to be the embodiment of that unity independent of, and superior to, the nation itself, from which it was but a parasitic excrescence. While the merely repressive organs of the old governmental power were to be amputated, its legitimate functions were to be wrested from an authority usurping pre-eminence over society itself, and restored to the responsible agents of society. Instead of deciding once in three or six years which member of the ruling class was to misrepresent the people in Parliament, universal suffrage was to serve the people, constituted in the Communes, as individual suffrage serves every other employer in the search for the workmen and managers in his business. And it is well known that companies, like individuals, in matters of real business generally know how to put the right man in the right place, and, if they for once make a mistake, to redress it promptly. On the other hand, nothing could be more foreign to the spirit of the Commune that to supersede universal suffrage by hierarchic investiture.

It is generally the fate of completely new historical creations to be mistaken for the counterpart of older and even defunct forms of social life, to which they may bear a certain likeness. Thus, this new Commune, which breaks the modern State power, has been mistaken for a reproduction of the mediaeval Communes, which first preceded, and afterwards became the substratum of, that very State power. The Communal Constitution has been mistaken for an attempt to break up into a federation of small States, as dreamt of by Montesquieu and the Girondins, that unity of great nations which, if originally brought about by political force, has now become a powerful coefficient of social production. The antagonism of the Commune against the State power has been mistaken for an exaggerated form of the ancient struggle against over-centralisation. Peculiar historical circumstances may have prevented the classical development, as in France, of the bourgeois form of government, and may have allowed, as in England, to complete the great central State organs by corrupt vestries, jobbing councillors, and ferocious poor-law guardians in the towns, and virtually hereditary magistrates in the counties. The Communal Constitution would have restored to the social body all the forces hitherto absorbed by the State parasite feeding upon, and clogging the free movement of, society. By this one act it would have initiated the regeneration of France. The provincial French middle class saw in the Commune an attempt to restore the sway their order had held over the country under Louis Philippe, and which, under Louis Napoleon, was supplanted by the pretended rule of the country over the towns. In reality, the Communal Constitution brought the rural producers under the intellectual lead of the central towns of their districts, and these secured to them, in the working men, the natural trustees of their interests. The very existence of the Commune involved, as a matter of course, local municipal liberty, but no longer as a check upon the, now superseded, State power. It could only enter into the head of a Bismarck, who, when not engaged on his intrigues of blood and iron, always likes to resume his old trade, so befitting his mental calibre, of contributor to *Kladderadatsch* (the Berlin *Punch*), it could only enter into such a head, to ascribe to the Paris Commune aspirations after that caricature of the old French municipal organisation of 1791, the Prussian municipal constitution which degrades the town governments to mere secondary wheels in the police-machinery of the Prussian State. The Commune made that catchword of bourgeois revolutions, cheap government, a reality, by destroying the two greatest sources of expenditure—the standing army and State functionarism. Its very existence presupposed the non-existence of monarchy, which, in Europe at least, is the normal incumbrance and indispensable cloak of class-rule. It supplied the Republic with the basis of really democratic institutions. But neither cheap Government nor the "true Republic" was its ultimate aim; they were its mere concomitants.

The multiplicity of interpretations to which the Commune has been subjected, and the multiplicity of interests which construed it in their favour, show that it was a thoroughly expansive political form, while all previous forms of government had been emphatically repressive. Its true secret was this. It was essentially a working-class government, the produce of the struggle of the producing against the appropriating class, the political form at last discovered under which to work out the economic emancipation of labour.

Except on this last condition, the Communal Constitution would have been an impossibility and a delusion. The political rule of the producer cannot coexist with the perpetuation of his social slavery. The Commune was therefore to serve as a lever for uprooting the economical foundations upon which rests the existence of classes, and therefore of class-rule. With labour emancipated, every man becomes a working man, and productive labour ceases to be a class attribute.

It is a strange fact. In spite of all the tall talk and all the immense literature, for the last sixty years, about Emancipation of Labour, no sooner do the working men anywhere take the subject into their own hands with a will, than uprises at once all the apologetic phraseology of the mouthpieces of present society with its two poles of Capital and Wages Slavery (the landlord now is but the sleeping partner of the capitalist), as if capitalist society was still in its purest state of virgin innocence, with its antagonisms still undeveloped, with its delusions still unexploded, with its prostitute realities not yet laid bare. The Commune, they exclaim, intends to abolish property, the basis of all civilisation! Yes, gentlemen, the Commune intended to abolish that class-property which makes the labour of the many the wealth of the few. It aimed at the expropriation of the expropriators. It wanted to make individual property a truth by transforming the means of production, land and capital, now chiefly the means of enslaving and exploiting labour, into mere instruments of free and associated labour.—But this is Communism, "impossible" Communism! Why, those members of the ruling classes who are intelligent enough to perceive the impossibility of continuing the present system—and they are many—have become the obtrusive and full-mouthed apostles of co-operative production. If co-operative production is not to remain a sham and a snare; if it is to supersede the Capitalist system; if united co-operative societies are to regulate national production upon a common plan, thus taking it under their own control, and putting an end to the constant anarchy and periodical convulsions which are the fatality of Capitalist production—what else, gentlemen, would it be but Communism, "possible" Communism?

The working class did not expect miracles from the Commune. They have no ready-made utopias to introduce *par décret du peuple*. They know that in order to work out their own emancipation, and along with it that higher form to which present society is irresistibly tending by its own economical agencies, they will have to pass through long struggles, through a series of historic processes, transforming circumstances and men. They have no ideals to realise, but to set free the elements of the new society with which old collapsing bourgeois society itself is pregnant. In the full consciousness of their historic mission, and with the heroic resolve to act up to it, the working class can afford to smile at the coarse invective of the gentlemen's gentlemen with the pen and inkhorn, and at the didactic patronage of well-wishing bourgeois-doctrinaires, pouring forth their ignorant platitudes and sectarian crotchets in the oracular tone of scientific infallibility.

When the Paris Commune took the management of the revolution in its own hands; when plain working men for the first time dared to infringe upon the Governmental privilege of their "natural superiors," and, under circumstances of unexampled difficulty, performed their work modestly, conscientiously, and efficiently,—performed it at salaries the highest of which barely amounted to one-fifth of what, according to high scientific authority,[9] is the minimum required for a secretary to a certain metropolitan school board,—the old world writhed in convulsions of rage at the sight of the Red Flag, the symbol of the Republic of Labour, floating over the Hôtel de Ville.

And yet, this was the first revolution in which the working class was openly acknowledged as the only class capable of social initiative, even by the great bulk of the Paris middle class—shopkeepers, tradesmen, merchants—the wealthy capitalists alone excepted. The Commune had saved them by a sagacious settlement of that ever-recurring cause of dispute among the middle classes themselves—the debtor and creditor accounts.[1] The same portion of the middle class, after they had assisted in putting down the working men's insurrection of June, 1848, had been at once unceremoniously sacrificed to their creditors by the then Constituent Assembly. But this was not their only motive for now rallying round the working class. They felt that there was but one alternative—the Commune, or the Empire—under whatever name it might reappear. The Empire had ruined them economically by the havoc it made of public wealth,

9. Professor Huxley. [*Engels, German edition of 1871*]
1. On April 18, the Commune promulgated a decree postponing payments on debt obligations for three years.

by the wholesale financial swindling it fostered, by the props it lent to the artificially accelerated centralisation of capital, and the concomitant expropriation of their own ranks. It had suppressed them politically, it had shocked them morally by its orgies, it had insulted their Voltairianism by handing over the education of their children to the *frères Ignorantins*, it had revolted their national feeling as Frenchmen by precipitating them headlong into a war which left only one equivalent for the ruins it made—the disappearance of the Empire. In fact, after the exodus from Paris of the high Bonapartist and capitalist *bohème*, the true midle-class Party of Order came out in the shape of the "Union Républicaine," enrolling themselves under the colours of the Commune and defending it against the wilful misconstruction of Thiers. Whether the gratitude of this great body of the middle class will stand the present severe trial, time must show.

The Commune was perfectly right in telling the peasants that "its victory was their only hope." Of all the lies hatched at Versailles and re-echoed by the glorious European penny-a-liner, one of the most tremendous was that the Rurals represented the French peasantry. Think only of the love of the French peasant for the men to whom, after 1815, he had to pay the milliard of indemnity. In the eyes of the French peasant, the very existence of a great landed proprietor is in itself an encroachment on his conquests of 1789. The bourgeois, in 1848, had burdened his plot of land with the additional tax of forty-five cents in the franc; but then he did so in the name of the revolution; while now he had fomented a civil war against the revolution, to shift on to the peasant's shoulders the chief load of the five milliards of indemnity to be paid to the Prussian. The Commune, on the other hand, in one of its first proclamations, declared that the true originators of the war would be made to pay its cost. The Commune would have delivered the peasant of the blood tax,—would have given him a cheap government, —transformed his present blood-suckers, the notary, advocate, executor, and other judicial vampires, into salaried communal agents, elected by, and responsible to, himself. It would have freed him of the tyranny of the *garde champêtre*, the gendarme, and the prefect; would have put enlightenment by the schoolmaster in the place of stultification by the priest. And the French peasant is, above all, a man of reckoning. He would find it extremely reasonable that the pay of the priest, instead of being extorted by the taxgatherer, should only depend upon the spontaneous action of the parishioners' religious instincts. Such were the great immediate boons which the rule of the Commune—and that rule alone—held out to the French peasantry. It is, therefore, quite superfluous here to expatiate upon the more complicated but vital problems which the Commune alone was able, and at the same time compelled, to solve in favour of the peasant, *viz.*, the hypothecary debt, lying like an incubus upon his parcel of soil, the *prolétariat foncier* (the rural proletariat), daily growing upon it, and his expropriation from it enforced, at a more and more rapid rate, by the very development of modern agriculture and the competition of capitalist farming.

The French peasant had elected Louis Bonaparte president of the Republic; but the Party of Order created the Empire. What the French peasant really wants he commenced to show in 1849 and 1850, by opposing his *maire* to the Government's prefect, his schoolmaster to the Government's priest, and himself to the Government's gendarme. All the laws made by the Party of Order in January and February, 1850, were avowed measures of repression against the peasant. The peasant was a Bonapartist, because the great Revolution, with all its benefits to him, was, in his eyes, personified in Napoleon. This delusion, rapidly breaking down under the Second Empire (and in its very nature hostile to the Rurals), this prejudice of the past, how could it have withstood the appeal of the Commune to the living interests and urgent wants of the peasantry?

The Rurals—this was, in fact, their chief apprehension—knew that three months' free communication of Communal Paris with the provinces would bring about a general rising of the peasants, and hence their anxiety to establish a police blockade around Paris, so as to stop the spread of the rinderpest.

If the Commune was thus the true representative of all the healthy elements of French society, and therefore the truly national Government, it was, at the same time, as a working men's Government, as the bold champion of the emancipation of labour, emphatically international. Within sight of the Prussian army, that had annexed to Germany two French provinces, the Commune annexed to France the working people all over the world.

The Second Empire had been the jubilee of cosmopolitan blacklegism, the rakes of all countries rushing in at its call for a share in its orgies and in the plunder of the French people. Even at this moment the right hand of Thiers is Ganesco, the foul Wallachian, and his left hand is Markovsky, the Russian spy. The Commune admitted all foreigners to the honour of dying for an immortal cause. Between the foreign war lost by their treason, and the civil war fomented by their conspiracy with the foreign invader, the bourgeoisie had found the time to display their patriotism by organising police-hunts upon the Germans in France. The Commune made a German working man its Minister of Labour. Thiers, the bourgeoisie, the Second Empire, had continually deluded Poland by loud professions of sympathy, while in reality betraying her to, and doing the dirty work of, Russia. The Commune honoured the heroic sons of Poland by placing them at the head of the defenders of Paris. And, to broadly mark the new era of history it was conscious of initiating, under the eyes of the conquering Prussians, on the one side, and of the Bonapartist army, led by Bonapartist generals, on the other, the Commune pulled down that colossal symbol of martial glory, the Vendôme column.

The great social measure of the Commune was its own working existence. Its special measures could but betoken the tendency of a government of the people by the people. Such were the abolition of the nightwork of journeymen bakers; the prohibition, under penalty, of the employers' practice to reduce wages by levying upon their work-people fines under manifold pretexts,—a process in which the employer combines in his own person the parts of legislator, judge, and executor, and filches the money to boot. Another measure of this class was the surrender, to associations of workmen, under reserve of compensation, of all closed workshops and factories, no matter whether the respective capitalists had absconded or preferred to strike work.

The financial measures of the Commune, remarkable for their sagacity and moderation, could only be such as were compatible with the state of a beseiged town. Considering the colossal robberies committed upon the city of Paris by the great financial companies and contractors, under the protection of Haussmann,[2] the Commune would have had an incomparably better title to confiscate their property than Louis Napoleon had against the Orleans family. The Hohenzollern and the English oligarchs, who both have derived a good deal of their estates from Church plunder, were, of course, greatly shocked at the Commune clearing but 8,000 f. out of secularisation.

While the Versailles Government, as soon as it had recovered some spirit and strength, used the most violent means against the Commune; while it put down the free expression of opinion all over France, even to the forbidding of meetings of delegates from the large towns; while it subjected Versailles and the rest of France to an espionage far surpassing that of the Second Empire; while it burned by its gendarme inquisitors all papers printed at Paris, and sifted all correspondence from and to Paris; while in the National Assembly the most timid attempts to put in a word for Paris were howled down in a manner unknown even to the *Chambre introuvable* of 1816; with the savage warfare of Versailles outside, and its attempts at corruption and conspiracy inside Paris—would the

2. During the Second Empire, Baron Haussmann was Prefect of the Department of the Seine, that is, of the City of Paris. He introduced a number of changes in the layout of the city for the purpose of facilitating the crushing of workers' insurrections. [*V. I. Lenin, 1905 Russian translation*]

Commune not have shamefully betrayed its trust by affecting to keep up all the decencies and appearances of liberalism as in a time of profound peace? Had the Government of the Commune been akin to that of M. Thiers, there would have been no more occasion to suppress Party-of-Order papers at Paris than there was to suppress Communal papers at Versailles.

It was irritating indeed to the Rurals that at the very same time they declared the return to the church to be the only means of salvation for France, the infidel Commune unearthed the peculiar mysteries of the Picpus nunnery, and of the Church of Saint Laurent. It was a satire upon M. Thiers that, while he showered grand crosses upon the Bonapartist generals in acknowledgement of their mastery in losing battles, signing capitulations, and turning cigarettes at Wilhelmshöhe, the Commune dismissed and arrested its generals whenever they were suspected of neglecting their duties. The explusion from, and arrest by, the Commune of one of its members who had slipped in under a false name, and had undergone at Lyons six days' imprisonment for simple bankruptcy, was it not a deliberate insult hurled at the forger, Jules Favre, then still the foreign minister of France, still selling France to Bismarck, and still dictating his orders to that paragon Government of Belgium? But indeed the Commune did not pretend to infallibility, the invariable attribute of all governments of the old stamp. It published its doings and sayings, it initiated the public into all its shortcomings.

In every revolution there intrude, at the side of its true agents, men of a different stamp; some of them survivors of and devotees to past revolutions, without insight into the present movement, but preserving popular influence by their known honesty and courage, or by the sheer force of tradition; others mere bawlers, who, by dint of repeating year after year the same set of stereotyped declamations against the Government of the day, have sneaked into the reputation of revolutionists of the first water. After the 18th of March, some such men did also turn up, and in some cases contrived to play pre-eminent parts. As far as their power went, they hampered the real action of the working class, exactly as men of that sort have hampered the full development of every previous revolution. They are an unavoidable evil: with time they are shaken off; but time was not allowed to the Commune.

Wonderful, indeed, was the change the Commune had wrought in Paris! No longer any trace of the meretricious Paris of the Second Empire. No longer was Paris the rendezvous of British landlords, Irish absentees,[3] American ex-slaveholders and shoddy men, Russian ex-serf-owners, and Wallachian boyards. No more corpses at the morgue, no nocturnal burglaries, scarcely any robberies; in fact,

3. *Absentees*: Big landlords who hardly ever visited their estates.

for the first time since the days of February, 1848, the streets of Paris were safe, and that without any police of any kind. "We," said a member of the Commune, "hear no longer of assassination, theft and personal assault; it seems indeed as if the police had dragged along with it to Versailles all its Conservative friends." The *cocottes* had refound the scent of their protectors—the absconding men of family, religion, and, above all, of property. In their stead, the real women of Paris showed again at the surface—heroic, noble, and devoted, like the women of antiquity. Working, thinking, fighting, bleeding Paris—almost forgetful, in its incubation of a new society, of the cannibals at its gates—radiant in the enthusiasm of its historic intiative!

Opposed to this new world at Paris, behold the old world at Versailles—that assembly of the ghouls of all defunct *régimes*, Legitimists and Orleanists, eager to feed upon the carcass of the nation, —with a tail of antediluvian Republicans, sanctioning, by their presence in the Asssembly, the slaveholders' rebellion, relying for the maintenance of their Parliamentary Republic upon the vanity of the senile mountebank at its head, and caricaturing 1789 by holding their ghastly meetings in the *Jeu de Paume*.[4] There it was, this Assembly, the representative of everything dead in France, propped up to the semblance of life by nothing but the swords of the generals of Louis Bonaparte. Paris all truth, Versailles all lie; and that lie vented through the mouth of Thiers.

Thiers tells a deputation of the mayors of the Seine-et-Oise,— "You may rely upon my word, which I have *never* broken!" He tells the Assembly itself that "it was the most freely elected and most Liberal Assembly France ever possessed"; he tells his motley soldiery that it was "the admiration of the world, and the finest army France ever possessed"; he tells the provinces that the bombardment of Paris by him was a myth: "If some cannonshots have been fired, it is not the deed of the army of Versailles, but of some insurgents trying to make believe that they are fighting, while they dare not show their faces." He again tells the provinces that "the artillery of Versailles does not bombard Paris, but only cannonades it." He tells the Archbishop of Paris that the pretended executions and reprisals (!) attributed to the Versailles troops were all moonshine. He tells Paris that he was only anxious "to free it from the hideous tyrants who oppress it," and that, in fact, the Paris of the Commune was "but a handful of criminals."

The Paris of M. Thiers was not the real Paris of the "vile multitude," but a phantom Paris, the Paris of the *francs-fileurs*,[5] the

---

4. *Jeau de Paume*: The tennis court where the National Assembly of 1789 adopted its famous decisions. [*Engels,* *German edition of 1871*]

5. *Francs-fileurs*: Absconders.

Paris of the Boulevards, male and female—the rich, the capitalist, the gilded, the idle Paris, now thronging with its lackeys, its black-legs, its literary *bohême*, and its *cocottes* at Versailles, Saint-Denis, Rueil, and Saint-Germain; considering the civil war but an agree-able diversion, eyeing the battle going on through telescopes, count-ing the rounds of cannon, and swearing by their own honour and that of their prostitutes, that the performance was far better got up than it used to be at the Porte St. Martin. The men who fell were really dead; the cries of the wounded were cries in good earnest; and, besides, the whole thing was so intensely historical.

This is the Paris of M. Thiers, as the emigration of Coblenz was the France of M. de Calonne.

IV

The first attempt of the slaveholders' conspiracy to put down Paris by getting the Prussians to occupy it, was frustrated by Bis-marck's refusal. The second attempt, that of the 18th of March, ended in the rout of the army and the flight to Versailles of the Government, which ordered the whole administration to break up and follow in its track. By the semblance of peace-negotiations with Paris, Thiers found the time to prepare for war against it. But where to find an army? The remnants of the line regiments were weak in number and unsafe in character. His urgent appeal to the provinces to succour Versailles, by their National Guards and volun-teers, met with a flat refusal. Brittany alone furnished a handful of *Chouans* fighting under a white flag, every one of them wearing on his breast the heart of Jesus in white cloth, and shouting *"Vive le Roi!"* (Long live the King!) Thiers was, therefore, compelled to collect, in hot haste, a motley crew, composed of sailors, marines, Pontifical Zouaves, Valentin's gendarmes, and Pietri's *sergents-de-ville* and *mouchards*. This army, however, would have been ridicu-lously ineffective without the instalments of imperialist war-prison-ers, which Bismarck granted in numbers just sufficient to keep the civil war a-going, and keep the Versailles Government in abject dependence on Prussia. During the war itself, the Versailles police had to look after the Versailles army, while the gendarmes had to drag it on by exposing themselves at all posts of danger. The forts which fell were not taken, but bought. The heroism of the Feder-als convinced Thiers that the resistance of Paris was not to be broken by his own strategic genius and the bayonets at his disposal.

Meanwhile, his relations with the provinces became more and more difficult. Not one single address of approval came in to glad-den Thiers and his Rurals. Quite the contrary. Deputations and addresses demanding, in a tone anything but respectful, conciliation with Paris on the basis of the unequivocal recognition of the Republic, the acknowledgement of the Communal liberties, and the dissolution of the National Assembly, whose mandate was extinct, poured in from all sides, and in such numbers that Dufaure, Thiers' Minister of Justice, in his circular of April 23 to the public prosecutors, commanded them to treat "the cry of conciliation" as a crime! In regard, however, of the hopeless prospect held out by his campaign, Thiers resolved to shift his tactics by ordering, all over the country, municipal elections to take place on the 30th of April, on the basis of the new municipal law dictated by himself to the National Assembly. What with the intrigues of his prefects, what with police intimidation, he felt quite sanguine of imparting, by the verdict of the provinces, to the National Assembly that moral power it had never possessed, and of getting at last from the provinces the physical force required for the conquest of Paris.

His banditti-warfare against Paris, exalted in his own bulletins, and the attempts of his ministers at the establishment, throughout France, of a reign of terror, Thiers was from the beginning anxious to accompany with a little by-play of conciliation, which had to serve more than one purpose. It was to dupe the provinces, to inveigle the middle-class element in Paris, and, above all, to afford the professed Republicans in the National Assembly the opportunity of hiding their treason against Paris behind their faith in Thiers. On the 21st of March, when still without an army, he had declared to the Assembly: "Come what may, I will not send an army to Paris." On the 27th March he rose again: "I have found the Republic an accomplished fact, and I am firmly resolved to maintain it." In reality, he put down the revolution at Lyons and Marseilles[6] in the name of the Republic, while the roars of his Rurals drowned the very mention of its name at Versailles. After this exploit, he toned down the "accomplished fact" into an hypothetical fact. The Orleans princes, whom he had cautiously warned off Bordeaux, were now, in flagrant breach of the law, permitted to intrigue at Dreux. The concessions held out by Thiers in his interminable interviews with the delegates from Paris and the provinces, although constantly varied in tone and colour, according to time and circumstances, did in fact never come to more than the prospective restriction of revenge to the "handful of criminals implicated in the murder of Lecomte and Clément Thomas," on the well-understood premise that Paris and France were unreservedly to accept M. Thiers himself as the best of possible Republics, as he, in 1830, had done with Louis Philippe. Even these concessions he not only took

6. A few days after March 18, 1871, revolutionary outbreaks occurred in Lyons and Marseilles aimed at the proclamation of Communes. The movement was crushed by the Thiers government.

care to render doubtful by the official comments put upon them in the Assembly through his Ministers. He had his Dufaure to act. Dufaure, this old Orleanist lawyer, had always been the justiciary of the state of siege, as now in 1871, under Thiers, so in 1839 under Louis Philippe, and in 1849 under Louis Bonaparte's presidency. While out of office he made a fortune by pleading for the Paris capitalists, and made political capital by pleading against the laws he had himself originated. He now hurried through the National Assembly not only a set of repressive laws which were, after the fall of Paris, to extirpate the last remnants of Republican liberty in France; he foreshadowed the fate of Paris by abridging the, for him, too slow procedure of courts-martial, and by a new-fangled, Draconic code of deportation. The Revolution of 1848, abolishing the penalty of death for political crimes, has replaced it by deportation. Louis Bonaparte did not dare, at least not in theory, to re-establish the *régime* of the guillotine. The Rural Assembly, not yet bold enough even to hint that the Parisians were not rebels, but assassins, had therefore to confine its prospective vengeance against Paris to Dufaure's new code of deportation. Under all these circumstances Thiers himself could not have gone on with his comedy of conciliation, had it not, as he intended it to do, drawn forth shrieks of rage from the Rurals, whose ruminating mind did neither understand the play, nor its necessities of hypocrisy, tergiversation, and procrastination.

In sight of the impending municipal elections of the 30th April, Thiers enacted one of his great conciliation scenes on the 27th April. Amidst a flood of sentimental rhetoric, he exclaimed from the tribune of the Assembly: "There exists no conspiracy against the Republic but that of Paris, which compels us to shed French blood. I repeat it again and again. Let those impious arms fall from the hands which hold them, and chastisement will be arrested at once by an act of peace excluding only the small number of criminals." To the violent interruption of the Rurals he replied: "Gentlemen, tell me, I implore you, am I wrong? Do you really regret that I could have stated the truth that the criminals are only a handful? Is it not fortunate in the midst of our misfortunes that those who have been capable to shed the blood of Clément Thomas and General Lecomte are but rare exceptions?"

France, however, turned a deaf ear to what Thiers flattered himself to be a parliamentary siren's song. Out of 700,000 municipal councillors returned by the 35,000 communes still left to France, the united Legitimists, Orleanists and Bonapartists did not carry 8,000. The supplementary elections which followed were still more decidedly hostile. Thus, instead of getting from the provinces the badly-needed physical force, the National Assembly lost even its last claim to moral force, that of being the expression of the universal suffrage of the country. To complete the discomfiture, the newly-chosen municipal councils of all the cities of France openly threatened the usurping Assembly at Versailles with a counter Assembly at Bordeaux.

Then the long-expected moment of decisive action had at last come for Bismarck. He peremptorily summoned Thiers to send to Frankfort plenipotentiaries for the definitive settlement of peace. In humble obedience to the call of his master, Thiers hastened to depatch his trusty Jules Favre, backed by Pouyer-Quertier. Pouyer-Quertier, an "eminent" Rouen cotton-spinner, a fervent and even servile partisan of the Second Empire, had never found any fault with it save its commercial treaty with England, prejudicial to his own shop-interest. Hardly installed at Bordeaux as Thiers' Minister of Finance, he denounced that "unholy" treaty, hinted at its near abrogation, and had even the effrontery to try, although in vain (having counted without Bismarck), the immediate enforcement of the old protective duties against Alsace, where, he said, no previous international treaties stood in the way. This man, who considered counter-revolution as a means to put down wages at Rouen, and the surrender of French provinces as a means to bring up the price of his wares in France, was he not *the one* predestined to be picked out by Thiers as the helpmate of Jules Favre in his last and crowning treason?

On the arrival at Frankfort of this exquisite pair of plenipotentiaries, bully Bismarck at once met them with the imperious alternative: Either the restoration of the Empire, or the unconditional acceptance of my own peace terms! These terms included a shortening of the intervals in which the war indemnity was to be paid and the continued occupation of the Paris forts by Prussian troops until Bismarck should feel satisfied with the state of things in France; Prussia thus being recognised as the supreme arbiter in internal French politics! In return for this he offered to let loose, for the extermination of Paris, the captive Bonapartist army, and to lend them the direct assistance of Emperor William's troops. He pledged his good faith by making payment of the first instalment of the indemnity dependent on the "pacification" of Paris. Such a bait was, of course, eagerly swallowed by Thiers and his plenipotentiaries. They signed the treaty of peace on the 10th of May, and had it endorsed by the Versailles Assembly on the 18th.

In the interval between the conclusion of peace and the arrival of the Bonapartist prisoners, Thiers felt the more bound to resume his comedy of conciliation, as his Republican tools stood in sore need of a pretext for blinking their eyes at the preparations for the carnage of Paris. As late as the 8th of May he replied to a deputation of middle-class conciliators: "Whenever the insurgents will make up their minds for capitulation, the gates of Paris shall be flung wide open during a week for all except the murderers of Generals Clément Thomas and Lecomte."

A few days afterwards, when violently interpellated on these promises by the Rurals, he refused to enter into any explanations; not, however, without giving them this significant hint. "I tell you there are impatient men amongst you, men who are in too great a hurry. They must have another eight days; at the end of these eight days there will be no more danger, and the task will be proportionate to their courage and to their capacities." As soon as MacMahon was able to assure him that he could shortly enter Paris, Thiers declared to the Assembly that "he would enter Paris with the *laws* in his hands, and demand a full expiation from the wretches who had sacrificed the lives of soldiers and destroyed public monuments." As the moment of decision drew near he said—to the Assembly, "I shall be pitiless!"—to Paris, that it was doomed; and to his Bonapartist banditti, that they had State licence to wreak vengeance upon Paris to their hearts' content. At last, when treachery had opened the gates of Paris to General Douay, on the 21st of May, Thiers, on the 22nd, revealed to the Rurals the "goal" of his conciliation comedy, which they had so obstinately persisted in not understanding. "I told you a few days ago that we were approaching *our goal*; today I come to tell you *the goal* is reached. The victory of order, justice and civilisation is at last won!"

So it was. The civilisation and justice of bourgeois order comes out in its lurid light whenever the slaves and drudges of that order rise against their masters. Then this civilisation and justice stand forth as undisguised savagery and lawless revenge. Each new crisis in the class struggle between the appropriator and the producer brings out this fact more glaringly. Even the atrocities of the bourgeois in June, 1848, vanish before the ineffable infamy of 1871. The self-sacrificing heroism with which the population of Paris—men, women and children—fought for eight days after the entrance of the Versaillese, reflects as much the grandeur of their cause, as the infernal deeds of the soldiery reflect the innate spirit of that civilisation of which they are the mercenary vindicators. A glorious civilisation, indeed, the great problem of which is how to get rid of the heaps of corpses it made after the battle was over!

To find a parallel for the conduct of Thiers and his blood-hounds we must go back to the times of Sulla and the two Triumvirates of Rome. The same wholesale slaughter in cold blood; the same disregard, in massacre, of age and sex; the same system of torturing prisoners; the same proscriptions, but this time of a whole class; the same savage hunt after concealed leaders, lest one might escape; the same denunciations of political and private enemies; the same indifference for the butchery of entire strangers to the feud. There is but this difference, that the Romans had no *mitrailleuses* for the despatch, in the lump, of the proscribed, and that they had not "the law in their hands," nor on their lips the cry of "civilisation."

And after those horrors, look upon the other, still more hideous, face of that bourgeois civilisation as described by its own press!

"With stray shots," writes the Paris correspondent of a London Tory paper, "still ringing in the distance, and untended wounded wretches dying amid the tombstones of Père la Chaise—with 6,000 terror-stricken insurgents wandering in an agony of despair in the labyrinth of the catacombs, and wretches hurried through the streets to be shot down in scores by the *mitrailleuse*—it is revolting to see the *cafés* filled with the votaries of absinthe, billiards, and dominoes; female profligacy perambulating the boulevards, and the sound of revelry disturbing the night from the *cabinets particuliers* of fashionable restaurants." M. Edouard Hervé writes in the *Journal de Paris*, a Versaillist journal suppressed by the Commune: "The way in which the population of Paris (!) manifested its satisfaction yesterday was rather more than frivolous, and we fear it will grow worse as time progresses. Paris has now a *fête* day appearance, which is sadly out of place; and, unless we are to be called the *Parisiens de la décadence*, this sort of thing must come to an end." And then he quotes the passage from Tacitus: "Yet, on the morrow of that horrible struggle, even before it was completely over, Rome—degraded and corrupt—began once more to wallow in the voluptuous slough which was destroying its body and polluting its soul—*alibi proelia et vulnera*; *alibi balnea popinaeque* (here fights and wounds, there baths and restaurants)." M. Hervé only forgets to say that the "population of Paris" he speaks of is but the population of the Paris of M. Thiers—the *francs-fileurs* returning in throngs from Versailles, Saint-Denis, Rueil and Saint-Germain—*the* Paris of the "Decline."

In all its bloody triumphs over the self-sacrificing champions of a new and better society, that nefarious civilisation, based upon the enslavement of labour, drowns the moans of its victims in a hue-and-cry of calumny, reverberated by a worldwide echo. The serene working men's Paris of the Commune is suddenly changed into a pandemonium by the bloodhounds of "order." And what does this tremendous change prove to the bourgeois mind of all countries? Why, that the Commune has conspired against civilisation! The Paris people die enthusiastically for the Commune in numbers unequalled in any battle known to history. What does that prove? Why, that the Commune was not the people's own government but the usurpation of a handful of criminals! The women of Paris joyfully give up their lives at the barricades and on the place of execution. What does this prove? Why, that the demon of the Commune has changed them into Megaeras and Hecates! The moderation of the Commune during two months of undisputed sway is equalled only by the heroism of its defence. What does that prove? Why, that for months the Commune carefully hid, under a mask of moderation and humanity, the blood-thirstiness of its fiendish instincts, to be let loose in the hour of its agony!

The working men's Paris, in the act of its heroic self-holocaust, involved in its flames buildings and monuments. While tearing to pieces the living body of the proletariat, its rulers must no longer expect to return triumphantly into the intact architecture of their abodes. The Government of Versailles cries, "Incendiarism!" and whispers this cue to all its agents, down to the remotest hamlet, to hunt up its enemies everywhere as suspect of professional incendiarism. The bourgeoisie of the whole world, which looks complacently upon the wholesale massacre after the battle, is convulsed by horror at the desecration of brick and mortar!

When governments give state-licences to their navies to "kill, *burn* and destroy," is that a licence for incendiarism? When the British troops wantonly set fire to the Capitol at Washington and to the summer palace of the Chinese Emperor, was that incendiarism? When the Prussians, not for military reasons, but out of the mere spite of revenge, burned down, by the help of petroleum, towns like Châteaudun and innumerable villages, was that incendiarism? When Thiers, during six weeks, bombarded Paris, under the pretext that he wanted to set fire to those houses only in which there were people, was that incendiarism?—In war, fire is an arm as legitimate as any. Buildings held by the enemy are shelled to set them on fire. If their defenders have to retire, they themselves light the flames to prevent the attack from making use of the buildings. To be burnt down has always been the inevitable fate of all buildings situated in the front of battle of all the regular armies of the world. But in the war of the enslaved against their enslavers, the only justifiable war in history, this is by no means to hold good! The Commune used fire strictly as a means of defence. They used it to stop up to the Versailles troops those long, straight avenues which Haussmann had expressly opened to artillery-fire; they used it to cover their retreat, in the same way as the Versaillese, in their advance, used their shells which destroyed at least as many buildings as the fire of the Commune. It is a matter of dispute, even now, which buildings were set fire to by the defence, and which by the attack. And the defence resorted to fire only then, when the Versaillese troops had already commenced their wholesale murdering of prisoners.—Besides, the Commune had, long before, given full public notice that, if driven to extremities, they would bury themselves under the ruins of Paris, and make Paris a second Moscow, as the Government of Defence, but only as a cloak for its treason, had promised to do. For this purpose Trochu had found them the petroleum. The Commune knew that its opponents cared nothing for the lives of the Paris people, but cared much for their own Paris buildings. And Thiers, on the other hand, had given them notice that he would be implacable in his vengeance. No sooner had he got his army ready on one side, and the Prussians shutting up the trap on the other, than he proclaimed: "I shall be pitiless! The expiation will be complete, and justice will be stern!" If the acts of the Paris working men were vandalism, it was the vandalism of defence in despair, not the vandalism of triumph, like that which the Christians perpetrated upon the really priceless art treasures of heathen antiquity; and even that vandalism has been justified by the historian as an unavoidable and comparatively trifling concomitant to the titanic struggle between a new society arising and an old one breaking down. It was still less the vandalism of Haussmann, razing historic Paris to make place for the Paris of the sightseer!

But the execution by the Commune of the sixty-four hostages, with the Archbishop of Paris at their head! The bourgeoisie and its army in June, 1848, re-established a custom which had long disappeared from the practice of war—the shooting of their defenceless prisoners. This brutal custom has since been more or less strictly adhered to by the suppressors of all popular commotions in Europe and India; thus proving that it constitutes a real "progress of civilisation!" On the other hand, the Prussians, in France, had re-established the practice of taking hostages—innocent men, who, with their lives, were to answer to them for the acts of others. When Thiers, as we have seen, from the very beginning of the conflict, enforced the humane practice of shooting down the Communal prisoners, the Commune, to protect their lives, was obliged to resort to the Prussian practice of securing hostages. The lives of the hostages had been forfeited over and over again by the continued shooting of prisoners on the part of the Versaillese. How could they be spared any longer after the carnage with which MacMahon's praetorians[7] celebrated their entrance into Paris? Was even the last check upon the unscrupulous ferocity of bourgeois governments— the taking of hostages—to be made a mere sham of? The real murderer of Archbishop Darboy is Thiers. The Commune again and again had offered to exchange the archbishop, and ever so many priests in the bargain, against the single Blanqui, then in the hands of Thiers. Thiers obstinately refused. He knew that with Blanqui he

7. Here "praetorians" refers to the Versailles army.

would give to the Commune a head; while the archbishop would serve his purpose best in the shape of a corpse. Thiers acted upon the precedent of Cavaignac. How, in June, 1848, did not Cavaignac and his men of order raise shouts of horror by stigmatising the insurgents as the assassins of Archbishop Affre! They knew perfectly well that the archbishop had been shot by the soldiers of order. M. Jacquemet, the archbishop's vicar-general, present on the spot, had immediately afterwards handed them in his evidence to that effect.

All this chorus of calumny, which the Party of Order never fail, in their orgies of blood, to raise against their victims, only proves that the bourgeois of our days considers himself the legitimate successor to the baron of old, who thought every weapon in his own hand fair against the plebeian, while in the hands of the plebeian a weapon of any kind constituted in itself a crime.

The conspiracy of the ruling class to break down the Revolution by a civil war carried on under the patronage of the foreign invader —a conspiracy which we have traced from the very 4th of September down to the entrance of MacMahon's praetorians through the gate of St. Cloud—culminated in the carnage of Paris. Bismarck gloats over the ruins of Paris, in which he saw perhaps the first instalment of that general destruction of great cities he had prayed for when still a simple Rural in the Prussian *Chambre introuvable* of 1849. He gloats over the cadavers of the Paris proletariat. For him this is not only the extermination of revolution, but the extinction of France, now decapitated in reality, and by the French Government itself. With the shallowness characteristic of all successful statesmen, he sees but the surface of this tremendous historic event. Whenever before has history exhibited the spectacle of a conqueror crowning his victory by turning into, not only the gendarme, but the hired bravo of the conquered Government? There existed no war between Prussia and the Commune of Paris. On the contrary, the Commune had accepted the peace preliminaries, and Prussia had announced her neutrality. Prussia was, therefore, no belligerent. She acted the part of a bravo, a cowardly bravo, because incurring no danger; a hired bravo, because stipulating beforehand the payment of her blood-money of 500 millions on the fall of Paris. And thus, at last, came out the true character of the war, ordained by Providence as a chastisement of godless and debauched France by pious and moral Germany! And this unparalled breach of the law of nations, even as understood by the old-world lawyers, instead of arousing the "civilised" Governments of Europe to declare the felonious Prussian Government, the mere tool of the St. Petersburg Cabinet, an outlaw amongst nations, only incites them to consider whether the few victims who escape the double cordon around Paris are not to be given up to the hangman at Versailles!

That after the most tremendous war of modern times, the conquering and the conquered hosts should fraternise for the common massacre of the proletariat—this unparalleled event does indicate, not, as Bismarck thinks, the final repression of a new society upheaving, but the crumbling into dust of bourgeois society. The highest heroic effort of which old society is still capable is national war; and this is now proved to be a mere governmental humbug, intended to defer the struggle of classes, and to be thrown aside as soon as that class struggle bursts out into civil war. Class rule is no longer able to disguise itself in a national uniform; the national Governments are *one* as against the proletariat!

After Whit-Sunday, 1871, there can be neither peace nor truce possible between the working men of France and the appropriators of their produce. The iron hand of a mercenary soldiery may keep for a time both classes tied down in common oppression. But the battle must break out again and again in ever-growing dimensions, and there can be no doubt as to who will be the victor in the end, —the appropriating few, or the immense working majority. And the French working class is only the advanced guard of the modern proletariat.

While the European governments thus testify, before Paris, to the international character of class-rule, they cry down the International Working Men's Association—the international counter-organisation of labour against the cosmopolitan conspiracy of capital —as the head fountain of all these disasters. Thiers denounced it as the despot of labour, pretending to be its liberator. Picard ordered those abroad should be cut off; Count Jaubert, Thiers' mummified accomplice of 1835, declares it the great problem of all civilised that all communications between the French Internationals and governments to weed it out. The Rurals roar against it, and the whole European press joins the chorus. An honourable French writer, completely foreign to our Association, speaks as follows:— "The members of the Central Committee of the National Guard, as well as the greater part of the members of the Commune, are the most active, intelligent, and energetic minds of the International Working Men's Association; . . . men who are thoroughly honest, sincere, intelligent, devoted, pure, and fanatical in the *good* sense of the word." The police-tinged bourgeois mind naturally figures to itself the International Working Men's Association as acting in the manner of a secret conspiracy, its central body ordering, from time to time, explosions in different countries. Our Association is, in fact, nothing but the international bond between the most advanced working men in the various countries of the civilised world. Whenever, in whatever shape, and under whatever conditions the class struggle obtains any consistency, it is but natural that members of our Association should stand in the foreground. The soil out of which it grows is modern society itself. It cannot be stamped out by any amount of carnage. To stamp it out, the Governments would have to stamp out the despotism of capital over labour—the condition of their own parasitical existence.

Working men's Paris, with its Commune, will be for ever celebrated as the glorious harbinger of a new society. Its martyrs are enshrined in the great heart of the working class. Its exterminators history has already nailed to that eternal pillory from which all the prayers of their priests will not avail to redeem them.

Notes

I

"The column of prisoners halted in the Avenue Uhrich, and was drawn up, four or five deep, on the footway facing to the road. General Marquis de Galliffet and his staff dismounted and commenced an inspection from the left of the line. Walking down slowly and eyeing the ranks, the General stopped here and there, tapping a man on the shoulder or beckoning him out of the rear ranks. In most cases, without further parley, the individual thus selected was marched out into the centre of the road, where a small supplementary column was, thus, soon formed. . . . It was evident that there was considerable room for error. A mounted officer pointed out to General Galliffet a man and woman for some particular offence. The woman, rushing out of the ranks, threw herself on her knees, and, with outstretched arms, protested her innocence in passionate terms. The General waited for a pause, and then with most impassible face and unmoved demeanour, said, 'Madame, I have visited every theatre in Paris, your acting will have no effect on me' (*'ce n'est pas la peine de jouer la comédie'*). . . . It was not a good thing on that day to be noticably taller, dirtier, cleaner, older, or uglier than one's neighbours. One individual in particular struck me as probably owing his speedy release from the ills of this world to his having a broken nose. . . Over a hundred being thus chosen, a firing party told off, and the column resumed its march, leaving them behind. A few minutes afterwards a dropping fire in our rear commenced, and continued for over a quarter of an hour. It was the execution of these summarily-convicted wretches."—*Paris Correspondent Daily News*, June 8th.—This Galliffet, "the kept man of his wife, so notorious for her shameless exhibitions at the orgies of the Second Empire," went, during the war, by the name of the French "Ensign Pistol."

"The *Temps* which is a careful journal, and not given to sensation, tells a dreadful story of people imperfectly shot and buried before life was extinct. A greater number were buried in the square round St. Jacques-la Bouchière; some of them very superficially. In the daytime the roar of the busy streets prevented any notice being taken; but in the stillness of the night the inhabitants of the houses in the neighbourhood were roused by distant moans, and in the morning a clenched hand was seen protruding through the soil. In consequence of this, exhumations were ordered to take place. . . . That many wounded have been buried alive I have not the slightest doubt. One case I can vouch for. When Brunel was shot with his mistress on the 24th ult. in the courtyard of a house in the Place Vendôme, the bodies lay there until the afternoon of the 27th. When the burial party came to remove the corpses, they found the woman living still and took her to an ambulance. Though she had received four bullets she is now out of danger."—*Paris Correspondent Evening Standard* June 8th.

II

The following letter appeared in the London *Times* of June 13th:

To the Editor of the *Times*:

Sir,—On June 6, 1871, M. Jules Favre issued a circular to all the European Powers, calling upon them to hunt down the International Working Men's Association. A few remarks will suffice to characterise that document.

In the very preamble of our statutes it is stated that the International was founded "September 28, 1864, at a public meeting held at St. Martin's Hall, Long Acre, London." For purposes of his own Jules Favre puts back the date of its origin behind 1862.

In order to explain our principles, he professes to quote "their (the International's) sheet of the 25th of March, 1869." And then what does he quote? The sheet of a society which is not the International. This sort of manoeuvre he already recurred to when, still a comparatively young lawyer, he had to defend the *National* newspaper, prosecuted for libel by Cabet. Then he pretended to read extracts from Cabet's pamphlets while reading interpolations of his own—a trick exposed while the Court was sitting, and which, but for the indulgence of Cabet, would have been punished by Jules Favre's expulsion from the Paris bar. Of all the documents quoted by him as documents of the International, not one belongs to the International. He says, for instance, "The Alliance declares itself Atheist, says the General Council, constituted in London in July 1869." The General Council never issued such a document. On the contrary, it issued a document which quashed the original statutes of the "Alliance"—L'Alliance de la Démocratie Socialiste at Geneva—quoted by Jules Favre.

Throughout his circular, which pretends in part also to be directed against the Empire, Jules Favre repeats against the International but the police inventions of the public prosecutors of the Empire, which broke down miserably even before the law courts of that Empire.

It is known that in its two addresses (of July and September last) on the late war, the General Council of the International denounced the Prussian plans of conquest against France. Later on, Mr. Reitlinger, Jules Favre's private secretary, applied, though of course in vain, to some members of the General Council for getting up by the Council a demonstration against Bismarck, in favour of the Government of National Defence; they were particularly requested not to mention the republic. The preparations for a demonstration with regard to the expected arrival of Jules Favre in London were made—certainly with the best of intentions—in spite of the General Council, which, in its address of the 9th of September, had distinctly forewarned the Paris workmen against Jules Favre and his colleagues.

What would Jules Favre say if, in its turn, the International were to send a circular on Jules Favre to all the Cabinets of Europe, drawing their particular attention to the documents published at Paris by the late M. Millière?[8]

I am, Sir, your obedient servant,

John Hales,

Secretary to the General Council of the International Working Men's Association.

London, June 12th, 1871.

In an article on "The International Society and its aims," that pious informer, the London *Spectator* (June 24), amongst other similar tricks, quotes, even more fully than Jules Favre has done, the above document of the "Alliance" as the work of the International, and that eleven days after the refutation had been published in the *Times*. We do not wonder at this. Frederick the Great used to say that of all Jesuits the worst are the Protestant ones.

8. See p. 539, above. [*R. T.*]

On Imperialism in India

KARL MARX

Marx's way of analyzing the problems of an Asian society under European imperial rule is reflected in these two articles which he wrote in English for *The New York Daily Tribune* and which were printed in its issues of June 25 and August 8, 1853. Of special interest in the analysis is the conception he entertained of Oriental despotism as an antique form of class society with a ruling bureaucracy based on large-scale irrigation works. We may note, too, his assumption that it was the fate of non-Western societies like that of India to go the way of bourgeois development as seen in modern Europe.

The British Rule in India

London, Friday, June 10, 1853

Hindostan is an Italy of Asiatic dimensions, the Himalayas for the Alps, the Plains of Bengal for the Plains of Lombardy, the Deccan for the Appenines, and the Isle of Ceylon for the Island of Sicily. The same rich variety in the products of the soil, and the same dismemberment in the political configuration. Just as Italy has, from time to time, been compressed by the conqueror's sword into different national masses, so do we find Hindostan, when not under the pressure of the Mohammedan, or the Mogul,[1] or the Briton, dissolved into as many independent and conflicting States as it numbered towns, or even villages. Yet, in a social point of view, Hindostan is not the Italy, but the Ireland of the East. And this strange combination of Italy and of Ireland, of a world of voluptuousness and of a world of woes, is anticipated in the ancient traditions of the religion of Hindostan. That religion is at once a religion of sensualist exuberance, and a religion of self-torturing asceticism; a religion of the Lingam[2] and of the Juggernaut; the religion of the Monk, and of the Bayadere.

1. *Mogul* dynasty: Moslem dynasty founded by Babur in 1526.
2. *Lingam*: Phallic emblem of the Hindu god Shiva. *Juggernaut* (Jaganath): An avatar of the god Vishnu.

I share not the opinion of those who believe in a golden age of Hindostan, without recurring, however, like Sir Charles Wood, for the confirmation of my view, to the authority of Khuli-Khan. But take, for example, the times of Aurung-Zebe;[3] or the epoch, when the Mogul appeared in the North, and the Portuguese in the South; or the age of Mohammedan invasion, and of the Heptarchy[4] in Southern India; or, if you will, go still more back to antiquity, take the mythological chronology of the Brahmin[5] himself, who places the commencement of Indian misery in an epoch even more remote than the Christian creation of the world.

There cannot, however, remain any doubt but that the misery inflicted by the British on Hindostan is of an essentially different and infinitely more intensive kind than all Hindostan had to suffer before. I do not allude to European despotism, planted upon Asiatic despotism, by the British East India Company,[6] forming a more monstrous combination than any of the divine monsters startling us in the temple of Salsette.[7] This is no distinctive feature of British colonial rule, but only an imitation of the Dutch, and so much so that in order to characterise the working of the British East India Company, it is sufficient to literally repeat what Sir Stamford Raffles, the *English* Governor of Java, said of the old Dutch East India Company:

"The Dutch Company, actuated solely by the spirit of gain, and viewing their subjects with less regard or consideration than a West India planter formerly viewed a gang upon his estate, because the latter had paid the purchase money of human property, which the other had not, employed all the existing machinery of despotism to squeeze from the people their utmost mite of contribution, the last dregs of their labour, and thus aggravated the evils of a capricious and semi-barbarous Government, by working it with all the practised ingenuity of politicians, and all the monopolising selfishness of traders."

All the civil wars, invasions, revolutions, conquests, famines, strangely complex, rapid and destructive as the successive action in Hindostan may appear, did not go deeper than its surface. England

---

3. *Aurung-Zebe*: Mogul emperor (1659–1707) who attempted to suppress Hinduism.
4. The *Heptarchy* (Seven Governments): The conventional designation in English history of the seven Saxon Kingdoms (sixth to eighth century). Marx by analogy uses this term here to denote the feudal dismemberment of the Deccan before its conquest by the Moslems.
5. *Brahmin*: A Hindu of the highest caste.
6. The *British East India Company*

was organised in 1600 for the purpose of carrying on a monopoly trade with India. Under cover of the Company's "trading" operations the English capitalists conquered the country and governed it for decades. During the Indian uprising of 1857–1859 the Company was dissolved and the British Government began to rule India directly.
7. *The temple of Salsette*: A cave temple situated on the island of that name near the city of Bombay. It contains a huge number of carvings, chiselled in stone like the entire temple itself.

has broken down the entire framework of Indian society, without any symptoms of reconstitution yet appearing. This loss of his old world, with no gain of a new one, imparts a particular kind of melancholy to the present misery of the Hindoo, and separates Hindostan, ruled by Britain, from all its ancient traditions, and from the whole of its past history.

There have been in Asia, generally, from immemorial times, but three departments of Government: that of Finance, or the plunder of the interior; that of War, or the plunder of the exterior; and, finally, the department of Public Works. Climate and territorial conditions, especially the vast tracts of desert, extending from the Sahara, through Arabia, Persia, India and Tartary, to the most elevated Asiatic highlands, constituted artificial irrigation by canals and waterworks the basis of Oriental agriculture. As in Egypt and India, inundations are used for fertilising the soil of Mesopotamia, Persia, etc.; advantage is taken of a high level for feeding irrigative canals. This prime necessity of an economical and common use of water, which, in the Occident, drove private enterprise to voluntary association, as in Flanders and Italy, necessitated, in the Orient where civilisation was too low and the territorial extent too vast to call into life voluntary association, the interference of the centralising power of Government. Hence an economical function devolved upon all Asiatic Governments the function of providing public works. This artificial fertilisation of the soil, dependent on a Central Government, and immediately decaying with the neglect of irrigation and drainage, explains the otherwise strange fact that we now find whole territories barren and desert that were once brilliantly cultivated, as Palmyra, Petra, the ruins in Yemen, and large provinces of Egypt, Persia and Hindostan; it also explains how a single war of devastation has been able to depopulate a country for centuries, and to strip it of all its civilisation.

Now, the British in East India accepted from their predecessors the department of finance and of war, but they have neglected entirely that of public works. Hence the deterioration of an agriculture which is not capable of being conducted on the British principle of free competition, of *laissez-faire* and *laissez-aller*. But in Asiatic empires we are quite accustomed to see agriculture deteriorating under one government and reviving again under some other government. There the harvests correspond to good or bad government, as they change in Europe with good or bad seasons. Thus the oppression and neglect of agriculture, bad as it is, could not be looked upon as the final blow dealt to Indian society by the British intruder, had it not been attended by a circumstance of quite different importance, a novelty in the annals of the whole Asiatic world. However changing the political aspect of India's past must appear, its social condition has remained unaltered since its remotest antiquity, until the first decennium of the 19th century. The hand-loom and the spinning-wheel, producing their regular myriads of spinners and weavers, were the pivots of the structure of that society. From immemorial times, Europe received the admirable textures of Indian labour, sending in return for them her precious metals, and furnishing thereby his material to the goldsmith, that indispensable member of Indian society, whose love of finery is so great that even the lowest class, those who go about nearly naked, have commonly a pair of golden ear-rings and a gold ornament of some kind hung round their necks. Rings on the fingers and toes have also been common. Women as well as children frequently wore massive bracelets and anklets of gold or silver, and statuettes of divinities in gold and silver were met with in the households. It was the British intruder who broke up the Indian hand-loom and destroyed the spinning wheel. England began with driving the Indian cottons from the European market; it then introduced twist into Hindostan and in the end inundated the very mother country of cotton with cottons. From 1818 to 1836 the export of twist from Great Britain to India rose in the proportion of 1 to 5,200. In 1824 the export of British muslins to India hardly amounted to 1,000,000 yards while in 1837 it surpassed 64,000,000 yards. But at the same time the population of Dacca decreased from 150,000 inhabitants to 20,000. This decline of Indian towns celebrated for their fabrics was by no means the worst consequence. British steam and science uprooted, over the whole surface of Hindostan, the union between agricultural and manufacturing industry.

These two circumstances—the Hindoo, on the one hand, leaving, like all Oriental peoples, to the central government the care of the great public works, the prime condition of his agriculture and commerce, dispersed, on the other hand over the surface of the country, and agglomerated in small centres by the domestic union of agricultural and manufacturing pursuits—these two circumstances had brought about, since the remotest times, a social system of particular features—the so-called *village system*, which gave to each of these small unions their independent organisation and distinct life. The peculiar character of this system may be judged from the following description, contained in an old official report of the British House of Commons on Indian affairs:

"A village, geographically considered, is a tract of country comprising some hundred or thousand acres of arable and waste lands; politically viewed it resembles a corporation or township. Its proper establishment of officers and servants consists of the following descriptions: the *potail*, or head inhabitant, who has generally the superintendence of the affairs of the village, settles the disputes of the inhabitants, attends to the police, and performs the duty of collecting the revenue within his village, a duty which his personal influence and minute acquaintance with the situation and concerns of the people render him the best qualified for this charge. The *kurnum* keeps the accounts of cultivation, and registers everything connected with it. The *Tallier* and the *totie*, the duty of the former of which consists in gaining information of crimes and offences, and in escorting and protecting persons travelling from one village to another; the province of the latter appearing to be more immediately confined to the village, consisting, among other duties, in guarding the crops and assisting in measuring them. The *boundary man*, who preserves the limits of the village, or gives evidence respecting them in cases of dispute. The Superintendent of Tanks and Watercourses distributes the water for the purposes of agriculture. The Brahmin, who performs the village worship. The schoolmaster, who is seen teaching the children in a village to read and write in the sand. The calendar-Brahmin, or astrologer, etc. These officers and servants generally constitute the establishment of a village; but in some parts of the country it is of less extent; some of the duties and functions above described being united in the same person; in others it exceeds the above-named number of individuals. Under this simple form of municipal government, the inhabitants of the country have lived from time immemorial. The boundaries of the villages have been but seldom altered; and though the villages themselves have been sometimes injured, and even desolated by war, famine or disease, the same name, the same limits, the same interests, and even the same families, have continued for ages. The inhabitants gave themselves no trouble about the breaking up and divisions of kingdoms; while the village remains entire, they care not to what power it is transferred, or to what sovereign it devolves; its internal economy remains unchanged. The *potail* is still the head inhabitant, and still acts as the petty judge or magistrate, and collector or rentor of the village."

These small stereotype forms of social organism have been to the greater part dissolved, and are disappearing, not so much through the brutal interference of the British tax-gatherer and the British soldier, as to the working of English steam and English free trade. Those family-communities were based on domestic industry, in that peculiar combination of hand-weaving, hand-spinning and hand-tilling agriculture which gave them self-supporting power. English interference having placed the spinner in Lancashire and the weaver in Bengal, or sweeping away both Hindoo spinner and weaver, dissolved these small semi-barbarian, semi-civilised communities, by blowing up their economical basis, and thus produced the greatest, and, to speak the truth, the only *social* revolution ever heard of in Asia.

Now, sickening as it must be to human feeling to witness those myriads of industrious patriarchal and inoffensive social organisations disorganised and dissolved into their units, thrown into a sea of woes, and their individual members losing at the same time their ancient form of civilisation, and their hereditary means of subsistence, we must not forget that these idyllic village communities, inoffensive though they may appear, had always been the solid foundation of Oriental despotism, that they restrained the human mind within the smallest possible compass, making it the unresisting tool of superstition, enslaving it beneath traditional rules, depriving it of all grandeur and historical energies. We must not forget the barbarian egotism which, concentrating on some miserable patch of land, had quietly witnessed the ruin of empires, the perpetration of unspeakable cruelties, the massacre of the population of large towns, with no other consideration bestowed upon them than on natural events, itself the helpless prey of any aggressor who deigned to notice it at all. We must not forget that this undignified, stagnatory, and vegetative life, that this passive sort of existence evoked on the other part, in contradistinction, wild, aimless, unbounded forces of destruction and rendered murder itself a religious rite in Hindostan. We must not forget that these little communities were contaminated by distinctions of caste and by slavery, that they subjugated man to external circumstances instead of elevating man to be the sovereign of circumstances, that they transformed a self-developing social state into never changing natural destiny, and thus brought about a brutalising worship of nature, exhibiting its degradation in the fact that man, the sovereign of nature, fell down on his knees in adoration of *Hanuman*, the monkey, and *Sabbala*, the cow.

England, it is true, in causing a social revolution in Hindostan, was actuated only by the vilest interests, and was stupid in her manner of enforcing them. But that is not the question. The question is, can mankind fulfill its destiny without a fundamental revolution in the social state of Asia? If not, whatever may have been the crimes of England she was the unconscious tool of history in bringing about that revolution.

Then, whatever bitterness the spectacle of the crumbling of an ancient world may have for our personal feelings, we have the right, in point of history, to exclaim with Goethe:

> "Sollte diese Qual uns quälen,
> Da sie unsre Lust vermehrt,
> Hat nicht Myriaden Seelen
> Timur's Heerschaft aufgezehrt?"[8]

8. Should this torture then torment us / Since it brings us greater pleasure? / Were not through the rule of Timur / Souls devoured without measure? (Goethe, *Westöstlicher Diwan. An Suleika*)

The Future Results of British Rule in India

London, Friday, July 22, 1853

How came it that English supremacy was established in India? The paramount power of the Great Mogul was broken by the Mogul Viceroys. The power of the Viceroys was broken by the Mahrattas.[9] The power of the Mahrattas was broken by the Afghans, and while all were struggling against all, the Briton rushed in and was enabled to subdue them all. A country not only divided between Mohammedan and Hindoo, but between tribe and tribe, between caste and caste; a society whose framework was based on a sort of equilibrium, resulting from a general repulsion and constitutional exclusiveness between all its members. Such a country and such a society, where they not the predestined prey of conquest? If we knew nothing of the past history of Hindostan, would there not be the one great and incontestable fact, that even at this moment India is held in English thraldom by an Indian army maintained at the cost of India? India, then, could not escape the fate of being conquered, and the whole of her past history, if it be anything, is the history of the successive conquests she has undergone. Indian society has no history at all, at least no known history. What we call its history, is but the history of the successive intruders who founded their empires on the passive basis of that unresisting and unchanging society. The question, therefore, is not whether the English had a right to conquer India, but whether we are to prefer India conquered by the Turk, by the Persian, by the Russian, to India conquered by the Briton.

England has to fulfil a double mission in India: one destructive, the other regenerating—the annihilation of old Asiatic society, and the laying of the material foundations of Western society in Asia.

Arabs, Turks, Tartars, Moguls, who had successively overrun India, soon became *Hindooised*, the barbarian conquerors being, by an eternal law of history, conquered themselves by the superior civilisation of their subjects. The British were the first conquerors superior, and therefore, inaccessible to Hindoo civilisation. They destroyed it by breaking up the native communities, by uprooting the native industry, and by levelling all that was great and elevated in the native society. The historic pages of their rule in India report hardly anything beyond that destruction. The work of regeneration

9. *Mahrattas:* A group of peoples in Central India which rose against the Mohammedans and in the beginning of the eighteenth century formed a confederation of feudal princedoms.

hardly transpires through a heap of ruins. Nevertheless it has begun.

The political unity of India, more consolidated, and extending farther than it ever did under the Great Moguls, was the first condition of its regeneration. That unity, imposed by the British sword, will now be strengthened and perpetuated by the electric telegraph. The native army, organised and trained by the British drill-sergeant, was the *sine qua non* of Indian self-emancipation, and of India ceasing to be the prey of the first foreign intruder. The free press, introduced for the first time into Asiatic society, and managed principally by the common offspring of Hindoo and Europeans, is a new and powerful agent of reconstruction. The *Zemindars*[1] and *Ryotwar*[2] themselves, abominable as they are, involve two distinct forms of private property in land—the great *desideratum* of Asiatic society. From the Indian natives, reluctantly and sparingly educated at Calcutta, under English superintendence, a fresh class is springing up, endowed with the requirements for government and imbued with European science. Steam has brought India into regular and rapid communication with Europe, has connected its chief ports with those of the whole south-eastern ocean, and has revindicated it from the isolated position which was the prime law of its stagnation. The day is not far distant when, by a combination of railways and steam vessels, the distance between England and India, measured by time, will be shortened to eight days, and when that once fabulous country will thus be actually annexed to the Western world.

The ruling classes of Great Britain have had, till now, but an accidental, transitory and exceptional interest in the progress of India. The aristocracy wanted to conquer it, the moneyocracy to plunder it, and the millocracy to undersell it. But now the tables are turned. The millocracy have discovered that the transformation of India into a reproductive country has become of vital importance to them, and that, to that end, it is necessary, above all, to gift her with means of irrigation and of internal communication. They intend now drawing a net of railways over India. And they will do it. The results must be inappreciable.

It is notorious that the productive powers of India are paralysed by the utter want of means for conveying and exchanging its various produce. Nowhere, more than in India, do we meet with social destitution in the midst of natural plenty, for want of the means of exchange. It was proved before a Committee of the British House

1. *Zemindars*: New big landowners who were established by the British from among former tax collectors and merchant-usurers through the expropriation of the Indian peasantry. The zemindar system was widespread in Northeast India.

2. *Ryotwar*: A system of renting land to peasants for an unlimited period of time. Introduced by the British in the South of India, it permitted the British authorities to let land to peasants on extremely onerous terms.

of Commons, which sat in 1848, that "when grain was selling from
6s. to 8s. a quarter at Kandeish, it was sold at 64s. to 70s. at Poonah,
where the people were dying in the streets of famine, without the
possibility of gaining supplies from Kandeish, because the clay-roads
were impracticable."

The introduction of railways may be easily made to subserve agricultural purposes by the formation of tanks, where ground is
required for embankment, and by the conveyance of water along
the different lines. Thus irrigation, the *sine qua non* of farming in
the East, might be greatly extended, and the frequently recurring
local famines, arising from the want of water, would be averted.
The general importance of railways, viewed under this head, must
become evident, when we remember that irrigated lands, even in
the district near Ghauts, pay three times as much in taxes, afford
ten or twelve times as much employment, and yield twelve or
fifteen times as much profit, as the same area without irrigation.

Railways will afford the means of diminishing the amount and
the cost of the military establishments. Col. Warren, Town Major
of the Fort St. William, stated before a Select Committee of the
House of Commons:

"The practicability of receiving intelligence from distant parts of
the country in as many hours as at present it requires days and even
weeks, and of sending instructions with troops and stores, in the
more brief period, are considerations which cannot be too highly
estimated. Troops could be kept at more distant and healthier stations than at present, and much loss of life from sickness would by
this means be spared. Stores could not to the same extent be
required at the various dépôts, and the loss by decay, and the
destruction incidental to the climate, would also be avoided. The
number of troops might be diminished in direct proportion to their
effectiveness."

We know that the municipal organisation and the economical
basis of the village communities has been broken up, but their
worst feature, the dissolution of society into stereotyped and disconnected atoms, has survived their vitality. The village isolation produced the absence of roads in India, and the absence of roads perpetuated the village isolation. On this plan a community existed
with a given scale of low conveniences, almost without intercourse
with other villages, without the desires and efforts indispensable to
social advance. The British having broken up this self-sufficient *iner-
tia* of the villlages, railways will provide the new want of communication and intercourse. Besides, "one of the effects of the railway
system will be to bring into every village affected by it such knowledge of the contrivances and appliances of other countries, and such
means of obtaining them, as will first put the hereditary and stipen-

diary village artisanship of India to full proof of its capabilities, and then supply its defects." (Chapman, *The Cotton and Commerce of India.*)

I know that the English millocracy intend to endow India with railways with the exclusive view of extracting at diminished expenses the cotton and other raw materials for their manufactures. But when you have once introduced machinery into the locomotion of a country, which possesses iron and coals, you are unable to withhold it from its fabrication. You cannot maintain a net of railways over an immense country without introducing all those industrial processes necessary to meet the immediate and current wants of railway locomotion, and out of which there must grow the application of machinery to those branches of industry not immediately connected with railways. The railway-system will therefore become, in India, truly the forerunner of modern industry. This is the more certain as the Hindoos are allowed by British authorities themselves to possess particular aptitude for accommodating themselves to entirely new labour, and acquiring the requisite knowledge of machinery. Ample proof of this fact is afforded by the capacities and expertness of the native engineers in the Calcutta mint, where they have been for years employed in working the steam machinery, by the natives attached to the several steam engines in the Hurdwar coal districts and by other instances. Mr. Campbell himself, greatly influenced as he is by the prejudices of the East India Company, is obliged to avow "that the great mass of the Indian people possesses a great *industrial energy*, is well fitted to accumulate capital, and remarkable for a mathematical clearness of head, and talent for figures and exact sciences." "Their intellects," he says, "are excellent." Modern industry, resulting from the railway-system, will dissolve the hereditary divisions of labour, upon which rest the Indian castes, those decisive impediments to Indian progress and Indian power.

All the English bourgeoisie may be forced to do will neither emancipate nor materially mend the social condition of the mass of the people, depending not only on the development of the productive powers, but on their appropriation by the people. But what they will not fail to do is to lay down the material premises for both. Has the bourgeoisie ever done more? Has it ever affected a progress without dragging individuals and peoples through blood and dirt, through misery and degradation?

The Indians will not reap the fruits of the new elements of society scattered among them by the British bourgeoisie, till in Great Britain itself the now ruling classes shall have been supplanted by the industrial proletariat, or till the Hindoos themselves shall have grown strong enough to throw off the English yoke altogether. At all events, we may safely expect to see, at a more or less remote period, the regeneration of that great and interesting country, whose gentle natives are, to use the expression of Prince Soltykov, even in the most inferior classes, *"plus fins et plus adroits que les Italiens,"*[3] whose submission even is counterbalanced by a certain calm nobility, who, notwithstanding their natural languor, have astonished the British officers by their bravery, whose country has been the source of our languages, our religions, and who represent the type of the ancient German in the *Jat*[4] and the type of the ancient Greek in the Brahmin.

I cannot part with the subject of India without some concluding remarks.

The profound hypocrisy and inherent barbarism of bourgeois civilisation lies unveiled before our eyes, turning from its home, where it assumes respectable forms, to the colonies, where it goes naked. They are the defenders of property, but did any revolutionary party ever originate agrarian revolutions like those in Bengal, in Madras, and in Bombay? Did they not, in India, to borrow an expression of that great robber, Lord Clive himself, resort to atrocious extortion, when simple corruption could not keep pace with their rapacity? While they prated in Europe about the inviolable sanctity of the national debt, did they not confiscate in India the dividends of the *rajahs*, who had invested their private savings in the Company's own funds? While they combatted the French revolution under the pretext of defending "our holy religion," did they not forbid, at the same time, Christianity to be propagated in India, and did they not, in order to make money out of the pilgrims streaming to the temples of Orissa and Bengal, take up the trade in the murder and prostitution perpetrated in the temple of Juggernaut? These are the men of "Property, Order, Family, and Religion."

The devastating effects of English industry, when contemplated with regard to India, a country as vast as Europe, and containing 150 millions of acres, are palpable and confounding. But we must not forget that they are only the organic results of the whole system of production as it is now constituted. That production rests on the supreme rule of capital. The centralisation of capital is essential to the existence of capital as an independent power. The destructive influence of that centralisation upon the markets of the world does but reveal, in the most gigantic dimensions, the inherent organic laws of political economy now at work in every civilised town. The bourgeois period of history has to create the material basis of the new world—on the one hand the universal intercourse founded upon the mutual dependency of mankind, and the means of that intercourse; on the other hand the development of the productive

3. Marx quotes from A. D. Soltykov's book *Lettres sur l'Inde*, Paris, 1848.   4. *Jats*: A caste in Northwest India.

powers of man and the transformation of material production into a scientific domination of natural agencies. Bourgeois industry and commerce create these material conditions of a new world in the same way as geological revolutions have created the surface of the earth. When a great social revolution shall have mastered the results of the bourgeois epoch, the market of the world and the modern powers of production, and subjected them to the common control of the most advanced peoples, then only will human progress cease to resemble that hideous pagan idol, who would not drink the nectar but from the skulls of the slain.

On Social Relations in Russia

FRIEDRICH ENGELS

Russian radicals in the second half of the nineteenth century showed an increasingly intense interest in Marxism, and Marx noted in a letter of 1880 that in Russia "*Capital* is more read and appreciated than anywhere else." Until the 1890's, however, the Russian socialist movement was largely Populist (*narodnik*), believing that in pre-bourgeois Russia there could be an early socialist revolution based on peasant rather than proletarian masses and using the archaic village commune as the nucleus of a future Russian socialist society. Leading Russian Populists occasionally wrote to Marx and Engels, either to elicit their views on the Russian situation or to defend their own views. One of them, Pyotr Tkachov, wrote an "Open Letter" to Engels in 1874, and Engels' reply, in the form of the essay printed here, is the fullest statement of his own and Marx's appraisal of Russian society in the late nineteenth century and the prospects for revolution there. Engels' essay was published in 1875 as a separate pamphlet.

On the subject matter proper, Mr. Tkachov tells the German workers that as regards Russia I possess not even a "little knowledge," possess nothing but "ignorance"; and he feels himself, therefore, obliged to explain to them the real state of affairs, and in particular the reasons why just at the present time a social revolution could be made in Russia with the greatest of ease, much more easily than in Western Europe.

"We have no urban proletariat, that is undoubtedly true; but, then, we also have no bourgeoisie; . . . our workers will have to fight only against the *political power*—the *power of capital* is with us still only in embryo. And you, sir, are undoubtedly aware that the fight against the former is much easier than against the latter."

The revolution which modern socialism strives to achieve is, briefly, the victory of the proletariat over the bourgeoisie, and the establishment of a new organisation of society by the destruction of all class distinctions. This requires not only a proletariat that carries out this revolution, but also a bourgeoisie in whose hands the productive forces of society have developed so far that they allow of the final destruction of class distinctions. Among savages and semi-savages there likewise often exist no class distinctions, and every people has passed through such a state. It could not occur to us to re-establish this state, for the simple reason that class distinctions necessarily emerge out of it as the productive forces of society develop. Only at a certain level of development of the productive forces of society, an even very high level for our modern conditions, does it become possible to raise production to such an extent that the abolition of class distinctions can be a real progress, can be lasting without bringing about stagnation or even decline in the mode of social production. But the productive forces have reached this level of development only in the hands of the bourgeoisie. The bourgeoisie, therefore, in this respect also is just as necessary a precondition of the socialist revolution as the proletariat itself. Hence a man who will say that this revolution can be more easily carried out in a country, because, *although* it has no proletariat, it has no bourgeoisie *either*, only proves that he has still to learn the ABC of socialism.

The Russian workers—and these workers are, as Mr. Tkachov himself says, "tillers of the soil and as such not proletarians but *owners*—have, therefore, an easier task because they do not have to fight against the power of capital, but "only against the political power," against the Russian state. And this state "appears only at a distance as a power; . . . it has no roots in the economic life of the people; it does not embody the interests of any particular estate. . . . In your country the state is no imaginary power. It stands four square on the basis of capital; it embodies in itself [!!] certain economic interests. . . . In our country the situation is just the reverse —the form of our society owes its existence to the state, to a state hanging in the air, so to speak, one that has nothing in common with the existing social order, and that has its roots in the past, but not in the present."

Let us waste no time over the confused notion that the economic interests need the state, which they themselves create, in order to acquire a *body*, or over the bold contention that the Russian "form of society (which, of course, must include also the communal property of the peasants) owes its existence to the state," or over the contradiction that this same state "has nothing in common" with the existing social order which is supposed to be its very own creation. Let us rather examine at once this "state hanging in the air," which does not represent the interests of even a single estate.

In European Russia the peasants possess 105 million dessiatins, the nobility (as I shall here term the big landowners for the sake of brevity) 100 million dessiatins of land, of which about half belong to 15,000 nobles, who consequently each possess on the average 3,-300 dessiatins. The land of the peasants is, therefore, only a trifle bigger than that of the nobles. So you see, the nobles have not the slightest interest in the existence of the Russian state, which protects them in the possession of half the country! To continue. The peasants, from their half, pay 195 million rubles land tax annually, the nobles—13 million! The lands of the nobles are on the average twice as fertile as those of the peasants, because during the settlement for the redemption of the *corvée* the state not only took the greater part but also the best part of the land from the peasants and gave it to the nobles, and for this worst land the peasants had to pay the nobility the price of the best. And the Russian nobility has no interest in the existence of the Russian state!

The peasants—taken in the mass—have been put by the redemption into a most miserable and wholly untenable position. Not only has the greatest and best part of their land been taken from them, so that in all the fertile parts of the country the peasant land is far too small—under Russian agricultural conditions—for them to be able to make a living from it. Not only were they charged an excessive price for it, advanced to them by the state and for which they now have to pay interest and instalments on the principal to the state. Not only is almost the whole burden of the land tax thrown upon them, while the nobility escapes almost scot-free—so that the land tax alone consumes the entire ground rent value of the peasant land and more, and all further payments which the peasant has to make and which we will speak of immediately are direct deductions from that part of his income which represents his wages. Then, in addition to the land tax, to the interest and amortisation payments on the money advanced by the state, since the recent introduction of local administration, there are the provincial and district imposts as well. The most essential consequence of this "reform" was fresh tax burdens for the peasant. The state retained its revenues in their entirety, but passed on a large part of its expenditure to the provinces and districts, which imposed new taxes to meet them, and in Russia it is the rule that the higher estates are almost tax exempt and the peasant pays almost everything.

Such a situation is as if specially created for the usurer, and with the almost unequalled talent of the Russians for trading on a lower level, for taking full advantage of favourable business situations and the swindling inseparable from this—Peter I long ago said that one Russian could get the better of three Jews—the usurer everywhere makes his appearance. When taxes are about to fall due, the usurer, the kulak—frequently a rich peasant of the same village community—comes along and offers his ready cash. The peasant must have the money at all costs and is obliged to accept the conditions of the usurer without demur. But this only gets him into a tighter fix, and he needs more and more ready cash. At harvest time the grain dealer arrives; the need for money forces the peasant to sell a part of the grain which he and his family require for their subsistence. The grain dealer spreads false rumours which lower prices, pays a low price and often even part of this in all sorts of high-priced goods; for the truck system is also highly developed in Russia. It is quite obvious that the great corn exports of Russia are based directly on the starvation of the peasant population. Another method of exploiting the peasant is the following: a speculator rents domain land from the government for a long term of years, and cultivates it himself as long as it yields a good crop without manure; then he divides it up into small plots and lets out the exhausted land at high rents to neighbouring peasants who cannot manage on the income from their allotment. Here we have exactly the Irish middlemen, just as above the English truck system. In short, there is no country in which, in spite of the pristine savagery of bourgeois society, capitalistic parasitism is so developed, so covers and entangles the whole country, the whole mass of the population, with its nets as in Russia. And all these bloodsuckers of the peasants are supposed to have no interest in the existence of the Russian state, whose laws and law courts protect their sleek and profitable practices!

The big bourgeoisie of Petersburg, Moscow, Odessa, which has developed with unheard-of rapidity during the last decade, chiefly due to the railways, and which cheerfully "went smash" along with the rest during the last swindle years, the grain, hemp, flax and tallow exporters, whose whole business is built up on the misery of the peasant, the entire Russian large-scale industry, which only exists thanks to the protective tariffs granted it by the state—have all these important and rapidly growing elements of the population no interest in the existence of the Russian state? To say nothing of the countless army of officials, which swarms over Russia and plunders it and here constitutes a real social estate. And when Mr. Tkachov assures us that the Russian state has "no roots in the economic life of the people," that "it does not embody the interests of any particular estate," that it "hangs in the air," methinks it is not the Russian state that hangs in the air, but rather Mr. Tkachov.

It is clear that the condition of the Russian peasants since the emancipation from serfdom has become intolerable and cannot be maintained much longer, and that for this reason alone if for no other a revolution is in the offing in Russia. The question is only: what can be, what will be the result of this revolution? Mr. Tkachov says it will be a social one. This is pure tautology. Every real revolution is a social one, in that it brings a new class to power and allows it to remodel society in its own image. But he wants to say it will be a socialist one, it will introduce into Russia the form of society aimed at by West European socialism, even before we in the West succeed in doing so—and that in a condition of society in which both proletariat and bourgeoisie appear only sporadically and at a low stage of development. And this is supposed to be possible because the Russians are, so to speak, the chosen people of socialism, and have artels and common ownership of land.

The artel, which Mr. Tkachov mentions only incidentally, but which we include here because since the time of Herzen it has played a mysterious role with many Russians—the artel in Russia is a widespread form of association, the simplest form of free co-operation, such as is to be found for hunting among hunting tribes. Word and content are not of Slavic but of Tatar origin. Both are to be found among the Kirghiz, Yakuts, etc., on the one hand, and among the Lapps, Samoyeds and other Finnish peoples, on the other.[1] That is why the artel developed originally in the North and East, by contact with Finns and Tatars, not in the South-West. The severe climate makes necessary industrial activity of various kinds, and so the lack of urban development and of capital is replaced, as far as possible, by this form of co-operation. One of the most characteristic features of the artel, the collective responsibility of its members for one another to third parties, was based originally on blood relationship, like the mutual liability [Gewere] of the ancient Germans, the blood vengeance, etc. Moreover, in Russia the word artel is used for every form of not only collective activity but also collective institution. The *Bourse* is also an artel. In workers' artels, an elder (*starosta, starshina*) is always chosen who fulfils the functions of treasurer, bookkeeper, etc., and of manager as far as necessary and receives a special salary. Such artels are formed:

1. For temporary enterprises, after the completion of which they dissolve;

2. For the members of one and the same trade, for instance, porters, etc.;

3. For permanent enterprises, industrial in the proper sense of the word.

They are established by a contract signed by all the members. Now if these members cannot bring together the necessary capital, as very often happens, for instance, in the case of cheeseries and fisheries (for nets, boats, etc.), the artel falls a prey to the usurer, who advances the amount lacking at high interest, and thereafter pockets

1. On the artel, compare *inter alia: Sbornik materialov ob artelyakh v Rossii* [*Collection of Material on Artels in Russia*], St. Petersburg 1873, Part 1. [*Engels*]

the greater part of the income from work. Still more shamefully exploited, however, are the artels which hire themselves in a body to an employer as wage labourers. They direct their industrial activity themselves and thus save the capitalist the cost of supervision. The latter lets to the members huts to live in and advances them the means of subsistence, which in turn gives rise to the most disgraceful truck system. Such is the case with the lumbermen and tar distillers in the Archangel *gubernia*, and in many trades in Siberia, etc. (*Cf.* Flerovsky, *Polozheniye rabochevo klassa v Rossii. [The Condition of the Working Class in Russia]*, St. Petersburg 1869.) Here then the artel serves to considerably *facilitate* the exploitation of the wage-worker by the capitalist. On the other hand, there are also artels which themselves employ wage-workers, who are *not* members of the association.

It is thus seen that the artel is a co-operative society which has arisen spontaneously and is, therefore, still very undeveloped, and as such neither exclusively Russian nor even Slavic. Such societies are formed wherever the need for them exists. For instance, in Switzerland among the dairy farmers, in England among the fishermen, where they even assume a great variety of forms. The Silesian navvies (Germans, not Poles), who built so many German railways in the forties, were organised in complete artels. The predominance of this form in Russia proves, it is true, the existence in the Russian people of a strong impulse to associate, but is far from proving their ability to jump, with the aid of this impulse, from the artel straight into the socialist order of society. For that, it is necessary above all that the artel itself should be capable of development, that it shed its primitive form, in which, as we saw, it serves the workers less than it does capital, and rise *at least* to the level of the West European co-operative societies. But if we are to believe Mr. Tkachov for once (which, after all that has preceded, is certainly more than risky), this is by no means the case. On the contrary, he assures us with a pride highly indicative of his standpoint: "As regards the co-operative and credit associations on the German [!] model, recently artificially transplanted to Russia, these have met with complete indifference on the part of the majority of our workers and have been a failure almost everywhere." The modern co-operative society has at least proved that it can run large-scale industry profitably on its own account (spinning and weaving in Lancashire). The artel is so far not only incapable of doing this; it must of necessity even be destroyed by big industry if it does not develop further.

The communal property of the Russian peasants was discovered about the year 1845 by the Prussian Government Councillor Haxthausen and trumpeted to the world as something absolutely wonderful, although Haxthausen could still have found survivals enough of it in his Westphalian homeland, and, as a government official, it was even part of his duty to know them thoroughly. It was from Haxthausen that Herzen, himself a Russian landowner, first learned that his peasants owned the land in common, and he made use of the fact to describe the Russian peasants as the true vehicles of socialism, as born Communists in contrast to the workers of the aging, decayed European West, who would first have to go through the ordeal of acquiring socialism artificially. From Herzen this knowledge came to Bakunin, and from Bakunin to Mr. Tkachov. Let us hear the latter:

"Our people . . . in its great majority . . . is permeated with the principles of common ownership; it is, if one may use the term, instinctively, traditionally communist. The idea of collective property is so closely interwoven with the whole world outlook [we shall see immediately how far the world of the Russian peasant extends] of the Russian people that today, when the government begins to understand that this idea is incompatible with the principles of a 'well-ordered' society, and in the name of these principles wishes to impress the idea of individual property on the consciousness and life of the people, it can succeed in doing so only with the help of the bayonet and the knout. It is clear from this that our people, despite its ignorance, is much nearer to socialism than the peoples of Western Europe, although the latter are more educated."

In reality communal ownership of the land is an institution which is to be found among all Indo-Germanic peoples on a low level of development, from India to Ireland, and even among the Malays, who are developing under Indian influence, for instance, in Java. As late as 1608, in the newly conquered North of Ireland, the legally established communal ownership of the land served the English as a pretext for declaring the land as ownerless and as escheated to the Crown. In India a whole series of forms of communal property has been in existence down to the present time. In Germany it was general; the communal lands still to be found here and there are a relic of it; and often still distinct traces of it, temporary divisions of the communal lands, etc., are also to be found, especially in the mountains. More exact references and details with regard to old German communal ownership may be consulted in the various writings of *Maurer*, which are classic on this question. In Western Europe, including Poland and Little Russia, at a certain stage in the social development, this communal ownership became a fetter, a brake on agricultural production, and was more and more eliminated. In Great Russia (that is, Russia proper), on the other hand, it has persisted until today, thereby proving in the first place that here agricultural production and the social conditions in the countryside corresponding to it are still very undeveloped, as is actually the case. The Russian peasant lives and has his being only in his village community; the rest of the world exists for him only in so far as it interferes with his village community. This is so much the case that in Russia the same word, *mir*, means, on the one hand, "world" and, on the other, "peasant community." *Ves mir*, the whole world, means to the peasant the meeting of the community members. Hence, when Mr. Tkachov speaks of the *"world outlook"* of the Russian peasants, he has obviously translated the Russian *mir* incorrectly. Such a complete isolation of the individual communities from one another, which creates throughout the country similar, but the very opposite of common, interests, is the natural basis for *Oriental despotism*, and from India to Russia this form of society, wherever it prevailed, has always produced it, and always found its complement in it. Not only the Russian state in general, but even its specific form, tsarist despotism, instead of hanging in the air, is the necessary and logical product of Russian social conditions with which, according to Mr. Tkachov, it has "nothing in common"! Further development of Russia in a *bourgeois* direction would here also destroy communal property little by little, without any need for the Russian government to intervene with "bayonet and knout." And this all the more because the communally owned land in Russia is not cultivated by the peasants in common so that the product may then be divided, as is still the case in some districts in India; on the contrary, from time to time the land is divided up among the various heads of families, and each cultivates his allotment for himself. Consequently, great differences in degree of prosperity are possible among the members of the community, and actually exist. Almost everywhere there are a few rich peasants among them—here and there millionaires—who play the usurer and suck the blood of the mass of the peasants. No one knows this better than Mr. Tkachov. While he wants the German workers to believe that the "idea of collective ownership" can be driven out of the Russian peasants, these instinctive, traditional Communists, only by bayonet and knout, he writes on page 15 of his Russian pamphlet: 'Among the peasants a class of *usurers* (*kulaks*) is making its way, a class of people who *buy up* and *rent* the lands of peasants and nobles—a muzhik aristocracy." These are the same kind of bloodsuckers as we described more fully above.

What dealt the severest blow to communal ownership was again the redemption of the *corvée*. The greater and better part of the land was allotted to the nobility; for the peasant there remained scarcely enough, often not enough, to live on. In addition the forests were given to the nobles; the wood for fuel, implements and building, which the peasant formerly might fetch there for nothing, he has now to buy. Thus the peasant has nothing now but his house and the bare land, without means to cultivate it, and on the average without enough land to support him and his family from one harvest to the next. Under such conditions and under the pressure of taxes and usurers, communal ownership of the land is no longer a blessing; it becomes a fetter. The peasants often run away from it, with or without their families, to earn their living as migratory labourers, and leave their land behind them.[2]

It is clear that communal ownership in Russia is long past its period of florescence and to all appearances is moving towards its disintegration. Nevertheless, the possibility undeniably exists of raising this form of society to a higher one, if it should last until circumstances are ripe for that, and if it shows itself capable of development in such manner that the peasants no longer cultivate the land separately, but collectively;[3] of raising it to this higher form without it being necessary for the Russian peasants to go through the intermediate stage of bourgeois small holdings. This, however, can only happen if, before the complete break-up of communal ownership, a proletarian revolution is successfully carried out in Western Europe, creating for the Russian peasant the preconditions requisite for such a transition, particularly the material conditions which he needs if only to carry through the revolution necessarily connected therewith of his whole agricultural system. It is, therefore, sheer bounce for Mr. Tkachov to say that the Russian peasants, although "owners," are "nearer to socialism" than the propertyless workers of Western Europe. Quite the opposite. If anything can still save Russian communal ownership and give it a chance of growing into a new, really viable form, it is a proletarian revolution in Western Europe.

Mr. Tkachov treats the political revolution just as lightly as he does the economic one. The Russian people, he relates, "protests incessantly" against its enslavement, now in form of "religious sects ... refusal to pay taxes ... robber bands (the German workers will be glad to know that, accordingly, Schinderhannes[4] is the father of German Social-Democracy) ... incendiarism ... revolts ... and hence the Russian people may be termed an instinctive revolutionist." And thus Mr. Tkachov is convinced that "it is only necessary

---

2. On the position of the peasants compare *inter alia* the official report of the government commission on agricultural production (1873), and further, Skaldin, *V zakholustye i v stolitse* [*In the Backwoods and in the Capital*], St. Petersburg 1870; the latter publication by a liberal conservative. [*Engels*]

3. In Poland, particularly in the Grodno *gubernia*, where the nobility for the most part was ruined by the rebellion of 1863, the peasants now frequently buy or rent estates from the nobles and cultivate them unpartitioned and *on their collective account*. And these peasants have not had communal ownership for centuries and are not Great Russians, but Poles, Lithuanians and Byelorussians. [*Engels*]

4. *Schinderhannes*: nickname of Johann Bückler, a well-known German robber.

to evoke an outburst in a number of places at the same time of all the accumulated bitterness and discontent, which is always seething in the breast of our people." Then "the union of the revolutionary forces will come about *of itself*, and the fight ... must end favourably for the people's cause. Practical necessity, the instinct of self-preservation," will then achieve quite of itself "a firm and indissoluble alliance among the protesting village communities."

It is impossible to conceive of a revolution on easier and more pleasant terms. One starts shooting, at three or four places simultaneously, and the "instinctive revolutionist," "practical necessity" and the "instinct of self-preservation" do the rest "of themselves." Being so dead easy, it is simply incomprehensible why the revolution has not long ago been made, the people liberated and Russia transformed into the model socialist country.

Actually, it is quite a different matter. The Russian people, this instinctive revolutionist, has, true enough, made numerous isolated peasant revolts against the *nobility* and against individual officials, but *never against the tsar*, except when *a false tsar* put himself at its head and claimed the throne. The last great peasant rising, under Catherine II, was only possible because Yemelyan Pugachov claimed to be her husband, Peter III, who allegedly had not been murdered by his wife, but dethroned and clapped in prison, and who had now escaped. The tsar is, on the contrary, the earth god of the Russian peasant: *Bog vysoko, tsar daleko*—God is on high and the tsar far away, is his cry in the hour of need. There is no doubt that the mass of the peasant population, especially since the redemption of the *corvée*, has been reduced to a condition which more and more forces on it a fight also against the government and the tsar; but Mr. Tkachov will have to try to sell his fairy-tale of the "instinctive revolutionist" somewhere else.

And then, even *if* the mass of the Russian peasants were ever so instinctively revolutionary, even *if* we imagined that revolutions could be made to order, just as one makes a piece of flowered calico or a teakettle—even then I ask, is it permissible for one over twelve years of age to imagine the course of a revolution in such an utterly childish manner as is the case here? And remember further that this was written after the first revolution made on this Bakunin model —the Spanish one of 1873—had so brilliantly failed. There, too, they let loose at several places simultaneously. There too it was calculated that practical necessity and the instinct of self-preservation would of themselves bring about a firm and indissoluble alliance between the protesting communities. And what happened? Every village community, every town only defended itself, there was no question of mutual assistance, and with only three thousand men Pavia overcame one town after another in a fortnight and put an end to the entire anarchist glory. (*Cf.* my *Bakuninists at Work,* where this is described in detail.)

Russia undoubtedly is on the eve of a revolution. Her financial affairs are in extreme disorder. Taxes cannot be screwed any higher, the interest on old state loans is paid by means of new loans, and every new loan meets with greater difficulties; money can now only be raised under the pretext of building railways! The administration, as of old, corrupt from top to bottom, the officials living more from theft, bribery and extortion than on their salaries. The entire agricultural production—by far the most essential for Russia— completely dislocated by the redemption settlement of 1861; the big landowners without sufficient labour power, the peasants without sufficient land, oppressed by taxation and sucked dry by usurers, agricultural production declining from year to year. The whole held together with great difficulty and only outwardly by an Oriental despotism whose arbitrariness we in the West simply cannot imagine; a despotism which not only from day to day comes into more glaring contradiction with the views of the enlightened classes and in particular with those of the rapidly developing bourgeoisie of the capital, but which, in the person of its present bearer, has lost its head, one day making concessions to liberalism and the next, frightened, cancelling them again and thus bringing itself more and more into disrepute. With all that a growing recognition among the enlightened strata of the nation concentrated in the capital that this position is untenable, that a revolution is impending, and the illusion that it will be possible to guide this revolution into a smooth, constitutional channel. Here all the conditions of a revolution are combined, of a revolution which, started by the upper classes of the capital, perhaps even by the government itself, must be rapidly carried further, beyond the first constitutional phase, by the peasants; of a revolution which will be of the greatest importance for the whole of Europe if only because it will destroy at one blow the last, so far intact, reserve of the entire European reaction. This revolution is surely approaching. Only two events could still delay it: a successful war against Turkey or Austria, for which money and firm alliances are necessary, or—a premature attempt at insurrection, which would drive the possessing classes back into the arms of the government.

PART V

The Later Engels: Elaboration and Popularization

Speech at the Graveside of Karl Marx

FRIEDRICH ENGELS

Marx died on March 14, 1883. Three days later Engels delivered this graveside speech in English at Highgate Cemetery, London, where Marx was buried.

On the 14th of March, at a quarter to three in the afternoon, the greatest living thinker ceased to think. He had been left alone for scarcely two minutes, and when we came back we found him in his armchair, peacefully gone to sleep—but for ever.

An immeasurable loss has been sustained both by the militant proletariat of Europe and America, and by historical science, in the death of this man. The gap that has been left by the departure of this mighty spirit will soon enough make itself felt.

Just as Darwin discovered the law of development of organic nature, so Marx discovered the law of development of human history: the simple fact, hitherto concealed by an overgrowth of ideology, that mankind must first of all eat, drink, have shelter and clothing, before it can pursue politics, science, art, religion, etc.; that therefore the production of the immediate material means of subsistence and consequently the degree of economic development attained by a given people or during a given epoch form the foundation upon which the state institutions, the legal conceptions, art, and even the ideas on religion, of the people concerned have been evolved, and in the light of which they must, therefore, be explained, instead of *vice versa*, as had hitherto been the case.

But that is not all. Marx also discovered the special law of motion governing the present-day capitalist mode of production and the bourgeois society that this mode of production has created. The discovery of surplus value suddenly threw light on the problem, in trying to solve which all previous investigations, of both bourgeois economists and socialist critics, had been groping in the dark.

Two such discoveries would be enough for one lifetime. Happy the man to whom it is granted to make even one such discovery. But in every single field which Marx investigated—and he investigated very many fields, none of them superficially—in every field, even in that of mathematics, he made independent discoveries.

Such was the man of science. But this was not even half the man. Science was for Marx a historically dynamic, revolutionary force. However great the joy with which he welcomed a new discovery in some theoretical science whose practical application perhaps it was as yet quite impossible to envisage, he experienced quite another kind of joy when the discovery involved immediate revolutionary changes in industry, and in historical development in general. For example, he followed closely the development of the discoveries made in the field of electricity and recently those of Marcel Deprez.

For Marx was before all else a revolutionist. His real mission in life was to contribute, in one way or another, to the overthrow of capitalist society and of the state institutions which it had brought into being, to contribute to the liberation of the modern proletariat, which *he* was the first to make conscious of its own position and its needs, conscious of the conditions of its emancipation. Fighting was his element. And he fought with a passion, a tenacity and a success such as few could rival. His work on the first *Rheinische Zeitung* (1842), the Paris *Vorwärts*[1] (1844), the *Deutsche Brüsseler Zeitung* (1847), the *Neue Rheinische Zeitung* (1848–49), the *New York Tribune* (1852–61), and in addition to these a host of militant pamphlets, work in organisations in Paris, Brussels and London, and finally, crowning all, the formation of the great International Working Men's Association—this was indeed an achievement of which its founder might well have been proud even if he had done nothing else.

And, consequently, Marx was the best hated and most calumniated man of his time. Governments, both absolutist and republican, deported him from their territories. Bourgeois, whether conservative or ultra-democratic, vied with one another in heaping slanders upon him. All this he brushed aside as though it were cobweb, ignoring it, answering only when extreme necessity compelled him. And he died beloved, revered and mourned by millions of revolutionary fellow workers—from the mines of Siberia to California, in all parts of Europe and America—and I make bold to say that though he may have had many opponents he had hardly one personal enemy.

His name will endure through the ages, and so also will his work!

1. *Vorwärts* (*Forward*): A radical newspaper of the German Socialists in emigration, one of whose contributors was Karl Marx. It appeared in German at Paris in 1844.

Socialism: Utopian and Scientific

FRIEDRICH ENGELS

At the request of his friend Paul Lafargue, Engels arranged three general chapters of *Anti-Dühring* as a pamphlet dealing with the origins of Marxism and summarizing its view of history. Originally published in French in 1880, *Socialism: Utopian and Scientific* soon appeared in many other languages and became, along with the *Communist Manifesto*, the most influential popular presentation of the Marxist position in the late nineteenth century. The text given here is that of the authorized English edition of 1892.

I

Modern socialism is, in its essence, the direct product of the recognition, on the one hand, of the class antagonism existing in the society of today between proprietors and non-proprietors, between capitalists and wage-workers; on the other hand, of the anarchy existing in production. But, in its theoretical form, modern socialism originally appears ostensibly as a more logical extension of the principles laid down by the great French philosophers of the eighteenth century. Like every new theory, modern socialism had, at first, to connect itself with the intellectual stock-in-trade ready to its hand, however deeply its roots lay in material economic facts.

The great men, who in France prepared men's minds for the coming revolution, were themselves extreme revolutionists. They recognised no external authority of any kind whatever. Religion, natural science, society, political institutions—everything was subjected to the most unsparing criticism: everything must justify its existence before the judgement-seat of reason or give up existence. Reason became the sole measure of everything. It was the time when, as Hegel says, the world stood upon its head;[1] first in the

1. This is the passage on the French Revolution: "Thought, the concept of law, all at once made itself felt, and against this the old scaffolding of wrong could make no stand. In this conception of law, therefore, a constitu- tion has now been established, and henceforth everything must be based upon this. Since the sun had been in the firmament, and the planets circled round him, the sight had never been seen of man standing upon his

sense that the human head, and the principles arrived at by its thought, claimed to be the basis of all human action and associations; but by and by, also, in the wider sense that the reality which was in contradiction to these principles had, in fact, to be turned upside down. Every form of society and government then existing, every old traditional notion was flung into the lumber-room as irrational; the world had hitherto allowed itself to be led solely by prejudices; everything in the past deserved only pity and contempt. Now, for the first time, appeared the light of day, the kingdom of reason; henceforth superstition, injustice, privilege, oppression, were to be superseded by eternal truth, eternal Right, equality based on Nature and the inalienable rights of man.

We know today that this kingdom of reason was nothing more than the idealised kingdom of the bourgeoisie; that this eternal Right found its realisation in bourgeois justice; that this equality reduced itself to bourgeois equality before the law; that bourgeois property was proclaimed as one of the essential rights of man; and that the government of reason, the Contrat Social of Rousseau, came into being, and only could come into being, as a democratic bourgeois republic. The great thinkers of the eighteenth century could, no more than their predecessors, go beyond the limits imposed upon them by their epoch.

But, side by side with the antagonism of the feudal nobility and the burghers, who claimed to represent all the rest of society, was the general antagonism of exploiters and exploited, of rich idlers and poor workers. It was this very circumstance that made it possible for the representatives of the bourgeoisie to put themselves forward as representing not one special class, but the whole of suffering humanity. Still further. From its origin the bourgeoisie was saddled with its antithesis: capitalists cannot exist without wage-workers, and, in the same proportion as the mediaeval burgher of the guild developed into the modern bourgeois, the guild journeyman and the day-labourer, outside the guilds, developed into the proletarian. And although, upon the whole, the bourgeoisie, in their struggle with the nobility, could claim to represent at the same time the interests of the different working classes of that period, yet in every great bourgeois movement there were independent outbursts

---

head—*i.e.*, on the Idea—and building reality after this image. Anaxagoras first said that the Nous, reason, rules the world; but now, for the first time, had man come to recognise that the Idea must rule the mental reality. And this was a magnificent sunrise. All thinking beings have participated in celebrating this holy day. A sublime emotion swayed men at that time, an enthusiasm of reason pervaded the world, as if now had come the reconciliation of the Divine Principle with the world." [Hegel: *Philosophy of History*, 1840, p. 535.] Is it not high time to set the anti-Socialist law in action against such teachings, subversive and to the common danger, by the late Professor Hegel? [*Engels*] of that class which was the forerunner, more or less developed, of the modern proletariat. For example, at the time of the German Reformation and the Peasants' War, the Anabaptists and Thomas Münzer; in the great English Revolution, the Levellers; in the great French Revolution, Babeuf.

There were theoretical enunciations corresponding with these revolutionary uprisings of a class not yet developed; in the sixteenth and seventeenth centuries, Utopian pictures of ideal social conditions;[2] in the eighteenth, actual communistic theories (Morelly and Mably). The demand for equality was no longer limited to political rights; it was extended also to the social conditions of individuals. It was not simply class privileges that were to be abolished, but class distinctions themselves. A communism, ascetic, denouncing all the pleasures of life, Spartan, was the first form of the new teaching. Then came the three great Utopians: Saint-Simon, to whom the middle-class movement, side by side with the proletarian, still had a certain significance; Fourier; and Owen, who in the country where capitalist production was most developed, and under the influence of the antagonisms begotten of this, worked out his proposals for the removal of class distinction systematically and in direct relation to French materialism.

One thing is common to all three. Not one of them appears as a representative of the interests of that proletariat which historical development had, in the meantime, produced. Like the French philosophers, they do not claim to emancipate a particular class to begin with, but all humanity at once. Like them, they wish to bring in the kingdom of reason and eternal justice, but this kingdom, as they see it, is as far as heaven from earth, from that of the French philosophers.

For, to our three social reformers, the bourgeois world, based upon the principles of these philosophers, is quite as irrational and unjust, and, therefore, finds its way to the dust-hole quite as readily as feudalism and all the earlier stages of society. If pure reason and justice have not, hitherto, ruled the world, this has been the case only because men have not rightly understood them. What was wanted was the individual man of genius, who has now arisen and who understands the truth. That he has now arisen, that the truth has now been clearly understood, is not an inevitable event, following of necessity in the chain of historical development, but a mere happy accident. He might just as well have been born 500 years earlier, and might then have spared humanity 500 years of error, strife, and suffering.

We saw how the French philosophers of the eighteenth century,

2. Engels refers here to the works of the Utopian Socialists Thomas More (sixteenth century) and Tommaso Campanella (seventeenth century).

the forerunners of the Revolution, appealed to reason as the sole judge of all that is. A rational government, rational society, were to be founded; everything that ran counter to eternal reason was to be remorselessly done away with. We saw also that this eternal reason was in reality nothing but the idealised understanding of the eighteenth century citizen, just then evolving into the bourgeois. The French Revolution had realised this rational society and government.

But the new order of things, rational enough as compared with earlier conditions, turned out to be by no means absolutely rational. The state based upon reason completely collapsed. Rousseau's Contrat Social had found its realisation in the Reign of Terror, from which the bourgeoisie, who had lost confidence in their own political capacity, had taken refuge first in the corruption of the Directorate, and, finally, under the wing of the Napoleonic despotism. The promised eternal peace was turned into an endless war of conquest. The society based upon reason had fared no better. The antagonism between rich and poor, instead of dissolving into general prosperity, had become intensified by the removal of the guild and other privileges, which had to some extent bridged it over, and by the removal of the charitable institutions of the Church. The "freedom of property" from feudal fetters, now veritably accomplished, turned out to be, for the small capitalists and small proprietors, the freedom to sell their small property, crushed under the overmastering competition of the large capitalists and landlords, to these great lords, and thus, as far as the small capitalists and peasant proprietors were concerned, became "freedom *from* property." The development of industry upon a capitalistic basis made poverty and misery of the working masses conditions of existence of society. Cash payment became more and more, in Carlyle's phrase, the sole nexus between man and man. The number of crimes increased from year to year. Formerly, the feudal vices had openly stalked about in broad daylight; though not eradicated, they were now at any rate thrust into the background. In their stead, the bourgeois vices, hitherto practised in secret, began to blossom all the more luxuriantly. Trade became to a greater and greater extent cheating. The "fraternity" of the revolutionary motto was realised in the chicanery and rivalries of the battle of competition. Oppression by force was replaced by corruption; the sword, as the first social lever, by gold. The right of the first night was transferred from the feudal lords to the bourgeois manufacturers. Prostitution increased to an extent never heard of. Marriage itself remained, as before, the legally recognised form, the official cloak of prostitution, and, moreover, was supplemented by rich crops of adultery.

In a word, compared with the splendid promises of the philosophers, the social and political institutions born of the "triumph of reason" were bitterly disappointing caricaturers. All that was wanting was the men to formulate this disappointment, and they came with the turn of the century. In 1802 Saint-Simon's Geneva letters appeared; in 1808 appeared Fourier's first work, although the groundwork of his theory dated from 1799; on January 1, 1800, Robert Owen undertook the direction of New Lanark.

At this time, however, the capitalist mode of production, and with it the antagonism between the bourgeoisie and the proletariat, was still very incompletely developed. Modern industry, which had just arisen in England, was still unknown in France. But modern industry develops, on the one hand, the conflicts which make absolutely necessary a revolution in the mode of production, and the doing away with its capitalistic character—conflicts not only between the classes begotten of it, but also between the very productive forces and the forms of exchange created by it. And, on the other hand, it develops, in these very gigantic productive forces, the means of ending these conflicts. If, therefore, about the year 1800, the conflicts arising from the new social order were only just beginning to take shape, this holds still more fully as to the means of ending them. The "have-nothing" masses of Paris, during the Reign of Terror, were able for a moment to gain the mastery, and thus to lead the bourgeois revolution to victory in spite of the bourgeoisie themselves. But, in doing so, they only proved how impossible it was for their domination to last under the conditions then obtaining. The proletariat, which then for the first time evolved itself from these "have-nothing" masses as the nucleus of a new class, as yet quite incapable of independent political action, appeared as an oppressed, suffering order, to whom, in its incapacity to help itself, help could, at best, be brought in from without or down from above.

This historical situation also dominated the founders of socialism. To the crude conditions of capitalistic production and the crude class conditions corresponded crude theories. The solution of the social problems, which as yet lay hidden in undeveloped economic conditions, the Utopians attempted to evolve out of the human brain. Society presented nothing but wrongs; to remove these was the task of reason. It was necessary, then, to discover a new and more perfect system of social order and to impose this upon society from without by propaganda, and wherever it was possible, by the example of model experiments. These new social systems were foredoomed as Utopian; the more completely they were worked out in detail, the more they could not avoid drifting off into pure phantasies.

These facts once established, we need not dwell a moment longer upon this side of the question, now wholly belonging to the past. We can leave it to the literary small fry to solemnly quibble over these phantasies, which today only make us smile, and to crow over the superiority of their own bald reasoning, as compared with such "insanity." For ourselves, we delight in the stupendously grand thoughts and germs of thought that everywhere break out through their phantastic covering, and to which these Philistines are blind.

Saint-Simon was a son of the great French Revolution, at the outbreak of which he was not yet thirty. The Revolution was the victory of the third estate, *i.e.*, of the great masses of the nation, *working* in production and in trade, over the privileged *idle* classes, the nobles and the priests. But the victory of the third estate soon revealed itself as exclusively the victory of a small part of this "estate," as the conquest of political power by the socially privileged section of it, *i.e.*, the propertied bourgeoisie. And the bourgeoisie had certainly developed rapidly during the Revolution, partly by speculation in the lands of the nobility and of the Church, confiscated and afterwards put up for sale, and partly by frauds upon the nation by means of army contracts. It was the domination of these swindlers that, under the Directorate, brought France to the verge of ruin, and thus gave Napoleon the pretext for his *coup d'état*.

Hence, to Saint-Simon the antagonism between the third estate and the privileged classes took the form of an antagonism between "workers" and "idlers." The idlers were not merely the old privileged classes, but also all who, without taking any part in production or distribution, lived on their incomes. And the workers were not only the wage-workers, but also the manufacturers, the merchants, the bankers. That the idlers had lost the capacity for intellectual leadership and political supremacy had been proved, and was by the Revolution finally settled. That the non-possessing classes had not this capacity seemed to Saint-Simon proved by the experiences of the Reign of Terror. Then, who was to lead and command? According to Saint-Simon, science and industry, both united by a new religious bond, destined to restore that unity of religious ideas which had been lost since the time of the Reformation—a necessarily mystic and rigidly hierarchic "new Christianity." But science, that was the scholars; and industry, that was, in the first place, the working bourgeois, manufacturers, merchants, bankers. These bourgeois were, certainly, intended by Saint-Simon to transform themselves into a kind of public officials, of social trustees; but they were still to hold, *vis-à-vis* of the workers, a commanding and economically privileged position. The bankers especially were to be called upon to direct the whole of social production by the regulation of credit. This conception was in exact keeping with a time in which modern industry in France and, with it, the chasm between bourgeoisie and proletariat was only just coming into existence. But what Saint-Simon especially lays stress upon is this: what interests him first, and above all other things, is the lot of the class that is the most numerous and the most poor (*"la classe la plus nombreuse et la plus pauvre"*).

Already in his Geneva letters, Saint-Simon lays down the proposition that "all men ought to work." In the same work he recognises also that the Reign of Terror was the reign of the non-possessing masses. "See," says he to them, "what happened in France at the time when your comrades held sway there: they brought about a famine." But to recognise the French Revolution as a class war, and not simply one between nobility and bourgeoisie, but between nobility, bourgeoisie, and the non-possessors, was, in the year 1802, a most pregnant discovery. In 1816, he declares that politics is the science of production, and foretells the complete absorption of politics by economics. The knowledge that economic conditions are the basis of political institutions appears here only in embryo. Yet what is here already very plainly expressed is the idea of the future conversion of political rule over men into an administration of things and a direction of processes of production—that is to say, the "abolition of the state," about which recently there has been so much noise.

Saint-Simon shows the same superiority over his contemporaries, when in 1814, immediately after the entry of the allies into Paris, and again in 1815, during the Hundred Days' War, he proclaims the alliance of France with England, and then of both these countries with Germany, as the only guarantee for the prosperous development and peace of Europe. To preach to the French in 1815 an alliance with the victors of Waterloo required as much courage as historical foresight.

If in Saint-Simon we find a comprehensive breadth of view, by virtue of which almost all the ideas of later Socialists that are not strictly economic are found in him in embryo, we find in Fourier a criticism of the existing conditions of society, genuinely French and witty, but not upon that account any the less thorough. Fourier takes the bourgeoisie, their inspired prophets before the Revolution, and their interested eulogists after it, at their own word. He lays bare remorselessly the material and moral misery of the bourgeois world. He confronts it with the earlier philosophers' dazzling promises of a society in which reason alone should reign, of a civilisation in which happiness should be universal, of an illimitable human perfectibility, and with the rose-coloured phraseology of the bourgeois ideologists of his time. He points out how everywhere the most pitiful reality corresponds with the most high-sounding phrases, and he overwhelms this hopeless fiasco of phrases with his mordant sarcasm.

Fourier is not only a critic; his imperturbably serene nature makes him a satirist, and assuredly one of the greatest satirists of all time. He depicts, with equal power and charm, the swindling speculations that blossomed out upon the downfall of the Revolution, and the shopkeeping spirit prevalent in, and characteristic of, French commerce at that time. Still more masterly is his criticism of the bourgeois form of the relations between the sexes, and the position of woman in bourgeois society. He was the first to declare that in any given society the degree of woman's emancipation is the natural measure of the general emancipation.

But Fourier is at his greatest in his conception of the history of society. He divides its whole course, thus far, into four stages of evolution—savagery, barbarism, the patriarchate, civilisation. The last is identical with the so-called civil, or bourgeois, society of today— *i.e.*, with the social order that came in with the sixteenth century. He proves "that the civilised stage raises every vice practised by barbarism in a simple fashion into a form of existence, complex, ambiguous, equivocal, hypocritical"—that civilisation moves in "a vicious circle," in contradictions which it constantly reproduces without being able to solve them; hence it constantly arrives at the very opposite to that which it wants to attain, or pretends to want to attain, so that, e.g., "under civilisation poverty is born of superabundance itself."

Fourier, as we see, uses the dialectic method in the same masterly way as his contemporary, Hegel. Using these same dialectics, he argues against the talk about illimitable human perfectibility, that every historical phase has its period of ascent and also its period of descent, and he applies this observation to the future of the whole human race. As Kant introduced into natural science the idea of the ultimate destruction of the earth, Fourier introduced into historical science that of the ultimate destruction of the human race.

Whilst in France the hurricane of the Revolution swept over the land, in England a quieter, but not on that account less tremendous, revolution was going on. Steam and the new tool-making machinery were transforming manufacture into modern industry, and thus revolutionising the whole foundation of bourgeois society. The sluggish march of development of the manufacturing period changed into a veritable storm and stress period of production. With constantly increasing swiftness the splitting-up of society into large capitalists and non-possessing proletarians went on. Between these, instead of the former stable middle class, an unstable mass of artisans and small shopkeepers, the most fluctuating portion of the population, now led a precarious existence.

The new mode of production was, as yet, only at the beginning of its period of ascent; as yet it was the normal, regular method of production—the only one possible under existing conditions. Nevertheless, even then it was producing crying social abuses—the herding together of a homeless population in the worst quarters of the large towns; the loosening of all traditional moral bonds, of patriarchal subordination, of family relations; overwork, especially of women and children, to a frightful extent; complete demoralisation of the working class, suddenly flung into altogether new conditions, from the country into the town, from agriculture into modern industry, from stable conditions of existence into insecure ones that changed from day to day.

At this juncture there came forward as a reformer a manufacturer 29 years old—a man of almost sublime, childlike simplicity of character, and at the same time one of the few born leaders of men. Robert Owen had adopted the teaching of the materialistic philosophers: that man's character is the product, on the one hand, of heredity; on the other, of the environment of the individual during his lifetime, and especially during his period of development. In the industrial revolution most of his class saw only chaos and confusion, and the opportunity of fishing in these troubled waters and making large fortunes quickly. He saw in it the opportunity of putting into practice his favourite theory, and so of bringing order out of chaos. He had already tried it with success, as superintendent of more than five hundred men in a Manchester factory. From 1800 to 1829, he directed the great cotton mill at New Lanark, in Scotland, as managing partner, along the same lines, but with greater freedom of action and with a success that made him a European reputation. A population, originally consisting of the most diverse and, for the most part, very demoralised elements, a population that gradually grew to 2,500, he turned into a model colony, in which drunkenness, police, magistrates, lawsuits, poor laws, charity, were unknown. And all this simply by placing the people in conditions worthy of human beings, and especially by carefully bringing up the rising generation. He was the founder of infant schools, and introduced them first at New Lanark. At the age of two the children came to school, where they enjoyed themselves so much that they could scarcely be got home again. Whilst his competitors worked their people thirteen or fourteen hours a day, in New Lanark the working-day was only ten and a half hours. When a crisis in cotton stopped work for four months, his workers received their full wages all the time. And with all this the business more than doubled in value, and to the last yielded large profits to its proprietors.

In spite of all this, Owen was not content. The existence which he secured for his workers was, in his eyes, still far from being worthy of human beings. "The people were slaves at my mercy." The relatively favourable conditions in which he had placed them were still far from allowing a rational development of the character and of the intellect in all directions, much less of the free exercise of all their faculties. "And yet, the working part of this population of 2,500 persons was daily producing as much real wealth for society as, less than half a century before, it would have required the working part of a population of 600,000 to create. I asked myself, what became of the difference between the wealth consumed by 2,500 persons and that which would have been consumed by 600,000?"[3]

The answer was clear. It had been used to pay the proprietors of the establishment 5 per cent on the capital they had laid out, in addition to over £300,000 clear profit. And that which held for New Lanark held to a still greater extent for all the factories in England. "If this new wealth had not been created by machinery, imperfectly as it has been applied, the wars of Europe, in opposition to Napoleon, and to support the aristocratic principles of society, could not have been maintained. And yet this new power was the creation of the working class."[4] To them, therefore, the fruits of this new power belonged. The newly-created gigantic productive forces, hitherto used only to enrich individuals and to enslave the masses, offered to Owen the foundations for a reconstruction of society; they were destined, as the common property of all, to be worked for the common good of all.

Owen's communism was based upon this purely business foundation, the outcome, so to say, of commercial calculation. Throughout, it maintained this practical character. Thus, in 1823, Owen proposed the relief of the distress in Ireland by communist colonies, and drew up complete estimates of costs of founding them, yearly expenditure, and probable revenue. And in his definite plan for the future, the technical working out of details is managed with such practical knowledge—ground plan, front and side and bird's-eye views all included—that the Owen method of social reform once accepted, there is from the practical point of view little to be said against the actual arrangement of details.

His advance in the direction of communism was the turning-point in Owen's life. As long as he was simply a philanthropist, he was rewarded with nothing but wealth, applause, honour, and glory. He was the most popular man in Europe. Not only men of his own class, but statesmen and princes listened to him approvingly. But when he came out with his communist theories that was quite another thing. Three great obstacles seemed to him especially to block the path to social reform: private property, religion, the pres-

---

3. From "The Revolution in Mind and Practice," p. 21, a memorial addressed to all the "red Republicans, Communists and Socialists of Europe," and sent to the provisional government of France, 1848, and also "to Queen Victoria and her responsible advisers." [*Engels*]

4. Note, *l.c.*, p. 22. [*Engels*]

ent form of marriage. He knew what confronted him if he attacked these—outlawry, excommunication from official society, the loss of his whole social position. But nothing of this prevented him from attacking them without fear of consequences, and what he had foreseen happened. Banished from official society, with a conspiracy of silence against him in the press, ruined by his unsuccessful communist experiments in America, in which he sacrificed all his fortune, he turned directly to the working class and continued working in their midst for thirty years. Every social movement, every real advance in England on behalf of the workers links itself on to the name of Robert Owen. He forced through in 1819, after five years' fighting, the first law limiting the hours of labour of women and children in factories. He was president of the first Congress at which all the Trade Unions of England united in a single great trade association. He introduced as transition measures to the complete communistic organisation of society, on the one hand, co-operative societies for retail trade and production. These have since that time, at least, given practical proof that the merchant and the manufacturer are socially quite unnecessary. On the other hand, he introduced labour bazaars for the exchange of the products of labour through the medium of labour-notes, whose unit was a single hour of work; institutions necessarily doomed to failure, but completely anticipating Proudhon's bank of exchange of a much later period, and differing entirely from this in that it did not claim to be the panacea for all social ills, but only a first step towards a much more radical revolution of society.

The Utopians' mode of thought has for a long time governed the socialist ideas of the nineteenth century, and still governs some of them. Until very recently all French and English Socialists did homage to it. The earlier German communism, including that of Weitling, was of the same school. To all these socialism is the expression of absolute truth, reason and justice, and has only to be discovered to conquer all the world by virtue of its own power. And as absolute truth is independent of time, space, and of the historical development of man, it is a mere accident when and where it is discovered. With all this, absolute truth, reason, and justice are different with the founder of each different school. And as each one's special kind of absolute truth, reason, and justice is again conditioned by his subjective understanding, his conditions of existence, the measure of his knowledge and his intellectual training, there is no other ending possible in this conflict of absolute truths than that they shall be mutually exclusive one of the other. Hence, from this nothing could come but a kind of eclectic, average socialism, which, as a matter of fact, has up to the present time dominated the minds of most of the socialist workers in France and England. Hence, a mish-mash allowing of the most manifold shades of opinion; a mish-mash of such critical statements, economic theories, pictures of future society by the founders of different sects, as excite a minimum of opposition; a mish-mash which is the more easily brewed the more the definite sharp edges of the individual constituents are rubbed down in the stream of debate, like rounded pebbles in a brook.

To make a science of socialism, it had first to be placed upon a real basis. ·

II

In the meantime, along with and after the French philosophy of the eighteeenth century had arisen the new German philosophy, culminating in Hegel. Its greatest merit was the taking up again of dialectics as the highest form of reasoning. The old Greek philosophers were all born natural dialecticians, and Aristotle, the most encyclopaedic intellect of them, had already analysed the most essential forms of dialectic thought. The newer philosophy, on the other hand, although in it also dialectics had brilliant exponents (e.g., Descartes and Spinoza), had, especially through English influence, become more and more rigidly fixed in the so-called metaphysical mode of reasoning, by which also the French of the eighteenth century were almost wholly dominated, at all events in their special philosophical work. Outside philosophy in the restricted sense, the French nevertheless produced masterpieces of dialectics. We need only call to mind Diderot's *Le Neveu de Rameau* and Rousseau's *Discours sur l'origine et les fondements de l'inégalité parmi les hommes*. We give here, in brief, the essential character of these two modes of thought.

When we consider and reflect upon Nature at large or the history of mankind or our own intellectual activity, at first we see the picture of an endless entanglement of relations and reactions, permutations and combinations, in which nothing remains what, where and as it was, but everything moves, changes, comes into being and passes away. We see, therefore, at first the picture as a whole, with its individual parts still more or less kept in the background; we observe the movements, transitions, connections, rather than the things that move, combine and are connected. This primitive, naïve but intrinsicially correct conception of the world is that of ancient Greek philosophy, and was first clearly formulated by Heraclitus: everything is and is not, for everything is fluid, is constantly changing, constantly coming into being and passing away.

But this conception, correctly as it expresses the general character of the picture of appearances as a whole, does not suffice to explain the details of which this picture is made up, and so long as we do not understand these, we have not a clear idea of the whole picture. In order to understand these details we must detach them from their natural or historical connection and examine each one separately, its nature, special causes, effects, etc. This is, primarily, the task of natural science and historical research: branches of science which the Greeks of classical times, on very good grounds, relegated to a subordinate position, because they had first of all to collect materials for these sciences to work upon. A certain amount of natural and historical material must be collected before there can be any critical analysis, comparison, and arrangement in classes, orders, and species. The foundations of the exact natural sciences were, therefore, first worked out by the Greeks of the Alexandrian period,[5] and later on, in the Middle Ages, by the Arabs. Real natural science dates from the second half of the fifteenth century, and thence onward it had advanced with constantly increasing rapidity. The analysis of Nature into its individual parts, the grouping of the different natural processes and objects in definite classes, the study of the internal anatomy of organic bodies in their manifold forms— these were the fundamental conditions of the gigantic strides in our knowledge of Nature that have been made during the last four hundred years. But this method of work has also left us as legacy the habit of observing natural objects and processes in isolation, apart from their connection with the vast whole; of observing them in repose, not in motion; as constants, not as essentially variables; in their death, not in their life. And when this way of looking at things was transferred by Bacon and Locke from natural science to philosophy, it begot the narrow, metaphysical mode of thought peculiar to the last century.

To the metaphysician, things and their mental reflexes, ideas, are isolated, are to be considered one after the other and apart from each other, are objects of investigation fixed, rigid, given once for all. He thinks in absolutely irreconcilable antitheses. "His communication is 'yea, yea; nay, nay'; for whatsoever is more than these cometh of evil." For him a thing either exists or does not exist; a thing cannot at the same time be itself and something else. Positive and negative absolutely exclude one another; cause and effect stand in a rigid antithesis one to the other.

At first sight this mode of thinking seems to us very luminous, because it is that of so-called sound common sense. Only sound com-

5. The *Alexandrian period* of the development of science comprises the period extending from the third century B.C. to the seventh century A.D. It derives its name from the town of Alexandria in Egypt, which was one of the most important centres of international economic intercourse at that time. In the Alexandrian period, mathematics (Euclid and Archimedes), geography, astronomy, anatomy, physiology, etc., attained considerable development.

mon sense, respectable fellow that he is, in the homely realm of his own four walls, has very wonderful adventures directly he ventures out into the wide world of research. And the metaphysical mode of thought, justifiable and necessary as it is in a number of domains whose extent varies according to the nature of the particular object of investigation, sooner or later reaches a limit, beyond which it becomes one-sided, restricted, abstract, lost in insoluble contradictions. In the contemplation of individual things, it forgets the connection between them; in the contemplation of their existence, it forgets the beginning and end of that existence; of their repose, it forgets their motion. It cannot see the wood for the trees.

For everyday purposes we know and can say, e.g., whether an animal is alive or not. But, upon closer inquiry, we find that this is, in many cases, a very complex question, as the jurists know very well. They have cudgelled their brains in vain to discover a rational limit beyond which the killing of the child in its mother's womb is murder. It is just as impossible to determine absolutely the moment of death, for physiology proves that death is not an instantaneous, momentary phenomenon, but a very protracted process.

In like manner, every organic being is every moment the same and not the same; every moment it assimilates matter supplied from without, and gets rid of other matter; every moment some cells of its body die and others build themselves anew; in a longer or shorter time the matter of its body is completely renewed, and is replaced by other molecules of matter, so that every organic being is always itself, and yet something other than itself.

Further, we find upon closer investigation that the two poles of an antithesis, positive and negative, e.g., are as inseparable as they are opposed, and that despite all their opposition, they mutually interpenetrate. And we find, in like manner, that cause and effect are conceptions which only hold good in their application to individual cases; but as soon as we consider the individual cases in their general connection with the universe as a whole, they run into each other, and they become confounded when we contemplate that universal action and reaction in which causes and effects are eternally changing places, so that what is effect here and now will be cause there and then, and *vice versa.*

None of these processes and modes of thought enters into the framework of metaphysical reasoning. Dialectics, on the other hand, comprehends things and their representations, ideas, in their essential connection, concatenation, motion, origin, and ending. Such processes as those mentioned above are, therefore, so many corroborations of its own method of procedure.

Nature is the proof of dialectics, and it must be said for modern science that it has furnished this proof with very rich materials increasing daily, and thus has shown that, in the last resort, Nature works dialectically and not metaphysically; that she does not move in the eternal oneness of a perpetually recurring circle, but goes through a real historical evolution. In this connection Darwin must be named before all others. He dealt the metaphysical conception of Nature the heaviest blow by his proof that all organic beings, plants, animals, and man himself, are the products of a process of evolution going on through millions of years. But the naturalists who have learned to think dialectically are few and far between, and this conflict of the results of discovery with preconceived modes of thinking explains the endless confusion now reigning in theoretical natural science, the despair of teachers as well as learners, of authors and readers alike.

An exact representation of the universe, of its evolution, of the development of mankind, and of the reflection of this evolution in the minds of men, can therefore only be obtained by the methods of dialectics with its constant regard to the innumerable actions and reactions of life and death, of progressive or retrogressive changes. And in this spirit the new German philosophy has worked. Kant began his career by resolving the stable solar system of Newton and its eternal duration, after the famous initial impulse had once been given, into the result of a historic process, the formation of the sun and all the planets out of a rotating nebulous mass. From this he at the same time drew the conclusion that, given this origin of the solar system, its future death followed of necessity. His theory half a century later was established mathematically by Laplace, and half a century after that the spectroscope proved the existence in space of such incandescent masses of gas in various stages of condensation.

This new German philosophy culminated in the Hegelian system. In this system—and herein is its great merit—for the first time the whole world, natural, historical, intellectual, is represented as a process, i.e., as in constant motion, change, transformation, development; and the attempt is made to trace out the internal connection that makes a continuous whole of all this movement and development. From this point of view the history of mankind no longer appeared as a wild whirl of senseless deeds of violence, all equally condemnable at the judgement-seat of mature philosophic reason and which are best forgotten as quickly as possible, but as the process of evolution of man himself. It was now the task of the intellect to follow the gradual march of this process through all its devious ways, and to trace out the inner law running through all its apparently accidental phenomena.

That the Hegelian system did not solve the problem it propounded is here immaterial. Its epoch-making merit was that it propounded the problem. This problem is one that no single individual will ever be able to solve. Although Hegel was—with Saint-Simon —the most encyclopaedic mind of his time, yet he was limited, first, by the necessarily limited extent of his own knowledge and, second, by the limited extent and depth of the knowledge and conceptions of his age. To these limits a third must be added. Hegel was an idealist. To him the thoughts within his brain were not the more or less abstract pictures of actual things and processes, but, conversely, things and their evolution were only the realised pictures of the "Idea," existing somewhere from eternity before the world was. This way of thinking turned everything upside down, and completely reversed the actual connection of things in the world. Correctly and ingeniously as many individual groups of facts were grasped by Hegel, yet, for the reasons just given, there is much that is botched, artificial, laboured, in a word, wrong in point of detail. The Hegelian system, in itself, was a colossal miscarriage—but it was also the last of its kind. It was suffering, in fact, from an internal and incurable contradiction. Upon the one hand, its essential proposition was the conception that human history is a process of evolution, which, by its very nature, cannot find its intellectual final term in the discovery of any so-called absolute truth. But, on the other hand, it laid claim to being the very essence of this absolute truth. A system of natural and historical knowledge, embracing everything, and final for all time, is a contradiction to the fundamental law of dialectic reasoning. This law, indeed, by no means excludes, but, on the contrary, includes the idea that the systematic knowledge of the external universe can make giant strides from age to age.

The perception of the fundamental contradiction in German idealism led necessarily back to materialism, but, *nota bene*, not to the simply metaphysical, exclusively mechanical materialism of the eighteenth century. Old materialism looked upon all previous history as a crude heap of irrationality and violence; modern materialism sees in it the process of evolution of humanity, and aims at discovering the laws thereof. With the French of the eighteenth century, and even with Hegel, the conception obtained of Nature as a whole, moving in narrow circles, and for ever immutable, with its eternal celestial bodies, as Newton, and unalterable organic species, as Linnaeus, taught. Modern materialism embraces the more recent discoveries of natural science, according to which Nature also has its history in time, the celestial bodies, like the organic species that, under favourable conditions, people them, being born and perishing. And even if Nature, as a whole, must still be said to move in recurrent cycles, these cycles assume infinitely larger dimensions. In both aspects, modern materialism is essentially dialectic, and no longer requires the assistance of that sort of philosophy which, queen-like, pretended to rule the remaining mob of sciences. As soon as each special science is bound to make clear its position in the great totality of things and of our knowledge of things, a special science dealing with this totality is superfluous or unnecessary. That which still survives of all earlier philosophy is the science of thought and its laws—formal logic and dialectics. Everything else is subsumed in the positive science of Nature and history.

Whilst, however, the revolution in the conception of Nature could only be made in proportion to the corresponding positive materials furnished by research, already much earlier certain historical facts had occured which led to a decisive change in the conception of history. In 1831, the first working-class rising took place in Lyons; between 1838 and 1842, the first national working-class movement, that of the English Chartists, reached its height. The class struggle between proletariat and bourgeoisie came to the front in the history of the most advanced countries in Europe, in proportion to the development, upon the one hand, of modern industry, upon the other, of the newly-acquired political supremacy of the bourgeoisie. Facts more and more strenuously gave the lie to the teachings of bourgeois economy as to the identity of the interests of capital and labour, as to the universal harmony and universal prosperity that would be the consequence of unbridled competition. All these things could no longer be ignored, any more than the French and English socialism, which was their theoretical, though very imperfect, expression. But the old idealist conception of history, which was not yet dislodged, knew nothing of class struggles based upon economic interests, know nothing of economic interests; production and all economic relations appeared in it only as incidental, subordinate elements in the "history of civilisation."

The new facts made imperative a new examination of all past history. Then it was seen that *all* past history, with the exception of its primitive stages, was the history of class struggles; that these warring classes of society are always the products of the modes of production and of exchange—in a word, of the *economic* conditions of their time; that the economic structure of society always furnishes the real basis, starting from which we can alone work out the ultimate explanation of the whole superstructure of juridical and political institutions as well as of the religious, philosophical, and other ideas of a given historical period. Hegel had freed history from metaphysics—he had made it dialectic; but his conception of history was essentially idealistic. But now idealism was driven from its last refuge, the philosophy of history; now a materialistic treatment of history was propounded, and a method found of explaining man's "knowing" by his "being," instead of, as heretofore, his "being" by his "knowing."

From that time forward socialism was no longer an accidental discovery of this or that ingenious brain, but the necessary outcome of the struggle between two historically developed classes—the proletariat and the bourgeoisie. Its task was no longer to manufacture a system of society as perfect as possible, but to examine the historico-economic succession of events from which these classes, and their antagonism had of necessity sprung, and to discover in the economic conditions thus created the means of ending the conflict. But the socialism of earlier days was as incompatible with this materialistic conception as the conception of Nature of the French materialists was with dialectics and modern natural science. The socialism of earlier days certainly criticised the existing capitalistic mode of production and its consequences. But it could not explain them, and, therefore, could not get the mastery of them. It could only simply reject them as bad. The more strongly this earlier socialism denounced the exploitation of the working class, inevitable under capitalism, the less able was it clearly to show in what this exploitation consisted and how it arose. But for this it was necessary—(1) to present the capitalistic method of production in its historical connection and its inevitableness during a particular historical period, and therefore, also, to present its inevitable downfall; and (2) to lay bare its essential character, which was still a secret. This was done by the discovery of *surplus value*. It was shown that the appropriation of unpaid labour is the basis of the capitalist mode of production and of the exploitation of the worker that occurs under it; that even if the capitalist buys the labour power of his labourer at its full value as a commodity on the market, he yet extracts more value from it than he paid for; and that in the ultimate analysis this surplus value forms those sums of value from which are heaped up the constantly increasing masses of capital in the hands of the possessing classes. The genesis of capitalist production and the production of capital were both explained.

These two great discoveries, the materialistic conception of history and the revelation of the secret of capitalistic production through surplus value, we owe to Marx. With these discoveries socialism became a science. The next thing was to work out all its details and relations.

III

The materialist conception of history starts from the proposition that the production of the means to support human life and, next to production, the exchange of things produced, is the basis of all social structure; that in every society that has appeared in history, the manner in which wealth is distributed and society divided into classes or orders is dependent upon what is produced, how it is produced, and how the products are exchanged. From this point of view the final causes of all social changes and political revolutions are to be sought, not in men's brains, not in men's better insight into eternal truth and justice, but in changes in the modes of production and exchange. They are to be sought not in the *philosophy*, but in the *economics* of each particular epoch. The growing perception that existing social institutions are unreasonable and unjust, that reason has become unreason and right wrong,[6] is only proof that in the modes of production and exchange changes have silently taken place with which the social order, adapted to earlier economic conditions, is no longer in keeping. From this it also follows that the means of getting rid of the incongruities that have been brought to light must also be present, in a more or less developed condition, within the changed modes of production themselves. These means are not to be invented by deduction from fundamental principles, but are to be discovered in the stubborn facts of the existing system of production.

What is, then, the position of modern socialism in this connection?

The present structure of society—this is now pretty generally conceded—is the creation of the ruling class of today, of the bourgeoisie. The mode of production peculiar to the bourgeoisie, known, since Marx, as the capitalist mode of production, was incompatible with the feudal system, with the privileges it conferred upon individuals, entire social ranks and local corporations, as well as with the hereditary ties of subordination which constituted the framework of its social organisation. The bourgeoisie broke up the feudal system and built upon its ruins the capitalist order of society, the kingdom of free competition, of personal liberty, of the equality, before the law, of all commodity owners, of all the rest of the capitalist blessings. Thenceforward the capitalist mode of production could develop in freedom. Since steam, machinery, and the making of machines by machinery transformed the older manufacture into modern industry, the productive forces evolved under the guidance of the bourgeoisie developed with a rapidity and in a degree unheard of before. But just as the older manufacture, in its time, and handicraft, becoming more developed under its influence, had come into collision with the feudal trammels of the guilds, so now modern industry, in its more complete development, comes into collision with the bounds within which the capitalistic mode of production holds it confined. The new productive forces have already outgrown the capitalistic mode of using them. And this conflict between productive forces and modes of production is not a conflict

6. Mephistopheles, in Goethe's *Faust*.

engendered in the mind of man, like that between original sin and divine justice. It exists, in fact, objectively, outside us, independently of the will and actions even of the men that have brought it on. Modern socialism is nothing but the reflex, in thought, of this conflict in fact; its ideal reflection in the minds, first, of the class directly suffering under it, the working class.

Now, in what does this conflict consist?

Before capitalistic production, i.e., in the Middle Ages, the system of petty industry obtained generally, based upon the private property of the labourers in their means of production; in the country, the agriculture of the small peasant, freeman or serf; in the towns, the handicrafts organised in guilds. The instruments of labour—land, agricultural implements, the workshop, the tool—were the instruments of labour of single individuals, adapted for the use of one worker, and, therefore, of necessity, small, dwarfish, circumscribed. But, for this very reason they belonged, as a rule, to the producer himself. To concentrate these scattered, limited means of production, to enlarge them, to turn them into the powerful levers of production of the present day—this was precisely the historic role of capitalist production and of its upholder, the bourgeoisie. In the fourth section of *Capital*[7] Marx has explained in detail how since the fifteenth century this has been historically worked out through the three phases of simple co-operation, manufacture and modern industry. But the bourgeoisie, as is also shown there, could not transform these puny means of production into mighty productive forces without transforming them, at the same time, from means of production of the individual into *social* means of production only workable by a collectivity of men. The spinning-wheel, the hand-loom, the blacksmith's hammer, were replaced by the spinning-machine, the power-loom, the steam-hammer; the individual workshop, by the factory implying the co-operation of hundreds and thousands of workmen. In like manner, production itself changed from a series of individual into a series of social acts, and the products from individual to social products. The yarn, the cloth, the metal articles that now came out of the factory, were the joint product of many workers, through whose hands they had successively to pass before they were ready. No one person could say of them; "I made that; this is *my* product."

But where, in a given society, the fundamental form of production is that spontaneous division of labour which creeps in gradually and not upon any preconceived plan, there the products take on the form of *commodities*, whose mutual exchange, buying and selling, enable the individual producers to satisfy their manifold wants. And this was the case in the Middle Ages. The peasant, e.g., sold to the

7. See pp. 272–291, above. [*R. T.*]

artisan agricultural products and bought from him the products of handicraft. Into this society of individual producers, of commodity producers, the new mode of production thrust itself. In the midst of the old division of labour, grown up spontaneously and upon *no definite plan*, which had governed the whole of society, now arose division of labour upon a *definite* plan, as organised in the factory; side by side with *individual* production appeared *social* production. The products of both were sold in the same market, and, therefore, at prices at least approximately equal. But organisation upon a definite plan was stronger than spontaneous division of labour. The factories working with the combined social forces of a collectivity of individuals produced their commodities far more cheaply than the individual small producers. Individual production succumbed in one department after another. Socialised production revolutionised all the old methods of production. But its revolutionary character was, at the same time, so little recognised that it was, on the contrary, introduced as a means of increasing and developing the production of commodities. When it arose, it found ready-made, and made liberal use of, certain machinery for the production and exchange of commodities: merchants' capital, handicraft, wage-labour. Socialised production thus introducing itself as a new form of the production of commodities, it was a matter of course that under it the old forms of appropriation remained in full swing, and were applied to its products as well.

In the mediaeval stage of evolution of the production of commodities, the question as to the owner of the product of labour could not arise. The individual producer, as a rule, had, from raw material belonging to himself, and generally his own handiwork, produced it with his own tools, by the labour of his own hands or of his family. There was no need for him to appropriate the new product. It belonged wholly to him, as a matter of course. His property in the product was, therefore, based *upon his own labour*. Even where external help was used, this was, as a rule, of little importance, and very generally was compensated by something other than wages. The apprentices and journeymen of the guilds worked less for board and wages than for education, in order that they might become master craftsmen themselves.

Then came the concentration of the means of production and of the producers in large workshops and manufactories, their transformation into actual socialised means of production and socialised producers. But the socialised producers and means of production and their products were still treated, after this change, just as they had been before, i.e., as the means of production and the products of individuals. Hitherto, the owner of the instruments of labour had himself appropriated the product, because, as a rule, it was his own product and the assistance of others was the exception. Now the owner of the instruments of labour always appropriated to himself the product, although it was no longer *his* product but exclusively the product of the *labour of others*. Thus, the products now produced socially were not appropriated by those who had actually set in motion the means of production and actually produced the commodities, but by the *capitalists*. The means of production, and production itself, had become in essence socialised. But they were subjected to a form of appropriation which presupposes the private production of individuals, under which, therefore, everyone owns his own product and brings it to market. The mode of production is subjected to this form of appropriation, although it abolishes the conditions upon which the latter rests.[8]

This contradiction, which gives to the new mode of production its capitalistic character, *contains the germ of the whole of the social antagonisms of today*. The greater the mastery obtained by the new mode of production over all important fields of production and in all manufacturing countries, the more it reduced individual production to an insignificant residuum, *the more clearly was brought out the incompatibility of socialised production with capitalistic appropriation*.

The first capitalists found, as we have said, alongside of other forms of labour, wage-labour ready-made for them on the market. But it was exceptional, complementary, accessory, transitory wage-labour. The agricultural labourer, though, upon occasion, he hired himself out by the day, had a few acres of his own land on which he could at all events live at a pinch. The guilds were so organized that the journeyman of today became the master of tomorrow. But all this changed as soon as the means of production became socialised and concentrated in the hands of capitalists. The means of production, as well as the product, of the individual producer became more and more worthless; there was nothing left for him but to turn wage-worker under the capitalist. Wage-labour, aforetime the exception and accessory, now became the rule and basis of all production; aforetime complementary, it now became the sole remaining function of the workers. The wage-worker for a time became a wage-worker for life. The number of these permanent wage-workers was further enormously increased by the breaking-up of the feudal

8. It is hardly necessary in this connection to point out that, even if the *form* of appropriation remains the same, the *character* of the appropriation is just as much revolutionised as production is by the changes described above. It is, of course, a very different matter whether I appropriate to myself my own product or that of another. Note in passing that wage-labour, which contains the whole capitalistic mode of production in embryo, is very ancient; in a sporadic, scattered form it existed for centuries alongside of slave-labour. But the embryo could duly develop into the capitalistic mode of production only when the necessary historical preconditions had been furnished. [*Engels*]

system that occurred at the same time, by the disbanding of the retainers of the feudal lords, the eviction of the peasants from their homesteads, etc. The separation was made complete between the means of production concentrated in the hands of the capitalists, on the one side, and the producers, possessing nothing but their labour-power, on the other. *The contradiction between socialised production and capitalistic appropriation manifested itself as the antagonism of proletariat and bourgeoisie.*

We have seen that the capitalistic mode of production thrust its way into a society of commodity-producers, of individual producers, whose social bond was the exchange of their products. But every society based upon the production of commodities has this peculiarity: that the producers have lost control over their own social inter-relations. Each man produces for himself with such means of production as he may happen to have, and for such exchange as he may require to satisfy his remaining wants. No one knows how much of his particular article is coming on the market, nor how much of it will be wanted. No one knows whether his individual product will meet an actual demand, whether he will be able to make good his costs of production or even to sell his commodity at all. Anarchy reigns in socialised production.

But the production of commodities, like every other form of production, has its peculiar, inherent laws inseparable from it; and these laws work, despite anarchy, in and through anarchy. They reveal themselves in the only persistent form of social inter-relations, i.e., in exchange, and here they affect the individual producers as compulsory laws of competition. They are, at first, unknown to these producers themselves, and have to be discovered by them gradually and as the result of experience. They work themselves out, therefore, independently of the producers, and in antagonism to them, as inexorable natural laws of their particular form of production. The product governs the producers.

In mediaeval society, especially in the earlier centuries, production was essentially directed towards satisfying the wants of the individual. It satisfied, in the main, only the wants of the producer and his family. Where relations of personal dependence existed, as in the country, it also helped to satisfy the wants of the feudal lord. In all this there was, therefore, no exchange; the products, consequently, did not assume the character of commodities. The family of the peasant produced almost everything they wanted: clothes and furniture, as well as means of subsistence. Only when it began to produce more than was sufficient to supply its own wants and the payments in kind to the feudal lord, only then did it also produce commodities. This surplus, thrown into socialised exchange and offered for sale, became commodities.

The artisans of the towns, it is true, had from the first to produce for exchange. But they, also, themselves supplied the greatest part of their own individual wants. They had gardens and plots of land. They turned their cattle out into the communal forest, which, also, yielded them timber and firing. The women spun flax, wool, and so forth. Production for the purpose of exchange, production of commodities, was only in its infancy. Hence, exchange was restricted, the market narrow, the methods of production stable; there was local exclusiveness without, local unity within; the Mark in the country; in the town, the guild.

But with the extension of the production of commodities, and especially with the introduction of the capitalist mode of production, the laws of commodity production, hitherto latent, came into action more openly and with greater force. The old bonds were loosened, the old exclusive limits broken through, the producers were more and more turned into independent, isolated producers of commodities. It became apparent that the production of society at large was ruled by absence of plan, by accident, by anarchy; and this anarchy grew to greater and greater height. But the chief means by aid of which the capitalist mode of production intensified this anarchy of socialised production was the exact opposite of anarchy. It was the increasing organisation of production, upon a social basis, in every individual productive establishment. By this, the old, peaceful, stable condition of things was ended. Wherever this organisation of production was introduced into a branch of industry, it brooked no other method of production by its side. The field of labour became a battle-ground. The great geographical discoveries, and the colonisation following upon them, multiplied markets and quickened the transformation of handicraft into manufacture. The war did not simply break out between the individual producers of particular localities. The local struggles begot in their turn national conflicts, the commercial wars of the seventeenth and eighteenth centuries.

Finally, modern industry and the opening of the world market made the struggle universal, and at the same time gave it an unheard-of virulence. Advantages in natural or artificial conditions of production now decide the existence or non-existence of individual capitalists, as well as of whole industries and countries. He that falls is remorselessly cast aside. It is the Darwinian struggle of the individual for existence transferred from Nature to society with intensified violence. The conditions of existence natural to the animal appear as the final term of human development. The contradiction between socialised production and capitalistic appropriation now presents itself as *an antagonism between the organisation of production in the individual workshop and the anarchy of production in society generally.*

The capitalistic mode of production moves in these two forms of the antagonism immanent to it from its very origin. It is never able to get out of that "vicious circle" which Fourier had already discovered. What Fourier could not, indeed, see in his time is that this circle is gradually narrowing; that the movement becomes more and more a spiral, and must come to an end, like the movement of the planets, by collision with the centre. It is the compelling force of anarchy in the production of society at large that more and more completely turns the great majority of men into proletarians; and it is the masses of the proletariat again who will finally put an end to anarchy in production. It is the compelling force of anarchy in social production that turns the limitless perfectibility of machinery under modern industry into a compulsory law by which every individual industrial capitalist must perfect his machinery more and more, under penalty of ruin.

But the perfecting of machinery is making human labour superfluous. If the introduction and increase of machinery means the displacement of millions of manual by a few machine-workers, improvement in machinery means the displacement of more and more of the machine-workers themselves. It means, in the last instance, the production of a number of available wage-workers in excess of the average needs of capital, the formation of a complete industrial reserve army, as I called it in 1845, available at the times when industry is working at high pressure, to be cast out upon the street when the inevitable crash comes, a constant dead weight upon the limbs of the working class in its struggle for existence with capital, a regulator for the keeping of wages down to the low level that suits the interests of capital. Thus it comes about, to quote Marx, that machinery becomes the most powerful weapon in the war of capital against the working class; that the instruments of labour constantly tear the means of subsistence out of the hands of the labourer; that the very product of the worker is turned into an instrument for his subjugation. Thus it comes about that the economising of the instruments of labour becomes at the same time, from the outset, the most reckless waste of labour power, and robbery based upon the normal conditions under which labour functions; that machinery, "the most powerful instrument for shortening labour time, becomes the most unfailing means for placing every moment of the labourer's time and that of his family at the disposal of the capitalist for the purpose of expanding the value of his capital." (*Capital*, English edition, p. 406.)[9] Thus it comes

9. See p. 294, above. [*R. T.*]

about that the overwork of some becomes the preliminary condition for the idleness of others, and that modern industry, which hunts after new consumers over the whole world, forces the consumption of the masses at home down to a starvation minimum, and in doing thus destroys its own home market. "The law that always equilibrates the relative surplus population, or industrial reserve army, to the extent and energy of accumulation, this law rivets the labourer to capital more firmly than the wedges of Vulcan did Prometheus to the rock. It establishes an accumulation of misery, corresponding with accumulation of capital. Accumulation of wealth at one pole is, therefore, at the same time, accumulation of misery, agony of toil, slavery, ignorance, brutality, mental degradation, at the opposite pole, i.e. on the side of the class that produces *its own product in the form of capital*." (*Capital*, p. 661.)[1] And to expect any other division of the products from the capitalistic mode of production is the same as expecting the electrodes of a battery not to decompose acidulated water, not to liberate oxygen at the positive, hydrogen at the negative pole, so long as they are connected with the battery.

We have seen that the ever-increasing perfectibility of modern machinery is, by the anarchy of social production, turned into a compulsory law that forces the individual industrial capitalist always to improve his machinery, always to increase its productive force. The bare possibility of extending the field of production is transformed for him into a similar compulsory law. The enormous expansive force of modern industry, compared with which that of gases is mere child's play, appears to us now as a *necessity* for expansion, both qualitative and quantitative, that laughs at all resistance. Such resistance is offered by consumption, by sales, by the markets for the products of modern industry. But the capacity for extension, extensive and intensive, of the markets is primarily governed by quite different laws that work much less energetically. The extension of the markets cannot keep pace with the extension of production. The collision becomes inevitable, and as this cannot produce any real solution so long as it does not break in pieces the capitalist mode of production, the collisions become periodic. Capitalist production has begotten another "vicious circle."

As a matter of fact, since 1825, when the first general crisis broke out, the whole industrial and commercial world, production and exchange among all civilised peoples and their more or less barbaric hangers-on, are thrown out of joint about once every ten years. Commerce is at a standstill, the markets are glutted, products accumulate, as multitudinous as they are unsaleable, hard cash disappears, credit vanishes, factories are closed, the mass of the workers are in want of the means of subsistence, because they have pro-

1. See pp. 310–311, above. [R. T.]

duced too much of the means of subsistence; bankruptcy follows upon bankruptcy, execution upon execution. The stagnation lasts for years; productive forces and products are wasted and destroyed wholesale, until the accumulated mass of commodities finally filters off, more or less depreciated in value, until production and exchange gradually begin to move again. Little by little the pace quickens. It becomes a trot. The industrial trot breaks into a canter, the canter in turn grows into the headlong gallop of a perfect steeplechase of industry, commercial credit, and speculation which finally, after breakneck leaps, ends where it began—in the ditch of a crisis. And so over and over again. We have now, since the year 1825, gone through this five times, and at the present moment (1877) we are going through it for the sixth time. And the character of these crises is so clearly defined that Fourier hit all of them off when he described the first as "*crise pléthorique*," a crisis from plethora.

In these crises, the contradiction between socialised production and capitalist appropriation ends in a violent explosion. The circulation of commodities is, for the time being, stopped. Money, the means of circulation, becomes a hindrance to circulation. All the laws of production and circulation of commodities are turned upside down. The economic collision has reached its apogee. *The mode of production is in rebellion against the mode of exchange.*

The fact that the socialised organisation of production within the factory has developed so far that it has become incompatible with the anarchy of production in society, which exists side by side with and dominates it, is brought home to the capitalists themselves by the violent concentration of capital that occurs during crises, through the ruin of many large, and a still greater number of small, capitalists. The whole mechanism of the capitalist mode of production breaks down under the pressure of the productive forces, its own creations. It is no longer able to turn all this mass of means of production into capital. They lie fallow, and for that very reason the industrial reserve army must also lie fallow. Means of production, means of subsistence, available labourers, all the elements of production and of general wealth, are present in abundance. But "abundance becomes the source of distress and want" (Fourier), because it is the very thing that prevents the transformation of the means of production and subsistence into capital. For in capitalistic society the means of production can only function when they have undergone a preliminary transformation into capital, into the means of exploiting human labour power. The necessity of this transformation into capital of the means of production and subsistence stands like a ghost between these and the workers. It alone prevents the coming together of the material and personal levers of production;

it alone forbids the means of production to function, the workers to work and live. On the one hand, therefore, the capitalistic mode of production stands convicted of its own incapacity to further direct these productive forces. On the other, these productive forces themselves, with increasing energy, press forward to the removal of the existing contradiction to the abolition of their quality as capital, to the *practical recognition of their character as social productive forces.*

This rebellion of the productive forces, as they grow more and more powerful, against their quality as capital, this stronger and stronger command that their social character shall be recognised, forces the capitalist class itself to treat them more and more as social productive forces, so far as this is possible under capitalist conditions. The period of industrial high pressure, with its unbounded inflation of credit, not less than the crash itself, by the collapse of great capitalist establishments, tends to bring about that form of the socialisation of great masses of means of production which we meet with in the different kinds of joint-stock companies. Many of these means of production and of distribution are, from the outset, so colossal that, like the railways, they exclude all other forms of capitalistic exploitation. At a further stage of evolution this form also becomes insufficient. The producers on a large scale in a particular branch of industry in a particular country unite in a trust, a union for the purpose of regulating production. They determine the total amount to be produced, parcel it out among themselves, and thus enforce the selling price fixed beforehand. But trusts of this kind, as soon as business becomes bad, are generally liable to break up, and on this very account compel a yet greater concentration of association. The whole of the particular industry is turned into one gigantic joint-stock company; internal competition gives place to the internal monopoloy of this one company. This has happened in 1890 with the English alkali production, which is now, after the fusion of 48 large works, in the hands of one company, conducted upon a single plan, and with a capital of £6,000,000.

In the trusts, freedom of competition changes into its very opposite—into monopoly; and the production without any definite plan of capitalistic society capitulates to the production upon a definite plan of the invading socialistic society. Certainly this is so far still to the benefit and advantage of the capitalists. But in this case the exploitation is so palpable that it must break down. No nation will put up with production conducted by trusts, with so barefaced an exploitation of the community by a small band of dividend-mongers.

In any case, with trusts or without, the official representative of capitalist society—the state—will ultimately have to undertake the direction of production.[2] This necessity for conversion into state property is felt first in the great institutions for intercourse and communication—the post office, the telegraphs, the railways.

If the crises demonstrate the incapacity of the bourgeoisie for managing any longer modern productive forces, the transformation of the great establishments for production and distrubution into joint-stock companies, trusts and sttae property shows how unnecessary the bourgeoisie are for that purpose. All the social functions of the capitalist are now performed by salaried employees. The capitalist has no further social function than that of pocketing dividends, tearing off coupons, and gambling on the Stock Exchange, where the different capitalists despoil one another of their capital. At first the capitalistic mode of production forces out the workers. Now it forces out the capitalists, and reduces them, just as it reduced the workers, to the ranks of the surplus population, although not immediately into those of the industrial reserve army.

But the transformation, either into joint-stock companies and trusts, or into state ownership, does not do away with the capitalistic nature of the productive forces. In the joint-stock companies and trusts this is obvious. And the modern state, again, is only the organisation that bourgeois society takes on in order to support the external conditions of the capitalist mode of production against the encroachments as well of the workers as of individual capitalists. The modern state, no matter what its form, is essentially a capitalist machine, the state of the capitalists, the ideal personification of the total national capital. The more it proceeds to the taking over of productive forces, the more does it actually become the national capitalist, the more citizens does it exploit. The workers remain wage-workers—proletarians. The capitalist relation is not done away with. It is rather brought to a head. But, brought to a head, it top-

2. I say "have to." For only when the means of production and distribution have *actually* outgrown the form of management by joint-stock companies, and when, therefore, the taking them over by the state has become *economically* inevitable, only then—even if it is the state of today that effects this—is there an economic advance, the attainment of another step preliminary to the taking over of all productive forces by society itself. But of late, since Bismarck went in for state ownership of industrial establishments, a kind of spurious socialism has arisen, degenerating, now and again, into something of flunkeyism, that without more ado declares *all* state ownership, even of the Bismarckian sort, to be socialistic. Certainly, if the taking over by the state of the tobacco industry is socialistic, then Napoleon and Metternich must be numbered among the founders of socialism. If the Belgian state, for quite ordinary political and financial reasons, itself constructed its chief railway lines; if Bismarck, not under any economic compulsion, took over for the state the chief Prussian lines, simply to be the better able to have them in hand in case of war, to bring up the railway employees as voting cattle for the government, and especially to create for himself a new source of income independent of parliamentary votes—this was, in no sense, a socialistic measure, directly or indirectly, consciously or unconsciously. Otherwise, the Royal Maritime Company, the Royal porcelain manufacture, and even the regimental tailor shops of the Army would also be socialistic institutions, or even, as was seriously proposed by a sly dog in Frederick William III's reign, the taking over by the state of the brothels. [*Engels*]

ples over. State ownership of the productive forces is not the solution of the conflict, but concealed within it are the technical conditions that form the elements of that solution.

This solution can only consist in the practical recognition of the social nature of the modern forces of production, and therefore in the harmonising of the modes of production, appropriation, and exchange with the socialised character of the means of production. And this can only come about by society openly and directly taking possession of the productive forces which have outgrown all control except that of society as a whole. The social character of the means of production and of the products today reacts against the producers, periodically distrupts all production and exchange, acts only like a law of Nature working blindly, forcibly, destructively. But with the taking over by society of the productive forces, the social character of the means of production and of the products will be utilised by the producers with a perfect understanding of its nature, and instead of being a source of disturbance and periodical collapse, will become the most powerful lever of production itself.

Active social forces work exactly like natural forces: blindly, forcibly, destructively, so long as we do not understand, and reckon with, them. But when once we understand them, when once we grasp their action, their direction, their effects, it depends only upon ourselves to subject them more and more to our own will, and by means of them to reach our own ends. And this holds quite especially of the mighty productive forces of today. As long as we obstinately refuse to understand the nature and the character of these social means of action—and this understanding goes against the grain of the capitalist mode of production and its defenders—so long these forces are at work in spite of us, in opposition to us, so long they master us, as we have shown above in detail.

But when once their nature is understood, they can, in the hands of the producers working together, be transformed from master demons into willing servants. The difference is as that between the destructive force of electricity in the lightning of the storm, and electricity under command in the telegraph and the voltaic arc; the difference between a conflagration, and fire working in the service of man. With this recognition, at last, of the real nature of the productive forces of today, the social anarchy of production gives place to a social regulation of production upon a definite plan, according to the needs of the community and of each individual. Then the capitalist mode of appropriation, in which the product enslaves first the producer and then the appropriator, is replaced by the mode of appropriation of the products that is based upon the nature of the modern means of production; upon the one hand, direct social appropriation, as means to the maintenance and extension of production—on the other, direct individual appropriation, as means of subsistence and of enjoyment.

Whilst the capitalist mode of production more and more completely transforms the great majority of the population into proletarians, it creates the power which, under penalty of its own destruction, is forced to accomplish this revolution. Whilst it forces on more and more the transformation of the vast means of production, already socialised, into state property, it shows itself the way to accomplishing this revolution. *The proletariat seizes political power and turns the means of production into state property.*

But, in doing this, it abolishes itself as proletariat, abolishes all class distinctions and class antagonisms, abolishes also the state as state. Society thus far, based upon class antagonisms, had need of the state. That is, of an organisation of the particular class which was *pro tempore* the exploiting class, an organisation for the purpose of preventing any interference from without with the existing conditions of production, and, therefore, especially, for the purpose of forcibly keeping the exploited classes in the condition of oppression corresponding with the given mode of production (slavery, serfdom, wage-labour). The state was the official representative of society as a whole; the gathering of it together into a visible embodiment. But it was this only in so far as it was the state of that class which itself represented, for the time being, society as a whole: in ancient times, the state of slaveowning citizens; in the Middle Ages, the feudal lords; in our own time, the bourgeoisie. When at last it becomes the real representative of the whole of society, it renders itself unnecessary. As soon as there is no longer any social class to be held in subjection; as soon as class rule, and the individual struggle for existence based upon our present anarchy in production, with the collisions and excesses arising from these, are removed, nothing more remains to be repressed, and a special repressive force, a state, is no longer necessary. The first act by virtue of which the state really constitutes itself the representative of the whole of society—this is, at the same time, its last independent act as a state. State interference in social relations becomes, in one domain after another, superfluous, and then dies out of itself; the government of persons is replaced by the administration of things, and by the conduct of processes of production. The state is not "abolished." *It dies out.* This gives the measure of the value of the phrase *"a free state,"* both as to its justifiable use at times by agitators, and as to its ultimate scientific insufficiency; and also of the demands of the so-called anarchists for the abolition of the state out of hand.

Since the historical appearance of the capitalist mode of production, the appropriation by society of all the means of production has often been dreamed of, more or less vaguely, by individuals, as well as by sects, as the ideal of the future. But it could become possible, could become a historical necessity, only when the actual conditions for its realisation were there. Like every other social advance, it becomes practicable, not by men understanding that the existence of classes is in contradiction to justice, equality, etc., not by the mere willingness to abolish these classes, but by virtue of certain new economic conditions. The separation of society into an exploiting and an exploited class, a ruling and an oppressed class, was the necessary consequence of the deficient and restricted development of production in former times. So long as the total social labour only yields a product which but slightly exceeds that barely necessary for the existence of all; so long, therefore, as labour engages all or almost all the time of the great majority of the members of society—so long, of necessity, this society is divided into classes. Side by side with the great majority, exclusively bond slaves to labour, arises a class freed from directly productive labour, which looks after the general affairs of society: the direction of labour, state business, law, science, art, etc. It is, therefore, the law of division of labour that lies at the basis of the division into classes. But this does not prevent this division into classes from being carried out by means of violence and robbery, trickery and fraud. It does not prevent the ruling class, once having the upper hand, from consolidating its power at the expense of the working class, from turning its social leadership into an intensified exploitation of the masses.

But if, upon this showing, division into classes has a certain historical justification, it has this only for a given period, only under given social conditions. It was based upon the insufficiency of production. It will be swept away by the complete development of modern productive forces. And, in fact, the abolition of classes in society presupposes a degree of historical evolution at which the existence, not simply of this or that particular ruling class, but of any ruling class at all, and, therefore, the existence of class distinction itself has become an obsolete anachronism. It presupposes, therefore, the development of production carried out to a degree at which appropriation of the means of production and of the products, and, with this, of political domination, of the monopoly of culture, and of intellectual leadership by a particular class of society, has become not only superfluous but economically, politically, intellectually, a hindrance to development.

This point is now reached. Their political and intellectual bankruptcy is scarcely any longer a secret to the bourgeoisie themselves. Their economic bankruptcy recurs regularly every ten years. In every crisis, society is suffocated beneath the weight of its own productive forces and products, which it cannot use, and stands helpless, face to face with the absurd contradiction that the producers have nothing to consume, because consumers are wanting. The expansive force of the means of production bursts the bonds that the capitalist mode of production had imposed upon them. Their deliverance from these bonds is the one precondition for an unbroken, constantly accelerated development of the productive forces, and therewith for a practically unlimited increase of production itself. Nor is this all. The socialised appropriation of the means of production does away, not only with the present artificial restrictions upon production, but also with the positive waste and devastation of productive forces and products that are at the present time the inevitable concomitants of production, and that reach their height in the crises. Further, it sets free for the community at large a mass of means of production and of products, by doing away with the senseless extravagance of the ruling classes of today and their political representatives. The possibility of securing for every member of society, by means of socialised production, an existence not only fully sufficient materially, and becoming day by day more full, but an existence guaranteeing to all the free development and exercise of their physical and mental faculties—this possibility is now for the first time here, but *it is here*.[3]

With the seizing of the means of production by society, production of commodities is done away with, and, simultaneously, the mastery of the product over the producer. Anarchy in social production is replaced by systematic, definite organisation. The struggle for individual existence disappears. Then for the first time man, in a certain sense, is finally marked off from the rest of the animal kingdom, and emerges from mere animal conditions of existence into really human ones. The whole sphere of the conditions of life which environ man, and which have hitherto ruled man, now comes under the dominion and control of man, who for the first time becomes the real, conscious lord of Nature, because he has now become master of his own social organisation. The laws of his own social action, hitherto standing face to face with man as laws of Nature foreign to, and dominating him, will then be used with full understanding, and so mastered by him. Man's own social organisation, hitherto confronting him as a necessity imposed by Nature and history, now becomes the result of his own free action. The extraneous objective forces that have hitherto governed history pass under the control of man himself. Only from that time will man

3. A few figures may serve to give an approximate idea of the enormous expansive force of the modern means of production, even under capitalist pressure. According to Mr. Giffen, the total wealth of Great Britain and Ireland amounted, in round numbers in

    1814 to £2,200,000,000.
    1865 to £6,100,000,000.

    1875 to £8,500,000,000.

As an instance of the squandering of means of production and of products during a crisis, the total loss in the German iron industry alone, in the crisis 1873–78, was given at the second German Industrial Congress (Berlin, February 21, 1878) as £22,750,000. [*Engels*]

himself, more and more consciously, make his own history—only from that time will the social causes set in movement by him have, in the main and in a constantly growing measure, the results intended by him. It is the ascent of man from the kingdom of necessity to the kingdom of freedom.

Let us briefly sum up our sketch of historical evolution.

I. *Mediaeval Society.* Individual production on a small scale. Means of production adapted for individual use; hence primitive, ungainly, petty, dwarfed in action. Production for immediate consumption, either of the producer himself or of his feudal lord. Only where an excess of production over this consumption occurs is such excess offered for sale, enters into exchange. Production of commodities, therefore, only in its infancy. But already it contains within itself, in embryo, *anarchy in the production of society at large.*

II. *Capitalist Revolution.* Transformation of industry, at first by means of simple co-operation and manufacture. Concentration of the means of production, hitherto scattered, into great workshops. As a consequence, their transformation from individual to social means of production—a transformation which does not, on the whole, affect the form of exchange. The old forms of appropriation remain in force. The capitalist appears. In his capacity as owner of the means of production, he also appropriates the products and turns them into commodities. Production has become a *social* act. Exchange and appropriation continue to be *individual* acts, the acts of individuals. *The social product is appropriated by the individual capitalist.* Fundamental contradiction, whence arise all the contradictions in which our present-day society moves, and which modern industry brings to light.

A. Severance of the producer from the means of production. Condemnation of the worker to wage-labour for life. *Antagonism between the proletariat and the bourgeoisie.*

B. Growing predominance and increasing effectiveness of the laws governing the production of commodities. Unbridled competition. *Contradiction between socialised organisation in the individual factory and social anarchy in production as a whole.*

C. On the one hand, perfecting of machinery, made by competition compulsory for each individual manufacturer, and complemented by a constantly growing displacement of labourers. *Industrial reserve army.* On the other hand, unlimited extension of production, also compulsory under competition, for every manufacturer. On both sides, unheard-of development of productive forces, excess of supply over demand, over-production, glutting of the markets, crises every ten years, the vicious circle: excess here, of means of production and products—excess there, of labourers, without employment and without means of existence. But these two levers of production and of social well-being are unable to work together, because the capitalist form of production prevents the productive forces from working and the products from circulating, unless they are first turned into capital—which their very superabundance prevents. The contradiction has grown into an absurdity. *The mode of production rises in rebellion against the form of exchange.* The bourgeoisie are convicted of incapacity further to manage their own social productive forces.

D. Partial recognition of the social character of the productive forces forced upon the capitalists themselves. Taking over of the great institutions for production and communication, first by joint-stock companies, later on by trusts, then by the state. The bourgeoisie demonstrated to be a superfluous class. All its social functions are now performed by salaried employees.

III. *Proletarian Revolution.* Solution of the contradictions. The proletariat seizes the public power, and by means of this transforms the socialised means of production, slipping from the hands of the bourgeoisie, into public property. By this act, the proletariat frees the means of production from the character of capital they have thus far borne, and gives their socialised character complete freedom to work itself out. Socialised production upon a predetermined plan becomes henceforth possible. The development of production makes the existence of different classes of society thenceforth an anachronism. In proportion as anarchy in social production vanishes, the political authority of the state dies out. Man, at last the master of his own form of social organisation, becomes at the same time the lord over Nature, his own master—free.

To accomplish this act of universal emancipation is the historical mission of the modern proletariat. To thoroughly comprehend the historical conditions and thus the very nature of this act, to impart to the new oppressed proletarian class a full knowledge of the conditions and of the meaning of the momentous act it is called upon to accomplish, this is the task of the theoretical expression of the proletarian movement, scientific socialism.

Letters on Historical Materialism

FRIEDRICH ENGELS

Because of his preoccupation with *Capital* and for other reasons, Marx in his later years failed to produce a detailed and comprehensive formulation of the materialist conception of history. Engels attempted to make good this deficiency with the sketch of the conception presented in *Socialism: Utopian and Scientific*, and by offering clarifications on important particular points in these letters. Of special note are his discussions of ideology and his effort to guard against an oversimplified interpretation of the doctrine of economic determinism in history.

To Joseph Bloch

London, September 21–22, 1890

According to the materialist conception of history, the *ultimately* determining element in history is the production and reproduction of real life. More than this neither Marx nor I have ever asserted. Hence if somebody twists this into saying that the economic element is the *only* determining one, he transforms that proposition into a meaningless, abstract, senseless phrase. The economic situation is the basis, but the various elements of the superstructure: political forms of the class struggle and its results, to wit: constitutions established by the victorious class after a successful battle, etc., juridical forms, and then even the reflexes of all these actual struggles in the brains of the participants, political, juristic, philosophical theories, religious views and their further development into systems of dogmas, also exercise their influence upon the course of the historical struggles and in many cases preponderate in determining their *form*. There is an interaction of all these elements in which, amid all the endless host of accidents (that is, of things and events, whose inner connection is so remote or so impossible of proof that we can regard it as non-existent, as negligible) the economic move-

640

ment finally asserts itself as necessary. Otherwise the application of the theory to any period of history one chose would be easier than the solution of a simple equation of the first degree.

We make our history ourselves, but, in the first place, under very definite assumptions and conditions. Among these the economic ones are ultimately decisive. But the political ones, etc., and indeed even the traditions which haunt human minds also play a part, although not the decisive one. The Prussian state also arose and developed from historical, ultimately economic causes. But it could scarcely be maintained without pedantry that among the many small states of North Germany, Brandenburg was specifically determined by economic necessity to become the great power embodying the economic, linguistic and, after the Reformation, also the religious difference between North and South, and not by other elements as well (above all by its entanglement with Poland, owing to the possession of Prussia, and hence with international political relations—which were indeed also decisive in the formation of the Austrian dynastic power). Without making oneself ridiculous it would be a difficult thing to explain in terms of economics the existence of every small state in Germany, past and present, or the origin of the High German consonant shifts, which widened the geographical wall of partition, formed by the mountains from the Sudetic range to the Taunus, to the extent of a regular fissure across all Germany.

In the second place, however, history is made in such a way that the final result always arises from conflicts between many individual wills, of which each again has been made what it is by a host of particular conditions of life. Thus there are innumerable intersecting forces, an infinite series of parallelograms of forces which give rise to one resultant—the historical event. This may again itself be viewed as the product of a power which works as a whole, *unconsciously* and without volition. For what each individual wills is obstructed by everyone else, and what emerges is something that no one willed. Thus past history proceeds in the manner of a natural process and is essentially subject to the same laws of motion. But from the fact that individual wills—of which each desires what he is impelled to by his physical constitution and external, in the last resort economic, circumstances (either his own personal circumstances or those of society in general)—do not attain what they want, but are merged into a collective mean, a common resultant, it must not be concluded that their value is equal to zero. On the contrary, each contributes to the resultant and is to this degree involved in it.

I would furthermore ask you to study this theory from its original sources and not at second-hand; it is really much easier. Marx hardly wrote anything in which it did not play a part. But especially *The Eighteenth Brumaire of Louis Bonaparte* is a most excellent example of its application. There are also many allusions in *Capital*. Then may I also direct you to my writings: *Herr Eugen Dühring's Revolution in Science* and *Ludwig Feuerbach and the End of Classical German Philosophy*, in which I have given the most detailed account of historical materialism which, as far as I know, exists.

Marx and I are ourselves partly to blame for the fact that the younger people sometimes lay more stress on the economic side than is due to it. We had to emphasise the main principle *vis-à-vis* our adversaries, who denied it, and we had not always the time, the place or the opportunity to allow the other elements involved in the interaction to come into their rights. But when it was a case of presenting a section of history, that is, of a practical application, it was a different matter and there no error was possible. Unfortunately, however, it happens only too often that people think they have fully understood a new theory and can apply it without more ado from the moment they have mastered its main principles, and even those not always correctly. And I cannot exempt many of the more recent "Marxists" from this reproach, for the most amazing rubbish has been produced in this quarter, too.

To Conrad Schmidt

London, October 27, 1890

I am taking advantage of the first free moments to reply to you. I think you would do very well to take the post in Zurich. You could always learn a good deal about economics there, especially if you bear in mind that Zurich is after all only a third-rate money and speculation market, so that the impressions which make themselves felt there are weakened by twofold or threefold reflection or are deliberately distorted. But you will get a practical knowledge of the mechanism and be obliged to follow the stock-exchange reports from London, New York, Paris, Berlin and Vienna at first hand, and thus the world market, in its reflex as money and stock market, will reveal itself to you. Economic, political and other reflections are just like those in the human eye: they pass through a condensing lens and therefore appear upside down, standing on their heads. Only the nervous apparatus which would put them on their feet again for representation is lacking. The money market man sees the movement of industry and of the world market only in the inverted reflection of the money and stock market and so effect becomes cause to him. I noticed that already in the forties in Manchester the London stock-exchange reports were utterly useless for understanding the course of industry and its periodical maxima and minima because these gentry tried to explain everything from crises on the money market, which of course were generally only symptoms. At that time the point was to disprove temporary overproduction as the origin of industrial crises, so that the thing had in addition its tendentious side, provocative distortion. This point now ceases to exist—for us, at any rate, for good and all—added to which it is indeed a fact that the money market can also have its own crises, in which direct disturbances of industry play only a subordinate part or no part at all. Here there is still much, especially in the history of the last twenty years, to be established and examined.

Where there is division of labour on a social scale there the different labour processes become independent of each other. In the last instance production is the decisive factor. But as soon as trade in products becomes independent of production proper, it follows a movement of its own, which, while it is governed as a whole by production, still in particular respects and within this general dependence follows laws of its own contained in the nature of this new factor; this movement has phases of its own and in its turn reacts on the movement of production. The discovery of America was due to the thirst for gold which had previously driven the Portuguese to Africa (compare Soetbeer's *Production of Precious Metals*), because the enormously extended European industry of the fourteenth and fifteenth centuries and the trade corresponding to it demanded more means of exchange than Germany, the great silver country from 1450 to 1550, could provide. The conquest of India by the Portuguese, Dutch and English between 1500 and 1800 had *imports* from India as its object—nobody dreamt of exploring anything there. And yet what a colossal reaction these discoveries and conquests, solely conditioned by the interests of trade, had upon industry: it was only the need for *exports to* these countries that created and developed large-scale industry.

So it is, too, with the money market. As soon as trade in money becomes separate from trade in commodities it has—under certain conditions imposed by production and commodity trade and within these limits—a development of its own, special laws determined by its own nature and separate phases. If to this is added that money trade, developing further, comes to include trade in securities and that these securities are not only government papers but also industrial and transport stocks, so that money trade conquers the direct control over a portion of the production by which, taken as a whole, it is itself controlled, then the reaction of money trading on production becomes still stronger and more complicated. The traders in money are the owners of railways, mines, iron works, etc. These means of production take on a double aspect; their operation has to be directed sometimes in the interests of direct production but sometimes also according to the requirements of the shareholders, so far as they are money traders. The most striking example of this is the North American railways, whose operation is entirely dependent on the daily stock-exchange operations of a Jay Gould or a Vanderbilt, etc., these having nothing whatever to do with the particular railway concerned and its interests as a means of communication. And even here in England we have seen contests lasting for tens of years between different railway companies over the boundaries of their respective territories—contests in which an enormous amount of money was thrown away, not in the interests of production and communication but simply because of the rivalry which usually only had the object of facilitating the stock-exchange dealings of the shareholding money traders.

With these few indications of my conception of the relation of production to commodity trade and of both to money trading, I have answered, in essence, your questions about historical materialism generally. The thing is easiest to grasp from the point of view of the division of labour. Society gives rise to certain common functions which it cannot dispense with. The persons appointed for this purpose form a new branch of the division of labour *within society*. This gives them particular interests, distinct, too, from the interests of those who empowered them; they make themselves independent of the latter and—the state is in being. And now things proceed in a way similar to that in commodity trade and later in money trade: the new independent power, while having in the main to follow the movement of production, reacts, by virtue of its inherent relative independence, that is, the relative independence once transferred to it and gradually further developed, in its turn upon the conditions and course of production. It is the interaction of two unequal forces: on the one hand, the economic movement, on the other, the new political power, which strives for as much independence as possible, and which, having once been established, is endowed with a movement of its own. On the whole, the economic movement gets its way, but it has also to suffer reactions from the political movement which it itself established and endowed with relative independence, from the movement of the state power, on the one hand, and of the opposition simultaneously engendered, on the other. Just as the movement of the industrial market is, in the main and with the reservations already indicated, reflected in the money market and, of course, in *inverted* form, so the struggle between the classes already existing and already in conflict with one another is reflected in the struggle between government and opposition, but also in inverted form, no longer directly but indirectly, not as a class struggle but as a fight for political principles, and so distorted that it has taken us thousands of years to get behind it.

The reaction of the state power upon economic development can be one of three kinds: it can run in the same direction, and then development is more rapid; it can oppose the line of development, in which case nowadays state power in every great people will go to pieces in the long run; or it can cut off the economic development from certain paths, and prescribe certain others. This case ultimately reduces itself to one of the two previous ones. But it is obvious that in cases two and three the political power can do great damage to the economic development and result in the squandering of great masses of energy and material.

Then there is also the case of the conquest and brutal destruction of economic resources, by which, in certain circumstances, a whole local or national economic development could formerly be ruined. Nowadays such a case usually has the opposite effect, at least among great peoples: in the long run the vanquished often gains more economically, politically and morally than the victor.

Similarly with law. As soon as the new division of labour which creates professional lawyers becomes necessary, another new and independent sphere is opened up which, for all its general dependence on production and trade, still has also a special capacity for reacting upon these spheres. In a modern state, law must not only correspond to the general economic condition and be its expression, but must also be an *internally coherent* expression which does not, owing to inner contradictions, reduce itself to nought. And in order to achieve this, the faithful reflection of economic conditions suffers increasingly. All the more so the more rarely it happens that a code of law is the blunt, unmitigated, unadulterated expression of the domination of a class—this in itself would offend the "conception of right." Even in the *Code Napoléon* the pure, consistent conception of right held by the revolutionary bourgeoisie of 1792–96 is already adulterated in many ways, and, in so far as it is embodied there, has daily to undergo all sorts of attenuations owing to the rising power of the proletariat. Which does not prevent the *Code Napoléon* from being the statute book which serves as a basis for every new code of law in every part of the world. Thus to a great extent the course of the "development of right" only consists, first, in the attempt to do away with the contradictions arising from the direct translation of economic relations into legal principles, and to establish a harmonious system of law, and then in the repeated breaches made in this system by the influence and pressure of further economic development, which involves it in further contradictions. (I am speaking here only of civil law for the moment.)

The reflection of economic relations as legal principles is necessarily also a topsy-turvy one: it goes on without the person who is acting being conscious of it; the jurist imagines he is operating with *a priori* propositions, whereas they are really only economic reflexes; so everything is upside down. And it seems to me obvious that this inversion, which, so long as it remains unrecognised, forms what we call *ideological conception*, reacts in its turn upon the economic basis and may, within certain limits, modify it. The basis of the law of inheritance—assuming that the stages reached in the development of the family are equal—is an economic one. Nevertheless, it would be difficult to prove, for instance, that the absolute liberty of the testator in England and the severe restrictions imposed upon him in France are only due in every detail to economic causes. Both react back, however, on the economic sphere to a very considerable extent, because they influence the distribution of property.

As to the realms of ideology which soar still higher in the air, religion, philosophy, etc., these have a prehistoric stock, found already in existence by, and taken over in, the historic period, of what we should today call bunk. These various false conceptions of nature, of man's own being, of spirits, magic forces, etc., have for the most part only a negative economic basis; the low economic development of the prehistoric period is supplemented and also partially conditioned and even caused by the false conceptions of nature. And even though economic necessity was the main driving force of the progressive knowledge of nature and becomes ever more so, it would surely be pedantic to try and find economic causes for all this primitive nonsense. The history of science is the history of the gradual clearing away of this nonsense or of its replacement by fresh but always less absurd nonsense. The people who attend to this belong in their turn to special spheres in the division of labour and appear to themselves to be working in an independent field. And to the extent that they form an independent group within the social division of labour, their productions, including their errors, react back as an influence upon the whole development of society, even on its economic development. But all the same they themselves are again under the dominating influence of economic development. In philosophy, for instance, this can be most readily proved for the bourgeois period. Hobbes was the first modern materialist (in the eighteenth century sense) but he was an absolutist in a period when absolute monarchy was at its height throughout the whole of Europe and when the fight of absolute monarchy versus the people was beginning in England. Locke, both in religion and politics, was the child of the class compromise of 1688. The English deists and their more consistent continuators, the French materialists, were the true philosophers of the bourgeoisie, the French even of the bourgeois revolution. The German Philistine runs through German philosophy from Kant to Hegel, sometimes positively and sometimes negatively. But the philosophy of every epoch, since it is a definite sphere in the division of labour, has as its presupposition certain definite thought material handed down to it by its predecessors, from which it takes its start. And that is why economically backward countries can still play first fiddle in philosophy: France in the eighteenth century compared with England, on whose philosophy the French based themselves, and later Germany relatively to both. But in France as well as Germany philosophy and the general blossoming of literature at that time were the result of a rising economic development. I consider the ultimate supremacy of economic development established in these spheres too, but it comes to pass within the conditions imposed by the particular sphere itself: in philosophy, for instance, through the operation of economic influences (which again generally act only under political, etc., disguises) upon the existing philosphic material handed down by predecessors. Here economy creates nothing anew, but it determines the way in which the thought material found in existence is altered and further developed, and that too for the most part indirectly, for it is the political, legal and moral reflexes which exercise the greatest direct influence upon philosophy.

About religion I have said what was most necessary in the last section on Feuerbach.

If therefore Barth supposes that we deny any and every reaction of the political, etc., reflexes of the economic movement upon the movement itself, he is simply tilting at windmills. He has only got to look at Marx's *Eighteenth Brumaire*, which deals almost exclusively with the *particular* part played by political struggles and events; of course, within their *general* dependence upon economic conditions. Or *Capital*, the section on the working day, for instance, where legislation, which is surely a political act, has such a trenchant effect. Or the section on the history of the bourgeoisie. (Chapter XXIV.) Or why do we fight for the political dictatorship of the proletariat if political power is economically impotent? Force (that is, state power) is also an economic power!

But I have no time to criticise the book now. I must first get volume III[1] out and besides I think that Bernstein, for instance, could deal with it quite effectively.

What these gentlemen all lack is dialectics. They always see only here cause, there effect. That this is a hollow abstraction, that such metaphysical polar opposites exist in the real world only during crises, while the whole vast process goes on in the form of interaction—though of very unequal forces, the economic movement being by far the strongest, most primeval, most decisive—that here everything is relative and nothing absolute—this they never begin to see. Hegel has never existed for them.

1. A reference to Volume III of Marx's *Capital*.

To Franz Mehring

London, July 14, 1893

Today is my first opportunity to thank you for the *Lessing Legend* you were kind enough to send me. I did not want to reply with a bare formal acknowledgement of receipt of the book but intended at the same time to tell you something about it, about its contents. Hence the delay.

I shall begin at the end—the appendix on historical material-ism,[2] in which you have lined up the main things excellently and for any unprejudiced person convincingly. If I find anything to object to it is that you give me more credit than I deserve, even if I count in everything which I might possibly have found out for myself—in time—but which Marx with his more rapid *coup d'œil*[3] and wider vision discovered much more quickly. When one has the good fortune to work for forty years with a man like Marx, one does not usually get the recognition one thinks one deserves during his lifetime. Then, if the greater man dies, the lesser easily gets over-rated and this seems to me to be just my case at present; history will set all this right in the end and by that time one will have qui-etly turned up one's toes and not know anything any more about anything.

Otherwise there is only one point lacking, which, however, Marx and I always failed to stress enough in our writings and in regard to which we are all equally guilty. That is to say, we all laid, and *were bound* to lay, the main emphasis, in the first place, on the *deriva-tion* of political, juridical and other ideological notions, and of actions arisng through the medium of these notions, from basic eco-nomic facts. But in so doing we neglected the formal side—the ways and means by which these notions, etc., come about—for the sake of the content. This has given our adversaries a welcome opportunity for misunderstandings and distortions, of which Paul Barth is a striking example.

Ideology is a process accomplished by the so-called thinker con-sciously, it is true, but with a false consciousness. The real motive forces impelling him remain unknown to him; otherwise it simply would not be an ideological process. Hence he imagines false or seeming motive forces. Because it is a process of thought he derives its form as well as its content from pure thought, either his own or that of his predecessors. He works with mere thought material, which he accepts without examination as the product of thought,

2. Mehring's article "Über den histori-schen Materialismus" ("On Historical Materialism") was printed in 1893 as an appendix to his book *Die Lessing Legende* (*The Lessing Legend*).
3. Grasp.

and does not investigate further for a more remote source independent of thought; indeed this is a matter of course to him, because, as
all action is *mediated* by thought, it appears to him to be ultimately *based* upon thought.

The ideologist who deals with history (history is here simply
meant to comprise all the spheres—political, juridical, philosophical,
theological—belonging to *society* and not only to nature) thus possesses in every sphere of science material which has formed itself
independently out of the thought of previous generations and has
gone through its own independent process of development in the
brains of these successive generations. True, external facts belonging
to one or another sphere may have exercised a codetermining influence on this development, but the tacit presupposition is that these
facts themselves are also only the fruits of a process of thought, and
so we still remain within that realm of mere thought, which apparently has successfully digested even the hardest facts.

It is above all this appearance of an independent history of state
constitutions, of systems of law, of ideological conceptions in every
separate domain that dazzles most people. If Luther and Calvin
"overcome" the official Catholic religion or Hegel "overcomes"
Fichte and Kant or Rousseau with his republican *contrat social*
indirectly overcomes the constitutional Montesquieu, this is a process which remains within theology, philosophy or political science,
represents a state in the history of these particular spheres of
thought and never passes beyond the sphere of thought. And since
the bourgeois illusion of the eternity and finality of capitalist production has been added as well, even the overcoming of the mercantilists by the physiocrats and Adam Smith is accounted as a sheer
victory of thought; not as the reflection in thought of changed economic facts but as the finally achieved correct understanding of
actual conditions subsisting always and everywhere—in fact, if
Richard Coeur de Lion and Philip Augustus had introduced free
trade instead of getting mixed up in the crusades we should have
been spared five hundred years of misery and stupidity.

This aspect of the matter, which I can only indicate here, we
have all, I think, neglected more than it deserves. It is the old story:
form is always neglected at first for content. As I say, I have done
that too and the mistake has always struck me only later. So I am
not only far from reproaching you with this in any way—as the
older of the guilty parties I certainly have no right to do so; on the
contrary. But I would like all the same to draw your attention to
this point for the future.

Hanging together with this is the fatuous notion of the ideologists that because we deny an independent historical development
to the various ideological spheres which play a part in history we

also deny them any *effect upon history*. The basis of this is the common undialectical conception of cause and effect as rigidly opposite poles, the total disregarding of interaction. These gentlemen often almost deliberately forget that once a historic element has been brought into the world by other, ultimately economic causes, it reacts, can react on its environment and even on the causes that have given rise to it. For instance, Barth on the priesthood and religion, on your page 475. I was very glad to see how you settled this fellow whose banality exceeds all expectations; and him they make professor of history in Leipzig! I must say that old man Wachsmuth—also rather a bonehead but greatly appreciative of facts—was quite a different chap.

As for the rest, I can only repeat about the book what I repeatedly said about the articles when they appeared in the *Neue Zeit*: it is by far the best presentation in existence of the genesis of the Prussian state. Indeed I may well say that it is the only good presentation, correctly developing in most matters their interconnection down to the veriest details. One regrets only that you were unable to include the entire further development down to Bismarck and one hopes involuntarily that you will do this another time and present a complete coherent picture, from the Elector Frederick William down to old William. You have already made your preliminary investigations and, in the main at least, they are as good as finished. The thing has to be done sometime anyhow before the shaky old shanty comes tumbling down. The dissipation of the monarchical-patriotic legends, while not directly a necessary precondition for the abolition of the monarchy which screens class domination (inasmuch as a *pure*, bourgeois republic in Germany will be outstripped by events before it will have come into existence) will nevertheless be one of the most effective levers for that purpose.

Then you will have more space and opportunity to depict the local history of Prussia as part of the general misery that Germany has gone through. This is the point where I depart somewhat here and there from your view, especially in the conception of the preconditions for the dismemberment of Germany and of the failure of the bourgeois revolution in Germany during the sixteenth century. When I get down to reworking the historical introduction to my *Peasant War*, which I hope will be next winter, I shall be able to develop there the points in question. Not that I consider those you indicated incorrect, but I put others alongside of them and group them somewhat differently.

On the Origin of the State

FRIEDRICH ENGELS

In *Ancient Society, or Researches in the Lines of Human Progress from Savagery Through Barbarism to Civilization* (1877), the American anthropologist Lewis H. Morgan propounded a matrilineal theory of the origins of human society. His account of a stateless primitive society founded on communal property appeared to Marx and Engels to have (as Engels later put it) the same significance for the history of primitive society as Darwin's theory of evolution had for biology and Marx's theory of surplus value had for political economy. Marx planned to write a study based on Morgan's researches, and made extensive extracts from and notes on *Ancient Society* for this purpose. Using Marx's materials as well as the original sources, Engels in 1884 wrote his monograph on *The Origin of the Family, Private Property and the State*, from which this account of the origin of the state is taken.

---

* * * Above we discussed separately each of the three main forms in which the state was built up on the ruins of the gentile constitution. Athens represented the purest, most classical form. Here the state sprang directly and mainly out of the class antagonisms that developed within gentile society. In Rome gentile society became an exclusive aristocracy amidst numerous plebs, standing outside of it, having no rights but only duties. The victory of the plebs burst the old gentile constitution asunder and erected on its ruins the state, in which both the gentile aristocracy and the plebs were soon wholly absorbed. Finally, among the German vanquishers of the Roman Empire, the state sprang up as a direct result of the conquest of large foreign territories, which the gentile constitution had no means of ruling. As this conquest did not necessitate either a serious struggle with the old population or a more advanced division of labour, and as conquered and conquerors were almost at the same stage of economic development and thus the economic basis of society remained the same as before, therefore, the gentile consti-

tution could continue for many centuries in a changed, territorial form, in the shape of a Mark constitution, and even rejuvenate itself for a time in enfeebled form in the noble and patrician families of later years, and even in peasant families, as in Dithmarschen.[1]

The state is, therefore, by no means a power forced on society from without; just as little is it "the reality of the ethical idea," "the image and reality of reason," as Hegel maintains. Rather, it is a product of society at a certain stage of development; it is the admission that this society has become entangled in an insoluble contradiction with itself, that it is cleft into irreconcilable antagonisms which it is powerless to dispel. But in order that these antagonisms, classes with conflicting economic interests, might not consume themselves and society in sterile struggle, a power seemingly standing above society became necessary for the purpose of moderating the conflict, of keeping it within the bounds of "order"; and this power, arisen out of society, but placing itself above it, and increasingly alienating itself from it, is the state.

In contradistinction to the old gentile organisation, the state, first, divides its subjects *according to territory*. As we have seen, the old gentile associations, built upon and held together by ties of blood, became inadequate, largely because they presupposed that the members were bound to a given territory, a bond which had long ceased to exist. The territory remained, but the people had become mobile. Hence, division according to territory was taken as the point of departure, and citizens were allowed to exercise their public rights and duties wherever they settled, irrespective of gens and tribe. This organisation of citizens according to locality is a feature common to all states. That is why it seems natural to us; but we have seen what long and arduous struggles were needed before it could replace, in Athens and Rome, the old organisation according to gentes.

The second is the establishment of a *public power* which no longer directly coincided with the population organising itself as an armed force. This special public power is necessary, because a self-acting armed organisation of the population has become impossible since the cleavage into classes. The slaves also belonged to the population; the 90,000 citizens of Athens formed only a privileged class as against the 365,000 slaves. The people's army of the Athenian democracy was an aristocratic public power against the slaves, whom it kept in check; however, a gendarmerie also became necessary to keep the citizens in check, as we related above. This public power exists in every state; it consists not merely of armed people but also of material adjuncts, prisons and institutions of coercion of all

1. The first historian who had at least an approximate idea of the nature of the gens was Niebuhr, thanks to his knowledge of the Dithmarschen families—to which, however, he also owes the errors he mechanically copied from there. [*Engels*]

kinds, of which gentile society knew nothing. It may be very insignificant, almost infinitesimal, in societies where class antagonisms are still undeveloped and in out-of-the-way places as was the case at certain times and in certain regions in the United States of America. It grows stronger, however, in proportion as class antagonisms within the state become more acute, and as adjacent states become larger and more populated. We have only to look at our present-day Europe, where class struggle and rivalry in conquest have screwed up the public power to such a pitch that it threatens to devour the whole of society and even the state.

In order to maintain this public power, contributions from the citizens become necessary—*taxes*. These were absolutely unknown in gentile society; but we know enough about them today. As civilisation advances, these taxes become inadequate; the state makes drafts on the future, contracts loans, *public debts*. Old Europe can tell a tale about these, too.

In possession of the public power and of the right to levy taxes, the officials, as organs of society, now stand *above* society. The free, voluntary respect that was accorded to the organs of the gentile constitution does not satisfy them, even if they could gain it; being the vehicles of a power that is becoming alien to society, respect for them must be enforced by means of exceptional laws by virtue of which they enjoy special sanctity and inviolability. The shabbiest police servant in the civilised state has more "authority" than all the organs of gentile society put together; but the most powerful prince and the greatest statesman, or general, of civilisation may well envy the humblest gentile chief for the uncoerced and undisputed respect that is paid to him. The one stands in the midst of society, the other is forced to attempt to represent something outside and above it.

As the state arose from the need to hold class antagonisms in check, but as it arose, at the same time, in the midst of the conflict of these classes, it is, as a rule, the state of the most powerful, economically dominant class which, through the medium of the state, becomes also the politically dominant class, and thus acquires new means of holding down and exploiting the oppressed class. Thus, the state of antiquity was above all the state of the slave owners for the purpose of holding down the slaves, as the feudal state was the organ of the nobility for holding down the peasant serfs and bondsmen, and the modern representative state is an instrument of exploitation of wage labour by capital. By way of exception, however, periods occur in which the warring classes balance each other so nearly that the state power, as ostensible mediator, acquires, for the moment, a certain degree of independence of both. Such was the absolute monarchy of the seventeenth and eighteenth centuries, which held the balance between the nobility and the class of burghers; such was the Bonapartism of the First, and still more of the Second French Empire, which played off the proletariat against the bourgeoisie and the bourgeoisie against the proletariat. The latest performance of this kind, in which ruler and ruled appear equally ridiculous, is the new German Empire of the Bismarck nation: the capitalists and workers are balanced against each other and equally cheated for the benefit of the impoverished Prussian cabbage Junkers.

In most of the historical states, the rights of citizens are, besides, apportioned according to their wealth, thus directly expressing the fact that the state is an organisation of the possessing class for its protection against the non-possessing class. It was so already in the Athenian and Roman classification according to property. It was so in the mediaeval feudal state, in which the alignment of political power was in conformity with the amount of land owned. It is seen in the electoral qualifications of the modern representative states. Yet this political recognition of property distinctions is by no means essential. On the contrary, it marks a low stage of state development. The highest form of the state, the democratic republic, which under our modern conditions of society is more and more becoming an inevitable necessity, and is the form of state in which alone the last decisive struggle between proletariat and bourgeoisie can be fought out—the democratic republic officially knows nothing any more of property distinctions. In it wealth exercises its power indirectly, but all the more surely. On the one hand, in the form of the direct corruption of officials, of which America provides the classical example; on the other hand, in the form of an alliance between government and Stock Exchange, which becomes the easier to achieve the more the public debt increases and the more joint-stock companies concentrate in their hands not only transport but also production itself, using the Stock Exchange as their centre. The latest French republic as well as the United States is a striking example of this; and good old Switzerland has contributed its share in this field. But that a democratic republic is not essential for this fraternal alliance between government and Stock Exchange is proved by England and also by the new German Empire, where one cannot tell who was elevated more by universal suffrage, Bismarck or Bleichröder. And lastly, the possessing class rules directly through the medium of universal suffrage. As long as the oppressed class, in our case, therefore, the proletariat, is not yet ripe to emancipate itself, it will in its majority regard the existing order of society as the only one possible and, politically, will form the tail of the capitalist class, its extreme Left wing. To the extent, however, that this class matures for its self-emancipation, it constitutes itself as its own party and elects its own representatives, and not those of the capitalists. Thus, universal suffrage is the gauge of the maturity of the working class. It cannot and never will be anything more in the present-day state; but that is sufficient. On the day the thermometer of universal suffrage registers boiling point among the workers, both they and the capitalists will know what to do.

The state, then, has not existed from all eternity. There have been societies that did without it, that had no conception of the state and state power. At a certain stage of economic development, which was necessarily bound up with the cleavage of society into classes, the state became a necessity owing to this cleavage. We are now rapidly approaching a stage in the development of production at which the existence of these classes not only will have ceased to be a necessity, but will become a positive hindrance to production. They will fall as inevitably as they arose at an earlier stage. Along with them the state will inevitably fall. The society that will organise production on the basis of a free and equal association of the producers will put the whole machinery of state where it will then belong: into the Museum of Antiquities, by the side of the spinning wheel and the bronze axe.

Thus, from the foregoing, civilisation is that stage of development of society at which division of labour, the resulting exchange between individuals, and commodity production, which combines the two, reach their complete unfoldment and revolutionise the whole hitherto existing society.

Production at all former stages of society was essentially collective and, likewise, consumption took place by the direct distribution of the products within larger or smaller communistic communities. This production in common was carried on within the narrowest limits, but concomitantly the producers were masters of their process of production and of their product. They knew what became of the product: they consumed it, it did not leave their hands; and as long as production was carried on on this basis, it could not grow beyond the control of the producers, and it could not raise any strange, phantom powers against them, as is the case regularly and inevitably under civilisation.

But, slowly, division of labour crept into this process of production. It undermined the collective nature of production and appropriation, it made appropriation by individuals the largely prevailing rule, and thus gave rise to exchange between individuals—how, we examined above. Gradually, the production of commodities became the dominant form.

With the production of commodities, production no longer for one's own consumption but for exchange, the products necessarily pass from hand to hand. The producer parts with his product in the course of exchange; he no longer knows what becomes of it. As soon as money, and with it the merchant, steps in as a middleman between the producers, the process of exchange becomes still more complicated, the ultimate fate of the product still more uncertain. The merchants are numerous and none of them knows what the other is doing. Commodities now pass not only from hand to hand, but also from market to market. The producers have lost control of the aggregate production of the conditions of their own life, and the merchants have not acquired it. Products and production become the playthings of chance.

But chance is only one pole of an interrelation, the other pole of which is called necessity. In nature, where chance also seems to reign, we have long ago demonstrated in each particular field the inherent necessity and regularity that asserts itself in this chance. What is true of nature holds good also for society. The more a social activity, a series of social processes, becomes too powerful for conscious human control, grows beyond human reach, the more it seems to have been left to pure chance, the more do its peculiar and innate laws assert themselves in this chance, as if by natural necessity. Such laws also control the fortuities of the production and exchange of commodities; these laws confront the individual producer and exchanger as strange and, in the beginning, even as unknown powers, the nature of which must first be laboriously investigated and ascertained. These economic laws of commodity production are modified at the different stages of development of this form of production; on the whole, however, the entire period of civilisation has been dominated by these laws. To this day, the product is master of the producer; to this day, the total production of society is regulated, not by a collectively thought-out plan, but by blind laws, which operate with elemental force, in the last resort in the storms of periodic commercial crises.

We saw above how human labour power became able, at a rather early stage of development of production, to produce considerably more than was needed for the producer's maintenance, and how this stage, in the main, coincided with that of the first appearance of the division of labour and of exchange between individuals. Now, it was not long before the great "truth" was discovered that man, too, may be a commodity; that human power may be exchanged and utilised by converting man into a slave. Men had barely started to engage in exchange when they themselves were exchanged. The active became a passive, whether man wanted it or not.

With slavery, which reached its fullest development in civilisation, came the first great cleavage of society into an exploiting and an exploited class. This cleavage has continued during the whole period of civilisation. Slavery was the first form of exploitation, peculiar to the world of antiquity; it was followed by serfdom in the Middle Ages, and by wage labour in modern times. These are the three great forms of servitude, characteristic of the three great epochs of civilisation; open, and, latterly, disguised slavery, are its steady companions.

The stage of commodity production, with which civilisation began, is marked economically by the introduction of 1) metal money and, thus, of money capital, interest and usury; 2) the merchants acting as middlemen between producers; 3) private ownership of land and mortgage; 4) slave labour as the prevailing form of production. The form of the family corresponding to civilisation and under it becoming the definitely prevailing form is monogamy, the supremacy of the man over the woman, and the individual family as the economic unit of society. The cohesive force of civilised society is the state, which in all typical periods is exclusively the state of the ruling class, and in all cases remains essentially a machine for keeping down the oppressed, exploited class. Other marks of civilisation are: on the one hand fixation of the contrast between town and country as the basis of the entire division of social labour; on the other hand, the introduction of wills, by which the property holder is able to dispose of his property even after his death. This institution, which was a direct blow at the old gentile constitution, was unknown in Athens until the time of Solon; in Rome it was introduced very early, but we do not know when.[2] Among the Germans it was introduced by the priests in order that the good honest German might without hindrance bequeath his property to the Church.

With this constitution as its foundation civilisation has accomplished things with which the old gentile society was totally unable to cope. But it accomplished them by playing on the most sordid instincts and passions of man, and by developing them at the expense of all his other faculties. Naked greed has been the moving spirit of civilisation from the first day of its existence to the present time; wealth, more wealth and wealth again; wealth, not of society, but of this shabby individual was its sole and determining aim. If, in the pursuit of this aim, the increasing development of science and

2. Lassalle's *Das System der erworbenen Rechte* (*System of Acquired Rights*) turns, in its second part, mainly on the proposition that the Roman testament is as old as Rome itself, that in Roman history there was never "a time when testaments did not exist": that the testament arose rather in pre-Roman times out of the cult of the dead. As a confirmed Hegelian of the old school, Lassalle derived the provisions of the Roman law not from the social conditions of the Romans, but from the "speculative conception" of the will, and thus arrived at this totally unhistoric assertion. This is not to be wondered at in a book that from the same speculative conception draws the conclusion that the transfer of property was purely a secondary matter in Roman inheritance. Lassalle not only believes in the illusions of Roman jurists, especially of the earlier period, but he even excels them. [*Engels*]

repeated periods of the fullest blooming of art fell into its lap, it was only because without them the ample present-day achievements in the accumultion of wealth would have been impossible.

Since the exploitation of one class by another is the basis of civilisation, its whole development moves in a continuous contradiction. Every advance in production is at the same time a retrogression in the condition of the oppressed class, that it, of the great majority. What is a boon for the one is necessarily a bane for the other; each new emancipation of one class always means a new oppression of another class. The most striking proof of this is furnished by the introduction of machinery, the effects of which are well known today. And while among barbarians, as we have seen, hardly any distinction could be made between rights and duties, civilisation makes the difference and antithesis between these two plain even to the dullest mind by assigning to one class pretty nearly all the rights, and to the other class pretty nearly all the duties.

But this is not as it ought to be. What is good for the ruling class should be good for the whole of the society with which the ruling class identifies itself. Therefore, the more civilisation advances, the more it is compelled to cover the ills it necessarily creates with the cloak of love, to embellish them, or to deny their existence; in short, to introduce conventional hypocrisy—unknown both in previous forms of society and even in the earliest stages of civilisation —that culminates in the declaration: The exploiting class exploits the oppressed class solely and exclusively in the interest of the exploited class itself; and if the latter fails to appreciate this, and even becomes rebellious, it thereby shows the basest ingratitude to its benefactors, the exploiters.[3]

And now, in conclusion, Morgan's verdict on civilisation: "Since the advent of civilisation, the outgrowth of property has been so immense, its forms so diversified, its uses so expanding and its management so intelligent in the interests of its owners that it *has become*, on the part of the people, *an unmanageable power. The human mind stands bewildered in the presence of its own creation.* The time will come, nevertheless, when human intelligence will rise to the mastery over property, and define the relations of the state to the property it protects, as well as the obligations and the limits of the rights of its owners. The interests of society are paramount to individual interest, and the two must be brought into just and har-

3. I had intended at the outset to place the brilliant critique of civilisation, scattered through the works of Fourier, by the side of Morgan's and my own. Unfortunately, I cannot spare the time. I only wish to remark that Fourier already considered monogamy and property in land as the main characteristics of civilisation, and that he described it as a war of the rich against the poor. We also find already in his work the deep appreciation of the fact that in all imperfect societies, those torn by conflicting interests, the individual families (*les families incohérentes*) are the economic units. [*Engels*]

monious relation. A mere property career is not the final destiny of mankind, if progress is to be the law of the future as it has been of the past. The time which has passed away since civilisation began is but a fragment of the past duration of man's existence; and but a fragment of the ages yet to come. The dissolution of society bids fair to become the termination of a career of which property is the end and aim, because such a career contains the elements of self-destruction. Democracy in government, brotherhood in society, equality in rights and privileges, and universal education, foreshadow the next higher plane of society to which experience, intelligence and knowledge are steadily tending. *It will be a revival, in a higher form, of the liberty, equality and fraternity of the ancient gentes.*" (Morgan, *Ancient Society*, p. 552.)

Versus the Anarchists

FRIEDRICH ENGELS

The issue between Marxism and Anarchism has often been defined in terms of two opposing beliefs as to the grand strategy of socialist revolution—with Marxists taking the position that state power must be seized and employed for the transformation of society and Anarchists (such as Bakunin) holding that state power must be destroyed in the very process of the revolution. Underlying that important disagreement, as Engels made plain in this letter of January 24, 1872, to Theodor Cuno, is a still more fundamental theoretical divergence that turns on differing definitions of what is to be regarded as the "main evil" in society—capital or state power.

Letter to Theodor Cuno

London, January 24, 1872

Bakunin, who up to 1868 had intrigued against the International, joined it after he had suffered a fiasco at the Berne Peace Congress[1] and at once began to conspire *within it* against the General Council. Bakunin has a peculiar theory of his own, a medley of Proudhonism and communism, the chief point of which is, in the first place, that he does not regard capital—and therefore the class antagonism between capitalists and wage-workers which has arisen through social development—but the *state* as the main evil to be abolished. While the great mass of the Social-Democratic workers hold our view that the state power is nothing more than the organisation with which the ruling classes—landlords and capitalists—have provided themselves in order to protect their social privileges, Bakunin maintains that it is the *state* which has created capital, that the capitalist has his capital *only by the grace of the state*. As, therefore, the state is the chief evil, it is above all the state which must be done away with and then capitalism will go to blazes of itself. We, on the contrary, say: Do away with capital, the

1. The reference is to the Berne Congress of the bourgeois League of Peace and Freedom, in which Bakunin took a leading part until October 1868.

concentration of all means of production in the hands of the few, and the state will fall of itself. The difference is an essential one: Without a previous social revolution the abolition of the state is nonsense; the abolition of capital *is* precisely the social revolution and involves a change in the whole mode of production. Now then, inasmuch as to Bakunin the state is the main evil, nothing must be done which can maintain the existence of the state, that is, of any state, whether it be a republic, a monarchy or anything else. Hence *complete abstention from all politics.* To commit a political act, and especially to take part in an election, would be a betrayal of principle. The thing to do is to carry on propaganda, heap abuse upon the state; organise, and when ALL the workers are won over, that is, the majority, depose all the authorities, abolish the state and replace it by the organisation of the International. This great act, with which the millennium begins, is called *social liquidation.*

All this sounds extremely radical, and is so simple that it can be learnt by heart in five minutes; that is why this theory of Bakunin's has speedily found favour in Italy and Spain among young lawyers, doctors and other doctrinaires. But the mass of the workers will never allow itself to be persuaded that the public affairs of their countries are not also their own affairs, they are by nature *political* and whoever tries to make out to them that they should leave politics alone will in the end be left alone. To preach to the workers that they should in all circumstances abstain from politics is to drive them into the arms of the priests or the bourgeois republicans.

Now, as the International, according to Bakunin, was not formed for political struggle but in order that it may at once replace the old state organisation as soon as social liquidation takes place, it follows that it must come as near as possible to the Bakuninist ideal of the society of the future. In this society there will above all be no *authority*, for authority=state=an absolute evil. (Indeed, how these people propose to run a factory, operate a railway or steer a ship without having in the last resort one deciding will, without single management, they of course do not tell us.) The authority of the majority over the minority also ceases. Every individual and every community is autonomous; but as to how a society, even of only two people, is possible unless each gives up some of his autonomy, Bakunin again maintains silence. * * *

On Authority

FRIEDRICH ENGELS

In this article written in October, 1872, and originally published in Italian in the collection *Almanacco Repubblicano* for 1874, Engels continued the debate against the Anarchists. Of special note is his argument that revolution itself is "certainly the most authoritarian thing there is," and his further contention, which seems inconsistent with some of what we know of the thinking of Marx, that machine industry is inherently "despotic" in relation to the workers.

A number of Socialists have latterly launched a regular crusade against what they call the *principle of authority*. It suffices to tell them that this or that act is *authoritarian* for it to be condemned. This summary mode of procedure is being abused to such an extent that it has become necessary to look into the matter somewhat more closely. Authority, in the sense in which the word is used here, means: the imposition of the will of another upon ours; on the other hand, authority presupposes subordination. Now, since these two words sound bad and the relationship which they represent is disagreeable to the subordinated party, the question is to ascertain whether there is any way of dispensing with it, whether—given the conditions of present-day society—we could not create another social system, in which this authority would be given no scope any longer and would consequently have to disappear. On examining the economic, industrial and agricultural conditions which form the basis of present-day bourgeois society, we find that they tend more and more to replace isolated action by combined action of individuals. Modern industry with its big factories and mills, where hundreds of workers supervise complicated machines driven by steam, has superseded the small workshops of the separate producers; the carriages and wagons of the highways have been substituted by railway trains, just as the small schooners and sailing feluccas have been by steam-boats. Even agriculture falls increasingly under the dominion of the machine and of steam, which slowly but relentlessly put in the place of the small proprietors big capitalists, who with the aid of hired workers cultivate vast stretches of land. Everywhere combined action, the complication of processes dependent upon each other, displaces independent action by individuals. But whoever mentions combined action speaks of organisation; now, is it possible to have organisation without authority?

Supposing a social revolution dethroned the capitalists, who now exercise their authority over the production and circulation of wealth. Supposing, to adopt entirely the point of view of the anti-authoritarians, that the land and the instruments of labour had become the collective property of the workers who use them. Will authority have disappeared or will it only have changed its form? Let us see.

Let us take by way of example a cotton spinning mill. The cotton must pass through at least six successive operations before it is reduced to the state of thread, and these operations take place for the most part in different rooms. Furthermore, keeping the machines going requires an engineer to look after the steam engine, mechanics to make the current repairs, and many other labourers whose business it is to transfer the products from one room to another, and so forth. All these workers, men, women and children, are obliged to begin and finish their work at the hours fixed by the authority of the steam, which cares nothing for individual autonomy. The workers must, therefore, first come to an understanding on the hours of work; and these hours, once they are fixed, must be observed by all, without any exception. Thereafter particular questions arise in each room and at every moment concerning the mode of production, distribution of materials, etc., which must be settled at once on pain of seeing all production immediately stopped; whether they are settled by decision of a delegate placed at the head of each branch of labour or, if possible, by a majority vote, the will of the single individual will always have to subordinate itself, which means that questions are settled in an authoritarian way. The automatic machinery of a big factory is much more despotic than the small capitalists who employ workers ever have been. At least with regard to the hours of work one may write upon the portals of these factories: *Lasciate ogni autonomia, voi che entrate!*[1] If man, by dint of his knowledge and inventive genius, has subdued the forces of nature, the latter avenge themselves upon him by subjecting him, in so far as he employs them, to a veritable despotism independent of all social organisation. Wanting to abolish authority in large-scale industry is tantamount to wanting to abolish industry itself, to destroy the power loom in order to return to the spinning wheel.

Let us take another example—the railway. Here too the co-opera-

1. "Leave, ye that enter in, all autonomy behind!"

tion of an infinite number of individuals is absolutely necessary, and this co-operation must be practised during precisely fixed hours so that no accidents may happen. Here, too, the first condition of the job is a dominant will that settles all subordinate questions, whether this will is represented by a single delegate or a committee charged with the execution of the resolutions of the majority of persons interested. In either case there is very pronounced authority. Moreover, what would happen to the first train dispatched if the authority of the railway employees over the Hon. passengers were abolished?

But the necessity of authority, and of imperious authority at that, will nowhere be found more evident than on board a ship on the high seas. There, in time of danger, the lives of all depend on the instantaneous and absolute obedience of all to the will of one.

When I submitted arguments like these to the most rabid anti-authoritarians the only answer they were able to give me was the following: Yes, that's true, but here it is not a case of authority which we confer on our delegates, *but of a commission entrusted*! These gentlemen think that when they have changed the names of things they have changed the things themselves. This is how these profound thinkers mock at the whole world.

We have thus seen that, on the one hand, a certain authority, no matter how delegated, and, on the other hand, a certain subordination, are things which, independently of all social organisation, are imposed upon us together with the material conditions under which we produce and make products circulate.

We have seen, besides, that the material conditions of production and circulation inevitably develop with large-scale industry and large-scale agriculture, and increasingly tend to enlarge the scope of this authority. Hence it is absurd to speak of the principle of authority as being absolutely evil, and of the principle of autonomy as being absolutely good. Authority and autonomy are relative things whose spheres vary with the various phases of the development of society. If the autonomists confined themselves to saying that the social organisation of the future would restrict authority solely to the limits within which the conditions of production render it inevitable, we could understand each other; but they are blind to all facts that make the thing necessary and they passionately fight the word.

Why do the anti-authoritarians not confine themselves to crying out against political authority, the state? All Socialists are agreed that the political state, and with it political authority, will disappear as a result of the coming social revolution, that is, that public functions will lose their political character and be transformed into the simple administrative functions of watching over the true interests of society. But the anti-authoritarians demand that the authoritarian political state be abolished at one stroke, even before the social conditions that gave birth to it have been destroyed. They demand that the first act of the social revolution shall be the abolition of authority. Have these gentlemen ever seen a revolution? A revolution is certainly the most authoritarian thing there is; it is the act whereby one part of the population imposes its will upon the other part by means of rifles, bayonets and cannon—authoritarian means, if such there be at all; and if the victorious party does not want to have fought in vain, it must maintain this rule by means of the terror which its arms inspire in the reactionaries. Would the Paris Commune have lasted a single day if it had not made use of this authority of the armed people against the bourgeois? Should we not, on the contrary, reproach it for not having used it freely enough?

Therefore, either one of two things: either the anti-authoritarians don't know what they are talking about, in which case they are creating nothing but confusion; or they do know, and in that case they are betraying the movement of the proletariat. In either case they serve the reaction.

On Morality

FRIEDRICH ENGELS

Value judgments resting on moral convictions abound in Marx and Engels. Thus they not only analyze exploitation and the division of labour in society, but morally condemn these phenomena as evil. Yet, there is almost no abstract discussion of ethics in their voluminous writings. An exception is this passage from *Anti-Dühring*, frequently cited as an authoritative statement of the view of Marx and Engels on the nature of morality. The mode of reasoning seems more distinctively characteristic of Engels' mind, however, than of Marx's.

---

* * * If, then, we have not made much progress with truth and error, we can make even less with good and evil. This opposition manifests itself exclusively in the domain of morals, that is, a domain belonging to the history of mankind, and it is precisely in this field that final and ultimate truths are most sparsely sown. The conceptions of good and evil have varied so much from nation to nation and from age to age that they have often been in direct contradiction to each other.

But all the same, someone may object, good is not evil and evil is not good; if good is confused with evil there is an end to all morality, and everyone can do as he pleases. This is also, stripped of all oracular phrases, Herr Dühring's opinion. But the matter cannot be so simply disposed of. If it were such an easy business there would certainly be no dispute at all over good and evil; everyone would know what was good and what was bad. But how do things stand today? What morality is preached to us today? There is first Christian-feudal morality, inherited from earlier religious times; and this is divided, essentially, into a Catholic and a Protestant morality, each of which has no lack of subdivisions, from the Jesuit-Catholic and Orthodox-Protestant to loose "enlightened" moralities. Alongside these we find the modern-bourgeois morality and beside it also the proletarian morality of the future, so that in the most advanced European countries alone the past, present and future provide three great groups of moral theories which are in force simultaneously and alongside each other. Which, then, is the true one? Not one of them, in the sense of absolute finality; but certainly that morality contains the maximum elements promising permanence which, in the present, represents the overthrow of the present, represents the future, and that is proletarian morality.

But when we see that the three classes of modern society, the feudal aristocracy, the bourgeoisie and the proletariat, each have a morality of their own, we can only draw the one conclusion: that men, consciously or unconsciously, derive their ethical ideas in the last resort from the practical relations on which their class position is based—from the economic relations in which they carry on production and exchange.

But nevertheless there is quite a lot which the three moral theories mentioned above have in common—is this not at least a portion of a morality which is fixed once and for all? These moral theories represent three different stages of the same historical development, have therefore a common historical background, and for that reason alone they necessarily have much in common. Even more. At similar or approximately similar stages of economic development moral theories must of necessity be more or less in agreement. From the moment when private ownership of movable property developed, all societies in which this private ownership existed had to have this moral injunction in common: Thou shalt not steal. Does this injunction thereby become an eternal moral injunction? By no means. In a society in which all motives for stealing have been done away with, in which therefore at the very most only lunatics would ever steal, how the preacher of morals would be laughed at who tried solemnly to proclaim the eternal truth: Thou shalt not steal!

We therefore reject every attempt to impose on us any moral dogma whatsoever as an eternal, ultimate and forever immutable ethical law on the pretext that the moral world, too, has its permanent principles which stand above history and the differences between nations. We maintain on the contrary that all moral theories have been hitherto the product, in the last analysis, of the economic conditions of society obtaining at the time. And as society has hitherto moved in class antagonisms, morality has always been class morality; it has either justified the domination and the interests of the ruling class, or, ever since the oppressed class became powerful enough, it has represented its indignation against this domination and the future interests of the oppressed. That in this process there has on the whole been progress in morality, as in all other branches of human knowledge, no one will doubt. But we have not yet passed beyond class morality. A really human morality which stands above class antagonisms and above any recollection of them becomes possible only at a stage of society which has not only overcome class antagonisms but has even forgotten them in practical life. And now one can gauge Herr Dühring's presumption in advancing his claim, from the midst of the old class society and on the eve of a social revolution, to impose on the future classless society an eternal morality independent of time and changes in reality. Even assuming—what we do not know up to now—that he understands the structure of the society of the future at least in its main outlines. * * *

Bibliographic Note

The literature on classical Marxism and its founders is very large and constantly growing. Many new studies have appeared in recent years as a result of the discovery of the early Marx and the controversy over the place of "original Marxism" in the development of Marx's thought and, more broadly, in intellectual history. This bibliographic note makes no pretense to being an exhaustive guide even to the books available in English on classical Marxism. It is a small personal selection of studies that may be useful for further reading on Marx and Engels and their thought. (Books marked with an asterisk are available as paperbacks.)

BIOGRAPHICAL

The standard Marxist biography of Marx is *Franz Mehring, *Karl Marx: The Story of His Life* (New York, 1957) (Michigan). The comparable biography of Engels is Gustav Mayer, *Friedrich Engels: A Biography* (New York, 1936). See also Steven Marcus, *Engels, Manchester and the Working Class* (New York, 1971). Other biographical studies of Marx include: Otto Rühle, *Karl Marx: His Life and Work* (London, 1929); *Isaiah Berlin, *Karl Marx: His Life and Environment* (New York, 1959) (Oxford); *Leopold Schwarzschild, *The Red Prussian* (New York, 1958) (Grosset & Dunlap); Boris Nicolaevsky and O. Mänchen-Helfen, *Karl Marx: Man and Fighter* (Philadelphia, 1936); and David McLellan, *Marx Before Marxism* (New York, 1970).

SOCIALIST THOUGHT BEFORE MARXISM

On classical Marxism's background in earlier modern socialist theories: G. D. H. Cole, *History of Socialist Thought*, Volume I, *The Forerunners 1789–1850* (New York, 1953); *J. L. Talmon, *The Origins of Totalitarian Democracy* (New York, 1970) (Norton); *George Lichtheim, *The Origins of Socialism* (New York, 1969) (Praeger); and *Martin Buber, *Paths in Utopia* (Boston, 1949) (Beacon).

THE EARLY MARX

On Marxism's background in German philosophy, the interpretation of the early Marx, and the alienation theme in Marxism: *Louis Dupré, *The Philosophical Foundations of Marxism* (New York, 1966) (Harcourt Brace Jovanovich); *Herbert Marcuse, *Reason and Revolution: Hegel and the Rise of Social Theory* (Boston, 1960) (Beacon); William J. Brazill, *The Young Hegelians* (New Haven, 1970); Eugene Kamenka, *The Philosophy of Ludwig Feuerbach* (New York, 1970); *Erich Fromm, *Marx's Concept of Man* (New York, 1961) (Unger); *Gajo Petrović, *Marx in the Mid-Twentieth Century: A Yugoslav Philosopher Reconsiders Karl Marx's Writings* (Garden City, N.Y., 1967) (Anchor); *Shlomo Avineri, *The Social and Political Thought of Karl Marx* (New York, 1968) (Cambridge); *Sidney Hook, *From Hegel to Marx: Studies in the Intellectual Development of Karl Marx* (New York, 1950) (Michigan); *N. Lobkowicz, ed., *Marx and the Western World* (South Bend, Ind., 1967) (Notre Dame); *Louis Althusser, *For Marx* (New York, 1970) (Vintage); and *Robert C. Tucker, *Philosophy and Myth in Karl Marx*, revised edition (New York, 1972) (Cambridge).

HISTORICAL MATERIALISM AND THE CRITIQUE OF CAPITALISM

On classical Marxist theory in its development from 1848: G. D. H. Cole, *History of Socialist Thought*, Vol. II, *Marxism and Anarchism 1850–1890* (New York, 1954); *George Lichtheim, *Marxism: An Historical and Critical Study* (New York, 1961) (Praeger); *Alfred G. Meyer, *Marxism: The Unity of Theory and Practice* (Ann Arbor, 1963) (Michigan); *M. M. Bober, *Karl Marx's Interpretation of History* (New York, 1950) (Norton); *Ralf Dahrendorf, *Class and*

Class Conflict in Industrial Society (Stanford, Calif., 1959) (Stanford); *Edwin R. A. Seligman, *The Economic Interpretation of History* (New York, 1907) (Columbia); *Paul Sweezy, *The Theory of Capitalist Development: Principles of Marxian Political Economy* (New York, 1956) (Monthly Review); A. D. Lindsay, *Karl Marx's Capital: An Introductory Essay* (London, 1947); *Karl Kautsky, *The Class Struggle* (New York, 1971) (Norton); Karl Korsch, *Karl Marx* (London, 1938); *Robert C. Tucker, *Philosophy and Myth in Karl Marx*, revised edition (New York, 1972) (Cambridge), and *The Marxian Revolutionary Idea* (New York, 1969) (Norton).

THE REVOLUTIONARY POLITICS OF MARX AND ENGELS

On revolutionary strategy and tactics according to classical Marxism, the relations of Marxism and anarchism, and the involvement of Marx and Engels in the socialist and revolutionary politics of the middle and later nineteenth century: G. D. H. Cole, *History of Socialist Thought*, Vol. II, *Marxism and Anarchism 1850–1890* (New York, 1954); J. Hampden Jackson, *Marx, Proudhon and European Socialism* (London, 1957); *James Joll, *The Anarchists* (New York, 1966) (Grosset & Dunlap), and *The Second International 1889–1914* (New York, 1955) (Harper & Row); *Arthur Rosenberg, *Democracy and Socialism* (Boston, 1965) (Beacon); Bertram D. Wolfe, *Marxism: One Hundred Years in the Life of a Doctrine* (New York, 1964); *George Lichtheim, *Marxism: An Historical and Critical Study* (New York, 1961) (Praeger); and *Robert C. Tucker, *The Marxian Revolutionary Idea* (New York, 1969) (Norton).

Index

Abstracting, 101–2
Abstractions, 87–89, 100
Accumulated labour
  in bourgeois society, 34
  capital and, 176, 178, 180, 185
  in communist society, 347
Activity, 71–72, 75–76
Actuality, 97
"Address of the Central Committee to the Communist League" (Marx and Engels), 363–73
Aeschylus, 15
Agriculture, 235
  Asian, 579–80
  capitalist accumulation and, 314–15
  decline of Roman Empire and, 117
  feudal, 117
  liberation and development of, 133
  Roman conquests and, 116
Aiken, 148
Ailly, Pierre d', 522
Alexander the Great, 144
Alienated labour, *see* Labour, alienated
Alienation
  class and, 104–6
  economic, 71
  religion and, 58, 60, 64, 71
Allgemeine Augsburger Zeitung, 4
Allgemeine Literatur-Zeitung, 54n, 85n
Alsace-Lorraine, 414, 527
Amalfi, 151
Anarchists, 660–61
Anecdotis (Ruge), 54, 84
Animals, 61–62
Annulment, 98–105
Anti-Corn Law League, 140
Anti-Dühring (Engels), 321
Antipatros, 294
Appearance, 97
Apprentices, feudal, 117
  patriarchal relationship between masters and, 141
Aristocracy
  democracy and, 124
  French, 138
  honor and loyalty under, 137
Aristotle, 78, 229n–230n, 294, 616
Art
  ethical mind and, 97
  as mode of production, 71
  religion and, 87, 97
Asiatic mode of production, 5
Assemblée Nationale, 496
Atelier, 393
Atheism
  communism and, 71, 78–79
  humanism and, 98
  as mediation, 78
  and the state, 34

Aurelle de Paladines, Louis d', 544–45, 547
Australia, 6
Austria, 19, 420
Austro-Prussian War (1866), 529–31, 537–39
Authority, 662–65
Avignon, 282

Babeuf, François Nöel, 359, 607
Bacon, Francis, 617
Baking industry, 256–58, 263
Bakunin, Mikhail, 595, 660–61
Banks, 148
Baraguey d'Hilliers, Achille, 489, 498
Barbarians, 116–17
Barbon, Nicholas, 199n, 200n, 201
Barbès, Armand, 427
Baroche, Pierre-Jules, 475, 485, 489, 493
Barrot, Odilon, 422, 453–55, 457, 469–70, 479, 490, 497, 498, 505
Barth, Paul, 647
Bauer, Bruno, 53n, 54n, 110
  on dialectic, 83–84
  on Jewish question, 24–30, 33, 35–36, 38, 40, 45, 48–49
  on nature, 134
  polemic against, 104–6
Baze, Jean-Didier, 497
Beaumont, Gustave de, 29n, 37
Bebel, August, 399, 416
Bedau, Gen. Marie-Alphonse, 458, 490
Being
  becoming as, 102
  essence and, 100
  natural and species-, 94
  objective, 94
  other-, 96
  thinking and, 72
Belgium, 420
Benoît d'Azy, Denis, 492, 496
Bernard, Col., 450
Bernstein, Eduard, 399, 647
Berryer, Antoine, 475, 490, 496, 498, 502
  accusations against, 499
Beslay, Charles, 542–43
Big industry
  abolition of private property and, 154
  capital determined by, 150
  class created by, 149–50
  communications and, 149
  contradiction between means of production and private property in, 153–54
  crafts destroyed by, 149

671

THE MOUNTAINS WAIT

THE MOUNTAINS WAIT

THEODOR BROCH

ILLUSTRATED BY ROCKWELL KENT

Saint Paul
WEBB BOOK PUBLISHING COMPANY
1942

CONTENTS

CONTENTS

THE MOUNTAINS WAIT

I — NARVIK

The mountains had closed behind us. After a night of strenuous climbing we had reached the plains between the snow-capped peaks and the last of winter ice slowly melting in the shadows behind them. The Laplander boy who was guiding me through the mountains to Sweden said we could take a breath now. There was no longer any danger of being overtaken.

We had come from a ravaged and looted land. We had seen our country invaded and occupied by hordes of men in green uniforms. The last front in northern Norway where the Germans had suffered their first defeat of the war had been given up. Narvik had been evacuated by the British and our other Allied friends. They were on their way to France to try to stop the deluge before the gates of Paris. We had left behind burning cities and a confused people.

Three days before from Harstad, a little town on Norway's largest island, Ellen and I and our little girl,

1

Siri, had sailed into the fjords in a small craft manned by an old fisherman and his young son. I was being sought by the Germans throughout northern Norway. The sheriffs of the district and the German patrols had been ordered to return me to Narvik. I was said to be a British spy.

As Mayor of occupied Narvik, I had negotiated with the Germans. We had not always agreed too well. I had sent information to the British warships, and their heavy guns had silenced the German positions. Norwegian and Allied troops had recaptured the city and had held it for a week, but had been forced to give it up. Now the Germans were in control of all Norway.

In a little cabin deep in a fjord arm near the Swedish border I had been forced to leave Ellen and Siri with friends, and to go on alone with a Lap guide into the mountains toward Sweden.

Now we stood beside a cairn on a mountain crag. The cairn marked the Swedish border. We threw down our knapsacks and took a brief rest.

Before going on I looked for a long time on what I could yet see of Norway. The ocean was no longer visible. Mountains stretched on all sides, with snow and green moss scattered between. Mountain streams shone like silver ribbons. The lakes were open, but ice bordered the shores. The wild heather had already colored its small, hard flowers, and but for them the dominating tone was gray.

It was a harsh land we had, but never had it been so delightful, so desirable as now. Our best men had

already been driven abroad. Our ships had been sunk or had sailed away. All along the border were young men like myself. Thousands more would follow. We had to leave to learn the one craft we had neglected.

We had built good homes in the mountains, but we had neglected to fence them properly. Now strangers had taken over our land. They would loot and pluck it clean before we returned. But the country itself they could not spoil. The sea and the fjords and the mountains—to these we alone could give life. We were coming back. The mountains would wait for us.

Now the summer would come to the Northland but I would not be there. It was June, 1940.

I remembered that it was almost ten years to the day since we—Ellen and I—had come up here to build a life together. The time had passed rapidly, although much had happened in these years. It was in June that we had arrived, June, 1930.

We came from friendships and restaurants, from student debates on Freud and Marx and resolutions proposing the reform of the world. I was a young lawyer, she a young housewife, without too much housekeeping to do. We came from great dreams, and difficulties with the rent. We came from the nation's Capital.

Two days before, in Oslo, we had taken the train for Narvik through Sweden. We could have taken a train to Trondheim and a steamer from there up the coast, but it would have been more expensive and we would not have had the trip abroad. Now we were approach-

ing our destination. The train had worked its way up along evenly-climbing slopes on the Swedish side of the border. Already, through a cleft in the mountain below us, we could see the distant blue-green ocean. Down there lay Narvik.

The last mile or two we sat in silence looking down upon the fjord. The scene came and went in panorama as the many tunnels opened the way for the train on its steep and winding road. Coming out of the last tunnel, we saw the whole town in sharp focus as if it lay under a magnifying glass. Even so, it was smaller than I had imagined.

— Could anything ever happen in such a sleepy little town? — I mused aloud.

"It certainly is a beautiful town," Ellen said encouragingly, "and at least it is smiling in its sleep."

To us the trip was more than an excursion. We had come to stay, to build a home and a law practice in a young and vigorous country. Here, I had thought, a young lawyer would not have to lick stamps for ten years before being permitted to write the letter itself. But now I was not so sure. A silent anxiety crept over me at the thought of beginning a new life.

Had my imagination created a fairyland, I wondered.

True, our conquest of Narvik was disguised under the pretext of a summer visit to my parents, who had arrived the previous fall. This arrangement somewhat reduced both the glory and the risk of our adventure. My father was Colonel of the Northern Hålogoland Regiment with headquarters in Narvik. In a year or two

4

he might be ordered south again, if he should survive
and a colleague down south should not.

There were still remnants of winter in the mountains,
but down by the fjord the birches welcomed us in a
veil of new, light-green spring. As we stepped off the
train the Station Master came toward us without his
overcoat, as though in demonstration of the fact that
the tourist season was about to begin.

Although we knew that we were more than welcome,
we planned to take as little advantage of the Colonel
as possible and rather specialize on the parents. And
there on the station platform they were, Father in uniform, Mother in a new hat.

A taxi brought us across the town to the Regimental
Headquarters on the hill not far from the white frame
City Hospital.

The welcome was everywhere evident—in the vases
of flowers in the guest room, in the silver coffeepot
gleaming on the table in the living room downstairs, in
my favorite cookies, prepared in abundance. For the
first time in many years I was going to live at home.

Like many students from conservative environments,
I felt it my duty during my University years to revolt against tradition and old-fashioned ideas. I had
lived alone on the wrong side of town and supported
myself by selling advertising for magazines of poor
circulation. Father had learned to look upon the world
and his children with that magnanimity of spirit with
which nature seems to endow fathers as a protective
shield in their relations with rebellious sons.

As the days passed we were introduced to the quiet little town. The introduction was made with great thoroughness, until we felt that we had eaten roast beef and canned pineapple in all the best houses in the city. We met the Director of the Swedish Iron Ore Company, the City and District Judges, the Doctors, the Parson, the Veterinarian, the Police Chief, and the higher officials of the Railroad—all friendly and well-meaning people. And yet it seemed that these men and women were not the city. They were all, more or less, people in transit. Soon they would be on their ways again. They had come from the Outside and their dream was to move south once more.

Of course, they admitted, Narvik was a beautiful place to live, especially at midsummer. The mountains, the ocean, the ever-changing colors were breath-taking. But, after all, there was a saying up here that summer came only every fourth year, and, as we certainly would learn for ourselves, the winters were dark and burdensome, and the distance from Oslo and the other great cities was altogether too great. Here there was no theater, no art gallery, no symphony concerts, not even a lively cafe where interesting people gathered.

We asked about the other side of town life, the people who had built it and who made their homes here.

The workers on the railroad and at the Iron Company constituted the mainstay of the town. They were all organized and the Labor Union possessed the only great hall in town. There the City Council held its meetings and traveling stock companies staged their

6

plays. There was perhaps some truth in the statement that the city spirit was dominated from the Labor Union Center. The town had been governed by Labor from its very beginning. Young and vigorous as it was, it had not much in the way of tradition, but it did have a history of its own.

In the nineties a British company had begun to buy up the land with a view to exploiting the Swedish iron-ore deposits. The plan was to build a railroad through the mountains, across the narrowest part of Norway, to the half-moon-shaped bay below Fagernes Mountain, where a peninsula extends into the Ofotfjord. Streets were laid out for a city to be called Victoria Harbor.

A great construction gang, supplemented by peasant boys and fishermen, worked for months in the mountains. Then the company went bankrupt. When, one Friday, the wages stopped, the job was deserted, and tools and equipment were left scattered about. The project was abandoned. The right of way reverted to the elements. The doors of the empty barracks swung on screaming hinges.

Then the Norwegian Government took it over and completed the railroad from the Swedish border down to the harbor. The city was built and named Narvik after the lonely homestead and small trading post that lay inside the tip of the half moon.

A railroad station was built on the other side of the peninsula for passenger traffic, but the heavy ore trains moved slowly through the center of town, cutting it in two.

7

Oscarsborg, the business district, lay on the side toward the mountain. Along the low, forested ridge on the outside of the peninsula, protected from the cold winds of the open fjord, lay Frydenlund, the best residential section. The Parkway was the finest street in Frydenlund, and on it were the great one-family houses of the Company officers and engineers.

Most houses in town, however, were two-family dwellings built by the workers themselves. The owners lived on the second floors and rented the best rooms until the mortgages were reduced. All the houses had small, fenced "rose gardens" in which the owners took great pride. In northern Norway all garden flowers are called roses because of their size and rarity. The wild flowers are usually small, with strong fragrance and vivid coloring.

In the Frydenlund park stood the town's great stone church. It had been designed by a famous architect, who had planned it to be viewed from the south, so that the tower with its slender spire stood between the heavy dome of Fagernes Mountain and the leaning horn of Rombakstötta.

The Market Place was at Oscarsborg, a large open quadrangle faced by the old Post Office and Telegraph Building, with enclosed market stalls built into the hill beneath it. When we arrived, the Market Place was still under construction. The town's wealthy but unpopular banker had donated a fountain which was to be inscribed with a copper plate. The city fathers accepted the fountain but declined the copper plate.

The bridge led directly from the Market Place. Its beautiful bronze lampposts were not held in too high favor by the townspeople. They had been bought secondhand from a small town in the South which had installed larger ones.

The railroad tracks ran under the bridge, extending in a fanwise net towards the harbor. Between the tracks lay the ore heaps in huge, prim cones. From the bridge the great steamers in the harbor were barely visible, but the roaring rumble of the ore streaming into the hulls could be heard day and night.

Across the harbor was a wooded ridge above which a mountain towered. The top of the mountain resembled the profile of a woman. It was called the Sleeping Queen. A veil of ice and snow always lay over the forehead and eyes, but the nose, a bit on the long side, remained snow-bare until late August.

Above the Market Place was the City Hall. It had originally been a hotel with gay life and illegal brandy. It retained its tower at the corner and the huge, drafty windows on the first floor. Here the Municipal Court had been installed, where the town drunks were sentenced. On the second floor was the Mayor's office, and in the attic the Taxation Division wrestled with the problem of the city's ever-rising taxes.

Such was the city, simple and surveyable. One never ran the risk of getting lost in it. At a dinner party on the Parkway we were told that the citizens were just as simple. I asked whether this hard land did not make its imprint upon the people.

9

"Yes, the girls are wild during the summer," the regimental lieutenant said encouragingly. "They become playful from the long Midnight Sun."

"Oh, I rather think it comes from eating too much fish," his blond wife, my dinner partner, interrupted with a laugh. "The farther north they live, the more fish they eat."

"And where do you come from?" I asked.

She laughed again and said she was born in Hammerfest not far from North Cape. I was more cautious the rest of the evening.

It was self-evident that Narvik was a democratic town without any truly wealthy people. The merchants went bankrupt each time there was a depression and started all over again. The higher officials, the physicians, the dentists, and the lawyers used their money to heat their large homes during the winters, or they put it aside with the idea of moving south again.

The city itself was clean and orderly. Each evening, after supper, which was taken at eight o'clock, we went for a walk, usually on Street 1. The name of the main street was King's Street, when one wanted to be correct, but its common name was just Street 1. When the city was built the streets were given numbers before they were named, and the numbers stuck.

On calm and clear evenings there were always people walking up and down Street 1, people with children, walking sticks, and dignity, or only with dignity. The walking tempo was slow and sedate; no one was rushed for time, no one was going anywhere in particular, and

the street lasted longer at a slower pace. And one always greeted with the hat. God, how one greeted with the hat! Not only to ladies or elderly gentlemen, but to everyone. All the men agreed that this hat-greeting procedure was a silly custom that should be abolished, yet no one had the courage to flout tradition.

Psychologically, this irrational slavery to traditional "dignity" may have covered a certain shy reticence. There was, for instance, the young red-haired girl in the tobacco store on the corner of the Market Place. For ten years I was to buy tobacco and razor blades over her counter. We exchanged objective remarks on the state of the weather, the quality of tobacco, and the efficacy of throat tablets. For herself, she preferred the fresh air of Street 1, and thus became one of the many reasons that I wore out my hats in quick succession. Yet, through all those years and hats, she never honored me with more than a barely visible puckering of the lips in what might have been construed as a vague smile of condescension. At first I thought she was supercilious, yet I must be a good customer since my purchases of tobacco were on the upward trend. Then I became fearful lest she thought I was teasing her, though her change was as correct as her advice on tobacco. As the years went by, her correct smile remained the same enigma of friendly condescension. Finally, I realized that it was in this manner that decent people with mutual respect greeted one another in a decent town.

These evening promenades were not completely devoid of purpose. Every Friday night the express steam-

er, *Nord Norge,* the city's own boat, departed for the
South. The Ofoten Steamship Line had given painful
birth to a little fleet of ships plying the broad fjord in
from Lofoten to Narvik. *Nord Norge* was the pride
and prize of this community effort. She sailed the express route to Trondheim and return. Except for the
Iron Ore Railway into Sweden, Narvik, like all towns
in northern Norway, depended upon sea communications. Great and small steamship companies fought for
the best places of call. Most of these companies had
subsidies, which gave the Government control over the
communications. The system worked for equity in
bringing the mail in a short time into the most distant
places in the isolated fjords.

The fact that the regular express steamers never called at Narvik remained always an open wound. The
daily express communications from Bergen or Trondheim bypassed Narvik in order to save some expensive
seven or eight hours from the running time across the
Ofotfjord via North Cape to Kirkenes, near the border
of Finland. Narvik, with its ten thousand people, was,
after all, only two hundred souls behind Tromsö, its
neighbor city in the North. But the citizens of Narvik
took consolation from *Nord Norge,* their own steamer.

Town officials and business men sailed away and returned on *Nord Norge.* The Town Singers in white
caps and blue jackets often enlivened the scene. Sea
gulls screamed above the ships in the harbor, and there
was the smell of seaweed and tar. Perhaps the Band
was on hand to play a Sousa march.

The pier was always a focal point of activity, and the stroll down Street 1 often led to it. "The whole town stood on the dock or in open windows waving good-bye," a poet of the local press had written in one of his spring poems.

There were three newspapers in the city. Their schedule of publication was so arranged that the editors might attack one another in turn. On only one point was there complete agreement: that Narvik was the harbor of the world. Unsung and hidden away, it lay like an outpost toward the silent arctic in the service of mankind. Rocked on the swells of the warm gulf stream, the ships kept coming to load the heavy ore, the basic metal for the plowshare that was destined to turn the furrow of civilization. Each of the newspapers had its own house poet. One of them specialized on early spring.

It is somewhat of an exaggeration to speak of spring in northern Norway. Winter clothing was needed the whole of June. But one morning summer definitely arrived. A calm and comfortable warmth filled the air. A shining transparence spread itself over the heavens, making a thousand different colors come to life in the mountains, the fields, and out on the ocean, until sea and horizon merged in a far-distant embrace. This was the prelude to one long continuous summer day that would last without sundown until the first chill of autumn in mid-August. The Nordic summer had come at last, with sun, day and night; and Nature, in man and beast, drank of its light and warmth. It seemed

13

that life received this re-creating miracle with all its senses open before the long winter night would again close in.

This was our first summer in northern Norway and we had to take it all in. We had to climb the mountains, wade in ice and snow, hike over the lonely plains with deep and silent lakes, dark with the mysteries of winter and spring. And we had to take a boat trip to the islands in the fjord.

There were three boats. We were to row for an hour or so from the boat harbor north of town to Øyjord, a small peninsula on the other side of Rombaksfjord, where there were some low, wooded cliffs, ideal for picnicking.

Mr. and Mrs. Einar Mosling were the host and hostess. He was the proprietor of the bookstore and represented the only old family in town. Hardly more than a generation ago there was only the one lonely farm in Narvik, on the inside of the half-moon-shaped harbor. On this fertile, flat soil there had been a habitation since time immemorial. Two generations ago a trading post had appeared where people from inner Ofoten brought their wares and bought their necessities. The Moslings were known as old and fair tradespeople even at that early date. Then the town came. The good soil was turned into streets with new houses, shops multiplied, and business dealings became more complex. The last generation retained nothing more than the name and a bookstore. The bookstore was the only one in town and the business of being a bookseller might have been

14

quite good. Mr. Mosling, however, was all things besides, and Dutch Vice-Consul too. Since we were newcomers and from the Colonel's house, we were placed in the host's boat.

The second boat was that of Dr. Paus, who came from the seacoast north of Bergen, where people have sharp gutturals and sharp elbows. Mrs. Paus had been something of a beauty but was consistently having a child. With the doctor and his large family were Engineer and Mrs. Toft. He was Administrative Counselor of the Railroad and might become District Superintendent when the incumbent got a stroke. Mrs. Toft was president of the local Red Cross.

In the third boat sat Lawyer Nils K. Nilsen, with whom I had visited on an earlier occasion. He had minced no words in warning me that it would not be wise to try to start a lawyer's practice in Narvik, if one had not been born in the high North. Today he wore a sport suit complete with leggings and a curved pipe. His facial expression indicated that he did not think our presence quite necessary for a successful picnic.

Our boats slid smoothly across the mirror-like sea between the islands. The oars squeaked a little until we poured water on them. The contours of the mountains were sharply silhouetted against the bright blue sky. The sun was still fairly high, but had begun to take on the glowing reddish-purple hue.

The odor of seaweed mixed with the smell of tar from the boat. Sea gulls sailed through the air, now and then diving to catch a fish or a floating piece of

green growth. Their hoarse screams filled out the tonal quality of the sea symphony. The picture of the rugged mountains in the strangely glowing light is not complete without this smell of sea and shore, this sound of bird and ocean, the regularly beating breath of the sea as it licks the wet stones on the shore. In the crystal clear water sea plants rose and fell in slow rhythm. We rowed through narrow inlets between naked stone islands. Farther in, we met heather and wild flowers and crooked pine trees that storm and sea had given fantastic shapes.

At Øyjord we beached the boats and built a fire. The children played with shells and sea-worn stones. Others played games. The men were put to work. The Moslings said that there was enough food, so that only two fishermen would be needed to get the catch for supper. Salt-water fishing is not regarded as either an art or a sport, so Engineer Toft took me, as the newcomer, along with him in the smallest skiff.

It was fairly obvious that he had been taking my measure. He said he understood that I had taken an active part in student politics at the University, and on the Red left wing at that. I saw no reason to deny it.

In his young days he had been a radical himself, he confided, a Red firebrand. But life had taught him a few lessons.

I am afraid my smile was a bit cynical. Perhaps he realized that his opening had been a little on the arrogant side.

"Let me put it this way," he said. "One doesn't be-

come wiser as time passes on. Rather, things seem to
become more complex and difficult."

"We who are young don't think that life is easy, either," I answered, "but we do think that improvement
is possible."

"Granted. But it is hopeless to try to impress a new
and alien pattern upon society. Men must first be re-
formed themselves."

"But the majority of people are more or less what
their environment makes them. If we could create more
secure and fair social conditions, perhaps even people
might be improved in quality."

"And so you want to abolish capitalism and militar-
ism in order to build a community of fraternity and
eternal peace?"

I was inclined to let it stand at that. "Something in
that direction, yes." The discussion was too general to
be of interest.

We continued to fish in silence.

When we returned to the party on shore, the ladies
held the preposterous view that it would take too long
to fry our catch. Sandwiches, cakes, and coffee must
suffice, they said. Of course, the ladies won.

The sun had just barely touched the mountain peaks
and was ascending again. The light was soft, and in
the quiet we could hear the sea and the gulls. An intoxicating tension filled the air. How was it going to be
possible to sleep through these sunlit nights?

During the evening Mr. Nilsen, the lawyer, made me
the object of his special attention. He realized that I

17

had made up my mind to open a law office and, even though there would be few spoils to share, he wanted to bid me welcome as a colleague.

He asked me how I intended to begin.

— Well, I would hang out my shingle and see what happened. Perhaps I would even move about a bit among the people until they showed an inclination to come to me. I was even contemplating an office day once a week in Ballangen, the small mining town on the south side of the fjord. It might be easier to become known in a place even smaller than Narvik. —

— Most certainly a good idea, but it would take patience. —

I had to admit that patience was not one of my strong points, but said that I at least intended to try.

Mr. Nilsen was silent for a while, seemingly lost in contemplation of the awe-inspiring scene. Then he made a suggestion, as though he had just thought of it.

— Since I was going to stay here anyway, perhaps I would like to start as a junior partner in his office. There would be a monthly salary, and it would rise as I became more experienced. —

The proposal caught me somewhat off guard. But this was marvelous! It would mean security, and no starting expense. I could begin working at once, with nothing to worry about. I thanked him, and said I would think it over.

On the way home the reddish tone above the mountains had again given way to a white light. Another working day was at hand. And certainly this was a

land to work in. Perhaps, all things considered, the thrill of the struggle would be worth more than security. And that, after all, had been our real reason for coming up here.

II — LAW AND ORDER

ACCEPTING a junior partnership with a fixed salary certainly seemed to be the most sensible thing to do, but it did not appeal to us. We went for many long walks discussing our poor chances of establishing an independent law practice in Narvik and from these walks we at least learned something of the surrounding country. The road into the Beidsfjord was the only one that led to any particular destination. A little village lay at the foot of the fjord.

Ellen said that we must become acquainted with the natives. The people of the Parkway did not look as though they had a great need for lawyers, and, if any of them wanted a divorce, it was unlikely that they would come to me.

Halfway into the fjord I recalled that there was at least one native we might try to meet when we had come this far. It was from somewhere around here that one could get a view of the troll on the opposite side of the

narrow fjord. It was a tall moss-covered stone close
to the shore line, and would have the exact likeness of a
giant with a hanging jaw, if one got hold of him from
the right angle. It was one of the tourist attractions.
We walked back and forth at the turn of the road from
where one should look. There was nothing to see. We
did not want to be taken for tourists and so did not inquire from people who passed by. At length we did
shout across the narrow fjord to an old fisherman who
could have no interest in us anyhow. He did not answer but merely scrutinized us from the shore. We
shouted again. Then we discovered that it was unnecessary. It was the Beidsfjord Troll himself.

We agreed that it would be wise to make a humble
beginning. At a party a few days before, the old District Judge had lamented the fact that he must hold
court in many different places during the summer and
that he was without a secretary. Members of his office
staff had shown no inclination to sacrifice their vacations
even though justice was threatened. Could I come to
the rescue? The position carried no salary, but I might
learn a few things. Ellen agreed that this was probably
the proper start, and that perhaps my association with
the District Court would tend to offset my youthful appearance in the minds of the people in connection with
matters of law and order.

Thus it happened that I became a member of the
Court party which for fourteen days was out to establish
justice throughout the district. I carried the Judge's
wooden box, which contained the law books and the

21

public records. I was to be of general usefulness to the Judge and to act as Court Reporter, and I was also expected to supply a certain amount of entertainment.

It was just as well, I thought, that my friends in Oslo could not hear me. It was not easy to disregard either tradition or the wooden box of court records, but I felt that the latter was really heavier than need be. It was a massive box, heavy even without the books. There was a new set of lighter leather bags available, imprinted with the Royal Seal, but the father of the District Judge had been District Judge before him, and *he* had used the wooden box to house the statutes and the ink bottles, so there was no help for it.

Most of the journeys were made in the small, overworked steamboats which zigzagged hither and yon throughout the fjords. A case of oleomargarine would be left on the dock on the south side of the fjord, a barrel of syrup at the grocery store on the north side, plus mail bags with the Royal Lion insignia. Farther south a case of canned fruit might be unloaded.

Our first port of call was Sjomen, an arm of the fjord that cuts through the mountain range south of Narvik.

The Court was called to order in the white-painted schoolhouse by the church. The litigant was a sewing machine company of Oslo. It was represented by an attorney from Narvik. The defendant was one Hans Nilsen Frostisen, who was his own lawyer.

He had bought an electric sewing machine on time payments from a traveling salesman who had been around during the last Lofot fishing season. Admitted-

ly there was no electricity on his farm, but the agent had explained that one would have to take into consideration what would be likely to happen. Before he had paid up his contract the wonder of electricity would, most certainly, have found its way even to Sör-Sjomen, the agent had assured him. The most reassuring rumors were abroad, even down to distant Oslo, that rural electrification would soon cover even this fjord district. The payments were small, but many. And as to the risk, that was negligible. As the agent had said, he did not risk anything further than that the sewing machine would be taken back and, then, it would not be his anyhow till he had paid for it. And now he had not met his payments. In fact, he had not gone any further than the cash amount given in down payment out in Lofoten and one of the monthly payments. That had been almost a year ago.

"Now, it is a fact that Hans Nilsen Frostisen did sign a contract with regard to that sewing machine, didn't he?" asked the Judge.

The old farmer admitted signing the contract, but said that he had no more money and could not meet the payments.

— But under such circumstances he could not expect to keep the sewing machine? —

— No, he didn't expect that. In fact, he had boarded it up in the very same box and carried it in his rowboat over to the mail pier to be returned. He would call the postmaster as witness of this fact. But now the sewing machine people would take his homestead, the

very farm of Frostisen which had been in his family's possession for two hundred years. —

The lawyer for the company referred to the contract. The legal conditions of a sale were established. The company was merely interested in getting its payments. It wanted only a judgment for payment of the contracted obligation. If, later, it asked for security in the form of a mortgage on the farm, such a procedure would not exceed the rights of the firm in question.

"What is your answer to all this, Mr. Nilsen?" the District Judge inquired in a friendly tone.

"They may take the machine, they may put me in jail, but they must not take the homestead," he answered.

"There is no question of prison or homestead. I don't think you get the point, Mr. Nilsen," the Judge broke in. His patience appeared to be wearing thin.

"I know I am an unlearned and simple-minded man, Your Honor, but I do understand that they are out to get the farm."

The old farmer walked across the floor and pointed toward the other side of the narrow fjord. On a light green strip of land some gray old houses were visible between white-stemmed birches which stood like sentinels on watch against the threatening mountain cliffs that overhung the farm on three sides. From between two somber ridges a glacier protruded like a huge, ice-cold tongue, bluish-green on the sides. It looked as if it were drooling oversized drops into the river, which, in one great fall, crashed straight down into the sea.

"Do I have the permission of the Court to tell the history of that old homestead under the glacier?" he asked.

"If it has anything to do with this lawsuit." The Judge could not find it in his heart to stop the old man.

"That is for the Court to decide. It may be somewhat distant in time. My grandfather was twelve years old when it happened. The avalanche struck and carried all the houses and everything alive with it into the sea. He and his mother were down by the fjord and got safely into a boat. His father, a child in his arms, had almost reached the shore when the avalanche took him. In the barn were a maid and two small girls. They were killed, too. That was the second time it happened, but each time the rest of our family moved back."

"But what has that to do with the present lawsuit?"

"Only this, that I can not lose the farm. You must not take Frostisen away from us, do you hear?"

The man was calmed down and the Court proceeded.

It is possible that Hans Nilsen Frostisen at the next Lofot fishing season wasted all his cash on a silver brooch and dress material for his wife, but the gray old homestead is still there, and his family will in all likelihood stay there till the avalanche strikes again.

The next case concerned the theft of a windbreaker with leather lapels. It had not been much of a garment at best, but, as the injured party said, a man must be able to hang his coat in his own forests without running the risk of being robbed. The defendant was now em-

ployed in the woods on the other side of the mountain
and had tramped the whole night in order to be in court
in time to hear his sentence. He agreed in principle
but insisted that he was without guilt. In the first place,
he had found the jacket on the ground, and, secondly,
the sleeves had been too long. He had not intended to
keep it and had merely forgotten to return it before the
sheriff had arrived.

The defense lawyer held that it did not appear that
public security in Sjomen was seriously endangered.
The defendant received a light sentence, and the owner
of the jacket the suggestion that it would be safer in his
own closet, and that, besides, it might fit the next man
who found it.

Most of the cases seemed to be more largely concerned with principle than with any great loss of
property. As we sat in the schoolroom with flies humming at the windows, and the solemn District Judge
facing the serious audience along the walls from his
seat behind the huge, ink-stained table, there seemed to
be something inevitable and foreordained in the simple
decisions that were dictated into the Court records.

Respect for law and order is old and ingrown in Norway. The unity of the nation and the inviolability of
the laws are basic traditions. The sagas of the Norse
kings are learned by the children with their ABC's and
fire them with an almost excessive sense of national
romanticism. The extent of the fascination of the sagas
for the children's minds I rediscovered during the
Court's travels.

It happened at Liland, on the north side of the fjord. Liland is an open, pleasant sea village with relatively large houses. The County Sheriff lives there, and the King's Highway runs as a main thoroughfare the length of the county. The highway follows the shore line, bending and unbending through the widely scattered farms. Where the side road comes up from the steamship pier one finds a country grocery store, the windows plastered with notices about taxes and military service, county council meetings, and public dances. A little farther up, on the other side of the road, stands the "hotel," the ancestral home of two spinsters who found it too large for their needs and so let rooms to respectable tourists. Next to it is the schoolhouse.

The local steamer had arrived ahead of schedule. There had been no cases of oleomargarine to be left at the pier on the south side. No business was scheduled for the afternoon, but we were to hold a brief legal hearing in the evening. The midwife of the valley had accused the postmaster of reading her mail, and he had sued her for libel.

It was the first day of Court of the second week of travel. The Judge was taking his midday nap in the hotel. We had eaten an early dinner and school was still in session. Some of the witnesses were loitering outside the schoolhouse, where the ground was worn from the bare feet of the children, leaving the grass growing only along the fence and the schoolhouse walls. The County Sheriff had found himself a seat on the ground and pondered with closed eyes the welfare of

the community. He had left his cap at home and hence was not in uniform, but a heavy leather bag revealed the fact that he was out on legal business.

The sunshine was warm and enjoyable as I lay down in the grass next to a young fellow from the village store, who had been called as a witness. We were too lazy to be formal and simply enjoyed the warm rays of the sun against the schoolhouse wall. Through the open windows we could hear the friendly, slightly droning voice of the teacher and the quick answers from the pupils. He made them repeat the old dictum of the saga: "On Law the Land must be built." It seemed to be the history lesson for the day, or perhaps it was nothing more than an additional attraction, since it happened to be the day when the Court was in session in the village. Whatever it was, we heard about the Constitution and the unity of the nation.

"Ten legal codes existed in Norway before it became unified into one nation," the teacher proclaimed, perhaps more for the benefit of his public out-of-doors than for the edification of the pupils, who seemed not too impressed. We heard the scraping of a knife into a desk, and the protesting voice of a girl who had been taken by the hair and was calling for law and protection.

"Who gathered Norway into one realm?" The teacher found the time appropriate to call forth a little active knowledge.

"Harald the Fairhaired, in the Battle of Hafrsfjord," the children shouted in happy unison. The problem seemed to be too simple and evidently did not warrant

the disturbance of the midday restfulness of the village. The floor was given to a young girl, probably one in the first row accustomed to answer whenever there was to be a special demonstration of wisdom.

The clear, girlish voice came through the open window, breaking the dull sleepiness of the summer day. At first there was a certain stiff formality as the utterances echoed the printed words of the textbook. The saga was about King Harald, who had given an oath that he would let his hair and beard grow until Norway had become united into one Kingdom. He sailed down the coast and engaged the fleet of the combined lords and local kings in the Hafrsfjord, right outside the site of the present city of Stavanger.

"What was the date of that battle, Ingeborg?" the teacher asked.

"In the year 872 Norway was united," answered Ingeborg, changing the subject, "and Queen Gyda got permission to cut the King's hair, and since that time the country has remained one realm."

"You are a very clever girl, Ingeborg. Now, perhaps, you can tell us something about how Norway became christianized?"

Again she repeated sentences from the history text, but soon found that method too slow, and continued her story in a lively and self-assured voice. She told how several of the kings had sailed abroad on all kinds of martial business and how they learned about Christianity and wanted to try it out at home.

Among them was Olav Trygvason, who had lived in

exile with his mother since he was a little boy and had
become a Christian but remained at the same time a
great warrior. When he returned home he built churches and made people believe in God and put hot dishes
on the stomachs of those who would not.

"I think you can skip that, Ingeborg," the teacher
interrupted. "Perhaps we can not take the saga quite
literally."

Ingeborg had some difficulty in letting go of Olav
Trygvason, who admittedly had not met with too much
success in this line of business. To make up for it,
however, he had many other virtues, and really did not
have the time to christianize the country, since he had
to be with his warriors.

"But Christianity, Ingeborg."

"Oh, yes. Olav Trygvason was killed in the battle
of Svolder in the year 1000, when the enemy trapped
him. Afterwards Norway had another king named Olav
and he took time out to christianize the country. But
the landowners murdered him in battle at Stiklestad in
the year 1030. Later on they were sorry and built a
church on the spot where he fell. After he died he did
miracles and they called him St. Olav and then all the
people of Norway put their faith in God."

Ingeborg was out of breath but managed to arrive
at a happy ending before the teacher's wife, from her
kitchen on the second floor, rang the bell, dismissing
school for the day. The teacher was in no hurry today, however, as the Court was evidently not yet ready
to take over the schoolhouse. He took advantage of

the opportunity to emphasize the relationship between Authority and God—His Law in Heaven and the King's Law in Norway—and said that we all would be better off if we obeyed them both. The children streamed out into the sunshine. We heard Ingeborg's voice all over the playground. This was her day. Her small, stiff braids stuck straight out in the air from sheer excitement.

"As to Authorities, the good Lord sometimes makes use of strange specimens," the grocery clerk remarked.

I thought he had been napping in the grass next to me, but even he had evidently been kept awake by Ingeborg with the braids and the hero-kings.

"Out in Svolvær we once had a mad police captain who arrested people for drinking from bottles," he said. "If they drank from glasses it was all right, but poor devils who drank from bottles were locked up. That was when the new laws came to Lofoten regulating the fisheries, so there was ample reason to arrest people anyhow, but that bloodhound of a police captain was too much of a good thing. At length the people took their revenge. When the fishing went bad and they all went around in Svolvær sucking their thumbs and cursing, they threw codfish heads against his windows."

"What good did that do?" I asked. "He was not to blame for the poor fishing."

"Well, there is no Authority except by the Will of God," the boy answered, spitting far into the grass. Suddenly he relented. "It wasn't nice, was it? But it didn't happen again. Fishing was good the next year."

31

"And I thought you people had such deep respect for the law," I said. "I had planned to practice law in Narvik myself when this District Court is over."

"Oh, we keep within the law most of the time, but we don't like being bossed around as we were in olden days." He gave me a telling smile. "But we do want justice and order. When I get around to it, I may have a little lawsuit myself. My neighbor has a queer notion about his boundary line. Some people must be lawyers, I suppose," he added good-naturedly.

The traveling District Court was not without its charm. Here in northern Norway, where distances are great and hotel accommodations not always too good, these legal journeys had created their own forms, blending into the social life as part of a living tradition.

The Court sessions were held in city halls, in schoolrooms, or in Labor Union halls. Members of the Court lived in the nearest hotel, such as it was, or on farms accustomed to receiving travelers. The District Judge had the same room on each occasion and the defense lawyers and the secretary theirs, as a rule sharing it with the youngest lawyer.

At dinner the meat platter went first to the Judge, who sat at the head of the table beneath the picture of King Haakon in its gilded and fly-specked frame. The party passed through the doors in order of age, the eldest first. Titles were always used before names except in the case of the District Judge himself, who remained nameless and was referred to only in the third person, even when addressed directly.

The conversation also had its own form. The District Judge was old and insisted upon his dignity. The stories kept within a certain moral standard, although the limit was somewhat flexible. The supply was not impressive.

As a new member of the party I was looked upon as a kind of fresh breath from Oslo and the University. Of course, the Judge said, things down there were not what they had been in his young days. Quite the contrary, from what he had heard. In those days there was dignity in the student life. The young student swung his glass or his girl with cultured restraint and fought for ideals under a lofty heaven. Ideals were pure and the fight was noble.

I admitted that our modern student life was more earthy. The competition was severe. Positions did not stand waiting for us and our ideals were turned more towards practical life.

"Politics, I suppose you mean," the Judge said, somewhat testily.

"Yes, politics particularly. Most of us were radicals —socialists, bolshevists, anticlerics, and prohibitionists." I thought it opportune to nail to the mast all the pirate colors I could hit upon.

"Yes, yes," he said, rather wearily, I thought, "but what of the student life itself?"

"Well, we lived in cheap rooming houses and studied expensive textbooks. We went to bed late and tried to get up early in order to secure a reading desk in the University study rooms. We heard lectures from pro-

fessors who were not occupied with other scientific enterprises. We sat in student cafes in the University basement where the coffee came from the city waterworks and the Danish pastry from Osterhaugsgaten's Lumberyards."

"What do you mean?"

"Oh, it's only a standard joke. The coffee was thin and the cakes dry as sawdust, but cheap."

"But you had no festivals and discussions?"

"Of course. An endless variety of clubs and forums where we took up all kinds of questions, some old and dignified but most new and offensive. We debated social and political issues, religion, sex, and psychology."

"But is there nothing left of the old student humor which characterized our group and made us go out to meet life with a smile when we were young? Didn't you make fun of your professors?"

"Certainly, but the professors were not too original or queer any more, at least not the young ones with whom we worked. They cut their hair and pressed their trousers. But even so we did our best. Off and on we staged a University show with a masculine ballet and student satire."

"You did? And you made satirical attacks on the educational set-up, just as we used to? In what way?"

I racked my brains to recall some of those stupid student reviews. They were no longer regarded as outstanding events in the hard and examination-ridden student life of modern Oslo. Our days had been filled

with heated discussions of the new and influential ideas. The old-fashioned student witticisms were like stale beer. The students no longer felt themselves to be the cream of a privileged class. We started from the ground. We were about to build something new and we did not know exactly what to do with the old. Perhaps we did not even see clearly what we wanted to build. We did realize, however, that we were destined to struggle our way through a world of appalling difficulties. Our wit had a bitter touch. We smiled, but our smiles at times may have been a little cynical. It was not that we felt superior in comparison with our fathers' simple-minded humor; we just felt different. We, too, were out to conquer the world. Perhaps we were not such happy warriors, but the world had become a heavier load to carry.

It was impossible to get the feel of this change across to the old official. He would not understand, and would probably only come to believe that we were even more insane and lost than he had pictured us.

— Could I recall any of those innocent student witticisms? —

In despair I glanced at the thick volumes in the wooden box, those bone-dry textbooks on Law. There was the *Mortgage Law* by Professor Hagerup. Hadn't there been something about old, boring Hagerup? Not very amusing, to be sure, but quite innocent.

"At a law school banquet we put on a sketch from the Roman Law: the slave Crassus indicted for manslaughter."

35

"Good! That's what I mean."

"But he refused to confess. He was threatened with snakes and burning oil. Still he refused. At length a new instrument of torture was carried in and placed on a red velvet pillow. The slave Crassus shivered till his teeth chattered. The procession marched forward until it came before the bar. The Judge commanded the defendant to scrutinize the object on the pillow. It was a book. The slave Crassus screamed a confession. It was Hagerup's volume on Mortgage Law."

"Excellent! And they say that you modern students lack humor. I begin to regain my faith in our youth. But it is unfortunate that the youth of today has so little of optimism and conviction. In my time our idealism came from healthier and stronger sources. We believed in the goodness of mankind and the victory of the human spirit. We never got lost in the mire of petty politics. We moved among the stars in an evolutionary heaven."

— And there you are still hanging, — I thought to myself, — even though the earth in the meantime has evolved through one long war and is already approaching the next. —

But I held my tongue. It was an unspoken rule that the Judge should have the last word. While I had no desire to seek popularity with the authorities I did wish to be tolerated in the first-class smoking room of A Deck.

When we arrived back in Narvik, having created justice throughout the District for a long time to come, I went to the sign painter on Street 3 and ordered a great

36

white shingle with name and title. Then Ellen and I went on a tour of inspection to find suitable offices. We found them on the top floor of the brick building in the center of town. There were, of course, other brick buildings in Narvik, but Danielsen's brick building was the largest. It was only three stories high, but its red brick and green window frames dominated the scene. In the building there were both a bank and a clothing shop, the latter the largest in town, belonging to Mr. Danielsen himself. On the second floor the town's best physicians had their offices.

Mr. Danielsen was one of the town's more colorful characters and usually stood in the doorway of his establishment, immaculate, elegant, and affable, to greet and be greeted by all who passed. To be a tenant of Mr. Danielsen was not without a certain prestige, a prestige which had been fostered by the proprietor himself until it had finally come to be accepted by the townspeople with benevolent tolerance. For the prestige, no extra charge was made in the rent.

III — WE PRACTICE LAW

FROM our new office windows we enjoyed a glorious view of the harbor and the rugged mountains to the south of town. The first days we only sat—from 9:30 A.M. until 2:30 P.M. and from 4:30 P.M. until 7 P.M., except Saturday afternoon, as announced on the shingle. We wondered whether everyone in town was going to pay as little attention to it as the Sleeping Queen, who lay in solemn dignity across the harbor.

Ellen sat in the reception room at the reconditioned typewriter. The furnishings of the lawyer's office itself looked a little too new and unused by contrast.

Much of the time I stood in the open door chatting with the typist, but at the same time giving an impression of brisk activity. Ellen took letters, mostly to our friends in Oslo. They certainly were going to be astonished at this sudden friendliness at midsummer. But in this way we managed to see other papers around us than the inescapable bills for office equipment. We inserted

announcements in all three of the town's papers, and the editors printed short news notes about the friendly young man from Oslo who was opening a law office.

Then things began to happen. Clients arrived in numbers beyond all expectations. People came all the time—or almost every day: townspeople and people from the district, for the most part older people.

Cases came in at a great rate, mostly very old cases. An article for young lawyers that I had read had been correct in saying that no great amount of success is needed before a special type of client will flock to a new law office. More papers were in evidence, fat files of completely impossible things, cases which all lawyers for miles around had lost before all the courts that would permit them a hearing. At length I began to inquire whether other lawyers had had the cases before.

"Well, they are all of the same wool."

— And here sits a lamb, — I mused.

It was imperative, however, not to lose patience, whether it was the woman who fancied people were spitting after her in the street, or the man who had not received any inheritance in spite of the fact that he had defrayed the costs of putting the inheritance uncle in the grave with special handles on the casket and a heavy tombstone to top it all off. The estate didn't balance, the court had said; there was no inheritance.

— But wasn't it a bloody shame to have the deceased parade around, deeply beloved as an inheritance uncle for fifty years, and then, when he finally did pass away —no inheritance? —

39

The problem was to get such people out of the office. I did not see my way clear to pay them for this service, although many times the temptation was strong to do so.

What we needed were some real cases, with all justice on the side of our client, all injustice and all the money, or at least almost all, on the other side, and involving problems not impossible of solution. A widow of Sarepta fighting for her urn, perhaps, or orphaned sons struggling for their ancestral farm even if it was located in Ballangen. Alas, such cases were not plentiful. The world admittedly was full of injustice, but wherever the victims did go to wring their hands during that excellent summer of 1930, they did not find their way to the third floor of Danielsen's brick building.

Patience, of course, would win, but it might not be unwise to go to the mountain, since it was by now an established fact that the mountain was not coming to Mohammed. I, therefore, put into effect my plan to keep office hours every Saturday in Ballangen. The express steamer went out from Narvik on Friday nights, bringing me to Ballangen in an hour and a half. But it took most of Sunday to get back to town. After crisscrossing the fjord as many times as was theoretically and practically possible, unloading a Laplander here and a package there, I usually managed to get home for a late Sunday dinner.

For the better part of a year I kept Saturday office in the back room of Widow Carlsen's hotel in Ballangen. The arrangement did not yield much wealth nor great experience but it was not without some benefits. I mixed

with the people and at length felt that I *knew* Ballangen. According to the census, Ballangen consisted of 3,000 souls, but that figure included the whole country to the south of the fjord. And from out there people could, if need be, travel with greater ease to a lawyer in Narvik. The village proper, situated at the foot of the fjord, is nothing but a cluster of homes with a few hundred sleepy but good souls. But three miles up in the valley lies Björkåsen where there are sulphur mines and life and almost a thousand inhabitants. In addition, there was Milk Valley, occupied by Laplanders with small farms and big families.

Almost all the people in the country districts of northern Norway have farms, at least on the side. The miners have their farms, and even the majority of the fishermen can not do without their plots of ground. Right up into naked, tree-bare Finmark, agriculture remains, in spite of all, the one sure source of livelihood. The potatoes never fail, and there is always some hay for the cattle, even though the corn needed for feed must be imported.

In Mrs. Carlsen's back room I was introduced to the social and political problems of this valley community. The workers formed the strongest group even though the two or three other political groups retained a plurality on the County Council. The political situation was in many respects identical with that in many other places throughout the country or with that of the National scene. In Parliament, the small center party, the Left, sat in power with a National Cabinet. And in Ballangen, Post

Carlsen, the Postmaster, was Mayor. Mr. Carlsen was a man of humor and tolerance, by his own statement, a virtue of necessity. There would soon be barely enough Liberals left for a bridge foursome, yet they were the only ones who knew how to run the community.

The Township is a real force in such a small society. If unemployment strikes, the Township provides extra work; it is duty-bound to care for its people. It extends credit in dealings with respect to the Land Bank, the hospital, and even down to the cabinetmaker who builds caskets.

"Communal self-government is a fine idea," Post Carlsen commented, "even though it is slavery to those who sit at the top."

"But why did you accept such a job with no pay and all trouble?"

"Well, my party nominated me, and after all someone must be Mayor. My father lived here before me and my children will perhaps continue to live and work in Ballangen. This is our history and it is fun to have a part in its making. Nothing much happens here in Ballangen, but it is not without interest to have a place in the game. After a while one gets pretty good at playing one's cards."

He explained the set-up of the game.

The Township played with the Government as its partner. The State was distant and vague, and its cards lay on the table and were played by the Township. The State held the trump cards. Without its authority and resources the play could not continue.

42

The other players were the Co-operative and the Mining Company. The Co-operative meant the miners and most of the peasants in the immediate neighborhood. The private merchants were without financial resources and there was no bank in the community. Anyone could buy at the Co-operative store, but only members participated in the bonus. Because of its well-knit organization the Co-operative had a certain political importance. It did not hold much of a hand, but its cards were played with passion and optimism.

Who was really behind the cards of the fourth player, the Mining Company, was never clearly brought out. At first it had played for large stakes, but later only to keep things going. On solemn occasions statements were issued to the effect that all that mattered was to keep the mines open for the employes, and in that manner it appeared to join the interests of the Co-operative. It was felt in some quarters that another reason for their continued operation was to protect what was left of the original investment.

Björkåsen Mines had originally been a stock company. It had gone bankrupt and had been reconstructed several times. The holders of the mortgages in the company's properties were the real owners, even though it never seemed possible to get to the bottom of those property rights. The Company never paid income taxes, as it never showed a profit, and yet the sulphur went out of the valley in a now thin, now heavy, but never-ending stream. The little engine kept steaming asthmatically up and down from the mines in Björkåsen to

the loading piers at Ballangen. Back and forth, puffing and wheezing, always on the verge of capsizing on the sharp curves but never quite succeeding. By sheer force of custom the lilliputian train seemed always to get through, arriving safely all out of breath at the warehouses next to the pier. There were no accidents save when a cow or sheep, off and on, went through a fence to let itself be run down by the locomotive.

"The peasants evidently train their cattle for this particular purpose," the Mining Director used to complain when we came to his office with our clients' claims.

"Oh, no, we are really afraid that our cattle may get your whole train in the wrong throat and contract stomach infection from sulphur," was the client's common retort.

Compensation for lost cattle was made at fixed prices and usually did not require legal assistance. A lawyer was needed only when the cow was with calf and, therefore, warranted a somewhat higher price. Naturally enough, it usually happened to be a pregnant and slightly absent-minded cow which had the misfortune to be on the wrong side of the fence. It was, therefore, a rather simple matter to figure out the compensation; "One cow, 'Litagod' and practically one calf." The Company usually paid. The Director was a humane man with a keen sense of humor, but he limited himself to *one* calf.

One thrifty little Laplander from Milk Valley vociferously claimed twins, and was deterred from taking the case to court only by the expense involved. His sense

of injury and desire for satisfaction were in no way lessened when the Mining Director, in exasperation, finally said, "You had better watch your wife, my dear man. Even she might find a hole in the fence one of these days."

I was to have much to do with Laplanders during the next ten years, so it was fortunate that I had the opportunity, while in Ballangen, of learning something about them. As farmers they are not successful, but in the mines and at hard labor they get along fairly well. They live in the present moment and share with all primitive races a dislike of any long-range planning. They need a driving force since they have lost for all time the natural freedom of their primitive reindeer existence. Tuberculosis has wrought havoc among the Laplanders of northern Norway. Approximately twenty thousand are left, and it is safe to assume that that number will remain fairly constant. Social and medical welfare work have corrected the worst defects. There are no laws of discrimination against the Laplanders and they have not been made the victims of any race prejudice. There is, perhaps, a touch of condescension in dealings with them, which can be bad enough, but this attitude does not apply to the individual Laplander of proven ability in society.

"You can even marry a Lap girl," said Post Carlsen, "if you can find one who is attractive enough."

The reindeer Laplanders are proud of their origin. They call themselves *Samer* and retain their native, original language. They wear their own picturesque

clothes, baggy blouses, called *kofte*, made either of leather with the fur on the outside, or of black cloth, gaily decorated with borders of red and green, and hung with tassels. The caps are of odd shapes, some resembling stars, others, small, broad skis, with tassels at the points. Each tribe has its own peculiar pattern.

The other Laplanders, who have settled among Norwegians, are called *Bulapper*, and they strive hard to conform to the modern mode of living. They have discarded the customary Laplander dress but keep the *komagers*, a soft leather moccasin without stiff soles or heels. Filled with a special kind of dry grass, they are the warmest footwear known. In the *komagers* the Laplanders glide with the greatest ease across the mountain plains, their bowlegs and crooked knees making them recognizable at great distances. Their knives dangle in their great sheaths and red tassels swing in the wind. Their round faces with the high cheek bones are brown and baked by sun and storm. A narrow mouth smiles a broad smile in a beardless face. Their teeth are, generally speaking, poor, from improper diet. The Laplanders are small of stature and narrow-skulled. They are a friendly people, mingling a sense of fantasy with limitless curiosity.

For the benefit of the tourist traffic they tend to exaggerate their supposed peculiarities and oddities, their superstitions, and magic. In any Laplander camp shown as a tourist attraction there will easily come to be too many reindeer in artistically overdone carvings on knives and utensils. The Laplanders have discovered

that tourists want things as fancy as possible. The things they make for their own use are often characterized by a truly artful simplicity.

So far as the mysterious magic is concerned, that is pretty well worn-out by this time. An ancient Lap woman in Milk Valley knew the art. She could *gane*, people said, putting disease and affliction on man and beast. But she never practiced except where love affairs were concerned.

I asked an intelligent old Laplander about these things. He was a retired teacher and a very happy person. With a somewhat sad smile he said he was proud of being a Laplander. But he wore neither *kofte* nor *komagers*.

"Why do you people always have to ask about these evil practices?" he asked. "With primitive life there are always certain mystical secrets. I do not know whether there is much in it, but there are many Laplanders who have the power to stop bleeding. The physicians don't believe it, but they do not object to our trying it, and the wound does not bleed any more."

We sat talking in Widow Carlsen's garden. Teacher Sarri wished to talk with me, if I could spare a moment from my office, so we had moved outdoors. I understood that he did not want to be regarded as a new client.

— If I were interested in business, there would soon be a case in Milk Valley. A young girl in trouble. The case would not be up for another month or so. And, if the fat son of the grocery owner came around, would I please tell him that I had already been engaged? It was

Inga in his neighbor's house. She was barely seventeen. —

And of young Inga's sad and short romance I was going to hear again and again until it was all concluded in a prosaic statement between stiff covers with an official stamp, reducing the whole dream about life and love to a monthly payment of ten dollars.

As time went on my Ballangen files, little by little, received legal material. Deeds were written, tax complaints were made out, and other legal statements were addressed to the authorities and the courts.

When former clients visited Narvik they usually called at my office, frequently bringing friends or relatives with them. Things began to shape up. Now it was ordinary people who came, persons who did not especially want to consult a lawyer but who had been forced by circumstances to do so. They were mostly minor cases and few of them went on to court.

Sometimes cases came to me from even other districts than Ballangen. One day toward fall a firm peasant woman entered the office. She wore her black Sunday dress and had a silk scarf about her head. It was difficult to get a clear picture of her case, but we took our time. At intervals, Ellen, who still served as office assistant, would come in with papers to sign. Instant silence broke our discussion and my wife-secretary disappeared in a hurry.

I took notes, and at the close of our conversation found it necessary to make a summary of the whole affair. Her name was Amanda and she was engaged to

the owner of Tykkskog in Kjeldbotn. The engagement had lasted for twenty years. One Saturday night many years ago Lars had proposed marriage, and he had made the proposal many times since. She had lived on the farm all that time. Marriage had not materialized. Now he was past eighty and sick in bed. The doctor had little hope, and Amanda did not know whether she should call the parson or the lawyer. She had come to the lawyer.

"And Lars Tykkskog is still of a sound mind and willing to sign such a will in the presence of witnesses?" I asked.

"Lars has promised me both the farm and marriage since I was eighteen."

"But does he remember this now?"

"Oh, yes, he remembers it all right. Now he even talks about the parson."

"Perhaps he wants to confess his sins?"

"No, he wants us to get married, but now I don't see that it makes any difference. If we are married, I will receive only half the property, as I would have to share it with a nephew of Lars who lives in Lofoten. A legal will would be better for me."

"And Lars wants me to come along?"

"He gave me a cow to get to town. I sold her to the butcher and the question now is whether you will come with me. We can catch the local steamer this after-noon, and you can return on the milk boat."

Amanda and I took the steamer to Kjeldbotn, which lies at the mouth of the fjord to the south of town. It

was late when we arrived and only a few persons were on the dock. The agent, observing that she had a strange gentleman companion, greeted Amanda politely. She acknowledged the greeting, but it was clear that she did not wish to enter into conversation. We marched silently along the main highway until we turned left on a trail leading up to the forest-clad ridge.

The midnight sun was gone, but its light touched the mountain peaks, causing the patches of snow to glow with a red-violet reflection. The pine woods were dark and colorless, but there was a delightful aroma of wild berries and heather. Suddenly the forest opened and there, on a slightly sloping plain, lay Tykkskog. The small unpainted house was next to the wooden fence. The barn, a little farther down, had once been red, but that was long ago. The buildings lay as though they had been created simultaneously with the mountains and the woods at the dawn of time.

Amanda had marched in silence like a soldier. She halted suddenly at the opening in the fence and dried her brow.

— Wasn't this a beauty spot? She had carried water from the pump back of the house every day for twenty years. She had cared for the cattle and baked the bread. The stove filled with heavy smoke when the wind blew against the cliff, but it was a good stove and always gave even heat. Tykkskog was the first place in the valley to see the sun after the winter darkness. It lay so high and free. It was the only place in the world for her. —

A bed was made for me in the main living room. We

could talk business tomorrow. Her sister and two of the neighbors would be over for breakfast. She had understood that the witnesses must not be relatives.

After coffee and breakfast, and more coffee when the neighbors came, we went in to see Lars. He was still alive. He looked more tired than sick, as though he had decided that his working days were over. We talked about the weather and the valley and the farm. Amanda moved cautiously towards the subject. Lars frowned so hard that wrinkles formed and disappeared in his strong old face. For a moment he seemed to be uncertain which of his promises he was about to be asked to keep. I thought it would be best to speak plainly.

— The fact of the matter was that Amanda had called me out from town. She told me that he wished to make his last will about the farm. It was, of course, not absolutely necessary to make any definite will at all. But, if he had arrived at a final decision, I would put into writing whatever he might dictate. Perhaps he wished to speak to me in private first? —

— Yes, that would probably be best. —

I felt that I sat alone with him for an eternity. Flies hummed against the nailed window, while from the open window to the south came the smell of new hay.

— It was true, he hadn't treated Amanda right. She had been wife on the farm all these years, but he had never gone through the wedding ceremony. He had promised that many, many times. —

— But why hadn't he gotten around to it? —

"Well, you see, Mister Lawyer," he said "once I was

51

going to marry the girl on the greatest farm in the valley, but her father objected. She moved into town and I stayed on out here. She was beautiful, small and blonde and full of life."

"Yes, but that must have been ages ago?"

— Yes, it had been a long time ago. Since then he had taken life pretty much as it came. And, since Amanda had not had any children anyhow, there hadn't been any great haste. Now it was perhaps too late to bother the parson. But he had certainly brought the farm into fine form; the fields were good and they were free from stones. He was about to leave it now and Amanda should have it all; that was correct enough. —

Finally the will was written. In as solemn terms as I could make myself adopt I wrote it on the excellent stamped paper I had brought along. There was both Royal Crown and official stamp on the document. If things had not been too orderly earlier, Lars was at least going to have his last will in decent form and order. The whole thing was somewhat involved, but no doubt remained as to who was going to inherit Tykkskog with all its rights and glories when the signer went to his just reward. He heard the solemn will and winked as the last sentence was read. The witnesses found everything in legal order and signed with great, clear hands. Amanda cried a little and the whole occasion was very formal and proper.

Again we had coffee, and Lars took a nap. The rest of us moved back to the main living room and continued our conversation about the valley. The Lofot fisheries

had been pretty poor this season, but the potatoes and the hay looked good. Finally, the witnesses departed.

Some hours still remained of the beautiful day, and I went for a walk. The mountains in northern Norway have a charm of their own. In the southern part of the country there are both plains and higher peaks, but here the forest limit is lower, and Nature gives one everything in one great glimpse: the distant ocean, the crooked pines, the white birches, the bare plateau with its quiet mountain lakes. The land stretches arms out into the ocean and embraces the quiet fjords where fishermen have lived for long generations.

There was something inevitable about the valley down there. It was exactly right that it should lie just where it did.

If I wanted to say good-bye to Amanda, I would have to turn back. It might be a good idea to try to get a little sleep before the milk boat left at 4 A.M.

It was arranged that Amanda should see me to the boat. She had to take care of the milk anyhow. I was up early without being called. Sleep was very light when no dark curtains covered the windows. The wooden bedstead was a trifle short and the cover was heavy. The aroma of coffee drifted in from the kitchen and I went out and poured myself a cup from the great copper kettle.

Amanda was in the barn. She sat milking when I came in, looking years younger in her working dress.

"Are you up already?" she said. "I had planned to bring you coffee in bed."

I told her I had helped myself and had come out to inspect the barn.

Everything looked clean and orderly. She rose and moved a few things. In front of an empty stall was a wooden vessel with salt which she placed on the shelf. She smiled an excuse.

"It is only the farewell meal of Dagros. Lars told me to feed her plenty of salt the last day, so that she might drink her stomach a little more round."

"What a pity you have to sell Dagros. Now you will have only three left," I said.

"Oh, Dagros is getting pretty old, and it is too much work with four. Personally, I prefer chickens and sheep."

We discussed all kinds of possible improvements as we walked down the trail. After some debate, she let me help her carry the milk bucket. At the highway there was one more bucket, so we had one each. Amanda was not so solemn now. She did not have city clothes on. She joked and said I might get a job as farm hand, if I failed as a lawyer. There could not be many such silly old girls in the valley or old bachelors with good estates and bad consciences. I said I thought she would need a farm hand under any circumstances. Did she have to carry this milk every morning? Hardly morning, in fact; even the birds sounded sleepy.

The milk had to go to the dairy in Narvik. But every second week the neighbor maid carried the milk cans from the crossroad. Then Amanda had to carry them only that far. She used to leave them in the evening.

"But doesn't it happen that the milk cans sometimes disappear?"

"Why? There is a name plate on each of them."

When we neared the dock, she suddenly grasped my can. I was not to carry it any longer.

"But that's silly. Give it to me."

"No. There are too many people here. They would think . . ."

"What could they possibly think? After all, when you have lived with Lars for twenty years, you might— I mean, you can certainly let me help you carry the milk."

"You don't understand."

"I'm afraid, I don't."

"Well, people might think that you are not a real lawyer, and you do look young, if you will pardon me for saying so."

She kept her burden. We said good-bye with austere formality. The little white boat *Haldis* lay at the dock, her motor idling. Almost on schedule we were on our way.

The milk route was a life necessity to the farmers along the fjord. It was the milk which produced cash for the needed everyday expenses plus the small luxuries, such as coffee, tobacco, and such magazines as limited budgets would permit. The income from milk was the steady source of cash; all other income was more or less sporadic.

The *Haldis* took passengers, and the fares were reasonable, when one took the distances into consideration.

She stopped at practically every farm along the fjord. What she lacked in beauty she made up in dependability. Even in wintry storms and high seas she kept her schedule. She was strong and seaworthy and had an engine that made itself both felt and known. Her explosive coughing shattered the eardrums, while her unbelievable vibration took toll of the nervous system. Sleep was out of the question. To read was impossible, and conversation difficult, if one did not want to exert oneself. The five or six hours in to Narvik was not a pleasure trip.

Soon milk cans filled the deck, and the passengers were driven down into the dim light of the cabin. The place was clean enough but smelled strongly of milk and oil and tobacco.

Despite the difficulties, we could not sit in silence for the entire trip. Most of those aboard were already acquainted. These northern fishermen and farmers have a keen sense of humor, but their sense of propriety dominates their conduct. They seemed a trifle on the cold side and somewhat dull, but then it was not regarded as good form to show too much curiosity. The Laplander who sat on his cheese barrel in the middle of the floor could not restrain his curiosity and finally asked, "Where do you come from?"

I thought I gave him complete and correct information, but he pursued every detail to its furthest point. The shaking of the boat and the noise under the deck made it difficult to talk. We had to shout to each other.

— So I was married? Why did I not have any children? Did I have much experience as a lawyer? —

Haldis suddenly dove to the side and we had to hang on to our seats, but the Laplander did not lose the thread of the conversation. His teeth clattered so wildly that I was afraid they would break, and they looked new. He was aware of the danger himself and put them into his pocket before continuing with his examination.

Across from me sat an elderly and dignified peasant. He had kept silent the whole time. Now he moved over to my bench and proposed that we go up for a breath of fresh air. We sat on milk cans in the stern of the boat.

He understood that I was new in the fjord and that I came from Oslo. He had lived up here all his life. To-day he was on his way to Narvik to attend the annual meeting of the Co-owners' Dairy.

I expressed an interest in its organization, but hardly realized what I was letting myself in for.

He explained in detail how communications and co-operation had begun to bring confidence and continuity to the hard and insecure life along the coast. Poverty and mutual distrust had been the bane of the peasants for years. At last they had discovered the need for co-operative effort. Small co-owners' dairies were being organized throughout the region and they were bringing profit to the farms and security to the farmers. They were built on the pledges of members to sell all their market milk to the dairy. A stable production meant a stable price level.

The greatest weakness thus far was that there existed no nation-wide organization such as was enjoyed by the great consumer Co-operative.

He stood prophetic before his audience of old milk cans and sleepy me.

"We see our way now. It is going to be possible to increase the efficiency and raise the living standards of the peasants, but the Government must use its authority to get them organized. The industrial workers went ahead with their organizing in the face of Government opposition until the trade unions became recognized and finally received the blessing of the State. Our peasants are more individualistic and the development will be somewhat different, but it will come. And then the fishermen will come along. When the co-operatives and the trade unions include workers, peasants, and fishermen, this is going to be a fine country. My brother gave up hope and emigrated to America, but I still believe this country can become a good place for the common people.

"My name is Trondsen. I hope I have not bothered you too much, Mr. Lawyer," he wound up. "People out in my valley call me Endless Trondsen."

I assured him that he had never had a more interested audience and that I, too, believed in co-operation and progress. I told him that we city students had some understanding of the struggles and visions of the labor movement and that in them we found a new concept of society and were enthusiastic about it. The problems of the peasants, however, were more distant to us, shrouded somewhat in a cloud of old-fashioned national romanticism. But perhaps milk prices and meat control were just as important as peasant dances.

"At least to us they are," he said. "The struggle for survival these days tends to become so hard that there is little energy left for other things."

We had talked ourselves in to Narvik, and Trondsen promised to pay me a visit, which he did some weeks later, with a small legal matter.

At length a certain order and meaning began to characterize the work in the little office. It became alive with human destinies, and a new life opened before us. Had it not been for the necessity of bringing a certain business-like balance to our books, we would have been perfectly happy. The summer went into fall and the darkness grew on us. It was not easy to keep the belief that we were necessary in this land of the Northern Lights. Law and order seemed to take care of themselves pretty well without our help.

In some fashion we managed to struggle through. We had our own apartment, furnished on the installment plan. Occasionally we took a few small cases to court, we got a father of sorts to the girl born to Inga in Ballangen, but no really important cases came our way.

Ellen continued to pound the typewriter and often expressed mixed feelings of weariness and optimism at the growing stack of papers. Business must be improving, she thought. I quoted the words of the old farmer when he presented his wife to the King, "Not much to brag about, Your Majesty."

Then I got my great case. It is said that every young man gets one great chance. This was mine. The case itself was rather ridiculous. At least there was no connec-

tion between the point at issue and the passions it aroused. The town Banker had injured the honor of a Company Director and vice versa. The latter represented persecuted innocence; that is, he was our client.

Banker Ole Dahl was the town capitalist. He was the owner of all the great buildings in Street 1, at least the most important corner buildings with shops to either side. The economic life of the town had swung up and down, dependent as it was on one single industry. Off and on merchants went bankrupt and their property was sold at auction. The bank took over and the Banker had acquired quite an assortment of buildings. He was a very shrewd business man on behalf of both the bank and himself. Thirty years earlier he had been a carpet-bagger, visiting the temporary barracks which housed the railroad gangs. That was at the time when the railroad was built from Sweden. There had been a building boom. Much money came and went. Ole Dahl's genius was to see that the money always came and never went. He had had no schooling and his knowledge was entirely practical. In many ways he was the mightiest man in town. The bank was a savings bank, and, theoretically, the people with savings accounts had the authority and the State the control. But in one way or another it was Ole Dahl who held the wheel. This was most extraordinary, but Mr. Dahl himself was extraordinary. Right here in ultra-democratic, modern, radical Narvik he sat, a despot, both dangerous and mighty. He knew everything and everybody. He tyrannized the private merchants and bought up claims on the city. He

was a member of the City Council, but always with the minority. He had no connection with the Swedish Iron Ore Company. His private fortune was tied up in passive capital; he was only an employee of the bank even though he was its Chief. There was no real basis for his power, which, nevertheless, was real beyond any doubt. He was the Moloch in the town idyl, its feared and hated capitalist. The type itself could occur only in northern Norway, but there was a more redeeming side to his character that was most Northlandish. In spite of his avarice and his lust for power, he possessed a keen sense of humor and a certain charm coupled with an absolutely artistic sense for intrigue. The one bitter limitation in his life was his sense of inferiority; he knew he was not "fine" enough. He got no invitations from the cultured society. It might have been this feeling which caused his hatred of Director Plöen, who was one of the society leaders.

Certain arguments between them had been aired in the town papers and had gotten beyond control, so the gentlemen took legal action against each other. The police authorities had rejected their appeals, and they preferred their charges in the civil courts. The Banker retained the most famous lawyer in northern Norway, while the Director had only me, a choice made, no doubt, with certain misgivings.

The case itself was farce comedy. The town's labor population had no love for the Mining Director, but they wished all evil upon the head of the Banker. The business people were filled with secret glee and the Iron Ore

Company leaders looked down from their chilly heights upon a most refreshing spectacle. The court room in the City Hall was packed to overflowing for three consecutive days. The City Judge was disqualified in the opening skirmishes and the court proceedings were conducted by a judge from one of the neighboring towns.

As it happened, the accusations of the Banker, thanks to his acute imaginative malice, were rougher than those of the Director. It was really true that the Banker had exceeded the limits of legal slander while the Director had not. There was no need for extensive legal knowledge or brilliant court-room technique. It was necessary only to aim and fire, and that before an extremely receptive public. We won the case. The Banker was found guilty and received a fine, which, even though it was only for five dollars, broke his magic power in the town.

We bought a new typewriter and hired an office girl. The law office was successfully established.

IV — TOWN POLITICS

ALTHOUGH our victory in the "famous" lawsuit did not bring more work into the office, it did result in work for which we began to be paid. The merchants came with documents and bad debts, the Mining Company sent us some cases, and there were occasional calls from the little jail behind the City Hall on behalf of clients who wanted a defense lawyer. As time went on the legal work began to be routine, during the dark winter almost automatic.

Perhaps one is likely to overstress the importance of the dark period in which the sun disappears. The individual day during the three winter months without sun is really not much different from a cold gray day farther south. It is not completely dark, and there is a faint indication of daylight for several hours each day, even though it is necessary to use electric lights. And it is not so cold, after all. Thanks to the gulf stream, the coastal temperature rarely drops below 30°. For the

63

most part it is the dull monotony over a seemingly infinite number of days that makes the time seem so heavy.

Perhaps the monotony of the small town is universal, but it becomes a test of character when a colorless sky drops on one's head and dim mountain ranges seem to press in from all sides and the feeling of space is created only by the storms which rage in from the horizonless ocean and whine among the mountains. It is during the dark weeks that one learns to appreciate sturdy homes and pleasant firesides.

Many books are read during the long evenings of the long night. The dark period seems ideally suited to reading. No volumes are too thick, no topics too strange, to be of interest now. All the new Norwegian books were read as a matter of course—Knut Hamsun, Sigrid Undset, Olav Duun, Arnulf Øverland, and Herman Wildenvey. We also took a keen interest in foreign literature. Many American books appeared in Norwegian translations. We discussed Hemingway's simple and direct style and his indirect method of making his characters come alive. We liked Hemingway. His literary form was growing better and more sure, and yet we felt that his books and the problems he dealt with became steadily smaller. We debated the extent to which we might accept the realism of Sinclair Lewis as an accurate description of modern American life and how much should be credited to personal criticism of things he didn't like. Thornton Wilder's *Bridge of San Luis Rey* provided a topic of discussion for a long time.

Once a week we went to the movie theater and saw American films. We found it difficult to reconcile the picture our emigrants had painted for us about a toilsome and not too adventurous life in God's great, new country, with these black and white pictures of sinister gangsters and noble millionaires who married poor but blond secretaries.

And we played bridge, with some dispute as to the merits of Mr. Culbertson.

In spite of these activities, however, we had a surplus of time and a need for other interests. One of our best friends, a lean, good-humored instructor from Bergen whom we called "Bergenstick," maintained that it was lack of patience with bridge and a stomach that would not tolerate Scotch that drove me into politics. I was to learn that local politics could keep one's hands full.

At first I could not see much connection between the great political visions that had presented themselves during the student days in Oslo and the struggle for justice and power in the town of Narvik. The labor movement in Narvik was old and strong, both as a trade union and as a political force. All the workers of the Iron Ore Company and of the Railroad were organized, and most trade unions had collective membership in the Norwegian Labor Party. The Narvik group comprised more than a thousand members, and the Party, practically speaking, had a plurality on the City Council throughout the history of the town. The Party life consisted in its contact with the leadership in Oslo and discussion

of fundamental questions, in Trade Union matters, and, above all, in endless debates and small intrigues concerning local civic problems. Although the squabbles were usually tempests in a teapot the waves ran high.

I had been a member of the Labor Party youth organization since high school days, and again found it necessary to steer a course between the two common pitfalls, too much theorizing on the one hand and too many social evenings with coffee and *julekakke* on the other.

In Narvik there were still repercussions of the split between the Labor Party and the Moscow Communists. As early as 1922 the Norwegian Labor Party had rejected the thesis of the Third Internationale as presented by Moscow. I can still remember the heavy volume printed on cheap newsprint, its unspeakably bad translation bristling with technical and alien phrases. The problems were analyzed both as to fundamental theory and from the standpoint of dialectics, and all the dynamic elements had to be taken into consideration. Our discussions resolved themselves into debates for and against the power lines of Leninism. Although we were unwilling to accept the thesis, we were contemptuous of the designation "pink." In any event the Moscow Communists were now in a helpless minority and the sect had steadily shrunk, but there were still small groups here and there of stiff-necked "againsters."

As the Labor Party was in power it was only natural that there should be opposition from the Left on the part of the Narvik Communists who, though not very numerous, were extremely eager and tried to gain some hold

through the youth organizations. We had some great political fights.

In the spring of 1931 I was appointed the representative of the Youth Organization on the Governing Board of the Party, the mighty institution that laid out the course, nominated and criticized the Party representatives, and, in short, acted as the moving but perhaps somewhat too talkative force behind our city politics. Membership on the Governing Board totaled more than one hundred, and all members were voluble with personal opinions on all questions. It is quite probable that I did not take the matter very seriously. It was difficult for me to appreciate the importance of minor points in connection with the granting of beer licenses to the hotels, or the closing hours of the news kiosks, or whether the firemen should be exempted from the obligation of buying uniforms from money allotted them for that particular purpose.

In any event, I was put to work on *Vergerådet*, the civic committee which handled the intricate problems of broken homes and juvenile delinquency. I consoled myself with the thought that *Vergerådet*, too, had its mission. It was made up of elderly and dignified gentlemen, experienced and bearded, plus the Judge and Parson of the town, the two latter being members according to law.

Our work, as are practically all assignments in city government, was unpaid. The members were chosen by the City Council and were numbered in proportion to the strength of their respective parties: the Labor Party

had three, the Conservatives and the Liberals one representative each. Our group had been instructed to fight for the ideals of the labor movement, but the indifference of parents and the pranks of children did not seem to fall into different political or social categories. Neither in Norway as a whole, nor in Narvik, did we have any juvenile delinquency to speak of, but there were, of course, parents who neglected their children.

The City Judge and the Parson, as permanent members, gave continuity to the work of *Vergerådet*. They were kindly and humane men and their advice was generally followed. Frequently, after the meetings were over, the Judge, the Parson, and I remained in the Judge's office and talked at length of life and society. The office itself was old and dingy but it afforded a magnificent view of the rugged mountains to the north of the fjord. The Judge was a small and unpretending man with a keen mind, the Parson tall and aristocratic in appearance, a political conservative more tolerant of human beings than of ideas. I was subjected to much bantering about the "terrible" Labor Party in Narvik which was anti-clerical and yet had built the greatest and most beautiful church in northern Norway.

"We wish to be tolerant," I said, not knowing whether to take his words as complimentary or critical.

"I, too," answered the Parson, "and I want to tell you that even though people here, as in so many other places in the country, are poor churchgoers, that is no sign that the church is in danger. The workers here in Narvik still have church weddings and their children are bap-

tized and confirmed. Religious education in the schools is going forward rather than backward. There was a time when things looked pretty bad, and perhaps the church was partly to blame, but now the danger seems to be over."

"But perhaps the influence of the church over people and society is not as great as it was in earlier days?"

"True, and yet our spirit is more alive than ever. Here in Narvik, for instance, respect for the needy and the whole problem of social welfare has been handled to an extent that is absolutely marvelous."

"But you can not maintain that the church stands back of these new theories of social security and of society's responsibility to its unfortunates."

"Perhaps we should say that the spirit of brotherly love in human relations is even older than the theories you are talking about."

The Judge usually concluded these discussions with some sound remarks about the parallelogram of forces. The direction of development was a result of many forces. The social struggle within the country had not yet reached its conclusion; but, if one considered Sweden and Denmark as examples, the labor movement in Norway would still progress for some time and finally gain political responsibility and moderation together with political power.

We usually let the Judge have his last word.

Vergerådet was not the only responsibility with which I was entrusted. The following fall I was asked to start an evening school for labor youth, and in spite of the

fact that the teachers received no remuneration, an ample teaching staff was made up of volunteers from the high school and college. There were more Labor Party members among teachers in the high schools than in the grade schools. The main subjects taught were political science, social history, and English. The general results were satisfactory; at any rate, I learned a good deal myself.

It would soon be two years since we had arrived in Narvik, and we had grown rather easily into the life of the town. Glory and reward had not been great, but we were in satisfactory circumstances. We had good friends and good credit. When one knew it from the inside, the town was not so bad after all, and interesting things managed to happen with reasonable regularity.

Thus it also happened that one day we came to own our own home. It was a small yellow house with green window frames out on Framnes Peninsula. A little far out, perhaps, fifteen minutes' walk from the Market Place, but it had an open location on a hillside facing the harbor and was protected from the ocean. One reached it over a winding road which made a little S among small pine trees and white-stemmed birches. It was new and complete and modern, and the owner was going south. We took over the mortgage and the name "Kittenshill." From the corner window in the living room we had a magnificent view on two sides: the Sleeping Queen to the south, looking even longer in face from here than from downtown, and Fagernes Mountain to the east, hovering above the city. Straight ahead we had a full

view of the harbor, where we counted the ships every morning when we raised the curtains in the sleeping room upstairs.

That summer my parents left for Oslo, but before they left they had seen us settled at Kittenshill.

My father's successor was a certain Colonel Konrad Sundlo. We knew that he was a reactionary with political ambitions. He was not old-fashioned and high-minded in his conservatism like our ordinary politicians of the Right, but showed extreme sympathy for Fascism. Immediately upon arriving in town he had written articles for the local papers pointing out the Danger from the East. He had once been in Russia and knew some Russian and, therefore, regarded himself as an expert on the Red Peril. He was also anti-British and a Jew baiter. He spoke patronizingly in broad generalities of the working classes and at the same time attacked labor leaders and trade unionists.

It could not be said that he was forceful or dominating in appearance. Short and stocky, he had a flushed, rather formless face. His hobby was to popularize philosophy, and he attempted to redeem his slightly ridiculous personality through speechmaking on strong men and Viking exploits.

In the fall of the same year I became secretary of the Labor Party in Narvik, and, before I knew it, I was deep in city politics. The problems were not so ridiculous now. The endless debates concerning liquor licenses for the hotels continued, and in these discussions the roots of the labor movement history were laid bare.

Prohibition was defended not so much by teetotalers from personal conviction as by the old wheel horses of the labor movement. In earlier days they had seen their meetings broken up and their organization ruined by liquor and noise; they had seen money wasted in heavy drinking, so that union dues could not be paid. As a consequence they had come to hate with a fanatical hatred both the liquor interests and restaurants and bars serving liquor.

The prohibition which followed the first world war had long since been abolished, but the individual township retained the right to determine how the local liquor problem should be handled. The granting of liquor licenses to hotels and restaurants was passed upon by the City Council. A current question was whether the Government's wine monopoly should be permitted to open a store in the town and whether a plebiscite should be taken.

An open vote in the City Council gave the dry forces more than two thirds majority, but in a secret public plebiscite it was impossible to predict what the result might be. The debate was carried on with a certain dignity. Political parties as such took no official stand on the question, but the most eager representatives of the pros and cons wrote articles in the local newspapers. Most of the leaders of the Labor Party were dry, some fanatically so rather than from practical reasons.

The plebiscite was held and the wets won, but the City Council continued to deny the hotels licenses to serve anything stronger than beer.

"A perfect solution," said our friend Bergenstick, "even though the opposite might have been better, since, then, we would have had more tourists in the hotels and fewer drunks in the streets."

It was a solution of sorts. There were other problems to be solved and Narvik had its share of them. Unemployment began to increase. We began to feel the world depression. Narvik was very much like a seismograph in that respect. All economic tremors were instantly felt on the payrolls. First, the Mining Company cut down on overtime and then explained the dismissal notices which were soon to follow. The years from 1932 to 1936 were the worst. During 1932 the average unemployment for organized labor in Norway stood at 30 per cent. It was going to rise to 40 per cent before it began to drop again in 1935.

The depression did not strike everywhere with the same force. Cities with small businesses and home production came through best. Narvik was hard hit but managed to struggle through without any real suffering. But, when the bottom was reached, both public and private resources were exhausted. Shops had gone bankrupt and house after house had been sold at auction, even though the same people continued to live in them.

For more than two years conditions were bad, with about one third of the population partly or completely dependent upon public relief. The workers in the Swedish Iron Ore Company had agreed to work on a reduced time schedule in order to avoid further dismissals. The

Ore Company itself operated under a tremendous defi-
cit. The local income tax rose to 20 per cent, to which
was added the State income tax. But there was no destitution. There was no want of food or clothing or fuel,
and the people lived in the same houses as before. It
was not regarded as fair to buy a house which had been
taken over by the bank if the owner declared his intention of redeeming it.

It was not charity or private welfare that helped us
through the crisis; it was law and justice. But we did
engage in endless debates as to the form the assistance
should take. The Conservatives pointed out the dangers
in having the help come too easily. Something must
be asked in return, it was said, if the people were not
to lose their spirit and self-respect. A host of problems
presented themselves. Should work be demanded in return for help? Should the assistance be in the form of
cash, or in credit to be used for the purchase of the most
necessary things? The last conservative Cabinet in
Norway had even suggested that the acceptance of public help be coupled with the loss of certain civic rights.
The opposite point of view, however, had the support of
the people in the labor movement and also of the majority of the Liberals.

We were face to face with a social crisis which affected individuals impartially. There was no question of
blame or ill will. It was bad enough to lose work and
livelihood. To add shame to disaster would be too
much. The unemployed had rights and should not be
forced to stand as beggars before society. Society had

the duty of aiding its members. The Gordian Knot lay
in asking for work in return for help when there was
not work enough to go around.

It was truly a paradoxical situation. A thousand
tasks awaited accomplishment. Equipment stood idle
and material lay waiting, with empty hands stretched
toward them. Somewhere there had been a fatal weakness and resulting failure in the social and economic
structure. We thought we knew where that weakness
was, but it would take a long time to work it out. The
immediate situation was that there was not enough work
for everybody, and if people on relief were given regular jobs it would only mean that those already employed
would lose theirs. We persisted, however, in the belief
that assistance given should be looked upon as a loan
from society, to be repaid when the opportunity came,
a view which many on relief shared.

The fact that Norway did come through the crisis
with comparative ease was due to the traditions behind
Norwegian society. The social security apparatus functioned openly, so that everyone was able to understand
the difficulties and follow the process. According to
law, each town must see to it that no individual was
without life's necessities, whether the needy had civic
rights in that particular town or not. An intricate system of refunding rates had been established between the
Government and the local authorities, but it was the
responsibility of the individual towns and country communities to give needed help according to rates and
regulations they themselves determined. In Narvik the

rates were kept up, since they had to stand in reasonable relation to the level of living expenses in the town. In spite of all necessary reductions, the living standard of the town was higher than that of the coastal districts where the price of cod had dropped to one cent a pound.

The expenses of the city rose steadily, and ability to meet them declined as fast.

On the surface all was peaceful—too peaceful. Few ships were in the harbor and there was little activity in the Iron Company.

V — CITY HALL

IN THE midst of this period, to my complete surprise, I became Mayor of the town. The old Mayor had worked in the city government ever since the town had been established. Promotion had followed promotion until now he had reached the highest civic position, that of Supervisor of City Offices. As such, by law, he could not also retain the office of Mayor.

Elections had been held in the fall, and I had been elected to the City Council as one of the twenty-four representatives of the Labor Party. The new Council Members would not be inducted into office until after the first of the year, when the Mayor for the year would be elected by the Council itself. Each of the different party groups nominated its own candidate; but, as the Labor Party was strongest, its candidate would be elected. A contest was expected between the Railroad workers and the Company workers. There was always some rivalry between them and meetings were often long and warm.

Just before the Party meeting opened a group of the older leaders came to me and said that they had a plan that would simplify matters. I was to be the next Mayor.

"But that is impossible. I am too young, too new up here." I could think of many other reasons.

"Yes, but it is the simplest solution."

"Not for me," I answered.

The Party patriarch chewed a little.

"Well, men, we'd better begin the meeting," he said. Then to me, "Now you do as we decide. We know that you aren't thirty yet, and that you are a lawyer, and all sorts of things, but we will take the risk."

I was both a little angry and a little touched when the vote was cast and it became necessary for me to thank them for their confidence.

In the City Council itself there were no discussions. Each party nominated its own candidate and then mathematics took over. I promised that I would do my best.

The City Council was elected for three years, a body of forty-four serious councilmen and women whose chief interest was to try to direct the city government as well as possible. They elected an Executive Council whose responsibility it was to conduct all current business. The Executive Council held weekly meetings, but the Mayor called together the entire City Council for discussion of vital issues and whenever the budget was to be prepared and voted on. The City Council controlled the Executive Council and also elected the representatives to the key committees. The machinery was

rather slow-moving but it did its work smoothly and well. Not one dollar of public funds could be misused. All economic measures were open to public inspection. There were heated debates and much waste of time in misunderstandings and delays, but we usually found our way to the proper solution of our problems. In any case, this was our public democratic government and this was the way we built our nation.

The situation was becoming desperate and it was imperative that the town have more money. The Railroad and the Mining Company continued their layoffs, although they kept on the payrolls as long as possible the heads of families and those with long employment records. The young men were the first to go, and it was not pleasant to have to talk with these impatient boys and have nothing to tell them. They said that things could not continue longer in this manner. We agreed, but what was there to do? And yet there they stood, aggressive, forceful, eager, and at the same time willing to be reasonable.

"But we want work," they said. "You have been talking about a new hospital, about the school buildings that are overflowing, about the electric power plant that should be enlarged. The streets could be improved. The cliff down by the pier should be dynamited to straighten out the road. It has been planned for a long time. Why can't we begin now? The city is not finished. Can it not build and dynamite and improve and give us work?"

"Of course you are right," we answered. "There are

many things that should be done. But we have no money. We are trying everything. Give us more time."

And they would retort, "Time is the one thing we have too much of now."

Our best did not seem to be enough, so we sent delegates south to see what could be done. The Conservative group appointed an able man. The Supervisor of City Offices had been down to borrow money before. The three of us traveled the route between Oslo and Stockholm again and again, and, finally, there were some tangible results. In Stockholm we made an arrangement with the Swedish Iron Ore Company that it should pay a minimum annual tax which in slump years would be looked upon as an advance tax payment on future profits. At the Government offices in Oslo we presented plans for new schools, a new hospital, and the expansion of the electric power plant. What we needed was money to pay for the necessary work. We were not able to secure assistance for our most ambitious plans, but the cliff by the pier was dynamited away.

When the Labor Party came into power with a National Cabinet we were on hand again with our appeals for help. We thought our friends were sadly cautious. But Narvik was not the only city hit by the depression. We concentrated on our request for the new hospital and we did receive a promise of money from the National Hospitalization Agency.

It was the Assistant Mayor who *personified* the new hospital. He was Chairman of the Board of the old hospital and for years had fought for expansion. Henry

Ottemo was a stout and jovial railroad carpenter, but he did not joke about the new hospital. It must be built of concrete and must adjoin the old wooden building, which would be changed into a nurses' home. He knew exactly how things should be. Mrs. Ottemo complained that her husband studied heavy books in bed every evening, books on dishwashing machines, innerspring mattresses, stainless steel, and floor finishing. At last the long-cherished dream was to become reality. In co-operation with the Head Surgeon he pressed the demands through the Government offices—but there never seemed to be enough money on hand. Finally, the Head Surgeon lent his personal savings to the project in order to meet the building expense and balance the account.

The Head Surgeon was one of the forceful personalities who made the poor little town so rich. He worked long hours year in and year out with no vacations other than lone Sunday ski trips in the mountains. Occasionally he permitted himself a "vacation" to work for some months in a hospital abroad. From one such trip he returned to tell us the seeming fairy tale of the Mayo Clinic somewhere out on the prairies of the American Middle West. He was a magnificent surgeon. As a private person he was a bachelor and very reserved, but within the limits of his reserved nature we were the best of friends. We passed many pleasant evenings in heated discussion of our seemingly divergent philosophies of life. At bottom, we were not too far apart, although he was in fundamental disagreement with my political views, perhaps mostly for the reason that they

were those of the majority. It helped some that he got his new hospital.

And then, gradually, things began to return to normal. People were buying again. It was no longer only the city which used money. More ships could be counted in the harbor. The reduction arrangement of working hours in the Iron Company was canceled. The economic seismograph registered once more in the right direction. Things began to happen.

We began to build again, and building gave us deep satisfaction. We blasted mountains and hewed stone and fashioned dwellings for men. We altered the landscape for all time and impressed it with man's will. In form and color we gave of ourselves.

I remember the long discussions we had with our old architect. When we outlined plans for a new chapel that was to stand on a hill near the churchyard north of the town, he said that at last he knew just what we wanted him to do—to remove one mountain and design a new one. We laughed. It may be that we had expressed ourselves in that way, but what probably had happened was that the mountains had affected us, and not we the mountains. We wanted something impressive and worthy of its purpose, combining strength and dignity with loveliness and charm. We built our little stone chapel and it looked not too different from the building we had planned. It really belonged on its hill overlooking the sea and the mountains. The town had a beautiful cemetery. We wanted to express our love for the living by our respect for the dead.

The next three or four years were going to be the happiest in the city's history. It was not a boom time, no one got wealthy—limited opportunities and high taxes prevented that—but it was a period of healthy economic growth. There were, alas, too many holes to be plugged before we could feel the real security of good times. The social machinery had broken down at certain points and repairs had to be made before we could proceed with expansion, but improvements continued to come into existence. We got our School Dental Clinic, and prepared complete blueprints for a great new school building of brick. Private business firms also recovered, although there remained the crying need for capital and, to some extent perhaps, for courage and imagination.

The proposal was made that we might offer assistance to a few Jewish business people in Germany and give them a second chance in Narvik. The two or three Jewish families we already had in town distinguished themselves in no other ways than by working a little harder and selling their goods a little cheaper than their competitors. A little imported cleverness and initiative might not hurt.

The problem came up for discussion in the City Council, the issue being whether this Jewish relief proposal should be dominated by political or humanitarian motives. It was voted to underwrite a recommendation for immigration and a working permit for a small business concern in Narvik, and to give active assistance in the form of cheap electric rates.

Some weeks later a middle-aged German Jew appeared. The situation in his own *Vaterland* was not entirely hopeless as yet, and he thought that the storm of anti-Semitism would abate as it had done so often before. But one could not be sure, since extremely ugly things had already happened in Nazi Germany. Through friends who had traveled in northern Norway he had heard of our hospitable town and had come to pay us a visit.

He was polite, but somehow suspicious. Both the people and the region appeared to him to be a little too reserved and he seemed to be seeking the reason. I do not know whether he understood us, that we had no ulterior motives, and that there was no absolute need for us to invite someone to build a little button factory on the empty lot next to the oil station on the pier. As for his race, we felt that it had certain characteristics which might be stimulating to our sedate way of life. Our offer was meant purely as an expression of sympathetic friendship. He expressed his gratitude and said that he would return to Germany to get his family, but we never saw him again.

We were not always successful in our youthful enthusiasm for personal initiative and the need for taking long chances. Too often, young, unemployed families which we sent farming, returned with the smallest potatoes in the world and huge indebtedness.

We were more successful with Mrs. Polly, the not exactly young but extremely ambitious owner of the Royal Hotel, the second largest hotel in town. Grand

Hotel Phoenix was the largest, but its owner was not ambitious. Both were on the dilapidated side, that is the hotels. There were many complaints about the poor accommodations. Even the Grand had but one bath on each floor. The one on the ground floor leaked, and the one on the top floor was used by the proprietor himself, so it was only the one on the second floor that could really be used.

Mrs. Polly of the Royal sent us many letters, none of which resulted in money being placed at her disposal. Then Mrs. Polly visited us in person. She had had a new permanent and was brimming with enthusiasm and vitality. The tourist season was almost at hand. Would I not be interested in making it possible for foreigners to stay over night in the town? Did not the city think it was high time to become a little more modern and up-to-date? Only the other day a real English baronet had come in on the train only to find that every room was taken. He had to sleep in the maid's room.

— And the little blonde had to move out? — I asked.

— Well, that was the only objection the Baronet had voiced. —

We laughed and went at the problem. It was, of course, to the city's interest that these conditions be improved, but how?

— What if we built a truly Hotel Royal of concrete in functional architectural design, with baths and elevators, and a doorman in a burgundy uniform to match the draperies in the lobby? —

— And where would we secure the needed funds? —

— We might start a holding company. —

— But we would need money and good names. —

— All the merchants on Street 1 were interested. —

— Yes, but that didn't solve the problem of cash money. Even a holding company must have capital, at least to begin with. —

— Why not allocate public funds? —

— That idea was not especially new. Much Government money had already been invested in projects that seemed excellent, and yet the possibility of return in many cases was most uncertain. The inescapable result could only be that there would be criticism of the lack of business ability within the Administration. —

— Yes, but wasn't Narvik an exception? The Government had the Railroad and had secured for itself an annual minimum income from the Swedish Iron Ore Company. Wasn't that so? —

Well, we had ridden that horse for a long time, but we promised that we would try again. And so there was more pressure and more trips to the Capital. We had really begun to be experts in this line of business.

At Oslo I explained that, despite the alluring tourist advertising, the placards extolling the beauties of the Land of the Midnight Sun, there were no good hotels in that country. Tourists were invited and yet, when they arrived, they could not be offered proper sleeping accommodations. That this situation should exist in Narvik was especially unfortunate since it was the only town having railroad connections with the continent. Once again the argument struck home.

A sort of semipublic co-operative was established
within a framework of private capital. From the economic point of view the arrangement was rather complicated, but the new hotel that came into being was
beautiful and simple. It had the undivided blessing of
the town authorities and very limited liquor rights. The
opening ceremonies were impressive, with moving
speeches following the ice cream. Proper homage was
paid to Mrs. Polly. Irritating incidents and gray hairs
were forgotten. Madam was more blond than ever. At
last we were equipped to show our hospitality. Now
the tourists could come.

And come they did, mostly from continental Europe.
While they did not always have much money they did
not lack enthusiasm.

Shipping increased. The Iron Ore Company worked
night shifts during the dark season and the loading piers
were bright under flood lights. The Song of Work was
heard between the mountains. Once more the world
needed iron. Confidence has returned, the people said.

But most of the ships in the harbor flew red flags with
a black swastika.

VI — LOFOTEN

LOCAL self-government has been a living reality in Norway since 1837. For a century it has educated the people to political maturity and social responsibility. Each township is so small and transparent that our democracy has become simple and direct. It may be, however, that this local color in some respects tends to mark the borderlines a little too strongly.

In Narvik the people in the market place were as alert and disputatious in politics as the Greeks of ancient Athens. And the small but dignified town of Bodö was our Sparta.

Bodö was in reality a beautiful, idyllic town which could not help that it was centuries older than Narvik or that it was more fortunately situated in the direct line of communications along the outer coast. Bodö was the center of civil and legal administration for the Northland. Here the civil authorities lived and here also were the higher courts.

Of course, as Mayor of Narvik, I must not express too high an opinion of little Bodö, which, after all, had not half the population of Narvik and had a Railroad Committee which was one of our standing jokes. The committee was reorganized and somewhat rejuvenated every fourth year, but the good citizens of Narvik held that such changes might as well be made only once in twenty or fifty years, so slight was the probability that the railroad would ever come to Bodö.

Back of this seemingly good-natured banter there was more than mere local rivalry. The feeling covered a sore spot in our local self-government system. The burdens did tend to become uneven. A new city with a socially and economically young citizenship had to carry burdens out of all proportion to its developed ability. As an example, the Dröbak resort, with rich and pensioned skippers and merchants and few school children, could operate with a city income tax of five per cent, while in the industrial town of Narvik, where children were constantly being born, and where school buildings were always more or less crowded, it was necessary to make the tax about twenty per cent. A nation-wide system to even these differences in local taxation had been in the making for some time. Both in the Government itself and in the municipalities constructive forces were at work to correct the situation. And there were other points of difference, including the problems of communications.

These communication problems were not simple or easy to solve. For instance, there were the plans for

land connections southwards. The plan for a highway from Narvik to Bodö had been in the blueprint stage long before my time. Bodö did have some road connection with the rest of the country to the south, but to the north there was no road continuation. Now certain misguided souls wanted to put through the highway over the islands and the outer fjord districts so that it would not pass through Narvik. We, on our side, argued that a highway must be built for the benefit of all the people and not only for tourists who wished to save gasoline.

We held our meeting in the relatively neutral town of Svolvær. Shoemaker Pedersen of the Narvik City Council maintained that even the inhabitants of Bodö and Svolvær were reasonable human beings, and for this reason he had been given a seat on the communications committee where, it was felt, his illusions would be helpful or his eyes would be opened. The Narvik Chamber of Commerce was represented by Consul Mosling, who, as a burning local patriot, could be counted on to counterbalance Mr. Pedersen. The Mayors of the interested towns naturally would be called upon to present their arguments at the conference. We had chosen a week end in February, a time when the Lofot fisheries were busiest.

Svolvær received us with a blanket of wet snow over streets deep in mud. Its location close to the ocean tended to make the climate warmer than in the inner fjord districts. Sunshine was breaking through for the first time after the long dark period. The fishing operations were going on in East Lofoten, that year, which meant

90

that the bulk of the fish was lying closer to the mainland. Svolvær harbor was packed with fishing boats. We saw them seeking land as we neared the harbor: big motor-boats which carried the buyers, steamships with decks piled high with empty barrels for liver and roe, and thousands upon thousands of smaller craft, the whole an immense forest of ship masts.

A light fog had been half-swept away by a breeze at sunset, but the horizon was still mysteriously diffuse. It looked as though the fishing fleet was sailing in from the very heavens themselves. The coughing of individual motors was drowned in the common symphony of all the motors of the fleet.

Svolvær harbor was different each time I saw it. In some respects there was more of personality and changing mood in that little harbor between the rugged mountains in Lofoten than in any other place I know in the world. The scene could change from one of sleepy-eyed intimacy to stark and brutal drama, but the overall effect was always one of masculinity and virile strength. Its deepest essence was most clearly revealed in the nights of wintry hurricane roaring in from the sea. Just as the real feeling of the North is found in the long dark winter rather than in the light weeks of summer, so Lofoten is not a midsummer night's dream but rather a tower planted against storm, the Lofot Mountains defying a wild sea. From a distance the mountains appear impregnable, massive and solid in their great bulk; but, at closer view, narrow channels are visible between the rocky cliffs. Behind reefs and

cliffs there are calm harbors. Such a place is Svolvær.

Tossing craft swing in around the breakwater from the storm-ridden Vestfjord and anchor in its calm. The pier is a handshake and the town extends into the water bidding all its welcome. Above the cluster of wooden houses stretches the tower of the simple stone church, standing as if on tiptoe. The church is the pride of Svolvær and during the winter is floodlighted and serves as a landmark.

It took some time before we found a free place at the pier, and darkness fell before we disembarked. The lanterns were lit on all the boats and thousands of lights were glowing. It was Saturday night and over the harbor there were accordions and singing and festive release.

As we were not scheduled to meet till after the church service on Sunday, we sauntered around a while in the street from the pier to the market place. It was not cold, but the air was raw and it was more comfortable to keep in motion. The narrow street was packed with people, mostly young men in Sunday dress but for the heavy sea boots. Young girls chattered and threw their heads back in gay laughter. They were bareheaded, since they were out only to get some fresh air before bedtime. The movie theater played brief but numerous showings of cowboy films filled with action. From within came the sound of stamping of heavy boots, indicating that the hero had not come quickly enough to the rescue. But there were also other temptations. In the cafe windows were small placards, placed between the

glass and the freshly ironed curtains: *Stewed Prunes With Cream—5 cents*. The fishermen, tired of the monotany of sandwiches, coffee, and canned milk, felt little compunction in spending their money for this delicacy.

In the street I met young Oscar. I knew he had been excused from the trade school in Narvik so that he might make enough money to finish his training as an electrician. We had been good friends since the previous summer, when he had been judged not guilty in a paternity case.

He had been almost too innocent when he explained, somewhat regretfully, to the court that he was not the guilty one. I had had a blood test made and this had saved him.

He told me that his fishing boat had been lucky and that his share might amount to one hundred dollars.

"I suppose it's rather hard work?" I said.

"You mean the work out there at sea? Why, it's life itself!"

I invited him to have a glass of beer in the hotel, so that we might talk a while, but he asked to be excused. His clothes were filled with the odor of fish, so he had better keep out-of-doors. Besides, he had promised to take someone home. Well, good luck, and he must be careful, I told him. He couldn't expect that luck would always follow him.

"Oh, I have it in the blood, you know," he said as he went on his way.

When I reached the hotel, most of the delegates had arrived, and we had a pleasant social evening. After

all, there were many other problems in life than extending the highway down to little Bodö.

The hotel was built with one of its wings along the pier and the lights in the harbor could be seen from the windows. The odor of fish was almost as strong within as without. It was not of the fragrance of flowers, but it was an honest and decent odor and it somehow belonged there. After all, it was the proper odor for the season.

We heard the groaning of the sea. The radio had warned of storm. The day of rest tomorrow would spare lives. Perhaps the storm would have abated when work began once more. We could see the forest of masts waving to and fro even in the calm of the harbor. The moon sailed through torn skies and sharpened the contours of the mountain back of the town. Snow still remained at the mountain top giving a white background to the strange stone formation halfway up the slope. When seen from the harbor, this silhouette resembled the horns of a monstrous animal head which the fishermen called the Svolvær Goat. But the townspeople, who saw it from another side, explained to tourists that it was the Two Lovers who had stood there in stone since sin came into the world.

After general handshaking we sat down in the barroom around glasses. It was only natural that Lofot stories were told, stories of smart buyers outsmarted by still smarter fishermen.

A fish buyer from Kabelvåg began to tell about Draugen and the superstition among fishermen. Draugen

was Death in the Sea, the scream from overturned life-boats. Admittedly, very few could give a description of him, since Draugen sounded the last warning before the boat plunged into the depths. It had, however, happened that some had cheated him, and that half-drowned men had sometimes ridden overturned boats to safety. But such lucky fellows usually had little to tell. Perhaps, after a long period, they would talk, but then one could not tell how much to believe.

It was certain that Draugen was no shipmate to sit with on a capsized skiff. He wore oilskins like an ordinary fisherman, but his death-like skull shone in phosphor green, his eye sockets were empty, and his voice was the screech of an owl.

"You don't mean to tell me that people still believe in such things?" I asked.

"Oh, no, not any more. Since people began to use motorboats they have not talked very much about Draugen."

"You mean to say that people have become more modern together with their equipment?"

"Well, Draugen does not like the exhaust of the motors."

We laughed, and the conversation turned to the question of state subsidy to the fisheries. All other Norwegian industries had achieved a certain degree of security, some with, some without, assistance from the Government. But fishing, the most Norwegian of them all, still labored under great difficulties. When fishing was poor, the fishermen barely met the expenses of tackle

and equipment, and, when it was good, wholesale prices were forced so low that there was little profit. In recent years the Government had stepped in. The possibility of speculation was restricted, subsidies were provided for the purchase of tackle, and the export trade was made subject to regulation.

"The fishermen, too, must be organized," said an official of the Bureau of Fisheries who had taken part in the discussion. "That is the only way the living standards can be raised. It is slow, and it is not easy so far as the Lofot fishermen are concerned. People organize more quickly where they are permanently settled. But here they come from all parts of the country, they fish all over the Lofot Sea, and sell their catch at whichever harbor happens to be closest. The Government wants to see them organized, and it is certainly possible to bring it about."

"But what will happen to us poor fish buyers?" the fish merchant from Kabelvåg inquired.

"Perhaps you will have to exert yourselves a little," the official replied.

We smiled, but the man from Kabelvåg did not think it funny. He replied with irony.

"So you can even make politics out of herring and cod!" he said.

The conversation turned to the international political situation. The men were well informed and had followed with anxiety the insane developments in Germany, which they thought a kind of political epidemic. It had broken out in Italy first and there it might have been

stopped. Was it not true that the League of Nations had protested against the Fascist rape of Ethiopia? And, even though the League of Nations had little power, it still had a weapon in the form of sanctions, a weapon it had declared its willingness to use. As things stood, we in Norway took the economic sanctions seriously and paid dearly for it. Thousands of tons of fish which otherwise would have been sold to Italy were left lying to rot when the trade stopped because we strictly observed the appeal not to buy Italian goods. Had the Great Powers shown similar good faith in action, the whole catastrophe might have been averted.

"But why have you always been against military preparedness?" Kabelvåg was again on the offensive.

I felt it my turn to answer.

"The idea has been that the first world war should have been the absolutely final war. Groups have been at work in all countries to make this dream a reality. And these liberal groups and the different labor organizations the world over were really a guarantee that the peace would be kept. But, when the German democracy and the German labor movement were crushed, this basis for international peace disappeared. We realized that this approach was destroyed, and said so. We are now all agreed that we must strengthen our national defenses. The defense problem is no longer a political question. And the defense budget we have today is the largest in our history."

"Perhaps it is too late. Up here anyone may come and take us over."

Here I received assistance.

"These naked mountains up in the North? Who could possibly be interested in them? The struggle for life is so severe that certainly no one could possibly envy us. And how would they get here in the first place? There are no communications except by the ocean."

"They'd better wait until we've built that new highway."

"And about that we will fight tomorrow," said Bodö, as he rose from the table.

The highway meeting was not so bad after all. At least we did agree that there were several alternate routes possible. And, in the end, the Government would have to decide where the road was to go. Each of the committees felt that there would certainly be no question as to which was the most sensible route.

VII — THE GULLS FLY LOW

BACK in Narvik, we continued to talk about the crisis. It was an old habit. The true picture of the situation, however, was that we were enjoying the best period the town had ever experienced. The change had come gradually and was reflected in life and work even more than in mere money or high prices. Once more iron had become a precious metal.

Out in the yellow-painted house at Framnes we had almost all we could desire. At last even a little daughter arrived. We called her Siri.

Otherwise not much happened. The steady flow of days passed quietly and happily with pleasurable activity, their similarity serving only to fill the weeks and months with more contentment. The City Gardener planted flowers in the Market Place and the people did not disturb them. We loved life and the town and our country, and thought it perfectly natural that tourists should come to see its glories. Not all the tourists were

the most desirable, and they often had little cash; still, they were foreigners and added color to our existence.

At intervals some rather curious individuals came to town. In the late fall of 1938, the mad Major Quisling arrived on a visit. He had just resigned from active military service to devote himself to his philosophical and political studies and was to give a lecture in the Temperance Hall.

A rather large group attended. It had been a long time since a circus had been in town.

The speaker was late, giving us an opportunity to refresh our memories of his strange career. What one did not recall, his neighbor would relate as we sat on the hard wooden benches waiting for the show to begin.

After the last war he had been the Norwegian military attache in Moscow. He accompanied Nansen on his travels through the hunger districts and returned home at length with an anti-capitalistic point of view and a collection of antique Russian paintings, which he tried to sell through a Jewish art dealer with whom he was to have a long legal feud concerning the dealer's share. Major Quisling put his ideas at the disposal of the Labor Party and offered to organize Red Guards. When he was ignored by the Left he veered to the Right, where he had considerably more success.

Quisling was Minister for Defense in the only Fascist-minded Cabinet the country has ever had, an Agrarian Cabinet in the years 1931-1933. During this period he distinguished himself chiefly by being the victim of a nocturnal attack which was said to have been perpetrat-

ed upon him one night when he was alone in the Defense Ministry. We could not make much sense out
of his story that an invisible Bolshevik had thrown pepper in his face and hit him from behind with a blunt
instrument, with the result that he had fainted. Thanks
to his strong physical constitution, he had lost neither
life nor military secrets. He never succeeded in apprehending the assailant, but he did discover several points
to add to his propaganda against the Labor movement.
At length he severed all connection with the Agrarian
Party and for a brief period acted the lone, strong man,
until he attempted to stage a political comeback by
means of his own newly-created but hopelessly unpopular party "National Unity."

This was the "Pepper Minister" to hear whom we had
paid ten cents. It was not worth more. The only qualification he seemed to possess for the role of dictator and
Führer of the Norse race was a doughy face and a complete lack of humor. It certainly could not be said that
he did not take himself or life seriously. He began by
predicting the bankruptcy of the British Empire and
proceeded to bury international Jewish capitalism together with the rotten democratic system of government.
As for the Norwegian people, there was still hope, not
because of any intelligence or self-control they had thus
far shown, but because of racial qualities in the national
character. As yet, he said, we were still raving in the
night of liberalism, but before too long the strong, clear
day was sure to come.

We shook our heads and went for a stroll in Street 1,

to clear our minds in the fresh evening air. That paranoiac could thank the "night of liberalism" that he still was permitted to be loose. Probably not a single person in the audience really agreed with him.

We knew that he was publishing a weekly in Oslo and that he had small groups of adherents here and there in the country. The movement was without any political significance. It was a "defiance phenomenon" which, in difficult times, might fill a certain psychological need, but it was without any positive content. The "leaders" of National Unity were superannuated crackpots that the world had not appreciated. The "followers," such as they were, consisted of unmarried women of the critical age, and discontented youth without work. Two or three years earlier, when unemployment had been at its peak, Quisling had enjoyed his greatest vogue and had managed to poll between one and two per cent of the votes in the National election. Afterwards he had been on the down grade as the depression abated and life again became more normal. The minute Communist Party had a similar experience, even though it had more to offer than the Quisling group.

Once again we began to believe that life was not too complicated and that "normal" times really were the normal way of life. At intervals we had tremors of doubt; but, as long as one's wishful thinking and one's immediate environment approximately agreed, it was tempting to believe and act accordingly.

Iron ore passed steadily through the town. Work at the piers went on day and night; three steamers were

loaded simultaneously, while others lay waiting their turn in the harbor. Never had so much iron ore been shipped in the Ofotfjord as during that winter. But the local newspapers no longer printed poems about iron being made into plowshares and building materials.

We still counted the ships in the harbor every morning and automatically added the three by the pier, but there was not the same unmixed joy as before in watching the feverish activity.

Austria, Sudetenland, Czechoslovakia—with each annexation the iron-ore flow through the town assumed a darker and more sinister hue. But we told ourselves that we were without guilt. It was not our iron. We had no power over it. And anyway, what could we do?

The summer light returned, and with it our faith in beauty and life. Once more foreign guests came to admire our country and reservations had to be made far in advance for berths on the coastal steamers.

Later, we often discussed how strangely different the tourist traffic had been during that last summer. Could it be that the events themselves cast shadows backwards in our memory? No, there had been a definite and observable difference.

The German summer tourists of 1939 actually had money. The visitors were no longer young boys who tramped about with their songs and mandolins. Neither were they the usual grasshopper swarm from the *Kraft durch Freude* boats, those "tourists" who used to come ashore with wurst sandwiches, and who bought postcards and soap. The new German tourists traveled first class

and did not haggle over prices. They were mostly younger and middle-aged men of erect carriage who really knew how to appreciate our country's natural beauty, through fine telescopes. They seemed very studious about it.

In the late summer we were traveling, a party of lawyers and the District Judge, on the northbound express steamer. We were returning from a court session at Bodö. A party of German tourists was on board, including a widely-traveled and convivial *Herr Doktor* and his wife. The couple used every opportunity to gather small groups around the coffee table in the saloon to discuss German culture and intellectual life.

The Germany that had created Beethoven and Goethe was appealing to the land of Henrik Ibsen and Edvard Grieg. The German people were extending their open hand; why were we withholding ours?

We explained in equally friendly and polite terms that we had never harbored any dislike for the old German culture. We had believed in the Weimar Republic and we had shown our sympathy in many ways, but we did not understand the New Order. We hated brutality and intolerance.

The Doctor moved back in his easy chair. He must have answered similar remarks before.

— No, it might be true that we did not know too much about the New Germany. Actually there had not been much brutality and violence. There had been only a few skirmishes with certain cliques of Jews and Bolsheviks, who had failed to realize that the German people

had lost patience with them. Since we in Norway did not have such problems, it was only natural that we did not understand them. The Jews had multiplied like rabbits. They had taken over one industry or trade after another. The Bolsheviks had undermined public morals. The politicians had done nothing but talk and intrigue. The German nation had decided to determine its own destiny. Personally, the *Führer* loathed any use of violence. His only aim was to create order. He wanted peace and progress. The New Germany was filled with song and work. The people breathed a purer air. Unemployment was a thing of the dark past. Culture and intellectual life were blooming. —

When the Doctor ran out of breath his wife took over. Their enthusiasm was genuine enough.

We were polite and reserved, but curious. We admitted that we had not heard much about the intellectual life in the New Germany. The round and amiable Norwegian judge asked whether the lady could tell us a little about the new German authors. The New Order most certainly must have inspired new artists. In our own national history each epoch had its great names. Ibsen and Björnson had received State pensions in recognition of their work. How was it in Germany?

The question was innocent and without malice, but the faces of the Doctor and his wife became red and taut.

— No, he did not mean those who sat in . . . — The distressed Judge realized that he had again gotten off on the wrong foot and attempted to right matters.

— He had only wished to ask the lady to tell a little about the new German literature. —

The Doctor interrupted. He had regained his best bedside manner.

— The gentlemen must understand that the New Germany as yet was so much in its infancy that it had not advanced so far as the matter of books . . . the writing of books, — he corrected himself. — The new literature would come when Germany was ready, after other important matters had been settled. —

The Judge smiled with relief and we went on with our coffee.

The printed Nazi propaganda met with still less success in Norway. Through the mail we received pamphlets and circular letters containing simply-explained racial theories combined with flattering invitations to join in Nordic cultural fellowship.

We knew *one* thing, that Nazism was violence and oppression. Our periodicals had carried excellent analyses of the Nazi violence mentality that had created a machine which no one could stop, least of all its inventors.

And still we did not believe in a possible war, at least not in a war that would affect our national future. To play safe, however, additional funds were voted for national defense and the Government got without question whatever it requested. We were willing to pay fire insurance premiums according to traditional rates, but we did not believe that our own house would ever burn. We were out of the traffic, and mountains and graystone did not seem inflammable.

Nor did we believe in any danger from the East. Russia had her own ice-free harbors in the North. We were not immediate neighbors. Finland drove her narrow corridor between us. We had never been at war with Russia. The danger from the south was greater, but there was, thank God, an ocean between us and Hitler. We believed that we had good reason to feel fairly secure, especially since we were paying such extremely high taxes.

The Russian-German Pact came as a shock and the war as a tragedy that might have been prevented, although we did not know exactly how. Taxes continued to rise and placards were posted on public buildings warning us to be cautious and to keep silent. We began to doubt whether we really had very much to keep silent about.

Over the New Year holiday I went to Oslo in connection with the building of our new school. I found that all my old anti-militaristic friends had become interventionists in principle, if it could be said that any principles were sharply defined any more. All political matters had become inextricably tangled. We found ourselves on the same side as British imperialism. During the last months we had all helped to organize assistance for the Finnish people in their fight against the dream of our young days. It was certainly not easy any longer to see clearly either the principles or the lines. It appeared that we would have to build a new world view from the bottom up, to begin again with the simple and basic moral values like truth and justice, freedom

and mutual consideration. In our University days we had turned fine phrases to the effect that each generation must fight for its freedom anew. It now appeared that the phrases were going to be given very literal application.

When I returned to Narvik I learned that our Head Surgeon had volunteered at a frontline military hospital in Finland and that the Chief of Police had arrested the local representative of the Krupp Works. Engineer Möller was a spy. With German thoroughness he had kept a diary which showed that reports had been transmitted to a German center in Stockholm concerning the sailing dates of British iron-ore transports. Some of them had disappeared without a trace out in the ocean.

A German fish buyer had spent the winter in Narvik. Herr Koehln traveled all over the coast and we were convinced that he was also a spy, but the police were unable to get any evidence. The German Consul, Wusof, who lived at the Grand Hotel, was protected by his position. Mr. Gibbs, the British Consul, lived at the Royal. To people who insisted that all foreign consulates are equally evil in wartime, we pointed to these two men. The German Consul nosed about everywhere and invited as many people as possible to his table in order to learn Norwegian and Norwegian customs. Mr. Gibbs and his secretaries went back and forth to their offices with clock-like regularity and knew scarcely enough Norwegian to say *Skål*, not because they did not wish to talk to us, but because they did not wish to appear indiscreet.

On Christmas Eve Madame Polly gave a party to which the Finnish refugee children in the town and vicinity were invited. She was dressed and decorated in her best style. The Christmas tree itself was locked in an adjoining room until after dinner, when Consul Gibbs played Santa Claus, even though he refused to dress for the part. The whole city had sent gifts. It was a sad joy. Some of the Finnish children were accompanied by their mothers or older relatives, but few of them spoke anything but Finnish. We could not understand one another, the children were shy, and the mothers were tired, but the food and the sweets seemed to be enjoyed.

This year the winter darkness was more burdensome than usual. There were heavy snowfalls and the winter storms seemed never to end. The express steamers were as much as a whole day late and the local steamers frequently had to leave without making connections or getting the mail.

The somber atmosphere in the harbor grew ever more depressing. The ore boats lay waiting even after they had been loaded, as if they hesitated to go into the open sea. Then, usually on moonless nights, they would suddenly disappear, one nationality at a time.

Before the war the annual ore export had averaged between four and seven million tons. Two thirds of it had gone to Germany. Now, more British than German flags were to be seen. The Norwegian coast had many open stretches and the Germans evidently feared for their ships.

The Swedish ore port of Luleå in the Baltic is frozen

until late May, and the major part of the Swedish ore had always gone out of Narvik. When we met with the Swedes in conferences on taxation or labor problems they often chided us that we must not imagine ourselves indispensable to the ore export. Plans were afoot for the building of new icebreakers that would keep Luleå harbor open during the winter. It might even become feasible to transport the ore by rail to the harbors in southern Sweden. On such occasions we expressed a certain ironical gratitude over the fact that our beloved brother nation preferred to keep our workers occupied rather than their own. We knew that our position was fairly secure. The good Lord had in his inscrutable wisdom put the ore on the other side of the border but he had left the key on the outside. We had the *harbor*. From an economic point of view it would not be practicable to export the ore any other way, all the year round, nor was it technically probable. We had always been proud of the fortunate location of our harbor. Now we began to wonder whether, after all, we were so fortunate.

Steamers flying the flags of the belligerent nations lay side by side. In times like these the crews were forbidden to go ashore, but occasionally it happened that men did leave the ships.

One day in February I received an unexpected visitor. It was on the ninth, the day of the first return of the sun at the end of the winter darkness. The schools were closed, and the community had declared a local though unofficial holiday. The streets were crowded with people, their faces turned toward the sun. It rose in its full

size above the mountains, leaned for a minute against
the crooked nose of the Sleeping Queen, and floated free
a moment before it sank, seemingly tired after its exertion.

From my own office I had just called the City Hall.

— No, there was no mail today. It was really very
quiet this morning. Most of the clerks had gone into
town on some important business or other. —

I smiled as I hung up. Truly, the sun shone alike on
the just and the unjust.

The secretary announced that a young man wished a
private interview. He was German but easy to understand, she said with pride in her linguistic ability.

He was very young, barely twenty. He took a seat
in the client's chair across my desk.

— No, he had not come on any legal affair. But he
wanted first to know whether he might speak freely. —

Of course, I said.

— He had been given my name by some social democrat friends in Germany. As I would know they were
still active there. He had been put on duty aboard one
of the ore steamers, but this was to be his last trip. On
his return to Germany he would be drafted into the
army, but he did not believe in this war. He refused to
sacrifice his life to Hitler. He intended to desert his ship
here in Narvik. —

I asked him for his papers.

— That was exactly where the hitch came in. He had
neither identification papers nor passport. He would
like to hear my position in the matter. What were the

Norwegian Government agencies likely to do with him? —

I told him that he probably would be returned to his ship immediately. As he must realize, crew members from belligerent ships were not permitted ashore.

— Yes, he knew that. He had sneaked ashore to meet me. It might be possible that he could get back without detection. But, if he were to stay ashore, would he run the risk of being given up? —

— It was no easy matter. As he must understand, we on our side had to show some caution. We were neutral. —

— But others had entered the country. —

Only too well I knew that to be a fact. There were many Germans in the country. In earlier days we had welcomed the *Wandervögel* and tourists; now we had refugees, most of them without papers. Not long ago another man had deserted his ship. He had told me that he was an Austrian trade union official. His story was plausible. When the *Anschluss* broke in on his beloved Vienna, he had been discovered attempting to hide the trade union treasure, and had been put in a concentration camp. He had managed to escape, and had worked himself north to a Baltic port where friends had smuggled him on board a freighter bound for Narvik. We gave him money and bought him a ticket to Trondheim.

He had been invited by a student club to participate in a discussion on socialism and the modern labor movement. He had not shown much knowledge of the subject and when, later, he was discovered to be taking

an undue interest in the harbor works of Trondheim, he was arrested as a spy.

I related this incident to my new guest. He blushed, but looked me straight in the eye and assured me that he was no Nazi, that he had come this distance to be with a truly free people. He wanted my advice.

I called the Chief of Police. He said that he had orders to arrest all aliens without papers.

— But if it concerns a German sailor who refuses to fight Hitler's war? Would he be returned to his ship? —

— Hmmn. —

From his voice I could almost visualize our humane Chief of Police scratching his head.

— We must be careful, of course. We had run into trouble already. Political prisoners were not supposed to be given up. Each case must be decided strictly on its own merit. He could not make any statement beforehand. —

I repeated his answer to the German youth. He did not seem to be entirely satisfied, but he thanked me and reassured me of his admiration for the free Norwegian people.

— Perhaps we might meet again! —

During February and March we enjoyed some bright, quiet weeks. The latter part of the winter was usually calm. March was the best month for skiing. The mountains were a fairyland of light and the snow was heavy with ice crystals, ideal for sliding. Then the gray weather began to drift in from the ocean. The fishing ended

in April and the spring storms were at the door. Even the sea birds sought shelter.

"It is a sure omen of storm," the fishermen said, "when the sea gulls fly low."

VIII — THE NINTH OF APRIL

THE ninth of April was a Tuesday. That day the lightning struck and our world broke in pieces. It can not be said that it came without warning. We had seen the storm growing on the horizon but we had not realized that it would hit even us. We had had omens, but we had not interpreted them.

Afterwards we often talked of the day before the catastrophe. Dogs howl on many dark nights, but it is only after death has visited a house that the howls assume significance. Perhaps we recalled the day only because it was the last in a normal world.

Monday, as usual, had brought two days' mail from the South and there had been the regular busy tempo in the office. I was interrupted by a telephone call from the harbor. A British sea captain asked me to come down with a certificate of seaworthiness for the freighter S.S. *Romanby*. There had been a minor collision in the harbor the week before. I represented Lloyd's of

London and had arranged the details in connection with the repairs.

On the way I met a friend from the Customs Office. He had worked all night and was on his way home. A total of twenty-five iron-ore ships filled the harbor, roadstead, and piers. All had been inspected on arrival and their radio transmitters had been sealed. That morning a huge whaling ship, the *Jan Wellem,* had arrived from the north. He had been on board himself. It had exceptionally large food stores for being southward bound. Perhaps it had been chased into harbor by the British. He had not noticed anything unusual. The crew had been polite, but the cigars were bad.

I told him that I was going on board a British ship.

"Then you will at least get better cigars," he yawned, and was on his way.

I was taken to the ship by a ferryman who operated a kind of harbor taxi service.

— Business was not too bad. Tips were better since there were more British and fewer Germans, but there was not much of the traditional good spirit in the harbor. Everything was secretive. No one knew when the boats arrived or left. On the surface everything was peaceful. The ships lay side by side, flying the Union Jack or the Swastika, but they all had secret machines covered up on the foredeck. They kept their cannons under cover. Harbor police were to be seen on every side. There was much talk about spies, yet no one had been arrested since Möller, so things could not be so bad after all. But it was not pleasant any more. —

Aboard the S.S. *Romanby* I was invited to the Captain's cabin after we had inspected the repairs. He poured drinks.

"*Skål for Narvik,*" said the skipper by way of a toast. "You see I have already learned some Norwegian."

"And an essential part of it," I answered.

I gave the Captain his certificate and we sat down for a little farewell chat. We talked about the strange war and about Narvik.

"When things begin to happen will we be likely to get into trouble?" I asked.

The Captain quieted my fears.

"So far Great Britain has, perhaps, not done too much in the land fighting," he said, "but she still rules the sea. A freighter or two the Nazis might be able to sneak up along your neutral coast to Narvik, but warships which have to go out to sea will not get through. You may rest assured, there is no danger up here."

As I left I observed the huge Nazi whaling ship, *Jan Wellem*, riding at anchor at some distance. An oversized Swastika flew from the foremast. A little farther off lay the Norwegian *panzer* boats *Norge* and *Eidsvold*.

After office hours Ellen came to meet me. We were going to a movie. The official radio news bulletin was broadcast in the theatre at 7 P.M. The news report that evening was that the wreckage of a German transport, the *Rio de Janeiro*, had drifted ashore earlier in the day on the coast of southern Norway. With the wreckage were dead horses and drowned soldiers. The soldiers all appeared to have been young men and of

the same year classes. There was no official comment.

After the movie we had supper at the Hotel Royal, where we visited with Mrs. Polly. She told us that some of the naval officers from the Norwegian *panzer* boats had also been in for supper, but that, as soon as they heard the seven o'clock news, they had hurriedly left for the harbor. Several foreign journalists were staying at the hotel, two Americans and the English newspaper man, Giles Romilly, a nephew of Mr. Churchill. They had sat in the telephone booth all evening. The incident of the sunk German transport must have meant something, but no one seemed to know exactly what. Could it mean an attack on Great Britain?

We continued to talk war on the way home.

I repeated what the British sea captain had told me earlier in the day. Up here nothing could happen.

Before we put out the lights we went in to see Siri. She had, as usual, kicked off her covers and was sleeping peacefully in the least comfortable position. This night she had her head underneath her pillow in sweet company with Trine, the faithful but legless old doll.

Early the next morning we were awakened by a terrific blast. The whole house rocked. Ellen jumped up. What was it?

I said it was probably dynamiting down on the Iron Company grounds. It was 4:45 A.M. We'd better try to sleep some more.

Then came an even more terrifying explosion. The windows rattled.

"That's not from the Company, that's from the sea!"

I did not answer, but ran to the window and raised the curtains. The dawn was heavy with fog, and through it we saw tongues of flames. There was shooting in the harbor.

"Is it war?"

"It can't have anything to do with us," I said. "Some German ships must have been chased into the fjord by the British."

Then there was a new sea of fire and a tremendous explosion. We felt it rather than saw it.

Siri was stirring in her room. We heard her climbing over the bed rail. Then the tripping of small bare feet over the floor. She stood in the door.

"What is it?" And, as we didn't answer, "Is it Christmas?"

We had told her that there would be fireworks from the ships in the harbor on Christmas Eve.

Faces appeared in all the open windows. We shouted to one another. No one knew what it might be. A soldier came running from the guard post out on the peninsula.

— No, he didn't know for sure. Too much fog. They could not see. But the harbor had reported that the shooting came from the Germans. —

We dressed and went downstairs.

Germans shooting! We could not understand it.

We talked with the next-door neighbors, who were also dressed.

— How many soldiers did we have in town? —

— Not very many, it seemed. But inland, to the north

119

of the fjord, there was Elvegård training field, and there were some five hundred men there. —

It took some minutes to quiet Ellen and Siri before I ran down into town.

At the bridge there was a great number of Nazi soldiers. They had mounted their machine guns.

People filled the streets. They said the city had capitulated.

— Capitulated, what nonsense! —

— But the German flag flies in the Market Place. —

That was correct. A huge flag was flying over the Telegraph Building. I ran to the City Hall. A swastika flew there also. In the City Council room I found the caretaker. He said he had witnessed a strange performance in the Market Place a few minutes earlier. Hundreds of Germans had marched up from the piers and had hustled the Norwegian soldiers together in the Market Place. Then Colonel Sundlo and the Norwegian forces had marched over to the school on the other side of the town. But some of the Norwegian officers and half of the soldiers had fallen out of the lines before they reached the bridge and had gone up the street leading towards the Railroad Station. He had heard rifle shots from that direction. It appeared that Sundlo had surrendered his men and had ordered them to their quarters. Obviously, some of them had refused to obey the order and had bolted.

Later, German soldiers had arrived at the City Hall and had hoisted their flag on the mast. Both Grand and Royal Hotels were swarming with German officers. The

Telegraph Office and the Railroad Station were occupied. Further, he had nothing to report. Would there be office hours as usual?

— Yes, usual office hours. —

In the meantime the first office workers had appeared. I asked them to call all the members of the City Council, as well as the leaders of the most important institutions, the Railroad, the Iron Company, the Hospital, and the Telegraph Office. I also asked them to try to contact Colonel Sundlo, so that we might become oriented and decide what action to take.

From the corner windows of the City Hall we saw German soldiers hurrying about in all directions. They evidently knew what they were to do. They carried all kinds of strange weapons, and hand grenades dangled about their bodies as though they were walking Christmas trees.

The Hospital reported. It was packed with dead and wounded Norwegian navy boys and some Germans. Both the Norwegian warships had been sunk. It appeared that all the Norwegian Navy officers had been killed. The Commander in Chief of the local sea defenses, Per Askim, had just been brought in on a truck. They did not know whether he was alive.

Some Norwegian sailors had said that there had been five hundred men aboard the Norwegian men-of-war. Most of them must have been killed in the first half hour. The *Eidsvold* had stopped the German destroyer outside the harbor. A German officer in a motor launch had come over to arbitrate. He had demanded immediate and

complete surrender. Captain Willoch of the *Eidsvold* had radiophoned the demand to Commander Askim on the *Norge*. He had replied, "We will not surrender. We will fight."

The German officer had been given safe return passage; but, before he reached his ship, he had signaled the Norwegian decision by the means of a flash-pistol. Then torpedoes came out of the fog. Without having opportunity to fire a shot the *Eidsvold* was blown up in a single terrific explosion. Eight men were saved, no officers.

The survivors from the *Norge* reported that they had had warning a few hours earlier that a German naval squadron was steaming from the ocean into the fjord. The *Norge* had cleared the decks for action and had her 21-centimeter cannons in readiness. The first vague shadows that appeared in the harbor opening had been attacked immediately, but the heavy fog blanket prevented definite aim. A second later, the fog hid the opposing forces from each other. Aboard the *Norge* they realized that several enemy ships had already entered the harbor. One of these was next sighted alongside the steamship pier. The *Norge* opened fire but was hit herself by German torpedoes coming in from all directions. She sank within twenty seconds.

The Railroad Station reported that two trains had left for Sweden early in the morning, but the line had been disrupted. The ferries still operated. From both sides of the Narvik peninsula people were trying to get out of town.

Now the members of the City Council began to appear. We sat down at the long table with the green cover. Few words were spoken. The faces were ashen gray. We realized that something terrible had happened. We understood and yet could not understand. The military must have some information. We had better wait.

A sudden noise came from the staircase. There were calls for the Chief of Police and myself. We were to be escorted to the German Headquarters. The Chief of Police entered the room and we left together. At the main entrance German soldiers stood waiting for us. They were ridiculously erect. We were to come to the Grand Hotel.

— Why exactly to the Grand? — I thought.

The lobby was filled with German officers, most of them young. Consul Wusof steamed about, busy as a bee, his hands full of documents. He took time to explain to us that the General would soon arrive and that it would be his pleasure to introduce us to Lieutenant-General Edward Dietl.

"This is a very extraordinary situation, Mr. Mayor. The events took even me by complete surprise."

The Consul beamed an exalted smile and waved his documents.

— Then you have been exceedingly fast on your typewriter, you devil, — I thought, but we only sat down to wait.

Soon the General arrived in a taxi. Everybody stiffened a bit more. We were presented to him, and the General began to talk. He was tall, with a narrow, sharp

face and a slight stoop. A lieutenant tried to attract his attention; he had a Norwegian at his back.

"What is it?"

"It's only the cab driver who says the General did not pay his fare. We haven't got small Norwegian change, Herr General."

"Scandalous!"

The General was extremely apologetic for this oversight. The Chief of Police and I exchanged glances. They had murdered our navy boys in the harbor and had occupied our town, and now they apologized because they lacked change.

"Only an oversight, Herr Mayor."

We nodded.

The General was politeness itself.

"Let us hope we shall have more time later. We have just arrived. I want to make it clear from the start that we have come as friends, to protect your country against any further British breaks of your neutrality. The German *Wehrmacht* has taken over the protection of Oslo, Bergen, and Trondheim. We have encountered no armed resistance anywhere."

"But our navy men in the harbor?"

"Sad, isn't it?"

We did not answer.

"I can assure you, gentlemen, that we do not wish any bloodshed. I am happy to inform you that Norway is now occupied peacefully in the name of *Der Führer.*"

I looked towards the Chief of Police. He shrugged his shoulders in dismay, indicating that I should answer.

"We are not prepared to discuss the destiny of our nation with the General. Perhaps we should limit ourselves to our own town here?"

"Well, your Colonel showed good sense in not offering any resistance. He surrendered the city to me. As Commander in Chief of the occupation troops I am now in charge. I wish, however, to make it clear that the Civil Administration must continue as heretofore, at least insofar as it is in keeping with military expediency. We need a certain control of communications, and, for their own protection, the populace must be indoors at 8 P.M. That should be all. No, not quite, my troops need some shaving cream and similar articles. You must inform the local business people that they must accept German currency. To simplify matters, we have printed special reichsmarks. They are worth, let me see —"

The General examined some documents brought to him by his adjutant.

"Here it is. One reichsmark equals one krone and sixty öre. I think this will do for the present. I will be happy to see the gentlemen at a later occasion."

The General made a bow and turned to his staff. We were made to understand that we might go.

At the City Hall the officials were expecting us, Colonel Sundlo among them. No words seemed to have been uttered.

I told what I knew and reported on my conference with the German General. First we must try to get an idea of where we stood and then concentrate on the tasks nearest at hand.

Colonel Sundlo had better give his explanation first. The Colonel was calm and impassive.

— He could say only that he had been taken completely by surprise when the attack came and that he had found it useless to resist after the Norwegian warships had been sunk. He had from three to four hundred men ashore. The Germans were said to have ten thousand. —

— Had he contacted his superiors? —

— Yes, in the midst of the attack he had talked by telephone with the Headquarters at Harstad. —

— Had he received power to surrender the town? —

— Yes. Well—one might say that that question had been left somewhat at his own discretion. He wished to add, on his own behalf, that it seemed that the Norwegian military authorities did not completely understand the situation. —

— But what of the rest of the country? —

— It would appear that the leading cities in the southern part of the country had been taken. It was hopeless to resist. —

I begged my colleagues not to discuss that problem. We could not control the national destiny. We must limit ourselves to the pressing duties at Narvik.

Perhaps it would be best to have as many people as possible evacuate. In any case, the city authorities would have to take over the food administration. Many things might still happen.

Not much was said. Some further bits of information were reported. Mr. Toft, who recently had been made

head of the Ofoten Railroad, announced that they had managed to send out an extra train after the early morning express had left for Sweden. It had been packed with hundreds of civilians who lived in the vicinity of the railroad, but it had been stopped at Hundalen Station, since the Nordal viaduct was out of order. All evacuees would have to go by sea routes.

We decided upon an evacuation of as many civilians as possible. To avoid the risk of an unplanned flight Director Hoel of the Iron Company, the Chief of Police, and I were asked to prepare an appeal to the citizens. The city would also gather complete information on the food stores left in town. Hoarding must be prevented.

Later the same day, I was given an opportunity to make a statement over the local radio station. I explained that the railroad was not operating, but that boats might be used. Everyone must remain as calm as possible and not take too much luggage along. I wanted to add more but was cut off by the German censor.

Between one and two thousand citizens left town the first day, but it was impossible to carry out any detailed plan. There was no panic, but people left in complete uncertainty. We had no information as to what localities the Germans might declare forbidden zones. We feared for the northern district, since two German destroyers had gone in that direction at early dawn.

North of the city are two fjord arms. The ocean goes in to Rombakken in a long thin arm where the mountains stand almost vertically above unpopulated fjord shores. To the west of the Øyjord peninsula the

Herjangen fjord opens to a broad bosom. The inner fjord has forests and open fields. Here Bjerkvik lies, a friendly little village with a church and a large new school building. Three or four miles up in the valley lies Elvegårdsmoen, the military training camp. Hundreds of families left for Øyjordtangen. We received news that the summer cottages there were crowded and that transportation difficulties beyond that point were great. German troops were marching north. We got a telephone call through to Bjerkvik but the youthful telephone operator was confounded and did not know what to say.

The City Council room became a kind of headquarters. We sat at the long table and received reports.

The boats with evacuees had not returned. That was the first sign. There were free districts where our people began to make free decisions.

Oslo Radio announced that Quisling had been made Prime Minister, that all was quiet, and that we must cooperate with the Germans. The King and the Government had fled.

A round little woman came rolling in, completely out of breath.

— The German soldiers were buying up all the chocolate in her store and they paid only in funny little paper money. What was she to do? —

— There was nothing to do about it. But she might conceal the best chocolate. Sell candy in small bags. —

— Yes, but the money? —

— That's German money which the banks are compelled to exchange. —

128

The Head Surgeon on the phone: "Where shall we bury our dead?"

The merchants called. They could not ration food without regulations and cards. There must be law and rules. They had old customers who wished to buy.

— Calm down. Sell as little as possible. We will print cards. —

And the bakers called.

— The Germans are devouring all the pastry. —

— Let them eat. But don't bake any more. —

— Did the Mayor know where to get a pair of pants for a navy cook who had been blown ashore in his underwear? —

Odd calls.

"This is the Commerce Bank calling. Does the City not need more cash?"

"Yes, but wasn't a man from the City Treasurer's Office just in to get money?"

"True enough, but don't you want more? The money is being exchanged pretty fast."

"Of course. Thank you for calling. We will send for more immediately."

The citizens had heard they should not believe Oslo Radio. The Germans had taken over the station.

"Tromsö Station says we are at war."

The messenger boy we had sent to Øyjord returned.

"I took a row boat across," he reported. "The Germans had taken the ferry. People out there don't know what to do. The highway to the north is closed. The military camp at Elvegård is taken."

The man with the radio news came back.

"I got Stockholm. They announce that all leading harbor cities in Norway have been conquered and that there is confusion throughout the country. But Tromsö says that there was an all-night battle in Oslofjord and that the Capital was conquered from the air. Also that the King and the Government escaped and have ordered general mobilization."

— What shall we do with Øyjord? —

— Widow Johansen on Street 2 refuses to ration. —

— Evacuees are fleeing along the railroad tracks, but we have heard shooting from that direction. Shall we try to stop them? —

— Karlsen is drunk again and fought with a German soldier. They dragged him away. There are other drunks, too. —

— The Hospital has issued an emergency call for trucks. The cellar is full of corpses. But Commander Askim is pulling through. —

— The Germans have taken all trucks. —

For a while it appeared to be almost hopeless to try to put order into the chaos the men of the New Order had created. Then a few of us moved to an inner private office. We posted a sentinel at the door. All the errand boys in town were used as special official messengers. Our orders were in writing and signed.

The Liquor Store must be closed.

Disloyal merchants will have their stores confiscated.

Placards were posted announcing that advice on evacuation could be had at the City Hall. Admittedly we had

no other advice to give than to take things calmly till we could get more information.

People were sent to Øyjord carrying written powers of attorney.

The northern territory was banned, including both the railway to Sweden and the highway to Bjerkvik.

— Calm down. —

The day was a nightmare of activity and we thanked God for that.

How could it have happened? There was no time to contemplate and consider.

Norway was at war. In northern Norway a cannon had never been fired at a human target. But we were about to learn the lesson of war to the last bitter detail.

IX — THE BRITISH COME

W E SLEPT like logs that night and were still dazed when we were awakened by the first cannon shots the next morning. They came at the same hour as on the day before with the same heavy detonations. Again we heard Siri's tripping feet, this time before we were out of bed.

"Isn't it Christmas today either?"

"No, it is war."

"Is war nice?"

— No, war was not nice, but it was undeniably exciting. —

When we drew the curtains from the windows we saw fiery tongues all over the harbor. The clouds hung low but the fog was not quite as thick as on the previous day. Thunder came from the fjord and the harbor replied.

"Who is firing out there now?"

"I don't know. Whoever it is, they are friends, and their aim is excellent."

We saw direct hits on several of the ships in the harbor. The flames were so intense that the metal itself seemed to be burning.

Shells rained upon the harbor and debris from the mail pier sailed through the air and whistled above our home. For, a time we had to flee into the basement. It was a bit cold down there and we were in night clothes. I ran upstairs for some heavier clothing, but was fascinated by the sight from the windows. One of the German destroyers was afire from stem to stern. Its engines were still operating but it circled aimlessly without direction or plan.

From the basement, "Aren't you coming back? Siri is cold."

"I must see this. Our protectors are burning in the harbor."

"They won't stop burning if you bring our clothes."

But, after I had delivered the clothes and returned upstairs, there was nothing to be seen but smoky fog. The cannonading was withdrawing to the outer fjord. It lasted for hours. Even in the late forenoon, after we had started office work again in the City Hall, we could hear violent explosions from the outer fjord. But this time we knew what was happening.

The first of the wounded had told the story at the Hospital. British destroyers had entered the harbor opening before the Germans had discovered them. This time the British had let go first. The leader of the German destroyers was blown up and a Commodore Bonte had been killed. Wounded Germans had talked of his

loss as a terrible catastrophe, revealing that Mr. Bonte must have been of considerable importance.

This welcome news, however, did not greatly change the situation in the town. The people insisted on leaving. Most of the rowboats disappeared during the forenoon. Families in sports dress and with knapsacks could be seen everywhere going toward the water front and to the north of town. We were somewhat worried about this impromptu evacuation.

It might prove difficult for small boats to get through to the unoccupied territories. Now even the south side, called Ankenesstrand, had been taken over by the Germans, who had also confiscated the ferries.

We had to try to put the brakes on the evacuation. Panic must be prevented. We at the City Hall told the people that we had wives and children ourselves and that they would be among the last to go.

At the City Hall things began to move in a fairly orderly fashion. The Rationing Board worked under heavy pressure. Ration cards had been printed and the amounts fixed. The system was so devised that any further reductions which might become necessary could be effected without printing new cards. We had enough flour and canned goods. There were huge stores of fish waiting to be exported to Germany. Now the customers had put in a personal appearance. We lacked ice, however, and had to salt the fish. The result was not all that could be desired, even though the fish did taste better than it smelled. We were all to have salt fish for dinner every day during the two months of war to come.

Many committees were organized. A widow enlisted the aid of a group of young girls and organized a soup kitchen. Any one could eat there if he showed a reasonable need and secured a ticket book at the City Hall. Money was no issue, but there must be order.

From the Hospital came an emergency call for extra help and trucks. The dead were now lying way up into the cellar stairs.

"We do not have sufficient trucks."

"Make the Germans haul them away."

"They are their corpses anyway. Incidentally, we now know who Commodore Bonte was. The German surgeons here say he was their Supreme Naval Commander. He and his whole staff were blown to kingdom come this morning. They had ten destroyers when they arrived yesterday. Looks as though half of them are more or less destroyed already."

"Excellent. We will confer with the Germans about the dead ones."

Our own Red Cross had more than enough with its own. A complete reorganization had been necessary. The excellent ladies who had sewed and knitted and drunk coffee for the benefit of the cause through the years were of little help now. We needed young boys who would always be ready to go to work. The ladies shown on the Red Cross posters in white aprons, with little morphine syringes, would do no longer. Instead, we needed young fellows who were willing to go out when shots were fired and who knew how to use shovels and tarpaulins.

The new Red Cross Corps was organized into emergency patrols and a First Aid Station was equipped in an auditorium in the City Hall. Arne and Finn, two boys just out of trade school, became patrol leaders, and Deacon Njöten, the church sexton, supervised the First Aid Station. He was a quiet little man with a half-moon, reddish, innocent face. He had married a mighty and broad-bosomed school teacher and had never made any attempt to set the world on fire, but he was going to prove himself one of the most valuable men in town during the weeks to come.

Germans called frequently at the City Hall. They wanted the keys to the Prayer House, the Public Schools, and other institutions which they had requisitioned for quarters and military hospitals. They did not like to break into these buildings, they said.

We called upon the teachers in the high schools to serve as interpreters and we tried to get as much as possible in writing. It perhaps made little difference just how the Germans stole our property, but we felt that we should have some kind of form for the transactions. Also, we had to prevent panic, and we thought that the use of written documents might help bolster our self-respect in the face of the German lawlessness.

We knew that the Germans preferred to act through the Norwegian authorities. But, if they imagined that they could make us appear to be sharing their responsibility, they were badly mistaken. We made it a point to see that our citizens fully understood the true situation. Now we benefited to the full from the open-door

politics of a free people. We had no leaders but those who had been entrusted with power by the people.

The Germans had already posted placards in Norwegian text. The sentence construction was somewhat awkward and strange, but the contents were clear enough. The German *Wehrmacht* had come to protect us and would defend our land and people against all attacks, while we on our side would be shot as traitors if we attempted to do the same thing.

As things developed the German *Wehrmacht* did not have much time to spend on us the first few days.

"The first British attack has been victoriously repulsed, but it is not beyond the cowardly British to return," a strutting little German orderly confided to us. He was kept constantly running back and forth between the two hotels and the City Hall with requisitions and announcements. We called him *Sauerkraut*. We understood that the Germans were waiting for "the cowardly British." They kept up an incessant transport of heavy logs and rails out to Framnes peninsula and to the shores beyond.

At Kittenshill the neighborhood became so unattractive that we loaded bedding and jam jars on a sled and moved downtown. Siri thought it great fun to go on a picnic so early in the spring. But, when we told her that it might be sometime before we could return, she insisted on taking old Trine along. She wanted to bring all the toy animals from under the bed but finally limited herself to the ice bear called Truls. It would be too cold for the rest of the zoo.

From then on we stayed in three different places as the city was gradually evacuated, district by district. Most of the time we slept on the floor in the sitting room in a teacher's house. We did not think it wise to sleep on the second floor if there should be more shooting from the sea. The teacher and his wife slept in the dining room.

The day we moved into town an old railroad employe came to visit me. He was secretive and we went into a room where we could be alone. He told me that his telephone line did not pass through the Telephone Building, where the Germans had twenty-four-hour tapping service. He had access to a direct railroad telephone line which reached to the first station on the other side of the Swedish border. We went to his home and made immediate connection with the border village of Riksgrensen in Sweden. I got a Swedish officer on the line. We were both highly excited. I gave all the information I had.

— No, the Germans had no airplanes or heavy artillery. They numbered no more than five thousand men. —

He promised to try to get the information through to the Norwegian Government. We made a date for a later call, but, alas, the Germans had listening posts established throughout the whole line the next day.

Later in the day, we had an air alarm. The new sirens at the Iron Company and the Royal Hotel functioned perfectly, but not many people went into the cellars. It was an Allied air attack. We counted a total of seven planes, two of a peculiar type. Through my open win-

dow I heard some of the survivors from the *Norge* discuss their nationality. They decided the five were British and the two of the different type Norwegian. They seemed strangely outmoded.

There was firing from all directions. It was the first time any of us had seen tracer bullets. Between Fagernes Mountain and the Sleeping Queen the whole sky was filled with streaks of illumination. The airplanes took their time over the harbor. We saw bombs fall, not large but many. They hit the water between the ships. Three or four of the airplanes disappeared behind the mountains, but the rest turned and swooped low. The fire from the German anti-aircraft guns grew more intense. One of the old-fashioned planes kept swinging madly over one of the ships at anchor, like an angry old bird that refused to give up. Several bombs swirled around in the air. The sailor boys outside my window insisted they were cans like those used for meat balls on board their own ship.

"Do you believe that our people are making use of empty cans for homemade bombs?" I asked, as we heard one of the "bombs" land with a terrific noise directly on the deck of one of the ships.

"Good Lord, man, the meat balls must still have been inside," the sailor exclaimed.

Sadly enough, it was not one of the destroyers that was hit, but a Norwegian coast guard vessel on which the Germans had hoisted the Swastika since they had taken her over. All planes escaped to safety across the mountains. We breathed with relief.

The same day the Tromsö Radio Station broadcast an evacuation appeal to the populace of Narvik. New skirmishes might be expected at any moment, they warned. Now our people demanded that we take immediate action. If they were destined to lose their lives, it should not be by Norwegian meat balls and cooped up in a town with Germans and rotten fish.

There was nothing for it but to try our luck. I brought along the Chief of Police and a high school teacher whose special field was the German language. The others of us knew German, even though we did not speak it to perfection. We got an audience with General Dietl, who introduced us to his Adjutant, *Korvettenkapitän* Reichmann, a stunning, polite man with an ironhard face. His heels clicked like a pistol shot. We voiced our case and explained that there were still thousands of women and children left in town, that we were facing a shortage of food, and that it could not be in the interest of the Germans to detain them if there was to be more fighting for possession of the city.

"The British have already sustained one defeat. It is not likely they will return for another."

"But our citizens want to leave."

"We won't stand for any panic, gentlemen."

"There is no panic, but the people want to bring their families out into safety."

"They are safe here." The General turned his back.

"But —"

"The General has no more to say. Sorry, gentlemen, the General is exceedingly busy." *Korvettenkapitän*

Reichmann politely saw us to the door. He clicked his heels.

On our return from the Royal Hotel we were met by a crowd which had gathered in front of the City Hall. They saw us come and opened a way for us toward the stone balustrade. I turned and faced the questioning eyes and made some sort of a speech.

— We had done our utmost. The Germans refused to let anybody evacuate. We had to face things as they came. We must prove ourselves Norwegians and not behave like a flock of frightened chickens. Should there be any food shortage, we would starve together. —

Later in the evening I was called back to General Dietl at the Royal Hotel. He occupied the room which Consul Gibbs had lived in only a few days earlier. Captain Reichmann was again present. The General looked up from the maps spread before him.

"You have a nice city here, Mr. Mayor," he said.

"We used to like it," I answered.

"And what magnificent mountains! Beautiful Nature, excellent skiing terrain. Better than on the Swedish side. I once vacationed at Abisko, only fifteen miles across the border."

"The General wishes to confer with the Mayor about the conditions for the publication of a newspaper," Captain Reichmann interrupted.

"That is correct. I regret that I could not grant your request this morning, but we wish life to continue as normally as possible. Your people must return to work."

141

"The General means the ore export?"

"Well, that will begin again in good time. But all other work."

"The railroad and the ore export are the mainstay of our employment."

"You can fish."

"We have no boats."

"You can fish from the shores."

Herr Reichmann again interrupted.

"Herr General wants to say that all work must be started again insofar as the military operations will permit. This must be announced in a newspaper which you will be permitted to publish. All copy must be approved before you go to press."

"And we must encourage people to fish from the shores?"

"We will return to the details in proper time." The Captain was stiff.

The General was lost over his maps.

Captain Reichmann invited me to his private room.

General Dietl looked up.

"We will become friends, Mr. Mayor, later," he said, "when we learn to know each other better."

He spoke as though he were announcing an item fairly far down in the program, an item that might some day be of interest.

We left. It was the last time I saw him.

Captain Reichmann did his best to be friendly.

"You somehow have not complete confidence in us, have you, Mr. Mayor?" he said.

"We *are* enemies," I answered.

His face turned hard and white.

"Do you still listen to the English?"

"We listen to the Norwegian Government."

"There is no longer a Norwegian Government."

"We think there is."

"Do you think we can become friends on that basis?"

"I never said so."

"Your attitude will be changed. Do not our soldiers behave well?"

"You mean the first morning?"

"You know perfectly well what I mean. Have we looted anything in the town? Don't we pay for all we get?"

"Yes, with occupation currency."

"What's wrong with that, don't your banks have orders to exchange it?"

"And what are the banks going to do with it?"

"That will be taken care of in the final settlement. We will see to it that England pays. They started this war. You shall see that we are one day going to make England pay even you."

"The war is not over yet."

"It won't last many weeks now."

I rose.

"You mentioned we could publish a newspaper. What are the conditions?"

"No conditions, but we must see all copy."

"I will confer with our newspaper men and you will hear from us tomorrow."

The following day we had our manuscript finished. Part of it consisted of rules for rationing and part of it of appeals for unified sacrifice and co-operation, all held in a fairly general tone. We had attempted to use words with a double meaning, and hidden appeals were made in some places. Alas, most of the first ones were discovered and deleted. The Germans had good interpreters. I met two of them, Corporal Wiedener, who spoke excellent Danish, and a private who spoke Norwegian with an East Norwegian accent. The private was exceptionally slimy. It seemed to be of the utmost importance to him to show his friendliness. We did not return it. He had evidently received his share of Norwegian kindness already. From his accent we knew quite accurately where in our land he had been enjoying Norwegian hospitality as a "Vienna-child" after the last war.

The newspaper which finally resulted did not make too good reading, but it might perhaps do some good. It did not carry much news; but, on the other hand, it was not humiliating. It had a Norwegian profile and it was going to be the last Norwegian newspaper printed in Narvik.

But the citizens received accurate news as well. At the moment when Captain Reichmann was busying himself at the Grand Hotel with proofreading, typewritten radio news bulletins were circulating all over town. Fat little Instructor Tanke was the editor and publisher. His work was surrounded with the utmost secrecy and was painstakingly correct.

Now, at long last, we began to get a full and correct picture of what had happened on the war front in southern Norway. The Germans had already been made to pay severely. The first day a number of German warships had been sunk, among them the cruiser *Blücher* with the entire Gestapo force destined for the Norwegian scene. Thousand of corpses had been floating in Oslofjord.

Long after the fighting had begun the German ultimatum had been presented to the Norwegian Government.

— We must place our entire coast line at the disposal of Germany. We must surrender our airfields and our communications. The fortifications must be delivered intact. We must give up our merchant fleet and break all contact with the Western Powers as well as with the American continent. —

Together with this ultimatum the German Minister had delivered a personal message from Hitler to our King, "whom he highly respected." He wished the Norwegian King would appoint a more "co-operative" cabinet under the leadership of Major Quisling.

We heard that none of these demands had been given a moment's consideration. We heard of the courageous stand taken by the King and the Government and how the Norwegian Storting had met in the midst of the violent war zones and had authorized the King to continue the war, how other German diplomats in Oslo, at a moment when the diplomatic conferences were still in session, had led advance attack patrols north along the

highways with the intent of taking the King and the Government prisoners, and how the new Commander in Chief, General Ruge, with a band of fresh minutemen, had stopped them a few miles south of Elverum. His men were in the main farmers and lumberjacks who had volunteered the moment they heard of the German sneak attack.

We heard how Hitler had followed up his "respect" message to our King by having his bombers hunt him from place to place through Trysil before the Norwegian mobilization had become effective.

We could now follow the progress of the war. Front upon front became established. After three days there were six front lines. The King and the Government were still in mortal danger. Our boys fought in the forests, they fought in the mountains, they were giving their lives for the hard, beautiful land which we called ours. But they made the Germans pay dearly.

I can still see the faces of our young boys when they came stealing up the back stairs in the City Hall to read the news bulletins. They did not say very much. Their faces were emotionless, but their eyes spoke. They were like a scream or a prayer: *Weapons!*

X — THUNDER IN THE FJORD

WE DID not hear much about our own front up here. The naval battle of April tenth was already an old story. Via Swedish radio we heard that three of the British destroyers had been sunk, *Hardy*, *Hunter*, and *Hotspur*, but that two remaining had escaped. There were thus five Britishers to the ten in the German flotilla. The German victory did not seem too overwhelming.

But the radio did not mention the fighting in the mountains near the Swedish border at Björnefjell. A skier had brought in news about the fighting in that sector. It was evident that our local boys had not yet been able to establish contact with the other Norwegian forces. We were the forgotten war front.

The same evening German Headquarters asked for a copy of the City Roster. The protectors wanted a complete list of their protegees.

The following morning, Saturday, the 13th of April, came the first week end of the war. It was destined to

become Our Day. Our front sector was, after all, not forgotten or neglected. In the forenoon we heard the King broadcast a strong personal appeal to all Norwegians. He could not reveal where he was, but he was with the Crown Prince and the Government. They had all escaped a murderous bombing attack. He had seen defenseless cities bombed by the Germans. He encouraged his people to continue resistance and to fight.

Early in the afternoon we heard heavy gunfire again from the outer fjord, increasing in violence. The German-occupied sectors of the town were evacuated and the Alpines marched out toward the north side. Troops were left behind to defend the harbor and to hold the Telegraph Office.

A young fellow came running from the direction of Framnes. It was my friend Oscar.

The Germans had chased him away from the sea view, but he had seen the whole fjord swarming with ships. The whole British fleet must be there. Among them was a colossus of a warship.

I thanked him. "Now we are getting some real benefit of your curiosity," I said. "Call again."

No German orderlies with requisitions appeared on that day. It was hard to buckle down to work. We were tense and watchful. We could not see much of what was taking place in the fjord, but we did hear that the center of the fighting was moving closer. Some shells flew in over the harbor, and several struck in the city proper. We stood at the windows. We ran through the streets. We hid behind the corners when we heard the shell

splinters whine through the air. Women and children were placed in the comparative safety of the cellars and basements. An underpass was under construction beneath the Iron Ore Company. It was only partly completed and the raw-cut cliff walls lacked their concrete finish. Water was continuously streaming down the walls, and the floor was only loose planks. But it was said to be bombproof and, it could accommodate one thousand people. That day it became very popular.

There was also an excellent basement underneath the Fire Station behind the City Hall. A double shift was kept working there, day and night. We dug two cellars, one under the other. They were strengthened by pillars and equipped with lights and benches.

For those of us, however, who had any kind of excuse for staying up in the daylight world it was impossible to remain quiet. We were burning with impatience. Our destiny was being decided in the fjord. The shooting seemed never to come to an end. Oftentimes the blasts made one continuous sound effect. Then quiet reigned again. We could distinguish the heavy shots; these must come from the largest guns. The mountains hurled the sound like a ball back and forth among themselves. Once we counted the echoes up to seven.

We felt like the princess in the fairy tale about whom the princes were fighting. We felt the joy and the pride when the white prince rode in with victory and also the humility of being only a passive prize. The horrifying inactivity of it all!

We heard a deafening explosion from the harbor,

even though the thunderous cannonading itself was drawing northward. The deserted streets were again filled with people. We saw German soldiers come from Framnes forest on the opposite side of Hospital Hill. They were wet and weak. Many had thrown away their weapons. And we acknowledged for the first time a strange peculiarity of the human mind, a psychological reaction which many of us were to be given a chance to experience. After mortal danger the reaction takes the form of a psychic intoxication. Now we witnessed how the stone-like stares of the stiff German sailors were transformed into half-delirious laughter and smiles. Many of them went through the streets, arm in arm, singing. They stopped to chat with us. We were told that it was a British battleship which was out there on the warpath together with other British craft. The German squadron was at this moment engaged in a death struggle inside the narrow Rombaksfjord to the north.

When we told them that their number was up, they only smiled forlorn smiles and muttered *"Kamerad."* They were certainly no longer the *blitz* men. They looked rather like half-drowned cats nestling close to one another in order to keep warm. Nor were they any longer condescending in their attitude towards their "racial brethren" who had been so tragically led astray by the decadent democracies. Now they wished to be accepted because they were human beings like us and because it was good to be alive. They had lost their contact with their officers and their morale was gone.

Bands of beaten Germans continued to drift through

town and up Fagernes Mountain. Laboriously they
trampled a path for themselves, zigzagging their way
up the steep slope. Their dark rows stood against the
snow wall like curving snakes.

An old woman came down the hill with her mattress
on a sled. She owned a little cabin up on the ridge, but
now it was packed with Germans. She told us that they
had asked about the way to Sweden and that she had
pointed skywards. They could march endlessly in the
mountains before they discovered that there was no way
leading through.

There was not much life in our streets any more. It
was limited mainly to the German sentinels and an occasional truck with corpses under tarpaulins. The dead
came from the sea. Our own Red Cross patrols were
kept busy. There were as yet not many wounded among
the civilians. In emergencies our Red Cross workers
gave a hand to the enemy.

Even though I belonged only to the Red Cross reserve
I felt an urge to see things for myself. In any case,
observation might offer some relief from the nerve-
wracking impatience which burned us all. I put the Red
Cross band on my arm and went to the piers. Perhaps
there might still be some wounded there. At intervals
shells still burst in that vicinity.

In the street above the pier I found the doors of the
Seamen's Home standing open. All the rooms were
filled with bedding and German uniforms and articles.
On the tables were the remains of meals, but there was
not a living being in the entire building. It had been

used as a barracks by the invaders, and they must have left in great haste. On the shelf above one of the beds lay a diary and a pile of snapshots. I put them in my pocket and left the building.

The harbor itself was a ship graveyard with wreckage wherever one looked. Flocks of frightened sea gulls screamed in the air. Occasionally they dove hurriedly into the waters to nip at some of the strange objects that floated in the oily sea. The pier itself was a tragic sight. The new cold storage vault that we had built was gone except for some falling brick walls. The installation of the heavy machinery had never been completed. We had planned the dedication for the last days of April. The creamery on the other side of the square had also been hit. One wall had a gaping hole and all the windows were blown out, but the building itself might perhaps be repaired. The piers looked hopeless. The wooden planks of the old pier had been blasted away. The wooden pillars projected from the water like so many stumped teeth. The new pier was torn apart. The huge concrete block at the end had been cut in two as by a huge axe. Everywhere were strewn bits of wreckage. Parts from ships were thrown ashore among timber, logs, and cleft rocks. Whole parts of warships lay in silent testimony to the terrific force of naval artillery fire.

It was the strangest sight I had ever witnessed. I felt as though I were walking around the playground of a huge monster who had suddenly tired of his toys. The whole inside of a warship seemed strewn around. It was

like a gigantic jigsaw puzzle which had been left unfinished. One could, however, somehow guess that, if the parts were brought logically together again, they would make up a warship or, more accurately, one of those German destroyers which had brought to Narvik the chaos of the New Order. How these pieces had been clipped off and thrown around between our piers was a riddle that baffled me.

But we had long since stopped our wondering. Life had become very strange during these latter days. I know, however, that I should have been greatly surprised, if someone at that moment had told me that I was going to have the riddle solved a year and a half later, in the peaceful little town of Beloit, Wisconsin, and that I would find it in a book written by a German officer who even at that moment was watching my aimless wanderings along the destroyed pier. And yet it was thus that I got the explanation. One of the ten destroyer commanders, *Korvettenkapitän* Fritz Otto Busch was going to write a thick volume full of Nazi romanticism about the exploit: *Narvik - vom Heldenkampf deutscher Zerstörer.* And he was to send a copy to relatives in the United States from whom a Norwegian-American friend had borrowed it.

The solution itself was fantastic enough. It really was true that the broken mosaic by the pier that afternoon was made up of parts from one of the ten destroyers. She had been the last in line of the German squadron, and they themselves had called her "The Tactical No. 10." She had been mortally wounded in the harbor

battle of April tenth and had not been able to participate in the death struggle this fateful Saturday. When the naval battle began in the outer fjord she had been left deserted and tied to the pier. All things removable had been brought ashore and her crew and officers had taken up their position in the railroad tunnel above the pier. The destroyer had been changed into a huge floating mine loaded with depth charges ready to explode.

From the observation point up in the tunnel the Germans had followed the battle outside. They saw a British destroyer enter the harbor. She had obviously been hit during the battle and proceeded at slow speed, listing badly. Cautiously the crew maneuvered her between the wrecked ships till they could beach her in shallow water at Ankenes, to the south of the harbor, in full view of the town. The sea bottom was even there and it was low tide.

Then a second British destroyer entered the harbor. She was in battle trim and looked as though she were hunting more opponents. When she discovered the silent German destroyer along the pier she approached cautiously. A dynamite expert stole down from the tunnel. He started the timing device and escaped to safety. The mine was set for ten minutes. The British destroyer continued its approach. The distance to "The Tactical No. 10" was now only about two hundred yards and grew constantly less. Suddenly a shot burst from a German machine-gun nest planted among the wooden pillars beneath one of the iron-ore piers. The soldiers there had not been informed. The British changed their course

and were out of danger when the German ship exploded.

It was this terrifying explosion that we had heard earlier in the afternoon. As I stood on the shell-torn pier and prayed for telepathic powers to call our allies to land I did not know that one of their ships had already been there, that she had barely escaped a death trap, and that she had left again since she did not carry invasion troops.

I kept watch of the beached British destroyer across the harbor, not more than a mile or so away. She was not so badly damaged that she could not fire and she kept sending shells against the German machine-gun nest beneath the ore pier. I could see the propellers whip the water and I hoped each moment that she might get off again.

I might be running the risk of having the people over there take me for a German, so I kept the arm band with the cross turned towards the sea.

At last I tired of standing at the pier and turned to walk towards the shell-torn warehouses. Turning a corner, I ran into a German lieutenant. He had a revolver in his hand. His face was tense, his jaw jutted forward.

"I had you at dead aim all the time," he said. "If you had attempted to contact the gentlemen across the water, you would have been a dead man. I can assure you of one thing, and that is that your friends the British will never come!"

I shrugged my shoulders and went into town. I met one of our Red Cross cars in Street 1. It was packed with boys of the Fire Brigade, most of whom also func-

tioned as Red Cross helpers. The car they were using
had been put at their disposal by the Iron Ore Director.
It had been an elegant old automobile, with tasseled curtains at the windows; but, since it had been given hard
usage by our Red Cross after the war began, it was pretty badly battered. We drove around town for a while.
The city itself was deadly quiet. The cannon thunder
from the fjord had stopped. Off and on an explosion
came from the direction of Rombaksfjord.

As we drove past the Market Place we saw the Swastika still flying from the Telegraph Building. An idea
struck me. The German service chief was still on duty,
compelling Norwegian operators to make telegraph and
telephone connections.

It might prove helpful if it did not function too
well at this particular time. This was the only central
office and so far as we had been able to learn all the
German communication lines passed through it. It
might at least do no harm to create a little extra confusion. Something must develop very shortly. The way
had been blasted open for our allies.

We stopped and entered. Corporal Wiedener received us with a smile and his best Danish. He was obviously nervous. I made my face somber as a swastika and
assured him that the game was up. The city was once
more Norwegian. We were expecting the British in town
at any moment. They were already disembarking.

He was not feeling too good.

I continued.

— The German troops had fled the town. He could

see for himself through the windows that not a dog was left in the streets. —

The Corporal in his shocked fear dropped into the German: "Ach, but I am not a combatant, I am a telephone watchman."

"But you carry weapons."

He delivered his pistol, clicked his heels, and declared himself to be my personal prisoner.

I clicked my own heels a little to make it official. But I am afraid I scratched my head in a rather unmilitary fashion. What was I going to do with the poor devil? When I just asked him to disappear, the Corporal regained his dignity to a considerable extent and asked for a receipt for his pistol.

I became brusque once more and tried to look as mad as a colonel at morning parade.

— What? Did he not know the simplest war rules? Baggage checks are not issued in such instances! —

He left.

But I had to disappoint the Norwegian telephone operators by telling them that I had not told the gospel truth. Our troops were not yet in town. It was high time we were all off. The Germans might wish to continue the use of the station until the last minute and it would be best if there were no one to assist them.

"But there are more sentinels in the basement!"

"Oh! That's bad!" I said. Perhaps I had let myself in for something.

But even they let themselves be bluffed. They refused, however, to give up their weapons.

— Well, they could take their weapons along and march off. —

And off they went. We saw them march up towards the mountain. They had not gone far, however, before they met another group descending. They stopped. Then they all came storming back towards the Telegraph Building. We jumped into the car and drove off. They fired at us. The right window was smashed, but we escaped. The dignified old car cut the corners so fast that the curtains flew.

At the City Hall we waited deep into the night for the counter invasion. Reports kept coming in, but the invasion did not materialize. The electric lights went out. The power station in Rombakken had evidently been hit. We lit candles and continued with our work.

Two boys had watched the last phase of the battle in Rombaksfjord and brought in a report.

— Four German destroyers had been driven in there. One of them had laid itself crosswise, thus blocking the whole fjord, while the three had gone in to the foot where they had beached the ships and saved the crews.

— The blocking destroyer had fought to the end. She was laid in a narrow passage and the British were prevented from getting by as only one boat could pass through. The huge battleship that we had seen in the fjord had obviously been unable to get at them. Only the smaller British craft could get within shooting range. The first one which had attempted to force passage had her whole front shot off, but had continued to fight further inside the fjord. Then several British had forced

158

the blockade, and the Germans had been blasted beautifully by the British broadsides. Finally, the last German had been beached, whereupon the Germans blew up
all their own ships. —

"That was four. But they were ten when they arrived.
Let's do some arithmetic."

"Two were sunk in the harbor on April tenth, during
the first British attack, and several were hit. One of
them capsized at the pier the next morning. That was
the ship of big boss Bonte himself! That makes three in
the first battle. And today's harvest was four in Rombakken and another sank outside Framnes," said the
boy from Beidsfjord. "And we saw one go into Herjangen that went smack bang ashore on the rocks and
blew to bits."

"That makes it minus six as of today."

And I myself had seen the remains of one of the destroyers down on the piers this afternoon.

"That's minus seven today and minus three before.
That makes a perfect score!"

We sang *Tipperary*. That was the only English song
we knew by heart except for *My Wild Irish Rose*, which
did not seem to fit the occasion. We felt an urge to voice
our enthusiasm for the British.

What was going to happen next? We discussed all
the possibilities. At intervals we went out into the street
to take a look towards the fjord. The sky was gray and
we could not discover anything.

A fireman and I walked to the Royal Hotel from
where we could see over into Herjangen. We thought

we could see a smoke column on the far side of the fjord. That was all. But the hotel was not deserted as yet. The lobby was full of soldiers. They saw us also. Suddenly we seemed to be surrounded by a whole battalion. One of the men shouted that he was sure this was the fellow who had made Wiedener give up his weapons.

Then gun barrels prodded our backs and we were ordered to turn about. First we were going to be confronted with the Corporal at the Telegraph Office.

— Yes, I was that fellow! —

My companion explained that he had been on duty at the Fire Station all afternoon.

"There were some men with firemen's helmets, but this one was not among them," the Corporal explained with generosity, and they let my companion go.

I asked him to call home and tell them that I would perhaps be detained at my office for the night with the Rationing Board.

When my identity had been established I was marched with a guard to Captain Müller. I kept a reasonable and even pace with the gun barrels. By way of consolation I was informed that Captain Müller was the Chief of Espionage and Military Intelligence. He stayed at the Royal.

The Captain was sleepy and angry, but he placed me under arrest in the most correct form, and I was locked up in one of the rooms on the top floor of the hotel. The door was not locked but a sentinel was stationed outside.

XI — SECTION THIRTY-SIX

FOR the first time I spent a night in the Royal Hotel, which, in a measure, I had been instrumental in getting built. The room was delightful, and it was in no way the fault of the bed that I was unable to sleep.

I had hung my jacket over a chair. Some papers peeped out of one of the pockets, the book and photos I had found in the abandoned German quarters at the Seamen's Home. Even at 2 A.M. there was enough light for reading. The snapshots were of Norwegian soldiers. They must have been taken just before the war. Most likely they had been taken from Norwegian prisoners. But the book was German. It was a diary, half-filled with notes and observations. The German Gothic hand was a little difficult to decipher, but the handwriting was as clear as a pupil's just out of grammar school. DIARY OF KLAUS HERMAN KLAUSHAUSER it read in block letters on the front page. The first entry was dated *April 7, 1940. At high sea.*

From that night's reading I learned that Klaus was a very young man and that, although he was not afraid to fight against the whole world, he preferred to do his fighting on land. He did not reveal directly that he had been seasick on the way north, but his description of the twelve hundred and fifty mile sea voyage from Bremen to Narvik was limited to brief, staccato sentences telling of roaring waves crashing against the deck and the great congestion aboard the destroyer. In addition to crews of two hundred and fifty there were equal numbers of Alpine troops on each ship. Klaus himself appeared to be an Alpine from Steiermark. He made a comparison between the Norwegian landscape and the mountains of his home valley.

The departure from Bremen was mentioned. There had been neither father nor mother nor girls, promising to send him letters. But there had been a parade the evening of April sixth and speeches by the officers. The men had not been told where they were going but they had heard that they were about to have an opportunity to fight for the *Führer* in one of the most daring military expeditions of history.

They had talked among themselves in the hammocks in the narrow corridor of the destroyer about what adventures they were about to experience. Most of them guessed it was to be Scotland. It was not until the eighth of April that they were informed that the expedition was headed for Norway.

"We did not know very much about the country or about the people we were going to visit," Klaus wrote.

But a statement about Norway had been posted on the bulletin board, giving a detailed description, so that they might know everything about the Norwegians before their arrival.

"We learned that the people of Norway were honest and Nordic," he wrote, "and that they never locked their homes. They were slow, like our peasants in Friesland, and suspicious toward foreigners. They had lagged behind in modern progress and did not know anything worth mentioning about war. Also, they had been misled by British propaganda. Therefore, the German soldiers must behave as nicely as possible, especially toward women. We were going to take over Norway in order to protect the land and the people.

"That evening we all had beer, and one of our officers saluted the *Führer*, who had entrusted us with this crusade. We were to protect our racial brethren and bring the New Order to the Land of the Midnight Sun. We all held on to our chairs and roared '*Sieg Heil.*' "

Thus he had ended his writing for that evening.

There were a few pages about Narvik, but young Klaushauser had not been greatly impressed. Narvik! Why, it was only ocean and mountains and a mad people who did not know what was in their best interest.

I put the photos in my pocket and the diary underneath the mattress and tried to get some sleep. The whole thing was so completely ridiculous. We did not understand war and our homes were always unlocked! That was our guilt!

I felt ill, nauseated. Those heavy boots outside the

door somehow trampled on all the things we loved and worked for, on all justice and consideration for others, on all that was noble and beautiful, and on all the dreams of happiness and liberty that we cherished.

Could it be that all we had worked for had been only a passing dream, an escape from reality?

I got up and walked slowly about the room. From the window I could see the gray windswept farms across the fjord. Small, crooked birches stood around the homes. In the shallow soil the trees seemed to have braced themselves against the rocks in order to weather the storms.

No, we could not have done differently. Had we furnished enough weapons, all alone, to stop the demonic machine of Nazi violence from breaking over our homes, there would have been no homes left to defend.

I tried to open the windows to get some fresh air. They were tightly closed and made a noise. The sentinel opened the door and asked what was going on. I went back to bed. The German soldier remained standing in the open door leaning on his gun. He could not be twenty yet. I asked him.

— Eighteen. —

— And how long had he been a soldier? —

— He was a sailor, and his ship had been in the midst of it since last fall when Poland started the war. —

He was eager for conversation. The night had evidently been a little long for him, too.

We talked about everything between heaven and earth. Often his answers were as solemn and memor-

ized as from a confirmant on the church floor. *Der Führer hat es gesagt!* Thus the *Führer* had said.

His view of the world outside Germany could not possibly have been more distorted had he been given an imaginary picture of men on Mars and told they were his neighbors. As for Norway, he obviously thought it was a kind of half-colonized people exploited by international Jewish capitalism.

I told him a little about our country, our social reforms, and our neutrality policy, and asked him whether he thought these things could come from a half-civilized people?

He somehow withdrew, and answered that he had never had opportunity to get much education. Such questions his officer could answer.

His humbleness was genuine. He seemed to find some kind of satisfaction in a relentless self-immolation. And I caught myself admiring this soldier material. To what could one not drive these young men? I had seen the emigrating lemmings up in the mountains, tiny brown creatures that went in closed ranks led by a blind instinct straight through all dangers across rivers and into the sea. And if the waters were too broad for crossing they all drowned instead of turning back.

Now the brown pest had come in a new form. The little animal might be nice enough as an individual with its smooth, young skin, but the herd as a closed phalanx was quite another matter. One hoped it would not become necessary to kill them all off.

But, after all, this was scarcely the right moment to

165

ponder what was to be done with a beaten Germany. At the moment it was she who stood there with the gun in the open door, all powerful, and I who lay defenseless on the bed. And I certainly did not feel arrogant at this particular hour. Yet it seemed contrary to all natural laws that this ignorant enthusiast, this undeveloped youngster with a gun, should have power over me.

At last the chief of Nazi sentinels arrived and I was taken downstairs. They gave me something that was said to be coffee, although it did not bear much resemblance to our breakfast drink of the same name. Mrs. Polly's regime in the Royal Hotel was definitely a thing of the past.

Then I was placed in the lobby to wait for the prosecutor. My sentinel now spoke to me in completely frank comradeship and showed me a picture of his sweetheart in Germany.

The army lawyer was about my own age. I could see that he was not a man with an officer's training. He took down my explanation. I admitted the facts, but said that I had personally believed that the British were about to land. Corporal Wiedener had dressed up his account and reported my behavior as being far more threatening than was actually the case. When the evidence had been concluded the report was taken to the General for disposition.

I sat waiting. This part of the lobby was a kind of smoking room with a fireplace. It also served as a passage to the dining room. A steady stream of officers passed through. I heard them mention the British bat-

tleship *Warspite*. This was evidently the big ship we had seen during the naval engagement in the outer fjord. The destroyer beached on the other side, at Ankenes, seemed to be the *Cossack*, so far as they had heard. She had been refloated at early dawn. They were all more or less excited, even though it did appear that the morale had been re-established during the night, since nothing more had happened. They raged over the brutality of the British. Those *Schwein* had been firing at German sailors who were crawling ashore.

— They, of course, would have waited until the enemy had finished taking their position, — I thought.

When the prosecutor returned he was abrupt and a little nervous. He informed me that the General had found me guilty of violating §36 of the German Military Law having to do with sabotage of communications. Since I was a colleague I might read the law myself.

Section Thirty-Six was not inviting. It carried the death penalty. There was no alternative.

I looked up. The prosecutor smiled grimly.

"I take it you understand," he said.

I nodded.

And then he departed. I remained sitting in the same position. The room was a little chilly and there was a bad draft from the door. I thought the janitor had not made a very good fire this morning.

My guard peeped over my shoulder at the legal papers on the table. There were tears in his eyes as he turned aside.

Only then did I realize that the situation was serious,

even though it all seemed unreal in this well-known setting. The morning sun came through the window, flattering Mrs. Polly's burgundy draperies. The others of us on the building committee had to the last urged a more discreet color, but she had been firm and had shown us the doorman's uniform, already tailored.

Was this, then, really going to be the last day? I hoped it would be over soon. If I could be spared seeing anybody I could stand it. I must not think of those who were left behind. Now there was not much that I could do for them anyhow.

I don't know how long I sat there. In the late forenoon the prosecutor reappeared. He informed me that he had again conferred with the General and with some of the officers. Because of a plea from the City Council it had been proposed that I be pardoned and the General had finally given his consent. I must give my word of honor, however, to report to Captain Müller every day at 12 noon and at 6 P.M.

I promised.

When I returned to the City Hall I found the atmosphere gloomy. My colleagues had heard of my arrest and early in the morning had sent an appeal to the General. They stressed the fact that I spoke German and that I was indispensable to the civil administration.

I asked for a copy of the appeal. It might come in handy on some later occasion.

For the remainder of the forenoon, in spite of its being Sunday, we held an emergency meeting to consider rationing problems. A large part of our stores at the

piers had been destroyed during the naval battle of the previous day and we had to tighten the rations. This, however, did not constitute our only problem.

We still tried to operate on a monetary system but were very short of ready money. The money went only one way, from the buying public to the merchants. The latter did not wish to deposit it in the banks which were already bursting with occupation reichsmarks.

We discussed the possibility of printing our own local money. Either we must use the German currency in our own dealings or we must put new paper money onto the market. We invited some bankers in to advise us. We were especially concerned with the ethical side of the problem. Naturally, we wished to see as little as possible of the occupation money in circulation, but the main point at issue was whether or not it should be looked upon as money.

One of our revered city councilmen who was in the printing trade said, "These insulting slips of paper are shoved at us on bayonet points. We must refuse to accept them as money. If I didn't have to print them on a Saturday afternoon, they would cost no more than fifteen cents a pound."

But we could not begin with the question of whether they were real money or worthless paper. We had to consider the social side of the case. The moment such a mark note was forced upon us there had been given from the Norwegian side some service or value in return for it. The question was, then, whether the chance merchant or worker who was left with this mark note

169

must carry the loss alone or whether all should do their part in assuming it.

The question became clearer when we followed the logic of the Germans themselves. During the first week they used nothing but occupation marks. Later they threw bag after bag of the paper marks on the counter in the bank and disappeared with our currency. Since then they had used Norwegian money. Did it make any difference? The fact was that they were stealing from society as such, and that each and every one of us, therefore, must pay. Thus it was in Narvik, and the same thing was probably happening throughout the country. This was the problem which the whole world would have to face until these organized gangsters one day were stopped.

I reported an incident to illustrate my point of view. The previous Thursday the Germans had taken a bicycle from one of the messenger boys in the street. They explained that they were going to pay; but, as the boy fought for his bicycle, they gave him a receipt and sent him on his way, telling him to go to the Mayor at the City Hall and ask him to write a bill on the German Occupation Treasury. The boy came to me and we wrote a bill. When we came to the question of value, the boy, naturally enough, begged me to set a high price. I refused to exceed the purchase price.

"Why can't those *Schwein* pay?" he asked.

"It is not the Germans who are paying," I replied. "You know you will get nothing but occupation marks, and what will you do next?"

"I'll go straight to the Bank and change them."

"Exactly. And the Norwegian money in the bank is the savings we all have there."

"Damn it, what a mess things have gotten into!" he replied.

"You are certainly right about that," I sighed.

But then the problem arose as to what kind of money we were going to use. The city was now the only significant employer that still had work projects under way, with the digging of cellars and graves, repair jobs, and clean-up work. We thought we had sufficient funds, but money rolled out rapidly and very little came in. In a few days the City Treasury would be empty.

The banks reported that the City had large accounts outstanding but that we would have to accept either occupation money or a check.

We returned to first beginnings. It really made little difference what we used; but, since we could no longer have currency with the picture of our own chosen King, we certainly would not use the insulting German paper. We decided to print new money. We split a check for one hundred thousand kroner into printed five-krone checks. They became quite popular with the citizens and I do not doubt but that our distressed city did come out a few kroner to the good, since many of these bills were kept as souvenirs and disappeared from circulation.

Having settled this phase of the economic problem, we went on to rationing and employment. Not all things could be rationed. It was to be expected that the initial confidence in the new money would sink and that every-

body would attempt to buy something. Stocks were already so limited that difficulties might arise if we did not drastically curtail the buying power. It was still more important to keep alive the strong feeling of our unity in distress. If the liberation of the town were to be long delayed, the good morale we had might be destroyed through an ever-growing impatience with living conditions. It was of paramount importance to keep as many as possible employed. Work gave release and created community spirit.

Accordingly, we put into operation a plan for expanded activity in all fields. Our excellent old City Planning Engineer was appointed chief of the whole public works system. He did not need much sleep and worked, practically speaking, day and night. He worked out plans for the reinforcement of more cellars, the changing of public parks into potato fields, and the laying out of a new cemetery. We decided to take in more workers and more civil service employes, and at the same time expand the activities of the Red Cross and the Fire Department. As a counterbalance, all wages were regulated downward to a minimum, taking into consideration the family burden of each man. As for the people already on the city payroll, they were to be paid only a part of their regular salaries. Everyone was treated alike, not because of any fundamental principle, but simply because we were at war. Even though we had no weapons, we were not going to be deprived of feeling ourselves to be soldiers. We had finally realized that in totalitarian war all the people must do their

part and not only the young men with perfect physiques and good teeth.

I received a special salary of ten dollars a week during these months and it was quite sufficient. No one paid any rent. That would have been altogether too complicated as we all were kept moving from place to place. The half-rotten fish was cheap.

Yes, indeed, that Sunday we certainly put through a radical social revolution. Conservative Mr. Toft of the Railroad shook his head but admitted that under the circumstances there wasn't much else that we could do. Some days later he instituted the new system among his own employes.

That day, as I returned to our emergency quarters in the Headmaster's house for fish dinner, I was excited and in boundlessly high spirits. I was told that all these rationing nights could not be so dry and boring after all. I said that I had passed a rather interesting night, but that as a gentleman I could not discuss the details.

"Skinny little Mrs. Sivertsen is, after all, the only woman on the Rationing Board, isn't she?" the teacher's wife laughingly inquired.

I knew I was going to sleep like a stone that night. The moment I stretched out on the mattress in the corner it was as though I sank comfortably into a deep well. I saw the surface as a shining halo far above. Bubbles kept ascending. They hung together like section signs.

— §36, — I thought, and was asleep.

XII — LIVING WITH THE ENEMY

THE following week the General with his staff moved farther inland along the railroad line to Sweden. We received news that the Norwegian railroad stations in the mountains as well as the private ski huts were being used to quarter German soldiers. The city itself became a kind of outer front sector and we got an *Ortskommandant,* or city commander. I was introduced to the new commanding officer at the Grand Hotel, where he occupied a suite of offices on the first floor. The Grand Hotel was situated a little lower than the Royal and the offices of the commanding officer could not be hit directly by shelling from the sea. The British warships were continuously circling the Narvik peninsula and bombarded the German positions from time to time.

The new chief was Major Haüzel. One glance at him sufficed: he was no good. The type is well known, dominating and brutal, self-satisfied and condescending, with a peculiar, calculating suspicion which covers a secret

feeling of inferiority. The type dominates the new Germany. It is the unappreciated geniuses who have taken the power, and the power itself is glorious and mysterious. For lack of a better explanation, it is ascribed to Blood and Race. Not all the German officers are of the Major Haüzel type. If they were, the war could be won more easily.

The majority of them are brilliant technicians trained to severe discipline, and they now follow Hitler, as they once followed the Kaiser. In either event, it is a misjudged Germany for which they are fighting, and whether it is called *Grossdeutschland* or *das Herrenvolk* is quite irrelevant. As for the youngsters who have grown to maturity under Goebbel's supervision, the picture is different. They are healthy, well-trained boys who believe in the Blood God, since they know no other.

But Major Haüzel was a man who had followed the new Leader when he was still ridiculous, and such a faith has claim on reward. We guessed that he had been a sour and envious manual-training teacher when Nazism was still confined to the back streets. Now he had come into a dignified position and this dignity the world was going to learn to respect. He had an irritating way of circling a bony nicotine-stained index finger before one's face when he was giving his orders. He numbered them, *Ein, Zwei, Drei.* He always repeated the last sentence of each section, as if he wished to polish it so that it would stand indelibly in the mind of the mentally inferior listener. I, too, had to count numbers, but silently, in order not to lose my self-control.

When he smiled he was especially obnoxious. He had poor, hungry teeth. He showed them especially in emphasizing that point in the instruction relative to the dull and undeveloped Nordics, for whom, as members of his great race, there was still some hope.

At our first interview, he began with a brief review of the fundamentals of the relationship between the German *Wehrmacht* and the civilians in an occupied country. This philosophic German diatribe was followed by an enumeration of demands which were intended to suffice for the present.

Ein: Quarters must be provided for British sailors taken as prisoners off the ore ships. They need not be too good. The British prisoners had been incarcerated in the Public School, together with the group of Norwegian soldiers given up by Sundlo, but now the Germans needed more room, since the stay was likely to be long.

Zwei: Quarters must be arranged for German sailors of the merchant marine.

Drei: The Major himself needed a new uniform for use in milder weather. Spring would, one hoped, arrive, even in these latitudes.

We explained that there were no more quarters available. All public buildings had already been requisitioned except the City Hall and the Hospital. As for the uniform, we carried none in stock. The Major might try a tailor.

We wished to prevent as long as possible the taking over of private homes, so we found a restaurant in which to house the British prisoners. There was, however, no

building that would take care of the German sailors. They numbered about five hundred. Finally, we had to open the beautiful new church in the park at Frydenlund.

We carried on our negotiations through one of the German captains old in the ore trade at Narvik. He deplored the fact that he had received orders to requisition the church. He confided to us that he personally was a religious man, and we made a gentleman's agreement with him. We furnished hay mattresses for his people, and he promised to protect the church property, not to desecrate the altar with guns or foodstuffs, and to do his best to prevent the installation of anti-aircraft guns in the steeple.

As for the tailor, I committed a tactical blunder. I took him personally to the Major's quarters, to which we were shown by a sentinel. It might be of interest to find out how he had arranged matters for himself.

We were led to a house hidden by a hill down near the Railroad Station. The owners had been moved out. The Major took full advantage of the situation to show his patronizing attitude. He kept us waiting for as long a period as fitted his dignity, taking his meal and his after-luncheon rest. The house had been carefully chosen, since it was well protected against fire from the sea. After the audience we were dismissed with a condescending gesture. The samples shown by the tailor were of good English quality, but the uniform was never finished. The tailor constantly found causes for delay.

There would have been no need for our anxiety over

being the forgotten front. The British did not stint in their use of ammunition but they did take cautious aim, and, in the beginning, only the German positions were hit.

One night they annihilated a complete German sentry post near Vasvik, the little harbor on the north side of the peninsula with a pier for the ferry and fishing boats. The corpses lay for days before they were buried. The house which the soldiers had been occupying burned down and not much more than their bones were left. The Germans contended that such remains were not worth burial.

I heard several comments on the British shelling during the two daily visits I was forced to pay to Captain Müller's office.

— This was just the beginning. The English were certainly contemplating the utter destruction of the whole city. Only one salvation could be seen—German planes—and they would soon come. —

I begged them not to go out of their way on our behalf. The tone of our conversation became progressively more free. To begin with, I thought it was a Gestapo center; but, when I asked one of the young soldiers, he became so infuriated that I concluded it was a purely military office.

It was well equipped with radio transmitter, typewriters, and trunks built for index files. The walls were decorated with huge maps of Narvik and the Ofotfjord. They were by far the most detailed maps I had ever seen of Norwegian territory. The text was German. On one

general map a heavy black arrow in the fjord bore the legend *Der Weg nach Narvik*—the way to Narvik.

That week we completed our rationing system and put into effect our new wage policies.

The next Sunday forenoon we had our last contact with Major Haüzel. We were enjoying some tranquil hours in the City Hall bringing the records up-to-date— all important incidents and decisions were recorded and witnessed—when suddenly Sauerkraut came rattling in. Orders from the Major. He wanted a pair of first-class bedroom slippers delivered at once.

"Slippers, of all things!"

"Soft slippers with stiff toe caps and low heels."

We patiently explained to him that we did not carry slippers in the City Hall.

"But the Major expressly ordered me to come here to ask for them."

We offered Sauerkraut a cigaret and explained that today was Sunday and that it was absolutely impossible on the Sabbath to purchase a pair of slippers in the whole town of Narvik. We finally succeeded in convincing him, and he went on his way.

We had not finished the work with the records before we again heard the tramping of boots in the hallway. This time it was a lieutenant with a whole guard of soldiers.

"*Herr Ortskommandant* wishes, first, to inform you that the ordered articles must be delivered; secondly, that he must have them before 1 P.M. The Mayor knows his address."

The guard clicked all its heels. That was all!

We sat there, not knowing whether to laugh or to cry. They had taken the banks, the schools, and the church. And now slippers on Sunday! It was a humiliating kick in the pants. In this case, counting numbers did not help. We told one another all the jokes we remembered about slippers. It helped some. One of the boys had an uncle in the shoe business. He ran out and got a huge pair of slippers that had been used for advertising purposes, and we let the seven-year-old daughter of the janitor deliver them. The child thought it was great fun. She almost had to drag the slippers to the Major's residence.

As we had expected, the Lieutenant soon came rushing back with them. The slippers did not fit. They were too big. He had orders to return them to be exchanged for a pair many sizes smaller. The Major could not understand why such a pair had been sent. We could see, however, that the Lieutenant did.

— We were very sorry, but we did not know what size the Major wore. Perhaps the Lieutenant himself would exchange them since he undoubtedly had more knowledge of the Major's feet. —

He hesitated a while. He sent the soldiers out into the hallway. We offered him a cigar, and he shrugged his shoulders and decided to go. It might, after all, save him from another trip. He put the gigantic slippers under his arm and disappeared.

The following day Oscar dropped in again. He had heard of the slipper incident. It was all over town and

everyone enjoyed it. Could we make use of him for a trick or two? He had been spying a little on his own and had seen the Germans busy with something down by the shore where it was easy to make a landing. They were burying huge metal containers in the ground. He wished to tell some official about his findings. We went into a secret conference.

Offers to help came in constantly. A middle-aged seamstress offered to make British flags. They might come in handy if there were to be some kind of celebration in town in the near future. It was well that we did not know how long we were going to wait before we could make use of them. Every morning we said to ourselves, "Today something will happen," but as the days passed we became more patient. "Nothing this week. All right. But next week we shall be free again."

We were without news for several days when the power plant blew up. It took some time to get batteries; the Germans had taken all they could lay their hands on. But Instructor Tanke finally got a fresh supply and the news service again functioned.

We heard that fighting was still going on in all the valleys to the south. British troops had been landed at three points: at Åndalsnes on the west coast; in Namsos, north of Trondheim; and in Harstad, immediately north of Narvik, a little farther out among the islands in the ocean. Later bulletins told that French Alpine troops had also landed. On the southern front and around Namsos our Norwegian troops were fighting side by side with the British within a week after the war had touched

Norwegian soil. Farther north it was longer before Allied infantry came in contact with the enemy.

Norwegian soldiers were stationed on the mainland between Tromsö and Narvik. Although the military training camp at Elvegårdsmoen had been occupied the first day, there were Norwegian detachments at many points. The Sixth Division had been mobilized as a border patrol during the first Finnish-Russian war and a major part of it was still under arms. Their Chief, General Fleischer, was a strong and active-minded officer.

For the first three weeks the Norwegians fought alone. The mountains we knew from hunting and fishing trips in summer vacations now became names connected with bloody and bitter battles. The Germans had made good use of their treacherous beginning and had erected machine-gun posts before the Norwegian counterattack could be gotten under way. The German soldiers were obviously trained for mountain fighting. They had better weapons, and they fought from well-defended positions. But the Norwegian boys knew their mountains better, and they were their own. We got bulletins of victories, but the advance was slow, and the Norwegian forces did not arrive in time to save the small front sector in the mountains back of the town towards Sweden.

One morning we received a report that Norwegian prisoners were being brought down along the railroad tracks. They were the survivors of two hundred Norwegian soldiers who had refused to surrender on the first morning. I knew their commanding officer, Major Omdahl, and was permitted to visit him in the prison. We

were forced to carry on our conversation in German, but I did learn that he had managed to contact headquarters on the first day and that Sundlo had disobeyed instructions. The order had been to fight.

Even though we had received no news of Allied infantry activity, the British warships were active. The summer nights were growing steadily brighter and the Germans could never feel secure in their positions. They lay themselves as close as possible to the civilians. They used the little chapel on the outskirts of Northtown for a light artillery position and they installed their quarters and machine-gun nests directly between the homes in the town proper. The exchange of fire grew ever more intense.

One morning Sauerkraut arrived to take me to a new *Ortskommandant*. Now Major Haüzel, too, had moved farther up the railroad line. This time the commander was no more than a captain, *Korvettenkapitän* Boehme. But, even so, the change was for the better. He was more a sailor than a politician, and, also, he was one rank lower than his predecessor, a fact which we construed as a happy omen. The Germans evidently did not wish to be defeated under such a fine creature as a Major. We thought that argument pretty sound, and hoped that the defeat would begin to happen soon. We were growing impatient. Our homes had begun to be somewhat overpopulated. When the Germans, for greater protection, placed their gun positions between private houses, the houses were evacuated.

Captain Boehme gave us permission to visit the Eng-

lish prisoners. Their chief complaints were about the *ersatz* coffee and the "news" that the Germans were giving them.

— As for the coffee, I knew about that, but what kind of news was being circulated? —

— That the Norwegians resented English intervention and that nowhere in Norway was there any fighting going on. —

I outlined the true picture of the situation.

As nearly as I could determine I had been talking with Giles Romilly, the nephew of Mr. Churchill. He was in excellent humor but he looked considerably thinner than his famous uncle. I did not see him again. He had been unable to restrain himself, and had rejected with contempt the news reports brought to him by the sentinel that evening. The next day I was accused of talking politics with the prisoners, and further visits were denied.

I had looked in vain for Consul Gibbs and his staff among the prisoners. There had been unconfirmed rumors that they had been captured, but no one seemed to know their whereabouts. One chambermaid at the hotel had talked with Mr. Gibbs and his colleagues the morning of the invasion. They had come into the corridor in their robes when the firing began and asked what was going on. She had told them that she had heard in the kitchen that the Norwegian warships were firing on German men-of-war. As far as she could make out the British gentlemen had been busy destroying their secret papers right up to the moment when the Germans

arrived. They had just barely escaped. The Royal Hotel was one of the first buildings the Germans occupied. An officer and some soldiers had gone directly to the Consul's room. The maid had been called and they had held a revolver under her nose and one of the soldiers had threatened her in Norwegian. She had replied that she knew nothing, and the Germans seemed too busy with other things to detain her.

We continued to hope that the Consul and his party had escaped and reached Sweden.

On April 21 one of our special messengers reported that the British prisoners had been ordered to prepare to leave. They were under heavy guard, and it appeared that they were to be marched into the mountains. A moment later they came by. I waved to the Captain of the S.S. *Romanby* and he waved back. Among the German guards I recognized the young lover of liberty who had called upon me less than three months before with his plea to be allowed to remain in Norway.

A few days later Norwegian prisoners were also taken away from Narvik along the same railroad line on which they had been brought down.

One of the British destroyers accompanied this last prison transport by steaming in close to the shores of southern Rombaksfjord. Shells rained in from the fjord and the prisoners had to run for cover. Two Norwegian officers grasped the opportunity, jumped down the slope and ran at high speed towards the shore, where they were picked up by a boat lowered from the destroyer. We learned, too, that Major Omdahl had also escaped dur-

ing a snowstorm in the mountains and had reached the Norwegian forces in the North.

That evening we *skåled* for Major Omdahl with German beer. The Fire Brigade celebrated its anniversary in the station cellar. The city had prohibition, it was true; but, since it was only beer and stolen from the German stores, we let the law sleep for one evening. A depot in the harbor had been set on fire by British shells in the morning and the firemen had saved a considerable quantity of flour and had also picked up some of the German stores.

Otherwise, the local prohibition, voted at the beginning of the war, was rigidly enforced. Not a bottle of hard liquor was sold, even on a doctor's prescription. Only requests from the Hospital were delivered. All the best whiskey was sent there as the Germans raised their requisitions, and in inverse proportion to the number of troops stationed in town. At first they had asked for only the best brandy; but, later on, as nothing but younger officers stayed in town, the stars on the bottles also decreased in number.

As the shelling from the fjord grew in intensity the drunkenness among the Germans increased, and we descended still one more grade in the rank of our *Ortskommandant*. The last was a Lieutenant—even though he was *Oberleutnant*—Poetsch. Him we were going to keep.

Poetsch was twenty-nine years old and had been educated as an engineer, but he evidently had been through a more or less continuous military training since boy-

hood. He used both military and civil titles on his let-
terheads, requisitions, and military passes. Above all,
he was a soldier, and a strutting one, but not without humor. He did not unduly emphasize his dignity as master of the town except when he was issuing
disagreeable orders. Generally speaking, he was easy to
talk with except when we happened to touch on certain
issues. Then it was like clashing with a wall of prejudices that reached to high heaven. There was no shadow
of doubt in his mind about the righteousness of the German cause. Might was right, and might meant good guns
and well-trained soldiers. After the fall of Belgium and
Holland, when the German military machine rolled over
France and nothing seemed able to stop it, he walked
about in a state of emotional intoxication. Life was
wonderful!

The radio bulletins ascribed many of these first victories to Hitler's secret weapons. Under one of the British bombardments we sat side by side in an air shelter
and I asked him about these secret weapons. If they
really were in existence and were being used they could
not be entirely secret. Poetsch laughed.

— *Selbstverständlich*. He would be delighted to en-
tertain me with a military lecture; but, frankly, he had
not advanced to a sufficiently high rank to receive such
information. But he was not so sure that any new weapons had been put into use, as yet. The ones they had
were proving their excellence and they had plenty of
them. Oh, if only we could see how hopeless it was to
resist! Our people might march with the Germans to-

ward an epoch of world dominion such as history has never seen. Against them we faced only destructon. —

"Even if that were true," I said, "we have made our choice. But the war is not over yet. Perhaps it has not even gotten a good start."

He felt that I was hopeless. In his view I was a fairly agreeable young fellow, a little too old, perhaps, and completely misled by plutocratic propaganda, whatever that may have meant.

He allowed me quite a bit of freedom of action. I even received a personal pass permitting me to be on the streets after eight o'clock in the evening. I had used as an excuse my late evening work in the City Hall, which was true enough. He did not, however, trust me completely. And once or twice he discovered activities of which he disapproved. Fortunately, they were relatively innocent incidents. He learned, among other things, that we had ordered everyone to refrain from speaking to German soldiers except when it was absolutely necessary or when official business was being transacted. But the discovery of this order occurred on a day "filled with unique victories for the German Army," so he overlooked it.

When the *Kommandant* office itself was blown up by British shells, he came to the City Hall every day to issue military passes to Beidsfjord or to the outskirts of town, which had been declared forbidden zones. Some days he brought his "Treasurer" along. Twice a week the plunderings in town were made "legal" through refund payments in occupation currency.

Poetsch was always correct and smiling. Miss Hansen, our not exactly young typist, went so far as to say that this last *Kommandant* really was quite a nice person and that, after all, he probably was only acting under orders.

"Granted that he may be a fairly decent being," one of us coldly replied, "but don't forget that even a tiger has white teeth and isn't the less dangerous for that. Furthermore, it goes far beyond the mere fact of his doing his duty. He is our enemy with all his heart and soul. Each thought he thinks, each breath he breathes, is deadly poison to everything that we call freedom and justice."

"Well, I do not mean that he ought not to be shot even though he is a nice man," Miss Hansen said.

Our friendly relations with *Oberleutnant Diplom-Engineer* Poetsch had, from the very beginning, their clearly-defined limits. On the second day of his regime he found it necessary to exercise his authority. There had been intense firing from the fjord the night before we received important news from a Beidsfjord peasant who had been wounded by splinters and had come to the Hospital for treatment. He told us that Allied troops had arrived on the other side of the mountains and were quartered in the village of Håkvik.

The same morning Sauerkraut appeared on the scene again. He clicked his heels with extraordinary solemnity. *Herr Ortskommandant* requested the Mayor and the Chief of Police to come at once to his office.

When we arrived we found only the *Oberleutnant* and

189

not much of the *diplom-engineer*.

"Gentlemen," he said, "I have been ordered to inform you that during the night shots were fired in the streets at German soldiers. The perpetrators escaped. They were Norwegian civilians."

"But you took all weapons from us on the day of the invasion," we answered.

"That does not matter. The case is closed."

We thought the Lieutenant was having a joke at our expense. That Norwegians should have hidden weapons and ammunition all this time and then fire a few wild shots in the street and not even hit anyone—there was no logic in that.

The *Kommandant* rose and smiled a hard smile.

"I think the gentlemen do not quite understand the situation," he said, "the case is not open for discussion. I have orders from headquarters to submit a list of hostages who will vouch with their lives for the peace and order of the town. You may name five citizens. I must have their names immediately. Otherwise, we must select them ourselves."

The Chief of Police looked to me to give the answer. It was anything but an inviting task.

"You had better begin with us two," I said.

"And three more?"

"Well, we might take the City Engineer, the Head Surgeon at the Hospital, and the Norwegian Manager of the Swedish Iron Ore Company."

They were the best names in town, I thought, four of them at least.

We rose from our chairs, but the *Kommandant* had not finished. "That was *punkt ein. Punkt zwei* is the publication of this news. The gentlemen may personally arrange that matter. You will post public announcements in prominent places in town."

There is that index finger of Haüzel again, I thought. Weren't we through with that devil yet?

We left.

At the City Hall we printed announcements which recorded our conversation as accurately as possible. Perhaps we had emphasized the fact that the supposed firing in the streets had been brought to the *Kommandant's* attention by the German Headquarters in the mountains. But the Germans did not fail to see the irony. Later in the forenoon, we were ordered to remove the announcements. New placards were posted. The text was written by the *Kommandant* himself.

The same evening the hostages were called to his office and he delivered a speech to us. It came *punkt* by *punkt*. Afterwards, he tried to be friendly and dwelt upon the alibis of the British and the heroism of the Germans. The social atmosphere did not improve. He gave us cigarets imprinted with gold letters and filled with straw. We were not impressed. The conversation turned to the shelling of the town, which, it appeared, would be likely to be worse. We did manage to have some kind of conversation on that subject.

Poetsch asked me to stay after the meeting. He tried to let me know indirectly that he, personally, did not like to use harsh methods, but that he was under orders.

He wished to express his personal regrets.

"Completely superfluous," I answered, and offered him a cigaret with tobacco inside. They were no longer to be had in the stores, at least by the new customers.

There were several good reasons why a relatively friendly relation with the *Kommandant* might prove advantageous.

The next day Oscar turned up again at the City Hall. He was bubbling over with excitement. It was almost impossible to prevent him from exploding before we had found a soundproof room in the attic.

— He had been asked to convey greetings from a British Admiral, from Poles, and from Frenchmen. Soon there was going to be some real fireworks. Very soon. The Admiral had said so himself. 'All right,' Oscar had answered. And he had witnessed the execution of a dozen Germans behind a barn. The French had accomplished that. *Fini!* —

He was so enthusiastic that he attempted to tell all the stories at the same time.

"Please, please, calm down," I broke in, as I lit a cigaret with deliberate slowness, "and tell me only what you yourself have seen and heard. Only the truth and nothing but the truth, so help you God? You may recall, perhaps . . ."

Oscar smiled. He became a little less tense.

"Well, you remember we agreed that I should go to that lady who was to be my aunt in Beidsfjord. The German pass was all right and I came to her house that same evening. In the night I went on borrowed skis

192

across the mountains to Håkvik. There was only a little snow left in the valley, and I had to leave the skis in the forest. I did not see any soldiers but there were many evacuees from Narvik in Håkvik. There I got a boy to row me out to one of the biggest British warships. I said I had come to report from Narvik and that I had secret instructions from the Mayor and must speak to the Supreme Commander. And I will say that I got to talk with the boss himself. We sat in easy chairs in his cabin and exchanged news over grog and a cigar. I still have my cigar."

Oscar pulled a huge, fine cigar from his pocket.

"It had a band on it, but I threw that away so that the Germans would not become suspicious if I happened to be caught. A cigar—why any gentleman must be permitted to carry a cigar."

"But what did you two talk about?"

"Oh, first, I told everything I knew about Narvik and the Germans."

"Wait a minute, how could you understand each other?"

"Well, there was a young officer on board who had some knowledge of Norwegian, and I said 'Sir' and 'All right,' and we understood each other perfectly. I was to convey his greetings."

"Good, but what instructions did you get?"

"First, I was to ask whether you knew anything about the British Consul in Narvik, Mr. Gibbs, and his staff. They can not have left the town, because they have not sent word out.

"And then he asked me about *morale*. The officer hurried the translation so fast that at first I didn't get that. I thought he meant were the girls here very strict, and maybe I could have given him some information about that, too, but he wanted to know how we felt and on which side we stood. I asked him whether he didn't know that the King had declared war on Germany and that in the whole of Narvik only the nitwit Sundlo did not think that the Germans were so many swine. I told him that we were impatient as hell and eating rotten fish loaded with mustard. Then we shook hands and the Admiral asked me to come again, and I said 'All right, Sir.' "

"But what about those twelve Germans behind the barn?"

"You must be patient. I have just barely finished with the Admiral. As I said, he saw me to the side of the ship and I was put ashore near Sjomen, so I had to walk back to Håkvik. The same day Polish troops and French Alpines, or the Foreign Legion, appeared there. They said that I must not go back over the mountains to Beidsfjord."

"And it was there you learned French?" I asked.

"To be honest, I am no good at French, but they had brought a Norwegian lieutenant along from Harstad, who served as interpreter. I told him what the British Captain had said."

"You told me that he was an Admiral."

"Well, he was Captain of his own ship also, don't you see? Anyway, I was permitted to accompany the French

troops in the valley. They marched in single files on the edge of the forest, one on each side of the highway. Turning a curve, it happened! You remember that dam at the lower end of the biggest lake? There we were met by a small group of soldiers in Norwegian uniforms. The French had them encircled before they could say 'boo!' I shouted, 'Watch out, they are Norwegians!'

"But at that moment one of them fired his revolver and wounded one of the Frenchmen. The soldier himself dropped in the ditch, with a bullet in his head. The others instantly raised their hands. They spoke in German—one didn't have to be much of a professor to know that.

"The French took all their weapons and marched them a short distance down the road, turning into a farm where an old peasant woman waved as we passed. The prisoners were lined up behind the barn. The French officer asked the Norwegian lieutenant whether he was absolutely certain the uniforms were Norwegian. The Norwegian officer said that he was sure. The Frenchmen took the small metal identification tags which the Germans had around their necks. They turned pale but didn't say anything. The French officer saluted. One of the Germans took the scarf that he had around his neck and tied it over his eyes. The others did the same. One of them was working frantically at a knot when the shots went off. *'Fini!'* the Frenchman said. That means: 'Now we are through with those swine.'"

"Wasn't it hard to witness all that? You have never seen anyone die before, or have you?"

"I saw them carry home my dad when he drowned in Lofoten, but, of course, that was quite different. Yes, it was a little frightening."

"And how did you get farther?"

"Well, at the upper end of the lake the Frenchmen took up their positions, and I crossed the mountains alone. There were Germans in the woods, but I crept through. At one place I had to lie in a snow cave and act like a block of ice, and I was not far from becoming one. I finally reached Beidsfjord and there I picked up a milk can which I brought into Narvik."

"You have done a nice piece of work, Oscar. It is a pity that I can not tell the others about it but we had better keep this to ourselves. A man downtown will give you help. You shall meet him today. But, when the war is over, we will certainly have a celebration in your honor."

Oscar blushed like a young girl.

"Oh, it's nothing," he said.

We made a date for the next day. I hoped that in the meantime I could get some definite information about Mr. Gibbs. I had a notion where I might search for him.

Some days earlier I had heard two boys talking about a group of unshaved deaf-mutes who were living in a tool shed not far up in the mountains, no more than half an hour away. They played cards all day long. The Germans had lookouts both above and below. The British were firing intermittently at the enemy positions there, and some civilians had been wounded.

I talked to one of the boys, who gave me a detailed description of these silent men. The descriptions tallied, and I told him who I thought they were. He must help us bring them into town. He was delighted. He had a friend who owned a truck that had been used to transport corpses. We might use the truck.

That evening Consul Gibbs and his colleagues came into town under tarpaulins. We had a house ready for them. We had taken the home of the City Judge, since his family had left town on the morning of the invasion. We had hired both a cook and a maid. Clothes and whiskey awaited them on their arrival. As Consul, Mr. Gibbs enjoyed extraterritorial privileges so far as liquor was concerned.

The truck arrived with the honored guests: Consul Gibbs, Captain Thompson, Mr. E. Pegott, and a Commander whose name I never learned to pronounce correctly. They had lived in the tool shed for three weeks, surviving on canned foods. Captain Thompson knew Norwegian, but the others pretended to be deaf-mutes when people happened by. After the naval battle of April thirteenth the cabin had been packed with German sailors who raged and cursed at the British; and Consul Gibbs, shaking his head and smiling, had poured coffee for the uninvited guests. Typically good-natured and dumb Norwegians, the Germans must have thought. They had, however, enjoyed the coffee.

How the British officials had been able to continue the comedy for so long was beyond my imagination. Even minus their collars and with rough beards, the

197

consular personnel looked typically English. It is not easy to disguise gentlemen, but hot baths, shaves, and fresh clothes did make some difference.

We *skåled*, and I told them that the town counted it a great honor to have them as its guests. It was too bad that, for the time being, they would have to live behind drawn blinds.

On the door we placed a placard warning that contagious disease had put the house under quarantine. It worked. The Germans took over most of the houses in that quiet street, but they did not enter the infected home of the City Judge.

The following day I had an excellent map made for Oscar, but he did not appear at the meeting place. I returned to my office. A few minutes later word came that Gunnar, our intermediary, wished to see me immediately. I knew where to go. Gunnar was a Norwegian officer who lived as a civilian in town, but he had not laid aside his responsibilities with his uniform. He lived near the church and I found him at our usual meeting place in the church basement.

"It's about the young fellow you are using," he said. "He was to see me yesterday. He was dressed in knickers and a windbreaker, wasn't he?"

"Yes," I answered.

"I fear they have gotten him. A while ago a truck passed down the street. On the floor lay a boy dressed as I have described. His face was shot away. I could not tell for sure who it was, but thought it best to let you know."

Oscar killed—his face shot away! And I had sent him. No, it could not be! He carried no documents on his person.

"Let's wait a while to see. Don't let us talk any more about it now," I said.

I returned to my work, but I froze so that my whole body shivered.

Miss Hansen put her head inside the door.

"I forgot to tell you that a boy was here to see you. He reeked of fish."

"Beloved Hansen, where is he?"

"He took the back stairs to the attic."

Of course it was Oscar with a broad grin across a complete face. He had been delayed. He had to say good-bye to someone.

"Well, if it is a girl again, I give you up for hopeless."

"No, no girl, but I have made a date to go with a fellow who is driving a truckload of coffins to Beidsfjord. I did not think it wise to show myself in town before I went. The truck is outside the coffin factory up the street. I was scared. I thought you weren't coming."

Scared? Never in all my sinful life had I myself been so scared. I told him what Gunnar had feared. The body in the truck must have been that of a German scout who had been hit by shell-fire from the ships. We knew that the Germans used not only Norwegian uniforms but also civilian clothes.

I was not eager to send Oscar on his way, but he in-

sisted. I gave him his map and bade him farewell. He promised not to return for a while. That promise he kept. The next time I was to hear from him he was serving on board a Norwegian freighter off Canada.

XIII — THUNDER IN THE MOUNTAINS

DURING the next few days we were to hear more from our allies in Håkvik. They had brought up a howitzer on the other side of the mountain and sent heavy shells over the town from time to time. They obviously had established a lookout post on the mountain plateau across the harbor.

The first shots were wild, but those that followed were usually direct and meaningful. Once the range-finding equipment became accurate, more and more German quarters were destroyed. Admittedly, the civilians paid, for the Germans simply moved into new houses; but, as time went on, they felt less and less secure. At night we could hear the patrols singing in the streets, more often as a result of Norwegian brandy than of German courage. In constantly increasing numbers the Germans made use of Norwegian uniforms and civilian clothes. When we protested they pointed to the German emblem, or armband, with the inscription *Deutsche Wehrmacht*

and said, "It's easy enough to read, isn't it?"

"Certainly, at bayonet point," we retorted, "but scarcely from the destroyers out in the fjord."

When Finn and Arne sent their men up along the railroad line with food and medicines for the evacuated Norwegian families forced to stay in the mountain cottages, the German soldiers mingled with the Norwegian relief workers.

Even Allied shells could be discomfiting on the wrong side of the firing line, but that could not be helped. Our impatience had changed its character. We had come to understand what this war demanded. It would not do merely to rush ashore with guns blazing. Most of us would escape the gun fire. We must wait.

Shells are worse than bombs. They scream more fiercely and come over more regularly. One is given time to dread. The tunnel and the basements again became populated. The old told fairy tales to the young, but the children found what was happening above their heads more exciting and more unbelievable than the legends. Children were most frightened when they saw that their parents were frightened, and most mothers, consciously or unconsciously, realized it. It was the children who kept the women erect and calm, but it was also the children who bound us all to constant caution.

Naturally, we had our casualties among civilians. Accidents happened every day. A city janitor had his head blown off when a shell exploded in the Market Place. During the attack on the German positions at Framnes some of the shells exploded in the city itself.

One morning we heard a shrill scream directly above the City Hall and saw the shells bursting higher up in the city. From the windows we could see smoke from a little house in Street 3. We heard people down in the street shout, "That's Hårek Olsen's house. There were people in the kitchen."

I knew Hårek Olsen. He was a member of the Fire Brigade. In a few seconds a fire engine sped through the street. Soon some of the people returned from the scene.

Half of the house was shot away, but there had not been much of a fire. Yes, there had been people inside. Three young girls in the kitchen, two sisters and a girl friend from the neighbor's. Hårek had been the first to enter. There had been some blood splotches and a few garment fragments on one wall. That was all that was left of them. The father had recognized the garments.

Later in the day, I stopped in at the Fire Station. Olsen was at work again. There was not much that anyone could say in such circumstances, except to ask whether there was anything we could do for him. His white face, hard and tense, shone in the dim workroom. He thanked us, but said there was nothing he wanted except to work. The shell must have gone astray. No one ever heard him say a bitter word against the British.

The next Sunday something similar happened. Five or six women came to the City Hall to ask for food that they might take over to Øyjord. A few days before a motorboat had come from the city with provisions for the population there, but the German soldiers had stolen it.

"But why were not boys sent on this errand?" we

203

asked. "It is fatally dangerous to cross the fjord now."

"We tried," they said, "but the Germans refused to grant permission. They were afraid that boys might board the British ships. Finally we were permitted to take two rowboats, but only women could go. Most of us have children waiting for us back home."

We loaded the Red Cross wagon with the best provisions we had, flour, beans, and canned goods. We also had a small supply of chocolate for the children, and each of the mothers received a package. Then they left for the shore. Arne asked the station wagon to wait while he ran down to the apothecary shop to get some bottles of cod-liver oil.

He was hardly back when a boy came running over the bridge. He was headed for the City Hall and we heard him shout confused words of excitement.

"There's nothing left of them. They're all dead!"

I saw the men start to unload the wagon and I ran down, only to see it disappear at high speed, Arne and Finn on the running boards. A heap of tarpaulins bounced up and down in the empty truck.

The boy caught his breath enough to tell a fairly coherent story of what had happened. From a few hundred yards away he had seen a group of women by two rowboats. They had started to load packages into the boats. Suddenly the ships had opened fire. In quick succession two or three shells hit. He had thrown himself behind a huge stone by the road. When he looked up, the women were no longer there, but there were two oblong holes in the sand, a bloody mess, and bits of

clothing and flesh spread over a wide area. It was impossible to conceive that these bits had been human beings. He had seen heads without bodies.

The boy could not continue. He began to vomit.

We were still in the street when the Red Cross wagon returned. The driver asked for Mr. Njöten. The men did not know just what should be done. Mr. Njöten emerged from the first-aid station. We agreed he had better take some coffins along.

Later in the day we issued a sort of protocol. There were five caskets. They were numbered, and we indicated who was lying in each of them. But they were sealed before friends and relatives came for them.

We had meant to act in the most practical manner; but there should have been one more casket.

One of the carpenters employed at the reinforcement work in the church basement called later at the City Hall. He had heard that his daughter had been home to inquire about him. She had gone to stay with a family at Øyjord on the day of the invasion and he had felt happy that she was safe. Now he had heard news of the accident at Vasvik and he was anxious about her. She was his one child, only nineteen. Her name was Constance. I knew her. She had been in the group of women that had gone down to the rowboats. But her name was not on our list. I showed it to him. He smiled a smile of relief. But the smile suddenly froze when he saw the uncertainty on our faces. We told him to return to work while we started a search for Constance.

We realized that there had been a mistake. It had

205

been impossible to identify the dead or even to know exactly how many women had been in the group. Eye-witnesses thought they had seen five persons before the accident, but now it was too late to do anything. Later, Mr. Njöten told Constance's father that she must have drifted out to sea. The old carpenter wanted to drag for her. He begged for people to follow him at once, but we explained that we dared not risk any more lives. We would find Constance one day so that she might have a proper funeral.

At first we did not discuss the cause of the accident very much. Most of the men could not understand it. The distance had been little more than a mile. The men on the warships must have been able to ascertain that it was not Germans who were working by the two rowboats. We heard it said in the air-raid shelters that the shells must have come from one of the German guns up in the mountains. Some persons chose to believe this, or, rather, wanted to believe it. The atmosphere was dark and confused.

I felt that the situation must be growing steadily worse, if it could be believed that the shells had been German, when everyone who had seen the marks in the sand must know that the shells had come from the sea.

A group of us met to discuss the incident. We agreed that there was no reason to permit our people to believe that a German shell had caused the tragedy. In most respects the German weapons were superior to our own, but we did have one advantage. We could always dare to tell the truth. And even in this instance it must be

possible to make the people realize who was really to blame. The Germans not only walked about in Norwegian uniforms but they made use of civilian clothes and women's clothes when they patrolled the seashore and the railroad line. The British had learned of this deception. On the Sunday morning of the accident, however, real Norwegian women had been on the shore.

It was necessary to postpone the funeral for a few days. The Germans had promised to return the church to us. It had long since been agreed that the merchant-marine men quartered there should be shipped home to Germany via Sweden. Finally they were on their way. Since they were civilians, they had received Swedish visas. Later, we learned that a German U-boat crew had been smuggled through with them.

The church was packed for the funeral. The parson was living with a colony of evacuees somewhere up along the railroad line, so his assistant officiated. He was a small man with a crooked back, but as upright a human character as can be found among men. He tried to make his funeral sermon as subdued as possible, but behind his words there trembled a fire of intense emotion.

Most of the church windows had been blasted away, but the church itself was washed and decorated with the flowers of spring. Graves had been dug in the church garden outside, since the cemetery at the outskirts of Northtown was no longer accessible. The graves had been laid open by the shelling and our little stone chapel had been blown to bits. Debris covered the graveyard.

It was a sad funeral. Saddest of all was the father of

Constance. He did not even have a casket. The pastor performed a beautiful little ceremony in the memory of the young girl. Some flowers were taken from the wreaths to be thrown upon the sea as a last farewell.

On May thirteenth, Bjerkvik in Herjangen was recaptured by the French Foreign Legion. During the previous night there had been fierce bombardment from the ships. Tromsö Radio had warned the civilian population for days. We saw the village burn and hoped that the peasants had escaped to the woods. The same evening the radio announced Allied victories. Bjerkvik had been cleared of Germans, and Norwegian forces had recaptured several important positions in the mountains. The next few days we could hear the front creeping steadily in on both sides of town. We were losing more of our people, both soldiers and civilians, every day.

The tempo became intensified, even in the air. Until now, only a few planes had come over and they had been, for the most part, transport planes, dropping provisions and mail to the German forces.

During the entire siege of Narvik the German troops received mail twice a week. The mail bags floated slowly through the air fastened to small parachutes.

Sometimes the bags were rather heavy. The Germans said they contained Red Cross materials. On one occasion, when a parachute failed to open, a bag fell through the roof of a little house in Frydenlund into an old lady's bedroom. She awoke to find the room filled with cartridges.

Now it was mostly bombers that came over, huge,

208

gray birds of prey, fighting the ships. The battleship *Warspite* had long since left for more important theaters of war, but destroyers constantly roamed the fjord. Often they clung so close to shore that we could wave to them. On one occasion we thought we observed one of them flying a Polish flag.

The German bombers invariably arrived during mid-morning, having probably started at dawn from the German bases. Sometimes we watched aerial combat against the translucent spring sky. The British were obviously making use of a base south of Tromsö. The British planes were fighters, small, and with sharp wings. The Germans attempted to stay away from any dog-fights. They came bursting from the mountains in the direction of the Swedish border into the fjord, but they never succeeded in catching the ships off guard. The vessels were continuously on the move. We could see them rush at top speed, zigzagging towards the open water whenever the planes appeared, and the skies were dotted by smoke rings from the guns. Day after day the performance was repeated. On only one occasion did we see a German plane shot down.

Once, immediately above Framnes, we saw a bomber come down in a spin. It looked as if it had been mortally hit. But, as soon as it was out of the vision of the ships at sea, it leveled off, flew close to the housetops, and disappeared above the ridge.

We could not see the destroyers in the fjord; but, judging from the shelling and bombing, the plane could not have been far out from shore when it took the de-

stroyers by surprise. There were terrific explosions which boded ill for our friends. That evening the German officers boasted of sinking a Polish destroyer. Brandy flowed freely and we took advantage of the opportunity to strike a not unprofitable bargain involving a green necktie.

A young German lieutenant had visited all the stores in vain seeking a tie that matched his uniform. He was in charge of the gasoline supply service. We of the city had to beg for each barrel, since the Germans had taken all our gasoline at the first opportunity. Once before he had chided us on the city's poor stock of neckties. This evening he reiterated his keen disappointment.

He was in high humor and we said that we would propose a little deal. We would see that he got an exquisite green tie of the best British make if, in exchange, we got a four-door sedan. Several seized cars of this description stood behind the Royal Hotel. The lieutenant was willing, but he refused to allow any record to be made of the transaction.

Both the sedan and the necktie were put to use the same evening. We had our first ride in the sedan with the stout salesgirl from Danielsen's clothing store, who was still able, from hidden stocks, to supply the wants of her old customers.

The following day we used the car to bring guests to an illegal little celebration in the cellar underneath the Fire Station. It was the Seventeenth of May, Norway's Independence Day. We had been forbidden any kind of public gathering, but we might play music in

the homes and hoist the Norwegian flag, *Oberleutnant* Poetsch had announced when he called at the City Hall.

"So that the people out in the fjord may see that we feel happy and free?" we had asked.

"You people have still much to learn," the *Ortskommandant* said, shrugging his shoulders as he left.

No, we did not want music or flag ceremonies on this Seventeenth of May. In a way the Germans themselves took care of that for us. Early in the morning we discovered that they had fastened a huge swastika to a temporary flag pole raised between the cairn stones on the top of Fagernes Mountain. The ships used it as a target for shooting practice all day. White geysers of snow rose at each hit. The distance was more than five miles. In the afternoon a shell blasted the flag pole and the obnoxious flag disappeared.

It was then that we decided on a little celebration in spite of the German ban. We were the group from the City Hall, Mr. Njöten's Red Cross boys, and some members of the Fire Brigade. It was no real festival but we still had some of the German beer and a few cigarets.

— It looks like a scene from a Russian drama, — I thought, as I descended the ladder into the cellar and saw the flickering candles in empty bottles on the unfinished table tops.

We all felt the need of sitting quietly to talk about the things we were experiencing and getting them into some kind of perspective. We sat in the damp cellar and talked about our national history. It was as if we wished to rediscover our own identity and gain strength and

confidence from the living past. Ours were treasures that no one could take from us. We had the traditions of an age-old culture, and yet we felt that we were a young nation.

Our thoughts drifted to that one old man who, in his impressive, erect person, represented our nation and our history. We thought of our King. Ever since, thirty-five years before, he had been elected to the throne of Norway, we had thought of him as something to be taken for granted. He was a living part of our Constitution. Perhaps we had not even been conscious of our real affection for this kindly and simple man. His motto— *All for Norway*—was engraved on our money. We had seen it so often that we no longer associated anything specific with it. Now, that he was in mortal danger, we began to appreciate his lifelong contribution.

Through Tromsö Radio we had been able to follow him on his journey to the North. His travels lay through the cities and villages laid waste by German bombers. We proudly realized that so long as our King remained free, our flag was not stricken. We pledged him our undying allegiance.

We did not, of course, actually say things like these in that darkened room. The more dramatic the realities themselves became, the more inadequate and futile were words to express them. It was our inner mood that whispered this flaming confidence, and it lived in the dim light between us as well as in the songs we quietly hummed together.

On our way home we drifted through the streets in

small groups of two or three, so as not to attract undue attention. We met drunken German soldiers celebrating our Norwegian Independence Day by shooting at street cats scared out of their wits. It seemed that we always had to have some shooting going on about us. A whole night of undisturbed sleep none of us had enjoyed since April ninth.

The acrid odor of continuous fires, the loud noise of explosions, sleepless nights, and dazed minds character- ized these bright but chilly spring days of 1940. But we were most aware of the bursting shells. We learned to recognize the multiple sounds of modern warfare. We could distinguish the heavy drone of the big bombers from the lighter humming of the fighter planes. We knew the difference between the boom of the naval can- nons and the sound from the land batteries. The spitfire shrill of the machine guns sounded different when it came from the ships than when it sang between fighting planes over our heads. We heard bombs crash into the sea, leaving half-choked booms in the tense air. And all these sounds were thrown back into the mountains, each in its own fashion. If we were unable to identify any of them immediately we need but wait for the repeti- tion, since the echoes served only to emphasize their peculiarities. This knowledge was useful. We learned to take proper precautions. The piercing whistles from the howitzer at Håkvik put us on special alert, just as does a country telephone ringing one's own call signal.

The danger was not always proportionate to the vol- ume and strength of the sound. The rattling of shell

splinters sounded like soft rain, but it was a sound to watch out for. Many were wounded by those terrifying steel splinters with their sharp and jagged surfaces.

One night a new sound was introduced to the fearsome orchestra. Heavy explosions came from the direction of the Iron Ore Company by the piers. They were not preceded by any shrills and seemed to come out of nowhere. They were blasting explosions. At first we were unable to classify them but we soon learned their meaning. The Germans, realizing that they would be unable to hold the town, had begun to blow it up, just as they had blown up their own ships when the sea battle was lost, so that the enemy would have the least possible joy of victory.

Special blasting experts had been shipped in through Sweden in the guise of civilians. They were busy for a week, and we estimated that they destroyed property to the extent of a million dollars a night.

After a few days we succeeded in sending a message to the Swedish Government, advising that the first thing these special "Red Cross Workers" did when they arrived in Norway was to blow up the properties of the Swedish Iron Ore Company in Narvik.

At first the Germans refused to admit that they were committing these acts of sabotage. They blamed it on British shelling, but Director Hoel of the Company sent them lists of their crimes every morning and lodged a protest in the name of the Swedish company. They did not deem the protest worthy of an answer.

Day by day, Mr. Hoel continued to sit in his execu-

tive office. He was a powerful personality of about sixty with a heavy but friendly face. He had entered the company service as a young engineer and had supervised the building of these huge piers and workshops which now, step by step, were being blasted into a desolate waste of stone blocks and twisted iron. Each morning, when he looked out of his windows he could see another part of his life's work destroyed. And he would stand in frozen silence at the inconceivable wantonness of the Nazi demons. Every night between twelve and one o'clock the explosions began, and those who had beds to sleep in had to hold on so as not to be thrown out. Now there was some real point to sleeping on the floor.

One by one the expensive electric locomotives were blown up. The night the huge locomotive stalls went up into the air not a single window was left intact in Street 1. The next day the Polish howitzer set the Grand Hotel on fire and British shells hit the Royal. The Royal was not completely demolished but there were holes through the walls and the Germans hurriedly left it.

We investigated the quarters left by the Germans and found a number of things of interest. In one of the offices, papers were scattered about, pay roll lists, and various forms. One of the printed forms was for the recording of details in connection with suicides among German soldiers. We left them, hoping they might some day be filled out. But we took along some articles belonging to the English consular officials. We also picked up some good telescopes, and a kettleful of delightful partridge, evidently intended for the German officers.

That same evening the birds were served with cream gravy at the City Judge's home. Consul Gibbs sat at the head of the table, again in a freshly pressed suit. He promised me a dinner on board one of the British destroyers in the fjord, a promise which he fulfilled a few days later.

We made good use of the German telescopes. Observation posts were set up to follow the military operations. From Oscar's report I had a general idea of how the recapture was going to be effected. There would be a smashing attack and we had best stay out of the line of fire.

Even the Germans evidently expected something to happen. The *Ortskommandant* had lost most of his papers in the fire that swept the Grand Hotel. He had moved into a makeshift office in the Industrial High School opposite the City Hall, and the high degree of efficiency noticeably slackened.

It would be incorrect to say that the Germans had become frightened, but it was obvious that they no longer enjoyed acting the role of masters. They realized that Narvik was about to fall to the British, and the forms of the New Order fell apart, one by one. The *zahlmeister* no longer bothered to fill out the solemn-looking requisitions or to pay in *reichskredittenscheine* for what they looted. Even the illusion that it was British shells that exploded in the night they made no effort to maintain.

When the explosion experts carried their oblong boxes into the transformer station by the bridge we arrived on the scene with drawings and charts to prove that the

216

station had nothing to do either with the Iron Ore Company or with the railway, but that it served only the light system of the town itself. And the transformer escaped destruction that night from "the perfidious Albion."

In other ways, too, we could observe the deterioration of the German morale. They treated their own dead in a most appalling manner. One morning our cemetery registrar rushed in to report that the Germans had stuffed their dead into the sewers by the church and that they had taken a grave that was to have been used for a Norwegian funeral. They had crowded the twisted German corpses into a heap and thrown a little sand on them.

We played it up. We protested in the name of the German dead. We submitted a report of a Norwegian funeral for German soldiers in Beidsfjord, including the numbers of the hymns used on that occasion. And now they themselves stuffed their dead into the sewers! Lieutenant Poetsch was somewhat ashamed, though he thought we were making too much fuss about it. But the corpses were removed and the leader of the German funeral gang was sent to the City Hall to offer apologies. He was a small, pale-faced, fat creature under an oversized helmet. We were very angry, but his appearance and apology at least provided a kind of explanation.

Three times the *Kommandant* had picked a funeral patrol. The first had been wiped out during its work by the chapel. The second had been on its way in a truck with six German corpses when a shell from the ships had buried both the cargo and the patrol. Our

visitor was responsible for the third patrol. They were just returning with a fresh load from the positions at Framnes when they discovered the convenient newly-dug sewers in the park by the church and decided that it would be most practical not to drive any farther.

"But the Germans themselves set up the battery positions in the cemetery," we pointed out.

The tiny funeral director with the huge helmet insisted that he had not ordered them there. And we believed him.

The sewer incident did not stand alone. The treatment the Germans gave their dead revealed a cynicism that was depressing, but the wounded at Narvik were excellently cared for. The slightly wounded the Germans treated themselves in the hope of getting them back into service as quickly as possible. The severely wounded were sent to our Hospital.

Our energetic Head Surgeon performed marvelous medical feats, often remaining at the operating table the whole day. The Germans held him in such high regard that his name was removed from the list of hostages. They soon discovered that their own doctors were of poor quality. Their medical leader proved himself a thorough ruffian. When we pointed out to him that the Germans were breaking the international Red Cross laws by erecting gun positions in close proximity to the Hospital, he shrugged his shoulders and answered that the Hospital had an unfortunate location.

We received many small bits of information from the Hospital which served to complete the picture we al-

ready had of the enemy. The dying soldiers did not make confessions or reveal military secrets, but they did become more human as they neared the threshold of death themselves.

In the Hospital there was a little nurse with a great blond braid wrapped around her head. Perhaps her name really was Grete. At any rate, she spoke German not too badly. She was the object of constant proposals and when she was sure that the suitors were going to die pretty quickly she told them she would think it over.

The Germans really seemed to be in earnest, and to imagine that they were going to bring youthful Nordic Gretchens home with them. One young sub-lieutenant was especially serious. He quoted Heine and talked philosophy, but he could not for a moment believe that Germany could ever commit a wrong. He related that he was a medical student and that in two years he would start practicing in a little Bavarian village where his parents owned a great farm. He delivered eloquent philosophical sermonettes. He admitted that things looked pretty ugly and that we simple-minded Norwegians might find it difficult to grasp the New Order and the deeper meaning behind the invasion. What we were now witnessing, he said, was the birth pangs of a New Era. As in all such processes, it was a hideous and bloody spectacle, but when the struggle was over we should see a beautiful and well-formed child. Peace and order would follow. Blond men and women with strong wills would dominate the world. The women of Bavaria would be clothed in French silk and Irish linen and their

men would smoke real tobacco and they would go to movies and see American films. Perhaps even Heine would once again be recognized when the Jewish financial swindlers had been liquidated. A new, great, light-hearted, happy Germany was rising.

"But what of the rest of the world?" Grete had interrupted. "Besides, I have a sister who is a brunette."

"Even the others will become happy, since they were born to obey. Yes, all will be truly happy in this life, the only life there is. So happy," said the little lieutenant, and died.

The general picture, as pieced together from these incidents related by the nurses, indicated that the Austrian soldiers really felt a certain sense of shame, and that they were grateful for the kind treatment given them. The Germans, on the other hand, remained for the most part closed and hard. They did not talk much, but they protested violently against being placed in the rooms on the top floors.

I visited the Hospital almost every day and it was here that I first met Dr. Kant. He had arrived as a civilian via Sweden and had fussed and fretted about town for several days. We had heard that the German officers bent over backwards to please Dr. Kant, and that he lived alone. At the Hospital he consistently refused to become involved in any discussion of medical matters, although he visited all the rooms regularly and screamed *"Heil Hitler!"*

Dr. Kant was that type of sausage-German who bangs the table when he talks politics and pronounces

universal truths, and berates the waiters when there is either too much or too little foam on the beer. An Austrian soldier, who had lost his leg and was not too sure that the Germans would go to the expense of sending him home as return freight, whispered to us that Kant was from the Gestapo. His visit meant that the Devil was loose.

Whether they were related to the "Doctor's" inspiring energy or not, we received other warnings of coming events. Our freedom of mobility was put under new and more severe restrictions. People were driven from all houses that had an open view of the sea. Maps were posted announcing new forbidden zones. The proclamations contained mysterious threats against any trespassing of these areas. We knew perfectly well what they meant. The Germans had planted land mines along the shore in order to render landing attempts suicidal. The maps were dated May twenty-sixth.

On the following night, from an attic where we had posted a lookout, came the electrifying news that a whole fleet was steaming into the fjord. The ships were traveling in close formation and at high speed. They were accompanied by planes. It did not look like an ordinary patrol. The news was spread immediately through the secret channels. This time it appeared to be the real thing.

We had braced ourselves for a harassing test before the city again would be free, but the overwhelming fierceness of this attack was beyond either expectation or description. The night was one continuous explosion.

The British ships ran in from both sides of the Narvik peninsula. From the roof and the top floors of the Hospital we had veritable ringside seats. That particular night I had happened to call at a late hour and could follow the dramatic action as in a theater. Even curtains and wings were not missing from the awe-inspiring stage setting. The air was calm. The play of purple on the mountains was softened by light cotton clouds that seemed to cling to the peaks awhile before they let go and melted away into a quiet blue.

At first we thought the landing would be made to the south of the town. The houses on the opposite side of the harbor were kept under fierce British shellfire. Thank God, the civilians had been evacuated. We knew that some small detachments of Germans had been placed there. But tonight house after house was hit and took fire. Soon the burning houses formed a continuous wall of flame along the shore.

Then the shelling shifted to the north. A few shells burst above the public school buildings. I knew that Ellen and Siri were staying at the Headmaster's house by the public park. Accompanied by a friend, I commandeered an ambulance and drove to the house. The exodus was accomplished in a few minutes, despite the delay caused by the teacher's wife who insisted on bringing along her fat little dog, which was rushing about, insane with fright. Just as we returned to our observation post in the Hospital, the Headmaster's house was hit.

The shellfire was now concentrated on the north side of town, especially the vicinity of Vasvik harbor. Shells

flew like shafts of fire through the houses and we feared the worst, since only the lower part of town had been completely evacuated. The Germans had some small-caliber guns on the mountain slopes. On the Iron Ore Company grounds an anti-aircraft cannon was firing in the direction of Ankenesstrand. This meant that the Poles were working their way down towards the sea. Otherwise, the Germans were concentrating their fire on Øyjord peninsula. They did not seem to be so much concerned about the ships as about the troops on the other side. We saw a few direct hits on the homes around the small ferry dock. The German gunfire, however, grew steadily weaker. One by one their cannons were being silenced.

One of the British destroyers went close to shore a little inside Rombakken and opened fire against a wooded ridge that leveled off into the sea. Geysers of trees and earth shot into the air after each hit.

Then, just before the summer midnight, attacking troops came in small landing barges from the direction of Øyjord. We realized that there would be hand-to-hand fighting north of town. That area was free of land mines. We remained standing at the Hospital windows, shivering with excitement. Shell fragments spattered against the walls and made us duck, but we did not move away. The spectacle was too fascinating to miss.

Wounded soldiers crept out of their beds. Some British patients whom we had kept in a separate room also came limping out. We had reported them as hopeless, but there they were, and they brought along field glass-

es they had managed to keep hidden. The glasses circulated from nurses and doctors to us visitors and on to the German and British wounded. The Germans realized that they would be prisoners by morning and became more ill and more polite as the night wore on.

Now we saw the attacking troopers disembark. We could hear the machine guns and the quick explosion of hand grenades. For a while it looked as if the Germans would hold the forest, but suddenly their fire lessened. Within an hour after the landing the din abated. The recapture of Narvik had taken a good four hours.

We saw German soldiers withdraw to the south of town. A party crept out of the Telegraph Office and broke up into small groups. One by one we could see them moving down Street 1 and farther on towards Beidsfjord. The last group of Germans to leave town blew up the gun position on the Company grounds. It had stood in the vicinity of a huge coal supply which also caught fire. That was our last coal supply.

The next morning, except for the wounded in the Hospital, not a single German was left in town. But, as yet, our troops had not begun to move in. A strange mood of uncertainty lay over the city, and we were all extremely sleepy.

"You all look pale and happy, like a bride at the breakfast table," Mr. Njöten commented as he drove by with a load of German corpses he had picked up around the Railroad Station.

Later that forenoon I went for a walk in the direction of the cemetery. In a forest grove the French Foreign

Legionnaires lay in position. I waved my arms and aired my French, such as it was. A colossus of a professional warrior approached me. He said that they had been ordered to halt for a while. I had, therefore, better return to town and ask the people to remain quiet. The Legionnaires would be coming in very shortly. To make it quite certain he gave me a kiss of joy on both cheeks. Damn it, I thought, that those Germans have bought up all the shaving cream!

The Frenchmen came, graciously arriving second to the Norwegian troops, who had taken part in the storming of the town. The first blond Norwegian boy that marched into town was the young son of the town baker. We took him in a bannered car to his parents, who embraced him with dough sticking to their forearms. They had had no news of him since the start of the war.

Then we drove to the Judge's house to fetch Consul Gibbs and his colleagues. British, French, and Polish flags waved on the car. We drove up and down Street 1. The Norwegian flag again floated above the City Hall and it was more beautiful than ever before.

W XIV — ABANDONED VICTORY

E WERE free again. People emerged from the cellars, and there were smiles and hilarious reunions. The Day had arrived at last. It was a Sunday. The only pity was that we were so sleepy that we could not enjoy it to the full. Even so, there was not going to be much sleeping.

We inquired about all that had happened at the front. The Norwegian soldiers, who had been in the thick of the mountain fighting for weeks, gave vivid descriptions of the battles around the town. They had slept in snow huts and had gone without warm meals for days. Many casualties had been suffered from the German planes until they learned how to take cover, and the Germans had employed all kinds of trickery, including the wearing of Norwegian uniforms and the forced use of the civilian population. German misuse of civilians and of the Red Cross sign had been especially bad at Gratangen, where the Norwegians had sustained heavy losses.

In other battle zones, too, the civilians had suffered greatly. At Bjerkvik, the peasants had moved to the woods as a result of the radio warning; but, when nothing happened, they had gone back to their homes on the shore. Many were killed during the recapture.

The actual recapture of Narvik cost one hundred and fifty soldiers. The French Foreign Legion and the Norwegian forces shared equally in the losses. Miraculously, of the civilian population in town only a few were wounded, and but one man was killed, a young sailor who had been spared when the *Norge* went down on the ninth of April.

We visited the Foreign Legionnaires, who had taken over the earth caves which the Germans had dug at Framnes. They planned to establish new positions outside the town the same night. They were made up of soldiers of many nations and had come from the fighting in Africa to the war above the Arctic Circle. The Colonel himself was from Vienna. He was enjoying a cup of tea outdoors with his officers when we arrived. An upturned crate was being used for a table. We asked him whether there was anything we might do, at least to the extent of furnishing better quarters. He thanked us, but said that he preferred to sleep in the open with his soldiers. They had not brought any antiaircraft guns with them and thought it best to camp in the woods back of the town. He wished only some brandy for his wounded and graves for his dead.

Late the next evening a Mass was held in the church. Our young parson and the French army priest offici-

ated. Three coffins decked with flags were placed before the altar. They represented the fallen French, British, and Norwegians. In the cemetery there were rows of caskets. They were all placed in a common grave. Soldiers, officers, and civilians thronged the place. We did not know one another and had difficulties with our differences in language. Yet around this great open grave we felt as one great family. Its name was Liberty. It could be found all over the earth and it was powerful and numerous, if only it could find place and opportunity to muster its powers. Here, under the Midnight Sun, we had answered a common call and we had won our first land victory. The dead had not died in vain.

The following day we were given to understand that it would be wise to move women and children out of the town. The Germans had bombed Norwegian towns before, where there had been neither soldiers nor forts. Narvik would undoubtedly be attacked with the utmost fury.

It was hard to get boats, and people were not too willing to leave their homes, now that we had recaptured our town and again were free.

Commander Askim organized an air alarm system with the survivors from the *Norge* and the *Eidsvold*. The church bells were used as warning signals, the heavy bell for danger and the small one for the all-clear.

One night a French cannon exploded, and questions were raised about fifth columnists. We knew of no quislings except Sundlo, but perhaps the Germans had

left behind some spies in civilian clothes. We got news of one of them. Before the recapture of the town, an Austrian soldier had been befriended by a Norwegian family when he had insisted that he was an anti-Nazi. He declared that he would desert, and his Norwegian friends had given him a suit and hidden him in their cellar during the last days of the fighting. He had remained in town a few days after the liberation. Now he had disappeared.

The old trickery once more, playing on our good, dumb, democratic hearts!

Again we had contact with the world outside. One morning there was a long-distance call from the Norwegian War Department, now stationed at Tromsö. We received congratulations and instructions. I recognized the voice. It was my father's. He had arrived in the North with the Royal party.

Congratulations poured in. It was not in vain that we had been the first city to be recaptured by the Allies. From Tromsö came representatives of the Government Press Service. Again there were interviews and radio greetings. Swedish journalists arrived. They were especially interested in learning whether we had any quislings.

The incident concerning Consul Gibbs and the partridge was described in detail by the optimistic radio station at Tromsö. Everyone was supremely sure that final victory had been won in the Narvik sector.

We also had military visitors. A British General and an Admiral dropped in on the town. The Admiral was

a Lord and looked as friendly and as dignified as the distinguished gentleman on the label of old three-star brandy. The Foreign Legionnaires held a brief parade for the visitors in Vasvik. His Lordship was slightly impatient, as though the waiting tea was getting cold. German bombing planes circled above our heads. Had they known what distinguished persons we were on that battered ferry dock that morning, they most certainly would not have limited themselves to the bombing of ships. The guests departed safely and the Legionnaires returned to their positions.

Soon we could follow again the well-known drama in the fjord, the zigzagging destroyers in combat with the bombing hawks.

A few days later Polish officers and soldiers descended in triumph on the town. They had taken the mountain to the south. Beidsfjord had been cleared of Germans. Norwegians who had assisted the Poles said that they had fought like madmen. For them it had evidently been more important to kill Germans than to secure a strategic position.

"Here in Norway the Germans have behaved like angels," they said, "but just wait. If you have anything more to do with them, the picture will be different."

We were in a strange position. We heard that Bodö had been bombed and taken. The general military position throughout the country appeared to be hopeless. In certain southern districts, where small detachments refused to give up in the woods and on the mountains, guerilla warfare continued. But it could only be a ques-

tion of time before the Germans had "mopped up," as they loved to express themselves.

Admittedly, their attempt to use quislings had failed; there were not enough quislings. The Norwegian Administration at Oslo had been taken over by a Council of leading officials. Even that makeshift arrangement seemed to be but a mutual bargaining for time.

In the Narvik sector the picture was reversed. The remainder of General Dietl's army was deadlocked in the mountains along the Iron Ore Railroad behind the town. The Germans were flanked on three sides and would soon have to choose between annihilation and retreat into neutral Sweden, where they would be demobilized and interned. We knew that there were armed forces of considerable size across the border.

At first, we were a little bitter against our Swedish brethren, but later we understood better. Like ourselves, Sweden was ill-prepared. She was admittedly a greater nation, with a stronger military machine, but she had sent the main part of her munition supply to Finland the previous winter. Sweden could not have offered us any assistance.

Then the birds came over with eggs earmarked for Narvik. In the first serious air bombardment they attempted to destroy the offices of the civil administration. Because of broken windows and holes left by shell splinters from the Polish howitzer, we had moved our offices from the City Hall to the near-by Fire Station. The latter was a partly-finished brick building. The cellar and the first floor were completed, but during the depression

we had run out of funds, and, since the remainder of the building had been planned as a community hall, we had put our dreams into the drawer with the blueprints and put a temporary roof over the unfinished part.

Several hundred persons were in the air-raid cellar when the bombs fell. They exploded in the section across the railroad tracks. That block of houses went up in flames, but we succeeded in rescuing some of the wounded. With Finn, I drove a truck to the Hospital, carrying an old woman who had half a leg torn off, and an old acquaintance, an engineer who only a few moments earlier had been in our office. He complained of loss of sensibility in the lower part of his body, but spoke calmly and cheerfully during the trip to the Hospital. He died on arrival. His spine was broken.

We realized that we must evacuate as many people as possible. The boats we had commandeered held no more than twenty to thirty persons each. We telephoned all the sheriffs in the surrounding districts, but they could tell us only that all their boats had sailed away. The Chief of Police at Harstad promised to send some fishing vessels as soon as he could find them.

One night we held a meeting at the Iron Company office. It was located near the tunnel, which now was looked upon as the only safe place in town. During the meeting it was reported that an Englishman was outside and wished to come in. I went out to see him. He was a young man in a raincoat and a British helmet. He spoke Norwegian with an English accent. The visitor introduced himself as Lieutenant Job—Patrick Job. He

wanted to talk to us about the evacuation. He had boats.

I asked him to come in. If he had been sent from heaven he could not have appeared at a more opportune moment. He informed us in a strange, primitive Norwegian that he belonged to the Royal Navy but that he had been commissioned to work with the evacuation of civilians. He had rented half a hundred fishing vessels in Lofoten. The boats would come in the fjord in small groups of five or six. As identification signals they had red and white paint on the prows and flew the flags on the front instead of on the back masts. They had completed the civilian evacuation of Bodö. Now it was Narvik's turn. Seven vessels lay ready to sail at Øyjord; they would have to depart within two hours. It was now about midnight, but it was not easy to get people ready. He realized that the time was not too good, but speed was imperative. He must have three or four hundred women and children on board these boats.

He had seated himself on the side of the Director's desk and dangled his sea boots in seeming embarrassment as he talked. When he removed his helmet, he looked even younger, with his unruly blond hair and an open smile on a sunbaked face.

I suppose that most of us unconsciously compared him with the young officers who had just been driven out of Narvik. They had been hard-bitten warriors with plans of world conquest. Here was a college youth, still a trifle timid at being an officer. He had been put ashore to try to find ways and means to be of assistance.

This was the youth of that "decadent" England which took loss and defeat until it found a way to gain victory.

We asked him how the war was going.

"Absolutely rotten, but the problem now is how to get these boats going."

"Where are they bound?"

He did not know, but he had made arrangements with a man who sat with a telephone on a pier somewhere out in the fjord at a place called Kjeldbotn. The boats would pass and call to him, and he, having contact with the local sheriffs in the islands, would announce the destination to each individual boat.

We liked Patrick Job. We sent trucks to all the air-raid cellars and took out the women and children. Lieutenant Job went to Vasvik and waved a huge yellow flag. Boat after boat moved across the fjord and loaded its cargo of sleepy children and excited mothers. Each boat had a leader, who, during the voyage, was to make a complete list of his passengers and be responsible for them on arrival.

Job stood on the pier, smiled to the children, cursed the skippers, and waved his flag. We furnished the cargo, but it was considerably more than two hours before the last families had sent back the superfluous suitcases with table linen and silver spoons. Each woman could take along only what she herself could carry. The evacuation was to continue the next night.

On the way home we asked Job whether he had any quarters and luggage, and also where he had picked up his Norwegian, which was serviceable even though it

was not academically impeccable. He told us that on
his vacations he had often gone fishing along the Norwegian coast and had learned it from the fishermen.
He had had a sea-going sailboat before the war. He had
not arranged for any quarters and would like to get a
place to sleep. He had brought along a toothbrush and
had a pair of clean socks in his pocket.

The next day at noon we paid a visit to Consul Gibbs
in the City Judge's home, where we were met by an atmosphere of deep gloom. It was obvious that there had
been bad news. The news was confidential, but we understood that it had to do with the situation in Norway.

As we left, Job suggested that we go for a ride
through the town. There was no reason to take the sor-
rows in advance. We would hear soon enough, and
there was much to do in the meantime. And what did
a little bad news, more or less, matter?

We drove to the ore docks. The scene was one of utter chaos. There must have been more than thirty ship-
wrecks in the harbor, and the tops of masts and parts
of ships protruded from the water. Along the docks lay
more blasted and desolated ships. *Jan Wellem* lay with
less than half its hull above water. We went on board.
The spacious cabins were empty. There was not as much
as a pair of dirty socks left.

We returned to the office. The Administration must
be kept up to date. A meeting of the City Council was
to be held that day. The various arrangements and dis-
posals that had been made would have to be reported
for approval. In the midst of our meeting the heavy

church bell began to sound a warning of enemy bombers. But the planes were on their way to a destination farther north. It was going to be a quiet day, after all. Other places were about to taste the fury of Nazi destruction and desolation.

At the close of the meeting a Swedish journalist appeared with the message that the Swedish Red Cross was ready to receive Norwegian children. He had personally come through the German lines and told us that the Germans would permit groups of ten a day to pass through, including the grownups who were taking care of the children. The Germans were probably glad to have a little respite from the fighting. We knew they were hard pressed and were being forced to retreat farther and farther into the mountains. The spring thaw had come in the higher regions and the terrain was not too favorable for troops under fire. We organized special groups of evacuees to go inland, mostly persons with families or relatives in Sweden.

The Sunday following the recapture of Narvik we had our first spring day of 1940. It was almost hot, and the streets were snowbare and dry. The trees had gotten the faint green veil. It was the second of June. During the night we had evacuated the last children. I had waved good-bye to Ellen and Siri. They had carried one suitcase and a small bag of bedding, plus old Trine. Trine had a dirty bandage around her head and a big safety pin in her stomach to keep what was left of the sawdust inside. The children had been playing bombing attack in the park.

Well into the forenoon German planes came over.
There were twenty in all. These were the planes meant
for us. They circled in at a low altitude in the absolute
assurance that we were without anti-aircraft guns. The
ships had left. We could only sit and wait and take it.
We harbored no illusions. This time they had come to
destroy the town and "lower the morale." They started
with Street 1 and worked their way uptown. In Frydenlund they blasted the new Police Chamber, which was
housed in a private home near the church. They also
attempted to hit the entrance to the air-raid tunnel near
the Iron Company. Job coolly contributed the observation that, if it were hit, not one of the five hundred
persons inside would survive. The tunnel had no gates,
and the air pressure would hit inwardly. Even so, there
were no other shelters that were secure except against
splinters.

We stood the test. I inspected all the big cellars and I
saw no one who had lost his self-control. Calmness was
something we had continually stressed. When people
had come to the City Hall sobbing or whining they had
been kept in the corridors until they could control their
emotions. Now only men and unmarried or childless
women were left. The young girls who remained were
mostly nurses or volunteers in the public soup kitchens.

The more people there were in the air-raid shelters
the higher the spirits seemed to be. Some spoke as loudly as possible to prevent others from listening to the
screams of falling bombs and counting the explosions.

The bombing lasted for two hours. It seemed to be

mainly five-hundred-pound bombs that were dropping on us, interspersed with incendiaries. Fires started wherever they hit and the conflagration spread. Heavy aerial machine-gun fire accompanied the bombing. In a defenseless city machine-gun fire along with the bombing does produce its intended effect of utter helplessness. It seemed that there was no limit to the savagery the Germans were prepared to use on civilians.

At length the British fighting planes arrived and we had an opportunity to attempt to save what was still left of the town. To extinguish the conflagration was impossible. We could only try to limit the fire and remove as much furniture and food stores as was possible from the threatened houses. The fire leapt from building to building and the heat was so intense that all wooden material seemed to melt away. We hoped that the fire would be arrested at Danielsen's brick building, at least momentarily, so that we might use the fire hose more effectively, but the fire was too fierce. The windows were shattered and within a few seconds the fire raced through the building and started on the next.

We dynamited the last house by the Market Place and managed to save the northern part of town. Everyone who remained in the city took part in salvaging all kinds of movables, which were piled in the streets and parks—furniture and clothing, dentist chairs, canary birds, and canned goods. There was no looting.

The entire business district was destroyed. The State liquor store burned down with all doors locked. We did not permit one bottle to be spared. When matters

quieted somewhat, we counted our casualties. We had escaped miraculously. Only three persons had been killed. Because of the gradual intensification of bombing and incendiarism over several weeks, we had become quite efficient in taking precautionary measures. Not for one moment was there panic among our citizens.

In the midst of the conflagration we reported to Tromsö. My father was on the wire once more. I told him that Ellen had left and that she would attempt to communicate with him.

Bombing could never break us, but it did create a certain disturbance. In the air-raid shelters and in the tunnel the spirits were high, but people began to tire. Excitement keeps one's courage up, but as soon as the tension is relaxed the reaction sets in. Then one is overcome by a great weariness and can go to sleep anywhere.

That night Job sent a few boatloads of elderly people out of town.

Young men were going into military service; others, able to work, remained to repair the railroad and the public dock. We organized a Norwegian Military Police and had a Norwegian Commanding Officer.

The men of the Foreign Legion came into town only at intervals. One evening I met their Colonel in the street. He expressed his gratitude for some brandy we had sent him from the Hospital, and asked whether we could get him a new banner. The old one had been destroyed in battle. He provided a drawing to be used as a pattern, but it was anything but easy to find the proper material or someone to sew it. Finally, the wife

of one of the engineers contributed a formal dress that she thought might be changed into a Foreign Legion standard.

Strange indeed were the days that followed. The fighting in our own front sector progressed very satisfactorily, but the news from Belgium, Holland, and France was heartbreaking. Rumors began to spread that the Allied troops in the mountains were about to be evacuated. We refused to believe it. Half the victory was already won. The Germans were being pressed ever closer to the border. In this sector, at least, there would be a complete victory. A British General Staff officer came to inform himself of the spirit. We assured him that our spirit was good, but said that it would be even better if we had a battery of anti-aircraft guns. Other foreign officers arrived and asked strange questions. We began to put things together. The skipper of one of the evacuation boats returned and told us that the British had begun to embark at Harstad. Our officers had no information.

On the sixth of June, the Foreign Legion standard was completed. The formal dress was certainly going to a dance this time! The banner was rust red and green and carried the Legion's emblem on one side and a greeting from Narvik on the other. I looked up some fine French words in a dictionary. It would, perhaps, be quite proper to make a short speech. The Norwegian liaison officer assigned to the Legion dropped in and I asked his advice. He said he had information for us. The city was to be given up within the next twenty-four

hours. The Allies were withdrawing their troops. I gave him the banner and asked him to deliver it.

We sat around the office desks at the Fire Station. We did not say much. Someone asked whether the war was over, whether we had lost. We did not know. No, the war could not have been lost. We decided to empty the town and go north. The northernmost part of the country was still free.

Job returned. He told us that he had called all his ships back and that the next day would be the last.

I called Tromsö. I realized that it was impossible to make any further inquiries by telephone, but we did receive powers to continue the evacuation. My father had not had any word from Ellen and Siri. He implored me not to permit myself to be caught.

That night the Foreign Legion fought overtime along the length of the railroad line. We heard that Norwegian troops had counterattacked farther inland. The following morning the Legionnaires were in town. I met the Colonel at the dock. It was evident that he deplored the situation as though it had been a personal humiliation, but he remained a gentleman to the last. Our banner would fly in new battles, he said, and he wanted to make a return gift. He pointed to some fifty mules that had been used in munition transport. It was impossible to take the animals back to France. Perhaps we could take them over and, preferably, eat them as quickly as possible. Mule stew in hot sauce was not too bad, he said. We promised to do our best, although there were other tasks which required more immediate attention,

Perhaps it made no difference, but we made it a point of honor to maintain order to the last minute. The Hospital personnel, the parson, and a few other persons were to remain with the wounded. We had to bring the city records out. As much food as possible must also be taken along. We were interrupted by a last bombardment, but not many bombs were dropped on this trip. Job had set the deadline for departure at 8 P.M. He said he would accompany me in a small boat. The deadline was postponed to 10 P.M. There was a little time left for last-minute instructions, but the telephone went dead; the personnel at the station had gone. I threw the receiver on the desk. Our city was no longer functioning.

Job arrived in a truck and we drove the public archives down to the dock. There was a strong smell of soot and dirt in the air. Street 1 was a meaningless ruin. It was strange that so little could remain of the houses. There was nothing left but a layer of brown pulver and rubble, with chimneys standing here and there like barren trees in a nightmare. Bedding and crushed furniture littered the street.

When we arrived at the pier, most of the ships had gone. The last of the military were being shipped. We boarded a small boat and sailed out into the fjord.

Narvik—the young, vigorous town! Only two months ago we had been happy there. Perhaps we had failed to realize how fortunate we had been. Ten thousand citizens had lived there. Now but fifty remained. The smoke from the last scenes of the devastation drifted out toward us in a tired and hopeless farewell.

242

We traveled all night. Occasionally German planes circled overhead, but we knew we were not a significant target, so we moved steadily along. In the early morning we approached Harstad, the white little town on Norway's greatest island, Hindö, immediately north of Lofoten. Job informed me that the British Headquarters were there. He thought that they had already been given up, but some of their ships should still be there.

We entered the harbor as a huge troop transport was leaving, a black steamer as large as the Norwegian transatlantic liners. A British destroyer was drawing in its anchor. This was Lieutenant Job's ship. We drew alongside and he climbed on board. He asked us to wait. In a few moments he returned to the rail accompanied by the commanding officer. The officer expressed his gratitude for the treatment of the British Consul and his staff. Now they were outward bound for England. He had orders to take me along if I wished to come. It might be a wise thing to do, he added.

No, I must go North, I told him. Our Government was in Tromsö. I waved good-bye. Job threw his camel's-hair coat down to me. It was a kind of parka, the type worn by British naval officers.

The fishing boat cast off, and the destroyer lashed the water with its propellers.

We proceeded to town. Here and there we could see the effect of bombs, but the town was not badly damaged. We asked people on the dock whether many Narvik evacuees had arrived.

— Yes, but not during the last few days. —

A fisherman who made his boat fast next to ours told us that he was from Kjeldbotn. The evacuation boats from Narvik had sailed by there. They had seemed to steer north of Harstad. Many rumors were abroad. Had many been killed, he asked. Was there anything left of the town?

— Well, there were a few blocks of houses left, and we did not have too many dead. How had it been in Kjeldbotn? Had they seen the naval battles? —

He became excited.

— Yes, indeed! They fought right off the dock. A hailstorm of shell splinters had fallen inland. —

— Had there been any accidents? —

— No, nothing worth mentioning. Some cattle had been killed in the fields, and an old maid up on the ridge. She had been taking care of an old bachelor who had been dying for years. She was to inherit him, people said. There had been a last will. All in vain, now. —

"Her name was Amanda?" I said.

— Yes, something like that. Was I that well acquainted in Kjeldbotn? —

He wished us Godspeed, and we continued north. On our way we saw the destroyers far out at sea. They were westward bound.

About noon we arrived in Tromsö. The stevedores said that the King and the Cabinet had left during the night on board the last British man-of-war out of Tromsö but that some officers and officials had been left behind.

In the improvised Governmental offices everything was quiet. Only a few elderly officials remained, well-known names from Oslo. I delivered my report and was advised to go abroad. Two planes were scheduled to leave for Finland in the afternoon. Perhaps I might secure a place in one of them.

In the evacuated War Department I found a letter from my father with Ellen's new address.

— He had left for London with the Royal party. The war would be continued from abroad. —

Later, I met friends, among them Tor Gjesdal, who had visited Narvik as the representative of the Government Press Office.

— No, the war was anything but over. He had been too late to make the British destroyers. Now he was on his way to Finland. Did I wish to join him? —

And I met Viggo Hansteen, the attorney for the National Trade Unions. We were old friends. He intended to stay. He had had no military training and felt that he would be of greater use inside Norway. There were untold difficulties to be faced. Some had to be there to meet them. There was no question in his mind about his choice.

At first, my own course was not too clear. Perhaps one day I would be forced to leave, but just now it was impossible. There was endless confusion. I must find my family and some of our friends from Narvik. We must make some plans for the future. Our people were scattered all through the islands and in the fjords.

I met a young engineer from Narvik who had a car

and gasoline, and he expressed his willingness to take me with him. We ferried to the mainland and drove south. We slept for a few hours on a farm and continued our journey the next morning.

In the forenoon we made Sætermoen, which had been one of the most important inland military centers during the war. The British forces had had their air field in its vicinity. The field was now blown up and the depots were emptied, but groups of Norwegian soldiers drifted along the roads or sat on the side of the highways, waiting for the final demobilization order. They knew that the Norwegian Commander in Chief, General Ruge, had gone to arbitrate with the Germans. He had decided to remain with his soldiers.

There was no ammunition left. A friend from the Military Police told me that the boys had received the news the day before. They had already guessed as much.

There had never been much military enthusiasm among these sons of Northland farmers and fishermen; no one had imagined that the military conscription we had maintained would ever be put to use. But now they had wept in sheer anger. Some of them had shaken their fists in the faces of the officers, enraged because they could not fight on.

"But the British must have ammunition!" they cried.

There was small comfort for them in the reply that the British would now have to leave to defend their own country.

We had to move on. On the way to the Coast we drove

through an evacuated French camp. In contrast to the British, the French troops had not been able to bring themselves to destroy everything behind them. In Sallangen we saw an old factory building filled with food stores and uniforms being looted by Laplanders. We saw Laplander boys drinking brandy from French helmets. They literally waded in biscuits and strange cheeses. It was the only example of looting we observed throughout the whole war. Nauseated and sick, we drove on.

In the middle of the night we arrived at a ferry landing, where we left the car. A fisherman rowed us out to an island where Ellen and Siri were to have sought refuge. Perfect order was being maintained on the island. Ellen and Siri had reached it safely. The sheriff knew where each family was staying. We found the house, and got food and sleep.

After a rest of two days a small party of us sailed for Harstad. We had heard that as yet there were no soldiers there. We knew a few people in the town and obtained a cabin near-by where Ellen stayed with Siri while I visited with various groups from Narvik. Our plan was to open a Narvik office in Harstad. The public schools were being used as havens for refugees. Everyone was inquiring about families or relatives. Through the radio we had instituted a makeshift information service.

Harstad had been a military center throughout the war, but had never been the scene of any direct action. Even the German planes kept cautiously away from

247

Harstad, since the British had destroyers and anti-aircraft artillery stationed around the town.

We heard that Svolvær, too, was undamaged. The German fish buyer, Herr Köehln, had been extremely zealous, even though no occupation troops had appeared. He had tried to get in to Narvik but had been arrested by the Norwegian Police and returned to Svolvær. When he was informed that his Norwegian sweetheart had been taken into custody, he committed suicide, acting with typical German thoroughness and Aryan taste by placing his head under the circular saw in the prison carpenter shop.

Most of our beautiful coastal steamers had been sunk during the war. Whether or not they had been used as troop transports had made no difference. One of them had been bombed by German planes even though it carried wounded and flew Red Cross flags from all masts. The *Nord Norge*, the pride of Narvik, was also sunk. The steamship companies now began to lease fishing vessels to start the traffic anew.

Life along the coast was going to begin again, but no one knew under what conditions.

XV — ESCAPE

O N THE fifteenth of June we held a meeting in the ticket office on the dock at Harstad to discuss the problem of sending the evacuees home. The Narvik radio had ordered the workers to return. We felt that we had better await developments.

When I came out of the office, the dock was crowded with soldiers. One of the local steamers had arrived with troops. They wore Norwegian uniforms, but I recognized some of them as Germans I had seen at Narvik. I walked rapidly toward town.

Now I would have to make a definite decision in my own case.

Suddenly a squad of soldiers came alongside and stopped me. They took me to the Nobel Hotel, a three-story, wooden building close to the pier, and set me in a chair in the lobby. Captain Reichmann had spotted me from a hotel window and ordered that I be brought to him immediately.

The Captain himself came into the room, his face like a thundercloud.

"We have some very interesting information about you, Mr. Mayor," he said. "You are under arrest."

Between two soldiers I was taken into the dining room. A young officer placed himself at the door. I heard the Captain conferring with someone in the lobby about getting a prison cell for a British spy.

I tried to appear indifferent and calm. The little dining room was in a corner of the hotel and had windows to the street and to a back yard where there were small storage shacks. It was on the first floor. There was a high cellar beneath. I walked about the room and looked at the pictures on the walls. A lady with a parasol and a coquettish smile hung in a gold frame next to the window facing the back yard. The window was open. Across the room there was a bar, with bottles and postcards, and behind it I saw that there was a stairway leading down to the cellar. The two soldiers remained standing in the middle of the floor. I walked across the room and made another study of the lady beneath the sun umbrella. She had an idiotic smile. Next to the picture hung a mirror. I was pale, and my smile was not very convincing either. Down in the yard a young boy was opening a barrel. He looked up. I nodded as meaningfully as I could, and he understood that I wanted something. I managed to whisper down to him for God's sake to get me a taxi. It must wait for me in the second cross street to the north.

One of the sentries came over and closed the window.

I sat down at the bar and lit a cigaret. We could hear more soldiers drive up from the dock. They had apparently already gotten some trucks. The sentries became curious. They both turned their backs on me and looked out the windows to the street.

"Now or never," I thought, as I ran quickly around the bar. Like lightning I was down the cellar stairs. From the cellar into the yard took no time. Now, if only I didn't make a fatal mistake between the storehouses! I was lucky, and made it around the block and into the street on the other side. The car was waiting in the right spot. I threw myself on the floor and we sped away.

We picked up Ellen and Siri at the cabin. I made a brief explanation in a frantic hurry. The Narvik archives and an already-packed knapsack were flung into the car, and we were on our way with greater haste than dignity.

North of town there was a crossroad. Should we choose the shore route towards the sound to the mainland or the road leading across the islands toward the ocean? We chose the latter.

Half a year later I met a young flyer in the Royal Norwegian Legation in Washington who told me that he had been in Harstad on that same day. He said that the Germans had stopped all traffic across the sound and searched for us in vain in all boats headed for the mainland. We had been fortunate.

On the other side of Hindö we arranged with a fisherman to take us to an island still farther off shore. I knew there was no telephone there, but there was a small fishing harbor. An even, fine fog drifted in from the sea and

even a few hundred yards out we were lost from observ-
ers ashore. We rested a few hours above the little harbor, but as soon as a fishing vessel made a call I rushed
down to make an arrangement with the crew, in this
case an old man and a youngster.

— Would they take the three of us for a little sightseeing trip around Lofoten? I was a Life Insurance
Inspector. —

— Yes, they could do that. —

We traveled outward among still more distant islands. At a certain place we stopped to leave behind the
box of records for safekeeping and to give some orders.
Then we set the course south for Lofoten. It was a good
boat, with a well-kept cabin in the bow. There was a
small stove and a shining copper coffeepot. In the cup-
board were coffee and bread. Siri played on deck with
some of the great green glass balls that fishermen use to
keep their nets afloat. The sun shone over a calm sea. I
talked with the skipper.

This was a very special inspection trip that I was taking, I said.

He understood. But he did not have enough oil for
any extended trip, unless we stopped at Svolvær.

— No, I did not like Svolvær. Could we not go via
Vestfjorden into one of those deep fjords that go in almost to the Swedish border? —

— That would take a good ten hours, but it was possible, to be sure. —

Ellen wanted to know what we planned to do. Could
not she and Siri go ashore somewhere? It might be eas-

ier for me to get through alone. The Germans would
be everywhere by this time. A woman and a little girl
would make identification too easy. Siri was tired and
fretful. She wanted to go ashore. We had forgotten
Trine, which did not help matters. I said we had plenty
of time to devise a plan. This would probably be the
last trip we would have among the islands for a long
time. We might as well sit and enjoy it.

We passed through Troldfjorden. Tourists had come
from all over the world to see this crooked channel that
the ocean had washed into existence between the mountains. It was the most exquisite beauty spot in all Lofoten. Each moment the mountains seemed to be closing
in before us. But, suddenly, around a headland, the
fjord went on again, until, at last, there were no more
mountains. It was as if a curtain had gone up before an
orchestra of sea gulls. The open ocean lay before us,
somnolent and calm, breathing lightly in the red sunshine.

It was not long before we saw the mountains in
Lofoten proper.

I pointed out the Vågakallen to Siri.

— But it was nothing but a black mountain, —she
said.

— Yes, now it looked like that. But once upon a time,
very long ago, it had been a real giant, who played in the
sea and owned all the mountains up here. When he became old he decided to marry and settle down. He knew
of a beautiful maiden in the Helgeland mountains. She
was called Lekamöya, the playful maiden, and she was

the most beautiful woman on the whole coast. The Våga giant wanted her for his wife. But Hestmannen, the Horseman, a younger giant who rode a proud horse in the ocean, loved her too, and wanted to keep her for himself. When he heard that the old giant was going to propose to her, he realized that he must act with great haste. So the Horseman saddled his horse and rode south so furiously that the sea churned about him. Then the Våga giant saw that time was getting short and he became very angry. But he could not get under way so quickly, so he took his great bow and sent an arrow singing after Hestmannen. The arrow went through the Horseman's hat and carried it off, and it landed way out in the ocean.

— Of course, this was long, long ago, even before there were men or boats up here. But we could still see the angry Våga giant in the mountain, and, if we went farther south, we could see Hestmannen riding hatless in the sea, while his hat lies floating out on the ocean. That is a beautiful little island called Torghatten, and there is still a big hole through the mountain made by the arrow of the Våga giant. —

"Can't we go down and pick it up for him?" Siri asked, half asleep.

— No, we had no time now, and our boat was too small anyway. We had better come back at some later time and put things in order. The mountains would certainly wait for us. —

Toward morning we were deep in the fjord. We knew some people in here and thought we might make

a call at one of the tiny trading posts. The boat was anchored at a cliff point outside the harbor and I climbed a forested ridge and looked down into the village. A German sentinel was stationed on the dock. We had to go on. We decided to proceed deep into one of the numerous fjord arms, where nature is so wild that there are neither farms nor roads. I knew an old couple who lived there in a lonely cabin, from where it would be possible to get to Sweden. I had been in here once before on a fishing trip.

We found the right arm of the fjord, and the cabin lay there, small and gray, as always, at the foot of the mountain. We paid the skipper and bade him a grateful good-bye.

Yes, the people on the farm had heard that there was war and that the Germans had been evil. The old man would not have believed a word of it if he had not seen it with his own eyes. Once on a fishing trip out in the fjord he had come upon some soldiers in green uniforms. They had fired their guns at him and made a hell of a noise.

We asked him whether he could guide us to Sweden. No, he himself was too old to climb the mountain slopes, but he knew a Laplander boy who knew the way. It was anything, however, but a route for women or children. It would take three days to reach people on the other side of the border, and there were some very treacherous streams to cross. He would fetch the young Laplander, whose name was Leif.

The remainder of the day we rested. We did not say

much. Ellen wanted me to get started as quickly as possible. Siri was completely worn out and fell asleep in a chair. When the Laplander arrived we sent him down the fjord with a message to some friends. We needed food and equipment. Then we rested again, or we talked about ordinary things. There was much we wanted to say, but words did not come easily.

Towards evening the boy returned. He brought with him all we had asked for, and much more. There was a message also. Our friends advised me to go immediately. My name had been broadcast together with those of other Norwegians whom the Germans wanted detained. I need not fear, my friends said, they would take good care of Ellen and Siri.

The message made the decision for us, even though we had known that this would be the only way out. The knapsack was packed, with Job's coat on top. Leif carried a bag. We made hasty farewells and started the mountain climb.

It was a beautiful night, the weather clear and chilly, but I was tired and our progress was not fast. At intervals we made bonfires of heather and dwarf-birch. We tried to get snatches of sleep while the heat lasted, and then were on our way again. Leif was eighteen years old, but he had been twice to the Lofot fisheries. He was thin and sinewy, almost too good a marching companion. His father owned a farm with four cows. It must be his mother who was a Laplander, I thought. We kept up a little conversation to begin with; but, later, we just marched on and on in silence.

The next morning after ten hours of walking and climbing we reached the cairn marking the Swedish border.

Yes, the years had passed quickly, although much had happened. The time ahead might not move so rapidly.

Wearily I rose and adjusted my knapsack. I prized Job's coat, but my pleasure in possessing it did not lessen its weight. We continued our march into Sweden.

After two days of tramping we arrived at the first Swedish Laplander colony. These were real Laplanders with tents and reindeer. They were friendly and helpful, and directed us to a tourist cabin where Swedish relief organizations had deposited blankets and food stores with the order that no money was to be asked of refugees from Norway. The log cabin was large and comfortable. We met a dozen Norwegians who had already made their escape. Most of them had been soldiers. One had brought his sweetheart along. She cooked our meals and he was very proud. He had oiled his gun with fat and buried it behind the barn at home, he said. He might have need for it.

The following day we were taken to the nearest military post. The Norwegian soldiers had to be temporarily interned, but the others were permitted to proceed. I went to Stockholm.

A strange atmosphere permeated the Swedish capital. The city was just the same as before, except that the autos had small wood-burning stoves in the rear for fuel. The newspapers wrote about neutrality and

"gengas," the new wood-gas auto fuel. There were soldiers and officers in all the streets and Germans in the hotels. In the lobby of the Grand Hotel I saw Dr. Kant pounding the hotel desk and demanding his mail. One of the hotel employes said he was a well-known German business man with connections everywhere.

I had heard that Mrs. J. Borden Harriman, the American Minister to Norway, had arrived in Stockholm, and I met her at the Grand. Ever since she had come to Norway as American Minister in 1937 she had been known as one of our country's great foreign friends. I thought she might assist me in securing a visa to the United States. I was not disappointed.

It was not easy to travel across the world in wartime and preparations for the start seemed to take an eternity.

There were many Norwegians in Stockholm burning with a desire to get back to work. Some were officers and soldiers who had been through the fighting, others were officials and workers who had refused to work under German tyranny.

We learned the details of the battles in southern Norway. There had been furious fighting, and the Germans had lost sixty thousand men. British assistance had been sadly inadequate; only territorials had been sent. Often the men did not know how to handle the machine guns, and the young officers had been forced to take over. Behind each destroyed machine-gun nest there had been dead British officers. They had done their best.

We were received with the greatest friendliness by the Swedes. Before the war we had never felt any differences between our neighbors and ourselves. We had shared the same views and the same illusions. The old illusions we had lost and in their stead we had gained a new world-view that was, perhaps, both more and less than illusion. The war was not over, even though the whole of Europe seemed to be under Nazi domination. We believed in the coming victory over German tyranny, but we felt something besides. We had an inner certainty that, before the victory was won, the tidal wave would continue to rise, and that it would spread throughout the world. In the shadows cast by our burning cities we had divined the dark truth, unclear and terrifying, that not one country or one home would be spared. Yet, half-unconsciously, too, we understood that the day of reckoning would come. So great was the injustice that the whole of humanity would rise against it, or be obliged to bow its head and build new temples for it on the ruins of the old.

Through our legation in Stockholm we received word from our Government in London. Its attitude was the same as ours: everything or nothing! No way led back to Norway but the way of victory. Our statesmen and our seamen had saved our merchant fleet, and it was now in the fight on the side of Great Britain. Our gold reserves had been carried over the mountains through the bombing attacks to the west coast. From there it had gone on fishing vessels north to Tromsö and thence abroad. Every ounce had come out. Yes, we believed

in victory, in victory not only for our way of life, and in eventual liberty and peace, but in military victory for our weapons, the weapons which, as yet, we did not have.

Our calm Swedish friends told us that they loved us but that we were mad. Somewhat mad, we from the other side of the Kjölen Mountains had, perhaps, always been, but now, they said, we were war psychopaths. We had been taken by surprise from our bed and thrown into ice water, and it had been too much for us.

Perhaps we were out of our minds, yet the world itself did not seem very sane, and our experience had been of our world, the world of reality. Of course, we might have had to admit that, if it had been Sweden and not us that had been lying on the outside of that Scandinavian double bed, if it had been Sweden and not us that had been thrown out of it, we, too, perhaps, might still be neutral, even though we had always shown a greater tendency to madness.

Again it was the inactivity that was the worst. One did not know what to do. Then I met an old friend from Oslo. We talked under such circumstances that our conversation made a strong impression upon me. He had been one of the leaders in intellectual circles in Norway, after having lived twenty years in America. His rich experience, his radical views, and his strong personality had placed their imprint upon all the young students who had come under his influence. In earlier years his opinions and guidance had been an important factor in the shaping of my life. Now he lay on his

deathbed in Stockholm, ill of a brain disease. He had gone to Sweden for an operation just before the invasion. He advised me to go to America. In his opinion the United States would become the deciding power in this revolutionary era.

Other refugees from Norway told us that the civilian population was beginning to recover after the initial shock, that some people still believed that the Germans would act like civilized human beings, and that there were very few quislings.

From Norway came news of an organized underground movement. At first, it had been largely in the form of small, isolated groups which hid away weapons and smuggled out information and refugees. Now there were growing signs that an intensified active resistance was being organized to combat the German attempt to nazify the country.

Through the underground I managed to get word to Ellen that I had an opportunity to go to the United States, and that our Government in London had authorized the plan. The reply came through a few weeks later, just before I had to leave: "Godspeed. Will try to join you soon."

XVI — THREE SOLDIERS

BEFORE leaving Stockholm, I spent a whole night talking with three Norwegian boys in a small hotel room. They were very young, and all had served in the war in Norway. Two were students from the University of Oslo, one of them a small law student wearing heavy glasses, the other a tall, handsome medical student. The third was a fair-haired, stocky peasant boy from the coast north of Trondheim.

We chanced to meet in a restaurant and, later, walked together after a Norwegian meeting at which a member of our Government had spoken. I invited them to my room for a smoke and a glass of beer. We all felt a need for unburdening our minds.

I told them that I was on my way to America to enlist the aid of our kinsmen there in our cause, to report what had happened in Norway, and to tell them that, although we had been temporarily defeated, the fight would go on and that they need not be ashamed of the homeland.

The small student in glasses laughed bitterly.

"I'm afraid you can not use me as an example," he said. He looked searchingly at each of us. "I am utterly and completely ashamed. I have not been able to talk with anyone about my experience, but I can think of nothing else. Perhaps it would help if I talked about it."

We urged him to go ahead.

"Well," he went on, "I enlisted on the first day and was a soldier as long as it lasted. I didn't see any front-line fighting except on one occasion—and then I failed miserably."

There was a long pause before he continued. He forced himself to go on.

"During the retreat through the valley south of Dovre I volunteered on a special squad that was charged with holding a curve on the road until our troops could take positions farther up the valley. We must hold it for only one hour, but during that time no one must be allowed to get through. There were four of us, three privates and a lieutenant. He had a strong, tanned face, and I remember that he had lost his cap. We blocked the road with logs and then took cover above the highway. I mentioned the fact that I had competed in some shooting meets and was put in a front position. The rest lay in a slanting line above. The Lieutenant stood behind a pine tree between me and the next man, field glasses to his eyes.

"We were there for only a few minutes when we heard motorcycles coming up from below. The Lieutenant reported that he saw three of them. They were Germans,

apparently on a reconnaisance trip. None must be permitted to return. The entire value of our mission depended upon that. We must take accurate aim. He would give the order to fire.

"When the Germans discovered the barricade they slowed up. One of them stopped directly below me. He half turned his motorcycle. I had him at dead aim all the time. The other two rode slowly toward the barricade, and looked anxiously around. The first one must have seen us. He shouted a warning. My man threw himself into the ditch only a few yards below me.

" 'Fire!' the Lieutenant shouted.

"Shots went off all along the line. Both the Germans on the highway dropped dead. I touched the trigger but could not make myself press it. It was the first time I was shooting at a human being. He lay with his back toward me and had absolutely no chance.

" 'Hi!' I shouted, to give him an opportunity to turn and reach for his gun. He rolled over and remained seated on the shoulder of the road. When he saw me he raised his hands above his head. I bobbed my gun up and down to indicate he was to rise and come forward. He nodded, but, as he rose, he let one hand down, as though to steady himself. Instead, he reached for a hand grenade in his belt and when his hand went up again it let go an oblong object which came whistling toward us. It exploded right behind me. I heard a moan. It was our Lieutenant. His lower bowel had been ripped out. I saw blood and intestines streaming out as he leaned against the tree. From the road I heard the

motorcycle starting up. My glasses were knocked off by the explosion. When I got them on again the German was out of range.

"I crawled up to the pine tree. The Lieutenant lay with his head against the trunk. I knelt beside him and placed my jacket over his torn stomach. He lifted his hand and touched me. It was like a caress.

" 'You are a good fellow,' he whispered hoarsely, 'but you are no good in a war.' His face was drawn in terrible agony. The others came out and wanted to carry him back to the main force. There was an ambulance there. But the Lieutenant managed to whisper that we must hold the position for the full hour. From my place next to the stone I could see his face, ashen beneath the tan. He made an almost imperceptible sign with his head that I must keep my eyes forward. When I looked at him again his head had fallen to the side.

"We lay there an eternity and nothing more happened. At the end of the hour he was dead. We carried him on our guns through the woods.

"I was never sent back into the fighting. I was no good!

"The next week southern Norway was given up. I was near the Swedish border when our company was demobilized and I came across the border with some other boys. I have reported for service every day at the Norwegian office in Stockholm. There must be something I can do! I have not sent word home that I am still alive. I will never have peace but I must find a way to remove that blot, to prove that I am good for something."

Silence followed his story.

"You needn't feel ashamed," I finally said. "You were just like the rest of our nation. We are not adjusted to killing. We are a civilized people."

He shook his head and gave us a hopeless stare from behind his heavy glasses.

"It makes no difference what you call it. We lost our country because there were too many like me. It was men like the Lieutenant that we needed, not bookworms in glasses."

"You'll get your chance, you may be sure of that," the tall student interrupted. "We'll all be in it again. I, too, was through the whole affair. We fired incessantly, but still we had to withdraw. There was certainly no lack of will to fight, but, so far as I was concerned, I never felt that the enemy was anything personal. We just fired at those green uniforms as long as we could.

"It didn't become personal until it was all over. Details of the battles I don't recall, but I shall never forget one incident that occurred after the fighting was over. The communication line had been broken. We were without ammunition all day. In the evening we were told that we would have to surrender at dawn. I got some civilian clothing and escaped through the German lines. I, too, wanted to get to Sweden. I did not like the idea of surrendering, not least, perhaps, because I could not stand the thought of standing defeated before those arrogant Germans.

"The night before I crossed the border I walked alone through a dense forest. The moon was up and the forest

266

was calm, except for a slight stir in the treetops. Suddenly I smelled a strange odor. It reminded me of the frying odor from the student restaurant. I used to have my seat in the corner of the great Reading Room. You remember it opens toward the side of the building over the University kitchen.

"Then I saw the reflection of a fire between the trees. Soon I came to a clearing in the forest and there, in an open field, a little homestead was blazing. I did not see any human beings about, but the odor of burning flesh was strong.

"I climbed a fence and approached the place. A little log cabin and an old barn were being destroyed by an intense, smokeless fire. Then I discovered that there was a human being there. In the farmyard next to the pump an old peasant woman sat. A steel helmet and a can lay beside her. She had apparently tried to extinguish the fire but had given it up. Now she sat motionless with parted legs on the bare ground. Her face was blank and expressionless. I tried to talk to her. I told her she must not sit there like that. Her clothes might catch fire. She gave me no answer, but straightened her skirt with a thin, worn hand.

"I carried a can of water to the burning buildings, but they were beyond salvage. Then I discovered what was causing the odor. The buildings were full of German corpses. Some still had steel helmets on. They were glowing red. Some of the faces seemed to be grinning sardonically through the flames.

"I went back to the old woman and poured some of

267

the water over her. It seemed to help. A faint expression came over her face, some of the blankness went out of the stare. 'Lord Jesus, Lord Jesus,' she moaned. I helped her to her feet and steadied her into the field below the house. She tottered a bit, but kept her balance, and talked a little.

"She had lived on the farm with her two sons. When they heard about the war, they caught a bus going south down the valley, and she had not heard anything more of them. She had been alone right up to the day before yesterday, when some Norwegian soldiers had happened by. They had warned her that there would be shooting and that she had better move up into the mountains. She felt, however, that she was too old to flee to the woods, so she had just turned the cattle out. Yesterday there had been shooting all over the valley, but she had not seen any soldiers until late in the evening. Then some German soldiers had arrived with truckloads of corpses and had piled the dead men into the cabin and in the hay in the barn and set them afire. She had tried to put out the fire, and, when they held her back she splashed water on the soldiers. They had just laughed at her and taken a helmet that had belonged to one of the dead and pressed it down on her head, so that she could not see anything. When the houses were well on fire, the soldiers disappeared.

"I tried to get the woman to come along with me, but she asked where she could go. Then I had to leave her to make my own escape through the forest.

"It was not much of an incident, perhaps. The Ger-

mans had destroyed city after city. They had burned and looted the whole countryside. But this poor little farm made into a hideous funeral pyre and this hopelessly homeless old woman somehow awakened me. It suddenly became a personal necessity to get back to those woods and fight again. I don't know whether you understand what I mean, but that is the way I feel."

"I understand perfectly, and I feel the same way," said the heavy-set blond boy from Trondelag.

His broad dialect filled the little room. We had no lights, but an advertising sign on the roof outside threw great splashes of light through the window. He lowered his voice as he continued.

"I was called to the colors at New Year. We participated in maneuvers, first up in northern Norway, and, later, down by Trondheimsfjord. In the beginning of the war I took part in the fighting there. We met disaster from the start. The English came to Namsos. Their weapons were not much better than ours. There seemed to be no order to anything, and we doubted whether our officers had any real plans at all. The boys wanted to counterattack and retake Trondheim. The officers said we were not strong enough, we must wait for the British. But the British did not manage to hold even Steinkjær at the foot of the fjord. More and more Germans were shipped in. They kept the fjord the whole time and they dominated the air. Whatever we tried amounted to nothing. They destroyed all the cities we held down there. Steinkjær was blown to bits from the sea and Namsos was bombed from the air. I saw

both cities burn to the ground. I drove through Steinkjær just as the church was burning. I and my six brothers had all been baptized and confirmed in that church.

"I had a motorcycle and was serving as a messenger. It was plain hell. I was thus prevented from taking part in any of the fights, but in compensation I had the cycle and escaped towards the north when the British had evacuated and the fighting was off in that section. I took part in all the fighting throughout the Northland. I left the cycle on a dock at Mosjöen and shipped on board a fishing boat for Bodö. I remember it was the twenty-third of May. That was the day they annihilated that town. The German planes began with the hospital and then destroyed the rest of the city. I went north again to fight, but I had no hope of victory.

"We had some wonderful days in the mountains north of Narvik. We shot Germans like rabbits and took one snow-peaked mountain after another. But, inside, I knew it was all in vain. We could never win.

"But finally I had my experience too. A small thing, perhaps, but it changed my whole view. It happened the day we had to give up. I was at Sætermoen when General Ruge returned from his arbitrations with the Germans. The boys said that he had tried to keep the northernmost part of the country free. He had the respect of the Germans, they said. Everybody must respect General Ruge. We soldiers loved him. I did not believe that the Germans would offer us any concessions. They would grab our land as well as all the rest of the world. We could only hope that the next generation might, per-

haps, become brutalized enough to beat them.

"The General returned with just the message I had expected. We must surrender unconditionally.

"We stood on the old parade grounds for a last parade. We were going to be demobilized. The Germans would come the same evening to take over. We would be sent either to prison camps or back to our homes to work as slaves on our own farms.

"A hush settled over the grounds when the General appeared. We had not said much before, but now we were all breathlessly silent. His words were brief and definite, like a command, but they were also like a personal greeting and a friendly farewell to each one of us.

"He said that we could not fight any more for the time being, but that the war was not over. We would never be free merely by waiting for help from the outside. We were going to fight again. He implored us to remain faithful and to be ready for that day. He paused for an instant and a twitch crossed his fine face. I remember he said, 'Whether I am dead or alive I will be with you on that day.'

"I could not look at him any more, or I would have sobbed aloud. I tried to think of something else. I stood on the extreme end next to the fence towards the highway. Across the road a young girl was standing. She lived on a farm not far from our camp. Every morning she had come with a wheelbarrow filled with milk cans. I had helped her a few times but I had never talked with her and did not know her name. I had thought of her often and called her Solveig to myself. She saw

that I was looking at her. She was sobbing and made no attempt to hide it, but there was a strange glow on her face and she smiled as if she wished to share her faith with me. I glanced at the officers, who stood stiffly erect behind the little General, and I looked along the rows of boys. All the faces were shining. And then I knew that we were going to make it, anyhow. The men and the women were what really counted. The tools we could get. Life suddenly became very simple. We would do what the General said. We would be faithful and ready. We would not just wait. We were going to liberate ourselves! Our children would not have to do it. I would flee abroad and learn something, so that I might be ready for that day. Afterwards I would return to this very place. I knew of a sheltered spot in the valley that could be cleared. I would build a home there with Solveig. Our children would live there."

He smiled.

"Well, fellows, you know how one may dream of silly things when your heart is so full that it hurts. Anyway, I managed to escape to the mountains before the Germans marched in. I carried my gun until I had to surrender it to the Swedish border guard. I told him to keep it oiled so that it would not be rusty when I came back for it. He laughed and said it might well be that we would be fighting side by side on that day.

"I was kept in an internment camp for a while in northern Sweden, but a few days ago I got permission to come to Stockholm. I said I had a kind of aunt here. Now they tell me that our Government is planning an

air training school in Canada. Today I talked with some Norwegian officers, and they promised to send me over as soon as plans are a little further along.

"Defeat is not so bitter, after all, if one does not swallow it. And we are certainly not through with this party yet."

For a while we smoked in silence. We were so tired that we sat for a bit before breaking up. The flashes from the sign outside the window came and went with steady regularity, lighting up the young faces. It was almost morning. We said that we would meet again in Norway, but that we would return as other men. The change that we felt in process in us was, perhaps, only a beginning. The war would recreate us in its own image. How hard and brutal and unmindful of life and feeling had we to become before we could take our country back again? Perhaps it was just as well that we did not know the price, but we said that no matter how high it should be we would pay it. We got up and gave one another our hands in farewell, and each handshake was a promise.

XVII — LONG JOURNEY

AT LAST I had passport and visa and money and ticket. There was no other connection between Sweden and Russia than the air route from Stockholm to Moscow, but the best was good enough. There were ten of us in the plane, half of us Scandinavian, the rest Englishmen traveling the wrong way to get back home.

We left Stockholm early in the morning and arrived at Riga about noon. Russia had occupied the Baltic states a few days earlier. In Esthonia things looked quiet, but the stop was short and we had neither time nor opportunity to see very much. In the evening we landed at the Dynamo Airfield in Moscow.

Our tickets were paid in advance, with hotel accommodations and meal tickets. A somber seriousness lay over the Red capital. We had to wait more than a week for room on the Siberia Express. The official tourist bureau "Intourist" took care of us. We were well treated, but it did not appear that Moscow was greatly interested

in furthering the tourist trade. The visit to Russia was not a vacation trip but we felt considerably more secure.

Fifteen years earlier I had been in Moscow as a young student. Even at that time there had not been much comfort, but there had been more interest and fascination. There had been flying banners and optimism. A new and fuller way of life was just around the corner. There had been mass meetings with posters and songs. Now Moscow was characterized by a peculiar gray resoluteness. Soldiers filled the streets. Their equipment was excellent and they were better dressed than the common people, but they did not sing. It was as if they were preparing for a threatening danger without knowing from what corner it would strike. Now the imperative problems were machines and weapons, not principles and world revolution. The only land whose name had a good sound was the United States of America. But even in Moscow there were Germans in all the hotels.

Our meal tickets were issued for only a brief stay, but there was a demand for clothing, and by selling a topcoat and a swimming suit we got ample funds for our needs. In the stores there was nothing to be had except food and vodka.

The week after our arrival we were packed into the Siberia Express. It was a fast train, but the trip took nine days. The diner had an atmosphere of long-lost glory with tasseled curtains and waiters who asked whether we wanted chicken or fish, fruit or ice. The individual orders were carefully written up, whereupon we all got beef stew and pudding.

275

The days were long and dirty. We played cards or chess with one another and with Russian officers, who were friendly but indifferent. They refused to discuss politics, but wanted to buy our wrist watches.

Siberia looked better than its reputation. We could see few highways, but many airfields. Finally we traversed the seemingly endless continent and once more could see the ocean.

We knew that Vladivostok was a much sought-after city, but it was not apparent why. There was work in the vicinity and many projects seemed to be going forward, but there was neither joy nor enthusiasm. In Vladivostok we had to wait again. Here, too, the hotel was filled, but only with bedbugs; there were no Germans.

The Intourist representative who had accompanied us throughout the journey, and who functioned as interpreter, uncle, and propagandist, regretted that our trip through Soviet Russia had not been more comfortable. He said, however, that we would not find it any better on the Japanese steamer to Tsuruga. Uncle Intourist was not lying. At our parting he declined a tip with indignation, but accepted as a personal remembrance a suit of Swedish BVD's, and a safety razor.

It took us three days to reach Japan in a freighter that sailed down the Korean coast. We went on to Tokyo and Yokohama and there the traveling party was dissolved. It was difficult to get on. The steamers were overloaded. A hectic life pulsated everywhere in Japan. There was far more merchandise in the stores than there had been in Russia, but most of it was substitute for

something else. Once again we were to find Germans in the hotels.

If it had been difficult to grasp the Russian attitude, it was not going to be any easier to understand the Japanese. It was said in the consulates that, among the common people, whose standard of living was steadily on the decline, the war had long since lost its popularity. Year after year they had been sending their sons to China and had got nothing in return except victory bulletins and small white boxes, the latter presumably containing the ashes of the heroes. It was strictly forbidden, under threat of both temporal and eternal punishment, to open these boxes, but the whisper went from man to man that they contained nothing but sand from the beaches of Shanghai.

The newspapers dispensed the queerest forms of propaganda. The *Japan Advertiser* published a call to celebrate the Day of the Rabbits, "in the honor of these humble creatures that are giving their skins for the army and the fatherland and in that manner setting an example for the rest of us." In the streets young fanatics raved into loud-speakers against the alien civilization and the white devils.

Everywhere there was a strange mixture of mysticism and common sense. Workers clattered through the streets on wooden sandals to ultramodern workshops and factories. The women kept humbly three feet behind their husbands. They were dressed in their beautiful long kimonos bound with the insanely impractical stomach belts made up of yards and yards of stiff silk, but

they visited up-to-date sports arenas and went swimming without swimming suits in public mixed pools. The food seemed to come from laboratories rather than from primitive oriental kitchens. The most modern airplanes were equipped with the latest automatic safety devices and were decorated with symbols to keep evil spirits away. No, it certainly was not easy to understand the soul of modern Japan, which might also prove itself to be a substitute.

After waiting for three weeks, a Norwegian cargo liner arrived, on which I was able to book passage for Los Angeles. I was again on Norwegian ground. The ship had been at sea on the ninth of April. Confusing and contradictory orders had come through the radio. From Oslo there had been instructions to return home at once. From London and Stockholm came the call of the Nygårdsvold Cabinet to proceed to Allied or neutral harbors. Like all other Norwegian seamen, the officers and sailors on board had placed themselves at the disposal of the Norwegian Government. Scarcely any of them had heard from their families in Norway since the day of invasion.

The Pacific lived up to its name. We had a peaceful voyage.

Los Angeles, San Francisco—America! I knew no one, but it was going to be easy to make new friends. Perhaps, after all, it was not too different from the mental picture I had already formed of it. The superabundance and the wastefulness, the noise and the traffic, the sea of lights at night, the frightening dimensions of

everything—to a certain extent I found it depressing. I examined my heart. It was not envy, it was rather anxiety and fear, that all this practical wealth and all these tough-minded and busy people would refuse to believe in ghosts. It was not that one was not met by friendliness and personal good will; of these things there was almost too much. But how could one ever expect that this self-sustaining and self-sure continent would come to look upon that one insane military state in Central Europe as a threat to all free peoples everywhere?

I went north to Seattle and east from there, through the country where Norwegian immigrants had settled. The feeling was the same as it had been on the coast. Perhaps there was even more of friendliness and personal interest in those of us who had come from Norway because of the old memories of the people themselves. Their reaction was one of compassion.

— It was a pity that the war had engulfed us! —

And yet, I realized that, not so long ago, we, too, had held that view, exactly that view, so far as other countries were concerned. What could we expect of this great nation, where there was such an abundance of liberty and consumable goods and where the possibilities still seemed limitless?

This was Norwegian America. It extended along the coast of the state of Washington, over the mountains into Montana, across the prairies of the Dakotas, to the rich hills of Minnesota, Iowa, and Wisconsin. Everywhere there were Norwegian farmers and craftsmen. They had come here many years ago or their fathers

had settled here, because it was too narrow and there was too little soil between the mountains in the homeland. They had found more soil than they had dreamed of, and they had found security. They had become respected citizens with equal rights in great, rich America. And yet they loved Norway, the old Norway, as it stood before them, little, poor, and hard. Pictures of the small gray homesteads they came from hung on the walls, with memories of the Old Country, where poverty, in spite of everything, had had a certain dignity and peace.

Yes, the interest and the sympathy were there. They wanted to help, but they were not willing to risk the one thing they had crossed the ocean to get—security. Many of their forefathers had come in sailing vessels and had told of hazardous voyages. Europe was far, far away.

Some of them asked bluntly, "But you can not expect us to declare war and send our boys abroad?"

No, we did not expect anything. We could only tell them that we, too, had once held exactly the same opinion. Time would tell whether this was a war for the possession of certain harbors and territories or whether it was a war about oceans and continents and freedom on earth—and time had become immensely precious.

In the history of a nation, a few years, more or less, may, of course, not seem to matter very much. On the other hand, a nation never lives more than a few generations at any given time, and the individual man or woman really ought to have a little something to eat from day to day. Out here in the Middle West, with its thousands of square miles of heavy wheat, it was too easy to talk

in terms of generations and to say that the mills of the gods grind slowly.

And yet, it was a fountain of inspiration to meet this Norwegian America, these foreign countrymen. They gathered in their stark and sober churches and sat around the coffee cups in the bare church basements to hear about Norway. Their stolid faces were expressive only of work and toil, but their eyes shone. There was power in these faces, and goodness in the clear eyes. They had come to these wild prairies with empty hands, and they had helped to build an Empire. These were the same people we had at home. We would get our country back, more barren and poorer than ever before, but we would rebuild it more beautiful and free than it had ever been.

It was late fall when I arrived in Washington. I went to the Norwegian Legation, one of the most important centers for free, fighting Norway. There I met Commodore Askim, who, with his wife had come the other way around the world. Again his ship had been torpedoed and sunk; he had been fortunate. It seemed a miracle that our Government and its diplomatic service had succeeded so quickly in building a new Government apparatus outside the country, and in securing such accurate and detailed information through the newly-organized Information Service. Not all the news was good. The country *was* being looted. The Gestapo *was* very busy, attempting to nazify the people.

The temporary administrative Council in Oslo had been painstakingly re-formed with Quisling's men. All

the former political parties had been declared illegal except for Quisling's infinitesimal and insignificant group.

The civic administrations of the various localities were being liquidated as rapidly as sufficient numbers of traitors could be found. In Narvik, a railroad telegraph operator named Trældal had been "appointed" mayor. Trældal had always had Nazi sympathies, a view shared only by Sundlo, and had been shunned or ridiculed by the people.

The prisons were crowded and concentration camps had been built and were being used. Hundreds of our best people were in them.

Personally, I received bad news. Ellen had been taken by the Gestapo. She was not imprisoned, but was kept under surveillance.

Strangely, radios had not, as yet, been confiscated. The Germans evidently still thought it possible to win the people with their propaganda. It was, of course, forbidden to listen to foreign stations, but now the whole nation was made up of lawbreakers. We could still talk with Norway.

The stream of youth that fled in boats and across the mountains continued to grow. We heard that the underground was well organized and was functioning smoothly and well. The Home Front was no longer led by amateurs. The lessons of the New Order had been quickly learned. The newspapers told of avalanches in the mountains. Highways and railroads were being washed out. Even the mountains were growing impatient.

XVIII — NORWAY SAILS ON

EVEN while the fighting was raging in Norway the huge Norwegian merchant marine was conscripted to serve under a special commission appointed by the Government. Thus the Norwegian Shipping and Trade Mission, *Nortraship*, became the largest shipping organization in the world. A new administration was quickly set up, with major offices in London, Montreal, and New York. Approximately twenty-five thousand seamen and one thousand ships were thrown into the battle of transport and the race for time.

The New York office was completely organized and functioning smoothly when I called in December, 1940. The office was a scene of intense activity, and, despite the fact that the force comprised more than one hundred officials and office workers, there was a shortage of technical help. Our ships, most of them modern, sailed all the seven seas. They had been our pride, and represented a large share of our wealth; they had given to

our relatively poor nation the necessary income for maintaining our high living standard and our culture. The Norwegian merchant marine was built for peaceful competition in world trade; but, whenever the freedom of the seas had been challenged, our ships had been of vital importance. The first World War had cost Norway more than half of her pre-war tonnage, a loss greater than that of any of the belligerent nations. Now, with our country conquered and occupied by the enemy, it was our merchant marine that gave us a position which counted among our Allies. The course was so precarious, the danger so great, that only realities mattered. Two hundred and seventy-two fast oil tankers was a contribution that did count. I looked at the charts and at pictures of our finest ships, many of them already marked with black crosses.

I met seamen waiting to make the next trip across the treacherous Atlantic. One evening a group of us chanced to meet and sit together in a restaurant on the Battery. It was not the best place in the world for quiet conversation. Sailors with too many loose nickels kept the music box working overtime. This nuisance was a huge monster of a thing, shrill both in sound and color. I thought it must have some kind of internal fountain that pumped colored water through glass tubes. It was not exactly the kind of thing that made foreigners love America.

The boys preferred not to talk of their torpedo sinkings. When, once in a while, they did have a peaceful night ashore, they said, why spoil it?

"But I do remember one funny thing," a stocky bos'n said. He smiled over his glass of beer. "We had been in a life boat for five days, three days without water. The U-boat had machine-gunned us and had riddled the water tank and destroyed the motor. We rowed until we were exhausted, and after that we drifted. Some one began to talk about beer in great, round barrels; light, fresh beer that bubbled with fine pearls coming up from the bottom. Someone else said we had better get a taxi and be on our way; perhaps there were some new regulations on closing hours; one could never tell with a war on. We begged him to shut up. But after a while we were all agreed that the most sensible thing to do was to call the taxi and get something to eat and drink. We actually imagined that the taxi stood waiting for us, with the taximeter humming. That was funny!"

"And then?"

"Well, that was all that was funny about it."

"And then you were saved?"

"No, not until the next day. We were picked up by a British destroyer, but not before three of the fellows had jumped overboard to—the taxi. I might have jumped myself, but the machinist's mate hit me on the head with the baler. That really helped the thirst. He always had been a teetotaller. Fine fellow, though. He was torpedoed during the last war, too.

"We go out again tomorrow. What do you think of the situation in Norway? Whenever I sit down to bacon and eggs in the mess room and think of those at home, the food chokes me."

We talked of the Home Front. We resented the fact that some newspapers had referred to it as passive resistance. Except for the lack of weapons, the resistance itself was certainly active enough. Quisling and the Germans had liquidated all the old political parties; youth and sports organizations had been taken over; but the New Order was meeting sabotage and resistance from all sides. The prisons were already filled with good Norwegians. At that, it appeared that the nazification was in its relatively innocent beginnings. We had reports that constantly new groups of the Gestapo were coming into the country. The Trade Union was likely to be hit next. Earlier in the fall, decrees had prohibited workers engaged in agriculture, lumbering, fishing, and shipping from changing jobs or moving from the country into the towns. The food situation was becoming steadily worse. Sooner or later there would be starvation.

"*We* can certainly take it," said the bos'n when we rose to go, "but what we fear is that we will have to go to the graveyards to find our families when we go home."

That attitude prevails among all Norwegian seamen. They are harder and tougher than landsmen, but they are also more emotional and sentimental. The heavy, monotonous routine, broken by moments of high excitement and utmost danger, makes for a strange dualism. The long and lonely watches filled with daydreams and anxiety for those at home, the U-boat psychosis, and the horrors in the life boats, combine to produce a special, peculiar reaction. The sailors do their work, not consciously realizing the unequal burden the war has placed

upon them; but, on the other hand, the distress and want of those at home press even stronger on their nerves. To us ashore there seems to be abundant time for preparation, but to those on ships there is always need for haste. They bring the rich, heavy cargos to England and other of our Allies, but never any food to the homeland. The morale of the sailors is largely a question of understanding their problem. But perhaps it is a question, too, of whether we on land can measure up to them.

I was invited to return to the Middle West, and visited all the more important Norwegian centers as well as filling many lecture engagements. Our kinsmen seemed to feel a little less pity for us now and a little more anxiety on their own behalf. Still, the feeling that they were spectators at a seemingly unexplainable accident persisted.

Dramatization of the fact that their old Norway had been brought into the focus of world-wide attention was often a little too dominant. Many times I was to meet with such statements as, "You probably saw me at your lecture last night. I have an aunt in Bodö. Of course the Germans have shot her by now." When I offered the consolation that not too many civilians had been shot, the reaction was often one of wounded pride. Of course the aunt had been shot!

On the whole, however, the feeling of sympathy and a desire to help was stronger and more frequent than the dramatization of the sensational. The relationship between the emigrants and those at home had always been close, and, like the gulf stream, the material benefits of the connection seemed always to have moved in

one direction. With "America money" many families in Norway had built that new home or repaired the old.

Immediately after the invasion, committees for Norwegian Relief were organized throughout the United States. The collection of funds and materials was limited only by the difficulties of sending them abroad.

In spite of its isolation, however, news—the real news —came in a steady stream from Norway, and there were, occasionally, letters. They had been opened and censored, but at least they were signs of life.

Ellen and I, on our excursion through the fjords, had talked of ways we might keep in touch with each other if we could not write letters directly. We made up a code based on memories we shared. I was to be a sailor with a large family. We created aunts and uncles all over Norway, and they happened to live in rather important places. Crabbed old Uncle Eric was Gestapo. As was natural, he became more and more disagreeable and suspicious in his old age, and tolerated no liberty for the young. Ellen was his ward. There were also cousins and friends, who advised her to get away from his supervision.

It worked. None of this family detail was blacked out by the censors, and for a while I got a fairly clear idea of what was happening. Then the letters stopped, although other mail was still coming through. I feared the worst but hoped for the best.

I received greetings from friends in London and letters from my father. Things were taking shape. To move around had never been his greatest pleasure and

certainly working conditions were not the best for an elderly gentleman. He had always taken life as it came,
and now it was coming fast and furiously. During the
worst period of the bombing of London, Norway had
set up a new Government organization.

I lectured all winter. In February, 1941, at Sioux
Falls, South Dakota, I received a forwarded cable from
Stockholm. Ellen and Siri had crossed the border. They
would, if possible, be sent through Russia, Siberia, and
Japan, and thence to the United States. I read avidly
everything I could lay my hands on concerning developments in the Far East, and discovered at least one com-
forting journalist who was of the opinion that the situation there would remain unchanged until spring.

A month later, when I was in the Eastern states, I received a message through our legation in Tokyo, "Arriving San Francisco in fourteen days aboard Nitta
Maru—Ellen."

We met in Chicago. I thought them both a little pale,
but Siri had grown. She had been intensely interested
in all the strange things she had seen and experienced.
Norway was already far away. She did not remember
much about it. But Mother did.

They had lived for some time in the cabin at the base
of the mountain in the fjord arm. Then they had returned to Narvik, where they had lived with friends.
Many of the workers had been called back and were put
to work on the repair of the railroad and the docks. The
remaining houses were crowded and barracks were being built.

Kittenshill was still intact when they returned, but was occupied by German "actresses" imported a few weeks after the fighting ceased, to "bolster the morale of the German troops." She had been permitted to take Siri's clothes, but her own were being worn by the ladies. The house had been visited by notables. Reichskommissar Terboven had stayed there when he had been on an inspection tour of Narvik. That was the day that France had capitulated, and neighbors reported that there had been a great celebration in the actresses' house that night.

— But what about herself? What had happened to her? —

— At first they had paid no attention to her. A German officer had even given her a pass. But that had been a trap, for when she attempted to leave the country she had been arrested on the train and returned to Narvik. Her luggage had been ransacked and she had been stripped for inspection.

— They questioned her an entire day. Siri caused so many timely interruptions that the Germans finally put her in a soldier's bunk where she fell asleep. As for herself, she knew little, and of that little, the Germans got less. After a few weeks she received permission to go to Oslo, but her movements were watched. —

— How had she managed with money? — I asked.

— That had not been so difficult. The Germans had not been much interested in the money of private persons. They continued to print new Norwegian paper money and there was more money in the land than ever

before. On the other hand, there was less and less to buy. Even during the first winter there had been almost no meat. Everything was rationed, and it was comparatively simple to get money for the few things that could be had. People in distress were always helped. A kind of freemasonry had sprung up between all loyal Norwegians. No, there were not many quislings. None of our personal friends had gone over to the Nazis.

— A strange atmosphere had pervaded Oslo during the first winter. People generally did not know much. Perhaps we over here were somewhat better informed as to what had happened in Norway, but it had been a really great experience to see at first hand how the nation had reacted. It was as though a new kind of social organism was being formed below the surface. Everyone was engaged in secret activity. Illegal groups were at work everywhere. Very few understood the organization of the underground, but it seemed to be the same kind of system that one could read of in nineteenth-century Russian novels. Only the key men knew anything about the next floor up in the pyramid. Who was at the top, no one seemed to know.

— Hidden radio stations denounced the Germans unendingly and broadcast the names of those who had become traitors. Illegal newspapers carried news as well as the latest jokes about Quisling and Terboven. The Norwegian broadcast from London was a major event of each day.

— Ellen had been promised help in leaving the country, but even after she was out she did not know who

had arranged the escape. She was told to be ready for instant departure during a certain week. The day was not named. Even her immediate family must not be told of her intention to leave.

— One night she and Siri were hurriedly called for. On the trip through the country different means of transportation were used, a new man with each. The last part of the way they had walked. Near the border a boy appeared, and carried Siri through forests into Sweden.

— It sounded adventurous, perhaps? Actually, she had been tired and miserable, and Siri had been fussy.

— Across the border it seemed that the people were accustomed to this traffic. They were friendly and businesslike. In Stockholm she had met friends. The trip across Russia and Siberia had seemed endless, but, after all, she had only the one child. Other mothers had three and four. —

"And what do you think of America?" I asked.

"Oh, it is nice here, of course. Peaceful and beautiful. And so much of everything! But can it last? It *is* possible, you see, to get over here even in wartime. Do you think America will eventually come in? That is the big question at home."

"I don't know," I said, "although it may be that the question should be, '*When* will America get in?' If only it does not come too late! In Washington the feeling seems to be that Russia will be next. You got through Siberia just in time."

Now the three of us traveled in the Ford. We felt like

missionaries, or, at least, were treated as such. We carried a gospel, but were cautious with the commandments. The congregation would have to make its own interpretation and draw its own conclusions.

We had a good but not a peaceful life. Siri, especially, needed more regular hours. We were all happy in the fall of the year when we received orders to open a Norwegian office in Minneapolis, where a home could once again be established.

One of the first news items the office received for distribution was a brief message stating that Viggo Hansteen had been executed in Oslo. On the tenth of September he and a young worker, Rolf Vickström, had been condemned to death by a Nazi tribunal. They had been shot the same evening.

Later, we received more details. A strike had been called in certain German-controlled plants in Oslo, and the Germans had declared a state of civil emergency. Covered truckloads of prisoners were driven through the streets all day. Most of the labor leaders who were still free had been arrested, together with hundreds of others who could have had no possible connection with the strike—newspapermen, sports leaders, teachers, business men. Even the head of the University of Oslo had been taken.

Orders from the Gestapo came thick and fast. The great Employers' Association was ordered dissolved, as well as such apparently harmless organizations as the Salvation Army, the Boy Scouts, and the Girl Scouts. Groups organized for the sole purpose of reconstructing

bombed homes and aiding war-stricken families were ordered disbanded.

It was stated in the reports that Hansteen and Vickström were more or less chance victims of the German military court, but Hansteen's friends found it difficult to believe that it had been only accidental that he had been one of the first victims. Why, accidentally, one of the noblest; he, who, in the discussions between the labor organizations and the Reichskommissar, had proven himself so infinitely superior? All those present had made involuntary comparison between this upright, fair, quiet Norseman, and the raceless, hysterical gangster type that represented the *Herrenvolk* in Norway.

A few hours after the death sentence had been passed, the Oslo Radio announced that the executions had already taken place, no one knew where. But, in the concentration camps, where Norwegians, in mysterious ways, were better informed than those outside, the report was tapped out on the walls that the martyrs had been killed by revolver bullets in the neck in the cellar of the Government Building, and that shortly afterward the clothes of the murdered men had been sent to their families.

We were to receive more and more messages of this nature. During the winter, German attention was turned to the church and schools. The Nazis, working with Quisling, attempted to force passage of new laws affecting public education in Norway looking to complete nazification of our children and our young people. The invaders had already taken everything we owned. Now

they wanted to rob us of our greatest treasure, the minds of future Norway. The church leaders and the school authorities took an immediate and absolute stand against what they deemed the worst of all treachery.

The fight between the quislings and the clergy ended in a complete break with the Nazis. The Church of Norway was fighting for the children and was the only church in occupied Europe to voice a fearless condemnation of Hitler's pagan tyranny. The teachers, as one man, protested in indignation, and pledged themselves never to surrender their fidelity to the ideal of free and independent education as guaranteed by the Norwegian Constitution. Teachers by the hundreds were thrown into concentration camps, but neither inhuman brutality nor subtle flattery could break their spirit.

We received information about almost unbelievable acts of terrorism and heroic resistance that made us proud and humble, ill and happy at the same time. The Quisling Government had said that the Church was dead and had lost its connection with modern life, and with typical Nazi inconsistency had taken the golden cross from the old king sagas as its symbol—the so-called Sun Cross—indicating the bright, new era.

From other sources we learned that the wooden cross in the shadow of Calvary had indeed become a symbol, a symbol of pride and unyielding struggle. Never before had the Norwegian Church had such close contact with living reality.

XIX — THE SECOND FRONT

IN THE late winter I again went on a lecture tour, this time in Ohio and New York, where I had been asked to speak at several colleges. It was extremely interesting to observe how American students reacted to the problems of war and peace. Again I found the thinking identical with that with which Norway had soothed itself before April 9, 1940—a year and a half before.

After the lectures there were usually discussions, with questions and answers. The students said that they could well understand that we were unprepared, that we had too few weapons, but they could not understand how we could have been taken so completely by surprise.

It was not easy to give a logical and plausible answer, and, at first, my answers were, perhaps, not too convincing. But during the latter part of the tour it became less difficult. The events of December 7 at Pearl Harbor had occurred in the meantime.

Once more I was to see reactions identically dupli-

cated. When young minds face the necessity of changing their views they change them speedily and ruthlessly. Student convocations had always fascinated me with their inspiring challenge. The young eyes had never been indifferent, but now they glowed with fire. The cause had become their own.

One evening, after a meeting at a college in New York state, I was invited to the president's home for further discussion. Most of the faculty was present. An old professor told me that he thought I had a very accurate picture of the student mind. The overwhelming majority of students had been more or less passive in their attitude before December 7. Immediately afterward they all became interventionists. Many of them wanted to discontinue their studies at once, even though they were seniors and about to graduate in a few months. In their impatience they felt that the whole affair might blow over during the Christmas vacation.

The professor asked me whether I was pleased at what had happened, and then quickly begged me not to answer. It was an unfair question, he said. He would answer it himself.

— It was a shameful and almost dishonoring blow that America had received right between its self-confident eyes, and it had represented a terrible loss of life and material. But he was glad that the war had come to the American people in just that way.

— What if Japan had pursued a different course, and had first attacked Russia? America's foresighted President would still have been forced to take action.

But would such a step have had the united support of
the people? After the declaration had been signed and
the casualty lists began to come in, would there not have
been questions of doubt as to its necessity? It was not
pleasant to be hit first, but the attack had convinced
every citizen that America had no other guilt than the
same false illusions of peace that had paralyzed all
other liberty-loving nations. —

The kind old professor had seemed to be talking half
to himself, as if he needed to formulate his views of
this new situation which would dominate the life of his
generation. Now he addressed himself directly to me.

"You described in the auditorium tonight what happened in Norway and in Narvik. In one sense, it is the
same destiny that has struck all the civilized world. I
am an old humanist, and my work will, perhaps, not
have any importance for a long time to come. But I can
not but feel that we human beings, first and last, and
in spite of everything, are spiritual beings. Those who
share the same ideals form one people across all borderlines.

"We have all been taken by surprise by ships which
have come out of the fog and blasted our comfortable
world to bits. Now our turn, too, has come. From now
on it is probably America's war more than that of anyone else. America can lose it, finally and definitely, but
America can also win it.

"I suspect that our enemies made very careful studies before they attacked. They have discovered that
we are poorly armed. I suppose it must look that way.

I am not thinking purely of the military side; I don't know much about that. I am thinking of the young men who must fight this war. Our young people themselves are apparently poorly armed. They are happy, self-centered children of liberty and democracy. They are undisciplined and daring, and they may not know too much about what freedom essentially is, since they have never known anything else.

"But they have what it takes. Discipline and the use of weapons are, after all, only matters of technique. Modern American youth will never give up. Just because they have had so rich a life, we can depend upon them. Together with you of the other nations, we will see this thing through to victory. You may rest assured that Norway will be free again, and that you will go back to rebuild your little town."

In a better humor than I had been in for a long time I traveled west again. The next fall I returned to the same territory and met some of the same students again. They were not so impatient now. The war was no longer an adventure that would be over soon. This time they really meant business.

On this trip I used the opportunity to go to Canada and visited Toronto, where the Royal Norwegian Air Force had built Camp Little Norway.

To the citizens of Toronto it may, perhaps, be only another bothersome military encampment obstructing the view of Lake Ontario; but, to an exiled and homeless Norwegian, it is a glowing symbol that provides a thrilling experience from the moment he glimpses the Nor-

wegian flag flying over the gray barracks. Here are not
only office buildings and Government representatives,
but schools, workshops, and training fields where Norwegian youth works and learns.

The guide at the entrance stopped me with a challenge
in English. From his accent and his face I could tell
from just about what section of Norway he had come.
He grinned, and said that my accent was not entirely un-
familiar either.

Earnestness and order were the keynotes of the camp.
At the time I visited it, it was not yet two years old. It
had been established as an emergency measure. Planes
Norway had ordered from America before the war had
not been finished in time and the men had traveled halfway around the world to learn to fly them. Because
America was neutral, the camp was established across
the border.

The Norwegian Government in London had done
everything in its power to make possible adequate training facilities. Income from the Norwegian merchant
marine had provided the necessary funds, as it has for
all free Norwegian activities. It was money that had
cost lives, and everyone in the camp knew that the best
possible use must be made of it. The young fliers themselves wanted to help and taxed their earnings to raise
money for new equipment. The plane "Spirit of Little
Norway" was purchased from this fund.

Norwegians and friends throughout the western hem-
isphere came to its aid. A Norwegian plantation owner
in Guatemala regularly sent all the coffee the boys could

drink. Other Norwegians in South America sent planes. Norwegian-Americans in the United States formed a national organization with headquarters in Minneapolis to provide the little extras that the USO and American homes could give their own sons.

Never have I seen such grownup young boys.

"Yes, the material is good," the officer said, with ill-concealed pride.

They were all volunteers, and most of them had reached the camp under great difficulty and against heavy odds. Norway lies exactly halfway around the world and those who try to leave face the death penalty if they are caught. Hundreds have already been trained and they continue to come, but no one knows how many have been lost on the way.

We visited the barracks. Discipline was self-administered and military forms seemed to be used only for practical reasons. Orders were so quiet as to be almost inaudible. We had interrupted a singing of the camp's new battle song. The officer said they might continue.

The camp had a new song written by Sigmund Skard, a Norwegian librarian now in Washington, whom the war had made a poet. He had written of the long journeys the boys had made.

"And he certainly had some experience in traveling himself," said the officer. "Last year he came through Siberia with his wife and two sets of twins."

We listened to the song. They were practicing the English version so that their Canadian comrades and girl friends might understand it. A light-haired boy sat in

an upper bunk and acted as conductor, a toothbrush for a baton. The young voices filled the narrow barracks:

"Round the wide world, comrades, we have journeyed;
Birds alone can follow on our trail;
Now in eagle flocks we come returning;
Back to Norway like a thundercloud we sail.
    Norse men! On guard!
    Norse men! Strike hard!
Our singing propellers sing best
    As we storm from the west.

"Unarmed our kinsmen fight on in the homeland;
Shame to him who fails to do his share;
Behind a thousand miles of storm-lashed coastline,
Comrades! They are waiting for us there.
    Norse men! Set forth
    Your course to the North.
A storm-cloud now foams in the sky
    As we fly.

"Through the night our squadrons drive onward,
Like the lightning, swift descends our blow.
In the dawn we see peaks rise above the cloudbanks;
Norway, free as before, lies below.
    Norse hearts! Be still!
    We know what we will!
Thy future lies safe in our hand,
    Fatherland!"

More than a thousand boys have come around the earth to this training camp on Lake Ontario. Every one has a daring adventure behind and an adventure not less daring ahead. The chief is a man who seems to have been predestined for exactly this task: equally able in the air, at sports meets, or in ski competitions, and

as close to the classic Viking type as a cultured human being can come.

I was interested in meeting recruits who had arrived from Norway recently, but none who had escaped from Norway during the summer had as yet reached Toronto. Experience had shown that their number decreased during the short and light summer nights. One new recruit, however, was expected in a day or two. He had sailed a tiny sailing boat to England a few weeks earlier and had recently arrived in New York on a Norwegian freighter out of London. He had just crossed the border and, at the moment, was waiting for his Canadian visa at Niagara Falls. If I wished to interview him I could find him in one of the hotels there. He was using the name Sverre. He had parents and brothers in Oslo.

On the trip back to the United States I traveled with one of the student pilots. He was waiting for a broken arm to heal and had been given a brief vacation.

We met Sverre in Niagara Falls. With him was a young Norwegian American who had just arrived to volunteer in the Norwegian Air Force. He had recently been graduated from a college in Minnesota and wished to see Niagara Falls before going on to Toronto. We all went sightseeing. Sverre confided his disappointment. There was too much water and too little fall to suit his Norwegian taste.

When we had paid proper attention to the falls, we returned to the hotel for a chat. The newspapers contained reports of the raid at Dieppe in which Commandos and airmen from many of the United Nations

had participated. The student pilot related how the Norwegian flyers had distinguished themselves during that historic raid. He had already lost several friends over France, but he did not know what the Norwegian losses had been this time.

We listened to the news over the radio. It was bad, as usual. The Russians were making a desperate stand in the outskirts of Stalingrad. Their irresistible will to struggle and sacrifice made us all humble. It seemed to be the rule with this amazing, distant, fighting people, that their actions caused either offense and indignation or unbounded admiration. What could we not learn from their great faith and their unyielding will! They were fighting hard, and alone. The great armies in the British Isles lay idle. What had become of the Second Front?

The student pilot said that he had feared all summer that the Second Front would be opened before he had his wings, and, when he had broken his arm during an emergency landing, he had been completely sunk. He might as well have saved himself the despair, he said, for it did not appear that the Second Front would become a reality any time during the year. What were the Generals waiting for?

The college student ventured the opinion that they were wrangling and playing politics just like politicians everywhere. He asked us to speak English since he could not understand or use the Norwegian expressions that fitted the occasion. He had learned his Norwegian from his grandmother.

We asked Sverre what he thought and what the people in Norway were thinking. Were they impatient?

He was the youngest in the party, and somewhat bashful. First he tried to use his school English, but quickly dropped into Norwegian. He warmed to his subject and told us with eagerness how things had developed after the Germans had crushed the armed resistance. Impressions and incidents streamed from him in a topsy-turvy flow, almost as if he had forgotten that he had an audience. As his story poured forth his youthful face, resting in cupped hands supported by elbows on the table, became alive with character and maturity.

He related small humiliating incidents which carried pestilence into the gray everyday life at home; of the endless lines before the food stores where women and children stamped their feet to keep them warm in worn-out footwear; of German officers who whizzed through the streets in their commandeered cars, spattering bystanders with mud; and of their wives who sailed by the waiting lines and went directly to the specialty counters reserved for the superior race.

He told of the shocks that came at intervals when islands and villages were devastated in revenge for some minor incident, or new lists of respected Norwegian names were posted as "condemned for illegal and treacherous activities." He told stories of terror and torture that had found their way through prison walls. One's gorge rose in powerless indignation.

Yes, they *were* becoming impatient at home, but

he brought to us the message that they could take it!

In a manner, also, he could bring us greetings from the land itself. He had walked across all southern Norway to escape. He was one of four young men who had planned to make their get-away by sailing a small boat hidden in a fjord on the west coast. They were all from Oslo, but they had traveled alone to avert suspicion. And yet it had been evident that the people on all the farms where he had spent the nights seemed to understand. They had not said as much, but they had been exceptionally cordial and solemn when they bade farewell and asked him to take greetings where he was going. It had been the most beautiful hike he had ever made.

When he arrived at the western fjord, two of his companions were already there, but the third failed to arrive. They waited for several days; but, finally, had to set sail, since the moon was growing brighter.

In England, the other two had enlisted in the Royal Norwegian Navy which had recently put into service some excellent new ships. As for himself, his fondest dream had come true. He had had some basic technical training and was accepted in the Air Force.

He noticed that we were gazing at his face and again he became self-conscious and boyish.

We broke up, and I went out into the night. Sverre's story had made it all live again. I could see Norway before me. The thunder of Niagara made the illusion more real.

I saw the land lying there, waiting. The mountains

were already white. Autumn storms were singing through the forests. The woods glowed in brilliant colors and hoar frost lay on the fields in the early morning before the sun gained strength. Another winter was at the door, with starvation and cold.

This summer the people had been sure that help would come. The young men had used their fat rations to oil their hidden firearms. They took desperate chances in preparation and in sabotage. The finest flower of our youth lay in nameless graves or pined away behind barbed wire fences. Old people died without seeing the liberation come. The people worked as hard as ever, but now there was neither joy nor honor in their travail. In the blacked-out cities they waited as in a fever for the Day.

But there was the message that this young boy had carried from them, that they could take it, and that they knew that help would come when it was ready. The people at home trusted the leaders who now held the Destiny of Humanity in their hands.

We had always been a quiet people who had never shown much emotion. Even now, no one cried out. Not with despair but with impatient hope came the almost audible whisper, "How long must we wait?"

307

SCRAPBOOK: A selection of maps and photographs from the author's personal file and other sources.

*The Scandinavian peninsula, showing the location of important
cities.*

Narvik from above. Upper right, the Sleeping Queen.

Frydenlund in Narvik, the Church, and the Parkway. In the lower left corner is the Headmaster's house.

The Market Place was an open quadrangle with market stalls built into the side of the hill below the Post Office and Telegraph Building.

The City Hall had originally been a hotel. It retained its tower at the corner and the huge, drafty windows on the first floor.

313

Behind reefs and cliffs there are calm harbors. Such a place is Svolvær.

Above the cluster of wooden houses stretches the tower of the simple stone church, standing as if on tiptoe.

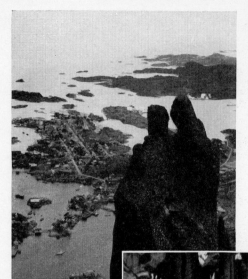

The Two Lovers, above Svolvær, who have stood in stone since sin came into the world. When seen from the harbor, the silhouette resembles the head of an animal which fishermen call the Svolvær Goat.

Fish-drying racks at Kabelvaag. Vaagakallen, in the background, resembles a fantastic giant when seen from the sea.

315

*A Lofoten fisher boy,
typical of Oscar in
the book.*

*Fishermen and nets,
Lofoten.*

316

Lieutenant - General Edward Dietl, chief of the German occupation forces in northern Norway.

The piers looked hopeless. Whole parts of ships were thrown ashore among timber, logs, and cleft rocks.

Detail of northern
Norway, showing
Narvik and the sur-
rounding towns,
fjords, and islands
in which much of
the action in the
book takes place.

In the sea battle of April 10, 1940, three British and two German ships were sunk and several were damaged.

The sea battle of April 13 ended in the destruction of the remaining destroyers of the German invasion fleet of ten.

Left, Norwegian emergency money. Right, an ordinary Norwegian ten krone note and a German occupation mark.

"The holder of this permit, the Mayor of Narvik, has permission to be on the streets of Narvik day or night."

The Polish howitzer set the Grand Hotel on fire and British shells hit the Royal. The Royal was not completely demolished, but there were holes through the walls and the Germans left it.

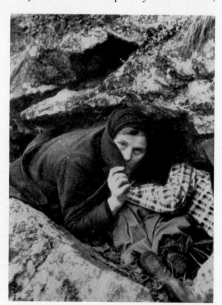

Bombing could not break us but it did cause a certain disturbance. Calmness was something we had continually stressed.

*The incendiaries started fires wherever they hit and the flames
spread. Everyone who remained in the city took part in the
salvaging.*

*To extinguish the conflagration was impossible. The heat was
so intense that all wooden material seemed to melt away.*

A new kind of social organism was being formed below the surface. Illegal groups were at work everywhere.

A picture taken at Grini concentration camp near Oslo and smuggled out of Norway. When the picture was taken there were eighteen concentration camps in Norway and ten more were being built. Grini is the largest.

Scenes at Camp
Little Norway,
Toronto. Clock-
wise: Induction.
"Round the wide
world, comrades,
we have jour-
neyed." Field
work. On the way.

*Thumbs up! Survivors from a torpedoed Norwegian freighter
who typify the spirit of the Norwegian Merchant Marine.*

*King Haakon's seventieth birthday on August 3, 1942, was cele-
brated the world over. In London the King and the Crown Prince
couple reviewed a parade in Hyde Park.*

325